THE SALES PROSPECTING & TERRITORY PLANNING DIRECTORY

THE SALES PROSPECTING & TERRITORY PLANNING DIRECTORY

The 4,000 Richest Organizations in North America

JOHN C. THOMAS
Editor

amacom
AMERICAN MANAGEMENT ASSOCIATION

This book is available at a special discount when ordered in
bulk quantities. For information, contact Special Sales
Department, AMACOM, a division of American Management
Association, 135 West 50th Street, New York, NY 10020.

ISBN 0-8144-7735-6
89-083381

Printing number

10 9 8 7 6 5 4 3 2 1

Contents

Introduction

The Sales Prospecting & Territory Planning Directory is a guide to the richest organizations in North America. It is your most complete source of information on more than 4,100 organizations with revenues above $250 million. We use the word *organizations* because in addition to listing publicly and privately held corporations in the United States and Canada—including more than 500 of their subsidiaries and divisions, as well as financial institutions and headquarters of foreign companies—we have included federal, state, local, and provincial (Canadian) government agencies and nonprofit organizations.

This mix of organizations, which you won't find in any other directory or listing, was conceived to provide businesspeople around the world with the ability to reach other businesspeople who make buying decisions. The importance of this mix is most apparent in Section 2, Organizations Listed by Revenue. This is where you'll see that eight of the top twenty organizations in North America are government agencies. In fact, although General Motors comes in as the number one organization in North America, the United States Department of the Navy is number two—and the state of California is number seven! This unique arrangement provides you with a new approach to tapping the enormous purchasing power of North America. The directory is the ideal companion for the business-to-business marketing and sales manager. It's also a valuable reference for CEOs, planning department staff, and librarians.

ARRANGEMENT

Organized for easy access, *The Sales Prospecting & Territory Planning Directory* has four sections: alphabetical, by revenue, geographic, and by industry. These provide you with the facts and figures you need on your most important sales prospects. The organization descriptions contain valuable information, including:

Organization Name. The organization may be a corporation that is publicly traded or privately held, a government unit, or a nonprofit organization. The organization name is found in each section of the directory. Each division or subsidiary has its own listing in Sections 1, 3, and 4 (see discussion below on revenue for treatment of divisions in Section 2).

Address. The organization's address includes street address, post office box, or both; the city name; the state or province (if Canada); and the Zip Code or Canadian postal code. Full addresses for organizations are found in Section 1 and Section 4.

Telephone. The organization's main telephone number is found in all four sections.

Major Group/Industry. There are twelve major groupings under which fifty-three industry names are found. Rather than use SIC codes in this directory, we have chosen easy-to-understand terms that reflect the diversity of today's business world, especially the growth in service industries.

Revenue. Each organization has an annual revenue amount shown in millions of U.S. dollars. Canadian organizations' revenues have been converted at $.85 per Canadian dollar, the exchange rate as this book went to press. Revenue is included in all sections of the directory. Section 2 ranks the organizations by revenue. Revenue information for subsidiaries and divisions is hard to retrieve and confirm for either privately held or publicly traded companies. When revenue information is not available, that organization is not included in Section 2. In all other sections NA (not available) appears in the revenue column.

Assets. Assets are shown in millions of U.S. dollars. Canadian organizations' assets are converted into U.S. dollars as their revenues were. Since assets are generally not a meaningful number for government agencies and nonprofit organizations, NM (not meaningful) is used in most of their listings. Occasionally, when information on assets is just not available, NA is used.

Employees. The number of employees is shown in thousands. For membership organizations, such as unions, *employee* stands for *membership*. For universities, *employees* stands for the total number of faculty and students.

EDITORIAL COMPILATION

The information provided in *The Sales Prospecting & Territory Planning Directory* was compiled primarily from annual reports with telephone interviews used to confirm some aspects of the data. We have attempted to provide complete, accurate, and current information. However, because of the possibilities for error in compiling a directory of this size, AMACOM Books does not assume liability for the accuracy of the information included. Once detected, however, errors will be corrected in the next edition. There is no charge for being listed in *The Sales Prospecting & Territory Planning Directory.*

ABOUT THE EDITOR

John C. Thomas has had fifteen years' experience in business-to-business sales and marketing in the information services and software industries including his position as vice president of sales for a division of CitiCorp. He is currently president of Thomas Information Group, Inc., a publisher of information products for sales and marketing professionals. In addition to this book he also has introduced the Thomas Sales Prospecting and Territory Planning Database.

How to Use This Book

To make *The Sales Prospecting & Territory Planning Directory* a practical and usable book, we have divided it into four sections: alphabetical, by revenue, geographic, and by industry.

ORGANIZATIONS LISTED ALPHABETICALLY

The first section lists more than 4,100 organizations alphabetically by organization name. It provides full detail on every organization, including address; telephone number; contact person (up to eighteen names for the 1,200 largest organizations); industry group; type of organization—private, public (if publicly held, includes exchange and ticker symbol), subsidiary, foreign, nonprofit, or government; a one-line description; revenues and assets; and number of employees.

The data provided in the alphabetical listing will help you to:

- Identify the top people in an organization

- Assess the buying power of an organization by revenues and assets

- Confirm whether a company is publicly owned or privately held

- Determine organization's type of business

ORGANIZATIONS LISTED BY REVENUE

Here you will find all the organizations from the alphabetical section (except for some subsidiaries and divisions for which revenue could not be confirmed) ranked by revenue. This list starts with the number one organization—General Motors—which earned $123,641 billion. Each entry includes organization name, address, and telephone number; annual revenue; assets; and number of employees.

By learning where an organization ranks among the top 4,100, you can:

- Identify key prospects

- Determine how much these key prospects have to spend

Table 1. Geographic Distribution of Organizations

United States	Number	United States	Number
Alabama	37	Ohio	177
Alaska	2	Oklahoma	29
Arizona	35	Oregon	28
Arkansas	16	Pennsylvania	183
California	403	Puerto Rico	3
Colorado	41	Rhode Island	17
Connecticut	132	South Carolina	16
Delaware	21	South Dakota	1
District of Columbia	96	Tennessee	45
Florida	90	Texas	273
Georgia	76	Utah	18
Hawaii	10	Vermont	4
Idaho	11	Virginia	84
Illinois	225	Washington	45
Indiana	51	West Virginia	7
Iowa	29	Wisconsin	68
Kansas	31	Wyoming	1
Kentucky	28		
Louisiana	32	United States	3608
Maine	7		
Maryland	41	Canadian Provinces	Number
Massachusetts	143		
Michigan	134	Alberta	48
Minnesota	81	British Columbia	35
Mississippi	11	Manitoba	17
Missouri	92	New Brunswick	5
Montana	2	Newfoundland	4
Nebraska	22	Nova Scotia	9
Nevada	12	Ontario	279
New Hampshire	10	Prince Edward Island	1
New Jersey	140	Quebec	97
New Mexico	5	Saskatchewan	9
New York	488		
North Carolina	53	Canada	504
North Dakota	2		

ORGANIZATIONS LISTED GEOGRAPHICALLY

Section 3 is arranged alphabetically by state/province name, and within each state/province, by Zip Code area (see Table 1 for a numerical breakdown of the geographic distribution of the organizations). Each entry includes annual revenue; organization name, address, and telephone number; and industry type. Canadian listings follow those for the U.S.

You'll want to use this section to:

- Identify companies by region, state, city, and Zip Code area

- Plan sales territories

- Build your own direct mail and telemarketing programs

ORGANIZATIONS LISTED BY INDUSTRY

The fourth section is arranged according to the fifty-three subclasses within these twelve major industry categories: financial, insurance, high tech, manufacturing, basic industries, business services, utilities, food processing and distribution, retail, consumer services, consumer products, government and nonprofit. Table 2 shows the number of organizations in each of the fifty-three divisions. Each entry includes organization name, address, and telephone number; assets; annual revenue; and number of employees. The total number of companies listed within each industry category also is provided.

The industry listing enables you to:

- Identify key prospects by line of business

- Target new organizations in existing industries

Table 2. Distribution by Major Group and Industry

Total Number of Organizations in Directory	4,112		Real Estate/Building	133
			Business Service	127
			Transport	55
INDUSTRY GROUP:			Accounting	20
			Consulting	34
Financial	513			
Banking	205		*Utilities*	206
Non-Bank Financial	115		Utility	206
Savings & Loan	92			
Securities	73		*Food Processing & Distribution*	251
Federal Government Financial	28		Beverage	18
			Food Processing	220
Insurance	189		Tobacco	13
Insurance	189			
			Retail	366
High Tech	405		Retail/Food	133
Aerospace	49		Retail/Merchandise	233
Electronics	128			
Instruments	24		*Consumer Services*	340
Computers/Office Equipment	128		Airline	23
Telecommunications	76		Consumer Service	8
			Drugs	43
Manufacturing	438		Food/Lodging	56
Appliances	26		Leisure Time	60
Automotive	108		Publishing/Communications	105
Conglomerate	21		Health Care	45
Packaging	22			
Machinery	16		*Consumer Products*	106
Manufacturing	209		Personal Care	31
Equipment	36		Apparel/Textiles	75
Basic Industries	507		*Government & Nonprofit*	388
Building Materials	54		Federal Government	60
Chemicals	94		State/Provincial Government	62
Metals/Mining	64		Local Government	105
Energy	168		Government Authority	3
Paper/Forest Products	71		Membership Organization	35
Steel	36		University	123
Tire/Rubber	20			
Business Service	403			
Oil Service	17			
Railroad	17			

Key to Abbreviations

ASE	American Stock Exchange	Merch	Merchandise
Assn	Association	Mkt	Marketing
Assoc	Associates	NA	Not Available
Auth	Authority	NASDAQ	traded over the counter
CEO	Chief Executive Officer	NM	Not Meaningful
CFO	Chief Financial Officer	Non-Bank	Non-Banking
Chr	Chair	Non-Prof	Non-Profit
Co	Company	NYSE	New York Stock Exchange
Com	Communications	Off	Office
Coop	Cooperative	Ops	Operations/Manufacturing
Corp	Corporation	Org	Organization
Emp	Employees	OTC	traded over the counter
Equip	Equipment	Par	Parent
Fin	Financial	PR	Public Relations
For	Foreign	Prd	Product
Furn	Furniture	Pres	President
Govt	Government	Prov	Province
Grp	Group	R&D	Research & Development
Inc	Incorporated	Rev	Revenue
Ind	Industry	Serv	Services
Intl	International	Sls	Sales
IR	Investor Relations	Sub	Subsidiary
IS	Information Systems	TOR	Toronto Stock Exchange
Ltd	Limited	Vch	Vice Chair
Mat	Materials	VP	Vice President

Section 1

Organizations Listed Alphabetically

Organizations Listed Alphabetically

Organization / Address / Phone	Descriptive Information	Revenue / ($ mil)	Assets / ($ mil)	Emp (thous)
A Mark Financial Corp 100 Wilshire Blvd Santa Monica, CA 90401 213-319-0200	Precious metals wholesaler. Type: Private Ind: Non-Bank Fin Grp: Financial Steven C Markoff, CEO	Rev: Assets: Emp:		1000 NA 1
AAR 1111 Nicholas Blvd Elk Grove, IL 60007 312-439-3939	Airline service company. Type: NYSE-AIR Ind: Business Service Grp: Business Service Ira Eichner, CEO	Rev: Assets: Emp:		384 329 4
Aaron Rents Inc 3001 N Fulton Drive NE Atlanta, GA 30363 404-231-0011	Rental company; office furniture. Type: OTC Ind: Appliances/Furn Grp: Manufacturing R Charles Loudermilk, CEO	Rev: Assets: Emp:		250 250 2
Aarque Companies Inc PO Box 310 Jamestown, NY 14702 716-664-6014	Metal fabricating. Type: Private Ind: Manufacturing Grp: Manufacturing R Quintus Anderson, CEO	Rev: Assets: Emp:		500 NA 3
Abbott Laboratories Inc One Abbott Park Road Abbott Park, IL 60064 312-937-6100	Prescription & over-the-counter drug company. Type: NYSE-ABT Ind: Drugs Grp: Consumer Service Robert A Schoellhorn, CEO Jack W Schuler, Pres James A Hanley, Tres Duane L Burnham, CFO Kenneth W Farmer, IS Robert S Janicki, R&D Richard B Hamilton, PR	Rev: Assets: Emp:		4937 4825 39
ABC Television Network Group Div 77 W 66th Street New York, NY 10023 212-456-7777	Television broadcasting & production division. Type: Private-Sub Par: Capital Cities--Amer Broadcasting Co In Ind: Publishing/Com Grp: Consumer Service John Sias, CEO	Rev: Assets: Emp:		NA NA NA
Abercrombie & Fitch Inc One Limited Parkway Columbus, OH 43230 614-479-6500	Operator of retail mens apparel retail stores. Type: Private-Sub Par: Limited Inc Ind: Retail/Merch Grp: Retail Thomas G Hopkins, CEO	Rev: Assets: Emp:		NA NA NA
Abitibi Price Ltd 2 First Canadian Place Toronto, ON M5X1A9 Can 416-369-6700	Forest products company; building materials. Type: TOR-ABY Ind: Paper/Forest Prd Grp: Basic Industries B K Koken, CEO Bernd K Koken, Chr John G Davis, VCh James Hone, Tres J Gordon Maw, CFO M Thomas Neill, R&D Allan Vatcher, Ops J Kenneth Stevens, VP William Wall, VP Sharon Paul, VP Michael Thompson, VP	Rev: Assets: Emp:		2809 2236 24
ACCO World Corp 22150 Sanders Road Northbrook, IL 60065 312-480-9700	Manufacturer of office products. Type: Private-Sub Par: American Brands Inc Ind: Publishing/Com Grp: Consumer Service Douglas K Chapman, CEO	Rev: Assets: Emp:		260 220 3
Ace Hardware Corp 2200 Kensington Court Oak Brook, IL 60521 312-990-6600	Operator of retailer hardware stores. Type: Private Ind: Retail/Merch Grp: Retail Roger Peterson, CEO	Rev: Assets: Emp:		1100 250 2
ACF Industries Inc 3301 Rider Trail S Earth City, MO 63045 314-344-4500	Manufacturer of railcars. Type: Private Ind: Railroad Grp: Business Service Carl C Icahn, CEO	Rev: Assets: Emp:		350 500 3
ACI Holdings Inc 1811 Quail Second Newport Beach, CA 92660 714-752-8576	Manufacturer of building materials; glass, wood. Type: Private-Sub-For Ind: Transport Grp: Business Service Hugh Davies, CEO	Rev: Assets: Emp:		500 250 3

Organizations Listed Alphabetically

Organization / Address / Phone	Descriptive Information	Revenue / ($ mil)	Assets / ($ mil)	Emp (thous)
Acklands Ltd 125 Higgins Avenue Winnipeg, MB R3B0B6 Can 204-956-0880	Operator of retail/wholesale automotive stores. Type: Private Ind: Automotive Grp: Manufacturing David Blank, CEO	Rev: Assets: Emp:	353 196 3	
Acme Markets Inc 124 N 15th Street Philadelphia, PA 19101 215-568-3000	Operator of retail food supermarkets. Type: Private-Sub Par: American Stores Co Ind: Retail/Food Grp: Retail Robert Neslund, CEO	Rev: Assets: Emp:	NA NA NA	
Acme Steel Co 13500 S Perry Avenue Chicago, IL 60627 312-849-2500	Metal forging & fabricating company. Type: OTC Ind: Manufacturing Grp: Manufacturing Brian W H Marsden, CEO	Rev: Assets: Emp:	350 250 3	
Acuson Corp 1220 Charleston Mountain View, CA 94043 415-969-9112	Manufacturer, medical imaging equipment. Type: NYSE-ACN Ind: Instruments Grp: High Tech Samuel H Maslak, CEO	Rev: Assets: Emp:	169 91 1	
Addington Resources Inc 9431 Route 60 Ashland, KY 41101 606-928-3433	Coal mining & minerals processing company. Type: OTC Ind: Metals/Mining Grp: Basic Industries C C Addington, CEO	Rev: Assets: Emp:	250 289 2	
Adia Services Inc 64 Willow Place Menlo Park, CA 94025 415-324-0696	Personnel agency; temporary & permanent placement. Type: OTC Ind: Business Service Grp: Business Service Yves J Paternot, CEO	Rev: Assets: Emp:	400 200 3	
ADM Milling Co 4550 W 109th Street Shawnee Mission, KS 66207 913-381-7400	Miller of flour & corn. Type: Private-Sub Par: Archer Daniels Midland Co Ind: Food Processing Grp: Food Processing H Hale, CEO	Rev: Assets: Emp:	NA NA NA	
ADT Inc One World Trade Center New York, NY 10048 215-558-1100	Security systems; guard service, electronic surveillance. Type: Private-Sub-For Ind: Electronics Grp: High Tech Raymond B Carey, CEO	Rev: Assets: Emp:	600 500 8	
Advance Publications 950 Fingerboard Road Staten Island, NY 10305 718-981-1234	Publisher of local newspapers. Type: Private Ind: Publishing/Com Grp: Consumer Service S I Newhouse Jr, CEO	Rev: Assets: Emp:	2500 NA 20	
Advanced Micro Devices Inc 901 Thompson Place PO Box 3453 Sunnyvale, CA 94088 408-732-2400	Manufacturer of integrated circuits. Type: NYSE Ind: Electronics Grp: High Tech W J Sanders III, CEO Anthony B Holbrook, Pres Richard Previte, CFO Joseph Proctor, IS Gene Conner, R&D Stephen Zelencik, Mkt Marvin Burkett, VP Stanley Winvick, VP	Rev: Assets: Emp:	1122 919 19	
Advest Inc 280 Turnbull Street Hartford, CT 06103 203-525-1421	Securities company. Type: Private Ind: Securities Grp: Financial Anthony LaCroix, CEO	Rev: Assets: Emp:	205 895 2	
Advo System Inc One Univac Lane Windsor, CT 06095 203-285-6100	Direct mail advertising company. Type: OTC Ind: Business Service Grp: Business Service Hugh R Beath, CEO	Rev: Assets: Emp:	500 300 6	
Aero Mexico SA 8390 NW 53rd Street Miami, FL 33166 305-591-1494	Airline company; national airline of Mexico. Type: Private-Sub-For Ind: Airline Grp: Consumer Service Gustavo Espinosa, CEO	Rev: Assets: Emp:	1650 NA 16	

Organizations Listed Alphabetically

Organization / Address / Phone	Descriptive Information	Revenue / ($ mil)	Assets / ($ mil)	Emp (thous)
Aero Products Inc 6101 Condor Drive Moorpark, CA 93021 805-864-5600	Manufacturer of electronic equipment. Type: Private-Sub Par: Litton Industries Inc Ind: Electronics Grp: High Tech Dudley Mahler, CEO	Rev: NA	Assets: NA	Emp: NA
Aerojet Inc 10300 N Torrey Pines Road La Jolla, CA 92037 619-455-8500	Aerospace technology company. Type: Private-Sub Par: GenCorp Inc Ind: Aerospace Grp: High Tech Roger Ramseier, CEO	Rev: NA	Assets: NA	Emp: NA
Aetna Life & Casualty Co 151 Farmington Avenue Hartford, CT 06156 203-273-0123	Life & casualty insurance company. Type: NYSE-AET Ind: Insurance Grp: Insurance James T Lynn, CEO Dean E Wolcott, Pres David Kocher, VCh Donald G Conrad, CFO Irwin Sitkin, IS Robert Nicholas, R&D Edward Jobe, VP John Donahue, VP Michael Mateja, VP Thomas Fay, IR Jason Wright, PR	Rev: 24296	Assets: 81415	Emp: 42
Aetna Life Insurance Co 145 King Street W Toronto, ON M5H3T7 Can 416-864-8000	Life insurance company. Type: Private-Sub-For Ind: Insurance Grp: Insurance Michael Stephen, CEO	Rev: 550	Assets: 1636	Emp: 1
Affiliated Foods Inc 100 Matt Gibbs Drive Keller, TX 76248 817-281-4417	Operator of retail food supermarkets. Type: Private Ind: Retail/Food Grp: Retail Don Smith, CEO	Rev: 1100	Assets: NA	Emp: 1
Affiliated Publications Inc 135 Morrissey Blvd Boston, MA 02107 617-929-2000	Newspaper & magazine publisher; radio station operator. Type: NYSE Ind: Publishing/Com Grp: Consumer Service William O Taylor, CEO John Giuggio, Pres Gerald Hobbs, VCh Arthur Kinsbury, CFO Robert Murphy, IS Catherine Henn, VP Richard Ockerbloom, VP Dan Orr, PR	Rev: 534	Assets: 425	Emp: 4
AFG Industries Inc 18200 Von Karman Avenue Suite700 Irvine, CA 92715 714-553-9026	Flat glass manufacturer. Type: Private Ind: Manufacturing Grp: Manufacturing R D Hubbard, CEO W G Basler, Pres G G Miller, CFO L C Kaufman, Sls	Rev: 500	Assets: 500	Emp: 3
AFL-CIO American Federation of Labor 815 Sixteenth Street NW Washington, DC 20006 202-637-5000	National labor union. Type: Membership Org Ind: Membership Org Grp: Govt & Non-Prof Lane Kirkland, CEO	Rev: 1000	Assets: NM	Emp: 5000
AG Processing Inc 11235 Davenport Street Omaha, NE 68154 402-334-8010	Food processing & distribution company. Type: Private Ind: Food Processing Grp: Food Processing Jim Lindsey, CEO James Yeates, Pres Kenneth Grubbe, CFO Anthony Porter, Mkt William C Lester, PR	Rev: 825	Assets: 250	Emp: 1
Agency Rent-A-Car Inc 30000 Aurora Road Solon, OH 44139 216-349-1000	Car rental company. Type: NASDAQ-AGNC Ind: Business Service Grp: Business Service Sam J Frankino, CEO Edward D Hammer, Tres Kenneth J Lorek, CFO Shirley J Koth, IS Louis H Rice, VP Edward D Paskel, VP Paul F Rochon, VP Timothy J Hlousek, VP Terry Holt, VP	Rev: 227	Assets: 351	Emp: 3
Agriculture Canada Sir John Carling Bldg 930 Carling Avenue Ottawa, ON K1A0C5 Can 613-995-8963	Federal government agency. Type: Federal Govt Ind: Federal Govt Grp: Govt & Non-Prof J J Noreau, CEO	Rev: 2040	Assets: NM	Emp: 11

Organizations Listed Alphabetically

Organization / Address / Phone	Descriptive Information	Revenue / ($ mil)	Assets / ($ mil)	Emp (thous)
Agropur Coop Agro Alimentaire Ltd 333 Lebeau Montreal, PQ H4N1S3 Can 514-332-2220	Agricultural cooperative; milk, dairy products. Type: Private-Coop Ind: Real Estate/Bldg Grp: Business Service Reynald Charest, CEO Michel Lemire, Pres R Claude Menard, CFO Andre Gauthier, VP	Rev: 695	Assets: 198	Emp: 2
Agway Inc PO Box 4933 Syracuse, NY 13221 315-477-7061	Manufacturer of farm supplies & petroleum products. Type: Private Ind: Manufacturing Grp: Manufacturing Ralph H Heffner, CEO Richard Call, VCh Robert Ryan, Tres Dennis J Lahood, IS Darwin Braund, R&D Margaret Hill, Mkt Richard K Arnold, IR Arthur J Fogerty, PR	Rev: 2894	Assets: 1497	Emp: 9
Ahmanson, H F & Co (Home Savings of Am) 3731 Wilshire Blvd Los Angeles, CA 90010 213-487-4277	Thrift institution. Type: NYSE-AHM Ind: Savings & Loan Grp: Financial Richard H Deihl, CEO Mario J Antoci, Pres Robert DeKruif, VCh R Calvin Wallace, CFO Warren L Androus, IS Charles W Seale, Mkt Charles Reed, VP Robert P Barbarwitz, VP Gayle Sweetland, IR	Rev: 3315	Assets: 40258	Emp: 9
Aid Association for Lutherans Inc 4321 N Ballard Road Appleton, WI 54919 414-734-5721	Fraternal life insurance society. Type: Private Ind: Insurance Grp: Insurance Richard L Gunderson, CEO	Rev: 1618	Assets: 6246	Emp: 1
Air Canada Ltd 500 Rene Levesque Blvd Montreal, PQ H2Z1X5 Can 514-879-7000	Worldwide airline. Type: TOR Ind: Airline Grp: Consumer Service Claude I Taylor, CEO Pierre Jeannniot, Pres L Desrochers, VCh W J Reid, CFO M E Fournier, Sls J Bourgeault, Mkt B Aubin, Ops W Wozniuk, VP G MacCormack, VP D Groom, VP L Cameron, VP B Gillies, VP	Rev: 2912	Assets: 2921	Emp: 24
Air Express International 120 Tokeneke Road Darien, CT 06820 203-655-7900	Air freight transport company. Type: ASE-AEX Ind: Transport Grp: Business Service Hendrik Hartong, CEO Guenter Rohrmann, Pres William E Reap, CFO Colin Cook, IS Robert J O'Connell, Sls Eileen Fetchick, PR	Rev: 500	Assets: 200	Emp: 3
Air Products & Chemicals Inc PO Box 538 Allentown, PA 18105 215-481-4911	Producer of industrial gases. Type: NYSE-APD Ind: Chemicals Grp: Basic Industries Dexter F Baker, CEO Leon C Holt, Pres Gerald A White, CFO Peter Mather, IS Brian M Rushton, R&D Robert Zamboldi, Sls Arnold Kaplan, VP Peter mather, VP Donald Shire, VP Richard Gray, VP W J Roberts, PR	Rev: 2432	Assets: 2999	Emp: 22
Airborne Freight Corp 3101 Western Avenue Seattle, WA 98121 206-285-4600	Air freight company. Type: NYSE-ABF Ind: Transport Grp: Business Service Robert S Cline, CEO Robert G Brazier, Pres Roy C Liljebeck, CFO David Billings, IS Raymond Barry, R&D Frank C Steele, Sls Kent Freudenberger, Mkt John Snyder, IR	Rev: 768	Assets: 329	Emp: 7
Akron, City of City Hall 166 S High Street Akron, OH 44308 216-375-2345	City government. Type: City Govt Ind: Local Govt Grp: Govt & Non-Prof D L Plusquellic, CEO	Rev: 250	Assets: NM	Emp: 3
AL Laboratories Inc One Executive Drive Fort Lee, NJ 07024 201-947-7774	Manufacturer & retailer, antibiotics & animal feed products. Type: NYSE Ind: Drugs Grp: Consumer Service E Sissener, CEO	Rev: 250	Assets: 200	Emp: 1
Alabama Power Co 600 N 18th Street Birmingham, AL 35291 205-250-1000	Electric power utility company. Type: Private-Sub Par: Southern Co Ind: Utility Grp: Utilities Joseph Farley, CEO	Rev: NA	Assets: NA	Emp: NA

Organizations Listed Alphabetically

Organization / Address / Phone	Descriptive Information	Revenue / ($ mil)	Assets / ($ mil)	Emp (thous)
Alabama, State of State Capitol Montgomery, AL 36136 205-261-2500	State government. Type: State Govt Ind: State/Prov Govt Grp: Govt & Non-Prof Guy Hunt, CEO	Rev: 8068	Assets: NM	Emp: 80
Alameda County 1221 Oak Street Oakland, CA 94612 415-272-6691	County government. Type: County Govt Ind: Local Govt Grp: Govt & Non-Prof Edward R Campbell, CEO	Rev: 950	Assets: NM	Emp: 6
Alamo Rent-a-Car Inc 110 SE Sixth Street Fort Lauderdale, FL 33301 305-522-0000	Nationwide automobile rental company. Type: Private Ind: Consumer Service Grp: Consumer Service Michael S Egan, CEO	Rev: 400	Assets: NA	Emp: 4
Alaska Air Group Inc 19300 S Pacific PO Box 68947 Seattle, WA 98168 206-433-3200	Regional airline. Type: NYSE-ALK Ind: Airline Grp: Consumer Service Bruce R Kennedy, CEO J Ray Vingo, CFO Steven G Hamilton, VP Marjorie Laws, VP Paul Nishimura, VP Louis G Cancelmi, PR	Rev: 814	Assets: 730	Emp: 6
Alaska, State of State Capitol Juneau, AK 99811 907-465-2111	State government. Type: State Govt Ind: State/Prov Govt Grp: Govt & Non-Prof Steve Cowper, CEO	Rev: 6726	Assets: NM	Emp: 26
Albany International Corp 1370 Broadway Menands, NY 12201 518-445-2200	Manufacturer of apparel products. Type: Private Ind: Apparel/Textiles Grp: Consumer Prd Frank McKone, CEO	Rev: 275	Assets: NA	Emp: 3
Alberici, J S Construction Co Inc 2150 Kienlen Avenue St Louis, MO 63121 314-261-2611	Heavy construction & commercial development company. Type: Private Ind: Real Estate/Bldg Grp: Business Service Raymond F Pieper, CEO	Rev: 500	Assets: NA	Emp: 2
Alberta & Southern Gas Co 425 1st Street SW Calgary, AB T2P3L8 Can 403-260-9911	Natural gas distribution company. Type: TOR Ind: Energy Grp: Basic Industries John E Gouldie, CEO	Rev: 932	Assets: 473	Emp: 1
Alberta Energy Co 10707 100th Avenue Edmonton, AB T5J3M1 Can 403-423-8333	Oil & gas exploration & production company. Type: TOR Ind: Energy Grp: Basic Industries David E Mitchell, CEO	Rev: 409	Assets: 1641	Emp: 1
Alberta Government Telephone Co 10020 100 Street Edmonton, AB T5J0N5 Can 403-425-2110	Telephone utility company; provincial government owned. Type: Prov Govt Ind: Telecom Grp: High Tech H Hobbs, CEO	Rev: 911	Assets: 2006	Emp: 11
Alberta Mortgage & Housing Corp 9405 50th Street Edmonton, AB T6B2T4 Can 403-468-3535	Consumer mortgage banker; provincial agency. Type: Prov Govt Ind: Non-Bank Fin Grp: Financial Joseph Engelman, CEO	Rev: 248	Assets: 3346	Emp: 1
Alberta Natural Gas Co 425 1st Street SW Calgary, AB T2P3L8 Can 403-260-9911	Natural gas distribution company. Type: Private-Sub-ForPar: Alberta & Southern Gas Co Ind: Energy Grp: Basic Industries J Gouldie, CEO	Rev: 298	Assets: 340	Emp: 2
Alberta Power Ltd 10035 105th Street Edmonton, AB T5J2V6 Can 403-420-5035	Electric power utility company. Type: Private-Sub Par: Atco Ltd Ind: Utility Grp: Utilities R Southern, CEO	Rev: 340	Assets: 1275	Emp: 2

Organizations Listed Alphabetically

Organization / Address / Phone	Descriptive Information	Revenue / ($ mil)	Assets / ($ mil)	Emp (thous)

Alberta Wheat Pool Ltd
505 2nd Street SW
Calgary, AB T2P2P5 Can
403-290-4910

Agricultural cooperative; wheat.
Type: Govt Corp
Ind: Food Processing   Grp: Food Processing
J W Madill, CEO   T Volk, CFO   G Dewar, Ops

Rev: 788
Assets: 1497
Emp: 2

Alberta, The University of
Administrative Bldg
Edmonton, AB T6G2E5 Can
403-432-3111

Major educational institution; university.
Type: University
Ind: University   Grp: Govt & Non-Prof
M Horowitz, CEO

Rev: 234
Assets: NM
Emp: 29

Alberto Culver Co
2525 Armitage Avenue
Melrose Park, IL 60160
312-450-3000

Manufacturer of personal health care products.
Type: NYSE
Ind: Personal Care   Grp: Consumer Prd
Leonard H Lavin, CEO   William J Cernugel, CFO   Nicholas Z Malham, IS
Thomas J Pallone, R&D   Timothy Croasdaile, IR

Rev: 605
Assets: 303
Emp: 5

Albertson's Inc
250 Parkcenter Blvd PO Box 20
Boise, ID 83726
208-385-6200

Supermarket retailing company.
Type: NYSE-ABS
Ind: Retail/Food   Grp: Retail
Warren E McCain, CEO   David I Connelly, Tres   A Craig Olsen, CFO
C Joyce Clint, IS   Pat Steele, R&D   Wally Jordan, Sls
James Reynolds, Mkt   Donald D Palmer, VP   Alec R Groth, VP
Gary G Michael, PR

Rev: 6773
Assets: 1591
Emp: 50

Albrecht, Fred W Grocery Co Inc
2700 Gilchrist
Akron, OH 44305
216-733-2861

Operator of retail food stores.
Type: Private
Ind: Retail/Food   Grp: Retail
Steven Albrecht, CEO

Rev: 275
Assets: NA
Emp: 3

Albuquerque, City of
City Hall
Albuquerque, NM 87103
505-768-3000

City government.
Type: City Govt
Ind: Local Govt   Grp: Govt & Non-Prof
Ken Schultz, CEO

Rev: 382
Assets: NM
Emp: 5

ALCAN Aluminum Co of Canada Ltd
1188 Sherbooke Street W
Montreal, PQ H3A3G2 Can
514-848-8000

Integrated manufacturer of aluminum.
Type: NYSE
Ind: Metals/Mining   Grp: Basic Industries
David M Culver, CEO   David Morton, Pres   Allan Hodgson, CFO
Ihor Suchoversky, IS   John Kelly, R&D   Roger Maggs, Mkt
Suresh Thadhani, VP   Maurice Taylor, VP   P K Pal, VP

Rev: 9165
Assets: 9153
Emp: 67

Alcatel Business Systems Inc
1623 Buckeye Drive
Milpitas, CA 95035
800-556-1234

Computer component manufacturer; maintenance, leasing.
Type: Private-Sub-For
Ind: Comput/Off Equip   Grp: High Tech
Donald E Lemon, CEO

Rev: 500
Assets: NA
Emp: 5

Alco Industries Inc
Route 363 & Betzwood Bridge
Valley Forge, PA 19482
215-666-0930

Diversified manufacturing company.
Type: OTC-AAHS
Ind: Manufacturing   Grp: Manufacturing
J H Kennedy, CEO   John F McNamara, Pres   Michael F Chapman, IS
Robert L Aitchison, Mkt   David B Kirkland, PR

Rev: 1732
Assets: 468
Emp: 6

Alco Standard Corp
825 Duportail Road PO Box 834
Valley Forge, PA 19087
215-296-8000

Distributor of paper, office equipment & food products.
Type: NYSE-ASN
Ind: Conglomerate   Grp: Manufacturing
Ray B Mundt, CEO   Richard C Gozon, Pres   William F Drake, VCh
O Gordon Brewer Jr, CFO   Maunallen Gregory, IS   Tinkham Veale, VP
George R Shelley, VP   Edward N Patrone, VP   David B Kirkland, PR

Rev: 3817
Assets: 1399
Emp: 16

Alden, John Financial Corp
7300 Corporate Center
Miami, FL 33126
305-470-3100

Property & casualty insurance company.
Type: Private
Ind: Insurance   Grp: Insurance
Glendon E Johnson, CEO

Rev: 1500
Assets: NA
Emp: 3

Organizations Listed Alphabetically

Organization / Address / Phone	Descriptive Information	Revenue / Assets / Emp ($ mil) ($ mil) (thous)		

Alexander & Alexander Service Inc
1211 Avenue of the Americas
New York, NY 10036
212-840-8500

Diversified financial services company.
Type: NYSE-AAL
Ind: Non-Bank Fin   Grp: Financial
Tinsley H Irvin, CEO   James D Berry, Pres   Kenneth Black, VCh
Paul E Rohner, CFO   Peter Densen, Mkt   William Wilson, VP
Ron Forest, VP   Peter Godsoe, VP   Robert H Moore, PR

Rev: 1228
Assets: 2635
Emp: 16

Alexander & Baldwin Inc
822 Bishop Street
Honolulu, HI 96801
808-525-6611

Ocean transport & real estate company.
Type: NASDAQ-ALEX
Ind: Business Service   Grp: Business Service
R J Pfeiffer, CEO   John C Couch, Pres   Frederick Fleischmann, VCh
G S Holaday, CFO   Don Fujimoto, IS   Judith Williams, R&D
John B Kelley, Mkt   R Dougal Crowe, VP   S Tim Soggin, VP
Howard Nakamura, VP   Marsha Petersen, IR   E S N Wong, PR

Rev: 702
Assets: 1070
Emp: 3

Alexander's Inc
500 Seventh Avenue
New York, NY 10018
212-869-0368

Department store retailing company.
Type: NYSE-ALX
Ind: Retail/Merch   Grp: Retail
Robin L Farkas, CEO

Rev: 700
Assets: NA
Emp: 9

Algoma Steel Ltd
503 Queen Street
Sault Ste Marie, ON P6A5P2 Can
705-945-2788

Manufacturer of steel products.
Type: Private-Sub   Par: Canadian Pacific Ltd
Ind: Steel   Grp: Basic Industries
John Macnamara, CEO   Peter M Nixon, Chr   Paul Finley, VCh
James Melville, Tres   Ross Cutmore, CFO   Paul Paciocco, R&D
Gerry Hudson, Sls   William Reed, Ops   Robert Turbin, VP
Gary Lucenti, VP

Rev: 1183
Assets: 1231
Emp: 11

Algonquin Gas Transmission Co
1284 Soldiers Field Road
Boston, MA 02173
617-254-4050

Natural gas & petroleum pipeline transmission.
Type: Private-Sub   Par: Dover Corp
Ind: Energy   Grp: Basic Industries
George Mazenec, CEO

Rev: NA
Assets: NA
Emp: NA

Alleco Inc
Allegheny Circle
Hyattsville, MD 20781
301-341-6000

Beverage bottler & distribution.
Type: OTC
Ind: Beverage   Grp: Food Processing
Morton M Lapides, CEO   Frank Silvestro, CFO   Liz Wright, IR
James A Hart, PR

Rev: 1000
Assets: 600
Emp: 4

Allegheny & Western Energy
1600 Kanawha Valley Bldg
Charleston, WV 25301
304-343-4327

Oil & natural gas production company.
Type: OTC
Ind: Energy   Grp: Basic Industries
John G McMillan, CEO

Rev: 250
Assets: 250
Emp: 1

Allegheny Corp
Park Avenue Plaza
New York, NY 10055
212-752-1356

Title, casualty & property insurance company.
Type: NYSE-Y
Ind: Non-Bank Fin   Grp: Financial
F M Kirby, CEO   John J Burns, Pres   John E Conway, CFO
David Cuming, VP   Theodore Somerville, VP   Pter Sismondo, VP

Rev: 1006
Assets: 1630
Emp: 9

Allegheny County Government
119 Courthouse Street
Pittsburgh, PA 15219
412-355-6940

County government.
Type: County Govt
Ind: Local Govt   Grp: Govt & Non-Prof
Tom Forester, CEO

Rev: 925
Assets: NM
Emp: 8

Allegheny International Inc
Two Oliver Plaza PO Box 456
Pittsburgh, PA 15230
412-562-4000

Manufacturer of household appliances & furniture.
Type: NYSE-AG
Ind: Appliances/Furn   Grp: Manufacturing
Oliver S Travers, CEO   Thomas Albani, Pres   James T Dougherty, VCh
Samuel H Iapalucci, CFO   Bernie Campbell, IS   Herbert Graves, Ops
K Wayne Long, VP   Edward Romanoff, PR

Rev: 968
Assets: 841
Emp: 12

Allegheny Ludlum Steel Corp
1000 Six PPG Plaza
Pittsburgh, PA 15222
412-394-2800

Specialty steel company.
Type: Private
Ind: Steel   Grp: Basic Industries
Richard P Simmons, CEO   Robert P Bozzone, Pres   James Murdy, CFO
Robert Rutherford, Mkt   Burt Delano, IR   Glen Swanson, PR

Rev: 1100
Assets: NA
Emp: 5

Organizations Listed Alphabetically

Organization / Address / Phone	Descriptive Information	Revenue / ($ mil)	Assets / ($ mil)	Emp (thous)
Allegheny Power System Inc 320 Park Avenue New York, NY 10022 212-752-2121	Electric utility company. Type: NYSE-AYP Ind: Utility Grp: Utilities Klaus Bergman, CEO Frank Eppich, VCh Nancy Campbell, Tres Alan J Noia, CFO H R McNutt, IS Marc Jansen, R&D Carlon D Kramer, VP Peter J Skrgic, VP Eileen Beck, VP Joseph L Bannon, PR	Rev: 2171	Assets: 1031	Emp: 6
Allen & Co Inc 711 Fifth Avenue New York, NY 10022 212-832-8000	Investment company. Type: Private Ind: Securities Grp: Financial Herbert A Allen, CEO	Rev: 275	Assets: 2200	Emp: 1
Allen Group Inc 534 Broad Hollow Road Melville, NY 11747 516-293-5500	Manufacturer of automobile parts. Type: NYSE-ALN Ind: Instruments Grp: High Tech Philip W Colburn, CEO	Rev: 344	Assets: 328	Emp: 5
Allergan Inc 2525 Dupont Drive Irvine, CA 92715 714-752-4500	Manufacturer of prescription & non-prescription drugs. Type: Private-Sub Par: Smithkline Beckman Corp Ind: Drugs Grp: Consumer Service William Shepherd, CEO	Rev: NA	Assets: NA	Emp: NA
Alliance Mutual Funds Inc 140 Broadway New York, NY 10005 800-221-5672	Mutual fund investment company. Type: Private Ind: Non-Bank Fin Grp: Financial George Hrabrosky, CEO	Rev: 300	Assets: 11000	Emp: 1
Alliance Ro-Na Home Inc 34 Henry Street St Jacobs, ON N0B2N0 Can 519-664-2252	Home hardware manufacturer. Type: Private-Sub-For Ind: Building Mat Grp: Basic Industries Andre Dion, CEO	Rev: 672	Assets: 170	Emp: 8
Allied Products Corp 10 S Riverside Chicago, IL 60606 312-454-1020	Manufacturer of equipment; farm machinery, presses. Type: NYSE-ADP Ind: Manufacturing Grp: Manufacturing S S Sherman, CEO Richard A Drexler, Chr Charles W Lunger, Pres Kenneth B Light, VCh James J Hayden, CFO Carolyn E Williams, R&D Martin A German, Mkt Robert Fleck, VP Bob Middlebrooks, VP Kenneth B Light, IR	Rev: 578	Assets: 441	Emp: 5
Allied Signal Aerospace Div 1000 Wilson Blvd Arlington, VA 22209 703-276-2000	Mfr of auxiliary power units, environmental cntl systems. Type: Private-Sub Par: Allied Signal Inc Ind: Aerospace Grp: High Tech Robert L Kirk, CEO	Rev: NA	Assets: NA	Emp: NA
Allied Signal Automotive Div 20650 Civic Center Southfield, MI 48086 313-827-5000	Manufacturer of automotive parts & components. Type: Private-Sub Par: Allied Signal Inc Ind: Automotive Grp: Manufacturing John Day, CEO	Rev: NA	Assets: NA	Emp: NA
Allied Signal Canada Inc 48 Clair Avenue W Mississauga, ON L4V3A3 Can 416-967-7211	Manufacturer of electronic & automotive parts. Type: Private-Sub-For Ind: Automotive Grp: Manufacturing William Tate, CEO	Rev: 565	Assets: 425	Emp: 5
Allied Signal Inc PO Box 4000R Morristown, NJ 07960 713-224-6611	Diversified aerospace & automobile component manufacturer. Type: NYSE-ALD Ind: Aerospace Grp: High Tech Edward L Hennessy, CEO Alan Belzer, Pres Robert L Kirk, VCh John W Barter, CFO Mary L Good, IS L J Colby Jr, R&D Roy Ekron, Sls Nicholas Cameron, Ops John B Fallon, VP Edward Callahan, VP G Peter D'Aloia, VP Dennis Signorovitch, IR David G Powell, PR	Rev: 11909	Assets: 10005	Emp: 110

Organizations Listed Alphabetically

Organization / Address / Phone	Descriptive Information	Revenue / ($ mil)	Assets / ($ mil)	Emp (thous)
Allied Stores Corp 1114 Avenue of the Americas New York, NY 10036 212-764-2000	Operator of retail department stores. Type: Private-Sub-For Ind: Retail/Merch Grp: Retail Robert Campeau, CEO Harold Leppo, Pres James Bloise, CFO Harold Leppo, Mkt Sandy Browning, PR	Rev: 4000	Assets: 5000	Emp: 25
Allied Van Lines Inc 2120 S 25th Street Broadview, IL 60153 312-681-8000	Household goods moving company. Type: Private Ind: Transport Grp: Business Service Roger Payton, CEO William J Welty, CFO Chuck Werner, IS Pat Bull, R&D Larry L Stein, Mkt Laura Ganson, PR	Rev: 600	Assets: 200	Emp: 5
Alling & Cory Corp 25 Verona Street Rochester, NY 14608 716-454-1880	Manufacturer of paper products. Type: Private Ind: Paper/Forest Prd Grp: Basic Industries Samuel T Hubbard, CEO	Rev: 350	Assets: NA	Emp: 1
Allis Chalmers Corp 1205 S 70th Street West Allis, WI 53214 414-475-2000	Business services; equipment repair. Type: NYSE Ind: Equipment Grp: Manufacturing John T Grigsby, CEO Wendell F Bueche, Chr Ronald J Burns, CFO Dennis Thisted, PR	Rev: 401	Assets: 10	Emp: 1
Allstate Insurance Co Canada 10 Allstate Parkway Markham, ON L3R 5P8 Can 416-477-6900	Property & casualty insurance company. Type: Private-Sub-For Ind: Insurance Grp: Insurance Terry Keleher, CEO	Rev: 320	Assets: 565	Emp: 2
Allstate Life Insurance Co Allstate Plaza S Northbrook, IL 60062 312-291-5000	Life insurance company. Type: Private-Sub Par: Sears Roebuck & Co Ind: Insurance Grp: Insurance Robert L Roberts, CEO Herbert E Lister, Chr Lawrence Williford, IR June Kramer, PR	Rev: 3354	Assets: 5972	Emp: 3
Alltel Corp 100 Executive Parkway Hudson, OH 44236 216-650-7000	Telephone utility company. Type: NYSE-AT Ind: Telecom Grp: High Tech Weldon W Case, CEO Joe T Ford, Chr Charles W Miller, VCh Max E Bobbitt, CFO Tom Orsini, R&D John T Dunbar, Ops George McConnaughey, VP Joseph Pordan, VP Dennis Ferra, VP	Rev: 1068	Assets: 2153	Emp: 8
Almac's Corp 1 Noyes Street E East Providence, RI 02916 401-438-2700	Operator of retail food stores. Type: Private Ind: Retail/Food Grp: Retail A W Pike, CEO	Rev: 500	Assets: NA	Emp: 2
Alpha Beta Co 777 S Harbor Blvd La Habra, CA 90631 714-738-2000	Operator of retail drugstores. Type: Private-Sub Par: American Stores Co Ind: Retail/Food Grp: Retail Donald Kohler, CEO	Rev: NA	Assets: NA	Emp: NA
Alpha Industries Inc 20 Sylvan Road Woburn, MA 01801 617-935-5150	Electronic component manufacturer. Type: ASE-BSE Ind: Electronics Grp: High Tech George S Kariotis, CEO	Rev: 200	Assets: 150	Emp: 2
Altus Bank 851 S Beltline Highway Mobile, AL 36606 205-473-0500	Thrift institution. Type: Private Ind: Savings & Loan Grp: Financial Chris C DeLaney, CEO	Rev: 274	Assets: 2774	Emp: 2
Alumax Inc 400 S El Camino San Mateo, CA 94402 415-348-3400	Manufacturer of aluminum products. Type: Private Ind: Metals/Mining Grp: Basic Industries Paul E Drack, CEO	Rev: 2200	Assets: 1800	Emp: 11

Organizations Listed Alphabetically

Organization / Address / Phone	Descriptive Information	Revenue / Assets / Emp ($ mil) ($ mil) (thous)		

Aluminum Co of America
1501 Alcoa Bldg
Pittsburgh, PA 15219
412-553-4545

Manufacturer of aluminum products.
Type: NYSE
Ind: Metals/Mining   Grp: Basic Industries
Paul H O'Neill, CEO   C Fred Fetterolf, Pres   James W Wirth, CFO
Joseph Muscari, IS   P Bridenbaugh, R&D   Doanld R Whitlow, VP
Vincent Scorsone, VP   Charles Ligon, VP   Ronald Hoffman, VP
Richard Fisher, VP   F Worth Hobbs, PR

Rev: 9795
Assets: 10538
Emp: 59

Alza Corp
950 Page Mill Road
Palo Alto, CA 94303
415-494-5222

Manufacturer of pharmaceutical products.
Type: ASE-AZA
Ind: Business Service   Grp: Business Service
Alejandro Zaffaroni, CEO

Rev: 84
Assets: 262
Emp: 1

AM International Inc
333 W Wacker Drive Suite 900
Chicago, IL 60606
312-558-1966

Office equipment company; duplicating, graphics.
Type: NYSE-AM
Ind: Business Service   Grp: Business Service
Merle H Banta, CEO   James P Corcoran, Tres   John H Shuey, CFO
R Troy Huggins, R&D   Marion G Durk, PR

Rev: 821
Assets: 777
Emp: 8

Amalgamated Clothing & Textile Workers
15 Union Square
New York, NY 10003
212-242-0700

National labor union.
Type: Membership Org
Ind: Membership Org   Grp: Govt & Non-Prof
Jack Sheinkman, CEO

Rev: 250
Assets: NM
Emp: 350

Amalgamated Sugar Co
First Security Bank Bldg
Ogden, UT 84401
801-399-3431

Producer of sugar.
Type: Private-Sub   Par: Valhi Corp
Ind: Food Processing   Grp: Food Processing
Harold C Simmons, CEO

Rev: 440
Assets: 750
Emp: 5

Amana Refrigeration Inc
Highway 220
Amana, IA 52204
319-622-5511

Refrigerator manufacturer & distributor.
Type: Private-Sub   Par: Raytheon Co
Ind: Appliances/Furn   Grp: Manufacturing
Henry Meyer, CEO

Rev: NA
Assets: NA
Emp: NA

AMAX Coal Industries Inc
Capital Center 251 N Illinois Street
Indianapolis, IN 46206
317-266-1500

Mining & minerals distribution company; coal.
Type: Private-Sub   Par: AMAX Inc
Ind: Metals/Mining   Grp: Basic Industries
Douglas Ashby, CEO

Rev: NA
Assets: NA
Emp: NA

AMAX Inc
200 Park Avenue
New York, NY 10166
212-856-4200

Mining & metals production company.
Type: NYSE
Ind: Metals/Mining   Grp: Basic Industries
Allen Born, CEO   Thomas A McKeever, VCh   Stephen C Knup, CFO
Joseph Rosio, IS   Stephen M Johnson, Mkt   Richard Kalaher, VP
M Badler, PR

Rev: 3944
Assets: 4076
Emp: 20

AmBase Corp (Home Group Inc)
59 Maiden Lane
New York, NY 10038
212-530-6800

Life & casualty insurance.
Type: NYSE-HME
Ind: Insurance   Grp: Insurance
Marshall Manley, CEO   Marshall Manley, Chr   Eben Pyne, VCh
Jack Plaxe, CFO   Hiram Moody, VP   Richard Braun, VP
Robert L Woodrum, PR

Rev: 2978
Assets: 13302
Emp: 8

AMC Entertainment Inc
106 W 14th Street
Kansas City, MO 64105
816-221-4000

Entertainment company; operator of movie theatres.
Type: ASE-AEN
Ind: Leisure Time   Grp: Consumer Service
Stanley H Durwood, CEO

Rev: 318
Assets: 300
Emp: 6

AMCA (Amer Can of Canada) Intl Ltd
1 International Blvd
Rexdale, ON M9W1A1 Can
416-432-2151

Manufacturer of fabricated building parts.
Type: Private-Sub   Par: Canadian Pacific Ltd
Ind: Packaging   Grp: Manufacturing
W Holland, CEO

Rev: 893
Assets: NA
Emp: 10

Amcast Industrial Corp
3931 S Dixie Avenue
Dayton, OH 45439
513-298-5251

Manufacturer of metal products; steel, aluminum.
Type: NYSE-AIZ
Ind: Manufacturing   Grp: Manufacturing
L W Ladehoff, CEO

Rev: 264
Assets: 200
Emp: 2

Organization / Address / Phone	Descriptive Information	Revenue / ($ mil)	Assets / ($ mil)	Emp (thous)
Amcena Inc 1114 Avenue of the Americas New York, NY 10036 212-391-4141	Operator of retail stores. Type: Private Ind: Retail/Merch Grp: Retail not available, CEO	Rev: Assets: Emp:	550 NA 5	
Amdahl Corp 1250 E Arques Avenue Sunnyvale, CA 94088 408-746-6000	Mainframe computer manufacturer. Type: ASE Ind: Comput/Off Equip Grp: High Tech John C Lewis, CEO John C Lewis, Chr E Joseph Zemke, Pres Eugene White, VCh Edward Thompson, CFO L Philip Lemay, IS Michael Clements, R&D E Ted Springstead, Mkt Bruce Beebe, VP William O'Connell, VP Anthony Pozos, VP R A Whitcomb, PR	Rev: Assets: Emp:	1802 1931 11	
AMDURA Corp(American Hoist & Derrick) 1800 Amhoist Tower 345 St Peter Street St Paul, MN 55102 612-293-4567	Manufacturer of industrial equipment. Type: NYSE-AHO Ind: Manufacturing Grp: Manufacturing Robert H Nassau, CEO	Rev: Assets: Emp:	258 205 2	
Amerada Hess Corp 1185 Avenue of the Americas New York, NY 10036 212-997-8500	International petroleum producer & marketer. Type: NYSE-AHC Ind: Energy Grp: Basic Industries Leon Hess, CEO Robert F Wright, Pres John B Hess, VCh G A Jamin, Tres H W McCollum, CFO Ronn Ellis, IS A A Bernstein, R&D M B Bianchi, Sls J B Collins, Mkt W Laidlaw, Ops R Stafford, VP Carl Tursi, PR	Rev: Assets: Emp:	4264 5372 8	
Amerco (U-Haul) Inc 2727 N Central Avenue Phoenix, AZ 85036 602-263-6011	U-haul vehicle rental. Type: Private Ind: Business Service Grp: Business Service Edward J Shoen, CEO	Rev: Assets: Emp:	750 NA 15	
America West Airlines Inc 4000 E Sky Harbor Blvd Phoenix, AZ 85034 602-894-0800	Regional airline. Type: NASDAQ-AWAL Ind: Airline Grp: Consumer Service Edward R Beauvais, CEO Michael J Conway, Pres A E Frei, CFO Jorge Franco, IS Leroy Paulson, R&D Mark J Coleman, Mkt Don Monteath, Ops Peter Otradovec, VP James Carr, VP Daphne Dicino, PR	Rev: Assets: Emp:	743 639 5	
American Brands Inc 1700 E Putnam Avenue PO Box 811 Old Greenwich, CT 06870 203-698-5000	Tobacco & consumer products. Type: NYSE-AMB Ind: Tobacco Grp: Food Processing William J Alley, CEO Thomas C Hays, Pres Paul Randour, VCh Arnold Henson, CFO Sebastian M Cicitta, IS Robert Rukeyser, Ops Robert Austin, VP Charles Mullen, VP Peter Reed, VP Dudley Bauerlein, VP Francis Bianca, VP Daniel Conforti, PR	Rev: Assets: Emp:	11980 12201 85	
American Breco Inc 1875 Century Park E Los Angeles, CA 90067 213-553-1009	Supermarkets, real estate & ranching. Type: Private Ind: Real Estate/Bldg Grp: Business Service Alfredo Brener, CEO	Rev: Assets: Emp:	750 NA 5	
American Building Maintenance Ind Inc 333 Fell Street San Francisco, CA 94102 415-864-5150	Commercial cleaning service company. Type: NYSE-ABM Ind: Business Service Grp: Business Service R David Anacker, CEO William C Banner, VCh David Hebble, CFO L Gayle Hutt, R&D Tony Vernava, Sls Theodore Rosenberg, VP Sherrill Sipes, VP John F Egan, VP	Rev: Assets: Emp:	582 172 32	
American Business Products Inc 2100 River Edge Parkway Suite 1200 Atlanta, GA 30328 404-953-8300	Manufacturer of office supplies. Type: NYSE-ABP Ind: Paper/Forest Prd Grp: Basic Industries W J Biggers, CEO Thomas R Carmody, Chr A J Wahn, Tres W C Downer, CFO Bobby Rogers, IS R A LeFeber, VP Dawn M Gray, VP	Rev: Assets: Emp:	358 152 4	

14

Organizations Listed Alphabetically

Organization / Address / Phone	Descriptive Information	Revenue / Assets / Emp ($ mil) ($ mil) (thous)		

American Capital Corp
2800 Post Oak Blvd
Houston, TX 77056
713-993-0500

Financial services & holding company.
Type: NYSE-ACA
Ind: Non-Bank Fin   Grp: Financial
George F Reed, CEO   Jack D Burstein, Chr   Steven R Cook, CFO

Rev: 99
Assets: 71
Emp: 1

American Carriers Inc
9393 W 110th Street
Overland Park, KS 66210
913-451-2811

Nationwide truck transport company.
Type: OTC
Ind: Transport   Grp: Business Service
Leon H Robertson, CEO   Burl G Cott, CFO   Gary Bailey, IS
Leo Blumenauer, Mkt   Linda Bastian, PR

Rev: 475
Assets: 250
Emp: 5

American Cast Iron Pipe Inc
2930 16th Street N
Birmingham, AL 35202
205-325-7701

Manufacturer of industrial products; pipe, tubing.
Type: Private
Ind: Manufacturing   Grp: Manufacturing
Paul Green, CEO

Rev: 275
Assets: NA
Emp: 2

American Cellular Communications Inc
1344 Capital Towers
Jackson, MS 39201
601-353-1300

Cellular phone sales & distribution.
Type: Private-Sub   Par: BellSouth Corp
Ind: Telecom   Grp: High Tech
Carroll McHenry, CEO

Rev: NA
Assets: NA
Emp: NA

American Continental Corp
2735 E Camelback Road
Phoenix, AZ 85106
602-957-7170

Thrift institution holding company.
Type: OTC
Ind: Savings & Loan   Grp: Financial
Charles H Keating, CEO   Judy Wisher, Pres   Andrew Ligget, CFO
Rob Symes, IS   Lori Fowler, PR

Rev: 800
Assets: 5000
Emp: 3

American Crystal Sugar Co
101 N Third Street
Moorhead, MN 56560
218-236-4400

Producer & distributor of packaged foods; sugar.
Type: Private
Ind: Food Processing   Grp: Food Processing
Ronald Hays, CEO

Rev: 550
Assets: NA
Emp: 2

American Cyanamid Co
One Cyanamid Plaza
Wayne, NJ 07470
201-831-2000

Pharmaceutical company.
Type: NYSE-ACY
Ind: Chemicals   Grp: Basic Industries
George J Sella, CEO   William A Liffers, Pres   Frank Atlee, VCh
Richard L Martino, CFO   Edward A Lustig, IS   Albert Costello, R&D
George Bywater, Sls   Frederick Armstrong, Mkt   W Perry Brown, Ops
Donald Droste, VP   M Artin Friedman, VP   Richard Martino, VP
Terence D Martin, VP   Joseph C Calitri, PR

Rev: 4592
Assets: 4593
Emp: 36

American Drug Stores Inc
1818 Swift Avenue
Oak Brook, IL 60521
312-572-5000

Operator of retail drugstores.
Type: Private-Sub   Par: American Stores Co
Ind: Retail/Food   Grp: Retail
Richard Scott, CEO

Rev: NA
Assets: NA
Emp: NA

American Electric Power Co Inc
1 Riverside Plaza
Columbus, OH 43215
614-223-1000

Utility holding company.
Type: NYSE-AEP
Ind: Utility   Grp: Utilities
W S White, CEO   Richard E Disbrow, Pres   Gerald Maloney, CFO
J A Valentine, IS   James Markowsky, R&D   Paul C Greiner, Mkt
Donald Macke, PR

Rev: 4841
Assets: 2762
Emp: 23

American Enterprise Institute
1150 Seventeenth Street NW
Washington, DC 20036
202-862-5800

Non profit special interest group.
Type: Federal Govt
Ind: Membership Org   Grp: Govt & Non-Prof
Christopher DeMuth, CEO

Rev: 500
Assets: NM
Emp: 2

American Express Co
American Express Tower World Financial Ctr
New York, NY 10285
212-640-2000

Diversified financial services company.
Type: NYSE-APX
Ind: Non-Bank Fin   Grp: Financial
Robert F Smith, CEO   Albert M Benezra, Pres   Robert A Savage, VCh
Howard L Clark Jr, CFO   Jerry Cole, R&D   Amos Z Bergner, VP
Robert Budenbender, VP   George Carmany, VP   Allan Langley, VP
John Junek, VP   William Bautz, VP   Harry L Freeman, IR
Lawrence Armour, PR

Rev: 22934
Assets: 142704
Emp: 100

Organizations Listed Alphabetically

Organization / Address / Phone	Descriptive Information	Revenue / Assets / Emp ($ mil) ($ mil) (thous)		

American Express Credit Corp
One Rodney Square
Wilmington, DE 19801
302-594-3350

Credit subsidiary of American Express.
Type: Private-Sub   Par: American Express Co
Ind: Non-Bank Fin   Grp: Financial
Ronald J Yoo, CEO   Vincent P Lisanke, Chr   Anthony J Gillespie, VCh
C J Martin, CFO   Walker C Thompson, VP   Jean G Webber, VP
Jay Stevelman, VP   Constance L Simmons, VP   Stephanie R Joseph, VP

Rev: 1224
Assets: 9800
Emp: 2

American Family Corp
1932 Wynnton Road
Columbus, GA 31909
404-323-3431

Television, communications, insurance & printing.
Type: NYSE-AFL
Ind: Non-Bank Fin   Grp: Financial
John B Amos, CEO   Salvador Diaz-Verson, Pres   Paul S Amos, VCh
Norman P Foster, CFO   Louis Hazouri, R&D   Leroy Paul, VP
John L Laska, VP

Rev: 2325
Assets: 6074
Emp: 3

American Fed of Musicians of US & Canada
1501 Broadway
New York, NY 10036
212-867-1330

National labor union.
Type: Membership Org
Ind: Membership Org   Grp: Govt & Non-Prof
Victor W Fuentealba, CEO

Rev: 250
Assets: NM
Emp: 250

American Fed of State, Cnty & Muni Emp
1625 L Street NW
Washington, DC 20036
202-429-1130

National labor union.
Type: Membership Org
Ind: Membership Org   Grp: Govt & Non-Prof
Gerald McEntee, CEO

Rev: 500
Assets: NM
Emp: 1100

American Federation of Government Emp
80 F Street NW
Washington, DC 20001
202-737-8700

National labor union.
Type: Membership Org
Ind: Membership Org   Grp: Govt & Non-Prof
Kenneth T Blaylock, CEO

Rev: 250
Assets: NM
Emp: 250

American Federation of Teachers
555 New Jersey Avenue NW
Washington, DC 20001
202-879-4400

National labor union.
Type: Membership Org
Ind: Membership Org   Grp: Govt & Non-Prof
Albert Shanker, CEO

Rev: 500
Assets: NM
Emp: 700

American Financial Corp
One E Fourth Street
Cincinnati, OH 45202
513-579-2121

Life insurance company.
Type: Private
Ind: Insurance   Grp: Insurance
Carl H Linder, CEO   Ronald F Walker, Pres   Fred Runk, CFO
Donald D Larson, IS   Pat Morgan, PR

Rev: 3000
Assets: 8000
Emp: 10

American General Corp
2929 Allen Parkway
Houston, TX 77019
713-522-1111

Life insurance & financial services.
Type: NYSE-AGC
Ind: Insurance   Grp: Insurance
Harold S Hook, CEO   Michael Poulos, Pres   Henry Romaine, VCh
Autin P Young, CFO   John Wesson, IS   Robert Marcotte, Mkt
Phillip Hardy, Ops   William Phelps, VP   Edwin Pfaff, VP

Rev: 3823
Assets: 30422
Emp: 18

American General Life & Accident Co
American General Plaza
Nashville, TN 37250
615-749-1000

Life insurance company.
Type: OTC
Ind: Insurance   Grp: Insurance
Carroll D Shanks, CEO   Harold S Hook, Chr   Michael J Poulos, Pres
Nick R Rasmussen, CFO   Ellis D Widner, IS   Barsa C Harclerode, PR

Rev: 741
Assets: 3472
Emp: 2

American Grain Inc
2829 Westtown Park
Des Moines, IA 50265
515-223-3700

Food products company; distribution & storage of grain.
Type: Private
Ind: Food Processing   Grp: Food Processing
Duane Swanson, CEO

Rev: 2750
Assets: NA
Emp: 1

American Greetings Corp
10500 American Road
Cleveland, OH 44144
216-252-7300

Manufacturer of greeting cards, gift wraps & gift items.
Type: OTC-AGREA
Ind: Leisure Time   Grp: Consumer Service
Irving I Stone, CEO   Morris Stone, VCh   Eugene Sherry, Tres
Henry Lowenthal, CFO   James Van Ardsdale, IS   Ray Kenny, R&D
William R Mason, Sls   Edward Fruchtenbaum, Mkt   William Powell, VP
James Van Arsdale, VP   Harvey Levin, VP   William Meyer, VP
John Hernandiz, IR   Roz O'Hearn, PR

Rev: 1275
Assets: 1088
Emp: 21

Organizations Listed Alphabetically

Organization / Address / Phone	Descriptive Information	Revenue ($ mil)	Assets ($ mil)	Emp (thous)
American Healthcare Management 14160 Dallas Parkway Dallas, TX 75240 214-387-9181	Hospital operating company. Type: ASE-AHI Ind: Health Care Grp: Consumer Service John A Bradley, CEO	Rev: 471 Assets: NA Emp: 8		
American Home Products Corp 685 Third Avenue New York, NY 10017 212-878-5000	Manufacturer of consumer drugs & personal care products. Type: NYSE Ind: Drugs Grp: Consumer Service John R Stafford, CEO Robert G Blount, VCh John F Simpson, IS John Horseman, VP Herbert Bly, VP Albert Pezzillo, VP Carol Emerling, PR	Rev: 5501 Assets: 4611 Emp: 45		
American International Group Inc 70 Pine Street New York, NY 10270 212-770-7000	Property & casualty insurance company. Type: NYSE-AIG Ind: Insurance Grp: Insurance Maurice R Greenberg, CEO Frank P Filipps, Tres Edward E Matthews, CFO Lawrence W English, IS Stephen Collesano, R&D John G Hughes, VP Michael Morrison, VP Howard I SMith, VP Stephen Y N Tse, VP Thomas Elliott, VP Lawrence W English, VP Gladys R Thomas, IR L Oakley Johnson, PR	Rev: 13613 Assets: 37409 Emp: 38		
American Maize Products Co 41 Harbor Drive Stamford, CT 06904 203-356-9000	Food products manufacturing company; corn, tobacco. Type: ASE-AZEA Ind: Food Processing Grp: Food Processing William Ziegler, CEO John McCormick, Pres Robert Britton, Tres Edward Norris, CFO Charles A Koons, R&D Fred M Ash, Mkt Edmund Herve, VP C Ziegler-Brighton, PR	Rev: 548 Assets: 420 Emp: 3		
American Management Corp 1777 N Kent Street Arlington, VA 22209 703-841-6000	Software & systems engineering services company. Type: OTC Ind: Comput/Off Equip Grp: High Tech Ivan Selin, CEO	Rev: 250 Assets: 150 Emp: 3		
American Mutual Liability Quannapowitt Parkway Wakefield, MA 01880 508-245-6000	Property & casualty insurance company. Type: Private-Mutual Ind: Insurance Grp: Insurance J John Wortman, CEO	Rev: 400 Assets: 800 Emp: 2		
American National Bank & Trust Co 33 N LaSalle Street Chicago, IL 60690 312-661-5000	Commercial bank. Type: Private-Sub Par: First Chicago Corp Ind: Banking Grp: Financial Michael E Tobin, CEO	Rev: 438 Assets: 4567 Emp: 3		
American National Insurance Co One Moody Plaza Galveston, TX 77550 409-763-4461	Life Insurance company. Type: OTC Ind: Insurance Grp: Insurance Robert L Moody, CEO Orson Clay, Chr Carl Robertson, VCh Vincent Soler, CFO	Rev: 934 Assets: 4303 Emp: 2		
American Overseas Marine Corp 116 E Howard Street Quincy, MA 02169 617-786-8300	Manufacturer of military equipment. Type: Private-Sub Par: General Dynamics Corp Ind: Manufacturing Grp: Manufacturing Bartholomew Fennick, CEO	Rev: NA Assets: NA Emp: NA		
American Petrofina Inc Fina Plaza Dallas, TX 75206 214-750-2400	Oil & natural gas production company. Type: ASE-APIA Ind: Energy Grp: Basic Industries Paul D Meek, CEO Ronald W Haddock, Chr Kenneth Perry, VCh S R West, CFO Phil Farr, IS Stuart Pearman, Mkt M J Couch, VP Christian Buggenhout, VP Jerry G Jenkins, VP Glenn Selvidge, VP Mark Palmer, PR	Rev: 2635 Assets: 2356 Emp: 4		
American Postal Workers Union 817 Fourteenth Street NW Washington, DC 20005 202-842-4200	National labor union. Type: Membership Org Ind: Membership Org Grp: Govt & Non-Prof Moe Biller, CEO	Rev: 250 Assets: NM Emp: 350		

Organizations Listed Alphabetically

Organization / Address / Phone	Descriptive Information	Revenue / Assets / Emp ($ mil) ($ mil) (thous)		

American President Companies Ltd
1800 Harrison Street
Oakland, CA 94612
415-272-8000

Ocean shipping transport company.
Type: NYSE-APS
Ind: Transport   Grp: Business Service
W B Seaton, CEO   J Hayashi, Pres   James S Marston, IS
Richard L Hill, R&D   Michael Goggins, Sls   Timothy J Rhein, Mkt
Mark Thompson, IR

Rev: 2131
Assets: 1711
Emp: 5

American President Trucking Co
1800 Harrison Street
Oakland, CA 94612
415-272-8000

Nationwide trucking company.
Type: Private-Sub   Par: American President Companies Ltd
Ind: Transport   Grp: Business Service
Robert Cross, CEO

Rev: NA
Assets: NA
Emp: NA

American Protection Industries Inc
12223 W Olympic Blvd
Los Angeles, CA 90064
213-442-5700

Manufacturer of security systems, Franklin Mint.
Type: Private
Ind: Consumer Service   Grp: Consumer Service
Neil Bersch, CEO

Rev: 750
Assets: NA
Emp: 5

American Restaurant Group Inc
450 Newport Centre Drive
Newport Beach, CA 92660
714-721-8000

Operator of restaurants.
Type: Private
Ind: Food/Lodging   Grp: Consumer Service
Anwar Soliman, CEO

Rev: 500
Assets: NA
Emp: 15

American Savings & Loan Assn Inc
222 N El Dorado Street
Stockton, CA 95202
209-948-1116

Thrift institution.
Type: Private
Ind: Savings & Loan   Grp: Financial
William J Popejoy, CEO   William G Lillis, Chr   Robert Hughes, CFO
Cheryl Bell, R&D   Cheryl Bell, Mkt   Claudia Dumitrescu, IR
Eleanor Jakab, PR

Rev: 500
Assets: 4000
Emp: 2

American Savings (UT) Assn Inc
77 W 200th S
Salt Lake City, UT 84101
801-483-5800

Thrift institution.
Type: Private
Ind: Savings & Loan   Grp: Financial
Edward W Clyde, CEO

Rev: 350
Assets: 3100
Emp: 1

American Savings Assn of Florida Inc
17801 NW 2nd Avenue
Miami, FL 33169
305-653-5353

Thrift institution.
Type: NYSE-AAA
Ind: Savings & Loan   Grp: Financial
Harris C Friedman, CEO

Rev: 350
Assets: 3500
Emp: 1

American Savings Bank (NY) Inc
1133 Avenue of the Americas
New York, NY 10036
212-575-7600

Thrift institution.
Type: NYSE-ASB
Ind: Savings & Loan   Grp: Financial
John T Morgan, CEO

Rev: 500
Assets: 4500
Emp: 2

American Seaway Foods Inc
22801 Aurora Road
Edford Heights, OH 44146
216-663-5500

Operator of retail food stores.
Type: Private
Ind: Retail/Food   Grp: Retail
Anthony Reagle, CEO

Rev: 550
Assets: NA
Emp: 2

American Security Bank NA
1501 Pennsylvania Avenue
Washington, DC 20013
202-624-4000

Commercial bank.
Type: NASDAQ-ASEC
Ind: Banking   Grp: Financial
Daniel J Callahan, CEO

Rev: 800
Assets: 6500
Emp: 2

American Standard Inc
40 W 40th Street
New York, NY 10018
212-703-5100

Manufacturer of plumbing, construction & building products.
Type: Private
Ind: Manufacturing   Grp: Manufacturing
William B Boyd, CEO   Gary J Biddle, IS   Lois Stewart, PR

Rev: 3500
Assets: 2200
Emp: 40

American Stores Co
5201 Amelia Earhart Drive
Salt Lake City, UT 84116
801-539-0112

Supermarket retailing company.
Type: NYSE-ASE
Ind: Retail/Food   Grp: Retail
L S Skaggs, CEO   Alan D Stewart, Pres   Dennis Eck, VCh
Victor Lund, CFO   John Womack, IS   H Prentice Merritt, R&D
Michael T Miller, VP   Jack Lunt, VP   Kent Anderson, VP
Richard Scott, VP   Scott Bergeson, VP   J Michael Holt, PR

Rev: 18478
Assets: 7010
Emp: 165

Organizations Listed Alphabetically

Organization / Address / Phone	Descriptive Information	Revenue / Assets / Emp ($ mil) ($ mil) (thous)		

American Telephone & Telegraph Co
550 Madison Avenue
New York, NY 10022
212-605-5500

National telecommunications company.
Type: NYSE-A
Ind: Telecom   Grp: High Tech
Robert E Allen, CEO   Randall Tobias, Pres   Charles Marshall, VCh
Morris Tannenbaum, CFO   William Garrett, IS   Ian Ross, R&D
William Marx, Mkt   Frank Blount, Ops   C Perry Colwell, VP
Marilyn Laurie, IR   Durke Stinson, PR

Rev: 35210
Assets: 35152
Emp: 304

American Television & Communications Inc
300 First Stamford Place
Stamford, CT 06902
203-328-0600

Cable television.
Type: OTC
Ind: Publishing/Com   Grp: Consumer Service
Joe Collins, CEO

Rev: 800
Assets: 600
Emp: 2

American Tobacco Co
Six Stamford Forum
Stamford, CT 06904
203-325-4900

Manufacturer & distributor of tobacco products.
Type: Private-Sub   Par: American Brands Inc
Ind: Tobacco   Grp: Food Processing
Charles Mullern, CEO

Rev: NA
Assets: NA
Emp: NA

American United Life Insurance Co
One American Square PO Box 368
Indianapolis, IN 46206
317-263-1877

Life insurance company.
Type: Private-Mutual
Ind: Insurance   Grp: Insurance
Jack E Reich, CEO   Jerry D Semler, Pres   Jack Huffford, Tres
James Murphy, CFO   Stephen Davis, IS   Doyle d Champion, Sls
Lewis F Born, Mkt

Rev: 856
Assets: 3361
Emp: 3

American Water Works Co Inc
1025 Laurel Oak Road
Voorhees, NJ 08043
609-346-8200

Holding company for water supply utilities.
Type: NYSE-AWK
Ind: Business Service   Grp: Business Service
James V LaFrankie, CEO   Loren Mellendorf, VCh   J James Barr, CFO
W Timothy Pohn, Sls   Robert Sievers, VP   Simon Stock, VP
George Johnstone, VP

Rev: 512
Assets: 1737
Emp: 4

AmeriFirst Federal Savings Miami Inc
One SE Third Avenue
Miami, FL 33131
305-577-1600

Thrift institution.
Type: NYSE-AMRI
Ind: Savings & Loan   Grp: Financial
Thomas R Bomar, CEO   Carlos Garcia-Velez, Pres   Robert W Benner, CFO
Joyce A Denny, IS   Vivian A Decker, Mkt   Robert Landau, IR
Bernard Lipskin, PR

Rev: 500
Assets: 4500
Emp: 2

Amerisure Companies
28 W Adams Avenue
Detroit, MI 48226
313-965-8600

Property & casualty insurance company.
Type: OTC
Ind: Insurance   Grp: Insurance
E L Cox, CEO

Rev: 500
Assets: 300
Emp: 2

Ameritech (Amer Information Tech Corp)
30 S Wacker Drive
Chicago, IL 60606
312-750-5000

Regional telecommunications company; telephone utility.
Type: NYSE-AIT
Ind: Telecom   Grp: High Tech
William L Weiss, CEO   Robert L Barnett, Pres   Carl G Koch, Tres
William H Springer, CFO   James R Heidenreich, IS   Gary G Drook, Mkt
John A Koten, IR   Beverly Hammond, PR

Rev: 9903
Assets: 19163
Emp: 77

Ameritech Communications Inc
500 W Madison
Chicago, IL 60606
312-906-4199

Regional telephone company.
Type: Private-Sub   Par: Ameritech (Amer Information Tech Corp)
Ind: Telecom   Grp: High Tech
Roger Plummer, CEO

Rev: NA
Assets: NA
Emp: NA

Ameritech Publishing Co
100 E Big Beaver Road
Troy, MI 48083
313-524-7300

Publishing company.
Type: Private-Sub   Par: Ameritech (Amer Information Tech Corp)
Ind: Publishing/Com   Grp: Consumer Service
Barry Allen, CEO

Rev: NA
Assets: NA
Emp: NA

Ameritrust Corp
900 Euclid Avenue
Cleveland, OH 44101
216-737-5000

Commercial bank.
Type: NASDAQ-AMTR
Ind: Banking   Grp: Financial
Jerry V Jarrett, CEO   James D Rode, Pres   John F Miller, VCh
James Otto, CFO   Robert Salipante, IS   Bruce H Akers, Mkt
Frederick Ramsey, VP   Peter Kratt, VP   Bruce H Akers, PR

Rev: 1052
Assets: 10738
Emp: 4

Organizations Listed Alphabetically

Organization / Address / Phone	Descriptive Information	Revenue / ($ mil)	Assets / ($ mil)	Emp (thous)
Ameron Inc 4700 Romona Blvd Monterey Park, CA 91754 213-268-4111	Pipe manufacturer; concrete, fiberglas. Type: NYSE-AMN Ind: Building Mat Grp: Basic Industries Lawrence R Tollenaere, CEO	Rev: 364	Assets: 312	Emp: 4
Ames Department Stores Inc 2418 Main Street Rocky Hill, CT 06067 203-563-8234	Department store retail company. Type: NYSE-ADD Ind: Retail/Merch Grp: Retail Peter B Hollis, CEO James T McKitrick, VCh Duane Wolter, CFO Richard Nawrot, IS Leslie Dietzman, Sls Vincent Osborne, Mkt Philip Chruse, VP Jeffrey Dentz, VP James Aglio, VP Catherine Leonard, PR	Rev: 3363	Assets: 1700	Emp: 21
Ametek Inc 410 Park Avenue 21st Floor New York, NY 10022 212-935-8640	Computer peripheral manufacturing company. Type: NYSE-AME Ind: Electronics Grp: High Tech John H Lux, CEO John P Dandalides, Pres Allan Kornfeld, CFO John K Whipple, IS Murray A Luftgass, R&D Robert A Russell, Mkt Neal Stark, VP Darrah Ribble, PR	Rev: 520	Assets: 448	Emp: 5
Amfac Inc 44 Montgomery Street PO Box 7813 San Francisco, CA 94120 415-772-3400	Hotel, real estate & food processing company; sugar. Type: NYSE-AMA Ind: Business Service Grp: Business Service Henry A Walker, CEO Richard L Griffith, Chr Thomas L Braje, CFO Keith V Mabee, PR	Rev: 2200	Assets: 1400	Emp: 19
Amgen Corp 1900 Oak Terrace Lane Thousand Oaks, CA 91320 805-499-5725	Biotechnology company; developer of human health care prd. Type: NASDAQ-AMGN Ind: Business Service Grp: Business Service George B Rathmann, CEO	Rev: 78	Assets: 207	Emp: 1
AMI American Medical International Inc 414 N Camden Drive Beverly Hills, CA 90210 213-278-6200	Operator of hospitals. Type: NYSE Ind: Business Service Grp: Business Service Royce Diener, CEO Royce Diener, Chr Gene E Burleson, Pres M Scott Athans, VCh Andre Dimitriadis, CFO Michael L Carrico, IS Ahmed Yehia, Mkt James Barker, VP Robert Bohlman, VP Michael Carrico, VP Suzanne Hovdey, IR Mick Taylor, PR	Rev: 3111	Assets: 832	Emp: 46
Amica Mutual Insurance Co 10 Weybosset Street Providence, RI 02940 401-521-9100	Property & casualty insurance company. Type: Private-mutual Ind: Insurance Grp: Insurance Joel N Tobey, CEO	Rev: 646	Assets: 1142	Emp: 2
Amoco Canada Petroleum Co 444 7th Avenue SW Calgary, AB T2P0Y2 Can 403-233-1313	Petroleum distribution & marketing company. Type: TOR Ind: Energy Grp: Basic Industries Patrick J Early, CEO T Don Stacey, Pres Norman Rubash, VCh David Morgenthaler, Tres William Bridgman, CFO R Donald Fullerton, VP Richard Brown, VP James Gaffney, VP	Rev: 1285	Assets: 1833	Emp: 2
Amoco Chemical Co 200 E Randolph Drive Chicago, IL 60601 312-856-6111	Producer of petroleum products & chemicals. Type: Private-Sub Par: Amoco Corp Ind: Energy Grp: Basic Industries Robert Caduiex, CEO	Rev: NA	Assets: NA	Emp: NA
Amoco Corp 200 E Randolph Drive Chicago, IL 60601 312-856-6111	Petroleum products company; production, distribution. Type: NYSE Ind: Energy Grp: Basic Industries Richard M Morrow, CEO H Laurence Fuller, Pres Frederick S Addy, CFO John Reid, IS Edward A Mason, R&D R J Rauscher, Mkt John Lyman, VP Richard Fischer, VP Wayne Anderson, VP Ronand Callahan, VP William Montgomery, VP R A Johnson, PR	Rev: 23919	Assets: 29919	Emp: 53
Amoskeag Co Prudential Center Boston, MA 02199 617-262-4000	Textile manufacuer, real estate, railroad operation. Type: OTC Ind: Apparel/Textiles Grp: Consumer Prd Joseph Ely, CEO	Rev: 1500	Assets: 1000	Emp: 25

Organizations Listed Alphabetically

Organization / Address / Phone	Descriptive Information	Revenue / ($ mil)	Assets / ($ mil)	Emp (thous)
AMP Inc 470 Friendship Road Harrisburg, PA 17109 717-564-0100	Manufacturer of electronic & electric connection devices. Type: NYSE-AMP Ind: Electronics Grp: High Tech Walter F Raab, CEO Benjamin Savidge, CFO Rudolf Gassner, IS August P Kastel, R&D Ted L Dalrymple, Mkt P G Guarneschelli, PR	Rev: 2670 Assets: 2376 Emp: 24		
AMP Packaging Systems Inc 700 E Jeffrey Way Round Rock, TX 78664 512-244-5110	Manufacturer of electronic devices. Type: Private-Sub Par: AMP Inc Ind: Electronics Grp: High Tech Carmen Burns, CEO	Rev: NA Assets: NA Emp: NA		
Ampco Pittsburgh Corp 700 Porter Bldg 600 Grant Street Pittsburgh, PA 15219 412-456-4400	Manufacturer of industrial equipment. Type: NYSE Ind: Manufacturing Grp: Manufacturing Marshall L Berkman, CEO	Rev: 251 Assets: 295 Emp: 3		
Ampex Corp 405 Park Avenue New York, NY 10022 212-759-6301	Manufacturer of TV & broadcast equipment, magnetic tape. Type: Private Ind: Publishing/Com Grp: Consumer Service Max O Mitchell, CEO	Rev: 600 Assets: NA Emp: 5		
AMR (American Airlines) Corp 4200 American Blvd Ft Worth, TX 76155 817-355-1234	International airline. Type: NYSE-AMR Ind: Airline Grp: Consumer Service Robert L Crandall, CEO Micheal Durham, Tres Donald J Carty, CFO Max D Hopper, IS Robert W Baker, R&D Michael Buckman, Sls Michael W Gunn, Mkt Richard Lempert, VP Gene Overbeck, VP Richard Pearson, VP Barbara Amster, VP Lowell C Duncan Jr, PR	Rev: 8824 Assets: 9722 Emp: 68		
Amsouth Bancorp Inc 1900 Fifth Ave N First Southern Bldg Birmingham, AL 35203 205-320-7151	Commercial bank. Type: NYSE-ASO Ind: Banking Grp: Financial John W Woods, CEO Dan L Hendley, Pres William A Powell, VCh Douglas B Nunnelly, CFO Linda Allison, IS Thomas M McCulley, Mkt Thomas J Tucker, VP Michael Underwood, VP Thomas M McCulley, IR Catherine Wiggins, PR	Rev: 797 Assets: 8313 Emp: 4		
Amstar Corp 1251 Avenue of the Americas New York, NY 10020 212-489-9000	Producer of packaged foods; sugar. Type: Private Ind: Food Processing Grp: Food Processing Howard B Wentz, CEO Duncan Kidd, CFO Joseph Forgione, IS Anthony Rizzuto, R&D Richard Grove, IR Lester McGuire, PR	Rev: 1250 Assets: 1500 Emp: 5		
Amsted Industries Inc 3700 Prudential Plaza Chicago, IL 60601 312-645-1700	Manufacturer of steel, iron pieces for railroad cars. Type: Private Ind: Manufacturing Grp: Manufacturing Robert H Wellington, CEO Gerald K Walter, CFO Ronald Nalepa, IS Jerry W Gura, PR	Rev: 1000 Assets: NA Emp: 10		
Amway Corp 7575 E Fulton Ada, MI 49301 606-676-6000	Manufacturer & direct marketer of personal care & home prod. Type: Private Ind: Retail/Merch Grp: Retail Jay Van Andel, CEO	Rev: 1500 Assets: NA Emp: 10		
Anacomp Inc 11550 N Meridian Street Indianapolis, IN 46032 317-844-9666	Microfilm equipment & computer service company. Type: NYSE-AAC Ind: Comput/Off Equip Grp: High Tech Louis P Ferrero, CEO	Rev: 300 Assets: 250 Emp: 2		
Anadarko Petroleum Corp 16855 Northchase Houston, TX 77251 713-875-1101	Exploration & development of oil & natural gas. Type: NYSE-APC Ind: Energy Grp: Basic Industries Robert J Allison, CEO	Rev: 333 Assets: 1490 Emp: 1		
Anaheim, City of City Hall Anaheim, CA 92803 714-999-5166	City government. Type: City Govt Ind: Local Govt Grp: Govt & Non-Prof Ben Bay, CEO	Rev: 339 Assets: NM Emp: 2		

Organizations Listed Alphabetically

Organization / Address / Phone	Descriptive Information	Revenue / Assets / Emp ($ mil) ($ mil) (thous)		

Analog Devices Inc
One Technology Way
Norwood, MA 02062
617-329-4700

Manufacturer of integrated circuits.
Type: NYSE-ADI
Ind: Electronics   Grp: High Tech
Ray Stata, CEO   Jerald Gishman, VCh   Joseph McDonough, Tres
Joseph M Hinchey, CFO   Dennis Buss, IS   Melvin Sallen, R&D
Douglas Newman, Mkt   Paul Brountas, VP   Kozo Imai, VP
Tom Urwin, VP

Rev: 439
Assets: 449
Emp: 5

Anchor Glass Container
1100 Anchor Street
Tampa, FL 33607
813-884-0000

Glass container manufacturing company.
Type: NASDAQ-AGLS
Ind: Packaging   Grp: Manufacturing
Vincent J Naimoli, CEO   Gary Matter, Tres   James H Smith, CFO
John Pearson, IS   Franklin E Whitmore, R&D   D Richard Barry, Mkt
Richard Dawson, VP   Edward Jonas, VP   James Luci, VP
Richard D Everett, IR

Rev: 978
Assets: 773
Emp: 8

Anchor Hocking Corp
109 N Broad Street
Lancaster, OH 43132
614-687-2111

Manufacturer of plastic & metal products; home,industrial.
Type: Private-Sub   Par: Newell Co
Ind: Manufacturing   Grp: Manufacturing
William R Cuthbert, CEO

Rev: 750
Assets: 500
Emp: 10

Anchor Savings Bank Inc
225 Main Street
Northport, NY 11768
516-295-0400

Thrift institution.
Type: NASDAQ-ABKR
Ind: Savings & Loan   Grp: Financial
Donald L Thomas, CEO   William G Schneider Jr, Pres   Eugene Schulz, VCh
John V Brull, CFO   Mitchell Levy, Mkt   Patricia Dawley, VP
Mitchell Levy, PR

Rev: 703
Assets: 7946
Emp: 2

Anchorage, City of
City Hall
Anchorage, AK 99519
907-264-4431

City government.
Type: City Govt
Ind: Local Govt   Grp: Govt & Non-Prof
Tom Fink, CEO

Rev: 790
Assets: NM
Emp: 4

Andersen Corp
Foot of 5th Avenue
Bayport, MN 55003
612-439-5150

Manufacturer, windows, patio doors.
Type: Private
Ind: Building Mat   Grp: Basic Industries
W Arvid Wellman, CEO

Rev: 1000
Assets: NA
Emp: 6

Andersons Inc
1200 Dussel Drive
Maumee, OH 43537
419-893-5050

Agribusiness, consumer products.
Type: Private
Ind: Food Processing   Grp: Food Processing
Richard P Anderson, CEO

Rev: 600
Assets: NA
Emp: 1

Andrew Corp
10500 W 153rd Street
Orland Park, IL 60462
312-349-3300

Electronic manufacturer; reconnaissance receiving equip.
Type: OTC
Ind: Electronics   Grp: High Tech
F English, CEO

Rev: 300
Assets: 200
Emp: 3

Angelica Corp
10178 Corporate Square Road
St Louis, MO 63132
314-991-2934

Manufacturer of business uniforms, laundry, retail stores.
Type: NYSE-AGL
Ind: Apparel/Textiles   Grp: Consumer Prd
Leslie F Loewe, CEO

Rev: 328
Assets: NA
Emp: 3

Anglo Canadian Telephone Co
8750 Cote De Liesse
Saint Laurent, PQ H4T1H3 Can
514-341-6321

Telephone utility company.
Type: Private-Sub
Ind: Telecom   Grp: High Tech
Charles R Lee, CEO   John M Edmiston, CFO   Ann E Hradsky, VP
Charles DeBlois, VP   Bernard Meier, VP

Rev: 1676
Assets: 3169
Emp: 22

Angus Petroleum Corp
350 Indiana Street
Golden, CO 80401
303-278-4300

Petroleum products exploration & distribution company.
Type: Private-Sub   Par: Pacific Gas & Electric Co
Ind: Energy   Grp: Basic Industries
Robert Kayser, CEO

Rev: NA
Assets: NA
Emp: NA

Organizations Listed Alphabetically

Organization / Address / Phone	Descriptive Information	Revenue / ($ mil)	Assets / ($ mil)	Emp (thous)
Anheuser Busch Companies Inc One Busch Place St Louis, MO 63118 314-577-2000	Largest U.S. nationwide brewer of beer. Type: NYSE-BUD Ind: Beverage Grp: Food Processing John L Haywood, CEO August A Busch III, Chr Thomas R Billen, CFO Kenn A Reynolds, R&D James Hunter, Sls Michael Roarty, Mkt James Young, Ops Jesse Aguirre, PR	Rev: 9705	Assets: 7110	Emp: 40
Anixter Brothers Inc 4711 Golf Road Skokie, IL 60076 312-677-2600	Manufacturer of telephone cable & equipment. Type: OTC Ind: Building Mat Grp: Basic Industries John A Pigott, CEO	Rev: 650	Assets: 600	Emp: 3
ANR Coal Co Crestar Bank Bldg 310 First Street Roanoke, VA 24011 703-983-0222	Coal mining & production company. Type: Private-Sub Par: Coastal Corp Ind: Metals/Mining Grp: Basic Industries James Paul, CEO	Rev: NA	Assets: NA	Emp: NA
ANR Pipeline Co 500 Renaissance Center Detroit, MI 48243 313-496-7075	Gas & oil pipeline transportation company. Type: Private-Sub Par: Coastal Corp Ind: Energy Grp: Basic Industries James Cordes, CEO	Rev: NA	Assets: NA	Emp: NA
Anschutz Corp 555 17th Street Denver, CO 80202 303-298-1000	Railroad & natural resource development company. Type: Private Ind: Energy Grp: Basic Industries Philip F Anschutz, CEO	Rev: 2250	Assets: NA	Emp: 20
Anthem Electronics Inc 1040 E Brokaw Road San Jose, CA 95431 408-295-4200	Manufacturer & distributor of electronic components. Type: NYSE-ATM Ind: Electronics Grp: High Tech Robert S Throop, CEO	Rev: 250	Assets: 200	Emp: 3
Anthony Industries Inc 4900 S Eastern Avenue Los Angeles, CA 90040 213-724-2800	Manufacturer of sporting equipment; swimming pools. Type: NYSE-ANT Ind: Leisure Time Grp: Consumer Service Bernard I Forester, CEO	Rev: 250	Assets: NA	Emp: 2
Anthony, C R Co Inc 701 N Broadway Oklahoma City, OK 73102 405-235-3711	Department stores. Type: Private Ind: Retail/Merch Grp: Retail John J Weisner, CEO	Rev: 500	Assets: NA	Emp: 5
Aon Corp (Combined Int'l) 123 N Wacker Drive Chicago, IL 60606 312-701-3000	Property & casualty insurance company. Type: NYSE-AOC Ind: Non-Bank Fin Grp: Financial W Clement Stone, CEO	Rev: 2732	Assets: 8266	Emp: 7
Apache Corp 1700 Lincoln Street Denver, CO 80203 303-837-5000	Oil & gas exploration & production company. Type: NYSE-APA Ind: Energy Grp: Basic Industries Raymond Plank, CEO	Rev: 500	Assets: 350	Emp: 2
Apex Corp 762 W Stewart Street Dayton, OH 45408 513-222-7871	Manufacturer of electrical equipment. Type: Private-Sub Par: Cooper Industries Inc Ind: Electronics Grp: High Tech Walter Callahan, CEO	Rev: NA	Assets: NA	Emp: NA
Apex Oil Co 8182 Maryland Avenue St Louis, MO 63105 314-889-9600	Distributor of petroleum products. Type: Private Ind: Energy Grp: Basic Industries John Hank, CEO	Rev: 3000	Assets: NA	Emp: 8
APL Corp 6917 Collins Avenue Miami, FL 33141 305-866-7771	Manufacturer of household products; paper, containers. Type: NYSE-APL Ind: Manufacturing Grp: Manufacturing Victor Posner, CEO	Rev: 1209	Assets: 584	Emp: 12

Organizations Listed Alphabetically

Organization / Address / Phone	Descriptive Information	Revenue / Assets / Emp ($ mil) ($ mil) (thous)		

Apollo Computer Inc
330 Billerica Road
Chelmsford, MA 01824
508-256-6600

Manufacturer of high performance computer systems.
Type: NASDAQ-APCI
Ind: Comput/Off Equip   Grp: High Tech
Thomas A Vanderslice, CEO   Roland Tampel, Pres   Richard Bond, CFO
Robert Elliott, IS   Michael S Gutman, R&D   Angelo Guadagno, Sls
Michael Gallup, Mkt   Mary Allard, IR   Joseph Nahil, PR

Rev: 654
Assets: 497
Emp: 4

Apple Computer Inc
20525 Mariani Avenue
Cupertino, CA 95014
408-996-1010

Manufacturer of desk top computers.
Type: NASDAQ-APPL
Ind: Comput/Off Equip   Grp: High Tech
John Sculley, CEO   Delbert W Yocam, Pres   John Louis Gassee, VCh
Deborah Coleman, CFO   Allan Loren, IS   Jean Louis Gasse, R&D
Chuck Boesenberg, Mkt   Jane Risser, IR   Barbara Krause, PR

Rev: 4071
Assets: 2082
Emp: 7

Applied Biosystems Inc
850 Lincoln Centre Drive
Foster City, CA 94404
415-570-6667

Chemical manufacturer, biotechnology research & equipment.
Type: NASDAQ-ABIO
Ind: Instruments   Grp: High Tech
Andre F Marion, CEO

Rev: 158
Assets: 151
Emp: 1

Applied Magnetics Corp
75 Robin Hill Road
Goleta, CA 93177
805-967-8227

Manufacturer of components for computer disk drives.
Type: NYSE-APM
Ind: Comput/Off Equip   Grp: High Tech
Harold R Frank, CEO

Rev: 300
Assets: NA
Emp: 3

Applied Materials Inc
3050 Bowers Avenue
Santa Clara, CA 95054
408-727-5555

Manufacturer of semiconductors.
Type: OTC
Ind: Electronics   Grp: High Tech
James C Morgan, CEO

Rev: 400
Assets: 200
Emp: 2

ARA Holding Co
1101 Market Street
Philadelphia, PA 19107
215-238-3000

Operator of food vending & institutional food services.
Type: Private
Ind: Business Service   Grp: Business Service
Joseph Neubauer, CEO   John Kallelis, IS   James Ksansnak, R&D
Thomas J Fitzgerald, Mkt   Harry R Belinger, IR   Alan K Campbell, PR

Rev: 4000
Assets: 1500
Emp: 110

Arbor Drugs Inc
1818 Maplelawn Drive
Troy, MI 48084
313-643-9420

Operator of retail drugstores.
Type: NASDAQ-ARBR
Ind: Retail/Merch   Grp: Retail
Eugene Applebaum, CEO

Rev: 300
Assets: 150
Emp: 4

Arcata Corp
601 California
San Francisco, CA 94108
415-781-4200

Book & magazine printing.
Type: Private
Ind: Publishing/Com   Grp: Consumer Service
Edward L Scarff, CEO

Rev: 750
Assets: NA
Emp: 10

Arch Mineral Corp
200 N Broadway
St Louis, MO 63102
314-231-1010

Mineral mining & processing company.
Type: Private
Ind: Metals/Mining   Grp: Basic Industries
William Heckman, CEO

Rev: 275
Assets: NA
Emp: 2

Archer Daniels Midland Co
4666 Faries Parkway
Decatur, IL 62626
217-424-5200

Producer of food products; food oils, flour, corn.
Type: NYSE
Ind: Food Processing   Grp: Food Processing
Dwayne O Andreas, CEO   James Randall, Pres   Richard E Burket, VCh
G Allen Andreas, Tres   Doug Schmalz, CFO   Ray Preiksaitis, IS
Thomas Duffield, VP   Dale Benson, VP   Richard Burket, IR
Judy Brackett, PR

Rev: 6798
Assets: 4398
Emp: 9

ARCO Chemical Co
3801 W Chester
Newtown Square, PA 15219
215-359-2000

International chemical company.
Type: Private-Sub   Par: Atlantic Richfield Co
Ind: Chemicals   Grp: Basic Industries
Harold A Sorgenti, CEO   Lodwrick M Cook, Chr   Robert Wycoff, Pres
James Morrison, VCh   Ronald Arnault, CFO   Mike Bowlin, VP
Kenneth Dickerson, VP   Camron Cooper, VP   Mike Bowlin, VP

Rev: 2500
Assets: 2500
Emp: 3

Organizations Listed Alphabetically

Organization / Address / Phone	Descriptive Information	Revenue / Assets / Emp ($ mil) ($ mil) (thous)		

Arden Group Inc
2020 S Central Avenue
Compton, CA 90220
213-638-2842

Food wholesale company.
Type: OTC
Ind: Retail/Food   Grp: Retail
Curtis H Palmer, CEO

Rev: 351
Assets: 250
Emp: 3

Argonaut Insurance Co
250 Middlefield Road
Menlo Park, CA 94025
415-326-0900

Property & casualty insurance company.
Type: OTC
Ind: Insurance   Grp: Insurance
Michael J Crall, CEO   Henry E Singleton, Chr   Charles E Rinsch, Pres
James Halliday, CFO

Rev: 350
Assets: 1500
Emp: 2

Aristech Chemical Corp
600 Grant Street
Pittsburgh, PA 15230
412-433-2747

Chemical company; polymers.
Type: NYSE-ARS
Ind: Chemicals   Grp: Basic Industries
Thomas Marshall, CEO   Craig R Andersson, Pres   Anthony F Mastro, CFO
Francis Meyer, IS   Edward J Nemeth, R&D   Robert J Kilpatrick, Mkt
Mary F Baits, IR   J Harry Varner, PR

Rev: 1000
Assets: NA
Emp: 6

Arix Corp
821 Fox Lane
San Jose, CA 95131
408-432-1200

Manufacturer of microcomputers.
Type: OTC
Ind: Comput/Off Equip   Grp: High Tech
Douglas Davis, CEO

Rev: 350
Assets: 200
Emp: 1

Arizona Bank Corp
101 N First Avenue
Phoenix, AZ 85002
602-262-2000

Commercial bank.
Type: NYSE-SPC
Ind: Banking   Grp: Financial
Robert L Matthews, CEO

Rev: 800
Assets: 6500
Emp: 2

Arizona Public Service Co
411 N Central Avenue
Phoenix, AZ 85072
602-250-1000

Electric utility company.
Type: Private-Sub   Par: Pinnacle West Capital
Ind: Utility   Grp: Utilities
O Mark DeMichele, CEO

Rev: 1442
Assets: 5991
Emp: 9

Arizona State University
Administrative Bldg
Tempe, AZ 85287
602-965-9011

Major educational institution; university.
Type: University
Ind: University   Grp: Govt & Non-Prof
J Russell Nelson, CEO

Rev: 196
Assets: 318
Emp: 45

Arizona, State of
State Capitol
Phoenix, AZ 85007
602-255-4900

State government.
Type: State Govt
Ind: State/Prov Govt   Grp: Govt & Non-Prof
Rose Mofford, CEO

Rev: 7324
Assets: NM
Emp: 53

Arkansas Best Corp
1000 S 21st Street
Fort Smith, AR 72901
501-785-6000

Furniture manufacturer & holding company.
Type: Private
Ind: Transport   Grp: Business Service
Robert A Young, CEO   H L Hembree, Chr   Don Neal, CFO
Jerry Yarbrough, IS   David Stubblefield, Mkt   Randall Loyd, PR

Rev: 750
Assets: 400
Emp: 8

Arkansas Power & Light Co
First Commercial Bldg 425 W Capitol
Little Rock, AR 72203
501-371-4000

Electric power utility.
Type: Private-Sub   Par: Entergy Corp (Middle South Utilities)
Ind: Utility   Grp: Utilities
Jerry L Maulden, CEO   R Drake Keith, Pres   Michael Bemis, VCh
Lee Randall, CFO   John Griffin, R&D   Kenneth Breeden, Mkt

Rev: 1357
Assets: 3928
Emp: 5

Arkansas, State of
State Capitol
Little Rock, AR 72201
501-371-3000

State government.
Type: State Govt
Ind: State/Prov Govt   Grp: Govt & Non-Prof
Bill Clinton, CEO

Rev: 4219
Assets: NM
Emp: 44

Arkla Inc
Arkla Bldg 525 Milam
Shreveport, LA 71101
318-226-2700

Production & distribution of natural gas.
Type: NYSE-ALG
Ind: Utility   Grp: Utilities
Thomas F McLarty, CEO   Carl S Quinn, Pres   Jim O Wilhite, VCh
William H Kelly, CFO   John Pronsky, R&D   James L Rutherford, Mkt
Rick Spurlock, VP   Jack Ellis, VP   James Bailey, VP
Bradford Keithley, VP

Rev: 1996
Assets: 3249
Emp: 6

Organizations Listed Alphabetically

Organization / Address / Phone	Descriptive Information	Revenue / Assets / Emp ($ mil) ($ mil) (thous)		
Arlington, City of City Hall Arlington, TX 76010 817-459-6121	City government. Type: City Govt Ind: Local Govt Grp: Govt & Non-Prof Richard Greene, CEO	Rev: Assets: Emp:	250 NM 3	
Armco Inc 300 Interpace Parkway Parsippany, NJ 07054 201-316-5200	Specialty steel manufacturer. Type: NYSE-AS Ind: Steel Grp: Basic Industries Robert E Boni, CEO Robert L Purdum, Pres Wallace B Askins, CFO William Monteith, IS David L Chalk, R&D A Lee Bland, PR	Rev: Assets: Emp:	3227 2788 16	
Armor All Products Corp 22 Corporate Park Drive Irvine, CA 92714 714-533-1003	Manufacturer of automotive appearance products. Type: Private-Sub Par: McKesson Corp Ind: Business Service Grp: Business Service Thomas W Field, CEO	Rev: Assets: Emp:	163 150 1	
Armour Food Co ConAgra Center One Central Park Plaza Omaha, NE 68102 402-978-4000	Manufacturer & distributor of packaged foods. Type: Private-Sub Par: Conagra Inc Ind: Food Processing Grp: Food Processing John Miller, CEO	Rev: Assets: Emp:	NA NA NA	
Armstrong Rubber Co 500 Sargent Drive New Haven, CT 06536 203-784-2200	Manufacturer of tires, rubber products. Type: Private-Sub-For Ind: Tire/Rubber Grp: Basic Industries Paul C James, CEO	Rev: Assets: Emp:	900 600 8	
Armstrong World Industries Inc W Liberty Street PO Box 3001 Lancaster, PA 17604 717-397-0611	Manufacturer of carpet & floor coverings. Type: NYSE-ACK Ind: Manufacturing Grp: Manufacturing William W Adams, CEO Robert Caldwell, VCh Charles A Walker, CFO Forbes H Burgess, IS Joseph Hennessey, R&D Frank Simpson, PR	Rev: Assets: Emp:	2680 2098 28	
Armtek Corp 500 Sargent Drive New Haven, CT 06511 203-784-2200	Manufacturer of heat transfer equipment, tubing. Type: NYSE Ind: Manufacturing Grp: Manufacturing Frank R O'Keefe, CEO Harley Rankin Jr, CFO John N Sievers, Mkt Robert H Jones, PR	Rev: Assets: Emp:	1200 1000 12	
Arrow Electronics Inc 25 Hubb Drive Melville, NY 11747 516-391-1300	Manufacturer of electronic components. Type: NYSE-ARW Ind: Electronics Grp: High Tech John C Waddell, CEO Stephen Kaufman, Chr Robert Klatell, VCh Dominic Polimeni, CFO Wesley Sagawa, Sls William Smith, Ops Robert McInerney, VP Don E Burton, VP Thomas Hallam, VP	Rev: Assets: Emp:	1006 530 5	
Arthur, Andersen & Co Inc 69 W Washington Chicago, IL 60602 312-580-0069	Major accounting firm. Type: Private Ind: Accounting Grp: Business Service Duane R Kullberg, CEO	Rev: Assets: Emp:	3000 NA 30	
Arthur, Young & Co Inc 277 Park Avenue New York, NY 10172 212-407-1500	Nationwide accounting firm. Type: Private Ind: Accounting Grp: Business Service William L Gladstone, CEO	Rev: Assets: Emp:	2000 NA 25	
Artra Group Inc 500 Central Avenue Winnetka, IL 60093 312-441-6650	Electronic instrument manufacturer. Type: NYSE-ATA Ind: Electronics Grp: High Tech John J Harvey, CEO	Rev: Assets: Emp:	204 150 2	
Arvin Industries Inc 1531 Thirteen Street Columbus, IN 47201 812-379-3000	Manufacturer of automotive parts; & replacement parts. Type: NYSE Ind: Automotive Grp: Manufacturing James K Baker, CEO L K Evans, Pres V William Hunt, VCh Haren B Thakor, CFO George Scheitlin, R&D Donald Scheidt, Sls Fred Meyer, PR	Rev: Assets: Emp:	1313 1058 17	

Organizations Listed Alphabetically

Organization / Address / Phone	Descriptive Information		Revenue / ($ mil)	Assets / ($ mil)	Emp (thous)

Asahi Chemical Industries
350 Fifth Avenue
New York, NY 10118
212-695-6720

Worldwide manufacturer of chemicals; US headquarters.
Type: Private-Sub-For
Ind: Chemicals   Grp: Basic Industries
Sukewuki Inaoa, CEO

Rev: 1100
Assets: NA
Emp: 1

Asamera Inc
144 4th Avenue SW
Calgary, AB T2P3N4 Can
403-269-5521

Oil & gas exploration & refining company.
Type: TOR
Ind: Energy   Grp: Basic Industries
Robert Welty, CEO

Rev: 306
Assets: 293
Emp: 1

Asarco Inc
180 Maiden Lane
New York, NY 10038
212-510-2000

Mining company; copper, zinc, lead.
Type: NYSE-AR
Ind: Metals/Mining   Grp: Basic Industries
Richard Osborne, CEO   Alexander Gillespie, VCh   Francis McAllister, CFO
Stephen McCandless, IS   Michael Varner, R&D   William Bennis, Sls
Robert Bothwell Jr, Mkt   George Anderson, VP   Robert J Muth, PR

Rev: 1988
Assets: 2223
Emp: 9

Ashland Coal Inc
2205 5th Street
Huntington, VA 25701
304-526-3333

Mining company; coal.
Type: Private-Sub   Par: Ashland Oil Inc
Ind: Metals/Mining   Grp: Basic Industries
William C Payne, CEO

Rev: 300
Assets: 250
Emp: 2

Ashland Oil Inc
1000 Ashland Drive
Russell, KY 41169
606-329-3333

International producer & marketer of petroleum products.
Type: NYSE-ASH
Ind: Energy   Grp: Basic Industries
John R Hall, CEO   Charles J Luellen, Pres   John A Brothers, VCh
Paul W Chellgren, CFO   Gaige R Paulsen, IS   William Voss, Sls
James Boyd, VP   John F Petus, VP   William Sawran, VP
Harry Zachem, VP   David D'Antoni, VP   J Dan Lacy, PR

Rev: 8196
Assets: 4254
Emp: 30

Ashton Tate Inc
20101 Hamilton Avenue
Torrance, CA 90502
213-329-8000

Manufacturer of computer software; database.
Type: NASDAQ-TATE
Ind: Comput/Off Equip   Grp: High Tech
Edward M Esber, CEO   Luther Nussbaum, Pres   George L Farinsky, CFO
Harvey Jeane, R&D   Lydia Dobyns, Sls   Joseph Brilando, Mkt
William Stow, VP   Stanley Witkow, VP   Paula Cowan, VP

Rev: 307
Assets: 305
Emp: 3

Ask Mr Foster Travel Inc
7833 Haskell Avenue
Van Nuys, CA 91406
818-988-0181

Operator of retail travel agencies.
Type: Private
Ind: Business Service   Grp: Business Service
Hans Belange, CEO

Rev: 550
Assets: NA
Emp: 2

Asplundh Tree Experts Inc
708 Blair Mill Road
Willow Grove, PA 19090
215-784-4200

Garden & tree service company.
Type: Private
Ind: Business Service   Grp: Business Service
Edward K Asplundh, CEO

Rev: 500
Assets: NA
Emp: 6

Associated Actors & Artistes of America
165 W 46th Street
New York, NY 10036
212-869-0358

National labor union.
Type: Membership Org
Ind: Membership Org   Grp: Govt & Non-Prof
Frederick O'Neil, CEO

Rev: 250
Assets: NM
Emp: 220

Associated Electric Co-op Inc
2814 S Golden
Springfield, MO 65801
417-881-1204

Producer & distributor of electric power to local utilities.
Type: Private
Ind: Utility   Grp: Utilities
Jerry Diddle, CEO

Rev: 550
Assets: NA
Emp: 2

Associated Food Stores Inc
1812 S Empire
Salt Lake City, UT 84104
801-973-4400

Operator of retail food stores.
Type: Private
Ind: Retail/Food   Grp: Retail
Gil Warner, CEO

Rev: 660
Assets: NA
Emp: 3

Associated Grocers Inc
3301 S Norfolk
Seattle, WA 98124
206-762-2100

Operator of food wholesale warehouses.
Type: Private
Ind: Retail/Food   Grp: Retail
Donald W Benson, CEO

Rev: 1100
Assets: NA
Emp: 2

Organizations Listed Alphabetically

Organization / Address / Phone	Descriptive Information	Revenue / Assets / Emp ($ mil) ($ mil) (thous)		

Organization / Address / Phone	Descriptive Information			
Associated Grocers of Colorado Inc 4891 Independence Suite 201 Wheatridge, CO 80033 303-297-9121	Grocery products distribution company. Type: Private Ind: Retail/Food Grp: Retail Charles New, CEO	Rev: Assets: Emp:	550 NA 1	
Associated Madison Asset Management Inc 200 Park Avenue New York, NY 10166 212-351-2600	Investment firm. Type: Private Ind: Non-Bank Fin Grp: Financial not available, CEO	Rev: Assets: Emp:	440 16500 1	
Associated Metals & Minerals Inc 3 N Corporate Park Drive White Plains, NY 10604 914-251-5400	Steel trading firm. Type: Private Ind: Metals/Mining Grp: Basic Industries Stefan E Eliel, CEO	Rev: Assets: Emp:	750 NA 1	
Associated Milk Producers Inc 6609 Blanco Road San Antonio, TX 78216 512-340-9100	Producer & marketer of dairy products. Type: Private Ind: Food Processing Grp: Food Processing Ira Rutherford, CEO Irving Elkin, Pres Harry Pickens, CFO Robert Seymour, IS James Eskin, PR	Rev: Assets: Emp:	3300 500 3	
Associated Wholesale Grocers Inc 5000 Kansas Avenue Kansas City, KS 66106 913-321-1313	Wholesaler of food & sundries for grocery stores. Type: Private Ind: Retail/Food Grp: Retail James L Baska, CEO	Rev: Assets: Emp:	1870 NA 2	
Associates Corp of America Inc 250 Carpenter Freeway Dallas, TX 75266 214-659-4000	Consumer finance company. Type: Private-Sub Par: Paramount Communications Corp Ind: Non-Bank Fin Grp: Financial R A Overcash, CEO	Rev: Assets: Emp:	1733 15000 7	
Assurance vie Desjardins Ltd 200 Avenue Des Commandeurs Levis, PQ G6V6R2 Can 418-835-2323	Life insurance company. Type: Private-Mutual Ind: Insurance Grp: Insurance Jean Claude Valand, CEO	Rev: Assets: Emp:	329 1057 1	
AST Research Inc 2121 Alton Avenue Irvine, CA 92713 714-863-1333	Manufacturer of micro computers. Type: NASDAQ-ASTA Ind: Comput/Off Equip Grp: High Tech Thomas Yien, CEO	Rev: Assets: Emp:	456 200 2	
Astec Industries Inc 4101 Jerome Avenue Chattanooga, TN 37407 615-867-4210	Manufacturer of construction equipment. Type: OTC Ind: Equipment Grp: Manufacturing J D Brock, CEO	Rev: Assets: Emp:	250 150 2	
Astoria Federal Savings Assn Inc 3716 30th Avenue Long Island City, NY 11103 718-545-4400	Thrift institution. Type: Private Ind: Savings & Loan Grp: Financial Henry Drewitz, CEO	Rev: Assets: Emp:	300 3084 1	
Astroline Corp 95 Walkers Brook Drive Reading, MA 01867 508-942-1600	Oil & petroleum trading company. Type: Private Ind: Energy Grp: Basic Industries Fred Boling, CEO	Rev: Assets: Emp:	2500 NA 1	
Atari Corp 1196 Borregas Avenue Sunnyvale, CA 94086 408-745-2000	Manufacturer of computer games, personal computers. Type: ASE-ATC Ind: Comput/Off Equip Grp: High Tech Jack Tramiel, CEO Sam Tramiel, Pres Gregory A Pratt, CFO	Rev: Assets: Emp:	452 NA 4	
Atco Ltd 909 11th Avenue SW Calgary, AB T2R1N6 Can 403-292-7500	Manufacturer of metal handling equipment. Type: TOR Ind: Machinery Grp: Manufacturing K Purdie, CEO	Rev: Assets: Emp:	1227 2737 5	

Organizations Listed Alphabetically

Organization / Address / Phone	Descriptive Information	Revenue / ($ mil)	Assets / ($ mil)	Emp (thous)
ATCOR Inc 16100 S Lathrop Avenue Harvey, IL 60426 312-339-1610	Manufacturer of industrial products; steel wire, cable. Type: Private-Sub Ind: Manufacturing Grp: Manufacturing Richard A Feletti, CEO	Rev: Assets: Emp:	500 250 4	
Athlone Industries Inc 200 Webro Road Parsippany, NJ 07540 201-887-9100	Manufacturer of specialty steel. Type: NYSE-ATH Ind: Steel Grp: Basic Industries Harold J Miller, CEO	Rev: Assets: Emp:	175 NA 2	
Atkinson, Guy F Co of California 10 W Orange Avenue S San Francisco, CA 94080 415-876-1000	Manufacturer of industrial equipment, electrical switches. Type: NASDAQ-ATKN Ind: Real Estate/Bldg Grp: Business Service Thomas W Halligan, CEO Thomas J Henderson, Chr Ray N Atkinson, Pres Chris V Braunlich, Tres James D Stevens, Sls William P Hart, Mkt John F Gibbons, VP Duane E Atkinson, VP Robert D Langford, VP Richard F Byers, VP John W Reece, VP Jack Agresti, VP David P Swearington, IR	Rev: Assets: Emp:	920 305 8	
Atlanta Gas Light Co 235 Peachtree NE Atlanta, GA 30302 404-584-4000	Natural gas utility company. Type: NYSE-ATG Ind: Utility Grp: Utilities David R Jones, CEO John D McHugh, VCh B Lloyd Fackler, CFO L Jay Hill, Mkt Thomas Bensen, Ops Richard Woodward, VP	Rev: Assets: Emp:	976 1221 4	
Atlanta, City of City Hall 68 Mitchell Street SW Atlanta, GA 30335 404-658-6100	City government. Type: City Govt Ind: Local Govt Grp: Govt & Non-Prof Andrew Young, CEO	Rev: Assets: Emp:	596 NM 7	
Atlantic Energy Co 1199 Black Horse Pike Pleasantville, NJ 08232 609-645-4100	Electric power utility. Type: NYSE-ATE Ind: Utility Grp: Utilities E Douglas Huggard, CEO Jerrold Jacobs, VCh J David McCann, Tres J G Salomone, CFO Henry Levari, R&D Joseph Kelley, Ops Henry Schwemm, VP Morgan T Morris, VP Bertram LeMunyon, VP Lance Cooper, VP	Rev: Assets: Emp:	676 1660 2	
Atlantic Financial Federal Inc 50 Monument Road Bala Cynwyd, PA 19004 215-668-6600	Thrift institution. Type: NASDAQ-ATLF Ind: Savings & Loan Grp: Financial Calvin D Baker, CEO Donald R Caldwell, Chr James Rizzo, VCh Richard Guttendorf, CFO Ronald Murray, IS James J Kinney, Mkt Joshua Thompson, VP James J Kinney, IR Bruce Boyle, PR	Rev: Assets: Emp:	764 7799 2	
Atlantic Mutual Insurance Co 45 Wall Street New York, NY 10005 212-943-1800	Property & casualty insurance company. Type: Private-Mutual Ind: Insurance Grp: Insurance Edward K Trowbridge, CEO	Rev: Assets: Emp:	652 1191 2	
Atlantic Packaging Products Ltd 111 Progress Avenue Scarborough, ON M1P2Y9 Can 416-298-8101	Manufacturer of paper packaging products; bags. Type: Private Ind: Packaging Grp: Manufacturing P Granovsky, CEO	Rev: Assets: Emp:	340 170 2	
Atlantic Richfield Co 515 S Flower Street Los Angeles, CA 90071 213-486-3511	International oil production & distribution company. Type: NYSE Ind: Energy Grp: Basic Industries Lodwrick M Cook, CEO Robert E Wycoff, Pres Ronald J Arnault, CFO	Rev: Assets: Emp:	18868 21514 27	
Atmos Energy Corp 5430 LBJ Freeway Dallas, TX 75240 214-934-9227	Natural gas distribution company. Type: NYSE-ATO Ind: Utility Grp: Utilities Charles K Vaughan, CEO	Rev: Assets: Emp:	323 600 2	

Organizations Listed Alphabetically

Organization / Address / Phone	Descriptive Information	Revenue / ($ mil)	Assets / ($ mil)	Emp (thous)
Auburn University Administrative Bldg Auburn University, AL 36849 205-826-4000	Major educational institution; university. Type: University Ind: University Grp: Govt & Non-Prof James E Martin, CEO	Rev: Assets: Emp:	171 330 21	
Audio/Video Affiliates Inc 2875 Needmore Road Dayton, OH 45414 513-274-3737	Operator of retail home electronics stores. Type: NYSE-AVA Ind: Retail/Merch Grp: Retail Stuart Rose, CEO	Rev: Assets: Emp:	200 150 2	
Audiovox Corp 150 Marcus Blvd Hauppauge, NY 11789 516-231-7750	Personal electronic retailing company; mobile phones. Type: ASE-VOX Ind: Retail/Merch Grp: Retail John J Shalam, CEO	Rev: Assets: Emp:	275 150 1	
Audits & Surveys Inc 650 Avenue of the Americas New York, NY 10011 212-627-9700	Engineering & consulting firm. Type: Private Ind: Business Service Grp: Business Service Solomon Dutka, CEO	Rev: Assets: Emp:	275 NA 4	
Augat Inc 89 Forbes Blvd Mansfield, MA 02048 617-543-4300	Electronic manufacturer. Type: NYSE-AUG Ind: Electronics Grp: High Tech Roger D Wellington, CEO	Rev: Assets: Emp:	321 278 4	
Aurora Eby Brown Co Inc 1001 Sullivan Aurora, IL 60505 312-897-8674	Producer & distributor of packaged food products. Type: Private Ind: Food Processing Grp: Food Processing William Wake, CEO	Rev: Assets: Emp:	550 NA 1	
Ausimont NV Inc 128 Technology Drive Waltham, MA 02154 617-899-3000	Manufacturer of specialty chemicals. Type: Private-Sub-For Ind: Chemicals Grp: Basic Industries Leonard Rosenblatt, CEO	Rev: Assets: Emp:	650 500 2	
Austin Co Inc 206 Cutler Street Corner Cutler & Hall Greeneville, TN 37743 615-638-4124	Producer & distributor of packaged food products. Type: Private Ind: Food Processing Grp: Food Processing Tom N Austin, CEO	Rev: Assets: Emp:	550 NA 1	
Austin Industries Inc 2949 Stemmons Freeway Dallas, TX 75247 214-630-5100	General contracting, construction. Type: Private Ind: Real Estate/Bldg Grp: Business Service William T Solomon, CEO	Rev: Assets: Emp:	500 NA 5	
Austin, City of City Hall Austin, TX 78767 512-499-2250	City government. Type: City Govt Ind: Local Govt Grp: Govt & Non-Prof Lee Cooke, CEO	Rev: Assets: Emp:	795 NM 9	
Auto Club of Michigan Inc 17000 Executive Plaza Drive Dearborn, MI 48126 313-336-1234	Property & casualty insurance company. Type: Private-Mutual Ind: Insurance Grp: Insurance John J Avignone, CEO	Rev: Assets: Emp:	733 1171 3	
Auto Owners Group Insurance Co 6101 Anacapri Blvd Lansing, MI 48917 517-323-1200	Property & casualty insurance company. Type: Private-Mutual Ind: Insurance Grp: Insurance R E Otto, CEO	Rev: Assets: Emp:	994 1724 3	
Auto Zone Corp 3030 Poplar Avenue Memphis, TN 38101 901-325-4600	Operator of automotive parts retail stores. Type: Private Ind: Retail/Merch Grp: Retail J R Hyde, CEO	Rev: Assets: Emp:	500 NA 5	

Organizations Listed Alphabetically

Organization / Address / Phone	Descriptive Information	Revenue ($ mil)	Assets ($ mil)	Emp (thous)
Autodesk Corp 2320 Marinship Way Sausalito, CA 94965 415-332-2344	Micro computer software developer & publisher. Type: NASDAQ-ACAD Ind: Comput/Off Equip Grp: High Tech Alvar Green, CEO	Rev: Assets: Emp:	117 170 2	
Automatic Data Processing Inc One ADP Blvd. Roseland, NJ 07068 201-994-5000	Payroll processing services. Type: NYSE-AUD Ind: Comput/Off Equip Grp: High Tech Josh S Weston, CEO Bill Turner, Pres Art Weinbach, CFO Bill Friel, R&D Bob Levenson, Mkt Arthur Weinbeck, VP Robert Casale, VP Robert Levenson, VP David L Perlman, VP Edward J Kanarkowski, PR	Rev: Assets: Emp:	1549 1653 23	
Automotive Aftermarket Co 707 Skokie Blvd Northbrook, IL 60026 312-272-9600	Manufacturer of motion control systems for automobiles. Type: Private-Sub Par: Parker Hannifin Corp Ind: Automotive Grp: Manufacturing Paul Schlloemer, CEO	Rev: Assets: Emp:	NA NA NA	
Automotive Carrier Div 4111 E Andover Road Bloomfield Hills, MI 48303 313-258-2000	Truck transportation services company. Type: Private-Sub Par: Ryder System Inc Ind: Transport Grp: Business Service Frederick Reinhardt, CEO	Rev: Assets: Emp:	NA NA NA	
AVCO Financial Services Inc 3349 Michelson Irvine, CA 92715 714-553-1200	Consumer financing & insurance. Type: Private-Sub Par: Textron Inc Ind: Non-Bank Fin Grp: Financial Carlton W Honebein, CEO Charles R Rinehart, Chr William A Barrett, VCh Ronald Bukow, CFO B F Dolan, VP Donald K Farrar, VP Gary L Fite, VP	Rev: Assets: Emp:	1047 4173 7	
Avery International Corp 150 N Orange Grove Blvd Pasadena, CA 91103 818-304-2000	Manufacturer of labels & adhesive materials. Type: NYSE-AVY Ind: Manufacturing Grp: Manufacturing Charles D Miller, CEO Nelson Peltz, Chr Peter W May, Pres Wayne H Smith, Tres R Gregory Jenkins, CFO Joseph A Michael, IS Alan Gotcher, R&D Diane B Dixon, Sls Charles Gilhuys, Ops Jerry Hostetter, IR Lynne Winters, PR	Rev: Assets: Emp:	1582 1119 12	
Avis Corp 900 Old Country Road Garden City, NY 11530 516-222-3000	International automobile rental & leasing company. Type: Private-Sub Par: PHH Group Inc Ind: Consumer Service Grp: Consumer Service Joseph V Vittoria, CEO	Rev: Assets: Emp:	1000 NA 13	
Avnet Inc 80 Cutter Mill Road Great Neck, NY 11021 516-466-7000	Distributor of electronic components & computer products. Type: NYSE-AVT Ind: Business Service Grp: Business Service Anthony R Hamilton, CEO Leon Machiz, Pres Albert Snider, VCh John Regazzi, CFO Anthony DeLuca, IS Edward Kaniger, Mkt Sam Farhy, Ops Daniel Robbin, VP Walter Hyjek, VP Miton Graham, VP Irwin Lubalin, PR	Rev: Assets: Emp:	1817 1153 11	
Avon Products Inc 9 W 57th Street New York, NY 10019 212-546-6015	Personal care products company. Type: NYSE Ind: Personal Care Grp: Consumer Prd Donald E Strange, CEO James E Preston, Chr Paul B MArkovits, Pres W Thomas Knight, VCh John Donaldson, CFO Raymond Perry, IS James P Steffenson, R&D Phyllis Davis, Sls Paul Markovits, Mkt Martha Worthing, VP Giovanni F Treccani, VP James Kehoe, VP John F Cox, PR	Rev: Assets: Emp:	3063 2460 28	
Avondale Industries Inc 5100 River Road New Orleans, LA 70094 504-436-2121	Diversified manufacturing company. Type: Private Ind: Manufacturing Grp: Manufacturing Al Bossier, CEO	Rev: Assets: Emp:	550 NA 5	

Organizations Listed Alphabetically

Organization / Address / Phone	Descriptive Information	Revenue / Assets / Emp ($ mil) ($ mil) (thous)		

Avtex Fibers Inc
Cassatt Road Bldg 200
Berwyn Park, PA 19312
215-251-7700

Manufacturer of textiles & apparel products.
Type: Private
Ind: Apparel/Textiles   Grp: Consumer Prd
John Gregg, CEO

Rev: 275
Assets: NA
Emp: 3

AVX Corp
60 Cuttermill Road
Great Neck, NY 11021
516-829-8500

Manufacturer of electronic parts & components.
Type: NYSE-AVX
Ind: Electronics   Grp: High Tech
Marshall D Butler, CEO

Rev: 271
Assets: 200
Emp: 2

Ayer, N W Inc
1345 Avenue of the Americas
New York, NY 10105
212-708-5000

Advertising agency.
Type: Private
Ind: Business Service   Grp: Business Service
Jerry Siano, CEO

Rev: 1100
Assets: NA
Emp: 2

Babcock & Wilcox Co
1010 Common Street
New Orleans, LA 70112
504-587-5400

Manufacturer of power generation systems & equipment.
Type: Private-Sub Par: McDermott International Inc
Ind: Manufacturing   Grp: Manufacturing
J Eckert, CEO

Rev: NA
Assets: NA
Emp: NA

Bacardi Import Corp
PO Box 3549
San Juan, PR 00936
809-795-1560

Distilled spirits & wine distributors.
Type: Private
Ind: Food Processing   Grp: Food Processing
Anwar Soliman, CEO

Rev: 750
Assets: NA
Emp: 2

Baddaur Inc
4300 New Getwell Street
Memphis, TN 38118
901-365-8880

Manufacturer of textile & apparel products.
Type: Private
Ind: Apparel/Textiles   Grp: Consumer Prd
Paul Baddaur, CEO

Rev: 275
Assets: NA
Emp: 2

Bain & Co
2 Copley Place
Boston, MA 02116
617-572-2000

Nationwide consulting company.
Type: Private
Ind: Consulting   Grp: Business Service
William Bain, CEO

Rev: 400
Assets: NA
Emp: 3

Baird & Warner Inc
200 W Madison
Chicago, IL 60606
312-368-1855

Construction & commercial building company.
Type: Private
Ind: Real Estate/Bldg   Grp: Business Service
Terry Schreiner, CEO

Rev: 550
Assets: NA
Emp: 2

Bairnco Corp
200 Park Avenue
New York, NY 10166
212-490-8722

Manufacturer of aerospace & electronic products.
Type: NYSE-BZ
Ind: Electronics   Grp: High Tech
Glen W Bailey, CEO   David C Bevan Jr, CFO   Ray Schumack, PR

Rev: 228
Assets: 297
Emp: 2

Baker Fentress & Co
200 W Madison Street
Chicago, IL 60606
312-236-9190

Investment management company.
Type: NYSE
Ind: Securities   Grp: Financial
James P Gorter, CEO

Rev: 200
Assets: 150
Emp: 1

Baker Hughes Co
3900 Essex Lane
Houston, TX 77027
713-439-8600

Oil exploration equipment manufacturer.
Type: NYSE-BHI
Ind: Oil Service   Grp: Business Service
James D Woods, CEO   Howard I Bull, VCh   Max L Lukens, CFO
Joel Staff, VP   Fanklin Myers, VP   Phillip Rice, VP
Ronald Turner, VP   G Finley, VP

Rev: 2316
Assets: 2118
Emp: 21

Baker Hughes Mining Equipment
455 Racetrack Road
Meadowlands, PA 15347
412-225-8016

Manufacturer of mining & drilling equipment.
Type: Private-Sub Par: Baker Hughes Co
Ind: Equipment   Grp: Manufacturing
Karl Schrock, CEO

Rev: NA
Assets: NA
Emp: NA

Baker International Corp
500 City Parkway W
Orange, CA 92668
714-634-2333

Manufacturer of equipment & service to the oil industry.
Type: Private-Sub Par: Baker Hughes Co
Ind: Oil Service   Grp: Business Service
F H Clarke, CEO   James D Woods, Chr   Max Lukens, CFO
Leroy Harmeyer, IS   Ronald Turner, IR   Wayne Bryant, PR

Rev: 1600
Assets: 1500
Emp: 20

Organizations Listed Alphabetically

Organization / Address / Phone	Descriptive Information	Revenue / Assets / Emp ($ mil) ($ mil) (thous)		

Baker, J Inc
65 Sprague Street
Boston, MA 02137
617-364-3000

Operator of retail stores; apparel, shoes.
Type: OTC
Ind: Retail/Merch   Grp: Retail
Sherman N Baker, CEO

Rev: 250
Assets: 200
Emp: 3

Baldor Electric Co
5711 S 7th Street
Fort Smith, AR 72902
501-646-4711

Manufacturer of industrial equipment; electrical motors.
Type: NYSE-BEZ
Ind: Electronics   Grp: High Tech
Roland S Boreham, CEO

Rev: 200
Assets: 200
Emp: 2

Balfour Maclaine Corp(former Kay Corp)
Wall Street Plaza
New York, NY 10005
212-269-0800

Import/export company; agricultural, metals, commodities.
Type: ASE-BML
Ind: Securities   Grp: Financial
Anthonie C van Ekris, CEO   Raymond Nessim, Pres   Thomas Hitselberger, VCh
Russell Diaz, CFO   Edward Rywalt, IS   Murray Ackerman, VP
William Ward, VP   Scott Spitzer, VP   Murray Ackerman, PR

Rev: 1042
Assets: 500
Emp: 1

Ball Corp
345 S High Street
Muncie, IN 47305
317-747-6100

Beverage can manufacturer.
Type: NYSE-BLL
Ind: Packaging   Grp: Manufacturing
Richard M Ringoen, CEO   Thomas D Bell, Pres   Delmont Davis, VCh
William L Peterson, CFO   Richard E Durbin, IS   Thomas Clark, R&D
Duane Emerson, VP   Roland Campbell, VP   Elizabeth Overrmyer, VP
R David Hoover, VP   John J Pruis, IR   Larry D Miller, PR

Rev: 1073
Assets: 877
Emp: 7

Bally Manufacturing Corp
8700 W Bryn Mawr Avenue
Chicago, IL 60631
312-399-1300

Leisure time service & manufacturing; hotels, gaming.
Type: NYSE
Ind: Leisure Time   Grp: Consumer Service
Robert E Mullane, CEO   Roger N Keesee, Pres   James M Rochford, VCh
Paul Johnson, CFO   Howard Polay, IS   Neil E Jenkins, VP
William H Peltier, VP   Charles T Powell, VP   James J Barrett, VP
Maurice J Ferchen, VP   William H Peltier, PR

Rev: 1941
Assets: 2867
Emp: 17

Baltimore Gas & Electric Co
Gas & Electric Bldg Charles Center
Baltimore, MD 21203
301-234-5000

Gas & electric utility.
Type: NYSE-BGE
Ind: Utility   Grp: Utilities
George V McGowan, CEO   Edward A Crooke, Pres   C W Shivery, CFO
Joseph Hunter, IS   Edwin W Skoglin, Mkt   Thomas Brady, VP
Jon Files, VP   Jeffrey Davis, VP   Gary Furman, IR
George W Gephart, PR

Rev: 1864
Assets: 5126
Emp: 9

Baltimore, City of
City Hall
Baltimore, MD 21202
301-396-4892

City government.
Type: City Govt
Ind: Local Govt   Grp: Govt & Non-Prof
Kurt L Schmoke, CEO

Rev: 1464
Assets: NM
Emp: 29

Banc One Corp
100 E Broad Street
Columbus, OH 43271
614-463-5944

Commercial bank.
Type: NYSE-ONE
Ind: Banking   Grp: Financial
John B McCoy, CEO   Frank E McKinney, Pres   R Patrick Handley, CFO
David Van Lear, IS   John F Fisher, R&D   John F Fisher, Mkt
John A Russell, IR   Johanna M White, PR

Rev: 2734
Assets: 25274
Emp: 17

Banc One Wisconsin
111 E Wisconsin Avenue
Milwaukee, WI 53202
414-765-3000

Commercial bank.
Type: OTC
Ind: Banking   Grp: Financial
George R Slater, CEO   Leila Fraser, Mkt   Nancy Kane, PR

Rev: 400
Assets: 4000
Emp: 2

Banca Serfin
88 Pine Street 24th Floor
New York, NY 10005
212-635-2300

Commercial bank.
Type: Private-Sub-For
Ind: Banking   Grp: Financial
Alfonso Maza, CEO

Rev: 440
Assets: 3500
Emp: 2

Banco Nacional de Mexico
375 Park Avenue
New York, NY 10022
212-838-8300

Commercial bank.
Type: Private-Sub-For
Ind: Banking   Grp: Financial
Alejandro Morales, CEO

Rev: 550
Assets: 4000
Emp: 2

Organizations Listed Alphabetically

Organization / Address / Phone	Descriptive Information	Revenue / ($ mil)	Assets / ($ mil)	Emp (thous)
Banco Popular de Puerto Rico Inc 4043 Broadway New York, NY 10032 212-928-8600	Commercial bank. Type: Private Ind: Banking Grp: Financial Rafael Carrion, CEO	Rev: Assets: Emp:	543 5707 7	
Bancorp Hawaii Inc 111 S King Street Honolulu, HI 96813 808-537-8111	Commercial bank. Type: NASDAQ-BNHI Ind: Banking Grp: Financial Frank J Manaut, CEO H Howard Stephenson, Pres Lawrence Johnson, VCh Richard J Dahl, CFO James Massey, IS David L Ramsour, R&D Daniel Bauer, Mkt William Huckins, VP Ruth Milyashiro, VP John Tsui, VP Piia Aarma, PR	Rev: Assets: Emp:	630 6635 3	
Bandag Inc Bandag Center Muscatine, IA 52761 319-262-1400	Manufacturer of rubber products. Type: NYSE-BDG Ind: Tire/Rubber Grp: Basic Industries Martin G Carver, CEO	Rev: Assets: Emp:	498 315 2	
Banister Continental Corp 9910 39th Avenue Edmonton, AB T5J2R4 Can 403-462-9430	Construction company; pipe line construction. Type: ASE Ind: Real Estate/Bldg Grp: Business Service R MacTavish, CEO	Rev: Assets: Emp:	311 213 1	
Bank Laurentienne du Canada 1981 McGill College Avenue Montreal, PQ H3A3K3 Can 514-284-3931	Thrift institution. Type: TOR Ind: Savings & Loan Grp: Financial Claude Castonguay, CEO	Rev: Assets: Emp:	416 4117 2	
Bank Leumi Trust Co 579 Fifth Avenue New York, NY 10017 212-382-4000	Commercial bank. Type: Private Ind: Banking Grp: Financial Meir Heth, CEO	Rev: Assets: Emp:	276 3140 3	
Bank of Boston Corp 100 Federal Street Boston, MA 02110 617-434-2200	Commercial bank. Type: NYSE-BKB Ind: Banking Grp: Financial Ira Stempanian, CEO William L Brown, Chr Ira Stepanian, Pres Alan L McKinnon, CFO Ira Jackson, IR Linda Hansus, PR	Rev: Assets: Emp:	5296 36060 20	
Bank of California (Mitsubishi Bank) 800 Wilshire Blvd Los Angeles, CA 90017 213-621-1200	Commercial bank. Type: Private-Sub-For Ind: Banking Grp: Financial Osamu Yamada, CEO	Rev: Assets: Emp:	583 6887 1	
Bank of Canada 234 Wellington Street Ottawa, ON K1A0G9 Can 613-563-8111	Canadian central bank; federal government. Type: Federal Govt Ind: Federal Govt Fin Grp: Financial John W Crow, CEO	Rev: Assets: Emp:	2040 NM 2	
Bank of Montreal 129 Rue St Jacques Montreal, PQ H2Y1L6 Can 514-877-7110	Commercial bank. Type: TOR-BMO Ind: Banking Grp: Financial W D Mulholland, CEO G L Reuber, Chr M W Barrett, Pres S M Davison, VCh K O Dorricott, CFO F A Comper, Ops M R P Rayfield, VP R G Rogers, VP A G McNally, VP D M Jones, VP R B Wells, VP S Zargham, VP	Rev: Assets: Emp:	6816 67073 34	
Bank of New England Corp 28 State Street Boston, MA 02109 617-742-4000	Commercial bank. Type: NYSE-NEB Ind: Banking Grp: Financial Walter J Connolly, CEO Peter H McCormick, Pres Joseph Whiteside, CFO Ray Dwyer, IS Elizabeth Segers, R&D Richard J Condon, Mkt Richard J Condon, IR Timothy Kilduff, PR	Rev: Assets: Emp:	3247 30110 18	

Organizations Listed Alphabetically

Organization / Address / Phone	Descriptive Information	Revenue / Assets / Emp ($ mil) ($ mil) (thous)		

Bank of New York Co
48 Wall Street
New York, NY 10286
212-495-1784

Commercial bank.
Type: NYSE-BK
Ind: Banking   Grp: Financial
Robert E Keilman, CEO   J Carter Bacot, Chr   Peter Herrick, Pres
Samuel Chevalier, VCh   Deno D Papageorge, CFO   David G Wertz, IS
Thomas J Dillman, R&D   Richard D Field, Mkt   Robert Keilman, VP
Charles E Rappold, VP   Richard D Field, VP   Owen A Brady, PR

Rev: 2620
Assets: 47388
Emp: 18

Bank of Nova Scotia Ltd
44 King Street W
Toronto, ON M5H 1H1 Can
416-866-6161

Commercial bank.
Type: Private
Ind: Banking   Grp: Financial
C E Ritchie, CEO

Rev: 5437
Assets: 60716
Emp: 26

Bank of Tokyo Trust
360 Madison Avenue
New York, NY 10017
212-766-3472

Commercial bank.
Type: Private-Sub-For
Ind: Banking   Grp: Financial
Hiroshi Hayashi, CEO   Tamotsu Yamaguchi, Chr   Yukio Yoshida, CFO
Yoji Izumi, IS   Tetsuya Nagase, Mkt   Norimichi Kanari, PR

Rev: 800
Assets: 7000
Emp: 1

Bank South Corp
55 Marietta Street
Atlanta, GA 30303
404-529-4521

Commercial bank.
Type: NASDAQ-BKSO
Ind: Banking   Grp: Financial
Robert P Guyton, CEO   Franklin Burke, VCh   Ralph Hutchins, CFO
Ina Beindorff, Mkt   Rod W Cook, VP   C Arnold Johnson, VP
H Thomas Miller, VP

Rev: 409
Assets: 4881
Emp: 2

BankAmerica Corp
Bank of America Center
San Francisco, CA 94104
415-622-3456

Commercial bank.
Type: NYSE-BA
Ind: Banking   Grp: Financial
A W Clausen, CEO   A W Clausen, Chr   Richard Rosenberg, VCh
Frank N Newman, CFO   Lewis W Coleman, IS   Robert Beck, Mkt
George Coombe, Ops   Michael Simmons, VP   George Cherrie, VP
Ronald E Rhody, IR   Art Miller, PR

Rev: 10182
Assets: 94647
Emp: 54

Bankers Trust New York Corp
280 Park Avenue
New York, NY 10017
212-250-2500

Commercial bank.
Type: NYSE
Ind: Banking   Grp: Financial
Charles S Sanford, CEO   Phillip M Hampton, VCh   William C Jennings, CFO
Carmine Vona, IS   James J Baechle, VP   Edward A Lesser, VP
Ralph L MacDonald, VP   Joseph A Manganello, VP   Eugene Shanks, VP
George Vojta, VP   Thomas A Parisi, PR

Rev: 5851
Assets: 57942
Emp: 13

Banks of Mid-America Inc
100 Broadway
Oklahoma City, OK 73125
405-231-6000

Commercial bank.
Type: NASDAQ-BOMA
Ind: Banking   Grp: Financial
Frank X Henke, CEO

Rev: 190
Assets: 2269
Emp: 2

Banner Industries Inc
25700 Science Park Drive
Beachwood, OH 44122
216-464-3650

Aerospace manufacturer; rubber, plastic components.
Type: NYSE-BNR
Ind: Automotive   Grp: Manufacturing
Jeffrey J Steiner, CEO   Samuel Krasney, VCh   Warren Persavich, Tres
Michael T Alcox, CFO   Sam Spector, R&D   Max Makowsky, Sls
Mark Wester, VP

Rev: 374
Assets: 1066
Emp: 5

Banque National de Paris
499 Park Avenue
New York, NY 10022
212-980-5185

Commercial bank.
Type: Private-Sub-For
Ind: Banking   Grp: Financial
Gerard Decourelle, CEO

Rev: 450
Assets: 3500
Emp: 1

Banta, George Corp
Harbor Place
Menasha, WI 54952
414-722-7777

Publishing company; college, novels, video.
Type: OTC
Ind: Business Service   Grp: Business Service
Harry W Earle, CEO

Rev: 300
Assets: 200
Emp: 3

Organizations Listed Alphabetically

Organization / Address / Phone	Descriptive Information	Revenue / Assets / Emp ($ mil) ($ mil) (thous)		

Barbecon Inc
20 Eglington Avenue W
Toronto, ON M4R 3G7 Can
416-488-3344

Manufacturer of paper products; envelopes.
Type: Private-Sub   Par: Abitibi Price Ltd
Ind: Paper/Forest Prd   Grp: Basic Industries
W Livingston, CEO

Rev: 255
Assets: 128
Emp: 1

Barclays American Corp
75 Wall Street
New York, NY 10265
212-412-4000

Commercial bank.
Type: Private-Sub-For
Ind: Banking   Grp: Financial
John Spencer, CEO   G M Keith, Chr   E D M Schachner, CFO
James L Downs, IS   Julie McGuire, PR

Rev: 550
Assets: 4500
Emp: 3

Barclays Bank of Canada Ltd
3500 Commerce Court W
Toronto, ON M5L1G2 Can
416-862-0594

Commercial bank.
Type: Private
Ind: Banking   Grp: Financial
William B Harris, CEO

Rev: 140
Assets: 1872
Emp: 1

Bard, C R Inc
730 Central Avenue
Murray Hill, NJ 07974
201-277-8000

Manufacturer of healthcare equipment & products.
Type: NYSE-BCR
Ind: Drugs   Grp: Consumer Service
Robert H McCaffrey, CEO   George T Maloney, Pres   William Longfield, VCh
George A Davis, CFO   Ronald J Brickley, IS   David Prigmore, Sls
Terence Brady, Mkt   Frank M Krakowski, VP   Eugene Schultz, VP
David B Thomas, VP   William Bopp, IR   George A Davis, PR

Rev: 758
Assets: 531
Emp: 8

Barnes Group Inc
123 Main Street
Bristol, CT 06010
203-583-7070

Automotive & aircraft parts manufacturer.
Type: NYSE-B
Ind: Manufacturing   Grp: Manufacturing
Wallace Barnes, CEO   William Fenoglio, Pres   Carlyle Barnes, VCh
George Crowley, Tres   A Stanton Wells, CFO   Robert O'Conner, R&D
Francis Boyle, VP   Jack William, VP   John Locher, VP

Rev: 496
Assets: 312
Emp: 5

Barnett Banks Inc
100 Laura Street
Jacksonville, FL 32202
904-791-7720

Commercial bank.
Type: NYSE-BBI
Ind: Banking   Grp: Financial
Charles E Rice, CEO   Albert D Ernest, Pres   Allen Lastinger, VCh
Stephen A Hansel, CFO   Roger H Wiegmann, IS   William M Fackler, Mkt
Earl B Hadlow, VP   Paul Kerins, VP   Bruce Anglin, VP
R David Barnett, VP   Russell S Hoadley, PR

Rev: 2546
Assets: 25748
Emp: 15

Baroid Corp
3000 North Belt E
Houston, TX 77032
713-987-4000

Oil & gas drilling service company.
Type: NYSE-BRC
Ind: Oil Service   Grp: Business Service
H C Simmons, CEO

Rev: 550
Assets: 600
Emp: 3

Bartlett Agricultural Enterprises Inc
4800 Main Street
Kansas City, MO 64112
816-753-6300

Producer of packaged food products.
Type: Private
Ind: Food Processing   Grp: Food Processing
Paul D Bartlett, CEO

Rev: 650
Assets: NA
Emp: 2

Barton Malow Co
27777 Franklin Road   American Ctr Bldg
Southfield, MI 48034
313-351-4000

Construction management, general contracting.
Type: Private
Ind: Real Estate/Bldg   Grp: Business Service
Ben C Maibach, CEO

Rev: 500
Assets: NA
Emp: 3

BASF Canada Inc
345 Carlington Drive
Toronto, ON M9W6N9 Can
416-675-3611

Diversified chemical manufacturing company.
Type: Private-Sub-For
Ind: Chemicals   Grp: Basic Industries
John H Tiarks, CEO

Rev: 298
Assets: 128
Emp: 1

BASF Corp
Nine Campus Drive
Parsippany, NJ 07054
201-397-2700

Diversified manufacturer of chemicals; US headquarters.
Type: Private-Sub-For
Ind: Chemicals   Grp: Basic Industries
Dieter Stien, CEO   Juergen F Strube, Chr   Frederick W Bernthal, CFO
Dieter Heuer, IS   Gerhard W Paul, R&D   Helmuth Von Moltke, IR
Liane B Kranhold, PR

Rev: 4070
Assets: 2200
Emp: 21

Organizations Listed Alphabetically

Organization / Address / Phone	Descriptive Information	Revenue / Assets / Emp ($ mil) ($ mil) (thous)		

Basic American Foods Inc
550 Kearny
San Francisco, CA 94108
415-981-5590

Food processing company; packaged foods.
Type: Private
Ind: Food Processing Grp: Food Processing
George Hume, CEO

Rev: 550
Assets: NA
Emp: 5

Basic American Medical Corp
4000 E Southport Road
Indianapolis, IN 46237
317-783-5461

Operator of hospitals, health care facilities.
Type: OTC
Ind: Health Care Grp: Consumer Service
Ethan Jackson, CEO

Rev: 284
Assets: 300
Emp: 4

Bassett Furniture Industries Inc
PO Box 626
Bassett, VA 24055
703-629-7511

Manufacturer of home furniture.
Type: OTC
Ind: Manufacturing Grp: Manufacturing
Robert H Spilman, CEO Bill M Brammer, CFO J R Meadors, Mkt
Tom E Prado, PR

Rev: 400
Assets: 250
Emp: 6

BAT US Inc
2000 Citizens Plaza
Louisville, KY 40202
502-581-8000

Diversified manufacturer of packaged goods; US headquarters.
Type: Private-Sub-For
Ind: Food Processing Grp: Food Processing
Henry F Frigon, CEO

Rev: 5500
Assets: NA
Emp: 16

Bateman Eichler Hill Richards Inc
700 S Flower Street
Los Angeles, CA 90017
213-683-3500

Investment firm; securities trading.
Type: Private
Ind: Securities Grp: Financial
Richard Capaibo, CEO

Rev: 220
Assets: 2200
Emp: 1

Bates, Ted Worldwide Inc
405 Lexington
New York, NY 10174
212-297-7000

Nationwide consulting company.
Type: Private
Ind: Business Service Grp: Business Service
Carl Speilvogel, CEO

Rev: 450
Assets: NA
Emp: 5

Bath Iron Works Inc
700 Washington
Bath, ME 04530
207-443-3311

Ship building company.
Type: Private
Ind: Manufacturing Grp: Manufacturing
William E Haggett, CEO

Rev: 750
Assets: NA
Emp: 7

Bathurst Paper Ltd
800 O Boul Dorchester
Montreal, PQ H3C2R5 Can
514-875-2160

Manufacturer of forest products; paper.
Type: Private-Sub Par: Consolidated Bathurst Inc
Ind: Paper/Forest Prd Grp: Basic Industries
W Turne, CEO

Rev: 425
Assets: 468
Emp: 3

Baton Rouge, City of
City Hall
Baton Rouge, LA 70821
504-389-3100

City government.
Type: City Govt
Ind: Local Govt Grp: Govt & Non-Prof
Pat Screen, CEO

Rev: 298
Assets: NM
Emp: 5

Battelle Memorial Institute Inc
505 King Avenue
Columbus, OH 43201
614-424-6424

Research & development firm.
Type: Private
Ind: Consulting Grp: Business Service
Douglas E Olesen, CEO

Rev: 700
Assets: NA
Emp: 10

Batterymarch Financial Management Inc
600 Atlantic Avenue
Boston, MA 02210
617-973-9300

Investment firm; pension management.
Type: Private
Ind: Non-Bank Fin Grp: Financial
Dean LeBaron, CEO

Rev: 20
Assets: 8600
Emp: 1

Battle Mountain Corp
333 Clay Street 42nd Floor
Houston, TX 77002
713-227-6330

Gold exploration & production.
Type: NYSE-BMG
Ind: Metals/Mining Grp: Basic Industries
Douglas J Bourne, CEO Karl E Elers, Pres George Mitchell, CFO
Robert Quinn, Sls Frank Schweitzer, Mkt John Sharpe, Ops
Richard Sumin, VP

Rev: 141
Assets: 206
Emp: 1

Organizations Listed Alphabetically

Organization / Address / Phone	Descriptive Information	Revenue / Assets / Emp ($ mil) ($ mil) (thous)		

Bausch & Lomb Inc
One Lincoln First Square
Rochester, NY 14601
716-338-6000

Manufacturer of contact lens & eye care products.
Type: NYSE-BOL
Ind: Instruments   Grp: High Tech
Daniel E Gill, CEO   Thomas C McDermott, Pres   W Richard Clark, VCh
Alan Resnick, Tres   Stephen P Kelbley, CFO   Diane C Harris, R&D
Stanley Merrell, VP   James E Kanaley, VP   Stephen Hellrung, VP
John Larson, VP   Franklin P Jepson, PR

Rev: 978
Assets: 1211
Emp: 10

Baxter Travenol Laboratories Inc
One Baxter Parkway
Deerfield, IL 60015
312-948-2000

Manufacturer of health care products.
Type: NYSE-BAX
Ind: Drugs   Grp: Consumer Service
Vernon R Loucks, CEO   Wilber H Gantz, Pres   Robert Simmons, VCh
Robert J Lambrix, CFO   Michael S Heschel, IS   Warren Johnson, Sls
James R Tobin, VP   Dale A Smith, VP   James Connelly, VP
Michael Estes, VP   Patrick Fortune, VP   Michael Hershel, VP
Roger F Lewis, IR   Chuck Thurman, PR

Rev: 6861
Assets: 8550
Emp: 64

Bay State Gas Co
120 Royall Street
Canton, MA 02021
617-828-8650

Natural gas utility company.
Type: NYSE-BGC
Ind: Utility   Grp: Utilities
Charles H Tenney, CEO

Rev: 350
Assets: NA
Emp: 2

Baybanks Inc
175 Federal Street
Boston, MA 02110
617-482-1040

Commercial bank.
Type: NASDAQ-BBNK
Ind: Banking   Grp: Financial
William M Crozier, CEO   William T Sandalls, Pres   Richard F Pollard, VCh
William T Sandalls Jr, CFO   Donald L Isaacs, IS   Ilene Beal, Sls
Donald Issacs, Mkt   Judith Benson, VP   James Kennedy, VP
Patrice Picard, VP   Joan Tonra, VP   Anne Connelly, VP
Robert M Sharkey, IR   Maureen Deyesso, PR

Rev: 1037
Assets: 8678
Emp: 6

Bayer USA
One Mellon Center
Pittsburgh, PA 15219
412-394-5500

Chemical company; polymers, organic, agrochemicals.
Type: Private-Sub-For
Ind: Chemicals   Grp: Basic Industries
Konrad Weis, CEO   Helge Wehmeier, Pres   Robert Coppenrath, VCh
Gerd D Mueller, CFO   Kurt Metelmann, Mkt   Gerald Wagner, VP
Vincent Kaseta, VP   Robert Crevels, VP   John McGlynn, VP
Michael Kochmann, VP   Elliot Schreiber, PR

Rev: 4719
Assets: 3627
Emp: 26

Bayerische Vereinsbank AG
335 Madison Avenue
New York, NY 10017
212-210-0300

Commercial bank.
Type: Private-Sub-For
Ind: Banking   Grp: Financial
Peter Koelle, CEO

Rev: 450
Assets: 3500
Emp: 1

Bayless, A J Markets Inc
2720 S Hardy Drive # 4
Tempe, AZ 85282
602-731-6800

Operator of retail food supermarkets.
Type: Private
Ind: Retail/Food   Grp: Retail
Richard Schaffer, CEO

Rev: 550
Assets: NA
Emp: 3

Bayliner Marine Corp
17825 59th Avenue NE
Arlington, WA 98223
206-435-5571

Manufacturer of pleasure power boats.
Type: Private
Ind: Leisure Time   Grp: Consumer Service
Jim Hoag, CEO

Rev: 550
Assets: NA
Emp: 4

BCE Development Ltd
Toronto Dominion Centre TD Tower
Toronto, ON M5K1A1 Can
416-369-2300

Real estate development company.
Type: Private-Sub   Par: Bell Canada Inc (BCE Inc)
Ind: Real Estate/Bldg   Grp: Business Service
John W Poole, CEO   Daniel O Jarvis, CFO   David R Podmore, R&D
J Stuart Spalding, VP   Donald H Weber, VP   Leslie E Linhart, VP
Brian E Richardson, VP   Josef J Fridman, VP   Leslie Boyd, IR

Rev: 730
Assets: 2290
Emp: 5

BCE PubliTech Inc
150 Bloor Street W
Toronto, ON M5S2X9 Can
416-964-1374

Printers of professional documents, directories.
Type: Private-Sub   Par: Bell Canada Inc (BCE Inc)
Ind: Publishing/Com   Grp: Consumer Service
Frank Allen, CEO

Rev: 659
Assets: 510
Emp: 6

Organizations Listed Alphabetically

Organization / Address / Phone	Descriptive Information	Revenue / ($ mil)	Assets / ($ mil)	Emp (thous)
BDM International Inc 7915 Jones Branch Drive McLean, VA 22102 703-821-5000	Nationwide consulting company. Type: Private Ind: Consulting Grp: Business Service Earl C Williams, CEO	Rev: Assets: Emp:	275 NA 4	
Bean, L L Corp Casco Street Freeport, ME 04033 207-865-4761	Retailer of apparel, sporting goods. Type: Private Ind: Retail/Merch Grp: Retail Leon A Gorman, CEO	Rev: Assets: Emp:	500 NA 3	
Bear Stearns Companies Inc 245 Park Avenue New York, NY 10167 212-272-2000	Brokerage & financial services. Type: NYSE-BSC Ind: Securities Grp: Financial Alan C Greenberg, CEO Alvin H Einbender, Pres John Rosenwald, VCh Michael Minnikes, Tres William J Montgoris, CFO W Ben Kuenemann, IS Livio Borghese, VP Vincent Mattone, VP Michael Tarnopol, VP Kenneth Edlow, VP Michael Abatemarco, VP Fabianne Gershon, IR Hanna Seachrist, PR	Rev: Assets: Emp:	1888 32171 4	
Bearings Inc 3600 Euclid Avenue PO Box 6925 Cleveland, OH 44115 216-881-2838	Manufacturer of bearings. Type: NYSE-BER Ind: Business Service Grp: Business Service John R Cunin, CEO George L LaMore, Pres John C Dannemiller, VCh Raymond E Smiley, CFO Bryan H Sanders, IS Fred L Mohr, Mkt Thomas Bradley, Ops	Rev: Assets: Emp:	543 223 4	
Beatrice Foods (BCI Holdings Inc) Two LaSalle Street Chicago, IL 60602 312-782-3820	Producer & distributor of packaged food products. Type: Private Ind: Food Processing Grp: Food Processing Frederick B Rentschler, CEO	Rev: Assets: Emp:	7500 5000 42	
Beazley, William Co Inc 97 Whitney Avenue New Haven, CT 06510 203-562-9801	Construction & commercial development company. Type: Private Ind: Real Estate/Bldg Grp: Business Service Robert W Scott, CEO	Rev: Assets: Emp:	550 NA 5	
Bechtel Group Inc 50 Beale Street San Francisco, CA 94105 415-768-1234	International construction & engineering company. Type: Private Ind: Real Estate/Bldg Grp: Business Service Stephen Bechtel Jr, CEO	Rev: Assets: Emp:	4500 NA 20	
Becker Milk Co 671 Warden Avenue Scarborough, ON M1L3Z7 Can 416-698-2591	Retail & wholesale dairy products company. Type: Private Ind: Food Processing Grp: Food Processing Frank Bazos, CEO	Rev: Assets: Emp:	340 170 3	
Beckman Instruments Inc 2500 Harbor Blvd Fullerton, CA 92635 714-871-4848	Manufacturer of bioanalytical software & supplies. Type: Private-Sub Par: Smithkline Beckman Corp Ind: Comput/Off Equip Grp: High Tech A Beckman, CEO	Rev: Assets: Emp:	800 500 7	
Becor Western Inc 1100 Milwaukee Avenue South Milwaukee, WI 53172 414-768-4000	Manufacturer of mining equipment. Type: NYSE-BCW Ind: Equipment Grp: Manufacturing Norris K Ekstrom, CEO	Rev: Assets: Emp:	400 NA 4	
Becton, Dickinson & Co One Becton Drive Franklin Lakes, NJ 07417 201-848-6800	Manufacturer of medical instruments & supplies. Type: NYSE-BDX Ind: Drugs Grp: Consumer Service Wesley J Howe, CEO Raymond V Gilmartin, Pres Robert P Denise, CFO Hank Willen, IS Donald S Hetzel, R&D Alfred Battaglia, VP E Ralph Biggadike, VP John W Galiardo, VP Ronald Jasper, IR James R Tobin, PR	Rev: Assets: Emp:	1709 2067 21	
Beech Aircraft Corp 9709 E Central Wichita, KS 67201 316-681-7111	Manufacturer of aircraft products. Type: Private-Sub Par: Raytheon Co Ind: Aerospace Grp: High Tech Max Bleck, CEO	Rev: Assets: Emp:	NA NA NA	

Organizations Listed Alphabetically

Organization / Address / Phone	Descriptive Information	Revenue / Assets / Emp ($ mil) ($ mil) (thous)		

Organization / Address / Phone	Descriptive Information	Rev:	Assets:	Emp:
Beef America Inc 7171 Mercy Road Omaha, NE 68106 402-397-2000	Meat packing, processing. Type: Private Ind: Food Processing Grp: Food Processing Michael M Erman, CEO	1000 NA 2		
Belcher Oil Co 8700 W Flagler Street Miami, FL 33174 305-551-5220	Oil & refining & marketing company. Type: Private-Sub Par: Coastal Corp Ind: Energy Grp: Basic Industries Dan Hill, CEO	NA NA NA		
Belk Store Services Inc 308 E Fifth Street Charlotte, NC 28231 704-372-8900	Operator of retail department stores. Type: Private Ind: Retail/Merch Grp: Retail John M Belk, CEO	1750 NA 30		
Bell & Howell Co 5215 Old Orchard Road Skokie, IL 60077 312-470-7100	Diversified manufacturing company; photographic devices. Type: Private Ind: Comput/Off Equip Grp: High Tech Gerald Schultz, CEO Jerome Herb, CFO Tom Jones, IS Ingeborg Marquardt, R&D Janie Lewis, PR	900 800 10		
Bell Atlantic Corp 1600 Market Street Philadelphia, PA 19103 215-963-6000	Regional telecommunication company; telephone utility. Type: NYSE-BEL Ind: Telecom Grp: High Tech Raymond W Smith, CEO Thomas E Bolger, Chr Raymond W Smith, Pres Carolyn Burger, Tres Philip A Campbell, CFO Joseph T Ambrozy, IS Bruce S Gordon, Mkt William Newport, VP John Kelleher, VP Edward Grogan, VP Christopher Clouser, IR Patricia Seif, PR	10880 24729 81		
Bell Atlantic Enterprises Co 1880 JFK Blvd Philadelphia, PA 19103 215-963-6666	Communications equipment & services company. Type: Private-Sub Par: Bell Atlantic Corp Ind: Telecom Grp: High Tech James Cullen, CEO	NA NA NA		
Bell Canada Inc (BCE Inc) 1050 Beaver Hall Hill Montreal, PQ H3C3G4 Can 514-870-1511	National telephone utility company. Type: TOR Ind: Telecom Grp: High Tech J Thackray, CEO	5421 11482 110		
Bell Helicopter Textron Inc 600 E Hearst Blvd Hearst, TX 76053 817-280-2011	Manufacturer of helicopters & parts. Type: Private-Sub Par: Textron Inc Ind: Aerospace Grp: High Tech Leornard Horner, CEO	NA NA NA		
Bell Industries Inc 11812 San Vicente Blvd Los Angeles, CA 90049 213-826-6778	Distributor of electronic parts, equipment. Type: NYSE-BI Ind: Electronics Grp: High Tech Theodore Williams, CEO	450 NA 4		
Bell Laboratories of AT&T 600 Mountain Avenue Murray Hill, NJ 07974 201-582-3000	Phone utility company, research laboratories. Type: Private-Sub Par: American Telephone & Telegraph Co Ind: Consulting Grp: Business Service Ian Roth, CEO	2000 NA 20		
Bell Telephone of Pennsylvania One Parkway Philadelphia, PA 19102 215-466-9900	Telephone utility company. Type: Private-Sub Par: Bell Atlantic Corp Ind: Telecom Grp: High Tech Robert Valentini, CEO	NA NA NA		
BellSouth Advertising & Publishing Corp 59 Executive Park S Atlanta, GA 30329 404-982-7400	Advertising & publishing company. Type: Private-Sub Par: BellSouth Corp Ind: Publishing/Com Grp: Consumer Service Donald Bullett, CEO	NA NA NA		

Organizations Listed Alphabetically

Organization / Address / Phone	Descriptive Information	Revenue / Assets / Emp ($ mil) ($ mil) (thous)		

Organization / Address / Phone	Descriptive Information			
BellSouth Corp 1155 Peachtree Street NE Atlanta, GA 30367 404-249-2000	Regional telecommunications company; telephone utility. Type: NYSE-BLS Ind: Telecom Grp: High Tech John L Clendenin, CEO F Duane Ackerman, Pres Arlen G Yokley, Tres Harvey R Holding, CFO John R Gunter, IS Jere A Drummond, Mkt John B White Jr, VP Richard L McGuire, VP Malcolm L Campbell, VP Patrick Casey, VP C Richard Yarbrough, PR	Rev: Assets: Emp:	13687 28472 101
BellSouth Financial Services Corp 1800 Century Blvd Atlanta, GA 30345 404-329-4200	Financial services company. Type: Private-Sub Par: BellSouth Corp Ind: Non-Bank Fin Grp: Financial R Dykes, CEO	Rev: Assets: Emp:	NA NA NA
BellSouth Services Inc 3535 Colonade Parkway Birmingham, AL 35243 205-321-1000	Telecommunication services company. Type: Private-Sub Par: BellSouth Corp Ind: Telecom Grp: High Tech Hugh B Jacks, CEO	Rev: Assets: Emp:	NA NA NA
Belo, A H Corp Communications Center Dallas, TX 75265 214-745-8730	Newspaper publisher & TV station operator. Type: NYSE-BLC Ind: Publishing/Com Grp: Consumer Service Robert W Decherd, CEO	Rev: Assets: Emp:	385 720 2
Beloit Corp One St Lawrence Avenue Beloit, WI 53511 608-365-3311	Manufacturer of industrial machinery. Type: Private-Sub Par: Harnischfeger Corp Ind: Manufacturing Grp: Manufacturing John McKay, CEO	Rev: Assets: Emp:	NA NA NA
Bemis Co Inc 800 Northstar Center Minneapolis, MN 55402 612-340-6000	Packaging manufacturing company. Type: NYSE-BMS Ind: Manufacturing Grp: Manufacturing Howard Culter, CEO John H Roe, Pres Edward S McBride, VCh Benjamin R Field III, CFO Thomas J Barrett, IS John Dempsey, R&D Lisa Liken, VP Scott Johnson, VP Lisa D Locken, PR	Rev: Assets: Emp:	1069 595 8
Beneficial Corp 1100 Carr Road Wilmington, DE 19899 302-798-0800	Consumer finance company. Type: Private Ind: Non-Bank Fin Grp: Financial Finn M W Caaspersen, CEO David J Farris, Pres William H Ely, Tres Andrew C Halvorsen, CFO J Edward Kerwan, IS Jeffry Adelman, Mkt Thomas McGough, VP Maryann Schneider, VP James Gilliam, VP Deborah Veasy, PR	Rev: Assets: Emp:	1418 7544 7
Bergen Brunswig Corp 4000 Metropolitan Drive Orange, CA 92668 714-385-4000	Distributor of pharmaceutical, health care & video cass. Type: ASE-BBCB Ind: Drugs Grp: Consumer Service Emil P Martini, CEO Robert E Martini, Pres Dwight A Steffensen, VCh Michael W Fipps, Tres George E Reinhardt Jr, CFO Anthony Vallario, IS Gary Rockhold, VP Jerold O Gutman, VP	Rev: Assets: Emp:	3486 889 6
Bergner, P A & Co Inc 331 W Wisconsin Milwaukee, WI 53203 414-347-4141	Operator of retail merchandise stores. Type: Private Ind: Retail/Merch Grp: Retail Allan Anderson, CEO	Rev: Assets: Emp:	550 NA 5
Berkley, W R Insurance Co 165 Mason Street Greenwich, CT 06836 203-629-2880	Property & casualty insurance company. Type: NASDAQ-BKLY Ind: Insurance Grp: Insurance William R Berkley, CEO Warren E Buffet, Chr Charles T Munger, VCh Marc D Hamburg, Tres Daniel J Jadsich, CFO Robert H Bird, Sls Michael Goldberg, Mkt J Verne McKenzie, VP Michael Goldberg, VP Stanford Lipsey, VP	Rev: Assets: Emp:	534 1232 2
Berkshire Hathaway Inc 1440 Kiewit Plaza Omaha, NE 68131 402-346-1400	Publishing company; newspapers. Type: NYSE-BRK Ind: Insurance Grp: Insurance Warren E Buffet, CEO J Verne McKenzie, CFO J Verne McKenzie, PR	Rev: Assets: Emp:	2333 6817 25

Organizations Listed Alphabetically

Organization / Address / Phone	Descriptive Information	Revenue / Assets / Emp ($ mil) ($ mil) (thous)		

Bernard, Chaus Inc
1410 Broadway
New York, NY 10018
212-354-1280

Manufacturer of women's apparel.
Type: NYSE-CHS
Ind: Apparel/Textiles   Grp: Consumer Prd
Bernard Chaus, CEO

Rev: 280
Assets: 150
Emp: 3

Berrie, Russ & Co Inc
111 Bauer Drive
Oakland, NJ 07436
201-891-7500

Manufacturer of gift items for retail stores.
Type: NYSE-RUS
Ind: Leisure Time   Grp: Consumer Service
Russell Berrie, CEO

Rev: 278
Assets: 212
Emp: 3

Best Buy Co
4400 W 78th Street
Minneapolis, MN 55435
612-831-4552

Operator of retail electronic & applicance stores.
Type: NYSE
Ind: Retail/Merch   Grp: Retail
Richard M Schulze, CEO

Rev: 400
Assets: 300
Emp: 2

Best Foods Baking Group Inc
Greenbrook Corporate Ctr 100 Passaic Ave
Fairfield, NJ 07006
201-808-3000

Producer & distributor of bakery products & pasta.
Type: Private-Sub Par: CPC International Inc
Ind: Food Processing   Grp: Food Processing
Robert Snyder, CEO

Rev: NA
Assets: NA
Emp: NA

Best Products Co Inc
Parham Road at Interstate 95
Richmond, VA 23227
804-261-2000

Manufacturer of household appliances, electronics.
Type: Private
Ind: Retail/Merch   Grp: Retail
Ben Weinstein, CEO   Robert E R Huntley, Chr   William F Costello, Pres
James D Staudohar, CFO   Daniel J Rubin, IS   Fred A Wollenberg, Mkt
Mark M Murphy, PR

Rev: 2000
Assets: 1000
Emp: 15

Best Western International Assn Inc
6201 N 24th Parkway
Phoenix, AZ 85016
602-957-4200

Nationwide operator & franchisor of hotels & motels.
Type: Private
Ind: Food/Lodging   Grp: Consumer Service
Ron Evans, CEO

Rev: 1100
Assets: NA
Emp: 1

Bethlehem Steel Corp
701 E Third Street
Bethlehem, PA 18016
215-694-2424

Integrated steel manufacturer.
Type: NYSE-BS
Ind: Steel   Grp: Basic Industries
Walter F Williams, CEO   D Sheldon Arnot, Pres   Gary L Millenbruch, CFO
George T Fugere, IS   Malcolm Roberts, R&D   C Adams Moore, Sls
James C Vanvliet, Mkt   Lonnie Arnett, VP   Roger Penny, VP
Larry Adams, VP   John Jordan, VP   Henry Von Spreckelsen, PR

Rev: 5489
Assets: 4449
Emp: 45

Betz Laboratories Inc
4636 Somerton Road
Trevose, PA 19047
215-355-3300

Manufacturer of specialty chemicals for water treatment.
Type: NASDAQ-BETZ
Ind: Chemicals   Grp: Basic Industries
John F McCaughan, CEO   William C Brafford, VCh   William R Cook, CFO
James T Egan, IS   Dr Richard E Fruit, R&D   Richard A Heal, Sls
Dr Hillel Lieberman, Mkt   William Maguire, Ops   B C Moore, VP
Edward Ross, VP   Thomas Smith, VP

Rev: 448
Assets: 319
Emp: 3

Beverly Enterprises Inc
99 S Oakland Avenue
Pasadena, CA 91101
818-793-2911

Operator of nursing centers & retirement facilities.
Type: NYSE
Ind: Business Service   Grp: Business Service
Robert VanTuyle, CEO   David Banks, Pres   William M Wright, CFO
Larry B Cornish, VP

Rev: 2025
Assets: 1845
Emp: 106

Bexar County Government
Bexar County Courthouse
San Antonio, TX 78205
512-220-2496

County government.
Type: County Govt
Ind: Local Govt   Grp: Govt & Non-Prof
Tom Vickers, CEO

Rev: 330
Assets: NM
Emp: 3

BHP Australia (Broken Hill) Inc
550 California Street
San Francisco, CA 94104
415-981-1515

Mining & minerals processing company; US headquarters.
Type: Private-Sub-For
Ind: Metals/Mining   Grp: Basic Industries
James T Curry, CEO

Rev: 9900
Assets: NA
Emp: 42

BIC Corp
Wiley Street
Milford, CT 06460
203-783-2000

Manufacturer of personal care products & pens.
Type: ASE-BIC
Ind: Manufacturing   Grp: Manufacturing
Marcel L Bich, CEO

Rev: 295
Assets: 243
Emp: 2

Organizations Listed Alphabetically

Organization / Address / Phone	Descriptive Information	Revenue / ($ mil)	Assets / ($ mil)	Emp (thous)
BID Building Materials Canada 312 Dolomite Drive Downsview, ON M3J3A2 Can 416-661-5950	Building materials manufacturer. Type: Private Ind: Building Mat Grp: Basic Industries C Copeland, CEO	Rev: 340	Assets: 170	Emp: 4
Big B Inc 2600 Morgan Road SE Bessemer, AL 35023 205-424-3421	Operator of retail discount drugstores. Type: NASDAQ-BIGB Ind: Retail/Merch Grp: Retail Joseph Bruno, CEO	Rev: 271	Assets: 150	Emp: 2
Big Bear Inc 770 Goodale Blvd Columbus, OH 43212 614-464-6500	Operator of supermarket retail stores. Type: OTC Ind: Retail/Food Grp: Retail Michael J Knilans, CEO	Rev: 900	Assets: 500	Emp: 9
Big Three Industries Inc 3535 W 12th Street Houston, TX 77008 713-868-0333	Manufacturer of oil exploration & production equipment. Type: OTC Ind: Oil Service Grp: Business Service Mike V Breber, CEO William M Boren, Pres Gary Petry, IS Roy Miller, R&D James Fry, PR	Rev: 650	Assets: 1000	Emp: 5
Big V Supermarkets Inc 176 N Main Street Florida, NY 10921 914-651-4411	Retail supermarkets. Type: Private Ind: Retail/Food Grp: Retail David G Bronstein, CEO	Rev: 600	Assets: NA	Emp: 3
Bindley Western Industries 4212 W 71st Street Indianapolis, IN 46268 317-298-9900	Wholesale drugs & sundries. Type: OTC-BIND Ind: Manufacturing Grp: Manufacturing William E Bindley, CEO C Richard Zartman, Pres Thomas J Salentine, CFO James P Keller, IS Ronald E Wightman, Mkt Sue Goebel, PR	Rev: 1275	Assets: 264	Emp: 2
Binswanger Co Inc 1635 Market Philadelphia, PA 19103 215-448-6000	Construction & real estate development company. Type: Private Ind: Real Estate/Bldg Grp: Business Service Frank Binswange, CEO	Rev: 550	Assets: NA	Emp: 1
Birks, Henry & Sons Ltd 50 Rideau Street Ottawa, ON K1N5W9 Can 613-236-3641	Operator of retail stores; jewelry, silverware & glassware. Type: Private Ind: Retail/Merch Grp: Retail H Birks, CEO	Rev: 314	Assets: 234	Emp: 5
Birmingham Steel Corp 3000 Riverchase Galleria Birmingham, AL 35201 205-985-9290	Operator of mini steel mills. Type: NYSE-BIR Ind: Steel Grp: Basic Industries James A Todd, CEO	Rev: 400	Assets: NA	Emp: 3
Birmingham, City of City Hall 710 N 20th Street Birmingham, AL 35203 205-254-2277	City government. Type: City Govt Ind: Local Govt Grp: Govt & Non-Prof Richard Arrington, CEO	Rev: 237	Assets: NM	Emp: 3
BJ Titan & BJ Services Inc 5500 NW Central Drive Houston, TX 77092 713-439-8600	Provides products & services to the petroleum industry. Type: Private-Sub Par: Baker Hughes Co Ind: Oil Service Grp: Business Service J Stewart, CEO	Rev: NA	Assets: NA	Emp: NA
Black & Decker Corp 701 E Joppa Road Towson, MD 21204 301-583-3900	Manufacturer of power equipment & tools, hand tools. Type: NYSE-BDK Ind: Manufacturing Grp: Manufacturing Nolan D Archibald, CEO Dennis Heiner, Pres George Sherman, VCh William E Stevens, CFO James Barcus Jr, IS Francis Rosenthal, R&D Roger Thomas, Mkt Gary DiCamillo, VP Barbara Lucas, VP Stephan Page, VP Francis Rosenthal, VP Barbara B Lucas, PR	Rev: 2281	Assets: 1825	Emp: 23

Organization / Address / Phone	Descriptive Information	Revenue / Assets / Emp ($ mil) ($ mil) (thous)		

Black & Veatch Inc
1500 Meadow Lake Drive
Kansas City, MO 64114
913-339-2000

Engineering & survey consulting company.
Type: Private
Ind: Consulting   Grp: Business Service
John H Robinson, CEO

Rev: 275
Assets: NA
Emp: 3

Blair Corp
220 Hickory Street
Warren, PA 16366
814-723-3600

Catalogue & direct mail sales of apparel & furniture.
Type: ASE
Ind: Retail/Merch   Grp: Retail
M McComas, CEO

Rev: 500
Assets: 159
Emp: 4

Blair, John & Co
1290 Avenue of the Americas
New York, NY 10104
212-603-5000

Communications company; radio stations.
Type: Private
Ind: Business Service   Grp: Business Service
J Blair, CEO

Rev: 750
Assets: NA
Emp: 7

Block Drug Co Inc
257 Cornelison Avenue
Jersey City, NJ 07302
201-434-3000

Manufacturer of prescription drug products.
Type: NASDAQ-BLOCA
Ind: Personal Care   Grp: Consumer Prd
Leonard Block, CEO   James A Block, Pres   Thomas Block, Tres
Gilbert Seymann, IS   Michael Alfano, R&D   Peter C Mann, Sls
Donald H LeSier, Mkt   John Peters, VP   Melvin Knopp, VP

Rev: 369
Assets: 356
Emp: 3

Block, H & R Inc
4410 Main Street
Kansas City, MO 64111
816-753-6900

Service company engaged in tax return preparation.
Type: NYSE-HRB
Ind: Business Service   Grp: Business Service
Henry W Block, CEO   Jerome Grossman, VCh   Donald Ayers, CFO
James Moran, R&D   Thomas M Bloch, VP   William Ross, VP
Ozzie Wenich, VP   Everett Canfield, VP   Steven R Dickey, VP

Rev: 794
Assets: 677
Emp: 4

Blockbuster Entertainment Inc
10460 Miller Road
Dallas, TX 75238
214-341-7700

Operator of video cassette rental & sales stores.
Type: NYSE
Ind: Retail/Merch   Grp: Retail
W Huizenga, CEO

Rev: 300
Assets: 100
Emp: 1

Blount Inc
4520 Executive Park Drive
Montgomery, AL 36116
205-244-4000

Manufacturer of industrial building products, equipment.
Type: ASE-BLT
Ind: Building Mat   Grp: Basic Industries
Winton M Blount, CEO   R William Van Sant, Pres   Ronald K Gorland, Tres
J Lee Ledbetter, CFO   Ross K Henderson, IS   Peter C Robinson, Mkt
James S Osterman, VP   Ben R Yorks, VP   Arlen L Chaney, VP
James Terry Honan, VP   Victor C Pozzo, VP   Charles R Barnette, PR

Rev: 1134
Assets: 665
Emp: 6

Blue Bell Inc
335 Church Center
Greensboro, NC 27401
919-373-3400

Manufacturer of apparel products.
Type: Private
Ind: Apparel/Textiles   Grp: Consumer Prd
Macky McDonald, CEO

Rev: 1100
Assets: NA
Emp: 5

Blue Cross Blue Shield of Alabama Inc
450 Riverchase Parkway E
Birmingham, AL 35298
205-988-2100

Medical insurance company.
Type: Private
Ind: Insurance   Grp: Insurance
William H Mandy, CEO

Rev: 1100
Assets: 2856
Emp: 5

Blue Cross Blue Shield of Illinois Inc
233 N Michigan Avenue
Chicago, IL 60601
312-938-7500

Medical insurance company.
Type: Private
Ind: Insurance   Grp: Insurance
S Martin Hickman, CEO

Rev: 1320
Assets: 3428
Emp: 4

Blue Cross Blue Shield of Massachusetts
100 Summer Street
Boston, MA 02110
617-956-2000

Medical insurance company.
Type: Private
Ind: Insurance   Grp: Insurance
John Larkin Thompson, CEO

Rev: 2750
Assets: 7140
Emp: 7

Blue Cross Blue Shield of Michigan Inc
600 E Lafayette
Detroit, MI 48226
313-225-8000

Medical insurance company.
Type: Private
Ind: Insurance   Grp: Insurance
Richard Wittmer, CEO

Rev: 4950
Assets: 12852
Emp: 9

Organizations Listed Alphabetically

Organization / Address / Phone	Descriptive Information		Revenue / Assets / Emp ($ mil) ($ mil) (thous)

Blue Cross Blue Shield of Oregon Inc
100 SW Market Street
Portland, OR 97201
503-225-5221

Medical insurance company.
Type: Private
Ind: Insurance   Grp: Insurance
Solomon Menashe, CEO

Rev: 825
Assets: 2142
Emp: 2

Blue Cross Blue Shield of Pennsylvania
1333 Chestnut Street
Philadelphia, PA 19107
215-448-5000

Medical insurance company.
Type: Private
Ind: Insurance   Grp: Insurance
David Markson, CEO

Rev: 1320
Assets: 3103
Emp: 2

Blue Cross Blue Shield of Virginia Inc
2015 Staples Mill Road
Richmond, VA 23230
804-359-7000

Medical insurance company.
Type: Private
Ind: Insurance   Grp: Insurance
Norwood Davis, CEO

Rev: 1100
Assets: 2856
Emp: 2

Blunt Ellis & Loewi Inc
225 E Mason Street
Milwaukee, WI 53202
414-347-3400

Investment firm; securities trading.
Type: Private
Ind: Securities   Grp: Financial
Thomas S Franke, CEO

Rev: 220
Assets: 2200
Emp: 1

Boatmen's Bancshares Inc
One Boatmen's Plaza 800 Market Street
St Louis, MO 63101
314-425-7525

Commercial bank.
Type: NASDAQ-NMS
Ind: Banking   Grp: Financial
Donald N Brandin, CEO   Andrew B Craig III, Chr   Philip N McCarty, Tres
James Kienker, CFO   Robert Brubaker, IS   Larry D Bayliss, Mkt
Micheal H T Lynch, VP   Richard P Patterson, VP   Phillip E Peters, VP
Roy C Postel, VP   Marvin W Smith, VP   H Chandler, VP
John R Wells, IR   Larry D Bayliss, PR

Rev: 1066
Assets: 14676
Emp: 5

Boeing Aerospace Corp
20403 68th Street
Kent, WA 98031
206-773-2121

Manufacturer of missiles & military research.
Type: Private-Sub   Par: Boeing Corp
Ind: Aerospace   Grp: High Tech
M Miller, CEO

Rev: NA
Assets: NA
Emp: NA

Boeing Commercial Airplanes Inc
Eighth Street & Logan Avenue N
Renton, WA 98124
206-237-2121

Manufacturer of commercial airplanes.
Type: Private-Sub   Par: Boeing Corp
Ind: Aerospace   Grp: High Tech
D Thornton, CEO

Rev: NA
Assets: NA
Emp: NA

Boeing Corp
7755 E Marginal Way S
Seattle, WA 98108
206-655-2121

World's largest manufacturer of aircraft.
Type: NYSE
Ind: Aerospace   Grp: High Tech
Frank Shrontz, CEO   M T Stamper, VCh   H W Haynes, CFO
J Lang, IS   A O Welliver, R&D   B D Pineck, Mkt
D D Cruze, Ops   H B Hebeler, VP   Bill B May, VP
Harold E Carr, PR

Rev: 17340
Assets: 12608
Emp: 153

Boeing Helicopters Inc
Boeing Center
Philadelphia, PA 19142
215-591-2121

Manufacturers of helicopters.
Type: Private-Sub   Par: Boeing Corp
Ind: Aerospace   Grp: High Tech
Donald Chestnut, CEO

Rev: NA
Assets: NA
Emp: NA

Bohemia Inc
2280 Oakmont
Eugene, OR 97401
503-342-6262

Manufacturer of construction materials; treated wood.
Type: NASDAQ-BOHM
Ind: Building Mat   Grp: Basic Industries
Faye H Stewart, CEO

Rev: 306
Assets: 250
Emp: 2

Boise Cascade Canada Ltd
3300 Bloor Street W
Toronto, ON M8X2X2 Can
416-231-3010

Integrated forest products company.
Type: Private-Sub-For
Ind: Paper/Forest Prd   Grp: Basic Industries
John Forrest, CEO

Rev: 350
Assets: 425
Emp: 2

Organization / Address / Phone	Descriptive Information	Revenue / Assets / Emp ($ mil) ($ mil) (thous)		

Organization / Address / Phone	Descriptive Information			
Boise Cascade Corp One Jefferson Square Boise, ID 83728 208-384-6161	Integrated forest products company. Type: NYSE-BCC Ind: Paper/Forest Prd Grp: Basic Industries John B Fery, CEO Jon H Miller, Pres William Bridenbaugh, VCh George J Harad, CFO Rex L Dorman, IS E Thomas Edquist, Sls N David Spence, Ops K Peter Norie, VP Alex P Boorman, VP Vernon Veron, VP John Wasserlein, VP J Kirk Sullivan, VP Alice E Hennessey, IR Robert B Hayes, PR	Rev: Assets: Emp:	4095 3610 20	
Boise Cascade Office Products Corp 800 Bryn Mawr Avenue Itasca, IL 60143 312-773-6400	Manufacturer & distributor of office supplies. Type: Private-Sub Par: Boise Cascade Corp Ind: Business Service Grp: Business Service John Clute, CEO	Rev: Assets: Emp:	NA NA NA	
Bolt Beranek & Newman Inc 10 Fawcett Street Cambridge, MA 02238 617-873-2000	Consulting & computer software company. Type: NYSE-BBN Ind: Comput/Off Equip Grp: High Tech Stephen R Levy, CEO	Rev: Assets: Emp:	305 264 3	
Bombardier Inc 800 Boul Dorchester 1700 Montreal, PQ H3B1Y8 Can 514-861-9481	Aerospace manufacturer; aircraft, subway equipment. Type: MON Ind: Manufacturing Grp: Manufacturing Laurent Beaudoin, CEO Raymond Royer, Pres J R Andre' Bombardier, VCh Paul Larose, CFO Robert Brown, R&D Claude Malette, Mkt Michael O'Bree, VP Pierre Poitras, VP Jean Rivard, VP Marie Claire Simoneau, VP	Rev: Assets: Emp:	1187 740 10	
Bonneville Power Administration 905 NE Eleventh Portland, OR 97232 503-230-5000	Government authority producer of electric power. Type: Govt Authority Ind: Govt Authority Grp: Govt & Non-Prof James J Jura, CEO	Rev: Assets: Emp:	2050 NM 5	
Booz, Allen & Hamilton Inc 101 Park Avenue New York, NY 10178 212-697-1900	Nationwide management consulting firm. Type: Private Ind: Consulting Grp: Business Service R M McCullough, CEO	Rev: Assets: Emp:	500 NA 4	
Borden Chemicals & Plastics Inc Highway 73 & 30 Geismar, LA 70734 504-673-6121	Manufacturer of specialty chemicals. Type: Private-Sub Par: Borden Inc Ind: Chemicals Grp: Basic Industries Wayne Leonard, CEO	Rev: Assets: Emp:	400 NA 4	
Borden Inc 277 Park Avenue New York, NY 10172 212-573-4000	Consumer food products & industrial chemical company. Type: NYSE-BN Ind: Food Processing Grp: Food Processing Romeo J Ventres, CEO David A Kelly, Tres Lawrence O Doza, CFO Allan L Miller, IS Alfred Cummin, R&D James T McCrory, PR	Rev: Assets: Emp:	7244 4440 33	
Borg Warner Acceptance Corp 225 N Michigan Chicago, IL 60601 312-329-6500	Financial subsidiary of Borg Warner Corp. Type: Private-Sub Par: Borg Warner Corp Ind: Non-Bank Fin Grp: Financial C E Johnson, CEO	Rev: Assets: Emp:	800 7000 3	
Borg Warner Corp 200 S Michigan Avenue Chicago, IL 60604 312-322-8500	Manufacturer of automotive parts & components. Type: Private Ind: Manufacturing Grp: Manufacturing James F Bere, CEO Donald C Trauscht, CFO Timothy M Wood, IS Patricia Yoxall, PR	Rev: Assets: Emp:	3800 3000 60	
Borman's Inc 18718 Borman Avenue Detroit, MI 48232 313-270-1000	Operator of retail supermarkets. Type: NYSE-BRF Ind: Retail/Food Grp: Retail Paul Borman, CEO	Rev: Assets: Emp:	1050 600 11	
Boston Companies Inc One Boston Place Boston, MA 02108 800-225-5267	Investment firm. Type: Private Ind: Non-Bank Fin Grp: Financial George Phillips, CEO	Rev: Assets: Emp:	300 11000 1	

Organizations Listed Alphabetically

Organization / Address / Phone	Descriptive Information	Revenue ($ mil)	Assets ($ mil)	Emp (thous)
Boston Consulting Group Inc Exchange Place Boston, MA 02109 617-973-1200	Nationwide consulting company. Type: Private Ind: Consulting Grp: Business Service John Clarkson, CEO	Rev: Assets: Emp:		300 NA 3
Boston Edison Co 800 Boylston Street Prudential Center Boston, MA 02199 617-424-2000	Electric power utility. Type: NYSE-BSE Ind: Utility Grp: Utilities Stephen J Seeney, CEO Bernard Reznicek, Pres William Harrington, VCh Robert Weafer, CFO Arthur Phillips, IS Joel Kamya, Ops Cameron Daley, VP Douglas Bauer, VP Ralph Bird, VP Thomas May, VP Eleanor Daly, VP L Carlisle Gustin, VP	Rev: Assets: Emp:		1203 2817 4
Boston Safe Deposit & Trust Co One Boston Place Boston, MA 02106 617-722-7000	Commercial bank. Type: NYSE-SLH Ind: Banking Grp: Financial James N VonGermeten, CEO	Rev: Assets: Emp:		1500 12000 3
Boston University Commonwealth Avenue Boston, MA 02215 617-353-2000	Major educational institution; university. Type: University Ind: University Grp: Govt & Non-Prof John Silber, CEO	Rev: Assets: Emp:		257 211 31
Boston, City of City Hall Boston, MA 02201 617-725-4500	City government. Type: City Govt Ind: Local Govt Grp: Govt & Non-Prof Raymond L Flynn, CEO	Rev: Assets: Emp:		1179 NM 21
Bow Valley Industries Ltd 321 6th Avenue SW Calgary, AB T2P3R2 Can 403-261-6100	Oil & gas exploration & production company. Type: ASE Ind: Energy Grp: Basic Industries Darryl Seaman, CEO	Rev: Assets: Emp:		468 935 2
Bowater Inc One Parklands Drive PO Box 401 Darien, CT 06820 203-656-7200	Producer of newsprint & computer business paper. Type: NYSE Ind: Paper/Forest Prd Grp: Basic Industries Anthony P Gammie, CEO John P Fucigna, Tres Richard D McDonough, CFO Ronald W Toelle, R&D Donald J D'Antuono, VP Robert Lancaster, VP Arthur H King, PR	Rev: Assets: Emp:		1410 1881 5
Bowery Savings Bank Inc 100 E 42nd Street New York, NY 10017 212-953-8400	Thrift institution. Type: Private Ind: Savings & Loan Grp: Financial Donald S Rice, CEO	Rev: Assets: Emp:		700 7000 2
Boys Market Inc 5531 Monte Vista Los Angeles, CA 90042 213-258-8080	Operator of retail food stores. Type: Private Ind: Retail/Food Grp: Retail Alfredo Breno, CEO	Rev: Assets: Emp:		550 NA 4
Bozell Jacobs Kenyon Inc 40 W 23rd Street New York, NY 10010 212-727-5000	Nationwide advertising agency. Type: Private Ind: Business Service Grp: Business Service Charles Peebler, CEO	Rev: Assets: Emp:		1650 NA 4
BP Petroleum Canada Ltd 333 5th Avenue SW Calgary, AB T2P3B6 Can 403-237-1234	Petroleum exploration, production & marketing company. Type: TOR-BPC Ind: Energy Grp: Basic Industries D S Harvie, CEO	Rev: Assets: Emp:		282 747 2
Bradford, J C & Co 330 Commerce Street Nashville, TN 37201 615-748-9000	Investment firm; securities trading. Type: Private Ind: Securities Grp: Financial J C Bradford, CEO	Rev: Assets: Emp:		220 2200 1

Organizations Listed Alphabetically

Organization / Address / Phone	Descriptive Information	Revenue / ($ mil)	Assets / ($ mil)	Emp (thous)
Bradlees Stores Inc 1 Bradley Circle Braintree, MA 02184 617-770-8000	Operator of discount retail department stores. Type: Private Ind: Retail/Merch Grp: Retail Avram J Goldberg, CEO	Rev: Assets: Emp:		990 NA 13
Bramalea Ltd 1867 Yonge Street Toronto, ON M4S1Y9 Can 416-487-3861	Construction & development company. Type: Private-Sub Par: Trizec Corp Ind: Real Estate/Bldg Grp: Business Service William G Davis, CEO Benjamen Swirsky, Chr Kenneth Lusk, VCh Peter Goring, Tres Stewart D Davidson, CFO Dag Nisbeth, R&D	Rev: Assets: Emp:		685 3506 3
Braman Enterprises Inc 2044 Biscayne Blvd Miami, FL 33137 305-576-6900	Operator of automobile dealerships. Type: Private Ind: Consumer Service Grp: Consumer Service Norman Braman, CEO	Rev: Assets: Emp:		750 NA 1
Brand Companies Inc 1420 Renaissance Drive Park Ridge, IL 60068 312-298-1200	Manufacturer of pipe equipment. Type: OTC Ind: Equipment Grp: Manufacturing Eugene Barrett, CEO	Rev: Assets: Emp:		300 150 1
Braniff Airline Corp 7701 Lemmon Avenue Dallas, TX 75209 214-358-6011	Regional airline. Type: OTC-BAIR Ind: Airline Grp: Consumer Service J Patrick Foley, CEO Mark Osterberg, CFO Roger Leonard, IS Robert L Fornaro, Mkt Irma Ellis, PR	Rev: Assets: Emp:		250 100 2
Branitek Inc 6555 Ambercorn Savannah, GA 31405 912-354-4885	Manufacturer of paper products, bags, cartons, lumber. Type: Private-Sub Par: Union Camp Corp Ind: Packaging Grp: Manufacturing C Abarr, CEO	Rev: Assets: Emp:		NA NA NA
Brascan Ltd 4800 Commerce Court W Toronto, ON M5L1B7 Can 416-363-9491	Diversified energy development & investment company. Type: TOR-BLA Ind: Energy Grp: Basic Industries Peter F Bronfman, CEO J Trevor Eyton, Chr Paul Marshall, VCh Jack L Cockwell, CFO Robert Yeoman, R&D Lowell Allen, Mkt Gillian Churchill, VP F Morton, VP Anne Arone, VP Edward Kress, VP Rose Mary Rosada, VP	Rev: Assets: Emp:		7491 4126 1
Brendle's Inc 1919 N Bridges Street Elkin, NC 28621 919-835-3400	Operator of retail stores; toys, hobbies, sporting goods. Type: NASDAQ-BRDL Ind: Retail/Merch Grp: Retail J Harold Brendles, CEO	Rev: Assets: Emp:		261 150 3
Brenlin Corp 705 Akron Center Akron, OH 44308 216-762-2420	Metal fabricating & steel processing. Type: Private Ind: Steel Grp: Basic Industries David L Brennan, CEO	Rev: Assets: Emp:		700 NA 3
Bridgestone Tire USA Inc 2000 W 190th Street Torrance, CA 90509 213-320-6031	Manufacturer of automobile tires; US headquarters. Type: Private-Sub-For Ind: Tire/Rubber Grp: Basic Industries Jim McCann, CEO	Rev: Assets: Emp:		1100 NA 2
Briggs & Stratton Corp 12301 W Wirth Street Wauwatosa, WI 53222 414-259-5333	Automobile component parts manufacturer. Type: NYSE-BGG Ind: Machinery Grp: Manufacturing Frederick P Stratton, CEO George A Senn, Pres Robert H Eldridge, CFO Larry G Salsbury, IS Robert Catterson, R&D Douglas W Anderson, Sls Stephen H Rugg, Mkt Charles L Fricke, VP William Schneider, VP George Thompson III, PR	Rev: Assets: Emp:		914 511 10
Brigham Young University Administrative Bldg Provo, UT 84602 801-378-4418	Major educational institution; university. Type: University Ind: University Grp: Govt & Non-Prof Jeffrey R Holland, CEO	Rev: Assets: Emp:		330 396 29

Organizations Listed Alphabetically

Organization / Address / Phone	Descriptive Information	Revenue / Assets / Emp ($ mil) ($ mil) (thous)		

Bright Banc Savings Assn Inc
2355 Stemmons Freeway
Dallas, TX 75207
214-638-9500

Thrift institution.
Type: Private
Ind: Savings & Loan   Grp: Financial
James B Reeder, CEO

Rev: 550
Assets: 5500
Emp: 2

Brink's Inc
Thorndal Circle
Darien, CT 06820
203-655-8781

Security transportation services.
Type: Private-Sub   Par: Pittston Co
Ind: Transport   Grp: Business Service
Gary Garton, CEO

Rev: NA
Assets: NA
Emp: NA

Brintec Systems Corp
1600 W Main Street
Willimantic, CT 06226
203-456-8000

Manufacturer of telecommunications equipment; wire, parts.
Type: NASDAQ-BRIX
Ind: Telecom   Grp: High Tech
Peter Petruchik, CEO

Rev: 300
Assets: 300
Emp: 4

Bristol Meyers Canada Inc
390 Bay Street
Toronto, ON M5H2Y2 Can
416-362-4281

Manufacturer of consumer products; food, personal care.
Type: Private-Sub-For
Ind: Food Processing   Grp: Food Processing
Richard Gelb, CEO

Rev: 298
Assets: 213
Emp: 2

Bristol Meyers Co
345 Park Avenue
New York, NY 10154
212-546-4000

Manufacturer of personal care products.
Type: NYSE-BMY
Ind: Drugs   Grp: Consumer Service
Ray C Adam, CEO   Richard L Gelb, Chr   William Miller, VCh
Michael E Autera, CFO   Frederick S Nelson, IS   Guilio Vita, R&D
Marvin A Koslow, Mkt   William Flatley, VP   Wayne Davidson, VP
Charles Heimbold, VP   Joseph Maroun, VP   Julius L Pericola, VP
Thomas D McCann, IR   John Weissberg, PR

Rev: 5973
Assets: 5190
Emp: 35

British Col Hydro & Power Authority Ltd
970 Burrard Street
Vancouver, BC V6Z1Y3 Can
604-663-2212

Electric power utility.
Type: TOR
Ind: Utility   Grp: Utilities
C Johnson, CEO

Rev: 1689
Assets: 8332
Emp: 6

British Columbia Railway Co
221 W Esplanade
Vancouver, BC V7M1A5 Can
604-986-2012

Railroad transportation company.
Type: Prov Govt
Ind: Railroad   Grp: Business Service
J Hyland, CEO

Rev: 298
Assets: 1190
Emp: 3

British Columbia Telephone Ltd
3777 Kingsway
Burnaby, BC V5H3Z7 Can
604-432-2151

Telephone utility company.
Type: Private-Sub   Par: Anglo Canadian Telephone Co
Ind: Telecom   Grp: High Tech
Gordon F MacFarlane, CEO   Brian A Canfield, VCh   J Neil Stewart, Tres
D Barry McNeil, CFO   Donald Calder, IS   Colin Patterson, R&D
E Lynn Patterson, Ops   Roy Osing, VP   Betty Rumford, VP
K Donald Morrison, VP

Rev: 1332
Assets: 2723
Emp: 15

British Columbia, The University of
2075 Wesbrook Mall
Vancouver, BC V6T1W5 Can
604-228-2211

Major educational institution; university.
Type: University
Ind: University   Grp: Govt & Non-Prof
D W Strangway, CEO

Rev: 327
Assets: NM
Emp: 28

British Petroleum America
200 Public Square
Cleveland, OH 44114
216-586-4141

International oil company; US headquarters.
Type: Private-Sub-For
Ind: Energy   Grp: Basic Industries
James H Ross, CEO   E J P Browne, CFO   D J H Smith, R&D
N D Muir, IR   J F Andes, PR

Rev: 11000
Assets: 24000
Emp: 47

Brookings Institution
1775 Massachusetts Avenue NW
Washington, DC 20036
202-797-6000

Non-profit special interest group.
Type: Federal Govt
Ind: Membership Org   Grp: Govt & Non-Prof
Bruce K MacLaury, CEO

Rev: 500
Assets: NM
Emp: 2

Organizations Listed Alphabetically

Organization / Address / Phone	Descriptive Information	Revenue / Assets / Emp ($ mil) ($ mil) (thous)
Brooklyn Union Gas Co 195 Montague Street Brooklyn, NY 11201 718-403-2000	Natural gas utility. Type: NYSE-BU Ind: Utility Grp: Utilities Edwin S Larson, CEO Robert Catell, VCh Craig Mathews, CFO Joseph Pinnola, IS Helmut Peter, R&D Maurice Shaw, Mkt Richard Coddington, VP Richard Desmond, VP James Dunlop, VP Vincent Enright, VP Edward Sondey, VP	Rev: 899 Assets: 1257 Emp: 4
Brooks Fashion Stores Inc 370 Seventh Avenue New York, NY 10001 212-714-8600	Manufacturer of apparel; operator of retail clothing stores. Type: Private Ind: Retail/Merch Grp: Retail James Knape, CEO	Rev: 275 Assets: NA Emp: 2
Brookshire Grocery Co 1600 SW Route 323 Tyler, TX 75703 214-534-3000	Supermarket chain. Type: Private Ind: Retail/Food Grp: Retail Brook G Brookshire, CEO	Rev: 750 Assets: NA Emp: 5
Broward County Government 115 S Andrews Avenue Fort Lauderdale, FL 33301 305-357-7000	County government. Type: County Govt Ind: Local Govt Grp: Govt & Non-Prof Sylvia Poiter, CEO	Rev: 675 Assets: NM Emp: 5
Brown & Root Inc 4100 Clinton Drive Houston, TX 77020 713-676-3011	Construction company. Type: Private-Sub Par: Halliburton Co Ind: Real Estate/Bldg Grp: Business Service Louis Austin, CEO	Rev: 500 Assets: NA Emp: 2
Brown Brothers Harriman & Co 59 Wall Street New York, NY 10005 212-483-1818	Investment banking firm. Type: Private Ind: Securities Grp: Financial Terence Farley, CEO	Rev: 400 Assets: 2200 Emp: 1
Brown Forman Inc 850 Dixie Highway Louisville, KY 40210 502-585-1100	Distiller & importer of alcoholic beverages. Type: ASE-BFDA Ind: Beverage Grp: Food Processing W L Lyons Brown, CEO Owsley Brown, Pres Christopher A Sailer, Tres Clifford Rompf Jr, CFO Robert S Lyons, IS Charles Staff, R&D Daniel Schusterman, Sls Stephen B Kauffman, Mkt Lois Musselman, VP Russell Buzby, VP John S Moremen, VP Lois Musselman, PR	Rev: 1355 Assets: 932 Emp: 9
Brown Group Inc 8400 Maryland Avenue St Louis, MO 63105 314-854-4000	Manufacturer of shoes; retail stores. Type: NYSE-BG Ind: Apparel/Textiles Grp: Consumer Prd B A Bridgewater, CEO Richard L Anderson, Pres Harry E Rich, CFO Donald G Lenoard, IS Robert D Pickle, VP William Frederick, VP David L Bowman, PR	Rev: 1707 Assets: 728 Emp: 30
Brown, Alex & Sons Inc 135 E Baltimore Street Baltimore, MD 21202 301-727-1700	Investment banking, security agents. Type: NASDAQ-ABSB Ind: Securities Grp: Financial Benjamin H Griswold, CEO	Rev: 244 Assets: 861 Emp: 1
Browning Ferris Industries Inc 757 N Eldridge Houston, TX 77253 713-870-8100	Waste disposal company. Type: NYSE-BFI Ind: Business Service Grp: Business Service William D Ruckelshaus, CEO John E Drury, Pres Harry J Phillips, VCh Oscar Holland, CFO Sam Baty, IS Robert Lary, R&D Edward J Crane, Sls Norman A Myers, Mkt Stephen L Thomas, Ops Gerald Burger, VP Peter Block, IR Don L Fitch, PR	Rev: 2067 Assets: 1872 Emp: 20
Bruncor Inc 1 Brunswick Square St John, NB E2L4K2 Can 506-694-6330	Diversified manufacturing company. Type: TOR Ind: Manufacturing Grp: Manufacturing Kenneth Cox, CEO	Rev: 340 Assets: 808 Emp: 3

Organizations Listed Alphabetically

Organization / Address / Phone	Descriptive Information	Revenue / Assets / Emp ($ mil) ($ mil) (thous)		

Organization / Address / Phone	Descriptive Information			
Bruno's Inc 300 Research Parkway Birmingham, AL 35211 205-940-9400	Retail food supermarkets & drugstores. Type: OTC Ind: Retail/Food Grp: Retail Angelo J Bruno, CEO Lee J Bruno, Pres Ronald Bruno, VCh Glenn Griffin, CFO Paul Garrison, Mkt William White, VP	Rev: Assets: Emp:	1982 592 6	
Brunswick Corp One Brunswick Plaza Skokie, IL 60077 312-470-4700	Manufacturer of leisure & recreation products. Type: NYSE-BC Ind: Leisure Time Grp: Consumer Service Jack F Reichert, CEO John Charvat, VCh Frederick Florjancic, CFO Justin Murrish, IS Eugene Fisher, Mkt Jack Singleton, VP Dianne Yaconetti, VP Thomas Weight, VP Ross H Stemer, PR	Rev: Assets: Emp:	3282 2092 29	
Brunswick Mining & Smelting Corp Commerce Court W Toronto, ON M5L1B6 Can 506-522-2100	Operator of mines & smelting plants. Type: Private-Sub Par: Noranda Inc Ind: Metals/Mining Grp: Basic Industries Mike Street, CEO	Rev: Assets: Emp:	255 340 3	
Brush Wellman Inc 1200 Hanna Bldg Cleveland, OH 44115 216-443-1000	Manufacturer of specialty metals. Type: NYSE-BW Ind: Metals/Mining Grp: Basic Industries Raymond A Foos, CEO	Rev: Assets: Emp:	346 358 3	
Budget Rent-a-Car Inc 200 N Michigan Avenue Chicago, IL 60601 312-580-5000	Automobile rental company. Type: NASDAQ-BDGT Ind: Consumer Service Grp: Consumer Service Morris Belzberg, CEO	Rev: Assets: Emp:	512 500 5	
Buena Vista International Inc 350 S Buena Vista Street Burbank, CA 91521 818-560-1000	Producer of motion pictures & television programs. Type: Private-Sub Par: Disney, Walt Co Ind: Leisure Time Grp: Consumer Service William Mechanic, CEO	Rev: Assets: Emp:	NA NA NA	
Buena Vista Pictures Distribution Inc 350 S Buena Vista Street Burbank, CA 91521 818-560-5000	Distributor of motion picture & television programs. Type: Private-Sub Par: Disney, Walt Co Ind: Leisure Time Grp: Consumer Service Richard Cook, CEO	Rev: Assets: Emp:	NA NA NA	
Buffalo, City of City Hall Buffalo, NY 14202 716-855-4841	City government. Type: City Govt Ind: Local Govt Grp: Govt & Non-Prof James Griffin, CEO	Rev: Assets: Emp:	510 NM 10	
Buick Motor Division 902 E Hamilton Avenue Flint, MI 48550 313-236-0444	Manufacturer of automobiles. Type: Private-Sub Par: General Motors Corp Ind: Automotive Grp: Manufacturing Edward Mertz, CEO	Rev: Assets: Emp:	NA NA NA	
Builder Marts of America Inc 1 Independence Pointe Greenville, SC 29615 803-297-6101	Wholesale building materials. Type: Private Ind: Retail/Merch Grp: Retail Richard E Ingram, CEO	Rev: Assets: Emp:	500 NA 4	
Builders Square Inc 100 Crossroads San Antonio, TX 78201 512-731-0500	Retail merchandise stores; building supplies, hardware. Type: Private-Sub Par: K Mart Corp Ind: Retail/Merch Grp: Retail Frank Denny, CEO	Rev: Assets: Emp:	750 NA 7	
Bulova Watch Co Inc One Bulova Avenue Woodside, NY 11377 718-204-3300	Manufacturer & wholesaler of watches. Type: Private-Sub Par: Loews Corp Ind: Manufacturing Grp: Manufacturing Andrew Tisch, CEO	Rev: Assets: Emp:	NA NA NA	
Bunge Corp 1 Chase Manhattan Plaza New York, NY 10005 212-943-6600	Food processing & distribution company. Type: Private Ind: Food Processing Grp: Food Processing John E Kline, CEO	Rev: Assets: Emp:	5500 NA 3	

Organizations Listed Alphabetically

Organization / Address / Phone	Descriptive Information	Revenue / ($ mil)	Assets / ($ mil)	Emp (thous)
Burlington Coat Factory Inc Route 130 Burlington, NJ 08016 609-387-7800	Manufacturer of clothing; retail stores. Type: NYSE-BCF Ind: Apparel/Textiles Grp: Consumer Prd Monroe G Milstein, CEO	Rev: 282 Assets: NA Emp: 3		
Burlington Industries Inc 3330 W Friendly Avenue Greensboro, NC 27410 919-379-2000	Manufacturer of textile products. Type: Private Ind: Apparel/Textiles Grp: Consumer Prd Frank S Greenberg, CEO Donald R Hughes, CFO Roger F Anthony, IS J Kenneth Lesley, IR C R Windham, PR	Rev: 3000 Assets: 2300 Emp: 25		
Burlington Northern Inc 3800 Continental Plaza Fort Worth, TX 76102 817-878-2000	Gas & oil exploration, production, distributor. Type: NYSE-BNI Ind: Railroad Grp: Business Service Richard M Bressler, CEO Gerald Grinsten, Pres Zane E Barnes, VCh Luino Dell'Osso Jr, CFO Mary Garst, VP Charles Harper, VP Christopher T Bayley, IR Ronald H Reimann, PR	Rev: 4701 Assets: 6330 Emp: 39		
Burlington Resources 999 Third Avenue Seattle, WA 98104 206-467-3838	Transporter of natural gas via pipelines; forest products. Type: NYSE-BNI Ind: Energy Grp: Basic Industries Richard M Bressler, CEO	Rev: 1500 Assets: NA Emp: 15		
Burnett, Leo Co Inc 35 W Wacker Chicago, IL 60601 312-565-5959	Nationwide advertising agency. Type: Private Ind: Business Service Grp: Business Service Kapp Adams, CEO	Rev: 2200 Assets: NA Emp: 4		
Burns Food Ltd 150 6th Avenue SW Calgary, AB T2P3X4 Can 403-265-8140	Wholesale grocery products dealer. Type: TOR Ind: Retail/Merch Grp: Retail Ronald Jacobson, CEO	Rev: 680 Assets: NA Emp: 3		
Burns Fry Ltd First Canadian Place Toronto, ON M5X1H3 Can 416-365-4000	Investment company; brokerage. Type: Private Ind: Securities Grp: Financial Latham C Burns, CEO	Rev: 263 Assets: 1616 Emp: 2		
Busch Agricultural Resources Inc 12855 Flushing Meadow Drive St Louis, MO 63131 314-822-6565	Agriculture, grower of hops, supplies for beer production. Type: Private-Sub Par: Anheuser Busch Companies Inc Ind: Food Processing Grp: Food Processing Raymond Goff, CEO	Rev: NA Assets: NA Emp: NA		
Businessland Inc 1001 Ridder Park Drive San Jose, CA 95131 408-437-4156	Operator or retail computer stores. Type: NYSE-BLI Ind: Retail/Merch Grp: Retail David A Norman, CEO	Rev: 750 Assets: NA Emp: 9		
Butler Manufacturing Co BMA Tower Kansas City, MO 64141 816-968-3000	Manufacture of systems & components for buildings. Type: NASDAQ-BTLR Ind: Manufacturing Grp: Manufacturing Robert H West, CEO Donald H Pratt, Pres Leslie V Rist, CFO Richard Ballentine, VP Dennis S Brown, VP Donald Pratt, PR	Rev: 646 Assets: 266 Emp: 4		
Butler Paper Co 23 Inverness Way E Englewood, CO 80155 303-790-8343	Manufacturer of paper. Type: Private-Sub Par: Great Northern Nekoosa Corp Ind: Paper/Forest Prd Grp: Basic Industries Francis G Walker, CEO	Rev: 250 Assets: NA Emp: 2		
Butt, H E Grocery Co 646 S Main Street San Antonio, TX 78204 512-270-8000	Operator of wholesale grocery distribution businesses. Type: Private Ind: Retail/Food Grp: Retail Charles C Butt, CEO	Rev: 2250 Assets: NA Emp: 15		

Organizations Listed Alphabetically

Organization / Address / Phone	Descriptive Information	Revenue / ($ mil)	Assets / ($ mil)	Emp (thous)
Cablec Corp 17 Squadron Blvd New City, NY 10956 914-634-0100	Steel manufacturing & distribution company. Type: Private Ind: Steel Grp: Basic Industries Harry Shell, CEO	Rev: Assets: Emp:	550 NA 5	
Cablevision Systems Inc One Media Crossways Woodbury, NY 11797 516-364-8450	Operator of cable television systems. Type: ASE-CVC Ind: Publishing/Com Grp: Consumer Service Charles F Dolan, CEO John Tatta, Pres William Bell, VCh Barry J O'Leary, CFO James Dolan, Sls Sheila Mahony, Mkt Francis Randolph, VP James Kofalt, VP Daniel Sweeney, VP Jerry Shaw, VP	Rev: Assets: Emp:	493 1171 2	
Cabot Corp 950 Winter Street Waltham, MA 02154 617-890-0200	Oil & natural gas exploration & production company. Type: NYSE-CBT Ind: Energy Grp: Basic Industries Samuel W Bodman, CEO Fred A Conti, CFO Richard K Hayden, IS James D Bittner, R&D Mario Cornacchio, PR	Rev: Assets: Emp:	1500 1800 9	
Cadillac Fairview Corp Cadillac Fairview Tower Toronto, ON M5H3R4 Can 416-598-8200	Real estate management & development company. Type: TOR Ind: Real Estate/Bldg Grp: Business Service Jack Lawrence, CEO	Rev: Assets: Emp:	579 3521 4	
Cadillac Motor Car Division 2860 Clark Avenue Detroit, MI 48232 313-554-6112	Manufacturer of automobiles. Type: Private-Sub Par: General Motors Corp Ind: Automotive Grp: Manufacturing John Grettenberger, CEO	Rev: Assets: Emp:	NA NA NA	
CAE Industries Ltd 3060 Royal Bank Plaza Toronto, ON M5J2J1 Can 416-865-0070	Diversified manufacturer of machinery & electronic equip. Type: TOR Ind: Manufacturing Grp: Manufacturing R Fraser Elliott, CEO David H Race, Chr C Douglas Reekie, VCh David Adams, Tres John E Caldwell, CFO John G MacKay, Ops Frederick Fraser, VP David A Lazzarato, VP	Rev: Assets: Emp:	712 986 7	
Caesars New Jersey 2100 Pacific Avenue Atlantic City, NJ 08401 609-348-4411	Gambling casino operator. Type: ASE Ind: Leisure Time Grp: Consumer Service Henry Gluck, CEO Henry Gluck, Chr Terrence Lanni, Pres M Peter Schweitzer, VCh Roger Lee, CFO Warren Salisbury, VP Edwin Getz, VP Joseph LaGumina, VP	Rev: Assets: Emp:	343 300 3	
Caesars World Inc 1801 Century Park E Suite 2600 Los Angeles, CA 90067 213-552-2711	Gambling casino & hotel company. Type: NYSE-CAW Ind: Leisure Time Grp: Consumer Service Henry Gluck, CEO J Terrence Lanni, Pres Roger Lee, CFO Charles J Monahan, Mkt Jack Leone, IR	Rev: Assets: Emp:	902 831 11	
Cain Chemical Corp 11 Greenwood Plaza Houston, TX 77046 713-622-2246	Manufacturer of chemical products. Type: Private-Sub Ind: Chemicals Grp: Basic Industries Roger Hirl, CEO	Rev: Assets: Emp:	1100 NA 3	
Caisse de Depot du Quebec Ltd 1981 Avenue McGill College Montreal, PQ H3A3C7 Can 514-842-3261	Diversified financial company. Type: Private Ind: Non-Bank Fin Grp: Financial Jean Campeau, CEO	Rev: Assets: Emp:	2253 25550 3	
Cajun Electric Power Cooperative Inc 10719 Airline Highway Baton Rouge, LA 70895 504-291-3060	Producer of electric power for use by local utilities. Type: Private Ind: Utility Grp: Utilities David Lee Moore, CEO	Rev: Assets: Emp:	275 NA 1	
Calcot Ltd Inc 1601 Brundage Lane Bakersfield, CA 93307 805-327-5961	Food processing & distribution company. Type: Private Ind: Food Processing Grp: Food Processing T W Smith, CEO	Rev: Assets: Emp:	1100 NA 2	

Organizations Listed Alphabetically

Organization / Address / Phone	Descriptive Information	Revenue / Assets / Emp ($ mil) ($ mil) (thous)	
Caldor Inc 20 Glover Avenue Norwalk, CT 06850 203-846-1641	Operator of retail department stores. Type: Private-Sub Par: May Department Stores Co Ind: Retail/Merch Grp: Retail Don Clarke, CEO	Rev: Assets: Emp:	NA NA NA
Calgary Cooperative Assn Ltd 8818 Macleod Trail SE Calgary, AB T2H0M5 Can 403-253-0345	Agricultural cooperative. Type: Private Ind: Retail/Food Grp: Retail Bruno Friesen, CEO	Rev: Assets: Emp:	382 86 3
Calgary, The University of 2500 University Drive NW Calgary, AB T2N1N4 Can 403-220-5110	Major educational institution; university. Type: University Ind: University Grp: Govt & Non-Prof N E Wagner, CEO	Rev: Assets: Emp:	234 NM 21
Calgon Carbon 400 Media Drive Robinson Twnshp, PA 15205 412-787-6700	Manufacturer of carbon & carbon products. Type: OTC Ind: Manufacturing Grp: Manufacturing Arthur L Goeschel, CEO	Rev: Assets: Emp:	200 200 1
California & Hawaiian Sugar Inc 1390 Willow Pass Road Concord, CA 94111 415-356-6000	Producer of packaged food products; sugar. Type: Private Ind: Food Processing Grp: Food Processing Harold Somerset, CEO Gary Nelson, CFO	Rev: Assets: Emp:	825 250 3
California Almond Growers Inc 1802 C Street Sacramento, CA 95814 916-442-0771	Agricultural cooperative food production; almonds, nuts. Type: Private Ind: Food Processing Grp: Food Processing Roger Baccigaluppi, CEO	Rev: Assets: Emp:	550 NA 3
California Federal S & L Assn Inc 5670 Wilshire Blvd Los Angeles, CA 90036 213-932-4321	Thrift institution. Type: NYSE-CAL Ind: Savings & Loan Grp: Financial John R Torell, CEO George P Rutland, Chr John Torell, Pres Stephen Natcher, VCh Jerry A St Dennis, CFO Edward E Wendt, IS James R Wegge Jr, R&D William F Watt, Mkt Peter Wyman, VP Douglas Wallis, VP Thomas Smith, VP James F Hurley, IR	Rev: Assets: Emp:	2816 27482 6
California First Bank Inc 350 California Street San Francisco, CA 94104 415-445-0200	Commercial bank. Type: Private-Sub-For Ind: Banking Grp: Financial Toshio Nagamura, CEO Seishichi Itoh, Chr Kasuzuke Naito, CFO Larry Murphy, IS Don Kinnaird, Mkt Mike Colwell, PR	Rev: Assets: Emp:	600 6000 4
California Public Emp Retirement System 400 P Street Sacramento, CA 95814 916-445-7700	State employees investment fund. Type: State Govt Ind: Non-Bank Fin Grp: Financial Dale Hanson, CEO	Rev: Assets: Emp:	3821 41249 2
California State Auto Association 100 Van Ness Avenue San Francisco, CA 94102 415-565-2012	Property & casualty insurance company. Type: Private-Mutual Ind: Insurance Grp: Insurance Alfred F Federico, CEO	Rev: Assets: Emp:	1096 1932 3
California State Univ Fullerton 800 N State College Blvd Fullerton, CA 92634 714-773-2011	Major educational institution; university. Type: University Ind: University Grp: Govt & Non-Prof Jewell Plummer Cobb, CEO	Rev: Assets: Emp:	110 84 26
California State Univ Long Beach 1250 Bellflower Blvd Long Beach, CA 90840 213-498-4158	Major educational institution; university. Type: University Ind: University Grp: Govt & Non-Prof Curtis L McCray, CEO	Rev: Assets: Emp:	139 271 36
California State Univ Los Angeles 5151 State University Drive Los Angeles, CA 90032 213-224-0111	Major educational institution; university. Type: University Ind: University Grp: Govt & Non-Prof James M Rosser, CEO	Rev: Assets: Emp:	108 132 23

Organizations Listed Alphabetically

Organization / Address / Phone	Descriptive Information	Revenue / Assets / Emp ($ mil) ($ mil) (thous)		

California State Univ Northridge
1811 Nordhoff Street
Northridge, CA 91330
213-885-1200

Major educational institution; university.
Type: University
Ind: University   Grp: Govt & Non-Prof
James Cleary, CEO

Rev: 120
Assets: 86
Emp: 30

California State Univ Sacramento
6000 J Street
Sacramento, CA 95819
916-454-6011

Major educational institution; university.
Type: University
Ind: University   Grp: Govt & Non-Prof
Ronald R Gerth, CEO

Rev: 110
Assets: 106
Emp: 26

California State University System
400 Golden Shore
Long Beach, CA 90802
213-590-5731

Major educational institution; university system.
Type: University
Ind: University   Grp: Govt & Non-Prof
W Ann Reynolds, CEO

Rev: 660
Assets: 660
Emp: 210

California, State of
State Capitol
Sacramento, CA 95814
916-322-9900

State government.
Type: State Govt
Ind: State/Prov Govt   Grp: Govt & Non-Prof
George Deukmejian, CEO

Rev: 73542
Assets: NM
Emp: 328

Calmat Co
3200 San Fernando Road
Los Angeles, CA 90065
213-258-2777

Regional producer of aggregate, asphalt & concrete.
Type: NYSE-CZM
Ind: Building Mat   Grp: Basic Industries
William Jenkins, CEO   A Frederick Gerstell, Chr   Thomas J Kelleher, Tres
Ronald C Hadfield, CFO   Wilbur G Jager, Mkt   Brian W Ferris, VP
John G S Mills, VP   David S Cahn, VP   Gene R Block, VP
Scott J Wilcott, VP   Thomas M Linden, VP

Rev: 661
Assets: 765
Emp: 3

Camco Inc
2645 Skymark Avenue
Mississauga, ON L4W4H2 Can
416-629-3000

Manufacturer of major appliances.
Type: Private-Sub Par: General Electric Canada Co
Ind: Appliances/Furn   Grp: Manufacturing
C Harper, CEO

Rev: 468
Assets: 213
Emp: 5

Cameron Iron Works Inc
13013 Northwest Freeway
Houston, TX 77040
713-939-2211

Manufacturer of tools for the exploration of oil & gas.
Type: NYSE
Ind: Oil Service   Grp: Business Service
Philip Burguieres, CEO   K Hardcastle, VCh   Norman Nolen, Tres
John D Deakins, CFO   N A Wilkinson, R&D   M E Eagles, Mkt
C King, VP   Neal Sutton, VP   J Hiett Ives, PR

Rev: 502
Assets: 757
Emp: 7

Campbell Soup Co
Campbell Place
Camden, NJ 08103
609-342-4800

Manufacturer of packaged foods.
Type: NYSE-CPB
Ind: Food Processing   Grp: Food Processing
R Gordon McGovern, CEO   Robert Norris, Tres   Edwin L Harper, CFO
Harry Wallaesa, IS   James R Kirkman, R&D   Carl V Stinnett, Mkt
T Forrest Fisher, VP   Donna Eaton, VP   Arnold Denton, VP
Paul N Mulcahy, VP   C Scott Rombach, IR   James H Moran, PR

Rev: 4869
Assets: 3610
Emp: 48

Campbell Soup Co Canada
60 Birmingham Street
Toronto, ON M8V2B8 Can
416-251-1131

Food processor; soups, packaged foods, frozen foods.
Type: TOR-CSC
Ind: Food Processing   Grp: Food Processing
G J Arnold, CEO

Rev: 302
Assets: 147
Emp: 2

Campbell Taggert Inc
6211 Lemmon Avenue
Dallas, TX 75209
214-358-9211

Food products manufacturing & distribution company.
Type: Private-Sub Par: Anheuser Busch Companies Inc
Ind: Food Processing   Grp: Food Processing
Patrick Stokes, CEO

Rev: NA
Assets: NA
Emp: NA

Campeau Corp
40 King Street
Toronto, ON M5H3Y8 Can
416-868-6460

Real estate development & retailing company.
Type: TOR
Ind: Real Estate/Bldg   Grp: Business Service
Robert Campeau, CEO   Ronald Tysoe, Pres   Russell Davis, CFO
James Zimmerman, Mkt   Thomas Cody, Ops   Paul D Campbell, VP
Jean Martineau, VP   Terrence Partington, VP   John Boorn, VP
Lenard McQuarrie, VP   John Burden, VP

Rev: 7368
Assets: 12151
Emp: 110

Organizations Listed Alphabetically

Organization / Address / Phone	Descriptive Information	Revenue / Assets / Emp ($ mil) ($ mil) (thous)		

Organization / Address / Phone	Descriptive Information			
Canada Cement Lafarge Ltd 606 Rue Cathcart Montreal, PQ H3B1L7 Can 514-861-1411	Manufacturer of cement & concrete products. Type: TOR Ind: Building Mat Grp: Basic Industries John Redfern, CEO	Rev: Assets: Emp:	838 638 6	
Canada Life Assurance Co 330 University Avenue Toronto, ON M5G1R8 Can 416-597-1456	Life insurance company. Type: Private Ind: Insurance Grp: Insurance E H Crawford, CEO E H Crawford, Chr D A Nield, Pres J G Fleming, CFO D Loney, Mkt H McCubbin, Ops A Symons, VP N Daly, VP J Fleming, VP	Rev: Assets: Emp:	3170 9661 3	
Canada Mortgage & Housing Corp 682 Montreal Road Ottawa, ON K1A0P7 CAN 613-748-2000	Home mortgage agency of the federal government. Type: Federal Govt Ind: Federal Govt Grp: Govt & Non-Prof Robert Jarvis, CEO	Rev: Assets: Emp:	758 8109 3	
Canada Packers Inc 30 St Clair Avenue W Toronto, ON M4V3A2 Can 416-869-6049	Operator of agricultural & food processing businesses. Type: TOR-CK Ind: Food Processing Grp: Food Processing James D Hunter, CEO Leo J Duchaine, Tres A Roger Porretti, CFO Sitaramaiah Atluru, R&D Edward J Roberts, VP David J Sommerville, VP L Richardson Symmes, VP Arthur F Devlin, VP Alistair M MacKenzie, VP	Rev: Assets: Emp:	2739 711 12	
Canada Post Corp Sir Alexander Campbell Bldg Ottawa, ON K1A0B1 Can 613-952-1524	Federal government agency. Type: Federal Govt Ind: Federal Govt Grp: Govt & Non-Prof Sylvain Cloutier, CEO	Rev: Assets: Emp:	2525 2235 61	
Canada Safeway Ltd 1015 4th Street SW Calgary, AB T2P2S6 Can 403-260-8600	Operator of retail grocery supermarkets. Type: TOR Ind: Retail/Food Grp: Retail Bill Sexsmith, CEO	Rev: Assets: Emp:	3291 821 22	
Canada Trust Financial Services Co 320 Bay Street Toronto, ON M5H2P6 Can 416-869-6100	Consumer financial services; mortgages, savings. Type: Private Ind: Non-Bank Fin Grp: Financial Peter C Laurice, CEO	Rev: Assets: Emp:	2468 21707 11	
Canada Trust Realtors Ltd 320 Bay Street Toronto, ON M5H2P6 Can 416-361-8657	Nationwide network of real estate sales offices. Type: Private Ind: Real Estate/Bldg Grp: Business Service John Schucht, CEO	Rev: Assets: Emp:	213 NA 4	
Canadian Commerical Corp 50 O'Conner Street Ottawa, ON K1A0S6 Can 613-996-0034	Canadian federal government industrial development agency. Type: Federal Govt Ind: Federal Govt Fin Grp: Financial Hugh Mullington, CEO	Rev: Assets: Emp:	659 420 1	
Canadian Department of Defense 101 Colonel By Drive Ottawa, ON K1A0K2 Can 613-995-2534	Federal government agency. Type: Federal Govt Ind: Federal Govt Grp: Govt & Non-Prof D B Dewar, CEO	Rev: Assets: Emp:	20298 NM 120	
Canadian Imperial Bank of Commerce Ltd Commerce Court W Toronto, ON M5L1A2 Can 416-980-2211	Commercial bank. Type: TOR-CM Ind: Banking Grp: Financial R D Fullerton, CEO F H Logan, VCh P G S Cantor, CFO J G Bickford, IS B Gestrin, Sls F D A Boal, Ops G Lewis, VP J Myers, VP A Flood, VP L Ronald, VP	Rev: Assets: Emp:	7854 80485 36	
Canadian Marconi Co 2442 Trenton Montreal, PQ H3P1Y9 Can 514-341-7630	Manufacturer of electronic components; solid state devices. Type: ASE Ind: Electronics Grp: High Tech J Grandy, CEO	Rev: Assets: Emp:	255 170 2	

Organizations Listed Alphabetically

Organization / Address / Phone	Descriptive Information	Revenue / ($ mil)	Assets / ($ mil)	Emp (thous)
Canadian National Railway 935 De la Gauchetiere Street W Montreal, PQ H3C3N4 Can 514-399-5430	Nationwide railroad transportation company. Type: TOR Ind: Railroad Grp: Business Service R E Lawless, CEO G C Church, Tres T Cedraschi, CFO P A Clarke, Mkt M A Blackwell, VP R Boudreau, VP F D Campbell, VP A E Deegan, VP A J Gillies, VP B E Horsman, VP J P Kelsall, IR B E Ducey, PR	Rev: 3975	Assets: 5870	Emp: 44
Canadian Occidental Petroleum Ltd 1500 635 8th Avenue SW Calgary, AB T2P3Z1 Can 403-234-6700	Petroleum exploration, production & marketing company. Type: TOR-CXY Ind: Energy Grp: Basic Industries Ray R Irani, CEO J Angus McKee, Chr Jerry Wright, VCh Victor Zaleschuk, CFO Keith E Peterson, R&D George Putnam, Mkt Charles Mikkelborg, VP Thomas Sugalski, VP H Thomas Irwin, VP	Rev: 629	Assets: 1153	Emp: 1
Canadian Pacific Express Ltd 2255 Sheppard Avenue E Toronto, ON M2J1W7 Can 416-498-8850	Transportation company; trucking. Type: Private-Sub Par: Canadian Pacific Ltd Ind: Transport Grp: Business Service William Wiley, CEO	Rev: 383	Assets: 213	Emp: 3
Canadian Pacific Forest Products Ltd Neebling Avenue Thunder Bay, ON P7C4W3 Can 807-475-2110	Forest products company. Type: TOR Ind: Paper/Forest Prd Grp: Basic Industries Cecil S Flenniken, CEO	Rev: 2555	Assets: 2358	Emp: 17
Canadian Pacific Ltd 910 Reel Street Windsor Station Montreal, PQ H3C3E4 Can 514-395-5151	Diversified company; oil, forest products, hotel, commnctns. Type: NYSE-CP Ind: Railroad Grp: Business Service Robert W Campbell, CEO W Stinson, Chr R Gamey, VCh G Michaels, CFO D toole, R&D N Wale, Mkt W Fatt, VP J Thomson, VP C Munro, VP J Hankinson, VP	Rev: 10214	Assets: 15003	Emp: 76
Canadian Tire Co 2180 Yonge Street Toronto, ON M4P2V8 Can 416-480-3000	Manufacturer & retailer of automotive tires. Type: TOR-CTR Ind: Retail/Merch Grp: Retail Hugh L Macaulay, CEO Dean Groussman, Chr Gerald S Kishner, CFO V Henning Mikkelsen, IS W Rae Cowan, Mkt Clive Minto, VP Peter Lige', VP Howard F Board, VP Steven Bochen, VP	Rev: 2245	Assets: 1301	Emp: 6
Canadian Utilities Ltd 10035 105 Street Edmonton, AB T5J2V6 Can 403-420-7121	Electric power utility holding company. Type: Private-Sub Par: Atco Ltd Ind: Utility Grp: Utilities R Southern, CEO	Rev: 978	Assets: 2231	Emp: 1
Canadian Western Natural Gas Co 909 11 Avenue SW Calgary, AB T2R1L8 Can 403-245-7110	Utility company; natural gas distribution & transmission. Type: Private-Sub Par: Atco Ltd Ind: Utility Grp: Utilities R Southern, CEO	Rev: 255	Assets: 340	Emp: 1
Canadian Wheat Board 423 Main Street Winnipeg, MB R3C2P5 Can 204-983-0239	Agricultural cooperative; wheat. Type: Federal Govt Ind: Federal Govt Grp: Govt & Non-Prof W E Jarvis, CEO David Offert, Tres B Oleson, CFO G P Machej, Mkt R L Kristjanson, VP F M Hetland, VP R H Klassen, VP L C Evans, VP	Rev: 1750	Assets: 3488	Emp: 1
Canam Manac Group Inc 11535 lre Avenue Bureau 700 Ville St Georges, PQ G5Y2C7 Can 418-228-8031	Steel fabrication & natural gas distribution company. Type: TOR-CAM Ind: Automotive Grp: Manufacturing Marcel Dutil, CEO Paul Gauthier, VCh Real Sureau, CFO Richard Vincent, R&D Pierre Tanguay, VP Robert Drolet, VP Jasmin Gosselin, VP Claude Saulnier, VP	Rev: 547	Assets: 562	Emp: 5

Organizations Listed Alphabetically

Organization / Address / Phone	Descriptive Information	Revenue ($ mil)	Assets ($ mil)	Emp (thous)
Canfor Corp 3000 Four Bentall Ctr 1055 Dunsmuir Street Vancouver, BC V6C1N5 Can 604-661-5241	Forest products company; lumber, building materials. Type: TOR Ind: Paper/Forest Prd Grp: Basic Industries Peter J G Bentley, CEO Roy A Bickell, Pres Mark H Gunther, VCh Janet K Pau, Tres Gordon Armstrong, CFO Christer Arnesen, Sls Peter Ashby, Mkt W Bert Gayle, Ops Ray B Haslam, VP William Hughes, VP	Rev: Assets: Emp:	921 986 4	
Canon USA Inc One Cannon Plaza Lake Success, NY 11042 516-488-6700	Manufacturer of electronic office equipment; US hq. Type: Private-Sub-For Ind: Comput/Off Equip Grp: High Tech Hideharu Takemoto, CEO	Rev: Assets: Emp:	2200 NA 4	
Canpotex Ltd 111 2nd Avenue S Saskatoon, SK S7K1K6 Can 306-931-2200	Manufacturer of fertilizer products. Type: TOR Ind: Chemicals Grp: Basic Industries E Ededahl, CEO	Rev: Assets: Emp:	324 73 1	
Canron Ltd 1 First Canadian Place Toronto, ON M5X1A4 Can 416-364-6600	Manufacturer of fabricated building parts, structural steel. Type: TOR Ind: Manufacturing Grp: Manufacturing James T Black, CEO William Cullens, Chr Carol Towner, CFO Jacques Robert, Ops Norman Dickenson, VP Gerald Lefebvre, VP William D Moncur, VP	Rev: Assets: Emp:	449 215 4	
Cansulex Ltd 1066 W Hastings Street Vancouver, BC V6E3X1 Can 604-688-1501	Manufacturer of sulphur products. Type: TOR Ind: Chemicals Grp: Basic Industries Robert Phillips, CEO	Rev: Assets: Emp:	292 170 1	
Canteen Inc 222 N LaSalle Street Chicago, IL 60601 312-701-2000	Operator of retail food vending & institutional catering. Type: Private-Sub Par: TW Service Inc Ind: Food/Lodging Grp: Consumer Service Richard Carlson, CEO	Rev: Assets: Emp:	NA NA NA	
Canterra Energy Ltd 505 5th Street SW Calgary, AB T2P2K7 Can 403-267-9111	Oil & gas exploration & distribution company. Type: TOR Ind: Energy Grp: Basic Industries Bernard Isautier, CEO	Rev: Assets: Emp:	383 2550 2	
Cantrex Group Inc 4445 Garend Street Montreal, PQ H4R2H7 Can 514-335-0260	Marketing company; advertising, direct mail. Type: MON Ind: Business Service Grp: Business Service Marc Bureau, CEO	Rev: Assets: Emp:	425 213 2	
Capital Cities--Amer Broadcasting Co Inc 77 W 66th Street New York, NY 10023 212-456-7777	Media company; TV broadcasting, newspapers, TV & radio. Type: NYSE-CCB Ind: Publishing/Com Grp: Consumer Service Thomas S Murphy, CEO Daniel B Burke, Pres John B Fairchild, VCh Ronald J Doerfler, CFO Ann Maynard Gray, IS Phillip Beuth, Sls John Frisoli, Mkt John Sias, VP Michael Mallardi, VP Jeffrey Ruthizer, VP Phillip Farnsworth, VP Patricia J Matson, PR	Rev: Assets: Emp:	4773 6089 20	
Capital Group Inc 333 S Hope Street Los Angeles, CA 90071 213-486-9200	Mutual fund & pension fund investment firm. Type: Private Ind: Non-Bank Fin Grp: Financial Michael Shanahan, CEO	Rev: Assets: Emp:	550 27500 2	
Capital Holding Co 680 Fourth Avenue PO Box 32830 Louisville, KY 40232 502-560-2000	Life insurance holding company. Type: NYSE-CPH Ind: Non-Bank Fin Grp: Financial Irving W Bailey, CEO John A Franco, Pres Theodore S Rosky, CFO John D Loewenberg, IS David E Sams Jr, Mkt William Gibbons, VP Barbara Laski, VP R Brayton Bowen, VP William Bosles, VP William Gibbons, PR	Rev: Assets: Emp:	2046 12963 8	

Organizations Listed Alphabetically

Organization / Address / Phone	Descriptive Information	Revenue / ($ mil)	Assets / ($ mil)	Emp (thous)
Capitol Federal Savings (Kansas) Inc 700 Kansas Avenue Topeka, KS 66603 913-235-1341	Thrift institution. Type: Private Ind: Savings & Loan Grp: Financial Henry A Bubb, CEO	Rev: Assets: Emp:		350 3000 1
Cara Operations Ltd 238 Bloor Street W Toronto, ON M5S1T8 Can 416-962-4571	Operator of retail restaurants & catering services. Type: TOR Ind: Food/Lodging Grp: Consumer Service Paul Phelen, CEO	Rev: Assets: Emp:		468 298 6
Cardinal Industries Inc 2040 S Hamilton Columbus, OH 43232 614-861-3211	Construction engineering & development company. Type: Private Ind: Real Estate/Bldg Grp: Business Service Austin Guirlinger, CEO	Rev: Assets: Emp:		550 NA 5
Caremark Inc 4340 Von Karman Newport Beach, CA 92660 714-851-2311	Specialized medical services. Type: NASDAQ-CMRK Ind: Retail/Merch Grp: Retail James M Sweeney, CEO	Rev: Assets: Emp:		200 150 1
Cargill Inc 15407 McGinty Road W Minnetonka, MN 55345 612-475-7575	International grain trading, storage & shipping company. Type: Private Ind: Food Processing Grp: Food Processing Whitney MacMillan, CEO	Rev: Assets: Emp:		40000 NA 45
Cargill Ltd 240 Graham Avenue Winnipeg, MB R3C4C5 Can 204-947-0141	Worldwide wheat wholesale, storage & transportation company. Type: Private-Sub-For Ind: Food Processing Grp: Food Processing Kerry Hawkins, CEO	Rev: Assets: Emp:		947 274 1
Carling O'Keefe Breweries Canada Ltd 1 Carling Drive Rexdale, ON M2P2C4 Can 416-675-3960	Food products company; beer. Type: Private-Sub-For Ind: Beverage Grp: Food Processing P Des Marais, CEO	Rev: Assets: Emp:		468 425 4
Carlisle Companies Inc 250 E Fifth Street Cincinnati, OH 45202 513-241-2500	Manufacturer of rubber & plastic products. Type: NYSE-CSL Ind: Tire/Rubber Grp: Basic Industries Malcolm C Myers, CEO Robert J Deffeyes, Pres Jerome H Eichert, CFO Gerald L Doerger, PR	Rev: Assets: Emp:		500 NA 5
Carlson Companies Inc 12755 Highway 55 Minneapolis, MN 55441 612-540-5000	International diversified services company. Type: Private Ind: Food Processing Grp: Food Processing Curtis L Carlson, CEO	Rev: Assets: Emp:		4000 NA 50
Carlson Marketing Group Ltd 5353 Dundas Street W Toronto, ON M9B6H8 Can 416-236-1991	Advertising services; direct mail. Type: Private-Sub-For Ind: Business Service Grp: Business Service E C Gage, CEO	Rev: Assets: Emp:		255 85 1
Carnegie Natural Gas Co 800 Regis Avenue Pittsburgh, PA 15236 412-655-8510	Natural gas transmission, exploration & producing company. Type: Private-Sub Par: USX Corp Ind: Energy Grp: Basic Industries D Casaday, CEO	Rev: Assets: Emp:		NA NA NA
Carnival Cruise Lines Inc 3915 Biscayne Blvd Miami, FL 33137 305-599-2600	Owner & operator of cruise ships. Type: ASE-CCL Ind: Leisure Time Grp: Consumer Service Ted Arison, CEO	Rev: Assets: Emp:		900 NA 10
Carolina Freight Corp NC Highway 150 E Cherryville, NC 28021 704-435-6811	Trucking transport company. Type: NYSE-CAO Ind: Transport Grp: Business Service K G Younger, CEO Kenneth E Mayhew Jr, Pres Carlisle Jackson, Tres Carlisle Jackson, CFO P E Huffstetler, IS James R Eaton, Mkt James D Carlton, Ops Palmer E Huffstetler, IR James R Eaton, PR	Rev: Assets: Emp:		651 347 10

Organizations Listed Alphabetically

Organization / Address / Phone	Descriptive Information	Revenue / ($ mil)	Assets / ($ mil)	Emp (thous)
Carolina Power & Light Co 411 Fayetteville Street Mall Raleigh, NC 27602 919-836-6111	Electric power utility. Type: NYSE Ind: Utility Grp: Utilities Sherwood H Smith, CEO William E Graham Jr, Pres Edwin Utley, VCh Edward G Lilly Jr, CFO R T Dwyer III, IS Charles Barham, VP James Davis, VP Lynn Eury, VP M McDuffie, VP Wilson Morgan, VP Paul S Bradshaw, VP Albert L Morris Jr, IR S M Henry Brown Jr, PR	Rev: Assets: Emp:	2273 7504 10	
Carolina Telephone & Telegraph Co 720 Western Blvd Tarboro, NC 27886 919-823-9900	Telephone utility company. Type: Private-Sub Par: United Telecommunications Inc Ind: Telecom Grp: High Tech Wayne Peterson, CEO	Rev: Assets: Emp:	NA NA NA	
Carpenter Technology Corp 101 W Bern Street Reading, PA 19603 215-371-2000	Manufacturer & fabricator of metals. Type: NYSE-CRS Ind: Manufacturing Grp: Manufacturing Paul R Roedel, CEO Adolph J Lena, Pres John A Schuler, CFO Donald R Mikes, IS Edward Gilbert, R&D Robert W Cardy, Mkt John McHale, VP Daniel Rothermel, VP Robert Holmes, PR	Rev: Assets: Emp:	556 635 4	
Carpenter, E R Corp 5016 Monument Avenue Richmond, VA 23230 804-359-0800	Manufacturer of plastic foams. Type: Private Ind: Building Mat Grp: Basic Industries Stanley F Pauley, CEO	Rev: Assets: Emp:	500 NA 5	
Carrier Corp 6304 Carrier Parkway Syracuse, NY 13221 315-432-6000	Manufacturer of air conditioning systems. Type: Private-Sub Par: United Technologies Corp Ind: Appliances/Furn Grp: Manufacturing W Wilson, CEO	Rev: Assets: Emp:	NA NA NA	
Carroll McEntee & McGinley Inc 40 Wall Street New York, NY 10005 212-825-6780	Investment firm; securities trading. Type: Private Ind: Securities Grp: Financial Tom Basile, CEO	Rev: Assets: Emp:	330 3300 1	
Carson, Pirie, Scott & Co One S State Street Chicago, IL 60603 312-641-7000	Retailing; department & specialty stores. Type: NYSE-CRN Ind: Retail/Merch Grp: Retail Peter S Willmott, CEO Bruce R Rismiller, VCh Susan T Congalton, CFO H Lynn Hazlett, IS Clifford Bown, Ops Kate Leatham, VP Barry Parker, VP	Rev: Assets: Emp:	1023 666 18	
Carter Hawley Hale Stores Inc 550 S Flower Street Los Angeles, CA 90071 213-620-0150	Retail stores; apparel, home furnishings & furniture. Type: NYSE Ind: Retail/Merch Grp: Retail Philip M Hawley, CEO Waldo H Burnside, Pres John F Busey, Tres J M Gaileys, CFO Serena S Kokjer, IS Arthur Coons, Mkt Lloyd E Ellis, VP Edwin Holman, VP Larry Peterson, VP Thomas E Brown, VP Bill Dombrowski, IR E Harlin Smith, PR	Rev: Assets: Emp:	2617 1672 33	
Carter Wallace Inc 767 Fifth Avenue New York, NY 10153 212-758-4500	Manufacturer of health care & consumer products. Type: NYSE Ind: Drugs Grp: Consumer Service Henry H Hoyt, CEO Charles O Hoyt, VCh Paul Veteri, CFO	Rev: Assets: Emp:	514 400 3	
Carteret Savings Bank Corporated 200 South Street Morristown, NJ 07960 201-326-1000	Thrift institution. Type: NYSE-CBC Ind: Savings & Loan Grp: Financial Robert B O'Brien, CEO Robert J Mueller, Pres Dennis M Mahoney, CFO James M Krupinski, IS Frank A Willis, PR	Rev: Assets: Emp:	700 6000 2	
Cascades Inc 404 Rue Marie Victorin Kingsey Falls, PQ J0A1B0 Can 819-363-2245	Pulp & paper manufacturer. Type: TOR-CAS Ind: Packaging Grp: Manufacturing Bernard Lemaire, CEO Laurent LeMaire, Pres Alain Lemaire, VCh Fernand Cloutier, CFO Jacques Aubert, VP	Rev: Assets: Emp:	501 458 3	

Organizations Listed Alphabetically

Organization / Address / Phone	Descriptive Information	Revenue / ($ mil)	Assets / ($ mil)	Emp (thous)
Casey's General Stores Inc 1277 NE Broadway Des Moines, IA 50313 515-263-3700	Operator of gasoline stations & convenience stores. Type: NASDAQ-CASY Ind: Retail/Food Grp: Retail Donald F Lambarti, CEO	Rev: Assets: Emp:	419 200 4	
Castle & Cooke Inc 10900 Wilshire Blvd Los Angeles, CA 90071 213-824-1500	Food products company; Dole pineapple, raisins, real estate. Type: NYSE-CKE Ind: Food Processing Grp: Food Processing David H Murdock, CEO Raymond Henze, VCh William J Haain, CFO Harry E Stephens III, IS Thomas Leppert, Mkt Antony Lundy, VP Leo Korman, VP George Horne, VP Alan Sellers, VP	Rev: Assets: Emp:	2469 1922 42	
Castle, A M & Co 3400 N Wolf Road Franklin Park, IL 60131 312-455-7111	Wholesale metals company; steel, aluminum, nickel. Type: ASE-CAS Ind: Metals/Mining Grp: Basic Industries Michael Simpson, CEO	Rev: Assets: Emp:	375 300 2	
Catalyst Energy Development Inc 245 Park Avenue New York, NY 10167 212-949-0040	Producer of energy; alternative generation technology. Type: NYSE-CE Ind: Utility Grp: Utilities James J Lowrey, CEO	Rev: Assets: Emp:	400 1200 1	
Caterpillar Inc 100 NE Adams Street Peoria, IL 61629 309-675-1000	Manufacturer of industrial & construction equipment. Type: NYSE Ind: Equipment Grp: Manufacturing George A Schaefer, CEO Peter Donis, Pres Donald Fites, VCh Frank M Grimsley, CFO D Fieldcamp, IS Charles Fangman, R&D John N Hanson, Mkt Glen A Barton, VP Donald Coonan, VP Robert C Dryden, VP Charles Fangman, VP James Wogsland, VP Pierre Guerindon, VP Byron Dehaan, PR	Rev: Assets: Emp:	10435 9686 58	
Caterpillar of Canada Ltd 1550 Caterpillar Road Mississauga, ON L4X1E7 Can 416-846-3222	Manufacturer of industry construction equipment. Type: Private-Sub-For Ind: Equipment Grp: Manufacturing D Mckie, CEO	Rev: Assets: Emp:	301 113 1	
Cato Corp 8100 Denmark Road Charlotte, NC 28234 704-554-8510	Retailer of women's apparel. Type: OTC Ind: Retail/Merch Grp: Retail Wayland Cato, CEO	Rev: Assets: Emp:	250 150 22	
Cavenham (USA) Inc 25 Old Kings Highway N Darien, CT 06820 203-655-6211	Diversified manufacturer of consumer goods & services; US hq. Type: Private-Sub-For Ind: Retail/Merch Grp: Retail Floyd Hall, CEO	Rev: Assets: Emp:	2750 500 21	
CB & T Bancshares Inc 1148 Broadway Columbus, GA 31901 404-649-2387	Commercial bank. Type: NASDAQ-CBTB Ind: Banking Grp: Financial James H Blanchard, CEO	Rev: Assets: Emp:	251 1957 2	
CB Pak Inc 800 Boul Dorchester Montreal, PQ H3C2R5 Can 516-875-2160	Manufacturer of packaging materials; boxes, fiberboard. Type: Private-Sub Par: Consolidated Bathurst Inc Ind: Packaging Grp: Manufacturing Oscar Strangeland, CEO	Rev: Assets: Emp:	425 425 6	
CBI Industries Inc 800 Jorie Blvd Oak Brook, IL 60522 312-572-7000	Petroleum industry service & equipment company. Type: NYSE-CBH Ind: Oil Service Grp: Business Service William A Pogue, CEO J E Jones, Pres Lewis Akin, VCh G L Schueppert, CFO Robert Daniels, IS Jon Hagstrom, R&D James Mansell, Mkt Buel Adams, VP Hugh Fewin, VP C Graham Harper, PR	Rev: Assets: Emp:	1376 1343 15	

Organizations Listed Alphabetically

Organization / Address / Phone	Descriptive Information	Revenue / Assets / Emp ($ mil) ($ mil) (thous)		

CBS Inc
51 W 52nd Street
New York, NY 10019
212-975-4321

Television broadcasting company; radio & TV stations.
Type: NYSE-CBS
Ind: Publishing/Com   Grp: Consumer Service
William S Paley, CEO   Laurence Tisch, Chr   Gene Jankowski, Pres
Peter W Keegan, CFO   Peter J Schementi, IS   Thomas F Leahy, Mkt
Edward Grebow, Ops   Louis Rauchenberger, VP   John Showalter, VP
Jay Kriegel, VP   Howard Stringer, VP   Alice Henderson, PR

Rev: 2778
Assets: 4407
Emp: 20

CC Industries Inc
300 W Washington
Chicago, IL 60606
312-236-6300

Home furnishings,paper, real estate development.
Type: Private
Ind: Real Estate/Bldg   Grp: Business Service
Neele E Stearns, CEO

Rev: 500
Assets: NA
Emp: 5

CCL Industries Ltd
235 Yorkland Blvd
Willowdale, ON M2J4Y8 Can
416-756-8500

Manufacturer of personal care products.
Type: TOR-CCQB
Ind: Personal Care   Grp: Consumer Prd
Gordon S Lang, CEO   Wayne McLeod, Pres   Edward G Johnston, VCh
Mel Snider, CFO   Ronald Sloan, IS   Larry Eddy, R&D
Perry Nelson, VP   Gary Ullman, VP   Douglas Chafee, VP

Rev: 720
Assets: 496
Emp: 6

CDI Corp
10 Penn Center
Philadelphia, PA 19103
215-561-1750

Personnel services firm; temporary help, recruiting.
Type: NYSE-CDI
Ind: Business Service   Grp: Business Service
Walter R Garrison, CEO

Rev: 734
Assets: NA
Emp: 8

Ceco Corp
1400 Kensington Avenue
Oak Brook, IL 60522
312-789-1400

Building materials.
Type: Private
Ind: Building Mat   Grp: Basic Industries
Erwin E Schulze, CEO

Rev: 500
Assets: NA
Emp: 5

Celanese Canada Inc
800 Boul Dorchester 0
Montreal, PQ H3B1X9 Can
514-871-5511

Specialty chemical company.
Type: TOR
Ind: Chemicals   Grp: Basic Industries
Pierre Cote, CEO

Rev: 298
Assets: 219
Emp: 2

Celanese Corp (Hoechst)
Route 202-206 N
Somerville, NJ 08876
201-231-2000

Diversified manufacturer of chemicals; US headquarters.
Type: Private-Sub-For
Ind: Chemicals   Grp: Basic Industries
Ernest Drew, CEO

Rev: 3190
Assets: 2400
Emp: 21

Celeron Corp
2400 MCorp Plaza
Houston, TX 77053
713-750-4552

Petrochemical company.
Type: Private-Sub   Par: Goodyear Tire & Rubber Co
Ind: Chemicals   Grp: Basic Industries
Robert Milk, CEO

Rev: 1000
Assets: NA
Emp: 4

Cenex Corp
5500 Cenex Drive
Inver Grove Heights, MN 55075
612-451-5151

Operator of retail food stores.
Type: Private
Ind: Retail/Food   Grp: Retail
Noel Estenson, CEO

Rev: 1100
Assets: NA
Emp: 2

Centel Corp
O'Hare Plaza 8725 Higgins Road
Chicago, IL 60631
312-399-2500

Telephone, cellular phone & cable television operator.
Type: NYSE-CNT
Ind: Telecom   Grp: High Tech
John P Frazee, CEO   James Lovell, Pres   J Stephen Vanderwoude, VCh
Eugene Irminger, CFO   A Allan Kurtze, R&D   Samuel Leftwich, VP
William Leggett, VP   David Bohmer, VP   John Brindley, VP
James Vodak, VP

Rev: 1095
Assets: 3753
Emp: 13

Centerior Energy Corp
55 Public Square
Cleveland, OH 44101
216-622-9800

Electric utility holding company.
Type: NYSE-CX
Ind: Utility   Grp: Utilities
Richard A Miller, CEO   Robert J Farling, Pres   Murray Edelman, VCh
Edgar H Maugans, CFO   Joseph M Stricker, IS   Lyman Phillips, Sls
Paul M Smart, Mkt   Paul G Busby, VP   Victor F Greenslade, VP
E Lyle Pepin, VP   Gary Hawkinson, VP   Stephen G Lorton, PR

Rev: 2038
Assets: 11573
Emp: 9

Organizations Listed Alphabetically

Organization / Address / Phone	Descriptive Information	Revenue / Assets / Emp ($ mil) ($ mil) (thous)		

Centerre Trust Co
One Boatmans Plaza 800 Market Street
St Louis, MO 63101
314-231-9300

Commercial bank.
Type: Private
Ind: Banking   Grp: Financial
Andrew Craig, CEO   Clarence C Barksdale, Chr   John Peters MacCarthy, Pres
Dan L Huffer, CFO   W Le Grande Rives, IS   Angela Rightnowar, R&D
Timothy D Blair, PR

Rev: 1100
Assets: 11000
Emp: 4

Centex Corp
3333 Lee Parkway
Dallas, TX 75219
214-559-6500

Residential & commercial construction & bldg products.
Type: NYSE-CTX
Ind: Business Service   Grp: Business Service
Paul R Seegers, CEO   Laurence E Hirsch, Pres   Lawrence Restall, Tres
David W Quinn, CFO   Thomas E Chapman, IS   Raymond G Smerge, VP
John G Jones, VP   Rodney E Cummickel, VP   Sheila E Gallagher, PR

Rev: 1460
Assets: 1039
Emp: 5

Centocor Inc
244 Great Valley Parkway
Malvern, PA 19355
215-296-4488

Manufacturer healthcare, diagnostic equipment.
Type: NASDAQ-CNTO
Ind: Business Service   Grp: Business Service
Hubert J P Schoemaker, CEO

Rev: 60
Assets: 153
Emp: 1

Central & South West Corp
2121 San Jacinto Street
Dallas, TX 75201
214-754-1000

Electric utility holding company.
Type: NYSE-CSR
Ind: Utility   Grp: Utilities
Merle L Borchelt, CEO   Durwood Chalker, Chr   E R Brooks, VCh
William F Malek, CFO   Mike Intille, IS   Ed Gastineau, R&D
Jane Kilby, Mkt   Glenn Rosilier, VP   Verla Campbell, VP
Paul Douty, VP   Gerald R Hunter, PR

Rev: 2512
Assets: 8110
Emp: 10

Central Bancorp Inc
Fifth & Main Streets
Cincinnati, OH 45202
513-651-8000

Commercial bank.
Type: OTC
Ind: Banking   Grp: Financial
Oliver W Birckhead, CEO

Rev: 500
Assets: 5000
Emp: 3

Central Bancshares Inc
701 S 20th Street
Birmingham, AL 35233
205-933-3000

Commercial bank.
Type: NASDAQ-CBSS
Ind: Banking   Grp: Financial
Terrence C Brannon, CEO   Harry B Brock Jr, Chr   Byrd Williams, Pres
D Paul Jones, VCh   Roy Gillia, CFO   Mark Faircloth, Sls
Charles Bretz, Mkt   Terence Brannon, VP   Joanne Bruno, PR

Rev: 401
Assets: 4109
Emp: 3

Central Capital Corp
1801 Hollis Street
Halifax, NS B3J3N4 Can
902-420-2000

Diversified financial company.
Type: TOR-CEH
Ind: Non-Bank Fin   Grp: Financial
Struan Robertson, CEO   C W Cole, Chr   David A Rattee, CFO
W Thomas Hodgson, Mkt   Alan J Lenczner, VP   Denis H Nixon, VP
David A Ogilvie, VP   Suzan M Maclean, VP   John F Ellis, VP
Isabella Smejda, VP

Rev: 1494
Assets: 13622
Emp: 4

Central Fidelity Banks Inc
Broad at Third Street
Richmond, VA 23261
804-782-4000

Commercial bank.
Type: NASDAQ-CFBS
Ind: Banking   Grp: Financial
Carroll L Saine, CEO   Lewis Miller, Pres   John T Percy, VCh
Howard B Silvis, CFO   Jay Livingston, Mkt

Rev: 446
Assets: 4731
Emp: 3

Central Guaranty Trust Ltd
366 Bay Street
Toronto, ON M5H2W5 Can
416-345-4000

Consumer savings & mortgage company.
Type: Private
Ind: Securities   Grp: Financial
W Thomas Hodgson, CEO

Rev: 850
Assets: 5100
Emp: 3

Central Hudson Gas & Electric Co
284 South Avenue
Poughkeepsie, NY 12601
914-452-2000

Electric & gas utility.
Type: NYSE
Ind: Utility   Grp: Utilities
John E Mack, CEO   Paul Ganci, VCh   L Wallace Cross, CFO
Carl Meyer, R&D   Herbert Round, Ops   James E Smith, VP
Charles Denny, VP

Rev: 438
Assets: 1046
Emp: 2

Organization / Address / Phone	Descriptive Information	Revenue / Assets / Emp ($ mil) ($ mil) (thous)		
Central Illinois Light Co 300 Liberty Street Peoria, IL 61602 309-672-5271	Electric power utility. Type: Private-Sub Par: Cilcorp Inc Ind: Utility Grp: Utilities R O Viets, CEO Donald G Raymer, Chr William A Koertner, Tres Robert W Jackson, CFO Lowell A Dodd, VP Robert G Lane, VP William A Morgan, VP Clyde S Heaton, PR	Rev: Assets: Emp:	434 924 2	
Central Illinois Public Service Co 607 E Adams Street Springfield, IL 62739 217-523-3600	Electric power utility company. Type: NYSE Ind: Utility Grp: Utilities Donald G Raymer, CEO Clifford Greenwalt, VCh William A Koertner, Tres Robert W Jackson, CFO Lowell A Dodd, R&D J Kay Smith, VP Craig D Nelson, VP John Fiaush, VP	Rev: Assets: Emp:	616 1678 3	
Central Louisiana Electric Co 2030 Donahue Ferry Road Pineville, LA 71360 318-484-7400	Electric utility company. Type: NYSE-CNL Ind: Utility Grp: Utilities Scott O Brame, CEO	Rev: Assets: Emp:	920 NA 5	
Central Maine Power Inc Edison Drive Augusta, ME 04336 207-623-3521	Electric utility company. Type: NYSE-CTP Ind: Utility Grp: Utilities Matthew Hunter, CEO David Marsh, CFO Lynn K Goldfarb, Mkt Douglas Stevenson, VP Gerald C Poulin, VP	Rev: Assets: Emp:	654 1211 3	
Central Newspapers Inc 307 N Pennsylvania Street Indianapolis, IN 46204 317-633-9027	Newspaper publishing company. Type: Private Ind: Publishing/Com Grp: Consumer Service Frank E Russell, CEO	Rev: Assets: Emp:	500 NA 5	
Central Power & Light Co 120 N Chaparral Street Corpus Christi, TX 78403 512-881-5300	Electric power utility. Type: Private-Sub Par: Central & South West Corp Ind: Utility Grp: Utilities T V Shockley, CEO	Rev: Assets: Emp:	812 3000 3	
Central Soya Co 1300 Fort Wayne National Bank Bldg Fort Wayne, IN 46802 219-425-5100	Producer & distributor of agricultural products. Type: Private Ind: Food Processing Grp: Food Processing David Swanson, CEO Thomas C Griffith, Pres William L Benford, CFO Dan Smith, IS Harley J Donnell, R&D Barry Collinsworth, PR	Rev: Assets: Emp:	1650 500 3	
Centrust Savings Bank Inc 101 E Flagler Street Miami, FL 33131 305-376-5000	Thrift institution. Type: ASE-AMS Ind: Savings & Loan Grp: Financial David L Paul, CEO Alfred L Teti, Pres James P Gross, CFO Paul J Repecki, IS John S Harris, Mkt	Rev: Assets: Emp:	750 7500 2	
Century 21 Canada Ltd 135-10551 Shellbridge Way Richmond, BC V6X2W9 Can 604-273-2721	Nationwide network of real estate sales offices. Type: Private Ind: Real Estate/Bldg Grp: Business Service Peter Thomas, CEO	Rev: Assets: Emp:	255 NA 6	
Century Communications Inc 65 Locust Avenue New Canaan, CT 06840 203-966-8746	Manfacturer of telecommunication systems. Type: OTC Ind: Publishing/Com Grp: Consumer Service Leonard Tow, CEO	Rev: Assets: Emp:	150 300 1	
Century Telephone Enterprises Inc 520 Riverside Drive Monroe, LA 71201 318-388-9000	Telephone utility holding company; local phone companies. Type: NYSE-CTL Ind: Telecom Grp: High Tech Clarke M Williams, CEO	Rev: Assets: Emp:	250 400 3	
Certainteed Corp 750 E Swedesford Road Valley Forge, PA 19482 215-341-7000	Diversified products for the home building industry. Type: NYSE Ind: Building Mat Grp: Basic Industries Michel L Besson, CEO Myron P Simmons, Pres Michael Walsh, Tres Michel J Lecomte, CFO Theodore F Merkel, IS Dottie Wackerman, PR	Rev: Assets: Emp:	1267 1108 8	

Organizations Listed Alphabetically

Organization / Address / Phone	Descriptive Information	Revenue / Assets / Emp ($ mil) ($ mil) (thous)		

| Certified Grocers Midwest Inc
4800 S Central
Chicago, IL 60638
312-585-7000 | Operator of retail food stores.
Type: Private
Ind: Retail/Food Grp: Retail
Harold Greenberg, CEO | Rev:
Assets:
Emp: | 1100
NA
2 |

Certified Grocers of America Inc
2601 S Eastern Avenue
Los Angeles, CA 90040
213-726-2601

Operator of retail grocery stores.
Type: Private
Ind: Retail/Food Grp: Retail
Bill Christie, CEO

Rev: 2750
Assets: NA
Emp: 3

Cessna Aircraft Corp
5800 E Pawnee Road
Wichita, KS 67218
316-685-9111

Light aircraft manufacturing company.
Type: Private-Sub Par: General Dynamics Corp
Ind: Aerospace Grp: High Tech
Russell Meyer, CEO

Rev: NA
Assets: NA
Emp: NA

Cetus Corp
1400 53rd Street
Emeryville, CA 94608
415-420-3300

Biotechnology research company.
Type: NASDAQ-CTUS
Ind: Business Service Grp: Business Service
Ronald E Cape, CEO

Rev: 45
Assets: 274
Emp: 1

CF & I Steel Corp
225 Canal Street
Pueblo, CO 81002
303-561-6000

Manufacturer of construction & steel products.
Type: OTC
Ind: Manufacturing Grp: Manufacturing
C Nevin, CEO

Rev: 350
Assets: 200
Emp: 2

CF AirFreight Inc
3350 W Bayshore Road
Palo Alto, CA 94303
415-855-9100

Air freight transportation company.
Type: Private-Sub Par: Consolidated Freightways Inc
Ind: Transport Grp: Business Service
Donald Berger, CEO

Rev: NA
Assets: NA
Emp: NA

CF Industries Inc
Salem Lake Drive
Long Grove, IL 60047
312-438-9500

Manufacturer of specialty chemicals.
Type: Private
Ind: Chemicals Grp: Basic Industries
Robert C Liuzzi, CEO Lawrence H Devereux, CFO Wayne E Brown, IS
John H Sultenfuss, Mkt Daniel R Van Tassel, IR Rosemary L O'Brien, PR

Rev: 1100
Assets: 1000
Emp: 2

Chaco Energy Co
400 N Olive Street
Dallas, TX 75201
214-812-8200

Electrical utility power production company.
Type: Private-Sub Par: Texas Utilities Co
Ind: Energy Grp: Basic Industries
Michael Spence, CEO

Rev: NA
Assets: NA
Emp: NA

Champion Enterprises Inc
5573 North Street
Dryden, MI 48428
313-796-2145

Manufacturer of mobile homes & recreational vehicles.
Type: ASE-CHB
Ind: Automotive Grp: Manufacturing
Stanley R Day, CEO

Rev: 350
Assets: NA
Emp: 3

Champion International Corp
One Champion Plaza
Stamford, CT 06921
203-358-7000

Manufacturer of forest products; paper, building supplies.
Type: NYSE
Ind: Paper/Forest Prd Grp: Basic Industries
Andrew C Sigler, CEO L C Heitz, Pres Aubrey L Cole, VCh
Frank Kneisel, Tres Gerald J Beiser, CFO Bartley L Reitz, IS
Howard J Gidez, Mkt Kenwood Nichols, VP Mark Fuller, VP
William Burchfield, VP William Haselton, VP Robert Turner, IR
Kim Scoffield, PR

Rev: 5129
Assets: 6700
Emp: 30

Champion Spark Plug Co
One Seagate
Toledo, OH 43604
419-247-1600

Manufacturer of spark plugs, automotive parts.
Type: NYSE
Ind: Electronics Grp: High Tech
O Lee Henry, CEO John Zimmerman, Tres Thomas G Kress, CFO
Richard L Black, R&D R E Fishbaugh, Sls R N Polcok, Mkt
Paul E Boehk, VP Daniel Tribble, VP Richard C Lappin, VP
R J Mougey Jr, PR

Rev: 738
Assets: 576
Emp: 13

Channel Home Centers Inc
945 Route 10
Whippany, NJ 07981
201-887-7000

Home improvement centers.
Type: Private
Ind: Retail/Merch Grp: Retail
Leon Berger, CEO

Rev: 750
Assets: NA
Emp: 10

Organizations Listed Alphabetically

Organization / Address / Phone	Descriptive Information	Revenue / ($ mil)	Assets / ($ mil)	Emp (thous)
Chaparral Steel 300 Ward Road Midlothian, TX 76065 214-775-8241	Operator of mini steel mills. Type: NYSE Ind: Steel Grp: Basic Industries Robert D Rogers, CEO	Rev: Assets: Emp:	400 300 1	
Charlotte, City of City Hall 600 E Trade Street Charlotte, NC 28202 704-336-2244	City government. Type: City Govt Ind: Local Govt Grp: Govt & Non-Prof Sue Myrick, CEO	Rev: Assets: Emp:	250 NM 4	
Charming Shoppes Inc 450 Winks Lane Bensalem, PA 19020 215-245-9100	Women's clothing retail store operator. Type: NASDAQ Ind: Retail/Merch Grp: Retail David V Wachs, CEO Ellis Wachs, Pres Steven Sidewater, VCh Ivan Szeftel, CFO Howard Edels, IS Moredhay Kafrey, Sls Samuel Sidewater, Mkt Anthony Desabato, VP Bernard Brodsky, VP Lionel Savadove, VP	Rev: Assets: Emp:	725 407 6	
Charter Co One E Fourth Street Cincinnati, OH 45202 513-579-2482	Residual fuel oil sales to utilities & sale of crude oil. Type: NYSE-CHR Ind: Energy Grp: Basic Industries Carl H Linder, CEO D Thomas Moody, Chr Larry W Singleton, CFO James N Wilke, IS David K Leininger, R&D	Rev: Assets: Emp:	480 295 2	
Charter Medical Corp 577 Mulberry Street Macon, GA 31298 912-742-1161	Manages hospitals. Type: Private Ind: Business Service Grp: Business Service William A Fickling, CEO C Michael Ford, CFO Darryl Bollinger, IS Robert O Friedel, R&D Christian L Mazzola, Mkt Benjamin G Porter, PR	Rev: Assets: Emp:	1200 NA 12	
Charter Power Systems 3043 Walton Road Plymouth Meeting, PA 19462 215-828-9000	Manufacturer of batteries, battery power systems. Type: ASE Ind: Electronics Grp: High Tech Merrill M Halpern, CEO	Rev: Assets: Emp:	200 250 2	
Chase Enterprises Inc One Commercial Plaza Hartford, CT 06103 203-549-1674	Real estate, communications & insurance. Type: Private Ind: Real Estate/Bldg Grp: Business Service David Chase, CEO	Rev: Assets: Emp:	500 NA 5	
Chase Manhattan Bank Inc One Chase Manhattan Plaza New York, NY 10081 212-552-2222	Commercial bank. Type: NYSE-CMB Ind: Banking Grp: Financial W C Butcher, CEO Thomas G Labrecque, Pres R J Boyle, VCh L J Stephens, Tres Michael P Esposito, CFO Michael Urkowitz, IS Gerald Weiss, R&D A Wright Elliott, Sls A F Ryan, Mkt R R Douglas, VP R L Huber, VP R G Murphy, VP H F Fierce, VP M F Dacey, VP P Larr, VP A Wright Elliott, IR Fraser P Seitel, PR	Rev: Assets: Emp:	12375 97455 42	
Chem-Nuclear Systems Inc 220 Stoneridge Drive Columbia, SC 29210 803-256-0450	Disposal company for industrial chemical waste. Type: Private-Sub Par: Waste Management Inc Ind: Business Service Grp: Business Service Victor Barnett, CEO	Rev: Assets: Emp:	NA NA NA	
Chemcentral Corp 7050 W 71st Street Chicago, IL 60638 312-594-7000	Chemical distributing. Type: Private Ind: Chemicals Grp: Basic Industries H Daniel Wenstrup, CEO	Rev: Assets: Emp:	500 NA 1	
Chemed 1200 Dubois Tower Cincinnati, OH 45202 513-762-6900	Specialty chemical company. Type: NYSE-CHE Ind: Chemicals Grp: Basic Industries Edward L Hutton, CEO	Rev: Assets: Emp:	600 NA 6	

Organizations Listed Alphabetically

Organization / Address / Phone	Descriptive Information	Revenue / Assets / Emp ($ mil) ($ mil) (thous)		

Chemical Leaman Corp
102 Pickering Way
Exton, PA 19353
215-363-4200

Truck transport company.
Type: OTC
Ind: Transport   Grp: Business Service
S F Niness, CEO   David R Hamilton, Chr   Charles Fernald Jr, CFO
Paul Wagner, IS   Nick Braden, Sls   Al Montgomery, Mkt
Debora Speier, PR

Rev: 250
Assets: 150
Emp: 2

Chemical New York Corp
277 Park Avenue
New York, NY 10172
212-310-6161

Commercial bank.
Type: NYSE-CHL
Ind: Banking   Grp: Financial
Walter V Shipley, CEO   Thomas S Johnson, Pres   Richard Simmons, VCh
Joseph Sponholz, CFO   William McDavid, VP   Richard Hulbert, VP
James Latchford, VP   John Wynne, VP   Charles G Salmans, IR
Kenneth B Herz, PR

Rev: 7644
Assets: 67349
Emp: 20

Chemical Systems Inc
PO Box 49028
San Jose, CA 95161
408-224-7796

Manufacturer of chemical products.
Type: Private-Sub   Par: United Technologies Corp
Ind: Chemicals   Grp: Basic Industries
S Berson, CEO

Rev: NA
Assets: NA
Emp: NA

Chemical Waste Corp
3001 Butterfield Road
Oak Brook, IL 60521
312-572-8800

Chemical & specialty waste removal company.
Type: NYSE-CHW
Ind: Business Service   Grp: Business Service
Jerry E Dempsey, CEO   Bruce Tobecksen, CFO   George Vander Velde, R&D
David L McEwan, Mkt   Victor Barnhart, VP   Joan Z Bernstein, VP
Raul Deju, VP   Samuel Garre, VP

Rev: 700
Assets: 876
Emp: 6

Chesapeake & Potomac Telephone Co
1710 H Street NW
Washington, DC 20006
202-887-0565

Telephone utility company.
Type: Private-Sub   Par: Bell Atlantic Corp
Ind: Telecom   Grp: High Tech
Thomas Gibbons, CEO

Rev: NA
Assets: NA
Emp: NA

Chesapeake Corp
1021 E Cary Street
Richmond, VA 23218
804-697-1000

Forest products company; packaging, building materials.
Type: NYSE-CSX
Ind: Paper/Forest Prd   Grp: Basic Industries
Sture G Olsson, CEO   J Carter Fox, Chr   Alvah H Eubank, Tres
Paul A Dresser Jr, CFO   Bruce N Parker, IS   Charles Cianciola, VP
Paul A Dresser, VP   Frederick Ernst, VP   J Paul Harper, VP
Samuel Taylor, VP   J P Causey, VP   Thomas Contrucci, IR
Walton Evans, PR

Rev: 711
Assets: 662
Emp: 7

Chesebrough Ponds Inc
33 Benedict Place
Greenwich, CT 06830
203-222-3000

Manufacturer of personal care products.
Type: OTC
Ind: Personal Care   Grp: Consumer Prd
Robert M Philips, CEO   Leo P Kroes, CFO   Michael Coughlin, IS
William H Schmitt, R&D   James W McCall, PR

Rev: 3400
Assets: 1500
Emp: 25

Chevrolet Motor Division
30007 Van Dyke Avenue
Warren, MI 48090
313-556-5000

Manufacturer of automobiles.
Type: Private-Sub   Par: General Motors Corp
Ind: Automotive   Grp: Manufacturing
Robert Burger, CEO

Rev: NA
Assets: NA
Emp: NA

Chevron Canada Ltd
1050 W Pender Street
Vancouver, BC V6E3T4 Can
604-668-5300

Petroleum exploration, production & marketing company.
Type: Private-Sub-For
Ind: Energy   Grp: Basic Industries
John McIntyre, CEO

Rev: 777
Assets: 830
Emp: 1

Chevron Canada Resources Ltd
500 5th Avenue SW
Calgary, AB T2P0L7 Can
403-234-5000

Oil & gas exploration, crude oil production.
Type: Private-Sub-For
Ind: Energy   Grp: Basic Industries
Gerald Henderson, CEO

Rev: 1190
Assets: 850
Emp: 2

Chevron Chemical Co
6001 Bollinger Canyon Road
San Ramon, CA 94583
415-842-1000

Producer of specialty chemicals.
Type: Private-Sub   Par: Chevron Corp
Ind: Chemicals   Grp: Basic Industries
R Davis, CEO

Rev: NA
Assets: NA
Emp: NA

Organizations Listed Alphabetically

Organization / Address / Phone	Descriptive Information	Revenue / ($ mil)	Assets / ($ mil)	Emp (thous)
Chevron Corp 225 Bush Street San Francisco, CA 94104 415-894-7700	Oil & natural gas production & marketing company. Type: NYSE-CHV Ind: Energy Grp: Basic Industries Robert W Davis, CEO J Dennis Bonney, VCh Leland C McGraw, CFO Marty L Klitten, IS Edwin R Lowry, R&D William Price, VP Lloyd Elkins, VP Roderick Hartung, VP Donald Henderson, VP Patricia E Yarrington, PR	Rev: Assets: Emp:	27722 33968 54	
Chevron Overseas Petroleum Co 6001 Bollinger Canyon Road San Ramon, CA 94583 415-842-1000	Petroleum & natural gas exploration & drilling company. Type: Private-Sub Par: Chevron Corp Ind: Energy Grp: Basic Industries J Silcox, CEO	Rev: Assets: Emp:	NA NA NA	
Chevron USA Inc 575 Market Street San Francisco, CA 94105 415-894-7700	Petroleum products distribution company. Type: Private-Sub Par: Chevron Corp Ind: Retail/Merch Grp: Retail Willis Price, CEO	Rev: Assets: Emp:	NA NA NA	
Chevy Chase Savings Bank Inc 8401 Connecticut Avenue Chevy Chase, MD 20815 301-986-7000	Thrift institution. Type: NYSE-BFS Ind: Savings & Loan Grp: Financial B Francis Saul, CEO	Rev: Assets: Emp:	350 3500 1	
Chicago Pacific Corp 200 S Michigan Avenue Chicago, IL 60604 312-435-7300	Durable goods; kitchen appliances. Type: NASDAQ-CPA Ind: Appliances/Furn Grp: Manufacturing Harvey Kapnick, CEO William Terpstra, CFO H Gordon Owens, IS William Schaefer, R&D Howard Baker, PR	Rev: Assets: Emp:	1400 1128 20	
Chicago, City of City Hall 121 N LaSalle Street Chicago, IL 60602 312-744-3300	City government. Type: City Govt Ind: Local Govt Grp: Govt & Non-Prof Richard Dailey, CEO	Rev: Assets: Emp:	2581 NM 43	
Child World Inc 25 Littlefield Street Avon, MA 02322 617-588-7300	Operator of retail stores; toys, games, furniture. Type: NASDAQ-CWLD Ind: Retail/Merch Grp: Retail Dennis H Barron, CEO	Rev: Assets: Emp:	807 400 4	
Chilewich Sons Inc 120 Wall Street New York, NY 10005 212-344-3400	Commodity trading, hides, cattle, meat company. Type: Private Ind: Food Processing Grp: Food Processing Simon Chilewich, CEO	Rev: Assets: Emp:	1000 NA 1	
Chili's Inc 6820 LBJ Freeway Dallas, TX 75240 214-980-9917	Operator of restaurants. Type: NYSE Ind: Food/Lodging Grp: Consumer Service Norman Brinker, CEO	Rev: Assets: Emp:	285 200 10	
Chips & Technologies Inc 3050 Zanker Road San Jose, CA 95035 408-434-0600	Manufacturer of semiconductors. Type: OTC Ind: Electronics Grp: High Tech Gordon Campbell, CEO	Rev: Assets: Emp:	218 100 2	
Chiquita Brands Inc 250 E Fifth Street Cincinnati, OH 45202 513-784-8000	Producer & distributor of bananas, pineapples. Type: Private-Sub Par: United Brands Co Ind: Food Processing Grp: Food Processing Keith Linder, CEO	Rev: Assets: Emp:	NA NA NA	
Chock-Full-O-Nuts Corp 370 Lexington Avenue New York, NY 10017 212-532-0300	Manufacturer of coffee products; operator of restaurants. Type: NYSE-CHF Ind: Food Processing Grp: Food Processing Leon Pordy, CEO	Rev: Assets: Emp:	200 200 3	
Chris-Craft Industries Inc 600 Madison Avenue New York, NY 10022 212-421-0200	Manufacturer of specialty films. Type: NYSE Ind: Publishing/Com Grp: Consumer Service Herbert J Siegel, CEO	Rev: Assets: Emp:	251 909 1	

Organizations Listed Alphabetically

Organization / Address / Phone	Descriptive Information	Revenue / ($ mil)	Assets / ($ mil)	Emp (thous)
Chrysler Canada Ltd 2450 Chrysler Center Windsor, ON N9A4H6 Can 519-973-2000	Automobile manufacturer. Type: TOR Ind: Automotive Grp: Manufacturing Maurice J Closs, CEO Ronald G Wigle, Tres Scott E Reed, CFO Clifford R Burnett, IS John B Damoose, Mkt Garnet W Fenn, VP Paul J McVittie, VP William Menchions, VP William J Fisher, IR Othmar M Stein, PR	Rev: 7368 Assets: 2656 Emp: 12		
Chrysler Corp 12000 Chrysler Drive Highland Park, MI 48203 313-956-5741	Automobile manufacturer. Type: NYSE-C Ind: Automotive Grp: Manufacturing Lee A Iacocca, CEO Robert A Lutz, Pres Gerald Greenwald, VCh Frederick Zuckerman, Tres Robert S Miller Jr, CFO Nick G Simonds, IS John D Withrow, R&D E T Pappert, Sls Bennett E Bidwell, Mkt Robert Perkins, VP William O'Brien, VP Christopher Steffen, VP Glenn White, VP Thomas Denomme, VP Michael K Morrison, IR John E Guiniven, PR	Rev: 35472 Assets: 48567 Emp: 130		
Chrysler Financial Corp 901 Wilshire Drive Troy, MI 48084 313-244-3060	Financial subsidiary of Chrysler Corp. Type: Private-Sub Par: Chrysler Corp Ind: Non-Bank Fin Grp: Financial J P Tierney, CEO	Rev: 2908 Assets: 25277 Emp: 6		
Chrysler/Plymouth Div 12000 Chrysler Drive Highland Park, MI 48288 313-956-5741	Automobile manufacturer. Type: Private-Sub Par: Chrysler Corp Ind: Automotive Grp: Manufacturing Joseph Campana, CEO	Rev: NA Assets: NA Emp: NA		
Chubb Corp 15 Mountain View Road Warren, NJ 07060 201-580-2000	Property & casualty insurance. Type: NYSE-CB Ind: Food/Lodging Grp: Consumer Service Henry U Harder, CEO Richard D Smith, Pres Dean R O'Hare, CFO John W Roblin III, IS Charles M Luchs, Mkt John P Matigan Jr, PR	Rev: 3980 Assets: 9741 Emp: 12		
Church & Dwight Co 469 N Harrison Princeton, NJ 08540 609-683-5900	Manufacturer of personal products. Type: OTC Ind: Personal Care Grp: Consumer Prd Dwight Menton, CEO	Rev: 400 Assets: 150 Emp: 1		
Church's Fried Chicken Inc 355 Spencer Lane San Antonio, TX 78201 512-735-9392	Fast food restaurants. Type: NYSE Ind: Food/Lodging Grp: Consumer Service Ernest E Renaud, CEO	Rev: 420 Assets: 301 Emp: 13		
Ciba Geigy USA Corp 444 Saw Mill River Parkway Ardsley, NY 10502 914-478-3131	Manufacturer of pharmaceuticals; US headquarters. Type: Private-Sub-For Ind: Drugs Grp: Consumer Service Richard Barth, CEO	Rev: 3300 Assets: NA Emp: 16		
CIGNA Corp One Logan Square Philadelphia, PA 19103 215-557-5000	Property & casualty insurance. Type: NYSE-CI Ind: Insurance Grp: Insurance Wilson H Taylor, CEO Robert D Kilpatrick, Chr Wilson H Taylor, Pres Paul H Rohrkemper, Tres James G Stewart, CFO J Raymond Caron, IS John K Leonard, Mkt Caleb L Fowler, VP Donald Levinson, VP Barry F Wiksten, VP Barry F Wiksten, IR Gloria C McNutt, PR	Rev: 17889 Assets: 55825 Emp: 49		
CIL Inc 90 Sheppard Avenue E North York, ON M2N6H2 Can 416-229-7000	Chemical company. Type: Private-Sub-For Ind: Manufacturing Grp: Manufacturing R C Hampel, CEO	Rev: 1139 Assets: 989 Emp: 6		
Cilcorp Inc 300 Liberty Street Peoria, IL 61602 309-672-5271	Electric utility holding company. Type: NYSE-CER Ind: Utility Grp: Utilities William R Vogelsang, CEO R W Slone, Chr Ronald Rainson, VCh Robert O Viets, CFO T S Romanowski, IS Wilma Sutton, Sls T S Kurtz, VP J L Johnson, VP J F Vergon, VP	Rev: 471 Assets: 1096 Emp: 2		

Organization / Address / Phone	Descriptive Information	Revenue / Assets / Emp ($ mil) ($ mil) (thous)		

Cincinnati Bell Inc
201 E Fourth Street
Cincinnati, OH 45202
513-397-9900

Telephone utility.
Type: NYSE-CSN
Ind: Telecom   Grp: High Tech
Dwight H Hibbard, CEO   John T LaMacchia, Pres   Raymond Clark, VCh
Dennis Sullivan, CFO   Ronald Hertel, R&D   Jeffrey Vorholt, VP
William Zimmer, VP   Charles Garber, VP

Rev: 738
Assets: 1253
Emp: 10

Cincinnati Financial Corp
6200 S Gilmore Road
Fairfield, OH 45014
513-870-2000

Diversified financial company.
Type: NASDAQ-CINF
Ind: Non-Bank Fin   Grp: Financial
John J Schiff, CEO   Robert B Morgan, Chr   Hayden D Davis, Pres
Larry R Plum, VCh   Robert J Driehaaus, CFO   Vincent Beckman, VP
William Zimmer, VP   Gregory Zeigler, VP   James Miller, VP

Rev: 910
Assets: 2117
Emp: 2

Cincinnati Gas & Electric Co
139 E Fourth Street
Cincinnati, OH 45202
513-381-2000

Electric & gas utility company.
Type: NYSE-CIN
Ind: Utility   Grp: Utilities
Jackson H Randolph, CEO   William L Sheafer, Tres   C Robert Everman, CFO
Milton L Van Schoik, IS   Earl A Borgmann, R&D   C Larry Schmidt, Ops
James Mayer, VP   Stephen Salay, VP

Rev: 1386
Assets: 3361
Emp: 5

Cincinnati Milacron Inc
4701 Marburg Avenue
Cincinnati, OH 45209
513-841-8100

Machine tool manufacturer.
Type: NYSE
Ind: Machinery   Grp: Manufacturing
James A D Geier, CEO   Daniel J Meyer, Pres   Robert Lienesch, Tres
William E Buchholz, CFO   Mary Jo Burnes, IS   Richard Messinger, R&D
D Michael Clabaug, Mkt   Christopher Cole, VP   David Entrekin, VP
John P Reading, PR

Rev: 857
Assets: 721
Emp: 8

Cincinnati, City of
City Hall 801 Plum Street
Cincinnati, OH 45202
513-352-3250

City government.
Type: City Govt
Ind: Local Govt   Grp: Govt & Non-Prof
Charles Luken, CEO

Rev: 431
Assets: NM
Emp: 6

Cineplex Odeon Corp
214 King Street W
Toronto, ON M5H3S6 Can
416-596-2200

Entertainment company; movie theatres.
Type: TOR
Ind: Leisure Time   Grp: Consumer Service
Garth Drabinsky, CEO

Rev: 592
Assets: 485
Emp: 3

Cintas Corp
11255 Reed Hartman Highway
Cincinnati, OH 45241
513-489-4000

Manufacturer of apparel products.
Type: NASDAQ-CTAS
Ind: Apparel/Textiles   Grp: Consumer Prd
Richard T Farmer, CEO

Rev: 205
Assets: 180
Emp: 3

CIP Inc
30 Carling Terrace
Montreal, PQ N0G2W0 Can
514-878-4811

Operator of broadcasting network; radio.
Type: Private-Sub   Par: Canadian Pacific Ltd
Ind: Publishing/Com   Grp: Consumer Service
C Flenniken, CEO

Rev: 1637
Assets: 1573
Emp: 8

Circle K Corp
1601 N Seventh Street
Phoenix, AZ 85006
602-253-9600

Operator of retail convenience stores.
Type: NYSE-CKP
Ind: Retail/Food   Grp: Retail
Karl Eller, CEO   Robert M Reade, Pres   Gehl P Babinec, VCh
Larry Zine, CFO   Renee Hornbaker, IS   David Maddox, R&D
Jack Nietzel, Mkt   Joel Sterrett, VP   Kris Jacober, PR

Rev: 2657
Assets: 1536
Emp: 25

Circuit City Stores Inc
2040 Thalbro Street
Richmond, VA 23230
804-257-4292

Retail stores for consumer electronics.
Type: NYSE-CC
Ind: Retail/Merch   Grp: Retail
Alan L Wurtzel, CEO   Richard L Sharp, Chr   William D Rivas, VCh
Michael T Chalifoux, CFO   Terry L Kelley, IS   Franklin Bell, VP

Rev: 1721
Assets: 587
Emp: 10

Circus Circus Enterprises Inc
2880 Las Vegas Blvd
Las Vegas, NV 89109
702-734-0410

Operates gambling casinos & hotels.
Type: NYSE-CIR
Ind: Leisure Time   Grp: Consumer Service
William G Bennett, CEO   Richard P Banis, Pres   Terry L Caudill, Tres
Glenn Schaeffer, CFO   Melvin Larson, Mkt   Mike Sloan, VP

Rev: 512
Assets: 524
Emp: 9

Organizations Listed Alphabetically

Organization / Address / Phone	Descriptive Information	Revenue / Assets / Emp ($ mil) ($ mil) (thous)		

CIT Group Financial Corp
650 CIT Drive
Livingston, NJ 07039
201-740-5000

Nationwide financial services company; consumer loans.
Type: Private-Sub
Ind: Non-Bank Fin   Grp: Financial
Albert R Gamper, CEO   Joseph Pollicino, Pres   Joseph Leone, CFO
Kailash Khanna, IS   Paul Scharpf, Sls   Donald Rapson, Mkt
George Fiore, VP

Rev: 1042
Assets: 9337
Emp: 4

Citadel Holding Corp(Fidelity Fed Svng)
600 N Brand Blvd
Glendale, CA 91209
213-956-7100

Thrift institution.
Type: ASE-CDL
Ind: Savings & Loan   Grp: Financial
Edward L Kane, CEO   James A Taylor, Chr   Samuel C McCarver, Pres

Rev: 384
Assets: 4642
Emp: 1

Citibank Arizona
3300 N Central Street
Phoenix, AZ 85012
602-248-2200

Commercial bank.
Type: Private-Sub   Par: Citicorp Inc
Ind: Banking   Grp: Financial
Michael Welborn, CEO

Rev: 500
Assets: 5000
Emp: 3

Citibank Canada Ltd
123 Front Street W
Toronto, ON M5J2M3 Can
416-947-5500

International commercial bank.
Type: Private-Sub-For
Ind: Banking   Grp: Financial
Frederick C Copeland, CEO

Rev: 360
Assets: 4167
Emp: 1

Citicorp Inc
399 Park Avenue
New York, NY 10043
212-559-1000

Commercial bank.
Type: NYSE
Ind: Banking   Grp: Financial
John S Reed, CEO   Paul Collins, Pres   Hans Angermuueller, VCh
Nancy Newcomb, CFO   Paul F Glaser, IS   Michael A Callan, VP
James D Farley, VP   Lawrence M Small, VP   Pamela Flaherty, VP
George L Davis, VP   David Gibson, VP   Sheridan Steinberg, IR
Amy Dates, PR

Rev: 32024
Assets: 207666
Emp: 89

Citicorp Savings Inc
399 Park Avenue
New York, NY 10043
212-559-1000

Thrift institution.
Type: Private-Sub   Par: Citicorp Inc
Ind: Savings & Loan   Grp: Financial
Ed Valencia, CEO

Rev: 1750
Assets: 17500
Emp: 4

Citizens & Southern Co
35 Broad Street NW
Atlanta, GA 30303
404-581-2121

Commercial bank.
Type: NASDAQ-CSOU
Ind: Banking   Grp: Financial
Bennett A Brown, CEO   Hugh M Chapman, Pres   James D Dixon, CFO
George Budd, IS   Harold Chandler, Mkt   Enoch Prow, IR
Scott Scredon, PR

Rev: 2090
Assets: 21098
Emp: 14

Citizens Fidelity Corp
Citizens Plaza
Louisville, KY 40296
502-581-2100

Commercial bank.
Type: Private-Sub   Par: PNC Financial Corp
Ind: Banking   Grp: Financial
J David Grissom, CEO

Rev: 700
Assets: 5000
Emp: 3

Citizens Savings Assn Inc
999 Brickell Avenue
Miami, FL 33131
305-577-0400

Thrift institution.
Type: NASDAQ-CSFC
Ind: Savings & Loan   Grp: Financial
Charles B Stuzin, CEO

Rev: 301
Assets: 2998
Emp: 2

Citizens Utilities Co
High Ridge Park
Stamford, CT 06905
203-427-8953

Utility holding company.
Type: NASDAQ-CITUA
Ind: Utility   Grp: Utilities
Ishier Jacobson, CEO

Rev: 302
Assets: 1033
Emp: 2

Citrus Hill Manufacturing Co
One Proctor & Gamble Plaza
Cincinnati, OH 45202
513-983-1100

Orange juice manufacturing company.
Type: Private-Sub   Par: Procter & Gamble Co
Ind: Food Processing   Grp: Food Processing
John Pepper, CEO

Rev: NA
Assets: NA
Emp: NA

Organizations Listed Alphabetically

Organization / Address / Phone	Descriptive Information	Revenue / Assets / Emp ($ mil) ($ mil) (thous)		

City Fed Financial Corp
Route 202-206 Bedminster One
Bedminster, NJ 07921
201-658-4100

Thrift institution.
Type: NASDAQ-CTYF
Ind: Savings & Loan   Grp: Financial
Gilbert G Roessner, CEO   Thomas P O'Toole, CFO   Michael Rust, VP
Ronald Tell, VP   Michael J Rust, PR

Rev: 1046
Assets: 10585
Emp: 5

City National Corp
400 N Roxbury Drive
Beverly Hills, CA 90210
213-550-5400

Commercial bank.
Type: OTC
Ind: Banking   Grp: Financial
Bram Goldsmith, CEO

Rev: 371
Assets: 4296
Emp: 2

City Public Service Inc
145 Nevarro Street
San Antonio, TX 78296
512-227-3211

Electric power utility company.
Type: Private
Ind: Utility   Grp: Utilities
Arthur VonRosenbert, CEO

Rev: 1100
Assets: NA
Emp: 5

Cityfed Financial Corp
293 S County Road
Palm Beach, FL 33480
407-655-5919

Holding company for financial institutions.
Type: NASDAQ-CTYF
Ind: Savings & Loan   Grp: Financial
Gilbert G Roessner, CEO

Rev: 1000
Assets: 10585
Emp: 5

Citytrust Bank Corp
961 Main Street
Bridgeport, CT 06601
203-384-5212

Commercial bank.
Type: NYSE-CYT
Ind: Banking   Grp: Financial
George F Taylor, CEO

Rev: 280
Assets: 2601
Emp: 2

Clabir Corp
10101 9th Street N
St Petersburg, FL 33716
813-577-5007

Manufacturer of industrial equipment.
Type: NYSE-CLG
Ind: Manufacturing   Grp: Manufacturing
Henry D Clarke, CEO

Rev: 350
Assets: 300
Emp: 3

Claiborne, Liz Co Inc
1441 Broadway
New York, NY 10018
212-354-4900

Designer & manufacturer of women's & men's apparel.
Type: NASDAQ-LIZC
Ind: Apparel/Textiles   Grp: Consumer Prd
Elizabeth Claiborne, CEO   Arthur Ortenberg, VCh   Walter L Krieger, CFO
Arthur Krulish, IS   Robert Bernard, Mkt   Harvey L Falk, Ops
Jon Margolis, VP   Robert Abajian, VP   Ellen Daniel, VP
Katherine Connors, IR   Cheryl Kaplan, PR

Rev: 1184
Assets: 629
Emp: 10

Clairol Inc
One Blachley Road
Stamford, CT 06922
203-632-1500

Manufacturer of personal care products; toiletries, shampoo.
Type: Private-Sub   Par: Bristol Meyers Co
Ind: Personal Care   Grp: Consumer Prd
Benjamin Brooks, CEO

Rev: NA
Assets: NA
Emp: NA

Clajon Production Corp
23 Desta Drive
Midland, TX 79705
915-683-4181

Natural resources development & energy company.
Type: Private
Ind: Energy   Grp: Basic Industries
Jamie Winkel, CEO

Rev: 825
Assets: NA
Emp: 1

Clarendon America Insurance Co
1100 N Market Street Wilmington Trust Ctr
Wilmington, DE 19801
302-656-0142

Property & casualty insurance company.
Type: OTC
Ind: Insurance   Grp: Insurance
Ralph Milo, CEO

Rev: 500
Assets: 500
Emp: 1

Clark Construction Enterprises Inc
7500 Old Georgetown Road
Bethesda, MD 20814
301-657-7100

Construction & commercial development company.
Type: Private
Ind: Real Estate/Bldg   Grp: Business Service
A James Clark, CEO

Rev: 1000
Assets: NA
Emp: 4

Clark Equipment Corp
100 N Michigan Street
South Bend, IN 46634
219-239-0100

Producer of industrial equipment, forklift vehicles.
Type: NYSE
Ind: Machinery   Grp: Manufacturing
Leo J McKernan, CEO   Thomas C Clark, VCh   William T Hjorth, CFO
Robert Barrett, IS   Gary Bello, R&D   Robert N Spolum, Mkt
Frank M Sims, VP   William Harper, VP

Rev: 1278
Assets: 951
Emp: 9

Organizations Listed Alphabetically

Organization / Address / Phone	Descriptive Information		Revenue / Assets / Emp ($ mil) ($ mil) (thous)		

Organization / Address / Phone	Descriptive Information				
Clark Oil & Refining Co 8182 Maryland St Louis, MO 63105 314-889-9600	Refiner & distributor of petroleum products. Type: Private Ind: Energy Grp: Basic Industries Ralph Cunningham, CEO		Rev: Assets: Emp:	3850 NA 3	
Clarkson Gordon Ltd 77 King Street W Toronto, ON M5K1J7 Can 416-864-1234	National accounting firm. Type: Private Ind: Accounting Grp: Business Service William Farlinger, CEO		Rev: Assets: Emp:	191 NM 3	
Cleveland Cliffs Inc 1100 Superior Avenue Cleveland, OH 44114 216-694-5700	Mining & shipping company; iron ore. Type: NYSE-CLF Ind: Metals/Mining Grp: Basic Industries M Thomas Moore, CEO John S Brinzo, CFO Peter Doyle, IS Thomas C Levan, R&D John L Kelley, IR David Gardner, PR		Rev: Assets: Emp:	350 NA 3	
Cleveland Electric Illuminating Co Illuminating Bldg Cleveland, OH 44113 216-447-3103	Electrical utility company. Type: Private-Sub Par: Centerior Energy Corp Ind: Utility Grp: Utilities Robert Farling, CEO		Rev: Assets: Emp:	NA NA NA	
Cleveland, City of City Hall 601 Lakeside Cleveland, OH 44114 216-664-2220	City government. Type: City Govt Ind: Local Govt Grp: Govt & Non-Prof George V Voinovich, CEO		Rev: Assets: Emp:	531 NM 10	
Climax Metals Co Amax Center Greenwich, CT 06836 203-629-6000	Producer & processor of metals. Type: Private-Sub Par: AMAX Inc Ind: Metals/Mining Grp: Basic Industries Stephen Johnson, CEO		Rev: Assets: Emp:	NA NA NA	
Clorox Co 1221 Broadway Oakland, CA 94612 415-271-7000	Manufacturer of household cleaning products. Type: NYSE-CLX Ind: Personal Care Grp: Consumer Prd C R Weaver, CEO John W Collins, Pres Lyle L Hoover, Tres William F Ausfahl, CFO Raymond H Johnson, IS Dr Sheldon Lewis, R&D Glynn M Phillips, Sls David L Goodman, Mkt Fred Reicker, IR David L Goodman, PR		Rev: Assets: Emp:	1260 1156 6	
Club Corp of America 2711 LBJ Freeway Suite 800 Dallas, TX 75234 214-243-6191	Athletic club & resorts. Type: Private Ind: Leisure Time Grp: Consumer Service Robert Dedman, CEO		Rev: Assets: Emp:	500 NA 6	
CML Group Inc 524 Main Street Acton, MA 01720 508-264-4155	Retail mail order, recreation & sporting goods. Type: NYSE-CML Ind: Retail/Merch Grp: Retail Charles M Leighton, CEO		Rev: Assets: Emp:	450 150 3	
CMS Energy-Consumers Power Co Fairlane Plaza S 300 Town Center Drive Dearborn, MI 48126 313-436-9261	Electric & natural gas utility holding company. Type: NYSE-CMS Ind: Utility Grp: Utilities William T McCormick, CEO Frederick W Buckman, Pres S Kinney Smith, VCh Thomas A McNish, Tres Victor J Fryling, CFO Roy A Wells, IS Gordon L Heins, R&D K E McGraw, Mkt Paul Elbart, Ops John W Clark, PR		Rev: Assets: Emp:	2943 8305 11	
CNA Financial Corp CNA Plaza Chicago, IL 60685 312-822-5000	Diversified insurance company, life & casualty. Type: Private-Sub Par: Loews Corp Ind: Insurance Grp: Insurance Laurence A Tisch, CEO		Rev: Assets: Emp:	8204 22941 17	

Organizations Listed Alphabetically

Organization / Address / Phone	Descriptive Information	Revenue / Assets / Emp ($ mil) ($ mil) (thous)		

CNW Corp
165 N Canal One NW Center
Chicago, IL 60606
312-559-7000

Railroad transportation company.
Type: NYSE-CNW
Ind: Railroad   Grp: Business Service
Robert Schmiege, CEO   John M Butler, CFO   Arthur Peters, Mkt
Robert Jahnke, Ops   James Daley, VP   James M Foote, PR

Rev: 995
Assets: 1727
Emp: 10

Co Steel Inc
1601 Hopkins Street
Whitby, ON L1N5R6 Can
416-686-2500

Basic steel manufacturing company.
Type: TOR
Ind: Manufacturing   Grp: Manufacturing
W J Sheilds, CEO

Rev: 694
Assets: 550
Emp: 3

Co-op Atlantic Ltd
123 Halifax Street
Moncton, NB E1C5NB Can
506-858-6000

Agricultural cooperative.
Type: Private-Coop
Ind: Food Processing   Grp: Food Processing
John Chisholm, CEO

Rev: 298
Assets: 85
Emp: 1

Co-operative Federee de Quebec Ltd
1055 Rue Marche Centrale
Montreal, PQ H2P2W2 Can
514-383-6450

Agricultural cooperative; livestock.
Type: Private-Coop
Ind: Food Processing   Grp: Food Processing
Alphonse Pelletier, CEO

Rev: 1057
Assets: 235
Emp: 5

Coachmen Industries Inc
601 E Beardsley Avenue
Elkhart, IN 46515
219-262-0123

Manufacturer of recreation vehicles.
Type: NYSE-COA
Ind: Automotive   Grp: Manufacturing
Thomas H Corson, CEO

Rev: 400
Assets: NA
Emp: 4

Coast Savings & Loan Assc Inc
1000 Wilshire Blvd
Los Angeles, CA 90017
213-688-2000

Thrift institution.
Type: NYSE-CSA
Ind: Savings & Loan   Grp: Financial
Ray Martin, CEO   Gerald D Barrone, Pres   Robert L Hunt II, CFO
William S Bradway, Mkt   Priscilla Finch, PR

Rev: 1110
Assets: 12647
Emp: 3

Coastal Corp
9 Greenway Plaza Coastal Tower
Houston, TX 77046
713-877-1400

Oil & gas production & transport, coal, trucking company
Type: NYSE-CGP
Ind: Energy   Grp: Basic Industries
Oscar S Wyatt, CEO   James R Paul, Pres   James Cordes, VCh
David A Arledge, CFO   Robert Holsclaw, IS   Jack Pester, Sls
Dan J Hill, Mkt   Kenneth Johnson, Ops   Jeffrey Connelly, VP
Robert Moss, VP   James Whalen, VP   W E Spencer, VP
Michael Beatty, VP   R W Wells, PR

Rev: 8187
Assets: 7865
Emp: 16

Cobe Laboratories Inc
1185 Oak Street
Denver, CO 80215
303-232-6800

Manufacturer of medical equipment.
Type: OTC
Ind: Health Care   Grp: Consumer Service
Robert Collins, CEO

Rev: 250
Assets: 200
Emp: 2

Coca Cola Bottling Co of New York
20 Horseneck Lane
Greenwich, CT 06830
203-625-4000

Beverage distribution company.
Type: Private
Ind: Food Processing   Grp: Food Processing
James Maloney, CEO

Rev: 500
Assets: NA
Emp: 2

Coca Cola Bottling of Chicago Inc
7400 N Oak Park Blvd
Chicago, IL 60648
312-775-0900

Beverage distribution company.
Type: Private
Ind: Food Processing   Grp: Food Processing
Marvin J Herb, CEO

Rev: 500
Assets: NA
Emp: 2

Coca Cola Consolidated
1900 Rerford Road
Charlotte, NC 28231
704-551-4400

Coca Cola bottlers.
Type: NASDAQ-COKE
Ind: Beverage   Grp: Food Processing
J Frank Harrison, CEO

Rev: 328
Assets: 150
Emp: 2

Coca Cola Corp
310 N Avenue NW One Coca Cola Plaza
Atlanta, GA 30313
404-676-2121

Manufacturer of soft drinks, orange juice, motion pictures.
Type: NYSE-KO
Ind: Beverage   Grp: Food Processing
Roberto C Goizueta, CEO   Donald R Keough, Pres   Phillip Carswell, Tres
Douglas Ivester, CFO   Hugh Switzer, IS   Robert Waltemyer, R&D
Ira C Herbert, Mkt   Susan Shaw, VP   M A Gianturco, VP
E Neville Isdell, VP   Carlton Curtis, IR   Randy Donaldson, PR

Rev: 8338
Assets: 7450
Emp: 40

Organizations Listed Alphabetically

Organization / Address / Phone	Descriptive Information	Revenue / ($ mil)	Assets / ($ mil)	Emp (thous)
Coca Cola Enterprises Inc One Coca Cola Plaza NW Atlanta, GA 30313 404-676-2100	Bottler & distributor of soft drinks. Type: NYSE-CCE Ind: Beverage Grp: Food Processing Donald R Keough, CEO Brian G Dyson, Chr H Richard Hiller, VCh Lawrence R Cowart, CFO James C Compton, IS Anton Amon, R&D Anton Amon, Ops James Stevens, VP P Michael Taschler, VP John Carew, VP W Lamar Chesney, VP T Michael Edwards, VP Jean-Michel Bock, PR	Rev: 3874 Assets: 4669 Emp: 11		
Coldwell Banker & Co 533 Fremont Avenue Los Angeles, CA 90071 213-402-5022	Real estate sales & mortgage operations company. Type: Private-Sub Par: Bristol Meyers Co Ind: Real Estate/Bldg Grp: Business Service Arthur J Hill, CEO	Rev: 144 Assets: NA Emp: NA		
Cole National Corp 29001 Cedar Road Cleveland, OH 44124 216-449-4100	Specialty retailing. Type: Private Ind: Retail/Merch Grp: Retail Jeffrey A Cole, CEO	Rev: 1250 Assets: NA Emp: 11		
Coleco Industries Inc 999 Quaker Lane S West Hartford, CT 06110 203-725-6000	Toy manufacturer. Type: NYSE-CLO Ind: Manufacturing Grp: Manufacturing J Brian Clarke, CEO Arnold C Greenberg, Chr J Brian Clarke, Pres Paul C Meyer, CFO Daniel W Robert, IS Michael S Bauer, Sls Robert A Jackman, Mkt Barbara C Wruck, PR	Rev: 185 Assets: NA Emp: 2		
Coleman Co 250 N St Francis Wichita, KS 67202 316-261-3211	Manufacturer of leisure time & recreational equipment. Type: NYSE-CLN Ind: Manufacturing Grp: Manufacturing Sheldon C Coleman, CEO Jon C Dell'Antonia, IS Charles McIlwaine, PR	Rev: 500 Assets: 500 Emp: 5		
Colgate Palmolive Co 300 Park Avenue New York, NY 10022 212-310-2000	Manufacturer of personal health care products. Type: NYSE-CL Ind: Personal Care Grp: Consumer Prd Reuben Mark, CEO Brian J Heidtke, Tres Robert M Agate, CFO Richard T Palmer, IS William Cooling, R&D Craig B Tate, Mkt Jules Blake, VP Robert S Roth, VP Robert A Murray, IR Katharine R Tarbox, PR	Rev: 4734 Assets: 3218 Emp: 25		
Collins & Aikman Corp 210 Madison Avenue New York, NY 10016 212-578-1200	Manufacturer of broadloom & commercial carpets, yarns. Type: OTC Ind: Manufacturing Grp: Manufacturing Alfred Crimmins, CEO	Rev: 1200 Assets: 750 Emp: 13		
Collins Foods International Inc 12655 W Jefferson Blvd Los Angeles, CA 90066 213-827-2300	Fast food & convenience restaurant operator. Type: NYSE-CF0 Ind: Food/Lodging Grp: Consumer Service James A Collins, CEO Richard Bermingham, Chr Rushton O Backer, VCh H William Glasner, CFO Ron Allans, Ops Thomas Gregory, VP LeMoyne Hammett, VP Kevin Perkins, VP Michael Minchin, VP Samuel Sibert, VP	Rev: 1024 Assets: 394 Emp: 13		
Collins, Barrow, Maheu, Noiseux Ltd 1400 777 8th Avenue SW Calgary, AB T2P3R5 Can 403-298-1500	National accounting firm. Type: Private Ind: Accounting Grp: Business Service Wesley Stritling, CEO	Rev: 85 Assets: NM Emp: 1		
Colonial Group Inc One Financial Center Boston, MA 02111 617-426-3750	Mutual fund investment company. Type: Private Ind: Non-Bank Fin Grp: Financial John A McNeice, CEO C Herbert Emilson, Pres Brian A Lajoie, Tres Davey O Stern, CFO Charles J Mohr, VP Arthur O Stern, VP Julian Daly, VP	Rev: 74 Assets: 82 Emp: 1		
Colonial Oil Industries Inc N Lathrop Avenue Savannah, GA 31402 912-236-1331	Distributor of petroleum products. Type: Private Ind: Energy Grp: Basic Industries Robert H Demery, CEO	Rev: 550 Assets: NA Emp: 1		

Organizations Listed Alphabetically

Organization / Address / Phone	Descriptive Information	Revenue / ($ mil)	Assets / ($ mil)	Emp (thous)
Colonial Penn Insurance Co 19th & Market Streets Philadelphia, PA 19181 215-988-8000	Property & casualty insurance company. Type: Private-Sub Par: FPL (Florida Power & Light) Group Inc Ind: Insurance Grp: Insurance Richard W Ohman, CEO	Rev: Assets: Emp:	486 873 2	
Colonial Pipeline Co Inc 3390 Peachtree Road Atlanta, GA 30326 404-261-1470	Natural gas pipeline transmission company. Type: Private Ind: Transport Grp: Business Service Don Brinkley, CEO	Rev: Assets: Emp:	550 NA 1	
Colorado Springs, City of City Hall Colorado Springs, CO 80901 303-578-6600	City government. Type: City Govt Ind: Local Govt Grp: Govt & Non-Prof Robert M Isacc, CEO	Rev: Assets: Emp:	458 NM 4	
Colorado, State of State Capitol Denver, CO 80203 303-866-5000	State government. Type: State Govt Ind: State/Prov Govt Grp: Govt & Non-Prof Roy Romer, CEO	Rev: Assets: Emp:	8200 NM 62	
Coloric Corp Washington & Heffner Streets Topton, PA 19562 215-682-4211	Manufacturer of major kitchen appliances. Type: Private-Sub Par: Raytheon Co Ind: Appliances/Furn Grp: Manufacturing David Dolak, CEO	Rev: Assets: Emp:	NA NA NA	
Colt Industries Inc 430 Park Avenue New York, NY 10022 212-940-0400	Industrial equipment manufacturer; automotive, aerospace. Type: Private Ind: Conglomerate Grp: Manufacturing David I Margolis, CEO Salvatore J Cozzolino, CFO John F Campbell, PR	Rev: Assets: Emp:	1750 1400 18	
Columbia Gas System Inc 20 Montchanin Road Wilmington, DE 19807 302-429-5000	Nationwide natural gas distribution company. Type: NYSE-CG Ind: Utility Grp: Utilities John H Croom, CEO Robert A Oswald, CFO Philip L Magley, IS Tejinder S Bindra, VP Joyce Hayes, VP Richard Lowe, VP Daniel L Bell, VP R Bruce Quayle, PR	Rev: Assets: Emp:	3128 5641 11	
Columbia Pictures 711 Fifth Avenue New York, NY 10022 212-751-4400	Motion picture production company. Type: NASDAQ-TRSP Ind: Leisure Time Grp: Consumer Service Victor A Kaufman, CEO Kenneth Williams, Tres Lawrence Ruisi, CFO Lewis J Korman, R&D Arnold Messer, Mkt M Jay Walkingshaw, VP Susan B Garelli, VP Ronald Jacobi, VP Victoria Shaw Cohen, VP Dawn Steel, VP Gary Lieberthal, VP	Rev: Assets: Emp:	1616 3565 10	
Columbia Savings (CA) Savings Assn Inc 8840 Wilshire Blvd Beverly Hills, CA 90211 213-657-6123	Thrift institution. Type: NYSE-CVS Ind: Savings & Loan Grp: Financial Abraham Spiegel, CEO Lawrence K Fish, Pres Bruce Nolan, IS Wendell Ruppe, Mkt Christopher Moore, VP Daniel Rohr, VP Leslie Hogan, PR	Rev: Assets: Emp:	1249 12744 3	
Columbia Savings (CO) Assn Inc 5850 S Ulster Circle E Englewood, CO 80111 303-773-3444	Thrift institution. Type: NASDAQ-FCLF Ind: Savings & Loan Grp: Financial Fred A Deering, CEO	Rev: Assets: Emp:	350 3500 1	
Columbia University 116th Street & Broadway New York, NY 10027 212-280-1754	Major educational institution; university. Type: University Ind: University Grp: Govt & Non-Prof Michael I Sovern, CEO	Rev: Assets: Emp:	431 409 21	
Columbus Southern Power Co 215 N Front Street Columbus, OH 43215 614-223-1000	Electric power company. Type: Private-Sub Par: American Electric Power Co Inc Ind: Utility Grp: Utilities W S White, CEO William Lhota, Pres John Brennan, VCh Peter DeMaria, CFO A Joseph Dowd, VP Gerald Maloney, VP Richard Disbrow, VP Richard McMorrow, VP Harry Post, VP	Rev: Assets: Emp:	778 2067 3	

Organizations Listed Alphabetically

Organization / Address / Phone	Descriptive Information	Revenue / ($ mil)	Assets / ($ mil)	Emp (thous)
Columbus, City of City Hall Columbus, OH 43215 614-222-7671	City government. Type: City Govt Ind: Local Govt Grp: Govt & Non-Prof Dana G Rinehart, CEO	Rev: Assets: Emp:		420 NM 6
Combustion Engineering Inc 900 Long Ridge Road PO Box 9308 Stamford, CT 06904 203-329-8771	Manufacturer of equipment for the power generation industry. Type: NYSE-CSP Ind: Electronics Grp: High Tech Charles E Gugel, CEO George Kimmel, Pres Charles Bernett, VCh Fred Jones, Tres Jeffrey S Rubin, CFO Robert E Kistner, IS Jack T Sanderson, R&D Dale E Smith, Ops Bernard Garry, VP William Connolly, VP William J Connolly, PR	Rev: Assets: Emp:		3484 2546 29
Comcast Corp 1414 S Penn Square Philadelphia, PA 19102 215-665-1700	Developer & operator of nationwide cable communications. Type: NASDAQ-CMCS Ind: Publishing/Com Grp: Consumer Service Ralph J Roberts, CEO Daniel Aaron, VCh Bernard Gallagher, Tres Julian Brodsky, CFO Brian Roberts, Mkt Jerome Purcell, VP Stanley Wang, VP Lawrence Smith, VP Robert Clasen, VP Stephen Backstrom, VP	Rev: Assets: Emp:		449 2371 3
Comdisco Inc 6111 N River Road Rosemont, IL 60018 312-698-3000	Computer leasing & maintenance company. Type: NYSE-CDO Ind: Business Service Grp: Business Service Kenneth N Pontikes, CEO William M Pontikes, Pres Raymond J Siegel, Tres John J Vosicky, CFO Richard Paulsen, IS Robert A Bardagy, Mkt Alan J Andreimi, VP Michael A Joseph, VP Vincent L Ricci, VP Daniel Geelan, VP Lisa Knauf, PR	Rev: Assets: Emp:		1309 3488 2
Comerica Inc 211 W Fort Street Detroit, MI 48226 313-222-3300	Commercial bank. Type: NASDAQ-CMCA Ind: Banking Grp: Financial Eugene A Miller, CEO Donald R Mandich, Chr John A Simonson, CFO Robert L Condon, IS Eliot R Stark, R&D James R Waterston, Mkt David O Taylor, PR	Rev: Assets: Emp:		1043 11145 7
Cominco Ltd 2600 - 200 Granville Street Vancouver, BC V6C2R2 Can 604-682-0611	Zinc & lead mining, smelting & refining company. Type: ASE-CLT Ind: Metals/Mining Grp: Basic Industries Norman B Keevil, CEO Robert Hallbauer, Chr John Anderson, Pres L Douglas Margerm, CFO Klaus Goeckmann, Mkt Dale W Massie, VP Robert R Stone, VP John M Van Brunt, VP	Rev: Assets: Emp:		1418 1798 9
Commerce Bancshares Inc 1000 Walnut Kansas City, MO 64199 816-234-2000	Commercial bank. Type: OTC Ind: Banking Grp: Financial James M Kemper, CEO David Kemper, Chr Warren Weaver, Pres James H Linn, VCh Charles Templer, CFO Jack McDonnell, IS Charles Erker, Mkt Russell Koos, VP Jeffrey Missman, VP Michael Petrie, VP George W Porter, VP J Hugh Shields, VP J Daniel Stinnett, VP Charles Erker, IR Warren Weaver, PR	Rev: Assets: Emp:		479 5444 4
Commerce Clearing House Inc 2700 Lake Cook Road Riverwoods, IL 60015 312-940-4600	Publisher of specialty business reference products. Type: OTC Ind: Publishing/Com Grp: Consumer Service Oakleigh B Thorne, CEO Richard Merrill, Chr Edward L Massie, Pres Bernard Elafros, CFO James McNeill, IS Fred Eickmeyer, Sls Victor F Bittner, Mkt Donald Izban, Ops Paul Alligood, VP Martin Bernstein, VP Bernard Elafros, VP John Randolph, PR	Rev: Assets: Emp:		625 355 7
Commercial Credit Corp 300 St Paul Place Baltimore, MD 21202 301-332-3000	Consumer lending company. Type: NYSE-CCC Ind: Non-Bank Fin Grp: Financial John Duvall, CEO Sanford I Weill, Chr James Dimon, CFO Edwin E Sherin, IS Francis J Partel Jr, Mkt Mary McDermott, PR	Rev: Assets: Emp:		1200 4900 5

Organizations Listed Alphabetically

Organization / Address / Phone	Descriptive Information	Revenue / Assets / Emp ($ mil) ($ mil) (thous)		

Commercial Federal Savings Assn Inc
2120 S 72nd Street
Omaha, NE 68124
402-554-9200

Thrift institution.
Type: NASDAQ-CFCN
Ind: Savings & Loan   Grp: Financial
William A Fitzgerald, CEO   Gene Boba, CFO   Areej B Rifat, IS
Marianne Simms, R&D   Roger Lewis, Mkt   Bob Cochrane, PR

Rev: 570
Assets: 6655
Emp: 2

Commercial Intertech
1775 Logan Avenue
Youngstown, OH 44501
216-746-8011

Manufacturers of hydraulic & filtration products.
Type: OTC
Ind: Machinery   Grp: Manufacturing
Paul Powers, CEO

Rev: 400
Assets: 250
Emp: 4

Commercial Metals Co
7800 Stemmons Freeway
Dallas, TX 75247
214-689-4300

Metals manufacturing & fabricating company.
Type: NYSE-CST
Ind: Manufacturing   Grp: Manufacturing
Stanley A Rabin, CEO   Moses Feldman, Pres   Lawrence A Engels, CFO
Craig Dow, IS   Walter Kammann, Ops   Bob Davis, PR

Rev: 1137
Assets: 337
Emp: 4

Commercial Union Assurance Group Ltd
Commercial Union Tower
Toronto, ON M5K1L9 Can
416-361-2500

Property & casualty insurance company.
Type: Private-Sub-For
Ind: Insurance   Grp: Insurance
K G Harris, CEO

Rev: 421
Assets: 774
Emp: 1

Commerical Union Insurance Co
One Beacon Street
Boston, MA 02108
617-725-6000

Property & casualty insurance company.
Type: OTC
Ind: Insurance   Grp: Insurance
Kenneth J Duffy, CEO

Rev: 658
Assets: 1167
Emp: 4

Commerzbank AG
55 Broadway
New York, NY 10004
212-208-6200

Commercial bank.
Type: Private-Sub-For
Ind: Banking   Grp: Financial
Albrecht Staerker, CEO

Rev: 450
Assets: 3500
Emp: 1

Commodore International
1200 Wilson Drive
West Chester, PA 19380
215-431-9100

Personal computer manufacturer.
Type: OTC
Ind: Comput/Off Equip   Grp: High Tech
Irving Gould, CEO

Rev: 250
Assets: 200
Emp: 3

Commonwealth Edison Co
One First National Plaza
Chicago, IL 60690
312-294-4321

Electric utility company.
Type: NYSE-CWE
Ind: Utility   Grp: Utilities
James J O'Conner, CEO   Bide L Thomas, Pres   Ernest M Roth, CFO
Paul J Fenoglio, IS   James W Johnson, R&D   John J Viera, Mkt
Dennis Galle, VP   J Stanley Graves, VP   Donald A Petkis, VP
John J Viera, VP   Donald A Petkus, PR

Rev: 5613
Assets: 17822
Emp: 18

Commonwealth Energy System
One Main Street
Cambridge, MA 02129
617-225-4000

Natural gas distributor & transmitter, holding company.
Type: NYSE-CES
Ind: Energy   Grp: Basic Industries
Gerald Anderson, CEO

Rev: 660
Assets: 600
Emp: 3

Commonwealth Holiday Inns Ltd
31 Sasken Drive
Rexdale, ON M9W1K8 Can
416-675-2030

Operator of nationwide hotel chain.
Type: Private-Sub   Par: Scott's Hospitality Inc
Ind: Food/Lodging   Grp: Consumer Service
Raymond Yelle, CEO

Rev: 255
Assets: 255
Emp: 10

Commonwealth Life Ins Co
Commonwealth Bldg PO Box 32800
Louisville, KY 40232
502-587-7371

Life insurance company.
Type: Private-Sub
Ind: Insurance   Grp: Insurance
Thomas H Schnick, CEO

Rev: 110
Assets: 2890
Emp: 2

Commtron Corp
1501 50th Street
Des Moines, IA 50265
515-226-3000

Wholesaler video tapes & electronics.
Type: ASE-CMR
Ind: Retail/Merch   Grp: Retail
Gary Rockhold, CEO

Rev: 450
Assets: 150
Emp: 1

Organizations Listed Alphabetically

Organization / Address / Phone	Descriptive Information	Revenue / ($ mil)	Assets / ($ mil)	Emp (thous)
Communications Workers of America 1925 K Street NW Washington, DC 20006 202-728-2300	National labor union. Type: Membership Org Ind: Membership Org Grp: Govt & Non-Prof Morton Bahr, CEO	Rev: Assets: Emp:		500 NM 700
Community Fed Savings (MO) Assn Inc 1 Community Federal Center St Louis, MO 63131 314-822-5000	Thrift institution. Type: Private Ind: Savings & Loan Grp: Financial Kenneth R Fiala, CEO	Rev: Assets: Emp:		500 5000 2
Community Psychiatric Centers Inc 517 Washington Street San Francisco, CA 94111 415-397-6151	Operator of hospitals & clinics. Type: NYSE-CMY Ind: Health Care Grp: Consumer Service Robert L Green, CEO James Conte, Pres Loren B Shook, VCh James P Smith, CFO Barry Dyches, R&D Richard Conte, Mkt Frances O'Shaughnessy, Ops Kay Seim, VP Jerald Bryant, VP Erick Agnew, VP David Wakefield, VP	Rev: Assets: Emp:		347 478 4
Compaq Computer Corp 20555 FM 149 Houston, TX 77070 713-370-0670	Manufacturer of personal computers. Type: NYSE-CPQ Ind: Comput/Off Equip Grp: High Tech Joseph R Canion, CEO James M Eckhart, Pres John Foster, Tres John F Gribi, CFO Gary Stimac, IS Jim Harris, R&D Ross Cooley, Sls Michael S Swavely, Mkt Eckhard Pfeiffer, Ops J Steven Flanagan, VP Robert Vieau, VP James D D'Arezzo, PR	Rev: Assets: Emp:		2066 1590 12
CompuServe Inc 5000 Arlington Center Blvd Columbus, OH 43220 614-457-8600	Computer information services company. Type: Private-Sub Par: Block, H & R Inc Ind: Comput/Off Equip Grp: High Tech Charles McCall, CEO	Rev: Assets: Emp:		NA NA NA
Computer Associates International Inc 125 Jericho Turnpike Jericho, NY 11753 516-333-6700	Computer software company. Type: NYSE-CA Ind: Comput/Off Equip Grp: High Tech Charles B Wang, CEO	Rev: Assets: Emp:		1030 NA 9
Computer Factory Inc 399 Executive Blvd Elmsford, NY 10523 914-347-5000	Retail store operator; personal computer & equipment. Type: NYSE-CFA Ind: Retail/Merch Grp: Retail Jay Gottlieb, CEO	Rev: Assets: Emp:		275 NA 3
Computer Innovations Distribution Inc 3415 American Drive Mississauga, ON L4V1T4 Can 416-793-9000	Personal computer retailer. Type: TOR Ind: Retail/Merch Grp: Retail Robert Kearny, CEO	Rev: Assets: Emp:		298 170 1
Computer Sciences Corp 2100 E Grand Avenue El Segundo, CA 90245 213-615-0311	Computer service; government contracts. Type: NYSE-CSC Ind: Comput/Off Equip Grp: High Tech William R Hoover, CEO George Barratt, CFO Robert T Knight, IS Lawrence Parkus, R&D Albert Gluckson, VP Van B Honeycutt, VP Walter J Culver, VP Denis M Crane, VP Lawrence Parkus, VP Bruce Plowman, IR	Rev: Assets: Emp:		1152 661 13
Computervision Corp 100 Crosby Drive Bedford, MA 01730 617-275-1800	Computer manufacturer, service. Type: NYSE-CVN Ind: Comput/Off Equip Grp: High Tech Martin Allen, CEO Joe M Henson, Chr Richard B Goldman, CFO Dwight Muller, IS Richard Snyder, R&D Donald Newman, IR Joe Gavaghan, PR	Rev: Assets: Emp:		500 431 5
COMSAT Communications Satellite Inc 950 L'Enfant Plaza SW Washington, DC 20024 202-863-6000	Telecommunications company; satellite. Type: NYSE-CQ Ind: Telecom Grp: High Tech Irving Goldstein, CEO	Rev: Assets: Emp:		359 1163 3

Organizations Listed Alphabetically

Organization / Address / Phone	Descriptive Information	Revenue / ($ mil)	Assets / ($ mil)	Emp (thous)
Comstock Group Inc 38 Old Ridgebury Road Danbury, CT 06810 203-792-9800	Real estate development company. Type: OTC Ind: Real Estate/Bldg Grp: Business Service Bertrand Geoffroy, CEO	Rev: Assets: Emp:		368 NA 5
Conagra Inc Conagra Center One Central Park Plaza Omaha, NE 68102 402-978-4000	Diversified company active in industries in the food chain. Type: NYSE Ind: Food Processing Grp: Food Processing Charles M Harper, CEO R F Morrison, VCh James P MacDonald, Tres L B Thomas, CFO Joseph V Petty, IS Robert J White, R&D L James Kennedy, Mkt Gerald B Vernon, VP David T Peters, VP Walter H Casey, VP John B Phillips, VP Walter H Casey, IR Lynn Phares, PR	Rev: Assets: Emp:		9475 3043 43
Concurrent Computer Corp 15 Main Street Holmdel, NJ 07733 201-946-8883	Computer manufacturer. Type: NASDAQ-CCUR Ind: Comput/Off Equip Grp: High Tech James K Sims, CEO	Rev: Assets: Emp:		278 200 3
Cone Mills Corp 1201 Maple Street Greensboro, NC 27405 919-379-6510	Textile manufacturers. Type: Private Ind: Apparel/Textiles Grp: Consumer Prd Dewey L Trogdon, CEO	Rev: Assets: Emp:		750 NA 10
Confederation Life Insurance Co 321 Bloor Street E Toronto, ON M4W1H1 Can 416-323-8111	Life insurance company. Type: Private-Mutual Ind: Insurance Grp: Insurance Patrick Burns, CEO	Rev: Assets: Emp:		2919 9173 5
Congress of the United States of America The Capitol Washington, DC 20515 202-224-3121	Legislative branch of the United States Federal Government. Type: Federal Govt Ind: Federal Govt Grp: Govt & Non-Prof D Quayle, CEO	Rev: Assets: Emp:		2139 NM 17
Connecticut Bank & Trust Co NA 1 Constitution Hartford, CT 06115 203-244-5000	Commercial bank. Type: OTC Ind: Banking Grp: Financial Gordon I Ulmer, CEO	Rev: Assets: Emp:		1500 1200 7
Connecticut General Life Ins Co 900 Cottage Grove Bloomfield, CT 06152 203-726-6000	Life insurance company. Type: NYSE Ind: Insurance Grp: Insurance Hartzel Z Lebed, CEO Thomas H Dooley, Chr R Chris Doerr, CFO Travers H Wills, IS David G Devereaux, Mkt Rick Goulart, IR Gloria McNutt, PR	Rev: Assets: Emp:		4692 26786 12
Connecticut Light & Power Co Selden Street Belden, CT 06037 203-665-5123	Electrical power utility company. Type: Private-Sub Par: Northeast Utilities Inc Ind: Utility Grp: Utilities W B Ellis, CEO	Rev: Assets: Emp:		NA NA NA
Connecticut Mutual Life Insurance Co 140 Garden Street Hartford, CT 06154 203-727-6500	Life insurance company. Type: Private Ind: Insurance Grp: Insurance Denis F Mullane, CEO S Ceaser Raboy, Pres Robert Dickson, VCh Albert E Reavill, CFO Robert T Lynn, IS Robin Moutrux, R&D Jerry J Coursey, Sls Donald H Pond Jr, Mkt Thomas Ungashick, VP Gerald Randall, VP Mary O'Conner, PR	Rev: Assets: Emp:		2039 11230 20
Connecticut Natural Gas Co 100 Columbus Blvd Hartford, CT 06144 203-727-3000	Distributor of natural gas. Type: NYSE-CTG Ind: Utility Grp: Utilities Robert Willis, CEO	Rev: Assets: Emp:		255 300 7
Connecticut, State of State Capitol Hartford, CT 06106 203-240-0555	State government. Type: State Govt Ind: State/Prov Govt Grp: Govt & Non-Prof William A O'Neill, CEO	Rev: Assets: Emp:		8599 NM 62

Organizations Listed Alphabetically

Organization / Address / Phone	Descriptive Information	Revenue / ($ mil)	Assets / ($ mil)	Emp (thous)
Connell Ltd (Avondale Foods) Ptr Inc 1 Mass Tech Center East Boston, MA 02128 617-567-2600	Metal recycling & industrial equipment. Type: Private Ind: Food Processing Grp: Food Processing Grover Connell, CEO	Rev: Assets: Emp:	1500 NA 5	
Connell Rice & Sugar Inc 45 Cardinal Drive Westfield, NJ 07092 201-233-0700	Heavy equipment leasing, food export & import. Type: Private Ind: Food Processing Grp: Food Processing Grover Connell, CEO	Rev: Assets: Emp:	1100 NA 2	
Conner Peripherals Corp 2221 Old Oakland Road San Jose, CA 95131 408-433-3340	Manufacturer of disk drives. Type: NASDAQ-CNNR Ind: Comput/Off Equip Grp: High Tech Finis Connor, CEO	Rev: Assets: Emp:	200 100 1	
Conoco Inc 1007 Market Street Wilmington, DE 19898 302-774-1000	Exploration & production of petroleum products. Type: Private-Sub Par: DuPont, E I DeNemours & Co Ind: Energy Grp: Basic Industries C Nicandros, CEO	Rev: Assets: Emp:	NA NA NA	
Consolidated Bathurst Inc 800 Rene Levesque Blvd W Montreal, PQ H3B1Y9 Can 514-875-2160	Forest products company; newsprint, paper. Type: Private-Sub Ind: Paper/Forest Prd Grp: Basic Industries T Oscar Strangeland, CEO Guy Coulombe, Pres Colin Fraser, Tres Jean-Jacques Carrier, CFO Timothy Wagg, R&D Bartley Duns, Sls M Strathy, Mkt Armand Legault, VP Ashok Narang, VP	Rev: Assets: Emp:	2016 1936 15	
Consolidated Beef Industries Inc 544 Acme Street Green Bay, WI 54302 414-437-4311	Meat packaging company. Type: Private Ind: Food Processing Grp: Food Processing Ronald Likas, CEO	Rev: Assets: Emp:	500 NA 1	
Consolidated Coal Co 1007 Market Street Wilmington, DE 19898 302-774-1000	Coal production company. Type: Private-Sub Par: DuPont, E I DeNemours & Co Ind: Metals/Mining Grp: Basic Industries B R Brown, CEO	Rev: Assets: Emp:	NA NA NA	
Consolidated Coal Corp 1800 Washington Road Pittsburgh, PA 15241 412-831-4000	Coal mining company. Type: Private Ind: Energy Grp: Basic Industries B R Brown, CEO	Rev: Assets: Emp:	825 NA 7	
Consolidated Edison New York Inc 4 Irving Place New York, NY 10003 212-460-4600	Electric power utility. Type: NYSE-ED Ind: Utility Grp: Utilities Arthur Hauspurg, CEO Eugene McGrath, Pres John V Thornton, VCh Raymond McCann, CFO Raymond P Priore, IS Robert A Bell, R&D John Dillon, Mkt Charles Soutar, Ops John Conway, VP Joseph Hydok, VP John Deegan, VP Edward Carey, VP Laurence Kleinman, IR Edward W Livingston, PR	Rev: Assets: Emp:	5109 9552 19	
Consolidated Freightways Inc 3240 Hillview Avenue Palo Alto, CA 94303 415-494-2900	Transportation company; trucking, air freight, ocean trans. Type: NYSE-CNF Ind: Transport Grp: Business Service Larry R Scott, CEO Raymond F O'Brien, Chr Norman R Benke, CFO Phillip Seeley, IS Roger Curry, Mkt Jim R Allen, PR	Rev: Assets: Emp:	2689 1536 29	
Consolidated Grain & Barge Co Inc 5100 Oakland Avenue St Louis, MO 63110 314-658-9200	Food processing & barge transport company. Type: Private Ind: Food Processing Grp: Food Processing Herb Jones, CEO	Rev: Assets: Emp:	550 NA 1	
Consolidated Natural Gas Co Four Gateway Center Pittsburgh, PA 15222 412-227-1000	Natural gas utility company. Type: NYSE Ind: Utility Grp: Utilities George A Davidson, CEO Ralbern Murray, VCh John Whitacre, Tres Lester D Johnson, CFO Raymond Ernest, Sls Thomas Stewart, VP David Weatherwax, VP	Rev: Assets: Emp:	2468 4109 8	

Organizations Listed Alphabetically

Organization / Address / Phone	Descriptive Information	Revenue / ($ mil)	Assets / ($ mil)	Emp (thous)
Consolidated Papers Inc 231 First Avenue N Wisconsin Rapids, WI 54494 715-422-3111	Manufacturer, enamel printing paper, cardboard, paper mill. Type: NASDAQ-CPER Ind: Paper/Forest Prd Grp: Basic Industries George W Mead, CEO Patrick F Brennan, Pres Leroy A Englehardt, CFO Gerald E Blum, IS H W Bennett, R&D G T Beckley, Mkt Daniel P Meyer, PR	Rev: Assets: Emp:		897 935 5
Consolidated Rail Corp (CONRAIL) Six Penn Center Philadelphia, PA 19103 215-977-4000	Railroad company. Type: NYSE Ind: Railroad Grp: Business Service James Hagen, CEO L Stanley Crane, Chr Richard D Sanford, Pres H William Brown, CFO Michael D Sims, IS Charles N Marshall, Mkt Saul Resnick, PR	Rev: Assets: Emp:		2689 1711 30
Consolidated Stores Corp 2020 Convair Avenue Columbus, OH 43207 614-224-1297	Regional discount chain; closeout merchandise. Type: NYSE-CNS Ind: Retail/Merch Grp: Retail James M Guinan, CEO Charles H Shenk, Pres Sheryl E Illnick, Tres William B Snow, CFO M Steven Bromet, IS Kent Larson, Sls Patricia L King, VP	Rev: Assets: Emp:		601 286 5
Constar International 835 Georgia Avenue Chattanooga, TN 37402 615-267-2973	Manufacturer of plastic products, consumer & industrial. Type: NYSE-CTR Ind: Manufacturing Grp: Manufacturing Charles F Casey, CEO James Baker, VCh James Goldman, CFO Thomas Judge, Mkt Roger Mulvihill, VP David Tatum, VP James B Baker, VP	Rev: Assets: Emp:		544 230 4
Constellation Operating Services Inc 250 W Pratt Street Baltimore, MD 21201 301-783-2827	Gas & electric utility company. Type: Private-Sub Par: Baltimore Gas & Electric Co Ind: Utility Grp: Utilities Donald Operating Services, CEO	Rev: Assets: Emp:		NA NA NA
Consumers Co-op Refineries Ltd 401 22nd Street E Saskatoon, SK S7K3M9 Can 306-244-3311	Operator of refineries; gas exploration & production. Type: Private-Sub Par: Federated Cooperatives Ltd Ind: Energy Grp: Basic Industries V Leland, CEO	Rev: Assets: Emp:		298 85 1
Consumers Distributing Co 62 Belfield Road Rexdale, ON M9W1G2 Can 416-245-4900	Catalog/direct mail retail sales company. Type: Private-Sub Par: Provigo Incorporated Ind: Retail/Merch Grp: Retail Pierre Lortie, CEO	Rev: Assets: Emp:		1105 425 11
Consumers Gas Ltd 1 First Canadian Place Toronto, ON M5X1C5 Can 416-864-3399	Natural gas distribution company. Type: Private-Sub Par: GW Utilities Ltd Ind: Energy Grp: Basic Industries R W Martin, CEO J L Aiken, VCh W C Currier, CFO J I Cuthill, R&D N B Loberg, Mkt C F Safrance, Ops R S Lougheed, VP R G Riedl, VP	Rev: Assets: Emp:		1417 1726 8
Consumers Packaging Inc 401 West Mall Etobicoke, ON M9C5J7 Can 416-232-3283	Manufacturer of packaging materials. Type: TOR-CGC Ind: Packaging Grp: Manufacturing William D Rooney, CEO Thomas Tinmouth, Chr Kenneth Grant, CFO David Jack, VP D Stewart Kennedy, VP James C Bacon, VP	Rev: Assets: Emp:		333 286 3
Contel Corp 245 Perimeter Ctr Parkway PO Box 105194 Atlanta, GA 30346 404-391-8000	Telecommunications company; telephone, data processing. Type: NYSE-CTC Ind: Telecom Grp: High Tech Charles Wohlstetter, CEO Donald W Weber, Chr Stuart Johnson, VCh Malcolm Holmes, CFO Michael B Esstman, IS John C McDonald, R&D Norman Brust, VP Norman Brust, IR Ken Bomar, PR	Rev: Assets: Emp:		2964 5865 23
Continental Airlines Corp 2929 Allen Parkway Houston, TX 77019 713-630-5000	International commercial airline. Type: Private-Sub Par: Texas Air Corp (Continental Airlines) Ind: Airline Grp: Consumer Service Joseph Carr, CEO	Rev: Assets: Emp:		NA NA NA

Organizations Listed Alphabetically

Organization / Address / Phone	Descriptive Information	Revenue / Assets / Emp ($ mil) ($ mil) (thous)		

Organization / Address / Phone	Descriptive Information	Rev:	Assets:	Emp:
Continental Assurance Co CNA Plaza Chicago, IL 60685 312-822-5000	Life insurance company. Type: NYSE Ind: Insurance Grp: Insurance Edward J Noha, CEO Dennis H Chookaszian, CFO Thomas P Ladd, IS Himanshu I Patel, R&D Philip L Engel, Mkt Susan H Hogan, IR Joyce Rice, PR	2323	6138	6
Continental Baking Co Checkerboard Square St Louis, MO 63164 314-982-1000	Bakers of bread & pastries; Hostess products, Wonder bread. Type: Private-Sub Par: Ralston Purina Co Ind: Food Processing Grp: Food Processing Jay Brown, CEO	NA	NA	NA
Continental Bancorp Inc 1500 Market Street Philadelphia, PA 19102 215-564-7000	Commercial bank. Type: NASDAQ-CPRB Ind: Banking Grp: Financial Roy Peraino, CEO	750	6000	3
Continental Bank Corp 231 S LaSalle Street Chicago, IL 60697 312-828-2345	Commercial bank. Type: NYSE-CBK Ind: Banking Grp: Financial Thomas C Theobald, CEO Thomas C Theobald, Chr Joseph Alaimo, Pres Edward S Bottum, VCh Hollis Rademacher, CFO Janet S Reed, IS William Kundert, Sls Roger H Sherman, Mkt Joseph Thompson, Ops Garry Scheuring, VP John V Egan, PR	3061	30578	8
Continental Cablevision Corp The Pilot House Boston, MA 02110 617-742-9500	Cable television systems operator. Type: Private Ind: Publishing/Com Grp: Consumer Service Amos B Hostetter, CEO	600	NA	5
Continental Companies Inc 3250 Mary Street Maimi, FL 33133 305-445-2493	Hotel management company. Type: Private Ind: Food/Lodging Grp: Consumer Service Sherwood M Weiser, CEO	500	NA	8
Continental Grain Co 277 Park Avenue New York, NY 10172 212-207-5100	International grain trading, storage & shipping company. Type: Private Ind: Food Processing Grp: Food Processing Donald Staheli, CEO	13000	NA	12
Continental International Corp 180 Maiden Lane New York, NY 10038 212-440-3980	Life & casualty insurance company. Type: NYSE-CIC Ind: Non-Bank Fin Grp: Financial John P Mascotte, CEO John Bretherick, Pres Frederic Marziano, VCh John H Loynes, CFO Kenneth Burk, IS Arthur O'Connor, Mkt Adrian Tocklin, Ops Wayne Fisher, VP Arthur O'Connor, PR	5878	13302	17
Control Data Corp 8100 34th Street S Minneapolis, MN 55440 612-853-8100	Computer manufacturing company. Type: NYSE-CDA Ind: Comput/Off Equip Grp: High Tech Robert M Price, CEO Lawrence Perlman, Pres Norbert Berg, VCh John K Buckner, CFO Robert M White, R&D James Ousley, Sls Catherine A Hapka, Mkt Emmanuel Otis, VP Kenneth Mellem, VP John Curran, VP Frank J Ryan, PR	3628	2534	34
Convergent Technologies Inc 2700 N First Street San Jose, CA 95150 408-434-2848	Computer manufacturer. Type: Private Ind: Comput/Off Equip Grp: High Tech Paul Ely Jr, CEO	400	295	15
Cook County Government County Bldg Chicago, IL 60602 312-443-5500	County government. Type: County Govt Ind: Local Govt Grp: Govt & Non-Prof George W Dunne, CEO	3900	NM	23

Organizations Listed Alphabetically

Organization / Address / Phone	Descriptive Information	Revenue / ($ mil)	Assets / ($ mil)	Emp (thous)
Cooke, Jack Kent Corp Kent Farms Middleburg, VA 22117 703-687-4000	Real estate development & sports entertainment company. Type: Private Ind: Real Estate/Bldg Grp: Business Service Jack Kent Cooke, CEO	Rev: Assets: Emp:		500 NA 1
Cooper Companies 3145 Porter Drive Palo Alto, CA 94304 415-856-5000	Manufacturer of medical instruments, equipment. Type: NYSE-COO Ind: Electronics Grp: High Tech Howard P Sturman, CEO Gary Singer, Pres Dennis L Winger, CFO Gene Elsbree, PR	Rev: Assets: Emp:		400 NA 4
Cooper Industries Inc First City Tower 1001 Fannin Street Houston, TX 77002 713-739-5400	Manufacturer of electrical equipment for power generation. Type: NYSE-CBE Ind: Equipment Grp: Manufacturing Robert Cizek, CEO Joseph Coppola, Pres Alan Reidel, VCh Dewain K Cross, CFO Carl Plesnicher, Sls Michael Sebastian, Ops H John Riley, VP Thomas Campbell, VP Laurence Polsky, VP	Rev: Assets: Emp:	4258 4384 46	
Cooper Tire & Rubber Co Western & Lima Streets Findley, OH 45839 419-423-1321	Tire manufacturer. Type: NYSE-CTB Ind: Tire/Rubber Grp: Basic Industries Edward E Brewer, CEO Ivan W Gorr, Pres William T Fitzgerald, VCh William Hattendorf, Tres J Alec Reinhardt, CFO Patrick W Rooney, Mkt John Fahl, VP William S Klein, VP Richard D Teeple, VP Karl W Klose, VP Arthur J Bakaitis, PR	Rev: Assets: Emp:	748 443 8	
Cooperators General Insurance Co 130 MacDonell Street Priority Square Guelph, ON N1H6P8 Can 519-824-4400	Property & casualty insurance company. Type: TOR Ind: Insurance Grp: Insurance Joseph Martin, CEO	Rev: Assets: Emp:	670 951 3	
Coopers & Lybrand Inc 1251 Avenue of the Americas New York, NY 10020 212-536-2000	Nationwide accounting firm. Type: Private Ind: Accounting Grp: Business Service Peter R Scanlon, CEO	Rev: Assets: Emp:		2500 NA 30
Coopers & Lybrand Ltd 145 King Street W Toronto, ON M5H1V8 Can 416-869-1130	National accounting firm. Type: Private Ind: Accounting Grp: Business Service Kenneth R Stevenson, CEO	Rev: Assets: Emp:		170 NM 3
Coopervision Inc 3145 Porter Drive Palo Alto, CA 94304 415-856-5000	Manufacturer of contact lenses. Type: OTC Ind: Instruments Grp: High Tech Arthur C Bass, CEO	Rev: Assets: Emp:	550 1000 5	
Coors, Aldolph Co 600 9th Street Golden, CO 80401 303-279-6565	Beer brewing & distribution. Type: OTC-ACCOB Ind: Beverage Grp: Food Processing William K Coors, CEO Jeffrey H Coors, Pres Joseph Coors, VCh Harold R Smethills, CFO Ed Crowe, IS Gary Truitt, Sls Robert Rechholtz, Mkt Marvin D Johnson, PR	Rev: Assets: Emp:	1522 1571 10	
Copperweld Corp Four Gateway Center Pittsburgh, PA 15222 412-263-3200	Manufacturer of tubing; copper. Type: NYSE-COS Ind: Metals/Mining Grp: Basic Industries John D Turner, CEO	Rev: Assets: Emp:		300 NA 3
Core Mark International Inc 13951 Bridgeport Road Richmond, BC V6V1J6 Can 604-273-7721	Operator of retail products stores; food, drugs. Type: TOR Ind: Retail/Food Grp: Retail Gerald J Bolduc, CEO L John Clark, Chr Anthony Regensburg, VCh Patrick Jones, CFO Gerald J Bolduc, IS Daniel Mohorc, Sls John DeMarco, Mkt Frank Udvare, Ops James Somerville, VP Gerald Sykes, VP	Rev: Assets: Emp:	2032 431 3	

Organizations Listed Alphabetically

Organization / Address / Phone	Descriptive Information	Revenue / ($ mil)	Assets / ($ mil)	Emp (thous)
Corestates Financial Corp Broad & Chestnut Streets Philadelphia, PA 19101 215-629-3869	Commercial bank. Type: NASDAQ-CSFN Ind: Banking Grp: Financial Terrence A Larsen, CEO Wilson D McElhinny, VCh Philip V Crane, CFO Robert M Evans, IS Robert N Gilmore, R&D Richard DeNatale, Mkt Robert D Murray, VP Thomas C DeBow, IR Gary Brooten, PR	Rev: 1630 Assets: 16430 Emp: 8		
Cornell University Administrative Bldg Ithaca, NY 14853 607-256-1000	Major educational institution; university. Type: University Ind: University Grp: Govt & Non-Prof Frank H T Rhodes, CEO	Rev: 484 Assets: 608 Emp: 24		
Corning Glass Works Inc Houghton Park Corning, NY 14831 607-974-9000	Specialty glass manufacturer. Type: NYSE-GLW Ind: Manufacturing Grp: Manufacturing James R Houghton, CEO Van C Campbell, VCh Richard B Klein, Tres James L Flynn, CFO Harvey Shrednick, IS David A Duke, R&D James Reisbeck, Mkt David Duke, VP Richard Dulude, VP David Van Allen, IR John Abrams, PR	Rev: 2122 Assets: 2898 Emp: 25		
Coronet Carpets Inc 1144 E Boul Magenta Farnham, PQ J2N2R4 Can 514-293-3155	Carpet manufacturer. Type: MON Ind: Apparel/Textiles Grp: Consumer Prd Harry McGee, CEO	Rev: 383 Assets: 170 Emp: 2		
Corpus Christi, City of City Hall Corpus Christi, TX 78469 512-880-3100	City government. Type: City Govt Ind: Local Govt Grp: Govt & Non-Prof Betty Turner, CEO	Rev: 250 Assets: NM Emp: 3		
Correctional Service of Canada 340 Laurier Ave W Sir Wilfrid Laurier Bldg Ottawa, ON K1A0P9 Can 613-993-7501	Federal government agency. Type: Federal Govt Ind: Federal Govt Grp: Govt & Non-Prof Ole Ingstrup, CEO	Rev: 1530 Assets: NM Emp: 11		
Corroon & Black Corp Wall Street Plaza New York, NY 10005 212-363-4100	Property & casualty insurance company. Type: NYSE-CBL Ind: Non-Bank Fin Grp: Financial Richard M Miller, CEO John Lambertson, VCh Stephen Crane, CFO Gerald Cusack, IS Richard Maxwell, Mkt Donald King, VP J Bransford Wallace, VP Joseph Oates, VP C Jackson Blair, VP	Rev: 425 Assets: 957 Emp: 4		
Coscan Development Corp 2 First Canadian Place Toronto, ON M5X1H9 Can 416-369-8200	Real estate development company. Type: Private Ind: Real Estate/Bldg Grp: Business Service Ross Cullingworth, CEO	Rev: 291 Assets: 656 Emp: 1		
Costco Wholesale 10829 120th Avenue NE Kirkland, WA 98033 206-828-8100	Wholesaler of groceries, appliances, furniture. Type: NASDAQ-COST Ind: Retail/Merch Grp: Retail Jeffrey Brotman, CEO	Rev: 2000 Assets: 1200 Emp: 5		
Cotter & Co 2740 N Clybourn Avenue Chicago, IL 60614 312-975-2700	Operator of retail stores. Type: Private Ind: Retail/Merch Grp: Retail Daniel Cotter, CEO	Rev: 2200 Assets: NA Emp: 3		
Coulter Electronics Corp 600 W 20th Street Hialeah, FL 33010 305-885-0131	Manufacturer of hematology analyzers, reagents. Type: Private Ind: Electronics Grp: High Tech Wallace H Coulter, CEO	Rev: 500 Assets: NA Emp: 5		
Country Companies 1701 Towanda Avenue Bloomington, IL 61701 309-557-2111	Property & casualty insurance company. Type: OTC Ind: Insurance Grp: Insurance John White, CEO	Rev: 400 Assets: 800 Emp: 2		

Organizations Listed Alphabetically

Organization / Address / Phone	Descriptive Information	Revenue ($ mil)	Assets ($ mil)	Emp (thous)
CountryMark Inc 4565 Columbus Price Delaware, OH 43105 614-548-8200	Manufacturer of specialty chemicals. Type: Private Ind: Chemicals Grp: Basic Industries Harry Ditty, CEO Robert Werner, CFO Thomas Scribner, IS Bill Cubbage, Mkt Robert Wolf, IR Jane Butler, PR	Rev: 1100 Assets: 250 Emp: 1		
Cowen & Co Financial Square New York, NY 10005 212-495-6000	Investment firm; securities trading. Type: Private Ind: Securities Grp: Financial Joseph Cowen, CEO	Rev: 330 Assets: 3300 Emp: 1		
Cox Enterprises Inc 1400 Lake Hearn Drive NE Atlanta, GA 30319 404-843-5000	Newspaper publisher & operator of broadcast & cable TV. Type: Private Ind: Publishing/Com Grp: Consumer Service James C Kennedy, CEO	Rev: 1750 Assets: NA Emp: 14		
CPC International Inc International Plaza Englewood Cliffs, NJ 07632 201-894-4000	Producer of food products. Type: NYSE-CPC Ind: Food Processing Grp: Food Processing James R Eiszner, CEO Charles Shoemate, Pres Richard Siebrasse, VCh Konrad Schlatter, CFO John Scott, Sls Andre Osser, Mkt Ivan Burns, VP Clifford Storms, VP Fred C Meendsen, VP Osvaldo Marinez, VP William Parker, PR	Rev: 4701 Assets: 3342 Emp: 39		
CPI Inc 1706 Washington Avenue St Louis, MO 63103 314-231-1575	Operator of photofinishing labs, studios. Type: NASDAQ-CPIC Ind: Leisure Time Grp: Consumer Service Milford Bohm, CEO	Rev: 328 Assets: 250 Emp: 5		
CPL Industries Inc 101 N Summit Street Tenafly, NJ 07670 201-568-2303	Manufacturer of consumer products. Type: Private-Sub Par: Colgate Palmolive Co Ind: Personal Care Grp: Consumer Prd Kenneth Snyder, CEO	Rev: NA Assets: NA Emp: NA		
Crane Co 757 Third Avenue New York, NY 10017 212-415-7300	Manufacturer of building products. Type: NYSE Ind: Manufacturing Grp: Manufacturing Robert S Evans, CEO Jack Barnes, VCh Eric Dalrymple, Tres R Kenneth Whitley, CFO J E Crismon, IS Thomas C Fish, Mkt Robert Muller, VP Richard Phillips, VP Michael Raithel, VP George H Broomfield, PR	Rev: 1313 Assets: 682 Emp: 10		
Crawford & Co 5620 Glenridge Road Atlanta, GA 30342 404-256-0830	Management services company. Type: NASDAQ-CRAW Ind: Business Service Grp: Business Service F Minx, CEO	Rev: 300 Assets: 200 Emp: 5		
Cray Research Inc 608 Second Avenue S Minneapolis, MN 55402 612-333-5889	Manufacturer of super computers. Type: NYSE-CYR Ind: Comput/Off Equip Grp: High Tech John A Rollwagen, CEO John A Rollwagen, Chr Marcelo Gumucio, Pres Andrew Scott, VCh John F Carlson, CFO Robert Ewald, IS Robert A Gartner, PR	Rev: 756 Assets: 991 Emp: 5		
Credit Agricole Mutuel Paris 520 Madison Avenue New York, NY 10022 212-418-2200	Commercial bank. Type: Private-Sub-For Ind: Banking Grp: Financial Michele Theveny, CEO	Rev: 450 Assets: 3500 Emp: 1		
Credit Lyonnais France 95 Wall Street New York, NY 10005 212-344-0500	Commercial bank. Type: Private-Sub-For Ind: Banking Grp: Financial Jean Cedelle, CEO	Rev: 450 Assets: 3500 Emp: 1		
Credithrift Financial Inc 601 NW 2nd Street Evansville, IN 47708 812-424-8031	Consumer credit company. Type: OTC Ind: Non-Bank Fin Grp: Financial W L Dixon, CEO	Rev: 523 Assets: 2772 Emp: 4		

Organizations Listed Alphabetically

Organization / Address / Phone	Descriptive Information	Revenue / ($ mil)	Assets / ($ mil)	Emp (thous)
Crestar Financial Corp (United VA) 919 E Main Street Richmond, VA 23261 804-782-5000	Commercial bank. Type: NASDAQ-CRFC Ind: Banking Grp: Financial Richard G Tilghman, CEO Samuel P Cardwell, Chr James M Wells, Pres Patrick D Giblin, CFO William Butler, VP C Garland Hagen, VP F Edward Harris, VP William C Harris, VP	Rev: Assets: Emp:	1016 10408 6	
Criterion Investment Management Inc 1000 Louisiana Suite 600 Houston, TX 77002 713-751-2400	Investment management holding company. Type: Private Ind: Non-Bank Fin Grp: Financial Crayton Lacey Baker, CEO	Rev: Assets: Emp:	42 11586 1	
Crompton & Knowles Inc One Station Place Stamford, CT 06902 203-353-5400	Specialty chemicals company. Type: NYSE-CNK Ind: Chemicals Grp: Basic Industries Vincent A Calarco, CEO	Rev: Assets: Emp:	350 NA 3	
Cross & Trecker Corp 505 N Woodward Avenue Bloomfield Hills, MI 48013 313-644-4343	Manufacturer, foundry equipment, tools. Type: NASDAQ-CTCO Ind: Equipment Grp: Manufacturing Russell A Hadden, CEO Richard T Lindgreen, Chr Walter Aspatore, VCh John Hinnendael, CFO Larry C Helber, Sls Donald Muench, Ops Roger John Lesinski, VP	Rev: Assets: Emp:	428 381 4	
Cross, A T Co One Albion Road Lincoln, RI 02865 401-333-1200	Manufacturer of high quality pens. Type: ASE-ATX Ind: Manufacturing Grp: Manufacturing Bradford R Boss, CEO	Rev: Assets: Emp:	232 176 2	
Crossland Savings Fed Savings Bank Inc 211 Montague Steet Brooklyn, NY 11201 718-780-0400	Thrift institution. Type: NYSE-CRL Ind: Savings & Loan Grp: Financial Maurice L Reissman, CEO Frank A Dellomo, VCh Donald White, CFO James Roarty, IS James Kerr, Mkt James Kerr, PR	Rev: Assets: Emp:	1374 15144 4	
Crowley Maritime Corp 101 California Street San Francisco, CA 94111 415-546-2500	Diversified maritime company. Type: Private Ind: Transport Grp: Business Service Thomas B Crowley, CEO	Rev: Assets: Emp:	1000 NA 5	
Crown American Corp 131 Market Street Johnstown, PA 15907 814-536-4441	Department stores, real estate company. Type: Private Ind: Real Estate/Bldg Grp: Business Service Frank J Pasquerilla, CEO	Rev: Assets: Emp:	750 NA 10	
Crown Central Petroleum Corp One N Charles Baltimore, MD 21201 301-539-7400	Petroleum refining & marketing company. Type: ASE-CNPA Ind: Energy Grp: Basic Industries Henry A Rosenberg, CEO James F Smith, Pres James King, VCh Ted M Jackson, CFO Kenneth Dalwig, IS Joseph P Candella, Mkt William Snyder, VP Bruce A Smith, VP William R Snyder, IR Melissa Scheitler, PR	Rev: Assets: Emp:	1149 443 6	
Crown Cork & Seal Co 9300 Ashton Road Philadelphia, PA 19136 215-698-5100	Manufacturer of packaging; cans, containers. Type: NYSE Ind: Packaging Grp: Manufacturing John F Connelly, CEO William Avery, Pres Henry E Butwel, CFO Merino Di Rugeris, IS Raymond H Shinn, R&D Michael McKenna, Sls Gary Munson, Mkt Mark Hartman, Ops Merino Di Rugeris, IR Gary Burgess, PR	Rev: Assets: Emp:	1834 1073 13	
Crown Crafts Inc Edmond Street Calhoun, GA 30701 404-629-7941	Manufacturer of lace curtains, comforters & accessories. Type: ASE-CRW Ind: Apparel/Textiles Grp: Consumer Prd Philip Bernstein, CEO	Rev: Assets: Emp:	150 100 2	

Organizations Listed Alphabetically

Organization / Address / Phone	Descriptive Information	Revenue / ($ mil)	Assets / ($ mil)	Emp (thous)
Crown Forest Industries Ltd 815 W Hastings Street Vancouver, BC V6C2Y4 Can 604-668-4242	Forest products company. Type: TOR Ind: Paper/Forest Prd Grp: Basic Industries W Sharkey, CEO	Rev: Assets: Emp:		876 717 5
Crown Henry & Co Inc 300 W Washington Chicago, IL 60606 312-236-6300	Manufacturer of paper products. Type: Private Ind: Paper/Forest Prd Grp: Basic Industries Lester Crown, CEO	Rev: Assets: Emp:		880 NA 4
Crown Life Insurance Co 120 Bloor Street E Toronto, ON M4W1B8 Can 416-928-4500	Life insurance company. Type: TOR Ind: Insurance Grp: Insurance R Frederick Richardsonn, CEO	Rev: Assets: Emp:		2944 7419 4
Crownx Inc 120 Bloor Street Toronto, ON M4W1B8 Can 416-928-7722	Life insurance company. Type: TOR-CRX Ind: Health Care Grp: Consumer Service David J Hennigar, CEO H Michael Burns, Pres Harold L Livergant, VCh A Hugh C Lewis, Tres Winston Ling, CFO Robert Granger, VP Edward Cannon, VP Barry Stephens, VP Len Koroneos, VP M Lynne Smith, VP	Rev: Assets: Emp:		2480 7641 30
CRS Sirrine Inc 1177 West Loop S Houston, TX 77027 713-552-2000	Design & construction service company. Type: NYSE-CRX Ind: Consulting Grp: Business Service Bruce Wilkenson, CEO Thomas Bullock, Chr Socrates Christopher, VCh Glenn Hobratscht, CFO Frank Perrone, VP Richard Daerr, VP	Rev: Assets: Emp:		478 186 3
Crum & Foster Inc 305 Madison Avenue Morristown, NJ 07960 201-285-7000	Property & casualty insurance company. Type: Private-Sub Par: Xerox Corp Ind: Insurance Grp: Insurance James A Stark, CEO	Rev: Assets: Emp:		3000 7500 8
Crystal Brands Inc Crystal Brands Road Southport, CT 06490 203-254-6200	Manufacturer & retailer of apparel products. Type: NYSE-CBR Ind: Apparel/Textiles Grp: Consumer Prd Richard F Kral, CEO	Rev: Assets: Emp:		400 300 3
CSA Press Inc 555 Main Street Hudson, MA 01749 508-568-0301	Publishing & printing house. Type: Private-Sub Par: Donnelley, R R & Sons Co Ind: Publishing/Com Grp: Consumer Service Jeffrey Fitzgerald, CEO	Rev: Assets: Emp:		NA NA NA
CSL Group Inc 759 Victoria Square Montreal, PQ H3C2R7 Can 514-288-0221	Transportation company; shipping. Type: TOR Ind: Transport Grp: Business Service Paul Martin, CEO	Rev: Assets: Emp:		349 207 5
CSX Corp One James Center Richmond, VA 23219 804-782-1400	Transportation company; railroad & ocean shipping. Type: NYSE-CSX Ind: Railroad Grp: Business Service Hays T Watkins, CEO John W Snow, Pres William H Sparrow, Tres James Ermer, CFO Ronald W Drucker, IS Alex J Mandl, R&D Thomas E Hoppin, IR Mark G Aron, PR	Rev: Assets: Emp:		7592 13026 54
CTS Corp 905 N West Blvd Elkhart, IN 46514 219-293-7511	Manufacturer of electronic products; industrial components. Type: NYSE-CTS Ind: Electronics Grp: High Tech George F Sommer, CEO	Rev: Assets: Emp:		325 300 2
Cubic Corp 9333 Balboa Avenue San Diego, CA 92123 619-277-6780	Manufacturer of electronic systems; defense, industry. Type: ASE-CUB Ind: Electronics Grp: High Tech Walter J Zable, CEO	Rev: Assets: Emp:		350 300 3

Organizations Listed Alphabetically

Organization / Address / Phone	Descriptive Information	Revenue / Assets / Emp ($ mil) ($ mil) (thous)		

Culbro Corp
387 Park Avenue S
New York, NY 10016
212-561-8700

Manufacturer of personal care products.
Type: NYSE-CUC
Ind: Food Processing   Grp: Food Processing
Edgar M Cullman, CEO   Edgar M Cullman Jr, Pres   William Lewis, CFO
John McLoughlin, PR

Rev: 942
Assets: 396
Emp: 5

Culinar Inc
2 Complexe Desjardins 2700
Montreal, PQ H5B1B2 Can
514-288-3101

Food products company.
Type: TOR
Ind: Food Processing   Grp: Food Processing
Jean Rene Halde, CEO

Rev: 441
Assets: 189
Emp: 5

Cullum Companies
14303 Inwood Road
Dallas, TX 75244
214-661-9700

Operator of retail food stores.
Type: Private
Ind: Retail/Food   Grp: Retail
Jack W Evans, CEO

Rev: 1000
Assets: NA
Emp: 10

Cumberland Farms Corp
777 Dedham Street
Canton, MA 02021
617-828-4900

Operator of retail convenience food stores.
Type: Private
Ind: Retail/Food   Grp: Retail
Demetrios B Haseotes, CEO

Rev: 2200
Assets: NA
Emp: 12

Cummins Engine Co Inc
500 Jackson Street PO Box 3005
Columbus, IN 47202
812-377-5000

Diesel engine manufacturer.
Type: NYSE-CUM
Ind: Automotive   Grp: Manufacturing
Henry B Schacht, CEO   James Henderson, Pres   John T Hackett, CFO
E Harold Davis, IS   Gary D Nelson, R&D   Theodore M Solso, Mkt
Kevin Sheehan, VP   George Fauerbach, VP   Wynne W Gulden, VP
Christine W Letts, PR

Rev: 3310
Assets: 2064
Emp: 26

Curry Corp
727 Central Avenue
Scarsdale, NY 10583
914-725-3500

Automobile dealerships.
Type: Private
Ind: Consumer Service   Grp: Consumer Service
Bernard F Curry, CEO

Rev: 500
Assets: NA
Emp: 1

Curtice Burns Inc
One Lincoln First Square
Rochester, NY 14603
716-325-1020

Manufacturer & marketer of food products.
Type: ASE-CBI
Ind: Food Processing   Grp: Food Processing
Ralph E Winsor, CEO   David McDonald, Chr   Roy Myers, VCh
William D Rice, CFO   Russell Appleyard, Mkt   J Willima Petty, VP

Rev: 695
Assets: 377
Emp: 6

Cuyahoga County Government
1219 Ontario Street
Cleveland, OH 44113
216-443-7000

County government.
Type: County Govt
Ind: Local Govt   Grp: Govt & Non-Prof
Timothy F Hagen, CEO

Rev: 1250
Assets: NM
Emp: 8

CVN Companies Inc
1405 N Xenium Lane
Minneapolis, MN 55441
612-559-8000

Retail goods distributors.
Type: OTC
Ind: Retail/Merch   Grp: Retail
Theodore Diekel, CEO

Rev: 700
Assets: 300
Emp: 4

CVS Inc
One CVS Drive
Woonsocket, RI 02895
401-765-1500

Operator of retail drugstores.
Type: Private-Sub   Par: Melville Corp
Ind: Retail/Merch   Grp: Retail
Harvey Rosenthal, CEO

Rev: NA
Assets: NA
Emp: NA

Cyanamid Canada Inc
2255 Sheppard Avenue E
Willowdale, ON M2J4Y5 Can
416-470-3600

Manufacturer of agricultural chemicals.
Type: Private-Sub-For
Ind: Chemicals   Grp: Basic Industries
W J Foran, CEO

Rev: 298
Assets: 170
Emp: 2

Cyclops Industries Inc
650 Washington Road
Pittsburgh, PA 15228
412-343-4000

Specialty steel manufacturer.
Type: NYSE-CYC
Ind: Steel   Grp: Basic Industries
William H Knoell, CEO   Susan Breon, PR

Rev: 900
Assets: NA
Emp: 7

Organizations Listed Alphabetically

Organization / Address / Phone	Descriptive Information	Revenue / ($ mil)	Assets / ($ mil)	Emp (thous)
Cypress Semiconductor Inc 3901 N First Street San Jose, CA 95134 408-943-2600	Manufacturer, semiconductors, integrated memory circuits. Type: NYSE-CY Ind: Electronics Grp: High Tech T J Rodgers, CEO	Rev: Assets: Emp:		139 245 2
Cyprus Minerals Co 9100 E Mineral Circle Englewood, CO 80155 303-643-5000	Diversified mining company; copper, gold, coal. Type: NYSE-CYM Ind: Energy Grp: Basic Industries Kenneth J Barr, CEO Donald Bellum, VCh Chester B Stone Jr, CFO A J West, IS H T Mulryan, Mkt James C Compton, VP F Steven Mooney, VP Thomas Williams, VP Phillip Wolf, VP William Lampard, VP Richard H Hagman, PR	Rev: Assets: Emp:		1327 1651 7
D'Arcy Masius Benton & Bowles Inc 909 Third Avenue New York, NY 10022 212-758-6200	Nationwide advertising agency. Type: Private Ind: Business Service Grp: Business Service Roy Bostock, CEO	Rev: Assets: Emp:		2750 NA 7
Dade County Government 111 NW First Street Miami, FL 33128 305-375-4176	County government. Type: County Govt Ind: Local Govt Grp: Govt & Non-Prof Stephen P Clark, CEO	Rev: Assets: Emp:		2300 NM 22
Daewoo Group 100 Daewoo Place Carlstadt, NJ 07072 201-896-2824	Manufacturer & importer of electronic equipment; US hdqtrs. Type: Private-Sub-For Ind: Manufacturing Grp: Manufacturing Hyo Bin Im, CEO	Rev: Assets: Emp:		1100 NA 2
Dai Ichi Kangyo Bank Ltd One World Trade Center New York, NY 10048 212-466-5200	Commercial bank. Type: Private-Sub-For Ind: Banking Grp: Financial Toshichi Hashimoto, CEO	Rev: Assets: Emp:		550 5000 2
Dain Bosworth Inc 100 Dain Tower Minneapolis, MN 55402 612-371-2711	Investment firm; securities trading. Type: Private Ind: Securities Grp: Financial Fred Friswold, CEO	Rev: Assets: Emp:		220 2200 1
Dairy Mart Convenience Stores Inc 240 South Road Enfield, CT 06082 203-741-3611	Operator of convienience stores & dairy plant. Type: NASDAQ-DMCV Ind: Retail/Merch Grp: Retail Charles Nirenberg, CEO	Rev: Assets: Emp:		717 400 6
Dairymen Inc 10140 Linn Station Road Louisville, KY 40223 502-426-6455	Producer & distributor of dairy products. Type: Private Ind: Food Processing Grp: Food Processing Jim McDowell, CEO James E Mueller, CFO David Lardner, IS Dr John Edwards, R&D Phillip L Kenney, Mkt James H Sumner, PR	Rev: Assets: Emp:		2420 250 4
Daiwa Bank & Trust Co 75 Rockefeller Plaza New York, NY 10019 212-399-2710	Commercial bank. Type: Private-Sub-For Ind: Banking Grp: Financial Hiroshi Ikeda, CEO	Rev: Assets: Emp:		450 3500 2
Daiwa Securities America Inc One World Fin Ctr 200 Liberty St Tower A New York, NY 10281 212-945-0100	Worlwide securities investment firm. Type: Private Ind: Securities Grp: Financial T Isoda, CEO	Rev: Assets: Emp:		330 3300 1
Dallas Corp 6750 LBJ Freeway Dallas, TX 75240 214-233-6611	Manufacturer of home building supplies. Type: NYSE-DLS Ind: Building Mat Grp: Basic Industries Robert C Haugh, CEO	Rev: Assets: Emp:		323 NA 2
Dallas County Government 411 Elm Street Dallas, TX 75202 214-749-8011	County government. Type: County Govt Ind: Local Govt Grp: Govt & Non-Prof Lee Jackson, CEO	Rev: Assets: Emp:		750 NM 5

Organizations Listed Alphabetically

Organization / Address / Phone	Descriptive Information	Revenue / ($ mil)	Assets / ($ mil)	Emp (thous)
Dallas, City of City Hall Dallas, TX 75201 214-670-4054	City government. Type: City Govt Ind: Local Govt Grp: Govt & Non-Prof Annette Strauss, CEO	Rev: Assets: Emp:		859 NM 14
Dan River Inc 2216 Memorial Drive Danville, VA 24541 804-799-7000	Manufacturer of apparel products. Type: Private Ind: Apparel/Textiles Grp: Consumer Prd L A Hudson, CEO	Rev: Assets: Emp:		500 NA 5
Dana Corp 4500 Dorr Street PO Box 1000 Toledo, OH 43697 419-535-4500	Automotive parts manufacturer. Type: NYSE-DCN Ind: Automotive Grp: Manufacturing Gerald B Mitchell, CEO Southwood Morcott, Pres Robert E Byrket, CFO Robert Cowie, PR	Rev: Assets: Emp:		4936 4786 40
Danaher Corp 3524 Water Street N Washington, DC 20007 202-333-1805	Manufacturer of automotive parts, components. Type: NYSE-DHR Ind: Manufacturing Grp: Manufacturing Steven M Rales, CEO Mitchell P Rales, Pres Arthur Byrne, VCh Teri Lynch, Tres Patrick W Allender, CFO C Scott Branan, VP James Ditkoff, VP Sandy Rogers, PR	Rev: Assets: Emp:		716 576 5
Darigold Inc 635 Elliott W Seattle, WA 98119 206-284-7220	Producer of packaged food products. Type: Private Ind: Food Processing Grp: Food Processing Louis Arrigoni, CEO	Rev: Assets: Emp:		825 NA 3
Dart Group Corp 3300 75th Avenue Landover, MD 20785 301-731-1200	Operator of retail auto parts stores. Type: NASDAQ-DART Ind: Retail/Merch Grp: Retail Herbert Haft, CEO	Rev: Assets: Emp:		406 250 5
Data General Corp 4400 Computer Drive Westboro, MA 01580 508-366-8911	Computer manufacturer; mini computers. Type: NYSE-DGN Ind: Comput/Off Equip Grp: High Tech Edson D DeCastro, CEO Ronald L Skates, Pres Ellen Richstone, Tres Michael B Evans, CFO James J Ryan, IS J Thomas West, R&D Frank Keaney, Sls Ward D MacKenzie, Mkt Michael Klatman, PR	Rev: Assets: Emp:		1365 1078 15
Datapoint Corp 9725 Datapoint Drive San Antonio, TX 78284 512-699-7000	Manufacturer of office equipment; computers, terminals. Type: NYSE Ind: Comput/Off Equip Grp: High Tech A B Edelman, CEO R J Potter, Chr J Novak, VCh B W Monroe, CFO L Wickwar, R&D D Bynum, Mkt C Temple, VP Y LeRoux, VP	Rev: Assets: Emp:		400 NA 4
Dataproducts Corp 6200 Canoga Avenue Woodland Hills, CA 91365 818-887-8000	Manufacturer of computer printers. Type: ASE-DPC Ind: Comput/Off Equip Grp: High Tech Jack C Davis, CEO	Rev: Assets: Emp:		400 NA 3
Dauphin Deposit Corp 213 Market Street Harrisburg, PA 17101 717-255-2121	Bank holding company. Type: NASDAQ-DAPN Ind: Banking Grp: Financial William King, CEO	Rev: Assets: Emp:		500 5000 2
Day & Zimmermann Inc 1818 Market Street Philadelphia, PA 19103 215-299-8000	Engineering, consulting, business services, real estate. Type: Private Ind: Consulting Grp: Business Service Harold L Yoh, CEO	Rev: Assets: Emp:		500 NA 6
Dayco Corp 33 W First Street Dayton, OH 45402 513-226-7000	Manufacturer of automotive parts. Type: Private-Sub Ind: Manufacturing Grp: Manufacturing Donald Ross, CEO	Rev: Assets: Emp:		350 250 4

Organizations Listed Alphabetically

Organization / Address / Phone	Descriptive Information	Revenue / Assets / Emp ($ mil) ($ mil) (thous)		

Dayton Hudson Corp
777 Nicollet Mall
Minneapolis, MN 55402
612-370-6948

National retailer.
Type: NYSE
Ind: Retail/Merch   Grp: Retail
Kenneth A Macke, CEO   Bruce G Allbright, Pres   James T Hale, VCh
Karl Emmerich, Tres   Willard C Shull, CFO   Ralph W Salo, VP
Willard C Shull, VP   Ann H Barkelew, VP   Larry E Carlson, VP
L Fred Hamacher, VP   William Harder, VP   Ann H Barkelew, PR

Rev: 12204
Assets: 6523
Emp: 150

Dayton Industries Inc
11516 N Port Washington Road
Mequon, WI 53092
414-241-6200

Diversified manufacturing company.
Type: Private-Sub   Par: Grainger, W W Inc
Ind: Manufacturing   Grp: Manufacturing
James Windsor, CEO

Rev: 250
Assets: NA
Emp: 2

DCNY Discount Corp of New York Inc
58 Pine Street
New York, NY 10005
212-248-8900

Investment firm; securities trading.
Type: NYSE-DCY
Ind: Securities   Grp: Financial
Edward J Sawicz, CEO

Rev: 178
Assets: 2386
Emp: 1

Dean Foods Co
3600 N River Road
Franklin Park, IL 60131
312-678-1680

Food products company; milk, dairy products.
Type: NYSE-DF
Ind: Food Processing   Grp: Food Processing
Kenneth J Douglas, CEO   Howard M Dean, Chr   Dale I Hecox, Tres
William D Fischer, CFO   John Brenner, IS   George A Muck, R&D
N Dale Finch, Mkt   Thomas L Rose, VP   Thomas A Ravencroft, VP
Terrence J Smith, VP   Roger W Huibregtse, VP   A S Watson, PR

Rev: 1552
Assets: 499
Emp: 7

Dean Witter Reynolds Inc
2 World Trade Center 66th Floor
New York, NY 10006
212-392-2222

Investment firm; nationwide retail brokerage.
Type: Private-Sub   Par: Sears Roebuck & Co
Ind: Securities   Grp: Financial
Philip Purlcell, CEO

Rev: 3500
Assets: 33000
Emp: 19

DeBartolo, Edward J Co Inc
7620 Market Street
Youngstown, OH 44512
216-758-7292

Real estate & operator of race tracks.
Type: Private
Ind: Retail/Food   Grp: Retail
Edward J DeBartolo, CEO

Rev: 1000
Assets: NA
Emp: 10

Deere & Co
John Deere Road
Moline, IL 61265
309-765-8000

Manufacturer of mobile power machinery;farming, building.
Type: NYSE-DE
Ind: Equipment   Grp: Manufacturing
Robert A Hanson, CEO   Hans W Becherer, Pres   Pierre Leroy, Tres
Eugene Schotanus, CFO   Robert A Bulen, IS   Paul F Ohman, R&D
David Stowe, VP   Thomas Gildehaus, VP   Joseph England, VP
Neil Christiansen, VP   Chester K Lasell, PR

Rev: 5365
Assets: 5245
Emp: 38

Deere, John Capital Corp
1 E First Street
Reno, NV 89501
702-786-5527

Finance subsidiary of parent corporation.
Type: Private-Sub   Par: Deere & Co
Ind: Non-Bank Fin   Grp: Financial
Robert A Hanson, CEO

Rev: 334
Assets: 2958
Emp: 1

Deere, John Ltd
Canal Bank Road
Welland, ON L3B3N3 Can
416-734-4501

Manufacturer of farming & construction equipment.
Type: Private-Sub-For
Ind: Equipment   Grp: Manufacturing
Stan Hiseler, CEO

Rev: 468
Assets: 425
Emp: 2

DeKalb Corp
3100 Sycamore Road
DeKalb, IL 60115
815-758-3461

Research, exploration of gas, manufacturer surgical equip.
Type: NASDAQ-SEEDB
Ind: Food Processing   Grp: Food Processing
Bruce P Bickner, CEO

Rev: 230
Assets: 203
Emp: 5

Del Monte Foods Corp
201 Alhambra Circle
Coral Gables, FL 33134
305-520-1000

Producer & distributor of packaged foods; fruit, pineapples.
Type: Private-Sub   Par: RJR Nabisco Inc
Ind: Food Processing   Grp: Food Processing
Robert Carbonell, CEO

Rev: NA
Assets: NA
Emp: NA

Delaware Management Investment Advisors
10 Penn Center Plaza
Philadelphia, PA 19103
215-988-1333

Investment firm; pension management.
Type: Private
Ind: Non-Bank Fin   Grp: Financial
John H Durham, CEO

Rev: 400
Assets: 15400
Emp: 1

Organization / Address / Phone	Descriptive Information	Revenue / Assets / Emp ($ mil) ($ mil) (thous)		

Organization / Address / Phone	Descriptive Information			
Delaware North Companies 700 Delaware Avenue Buffalo, NY 14209 716-881-6500	Airport & sports concessions, tracks, owners & operators. Type: Private Ind: Leisure Time Grp: Consumer Service Jeremy M Jacobs, CEO	Rev: Assets: Emp:	1500 NA 35	
Delaware, State of Legislative Hall Dover, DE 19901 302-736-4000	State government. Type: State Govt Ind: State/Prov Govt Grp: Govt & Non-Prof Michael Castle, CEO	Rev: Assets: Emp:	1907 NM 21	
Delchamps Inc 305 Delchamp Drive Mobile, AL 36602 205-433-0431	Operator of retail food stores. Type: NASDAQ-DLCH Ind: Retail/Food Grp: Retail Alfred Delchamps, CEO	Rev: Assets: Emp:	800 350 6	
Delco Electronics Co 700 E Firmin Kokomo, IN 46904 317-457-8461	Manufacturer of electronic automotive parts & components. Type: Private-Sub Par: General Motors Corp Ind: Automotive Grp: Manufacturing Donald Atwood, CEO	Rev: Assets: Emp:	NA NA NA	
Dell Computer Corp 9505 Arboretum Blvd Austin, TX 78759 512-338-4400	Manufacturer of personal computers. Type: NASDAQ-Dell Ind: Comput/Off Equip Grp: High Tech Michael Dell, CEO	Rev: Assets: Emp:	258 150 2	
Delmarva Power & Light Co 800 King Street Wilmington, DE 19899 302-429-3011	Electric utility company. Type: NYSE-DEW Ind: Utility Grp: Utilities Nevius M Curtis, CEO B Graham, Tres P Gerrittsen, CFO W Lyons, Ops	Rev: Assets: Emp:	768 1915 3	
Deloitte Haskins & Sells Ltd 95 Wellington Street W Toronto, ON M5J2P4 Can 416-861-9700	National accounting firm. Type: Private Ind: Accounting Grp: Business Service Giles Meikle, CEO	Rev: Assets: Emp:	170 NM 3	
Deloitte, Haskins & Sells Inc 1114 Avenue of the Americas New York, NY 10036 212-790-0500	Nationwide accounting firm. Type: Private Ind: Accounting Grp: Business Service J Michael Cook, CEO	Rev: Assets: Emp:	2000 NA 25	
Delta Air Lines Inc Hartsfield Atlanta Intl Airport Atlanta, GA 30320 404-765-2600	Nationwide airline. Type: NYSE Ind: Airline Grp: Consumer Service Ronald W Allen, CEO Hollis Harris, Pres Thomas Roeck Jr, CFO Robert Cowart, IS A H Kolakowski, Sls W Whitley Hawkins, Mkt Rex McCelland, Ops H Alger, VP Lawson Rollins, VP John Serger, VP W Suggs, VP James Taylor, VP James W Callison, IR Bill Berry, PR	Rev: Assets: Emp:	6915 5748 38	
Delta Woodside Industries Inc 233 N Main Street Greenville, SC 29601 803-232-8300	Textile manufacturing company. Type: NYSE-DLW Ind: Apparel/Textiles Grp: Consumer Prd E Erwin Maddrey, CEO	Rev: Assets: Emp:	500 500 4	
Deltic Farm & Lumber Co 200 Peach Street El Dorado, AR 71730 501-878-5194	Forest products company; lumber, building products. Type: Private-Sub Par: Murphy Oil Corp Ind: Paper/Forest Prd Grp: Basic Industries Harold Monzingo, CEO	Rev: Assets: Emp:	NA NA NA	
Deluxe Check Printers Inc 1080 W County Road F St Paul, MN 55126 612-483-7111	Bank check printing company. Type: NYSE-DLX Ind: Business Service Grp: Business Service Harold V Haverty, CEO Jerry K Twogood, VCh Charles M Osborne, CFO Steven R Jensen, IS Kenneth Chupita, R&D Terry J Egge, Sls W R Phillips Jr, Mkt Neil Beckwith, VP Lillard Christ, VP Terry Egge, VP Mark Grritton, VP Stuart Alexander, PR	Rev: Assets: Emp:	1196 786 17	

Organizations Listed Alphabetically

Organization / Address / Phone	Descriptive Information	Revenue / ($ mil)	Assets / ($ mil)	Emp (thous)
Democratic National Committee 430 S Capitol Street SE Washington, DC 20003 202-863-8000	Political party, national organization. Type: Federal Govt Ind: Membership Org Grp: Govt & Non-Prof Ronald H Brown, CEO	Rev: Assets: Emp:	1000 NM 5	
DeMoulas Super Markets Inc 875 East Street Tewksbury, MA 01876 508-851-7381	Grocery stores. Type: Private Ind: Retail/Food Grp: Retail T A DeMoulas, CEO	Rev: Assets: Emp:	1000 NA 9	
Denison Mines Ltd 3900 Royal Bank Plaza Toronto, ON M5J2K2 Can 416-865-1991	Energy resource company; uranium mines, oil & natural gas. Type: TOR Ind: Metals/Mining Grp: Basic Industries H E Roman-Barber, CEO	Rev: Assets: Emp:	360 1003 5	
Dennison Manufacturing Co 300 Howard Street Framingham, MA 01701 508-879-0511	Diversified manufacturing; printing, stationery, packaging. Type: NYSE-DSN Ind: Manufacturing Grp: Manufacturing Nelson S Gifford, CEO Nelson S Gifford, Chr John B Gray, Pres Henry Lewis, VCh Daniel J Sullivan, CFO Hugh McGlinchey, IS Bert E Conner Jr, Mkt Raymond F Richter, Ops Jonathan V Hubbard, PR	Rev: Assets: Emp:	722 516 8	
Denny's Inc 16700 Valley View Avenue La Mirada, CA 90637 714-739-8100	Nationwide operator of restaurants. Type: Private-Sub Par: TW Service Inc Ind: Food/Lodging Grp: Consumer Service Samuel Maw, CEO	Rev: Assets: Emp:	1650 NA 63	
Denver, City of City & County Bldg Denver, CO 80202 303-575-2721	City government. Type: City Govt Ind: Local Govt Grp: Govt & Non-Prof Federico Pena, CEO	Rev: Assets: Emp:	808 NM 11	
Department of Justice Canada 239 Wellington Street Justice Bldg Ottawa, ON K1A0H8 Can 613-995-2569	Federal government agency. Type: Federal Govt Ind: Federal Govt Grp: Govt & Non-Prof John C Tait, CEO	Rev: Assets: Emp:	510 NM 1	
Derlan Industries Inc 95 King Street E Toronto, ON M5C1G4 Can 416-364-5852	Diversified manufacturing company. Type: TOR Ind: Manufacturing Grp: Manufacturing D Coughlan, CEO	Rev: Assets: Emp:	340 213 5	
Des Moines, City of City Hall East First & Locust Streets Des Moines, IA 50307 515-283-4944	City government. Type: City Govt Ind: Local Govt Grp: Govt & Non-Prof John P Dorrian, CEO	Rev: Assets: Emp:	250 NM 2	
DeSoto Inc 1700 S Mount Prospect Road Des Plaines, IL 60017 312-391-9000	Paint manufacturer. Type: NYSE-DSO Ind: Building Mat Grp: Basic Industries Richard R Missar, CEO Nicholas Vittore, Tres William Lamey, CFO Harvey Beeferman, R&D T Farrell Shoffeitt, VP Jay Barreiro, VP	Rev: Assets: Emp:	403 219 2	
DeTomaso Industries 107 Monmouth Street Red Bank, NJ 07701 201-842-7200	Manufacturer of motorcycles, car bodies. Type: NASDAQ-DTOM Ind: Automotive Grp: Manufacturing Alejandro DeTomaso, CEO	Rev: Assets: Emp:	400 250 2	
Detroit Edison Co 2000 Second Avenue Detroit, MI 48226 313-237-8000	Electric utility company. Type: NYSE Ind: Utility Grp: Utilities Walter J McCarthy, CEO John E Lobbia, Pres Ernest L Grove, VCh Ronald Gresens, CFO Stanley Catola, R&D J Philip Lenihan, Mkt William Orser, Ops Willard Holland, VP Leon S Cohan, VP M Jane Kay, VP Saul Waldman, VP Susan Beale, VP Saul J Waldman, IR Bernadette Bland, PR	Rev: Assets: Emp:	3102 10060 10	

Organizations Listed Alphabetically

Organization / Address / Phone	Descriptive Information	Revenue / ($ mil)	Assets / ($ mil)	Emp (thous)
Detroit Medical Center Inc 4201 St Antoine Detroit, MI 48201 313-745-5192	Operator of hospitals & clinics. Type: Private Ind: Health Care Grp: Consumer Service Joseph Hudson, CEO	Rev: Assets: Emp:	989 NA 12	
Detroit, City of City & County Bldg 2 Woodward Ave Detroit, MI 48226 313-224-3400	City government. Type: City Govt Ind: Local Govt Grp: Govt & Non-Prof Coleman A Young, CEO	Rev: Assets: Emp:	1763 NM 19	
Deutsche Bank AG 9 W 57th Street New York, NY 10019 212-940-8000	Commercial bank. Type: Private-Sub-For Ind: Banking Grp: Financial Douglas Staecker, CEO	Rev: Assets: Emp:	450 3500 1	
Deutsche Bank Capital Corp 40 Wall Street New York, NY 10005 212-612-0600	Investment firm; securities trading. Type: Private Ind: Securities Grp: Financial Christian Streinger, CEO	Rev: Assets: Emp:	275 3300 1	
Dexter Corp One Elm Street Windsor Locks, CT 06096 203-627-9051	Manufacturer of industrial chemical coatings. Type: NYSE-DEX Ind: Chemicals Grp: Basic Industries David L Coffin, CEO K Grahame Walker, Pres Stephen Raffay, VCh Robert E McGill, CFO Alan Larese, IS Kathleen Burdett, VP Joseph Stokes, VP Michael Devaney, VP Robert E McGill, PR	Rev: Assets: Emp:	827 626 6	
DHL Airways/Worldwide Express Inc 333 Twin Dolphin Drive Redwood City, CA 94065 415-593-7474	Air express service company. Type: Private Ind: Transport Grp: Business Service Patrick Foley, CEO	Rev: Assets: Emp:	1500 NA 15	
Diamandis Communications Corp 1515 Broadway New York, NY 10036 212-719-6000	Producer & distributor of motion pictures. Type: Private Ind: Publishing/Com Grp: Consumer Service Peter Diamandis, CEO	Rev: Assets: Emp:	550 NA 1	
Diamond Bathurst Corp 4343 Anchor Place Parkway Tampa, FL 33634 813-884-0000	Diversified manufacturing company; US headquarters. Type: Private-Sub-For Ind: Manufacturing Grp: Manufacturing Vincent Naimoli, CEO	Rev: Assets: Emp:	550 250 5	
Diamond Shamrock R & M Corp 9830 Colonnade Blvd San Antonio, TX 78230 512-641-6800	Regional refiner & marketer of petroleum products. Type: NYSE-DRM Ind: Energy Grp: Basic Industries Roger R Hemminghaus, CEO Dewey Mark, Pres Robert Becker, CFO William Klesse, R&D A W O'Donnell, Mkt J E Prater, VP Harry Wright, VP Gary E Johnson, VP Robert Beadle, VP	Rev: Assets: Emp:	1804 843 4	
Diasonics Inc 230 Utah Avenue San Francisco, CA 94080 415-872-2722	Manufacturer of X-ray equipment. Type: ASE Ind: Health Care Grp: Consumer Service A S Waxman, CEO	Rev: Assets: Emp:	350 200 2	
Dibrell Brothers 512 Bridge Street Danville, VA 24541 804-792-7511	Manufacturing company. Type: NASDAQ-DBRL Ind: Manufacturing Grp: Manufacturing Richard Bridgeford, CEO	Rev: Assets: Emp:	685 500 5	
Dictaphone Corp 3191 Broadbridge Avenue Stratford, CT 06497 203-381-7000	Manufacturer of dictating equipment. Type: Private-Sub Par: Pitney Bowes Inc Ind: Comput/Off Equip Grp: High Tech George Harvey, CEO	Rev: Assets: Emp:	NA NA NA	
Diebold Inc 818 Mulberry Road SE Canton, OH 44711 216-489-4000	Manufacturer of safes & security devices. Type: NYSE-DBD Ind: Comput/Off Equip Grp: High Tech Robert W Mahoney, CEO	Rev: Assets: Emp:	451 455 5	

Organization / Address / Phone	Descriptive Information	Revenue / ($ mil)	Assets / ($ mil)	Emp (thous)
DiGiorgio Corp One Maritime Plaza San Francisco, CA 94111 415-765-0100	Food processing company. Type: NYSE-DIG Ind: Food Processing Grp: Food Processing Peter F Scott, CEO Benjamin Zdatny, Pres Christine D Timmerman, Tres Kent P Ainsworth, CFO Robert E Mellor, VP Lary L Davis, VP Norman P Adler, VP Kenneth T Foreman, VP Edward J Gallagher, VP Eugene P Lipka, VP Selma Silverman, IR	Rev: 1046 Assets: 226 Emp: 5		
Digital Communications Inc 1000 Alderman Drive Alpharetta, GA 30201 404-442-4000	Computer communications products. Type: NYSE-DCA Ind: Comput/Off Equip Grp: High Tech John C Bacon, CEO	Rev: 228 Assets: 252 Emp: 2		
Digital Equipment Corp 146 Main Street Maynard, MA 01754 617-493-5111	International manufacturer of computers. Type: NYSE-DEC Ind: Comput/Off Equip Grp: High Tech Kenneth H Olsen, CEO Winston R Hindle Jr, Pres Ilene Jacobs, Tres James M Osterhoff, CFO Rose Ann Giordano, IS Samuel H Fuller, R&D John F Smith, Sls John Shields, Mkt James Cudmore, Ops Robert Glorioso, VP David Grainger, VP William Hanson, VP William Hefner, VP Robert Hughes, VP William Johnson, VP Albert E Mullin Jr, PR	Rev: 11475 Assets: 10112 Emp: 122		
Digital Equipment of Canada Ltd 100 Herzberg Road Kanata, ON K2K2A6 Can 613-592-5111	Manufacturer of computers. Type: Private-Sub-For Ind: Comput/Off Equip Grp: High Tech not available, CEO	Rev: 680 Assets: 255 Emp: 3		
Dillard Department Stores Inc 900 W Capitol Avenue Little Rock, AR 72201 501-376-5200	Department store retail company. Type: ASE-DDSA Ind: Retail/Merch Grp: Retail William Dillard, CEO William Dillard Jr, Pres E Ray Kemp, VCh James I Freeman, CFO Corky Ritchie, IS Mike Dillard, Sls Alex Dillard, Mkt James Darr, Ops James Freeman, PR	Rev: 2558 Assets: 2068 Emp: 23		
Dillingham Corp 2 Embarcadero Drive San Francisco, CA 94111 415-362-1501	Construction & engineering company. Type: Private Ind: Real Estate/Bldg Grp: Business Service Donald K Stager, CEO	Rev: 1500 Assets: NA Emp: 5		
Dillon Co 700 E 30th Hutchinson, KS 67501 316-663-6801	Owner & operator of retail supermarkets. Type: Private-Sub Par: Kroger Co Ind: Retail/Food Grp: Retail David Dillon, CEO	Rev: 2000 Assets: NA Emp: 20		
Dillon Reed & Co Inc 535 Madison Avenue New York, NY 10022 212-906-7000	Investment firm; securities trading. Type: Private Ind: Securities Grp: Financial John Birkelund, CEO	Rev: 550 Assets: 5500 Emp: 1		
Dime Savings Bank of New York Inc 1225 Franklin Avenue Garden City, NY 11530 516-227-6030	Thrift institution. Type: NYSE-DME Ind: Savings & Loan Grp: Financial Harry W Albright, CEO Richard D Parsons, Pres Lawrence W Peters, VCh Dennis E Stark, CFO John J Heim, IS John J Monaghan, R&D Edward B Kramer, Mkt Edward B Kramer, PR	Rev: 1051 Assets: 12007 Emp: 6		
Dionex Corp 1228 Titan Way Sunnyvale, CA 94986 408-737-0700	Manufacturer of research instruments, industrial products. Type: OTC Ind: Instruments Grp: High Tech A B Bowman, CEO	Rev: 300 Assets: 200 Emp: 1		
Directories America Inc 7015 College Blvd Overland Park, KS 66211 913-491-7000	Publisher of phone directories. Type: Private-Sub Par: United Telecommunications Inc Ind: Publishing/Com Grp: Consumer Service Robert Johnson, CEO	Rev: NA Assets: NA Emp: NA		

Organizations Listed Alphabetically

Organization / Address / Phone	Descriptive Information	Revenue ($ mil)	Assets ($ mil)	Emp (thous)
Disney, Walt Co 500 Buena Vista Street Burbank, CA 91521 818-840-1000	Entertainment company; theme parks, films, products. Type: NYSE Ind: Leisure Time Grp: Consumer Service Michael D Eisner, CEO Frank Wells, Pres Roy E Disney, VCh John H Forsgren, Tres Gary L Wilson, CFO Bud Mathaisel, IS Erwin D Okun, VP Joe Shapiro, VP Neil R McCarthy, VP Doris A Smith, VP Erwin D Okun, IR	Rev: 3438 Assets: 5109 Emp: 39		
Disney, Walt World Inc Lake Buena Vista Buena Vista, FL 32830 407-824-4024	Operator of theme amusement parks & hotels. Type: Private-Sub Par: Disney, Walt Co Ind: Leisure Time Grp: Consumer Service Richard Nunis, CEO	Rev: NA Assets: NA Emp: NA		
Disneyland Inc 1313 Harbor Blvd Anaheim, CA 92802 714-824-4024	Operator of theme amusement park. Type: Private-Sub Par: Disney, Walt Co Ind: Leisure Time Grp: Consumer Service Richard Nunis, CEO	Rev: NA Assets: NA Emp: NA		
Diversified Energies Inc 201 S 7th Street Minneapolis, MN 55402 612-372-4664	Oil & gas exploration, development & distribution. Type: NYSE-DEI Ind: Utility Grp: Utilities Albert D Etchelecu, CEO Dan Dienstbier, VCh Lawrence E McNulty, Tres Curtis Peterson, CFO Gary Peterson, VP John D Somrock, VP Dwight Oglesby, VP Norman Jepsen, VP	Rev: 764 Assets: 819 Emp: 5		
Diversified Industries Inc 101 S Hanley Road St Louis, MO 63105 314-862-8200	Manufacturers of various metals. Type: NYSE-DMC Ind: Metals/Mining Grp: Basic Industries Ben Fixman, CEO	Rev: 250 Assets: 200 Emp: 3		
Dixie Yarns 1100 S Watkins Street Chattanooga, TN 37401 615-698-2501	Manufacturer of textile products. Type: NASDAQ-DXYN Ind: Apparel/Textiles Grp: Consumer Prd Daniel Frierson, CEO James C Fry, Pres Morgan M Schuessler, CFO Robert J Denton, IS Lyle Claiborne, R&D E Brian Gibson, IR Ray Jimison, PR	Rev: 600 Assets: 250 Emp: 10		
Doane Raymond Associates Ltd 2000 Barrington Street Halifax, NS B3J2P8 Can 902-421-1734	National accounting firm. Type: Private Ind: Accounting Grp: Business Service Glenn Williams, CEO	Rev: 128 Assets: NM Emp: 2		
Dobbs Houses Inc 5100 Poplar Avenue Memphis, TN 38137 901-766-3600	Operator of catering & restaurant businesses. Type: Private Ind: Food/Lodging Grp: Consumer Service Jimmy Dobbs, CEO	Rev: 500 Assets: NA Emp: 2		
Dodge Car & Truck Div 12000 Chrysler Drive Highland Park, MI 48288 313-956-5741	Car & truck manufacturer. Type: Private-Sub Par: Chrysler Corp Ind: Automotive Grp: Manufacturing Jerome York, CEO	Rev: NA Assets: NA Emp: NA		
Doe Run Co 11885 Lackland Road St Louis, MO 63146 314-991-7140	Lead mining & minerals processing company. Type: Private-Sub Par: Flour Corp Ind: Metals/Mining Grp: Basic Industries J Zelms, CEO	Rev: NA Assets: NA Emp: NA		
Dofasco Inc 1330 Burlington Street E Hamilton, ON L8N3J5 Can 416-544-3761	Steel manufacturing company. Type: TOR Ind: Steel Grp: Basic Industries Frank H Sherman, CEO Paul J Phoenix, Chr Bill P Solski, Tres Thomas Van Zuiden, CFO John W Craven, R&D William H Mulveney, Sls David H Samson, VP H Graham Wilson, VP John H McAllister, VP Noel G Thomas, VP L Allen Root, VP	Rev: 2535 Assets: 5069 Emp: 23		

Organizations Listed Alphabetically

Organization / Address / Phone	Descriptive Information	Revenue / Assets / Emp ($ mil) ($ mil) (thous)		

Dole Packaged Foods Inc
50 California Street
San Francisco, CA 94111
415-986-3000

Producer of canned & packaged fruit, nuts & juices.
Type: Private-Sub   Par: Castle & Cooke Inc
Ind: Food Processing   Grp: Food Processing
Harold Reed, CEO

Rev: NA
Assets: NA
Emp: NA

Dollar General Corp
427 Beech Street
Scottsville, KY 42164
502-237-5444

Retailing company; dry goods & clothing.
Type: NASDAQ-DOLR
Ind: Retail/Merch   Grp: Retail
Calister Turner, CEO

Rev: 590
Assets: 300
Emp: 7

Doman Industries Ltd
435 Trunk Road
Duncan, BC V9L9Z9 Can
604-748-3711

Manufacturer of lumber products.
Type: Private
Ind: Paper/Forest Prd   Grp: Basic Industries
Harbanse Doman, CEO

Rev: 340
Assets: 170
Emp: 1

Dome Petroleum Ltd
333 7th Avenue SW
Calgary, AB T2P2H8 Can
403-231-3000

Oil & gas exploration & production company.
Type: TOR
Ind: Energy   Grp: Basic Industries
J H MacDonald, CEO

Rev: 1266
Assets: 3529
Emp: 4

Dominicks Finer Foods Inc
555 N Northwest Road
Northlake, IL 60164
312-562-1000

Operator of retail food supermarkets.
Type: Private
Ind: Food Processing   Grp: Food Processing
Jim DiMatteo, CEO

Rev: 2000
Assets: NA
Emp: 10

Dominion Bankshares Inc
213 S Jefferson Street
Roanoke, VA 24040
703-563-7749

Commercial bank.
Type: NASDAQ-DMBK
Ind: Banking   Grp: Financial
Warner N Dalhouse, CEO   David L Caudill, Pres   Donald Kinzer, CFO
William Vance, IS   Susan L Koch, R&D   Carol S Jarratt, Mkt
George Yowell, VP   Byron L Yost, VP   Carlyle Stull, VP
Thompson Goodwin, VP   Lacy Edwards, VP   J Richard Carling, VP
Brenda McDaniel, PR

Rev: 898
Assets: 9204
Emp: 6

Dominion of Canada General Insurance Co
165 University Avenue
Toronto, ON M5H3B9 Can
416-362-7231

Property & casualty insurance company.
Type: TOR
Ind: Insurance   Grp: Insurance
Donald Waugh, CEO

Rev: 291
Assets: 491
Emp: 1

Dominion Resources Inc
701 E Byrd Street
Richmond, VA 23219
804-755-5700

Holding company for electric & natural gas utilities.
Type: NYSE-D
Ind: Utility   Grp: Utilities
William W Berry, CEO   Thomas E Capps, Pres   Ronald Leasburg, VCh
O James Peterson III, CFO   Billy Boykin, IS   Tyndall Baucom, VP
Everand Munsey, VP   J Kennerly Davis, VP   Patricia A Wilkerson, IR
Everard Munsey, PR

Rev: 3344
Assets: 9495
Emp: 15

Dominion Securities Inc
Commerce Court S
Toronto, ON M5L1A7 Can
416-864-4000

Investment company; brokerage.
Type: Private
Ind: Securities   Grp: Financial
James E Pitblado, CEO

Rev: 298
Assets: 255
Emp: 2

Dominion Textile Inc
1950 O Rue Sherbrooke
Montreal, PQ H3C3L1 Can
514-989-6000

Manufacturer of textile & apparel products.
Type: TOR-DOM
Ind: Apparel/Textiles   Grp: Consumer Prd
Thomas R Bell, CEO   Kenneth Doel, Tres   Milo A Smith, CFO
William N Gagnon, IS   Charles A McCrae, VP   Alex McAslan, VP
Sandy Mackay-Smith, VP   William Rusack, VP   Regean Claude, VP
Kay Craig, VP

Rev: 1034
Assets: 1228
Emp: 14

Domino's Pizza Inc
30 Frank Lloyd Wright Drive
Ann Arbor, MI 48105
313-668-4000

Pizza franchises.
Type: Private
Ind: Food/Lodging   Grp: Consumer Service
Thomas S Monaghan, CEO

Rev: 1000
Assets: NA
Emp: 15

Organizations Listed Alphabetically

Organization / Address / Phone	Descriptive Information	Revenue / Assets / Emp ($ mil) ($ mil) (thous)		

Domtar Inc
395 Boul de Maisonneuve O
Montreal, PQ H3C3M1 Can
514-848-5400

Manufacturer of specialty chemicals & building materials.
Type: NYSE-DTC
Ind: Chemicals   Grp: Basic Industries
James H Smith, CEO   Roger Ashby, Pres   Raymond Pinard, VCh
Derek Speirs, CFO   Steven Danyluk, R&D   W Boyd Henderson, Ops
Neil Martin, VP   Pierre Messier, VP   Gilles Pharand, VP
Bernard Sanssoucy, VP   Laurence Sellyn, VP

Rev: 2298
Assets: 2708
Emp: 16

Donaldson Co
1400 W 94th Street
Minneapolis, MN 55431
612-887-3131

Manufacturer of filter systems.
Type: NYSE-DCI
Ind: Manufacturing   Grp: Manufacturing
William A Hodder, CEO

Rev: 260
Assets: 200
Emp: 2

Donaldson, Lufkin & Jenrette Inc
140 Broadway
New York, NY 10005
212-504-3000

Investment firm; securities trading.
Type: Private
Ind: Securities   Grp: Financial
C John Charlsty, CEO

Rev: 2200
Assets: 20900
Emp: 3

Donnelley, R R & Sons Co
2223 Martin Luther King Drive
Chicago, IL 60616
312-326-8000

Publisher of business information.
Type: NYSE-DNY
Ind: Business Service   Grp: Business Service
John B Schwemm, CEO   John R Walter, Pres   Charles Haffner, VCh
Frank Jarc, CFO   Richard Brinkmann, IS   N Martellotto, R&D
Carl Doty, Ops   John A Capstick, VP   John S Oberhill, VP
Arthur C Prine Jr, IR   James T Ratcliffe, PR

Rev: 2878
Assets: 2346
Emp: 21

Donnelly Directory Corp
287 Bowman Avenue
Purchase, NY 10577
914-933-6400

Manufacturer of telephone directories, business directories.
Type: Private-Sub   Par: Dun & Bradstreet Corp
Ind: Publishing/Com   Grp: Consumer Service
Kenneth Johnson, CEO

Rev: NA
Assets: NA
Emp: NA

Donohue Inc
1150 Claire Fontaine
Quebec, PQ G1R5G4 Can
418-522-6471

Forest products company.
Type: TOR
Ind: Paper/Forest Prd   Grp: Basic Industries
Charles Albert Poissant, CEO   Paul Premont, Pres   P Denis Hamel, VCh
Richard Garneau, CFO   Gerard Arsenuault, R&D   J Andre Fortin, Sls
Andre Marcoux, Mkt   Jacques Massicotte, Ops

Rev: 551
Assets: 771
Emp: 4

Doskocil Companies Inc
321 N Main Street
Hutchinson, KS 67504
316-663-1000

Metal fabricating & construction company.
Type: NASDAQ-DOSK
Ind: Building Mat   Grp: Basic Industries
Larry D Doskocil, CEO

Rev: 275
Assets: 250
Emp: 1

Doubleday & Co Inc
245 Park Avenue
New York, NY 10167
212-984-7561

Consumer book publishing company.
Type: Private
Ind: Publishing/Com   Grp: Consumer Service
Robert Riger, CEO

Rev: 990
Assets: NA
Emp: 9

Douglas & Lomason Co
24600 Hallwood Court
Framingham, MI 48018
313-478-7800

Manufacturer of automotive parts.
Type: NASDAQ-DOUG
Ind: Automotive   Grp: Manufacturing
Harry Lomason, CEO

Rev: 300
Assets: 200
Emp: 4

Douglas Aircraft Co
3855 Lakewood Blvd
Long Beach, CA 90846
213-593-5511

Manufacturer of commercial & military aircraft.
Type: Private-Sub   Par: McDonnell Douglas Corp
Ind: Aerospace   Grp: High Tech
Robert Hood, CEO

Rev: NA
Assets: NA
Emp: NA

Dover Corp
277 Park Avenue
New York, NY 10172
212-826-7160

Elevator manufacturer.
Type: NYSE-DOV
Ind: Equipment   Grp: Manufacturing
Gary L Roubos, CEO   John F McNiff, CFO   Edward Kata, R&D
Cloyd Laporte, VP   Alfred Suesser, VP   John F McNiff, PR

Rev: 1956
Assets: 1366
Emp: 20

Dover Elevator International Inc
6750 Poplar Avenue
Memphis, TN 38138
601-342-4300

Manufacturer of elevators & elevator parts.
Type: Private-Sub   Par: Dover Corp
Ind: Equipment   Grp: Manufacturing
John B Apple, CEO

Rev: NA
Assets: NA
Emp: NA

Organizations Listed Alphabetically

Organization / Address / Phone	Descriptive Information	Revenue ($ mil)	Assets ($ mil)	Emp (thous)
Dow Chemical Canada Ltd 1086 Modeland Road Sarnia, ON N7T7K7 Can 519-339-3131	Diversified worldwide chemical company. Type: Private-Sub Ind: Chemicals Grp: Basic Industries David T Buzzelli, CEO	Rev: 1275	Assets: NA	Emp: 4
Dow Chemical Co 2030 Willard H Dow Center Midland, MI 48674 517-636-1000	Worldwide diversified chemical company. Type: NYSE-DOW Ind: Chemicals Grp: Basic Industries Paul F Oreffice, CEO Frank Popoff, Chr Joseph G Temple, VCh J Pedro Reinhard, Tres Enrique C Falla, CFO D P Sheetz, R&D Keith McKennon, VP T K Smith, PR	Rev: 16682	Assets: 16239	Emp: 56
Dow Corning Corp 2200 W Salzburg Road Auburn, MI 48611 517-496-4000	Manufacturer of specialty coatings & glass products. Type: Private Ind: Manufacturing Grp: Manufacturing Lawrence Reed, CEO Edward Steinhoff, CFO Robert E Chapman, IS Donald R Weyenberg, R&D John W Westcott, PR	Rev: 1500	Assets: 1500	Emp: 6
Dow Jones & Co 200 Liberty Street World Financial Center New York, NY 10281 212-416-2000	Publishing company; Wall Street Journal, Barron's, newspapers. Type: NYSE Ind: Publishing/Com Grp: Consumer Service Warren H Phillips, CEO Ray Shaw, Pres Kenneth L Burrenga, CFO William Dunn, IS Danforth W Austin, IR Jim Ambrosio, PR	Rev: 1603	Assets: 2112	Emp: 11
Downey Savings & Loan Assn Inc 3200 Bristol Street Costa Mesa, CA 92626 714-549-8811	Thrift institution. Type: Private Ind: Savings & Loan Grp: Financial Maurice L McAlister, CEO G H McQuarrie, Chr A J Morsillo, CFO R Silver, IS	Rev: 331	Assets: 4333	Emp: 1
DPL (Dayton Power & Light) Corp Courthouse Plaza SW Dayton, OH 45402 513-224-6000	Electric power utility. Type: NYSE-DPL Ind: Utility Grp: Utilities Peter H Forster, CEO Allen M Hill, Pres Robert E Buerger, VCh Paul Anderson, CFO Judy Lansaw, IS Stephen Koziar, Mkt Lloyd Lewis, VP	Rev: 1044	Assets: 2338	Emp: 4
Dr Pepper/Seven Up Inc 5523 E Mockingbird Lane Dallas, TX 75265 214-824-0331	Manufacturer of soft drinks & bottling company. Type: Private Ind: Beverage Grp: Food Processing John R Albers, CEO	Rev: 500	Assets: NA	Emp: 1
Dravo Corp One Oliver Plaza Pittsburgh, PA 15222 412-566-3000	Mining company; lime, crushed stone. Type: NYSE-DRV Ind: Manufacturing Grp: Manufacturing William G Roth, CEO	Rev: 1000	Assets: 500	Emp: 5
Dresdner Bank AG 60 Broad Street New York, NY 10004 212-425-4640	Commercial bank. Type: Private-Sub-For Ind: Banking Grp: Financial Winfried H Spaeh, CEO	Rev: 450	Assets: 3500	Emp: 1
Dress Barn Inc 88 Hamilton Avenue Stamford, CT 06904 203-327-4242	Operator of retail women's wear stores. Type: NASDAQ-DBRN Ind: Retail/Merch Grp: Retail Elliott S Jaffe, CEO	Rev: 200	Assets: 100	Emp: 3
Dresser Canada Inc 6688 Kitimat Road Mississauga, ON L5N1P8 Can 416-826-8411	Oil & gas exploration & distribution. Type: Private-Sub-For Ind: Energy Grp: Basic Industries B St John, CEO	Rev: 275	Assets: 196	Emp: 2

Organizations Listed Alphabetically

Organization / Address / Phone	Descriptive Information	Revenue / Assets / Emp	
		($ mil) ($ mil) (thous)	

Dresser Industries Inc
1600 Pacific Avenue
Dallas, TX 75201
214-740-6000

Manufacturer of equipment for oil & gas drilling.
Type: NYSE-DI
Ind: Oil Service   Grp: Business Service
John J Murphy, CEO   Bill D St John, VCh   Paul W Willey, Tres
David McElvain, CFO   William Bradford, Ops   Carroll Browning, VP
James Corboy, VP   George Korb, VP   Ralph Ytterberg, VP
Ardon Judd, VP   Gene Leeson, VP   Herbert M Ryan, PR

Rev: 3942
Assets: 2899
Emp: 31

Drexel Burnham Lambert Inc
60 Broad Street
New York, NY 10004
212-480-6000

Investment banking firm.
Type: Private
Ind: Securities   Grp: Financial
Frederick H Joseph, CEO

Rev: 3300
Assets: NA
Emp: 10

Dreyfus Corp
767 Fifth Avenue
New York, NY 10153
212-715-6000

Investment company; consumer mutual funds.
Type: NYSE-DRY
Ind: Non-Bank Fin   Grp: Financial
Howard Stein, CEO   Julien M Smerling, VCh   Alan Eisner, CFO
Monte J Gordon, R&D   Rolf Towe, VP   Mathew Baxter, VP
Robert F Dubuss, VP

Rev: 268
Assets: 763
Emp: 2

Drug Trading Co
1960 Eglington Avenue E
Scarborough, ON M1L2M5 Can
416-288-1100

Retail & wholesale company; toiletries, drugs.
Type: TOR
Ind: Retail/Merch   Grp: Retail
J Spence, CEO

Rev: 373
Assets: 213
Emp: 1

Drummond Coal Corp
530 Beacon Parkway
Birmingham, AL 35209
205-945-6500

Coal production.
Type: Private
Ind: Energy   Grp: Basic Industries
Garry N Drummond, CEO

Rev: 750
Assets: NA
Emp: 3

DSC Communications Corp
1000 Coit Road
Plano, TX 75075
214-519-3000

Manufacturer of communications equipment.
Type: NASDAQ-DSC
Ind: Consulting   Grp: Business Service
James L Donald, CEO

Rev: 340
Assets: 429
Emp: 3

DST Systems Inc
1004 Baltimore Avenue
Kansas City, MO 64105
816-221-5545

Manufacturer of motor vehicle parts.
Type: NASDAQ-DSTS
Ind: Telecom   Grp: High Tech
Thomas A McDonnell, CEO

Rev: 139
Assets: 184
Emp: 1

Dubuque Packing Co Inc
7171 Mercy Road
Omaha, NE 68106
402-397-2000

Food processing company; meat products.
Type: Private
Ind: Food Processing   Grp: Food Processing
Michael Erman, CEO

Rev: 880
Assets: NA
Emp: 3

Duchossois Industries Inc
845 Larch Avenue
Elmhurst, IL 60126
312-279-3600

Manufacturer of railroad equipment.
Type: Private
Ind: Manufacturing   Grp: Manufacturing
Richard L Duchossois, CEO

Rev: 750
Assets: NA
Emp: 8

Ducommun Inc
10824 Hope Street
Cypress, CA 90630
213-612-4200

Aerospace technologies & services company.
Type: ASE-DCO
Ind: Manufacturing   Grp: Manufacturing
Wallace Booth, CEO

Rev: 150
Assets: 100
Emp: 3

Duke Power Co
422 S Church Street
Charlotte, NC 28242
704-373-4011

Electric power utility.
Type: NYSE-DUK
Ind: Utility   Grp: Utilities
William S Lee, CEO   Douglas Booth, Pres   William Grigg, VCh
Richard Osborne, CFO   George E Stubbins, IS   Hal Tucker, R&D
Donald H Denton Jr, Mkt   Eugene C Sites, VP   Carolyn Duncan, VP
Shem Blackley, VP   J Kenneth Clark, VP   Steve Griffith, VP
J Kenneth Clark, IR   D E Hatley, PR

Rev: 3627
Assets: 8891
Emp: 21

Duke University
Administrative Bldg
Durham, NC 27706
919-684-8111

Major educational institution; university.
Type: University
Ind: University   Grp: Govt & Non-Prof
H Keith H Brodie, CEO

Rev: 404
Assets: 405
Emp: 13

Organizations Listed Alphabetically

Organization / Address / Phone	Descriptive Information	Revenue / ($ mil)	Assets / ($ mil)	Emp (thous)
Dun & Bradstreet Corp 299 Park Avenue New York, NY 10171 212-593-6800	Publisher of business credit & investment information. Type: NYSE-DNB Ind: Publishing/Com Grp: Consumer Service Charles W Moritz, CEO Robert E Weissman, Pres N Eugene Hardin, VCh Edwin A Bescherer Jr, CFO Michael S Field, IS George J Feeney, R&D Loraine Scarpa, Mkt Michael Brewer, VP John C Holt, VP David McBride, VP Volney Taylor, VP Robert S Diamond, IR William F Doescher, PR	Rev: Assets: Emp:	4267 5024 90	
Dun & Bradstreet Credit Services Co One Diamond Hill Road Murray Hill, NJ 07974 201-665-6660	Credit & financial services company. Type: Private-Sub Par: Dun & Bradstreet Corp Ind: Comput/Off Equip Grp: High Tech John Kunz, CEO	Rev: Assets: Emp:	NA NA NA	
Dunavant Enterprises Inc 3595 New Getwell Road Memphis, TN 38118 901-369-1500	International & domestic cotton merchandisers. Type: Private Ind: Apparel/Textiles Grp: Consumer Prd William B Dunavant Jr, CEO	Rev: Assets: Emp:	1500 NA 2	
Duplex Products Inc 1947 Bethany Road Sycamore, IL 60178 815-895-2100	Manufacturer of business forms, computer paper. Type: ASE-DPX Ind: Paper/Forest Prd Grp: Basic Industries L T Smith, CEO	Rev: Assets: Emp:	250 200 2	
DuPont Canada Ltd 6700 Century Avenue Mississauga, ON L5M2H3 Can 416-821-3300	International diversified chemical company. Type: TOR-DUP Ind: Chemicals Grp: Basic Industries J Edward Newall, CEO Paul M Costello, Tres Donald A S Ivison, CFO Gordon R Wittman, VP Finn Hovland, VP Arthur R Sawchuk, VP James M Stewart, VP John C Carson, VP F Gerald Fox, VP	Rev: Assets: Emp:	1171 649 4	
DuPont, E I DeNemours & Co 1007 Market Street Wilmington, DE 19898 302-774-1000	Worldwide chemical & natural resources company. Type: NYSE-DD Ind: Chemicals Grp: Basic Industries Richard E Heckert, CEO Edgar S Woolard Jr, Pres Elwood Blanchard, VCh John J Quindlen, CFO Raymond E Cairns Jr, IS Howard E Simmons, R&D Robert C Forney, VP Constantine Nicandros, VP H Rodney Sharp, VP Roger W Arrington, VP Louis Wonderly, VP John R Malloy, PR	Rev: Assets: Emp:	32917 30719 141	
Duquesne Light Co Inc 301 Grant Street Pittsburgh, PA 15279 412-393-6000	Electric utility company. Type: NYSE-DQU Ind: Utility Grp: Utilities Wesley W von Schack, CEO A William Stein, Tres James O Ellenberger, CFO David D Marshall, IS John D Sieber, R&D Roger Beck, Mkt John J Carey, Ops	Rev: Assets: Emp:	1063 3877 4	
Duracell Corp Berkshire Industrial Park Bethel, CT 06801 203-796-4000	Manufacturer of batteries & lighting products. Type: Private Ind: Electronics Grp: High Tech C Robert Kidder, CEO	Rev: Assets: Emp:	1500 NA 10	
Duriron Co 425 N Findley Street Dayton, OH 45401 513-226-4000	Manufacturer of corrosion resistant pumps, pipes, castings. Type: OTC Ind: Manufacturing Grp: Manufacturing J Haddock, CEO	Rev: Assets: Emp:	300 200 3	
Durr Fillauer Medical Inc 218 Commerce Street PO Box 951 Montgomery, AL 36104 205-241-8800	Distributor of pharmaceuticals, medical & surgical prod. Type: NASDAQ-DUFM Ind: Instruments Grp: High Tech W A Williamson Jr, CEO Charles Adair, Pres Robert Barnes, VCh Charles T Gross, Tres Richard Klein, CFO Robert Klebba, R&D John W Durr, VP M W Cotton, VP	Rev: Assets: Emp:	588 178 2	
Durwood Inc 106 W 14th Street Kansas City, MO 64105 816-221-4000	Construction & commercial building company. Type: Private Ind: Real Estate/Bldg Grp: Business Service Stanley Durwood, CEO	Rev: Assets: Emp:	880 NA 8	

Organizations Listed Alphabetically

Organization / Address / Phone	Descriptive Information	Revenue / ($ mil)	Assets / ($ mil)	Emp (thous)

DWG Corp
6917 Collins Avenue
Miami, FL 33141
305-866-7771

Liquified natural gas producing company.
Type: ASE-DWG
Ind: Energy   Grp: Basic Industries
Victor Posner, CEO   Russell A Boyle, Pres   Jack Coppersmith, CFO
Barry Graham, IS

Rev: 1200
Assets: 1000
Emp: 15

Dylex Ltd
637 Lakeshore Blvd W
Toronto, ON M5V1A8 Can
416-586-7000

Nationwide retailing organization.
Type: TOR
Ind: Retail/Merch   Grp: Retail
James F Kay, CEO   Wilfred Posluns, Chr   Irving Posluns, VCh
Donald Williams, CFO   David Beiles, R&D   Kenneth Axelrod, VP
Joel N Cooper, VP   Carol Cox, VP   Donald J Evans, VP

Rev: 1697
Assets: 595
Emp: 18

Dynalectron Corp
1313 Dolley Madison Blvd
McLean, VA 22101
703-264-0330

Aircraft maintenance & ground service company.
Type: Private
Ind: Electronics   Grp: High Tech
Dan Bannister, CEO

Rev: 750
Assets: 250
Emp: 15

Dynatech Corp
3 Executive Park
Burlington, MA 01803
617-272-3304

Electronic instrument manufacturer.
Type: NASDAQ-DYTC
Ind: Comput/Off Equip   Grp: High Tech
Warren M Rohsenow, CEO   J P Barger, Chr   Robert F Reno, CFO
R Claude Olier, IS   John Powers, R&D   Howard M Crow, VP
William w Welsh, VP   Terrence Kelly, VP   Joseph A Sciulli, VP
James Turner, VP   Dorothy Cooley, VP

Rev: 368
Assets: 254
Emp: 3

DynCorp Inc
1313 Dolly Madison Blvd
McLean, VA 22101
703-356-0480

Electrical contracting & technical services.
Type: Private
Ind: Manufacturing   Grp: Manufacturing
Dan Bannister, CEO

Rev: 750
Assets: NA
Emp: 10

Dyson Kissner Moran Corp
230 Park Avenue
New York, NY 10169
212-661-4600

Manufacturers of general industrial machinery.
Type: Private
Ind: Manufacturing   Grp: Manufacturing
John A Moran, CEO

Rev: 1000
Assets: NA
Emp: 5

E-Systems Inc
6250 LBJ Freeway
Dallas, TX 75266
214-661-1000

Manufacturer of electronic equipment for defense industry.
Type: NYSE-ESY
Ind: Electronics   Grp: High Tech
David R Tacke, CEO   P Gene Keiffer, Pres   A Lowell Lawson, VCh
Thomas D Kelly, CFO   Paul Pechersky, IS   Dr Samuel Musa, R&D
Eaton Adams, VP   James W Crowley, VP   Brian Cullen, VP
Dr Terry Heil, VP   Robert Kroeger, VP   James W Pope, VP
Joe W Russell, IR   John Kumpf, PR

Rev: 1443
Assets: 758
Emp: 17

E-Z Serve Inc
4001 Airport Freeway
Bedford, TX 76021
817-267-1777

Automobile & truck rental company.
Type: Private
Ind: Retail/Merch   Grp: Retail
Dale Ealvo, CEO

Rev: 550
Assets: 239
Emp: 5

Eagle Food Center Corp
801 E 1st Street
Milan, IL 61264
309-787-7700

Operator of retail food supermarkets.
Type: Private
Ind: Retail/Food   Grp: Retail
Pasquale V Petitti, CEO

Rev: 1000
Assets: NA
Emp: 10

Eagle Picher Industries Inc
580 Walnut Street
Cincinnati, OH 45202
513-721-7010

Manufacturer of automotive parts.
Type: OTC
Ind: Equipment   Grp: Manufacturing
Thomas E Petry, CEO   John Painter, VCh   David N Hall, CFO
Melvin F Chubb, Mkt   James M Dines, VP   James Baird, VP
John Powers, VP   Carroll Curless, VP   Ernest Hirsh, VP
J Rodman Nall, VP

Rev: 770
Assets: 583
Emp: 9

Organizations Listed Alphabetically

Organization / Address / Phone	Descriptive Information	Revenue / Assets / Emp
		($ mil) ($ mil) (thous)

Eastern Airlines Inc
Miami International Airport
Miami, FL 33148
305-873-2211

International airline.
Type: Private-Sub   Par: Texas Air Corp (Continental Airlines)
Ind: Airline   Grp: Consumer Service
Joe Leonard, CEO   Phil Bakes, Chr   Rolf Andresen, CFO
David Kunstler, R&D   Jose Smith, Sls   George Brennan, Mkt
Frank Causey, Ops   Edward Upton, VP   John Siefert, VP
Stephen Kolski, VP

Rev: 4402
Assets: 3673
Emp: 37

Eastern Enterprises Inc
9 Riverside Road
Weston, MA 02193
617-647-2300

Holding company for natural gas utility.
Type: NYSE-EFU
Ind: Utility   Grp: Utilities
William J Pruyn, CEO   Robert W Weining, Chr   Richard Clayton, VCh
John W Burns, Tres   Gail Deegan, CFO   John T McKenna, R&D
Chester Messer, Ops   L William Law, VP

Rev: 672
Assets: 1087
Emp: 4

Eastern Michigan University
Administrative Bldg
Ypsilanti, MI 48197
313-487-1849

Major educational institution; university.
Type: University
Ind: University   Grp: Govt & Non-Prof
John W Porter, CEO

Rev: 91
Assets: 128
Emp: 22

Eastern Utilities Associates Inc
One Liberty Square
Boston, MA 02109
617-357-9590

Electric power generation company.
Type: NYSE-EUA
Ind: Utility   Grp: Utilities
John F G Eichorn, CEO   Donald G Pardus, Pres   Robert E Maguire, VCh
Clifford J Herbert, Tres   Richard Burns, CFO   John Stevens, VP
William O'Conner, VP

Rev: 374
Assets: 1203
Emp: 1

Eastman Kodak Co
343 State Street
Rochester, NY 14650
716-724-4000

Manufacturer of photographic equipment, cameras, film.
Type: NYSE-EK
Ind: Leisure Time   Grp: Consumer Service
Colby H Chandler, CEO   Kay R Whitmore, Pres   C Michael Hamilton, Tres
Paul L Smith, CFO   Katherine M Hudson, IS   Edward Przybylowicz, R&D
David J Metz, VP   William L Sutton, VP   Peter Giles, VP
J Phillip Samper, VP   David J Metz, IR   Tom Levy, PR

Rev: 17034
Assets: 22964
Emp: 145

Eaton Corp
Eaton Center 1111 Superior Avenue
Cleveland, OH 44114
216-523-5000

Manufacturer of electric components for the auto industry.
Type: NYSE-ETN
Ind: Conglomerate   Grp: Manufacturing
James R Stover, CEO   John M Carmont, Tres   Stephen R Hardis, CFO
Floyd Wilkerson, IS   Warren Offutt, R&D   Richard T Sadler, VP
Marshall Wright, VP   Brock Haddox, VP   Patrick X Donavan, VP
Daniel J Brubeck, IR   Renald Romain, PR

Rev: 3469
Assets: 3034
Emp: 43

Ebasco Services Inc
Two World Trade Center
New York, NY 10048
212-839-1000

International building, engineering & consulting company.
Type: Private-Sub   Par: Enserch Corp
Ind: Consulting   Grp: Business Service
Richard Albosta, CEO

Rev: 900
Assets: NA
Emp: 5

Eby Brown Companies
1313 Timber Drive
Aurora, IL 60120
312-242-1919

Wholesale distributor of restaurant supplies,consumer goods.
Type: Private
Ind: Retail/Merch   Grp: Retail
Richard Wake, CEO

Rev: 750
Assets: NA
Emp: 1

Echlin Inc
100 Double Beach Road
Branford, CT 06405
203-481-5751

Manufacturer of parts & components for the auto industry.
Type: NYSE-ECH
Ind: Automotive   Grp: Manufacturing
Frederick J Mancheski, CEO   Daniel Carboni, VCh   Richard Wiscot, Tres
Andrew Mazzerella, CFO   Robert Tobey, R&D   John P Gethin, Mkt
Charles O'Conner, VP   Joseph Onorato, VP   Edward Shalagan, VP
Ralph Manning, VP   Kenneth Flynn, VP   Paul R Ryder, PR

Rev: 1294
Assets: 1087
Emp: 15

Eckerd, Jack Corp
8333 Bryan Dairy Road
Largo, FL 33543
813-397-7461

Operator of retail drugstores.
Type: Private
Ind: Retail/Merch   Grp: Retail
Stewart Turley, CEO

Rev: 3000
Assets: NA
Emp: 30

Organizations Listed Alphabetically

Organization / Address / Phone	Descriptive Information	Revenue / Assets / Emp		
		($ mil)	($ mil)	(thous)
Ecolab (Economics Laboratory) Inc Osborn Bldg St Paul, MN 55102 612-293-2233	Manufacturer of cleaning products. Type: NYSE-ECL Ind: Chemicals Grp: Basic Industries Pierson M Grieve, CEO Donald Rodel, VCh Brruce Bentcover, Tres Michael Shannon, CFO F William Tuominen, IS Jon Grunseth, Sls Kenneth Bjerk, Ops Allan Shuman, VP Roger Yeary, VP	Rev: Assets: Emp:	1212 943 12	
Econocom USA Inc 4385 Poplar Avenue Memphis, TN 38117 901-762-9200	Operator of retail merchandise stores. Type: Private Ind: Retail/Merch Grp: Retail Pierre Berberk, CEO	Rev: Assets: Emp:	550 NA 1	
Economical Group Ltd 10 Duke Street Kitchener, ON N2G4C1 Can 519-888-8200	Property & casualty insurance company. Type: Private Ind: Insurance Grp: Insurance P H Sims, CEO J Hill, Pres G S Cudlipp, CFO J Jensen, IS J H Bennett, R&D D L Kemp, Ops	Rev: Assets: Emp:	403 741 1	
Edgcomb Corp 30 Rockefeller Plaza New York, NY 10112 212-246-1000	Wholesale metal distribution company. Type: OTC Ind: Manufacturing Grp: Manufacturing Michael Scharf, CEO	Rev: Assets: Emp:	617 450 2	
Edison Brothers Stores Inc 501 N Broadway St Louis, MO 63178 314-331-6000	Operator of retail shoe stores & department stores. Type: NYSE-EBS Ind: Retail/Merch Grp: Retail Andrew E Newman, CEO	Rev: Assets: Emp:	1000 500 22	
Edwards, A G & Sons Inc One N Jefferson Avenue St Louis, MO 63103 314-289-3000	Securities & commodities brokerage firm. Type: NYSE-AGE Ind: Securities Grp: Financial Benjamin F Edwards, CEO Robert G Avis, Pres David Sisler, VCh Robert Bagby, CFO Ronald Buesinger, IS Terry Dessent, R&D Robert Dissett, Sls Michael Calabro, Ops	Rev: Assets: Emp:	501 1063 7	
EG & G Inc 45 William Street Wellesley, MA 02181 617-237-5100	Manufacturer of electronic equipment. Type: NYSE-EGG Ind: Electronics Grp: High Tech John M Kurarski, CEO Donald M Kerr, VCh John R Dolan, CFO Samuel Rubinovitz, IS William T Barrett, R&D James R Dubay, Sls Phillip Kautt, Mkt Richard Murphy, Ops Luciano Rossi, VP Louis Valente, VP Charles Williams, VP Peter F Chapski, PR	Rev: Assets: Emp:	1406 539 22	
Eighty Four Lumber Co Route 519 Eighty Four, PA 15384 412-228-8820	Retail building materials company. Type: Private Ind: Retail/Merch Grp: Retail Joseph Hardy, CEO	Rev: Assets: Emp:	1100 NA 5	
EL Financial Corp 165 University Avenue Toronto, ON M5H3B8 Can 416-868-1880	Diversified financial company. Type: Private Ind: Non-Bank Fin Grp: Financial Henry Jackman, CEO	Rev: Assets: Emp:	513 1312 1	
El Paso Electric Co Inc 303 N Oregon Street El Paso, TX 79901 915-543-5711	Electric power utility. Type: ASE Ind: Utility Grp: Utilities David H Wiggs, CEO Charles Mais, VCh Gary R Hedrick, Tres C R Becker, CFO Ignacio Troncoso, VP William J Johnson, VP	Rev: Assets: Emp:	639 1975 3	
El Paso Natural Gas Co One Paul Kayser Center El Paso, TX 79901 915-541-2600	Natural gas utility. Type: Private-Sub Par: Burlington Resources Ind: Utility Grp: Utilities Travis H Petty, CEO	Rev: Assets: Emp:	1447 3279 3	
El Paso Products Co Inc 5005 LBJ Freeway Occidental Tower Dallas, TX 75244 915-333-7200	Producer & distributor of packaged food products. Type: Private Ind: Food Processing Grp: Food Processing Andy Smith, CEO	Rev: Assets: Emp:	660 NA 2	

Organizations Listed Alphabetically

Organization / Address / Phone	Descriptive Information	Revenue / Assets / Emp ($ mil) ($ mil) (thous)		

El Paso, City of
Civic Center Plaza
El Paso, TX 79999
915-541-4766

City government.
Type: City Govt
Ind: Local Govt   Grp: Govt & Non-Prof
Jonathan Rogers, CEO

Rev: 250
Assets: NM
Emp: 2

Eldorado Nuclear Ltd
255 Albert Street
Ottawa, ON K1P6A9 Can
613-238-5222

Uranium ore mining company.
Type: Federal Govt
Ind: Metals/Mining   Grp: Basic Industries
Nicholas Ediger, CEO

Rev: 298
Assets: 765
Emp: 1

Electric Boat Div
75 Eastern Point Road
Groton, CT 06340
203-441-1000

Defense contractor; submarine manufacturing.
Type: Private-Sub Par: General Dynamics Corp
Ind: Manufacturing   Grp: Manufacturing
Robert Turner, CEO

Rev: NA
Assets: NA
Emp: NA

Electric Power Research Institute Inc
3412 Hillview Avenue
Palo Alto, CA 94304
415-855-2000

Non-profit research organization.
Type: Private
Ind: Membership Org   Grp: Govt & Non-Prof
Richard Balzhiser, CEO

Rev: 275
Assets: NA
Emp: 2

Electrolux US Inc
2300 Windy Ridge Parkway
Marietta, GA 30067
404-933-1000

Manufacturer & importer of vacuum cleaners; US headquarters.
Type: Private-Sub-For
Ind: Appliances/Furn   Grp: Manufacturing
Dennis Johnson, CEO

Rev: 2090
Assets: NA
Emp: 21

Electronic Data Systems Corp
7171 Forest Lane
Dallas, TX 75230
214-661-6000

Computer services & system integration company.
Type: NYSE-GME
Ind: Comput/Off Equip   Grp: High Tech
Les Alberthal, CEO   J Davis Hamlin, CFO   Jeff Heller, IS
Glen Self, R&D   Ron Verner, IR   Bill Wright, PR

Rev: 4844
Assets: 3416
Emp: 45

Electrospace Systems Inc
1301 E Collins Blvd
Richardson, TX 75083
214-470-2000

Manufacturer of electronic communication & navigation equip.
Type: Private-Sub Par: Chrysler Corp
Ind: Electronics   Grp: High Tech
James Lightner, CEO

Rev: NA
Assets: NA
Emp: NA

Elf Aquitaine Inc
High Ridge Road
Stamford, CT 06904
203-358-5000

Oil & gas exploration & production company; US headquarters.
Type: Private-Sub-For
Ind: Energy   Grp: Basic Industries
M Schneider Maunoury, CEO

Rev: 3850
Assets: NA
Emp: 8

Eljer Industries Inc
901 10th Street
Plano, TX 75074
214-881-7177

Manufacturer of plumbing, heating & ventilating equipment.
Type: NYSE-ELJ
Ind: Manufacturing   Grp: Manufacturing
D C Clark, CEO

Rev: 429
Assets: 197
Emp: 4

Ellis Don Ltd
2045 Oxford Street E
London, ON N6A4M6 Can
519-455-6770

Construction & building company.
Type: TOR
Ind: Real Estate/Bldg   Grp: Business Service
Donald Smith, CEO

Rev: 643
Assets: 196
Emp: 3

Elrick & Lavidge Inc
10 S Riverside Plaza
Chicago, IL 60606
312-726-0666

Marketing research firm.
Type: Private
Ind: Business Service   Grp: Business Service
Edward Schroder, CEO

Rev: 825
Assets: NA
Emp: 8

Emco Ltd
1108 Dundas Street E
London, ON N6A4N7 Can
519-451-1250

Building materials manufacturing company.
Type: TOR-EML
Ind: Building Mat   Grp: Basic Industries
John S Brant, CEO   Heath Gillam, Tres   W Wesley DeShane, CFO
Ross W MacDonald, R&D   Ronald M Clark, VP   James L Forgie, VP
R Douglas Roland, VP   Douglas E Speers, VP   Ian F Warburton, VP
Walter D LeGrow, IR

Rev: 1004
Assets: 572
Emp: 9

Organizations Listed Alphabetically

Organization / Address / Phone	Descriptive Information	Revenue / ($ mil)	Assets / ($ mil)	Emp (thous)
Emerson Electric Co 8000 W Florissant Avenue St Louis, MO 63136 314-553-2000	Manufacturer of electronic systems for the defense industry. Type: NYSE Ind: Electronics Grp: High Tech C F Knight, CEO W A Rutledge, Pres W C Bousquette, CFO D N Farr, R&D J F Bradley, Sls J G Berges, VP W L Davis, VP D O Gifford, VP P A Roberts, PR	Rev: 6652	Assets: 5027	Emp: 71
Emerson Radio Corp One Emerson Lane North Bergen, NJ 07047 201-854-6600	Manufacturer of electronic equipment for consumers/industry. Type: NYSE-EME Ind: Electronics Grp: High Tech William W Lane, CEO Edward Bohn, Tres Harold Falik, CFO Rudolph Malacrida, IS Tom Eishii, R&D John R Bond, Sls Edward Ryan, Mkt Donald Dvorkin, VP Harold Falk, VP Kunio Takei, VP Hachiro Masuda, VP Sharon Fenster, PR	Rev: 729	Assets: 255	Emp: 3
Emery Air Freight Corp Old Danbury Road Wilton, CT 06897 203-762-8601	Worldwide air courier & cargo company. Type: NYSE Ind: Transport Grp: Business Service Larry R Scott, CEO William F Souders, Chr Denis M McCarthy, Pres Daniel McCauley, VCh Arthur W Demelle, CFO Robert R Bohannon, IS Arthur C French, R&D Ton C M Heijmen, Mkt John Zarras, Ops John P Kelly, VP Tom A Teraoka, VP J Baxter Urist, VP Barbara C Graves, IR J Baxter Urist, PR	Rev: 1223	Assets: 733	Emp: 17
Emhart Corp 426 Colt Highway Farmington, CT 06032 203-678-3000	Manufacturer of electronic components & systems. Type: NYSE-EMH Ind: Manufacturing Grp: Manufacturing Peter L Scott, CEO William C Lichtenfels, Pres Richard Campbell, VCh Achim Knust, CFO David W Dandro, IS John Rydz, R&D Ralph Branca, Ops Richard L Cote, VP Fred Hollfelder, VP John F Budd Jr, PR	Rev: 2763	Assets: 2427	Emp: 33
Emigrant Savings Bank Inc 5 E 42nd Street New York, NY 10017 212-883-5800	Thrift institution. Type: Private Ind: Savings & Loan Grp: Financial Franklin R Saul, CEO	Rev: 550	Assets: 5500	Emp: 2
EMP Employers Mutual Casualty Ins Co 717 Mulberry Street Des Moines, IA 50309 515-280-2511	Property & casualty insurance company. Type: NASDAQ-EMCI Ind: Insurance Grp: Insurance Robb B Kelley, CEO	Rev: 118	Assets: 298	Emp: 1
Empire Co 115 King Street Stellarton, NS B0K1S0 Can 902-755-4440	Retail drugstores, real estate, financial, oil & gas. Type: TOR Ind: Automotive Grp: Manufacturing Donald R Sobey, CEO James W Gogan, Pres Paul D Sobey, VCh Chester D Thompson, CFO	Rev: 1193	Assets: 880	Emp: 4
Empire of America Fed Savings Bank Inc One Main Place Buffalo, NY 14202 716-845-7101	Thrift institution. Type: ASE-EOA Ind: Savings & Loan Grp: Financial Paul A Willax, CEO Daniel D Brown, Pres Gary M Crosby, CFO Richard J Troidl, IS Melissa J Bailey, R&D Bruce Long, Sls Carol G Corr, Mkt James Cassin, Ops Dennis W O'Neill, VP Mary Ann Lauricella, PR	Rev: 1090	Assets: 11281	Emp: 3
Employers of Texas Insurance Co 1301 Young Street Dallas, TX 75202 214-760-6100	Property & casualty insurance company. Type: OTC Ind: Insurance Grp: Insurance Dewey G Williams, CEO	Rev: 800	Assets: 800	Emp: 3
Employers Reinsurance Co 5200 Metcalf Avenue Overland Park, KS 66201 913-676-5200	Insurance company. Type: Private-Sub Par: General Electric Co Ind: Insurance Grp: Insurance Robert R Cross, CEO Michael G Fitt, Chr Delmar Burton, VCh Robert E Monroe, Tres Gary R Teaney, CFO James R Batterson, VP Michael Miller, VP Joseph Levin, VP Robert Breckenridge, VP Robert Cross, VP William Darrach, VP	Rev: 1425	Assets: 4293	Emp: 4

Organizations Listed Alphabetically

Organization / Address / Phone	Descriptive Information	Revenue / ($ mil)	Assets / ($ mil)	Emp (thous)
Employment & Immigration Canada Place du Portage Phase IV Hull, PQ K1A0J9 Can 819-994-6313	Federal government agency. Type: Federal Govt Ind: Federal Govt Grp: Govt & Non-Prof Arthur Kroeger, CEO	Rev: Assets: Emp:	4080 NM 24	
Encyclopedia Britannica Inc 310 S Michigan Chicago, IL 60604 312-347-7000	Publishers of reference books, educational services. Type: Private Ind: Publishing/Com Grp: Consumer Service Robert P Gwinn, CEO	Rev: Assets: Emp:	600 NA 2	
Energen Corp 2101 Sixth Avenue N Birmingham, AL 35203 205-326-2700	Natural gas pipeline company. Type: NYSE-EGN Ind: Energy Grp: Basic Industries Rex J Lysinger, CEO	Rev: Assets: Emp:	350 300 1	
Energy Services Co N Sandursky Street Mt Vernon, OH 43050 614-393-8200	Electrical supply company. Type: Private-Sub Par: Cooper Industries Inc Ind: Electronics Grp: High Tech Norman Shaman, CEO	Rev: Assets: Emp:	NA NA NA	
Energy, Mines & Resources Canada 580 Booth Street Ottawa, ON K1A0E4 Can 613-995-4510	Federal government agency. Type: Federal Govt Ind: Federal Govt Grp: Govt & Non-Prof Bruce Howe, CEO	Rev: Assets: Emp:	1020 NM 5	
Enfield Corp 1100 Eglinton Avenue E Toronto, ON M3C1H8 Can 416-445-7438	Holding company for manufacturing companies. Type: MON Ind: Manufacturing Grp: Manufacturing Michael Blair, CEO	Rev: Assets: Emp:	340 510 3	
Englehard Corp Menlo Park Edison, NJ 08818 201-632-6000	Manufacturer of specialty chemicals. Type: NYSE-EC Ind: Chemicals Grp: Basic Industries Reuben F Richards, CEO Orin R Smith, Chr Cyrus H Holley, Pres R Keith Elliott, CFO Stephen Pook, IS Harmon Garfinkel, R&D Donald LaTorre, VP Paul Norris, VP Francis X Vitale Jr, PR	Rev: Assets: Emp:	2351 1413 8	
Enron Canada Ltd 1300 700 9th Avenue SW Calgary, AB T2P3V4 Can 403-298-2690	Oil & natural gas exploration & production company. Type: Private-Sub-For Ind: Energy Grp: Basic Industries Brent Brown, CEO	Rev: Assets: Emp:	281 85 1	
Enron Corp 1400 Smith Street Houston, TX 77002 713-853-6161	Natural gas pipeline company; oil & gas exploration. Type: NYSE-ENE Ind: Utility Grp: Utilities Kenneth L Lay, CEO John M Seidl, Pres Richard Kinder, VCh Rodney Gray, Tres Jack I Tompkins, CFO J Ronald Knorpp, IS Louis Potempo, R&D Ross Workman, VP Donald H Gullquist, VP A Hardie Davis, IR Randal R Blauvelt, PR	Rev: Assets: Emp:	5708 8695 8	
Enron Oil & Gas Co 1400 Smith Street Houston, TX 77251 713-853-6161	Oil & gas exploration, production & marketing company. Type: Private-Sub Par: Enron Corp Ind: Energy Grp: Basic Industries Forrest Hogland, CEO	Rev: Assets: Emp:	NA NA NA	
Enserch Corp 300 S St Paul Dallas, TX 75201 214-651-8700	Oil & natural gas exploration & production company. Type: NYSE-ENS Ind: Utility Grp: Utilities Robert E Ebel, CEO W C McCord, Chr William T Satterwhite, VCh Albert Gallatin, Tres Sanford R Singer, CFO Robert H Goodman, R&D John Scarola, Ops Benjamin Brown, VP Robert Ebel, VP Michael Fortado, VP Benjamin A Brown, IR Crystal C Bell, PR	Rev: Assets: Emp:	2739 2970 19	
Enserch Exploration Inc 1817 Wood Street Dallas, TX 75201 214-748-1110	Oil & gas exploration & production company. Type: Private-Sub Par: Enserch Corp Ind: Energy Grp: Basic Industries Robert Fowler, CEO	Rev: Assets: Emp:	NA NA NA	

Organizations Listed Alphabetically

Organization / Address / Phone	Descriptive Information	Revenue / ($ mil)	Assets / ($ mil)	Emp (thous)

Ensite Ltd
2950 Metcalfe Street
Windsor, ON N8Y1W9 Can
519-257-4412

Automotive parts manufacturer.
Type: Private-Sub-For
Ind: Automotive   Grp: Manufacturing
L F Brown, CEO

Rev: 1150
Assets: 631
Emp: 3

Entergy Corp (Middle South Utilities)
225 Baronne Street
New Orleans, LA 70112
504-529-5262

Public utility holding company; electric power utilities.
Type: NYSE-MSU
Ind: Utility   Grp: Utilities
Edwin Lupberger, CEO   Edwin A Lupberger, Chr   John L Cowan, CFO
Robert D DeLoach, IS   Stephen Jenkins, Mkt   James Cain, VP
Jerry Jackson, VP   Jack L King, VP   Jerry Maulden, VP
Glenn Parsons, PR

Rev: 3565
Assets: 15942
Emp: 15

Entertainment Marketing Inc
10310 Harwin Drive
Houston, TX 77242
713-995-4433

Leasing company.
Type: ASE-EM
Ind: Comput/Off Equip   Grp: High Tech
Elias Zinn, CEO

Rev: 250
Assets: 200
Emp: 1

Entree Corp
111 E Wisconsin Avenue
Milwaukee, WI 53202
414-271-2768

Wholesale food processing company; meats, frozen foods.
Type: NASDAQ-FHFC
Ind: Food Processing   Grp: Food Processing
Donald Runge, CEO

Rev: 396
Assets: 200
Emp: 5

Envirodyne Industries
142 E Ontario
Chicago, IL 60611
312-649-0600

Manufacturer of plastics & industrial machinery.
Type: NASDAQ-ENVR
Ind: Manufacturing   Grp: Manufacturing
Ronald Linde, CEO   Lawrence C Henry, CFO   Helen Gallagher, IS
Maxine H Linde, IR   Alcie Stake, PR

Rev: 475
Assets: 400
Emp: 5

Environment Canada
10 Wellington Street
Hull, PQ K1A0H3 Can
819-997-2800

Federal government agency.
Type: Federal Govt
Ind: Federal Govt   Grp: Govt & Non-Prof
Genevieve Sainte-Marie, CEO

Rev: 1530
Assets: NM
Emp: 9

Epic Healthcare Group Inc
433 E Los Colinas Blvd Waterway Tower
Irving, TX 75039
214-869-0707

Operator of health care facilities; hospitals.
Type: Private
Ind: Health Care   Grp: Consumer Service
Ken S George, CEO

Rev: 1000
Assets: NA
Emp: 10

Epstein, A & Sons International Inc
600 W Fulton
Chicago, IL 60606
312-454-9100

Nationwide consulting company.
Type: Private
Ind: Consulting   Grp: Business Service
Sidney Epstein, CEO

Rev: 350
Assets: NA
Emp: 1

Equifax Inc
1600 Peachtree Street
Atlanta, GA 30302
404-885-8000

Computer services; credit information, service bureaus.
Type: NYSE-EFX
Ind: Comput/Off Equip   Grp: High Tech
J V White, CEO   C B Rogers, Pres   W N Aitken, VCh
H A Phillips, CFO   J A Baker, VP   J C Chartrand, VP
D F Walsh, VP   J O Perkins, VP   E T Merrigan, VP

Rev: 743
Assets: 421
Emp: 10

Equimark Corp
2 Oliver Plaza
Pittsburgh, PA 15222
412-288-5000

Commercial bank.
Type: NYSE-EQK
Ind: Banking   Grp: Financial
Alan Fellheimer, CEO   Claire W Gargalli, Pres   Stephen A Harrison, CFO
Leslie H Green, IS   Robert F Donovan, Mkt   Billie Brown, PR

Rev: 600
Assets: 6000
Emp: 2

Equitable BanCorp Inc
100 S Charles Street
Baltimore, MD 21201
301-547-4000

Commercial bank.
Type: NASDAQ-EBNC
Ind: Banking   Grp: Financial
H Grant Hathaway, CEO   Carl Stearn, Pres   John Evans, CFO
Peter M Martin, IS   Scott McBride, R&D   Joan Gillispie, Mkt
R Kenneth Rous, VP   Nancy Robertson, VP   Patricia Barry, IR
Janeallen Bowie, PR

Rev: 375
Assets: 5186
Emp: 3

Organizations Listed Alphabetically

Organization / Address / Phone	Descriptive Information	Revenue / ($ mil)	Assets / ($ mil)	Emp (thous)
Equitable Life Assurance Society Inc 1285 Avenue of the Americas New York, NY 10119 212-554-1234	Diversified financial company; life insurer. Type: NYSE Ind: Insurance Grp: Insurance E Rod Ross, CEO John Carter, Chr Harry D Garber, VCh Glenn H Gettier, CFO Lou Hughes, IS Michael S Martin, Mkt Brian Wruble, VP Benjamin D Holloway, VP Jeff R Hart, VP Donald Mooney, VP Gregory Good, IR Barbara Wilkoc, PR	Rev: 8898 Assets: 49288 Emp: 25		
Equitable Resources Co Inc 420 Blvd of the Allies Pittsburgh, PA 15219 412-261-3000	Natural gas production & gas utility. Type: NYSE-EQT Ind: Utility Grp: Utilities Donald I Moritz, CEO	Rev: 406 Assets: 1069 Emp: 2		
Equitable Variable Life 787 7th Avenue New York, NY 10019 212-554-4035	Life insurance company. Type: Private-Sub Par: Equitable Life Assurance Society Inc Ind: Insurance Grp: Insurance Robert Barth, CEO	Rev: 1800 Assets: 8000 Emp: 3		
Erbamont Inc 1266 Main Street Soundview Plaza Stamford, CT 06902 203-967-4882	Pharmaceutical company. Type: Private Ind: Drugs Grp: Consumer Service Powell Morione, CEO	Rev: 1100 Assets: NA Emp: 11		
Erie County Government 95 Franklin Street Buffalo, NY 14202 716-846-8500	County government. Type: County Govt Ind: Local Govt Grp: Govt & Non-Prof Roger Blackwell, CEO	Rev: 250 Assets: NM Emp: 2		
Erie Insurance Exchange Inc 100 Erie Insurance Place Erie, PA 16530 814-870-2000	Property & casualty insurance company. Type: Private-Mutual Ind: Insurance Grp: Insurance F William Hirt, CEO	Rev: 800 Assets: 1500 Emp: 3		
Ernst & Whinney Inc 2000 National City Bldg Cleveland, OH 44114 216-861-5000	Nationwide accounting firm. Type: Private Ind: Accounting Grp: Business Service Ray J Groves, CEO	Rev: 2000 Assets: NA Emp: 30		
ESI Energy Services Inc 100 Australian Avenue West Palm Beach, FL 33406 407-683-6996	Utility company. Type: Private-Sub Par: FPL (Florida Power & Light) Group Inc Ind: Energy Grp: Basic Industries J Bell, CEO	Rev: NA Assets: NA Emp: NA		
ESL Inc 495 Java Drive Sunnyvale, CA 94088 408-738-2888	Operator of radio & TV broadcasting stations. Type: Private-Sub Par: TRW Inc Ind: Publishing/Com Grp: Consumer Service Robert Kohler, CEO	Rev: NA Assets: NA Emp: NA		
Esprit de Corp Inc 900 Minnesota Street San Francisco, CA 94107 415-648-6900	Family apparel. Type: Private Ind: Apparel/Textiles Grp: Consumer Prd Corrado Federico, CEO	Rev: 1000 Assets: NA Emp: 2		
Esselte Corp 71 Clinton Road Garden City, NY 11530 516-741-1477	Manufacturer of office products, filing systems. Type: NYSE-EBS Ind: Manufacturing Grp: Manufacturing Sven Wallgren, CEO Hans Stahle, Pres John Bardner, VCh Hans Biorck, CFO Hans Biorck, VP Mark Tomasko, VP Eric Soderberg, VP Gerhard Lindholm, VP Joseph D Petitto, PR	Rev: 1401 Assets: 1073 Emp: 3		
Essex Group Inc 1601 Wall Street Fort Wayne, IN 46802 219-461-4000	Manufacturer of telecommunications products, wires, cables. Type: Private Ind: Manufacturing Grp: Manufacturing John M Bruce, CEO	Rev: 750 Assets: NA Emp: 5		

Organizations Listed Alphabetically

Organization / Address / Phone	Descriptive Information	Revenue / ($ mil)	Assets / ($ mil)	Emp (thous)
Esterline Corp 10800 NE 8th Street Bellevue, WA 98004 206-453-6000	Manufacturer of robot systems; factory, electronic assembly. Type: NYSE-ESL Ind: Equipment Grp: Manufacturing Wendell P Hurlbut, CEO	Rev: Assets: Emp:	260 190 2	
Ethan Allen Inc Ethan Allen Drive Danbury, CT 06810 203-743-8000	Manufacturer & retailer of furniture. Type: Private-Sub Par: Interco Inc Ind: Appliances/Furn Grp: Manufacturing Nathan Ancell, CEO	Rev: Assets: Emp:	250 NA 2	
Ethyl Corp 330 S Fourth Street Richmond, VA 23217 804-788-5000	Producer of performance chemicals. Type: NYSE-EY Ind: Chemicals Grp: Basic Industries Floyd D Gottwald, CEO Bruce C Gottwald, Pres Ray Wilkens, VCh Lloyd B Andrew, CFO Michael F Giesler, IS John T Marvel, R&D Roger Moser, Ops James Compass, VP Sampson Bass, VP A Prescott Rowe, PR	Rev: Assets: Emp:	2011 5251 10	
European American Bancorp EAB Plaza Uniondale, NY 11555 516-296-5000	Commercial bank. Type: NASDAQ Ind: Banking Grp: Financial Raymond J Dempsey, CEO Arnold Bartfeld, VCh Burt R Clark, CFO Rudolf P Guenzel, IS Thomas A Sawyer, Mkt Conrad Gunther, VP Edward Travaglianti, VP Thomas A Sawyer, PR	Rev: Assets: Emp:	540 5335 3	
Evans, Bob Farms Inc 3776 S High Street Columbus, OH 43207 614-491-2225	Food processor & restaurant operator. Type: NASDAQ-BOBE Ind: Food/Lodging Grp: Consumer Service Daniel E Evans, CEO Keith Bradbury, Tres Lawrence Carroll, CFO Larry Corbin, R&D	Rev: Assets: Emp:	395 219 12	
Everex Systems Inc 48431 Milmont Drive Fremont, CA 94538 415-498-1111	Manufacturer of personal computers. Type: OTC Ind: Comput/Off Equip Grp: High Tech Steven Hui, CEO	Rev: Assets: Emp:	400 300 2	
Everready Battery Corp Checkerboard Square St Louis, MO 63164 314-982-1000	Manufacturer of batteries. Type: Private-Sub Par: Ralston Purina Co Ind: Electronics Grp: High Tech J Patrick Mulcahy, CEO	Rev: Assets: Emp:	NA NA NA	
Excel Industries Inc 1120 N Main Street Elkhart, IN 46515 219-264-2131	Manufacturer of parts for auto industry; windows. Type: ASE-EXC Ind: Automotive Grp: Manufacturing James J Lohman, CEO	Rev: Assets: Emp:	250 200 2	
Excello Corp 850 Ladd Road Walled Lake, MI 48088 313-624-7800	Manufacturer of specialty industrial equipment. Type: Private Ind: Manufacturing Grp: Manufacturing Earl Slack, CEO	Rev: Assets: Emp:	1650 NA 18	
Executive Life Insurance Co PO Box 6090 Inglewood, CA 90312 213-312-1000	Life insurance company. Type: OTC Ind: Insurance Grp: Insurance Fred Carr, CEO Merle A Horst, CFO Raul A Cruz, IS Gary R Schulte, Mkt Allan L Chapman, PR	Rev: Assets: Emp:	2420 11400 2	
Exide Corp 101 Gibraltar Road Horsham, PA 19044 215-674-9500	Battery manufacturer. Type: Private Ind: Manufacturing Grp: Manufacturing Arthur Hawkins, CEO	Rev: Assets: Emp:	600 NA 6	
Export Development Corp 151 O'Connor Street Ottawa, ON K1P5T9 Can 613-598-2500	Export financing agency of the federal government. Type: Federal Govt Ind: Federal Govt Grp: Govt & Non-Prof Robert Richardson, CEO	Rev: Assets: Emp:	565 5893 1	

Organizations Listed Alphabetically

Organization / Address / Phone	Descriptive Information	Revenue / ($ mil)	Assets / ($ mil)	Emp (thous)
External Affairs Canada 125 Sussex Drive Lester B Pearson Bldg Ottawa, ON K1A0G2 Can 613-996-9134	Federal government agency. Type: Federal Govt Ind: Federal Govt Grp: Govt & Non-Prof James H Taylor, CEO	Rev: Assets: Emp:	1020 NM 4	
Exxon Corp 1251 Avenue of the Americas New York, NY 10020 212-333-1000	International integrated petroleum company. Type: NYSER-E Ind: Energy Grp: Basic Industries L G Rawl, CEO L R Raymond, Pres J Clark, VCh J F Bennett, CFO W B Nobles Jr, IS D R Clair, R&D E R Cattarulla, Mkt R S Lombard, VP H McBrayer, VP C Sitter, VP D McIvor, VP T Kirkley, VP E R Cattarulla, PR	Rev: Assets: Emp:	88563 74293 101	
Faberge Inc 725 5th Avenue New York, NY 10020 212-307-8000	Manufacturer of toiletries & apparel. Type: OTC Ind: Personal Care Grp: Consumer Prd Dan Manella, CEO Kenneth E Leccese, CFO Pat DeMartino, IS Harvey Schlissel, R&D Mark Goldston, Mkt Suzanne A Biallot, PR	Rev: Assets: Emp:	600 300 4	
Fabri Centers of America Inc 23550 Commerce Park Road Beachwood, OH 44122 216-464-2500	Operator of retail fabric stores. Type: NYSE-FCA Ind: Retail/Merch Grp: Retail Alan Rosskamm, CEO	Rev: Assets: Emp:	291 200 3	
Facet Enterprises Inc 7030 S Yale Tulsa, OK 74136 918-492-1800	Manufacturer & marketer of filtration products. Type: Private-Sub Par: Pennzoil Co Ind: Manufacturing Grp: Manufacturing James Malone, CEO	Rev: Assets: Emp:	NA NA NA	
Fairchild Industries Inc Dulles Airport 300 W Service Road Chantilly, VA 22021 703-478-5800	Manufacturer of electronics & aerospace equipment. Type: NYSE-FEN Ind: Aerospace Grp: High Tech Emanuel Fthenakis, CEO Paul E Wright, Pres Edward M Murchie, CFO Peter Marino, R&D Harold R Johnson, Mkt Jerry Lirette, VP Richard Orr, VP Thomas Spoehr, VP John McDonnell, VP James P Allen, VP Deborah M Tucker, PR	Rev: Assets: Emp:	539 441 5	
Fairfield Communities Inc 2800 Cantrell Road PO Box 3375 Little Rock, AR 72202 501-664-6000	Developer of master planned communities. Type: NYSE-FCI Ind: Real Estate/Bldg Grp: Business Service C Randolph Warner, CEO	Rev: Assets: Emp:	329 644 2	
Falconbridge Ltd Commerce Court W Toronto, ON M5L1B4 Can 416-863-7000	Mining company. Type: TOR Ind: Metals/Mining Grp: Basic Industries William James, CEO	Rev: Assets: Emp:	1139 2244 9	
Family Dollar Stores Inc 10401 Old Monroe Road Charlotte, NC 28212 704-847-6961	Operator of retail discount stores. Type: NYSE-FDO Ind: Retail/Merch Grp: Retail Leon Levine, CEO Ralph Dillon, Pres George R Mahoney, VCh C Martin Sowers, CFO Albert S Rorie, IS Richard Griner, Ops	Rev: Assets: Emp:	669 291 6	
Far West Savings Assn Inc 4001 MacArthur Blvd Newport Beach, CA 92660 714-833-8383	Thrift institution. Type: NYSE-FWF Ind: Savings & Loan Grp: Financial William Belzberg, CEO Fred Kayne, Chr Charles Green, CFO Cheryl Rastetter, Mkt Robert Suryn, IR	Rev: Assets: Emp:	400 4000 1	
Farah Inc 8889 Gateway W El Paso, TX 79985 915-593-4444	Manufacturer of men's clothing. Type: NYSE-FRA Ind: Apparel/Textiles Grp: Consumer Prd William F Farah, CEO	Rev: Assets: Emp:	350 250 4	

Organizations Listed Alphabetically

Organization / Address / Phone	Descriptive Information	Revenue / ($ mil)	Assets / ($ mil)	Emp (thous)
Farley Industries Inc 6300 Sears Tower 233 S Wacker Drive Chicago, IL 60606 312-876-1724	Manufacturer of apparel products & auto parts. Type: Private Ind: Manufacturing Grp: Manufacturing William Farley, CEO	Rev: Assets: Emp:	2000 NA 25	
Farm & Home Savings Assn Inc 221 W Cherry Street Nevada, MO 64772 417-667-3333	Thrift institution. Type: NASDAQ-FAHS Ind: Savings & Loan Grp: Financial Daniel C Arnold, CEO Donald F Roby, Pres Harry Gilbert, Tres Gerald Forrester, CFO Gerald Orman, IS Dale Buhl, Sls Joan McFarland, VP Jack W Eiffert, VP David A Todd, VP B J Figiel, VP Peggy Oglesby, PR	Rev: Assets: Emp:	312 3548 1	
Farm Credit Corp 434 Queen Street Ottawa, ON K1P6J9 Can 613-996-6606	Farm credit financing agency of the federal government. Type: Federal Govt Ind: Federal Govt Fin Grp: Financial James Hewitt, CEO	Rev: Assets: Emp:	411 4177 1	
Farm Fresh Inc 109 S Palm Norfolk, VA 23601 405-765-6656	Grocery stores. Type: Private Ind: Food Processing Grp: Food Processing Michael E Julian, CEO	Rev: Assets: Emp:	750 NA 5	
Farm House Foods Corp 111 E Wisconsin Avenue Suite 1900 Milwaukee, WI 53202 414-271-5050	Food processor & wholesaler. Type: NASDAQ-FHFC Ind: Retail/Merch Grp: Retail Donald E Runge, CEO John Sweet, CFO Beverly Hanke, VP Michael J McDonagh, VP Debbie McCoy, PR	Rev: Assets: Emp:	751 195 8	
Farmers Group Insurance Inc 4680 Wilshire Blvd Los Angeles, CA 90010 213-932-3200	Property & casualty insurance company. Type: NASDAQ-FGRP Ind: Insurance Grp: Insurance Leo E Denlea, Jr, CEO Robert McClintick, VCh Charles L Schultz, CFO Edward A Terhar, IS W H Braddock, Mkt Jason Katz, VP Maryann Seltzer, VP Darrell Norris, VP Tom Welch, IR Jeffrey C Beyer, PR	Rev: Assets: Emp:	1133 1528 16	
Farmers Union Central Exchange Inc 1180 N Concord South St Paul, MN 55075 612-451-1772	Manufacturer of agricultural equipment. Type: Private-Coop Ind: Energy Grp: Basic Industries Elroy Webster, CEO Noel Estenson, Chr David E Johnson, Pres Joel Koonce, CFO Joe Vossen, IS Maurice Miller, R&D Maurice Miller, PR	Rev: Assets: Emp:	1135 500 3	
Farmland Industries Inc 3315 N Oak Traffic Way Kansas City, MO 64116 816-459-6000	Refiner & distributor of petroleum products. Type: Private Ind: Energy Grp: Basic Industries James Rainey, CEO Garvin C Matthiesen, Pres Earl Knauss, CFO Ronald B Paul, IS Bill Matteson, PR	Rev: Assets: Emp:	4400 1000 6	
Farmstead Foods Corp East Main Street Albert Lea, MN 56007 507-377-4200	Meat processing company. Type: Private Ind: Food Processing Grp: Food Processing Lef DeNaumur, CEO	Rev: Assets: Emp:	750 NA 3	
Farwest Financial Corp 1800 Avenue of the Stars Los Angeles, CA 90067 213-277-3055	Financial investment firm. Type: OTC Ind: Savings & Loan Grp: Financial Fred Kayne, CEO	Rev: Assets: Emp:	450 4760 2	
Fay's Drug Co 7245 Henry Clay Blvd Liverpool, NY 13088 315-451-8000	Operator of retail drugstores. Type: NYSE-FAY Ind: Retail/Merch Grp: Retail Henry A Panasci, CEO	Rev: Assets: Emp:	527 300 6	

Organizations Listed Alphabetically

Organization / Address / Phone	Descriptive Information	Revenue / Assets / Emp ($ mil) ($ mil) (thous)		

FDL Foods Inc
701 E 16th Street
Dubuque, IA 52001
319-588-5400

Producer of packaged foods.
Type: Private
Ind: Food Processing Grp: Food Processing
Robert H Wallert, CEO

Rev: 825
Assets: NA
Emp: 4

Fedco Inc
9300 Santa Fe Street
Santa Fe Springs, CA 90670
213-946-2511

Operator of retail merchandise stores.
Type: Private
Ind: Retail/Merch Grp: Retail
Edward L Butterworth, CEO

Rev: 825
Assets: NA
Emp: 11

Fedders Corp
158 Highway 206 N
Peapack, NJ 07977
201-234-2100

Manufacturer of air conditioners.
Type: NYSE-FJQ
Ind: Appliances/Furn Grp: Manufacturing
Salvatore Giordano, CEO

Rev: 300
Assets: 200
Emp: 1

Federal Aviation Administration
800 Independence Avenue SW
Washington, DC 20591
202-366-4000

Federal government agency.
Type: Federal Govt
Ind: Federal Govt Grp: Govt & Non-Prof
T Allan McArtor, CEO

Rev: 5000
Assets: NM
Emp: 15

Federal Business Development Bank Ltd
800 Carre Victoria
Montreal, PQ H4Z 1L4 Can
514-283-5904

Business development agency of the federal government.
Type: Federal Govt
Ind: Federal Govt Fin Grp: Financial
D Lavigueur, CEO

Rev: 213
Assets: 1530
Emp: 1

Federal Deposit Insurance Corp
550 Seventeenth Street NW
Washington, DC 20429
202-393-8400

Federal government financial agency.
Type: Federal Govt
Ind: Federal Govt Fin Grp: Financial
L William Seidman, CEO

Rev: 5000
Assets: NM
Emp: 4

Federal Express Corp
2005 Corporate Avenue
Memphis, TN 38132
901-369-3600

Small package express delivery service company.
Type: NYSE-FDX
Ind: Business Service Grp: Business Service
Frederick W Smith, CEO James L Barksdale, Pres Fred Manske, VCh
David C Anderson, CFO Ron J Ponder, IS Thomas R Oliver, Sls
Carole A Presley, Mkt James Reidmeyer, Ops Theodore Weise, VP
Robert L Cox, VP Kenneth Masterson, VP Judith Rogala, VP
Carole A Presley, IR James E Coleman, PR

Rev: 3883
Assets: 3009
Emp: 49

Federal Home Life Insurance Co
6277 Sea Harbor Drive
Orlando, FL 32821
407-345-3020

Life insurance company.
Type: Private-Sub Par: Harcourt Brace Jovanovich Inc
Ind: Insurance Grp: Insurance
J William Brandner, CEO

Rev: NA
Assets: NA
Emp: NA

Federal Home Loan Bank Board
1700 G Street NW
Washington, DC 20052
202-377-6000

Federal government financial agency.
Type: Federal Govt
Ind: Federal Govt Fin Grp: Financial
M Danny Wall, CEO

Rev: 2000
Assets: NM
Emp: 10

Federal Industries Ltd
One Lombard Place S
Winnipeg, MB R3B0X3 Can
204-942-8161

Metals & minerals manufacturing company.
Type: TOR
Ind: Metals/Mining Grp: Basic Industries
Stewart A Searle, CEO Stewart Searle, Chr John Fraser, Pres
Gary Goertz, CFO Roy E Cook, R&D R J Vahsholtz, VP
John A Leitch, VP Larry Watson, VP Martin Freedman, VP
Harry Ethans, VP

Rev: 1623
Assets: 808
Emp: 15

Federal Mogul Corp
26555 Northwestern Highway
Southfield, MI 48034
313-354-7700

Manufacturer of precision parts & tools for automotive co.
Type: NYSE-FMO
Ind: Automotive Grp: Manufacturing
Thomas F Russell, CEO Dennis J Gormley, Pres Robert W Hague, CFO
Thomas English, IS Wayne G Smith, Sls Alan H Somershoe, Mkt
George Bashara, VP George Faulkner, VP Leonard Gay, VP
Lonnie Ross, PR

Rev: 1177
Assets: 811
Emp: 16

Organizations Listed Alphabetically

Organization / Address / Phone	Descriptive Information	Revenue ($ mil)	Assets ($ mil)	Emp (thous)

Federal National Mortgage Corp
3900 Wisconsin Avenue NW
Washington, DC 20016
202-537-7000

National mortgage issuer; packager & reseller of mortgages.
Type: NYSE-FNM
Ind: Non-Bank Fin   Grp: Financial
David O Maxwell, CEO   Roger E Birk, Pres   Samuel Alward, VCh
Bruce McMillen, CFO   David E Roberts, IS   Dennis Campbell, Mkt
Dale Riordan, VP   Michael Smilow, VP   Glenn Austin, VP
Dennis Campbell, VP   Dale P Riordan, PR

Rev: 10266
Assets: 112258
Emp: 5

Federal Paper Board Co Inc
75 Chestnut Ridge Road
Montvale, NJ 07645
201-391-1776

Packaging manufacturer.
Type: NYSE
Ind: Paper/Forest Prd   Grp: Basic Industries
John R Kennedy, CEO   Sidney J Pope, Tres   Thomas L Cox, CFO
Owen Cox, IS   Robert D Baldwin, Mkt   Donald J Gardner, VP
Jack E Spengler, VP   Quentin J Kennedy, VP

Rev: 1117
Assets: 1335
Emp: 5

Federal Reserve Bank of Atlanta Inc
104 Marietta Street
Atlanta, GA 30303
404-521-8500

Central bank of the U.S., regional headquarters.
Type: Federal Govt
Ind: Federal Govt Fin   Grp: Financial
Bradley Currey, CEO   Robert Forrestal, Chr   Jack Guynn, Pres
W Ronnie Caldwell, VCh   Patrick K Barron, CFO   Bobbie H McCrackin, IS
Sheila Tschinkel, R&D   John M Wallace, Mkt   H Terry Smith, VP
Francis Craven, VP   Anne DeBeer, VP

Rev: 934
Assets: 14294
Emp: 2

Federal Reserve Bank of Boston Inc
600 Atlantic Avenue
Boston, MA 02106
617-973-3000

Central bank of the U.S., regional headquarters.
Type: Federal Govt
Ind: Federal Govt Fin   Grp: Financial
George N Hatsopoulos, CEO

Rev: 1156
Assets: 17450
Emp: 2

Federal Reserve Bank of Chicago Inc
230 S LaSalle Street
Chicago, IL 60690
312-322-5111

Central bank of the U.S., regional headquarters.
Type: Federal Govt
Ind: Federal Govt Fin   Grp: Financial
Robert J Day, CEO   B F Backland, Chr   Marcus Alexander, VCh

Rev: 2469
Assets: 34695
Emp: 3

Federal Reserve Bank of Cleveland Inc
East 6th Street & Superior
Cleveland, OH 441141
216-579-2000

Central bank of the U.S., regional headquarters.
Type: Federal Govt
Ind: Federal Govt Fin   Grp: Financial
Charles W Parry, CEO   Lee W Hoskins, Pres   William H Hendricks, CFO
John M Davis, R&D   Lawrence Cuy, Mkt   John J Wixted, VP
Samuel Smith, VP   Andrew Bazar, VP   Andrew C Burkle, VP
Jill Goubeaux Clark, VP

Rev: 1114
Assets: 16294
Emp: 2

Federal Reserve Bank of Dallas Inc
400 S Akard Street
Dallas, TX 75202
214-651-6111

Central bank of the U.S., regional headquarters.
Type: Federal Govt
Ind: Federal Govt Fin   Grp: Financial
Bobby R Inman, CEO

Rev: 1258
Assets: 15185
Emp: 2

Federal Reserve Bank of Kansas City Inc
925 Grand Avenue
Kansas City, MO 64198
816-881-2000

Central bank of the U.S., regional headquarters.
Type: Federal Govt
Ind: Federal Govt Fin   Grp: Financial
Irvine O Hockaday, CEO

Rev: 751
Assets: 12690
Emp: 2

Federal Reserve Bank of Minneapolis Inc
250 Marquette Avenue
Minneapolis, MN 55480
612-340-2345

Central bank of the U.S., regional headquarters.
Type: Federal Govt
Ind: Federal Govt Fin   Grp: Financial
Michael W Wright, CEO

Rev: 312
Assets: 5473
Emp: 1

Federal Reserve Bank of New York Inc
33 Liberty Street
New York, NY 10045
212-720-5000

Central bank of the U.S., regional headquarters.
Type: Federal Govt
Ind: Federal Govt Fin   Grp: Financial
John R Opel, CEO

Rev: 6381
Assets: 99785
Emp: 4

Federal Reserve Bank of Philadelphia Inc
100 N Sixth Street
Philadelphia, PA 19105
215-574-6000

Central bank of the U.S., regional headquarters.
Type: Federal Govt
Ind: Federal Govt Fin   Grp: Financial
Nevius M Curtis, CEO   Edward G Boehne, Pres   William H Stone, VCh
Konstanty Adack, CFO   Richard W Lang, IS   Stephen A Meyer, R&D
Donald Dorcos, VP   Hilary Holloway, VP   Thomas Desch, VP
James Gaylord, VP

Rev: 572
Assets: 9116
Emp: 1

Organizations Listed Alphabetically

Organization / Address / Phone	Descriptive Information	Revenue / Assets / Emp ($ mil) ($ mil) (thous)		

Federal Reserve Bank of Richmond Inc
701 E Byrd Street
Richmond, VA 23219
804-643-1250

Central bank of the U.S., regional headquarters.
Type: Federal Govt
Ind: Federal Govt Fin   Grp: Financial
Robert A Georgine, CEO

Rev: 1513
Assets: 24861
Emp: 2

Federal Reserve Bank of San Francisco
101 Market Street
San Francisco, CA 94105
415-974-2000

Central bank of the U.S., regional headquarters.
Type: Federal Govt
Ind: Federal Govt Fin   Grp: Financial
Robert F Erburu, CEO

Rev: 2493
Assets: 34502
Emp: 3

Federal Reserve Bank of St Louis
411 Locust
St Louis, MO 63102
314-444-8444

Central bank of the U.S., regional headquarters.
Type: Federal Govt
Ind: Federal Govt Fin   Grp: Financial
Robert L Virgil, CEO

Rev: 574
Assets: 9329
Emp: 1

Federal Reserve System Headquarters
20th & Constitution Ave NW
Washington, DC 20551
202-452-3000

Central bank of the United States.
Type: Federal Govt
Ind: Federal Govt Fin   Grp: Financial
Alan Greenspan, CEO

Rev: 19526
Assets: 293674
Emp: 24

Federal Signal Corp
1415 W 22nd Street
Oak Brook, IL 60521
312-954-2000

Manufacturer of communications & signaling equipment.
Type: NYSE-FSS
Ind: Electronics   Grp: High Tech
Joseph J Ross, CEO

Rev: 400
Assets: 300
Emp: 3

Federated Cooperatives Ltd
401 22nd Street E
Saskatoon, SK S7K3M9 Can
306-244-3311

Agricultural cooperative; sawmill, plywood manufacturer.
Type: Private-Coop
Ind: Energy   Grp: Basic Industries
J Leland, CEO

Rev: 1214
Assets: 451
Emp: 2

Federated Department Stores Inc
Seven W Seventh Street
Cincinnati, OH 45202
513-579-7000

Nationwide operator of retail department stores.
Type: Private-Sub Par: Kellogg Co
Ind: Retail/Merch   Grp: Retail
John W Burden, CEO   James M Zimmerman, Pres   Thomas G Cody, VCh
Russell S Davis, CFO   Glen Griffith, IS   Donald J Stone, VP
Lawrence Stone, VP   Ronald Tysoe, VP   Thomas G Cody, IR
Patricia Ikeda, PR

Rev: 11118
Assets: 6009
Emp: 64

Federated Investment Corp
Federated Tower 1001 Liberty Center
Pittsburgh, PA 15222
412-288-1900

Investment company; personal & institutional funds.
Type: Private
Ind: Non-Bank Fin   Grp: Financial
John Donahue, CEO

Rev: 850
Assets: 44000
Emp: 3

Federated Mutual Insurance Co
121 E Park Square
Owatonna, MN 55060
507-455-5200

Property & casualty insurance company.
Type: Private-Mutual
Ind: Insurance   Grp: Insurance
Fred C Austin, CEO

Rev: 600
Assets: 1025
Emp: 2

Fednav Ltd
600 De La Gaucheitie 0062
Montreal, PQ H3B4M3 Can
514-878-6500

Deep sea equipment & transportation.
Type: MON
Ind: Transport   Grp: Business Service
Laurence Pathy, CEO

Rev: 340
Assets: 595
Emp: 1

Ferrell Companies Inc
One Liberty Plaza
Liberty, MO 64268
816-792-1600

Propane gas company.
Type: Private
Ind: Energy   Grp: Basic Industries
James E Ferrell, CEO

Rev: 750
Assets: NA
Emp: 3

Ferro Corp
1000 Lakeside Avenue
Cleveland, OH 44114
216-641-8580

Manufacturer of specialty chemicals & coatings.
Type: NYSE-FOE
Ind: Chemicals   Grp: Basic Industries
Adolph Posnick, CEO   Albert Bersticker, Pres   Hector R Ortino, CFO
Patrick H Cavanagh, IS   Roy Harrington, R&D   Werner Bush, VP
James Fisher, VP   John Goodger, VP   Roy Harrington, VP
David Woodbury, IR   J E Hugo, PR

Rev: 1009
Assets: 588
Emp: 8

Organizations Listed Alphabetically

Organization / Address / Phone	Descriptive Information	Revenue / Assets / Emp ($ mil) ($ mil) (thous)		

Organization / Address / Phone	Descriptive Information			
FGIC Inc 175 Water Street New York, NY 10038 212-607-3000	Municipal bond insurance company. Type: Private Ind: Insurance Grp: Insurance Gerald L Friedman, CEO	Rev: Assets: Emp:	250 958 1	
FHP International Corp 9900 Talbot Avenue Fountain Valley, CA 92728 714-963-7233	Operator of HMO facilities. Type: NASDAQ-FHPC Ind: Health Care Grp: Consumer Service R Gumbiuer, CEO	Rev: Assets: Emp:	504 182 1	
Fiberglas Canada Inc 4100 Yonge Street Willowdale, ON M2P2B6 Can 416-733-1600	Manufacturer of fiberglass products. Type: TOR Ind: Building Mat Grp: Basic Industries William McKee, CEO	Rev: Assets: Emp:	405 205 3	
Fidelcor Inc Broad & Walnut Streets Philadelphia, PA 19109 215-985-6000	Commercial bank. Type: NASDAQ-FICR Ind: Banking Grp: Financial Joseph Gallagher, CEO	Rev: Assets: Emp:	1300 13000 6	
Fidelity Brokerage Services Inc 161 Devonshire Street Boston, MA 02110 617-570-7000	Investment firm; securities trading. Type: Private Ind: Securities Grp: Financial Edward C Johnson, CEO	Rev: Assets: Emp:	275 2200 1	
Fidelity Investments Corp 82 Devonshire Street Boston, MA 02109 617-523-1919	Mutual fund investment company. Type: Private Ind: Non-Bank Fin Grp: Financial Edward C Johnson, CEO	Rev: Assets: Emp:	1000 85000 6	
Fiduciary Trust Co 2 World Trade Center New York, NY 10048 212-466-4100	Investment firm. Type: Private Ind: Non-Bank Fin Grp: Financial Laurence Huntington, CEO	Rev: Assets: Emp:	400 15400 1	
Fieldcrest Cannon Inc 326 E Stadium Drive Eden, NC 27288 919-627-3000	Manufacturer of household textile products. Type: NYSE Ind: Apparel/Textiles Grp: Consumer Prd Joseph P Ely, CEO C Edward Midgley, VCh W Randle Mitchell Jr, CFO R H Hair, IS W O Stone, R&D Robert B Dale, Mkt Robert E Dellinger, Ops M Kenneth Doss, VP W Giles Hunnings, VP Chris Kametches, VP Osborne L Raines, VP O L Raines Jr, PR	Rev: Assets: Emp:	1338 812 22	
Fifth Third BanCorp Inc 38 Fountain Square Cincinnati, OH 45263 513-579-5300	Commercial bank. Type: NASDAQ Ind: Banking Grp: Financial Clement L Buenger, CEO	Rev: Assets: Emp:	506 5246 3	
Figgie International Holding Inc 1000 Virginia Center Parkway Richmond, VA 23295 804-264-5600	Manufacturer of personal recreation & safety products. Type: NASDAQ-FIFIA Ind: Conglomerate Grp: Manufacturing Harry E Figgie, CEO Harry E Figgie Jr, Chr Zen Alexander, Mkt Donald Eagon, IR Richard G Bezjak, PR	Rev: Assets: Emp:	1201 1022 17	
Filene's Inc 426 Washington Street Boston, MA 02101 617-357-2978	Operator of retail department stores. Type: Private-Sub Par: Abbott Laboratories Inc Ind: Retail/Merch Grp: Retail David Mullen, CEO	Rev: Assets: Emp:	NA NA NA	
Financial Corp of America 18401 Von Karman Avenue Irvine, CA 92715 714-553-6900	Thrift institution. Type: NYSE-FIN Ind: Savings & Loan Grp: Financial William J Popejoy, CEO Victor H Indiek, CFO Layna J Browdy, IR	Rev: Assets: Emp:	3250 22000 6	
Financial Corp of Santa Barbara 3908 State Street Santa Barbara, CA 93102 805-682-2300	Thrift institution. Type: NYSE-FIGI Ind: Savings & Loan Grp: Financial Philip Brinkerhoff, CEO Arthur B Hall, CFO Mary Essary, IR	Rev: Assets: Emp:	400 5000 1	

Organizations Listed Alphabetically

Organization / Address / Phone	Descriptive Information	Revenue ($ mil)	Assets ($ mil)	Emp (thous)
Financial Trustco Capital Ltd 121 King Street W Toronto, ON M5H3T9 Can 416-366-8990	Consumer banking company. Type: Private Ind: Non-Bank Fin Grp: Financial Edward Clark, CEO	Rev: 263 Assets: 1831 Emp: 1		
Fine Homes International L P Inc 10 Stamford Plaza Stamford, CT 06901 203-356-1400	Real estate, brokerage & mortgage banking firm. Type: NYSE-FHI Ind: Real Estate/Bldg Grp: Business Service L J Biedeman, CEO	Rev: 800 Assets: 730 Emp: 6		
Finevest Services 191 Mason Street Greenwich, CT 06830 203-629-8750	Producer of packaged food products; private labels. Type: Private Ind: Food Processing Grp: Food Processing William R Berkley, CEO	Rev: 2000 Assets: NA Emp: 12		
Finning Ltd 555 Great Northern Way Vancouver, BC V5T1E2 Can 604-872-4444	Manufacturer of industrial equipment. Type: TOR Ind: Equipment Grp: Manufacturing D W Load, CEO P Von Der Porten, CFO C Cederberg, Sls J Shepard, Ops C Loyst, VP L Norlander, VP J Carthy, VP	Rev: 595 Assets: 558 Emp: 3		
Fireman's Fund Inc 777 San Marin Drive Novato, CA 94998 415-899-2000	Property & casualty insurance company. Type: NYSE-FFC Ind: Insurance Grp: Insurance John J Byrne, CEO Robert T Marto, CFO Virgil Pittman, IS Richard Dobson, R&D Edward Laugle, Mkt Ian Mitchell, VP Joseph W Brown, VP Donald McComber, VP LeRoy S Adams, VP Jean Baulis, IR Nancy Arvay, PR	Rev: 3704 Assets: 11190 Emp: 10		
Firestone Canada Inc 120 King Street W Hamilton, ON L8N4C6 Can 416-521-1111	Manufacturer of automotive tires & rubber products. Type: Private-Sub-For Ind: Tire/Rubber Grp: Basic Industries F Mitchell, CEO	Rev: 309 Assets: 256 Emp: 3		
Firestone Tire & Rubber Co 1200 Firestone Parkway Akron, OH 44317 216-379-7000	Manufacturer of tires & rubber products. Type: NYSE-FIR Ind: Tire/Rubber Grp: Basic Industries John Nevin, CEO Albert E Suter, Pres J Robert Anderson, CFO Laurance T Burden, IS James R Thomas, Sls Robert J Troyer, PR	Rev: 312 Assets: 730 Emp: 55		
First Alabama Bancshares PO Box 1448 Montgomery, AL 36102 205-832-8490	Commercial bank. Type: NASDAQ-FABC Ind: Banking Grp: Financial Joe M Hinds, CEO Terrell McCormick, Pres Dalton M Guthrie, VCh Joe Hinds, CFO	Rev: 474 Assets: 5174 Emp: 3		
First American Bank of Virginia Co 1970 Chain Bridge Road McLean, VA 22102 703-821-7777	Commercial bank. Type: Private-Sub Par: First American Bankshares Inc Ind: Banking Grp: Financial M L Drewer, CEO	Rev: 300 Assets: 3200 Emp: 2		
First American Bankshares Inc First American Bank Bldg Washington, DC 20005 202-383-1400	Commercial bank. Type: Private Ind: Banking Grp: Financial Robert G Stevens, CEO Gwain H Gillespie, CFO William S Ringler, IS Iris B Wordsworth, PR	Rev: 900 Assets: 8000 Emp: 6		
First American Corp First American Center Nashville, TN 37237 615-748-2100	Commercial bank. Type: NASDAQ-FATN Ind: Banking Grp: Financial Kenneth L Roberts, CEO Andrew G Higgins, Pres John C Fox, CFO Willis Rhodes, IS Frierson Craig, R&D Ken Mills, Mkt John Smithwick, VP Jack Stringham, VP Neil L Cunningham, IR Ellen Jones Pryor, PR	Rev: 699 Assets: 7204 Emp: 4		

Organizations Listed Alphabetically

Organization / Address / Phone	Descriptive Information	Revenue / ($ mil)	Assets / ($ mil)	Emp (thous)
First Bank System Inc 1200 First Bank Place E Minneapolis, MN 55402 612-370-5100	Commercial bank. Type: NYSE-FBS Ind: Banking Grp: Financial D H Ankeny, CEO Dennis E Evans, Pres Darrell Knudsen, VCh Gerald B Fischer, CFO Howard W Moody, IS Mary Ann Hansen, Mkt James E Ulland, IR K Rollag Wangstad, PR	Rev: Assets: Emp:	2441 24248 12	
First Boston Inc Park Avenue Plaza New York, NY 10055 212-909-2000	Investment banking firm. Type: NYSE Ind: Securities Grp: Financial Peter T Buchanan, CEO Alan Shoemaker, Pres John Toffolon, CFO F R Pete Talbott, IS William Galvin, Mkt Peter Anker, Ops John Baldwin, VP R Gamble Baldwin, VP Robert Baylis, VP Christopher Beale, VP Michael Beder, VP Richard Bott, VP William Galvin, IR Cecily Harrison, PR	Rev: Assets: Emp:	1323 36148 6	
First Brands Corp 39 Old Ridgebury Road Danbury, CT 06817 203-790-2900	Manufacturer of consumer products. Type: Private Ind: Personal Care Grp: Consumer Prd Alfred E Dudley, CEO	Rev: Assets: Emp:	1000 NA 5	
First Capital Holding Corp 1900 Avenue of the Stars Los Angeles, CA 90067 213-551-1000	Diversified financial services company. Type: Private Ind: Non-Bank Fin Grp: Financial Robert Weingarten, CEO	Rev: Assets: Emp:	250 750 1	
First Chicago Corp One First National Plaza Chicago, IL 60670 312-732-4000	Commercial bank. Type: NYSE-FNB Ind: Banking Grp: Financial Barry Sullivan, CEO Richard L Thomas, Pres William Bennett, VCh J Mikesell Thomas, CFO Robert Hokom, IS A D Frazier, Mkt David Vitale, VP Donald Hollis, VP Emile S Godfrey, PR	Rev: Assets: Emp:	4815 44432 16	
First Citizens Bank & Trust Co Martin Wilmington Road Raleigh, NC 27601 919-755-7215	Commercial bank. Type: NASDAQ-FCNC Ind: Banking Grp: Financial Lewis R Holding, CEO	Rev: Assets: Emp:	319 3218 3	
First City Bancorp of Texas Inc 400 First City Tower 1001 Fannin Street Houston, TX 77002 713-658-6873	Commercial bank. Type: NYSE-FBT Ind: Banking Grp: Financial A Robert Abboud, CEO Robert D Richley, Pres W L Medford, CFO Michael D Williams, IS Hugh J Barrett, Mkt James E Day, PR	Rev: Assets: Emp:	865 12195 7	
First City Financial Corp 777 Hornby Street 600 Vancouver, BC V6Z 1S4 Can 604-685-2489	Diversified financial company. Type: TOR-FCY Ind: Non-Bank Fin Grp: Financial Samuel Belzberg, CEO W Gordon Lancaster, VCh Lawrence Fox, CFO Marc Belzberg, R&D William Belzberg, Sls Hyman Belzberg, Mkt Ian Matheson, VP Aidan Hughes, VP Roger Franke, VP	Rev: Assets: Emp:	625 4225 7	
First City Industries Inc 8383 Wilshire Blvd Suite 800 Beverly Hills, CA 90211 213-852-0499	Land development company. Type: Private Ind: Manufacturing Grp: Manufacturing Keenan Burlhe, CEO	Rev: Assets: Emp:	750 1100 10	
First Colony Life Insurance Co PO Box 1280 Lynchburg, VA 24505 804-845-0911	Life insurance company. Type: OTC Ind: Insurance Grp: Insurance Ronald V Dolan, CEO	Rev: Assets: Emp:	777 2549 2	
First Commerce Corp 210 Baronne Street New Orleans, LA 70112 504-561-1371	Commercial bank. Type: NASDAQ-FCOM Ind: Banking Grp: Financial William Trotter, CEO Ian Arnof, Chr Michael Flick, CFO Dale Aronson, R&D M Braham Jue, Mkt Kathi Schroeder, PR	Rev: Assets: Emp:	300 3000 2	

Organizations Listed Alphabetically

Organization / Address / Phone	Descriptive Information	Revenue / Assets / Emp ($ mil) ($ mil) (thous)		

First Empire State Corp
One M & T Plaza
Buffalo, NY 14240
716-842-4200

Commerical bank.
Type: ASE-FES
Ind: Banking   Grp: Financial
Robert G Wilmers, CEO   James Vardon, CFO   Richard A Lammert, VP
Jeremy W P Wainwright, VP   Atwoods Collins, VP   Thomas F Keefe, VP

Rev: 537
Assets: 5908
Emp: 3

First Executive Corp
11444 W Olympic Blvd
Los Angeles, CA 90064
213-312-1000

Life insurance company.
Type: OTC
Ind: Non-Bank Fin   Grp: Financial
Fred Carr, CEO   Allan Chapman, VCh   Merle A Horst, CFO
Raul A Cruz, IS   Gary Schulte, Mkt   Robert Feigenbaum, Ops
William J Adams, VP

Rev: 3049
Assets: 18225
Emp: 1

First Federal of Michigan Inc
1001 Woodward Avenue
Detroit, MI 48226
313-965-1400

Thrift institution.
Type: NASDAQ-FFOM
Ind: Savings & Loan   Grp: Financial
James A Aliber, CEO   C Gene Harling, Pres   C Gene Harling, VCh
Richard W Neu, CFO   Allan D Breyer, IS   Kirk F Hartmann, R&D
Richard Platt, Mkt   Katherine N Anslow, PR

Rev: 1096
Assets: 11942
Emp: 3

First Federal Savings & Loan Assn Inc
One First Federal Plaza
Rochester, NY 14614
716-238-2100

Thrift institution.
Type: Private
Ind: Savings & Loan   Grp: Financial
Thomas N Borshoff, CEO

Rev: 550
Assets: 5500
Emp: 2

First Federal Savings of Pittsburgh Inc
300 Sixth Avenue
Pittsburgh, PA 15222
412-392-5500

Thrift institution.
Type: Private
Ind: Savings & Loan   Grp: Financial
Andrew R Evans, CEO

Rev: 400
Assets: 4000
Emp: 1

First Fidelity BanCorp Inc
550 Broad Street
Newark, NJ 07192
201-565-3200

Commercial bank.
Type: NYSE
Ind: Banking   Grp: Financial
Robert R Ferguson, CEO   Edward D Knapp, Pres   Leslie E Goodman, VCh
Frederick H Pennekamp, CFO   Jonathan J Palmer, Mkt   Frank Noonan, VP
Frederick H Pennekamp, VP   Wilbur Turnbill, VP   Richard T White, VP
J Roger Williams, VP   Harold Mortimer, VP   Susan Hails, IR
Paul J Levine, PR

Rev: 2806
Assets: 29777
Emp: 15

First Financial Management Corp
3 Corporate Square
Atlanta, GA 30329
404-321-0120

Data processing & computerized systems company.
Type: NASDAQ-FFMC
Ind: Comput/Off Equip   Grp: High Tech
Patrick Thomas, CEO

Rev: 400
Assets: 200
Emp: 3

First Florida Banks Inc
111 Madison Street
Tampa, FL 33602
813-224-1111

Commercial bank.
Type: OTC
Ind: Banking   Grp: Financial
A Bronson Thayer, CEO   John C Wulbern, Pres   Charles P Lykes, VCh
W H Thompson, CFO   Bruce L Lee, IS   Mark Gruetzmacher, Sls
Mark Gruetzmacher, Mkt   Frank DiMarco, Ops   James Warren, VP
Fred Byrne, VP   Frank Downs, VP

Rev: 479
Assets: 5132
Emp: 4

First Hawaiian Inc
165 S King Street
Honolulu, HI 96813
808-525-7000

Commercial bank.
Type: NASDAQ-FHWN
Ind: Banking   Grp: Financial
John D Bellinger, CEO

Rev: 396
Assets: 4239
Emp: 2

First Interstate BanCorp Inc
707 Wilshire Blvd
Los Angeles, CA 90054
213-614-6001

Commercial bank.
Type: NYSE-I
Ind: Banking   Grp: Financial
Joseph J Pinola, CEO   Dale Skurdahl, Tres   Don M Griffith, CFO
William Sudmann, R&D   John O Smith, Mkt   Andrew Studdert, Ops
Fredric Magner, VP   Jerry Jordan, VP   James M Large, VP
Richard Puz, VP   Patrick L Denny, VP   Paul D Minch, IR

Rev: 5932
Assets: 63703
Emp: 38

Organizations Listed Alphabetically

Organization / Address / Phone	Descriptive Information	Revenue / ($ mil)	Assets / ($ mil)	Emp (thous)
First Interstate Bank of Texas 1000 Louisiana Street Houston, TX 77002 713-224-6611	Commercial bank. Type: Private-Sub Ind: Banking Grp: Financial Jerome Williams, CEO Harold Leppo, Pres James Bloise, CFO Harold Leppo, Mkt Sandy Browning, PR	Rev: 1000 Assets: 10000 Emp: 4		
First Jersey National Corp 2 Montgomery Street Jersey City, NJ 07302 201-547-7000	Commercial bank. Type: OTC Ind: Banking Grp: Financial Thomas J Stanton, CEO	Rev: 500 Assets: 5000 Emp: 3		
First Kentucky National Corp 101 S Fifth Street Louisville, KY 40202 502-581-4498	Commercial bank. Type: NASDAQ-FKYN Ind: Banking Grp: Financial Steven Miles, CEO Morton Boyd, Pres George B Wombwell, CFO Michael L Douglas, IS Albert Bissmeyer III, Mkt Mary H Griffith, IR John Cooper, PR	Rev: 500 Assets: 5500 Emp: 5		
First Maryland BanCorp Inc 25 S Charles Street Baltimore, MD 21201 301-244-4000	Commercial bank. Type: Private-Sub-For Ind: Banking Grp: Financial Charles W Cole, CEO Robert W Schaefer, CFO Charles S Hooper, IS Joseph E Peters, Mkt Robert W Schaefer, IR Carroll S Jackson, PR	Rev: 660 Assets: 5881 Emp: 3		
First Minnesota Savings Bank Inc 77 S 7th Street Minneapolis, MN 55402 612-371-3700	Thrift institution. Type: Private Ind: Savings & Loan Grp: Financial Wilfred E Lingren, CEO	Rev: 400 Assets: 4000 Emp: 1		
First Mississippi Corp 70 North Street Jackson, MS 39202 601-948-7550	Mining & manufacturing company; chemicals, coal, gold. Type: NYSE-FRM Ind: Metals/Mining Grp: Basic Industries J Kelley Williams, CEO	Rev: 400 Assets: 500 Emp: 2		
First National Cincinnati Corp 425 Walnut Street Cincinnati, OH 45202 513-632-4000	Commercial bank. Type: NASDAQ-FNAC Ind: Banking Grp: Financial Oliver W Waddell, CEO Mark T Johnson, Pres Samuel M Cassidy, VCh Lester E Hilliard, Tres Gust Totlis, CFO Timothy J Fogarty, VP Phillip A Parker, VP	Rev: 531 Assets: 5214 Emp: 3		
First National Supermarkets Inc 17000 Rockside Maple Heights, OH 44137 216-587-7100	Operator of retail supermarkets. Type: Private Ind: Retail/Food Grp: Retail Richard J Bogomolny, CEO	Rev: 1650 Assets: NA Emp: 16		
First Nationwide Bank Inc 700 Market Street San Francisco, CA 94102 415-772-1400	Thrift institution. Type: Private-Sub Par: Ford Motor Co Ind: Savings & Loan Grp: Financial Robert E Lackovic, CEO John L Carr, Pres Joseph Mahoney, CFO William Banker, VP Kenneth Bourguignon, VP Will Caldwell, VP John Carr, VP	Rev: 2527 Assets: 34810 Emp: 4		
First of America Bank Corp 108 E Michigan Avenue Kalamazoo, MI 49007 616-383-9000	Commercial bank. Type: NASDAQ-FABK Ind: Banking Grp: Financial Daniel R Smith, CEO Richard F Chormann, Pres Richard D Klein, VCh Thomas Lambert, CFO Donald Kenney, IS Mary Beth Donovan, R&D John May Jr, Mkt Dean Williams, VP Dawn George, IR Melanie Bellon, PR	Rev: 885 Assets: 9769 Emp: 5		

Organizations Listed Alphabetically

Organization / Address / Phone	Descriptive Information	Revenue / ($ mil)	Assets / ($ mil)	Emp (thous)
First Options of Chicago Inc One Financial Place 440 S LaSalle Street Chicago, IL 60605 312-786-3000	Investment firm; securities trading. Type: Private Ind: Securities Grp: Financial Jim Porter, CEO	Rev: Assets: Emp:	330 3300 1	
First Pennsylvania Corp 1500 Market Street Philadelphia, PA 19101 215-786-5000	Commercial bank. Type: NYSE-FPA Ind: Banking Grp: Financial George A Butler, CEO Frank E Reed, Pres John Brine, CFO John Britt, IS Leslie Butler, Mkt David T Walker, VP Leslie Butler, VP A Bruce Crawley, IR Bill Kane, PR	Rev: Assets: Emp:	623 6407 4	
First Security Corp 79 S Main Street Salt Lake City, UT 84111 801-350-5325	Commercial bank. Type: NASDAQ-FSCO Ind: Banking Grp: Financial Spencer R Eccles, CEO Robert T Heiner, Pres Morgan J Evans, CFO T Eugene King, IS David R Dowdle, R&D Phillip F Hudson, Mkt Alan Behunin, IR Larry Brower, PR	Rev: Assets: Emp:	522 5159 3	
First Tennessee National Corp 165 Madison Avenue Memphis, TN 38103 901-523-5630	Commercial bank. Type: NASDAQ-FTEN Ind: Banking Grp: Financial Ronald Terry, CEO John P Dulin, Pres M List Underwood, Tres Susan Schmidt Bies, CFO Robert Young, IS J Terrence Lee, Mkt J Terrence Lee, IR Deborah Hallin, PR	Rev: Assets: Emp:	621 5800 4	
First Texas Financial Corp 14951 Dallas Parkway Dallas, TX 75240 214-960-4500	Thrift institution. Type: Private Ind: Savings & Loan Grp: Financial J Livingston Kosberg, CEO	Rev: Assets: Emp:	750 6000 4	
First Union National Bank Corp Two First Union Plaza Charlotte, NC 28288 704-374-6565	Commercial bank. Type: NYSE-FTU Ind: Banking Grp: Financial Edward E Crutchfield, CEO Ben T Craig, Pres B J Walker, VCh J Robert Lee, CFO Austin A Adams, IS Alvin T Sale, Mkt Barbara K Massa, IR Connie Fuller, PR	Rev: Assets: Emp:	2898 28978 16	
First Union Real Estate Inc 55 Public Square Cleveland, OH 44113 216-781-4030	Real estate investment company. Type: NYSE-FUR Ind: Real Estate/Bldg Grp: Business Service Donald S Schofield, CEO	Rev: Assets: Emp:	74 439 1	
First Virginia Banks Inc 6400 Arlington Blvd Falls Church, VA 22046 703-241-4000	Commercial bank. Type: NYSE-FVB Ind: Banking Grp: Financial Robert H Zalokar, CEO Paul H Geithner, Pres Harry Allen, VCh Ronald Locke, CFO Shirley Beavers, VP Raymond Brann, VP Hugh Campbell, VP A Paul Lanzillotta, VP Justin O'Donnell, VP	Rev: Assets: Emp:	482 4796 4	
First Wachovia Corp 301 N Main Street Winston-Salem, NC 27101 919-770-5000	Commercial bank. Type: NYSE-FW Ind: Banking Grp: Financial John G Medlin, CEO David L Cotterill, Pres L M Baker, VCh H Jack Runnion Jr, CFO Robert Copeland, Mkt G Prendergast, VP D Raymond Riddle, VP John McNair, VP Walter E Leonard, VP Thomas Boland, VP John H Arsmann III, IR Nancy Lovelace, PR	Rev: Assets: Emp:	2091 21815 14	
Firstar (First Wisconsin Corp) 777 E Wisconsin Avenue Milwaukee, WI 53202 414-765-4321	Commercial bank. Type: NYSE-FSR Ind: Banking Grp: Financial John H Hendee, CEO Roger L Fitzsimonds, Pres William H Risch, CFO Walter Fiorentini, IS Gerald Thorne, VP Howard Hopwood, VP Anne L Curley, PR	Rev: Assets: Emp:	850 7193 5	

Organizations Listed Alphabetically

Organization / Address / Phone	Descriptive Information	Revenue / ($ mil)	Assets / ($ mil)	Emp (thous)
Fischbach Corp 485 Lexington Avenue New York, NY 10017 212-986-4100	Mechanical & electrical contracting construction company. Type: Private Ind: Real Estate/Bldg　Grp: Business Service Jack Coppersmith, CEO　Alfred R Manville, Chr　Michael Appel, CFO Duane T O'Connor, Mkt　Edwin Wilinski, PR	Rev: Assets: Emp:	1375 500 16	
Fischer Francis Trees & Watts Inc 717 Fifth Avenue New York, NY 10022 212-350-8000	Investment firm. Type: Private Ind: Non-Bank Fin　Grp: Financial John Watts, CEO	Rev: Assets: Emp:	300 11000 1	
Fisher Controls International Inc 8000 Maryland Avenue Clayton, MO 63105 314-694-9900	Manufacturer of industrial process controls. Type: Private-Sub　Par: Monsanto Co Ind: Manufacturing　Grp: Manufacturing R Flynn, CEO	Rev: Assets: Emp:	NA NA NA	
Fisher Price Inc 636 Girard Avenue East Aurora, NY 14052 716-687-3000	Manufacturer of toys, childrens furniture & apparel. Type: Private-Sub　Par: Quaker Oats Co Ind: Manufacturing　Grp: Manufacturing R Bruce Sampsell, CEO	Rev: Assets: Emp:	NA NA NA	
Fisher Scientific Group Inc 11255 N Torrey Pines Road La Jolla, CA 92037 619-457-3565	Manufacturer of scientific & medical technology products. Type: NASDAQ-FSHG Ind: Instruments　Grp: High Tech Richard A Cramer, CEO　Harold Eastman, Pres　John Moynahan, Tres David A Bocchini, CFO　Jon A Jenkins, IS　Thomas Donahoe, VP Christopher Reinhard, VP　E Linwood Johnson, VP　Walter D Sanborn III, IR	Rev: Assets: Emp:	957 579 6	
Fisheries & Oceans Canada 200 Kent Street Centennial Towers Ottawa, ON K1A0E6 Can 613-993-0600	Federal government agency. Type: Federal Govt Ind: Federal Govt　Grp: Govt & Non-Prof Peter Meyboom, CEO	Rev: Assets: Emp:	1020 NM 6	
FL Industries Inc 220 S Orange Avenue Livingston, NJ 07039 201-535-9522	Diversified manufacturing company. Type: Private Ind: Manufacturing　Grp: Manufacturing Richard W Viser, CEO	Rev: Assets: Emp:	660 NA 6	
Fleet/Norstar Financial Corp 50 Kennedy Plaza Providence, RI 02903 401-278-5800	Commercial bank. Type: NYSE-FNG Ind: Banking　Grp: Financial J Terrence Murray, CEO　Richard Pannone, Tres　John W Flynn, CFO Michael R Zucchini, IS　Peter L Hood, Mkt　Andrew D Woodward, VP Irving J Gross, VP　H Jay Sarles, VP　John B Robinson, VP Robert L Mushkin, VP　Eugene T Mann, VP　Robert W Lougee Jr, PR	Rev: Assets: Emp:	3051 29052 15	
Fleetwood Enterprises Inc 3125 Myers Street Riverside, CA 92523 714-351-3500	Manufacturer of mobile homes, recreation vehicles, trailers. Type: NYSE-FLE Ind: Leisure Time　Grp: Consumer Service John C Cream, CEO　Glenn F Kummer, Pres　David R Mariner, Tres Paul M Bingham, CFO　John C Cola, IS　John Pollis, Sls Jim Sheldon, Mkt　L Bruce Boylen, VP　John A Nord, VP William A Lear, VP　Lawrence F Pittroff, VP　David R Marriner, IR	Rev: Assets: Emp:	1406 514 11	
Fleishman Kurth Malting Co 2100 S 43rd Street Milwaukee, WI 53219 414-384-7400	Manufacturer of consumer food products. Type: Private-Sub　Par: Archer Daniels Midland Co Ind: Food Processing　Grp: Food Processing John Busby, CEO	Rev: Assets: Emp:	NA NA NA	
Fleming Companies Inc 6301 Waterford Blvd Oklahoma City, OK 73126 405-840-7200	Wholesale food distribution company. Type: NYSE Ind: Business Service　Grp: Business Service R D Harrison, CEO　E Dean Werries, Chr　Lawrence M Jones, CFO Robert G Dolan Jr, IS　C A Vernon Jr, Mkt　Cheryl Mayfield-Hudak, PR	Rev: Assets: Emp:	10467 2559 25	

Organizations Listed Alphabetically

Organization / Address / Phone	Descriptive Information	Revenue / ($ mil)	Assets / ($ mil)	Emp (thous)
Fletcher Challenge Canada Ltd 700 W Georgia Street Vancouver, BC V7Y 1J7 Can 604-665-3821	Forest products. Type: TOR Ind: Paper/Forest Prd Grp: Basic Industries Kenneth P Benson, CEO Ian Donald, Chr Blair Beaton, CFO Ronald W Neil, VP James Rainer, VP	Rev: 1250	Assets: 1415	Emp: 7
Flextronics Inc 35325 Fircrest Newark, CA 94560 415-792-4177	Manufacturer of electronics Type: OTC Ind: Electronics Grp: High Tech Robert Todd, CEO	Rev: 200	Assets: 100	Emp: 3
Flightsafety International Inc LaGuardia Airport Marine Air Terminal Flushing, NY 11371 718-565-4100	Flight training company; services to aviation industry. Type: NYSE-FSI Ind: Business Service Grp: Business Service Albert L Ueltschi, CEO	Rev: 183	Assets: 451	Emp: 2
Flint Ink Corp 25111 Glendale Avenue Detroit, MI 48239 313-538-6800	Manufacturer of ink; specialty, newspaper inks. Type: Private Ind: Manufacturing Grp: Manufacturing Robert H Flint, CEO	Rev: 400	Assets: NA	Emp: 4
Florida East Coast Industries Inc One Malaga Street St Augustine, FL 32084 904-829-3421	Real estate, railroad transportation. Type: NYSE Ind: Railroad Grp: Business Service W L Thornton, CEO	Rev: 151	Assets: 561	Emp: 2
Florida Federal Savings & Loan Inc 360 Central Avenue St Petersburg, FL 33731 813-893-1131	Thrift institution. Type: NASDAQ-FLFE Ind: Savings & Loan Grp: Financial John W Sapanski, CEO Richard Prestera, IS Larry Byrd, Sls Dick Funsch, Mkt Jerry Jeter, VP Nancy Basham, VP Richard A Prestera, IR	Rev: 472	Assets: 5157	Emp: 2
Florida National Banks 225 Water Street Jacksonville, FL 32201 904-359-5020	Commercial bank. Type: NASDAQ-FNBF Ind: Banking Grp: Financial John D Uible, CEO E Bruce Bower, Pres Victoria W Miller, Tres James E Linkenauger, CFO Albert O Rebassa, IS David L Brown, Mkt John P Haley, VP R Dennis Burroughs, VP	Rev: 749	Assets: 7828	Emp: 5
Florida Power & Light Co 92 Flaglin Street Miami, FL 33174 305-552-3552	Electric power utility company. Type: Private-Sub Par: FPL (Florida Power & Light) Group Inc Ind: Utility Grp: Utilities John Hudiberg, CEO	Rev: NA	Assets: NA	Emp: NA
Florida Progress Corp 270 First Avenue S St Petersburg, FL 33701 813-895-1700	Electric power generation & distribution company. Type: NYSE-FPC Ind: Utility Grp: Utilities Andrew H Hines, CEO Jack B Critchfield, Pres Lee Scott, VCh Clarence W McKee, CFO Joseph Cronin, R&D	Rev: 2002	Assets: 4304	Emp: 8
Florida Rock Industries Inc 155 E 21st Street Jacksonville, FL 32206 904-355-1781	Manufacturer of building materials. Type: ASE-FPK Ind: Building Mat Grp: Basic Industries Edward L Baker, CEO	Rev: 475	Assets: 300	Emp: 4
Florida State University Administrative Bldg Tallahassee, FL 32306 904-644-2525	Major educational institution; university. Type: University Ind: University Grp: Govt & Non-Prof Bernard F Sliger, CEO	Rev: 156	Assets: 253	Emp: 23

Organizations Listed Alphabetically

Organization / Address / Phone	Descriptive Information	Revenue / Assets / Emp ($ mil) ($ mil) (thous)		

Florida, State of
State Capitol
Tallahassee, FL 32301
904-488-1234

State government.
Type: State Govt
Ind: State/Prov Govt   Grp: Govt & Non-Prof
Bob Martinez, CEO

Rev: 23940
Assets: NM
Emp: 139

Florsheim Shoe Co
130 Canal Street
Chicago, IL 60606
312-559-2500

Operator of retail shoe stores.
Type: Private-Sub   Par: Interco Inc
Ind: Retail/Merch   Grp: Retail
Ronald Mueller, CEO

Rev: NA
Assets: NA
Emp: NA

Flour Corp
3333 Michelson Drive
Irvine, CA 92730
714-975-2000

Worldwide construction company.
Type: NYSE-FLR
Ind: Real Estate/Bldg   Grp: Business Service
David S Tappan, CEO   Leslie G McCraw, Pres   Nad Peterson, VCh
Robert L Guyett, CFO   Gerald M Glenn, Mkt   Charles J Bradley, VP
Lawrence Fisher, VP   J Robert Fluor, VP   William Hofacre, VP
LArry Lineberger, VP   James O Rollans, IR   Lila Churney, PR

Rev: 5132
Assets: 2073
Emp: 18

Flow General Inc
7655 Old Springhouse Road
McLean, VA 22102
703-893-5915

Consulting & engineering company.
Type: NYSE-FGN
Ind: Consulting   Grp: Business Service
Robert E Wengler, CEO

Rev: 250
Assets: 200
Emp: 2

Flowers Industries Inc
PO Box 1338
Thomasville, GA 31799
912-226-9110

Food processing company; baked goods, frozen.
Type: NYSE-FLO
Ind: Food Processing   Grp: Food Processing
Amos R McMullian, CEO   Heeth Varnedoe III, Pres   Frederick Cooper, VCh
C Martin Wood III, CFO   Robert D Ayers, IS   Robert P Crozer, Mkt
B Scott Rich, VP   George Harrison, VP   Gerald Bussell, VP
Marta Jones, PR

Rev: 737
Assets: 434
Emp: 9

Fluke, John Manufacturing Co
6920 Seaway Blvd
Everett, WA 98203
206-347-6100

Manufacturer of electronic testing equipment.
Type: ASE-FKM
Ind: Electronics   Grp: High Tech
John M Fluke, CEO

Rev: 225
Assets: 200
Emp: 2

Fluorocarbon Co
27611 La Paz Road
South Laguna, CA 92677
714-831-5350

Manufacturer of molding equipment for plastics, rubber.
Type: NASDAQ-FCBN
Ind: Manufacturing   Grp: Manufacturing
Peter Chum, CEO

Rev: 250
Assets: 200
Emp: 2

Flying J Inc
990 S 50th W
West Brigham, UT 84302
801-734-9416

Integrated petroleum.
Type: Private
Ind: Energy   Grp: Basic Industries
O Jay Call, CEO

Rev: 1000
Assets: NA
Emp: 2

FMC Corp
200 E Randolph Drive
Chicago, IL 60601
312-861-6000

Manufacturer of machinery for defense & industrial use.
Type: NYSE-FMC
Ind: Equipment   Grp: Manufacturing
Robert H Malott, CEO   Raymond C Tower, Pres   Robert N Burt, VCh
Arthur D Lyons, CFO   Dan W Irwin, IS   Larry D Brady, R&D
Anthony G Tappin, Mkt   William F Beck, VP   W Glenn Bush, VP
Robert L Day, VP   Charles Fink, VP   William R Jenkins, PR

Rev: 3287
Assets: 2749
Emp: 24

Folger's Coffee Co
One Proctor & Gambel Plaza
Cincinnati, OH 45202
513-983-1100

Producer & distributor of coffee products.
Type: Private-Sub   Par: Procter & Gamble Co
Ind: Food Processing   Grp: Food Processing
John Pepper, CEO

Rev: NA
Assets: NA
Emp: NA

Food Emporium
400 Walnut Avenue
Bronx, NY 10454
212-579-3400

Operator of retail supermarkets.
Type: Private-Sub   Par: Great Atlantic & Pacific Tea Co
Ind: Retail/Food   Grp: Retail
Louis Ruggerio, CEO

Rev: 1000
Assets: NA
Emp: 10

Organizations Listed Alphabetically

Organization / Address / Phone	Descriptive Information	Revenue / ($ mil)	Assets / ($ mil)	Emp (thous)
Food Lion Inc 2110 Harrison Road PO Box 1330 Salisbury, NC 28145 704-633-8250	Retail food stores. Type: NASDAQ-FDLN Ind: Retail/Food Grp: Retail Ralph W Ketner, CEO Tom E Smith, Chr Jerry W Helms, Pres Brian P Woolf, CFO A E Benner Jr, IS Vincent Watkins, R&D John P Watkins, Mkt Mike Mozingo, PR	Rev: 3815	Assets: 1089	Emp: 36
Foodarama Supermarket Corp 303 W Main Street Freehold, NJ 07728 201-462-4700	Food supermarket retail company. Type: ASE-FSM Ind: Retail/Food Grp: Retail Joseph J Saker, CEO	Rev: 500	Assets: 300	Emp: 7
Foodmaker (Jack in the Box) Inc 9330 Balboa Avenue San Diego, CA 92112 619-571-2121	Operator of fast food restaurants. Type: Private Ind: Food/Lodging Grp: Consumer Service Jack Goodall, CEO	Rev: 825	Assets: NA	Emp: 26
Foote, Cone & Belding Inc 101 E Erie Street Foote Cone & Belding Ctr Chicago, IL 60611 312-751-7000	Advertising agency. Type: NYSE-FCB Ind: Business Service Grp: Business Service Norman W Brown, CEO	Rev: 520	Assets: 350	Emp: 4
Ford Credit Canada Ltd The Canadian Road Oakville, ON L6L4S9 Can 416-845-2511	Finance subsidiary of Ford Motor Canada. Type: Private-Sub-For Ind: Non-Bank Fin Grp: Financial George E Watts, CEO	Rev: 369	Assets: 3367	Emp: 1
Ford Credit Corp The American Road Dearborn, MI 48121 313-322-3000	Finance subsidiary of Ford Motor Company. Type: Private-Sub Par: Ford Motor Co Ind: Non-Bank Fin Grp: Financial William E Odom, CEO Kenneth Whipple, Pres Robert Warner, VCh Richard Bentley, CFO Leo Larkin, Mkt Raymond Maise, Ops	Rev: 6819	Assets: 56276	Emp: 9
Ford Div The American Road Dearborn, MI 48121 313-322-3000	Automobile manufacturer. Type: Private-Sub Par: Ford Motor Co Ind: Automotive Grp: Manufacturing Thomas Wagner, CEO	Rev: NA	Assets: NA	Emp: NA
Ford Electronics Manufacturing Corp 7455 Birchmount Road Markham, ON L3R 5C2 Can 416-475-8510	Electronics manufacturing subsidiary of Ford Motor Company. Type: Private-Sub-For Ind: Electronics Grp: High Tech Gary VanderHaagen, CEO	Rev: 351	Assets: 170	Emp: 2
Ford Motor Canada Ltd The Canadian Road Oakville, ON L6J5E4 Can 416-845-2511	Automobile manufacturer. Type: TOR Ind: Automotive Grp: Manufacturing Kenneth W Harrigan, CEO David B Carter, Tres Albert E Mathews, CFO Udo Kaul, Sls Jack Clissold, Mkt Robert Carter, VP Anthony Fredo, VP Donald McKenzie, VP David G Rehor, VP	Rev: 13552	Assets: 3067	Emp: 27
Ford Motor Co The American Road Dearborn, MI 48121 313-322-3000	International automobile manufacturer. Type: NYSE-F Ind: Automotive Grp: Manufacturing Donald E Petersen, CEO Harold A Poling, Pres William Clay Ford, VCh Stanley A Seneker, CFO Simon I Gilman, IS John P McTague, R&D Basil Couglin, Sls Robert L Rewey, Mkt John Betti, Ops Allan Gilmour, VP Louis Ross, VP Alexander Trotman, VP Kenneth Whipple, VP David W Scott, PR	Rev: 92446	Assets: 143367	Emp: 185
Ford Motor Insurance Co The American Road Dearborn, MI 48121 313-322-9045	Property & casualty insurance company. Type: Private-Sub Par: Ford Motor Co Ind: Insurance Grp: Insurance Ray Maise, CEO	Rev: 500	Assets: 1000	Emp: 2
Ford Motor Land Development Corp The American Road Dearborn, MI 48121 313-322-3000	Real estate developers. Type: Private-Sub Par: Ford Motor Co Ind: Real Estate/Bldg Grp: Business Service Wayne Doran, CEO	Rev: NA	Assets: NA	Emp: NA

Organizations Listed Alphabetically

Organization / Address / Phone	Descriptive Information	Revenue / Assets / Emp ($ mil) ($ mil) (thous)		

Ford, Henry Health Care Corp
2799 W Grand Blvd
Detroit, MI 48202
313-876-2600

Operator of hospitals & clinics.
Type: Private
Ind: Health Care   Grp: Consumer Service
Gail Warden, CEO

Rev: 1280
Assets: NA
Emp: 15

Foremost Insurance Co
5800 Foremost Drive
Grand Rapids, MI 49506
616-942-3000

Property & casualty insurance company.
Type: NASDAQ-FCOA
Ind: Insurance   Grp: Insurance
David G Frey, CEO   Richard L Antonini, Chr   John J Hannigan, VCh
F Robert Woudstra, CFO   David A Heatherly, VP   John H Blue, VP

Rev: 881
Assets: 814
Emp: 2

Forest City Enterprises Inc
10800 Brookpark Road
Cleveland, OH 44130
216-267-1200

Operator & builder of shopping centers.
Type: ASE-FCE
Ind: Real Estate/Bldg   Grp: Business Service
Albert B Ratner, CEO

Rev: 300
Assets: 200
Emp: 3

Forest Laboratories Inc
150 E 58th Street
New York, NY 10155
212-421-7850

Manufacturer of ethical drug products.
Type: ASE-FRX
Ind: Drugs   Grp: Consumer Service
Howard Solomon, CEO

Rev: 101
Assets: 194
Emp: 1

Formica Corp
155 Rt 46 W
Wayne, NJ 07470
201-890-9400

Manufacturer of resins.
Type: NYSE
Ind: Chemicals   Grp: Basic Industries
Gordon Sterling, CEO

Rev: 432
Assets: 250
Emp: 4

Fort Dodge Laboratories Inc
800 Fifth Street NW
Fort Dodge, IA 50501
515-955-4600

Manufacturer & marketer of prescription drugs.
Type: Private-Sub   Par: American Home Products Corp
Ind: Drugs   Grp: Consumer Service
Thomas Cocoran, CEO

Rev: NA
Assets: NA
Emp: NA

Fort Howard Paper Co
1919 S Broadway
Green Bay, WI 54307
414-435-8821

Forest products company; paper.
Type: Private
Ind: Paper/Forest Prd   Grp: Basic Industries
Paul J Schierl, CEO   William Dunn, CFO   Don Schneider, R&D
George Hartmann, Mkt   Jeffrey Eves, PR

Rev: 1750
Assets: 2000
Emp: 16

Fort Worth, City of
City Hall 1000 Throckmorton Street
Fort Worth, TX 76102
817-870-6117

City government.
Type: City Govt
Ind: Local Govt   Grp: Govt & Non-Prof
Bob Bolen, CEO

Rev: 338
Assets: NM
Emp: 5

Foster Wheeler Corp
Perryville Corporate Park
Clinton, NJ 08809
201-730-4000

Nationwide construction company.
Type: NYSE-FWC
Ind: Real Estate/Bldg   Grp: Business Service
Louis E Azzato, CEO   N William Atwater, VCh   David J Roberts, CFO
Henry Phillips, R&D   Alan K Hegedus, VP   Edward F Vitolo, PR

Rev: 1090
Assets: 1109
Emp: 18

Foster, L B Co
415 Holiday Drive
Pittsburgh, PA 15220
201-533-1100

Manufacture of tubular products.
Type: OTC-FSTRA
Ind: Business Service   Grp: Business Service
Joseph H Dugan, CEO

Rev: 262
Assets: 107
Emp: 1

Four Seasons Hotels Ltd
1165 Leslie Street
Toronto, ON M3C2K8 Can
416-449-1750

Operator of luxury hotels.
Type: TOR-FSH
Ind: Food/Lodging   Grp: Consumer Service
Isadore Sharp, CEO   H Roger Garland, VCh   Douglas Ludwig, CFO
Christopher Wallis, VP

Rev: 513
Assets: 167
Emp: 10

Fox & Lazo Inc
30 Washington Avenue
Haddonfield, NJ 08033
609-424-2800

Heavy construction & commercial building company.
Type: Private
Ind: Real Estate/Bldg   Grp: Business Service
Bill Fox, CEO

Rev: 935
Assets: NA
Emp: 2

Fox, G Co
960 Main Street
Hartford, CT 06115
203-522-1920

Operator of retail department stores.
Type: Private-Sub   Par: May Department Stores Co
Ind: Retail/Merch   Grp: Retail
Gerald Politzer, CEO

Rev: NA
Assets: NA
Emp: NA

Organizations Listed Alphabetically

Organization / Address / Phone	Descriptive Information	Revenue / ($ mil)	Assets / ($ mil)	Emp (thous)
Foxboro Co Bristol Park Foxboro, MA 02035 617-543-8750	Manufacturer of machine tools & automation systems. Type: NYSE-FOX Ind: Instruments Grp: High Tech Earle W Pitt, CEO Gary K Willis, Chr Gerald F Morris, CFO Peter Borrows, IS Peter F McCrea, R&D Richard McAllister, Mkt J C Fuller, VP Gerald A Gleason, VP Charles E Jordan, VP Richard J Kornblum, VP Glen W Peterson, IR Richard L Sherman, PR	Rev: 540 Assets: 472 Emp: 7		
FPI Fishery Products International Ltd 70 O'Leary Avenue St Johns, NF A1C5L1 Can 709-570-0000	Integrated seafood harvesting & processing company. Type: TOR-FPL Ind: Food Processing Grp: Food Processing Victor L Young, CEO	Rev: 312 Assets: 263 Emp: 9		
FPL (Florida Power & Light) Group Inc Golden Bear Plaza North Palm Beach, FL 33408 407-694-6300	Electric power utility. Type: NYSE-FPL Ind: Utility Grp: Utilities James L Broadhead, CEO John J Hudiberg, Chr Joe L Howard, VCh David K Baldwin, CFO Joe W Williams, Mkt Tom Petillo, VP Jack S Woodall, VP C O Woody, VP A F Bruns, PR	Rev: 5854 Assets: 11793 Emp: 19		
Franklin Life Insurance Co Franklin Square Springfield, IL 62713 217-528-2011	Life insurance company. Type: NYSE Ind: Insurance Grp: Insurance Howard C Humphrey, CEO Jack Watson, Pres Keith A Butler, IS Jack Watson, Mkt David G Vanselow, IR Mark Butler, PR	Rev: 1083 Assets: 11642 Emp: 4		
Franklin Mint Corp Baltimore Pike Media, PA 19063 215-459-6000	Manufacturer & marketer of novelty items, matched sets. Type: Private Ind: Retail/Merch Grp: Retail Stuart Resnick, CEO	Rev: 550 Assets: NA Emp: 5		
Franklin Resources Group Inc 777 Mariners Island Blvd San Mateo, CA 94404 415-570-3000	Mutual fund investment company. Type: NYSE-FT Ind: Non-Bank Fin Grp: Financial Charles B Johnson, CEO	Rev: 202 Assets: 177 Emp: 2		
Franklin Savings Assn Inc One Franklin Plaza Ottawa, KS 66067 913-242-6300	Thrift institution. Type: NASDAQ-FSAK Ind: Savings & Loan Grp: Financial Ernest M Fleischer, CEO Duane H Hall, Pres John Scowcroft, VCh Dennis J Katzer, CFO Jerry E Mayne, Mkt Nancy L Spavale, Ops Elizabeth M Kearns, VP Edward H Barnes, VP Jerry E Mayne, VP Larry H Powell, VP Marc Woodward, VP Alan D Beauchine, VP	Rev: 1059 Assets: 13419 Emp: 2		
Franklin, Benj Federal Savings Assn Inc 501 SE Hawthorne Blvd Portland, OR 97214 503-275-1201	Thrift institution. Type: NASDAQ-BENJ Ind: Savings & Loan Grp: Financial D Dale Weight, CEO G Dale Weight, Chr Donald McIntyre, VCh Ian D G McKechnie, CFO Lloyd Bell, IS Larry Brown, VP W Scott Couch, VP Gordon Crisman, VP Gary Cumpston, VP	Rev: 504 Assets: 5469 Emp: 2		
Fraternal Order of Police 2100 Gardiner Lane Louisville, KY 40205 502-452-2828	National labor union. Type: Membership Org Ind: Membership Org Grp: Govt & Non-Prof Dewey R Stokes, CEO	Rev: 250 Assets: NM Emp: 200		
Freedom Newspapers Inc 17666 Fitch Irvine, CA 92714 714-542-4415	Communications company; publisher of newspapers. Type: Private Ind: Publishing/Com Grp: Consumer Service D R Segal, CEO	Rev: 400 Assets: NA Emp: 5		
Freeman United Coal Mining Co 222 N LaSalle Street Chicago, IL 60601 312-263-4490	Coal mining & processing company. Type: Private-Sub Par: General Dynamics Corp Ind: Metals/Mining Grp: Basic Industries L Lincoln, CEO	Rev: NA Assets: NA Emp: NA		

Organizations Listed Alphabetically

Organization / Address / Phone	Descriptive Information	Revenue / ($ mil)	Assets / ($ mil)	Emp (thous)
Freeport McMoran Gold Inc 1615 Poydras Street New Orleans, LA 70112 504-582-4000	Gold mining company. Type: NYSE-FAU Ind: Metals/Mining Grp: Basic Industries Milton H Ward, CEO James Moffet, Chr Ronald Grossman, VCh Ronald P Malaya, CFO Thomas Gooding, IS Ronald Cambre, VP Louis Clinton, VP Thomas Egan, VP Robert Foster, VP Ronald Grossman, VP	Rev: Assets: Emp:		106 169 1
Freeport McMoran Inc 1615 Poydras Street New Orleans, LA 70161 504-582-4000	Mining company; copper, gold, uranium & natural resources. Type: NYSE-FTX Ind: Chemicals Grp: Basic Industries James R Moffett, CEO Milton H Ward, Pres Thomas Gooding, IS Roy A Pickren Jr, R&D Craig E Saporito, IR Jay Handelman, PR	Rev: Assets: Emp:		1945 3730 6
Fremont General Corp 1633 26th Street Suite 300 Santa Monica, CA 90404 213-483-0991	Property & casualty insurance company. Type: NASDAQ-FRMT Ind: Insurance Grp: Insurance L E McIntyre, CEO J McNeil, VCh K L Treffttzs, CFO E J Lieber, VP D C Ross, VP	Rev: Assets: Emp:		408 1240 2
Fresno, City of City Hall 2326 Fresno Street Fresno, CA 93721 209-488-1561	City government. Type: City Govt Ind: Local Govt Grp: Govt & Non-Prof Dale Doig, CEO	Rev: Assets: Emp:		250 NM 2
Friona Industries Inc PO Box 369 Friona, TX 79035 806-247-3991	Producer & distributor of packaged food products. Type: Private Ind: Food Processing Grp: Food Processing Danny Kendrick, CEO	Rev: Assets: Emp:		440 NA 1
Fruehauf Corp 10900 Harper Avenue Detroit, MI 48213 313-267-1000	Manufacturer of truck trailers, containers & auto parts. Type: NYSE-FTRB Ind: Automotive Grp: Manufacturing T Neal Combs, CEO Robert G Siefert, Pres Richard Darke, VCh John Garber, CFO John P Kenny, IS Edward J Hayes, R&D James McClain, Mkt John Utley, Ops Arnold McIlwain, VP Michael LaLonde, VP W Richard Smith, PR	Rev: Assets: Emp:		2094 1584 15
Fruit of the Loom Inc 233 S Wacker Drive 6300 Sears Tower Chicago, IL 60606 312-876-1724	Manufacturer of clothing. Type: ASE-FTL Ind: Apparel/Textiles Grp: Consumer Prd John B Holland, CEO Joseph Medalie, VCh Ralph Wakeland, CFO Joe Maresca, IS Juan Smith, R&D Leon Tonelson, Sls David Drescher, Mkt Edgar Davies, Ops Richard Landeau, VP Randall Koedyker, VP Lester Schwartz, PR	Rev: Assets: Emp:		1005 1830 15
Fuji Bank & Trust One World Trade Center New York, NY 10048 212-839-5600	Commercial bank. Type: Private Ind: Banking Grp: Financial Takao Oishi, CEO	Rev: Assets: Emp:		600 5000 3
Fuji Industries Inc 600 Third Avenue New York, NY 10016 212-943-4435	Manufacturer & importer of film & cameras; US headquarters. Type: Private-Sub-For Ind: Leisure Time Grp: Consumer Service not available, CEO	Rev: Assets: Emp:		1100 NA 2
Fujitsu Inc 19600 S Vermont Torrance, CA 90502 213-327-2151	Manufacturer & importer of electronic equipment; US hdqtrs. Type: Private-Sub-For Ind: Electronics Grp: High Tech K Yamagami, CEO	Rev: Assets: Emp:		1100 NA 2
Fuller, George A Co Inc 919 Third Avenue New York, NY 10022 212-355-2700	Construction & commercial building company. Type: Private Ind: Real Estate/Bldg Grp: Business Service Wilfred Mango, CEO	Rev: Assets: Emp:		1100 NA 2

Organizations Listed Alphabetically

Organization / Address / Phone	Descriptive Information	Revenue / ($ mil)	Assets / ($ mil)	Emp (thous)
Fuller, H B Co 2400 Energy Park Drive St Paul, MN 55108 612-645-3401	Specialty chemical manufacturer; adhesives, sealants. Type: NASDAQ-FULL Ind: Manufacturing Grp: Manufacturing Anthony L Andersen, CEO Vartkes Ehramjian, CFO John Bigalke, IS Rolf B Schubert, R&D Jerry McGinty, Sls Frank J Durham, Mkt Richard Johnson, PR	Rev: Assets: Emp:	685 434 5	
Fuqua Industries Inc 4900 Georgia Pacific Center Atlanta, GA 30303 404-658-9000	Manufacturer of consumer home equipment; lawn mowers. Type: NYSE-FQA Ind: Conglomerate Grp: Manufacturing J B Fuqua, CEO Lawrence P Klamon, Pres James M Bahin, CFO Samuel W Norwood, R&D Paul N Keil, VP Hiram Nowlan, VP James Foster, VP Mildred Hutcheson, VP Donna Browning, PR	Rev: Assets: Emp:	934 1146 16	
Furman-Selz Inc 230 Park Avenue New York, NY 10169 212-309-8200	Marketer of computer systems. Type: Private-Sub Par: Xerox Corp Ind: Comput/Off Equip Grp: High Tech Edward Hajim, CEO	Rev: Assets: Emp:	NA NA NA	
Furr's/Bishop's Cafeterias Inc 6901 Quaker Avenue Lubbock, TX 79493 806-792-7151	Operator of food & grocery stores. Type: NYSE Ind: Retail/Food Grp: Retail Jan Friederich, CEO	Rev: Assets: Emp:	300 200 10	
Furrs Inc 1708 Avenue G Lubbock, TX 79408 806-763-1931	Operator of retail food stores. Type: Private Ind: Retail/Food Grp: Retail Jan Friederich, CEO	Rev: Assets: Emp:	1250 NA 10	
G&G Shops Inc 520 Eighth Avenue New York, NY 10018 212-279-4961	Operator of retail women's apparel stores. Type: Private-Sub Par: Petrie Stores Corp Ind: Retail/Merch Grp: Retail Jay Gallin, CEO	Rev: Assets: Emp:	NA NA NA	
GAF Corp 1361 Alps Road Wayne, NJ 07470 201-628-3000	Manufacturer of building materials; roofing. Type: NYSE Ind: Building Mat Grp: Basic Industries Samuel J Heyman, CEO James T Sherwin, Pres Joel A Asen, CFO Matthew L Gooby, IS Carl Ekhardt, R&D Heinn Tomfohrde, VP Ed Novotny, PR	Rev: Assets: Emp:	837 1298 5	
Gainers Ltd 12425 66th Street Edmonton, AB T5J2H8 Can 403-471-0611	Manufacturer of meat packaging. Type: TOR Ind: Food Processing Grp: Food Processing Leo Bolanes, CEO	Rev: Assets: Emp:	318 170 2	
Galaxy Carpet Mills Inc 850 Arthur Avenue Elk Grove Village, IL 60007 312-593-0555	Manufacturer of carpeting. Type: ASE-GXY Ind: Appliances/Furn Grp: Manufacturing Irwin M Harvey, CEO	Rev: Assets: Emp:	275 150 3	
Gallo, Ernest & Julio Winery Inc 600 Yosemite Blvd Modesto, CA 95354 209-579-3111	Wine production. Type: Private Ind: Food Processing Grp: Food Processing Ernest Gallo, CEO	Rev: Assets: Emp:	1000 NA 5	
Gannett Co Inc 1100 Wilson Blvd Arlington, VA 22209 703-284-6000	Publishing company; newspapers, billboards, TV & radio. Type: NYSE-GCI Ind: Publishing/Com Grp: Consumer Service Allen H Neuharth, CEO John J Curley, Chr Douglas McCorkindale, CFO John Palm, IS Nancy Woodhull, R&D Cathleen P Black, Mkt Thomas Curley, VP Brian Donnelly, VP Millicent Feller, VP Mimi Feller, PR	Rev: Assets: Emp:	3314 3793 30	

Organizations Listed Alphabetically

Organization / Address / Phone	Descriptive Information		Revenue / ($ mil)	Assets / ($ mil)	Emp (thous)
GAP Stores Inc 900 Cherry Avenue San Bruno, CA 94066 415-952-4400	Nationwide operator of clothing stores. Type: NYSE-GPS Ind: Retail/Merch Grp: Retail Donald G Fisher, CEO Millard S Drexler, Pres Warren R Hashagen, Tres James V O'Donnell, CFO James A Carolan, IS J Neal Vantoosky, R&D George A Joseph, VP Steven B Kaplan, VP Jane P Metzroth, VP J Patrick Spainhour, VP Dexter C Tight, VP	Rev: Assets: Emp:	1252 481 14		
Gates Corp 900 S Broadway Denver, CO 80209 303-744-1911	Manufacturer of tires & rubber products. Type: Private Ind: Tire/Rubber Grp: Basic Industries Charles C Gates, CEO	Rev: Assets: Emp:	1250 NA 12		
Gates Learjet Corp 1255 E Aero Park Blvd Tucson, AZ 85706 602-745-5100	Manufacturer of jet airplanes Type: ASE-GLJ Ind: Aerospace Grp: High Tech Beverly Lancaster, CEO	Rev: Assets: Emp:	500 NA 2		
Gateway Foods Corp PO Box 1957 LaCrosse, WI 54602 608-785-1330	Operator of wholesale grocery distribution businesses. Type: Private Ind: Retail/Food Grp: Retail D B Reinhart, CEO	Rev: Assets: Emp:	2250 NA 6		
GATX Corp 120 S Riverside Plaza Chicago, IL 60606 312-621-6200	Rail car leasing & industrial tank storage company. Type: NYSE-GMT Ind: Business Service Grp: Business Service James J Glasser, CEO Frederick Ollett, Tres John Chlebowski, CFO Paul Heinen, Sls Roland Finkelman, Mkt	Rev: Assets: Emp:	587 2605 2		
Gaylord Container 500 Lakecook Road Deerfield, IL 60015 312-405-5500	Manufacturer of solid fiber products & corregated containers Type: ASE-GCR Ind: Manufacturing Grp: Manufacturing Marvin Pomertz, CEO	Rev: Assets: Emp:	380 200 3		
Gaz Metropolitain Inc 1717 Du Havre Montreal, PQ H2K2X3 Can 514-598-3444	Natural gas utility company. Type: Private-Sub Par: Noverco Inc Ind: Utility Grp: Utilities Pierre Martin, CEO	Rev: Assets: Emp:	808 1020 2		
GE Fanuc Automation Inc Routes 29 N & 606 Charlottsville, VA 22906 804-978-5000	Manufacturer of industrial control products. Type: Private-Sub Par: General Electric Co Ind: Equipment Grp: Manufacturing Robert Collins, CEO	Rev: Assets: Emp:	NA NA NA		
Gearhart Industries Inc 1100 Everman Road PO Box 1936 Fort Worth, TX 76101 817-293-1300	Manufacturer of oil field machinery & well head services. Type: NYSE-GOI Ind: Energy Grp: Basic Industries Marvin Gearhart, CEO	Rev: Assets: Emp:	297 355 4		
GEICO Corp Geico Plaza 5260 Western Avenue NW Washington, DC 20076 301-986-3000	Property & casualty insurance. Type: NYSE-GEC Ind: Insurance Grp: Insurance William B Snyder, CEO Eugene Meyung, Pres Olza Nicely, VCh Louis A Simpson, CFO James M Hitt, IS William E Roberts, Mkt Richard Lucas, VP James Regan, VP Louis Simpson, VP W Alvon Sparks, VP Walter R Smith, IR Jody Goulden, PR	Rev: Assets: Emp:	1557 3061 5		
Gelco Corp One Gelco Drive Eden Prairie, MN 55344 612-828-1000	Vehicle leasing company. Type: OTC Ind: Business Service Grp: Business Service Jim Rogers, CEO Richard W McFerran, CFO William J Clements, IS	Rev: Assets: Emp:	1000 2500 7		
GenCorp Inc 175 Ghent Road Akron, OH 44313 216-869-4200	Automobile tire & specialty chemical company. Type: NYSE-GY Ind: Tire/Rubber Grp: Basic Industries A William Reynolds, CEO Jack L Heckel, Pres Marvin Isles, VCh D Michael Steuert, CFO Russ Livigni, R&D Pat Servodidio, VP James Marlen, VP William Simon, VP Charles R Tilden, PR	Rev: Assets: Emp:	1891 1230 16		

Organization / Address / Phone	Descriptive Information	Revenue / Assets / Emp ($ mil) ($ mil) (thous)		

Organization / Address / Phone	Descriptive Information	Rev / Assets / Emp
Gendis Inc 1370 Sony Place Winnipeg, MB R3T1N5 Can 204-474-5200	Nationwide retailing company. Type: TOR Ind: Retail/Merch Grp: Retail Albert D Cohen, CEO G Allan Mackenzie, Pres Harry Cohen, VCh Patrick J Mathews, CFO H Murray Heselton, VP Edson Boyd, VP William Pounder, VP John Cohen, VP Harry B Cohen, VP Morley Cohen, VP	Rev: 575 Assets: 262 Emp: 7
General Accident Assurnace Co of Canada 2 First Canadian Place Toronto, ON M5H2T5 Can 416-368-4733	Property & casualty insurance company. Type: Private-Sub-For Ind: Insurance Grp: Insurance Leonard Latham, CEO	Rev: 366 Assets: 581 Emp: 1
General Accident Insurance Co 436 Walnut Street Philadelphia, PA 19105 215-625-1000	Property & casualty insurance company. Type: Private-Sub-For Ind: Insurance Grp: Insurance James C Corcoran, CEO George N Morris, Chr Walter E Farnam, Pres John J Naughton, Tres Frank J Coyne, VP John J DeStefano, VP M Edwin Leopold, VP Robert F Lewis, VP Diana M Childs, VP David O'Brien, VP	Rev: 1470 Assets: 4168 Emp: 4
General American Life Insurance Co 700 Market Street PO Box 396 St Louis, MO 63166 314-231-1700	Life insurance company. Type: Private-Mutual Ind: Insurance Grp: Insurance Richard A Liddy, CEO H Edwin Trusheim, Chr John W Barber, CFO Christopher Simons, IS Phillip A Schorr, Mkt John Nadeau, IR Warren Goodenough, PR	Rev: 1824 Assets: 4369 Emp: 4
General Aviation Services Co 2075 Diplomat Dallas, TX 75234 214-406-2000	Aviation transportation services. Type: Private-Sub Par: Ryder System Inc Ind: Business Service Grp: Business Service John Wallace, CEO	Rev: NA Assets: NA Emp: NA
General Binding Corp One GBC Plaza Northbrook, IL 60062 312-272-3700	Manufacturer of business machines & supplies. Type: OTC Ind: Comput/Off Equip Grp: High Tech William Lane, CEO	Rev: 300 Assets: 200 Emp: 4
General Chemical Canada Ltd 201 City Center Drive Mississauga, ON L5B3A3 Can 416-896-9595	Chemical manufacturer. Type: Private Ind: Chemicals Grp: Basic Industries H J N Lalonde, CEO	Rev: 340 Assets: 213 Emp: 3
General Cimema Corp 27 Boylston Street Chestnut Hill, MA 02167 617-232-8200	Operator of movie theatres & beverage bottler. Type: NYSE-GCN Ind: Beverage Grp: Food Processing Richard A Smith, CEO Robert J Tarr Jr, Pres Samuel Frankenheim, VCh J Atwood Ives, CFO Robert A Smith, R&D Peter Farwell, VP Eric Geller, VP Mayer Rabinowitz, VP Peter Farwell, IR Janine Dusossoit, PR	Rev: 2324 Assets: 1898 Emp: 26
General Cinema Beverages Inc 1300 Boylston Strett Chestnut Hill, MA 02167 617-739-2950	Independent bottler of Pepsi, Dr. Pepper, 7up. Type: Private-Sub Par: General Cimema Corp Ind: Beverage Grp: Food Processing Bert Einloth, CEO	Rev: NA Assets: NA Emp: NA
General Datacomm Industries Inc 1579 Straits Turnpike Middlebury, CT 06762 203-574-1118	Manufacturer of telecommunications systems. Type: NYSE-GDC Ind: Telecom Grp: High Tech Charles P Johnson, CEO	Rev: 240 Assets: 290 Emp: 3
General Development Corp 1111 S Bayshore Drive Miami, FL 33131 305-350-1200	Developer of planned communities. Type: NYSE-GDV Ind: Real Estate/Bldg Grp: Business Service David F Brown, CEO	Rev: 500 Assets: 600 Emp: 2

Organizations Listed Alphabetically

Organization / Address / Phone	Descriptive Information	Revenue / Assets / Emp ($ mil) ($ mil) (thous)		

General Dynamics Corp
Pierre Laclede Center
St Louis, MO 63105
314-889-8200

Manufacturer of defense equipment;aircraft, tanks, missiles.
Type: NYSE
Ind: Aerospace   Grp: High Tech
Stanley C Pace, CEO   Herbert F Rogers, Pres   Lester Crown, VCh
Standley H Hoch, CFO   Asaph H Hall, IS   Leonard Buchanan, R&D
David J Wheaton, Mkt   Ralph Hawes, VP   James Mellor, VP
Frederick S Wood, VP   Charles Anderson, VP   Robert A Morris, IR
Peter K Connelly, PR

Rev: 9551
Assets: 6118
Emp: 103

General Dynamics Services Corp
12101 Woodcrest Executive Drive
St Louis, MO 63141
314-851-4050

Manufacturer & servicer of electronic equipment.
Type: Private-Sub   Par: General Dynamics Corp
Ind: Electronics   Grp: High Tech
George Pishas, CEO

Rev: NA
Assets: NA
Emp: NA

General Dynamics Space Systems Div
5001 Kearny Villa Road
San Diego, CA 92123
619-573-8000

Manufacter & researcher of space launch vehicles.
Type: Private-Sub   Par: General Dynamics Corp
Ind: Aerospace   Grp: High Tech
A Lovelace, CEO

Rev: NA
Assets: NA
Emp: NA

General Electric Canada Co
2300 Meadowvale Blvd
Mississauga, ON L5N5P9 Can
416-858-5100

Manufacturer of industrial & consumer electric equipment.
Type: Private-Sub-For
Ind: Manufacturing   Grp: Manufacturing
William Blundell, CEO

Rev: 1436
Assets: 876
Emp: 10

General Electric Co
3135 Easton Turnpike
Fairfield, CT 06431
203-373-2431

Electrical equip, jet engines, TV network, financial serv.
Type: NYSE-GE
Ind: Electronics   Grp: High Tech
John F Welch, CEO   Paul W VanOrden, VCh   Dennis Dammerman, CFO
Edward J Skiko, IS   Walter L Robb, R&D   Nigel Andrews, Ops
Benjamen Heineman, VP   Frank Doyle, VP   Jack O Peiffer, VP
Joyce Hergenhan, PR

Rev: 50089
Assets: 110865
Emp: 298

General Electric Credit Corp
570 Lexington Avenue
New York, NY 10022
212-751-5315

Credit finance subsidiary of General Electric Corp.
Type: Private-Sub   Par: General Electric Co
Ind: Non-Bank Fin   Grp: Financial
Lawrence A Bossidy, CEO   Gary Wendt, Pres   Michael Carpenter, VCh
Leo Halloran, CFO   Silas Cathcart, VP   Michael G Fitt, VP
Burton A Colica, VP

Rev: 10655
Assets: 74645
Emp: 10

General Felt Industries Inc
Park 80 Plaza W
Saddle Brook, NJ 07662
201-843-0900

Manufacturer of carpet, accessories, furniture.
Type: Private
Ind: Apparel/Textiles   Grp: Consumer Prd
Rocco A Barbieri, CEO

Rev: 400
Assets: NA
Emp: 4

General Foods Corp
250 North Street
White Plains, NY 10625
914-335-2500

Consumer food products.
Type: Private-Sub   Par: Philip Morris Companies Inc
Ind: Food Processing   Grp: Food Processing
James Ferguson, CEO

Rev: NA
Assets: NA
Emp: NA

General Foods Ltd
95 Moatfield Drive
Don Mills, ON M3C3J5 Can
416-441-5000

Manufacturer of packaged foods.
Type: Private-Sub-For
Ind: Food Processing   Grp: Food Processing
R Hurlbut, CEO

Rev: 643
Assets: 392
Emp: 4

General Homes Corp
7322 SW Freeway
Houston, TX 77074
713-270-4177

Developer & builder of homes.
Type: NYSE
Ind: Real Estate/Bldg   Grp: Business Service
Jeffrey P Payson, CEO

Rev: 263
Assets: 438
Emp: 2

General Host Corp
22 Gate House Road PO Box 10045
Stamford, CT 06904
203-357-9900

Operator of retail stores.
Type: NYSE-GH
Ind: Retail/Food   Grp: Retail
Harris J Ashton, CEO   Robert Lovejoy, Tres   James Hull, CFO
Walter Rogers, Mkt   Robert Ench, VP

Rev: 467
Assets: 533
Emp: 6

Organizations Listed Alphabetically

Organization / Address / Phone	Descriptive Information	Revenue / ($ mil)	Assets / ($ mil)	Emp (thous)
General Instrument Corp 767 Fifth Avenue New York, NY 10153 212-207-6200	Manufacturer of electronic instruments. Type: NYSE Ind: Electronics Grp: High Tech Frank G Hickey, CEO George F Safiol, Pres Thomas DeFazio, Tres Gerard G Johnson, CFO Gerald Weinstein, IS Rein Narma, R&D Frederick Shuh, VP Richard Friedland, VP Harold M Krisbergh, VP Richard Smith, VP Edward R Kearney, PR	Rev: Assets: Emp:		1305 1309 29
General Mills Inc 9200 Wayzata Blvd Minneapolis, MN 55440 612-540-2311	Consumer food products marketer & restaurant operator. Type: NYSE-GIS Ind: Food Processing Grp: Food Processing H Brewster Atwater, CEO Mark H Willes, Pres David E Kelby, Tres F Caleb Blodgett, CFO Walter W Faster, R&D Edward K Bixby, Sls Joe R Lee, VP Steven M Rothschild, VP Arthur Schulze, VP James J Feeney, VP John L Frost, VP Dean Belbas, IR Austin P Sullivan, PR	Rev: Assets: Emp:		5179 2672 74
General Motors Acceptance Corp 3044 W Grand Blvd Detroit, MI 48202 313-556-5000	Finance subsidiary of General Motors Corporation. Type: Private-Sub Par: General Motors Corp Ind: Non-Bank Fin Grp: Financial Robert T O'Connell, CEO Keith L Jeffrey, Tres Terry R Holmes, CFO Paul B Clare, VP Harry W Yergey, VP	Rev: Assets: Emp:		10645 99041 10
General Motors Acceptance Corp Canada 3300 Bloor Street W Toronto, ON M8X2X5 Can 416-234-6616	Finance subsidiary of General Motors of Canada. Type: Private-Sub Ind: Non-Bank Fin Grp: Financial W James Watson, CEO	Rev: Assets: Emp:		703 6097 1
General Motors Corp 3044 W Grand Blvd Detroit, MI 48202 313-556-5000	Worldwide manufacturer of automobiles. Type: NYSE-GM Ind: Automotive Grp: Manufacturing Roger B Smith, CEO Robert C Stempel, Pres Donald Atwood, VCh Dr Robert A Frosch, R&D C N Moore, Sls John G Middlebrook, Mkt William Hogland, VP Lloyd Reuss, VP Robert Schultz, VP F Alan Smith, VP John F Smith, VP John W McNulty, PR	Rev: Assets: Emp:		123641 90571 766
General Motors of Canada Ltd 215 William Street E Oshawa, ON L1G1K7 Can 416-644-5000	Automobile manufacturer. Type: TOR Ind: Automotive Grp: Manufacturing George A Peapples, CEO Terry R Holmes, CFO Ross W McFarlane, R&D William Atkinson, Mkt Donald T Blight, Ops Robert Wilson, VP	Rev: Assets: Emp:		16414 1448 44
General Nutrition Inc 921 Penn Avenue Pittsburgh, PA 15222 412-288-4600	Operator of retail stores; health foods, vitamins. Type: NYSE-GNC Ind: Retail/Food Grp: Retail Jerry D Horn, CEO	Rev: Assets: Emp:		361 136 6
General Public Utilities Corp 100 Interpace Parkway Parsippany, NJ 07054 201-263-6500	Holding company for electric power utilities. Type: NYSE-GPU Ind: Utility Grp: Utilities William G Kuhns, CEO Michael Morrell, Tres John G Graham, CFO George Fair, IS Mary Nalewako, VP F Allen Donofrio, VP Mary Breslin, VP W L Gifford, IR Gary Plummer, PR	Rev: Assets: Emp:		2834 6415 4
General Re Corp Financial Centre PO Box 10351 Stamford, CT 06904 203-328-5000	Domestic property & casualty reinsurance company. Type: NYSE-GRN Ind: Insurance Grp: Insurance Ronald G Anderson, CEO Ronald E Ferguson, Chr John C Etling, VCh Louis Forgione, Tres Philip W Ness, Mkt Edmund F Rondepierre, IR Joan Burns, PR	Rev: Assets: Emp:		2736 9394 3
General Refractories Co 225 City Avenue Bala Cynwyd, PA 19004 215-667-7900	Manufacturer of industrial & commercial brick products. Type: NYSE-GRX Ind: Metals/Mining Grp: Basic Industries Raymond Perelman, CEO	Rev: Assets: Emp:		210 250 1

Organizations Listed Alphabetically

Organization / Address / Phone	Descriptive Information	Revenue / Assets / Emp ($ mil) ($ mil) (thous)		

General Signal Corp
High Ridge Park
Stamford, CT 06904
203-357-8800

Manufacturer of electronic instruments & control devices.
Type: NYSE-GSX
Ind:. Instruments   Grp: High Tech
Edmund M Carpenter, CEO   Joel Friedman, Pres   John Halter, VCh
Michael Jacquin, Tres   Theodore J Wiedemann, CFO   Nicholas D Guthrie, IS
J Robert Hipps, VP   Edgar J Smith, VP   Erwin Kantor, VP
Nino J Fernandez, PR

Rev: 1760
Assets: 1397
Emp: 21

General Trustco of Canada Ltd
120 Adelaide Street W
Toronto, ON M5H3Y3 Can
416-867-3200

Consumer banking company.
Type: Private-Sub
Ind: Non-Bank Fin   Grp: Financial
Marcel Cazavan, CEO   Maurice Myrand, Chr   Mark D Hayes, Tres
Michel Lavoie, Mkt   Gilles Vachon, VP   Pierre Arbour, VP
Jacques Custeau, VP

Rev: 497
Assets: 4204
Emp: 2

Generale Banque (Societe Generale)
12 E 49th Street
New York, NY 10017
212-418-8700

Commercial bank.
Type: Private-Sub-For
Ind: Banking   Grp: Financial
Alazar Dessi, CEO

Rev: 450
Assets: 3500
Emp: 1

Genesco Inc
Genesco Park
Nashville, TN 37202
615-367-7000

Shoe manufacturing & retail; clothing manufacturer.
Type: NYSE-GCO
Ind: Apparel/Textiles   Grp: Consumer Prd
William S Wire, CEO   Larry B Shelton, Pres   James S Gulmi, CFO
Richard Daniels, VP   James W O'Brien, VP   Robert Brosky, VP
Larry G Kinney, VP   M Wills Oglesby, VP

Rev: 463
Assets: 265
Emp: 6

Genetech Corp
460 Point San Bruno
S San Francisco, CA 94080
415-952-1000

Biotechnology research & products company.
Type: NYSE-GNE
Ind: Business Service   Grp: Business Service
Robert A Swanson, CEO

Rev: 262
Assets: 669
Emp: 2

Genetics Institute Inc
87 Cambridge Park Drive
Cambridge, MA 02140
617-876-1170

Research & development of biotechnology, pharmaceuticals.
Type: NASDAQ-GENI
Ind: Business Service   Grp: Business Service
Gabriel Schmergel, CEO

Rev: 30
Assets: 197
Emp: 1

Geneva Management Inc
1550 Wilson Blvd
Arlington, VA 22209
703-522-2300

Investment management company.
Type: Private
Ind: Business Service   Grp: Business Service
Donald Bavely, CEO

Rev: 550
Assets: NA
Emp: 1

Genicom Corp
One Genicom Drive
Waaynesboro, VA 229801
703-949-1000

Manufacturer of computer printers.
Type: OTC
Ind: Comput/Off Equip   Grp: High Tech
Curtis Powell, CEO

Rev: 300
Assets: 150
Emp: 4

Genlyte Group Inc
100 Lighting Way
Secaucus, NJ 07094
201-864-3000

Wholesale lighting fixtures manufacturer.
Type: OTC
Ind: Manufacturing   Grp: Manufacturing
Glenn Bailey, CEO

Rev: 450
Assets: 350
Emp: 4

Genovese Drug Stores Inc
80 Marcus Drive
Melville, NY 11747
516-420-1900

Operator of retail drugstores.
Type: ASE-GDXA
Ind: Retail/Merch   Grp: Retail
Leonard Genovese, CEO

Rev: 366
Assets: 200
Emp: 4

Genuine Parts Co
2999 Circle 75 Parkway
Atlanta, GA 30339
404-953-1700

Distributor of automotive parts.
Type: NYSE
Ind: Business Service   Grp: Business Service
Wilton Looney, CEO.   Larry L Prince, Pres   Edward Jones, VCh
Earl Dolive, CFO   Thomas Braswell, IS   Thomas Gallagher, VP
James Prince, VP   John Scalley, VP   William Valentine, VP
Lou Rice, PR

Rev: 2942
Assets: 1141
Emp: 15

Organization / Address / Phone	Descriptive Information	Revenue / ($ mil)	Assets / ($ mil)	Emp (thous)
George Washington University Administrative Bldg Washington, DC 20052 202-676-6000	Major educational institution; university. Type: University Ind: University Grp: Govt & Non-Prof Stephen J Trachtenberg, CEO	Rev: Assets: Emp:		245 256 21
Georgetown University 37th Street & O Street Washington, DC 20057 202-625-0100	Major educational institution; university. Type: University Ind: University Grp: Govt & Non-Prof Timothy S Healy, CEO	Rev: Assets: Emp:		253 255 16
Georgia Crown Distributing Corp 7 Crown Circle Columbus, GA 31908 404-568-4580	Liquor distributors. Type: Private Ind: Food Processing Grp: Food Processing Donald M Leegern, CEO	Rev: Assets: Emp:		500 NA 1
Georgia Federal Bank Inc 20 Marietta Street Atlanta, GA 30348 404-330-2440	Thrift institution. Type: Private-Sub Ind: Savings & Loan Grp: Financial Richard Jackson, CEO	Rev: Assets: Emp:		443 4365 2
Georgia Gulf Corp 400 Perimeter Terrace Atlanta, GA 30346 404-395-4500	Manufacturer of specialty chemicals. Type: Private Ind: Chemicals Grp: Basic Industries James R Kuse, CEO John D Bryan, Pres Jerry R Satrum, CFO Thomas G Simon, IS John F Walker, PR	Rev: Assets: Emp:		550 250 5
Georgia Kraft Corp 1700 Redmond Road Rome, GA 30161 404-232-0851	Manufacturer of packaging products. Type: Private Ind: Packaging Grp: Manufacturing Jim Emerson, CEO	Rev: Assets: Emp:		550 500 5
Georgia Pacific Corp 133 Peachtree Street NE Atlanta, GA 30303 404-521-4000	Forest products company; building materials, paper products. Type: NYSE-GP Ind: Paper/Forest Prd Grp: Basic Industries T Marshall Hahn, CEO Harold L Airington, Pres Ronald Hogan, VCh James C Van Meter, CFO Joseph H Joiner, IS Michael B Wilson, Sls Stephen K Jackson, Mkt James Taylor, VP Dewey Mobley, VP John Massaschi, VP Stephen Jackson, VP Donald Glass, VP Duncan Facey, VP Richard A Good, IR Beth Zoffmann, PR	Rev: Assets: Emp:		9509 7115 44
Georgia Power Co 333 Piedmont Avenue Atlanta, GA 30308 404-526-6000	Electric power utility company. Type: Private-Sub Par: Southern Co Ind: Utility Grp: Utilities A Dahlberg, CEO	Rev: Assets: Emp:		NA NA NA
Georgia State Unversity University Plaza Atlanta, GA 30303 404-658-2000	Major educational institution; university. Type: University Ind: University Grp: Govt & Non-Prof William M Suttles, CEO	Rev: Assets: Emp:		80 110 24
Georgia, State of State Capitol Atlanta, GA 30334 404-656-2000	State government. Type: State Govt Ind: State/Prov Govt Grp: Govt & Non-Prof Joe Frank Harris, CEO	Rev: Assets: Emp:		13455 NM 98
Gerber Products Co 445 State Street Fremont, MI 49412 616-928-2000	Baby foods & products. Type: NYSE Ind: Food Processing Grp: Food Processing David W Johnson, CEO Mathew Okkema, Tres Gordon Durkee, CFO John Kraley, IS George A Purvis, R&D Al Gorsky, Sls Robert Erber Jr, Mkt Kristina Kiley, VP David Hoogerwerf, VP Stephen Clark, VP Kenneth Peirce, VP L James Lovejoy, IR Steven Poole, PR	Rev: Assets: Emp:		1068 697 15
Gerber Scientific Co 83 Gerber Road W South Windsor, CT 06074 203-644-1551	Manufacturer of factory automation systems. Type: NYSE-GRB Ind: Instruments Grp: High Tech H Joseph Gerber, CEO	Rev: Assets: Emp:		299 245 2

Organizations Listed Alphabetically

Organization / Address / Phone	Descriptive Information	Revenue / ($ mil)	Assets / ($ mil)	Emp (thous)
Getty Petroleum Corp 125 Jericho Turnpike Jericho, NY 11753 516-338-6000	Petroleum products distribution & marketing company. Type: NYSE-GTY Ind: Energy Grp: Basic Industries Leo Liebowitz, CEO	Rev: Assets: Emp:	1041 1500 7	
GFI Knoll International Holdings Inc Park 80 Plaza W Saddlebrook, NJ 07662 201-843-0900	Manufacturer of apparel products. Type: Private Ind: Apparel/Textiles Grp: Consumer Prd Rocco Barbieri, CEO	Rev: Assets: Emp:	1650 NA 11	
Giant Eagle Inc 101 Cappa Drive Pittsburgh, PA 15238 412-963-6200	Operator of retail food supermarkets. Type: Private Ind: Retail/Food Grp: Retail David S Shapira, CEO	Rev: Assets: Emp:	1500 NA 14	
Giant Food Inc 6300 Sheriff Road Landover, MD 20785 301-341-4100	Retail food supermarkets. Type: ASE-GFSA Ind: Retail/Food Grp: Retail Isreal Cohen, CEO Alvin Dobbin, Pres David B Sykes, CFO Robert W Schoening, IS Terry A Gans, Sls Alvin Dobbin, Ops Ron Cooke, VP George Hannis, VP David Larson, VP Barry F Scher, PR	Rev: Assets: Emp:	2987 983 25	
Gibraltar Savings (CA) Inc 9111 Wilshire Blvd Beverly Hills, CA 90210 213-278-8720	Thrift institution. Type: NYSE Ind: Savings & Loan Grp: Financial James N Thayer, CEO John R Williamson, VCh Michael W Mooney, CFO Steven Hamburger, Mkt Dean Harrison, VP Linda K S Blount, IR	Rev: Assets: Emp:	1309 15011 3	
Gibraltar Savings (Texas) Assn Inc 13401 North Freeway Houston, TX 77060 713-872-3100	Thrift institution. Type: OTC Ind: Savings & Loan Grp: Financial Carl Webb, CEO	Rev: Assets: Emp:	1301 12724 3	
Gibson Greetings Inc 2100 Section Road Cincinnati, OH 45237 513-841-6600	Greeting card & gift wrap manufacturer. Type: NASDAQ-GIBG Ind: Retail/Merch Grp: Retail Thomas M Cooney, CEO	Rev: Assets: Emp:	404 326 4	
Gifford Hill & Co Inc 300 E John W Carpenter Freeway Irving, TX 75062 214-258-7000	Manufacturer of concrete & construction products. Type: OTC Ind: Building Mat Grp: Basic Industries Thomas Howard, CEO	Rev: Assets: Emp:	500 NA 3	
Gilbane Building Co 7 Jackson Way Providence, RI 02940 401-456-5800	Commercial construction company. Type: Private Ind: Real Estate/Bldg Grp: Business Service Paul J Choquette, CEO	Rev: Assets: Emp:	1000 NA 1	
Gilbert Associates Inc Morgantown Road Reading, PA 19603 215-775-2600	Engineering & consulting company. Type: OTC Ind: Real Estate/Bldg Grp: Business Service Alexander Smith, CEO	Rev: Assets: Emp:	265 200 4	
Gillett Group Inc 4400 Harding Road Nashville, TN 37205 615-292-0045	Meatpacking, broadcasting, resorts company. Type: Private Ind: Food Processing Grp: Food Processing George N Gillett Jr, CEO	Rev: Assets: Emp:	1250 NA 5	
Gillette Co Prudential Tower Bldg Boston, MA 02199 617-421-7000	Manufacturer of personal care products. Type: NYSE-GS Ind: Personal Care Grp: Consumer Prd Colman M Mockler, CEO Joseph F Turley, Pres Derwyn Phillips, VCh Lloyd Swan, Tres Thomas F Skelly, CFO Kevin Moody, IS John B Bush Jr, R&D Gaston Levy, VP John W Symons, VP David Fausch, IR David A Fausch, PR	Rev: Assets: Emp:	3581 2868 29	

Organizations Listed Alphabetically

Organization / Address / Phone	Descriptive Information	Revenue ($ mil)	Assets ($ mil)	Emp (thous)
Gitano Orit Imports Inc 1411 Broadway New York, NY 10018 212-819-0707	Manufacturer & marketer of clothing & apparel. Type: Private Ind: Apparel/Textiles Grp: Consumer Prd Haim Dabah, CEO	Rev: 550 Assets: NA Emp: 1		
Glatfelter, P H Co 228 S Main Street Spring Grove, PA 17362 717-225-4711	Manufacturer of paper products; office supplies, printing. Type: ASE-GLT Ind: Paper/Forest Prd Grp: Basic Industries T C Norris, CEO R W Wand, VCh M A Johnson, CFO R S Woods, VP	Rev: 569 Assets: 663 Emp: 3		
Gleason Corp 30 Corporate Woods Rochester, NY 14692 716-272-6000	Manufacturer of automotive & truck components. Type: NYSE-GLE Ind: Automotive Grp: Manufacturing James S Gleason, CEO	Rev: 250 Assets: 300 Emp: 3		
Glendale Federal Savings & Loan Assn 700 N Brand Blvd Glendale, CA 91203 818-500-2000	Thrift institution. Type: NYSE-GLN Ind: Savings & Loan Grp: Financial Raymond D Edwards, CEO Norman M Coulson, Chr Keith P Russell Jr, Pres Harold B Shore, VCh David T Hansen, CFO Roger Rittner, IR Rosanne O'Brien, PR	Rev: 2562 Assets: 23711 Emp: 8		
Glickenhaus & Co 6 E 43rd Street New York, NY 10017 212-953-7800	Investment firm; securities trading. Type: Private Ind: Securities Grp: Financial Seth Glickehaus, CEO	Rev: 275 Assets: 2200 Emp: 1		
Global Marine Inc 777 N Eldridge Road Houston, TX 77079 713-596-5100	Operates offshore oil & gas exploration. Type: NYSE Ind: Energy Grp: Basic Industries C Russell Luigs, CEO	Rev: 141 Assets: 696 Emp: 1		
Global Petroleum Corp 800 South Street Waltham, MA 02154 617-894-8800	Petroleum wholesaling. Type: Private Ind: Energy Grp: Basic Industries Alfred A Slifka, CEO	Rev: 1500 Assets: NA Emp: 1		
GNB Inc 1110 Highway 110 Mendota Heights, MN 55118 612-681-5000	Manufacturer of electronic equipment & components. Type: Private Ind: Electronics Grp: High Tech Graham Spurling, CEO	Rev: 440 Assets: NA Emp: 4		
Godiva Chocolatier Inc 450 Park Avenue New York, NY 10022 212-486-8750	Manufacturer of chocolate products. Type: Private-Sub Par: Campbell Soup Co Ind: Food Processing Grp: Food Processing Thomas Fey, CEO	Rev: NA Assets: NA Emp: NA		
Gold Kist Inc 244 Perimeter Center Parkway NE Atlanta, GA 30346 404-393-5000	Producer & distributor of citrus food products. Type: Private Ind: Food Processing Grp: Food Processing Don W Sands, CEO W W Gaston, Chr Peter J Gibbons, CFO T Ray Lollar, IS Jerry L Stewart, Mkt Paul G Brower, PR	Rev: 2200 Assets: 650 Emp: 11		
Golden Nugget Inc 129 Fremont Street Las Vegas, NV 89101 702-385-7111	Operator of gambling casinos & hotels. Type: NYSE-GNG Ind: Leisure Time Grp: Consumer Service Stephen A Wynn, CEO	Rev: 175 Assets: 1038 Emp: 2		
Golden State Foods Corp 234 E Colorado Pasadena, CA 91101 818-793-3135	Food processors, distributors for McDonalds. Type: Private Ind: Food Processing Grp: Food Processing James E Williams, CEO	Rev: 1000 Assets: NA Emp: 4		

Organizations Listed Alphabetically

Organization / Address / Phone	Descriptive Information	Revenue / ($ mil)	Assets / ($ mil)	Emp (thous)

Golden West Financial Corp
1901 Harrison Street
Oakland, CA 94612
415-446-6000

Thrift institution.
Type: NYSE-GDW
Ind: Savings & Loan   Grp: Financial
Herbert M Sandler, CEO   Marion O Sandler, Pres   Russell Kettell, VCh
J L Helvey, CFO   Theodore C Tomblinson, IS   James T Judd, Sls
J L Helvey, VP   Richard Crane, VP   David Foldman, VP
J L Helvey, IR

Rev: 1410   Assets: 16721   Emp: 2

Goldman, Sachs & Co
85 Broad Street
New York, NY 10004
212-902-1000

Investment banking firm.
Type: Private
Ind: Securities   Grp: Financial
John L Weinberg, CEO   Donald R Gant, Pres   Robert Mnuchin, VCh
Stephen Friedman, CFO   Howard Silverstein, VP

Rev: 4000   Assets: 51301   Emp: 7

Goldome Federal Savings Bank Inc
1 Fountain Plaza
Buffalo, NY 14203
716-847-5800

Thrift institution.
Type: OTC
Ind: Savings & Loan   Grp: Financial
Ross B Kenzie, CEO   Paul E Ruch, Pres   F William Bonito, CFO
Alan Pritchard, IS   Peter Ruddy, R&D   Edward K Duch Jr, Mkt
Marc Chodorow, PR

Rev: 1750   Assets: 17500   Emp: 5

Golub Corp
501 Duanesburg Road
Schenectady, NY 12306
518-355-5000

Grocery stores.
Type: Private
Ind: Retail/Food   Grp: Retail
Lewis Golub, CEO

Rev: 1000   Assets: NA   Emp: 10

Goodrich, B F Co
500 S Main Street
Arkon, OH 44318
216-374-3985

Manufacturer of rubber & chemical products.
Type: NYSE-GR
Ind: Tire/Rubber   Grp: Basic Industries
John D Ong, CEO   Leigh Carter, Pres   John Lauer, VCh
Robert A McMillan, Tres   D Lee Tobler, CFO   Matthew J Battista, IS
David C Bonner, R&D   H David Warren, VP   George K Sherwood, VP
Foster C Smith, IR   Robert S Jewell, PR

Rev: 2417   Assets: 2073   Emp: 12

Goodyear Canada Inc
10 Four Seasons Place
Islington, ON M9B6G2 Can
416-626-4611

Manufacturer of tire & rubber products.
Type: TOR
Ind: Tire/Rubber   Grp: Basic Industries
Scott H Buzby, CEO   Brian D Goard, Tres   Henry G Wolka, CFO
Richard Mendler, Mkt   Richard Archer, VP   Douglas Hamilton, VP
W Robert Hayward, VP   Gary K Dolson, PR

Rev: 664   Assets: 419   Emp: 6

Goodyear Tire & Rubber Co
1144 E Market Street
Akron, OH 44316
216-796-2121

Manufacturer of automobile tires & rubber products.
Type: NYSE
Ind: Tire/Rubber   Grp: Basic Industries
Robert E Mercer, CEO   Tom H Barrett, Pres   Jacques Sardas, VCh
Oren G Shaffer, CFO   Joseph H Gilchrist, IS   F Vincent Prus, R&D
Hoyt M Wells, Mkt   Stanley Michelick, VP   Robert Milk, VP
Eugene Culler, VP   William L Newkirk, PR

Rev: 10810   Assets: 8618   Emp: 114

Gordon Capital Corp
5401 Toronto Dominion Center
Toronto, ON M5K1E7 Can
416-364-9393

Investment company; brokerage.
Type: Private
Ind: Non-Bank Fin   Grp: Financial
James R Connacher, CEO

Rev: 255   Assets: 170   Emp: 1

Gordon Food Service Corp
333 50th Street SW
Grand Rapids, MI 49501
616-530-7000

Wholesale grocery distribution company.
Type: Private
Ind: Retail/Merch   Grp: Retail
Paul Gordon, CEO

Rev: 500   Assets: NA   Emp: 3

Gordon Jewelry Corp
820 Fannin Street
Houston, TX 77002
713-222-8080

Operator of retail jewelry stores.
Type: ASE-GOR
Ind: Retail/Merch   Grp: Retail
Aron S Gordon, CEO

Rev: 400   Assets: NA   Emp: 5

Gore, W L & Associates Inc
555 Paper Mill Road
Newark, DE 19711
302-738-4880

Manufacturer of textiles & apparel products.
Type: Private
Ind: Apparel/Textiles   Grp: Consumer Prd
Robert W Gore, CEO

Rev: 500   Assets: NA   Emp: 5

Organization / Address / Phone	Descriptive Information	Revenue / Assets / Emp ($ mil) ($ mil) (thous)		

Gould Inc
10 Gould Center
Rolling Meadows, IL 60008
312-640-4000

Manufacturer of electronic & electrical equipment.
Type: NYSE-GLD
Ind: Electronics   Grp: High Tech
James MacDonald, CEO   Jerry W Gaskin, CFO   Gerard F Corbett, PR

Rev: 1000
Assets: 1400
Emp: 11

Goulds Pumps Inc
240 Fall Street
Seneca Falls, NY 13148
315-568-2811

Manufacturer of pumps & equipment.
Type: NASDAQ-GULD
Ind: Manufacturing   Grp: Manufacturing
Robert L Tarnow, CEO

Rev: 454
Assets: 366
Emp: 4

Grace, W R & Co
1114 Avenue of the Americas
New York, NY 10036
212-819-5500

Worldwide chemical company.
Type: NYSE-GRA
Ind: Chemicals   Grp: Basic Industries
J Peter Grace, CEO   Charles Erhart, Pres   J P Bolduc, VCh
John F Spellman, CFO   George A Hvidsten, IS   F Peter Boer, R&D
Terence Daniels, Sls   Paul Paganucci, Mkt   Robert Samuels, VP
Frederick E Bona, PR

Rev: 5786
Assets: 5310
Emp: 46

Graco Inc
4050 Olson Memorial Highway
Minneapolis, MN 55442
612-623-6000

Manufacturer of pumps & fluid control devices.
Type: NYSE-GGG
Ind: Manufacturing   Grp: Manufacturing
David A Koch, CEO

Rev: 240
Assets: 200
Emp: 2

Grafton Group Ltd
9 Sunlight Park Road
Toronto, ON M4M3G1 Can
416-461-9411

Nationwide retailing company.
Type: TOR
Ind: Retail/Merch   Grp: Retail
W A Heaslip, CEO   G A Reynolds, CFO   R O Hutchinson, VP
N E Phillips, VP   B R Pestall, VP   A L Lucas, VP
J R Walker, VP

Rev: 543
Assets: 275
Emp: 4

Grainger, W W Inc
5500 W Howard Street
Skokie, IL 60077
312-982-9000

Distributor to the building industry.
Type: NYSE-GWW
Ind: Business Service   Grp: Business Service
David W Grainger, CEO   Wiley N Caldwell, Pres   Jere Fluno, VCh
Paul Wallace, CFO   Edward C Bender, IS   David K Barth, R&D
Micheal G Murray, Sls   John J Rozwat, Mkt   Paul J Wallace, VP
Neal Ormond, VP   Lee J Flory, IR   Gloria Sinclair, PR

Rev: 1535
Assets: 936
Emp: 7

Granada Corp
10900 Richmond Avenue
Houston, TX 77042
713-783-1310

Producer & distributor of packaged food products.
Type: Private
Ind: Food Processing   Grp: Food Processing
David Eller, CEO

Rev: 825
Assets: NA
Emp: 2

Grand Met USA Inc
100 Paragon Drive
Montvale, NJ 07645
201-573-4000

Diversified consumer products & services company; US hdqtrs.
Type: Private-Sub-For
Ind: Tobacco   Grp: Food Processing
Ian Martin, CEO

Rev: 2200
Assets: NA
Emp: 21

Grand Rapids, City of
City Hall 300 Monroe Street
Grand Rapids, MI 49503
616-456-3160

City government.
Type: City Govt
Ind: Local Govt   Grp: Govt & Non-Prof
Gerald Helmholdt, CEO

Rev: 250
Assets: NM
Emp: 2

Grand Trunk Corp
131 W Lafayette
Detroit, MI 48226
313-962-2260

Railroad holding company.
Type: Private-Sub-For
Ind: Railroad   Grp: Business Service
R Lawless, CEO   Gerald L Maas, Pres   Paul E Tatro, CFO
Robert A Walker, PR

Rev: 400
Assets: 500
Emp: 4

Grand Union Co
201 Willowbrook Blvd
Wayne, NJ 07470
201-890-6000

Operator of retail food supermarkets.
Type: Private
Ind: Retail/Food   Grp: Retail
Floyd Hall, CEO   Joseph J McCaig, Pres   Robert Terence Galvin, CFO
William Kinslow, IS   William Lehrburger, Mkt   Donald Vaillancourt, PR

Rev: 3100
Assets: 750
Emp: 25

Organizations Listed Alphabetically

Organization / Address / Phone	Descriptive Information	Revenue / ($ mil)	Assets / ($ mil)	Emp (thous)
Grant Thornton Inc Prudential Plaza Chicago, IL 60601 312-856-0001	Certified public accountants. Type: Private Ind: Accounting Grp: Business Service Burt Fisher, CEO	Rev: Assets: Emp:		250 NA 3
Graphic Communications Intl Union 1900 L Street NW Washington, DC 20036 202-461-1400	National labor union. Type: Membership Org Ind: Membership Org Grp: Govt & Non-Prof James J Norton, CEO	Rev: Assets: Emp:		250 NM 200
Graphic Industries Inc 2155 Monroe Drive NE Atlanta, GA 30324 404-874-3327	Commercial printing company. Type: NASDAQ-GRPH Ind: Business Service Grp: Business Service Mark Pope, CEO	Rev: Assets: Emp:		270 200 2
Graybar Electric Co Inc 34 N Meramec Avenue St Louis, MO 63177 314-727-3900	Electrical supplies & equipment wholesale company. Type: Private Ind: Electronics Grp: High Tech James L Hoagland, CEO	Rev: Assets: Emp:		2000 NA 5
Great American (AZ) First Savings Bank 3200 N Central Avenue Phoenix, AZ 85012 602-279-3456	Thrift institution. Type: Private Ind: Savings & Loan Grp: Financial Ronald Sheridan, CEO	Rev: Assets: Emp:		400 4000 1
Great American (CA) First Savings Bank 600 B Street San Diego, CA 92183 619-231-1885	Thrift institution. Type: NYSE-GTA Ind: Savings & Loan Grp: Financial Gordon C Luce, CEO Roger K Lindland, Pres Thomas Carter, VCh James A Krzeminski, CFO Rodney P Tompkins, IS Jan M Strode, Sls Marc W Sandstrom, Mkt William Chapman, VP Marc Sandstrom, VP Rodney Tomkins, VP John H Ruehlin, IR Kenneth G Ulrich, PR	Rev: Assets: Emp:		1601 16084 3
Great American Commmunications Co One E Fourth Street Cincinnati, OH 45202 513-579-2177	Television & radio broadcasting. Type: NASDAQ-GACC Ind: Publishing/Com Grp: Consumer Service Carl H Linder, CEO	Rev: Assets: Emp:		382 1965 3
Great Atlantic & Pacific Co of Canada 5559 Dundas Street W Toronto, ON M5W1A6 Can 416-239-7171	Operator of retail supermarkets. Type: Private-Sub-For Ind: Retail/Food Grp: Retail G Thomas, CEO	Rev: Assets: Emp:		1020 425 20
Great Atlantic & Pacific Tea Co 2 Paragon Drive PO Box 418 Montvale, NJ 07645 201-573-9700	Nationwide supermarket retailing company. Type: NYSE-GAP Ind: Retail/Food Grp: Retail James Wood, CEO Joseph H McCarthy, Pres James W Rowe, VCh Fred Corrado, CFO Eugene Bilenker, R&D John D Ryder, Mkt Joseph McCarthy, Ops Michael Larkin, VP Kenneth Green, VP George Graham, VP Clifford Horler, VP Michael J Rourke, PR	Rev: Assets: Emp:		10068 2640 92
Great Lakes Bancorp Inc One Great Lakes Plaza Ann Arbor, MI 48104 313-769-8300	Thrift institution. Type: NASDAQ-GLBC Ind: Savings & Loan Grp: Financial Roy E Weber, CEO Emerson Kampen, Chr Robert T Jeffares, CFO David A Hall, R&D B G McGuire, Sls Robert McDonald, Mkt John B Talpas, Ops Dennis Venters, VP	Rev: Assets: Emp:		334 3638 1
Great Lakes Chemical Corp Highway 52 NW West Lafayette, IN 47906 317-463-2511	Specialty chemical manufacturing company. Type: NYSE-GLK Ind: Chemicals Grp: Basic Industries Emerson Kampen, CEO Robert Jeffares, CFO Glenn Scuteri, IS John Little, R&D William Blake, Mkt David Bouchard, PR	Rev: Assets: Emp:		616 664 4

Organizations Listed Alphabetically

Organization / Address / Phone	Descriptive Information	Revenue / ($ mil)	Assets / ($ mil)	Emp (thous)

Great Lakes Forest Products Ltd
Neebing Avenue
Thunder Bay, ON P7C4W3 Can
807-475-2110

Forest products company; lumber, building materials.
Type: Private-Sub Par: Canadian Pacific Ltd
Ind: Paper/Forest Prd   Grp: Basic Industries
Charles Carter, CEO   Cecil S Flenniken, Chr   F D'arcy Quinn, Pres
Robert Chambers, VCh   Paul E Gagne, CFO   Keith Winrow, R&D
Norman W Lord, Sls   Sheila Britt, VP   Ronald Lehtovaara, VP
Jacques Beauchamp, VP   Francois Vachon, VP   Marc Regneir, VP

Rev: 638
Assets: 723
Emp: 5

Great Northern Nekoosa Corp
75 Prospect Street
Stamford, CT 06904
203-359-4000

Forest products manufacturing company; paper, newsprint.
Type: NYSE-GNN
Ind: Paper/Forest Prd   Grp: Basic Industries
William R Laidig, CEO   James Crump, Pres   Phillip Cannella, Tres
Douglas Wright, CFO   Richard W Fickey, IS   Raymond Taylor, VP
Francis G Walker, VP   Victor Mattson, VP   William Laimbeer, VP
Stephen Hill, PR

Rev: 3588
Assets: 3821
Emp: 20

Great West Life Assurance Co
100 Osborne Street N
Winnipeg, MB R3C3A5 Can
204-946-1190

Life insurance company.
Type: TOR
Ind: Insurance   Grp: Insurance
Kevin P Kavanagh, CEO   Orest Dackow, VCh   Jack A Miller, CFO
Robert Siddall, VP

Rev: 4221
Assets: 14669
Emp: 5

Great Western Financial Corp
8484 Wilshire Blvd
Beverly Hills, CA 90211
213-852-3411

Thrift institution.
Type: NYSE-GWF
Ind: Savings & Loan   Grp: Financial
James F Montgomery, CEO   John F Maher, Pres   Carl F Geuther, CFO
Joseph M Jackson, IS   Clifford A Miller, Mkt   Ian D Campbell, VP
Curtis J Crivellli, VP   J Lance Erikson, VP   William J Marchalk, VP
M M Pappas, VP   Joseph Jackson, VP   Ian D Campbell, PR

Rev: 3665
Assets: 32815
Emp: 13

Green Tree Acceptance Corp
345 St Peter Street
St Paul, MN 55102
612-293-3400

Servicing of sales contracts for manufactured homes.
Type: NYSE-GNT
Ind: Non-Bank Fin   Grp: Financial
Lawrence M Coss, CEO   John W Brink, CFO   Kenneth S Roberts, Mkt
Richard G Evans, VP   Robert Hegstrom, VP   Abdul Rajput, VP
Gregory Boyle, VP   Brian Hamblin, VP

Rev: 134
Assets: 645
Emp: 2

Green, B & Co Inc
3601 Washington Street
Baltimore, MD 21227
301-247-8300

Food wholesaling, grocery stores.
Type: Private
Ind: Retail/Food   Grp: Retail
Bernard Green, CEO

Rev: 600
Assets: NA
Emp: 1

Greenman Brothers Inc
105 Price Parkway
Farmingdale, NY 11735
516-293-5300

Toy retail & wholesale company.
Type: ASE-GMN
Ind: Retail/Merch   Grp: Retail
Bernard Greenman, CEO

Rev: 267
Assets: 150
Emp: 2

Greenwood Mills Corp
Greenwood Bldg
Greenwood, SC 29646
803-229-2571

Manufacturer of textile materials & apparel products.
Type: Private
Ind: Apparel/Textiles   Grp: Consumer Prd
J C Self, CEO

Rev: 250
Assets: NA
Emp: 3

Greif Brothers Corp
621 Pennsylvania Avenue
Delaware, OH 43015
614-363-1271

Manufacturer of packaging; paper, cardboard.
Type: OTC
Ind: Packaging   Grp: Manufacturing
John C Dempsey, CEO   John P Berg, Pres

Rev: 412
Assets: 267
Emp: 4

Grey Advertising Inc
777 3rd Avenue
New York, NY 10017
212-546-2000

Advertising agency.
Type: OTC
Ind: Consulting   Grp: Business Service
Edward Meyer, CEO

Rev: 450
Assets: 150
Emp: 3

Greyhound Corp
Greyhound Tower
Phoenix, AZ 85077
602-248-4000

Bus transportation & finance services company.
Type: NYSE
Ind: Business Service   Grp: Business Service
John W Teets, CEO   Ermo S Bartoletti, VCh   F Edward Lake, CFO
Harry Oakes, IS   John Meredith, R&D   Richard Zoller, VP
Armen Ervanaian, VP   Robert Lang, VP   Ronald Sustana, PR

Rev: 3305
Assets: 5034
Emp: 37

Organizations Listed Alphabetically

Organization / Address / Phone	Descriptive Information	Revenue / Assets / Emp ($ mil) ($ mil) (thous)		

Griffin Corp
780 Third Avenue
New York, NY 10017
212-753-1230

Entertainment company & operator of NJ gambling casinos.
Type: Private
Ind: Leisure Time   Grp: Consumer Service
Merv Griffin, CEO

Rev: 500
Assets: NA
Emp: 5

Grinnell Corp
Three Tyco Park
Exeter, NH 03833
603-778-9200

Manufacturer of electronic components & equipment.
Type: Private-Sub   Par: Tyco Laboratories Inc
Ind: Electronics   Grp: High Tech
Dennis Kozlowski, CEO

Rev: NA
Assets: NA
Emp: NA

Grocers Supply Co Inc
3131 E Holcombe
Houston, TX 77021
713-747-5000

Food wholesaling.
Type: Private
Ind: Retail/Food   Grp: Retail
Milton Levit, CEO

Rev: 1000
Assets: NA
Emp: 2

Grocery Supply Co Inc
130 Hillcrest Loop 301
Sulphur Springs, TX 75482
214-885-7621

Grocery products wholesale distribution company.
Type: Private
Ind: Retail/Food   Grp: Retail
Mike Mize, CEO

Rev: 550
Assets: NA
Emp: 2

Grossmans Inc
200 Union Street
Braintree, MA 02134
617-848-0100

Operator of retail home improvement stores.
Type: Private
Ind: Retail/Merch   Grp: Retail
Micheal Grossman, CEO

Rev: 1100
Assets: NA
Emp: 11

Group Olympia Ltd
2200 Avenue Pratte
St Simon de Bagot, PQ G2S4B6 Can
514-771-0400

Meat packing company.
Type: MON
Ind: Food Processing   Grp: Food Processing
Guy Bienvenue, CEO

Rev: 357
Assets: 170
Emp: 1

Groupe des Epiciers unis,Metro Richelieu
11011 Maurice Duplessis
Montreal, PQ H1C1V6 Can
514-643-1000

Diversified financial company.
Type: Private
Ind: Non-Bank Fin   Grp: Financial
Marcel Beaulieu, CEO

Rev: 1700
Assets: 850
Emp: 3

Groupe Pharmaceutique Focus Inc
5750 Boul Metropolitain E
Montreal, PQ H1S1A7 Can
514-254-4937

Manufacturer of pharmaceutical products.
Type: MON
Ind: Drugs   Grp: Consumer Service
Jean Francios Roy, CEO

Rev: 315
Assets: 95
Emp: 1

Groupe Ro-na Inc
1250 Nobel
Boucherville, PQ J4B5K1 Can
514-599-5100

Diversified manufacturing company.
Type: Private
Ind: Manufacturing   Grp: Manufacturing
Henri Drouin, CEO

Rev: 425
Assets: 213
Emp: 2

Groupe Videotron Ltee
2000 Rue Berri
Montreal, PQ H2L4V7 Can
514-281-1212

Diversified retail company.
Type: TOR
Ind: Retail/Merch   Grp: Retail
Andre Chagnon, CEO

Rev: 298
Assets: 213
Emp: 1

Groves, S J & Sons Co Inc
10000 Highway 55 W
Minneapolis, MN 55441
612-546-6943

Operator of retail merchandise stores.
Type: Private
Ind: Retail/Merch   Grp: Retail
Franklin N Groves, CEO

Rev: 550
Assets: NA
Emp: 5

Grow Group Inc
200 Park Avenue
New York, NY 10166
212-599-4400

Paint & special coatings manufacturing company.
Type: NYSE-GRO
Ind: Building Mat   Grp: Basic Industries
Russell Banks, CEO   John Gleason, VCh   John E Baker, CFO
Lloyd Frank, VP   Frank Esser, VP   W Horton Russell, VP
Judith Greer-Rudell, PR

Rev: 383
Assets: 223
Emp: 4

Growmark Inc
1701 Towanda Avenue
Bloomington, IL 61701
309-557-6000

Operator of retail stores.
Type: Private
Ind: Retail/Merch   Grp: Retail
Norm Jones, CEO

Rev: 2200
Assets: NA
Emp: 1

Organizations Listed Alphabetically

Organization / Address / Phone	Descriptive Information	Revenue / ($ mil)	Assets / ($ mil)	Emp (thous)
Grubb & Ellis Co 1 Montgomery Street San Francisco, CA 94104 415-956-1990	Real estate & property management & development company. Type: NYSE-GBE Ind: Real Estate/Bldg Grp: Business Service Harold Ellis, CEO	Rev: Assets: Emp:		250 300 3
Grumman Corp 1111 Stewart Avenue Bethpage, NY 11714 516-575-0574	Aerospace manufacturing company; aircraft, electronics. Type: NYSE-GQ Ind: Aerospace Grp: High Tech John D O'Brien, CEO Renso L Caporali, VCh Robert G Freese, CFO Robert Meyers, IS Richard Scheuing, R&D David L Walsh, Mkt Robert Bradshaw, VP Richard Anderson, VP Steven Dely, VP Thomas Genovese, VP Weyman B Jones, PR	Rev: Assets: Emp:		3649 2566 30
Gruntal & Co Inc 14 Wall Street New York, NY 10005 212-267-8800	Investment firm; securities trading. Type: Private Ind: Securities Grp: Financial Herbert A Allen, CEO	Rev: Assets: Emp:		275 2200 1
GSC Enterprises Inc 130 Hillcrest Sulphur Springs, TX 75482 214-885-7621	Food wholesalers. Type: Private Ind: Retail/Food Grp: Retail Michael K McKenzie, CEO	Rev: Assets: Emp:		500 NA 1
GTE Corp One Stamford Forum Stamford, CT 06904 203-965-2000	Telephone utilities, telephone/elec equip, finance companies Type: NYSE-GTE Ind: Telecom Grp: High Tech James L Johnson, CEO Charles Lee, Pres Bruce Carswell, VCh Nicholas Triviasonno, CFO Dennis Murphy, IS John C Redmond, R&D Claude Burleson, VP Marianne Drost, VP Bruce Haddad, VP Edward C MacEwen, IR Glenna Rogers, PR	Rev: Assets: Emp:		16460 31104 200
GTG Entertainment Co 150 E 52nd Street New York, NY 10022 212-888-7830	Entertainment company; radio & television broadcasting. Type: Private-Sub Par: Gannett Co Inc Ind: Leisure Time Grp: Consumer Service Steve Friedman, CEO	Rev: Assets: Emp:		NA NA NA
Guardian Industries Corp 43043 W Nine Mile Road Northville, MI 48167 313-349-6700	Manufacturer of flat glass. Type: Private Ind: Automotive Grp: Manufacturing William Davidson, CEO John C Angle, Chr Arthur V Ferrara, Pres Peter Hutchings, CFO Patrick McCloghrie, IS Robert Damon, R&D Mike Schiffman, Sls Harold C Kelshaw, IR Jeanne Berres, PR	Rev: Assets: Emp:		750 NA 7
Guardian Life Insurance Co of America 201 Park Avenue S New York, NY 10003 212-598-8000	Life insurance company. Type: Private-Mutual Ind: Insurance Grp: Insurance Arthur V Ferrara, CEO	Rev: Assets: Emp:		2876 4168 5
Guardian Savings (Texas) Assn Inc 5847 San Felipe Houston, TX 77057 713-784-4413	Thrift institution. Type: Private Ind: Savings & Loan Grp: Financial Robert F Parker, CEO	Rev: Assets: Emp:		300 3000 1
Guardsman Products Inc 2960 Lucerne Drive SE Grand Rapids, MI 49501 616-957-2600	Manufacturer of industrial coatings. Type: NYSE-GRV Ind: Chemicals Grp: Basic Industries Keith C VanderHyde, CEO	Rev: Assets: Emp:		1500 500 10
Guidance & Control Systems Div 5500 Canoga Avenue Woodland Hills, CA 91367 818-715-4040	Manufacturer of electronic defense systems. Type: Private-Sub Par: Litton Industries Inc Ind: Aerospace Grp: High Tech Larry Frame, CEO	Rev: Assets: Emp:		NA NA NA
Guilford Mills Inc 4925 W Market Street Greensboro, NC 27407 919-292-7550	Textile manufacturing company. Type: NYSE-GFD Ind: Apparel/Textiles Grp: Consumer Prd Charles A Hayes, CEO Paul R McGarr, CFO Michael Greenburg, Mkt Doug Galyon, PR	Rev: Assets: Emp:		550 300 6

Organizations Listed Alphabetically

Organization / Address / Phone	Descriptive Information	Revenue / ($ mil)	Assets / ($ mil)	Emp (thous)
Gulf Canada Ltd 401 9th Avenue SW Calgary, AB T2P2H7 Can 403-233-4000	Oil & gas exploration & production company. Type: TOR Ind: Energy Grp: Basic Industries S K McWalter, CEO J R Tysall, Tres A R Sello, CFO R J Rector, Mkt W G Russell, VP D R Motyka, VP J B Petrie, VP	Rev: Assets: Emp:	740 3159 18	
Gulf Power Co 75 N Pace Blvd Pensacola, FL 32520 904-444-6381	Electric power utility company. Type: Private-Sub Par: Southern Co Ind: Utility Grp: Utilities D McCrary, CEO	Rev: Assets: Emp:	NA NA NA	
Gulf States Toyota Corp 7701 Wilshire Place Drive Houston, TX 77040 713-744-3300	Automobile importers & retailers. Type: Private Ind: Automotive Grp: Manufacturing Jerry Pyle, CEO	Rev: Assets: Emp:	1500 NA 3	
Gulf States Utilities Co 350 Pine Street Beaumont, TX 77701 409-838-6631	Electric power utility. Type: NYSE-GSU Ind: Utility Grp: Utilities E Linn Draper, CEO Joseph L Donnelly, CFO Anthony Gabrielle, IS Edward Loggins, R&D Calvin J Hebert, Mkt Calvin J Hebert, PR	Rev: Assets: Emp:	1415 6858 5	
Gulfstream Aerospace Corp Savannah International Airport Savannah, GA 31402 912-964-3000	Manufacturer of corporate jet aircraft. Type: Private-Sub Par: Chrysler Corp Ind: Aerospace Grp: High Tech Allan Paulson, CEO	Rev: Assets: Emp:	NA NA NA	
GW Utilities Ltd One First Canadian Place Toronto, ON M4M1W7 Can 416-363-3300	Utility holding company. Type: TOR Ind: Utility Grp: Utilities Marshall Cohen, CEO	Rev: Assets: Emp:	680 1020 4	
Hadson Corp 101 Park Avenue Oklahoma City, OK 73126 405-235-9500	Oil & gas exploration company. Type: NYSE-HAD Ind: Energy Grp: Basic Industries Stephen W Houghton, CEO	Rev: Assets: Emp:	450 300 2	
HAL (Hawaiian Air) Inc 1164 Bishop Street Honolulu, HI 96813 808-525-5511	Regional airline. Type: ASE-HA Ind: Transport Grp: Business Service John H Magoon Jr, CEO Paul J Finazzo, Chr Richard R Anzai, CFO Lindsay Pollock, Mkt Clarence Lyman, PR	Rev: Assets: Emp:	354 167 3	
Hall, Frank B & Co Inc 549 Pleasantville Road Briarcliff Manor, NY 10510 914-769-9200	Insurance & brokerage services. Type: NYSE-FHB Ind: Insurance Grp: Insurance John A Addeo, CEO	Rev: Assets: Emp:	339 1237 4	
Halliburton Co 3600 Lincoln Plaza 500 N Akard Street Dallas, TX 75201 214-978-2600	Oil field, engineering & construction services. Type: NYSE-HAL Ind: Oil Service Grp: Business Service Thomas H Cruikshank, CEO Dale P Jones, VCh C Robert Fielder, Tres Lester L Coleman, CFO Thomas Woods, IS Guy T Marcus, Mkt Jack Skinner, Ops Don Woosley, VP Guy Marcus, VP Marion R Cracraft, IR Guy T Marcus, PR	Rev: Assets: Emp:	4839 4722 28	
Hallmark Cards Inc 2501 McGee Street Kansas City, MO 64108 816-274-5111	Manufacturer of greeting cards & gift items. Type: Private Ind: Retail/Merch Grp: Retail Irvine O Hockaday, CEO	Rev: Assets: Emp:	2250 NA 20	
Hallmark Electronics Corp 11333 Pagemille Dallas, TX 75243 214-343-5000	Operator of retail consumer electronic stores. Type: Private Ind: Retail/Merch Grp: Retail Jack Turpin, CEO	Rev: Assets: Emp:	500 NA 2	

Organizations Listed Alphabetically

Organization / Address / Phone	Descriptive Information	Revenue / ($ mil)	Assets / ($ mil)	Emp (thous)
Hamilton Bank Corp 1097 Commercial Avenue Lancaster, PA 17601 717-569-8731	Commercial bank. Type: Private-Sub Par: Corestates Financial Corp Ind: Banking Grp: Financial Wilson D McElhinny, CEO	Rev: 500 Assets: 4500 Emp: 2		
Hamilton Oil Corp 1560 Broadway Denver, CO 80202 303-863-3000	Exploration & development of oil & natural gas. Type: NASDAQ-HAML Ind: Energy Grp: Basic Industries Frederic C Hamilton, CEO	Rev: 195 Assets: 838 Emp: 1		
Hamilton Standard Inc One Hamilton Road Windsor, CT 06096 203-654-6000	Manufacturer of aerospace equipment. Type: Private-Sub Par: United Technologies Corp Ind: Aerospace Grp: High Tech T Stinson, CEO	Rev: NA Assets: NA Emp: NA		
Hancock Fabrics Inc 3406 W Main Street Tupelo, MS 38801 601-842-2834	Operator of wholesale & retail sewing & needlework stores. Type: NYSE Ind: Retail/Merch Grp: Retail Morris Jarvis, CEO	Rev: 300 Assets: 200 Emp: 3		
Hancock, John Mutual Life Insurance Co 200 Clarendon Street Boston, MA 02117 617-421-6000	Life insurance company. Type: Private Ind: Insurance Grp: Insurance E James Morton, CEO Stephen Brown, Pres Herbert F Gold, VCh William L Boyan, CFO Edward J Boudreau, IS Robert D Lowden, R&D John C Scully, Mkt David F D'Alessandro, VP Foster L Aborn, VP Diane M Capstaff, VP David D'Allessandro, IR Richard Bevilacqua, PR	Rev: 7926 Assets: 10067 Emp: 25		
Handleman Co 500 Kirts Blvd Troy, MI 48084 313-362-4400	Distributors of recorded music & books. Type: NYSE-HDL Ind: Business Service Grp: Business Service David Handleman, CEO Frank Hennessey, Chr Stephen Strome, VCh Louis Kircos, CFO Jerry Lauer, IS Sharon Hilliker, Sls Stephen Salsberg, Mkt	Rev: 532 Assets: 284 Emp: 3		
Handy & Harman Inc 850 Third Avenue New York, NY 10022 212-752-3400	Manufacturer & refiner of precious metal products. Type: NYSE-HNH Ind: Metals/Mining Grp: Basic Industries Richard N Daniel, CEO Stephen B Mudd, CFO Ronald A Flink, IS Donal A Corrigan, R&D Leo Demm, Sls George G Cimini, Mkt Sheila Sheehey, PR	Rev: 658 Assets: 466 Emp: 4		
Hanes Hosiery Inc 401 Hanes Mill Road Winston-Salem, NC 27102 919-744-2011	Manufacturer of underwear, pantyhose, socks. Type: Private-Sub Par: Sara Lee Corp Ind: Apparel/Textiles Grp: Consumer Prd Weldon Sceneck, CEO	Rev: NA Assets: NA Emp: NA		
Hanna, M A Corp 1301 E Ninth Street Cleveland, OH 44114 216-589-4000	Manufacturer of rubber products. Type: NYSE-MAH Ind: Tire/Rubber Grp: Basic Industries Martin D Walker, CEO Kenneth C Sprague, Chr Richard Ciecko, CFO Terrie Osuchowski, IS Greg Pesch, R&D Albert A Kopala, Sls Robert Rakstang, Mkt Kathy Faircloth, PR	Rev: 1000 Assets: 300 Emp: 8		
Hannaford Brothers 145 Pleasant Hill Road Scarborough, ME 04074 207-883-2911	Operator of retail supermarkets & drugstores. Type: NYSE-HRD Ind: Retail/Food Grp: Retail James L Moody, CEO	Rev: 1000 Assets: 500 Emp: 10		
Hanover Insurance Co 100 North Parkway Worcester, MA 01605 508-853-7200	Property & casualty insurance company. Type: OTC Ind: Insurance Grp: Insurance Frederick Fedeli, CEO William J O'Brien, Chr John E Sutton, VCh Joseph C Henry, CFO Thomas Van Burkel, IS J R Wintermuten, Mkt Roy Westran, VP John Wintermute, VP James Richardson, VP Patrick Finckler, VP Jim Durning, PR	Rev: 1581 Assets: 2649 Emp: 6		

Organizations Listed Alphabetically

Organization / Address / Phone	Descriptive Information	Revenue / ($ mil)	Assets / ($ mil)	Emp (thous)
Hanson Industries (Hanson Trust) Inc 100 Wood Avenue S Iselin, NJ 08830 201-549-7050	Diversified manufacturing company; US headquarters. Type: Private-Sub-For Ind: Manufacturing Grp: Manufacturing Gordon White, CEO William Landyt, CFO Edward D Collins, PR	Rev: Assets: Emp:	4180 3200 37	
Harbert Corp 1 Riverchase Parkway Birmingham, AL 35201 205-987-5500	Industrial construction company; highways, bridges. Type: Private Ind: Real Estate/Bldg Grp: Business Service John M Harbert, CEO	Rev: Assets: Emp:	500 NA 1	
Harcourt Brace Jovanovich Inc 6277 Sea Harbor Drive Orlando, FL 32821 305-345-2000	Book publishing, insurance services & amusement company. Type: NYSE-HBJ Ind: Publishing/Com Grp: Consumer Service William Jovanovich, CEO J William Brandner, Pres Robert E Evanson, VCh John F Berardi, CFO Bob W Blevins, IS Bruce C Starling, R&D Thomas Williamson, Sls Margaret Mary McQuinlan, VP Bill Barnet, VP Terry Campbell, VP Paul McCluskey, VP	Rev: Assets: Emp:	1782 3233 14	
Hardware Wholesalers Inc 6502 Nelson Road Fort Wayne, IN 46803 219-749-8531	Operator of retail hardware & home improvement stores. Type: Private Ind: Retail/Merch Grp: Retail Don Wolfe, CEO	Rev: Assets: Emp:	825 250 1	
Harken Energy Corp 4001 Airport Freeway Bedford, TX 76021 817-354-9944	Oil & gas exploration & refining company. Type: NASDAQ-HOGI Ind: Energy Grp: Basic Industries Alan Quasha, CEO	Rev: Assets: Emp:	747 500 1	
Harland, John H Co Inc 2939 Miller Road Decatur, GA 30035 404-981-9460	Check & business form printer. Type: NYSE-JH Ind: Business Service Grp: Business Service J William Robinson, CEO	Rev: Assets: Emp:	333 295 6	
Harlequin Enterprises Ltd 225 Duncan Mill Road Don Mills, ON M3B3K9 Can 416-445-5860	Publisher of consumer novels. Type: Private-Sub Par: Torstar Corp Ind: Publishing/Com Grp: Consumer Service Brian E Hickey, CEO	Rev: Assets: Emp:	298 NA 2	
Harley Davidson Inc 3700 W Juneau Avenue Milwaukee, WI 53201 414-342-4680	Manufacturer of motorcycles. Type: NYSE-HDI Ind: Automotive Grp: Manufacturing Vaughn L Beals, CEO Richard Teerlink, Pres Karen Jensen, IS Frank Cimermancic, R&D Darrell Fink, Sls Jerry Wilke, Mkt Kathryn Molling, IR Steve Piehl, PR	Rev: Assets: Emp:	550 400 4	
Harleysville Insurance Co 355 Maple Avenue Harleysville, PA 19438 215-256-5000	Property & casualty insurance company. Type: Private-Mutual Ind: Insurance Grp: Insurance Stephen R Smith, CEO	Rev: Assets: Emp:	450 850 2	
Harman International Industries Inc 1155 Connecticut Avenue Washington, DC 20036 202-955-6130	Manufacturer of consumer & industrial electronics. Type: NYSE-HAR Ind: Electronics Grp: High Tech Sidney Harman, CEO	Rev: Assets: Emp:	225 200 3	
Harnischfeger Corp 13400 Bishops Lane Brookfield, WI 53005 414-671-4000	Manufacturer of industrial equipment; mining, material hand. Type: NYSE-HPH Ind: Building Mat Grp: Basic Industries William W Goessel, CEO Jeffrey T Grade, Pres Francis M Corby Jr, CFO Howard Sutherland, IS Joseph A Devlin, Mkt Jose Yglesias, Ops James Benjamen, VP John Teitgen, VP Richard W Schulze, PR	Rev: Assets: Emp:	1187 1195 7	
Harper Group Inc 260 Townsend Road San Francisco, CA 94107 415-978-0600	International freight forwarding company. Type: NASDAQ-HARG Ind: Transport Grp: Business Service J Robinson, CEO	Rev: Assets: Emp:	283 250 2	

Organization / Address / Phone	Descriptive Information	Revenue / Assets / Emp ($ mil) ($ mil) (thous)		
Harris Corp 1025 W NASA Blvd Melbourne, FL 32919 305-727-9100	Manufacturer of telecommunications & electronic equipment. Type: NYSE-HRS Ind: Electronics Grp: High Tech John T Hartley, CEO Robert W Fay, Tres Bryan R Roub, CFO Herbert N McCauley, IS Fayette Brown III, R&D Raymond Oglethorpe, Mkt John E Cornell, VP Phillip Farmer, VP Frank J Lewis, VP Guy W Numann, VP Robert E Sullivan, VP Fayette Brown, VP James F Murphy, PR	Rev: Assets: Emp:	2099 1644 23	
Harris County Government 1001 Preston Road Houston, TX 77002 713-221-5000	County government. Type: County Govt Ind: Local Govt Grp: Govt & Non-Prof John Lindsey, CEO	Rev: Assets: Emp:	1200 NM 10	
Harris Trust & Savings Bank 111 W Monroe Street Chicago, IL 60690 312-461-2121	Commercial bank. Type: Private-Sub Ind: Banking Grp: Financial Kenneth West, CEO Phillip Delaney, Pres Donald S Hunt, VCh Richard L McAuliffe, CFO Rolland S Carlson, IS P David Hubbard, R&D Norwood Maddrey, Mkt Mary Ullrich, PR	Rev: Assets: Emp:	1165 11276 4	
Harris Wholesale Corp 2841 N Church Solon, NC 27802 919-977-1054	Wholesaler of drug store products. Type: Private Ind: Retail/Merch Grp: Retail Seth B Jarris, CEO	Rev: Assets: Emp:	1000 NA 1	
Harsco Corp 350 Poplar Church Road PO Box 8888 Wormleysburg, PA 17043 717-763-7064	Defense, industrial, commercial & construction systems. Type: NYSE-HSC Ind: Manufacturing Grp: Manufacturing Jeffrey J Burdge, CEO Malcolm W Gambill, Chr Louis Sheehan, Tres George F Rezich, CFO Ronald D Blystone, IS Jerome D Brady, Ops Roger Snodgrass, VP Demaris K Hetrick, PR	Rev: Assets: Emp:	1279 893 12	
Harte Hanks Communications Inc Harte Hanks Tower 200 Concord Plaza Drive San Antonio, TX 78216 512-344-8000	Cable television systems. Type: Private Ind: Publishing/Com Grp: Consumer Service Bob Marbut, CEO Larry D Franklin, Pres Richard L Ritchie, CFO Bill R Gulledge, IS Ann Downing, PR	Rev: Assets: Emp:	600 1000 7	
Hartford Life Insurance Co Hartford Plaza Hartford, CT 06115 203-547-5000	Life insurance company. Type: NYSE Ind: Insurance Grp: Insurance Robert S Lackey, CEO	Rev: Assets: Emp:	1189 3495 4	
Hartford National Corp 777 Main Street Hartford, CT 06115 203-728-2000	Commercial bank. Type: NASDAQ-HNAT Ind: Banking Grp: Financial Joel Alvord, CEO	Rev: Assets: Emp:	1100 12000 5	
Hartford Steam Boiler Inspection Inc One State Street Hartford, CT 06102 203-722-1866	Insurance, engineering, inspection services. Type: NASDAQ-HBOL Ind: Manufacturing Grp: Manufacturing Wilson Wilde, CEO Donald M Carlton, Chr P E Hudson, VCh F Scott LaGrone, CFO R Murray Wells, VP R G Baldwin, VP W E Corbett, VP James Dickerman, VP P Stan Dzierlenger, VP	Rev: Assets: Emp:	447 730 4	
Hartmarx Corp 101 N Wacker Drive Chicago, IL 60606 312-372-6300	Manufacturer & retail of men's & women's clothing. Type: NYSE Ind: Apparel/Textiles Grp: Consumer Prd Elbert O Hand, CEO Harvey A Weinberg, Chr Harvey Weinberg, VCh Jerome Dorf, CFO Guy Gunzberg, IS Frank A Brenner, Mkt Ralph Kaufman, VP Sherman Rosen, VP Patricia Plodzeen, PR	Rev: Assets: Emp:	1174 734 16	
Hartz Mountain Corp 700 S Fourth Street Harrison, NJ 07029 201-481-4800	Pet food, real estate & publishing company. Type: Private Ind: Food Processing Grp: Food Processing Leonard Stern, CEO	Rev: Assets: Emp:	1250 NA 5	

Organizations Listed Alphabetically

Organization / Address / Phone	Descriptive Information	Revenue / ($ mil)	Assets / ($ mil)	Emp (thous)
Harvard Industries Inc 4321 Semple Avenue St Louis, MO 63120 314-382-5590	Manufacturer of metal products; firearms, office furniture. Type: NASDAQ-HAVA Ind: Manufacturing Grp: Manufacturing William D Hurley, CEO J J Gagliardi, CFO George Tyrone, Mkt Lee Laino, PR	Rev: Assets: Emp:	600 400 4	
Harvard University Administrative Bldg Cambridge, MA 02138 617-495-1000	Major educational institution; university. Type: University Ind: University Grp: Govt & Non-Prof Derek Bok, CEO	Rev: Assets: Emp:	520 5100 19	
Harvest States Cooperatives Inc 1667 Snelling Avenue N St Paul, MN 55408 612-646-9433	Agricultural cooperative; grain products. Type: Private Ind: Food Processing Grp: Food Processing Ellen Hanson, CEO	Rev: Assets: Emp:	3300 NA 2	
Hasbro Inc 1027 Newport Avenue Pawtucket, RI 02862 401-727-5000	Toy manufacturer. Type: ASE-HAS Ind: Leisure Time Grp: Consumer Service Stephen Hassenfeld, CEO Alan Hassenfeld, Pres Barry J Alperin, VCh Nelson Chaffee, IS George Dunsay, R&D Lawrence Bernstein, Sls Alfred J Verrecchia, VP Lawrence B Bernstein, VP George R Ditomassi, VP Wayne Charness, PR	Rev: Assets: Emp:	1358 1112 8	
Hawaii, State of State Capitol Honolulu, HI 96813 808-548-2211	State government. Type: State Govt Ind: State/Prov Govt Grp: Govt & Non-Prof John Waihee, CEO	Rev: Assets: Emp:	2818 NM 48	
Hawaiian Electric Industries Inc 900 Richards Street Honolulu, HI 96813 808-543-5662	Electric power utility. Type: NYSE-HE Ind: Utility Grp: Utilities C Dudley Pratt, CEO Robert F Clarke, VCh Andrew Ing, Tres Glenn K Hong, CFO Harwood D Williamson, Ops Constance Lau, VP Betty Ann Splinter, VP	Rev: Assets: Emp:	732 2683 4	
Hawker Siddeley Canada Inc 7 King Street E Toronto, ON M5C1A3 Can 416-362-2941	Aerospace & defense systems manufacturing company. Type: TOR Ind: Manufacturing Grp: Manufacturing Peter Baxendell, CEO R D Cole, Chr J F Howard, VCh L Francoeur, CFO B R Bensly, Mkt W G Broley, VP A Johnson, VP K Miles, VP R Munro, VP F Sandford, VP	Rev: Assets: Emp:	331 208 3	
Haworth Corp One Haworth Center Holland, MI 49423 616-392-5961	Manufacturer of office furniture. Type: Private Ind: Appliances/Furn Grp: Manufacturing Richard G Haworth, CEO	Rev: Assets: Emp:	400 NA 4	
Hay Group Inc 229 S 18th Street Rittenhouse Square Philadelphia, PA 19103 215-875-2300	Nationwide consulting company. Type: Private Ind: Consulting Grp: Business Service Ken Shapiro, CEO	Rev: Assets: Emp:	300 NA 3	
Hayes Dana Inc 1 St Paul Street St Catharines, ON L2R 7K9 Can 416-687-4200	Manufacturer of automotive parts. Type: TOR Ind: Automotive Grp: Manufacturing Walter H Baum, CEO John Doddridge, Pres Donald Johnston, CFO George G Hough, VP Dean A Couch, VP Hugh Cosgrove, VP	Rev: Assets: Emp:	485 192 3	
HBE Corp 11330 Olive Street St Louis, MO 63141 314-567-9000	Industrial & commercial equipment renting & leasing. Type: Private Ind: Real Estate/Bldg Grp: Business Service Fred Kummer, CEO	Rev: Assets: Emp:	275 NA 2	

Organizations Listed Alphabetically

Organization / Address / Phone	Descriptive Information	Revenue / Assets / Emp ($ mil) ($ mil) (thous)	
HCB Contractors Inc 1401 Elm Street Suite 4600 Dallas, TX 75202 214-747-8541	General contracting, construction management. Type: Private Ind: Real Estate/Bldg Grp: Business Service Lawrence A Wilson, CEO	Rev: Assets: Emp:	750 NA 1
Health & Welfare Canada Brooke Claxton Bldg Tunney's Pasture Ottawa, ON K1A0K9 Can 613-957-2991	Federal government agency. Type: Federal Govt Ind: Federal Govt Grp: Govt & Non-Prof Maureen Law, CEO	Rev: Assets: Emp:	2040 NM 9
Health Tex Inc 33 Benedict Plaza Greenwich, CT 06830 203-661-2000	Manufacturer of apparel products. Type: Private Ind: Apparel/Textiles Grp: Consumer Prd Robert Phillips, CEO	Rev: Assets: Emp:	275 NA 3
Healthcare International Inc 9737 Great Hills Trail Austin, TX 78759 512-346-4300	Operator of healthcare hospitals & clinics. Type: ASE-HII Ind: Health Care Grp: Consumer Service James L Fariss, CEO	Rev: Assets: Emp:	400 400 4
Healthco International Inc 1125 Stuart Street Boston, MA 02116 617-423-6045	Wholesaler dental sypplies. Type: NASDAQ-HLCO Ind: Health Care Grp: Consumer Service Marvin Cyker, CEO	Rev: Assets: Emp:	444 300 3
HealthTrust Corp 4525 Harding Road Nashville, TN 37205 615-383-4444	Operator of hospitals & clinics. Type: Private Ind: Health Care Grp: Consumer Service R Clayton McWhorter, CEO	Rev: Assets: Emp:	1500 NA 20
Heard, Bill Enterprises Inc 2600 Cross Country Drive Columbus, GA 31907 404-561-6213	Operator of automobile dealerships, auto & truck leasing. Type: Private Ind: Automotive Grp: Manufacturing Bill Heard, CEO	Rev: Assets: Emp:	500 NA 1
Hearst Corp 959 8th Avenue New York, NY 10019 212-262-5700	Publisher of newspapers & operator of radio stations. Type: Private Ind: Publishing/Com Grp: Consumer Service Frank A Bennack, CEO	Rev: Assets: Emp:	2000 NA 15
Hechinger Co 3500 Pennsy Drive Landover, MD 20785 301-341-1000	Operator of retail hardware & lumber stores. Type: NASDAQ-HECH Ind: Retail/Merch Grp: Retail Richard England, CEO John Hechinger, Chr John Hechinger, Pres Stephen Bachand, VCh Lennie H Zallar, Tres W Clark McClelland, CFO Robert G DeMarco, IS Roger Wright, R&D	Rev: Assets: Emp:	1019 681 6
Hecht's Inc 685 N Glebe Road Arlington, VA 22203 703-558-1200	Operator of retail department stores. Type: Private-Sub Par: May Department Stores Co Ind: Retail/Merch Grp: Retail Irwin Zazulia, CEO	Rev: Assets: Emp:	NA NA NA
Heck's Inc Hub Industrial Park Nitro, WV 25143 304-755-8331	Operator of retail & wholesaler hardware stores. Type: NYSE-HEX Ind: Retail/Merch Grp: Retail Russell Issacs, CEO	Rev: Assets: Emp:	300 200 5
Hecla Mining Co 6500 Mineral Drive Coeur D'Alene, ID 83814 208-769-4107	Mining company; gold, silver. Type: NYSE-HL Ind: Metals/Mining Grp: Basic Industries Arthur Brown, CEO	Rev: Assets: Emp:	105 189 1
Heekin Can Inc 11310 Cornel Park Cincinnati, OH 45242 513-489-3200	Metal can manufacturer. Type: OTC Ind: Packaging Grp: Manufacturing H E Uehlein, CEO	Rev: Assets: Emp:	300 200 2

Organizations Listed Alphabetically

Organization / Address / Phone	Descriptive Information	Revenue / ($ mil)	Assets / ($ mil)	Emp (thous)
Hees Internationaal Corp 4400 Commerce Court W Toronto, ON M5L1K5 Can 416-865-0430	Commercial bank. Type: Private Ind: Non-Bank Fin Grp: Financial Willard L'Heureux, CEO	Rev: Assets: Emp:	230 3249 1	
Heileman, G Brewing Co Inc 100 Harborview Plaza LaCrosse, WI 54601 608-785-1000	Nationwide manufacturer of beer & snack products. Type: NYSE-GHB Ind: Beverage Grp: Food Processing Russell Cleary, CEO	Rev: Assets: Emp:	1500 1200 7	
Heilig Meyers Co 2235 Staples Mill Road Richmond, VA 23230 804-359-9171	Operator of retail home furnishing stores. Type: NYSE-HMY Ind: Retail/Merch Grp: Retail William C DeRusha, CEO	Rev: Assets: Emp:	352 150 3	
Heinz, H J Co 600 Grant Street Pittsburgh, PA 15219 412-456-5700	Manufacturer of packaged food products. Type: NYSE-HNZ Ind: Food Processing Grp: Food Processing Anthony J F O'Reilly, CEO Joseph Bogdanovich, Pres Paul F Renne, Tres Karl Von Der Heyden, CFO R Derek Findlay, R&D George Greer, Mkt R Derek Finlay, VP Paul Corddry, VP J Wray Connolly, VP Lee S Harrow, VP Lawrence McCabe, VP Thomas H McIntosh, VP D Edward I Smyth, PR	Rev: Assets: Emp:	5244 3605 39	
Heinz, H J Co of Canada 5650 Yonge Street Willowdale, ON M2M4G3 Can 416-226-5757	Manufacturer of packaged foods. Type: Private-Sub-For Ind: Food Processing Grp: Food Processing W Springer, CEO	Rev: Assets: Emp:	362 207 2	
Helene Curtis Industries Inc 325 N Wells Street Chicago, IL 60610 312-292-2121	Manufacturer of personal care products. Type: NYSE-HC Ind: Personal Care Grp: Consumer Prd Gerald S Gidwitz, CEO Charles G Cooper, VCh Robert Gray, Tres Lewis D Duberman, CFO Jack Calabro, Mkt Colin J Morgan, Ops Michael Goldman, VP Thomas Gildea, VP Robert Sack, VP Gilbert Smith, VP	Rev: Assets: Emp:	629 325 4	
Helmerich & Payne Inc Utica at 21st Street Tulsa, OK 74114 918-742-5531	Contract oil & gas drilling. Type: NYSE-HP Ind: Oil Service Grp: Business Service W H Helmerich, CEO	Rev: Assets: Emp:	160 576 1	
Helmsley Spear Co 60 E 42nd Street New York, NY 10165 212-687-6400	Commercial leasing, sales, consulting & management company. Type: Private Ind: Real Estate/Bldg Grp: Business Service Harry B Helmsley, CEO	Rev: Assets: Emp:	1800 NA 12	
Hendrick Management Corp 3400 South Blvd Charlotte, NC 28209 704-529-0578	Auto dealerships. Type: Private Ind: Real Estate/Bldg Grp: Business Service J R Hendrick, CEO	Rev: Assets: Emp:	500 NA 1	
Henley Group Inc Liberty Lane Hampton, NH 03842 603-926-5911	Holding company for Itel, Fisher Scientific, & Wheelabrator. Type: NASDAQ-HENG Ind: Business Service Grp: Business Service Michael D Dingman, CEO Paul Montrone, Pres Robert Barone, VCh Ron Simon, CFO William Buccella, R&D Harold Buirkle, Sls Christopher Reinhard, VP Walter Sanborn, VP Ronald Simon, VP David Summers, VP W D Sanborn III, PR	Rev: Assets: Emp:	1036 4503 2	
Henleys Group Ltd 800 Square Victoria Montreal, PQ H4Z1E9 Can 514-397-7640	Diversified manufacturing company. Type: Private Ind: Manufacturing Grp: Manufacturing David Henley, CEO	Rev: Assets: Emp:	714 NA 1	

Organizations Listed Alphabetically

Organization / Address / Phone	Descriptive Information	Revenue / Assets / Emp ($ mil) ($ mil) (thous)		

Hennepin County Government
Government Center
Minneapolis, MN 55487
612-348-3000

County government.
Type: County Govt
Ind: Local Govt   Grp: Govt & Non-Prof
John E Derus, CEO

Rev: 1400
Assets: NM
Emp: 9

Hercules Construction Co
8220 Delmar Blvd
St Louis, MO 63124
314-991-3730

Construction of commercial buildings.
Type: Private-Sub Par: Turner Corp
Ind: Real Estate/Bldg   Grp: Business Service
Peter Benoist, CEO

Rev: NA
Assets: NA
Emp: NA

Hercules Inc
Hercules Plaza 1313 N Market Street
Wilmington, DE 19894
302-594-5000

Specialty chemical manufacturing company.
Type: NYSE-HPC
Ind: Chemicals   Grp: Basic Industries
David S Hollingsworth, CEO   Fred L Buckner, Pres   Alexander Searle, Tres
Arden B Engebretsen, CFO   Ross O Watson, IS   Theodore Bednarski, R&D
Charles Gamble, VP   James Knox, VP   Daniel Desmond, VP

Rev: 2802
Assets: 3325
Emp: 23

Heritage Communications Inc
2195 Ingersoll Avenue
Des Moines, IA 50312
515-246-1440

Cable television
Type: Private
Ind: Publishing/Com   Grp: Consumer Service
James Hoak, CEO

Rev: 900
Assets: 700
Emp: 2

Heritage Today Corp
7224 Park Road
Charlotte, NC 28279
704-542-6000

Operator of religious television broadcasting network.
Type: Private
Ind: Publishing/Com   Grp: Consumer Service
Sam Johnson, CEO

Rev: 330
Assets: NA
Emp: 3

Hershey Foods Corp
100 Mansion Road E
Hershey, PA 17033
717-534-4000

Manufacturer of packaged food products; chocolate.
Type: NYSE-HSY
Ind: Food Processing   Grp: Food Processing
Richard A Zimmerman, CEO   Kenneth L Wolfe, Pres   William Lehr, VCh
Michael F Pasquale, CFO   Dr Barry Zoumas, R&D   John B Stiles, VP
Charles E Duroni, VP   Frank Cerminara, VP   Kenneth L Bowers, IR
John C Long, PR

Rev: 2168
Assets: 1765
Emp: 12

Hertz Corp
225 Brae Blvd
Park Ridge, NJ 07656
201-307-2000

Worldwide car & truck rental company.
Type: NYSE
Ind: Consumer Service   Grp: Consumer Service
Frank Olson, CEO   Craig R Koch, Pres   Brian J Kennedy, Mkt
Thomas W Jans, IR   Joseph M Russo, PR

Rev: 2000
Assets: 3400
Emp: 15

Hewlett Packard Canada Ltd
6877 Goreway Drive
Mississauga, ON L4V 1M8 Can
416-678-9430

Manufacturer of computers & electronic instrumentation.
Type: Private-Sub-For
Ind: Comput/Off Equip   Grp: High Tech
Malcolm Gissing, CEO

Rev: 298
Assets: 298
Emp: 1

Hewlett Parkard Co
3000 Hanover Street
Palo Alto, CA 94304
415-857-1501

Manufacturer of computers & electronic instrumentation.
Type: NYSE
Ind: Comput/Off Equip   Grp: High Tech
David Packard, CEO   John A Young, Chr   Dean O Morton, Pres
George Newman, Tres   Robert P Wayman, CFO   John L Doyle, IS
Charles W Richion, Sls   Richard Alberding, Mkt   Lewis Platt, VP
Willliam Craven, VP

Rev: 10070
Assets: 7497
Emp: 87

Hexcel Corp
650 California Street
San Francisco, CA 94108
415-828-4200

Specialty chemical manufacturer.
Type: NYSE-HXL
Ind: Chemicals   Grp: Basic Industries
Robert L Witt, CEO

Rev: 400
Assets: 300
Emp: 3

Hibernia Corp
313 Carondelet Street
New Orleans, LA 70130
504-586-5552

Commercial bank.
Type: NASDAQ-HIBCA
Ind: Banking   Grp: Financial
Martin C Miler, CEO   Thomas A Masilla Jr, Chr   Donald J Nalty, Pres
Charles L Petrey Jr, CFO   Gilbert H Vorhoff, R&D   Chris S Commons, Mkt
Chris S Commons, PR

Rev: 546
Assets: 5313
Emp: 3

Organizations Listed Alphabetically

Organization / Address / Phone	Descriptive Information	Revenue / Assets / Emp ($ mil) ($ mil) (thous)		

Highland Superstores Corp
909 N Sheldon Road
Plymouth, MI 48170
313-451-3200

Retail electronic appliances,video, stereo equipment stores.
Type: NASDAQ-HIGH
Ind: Retail/Merch   Grp: Retail
David Mondry, CEO

Rev: 911
Assets: 700
Emp: 5

Hill Financial Savings Assn Inc
400 Main Street
Red Hill, PA 18076
215-679-9506

Thrift institution.
Type: Private
Ind: Savings & Loan   Grp: Financial
Robert B Walker, CEO

Rev: 350
Assets: 3500
Emp: 1

Hill's Department Stores Inc
15 Dan Road
Canton, MA 02021
617-821-1000

Operator of retail discount department stores.
Type: NYSE-HDS
Ind: Retail/Merch   Grp: Retail
Stephen A Goldberger, CEO

Rev: 1671
Assets: 1000
Emp: 14

Hill's Pet Products Inc
400 W Eighth Street
Topeka, KS 66602
913-354-8523

Manufacturer of pet food.
Type: Private-Sub Par: Colgate Palmolive Co
Ind: Food Processing   Grp: Food Processing
Robert Wheeler, CEO

Rev: NA
Assets: NA
Emp: NA

Hillenbrand Industries Inc
Highway 46
Batesville, IN 47006
812-934-7000

Manufacturer of consumer products; luggage,security devices.
Type: NYSE-HB
Ind: Manufacturing   Grp: Manufacturing
Daniel A Hillenbrand, CEO   W August Hillenbrand, Pres   Lonnie Smith, VCh
Tom E Brewer, CFO   Steve Reiter, IS   Robyn Washburn, VP
Robert C Smith, PR

Rev: 884
Assets: 735
Emp: 8

Hillman Industries Inc
Grant Bldg
Pittsburgh, PA 15219
412-281-2620

Real estate development, office products, investment co.
Type: Private
Ind: Manufacturing   Grp: Manufacturing
Henry L Hillman, CEO

Rev: 1250
Assets: NA
Emp: 5

Hillsborough Holdings (Walter, Jim Corp)
1500 N Dale Mabry Highway
Tampa, FL 33607
813-871-4811

Construction company; home building & development.
Type: Private
Ind: Real Estate/Bldg   Grp: Business Service
Kenneth E Hyatt, CEO

Rev: 2500
Assets: 3000
Emp: 20

Hilton Hotels Corp
9336 Civic Center Drive
Beverly Hills, CA 90209
213-278-4321

Worldwide operator of hotels.
Type: NYSE
Ind: Food/Lodging   Grp: Consumer Service
Barron Hilton, CEO   Gregory R Dillon, VCh   Maurice J Scanlon, CFO
Sandra M Carpenter, IS   Joseph P Smyth, Mkt   Carl Mottek, Ops
John V Giovenco, VP   Leroy A Judge Jr, IR

Rev: 954
Assets: 1893
Emp: 18

Himont Inc
1313 N Market Street
Wilmington, DE 19894
302-594-5500

Manufacturing of chemical resins.
Type: NYSE-HMT
Ind: Chemicals   Grp: Basic Industries
Edwin Moler, CEO   Alex F Jiacco, Chr   R Michael Hendricks, Pres
Camillo J Difrancesco, CFO   Paolo Galli, R&D   Shelly Roth, PR

Rev: 600
Assets: 400
Emp: 1

Hiram Walker Gooderham Worts Ltd
2072 Riverside Road E
Windsor, ON N8Y4S5 Can
519-254-5171

Manufacturer of beverage products; liquor.
Type: Private-Sub-For
Ind: Food Processing   Grp: Food Processing
Clifford Hatch, CEO

Rev: 1309
Assets: NA
Emp: 6

Hitachi Sales Corp of America
401 W Artesia Blvd
Compton, CA 90220
213-537-8383

Manufacturer & importer of electronic equipment; US hdqtrs.
Type: Private-Sub-For
Ind: Electronics   Grp: High Tech
T Kataoka, CEO

Rev: 1100
Assets: NA
Emp: 2

Hoechst American Corp
1041 Route 202-206 N PO Box 2500
Somerville, NJ 08876
201-231-2000

Manufacturer & importer of automotive parts; US hdqtrs.
Type: Private-Sub-For
Ind: Chemicals   Grp: Basic Industries
Ernest Drew, CEO   Harry R Benz, CFO   E F Phares, IS
Dr Leon Starr, R&D   William S Kelly, PR

Rev: 1815
Assets: 1300
Emp: 11

Organizations Listed Alphabetically

Organization / Address / Phone	Descriptive Information	Revenue / ($ mil)	Assets / ($ mil)	Emp (thous)
Holiday (Inn) Corp 1023 Cherry Road Memphis, TN 38117 901-762-8600	Worldwide hotel chain. Type: NYSE-HIA Ind: Food/Lodging Grp: Consumer Service Michael D Rose, CEO D Michael Meeks, VCh Steve Bollenbach, CFO Richard L Nauman, IS Dwayne E Knapp, Mkt J W McCallister, VP Timothy Williams, VP Robert L Brannon, PR	Rev: Assets: Emp:	1597 2139 45	
Holiday Companies Inc 4567 W 80th Street Minneapolis, MN 55440 612-830-8700	Gasoline retailing, convenience stores. Type: Private Ind: Retail/Merch Grp: Retail Ronald Erickson, CEO	Rev: Assets: Emp:	1000 NA 5	
Hollinger Inc 10 Toronto Street Toronto, ON M5C2B7 Can 416-363-8721	Diversified manufacturing company. Type: TOR Ind: Manufacturing Grp: Manufacturing Conrad Black, CEO	Rev: Assets: Emp:	587 850 5	
Holly Corp 717 N Harwood Street Dallas, TX 75201 214-979-0210	Petroleum products refining & marketing company. Type: ASE-HOC Ind: Automotive Grp: Manufacturing Lamar Norsworthy, CEO E I Parsons, VCh James W Robertson, Tres Henry A Teicholz, CFO William Gray, Mkt Dewie O Stevenson, VP Gordon Bussey, VP Micke Mirbagheri, VP	Rev: Assets: Emp:	386 153 1	
Holly Farms Corp 1755-D Lynnfield Road Memphis, TN 38119 901-761-3610	Producer of consumer food products. Type: NYSE-HFF Ind: Retail/Food Grp: Retail Lewis K McKee, CEO R Lee Taylor II, Chr James Thompson, CFO John T Stout, Sls W F Bailey, Mkt Elbert L Thomas, VP Ted Bailey, PR	Rev: Assets: Emp:	1583 757 15	
Holman Enterprises Inc 7411 Maple Avenue Pennsauken, NJ 08109 609-663-5200	Auto dealerships, parts manufacturer. Type: Private Ind: Automotive Grp: Manufacturing Joseph S Holman, CEO	Rev: Assets: Emp:	750 NA 2	
Home Box Office Inc 1100 Avenue of the Amercias New York, NY 10036 212-522-1212	Owner & operator cable television station. Type: Private-Sub Par: Time Inc Ind: Publishing/Com Grp: Consumer Service Michael Fuchs, CEO	Rev: Assets: Emp:	NA NA NA	
Home Depot Inc 2727 Paces Ferry Road Atlanta, GA 30339 404-433-8211	Building material & hardware retailer. Type: NYSE-HD Ind: Retail/Merch Grp: Retail Bernard Marcus, CEO Arthur M Blank, Pres Ronald M Brill, CFO E Dennis Ross, IS Dick Hammill, Mkt Bill Hamlin, VP Dennis Ryan, VP Marshall L Day, VP Nathan Morton, VP Bruce Berg, VP Larry Mercer, VP	Rev: Assets: Emp:	1999 699 9	
Home Federal Savings & Loan Assn Inc 625 Broadway San Diego, CA 92101 619-699-8000	Thrift institution. Type: NYSE-HFD Ind: Savings & Loan Grp: Financial Kim Fletcher, CEO Robert F Adelizzi, Pres William D Nichol, CFO Edwin R Nichols, IS Bill N Kinter, Mkt Denise Botticelli, VP William Mayer, VP Sheree L Zizzi, IR	Rev: Assets: Emp:	1578 17009 5	
Home Interiors & Gifts Inc 4550 Spring Valley Road Dallas, TX 75381 214-386-1000	Wholesaler & retailer of home furnishings. Type: Private Ind: Retail/Merch Grp: Retail Donald J Carter, CEO	Rev: Assets: Emp:	400 NA 2	
Home Life Insurance Co 75 Wall Street New York, NY 10005 212-428-2000	Life insurance company. Type: Private-Mutual Ind: Insurance Grp: Insurance William B Wallace, CEO Kenneth C Nichols, Chr Sanford M Kimmel, CFO Gary Laughinghouse, IS Leonard J Ialeggio, Mkt Linda C Brett, IR Dora Mintz, PR	Rev: Assets: Emp:	1423 3542 3	

Organizations Listed Alphabetically

Organization / Address / Phone	Descriptive Information	Revenue / Assets / Emp ($ mil) ($ mil) (thous)		

Home Owners Federal S & L Assn
21 Milk Street
Boston, MA 02109
617-482-0630

Thrift institution.
Type: NYSEHFS
Ind: Savings & Loan   Grp: Financial
Bernard Grossman, CEO

Rev: 400
Assets: 4218
Emp: 2

Home Shopping Inc
12000 25th Court N
St Petersburg, FL 33716
813-572-8585

Retail discount merchandise.
Type: ASE-HSN
Ind: Retail/Merch   Grp: Retail
Roy M Speer, CEO   Lowell W Paxson, Pres   Nando DiFilippo, VCh
Les Paxson, CFO   Stella Tavilla, IS   Charles H Bohart, R&D
J Michael Reardon, Ops

Rev: 730
Assets: 540
Emp: 6

Homestake Mining Co
650 California Street
San Francisco, CA 94108
415-981-8150

Gold mining company.
Type: NYSE-HM
Ind: Metals/Mining   Grp: Basic Industries
Harry M Conger, CEO   D K Fagin, Pres   Jonathan J Williams, Tres
Richard W Stumbo Jr, CFO   R E Moulton, IS   R A Holway, Mkt
Lee A Graber, VP   Richard R Hinkel, VP   William Langston, VP
Robert L Watson, VP   Dennnis B Goldstein, VP

Rev: 433
Assets: 984
Emp: 2

Homestead Savings Fed Savings Assn Inc
5757 Geary Blvd
San Francisco, CA 94121
415-387-4300

Thrift institution.
Type: NYSE-HFL
Ind: Savings & Loan   Grp: Financial
Lawrence Weissberg, CEO   John P Halicky, CFO

Rev: 497
Assets: 5751
Emp: 2

Hon Industries Inc
414 E Third Street
Muscatine, IA 52761
319-264-7400

Diversified manufacturer of industrial products.
Type: NASDAQ-HONI
Ind: Manufacturing   Grp: Manufacturing
Stanley M Howe, CEO   Richard Stanley, VCh   John W Axel, CFO
Clare A Patterson, R&D   Clare Patterson, Ops   R Michael Derry, VP
Raymond E Lasell, VP   Melvin McMains, VP   Russell Woodward, VP
Richard Johnson, PR

Rev: 532
Assets: 276
Emp: 5

Honda Canada Inc
715 Milner Avenue
Scarborough, ON M1B2K8 Can
416-284-8110

Automobile marketing distribution company.
Type: Private-Sub-For
Ind: Automotive   Grp: Manufacturing
M Tsukamoto, CEO

Rev: 1034
Assets: 850
Emp: 1

Honda of America Corp
Honda Parkway
Marysville, OH 43040
513-642-5000

Manufacturer & importer of automobiles; US headquarters.
Type: Private-Sub-For
Ind: Automotive   Grp: Manufacturing
Hiroyuki Yoshino, CEO

Rev: 5500
Assets: NA
Emp: 16

Honeywell Bull (Cie des Machines Bull)
200 Smith Street
Waltham, MA 02154
617-895-6000

Manufacturer of computer equipment.
Type: Private-Sub-For
Ind: Comput/Off Equip   Grp: High Tech
Roland Pampel, CEO

Rev: 750
Assets: NA
Emp: 7

Honeywell Inc
Honeywell Plaza
Minneapolis, MN 55408
612-870-5200

International electronic controls corporation.
Type: NYSE-HON
Ind: Comput/Off Equip   Grp: High Tech
James J Renier, CEO   David Bergerson, VCh   Louis E Navin, CFO
Irma Wyman, IS   Gerald Dinneen, R&D   Richard Boyle, Mkt
Clint Larson, Ops   William Mackey, VP   Robert Mall, VP
Jerome Meyer, VP   Sigurd Ueland, VP   Mario P Santrizos, IR
Kathryn Tunheim, PR

Rev: 7148
Assets: 5089
Emp: 62

Honeywell Ltd
155 Gordon Baker Road
Willowdale, ON M2M3N7 Can
416-499-6111

Electronic controls manufacturer.
Type: Private-Sub-For
Ind: Comput/Off Equip   Grp: High Tech
Rodrigue J Bilodeau, CEO   Brian M McGourty, Chr   Michael A Rocca, CFO

Rev: 349
Assets: 205
Emp: 4

Hongkong & Shanghai Banking Corp
Five World Trade Center
New York, NY 10048
212-839-5000

Commercial bank.
Type: Private-Sub-For
Ind: Banking   Grp: Financial
James M C Morrow, CEO

Rev: 550
Assets: 4500
Emp: 1

Organizations Listed Alphabetically

Organization / Address / Phone	Descriptive Information	Revenue / Assets / Emp ($ mil) ($ mil) (thous)		

Hongkong Bank of Canada
885 W Georgia
Vancouver, BC V6C3E9 Can
604-685-1000

Commercial bank.
Type: Private-Sub-For
Ind: Banking   Grp: Financial
Jim Cleave, CEO

Rev: 250
Assets: 3045
Emp: 2

Honolulu, City of
City Hall
Honolulu, HI 96813
808-523-4111

City government.
Type: City Govt
Ind: Local Govt   Grp: Govt & Non-Prof
Frank F Fasi, CEO

Rev: 506
Assets: NM
Emp: 8

Hook SupeRX Stores Inc
PO Box 26285
Indianapolis, IN 46226
317-353-1451

Operator of retail drugstores.
Type: Private
Ind: Retail/Merch   Grp: Retail
Philip E Beekman, CEO

Rev: 1400
Assets: NA
Emp: 14

Horizon Bancorp Inc
225 South Street
Morristown, NJ 07960
201-539-7700

Commercial bank.
Type: Private
Ind: Banking   Grp: Financial
Roger Etherington, CEO

Rev: 400
Assets: 4000
Emp: 3

Horizon Industries Inc
S Industrial Blvd
Calhoun, GA 30701
404-629-7721

Textile manufacturer.
Type: OTC
Ind: Apparel/Textiles   Grp: Consumer Prd
Peter Spirer, CEO

Rev: 350
Assets: 200
Emp: 3

Hormel, George A & Co
501 Sixteenth Avenue NE
Austin, MN 55912
507-437-5611

Producer of packaged meats & foods.
Type: ASE-HRL
Ind: Food Processing   Grp: Food Processing
R L Knowlton, CEO   Robert Thatcher, Tres   Richard Schlange, CFO
Daniel Darveaux, IS   Forrest Dryden, R&D   William Hunter, Ops
Robert Wells, VP   Charles Nyberg, VP   Forrest Dryden, VP
David Larson, VP   V Allan Krejci, PR

Rev: 2293
Assets: 707
Emp: 7

Horn & Hardart Co
101 Convention Drive
Las Vegas, NV 89109
702-369-9500

Operator of restaurants & cafeterias.
Type: ASE-HOR
Ind: Food/Lodging   Grp: Consumer Service
Barry W Florescue, CEO

Rev: 499
Assets: 400
Emp: 6

Horsehead Industries Inc
204 E 39th Street
New York, NY 10016
212-972-2100

Industrial waste recycling company.
Type: Private
Ind: Business Service   Grp: Business Service
William E Flaherty, CEO

Rev: 750
Assets: NA
Emp: 3

Hospital Corp of America
One Park Plaza
Nashville, TN 37203
615-327-9551

Operator of hospitals & clinics.
Type: NYSE
Ind: Health Care   Grp: Consumer Service
Thomas F Frist, CEO   Jack Bovender, VCh   Roger E Mick, CFO
Thomas Cato, IS   Samuel Owen, R&D   Paul McKnight, VP
Donald Fish, VP   Vic Campbell, IR   Pamela Baesler, PR

Rev: 4111
Assets: 5388
Emp: 86

Hotel & Restrauant Employees Intl Union
1219 28th Street NW
Washington, DC 20007
202-393-4373

National labor union.
Type: Membership Org
Ind: Membership Org   Grp: Govt & Non-Prof
Edward T Hanley, CEO

Rev: 250
Assets: NM
Emp: 330

Houghton Mifflin Co
One Beacon Street
Boston, MA 02108
617-725-5000

Publisher of college & school textbooks.
Type: NYSE-HTN
Ind: Publishing/Com   Grp: Consumer Service
Harold T Miller, CEO   Robert Baker, Pres   Dennis Armes, VCh
Stephen Jaeger, CFO   Edward Sinni, IS   Claudia C Regan, Mkt
Claybourne White, VP   Paul D Weaver, VP   William Berman, VP

Rev: 368
Assets: 262
Emp: 2

House of Fabrics Inc
13400 Riverside Drive
Sherman Oaks, CA 91423
818-995-7000

Operator of retail fabric & sewing stores.
Type: NYSE-HF
Ind: Retail/Merch   Grp: Retail
Gary L Larkins, CEO

Rev: 338
Assets: 200
Emp: 3

Organizations Listed Alphabetically

Organization / Address / Phone	Descriptive Information	Revenue / ($ mil)	Assets / ($ mil)	Emp (thous)

Household International Inc
2700 Sanders Road
Prospect Heights, IL 60070
312-564-3663

Consumer financial services company.
Type: NYSE-HI
Ind: Conglomerate   Grp: Manufacturing
Donald C Clark, CEO   Edwin Hoffman, Pres   James Pinkerton, VCh
Donald Lohmann, CFO   David Barany, IS   Craig Wills, R&D
Robert F Logan, Sls   Theodore Thornton, VP   Serge Uccetta, VP
Colin Kelly, VP   Robert J Hartney, PR

Rev: 2352
Assets: 21032
Emp: 30

Household Manufacturing Corp
2700 Sanders Road
Prospect Heights, IL 60070
312-564-3910

Manufacturer of kitchen applicances, plumbing fixtures.
Type: NYSE-HH
Ind: Manufacturing   Grp: Manufacturing
Gary Dillon, CEO   William Chandler, CFO   Robert J Hartney, PR

Rev: 1000
Assets: 500
Emp: 10

Houston Community College
22 Waugh Drive
Houston, TX 77270
713-868-0700

Major educational institution; community college.
Type: University
Ind: University   Grp: Govt & Non-Prof
J B Whiteley, CEO

Rev: 72
Assets: 110
Emp: 28

Houston Industries Inc
611 Walker
Houston, TX 77002
713-228-2474

Diversified electric utility, electronic controls & finance.
Type: NYSE
Ind: Utility   Grp: Utilities
Don D Jordan, CEO   William A Cropper, Tres   Hollis R Dean, CFO
Robert Dyer, R&D   Gretchen H Denum, VP   Don D Sykora, VP
Hugh Rice Kelly, VP   Marc Killbride, VP   Kevin P Loughnane, VP
Rusfus S Scott, VP   Dan Bulla, PR

Rev: 3649
Assets: 10219
Emp: 10

Houston Lighting & Power Co
611 Walker Street
Houston, TX 77002
713-229-7267

Utility power utility company.
Type: Private-Sub   Par: Houston Industries Inc
Ind: Utility   Grp: Utilities
Don Jordan, CEO

Rev: 500
Assets: NA
Emp: 2

Houston, City of
City Hall
Houston, TX 77251
713-222-3141

City government.
Type: City Govt
Ind: Local Govt   Grp: Govt & Non-Prof
Kathryn J Whitmire, CEO

Rev: 1434
Assets: NM
Emp: 21

Hovnanian Enterprises Inc
10 Route 35
Red Bank, NJ 07701
201-747-7800

Developer of multi unit residental housing.
Type: ASE-HOV
Ind: Real Estate/Bldg   Grp: Business Service
Kevork S Hovnanian, CEO   Ara K Hovanian, Pres   Timothy P Mason, Tres
Paul W Buchanan, CFO   Stephen D Weinroth, VP   John J Schimpf, VP
Desmond P McDonald, VP

Rev: 301
Assets: 318
Emp: 2

Howard Savings Bank Inc
200 S Orange Avenue
Livingston, NJ 07039
201-533-7400

Thrift institution.
Type: NASDAQ-HWRD
Ind: Savings & Loan   Grp: Financial
Donald F McCormick, CEO   Leo J Rogers, Pres   Andrew Aldi, VCh
Joseph Wojak, CFO   John Petrillo, IS   Joseph Gershey, R&D
Jeffrey Haslett, Sls   Robert Dressel, Mkt   John Kuntz, VP
John Massarano, VP   Richard Bonnelli, VP   Walter Hausman, PR

Rev: 481
Assets: 5221
Emp: 2

Howell Corp
1010 Lamar
Houston, TX 77002
713-658-4000

Oil & gas exploration, refining, & pipeline company.
Type: NYSE-HWL
Ind: Energy   Grp: Basic Industries
Paul N Howell, CEO

Rev: 250
Assets: 300
Emp: 1

HR Textron Inc
25200 W Rye Canyon Road
Valencia, CA 91355
805-259-4030

Financial services company.
Type: Private-Sub   Par: Textron Inc
Ind: Non-Bank Fin   Grp: Financial
Richard Millman, CEO

Rev: NA
Assets: NA
Emp: NA

Hubbell Inc
584 Derby Milford Road
Orange, CT 06477
203-789-1100

Manufacturer of electrical equipment.
Type: ASE
Ind: Electronics   Grp: High Tech
G J Ratcliffe, CEO   Vincent Petrecca, VCh   James Biggart, Tres
Robert McRoberts, CFO   D G McNamara, IS   Edward Corner, R&D
Roger Search, VP   T R Conlin, PR

Rev: 614
Assets: 523
Emp: 5

Organizations Listed Alphabetically

Organization / Address / Phone	Descriptive Information	Revenue / ($ mil)	Assets / ($ mil)	Emp (thous)
Huber, J M Corp 333 Thornall Street Edison, NJ 08818 201-549-8600	Manufacturer, rubber, natural resources, energy. Type: Private Ind: Chemicals Grp: Basic Industries Michael W Huber, CEO	Rev: Assets: Emp:	500 NA 3	
Hudson Bay Mining & Smelting Co Toronto Dominion Center Toronto, ON M5K1B8 Can 416-362-2192	Mining & minerals processing company. Type: Private-Sub-For Ind: Metals/Mining Grp: Basic Industries Lloyd Nilson, CEO	Rev: Assets: Emp:	298 255 2	
Hudson Foods Inc 13th Street & Hudson Road Rogers, AR 72756 501-636-1100	Food processing company; beef, pork, chicken. Type: ASE-HDI Ind: Food Processing Grp: Food Processing James T Hudson, CEO	Rev: Assets: Emp:	450 250 5	
Hudson's Bay Co 401 Bay Street E Toronto, ON M5H2Y4 Can 416-861-6112	Operator of retail department stores. Type: TOR Ind: Retail/Merch Grp: Retail George J Kosich, CEO Donald S McGiverin, Chr Gary Lukassen, CFO Larry Rowe, IS Jerry Hartman, R&D John Cunningham, Ops Sheila Walters, VP Kenneth C Wong, VP A Rolph Huband, VP David Crisp, VP	Rev: Assets: Emp:	3971 2966 40	
Huffington, Roy M Inc 1100 Louisiana Houston, TX 77210 713-651-1600	Natural resource development & energy company. Type: Private Ind: Energy Grp: Basic Industries Roy M Huffington, CEO	Rev: Assets: Emp:	1100 NA 2	
Huffy Corp 7701 Byers Road Miamisburg, OH 45342 513-866-6251	Manufacturer of bicycles, sporting goods. Type: NYSE-HUF Ind: Leisure Time Grp: Consumer Service Harry A Shaw, CEO	Rev: Assets: Emp:	350 300 3	
Hughes Aircraft Co PO Box 45006 Los Angeles, CA 90045 213-568-6321	Manufacturer of aerospace electronic systems. Type: Private-Sub Par: General Motors Corp Ind: Aerospace Grp: High Tech Malcolm Currie, CEO	Rev: Assets: Emp:	NA NA NA	
Hughes Markets Inc 2716 San Fernando Los Angeles, CA 90065 213-227-8211	Dairy, grocery stores. Type: Private Ind: Retail/Food Grp: Retail Fred B McLaren, CEO	Rev: Assets: Emp:	1000 NA 5	
Hughes Supply Inc 521 W Central Blvd PO Box 2273 Orlando, FL 32802 305-841-4710	Distributor of products for the construction industry. Type: NYSE-HUG Ind: Appliances/Furn Grp: Manufacturing David H Hughes, CEO Alvin S Hall, VCh J Stephen Zepf, CFO Jasper L Holland, Mkt Kenneth H Stephens, Ops William C Weir, VP	Rev: Assets: Emp:	502 224 4	
Humana Inc Humana Bldg 500 W Main Street Louisville, KY 40202 502-580-1000	Operates hospitals & health facilities. Type: NYSE Ind: Health Care Grp: Consumer Service David A Jones, CEO Wendall Cherry, Pres William C Ballard Jr, CFO Fred Pirman Jr, IS Neal Westermeyer, Mkt George L Atkins, PR	Rev: Assets: Emp:	3435 3422 49	
Humiston Keeling Corp 233 E Erie Chicago, IL 60611 312-943-6066	Wholesale drug distribution company. Type: Private Ind: Retail/Merch Grp: Retail Burton H Olin, CEO	Rev: Assets: Emp:	400 NA 1	
Hunt Consolidated Oil Co 1401 Elm Street Dallas, TX 75202 214-744-7911	Petroleum & gas exploration & distribution. Type: Private Ind: Energy Grp: Basic Industries Ray L Hunt, CEO	Rev: Assets: Emp:	1000 NA 2	

Organizations Listed Alphabetically

Organization / Address / Phone	Descriptive Information	Revenue / Assets / Emp ($ mil) ($ mil) (thous)		

Hunt Corp
2450 S Tibbs Avenue
Indianapolis, IN 46241
317-241-6301

General contractors, construction management company.
Type: Private
Ind: Real Estate/Bldg   Grp: Business Service
Robert C Hunt, CEO

Rev: 1000
Assets: NA
Emp: 3

Hunt, J B Transportion Services Inc
Highway 71 N
Lowell, AR 72745
501-659-8800

Nationwide truck transport company.
Type: NASDAQ-JBHT
Ind: Transport   Grp: Business Service
J B Hunt, CEO   Kirk Thompson, Pres   Stephen Palmer, VCh
Bruce Jones, CFO   John Williams, IS   Paul Bergant, Mkt
Paul James, Ops   Bryan Hunt, VP   Bob Ralston, VP
Kirk Thompson, PR

Rev: 393
Assets: 301
Emp: 3

Huntington Bancshares Inc
41 S High Street
Columbus, OH 43260
614-476-8300

Commercial bank.
Type: NASDAQ-HBAN
Ind: Banking   Grp: Financial
Frank Wobst, CEO   A Zuheir Sofia, Pres   Ralph Fraiser, VCh
Kirk Simpson, CFO   James W Coons, Mkt   Lloyd Peele, VP
Leroy Sawatzky, VP   Richard Stage, VP   Dorothy R Brownley, PR

Rev: 901
Assets: 9506
Emp: 6

Huntsman Chemical & Oil Corp
2000 Eaglegate Tower 60 E S Temple
Salt Lake City, UT 84111
801-532-5200

Chemical & petroleum products company.
Type: Private
Ind: Chemicals   Grp: Basic Industries
John M Huntsman, CEO

Rev: 550
Assets: NA
Emp: 1

Husky Oil Ltd
707 8th Avenue SW
Calgary, AB T2P3G7 Can
403-298-6111

Petroleum products production & distribution company.
Type: Private-Sub
Ind: Energy   Grp: Basic Industries
Arthur R Price, CEO   Holland Berry, VCh   William Miller, CFO
Robert Phillips, Mkt   James Blair, VP   Robert Goods, VP
Murray Petersen, VP

Rev: 638
Assets: 1700
Emp: 2

Hutton, E F Group Inc
One Battery Park Plaza
New York, NY 10004
212-742-5000

Brokerage house.
Type: NYSE-EFH
Ind: Securities   Grp: Financial
Robert Fomon, CEO

Rev: 3000
Assets: 25000
Emp: 15

Hy Vee Food Stores Inc
1801 Osceola Avenue
Chariton, IA 50049
515-774-2121

Grocery stores.
Type: Private
Ind: Retail/Food   Grp: Retail
Ron Pearson, CEO

Rev: 1800
Assets: NA
Emp: 10

Hyatt Corp
200 W Madison
Chicago, IL 60606
312-750-1234

Worldwide operator of luxury hotels.
Type: Private
Ind: Food/Lodging   Grp: Consumer Service
Jay Pritzker, CEO

Rev: 2500
Assets: NA
Emp: 40

Hydro Quebec Ltd
75 Ouest Boul Rene Levesque
Montreal, PQ H2Z1A4 Can
514-289-2211

Electric power utility.
Type: Govt Corp
Ind: Utility   Grp: Utilities
Richard Drouin, CEO   Claude Boivin, Pres   John A Hanna, CFO
Maurice Huppe', R&D   Jacques Guevremont, Mkt   Jean Bernier, VP
Andre Delisle, VP   Rollande Montsion, VP   Jean-Claude Roy, VP
Benoit Michel, VP   Marcel Couture, PR

Rev: 4510
Assets: 26998
Emp: 19

Hyplains Dressed Beef Inc
2000 E Trail Street
Dodge City, KS 67801
316-227-7135

Producers & distributors of packaged foods; meat.
Type: Private
Ind: Food Processing   Grp: Food Processing
Don Mehesan, CEO

Rev: 275
Assets: NA
Emp: 1

Hyster Co Inc
2902 NE Wasco Street
Portland, OR 97232
503-280-7000

Manufacturer, fork lifts, metal handling equipment.
Type: Private
Ind: Equipment   Grp: Manufacturing
J Phillip Frazier, CEO

Rev: 750
Assets: NA
Emp: 5

Organizations Listed Alphabetically

Organization / Address / Phone	Descriptive Information	Revenue / ($ mil)	Assets / ($ mil)	Emp (thous)
Hyundai Auto Canada Inc 75 Frontenac Markham, ON L3R 6H2 Can 416-477-0202	Manufacturer & distributor of automobiles. Type: Private-Sub-For Ind: Automotive Grp: Manufacturing W I Lee, CEO	Rev: Assets: Emp:	377 184 1	
Hyundai USA Inc 7373 Hunt Avenue Garden Grove, CA 92642 714-890-6000	Manufacturer & importer of motor vehicles; US headquarters. Type: Private-Sub-For Ind: Automotive Grp: Manufacturing H W Baik, CEO	Rev: Assets: Emp:	2200 NA 4	
IBC Holdings (Interstate Bakeries Corp) 12 E Armour Blvd Kansas City, MO 64111 816-561-6600	Nationwide baking company; bread, cakes, food services. Type: Private Ind: Food Processing Grp: Food Processing Robert W Hatch, CEO R A Bevacqua, CFO B L Himes, IS Jan Van Lammeren, R&D John N Schwab, Mkt Linda Thompson, PR	Rev: Assets: Emp:	855 646 10	
IBM (Intl Business Mach) Canada Ltd 3500 Steeles Avenue E Markham, ON L3R 2Z1 Can 416-474-2111	Manufacturer of full line of computer equipment. Type: Private-Sub-For Ind: Comput/Off Equip Grp: High Tech L Lodge, CEO	Rev: Assets: Emp:	2638 2023 12	
IBM (Intl Business Mach) Corp Old Orchard Road Armonk, NY 10504 914-765-1900	Worldwide manufacturer of all ranges of computers. Type: NYSE-IBM Ind: Comput/Off Equip Grp: High Tech John F Ackers, CEO David E McKinney, Pres Frank A Metz Jr, CFO Ralph E Gomrory, R&D Terry R Lautenbach, Mkt C Michael Armstrong, VP George Conrades, VP Carl Conti, VP M Bernard Puckett, IR Marti Easterbrook, PR	Rev: Assets: Emp:	59681 73037 387	
IBP Corp IBP Avenue Dakota City, NE 68731 402-494-2061	Meat packing company. Type: Private-Sub Par: Occidental Petroleum Corp Ind: Food Processing Grp: Food Processing Robert Peterson, CEO	Rev: Assets: Emp:	9068 1154 18	
ICC Industries Inc 720 Fifth Avenue New York, NY 10019 212-903-1700	Manufacturer of chemicals. Type: Private Ind: Chemicals Grp: Basic Industries John Farber, CEO	Rev: Assets: Emp:	500 NA 2	
ICG Utilities Ltd 245 Yorkland Blvd Toronto, ON M2J1R1 Can 416-491-1880	Utility company; natural gas transmission & distribution. Type: Private-Sub Par: Inter City Gas Corp Ind: Utility Grp: Utilities Robert Graham, CEO	Rev: Assets: Emp:	510 638 1	
ICH Corp 4211 Norbourne Blvd Louisville, KY 40207 502-897-1861	Life & health insurance company. Type: ASE-ICH Ind: Non-Bank Fin Grp: Financial Robert T Shaw, CEO John W Gardiner, Pres Jack A Zimmer, Tres John T Hull, CFO C Fred Rice, Mkt Phillip Allen, Ops James R Kerber, VP Barth T Murphy, VP Thomas J Brophy, VP	Rev: Assets: Emp:	2885 9294 7	
ICI (Imperial Chemical) America Inc New Murphy Road & Concord Pike Wilmington, DE 19897 302-886-3000	Diversified chemical company; US headquarters. Type: Private-Sub-For Ind: Chemicals Grp: Basic Industries Harry Corless, CEO	Rev: Assets: Emp:	1650 NA 11	
ICN Pharmaceuticals Inc 3300 Hyland Avenue Costa Mesa, CA 92626 714-545-0100	Manufacturer, developer of drugs. Type: OTC Ind: Drugs Grp: Consumer Service Milan Panic, CEO	Rev: Assets: Emp:	166 465 2	
Idaho Power Co 1220 W Idaho Street Boise, ID 83707 208-383-2200	Electric power utility. Type: NYSE-IDA Ind: Utility Grp: Utilities Robert J O'Connor, CEO Wayne Anderson, Pres Joseph Marshall, VCh Dwayne D Hammond, CFO Larry G Teply, R&D Larry Gunnoe, Sls Clifford Bissell, VP Logan Lanham, VP Robert Stahman, VP	Rev: Assets: Emp:	412 1609 2	

Organizations Listed Alphabetically

Organization / Address / Phone	Descriptive Information	Revenue / ($ mil)	Assets / ($ mil)	Emp (thous)
Idaho, State of State Capitol Boise, ID 83720 208-334-2411	State government. Type: State Govt Ind: State/Prov Govt Grp: Govt & Non-Prof Cecil D Andrus, CEO	Rev: 1915	Assets: NM	Emp: 19
Ideal Basic Industries Corp 950 17th Street Denver, CO 80202 303-623-5661	Cement & cement products manufacturing company. Type: NYSE-IDL Ind: Building Mat Grp: Basic Industries Thomas E Bronson, CEO	Rev: 250	Assets: 250	Emp: 2
Idex Corp 630 Dundee Road Northbrook, IL 60062 312-498-7070	Manufacturer of fluid handling devices. Type: NYSE Ind: Manufacturing Grp: Manufacturing D Boyce, CEO	Rev: 250	Assets: 200	Emp: 3
Idle Wild Foods Inc 256 Franklin Street Worcester, MA 01604 617-757-7761	Meat processing company. Type: Private Ind: Food Processing Grp: Food Processing Anthony Geller, CEO	Rev: 1000	Assets: NA	Emp: 4
IDS Finacial Services Inc IDS Tower 10 Minneapolis, MN 55440 612-372-3131	Life insurance company. Type: NYSE Ind: Insurance Grp: Insurance James A Mitchell, CEO Harvey Golub, Chr David Hubers, CFO Roger Edgar, IS George Perry, R&D Jeffrey Stiefler, Mkt Carol Kerner, PR	Rev: 2326	Assets: 8963	Emp: 6
IE Industries Inc 200 First Street SE Cedar Rapids, IA 52401 319-398-4411	Electric power utility. Type: NYSE-IEL Ind: Utility Grp: Utilities Lee Liu, CEO	Rev: 250	Assets: 640	Emp: 2
Illinois Bell Telephone Co 212 W Washington Street Chicago, IL 60606 312-727-9411	Telephone utility company Type: Private-Sub Par: Ameritech (Amer Information Tech Corp) Ind: Telecom Grp: High Tech Frank Zimmerman, CEO	Rev: NA	Assets: NA	Emp: NA
Illinois Central Gulf Railroad Co 233 N Michigan Avenue Chicago, IL 60601 312-565-1600	Railroad transportation company. Type: NYSE-ICX Ind: Transport Grp: Business Service Harry Bruce, CEO G G Hester, Pres R P Bessette, CFO Henry Borgsmiller, IS G F Mohan, Mkt Frank J Allston, PR	Rev: 750	Assets: 1500	Emp: 5
Illinois Power Co 500 S 27th Street Decatur, IL 62525 217-424-6600	Electric power utility. Type: NYSE Ind: Utility Grp: Utilities Wendell J Kelley, CEO William Gerstner, VCh Larry D Haab, CFO Larry Altenbaumer, IS Porter Womeldorff, R&D Paul Lang, Mkt Larry Brodsky, VP Arthur Gray, VP Rodney Smith, PR	Rev: 1285	Assets: 6053	Emp: 5
Illinois State University School & North Streets Normal, IL 61761 309-438-2111	Major educational institution; university. Type: University Ind: University Grp: Govt & Non-Prof Thomas P Wallace, CEO	Rev: 112	Assets: 270	Emp: 24
Illinois Tool Works Inc 8501 W Higgins Road Chicago, IL 60631 312-693-3040	Manufacturer of tool systems. Type: NYSE-ITW Ind: Manufacturing Grp: Manufacturing John D Nichols, CEO Harold Byron SMith, Pres H Richard Crowther, VCh David Smith, CFO Donald VanErden, IS Thomas W Buckman, R&D John Deininger, Ops W James Farrell, VP John G Powers, VP Robert G Rettig, VP Steve Stefan, VP Stephen J Kaye, IR Michael H Hudson, PR	Rev: 1930	Assets: 1380	Emp: 14
Illinois, State of State House Springfield, IL 62706 217-782-2099	State government. Type: State Govt Ind: State/Prov Govt Grp: Govt & Non-Prof James R Thompson, CEO	Rev: 27399	Assets: NM	Emp: 155

Organizations Listed Alphabetically

Organization / Address / Phone	Descriptive Information	Revenue / ($ mil)	Assets / ($ mil)	Emp (thous)
Imasco Ltd 4 Westmont Square Montreal, PQ H3Z2S8 Can 514-937-9111	Manufacturer of personal care products. Type: TOR-IMS Ind: Personal Care Grp: Consumer Prd Purdy Crawford, CEO Jean Louis Mercier, Pres Torrance J Wylie, VCh Raymond Guyatt, CFO W John Bennett, Mkt William J Harris, VP Roy Schwartz, VP Robert Begin, VP Hugh McAdams, VP Norman Montcalm, VP	Rev: Assets: Emp:	5101 4514 60	
IMC Fertilizer Corp 2315 Sanders Road Northbrook, IL 60062 312-564-8600	Fertilizer manufacturing company. Type: Private-Sub Par: International Minerals & Chemical Corp Ind: Chemicals Grp: Basic Industries Billie Turner, CEO George D Kennedy, Chr Raymond F Bentele, VCh Daniel Feaker, Tres John F Sonderegger, CFO Donald Phillips, Sls A Jacqueline Dout, Ops	Rev: Assets: Emp:	1200 1000 6	
IMO Industries 3450 Princeton Pike Lawrenceville, NJ 08648 609-896-7600	Manufacturer of electronic instrumentation. Type: NYSE-IMD Ind: Electronics Grp: High Tech William J Holcombe, CEO	Rev: Assets: Emp:	650 550 4	
Imperial Bank Corp Century Blvd Los Angeles, CA 90009 213-417-5600	Commercial bank. Type: Private Ind: Banking Grp: Financial George M Eltinge, CEO	Rev: Assets: Emp:	178 2428 2	
Imperial Eastman Corp 6565 W Howard Niles, IL 60648 312-967-4500	Manufacturer of industrial fittings, piping, tubing etc. Type: OTC Ind: Manufacturing Grp: Manufacturing Jack Higgins, CEO	Rev: Assets: Emp:	500 500 5	
Imperial Holly Corp 1 Imperial Square Sugar Land, TX 77487 713-491-9181	Manufacturer of automotive products. Type: OTC Ind: Manufacturing Grp: Manufacturing I Kempner, CEO	Rev: Assets: Emp:	250 200 2	
Imperial Life Assurance Co 95 St Clair Avenue W Toronto, ON M4V1N7 Can 416-926-2600	Life insurance company. Type: TOR Ind: Insurance Grp: Insurance Robert StJacques, CEO	Rev: Assets: Emp:	1477 5180 4	
Imperial Oil Ltd 111 St Clair Avenue W Toronto, ON M5W1K3 Can 416-968-4111	Petroleum exploration, production & marketing company. Type: TOR Ind: Energy Grp: Basic Industries A R Haynes, CEO R B Peterson, Pres W J Young, CFO G L Munro, IS G Nuttall, R&D P J Dingle, Ops D D Baldwin, VP W West, VP R Walker, VP A Peterson, VP	Rev: Assets: Emp:	6124 7461 13	
Imperial Savings Assn Inc 9275 Sky Park Court San Diego, CA 92123 619-292-3000	Thrift institution. Type: NYSE-ICA Ind: Savings & Loan Grp: Financial Kenneth J Thygerson, CEO Kevin Villani, CFO	Rev: Assets: Emp:	972 10800 4	
Imperial Tobacco Ltd 3810 Rue St Antoine Montreal, PQ H4C1B5 Can 514-932-6161	Manufacturer of tobacco products; cigarettes. Type: Private-Sub Par: Imasco Ltd Ind: Tobacco Grp: Food Processing J Mercier, CEO	Rev: Assets: Emp:	1637 NA 7	
IMS International Inc 800 Third Avenue New York, NY 10022 212-371-2310	Market research company. Type: NASDAQ-IMSI Ind: Business Service Grp: Business Service Serge Okun, CEO	Rev: Assets: Emp:	500 400 6	
INA Life Insurance Co 1600 Arch Street Philadelphia, PA 19101 215-241-4000	Life insurance company. Type: OTC Ind: Insurance Grp: Insurance Robert F Rink, CEO	Rev: Assets: Emp:	478 2521 2	

Organizations Listed Alphabetically

Organization / Address / Phone	Descriptive Information	Revenue / ($ mil)	Assets / ($ mil)	Emp (thous)
Inacomp Computer Centers Inc 11550 N Meridian Street Indianapolis, IN 46240 317-844-9666	Manufacturer of microfilm equipment. Type: NYSE-AAC Ind: Comput/Off Equip Grp: High Tech Louis P Ferrero, CEO	Rev: Assets: Emp:	451 963 4	
Inco Ltd 1 First Canadian Place Toronto, ON M5X1C4 Can 416-361-7511	Mining company; nickel. Type: TOR Ind: Metals/Mining Grp: Basic Industries L Kowal, CEO	Rev: Assets: Emp:	2017 3307 19	
Indal Ltd 4000 Weston Road Weston, ON M9L2W8 Can 416-743-1400	Manufacturer of building products; doors, frames, windows. Type: TOR Ind: Building Mat Grp: Basic Industries Walter Stracey, CEO	Rev: Assets: Emp:	925 530 9	
Indian & Northern Affairs Canada 10 Wellington Street Hull, PQ K1A0H4 Can 819-997-0380	Federal government agency. Type: Federal Govt Ind: Federal Govt Grp: Govt & Non-Prof Harry Swain, CEO	Rev: Assets: Emp:	1020 NM 5	
Indiana Bell Telephone Co 240 N Meridian Street Indianapolis, IN 46204 317-265-2266	Telephone utility company. Type: Private-Sub Par: Ameritech (Amer Information Tech Corp) Ind: Telecom Grp: High Tech Ramon Humke, CEO	Rev: Assets: Emp:	NA NA NA	
Indiana Energy Inc 1630 N Meridian Street Indianapolis, IN 46202 317-926-3351	Natural gas utility company. Type: NYSE-IEI Ind: Utility Grp: Utilities Lawrence A Ferger, CEO	Rev: Assets: Emp:	250 600 2	
Indiana Farm Bureau Coop Assn Inc 120 E Market Street Indianapolis, IN 46204 317-631-8361	Agricultural cooperative; wholesale food supplier. Type: Private-Coop Ind: Food Processing Grp: Food Processing Phillip French, CEO Lloyd Arthur, Pres William Paddack, CFO Edward Bryan, IS Paul Weinstein, R&D Dean Denhart, Mkt Jeffrey D Harper, PR	Rev: Assets: Emp:	1320 250 1	
Indiana Michigan Power Co One Summit Square Fort Wayne, IN 46801 219-425-2111	Electric power utility company. Type: Private-Sub Ind: Utility Grp: Utilities W S White, CEO W A Black, Pres Milton Alexich, VCh Peter DeMaria, Tres Lenard Assante, CFO Joseph Vipperman, Mkt Joseph Dowd, VP Richard Disbrow, VP John Dolan, VP	Rev: Assets: Emp:	983 3993 4	
Indiana National Corp One Indiana Square Indianapolis, IN 46266 317-266-6000	Commercial bank. Type: NASDAQ-INAT Ind: Banking Grp: Financial Thomas M Miller, CEO David W Givens, Pres Andrew Paine, VCh Steven Schenck, CFO Percy Clark, IS Morris L Maurer, R&D Morris Maurer, VP Gerald L Rush, VP Steven Schenck, IR Jean Smith, PR	Rev: Assets: Emp:	545 5927 3	
Indiana University Bryan Hall Bloomington, IN 47405 812-332-0211	Major educational institution; university. Type: University Ind: University Grp: Govt & Non-Prof R R Gros Lewis, CEO	Rev: Assets: Emp:	315 572 34	
Indiana University at Indianapolis 355 N Lansing Indianapolis, IN 46202 317-635-8661	Major educational institution; university. Type: University Ind: University Grp: Govt & Non-Prof Gerald L Bepko, CEO	Rev: Assets: Emp:	278 290 26	
Indiana, State of State Capitol Indianapolis, IN 46204 317-232-4000	State government. Type: State Govt Ind: State/Prov Govt Grp: Govt & Non-Prof B Evan Bayh, CEO	Rev: Assets: Emp:	11256 NM 59	

Organizations Listed Alphabetically

Organization / Address / Phone	Descriptive Information	Revenue / ($ mil)	Assets / ($ mil)	Emp (thous)

Indianapolis, City of
City & County Bldg
Indianapolis, IN 46204
317-236-3600

City government.
Type: City Govt
Ind: Local Govt　　Grp: Govt & Non-Prof
William H Hudnut, CEO

Rev: 557
Assets: NM
Emp: 11

Industrial Alliance Life Insurance Co
1080 Schemin St Louis
Sillery, PQ G1K7M3 Can
418-463-5784

Life insurance company.
Type: Private
Ind: Insurance　　Grp: Insurance
Robert Begin, CEO　Raymond Garneau, Pres　J Marcel Boyer, VCh
Yvon Cote, CFO　Jacques Laverdure, IS　Normand Pepin, Mkt

Rev: 1487
Assets: 4389
Emp: 2

Industrial Automation Systems Group Inc
7300 Turfway Road
Florence, KY 41042
606-283-2202

Manufacturer of electronic equipment.
Type: Private-Sub　Par: Litton Industries Inc
Ind: Electronics　　Grp: High Tech
Gordon Palmer, CEO

Rev: NA
Assets: NA
Emp: NA

Industrial Bank of Japan Trust Co
245 Park Avenue
New York, NY 10067
212-557-3500

Commercial bank.
Type: Private-Sub-For
Ind: Banking　　Grp: Financial
Masahiro Takahashi, CEO

Rev: 650
Assets: 5500
Emp: 3

Industrial Machinery Corp
1800 Gardner Expressway
Quincy, IL 62301
217-222-5400

Manufacturer of industrial machinery.
Type: Private-Sub　Par: Cooper Industries Inc
Ind: Machinery　　Grp: Manufacturing
N Teshoian, CEO

Rev: NA
Assets: NA
Emp: NA

Information Resources Inc
150 N Clinton Street
Chicago, IL 60606
312-726-1221

Business information & computer software company.
Type: NASDAQ-IRIC
Ind: Comput/Off Equip　　Grp: High Tech
Magid Abraham, CEO　Gian Fulgoni, Chr　Gerald Eskin, VCh
Patricia Owens, CFO　Edgar Heinbach, IS　Randall S Smith, R&D
Brian Harris, VP　Edward S Berger, VP　Jeffrey Stamen, VP

Rev: 129
Assets: 151
Emp: 2

Ingersoll International Inc
707 Fulton Avenue
Rockford, IL 61103
815-987-6000

Diversified manufacturing company.
Type: Private
Ind: Manufacturing　　Grp: Manufacturing
Edson Gaylord, CEO

Rev: 550
Assets: NA
Emp: 5

Ingersoll-Rand Corp
200 Chestnut Ridge
Woodcliff Lake, NJ 07675
201-573-0123

Manufacturer of industrial pumps, motors, compressors.
Type: NYSE
Ind: Machinery　　Grp: Manufacturing
Theodore H Black, CEO　Thomas A Holmes, Chr　William Mulligan, VCh
Clyde H Folley, CFO　George Tabback, IS　James Odell, R&D
Frank DelleCave, VP　Frederick Hadfield, VP　David Lasier, VP
Thomas McBride, VP　Robert Ripston, VP　Richard Johnson, PR

Rev: 3021
Assets: 2483
Emp: 30

Ingles Markets Inc
Highway 70 E
Black Mountain, NC 28711
704-669-2941

Operator of retail food supermarkets.
Type: Private
Ind: Retail/Food　　Grp: Retail
Jack Fergason, CEO

Rev: 550
Assets: NA
Emp: 5

Inglis Ltd
1901 Minnesota Court
Mississauga, ON L5N3A7 Can
416-821-6400

Appliance manufacturers.
Type: TOR
Ind: Appliances/Furn　　Grp: Manufacturing
Stan Edwards, CEO

Rev: 360
Assets: 149
Emp: 3

Ingram Industries Inc
347 Redwood Drive
Nashville, TN 37217
615-793-5000

Marine transmission, oil, insurance, consumer products.
Type: Private
Ind: Personal Care　　Grp: Consumer Prd
E Bronson Ingram, CEO

Rev: 1250
Assets: NA
Emp: 7

Inland Container Corp
151 N Delaware
Indianapolis, IN 46206
317-262-0222

Manufacturer of paper products used for packages & cartons.
Type: Private-Sub　Par: Temple Inland Inc
Ind: Packaging　　Grp: Manufacturing
Ben Lancashire, CEO

Rev: NA
Assets: NA
Emp: NA

Organizations Listed Alphabetically

Organization / Address / Phone	Descriptive Information	Revenue / ($ mil)	Assets / ($ mil)	Emp (thous)
Inland Natural Gas Co 1066 W Hastings Street Vancouver, BC V6E3G3 Can 604-684-0484	Natural gas utility company. Type: TOR Ind: Utility Grp: Utilities Ronald Cliff, CEO	Rev: Assets: Emp:		255 383 1
Inland Real Estate Corp 2901 Butterfield Road Oak Brook, IL 60521 312-218-8000	Real estate management, insurance brokerage. Type: Private Ind: Real Estate/Bldg Grp: Business Service E J Morse, CEO	Rev: Assets: Emp:		500 NA 2
Inland Steel Industries Inc 30 W Monroe Street Chicago, IL 60603 312-346-0300	Basic steel manufacturer & operator of steel service ctrs. Type: NYSE Ind: Steel Grp: Basic Industries Frank W Luerssen, CEO Robert J Darnall, Pres Theodore A Myers, CFO William Sanders, IS Ian Hughes, R&D Robert E Powell, Sls Thomas Gleason, VP Clark Wagner, VP Judd Cool, VP Sam H Saran, PR	Rev: Assets: Emp:		4068 2925 21
Insilco Corp 1000 Research Parkway Meridan, CT 06450 203-634-2000	Steel & plastic manufacturer. Type: Private Ind: Manufacturing Grp: Manufacturing Donald J Harper, CEO John A McLendon, Pres Malcolm S Todt, CFO Richard Rees, IS Malcolm S Todt, PR	Rev: Assets: Emp:		750 700 10
Inspiration Resources Corp 250 Park Avenue New York, NY 10177 212-503-3100	Diversified natural resources & agricultural products. Type: NYSE-IRC Ind: Business Service Grp: Business Service Reuben F Richards, CEO Burton M Joyce, Pres Denis B Brady, CFO J Blair Howkins, R&D Gregor J Leinsdorf, Mkt Richard R Davies, VP J Blair Howkins, VP James M Simon, PR	Rev: Assets: Emp:		1436 842 6
Instrument Systems Inc 100 Jericho Quadrangle Jericho, NY 11753 516-938-5544	Manufacturer of electronic instrument systems. Type: ASE-ISY Ind: Electronics Grp: High Tech Harvey R Blau, CEO	Rev: Assets: Emp:		350 300 3
Integrated Resources 10 Union Square E New York, NY 10003 212-353-7000	Diversified financial company; life ins & money management Type: NYSE Ind: Non-Bank Fin Grp: Financial Selig A Zises, CEO Arthur H Goldberg, Pres Jay Zises, VCh Roderick Hoover, Tres Philip H Cohen, CFO Gerard Lavin, IS Jay D Chazanoff, Mkt Barton Sadowsky, VP Joel Paschow, VP Richard Ader, VP Frank Savage, VP David R Fluhrer, PR	Rev: Assets: Emp:		1111 6252 3
Intel Corp 3065 Bowers Avenue Santa Clara, CA 95052 408-987-8080	Manufacturer of computer chips. Type: NASDAQ Ind: Electronics Grp: High Tech Gordon E Moore, CEO Andrew S Grove, Chr Robert W Reed, CFO Carlene M Ellis, IS Gerhard H Parker, R&D Frank C Gill, Sls Ronald J Whittier, Mkt James W Jarrett, IR	Rev: Assets: Emp:		2875 3550 30
Intelligent Electronics Inc 35 E Uwchian Avenue Exton, PA 19341 215-524-1800	Wholesaler & franchiser of microcomputer products. Type: NASDAQ-INEL Ind: Comput/Off Equip Grp: High Tech Richard Sanford, CEO	Rev: Assets: Emp:		600 300 1
Intelsat Corp 3400 International Drive NW Washington, DC 20008 202-944-6800	Operator of communications satellites. Type: Private Ind: Telecom Grp: High Tech Bean Birch, CEO	Rev: Assets: Emp:		825 NA 2
Inter City Gas Corp 444 St Mary Avenue Winnepeg, MB R3C3T7 Can 204-944-9920	Natural gas distribution company. Type: TOR Ind: Energy Grp: Basic Industries Robert Graham, CEO	Rev: Assets: Emp:		1421 1687 6

Organizations Listed Alphabetically

Organization / Address / Phone	Descriptive Information	Revenue / ($ mil)	Assets / ($ mil)	Emp (thous)
Inter Exchange Auto Club of Southern Cal 2601 S Figueroa Street Los Angeles, CA 90007 213-741-3111	Property & casualty insurance company. Type: Private-Mutual Ind: Insurance Grp: Insurance Richard U Robison, CEO	Rev: Assets: Emp:		802 1424 3
Inter Regional Financial Corp 100 Dain Tower Minneapolis, MN 55402 612-371-7750	Financial services company. Type: NYSE Ind: Non-Bank Fin Grp: Financial Richard McFarland, CEO	Rev: Assets: Emp:		350 3500 3
Interco Inc 101 S Hanley Road St Louis, MO 63102 314-863-1100	Manufacturer & retailing company; apparel,shoes,furniture. Type: NYSE-ISS Ind: Apparel/Textiles Grp: Consumer Prd Harvey Saligman, CEO Harry M Krogh, Pres Ronald Aylward, VCh Robert Hensley, Tres Eugene F Smith, CFO Charles Rothschild, VP R Stuart Moore, VP Robert T Hensley, IR Russ Baumann, PR	Rev: Assets: Emp:		2012 1775 38
Intercontinental Hotels Corportion 100 Paragon Drive Montvale, NJ 07645 201-307-3300	International operator of hotels. Type: Private Ind: Food/Lodging Grp: Consumer Service Patrick Copeland, CEO	Rev: Assets: Emp:		550 NA 8
Interface Corporation Overland Hill Road LaGrange, GA 30241 404-882-1891	Manufacturer of industrial & commercial carpeting. Type: NASDAQ-IFSI Ind: Tire/Rubber Grp: Basic Industries R Anderson, CEO	Rev: Assets: Emp:		397 493 4
Intergraph Corp One Madison Industrial Park Huntsville, AL 35807 205-772-2000	Manufacturer of computer equipment. Type: NASDAQ-INGR Ind: Comput/Off Equip Grp: High Tech Richard H Lussier, CEO James W Meadlock, Chr Larry Lafter, CFO Nancy D Meadlock, IS Dr John Thorington Jr, R&D Richard Lussier, Sls Michael J Cunningham, VP Bruce J Brasseale, VP Edward F Boyle, VP Edward J Blaum, VP Allan B Wilson, VP Albert D Domine, VP Walter Thames, PR	Rev: Assets: Emp:		801 831 6
Interhome Energy Inc (Interprov Pipe) 324 8th Avenue SW Calgary, AB T2P2Z5 Can 403-232-5500	Natural gas pipeline transportation company. Type: TOR Ind: Energy Grp: Basic Industries Robert Heule, CEO	Rev: Assets: Emp:		729 2509 2
Interlake Corp 701 Harger Road Oak Brook, IL 60521 312-986-6600	Manufacturer of metalic powers. Type: NYSE Ind: Machinery Grp: Manufacturing Frederick C Langenbert, CEO Edward D Hopkins, Pres Raymond T Anderson, Tres John Schuster, R&D H Harry Henderson, Mkt David R Downs, VP Grant L Johnson, VP Wayne K Larson, IR H Harry Henderson, PR	Rev: Assets: Emp:		892 660 11
Intermark Inc 1020 Prospect Street La Jolla, CA 92038 619-459-3841	Operator of retail stores; sporting goods, nursery, imports. Type: ASE-IMI Ind: Retail/Merch Grp: Retail Charles R Scott, CEO	Rev: Assets: Emp:		721 400 7
International Aluminum Co 767 Monterey Pass Road Monterey Park, CA 91754 213-264-1670	Manufacturer of home improvement products, windows, doors. Type: NYSE Ind: Building Mat Grp: Basic Industries J Cunningham, CEO	Rev: Assets: Emp:		250 150 2
International Assn of Machinists 1300 Connecticut Avenue NW Washington, DC 20036 202-857-5200	National labor union. Type: Membership Org Ind: Membership Org Grp: Govt & Non-Prof William W Winpisinger, CEO	Rev: Assets: Emp:		500 NM 800
International Brotherhood Electrical Wkr 1125 Fifthteenth Street NW Washington, DC 20005 202-833-7000	National labor union. Type: Membership Org Ind: Membership Org Grp: Govt & Non-Prof J J Barry, CEO	Rev: Assets: Emp:		500 NM 1000

Organization / Address / Phone	Descriptive Information	Revenue / ($ mil)	Assets / ($ mil)	Emp (thous)
International Brotherhood of Teamsters 25 Louisiana Street NW Washington, DC 20001 202-624-6800	National labor union. Type: Membership Org Ind: Membership Org Grp: Govt & Non-Prof William J McCarthy, CEO	Rev: Assets: Emp:	1000 NM 2000	
International Controls Inc 5499 N Federal Boca Raton, FL 33431 305-997-7400	Manufacturer of automotive parts. Type: Private Ind: Automotive Grp: Manufacturing Arthur M Goldberg, CEO	Rev: Assets: Emp:	1000 500 8	
International Dairy Queen 5701 Green Valley Bloomington, MN 55437 612-830-0200	Fast food franchise company. Type: NASDAQ-INDQ Ind: Food/Lodging Grp: Consumer Service Michael Sullivan, CEO	Rev: Assets: Emp:	265 150 5	
International Data Corp 5 Speen Street Framingham, MA 01701 508-875-5000	Information services on information technology. Type: Private Ind: Publishing/Com Grp: Consumer Service Patrick J McGovern, CEO	Rev: Assets: Emp:	400 NA 4	
International Flavors & Fragrances Inc 521 W 57th Street New York, NY 10019 212-765-5500	Manufacturer of flavor for sale to food processors. Type: NYSE Ind: Personal Care Grp: Consumer Prd Eugene P Grisanti, CEO John P Winandy, CFO Ira Katz, R&D Ronald D Anderson, Sls Harry Fields, Mkt Van Vechten Sayre, PR	Rev: Assets: Emp:	840 882 4	
International Forest Products (Whonnock) 1055 Dunsmuir Street 34th Floor Vancouver, BC V7X1H7 Can 604-681-3221	Forest products company. Type: TOR Ind: Paper/Forest Prd Grp: Basic Industries W S Sauder, CEO	Rev: Assets: Emp:	326 261 2	
International Lease Finance Corp 8484 Wilshire Blvd Beverly Hills, CA 90211 213-658-7871	Leasing & sales of commercial aircraft. Type: NASDAQ-ILFC Ind: Business Service Grp: Business Service Leslie L Gonda, CEO	Rev: Assets: Emp:	213 1765 1	
International Minerals & Chemical Corp 2315 Sanders Road Northbrook, IL 60062 312-564-8600	Manufacturer of specialty chemicals. Type: NYSE-IGL Ind: Chemicals Grp: Basic Industries George D Kennedy, CEO John Sonderegger, CFO Ronald A Othick, IS Dr M B Ingle, R&D Elizabeth M Higashi, IR David A Prichard, PR	Rev: Assets: Emp:	1471 1794 10	
International Monitary Fund 700 Nineteenth Street NW Washington, DC 20431 202-623-7000	International financial agency. Type: Federal Govt Ind: Federal Govt Fin Grp: Financial Michel Camdessus, CEO	Rev: Assets: Emp:	2000 NM 4	
International Multifoods Corp Multifoods Tower PO Box 2942 Minneapolis, MN 55402 612-340-3300	Processor & distributor of food products. Type: NYSE-IMC Ind: Food Processing Grp: Food Processing Andre Gillet, CEO Anthony Luiso, Pres K Marvin Eberts Jr, CFO Paul A Taylor, IS John E Sampson, R&D Thomas P Brennan, VP Frank Bovino, VP Beverly Bajus, PR	Rev: Assets: Emp:	1874 716 9	
International Paper Co Two Manhattanville Road Purchase, NY 10577 914-397-1500	Worldwide forest products company. Type: NYSE-IP Ind: Paper/Forest Prd Grp: Basic Industries David W Oskin, CEO John A Georges, Chr John T Dillon, VCh Robert Butler, CFO David I J Wang, IS Eli Gonick, R&D Dana G Mead, Mkt John Nevin, Ops E William Boehmler, VP William Greener III, IR William P Fuller, PR	Rev: Assets: Emp:	9533 9462 55	
International Shipholding Corp 650 Poydras Street New Orleans, LA 70153 504-529-5461	Sea transportation, insurance & cargo handling company. Type: OTC Ind: Transport Grp: Business Service N W Johnsen, CEO	Rev: Assets: Emp:	300 200 1	

Organizations Listed Alphabetically

Organization / Address / Phone	Descriptive Information	Revenue / Assets / Emp ($ mil) ($ mil) (thous)	
International Technology Corp 23456 Hawthorne Blvd Torrance, CA 90505 213-378-9933	Environmental management services. Type: NYSE-ITX Ind: Business Service Grp: Business Service Murray H Hutchinson, CEO	Rev: Assets: Emp:	265 300 2
International Telecharge Corp 108 S Akard Dallas, TX 75222 214-744-0240	Telephone services & manufacturer of communication equipmnt. Type: ASE Ind: Telecom Grp: High Tech Edmund Tagg, CEO	Rev: Assets: Emp:	250 200 3
International Thomson Organisation Ltd 20 Queen Street W Toronto, ON M5H3R3 Can 416-977-8700	Publisher of newspaper, magazines, business information. Type: TOR Ind: Publishing/Com Grp: Consumer Service Lord Thomsom, CEO	Rev: Assets: Emp:	3987 3776 23
International Union Electronic & Elec 1126 16th Street NW Washington, DC 20036 202-296-1200	National labor union. Type: Membership Org Ind: Membership Org Grp: Govt & Non-Prof William H Bywater, CEO	Rev: Assets: Emp:	250 NM 200
International Union Operating Engineers 1125 17th Street NW Washington, DC 20036 202-429-9100	National labor union. Type: Membership Org Ind: Membership Org Grp: Govt & Non-Prof Larry Dugan, CEO	Rev: Assets: Emp:	300 NM 375
Interpublic Group of Companies Inc 1271 Avenue of the Americas New York, NY 10020 212-399-8000	Advertising agency holding company. Type: NYSE Ind: Business Service Grp: Business Service Philip H Geier, CEO Thomas J Volpe, Tres Eugene P Beard, CFO Arthur E Wilen, R&D Charles A Mittelstadt, Mkt Henry Strock, VP Donald F Connelly, VP Christopher Rudge, VP C Kent Kroeber, VP William S Keating, PR	Rev: Assets: Emp:	1192 1601 14
Interstate Johnson Lane Corp 2700 NCNB Plaza 101 S Tyron Street Charlotte, NC 28280 704-379-9000	Investment firm; securities trading. Type: Private Ind: Securities Grp: Financial J Craig Hill, CEO	Rev: Assets: Emp:	220 2200 1
Interstate Milk Producers Inc 1225 Industrial Highway Southampton, PA 18966 215-322-0200	Agricultural cooperative food production; dairy products. Type: Private Ind: Food Processing Grp: Food Processing Paul Hand, CEO	Rev: Assets: Emp:	550 NA 2
Interstate Power Co 1000 Main Street Dubuque, IA 52004 319-582-5421	Electric power & natural gas utility company. Type: NYSE-IPW Ind: Utility Grp: Utilities Wayne H Stoppelmoor, CEO	Rev: Assets: Emp:	274 540 2
Intertan Corp 2000 Two Tandy Center Fort Worth, TX 76102 817-332-7181	Operator of Radio Shack stores in Canada, Europe & Asia. Type: NYSE-ITN Ind: Retail/Merch Grp: Retail John V Roach, CEO	Rev: Assets: Emp:	600 400 6
Investors Group Inc One Canada Centre 447 Portage Winnipeg, MB R3C3B6 Can 204-943-0361	Diversified financial company. Type: TOR Ind: Non-Bank Fin Grp: Financial Robert H Jones, CEO	Rev: Assets: Emp:	252 1604 1
Investors Management Corp 5151 Glenwood Avenue Beta Center Raleigh, NC 27612 919-781-9310	Operator of restaurants. Type: Private Ind: Food/Lodging Grp: Consumer Service James H Maynard, CEO	Rev: Assets: Emp:	500 NA 10

Organizations Listed Alphabetically

Organization / Address / Phone	Descriptive Information	Revenue / ($ mil)	Assets / ($ mil)	Emp (thous)
Iowa Illinois Gas & Electric Inc 206 E Second Street Davenport, IA 52808 319-326-7111	Electric power & natural gas utility company. Type: NYSE-IWG Ind: Utility Grp: Utilities B C O'Brien, CEO J C Decker, Tres S J Bright, CFO J Averweg, R&D W T Green, Mkt J J Daniel, Ops H R Poe, VP J C Galt, VP C H Golliher, VP	Rev: Assets: Emp:	496 1242 2	
Iowa Public Service Co 401 Douglas Street Sioux City, IA 51102 712-277-7500	Electric power utility company. Type: NYSE-MWE Ind: Utility Grp: Utilities R E Christiansen, CEO	Rev: Assets: Emp:	600 1100 2	
Iowa Resources (Iowa Power & Light) Inc 666 Grand Avenue Des Moines, IA 50303 515-281-2900	Electric power utility. Type: OTC Ind: Utility Grp: Utilities Mark W Putney, CEO	Rev: Assets: Emp:	344 1168 2	
Iowa State University Administrative Bldg Ames, IA 50011 515-294-4111	Major educational institution; university. Type: University Ind: University Grp: Govt & Non-Prof Gordon P Eaton, CEO	Rev: Assets: Emp:	316 332 30	
Iowa, State of State Capitol Des Moines, IA 50319 515-281-5011	State government. Type: State Govt Ind: State/Prov Govt Grp: Govt & Non-Prof Terry E Branstad, CEO	Rev: Assets: Emp:	6603 NM 59	
Ipalco Enterprises Inc 25 Monument Circle Indianapolis, IN 46204 317-261-8261	Electric utility holding company. Type: OTC Ind: Utility Grp: Utilities Zane G Todd, CEO John R Hodowal, Tres John D Wilson, CFO Marcus Woods, VP John Breham, VP	Rev: Assets: Emp:	609 1752 2	
IPCO Corp 1025 Westchester Avenue White Plains, NY 10604 914-682-4500	Manufacturer & wholesaler of medical supplies. Type: NYSE-IHS Ind: Health Care Grp: Consumer Service Robert S Savin, CEO	Rev: Assets: Emp:	225 150 3	
IPSCO Inc Alberta Street N Regina, SK S4P3C7 Can 306-949-3530	Manufacturer of steel parts. Type: TOR Ind: Manufacturing Grp: Manufacturing R Phillips, CEO	Rev: Assets: Emp:	340 340 2	
Irvine Corp 550 Newport Center Newport Beach, CA 92660 714-720-2000	Real estate development & management. Type: Private Ind: Real Estate/Bldg Grp: Business Service Donald Bern, CEO	Rev: Assets: Emp:	600 NA 1	
Irving Bank Corp One Wall Street New York, NY 10005 212-635-1111	Commercial bank. Type: NYSE-V Ind: Banking Grp: Financial Joseph Rice, CEO Samuel F Chevalier, Pres Alvin L Begleiter, CFO James F Ganley, IS Stephan J Lovett, R&D H S Phillips, IR David Santos, PR	Rev: Assets: Emp:	2500 25000 11	
Island Creek Corp 2355 Harrodsburg Road Lexington, KY 40504 606-223-3636	Coal mining & processing company. Type: Private-Sub Par: Occidental Petroleum Corp Ind: Metals/Mining Grp: Basic Industries Sylvestor Ogden, CEO	Rev: Assets: Emp:	NA NA NA	
Israel Discount Bank 511 Fifth Avenue New York, NY 10017 212-551-8500	Commercial bank. Type: Private-Sub-For Ind: Banking Grp: Financial Aaron Kahana, CEO	Rev: Assets: Emp:	800 6000 4	

Organizations Listed Alphabetically

Organization / Address / Phone	Descriptive Information	Revenue / ($ mil)	Assets / ($ mil)	Emp (thous)

ISS International Service Corp
1430 Broadway
New York, NY 10018
212-382-9800

Cleaning services company.
Type: ASE-ISI
Ind: Business Service   Grp: Business Service
Henrik Slipsager, CEO

Rev: 250
Assets: 150
Emp: 4

Isuzu Motors USA Inc
300 Pellesseir Place
Whitter, CA 90601
213-949-0611

Importer & distributor of automobiles.
Type: Private-Sub-For
Ind: Automotive   Grp: Manufacturing
K Sakaino, CEO

Rev: 1650
Assets: NA
Emp: 2

Itel Corp
Two N Riverside Plaza
Chicago, IL 60606
312-902-1515

Leasing transportation equipment & financial services.
Type: NASDAQ-ITEL
Ind: Manufacturing   Grp: Manufacturing
Bernard F Brennan, CEO   Sam Zell, Chr   Rod Dammeyer, Pres
Gary Hill, CFO   John McNicholas, IS   Scott Williamson, R&D
Gloria Waber, Mkt   William G Wolfe, VP   Gloria Weaver, PR

Rev: 1644
Assets: 4001
Emp: 9

Itoh, C & Co Canada Ltd
200 Granville Street
Vancouver, BC V6C1S4 Can
604-683-5764

Import wholesale company; diversified goods.
Type: Private-Sub-For
Ind: Retail/Merch   Grp: Retail
K Nojima, CEO

Rev: 937
Assets: 425
Emp: 1

Itoh, C Trading Co USA
335 Madison Avenue
New York, NY 10017
212-818-8000

International trading company, U.S. headquarters.
Type: Private-Sub-For
Ind: Manufacturing   Grp: Manufacturing
M Murofushi, CEO

Rev: 1100
Assets: NA
Emp: 3

ITT Automotive Inc
505 N Woodward Avenue
Bloomfield Hills, MI 48013
313-540-9666

Manufacturer of automotive parts & components.
Type: Private-Sub   Par: ITT Corp
Ind: Automotive   Grp: Manufacturing
Ralph Reins, CEO

Rev: 2000
Assets: NA
Emp: 15

ITT Canada Ltd
Toronto Dominion Center
Toronto, ON M5K1H1 Can
416-863-9666

Manufacturer of electronic components & systems.
Type: Private-Sub-For
Ind: Electronics   Grp: High Tech
Thomas Savage, CEO

Rev: 298
Assets: 383
Emp: 3

ITT Corp
320 Park Avenue
New York, NY 10022
212-752-6000

Conglomerate; electrical components, automotive parts.
Type: NYSE-ITT
Ind: Conglomerate   Grp: Manufacturing
Rand V Araskog, CEO   D C Thomas, Pres   Howard Aibel, VCh
M Cabell Woodward Jr, CFO   James E Wynne, IS   Robert H Smith, R&D
Raymond Alleman, VP   D Travis Engen, VP   Juan C Capello, PR

Rev: 19355
Assets: 41941
Emp: 117

ITT Defense Technology Corp
1000 Wilson Blvd
Arlington, VA 22209
703-276-8300

Design & engineering company; defense technlogy.
Type: Private-Sub   Par: ITT Corp
Ind: Aerospace   Grp: High Tech
Travis Engen, CEO

Rev: 1500
Assets: NA
Emp: 10

ITT Financial Corportion
700 Community
St Louis, MO 63131
314-821-6060

Financial subsidiary of ITT Corporation.
Type: Private-Sub   Par: ITT Corp
Ind: Non-Bank Fin   Grp: Financial
Robert E Lewis, CEO   Melvin F Brown, VCh   W Gene Gerard, CFO
Earl Null, Sls   Walter Domeracki, Mkt   Thomas Wilshire, VP
Robert Slifka, VP   James Thompson, VP   Rihcard Schumacher, VP
Betty Wilson, VP

Rev: 1462
Assets: 8999
Emp: 7

ITT Fluid Technology Corp
444 Godwin Avenue
Midland Park, NJ 07432
201-444-6030

Developers of fluid technology.
Type: Private-Sub   Par: ITT Corp
Ind: Manufacturing   Grp: Manufacturing
Ray Gill, CEO

Rev: 500
Assets: NA
Emp: 4

IU International Corp
1500 Walnut Street
Philadelphia, PA 19102
302-571-5000

Trunking company.
Type: NYSE-IU
Ind: Business Service   Grp: Business Service
John Gilroy Christy, CEO   John A Moran, Chr   Louis A Guzzetti Jr, Pres
George E Fuehrer, CFO   Adam Friedman, PR

Rev: 1500
Assets: 900
Emp: 15

Organizations Listed Alphabetically

Organization / Address / Phone	Descriptive Information	Revenue / Assets / Emp ($ mil) ($ mil) (thous)		

Ivaco Inc
770 Rue Sherbrooke O
Montreal, PQ H3A1G1 Can
514-288-4545

Manufacturer of basic iron & steel.
Type: TOR
Ind: Steel   Grp: Basic Industries
Paul Ivanier, CEO   Sydney Ivanier, VCh   Albert Kassab, CFO
George Goldstein, Mkt   John Loveridge, VP

Rev: 1902
Assets: 827
Emp: 13

J & L Specialty Products Inc
1 PPG Plaza
Pittsburgh, PA 15230
412-338-1600

Manufacturer of stainless steel.
Type: Private
Ind: Steel   Grp: Basic Industries
James J Paulos, CEO

Rev: 750
Assets: NA
Emp: 2

Jackson National Life Ins Co
5901 Executive Drive
Lansing, MI 48911
517-394-3400

Life insurance company.
Type: OTC
Ind: Insurance   Grp: Insurance
A J Pasant, CEO

Rev: 1626
Assets: 3643
Emp: 4

Jackson, City of
City Hall
Jackson, MS 39202
601-630-1776

City government.
Type: City Govt
Ind: Local Govt   Grp: Govt & Non-Prof
Dale Danks, CEO

Rev: 250
Assets: NM
Emp: 2

Jacksonville Shipyards Inc
750 E Bay Street
Jacksonville, FL 32203
904-355-1711

Shipbuilding & ship repair company.
Type: Private-Sub   Par: Fruehauf Corp
Ind: Manufacturing   Grp: Manufacturing
A McIlwain, CEO

Rev: NA
Assets: NA
Emp: NA

Jacksonville, City of
City Hall 220 E Bay Street
Jacksonville, FL 32202
904-630-1776

City government.
Type: City Govt
Ind: Local Govt   Grp: Govt & Non-Prof
Tommy Hazouri, CEO

Rev: 1003
Assets: NM
Emp: 8

Jacobs Engineering Group Inc
251 S Lake Avenue
Pasadena, CA 91101
818-449-2171

Industrial construction & engineering company.
Type: ASE-JEC
Ind: Real Estate/Bldg   Grp: Business Service
Joseph J Jacobs, CEO

Rev: 800
Assets: 600
Emp: 6

Jacobson Stores Inc
1200 N West Avenue
Jackson, MI 49202
517-764-6400

Operator of retail apparel stores.
Type: NASDAQ-JCBS
Ind: Retail/Merch   Grp: Retail
J Russell Fowler, CEO

Rev: 357
Assets: 250
Emp: 5

Jafra Cosmetics Inc
2451 Townsgate
Westlake Village, CA 91361
805-496-1911

Manufacturer of cosmetics.
Type: Private-Sub   Par: Gillette Co
Ind: Personal Care   Grp: Consumer Prd
Denis Sanan, CEO

Rev: NA
Assets: NA
Emp: NA

Jaguar Cars Inc
600 Willow Tree Road
Leonia, NJ 07605
201-592-5200

Importer & distributor of automobiles.
Type: Private-Sub-For
Ind: Automotive   Grp: Manufacturing
Graham Whitehead, CEO

Rev: 550
Assets: NA
Emp: 1

James River Corp
Tredegar Street PO Box 2218
Richmond, VA 23217
804-644-5411

Manufacturer of paper products & packaging.
Type: NYSE-JR
Ind: Paper/Forest Prd   Grp: Basic Industries
Benton S Halsey, CEO   Robert C Williams, Pres   William Flaherty, Tres
David J McKittrick, CFO   James C Miller, IS   Ronald Estridge, R&D
Charles M Foster, VP   James Rogers, VP   Ronald Estredge, VP
Lawrence Morrow, VP   E Lee Showalter, VP   Stephen Garnett, IR
Robert J Sherry, PR

Rev: 5098
Assets: 5006
Emp: 34

Jamesway Corp
40 Hartz Way
Secaucus, NJ 07094
201-330-6000

Regional operator of discount department stores.
Type: NYSE-JMY
Ind: Retail/Merch   Grp: Retail
Herbert Fisher, CEO

Rev: 783
Assets: 400
Emp: 8

Organizations Listed Alphabetically

Organization / Address / Phone	Descriptive Information	Revenue / ($ mil)	Assets / ($ mil)	Emp (thous)
Janney Montgomery Scott Inc 5 Penn Center Plaza Philadelphia, PA 19103 215-665-6000	Investment firm; securities trading, retail brokerage. Type: Private Ind: Securities Grp: Financial Norman Wilde, CEO	Rev: Assets: Emp:		220 2200 1
Jannock Ltd 55 King Street W Toronto, ON M5K1B7 Can 416-364-8586	Manufacturer of pipe, tubing, & furnace products. Type: TOR Ind: Manufacturing Grp: Manufacturing George E Mara, CEO	Rev: Assets: Emp:		267 337 4
Jeep/Eagle Corp 12000 Chrysler Drive Highland Park, MI 48288 313-956-5741	Car & truck manufacturer. Type: Private-Sub Par: Chrysler Corp Ind: Automotive Grp: Manufacturing Joseph Cappy, CEO	Rev: Assets: Emp:		NA NA NA
Jefferson Pilot Corp 101 N Elm Street Greensboro, NC 27401 919-378-2011	Diversified insurance; title, life, prop & casualty. Type: NYSE-JP Ind: Non-Bank Fin Grp: Financial James G Babb, CEO W Roger Soles, Chr William Blackwell, Pres C Randolph Ferguson, VCh Thomas Fee, CFO John K Jones, IS Sherrill Hall, Mkt	Rev: Assets: Emp:		1223 4174 8
Jefferson Smurfit Corp 8182 Maryland Jefferson Smurfit Centre St Louis, MO 63105 314-746-1100	Manufacturer paperboard & packaging. Type: NASDAQ-JJSC Ind: Paper/Forest Prd Grp: Basic Industries Michael M J Smurfit, CEO James B Malloy, Pres Thomas A Reynolds, VCh Johm M Carroll, CFO Charles Bell, IS Dr Michael Davis, R&D Ron L Yates, Mkt Thomas Hardy, VP Richard Quina, VP Terry Ingram, PR	Rev: Assets: Emp:		1255 817 8
Jenn-Air Corp 3035 Shadeland Indianapolis, IN 46226 317-545-2271	Manufacturer of small appliances. Type: Private-Sub Par: Maytag Co Ind: Appliances/Furn Grp: Manufacturing Donald M Lorton, CEO	Rev: Assets: Emp:		NA NA NA
Jepson Corp 360 W Butterfield Road Elmhurst, IL 60126 312-834-3710	Manufacturer of appliances; air conditioners. Type: NYSE-JEP Ind: Appliances/Furn Grp: Manufacturing Robert Jepson, CEO Vernon Nagel, CFO Jeffrey Samuels, IS William Walker, R&D James Slazas, Sls Jeffrey Samuels, Mkt James Slazas, IR Pam Donofrio, PR	Rev: Assets: Emp:		600 400 6
Jerrico (Long John Silvers Res) Inc 101 Jerrico Drive Lexington, KY 40509 606-263-6000	Family restaurants. Type: NASDAQ-JERR Ind: Food/Lodging Grp: Consumer Service William E Anderson, CEO Warren W Rosenthal, Chr John E Tobe, Pres Larry D Bowles, Tres Gerald W Deitchle, CFO Ron W Cegnar, IS William P Connery, VP Robert L Sirkis, VP William G Mahoney, VP Howard J Singer, VP Bruce C Cotton, PR	Rev: Assets: Emp:		635 428 18
Jersey Central Power & Light Co Madison Avenue Morristown, NJ 07960 201-455-8200	Electric power utility company. Type: Private-Sub Par: General Public Utilities Corp Ind: Utility Grp: Utilities James Leva, CEO	Rev: Assets: Emp:		NA NA NA
Jersey City, City of City Hall Jersey City, NJ 07302 201-547-5202	City government. Type: City Govt Ind: Local Govt Grp: Govt & Non-Prof Anthony Cucci, CEO	Rev: Assets: Emp:		400 NM 3
Jetco Chemicals Inc 200 N 13th Street Corsicana, TX 75110 214-872-3011	Chemical manufacturer; cleaning products. Type: Private-Sub Par: Procter & Gamble Co Ind: Chemicals Grp: Basic Industries W Knodel, CEO	Rev: Assets: Emp:		NA NA NA

Organizations Listed Alphabetically

Organization / Address / Phone	Descriptive Information	Revenue / ($ mil)	Assets / ($ mil)	Emp (thous)
Jewel Food Stores 1955 W North Avenue Melrose Park, IL 60160 312-531-6000	Operator of retail food supermarkets. Type: Private-Sub Par: American Stores Co Ind: Retail/Food Grp: Retail James Henson, CEO	Rev: Assets: Emp:	NA NA NA	
Jim Beam Brands Inc 510 Lake Cook Road Deerfeild, IL 60015 312-948-0395	Liquor distilling & distributing company. Type: Private-Sub Par: American Brands Inc Ind: Beverage Grp: Food Processing Barry Berish, CEO	Rev: Assets: Emp:	NA NA NA	
Jimmy Dean Meat Co 1341 W Mockingbird Lane Dallas, TX 75247 214-638-1190	Manufacturer of meat food products. Type: Private-Sub Par: Sara Lee Corp Ind: Food Processing Grp: Food Processing Duane Getty, CEO	Rev: Assets: Emp:	NA NA NA	
Jitney Jungle Stores Inc 451 N Mill Street Jackson, MS 39207 601-948-0361	Grocery stores. Type: Private Ind: Retail/Merch Grp: Retail W H Holman, CEO	Rev: Assets: Emp:	500 NA 5	
JM Petroleum Corp 2323 Bryan Plaza of Americas Dallas, TX 75201 214-953-0330	Oil & petroleum trading company. Type: Private Ind: Energy Grp: Basic Industries James C Musselman, CEO	Rev: Assets: Emp:	600 NA 1	
JMB Institutional Realty 875 N Michigan Avenue Chicago, IL 60611 312-440-4800	Realty investment firm. Type: Private Ind: Non-Bank Fin Grp: Financial Neil Bluhm, CEO	Rev: Assets: Emp:	1500 15000 5	
Johnson & Higgins Inc 125 Broad Street New York, NY 10004 212-574-7000	Insurance company. Type: Private Ind: Insurance Grp: Insurance Robert V Hatcher, CEO	Rev: Assets: Emp:	750 2000 7	
Johnson & Johnson Corp One Johnson & Johnson Plaza New Brunswick, NJ 08933 201-524-0400	Worldwide manufacturer of health care products. Type: NYSE-JNJ Ind: Drugs Grp: Consumer Service James E Burke, CEO David Clare, Pres Robert Campbell, VCh Clark H Johnson, CFO Raymond Giovannelli, IS Robert Z Gussin, R&D Robert Larsen, Mkt Robert Wilson, VP J Taylor Woodward III, VP John Heldrich, VP Victor Dankis, VP Frank H Barker, IR Lawrence G Foster, PR	Rev: Assets: Emp:	9001 7119 81	
Johnson Coca Cola Bottling Inc PO Box 530 Chattanooga, TN 37421 615-899-3449	Soft drink bottler & distributor. Type: Private Ind: Beverage Grp: Food Processing Summerfield Johnston, CEO	Rev: Assets: Emp:	750 NA 5	
Johnson Controls Inc 5757 N Green Bay Avenue Milwaukee, WI 53201 414-228-1200	Energy systems controls & automotive components. Type: NYSE-JCI Ind: Instruments Grp: High Tech James H Keys, CEO John M Barth, VCh Stephen Roell, Tres James M Wade, CFO George Jacoby, R&D R Eugene Goodson, Mkt David Bigler, Ops Robert Gustine, VP J William Horton, VP George T Jacobi, VP William P Killian, VP Joseph W Lewis, VP Denise Zutz, PR	Rev: Assets: Emp:	3100 2013 29	
Johnson Worldwide Associates Inc 4041 N Main Street Racine, WI 53402 414-631-2000	Manufacturer of sporting goods. Type: NASDAQ-JWAI Ind: Leisure Time Grp: Consumer Service Samuel Johnson, CEO	Rev: Assets: Emp:	300 200 2	
Johnson, Axel & Co Inc 110 E 59th Street New York, NY 10022 212-758-3200	Petroleum & natural gas exploration & development. Type: Private Ind: Energy Grp: Basic Industries Vernon R Anderson, CEO	Rev: Assets: Emp:	1000 NA 1	

Organization / Address / Phone	Descriptive Information	Revenue / ($ mil)	Assets / ($ mil)	Emp (thous)
Johnson, S C & Son Inc 1525 Howe Street Racine, WI 53403 414-631-2000	Manufacturer of specialty chemicals. Type: Private Ind: Personal Care Grp: Consumer Prd Samuel C Johnson, CEO	Rev:	Assets:	Emp:
		2500	NA	12
Jones, Edward D & Co 201 Progress Parkway St Louis, MO 63043 314-851-2000	Investment firm; securities trading. Type: Private Ind: Securities Grp: Financial Ed Soule, CEO	Rev: 220	Assets: 2200	Emp: 1
Jordache Enterprises Inc 498 Seventh Avenue New York, NY 10018 212-279-7343	Manufacturer of apparel products; jeans, sportswear. Type: Private Ind: Apparel/Textiles Grp: Consumer Prd Aetan Mashiach, CEO	Rev: 825	Assets: NA	Emp: 3
Jordan Co 315 Park Avenue S New York, NY 10010 212-460-1920	Multicompany retail holding company. Type: Private Ind: Retail/Merch Grp: Retail John W Jordan, CEO	Rev: 750	Assets: NA	Emp: 7
Jorgensen, Earle M Corp 10700 Alameda Street Lynwood, CA 90262 213-567-1122	Manufacturer of steel & aluminum forgings. Type: NYSE-JOR Ind: Manufacturing Grp: Manufacturing Earle M Jorgensen, CEO	Rev: 400	Assets: 400	Emp: 4
Jostens Inc 5501 Norman Center Drive Minneapolis, MN 55437 612-830-3336	Manufacturer of jewelry & services for schools. Type: NYSE-JOS Ind: Manufacturing Grp: Manufacturing H William Lurton, CEO Robert W Leslie, Pres Rob L Prince, Tres Don C Lein, CFO Robb Prince, IS Louis G Foye, R&D Charles R Herrmann, Sls Roger D Peters, VP Larry R Stewart, VP James C Waggoner, VP Fred D Bjork, VP Gary L Buckmiller, VP Ellis F Bullock, PR	Rev: 560	Assets: 407	Emp: 7
Journal Communications Co Inc 333 W State Street Milwaukee, WI 53203 414-224-2000	Communications company; publisher of newspapers. Type: Private Ind: Publishing/Com Grp: Consumer Service Thomas J McCollow, CEO	Rev: 400	Assets: NA	Emp: 4
Joy Manufacturing Co 301 Grant Street Pittsburgh, PA 15219 412-562-4500	Industrial equipment manufacturing, mining. Type: Private Ind: Equipment Grp: Manufacturing Roy Wennerholm, CEO Otto Grieshaber, Pres Edmund J Freeman, CFO Mark E Broskey, PR	Rev: 650	Assets: 500	Emp: 5
JP Industries Inc 325 E Eisenhower Parkway Ann Arbor, MI 48108 313-663-6749	Manufacturer of plumbing & hardware supplies. Type: NYSE-JPI Ind: Building Mat Grp: Basic Industries John Psarouthakis, CEO	Rev: 550	Assets: 400	Emp: 3
JPM Industries Inc 7421 W 100th Place Bridgeview, IL 60455 312-598-1300	Commercial printing & insurance brokerage company. Type: NASDAQ-JPMI Ind: Publishing/Com Grp: Consumer Service Joseph McGivney, CEO	Rev: 200	Assets: 200	Emp: 1
JPS Textile Group Inc 555 N Pleasantberg Drive Greenville, SC 29607 803-271-9919	Manufacturer of carpet, elastics, yarn, apparel fibers. Type: Private Ind: Apparel/Textiles Grp: Consumer Prd Jerry E Hunter, CEO	Rev: 750	Assets: NA	Emp: 10
Justin Industries Inc 2821 W 7th Street Fort Worth, TX 76101 817-336-5125	Manufacturer of ceramic brick. Type: OTC Ind: Manufacturing Grp: Manufacturing John S Justin, CEO	Rev: 300	Assets: 150	Emp: 4

Organizations Listed Alphabetically

Organization / Address / Phone	Descriptive Information	Revenue / ($ mil)	Assets / ($ mil)	Emp (thous)
JWP Corp 2975 Westchester Avenue Purchase, NY 10577 914-935-4000	Maintenance & repair service company. Type: NYSE-JWP Ind: Business Service Grp: Business Service Andrew T Dwyer, CEO	Rev: Assets: Emp:		350 250 3
K & B Inc K & B Plaza 1055 St Charles Avenue New Orleans, LA 70130 504-586-1234	Operator of retail merchandise stores. Type: Private Ind: Retail/Merch Grp: Retail Sidney Besthoff, CEO	Rev: Assets: Emp:		550 NA 5
K & E Holding Inc 200 Park Avenue New York, NY 10017 212-880-2000	Nationwide consulting company. Type: Private Ind: Business Service Grp: Business Service not available, CEO	Rev: Assets: Emp:		275 NA 3
K Mart Canada Ltd 8925 Torbram Road Brampton, ON L6T4G1 Can 416-792-4400	Nationwide retail discount store operator. Type: Private-Sub-For Ind: Retail/Merch Grp: Retail B Fauber, CEO	Rev: Assets: Emp:		1278 530 33
K Mart Corp 3100 W Big Beaver Road Troy, MI 48084 313-643-1000	Nationwide operator of discount department stores. Type: NYSE-K Ind: Retail/Merch Grp: Retail Joseph E Antonini, CEO Richard S Miller, VCh Thomas Muraski, CFO D M Carlson, IS G H Nigolian, Sls Michael Wellman, Mkt Thomas Watkins, Ops Bernard Thomas, VP Thomas Nigolian, VP J L Moser, IR A Robert Stevenson, PR	Rev: Assets: Emp:		27301 12126 200
Kahn's & Co 3241 Spring Grove Avenue Cincinnati, OH 45225 513-541-4000	Manufacturer of food products. Type: Private-Sub Par: Sara Lee Corp Ind: Food Processing Grp: Food Processing Robert Huber, CEO	Rev: Assets: Emp:		NA NA NA
Kaiser Engineers Inc 1800 Harrison Street Oakland, CA 94623 415-268-6000	Construction engineering & management firm. Type: Private Ind: Real Estate/Bldg Grp: Business Service Ray List, CEO	Rev: Assets: Emp:		550 NA 2
Kaiser Permanente Medical One Kaiser Plaza Oakland, CA 94612 415-428-5000	Manufacturer of medical equipment. Type: Private Ind: Health Care Grp: Consumer Service James A Vohs, CEO Wayne R Moon, VCh Susan E Porth, CFO Alva Wheatley, R&D William O Slayman, Mkt Daniel O Wagstar, VP Robert Erickson, VP Scott Fleming, VP James A Lane, VP David L Pockell, VP	Rev: Assets: Emp:		5584 4161 50
Kaiser Technology Corp 300 Lakeside Drive Oakland, CA 94643 415-271-3300	Manufacturer, chemicals & aluminum. Type: Private-Sub Ind: Metals/Mining Grp: Basic Industries John M Seidl, CEO A Stephens Hutchcraft Jr, Pres John T LaDuc, Tres David G Schmidt, CFO John A Bonn, VP Edward J Coyne, VP James T Owen, VP Richard L Humphrey, VP Robert E Cole, VP Robert W Irelan, PR	Rev: Assets: Emp:		2219 2404 11
Kaman Corp 1332 Blue Hills Avenue PO Box 1 Bloomfield, CT 06002 203-243-8311	Diversified manufacturing company. Type: NASDAQ-KAMNA Ind: Conglomerate Grp: Manufacturing Charles H Kaman, CEO Harvey Levenson, VCh Robert Garneau, CFO Ronald M Galla, IS Fred Smith, Mkt Glenn Messemer, Ops Russell Jones, VP James A Morholt, VP J Kenneth Nasshan, VP Candace Clark, VP Raymond Picard, VP J Kenneth Nasshan, PR	Rev: Assets: Emp:		768 420 6
Kane Miller Corp 555 White Plains Road Tarrytown, NY 10591 914-631-6900	Meatpacking company. Type: Private Ind: Food Processing Grp: Food Processing Stanley B Kane, CEO	Rev: Assets: Emp:		500 NA 3

Organizations Listed Alphabetically

Organization / Address / Phone	Descriptive Information	Revenue / ($ mil)	Assets / ($ mil)	Emp (thous)
Kanematsu Gosho USA Inc 1133 Avenue of the Americas New York, NY 10036 212-704-9400	Diversified manufacturer & importer; US headquarters. Type: Private-Sub-For Ind: Manufacturing Grp: Manufacturing M Yosomiya, CEO	Rev: Assets: Emp:	3300 NA 8	
Kansas City Power & Light Co 1330 Baltimore Avenue Kansas City, MO 64105 816-556-2200	Electric power utility. Type: NYSE-KLT Ind: Utility Grp: Utilities David S Black, CEO A Drue Jennings, Chr J Robert Miller, VCh Louis Rasmussen, CFO Edwin McBurney, IS James Hogan, R&D J Michael Evans, Ops Samuel Cowley, VP Bernard J Beaudoin, VP William Miller, VP	Rev: Assets: Emp:	737 2647 3	
Kansas City Southern Industries Inc 114 W Eleventh Street Kansas City, MO 64105 816-556-0303	Railroad & real estate company. Type: NYSE-KSU Ind: Railroad Grp: Business Service James E Barnes, CEO Landon H Rowland, Chr William Deramus, Pres Thomas McDonnell, VCh Donald L Graf, CFO Albert Mauro, Ops Richard Bruening, VP John Deveney, VP Robert Haley, VP Anthony McCarthy, VP Sherry Cooper, VP Albert P Mauro, PR	Rev: Assets: Emp:	507 979 5	
Kansas City, City of City Hall Kansas City, MO 64106 816-274-2595	City government. Type: City Govt Ind: Local Govt Grp: Govt & Non-Prof Richard L Berkley, CEO	Rev: Assets: Emp:	503 NM 7	
Kansas Gas & Electric Co 120 E First Wichita, KS 67201 316-261-6611	Electric power & natural gas utility company. Type: NYSE-KGE Ind: Utility Grp: Utilities Wilson K Cadman, CEO W R Wittmer, Tres William Moore, CFO James Haines, VP Kent R Brown, VP Richard Haden, VP Robert Rives, VP	Rev: Assets: Emp:	526 2443 3	
Kansas Power & Light Co 818 Kansas Avenue Topeka, KS 66612 913-296-6300	Electric power utility. Type: NYSE-KAN Ind: Utility Grp: Utilities Charles W Battey, CEO David S Black, Chr William E Brown, Pres Steven L Kitchen, CFO Michael Blumenfeld, Mkt M Lee Brunton, Ops James Ingram, VP Norman Jackson, VP Richard LaGree, VP	Rev: Assets: Emp:	1166 1777 5	
Kansas, State of State Capitol Topeka, KS 66612 913-296-0111	State government. Type: State Govt Ind: State/Prov Govt Grp: Govt & Non-Prof Mike Hayden, CEO	Rev: Assets: Emp:	5872 NM 54	
Karcher, Carl Enterprises Inc 1200 N Harbor Blvd Anaheim, CA 92803 714-774-5796	Retail operator of fast food restaurants. Type: NYSE Ind: Food/Lodging Grp: Consumer Service Carl Karcher, CEO	Rev: Assets: Emp:	446 300 12	
Kash n Karry Food Stores Inc 6422 Harney Road Tampa, FL 33610 813-621-0200	Operator of retail food supermarkets. Type: Private Ind: Retail/Food Grp: Retail Ronald J Floto, CEO	Rev: Assets: Emp:	1000 NA 5	
Katy Industries Inc 853 Dundee Avenue Elgin, IL 60120 312-697-8900	Diversified consumer products & industrial equipment co. Type: NYSE-KT Ind: Conglomerate Grp: Manufacturing Jacob Saliba, CEO	Rev: Assets: Emp:	192 298 2	
Katz Communications Inc 1 Dag Hammarshield Plaza New York, NY 10017 212-572-5500	Operator of broadcasting stations; radio, TV. Type: Private Ind: Publishing/Com Grp: Consumer Service Jim Greenwald, CEO	Rev: Assets: Emp:	1100 NA 2	

Organizations Listed Alphabetically

Organization / Address / Phone	Descriptive Information	Revenue / ($ mil)	Assets / ($ mil)	Emp (thous)
Kaufman & Broad Inc 11601 Wilshire Blvd Los Angeles, CA 90025 213-312-5000	Home building company. Type: NYSE-BRO Ind: Real Estate/Bldg Grp: Business Service Eli Broad, CEO Bruce Karatz, Chr Robert Galloway, VCh Gordon Milne, Tres Jana Waring Greer, Mkt Guy Nafilyan, VP John E Polk, VP Alan R Markizon, VP Jana Waring Greer, IR	Rev: 903 Assets: 603 Emp: 3		
Kawasaki Industries USA Inc 9950 Jermino Road Irvine, CA 92718 714-770-0400	Manufacturer & importer of motorcycles; US headquarters. Type: Private-Sub-For Ind: Manufacturing Grp: Manufacturing M Yurikusa, CEO	Rev: 825 Assets: NA Emp: 5		
Kay Jewelers Corp 320 King Street Alexandria, VA 22314 703-683-3800	Retail jewelry stores. Type: NYSE-KJI Ind: Retail/Food Grp: Retail Anthonie C van Ekris, CEO Michael R Lavington, Pres Joe Bernstein, VCh Miguel Zarraga, Tres Roldan Fernandez, CFO William Heide, VP Ben Rifke, VP John Kosik, VP Harry Braverman, VP Timothy Braun, VP	Rev: 420 Assets: 275 Emp: 5		
KayBee Toys Inc 100 West Street Pittsfield, MA 01201 413-499-0086	Operator of retail toy stores. Type: Private-Sub Par: Melville Corp Ind: Retail/Merch Grp: Retail Saul Rubenstein, CEO	Rev: NA Assets: NA Emp: NA		
KDI Corp 5721 Dragon Way Cincinnati, OH 45227 513-272-1421	Manufacturer of electronic devices & systems. Type: NYSE-KDIC Ind: Electronics Grp: High Tech Eugene A Cafiero, CEO	Rev: 350 Assets: 300 Emp: 4		
Kearney, A T Inc 222 S Riverside Plaza Chicago, IL 60606 312-648-0111	Nationwide consulting company. Type: Private Ind: Consulting Grp: Business Service Fred Steingraber, CEO	Rev: 300 Assets: NA Emp: 3		
Keefe, Bruyette & Woods Inc Two World Trade Center Suite 8566 New York, NY 10048 212-323-8300	Investment firm; securities trading. Type: Private Ind: Securities Grp: Financial Gene S Bruyette, CEO	Rev: 220 Assets: 80 Emp: 1		
Keith, Ben E Co 600 E Nineth Street Fort Worth, TX 76102 817-332-9171	Operator of retail food stores. Type: Private Ind: Retail/Food Grp: Retail Ron Wallace, CEO	Rev: 550 Assets: NA Emp: 1		
Kellogg Co 235 Porter Street One Kellogg Square Battle Creek, MI 49016 616-966-2000	Producer of consumer food products. Type: NYSE-K Ind: Food Processing Grp: Food Processing William E LaMothe, CEO Robert Nichols, VCh John R Hinton, CFO Donald J Brett, IS Daryl Schaller, R&D Horst W Schroeder, Mkt Ross Buckland, VP Fred Buhler, VP W Lawrence Romans, VP Joseph M Stewart, PR	Rev: 4349 Assets: 3298 Emp: 23		
Kellwood Co 600 Kellwood Parkway Chesterfield, MO 63178 314-576-3100	Manufacturer of apparel, home fashion & camping products. Type: NYSE-KWD Ind: Apparel/Textiles Grp: Consumer Prd Fred W Wenzel, CEO William J McKenna, Chr Roger D Joseph, Tres James C Jacobsen, CFO Larry Carpenter, IS Bud Berman, R&D Lawrence E Hummel, VP Robert A Maddocks, VP Eugene D Johnson, VP Donna B Weaver, PR	Rev: 754 Assets: 447 Emp: 15		

Organizations Listed Alphabetically

Organization / Address / Phone	Descriptive Information	Revenue / Assets / Emp ($ mil) ($ mil) (thous)		

Kelly Services Corp
999 W Big Beaver Road
Troy, MI 48084
313-362-4444

Personnel & temporary help agencies.
Type: NASDAQ-NMS
Ind: Business Service   Grp: Business Service
William R Kelly, CEO   Terrence Adderly, Chr   Harley Furguson, IS
Joanne E Start, Sls   Joyce Furlong, Mkt   Angelo Agnello, VP
Carolyn R Fryar, VP   Stanley Mills, VP   Irene Adams Staskin, VP
Robert E Thompson, VP   Judith Allen, VP   Joyce Furlong, IR
Nora Pearson, PR

Rev: 1269
Assets: 326
Emp: 5

Kelly Springfield Tire Co
800 Kelly Road
Cumberland, MD 21502
301-777-6000

Manufacturer of tires.
Type: Private-Sub   Par: Goodyear Tire & Rubber Co
Ind: Tire/Rubber   Grp: Basic Industries
L DiPasqua, CEO

Rev: 1500
Assets: NA
Emp: 10

Kelly, Douglas & Co
808 Nelson Street
Vancouver, BC V6B3S1 Can
604-661-1200

Operator of retail food supermarkets.
Type: Private-Sub   Par: Weston, George Ltd
Ind: Retail/Food   Grp: Retail
R Addington, CEO

Rev: 1785
Assets: 404
Emp: 15

Kelsey Hayes Co
38481 Huron River Drive
Romulus, MI 48174
313-941-2000

Manufacturer of wheel & brake components for cars & trucks.
Type: Private-Sub   Par: Fruehauf Corp
Ind: Automotive   Grp: Manufacturing
Robert Seifert, CEO

Rev: NA
Assets: NA
Emp: NA

Kemper Corp
Route 22
Long Grove, IL 60049
312-540-2000

Insurance & financial services.
Type: NASDAQ-KEMC
Ind: Insurance   Grp: Insurance
Joseph E Luecke, CEO   Thomas Anderson, VCh   Donald R Clark, CFO
Robert W Tarjan, IS   Anthony Catania, R&D   Dee Milligan, Mkt
Walter White, VP   John Fitzpatrick, VP   John Burns, VP
Cherry Stoddard, VP   Charles F Johanns, IR   Pat Gould, PR

Rev: 3861
Assets: 12078
Emp: 16

Kendall Co
One Federal Street
Boston, MA 02110
617-574-7000

Manufacturer of surgical & medical supplies.
Type: Private-Sub   Par: Colgate Palmolive Co
Ind: Health Care   Grp: Consumer Service
J Dale Sherratt, CEO

Rev: 750
Assets: NA
Emp: 10

Kendavis Holding Co Inc
106 W Sixth Street
Fort Worth, TX 76102
817-335-5101

Manufacturer of industrial equipment.
Type: Private
Ind: Equipment   Grp: Manufacturing
Joe B Freeman, CEO

Rev: 550
Assets: NA
Emp: 5

Kennametal Inc
Route 981 at   Westmoreland County Airport
Latrobe, PA 15650
412-539-5000

Tools for machining metals; carbide, ceramics.
Type: NYSE-KMT
Ind: Equipment   Grp: Manufacturing
Quentin C McKenna, CEO   James E Morrison, Tres   William C Weaver, CFO
JOhn W Turko, IS   James W Heaton, R&D   Richard Hendricks, VP
Robert N Eslyn, VP   Robert McGeehan, VP   H Patrick Mahanes, VP
R Edwin Morgan, VP   Richard J Orwig, VP   Thomas McGuigan, IR

Rev: 420
Assets: 359
Emp: 5

Kent State University
Administrative Bldg
Kent, OH 44242
216-672-2121

Major educational institution; university.
Type: University
Ind: University   Grp: Govt & Non-Prof
Michael Schwartz, CEO

Rev: 114
Assets: 167
Emp: 22

Kentucky Fried Chicken Inc
1441 Gardiner Lane
Louisville, KY 40213
502-456-8300

Operator of fast food restaurants, franchises.
Type: Private-Sub   Par: PepsiCo Inc
Ind: Food/Lodging   Grp: Consumer Service
Richard Meyer, CEO

Rev: NA
Assets: NA
Emp: NA

Kentucky Power Co
1701 Central Avenue
Ashland, KY 41101
606-327-1111

Electric power utility company.
Type: Private-Sub   Par: American Electric Power Co Inc
Ind: Utility   Grp: Utilities
W S White, CEO   Robert Mathews, Pres   Coulter Boyle, VCh
Peter DeMaria, CFO   Richard Disbrow, R&D   John Dolan, Sls
Gerald Mahoney, Mkt   Joseph Vipperman, VP

Rev: 258
Assets: 600
Emp: 1

Organizations Listed Alphabetically

Organization / Address / Phone	Descriptive Information	Revenue / ($ mil)	Assets / ($ mil)	Emp (thous)
Kentucky Utilities Co One Quality Street Lexington, KY 40507 606-255-1461	Regional utility company. Type: NYSE-KU Ind: Utility Grp: Utilities John T Newton, CEO William Casebier, VCh Michael Whitley, CFO Lynwood Schrader, IS A Doyle Baker, R&D J W Spurrier, Sls O H Lewis, Mkt James Tipton, Ops	Rev: Assets: Emp:	560 1108 2	
Kentucky, State of State Capitol Frankfort, KY 40601 502-465-2500	State government. Type: State Govt Ind: State/Prov Govt Grp: Govt & Non-Prof Wallace Wilkinson, CEO	Rev: Assets: Emp:	7295 NM 71	
Kerr Glass Manufacturing Corp 1840 Century Park E Los Angeles, CA 90067 213-556-2200	Manufacturer of glass & plastic containers. Type: NYSE Ind: Packaging Grp: Manufacturing Roger Norsian, CEO	Rev: Assets: Emp:	350 200 3	
Kerr McGee Corp Kerr McGee Center PO Box 25861 Oklahoma City, OK 73125 405-270-1313	Diversified energy & chemical company. Type: NYSE Ind: Energy Grp: Basic Industries Frank A McPherson, CEO Frank A McPherson, Chr Jere W McKenny, Pres Dean McGee, VCh John C Linehan, CFO W Loy Johnson, IS Luke Corbett, R&D Robert Luke, Sls Kenneth Richards, Mkt Gene Ratcliff, VP W Loy Johnson, VP Tom McDaniel, VP Paul Reed, IR Annita M Bridges, PR	Rev: Assets: Emp:	2689 3123 10	
Ketchum & Co 77 Brant Avenue Clark, NJ 07066 201-815-2800	Wholesale company; drugs, personal care items. Type: ASE-KCH Ind: Retail/Merch Grp: Retail Jean Pierre Duche, CEO	Rev: Assets: Emp:	300 150 1	
Ketchum Communications Inc 300 Blvd of the Allies 6 PPG Place Pittsburgh, PA 15222 412-456-3500	Operator of broadcasting stations. Type: Private Ind: Publishing/Com Grp: Consumer Service William H Genge, CEO	Rev: Assets: Emp:	550 NA 1	
Key Pharmaceuticals Inc Galloping Hill Road Kenilworth, NJ 07033 201-298-4000	Manufacturer of pharmaceutical products. Type: Private-Sub Par: Schering Plough Corp Ind: Drugs Grp: Consumer Service Jean Garnier, CEO	Rev: Assets: Emp:	NA NA NA	
Keycorp Inc 60 State Street Albany, NY 12207 518-486-8500	Commercial bank. Type: NYSE-KEY Ind: Banking Grp: Financial Victor J Riley, CEO James J Miller, VCh Curtis M Carlson, CFO John P McNulty, R&D Allen J Volkenant, Mkt Vincent Ruede, VP Darrell Houston, VP William Stewart, IR Nancy Herron, PR	Rev: Assets: Emp:	1394 14646 8	
Keystone Consolidated Industries Inc 5430 LBJ Freeway Dallas, TX 75240 214-458-0028	Manufacturer of metal products; wire, bolts. Type: NYSE-KES Ind: Manufacturing Grp: Manufacturing Glenn R Simmons, CEO	Rev: Assets: Emp:	250 200 2	
Keystone International Inc 9600 W Gulf Drive Houston, TX 77040 713-466-1176	Manufacturer of liquid process control devices. Type: NYSE-KII Ind: Manufacturing Grp: Manufacturing Raymond A LeBlanc, CEO	Rev: Assets: Emp:	346 340 3	
Keystone Provident Life Insurance Co 99 High Street Boston, MA 02110 617-338-3500	Life insurance company. Type: OTC Ind: Insurance Grp: Insurance Robert G Sharp, CEO Lee Roberts, CFO Gerald Peters, IS Gerald L Johnson, Mkt Robert Stillman, PR	Rev: Assets: Emp:	1042 3836 2	
Kidd Creek Mines Ltd Commerce Court W Toronto, ON M5L1B4 Can 416-863-7000	Mining company; copper, zinc. Type: Private-Sub Par: Falconbridge Ltd Ind: Metals/Mining Grp: Basic Industries William James, CEO	Rev: Assets: Emp:	510 1020 3	

Organizations Listed Alphabetically

Organization / Address / Phone	Descriptive Information	Revenue / Assets / Emp ($ mil) ($ mil) (thous)		

Kidde Inc
Park 80 W Plaza Two
Saddlebrook, NJ 07662
201-368-9000

Industrial & commercial security systems, electrical equip.
Type: NYSE
Ind: Conglomerate   Grp: Manufacturing
Frederick Sullivan, CEO

Rev: 2500
Assets: 1750
Emp: 35

Kidder, Peabody & Co Inc
10 Hanover Square
New York, NY 10005
212-510-3000

Investment firm; consumer brokerage services.
Type: Private-Sub   Par: General Electric Co
Ind: Securities   Grp: Financial
Michael A Carpenter, CEO

Rev: 1650
Assets: 16500
Emp: 7

Kiewit, Peter & Sons Inc
1000 Kiewit Plaza
Omaha, NE 68131
402-342-2052

Diversified construction & coal mining company.
Type: Private
Ind: Real Estate/Bldg   Grp: Business Service
Walter Scott Jr, CEO

Rev: 4800
Assets: NA
Emp: 30

Kimball International Inc
1600 Royal Street
Jasper, IN 47546
812-482-1600

Manufacturer of office furniture & consumer durables.
Type: NASDAQ-KBAL
Ind: Manufacturing   Grp: Manufacturing
Thomas L Habig, CEO   Maurice R Kuper, Pres   James C Thyen, CFO
Norma L Kress, IS   Mathew A Slaats, R&D   John T Thyen, Mkt
Jack Schneider, PR

Rev: 530
Assets: 320
Emp: 8

Kimberly Clark Corp
PO Box 619100 DFW Airport Station
Dallas, TX 75261
214-830-1200

Manufacturer of paper products for personal use.
Type: NYSE-KMB
Ind: Paper/Forest Prd   Grp: Basic Industries
Darwin E Smith, CEO   James Bernd, VCh   Brendan M O'Neill, CFO
John Kohler, IS   James G Grosklaus, Mkt   Richard Sonnentag, Ops
Terrence Murray, VP   Burnell Schubbe, VP   Gilbert Zins, VP
Tina Barry, PR

Rev: 5394
Assets: 4268
Emp: 47

Kinder Care Centers Inc
2400 Presidents Drive
Montgomery, AL 36116
205-277-5090

Franchised day-care, nursery school providers.
Type: NASDAQ-KNDR
Ind: Business Service   Grp: Business Service
Perry Mendel, CEO   Richard Grassgreen, Pres   Charles B Paterson, VCh
Eddie O Nabors, CFO   Wayne N Nelluns, VP   Cheryl Davis, VP
L Wayne Drury, VP

Rev: 936
Assets: 6087
Emp: 15

King County Government
County Courthouse
Seattle, WA 98104
206-344-4100

County government.
Type: County Govt
Ind: Local Govt   Grp: Govt & Non-Prof
Tim Hill, CEO

Rev: 825
Assets: NM
Emp: 5

King Kullen Grocery Inc
1194 Prospect Street
Westbury, NY 11590
516-333-7100

Grocery stores.
Type: Private
Ind: Retail/Food   Grp: Retail
John B Cullen, CEO

Rev: 600
Assets: NA
Emp: 6

King World Productions Inc
430 Morris Turnpike
Short Hills, NJ 07078
201-522-0100

Distributes television programs to stations.
Type: NYSE-KWP
Ind: Leisure Time   Grp: Consumer Service
Roger King, CEO

Rev: 280
Assets: 117
Emp: 2

Kinney Shoe Corp
233 Broadway
New York, NY 10279
212-553-2000

Manufacturer & retailer of family shoes.
Type: Private-Sub   Par: Woolworth, F W Co
Ind: Retail/Merch   Grp: Retail
Harold Rowen, CEO

Rev: NA
Assets: NA
Emp: NA

Kinney Shoes of Canada Ltd
100 Mainshep Road
Weston, ON M9M1L5 Can
416-742-3590

Operator of retail shoe stores.
Type: Private-Sub-For
Ind: Retail/Merch   Grp: Retail
C Anderson, CEO

Rev: 367
Assets: 156
Emp: 5

KitchenAid Inc
701 Main Street
St Joseph, MI 49085
616-982-4500

Manufacturer of major home appliances
Type: Private-Sub   Par: Whirlpool Corp
Ind: Appliances/Furn   Grp: Manufacturing
Kenneth Kaminski, CEO

Rev: NA
Assets: NA
Emp: NA

Organizations Listed Alphabetically

Organization / Address / Phone	Descriptive Information	Revenue / ($ mil)	Assets / ($ mil)	Emp (thous)
KLA Instruments Corp 2051 Mission College Santa Clara, CA 95052 408-988-6100	Manufacturer of electronic testing & measuring equipment. Type: NASDAQ-KLAC Ind: Instruments Grp: High Tech Kenneth Levy, CEO	Rev: Assets: Emp:	113 135 1	
KN Energy Inc 12055 W Second Place Lakewood, CO 80215 303-989-1740	Natural gas distribution company. Type: NYSE-KNE Ind: Energy Grp: Basic Industries C W Battery, CEO	Rev: Assets: Emp:	335 650 3	
Knight Ridder Inc One Herald Plaza Miami, FL 33132 305-376-3800	Communications company;newspapers, TV, business information. Type: NYSE-KRI Ind: Publishing/Com Grp: Consumer Service James K Batten, CEO Richard G Capen, Pres Robert F Singleton, CFO Gary McCormick, IS Jerome S Tilis, Mkt John C Fontaine, VP Larry Jinks, VP James Knight, VP P Anthony Ridder, VP Frank N Hawkins Jr, PR	Rev: Assets: Emp:	2083 2357 20	
Knoll International Holdings 655 Madison Avenue New York, NY 10021 212-826-2400	Manufacturer of automotive parts. Type: Private Ind: Automotive Grp: Manufacturing Marshall S Cogan, CEO Rocco Barbieri, Pres Robert H Nelson, CFO Judith Woodfin, Mkt Judith Woodfin, PR	Rev: Assets: Emp:	1500 NA 20	
Kobe Steel Corp USA 535 Madison Avenue New York, NY 10022 212-751-9400	Manufacturer & importer of basic steel products; US hdqtrs. Type: Private-Sub-For Ind: Steel Grp: Basic Industries Koji Ouchi, CEO	Rev: Assets: Emp:	550 NA 1	
Koch Industries Inc 4111 E 37th Street N Wichita, KS 67220 316-832-5500	Diversified petroleum products company. Type: Private Ind: Manufacturing Grp: Manufacturing Charles Koch, CEO	Rev: Assets: Emp:	15000 NA 8	
Koenig & Strey Inc 999 Waukegan Road Glenview, IL 60025 312-729-6610	Real estate sales & management company. Type: Private Ind: Real Estate/Bldg Grp: Business Service Thomas Koenig, CEO	Rev: Assets: Emp:	550 NA 1	
Kohl's Food Stores 11100 W Burleigh Milwaukee, WI 53222 414-771-8000	Operator of retail supermarkets. Type: Private-Sub Par: Great Atlantic & Pacific Tea Co Ind: Retail/Food Grp: Retail Larry Zettle, CEO	Rev: Assets: Emp:	1000 NA 10	
Kohler Co Kohler Memorial Drive Kohler, WI 53044 414-457-4441	Plumbing equipment, engines, generators & hotels. Type: Private Ind: Manufacturing Grp: Manufacturing Herbert V Kohler Jr, CEO	Rev: Assets: Emp:	1000 NA 10	
Kohls Department Stores 2315 N 124th Street Brookfield, WI 53005 414-784-4480	Operator of retail department stores. Type: Private Ind: Retail/Merch Grp: Retail William Kellog, CEO	Rev: Assets: Emp:	400 NA 4	
Koll Co Inc 4343 Von Karment Newport Beach, CA 92660 714-833-3030	Real estate development, general contracting. Type: Private Ind: Real Estate/Bldg Grp: Business Service Donald M Koll, CEO	Rev: Assets: Emp:	500 NA 1	
Kollmorgen Corp 66 Gate House Road Stamford, CT 06902 203-327-7222	Motors, electronic instruments & interconnections. Type: NYSE-KOL Ind: Electronics Grp: High Tech Robert L Swiggett, CEO James P Thompson, Tres Edward M Felske, CFO Karl A Egerer, R&D Donald S Fisher, Sls George P Stephan, VP Jack Walnes, VP Robert Bollo, VP	Rev: Assets: Emp:	345 224 4	

Organizations Listed Alphabetically

Organization / Address / Phone	Descriptive Information	Revenue / Assets / Emp ($ mil) ($ mil) (thous)		

Koppers Co Inc
Coppers Bldg
Pittsburg, PA 15219
412-227-2000

Manufacturer of construction materials.
Type: NYSE-KOP
Ind: Chemicals   Grp: Basic Industries
Charles Pullin, CEO   Burnett G Bartley Jr, Pres   Thomas M St Clair, CFO
Dean F McAllister, IS   Charles Dorsey, R&D   Raymond R Wingard, Mkt
J Roger Beidler, PR

Rev: 1600
Assets: 1200
Emp: 12

Kraft Inc
2211 Sanders Road Kraft Court
Glenview, IL 60062
312-498-4000

Packaged goods company; food products.
Type: Private-Sub   Par: Philip Morris Companies Inc
Ind: Retail/Food   Grp: Retail
John M Richman, CEO   Michael A Miles, Pres   Gary P Caughlan, CFO
Edward S Fulkes, IS   Robert G McVicker, R&D   Joseph P Dirrett, Sls
Joel D Weiner, Mkt   Mardie MacKimm, PR

Rev: 10000
Assets: 6000
Emp: 45

Kraft Ltd
8600 Chermin Devonshire
Montreal, PQ H3C3J3 Can
514-341-5000

Manufacturer of packaged food products.
Type: Private-Sub-For
Ind: Food Processing   Grp: Food Processing
P Quinn, CEO

Rev: 700
Assets: 372
Emp: 3

Kroger Co
1014 Vine Street
Cincinnati, OH 45201
513-762-4000

Nationwide operator of retail supermarkets.
Type: NYSE-KR
Ind: Retail/Food   Grp: Retail
Lyle A Pichler, CEO   Lyle Everingham, Chr   Joseph A Pichler, Pres
Robert J Hodge, VCh   Lawrence Turner, Tres   William Sinkula, CFO
Jack Hudson, IS   Bill Doehm, R&D   Jack G Hudson, VP
Thomas E Murphy, VP   William Sinkula, VP   Paul Bernish, IR
Jack Partridge Jr, PR

Rev: 19100
Assets: 4200
Emp: 150

Krueger, W A Co
7301 E Helm Drive
Scottsdale, AZ 85260
602-948-5650

Commercial printing company.
Type: NASDAQ-KRUE
Ind: Business Service   Grp: Business Service
Jack Fowler, CEO

Rev: 400
Assets: 300
Emp: 3

Kruger Inc
3285 Rue Bedford
Montreal, PQ H3C2V2 CAN
514-737-1131

Manufacturer of newsprint, cardboard.
Type: Private-Sub-For
Ind: Paper/Forest Prd   Grp: Basic Industries
G Kruger, CEO

Rev: 510
Assets: 765
Emp: 6

Kyowa Bank Ltd
One World Trade Center
New York, NY 10048
212-432-6400

Commercial bank.
Type: Private-Sub-For
Ind: Banking   Grp: Financial
Y Yugihara, CEO

Rev: 450
Assets: 3500
Emp: 1

L'eggs Products Inc
5660 University Parkway
Winston-Salem, NC 27103
919-768-9540

Manufacturer of hosiery.
Type: Private-Sub   Par: Sara Lee Corp
Ind: Apparel/Textiles   Grp: Consumer Prd
John Piazza, CEO

Rev: NA
Assets: NA
Emp: NA

La Confederation Desjardins Du Quebec
One Complex Desjardins
Montreal, PQ H5B1E7 Can
514-281-8666

Diversified financial company.
Type: Private
Ind: Non-Bank Fin   Grp: Financial
Jocelyn Propeau, CEO

Rev: 2445
Assets: 25139
Emp: 24

LA Gear Inc
4221 Redwood Avenue
Los Angeles, CA 90066
213-822-1995

Manufacturer of recreational footwear.
Type: NYSE-LA
Ind: Apparel/Textiles   Grp: Consumer Prd
R Y Greenberg, CEO

Rev: 450
Assets: 300
Emp: 4

La Sauvegarde Assurance sur la vie Ltd
One Complex Desjardins S Tower 25th Floor
Montreal, PQ H5B1E2 Can
514-285-7700

Life insurance company.
Type: Private
Ind: Insurance   Grp: Insurance
Louis Phillippe Poulin, CEO

Rev: 167
Assets: 677
Emp: 1

La-Z-Boy Chair Co
1284 N Telegraph Road
Monroe, MI 48161
313-242-1444

Manufacturer of furniture, reclining chairs.
Type: NYSE-LZB
Ind: Appliances/Furn   Grp: Manufacturing
Charles T Knabusch, CEO

Rev: 553
Assets: 400
Emp: 4

Organizations Listed Alphabetically

Organization / Address / Phone	Descriptive Information	Revenue / ($ mil)	Assets / ($ mil)	Emp (thous)

Labatt, John Ltd
451 Ridout Street N
London, ON N6A5L3 Can
519-673-5050

Nationwide beverage company; beer.
Type: NYSE
Ind: Food Processing   Grp: Food Processing
Peter N T Widdrington, CEO   Edward Bradley, Pres   Robert Vaux, VCh
W James Emmerton, Tres   Paul L Meier, CFO   Dean C Kitts, Mkt
Larry J Innamen, VP   Robert F Dolan, VP   Sidney M Oland, VP

Rev: 4341
Assets: 2157
Emp: 18

Laborers' Intl Union of North America
905 Sixteenth Street NW
Washington, DC 20006
202-737-8320

National labor union.
Type: Membership Org
Ind: Membership Org   Grp: Govt & Non-Prof
Angelo Fosco, CEO

Rev: 250
Assets: NM
Emp: 450

Laclede Gas Co
720 Olive Street
St Louis, MO 63101
314-342-0500

Natural gas utility company.
Type: NYSE-LG
Ind: Utility   Grp: Utilities
Lee M Liberman, CEO

Rev: 450
Assets: 800
Emp: 2

Laclede Steel Co
Equitable Bldg 10 Broadway
St Louis, MO 63102
314-425-1400

Manufacturer of steel, carbon, wire products.
Type: OTC
Ind: Steel   Grp: Basic Industries
J McKinney, CEO

Rev: 350
Assets: 200
Emp: 3

Ladd Furniture Inc
One Plaza Center
High Point, NC 27261
919-889-0333

Manufacturer of furniture & home furnishing products.
Type: NASDAQ-LADF
Ind: Manufacturing   Grp: Manufacturing
Richard R Allen, CEO

Rev: 380
Assets: 173
Emp: 6

Ladd Petroleum Inc
830 Denver Club Bldg 518 17th Street
Denver, CO 80202
303-620-0100

Manufacturer of petroleum products.
Type: Private-Sub   Par: General Electric Co
Ind: Energy   Grp: Basic Industries
Ronald Spence, CEO

Rev: NA
Assets: NA
Emp: NA

Lafarge Corp
11130 Sunrise Valley Drive
Reston, VA 22091
703-264-3600

Concrete manufacturing & supply company.
Type: NYSE-LAF
Ind: Building Mat   Grp: Basic Industries
Bertrand Collomb, CEO   Robert W Murdoch, Pres   Francois Jaclot, CFO
Jean-Louis Nicolas, R&D   David Lovett, VP   John M Piecuch, VP
Jane Hainsworth, PR

Rev: 1309
Assets: 1199
Emp: 8

Laidlaw Industries Inc
15 Spinning Wheel Road
Hinsdale, IL 60521
312-439-6686

Operator of waste management systems & trucking.
Type: NASDAQ-LWSI
Ind: Business Service   Grp: Business Service
Michael DeGroote, CEO

Rev: 1200
Assets: 600
Emp: 5

Laidlaw Transportation Ltd
3221 N Service Road
Burlington, ON L7N3G2 Can
416-336-1800

Nationwide truck transportation company.
Type: NASDAQ-LDMFA
Ind: Transport   Grp: Business Service
Michael G DeGroote, CEO   Douglas Gowland, Pres   Kenneth Needler, VCh
Leslie Hawath, CFO   Victor Webster, Sls   Gary Degroote, VP
Robert Duncan, VP   Halliwell Soule, VP   Ivan Cairns, VP

Rev: 1006
Assets: 1391
Emp: 15

Lake Ontario Cement Ltd
2 Carlton Street
Toronto, ON M5B1J6 Can
416-977-0611

Building materials manufacturing company; cement.
Type: Private-Sub-For
Ind: Building Mat   Grp: Basic Industries
J Pal, CEO

Rev: 298
Assets: 255
Emp: 1

Lamar Life Insurance Corp
317 E Capitol Street
Jackson, MI 49201
601-949-3100

Life insurance company.
Type: NASDAQ-LLIC
Ind: Insurance   Grp: Insurance
Jack Dean, CEO

Rev: 250
Assets: 1200
Emp: 1

Lamb Technicon Inc
5663 E Nine Mile Road
Warren, MI 48091
313-497-6652

Diversified manufacturing company.
Type: Private
Ind: Manufacturing   Grp: Manufacturing
Carlo Clavenna, CEO

Rev: 550
Assets: NA
Emp: 2

Organizations Listed Alphabetically

Organization / Address / Phone	Descriptive Information	Revenue / ($ mil)	Assets / ($ mil)	Emp (thous)
Lamson & Sessions Co 25701 Science Park Drive Cleveland, OH 44122 216-464-3400	Manufacturer of aluminum castings & heat exchangers. Type: NYSE Ind: Manufacturing Grp: Manufacturing Russell Every, CEO	Rev: Assets: Emp:	400 250 3	
Lancaster Colony Corp 37 W Broad Street Columbus, OH 43215 614-224-7141	Diversified manufacturer of home products. Type: NASDAQ-LANC Ind: Manufacturing Grp: Manufacturing John J Gerlach, CEO	Rev: Assets: Emp:	453 286 5	
Lance Inc 8600 South Blvd Charlotte, NC 28210 704-554-1421	Producer of packaged food products. Type: NASDAQ-LNCE Ind: Food Processing Grp: Food Processing A T Sloan, CEO William Disher, Pres Paul A Stroup, VCh James Helms Jr, CFO John S Moore, VP Thomas B Horack, VP William B Meacham, VP Price Gwynn, VP	Rev: Assets: Emp:	408 256 3	
Land O'Lakes Inc 4001 Lexington Avenue North Arden Hills, MN 55126 612-481-2222	Food products company; dairy products. Type: Private Ind: Food Processing Grp: Food Processing Stanley Zylstra, CEO Ralph Hofstad, Chr Ronald Ostby, CFO Lavern Freeh, PR	Rev: Assets: Emp:	2180 750 6	
Land Systems Div 38500 Mound Road Sterling Heights, MI 48310 313-825-4000	Manufacturer of military tanks & heavy equipment. Type: Private-Sub Par: General Dynamics Corp Ind: Equipment Grp: Manufacturing Robert Truxell, CEO	Rev: Assets: Emp:	NA NA NA	
Landmark Communications Inc 150 Brambleton Avenue Norfolk, VA 23501 804-446-2000	Communications company; newspapers, TV. Type: Private Ind: Publishing/Com Grp: Consumer Service Frank Batten, CEO	Rev: Assets: Emp:	350 300 4	
Landmark Land Co Inc 100 Clock Tower Place Carmel, CA 93923 408-625-4060	Real estate development company. Type: ASE-LML Ind: Real Estate/Bldg Grp: Business Service Gerald G Barton, CEO Richard L Singleton, CFO Michael R Welch, IS	Rev: Assets: Emp:	500 2500 2	
Lands End Inc 1 Lands' End Lane Dodgeville, WI 53595 608-935-9341	Catalog retail mail order selling apparel, shoes, luggage. Type: NYSE-LE Ind: Retail/Merch Grp: Retail Gary C Comer, CEO	Rev: Assets: Emp:	456 151 2	
Lane Bryant Inc 11 W 42nd Street New York, NY 10036 212-930-9482	Operator of retail apparel stores; women's wear. Type: Private-Sub Par: Limited Inc Ind: Retail/Merch Grp: Retail Ira Quint, CEO	Rev: Assets: Emp:	NA NA NA	
Lane Co Inc East Franklin Avenue Altavista, VA 24517 804-369-5641	Furniture manufacturer. Type: Private Ind: Manufacturing Grp: Manufacturing Stewart Moore, CEO	Rev: Assets: Emp:	375 250 4	
Las Vegas, City of City Hall East Stewart Avenue Las Vegas, NV 89101 702-386-6241	City government. Type: City Govt Ind: Local Govt Grp: Govt & Non-Prof James Seastrand, CEO	Rev: Assets: Emp:	250 NM 3	
LaSalle Energy Corp 300 Crescent Court Suite 1320 Dallas, TX 75201 214-871-5333	Natural gas pipeline. Type: Private Ind: Energy Grp: Basic Industries Roy H Bettis, CEO	Rev: Assets: Emp:	1250 NA 2	
Lauder, Estee Cosmetics Ltd 161 Commander Blvd Scarborough, ON M1S3K9 Can 416-292-1111	Manufacturer of personal care products. Type: Private Ind: Personal Care Grp: Consumer Prd Leonard Lauder, CEO	Rev: Assets: Emp:	1488 595 5	

Organizations Listed Alphabetically

Organization / Address / Phone	Descriptive Information	Revenue / Assets / Emp ($ mil) ($ mil) (thous)		
Laurentian Bank of Canada 1981 Avenue McGill College Montreal, PQ H3A33a CAN 514-284-7967	Commercial bank. Type: Private Ind: Banking Grp: Financial Dominic D'Alessandro, CEO	Rev: Assets: Emp:	340 3400 2	
Laurentian General Insurance Co 507 Place D'Armes Montreal, PQ H2Y2W8 Can 514-842-6212	Property & casualty insurance company. Type: Private-Sub Ind: Insurance Grp: Insurance Claudee Castonguay, CEO	Rev: Assets: Emp:	276 969 1	
Laurentian Group Corp 500 Grande Allee Est Quebec, PQ G1R2J7 Can 418-647-5151	Life insurance company. Type: Private-Mutual Ind: Non-Bank Fin Grp: Financial Claude Castonguay, CEO	Rev: Assets: Emp:	1411 8244 7	
Laurentian Mutual Insurance Co 500 Grande Allee Est Quebec, PQ G1R2J7 Can 418-647-5255	Life insurance company. Type: Private-Mutual Ind: Insurance Grp: Insurance Claude Castomguay, CEO	Rev: Assets: Emp:	261 804 1	
Laval, Universite Cite Universitaire Quebec, PQ G1K7P4 Can 418-656-2131	Major educational institution; university. Type: University Ind: University Grp: Govt & Non-Prof Michel Gervais, CEO	Rev: Assets: Emp:	281 NM 31	
Lavalin Inc 1130 O Rue Sherbrooke Montreal, PQ H3A2R5 Can 514-288-1740	Engineering & construction services company. Type: Private Ind: Real Estate/Bldg Grp: Business Service Bernard LeMarre, CEO	Rev: Assets: Emp:	870 451 6	
Lavoro Banca Roma Ltd 25 W 51st Street New York, NY 10019 212-581-0710	Commercial bank. Type: Private-Sub-For Ind: Banking Grp: Financial Luiggi Sardelli, CEO	Rev: Assets: Emp:	450 3500 1	
Lawson Mardon Group Ltd 6711 Mississauga Road Suite 401 Mississauga, ON L5N2W3 Can 416-821-9711	Manufacturer of packaging. Type: TOR Ind: Packaging Grp: Manufacturing Lawrence Tapp, CEO	Rev: Assets: Emp:	880 707 7	
Lawyers Title Insurance Co 6630n W Broad Street Richmond, Va 23230 804-281-6700	Property title insurance company. Type: Private-Sub Par: Universal Leaf Tobacco Co Inc Ind: Insurance Grp: Insurance Robert Dawson, CEO	Rev: Assets: Emp:	NA NA NA	
Lazard Freres & Co 1 Rockefeller Plaza New York, NY 10020 212-489-6600	Investment banking firm. Type: Private Ind: Securities Grp: Financial Michele David Weill, CEO	Rev: Assets: Emp:	1000 10000 1	
Lazare Kaplan International Inc 529 Fifth Avenue New York, NY 10017 212-972-9700	Diamond marketing firm. Type: ASE Ind: Retail/Merch Grp: Retail M Templesman, CEO	Rev: Assets: Emp:	350 100 2	
LDI Corp 1375 E 9th Street Cleveland, OH 44114 216-687-0100	Data processing services company. Type: NASDAQ-LDIC Ind: Comput/Off Equip Grp: High Tech Robert Kendall, CEO	Rev: Assets: Emp:	270 125 2	
Le Groupe Ro Na Inc 1250 Nobel Boucherville, PQ J4B5K1 Can 514-599-5100	Building materials manufacturing company. Type: TOR Ind: Building Mat Grp: Basic Industries Andre Dion, CEO	Rev: Assets: Emp:	413 115 1	

Organizations Listed Alphabetically

Organization / Address / Phone	Descriptive Information	Revenue / ($ mil)	Assets / ($ mil)	Emp (thous)
Leaf Inc 2355 Waukegan Road Bannockburn, IL 60015 312-940-7500	Producer of packaged food products. Type: Private Ind: Food Processing Grp: Food Processing Jim Hanlon, CEO	Rev: Assets: Emp:	275 NA 3	
Lear Petroleum Corp 6688 N Central Expressway Dallas, TX 75206 214-363-6085	Natural gas exploration & production company. Type: NYSE-LPT Ind: Energy Grp: Basic Industries Joseph T Williams, CEO	Rev: Assets: Emp:	600 400 1	
Lear Siegler Seating Corp 21557 Telegraph Southfield, MI 48034 313-746-1500	Manufacturer of seating for auto companies. Type: Private Ind: Automotive Grp: Manufacturing Kenneth Way, CEO	Rev: Assets: Emp:	1000 NA 5	
Leaseway Transportation Corp 3700 Park East Drive Beachwood, OH 44122 216-464-3300	Nationwide truck transport company. Type: Private Ind: Transport Grp: Business Service Richard A Damsel, CEO Gerald C McDonough, Chr Dean Cole, IS Jackie Toth, R&D Charles Lounsbury, Mkt Karen A Lewicki, IR Frederick Andersky, PR	Rev: Assets: Emp:	1500 1100 20	
Lechmere Inc 275 Wildwood Street Woburn, MA 01801 617-935-8320	Operator of retail stores; small appliances. Type: Private-Sub Par: Dayton Hudson Corp Ind: Retail/Merch Grp: Retail George Scala, CEO	Rev: Assets: Emp:	NA NA NA	
Lee Apparel Inc 9001 W 67th Street Merriam, KS 66202 913-384-4000	Manufacturer of family apparel. Type: Private-Sub Par: VF Corp Ind: Apparel/Textiles Grp: Consumer Prd Richard Lamm, CEO	Rev: Assets: Emp:	NA NA NA	
Lee Enterprises Inc 130 E Second Street Davenport, IA 52801 319-383-2202	Newspaper publishing company. Type: NYSE-LEE Ind: Publishing/Com Grp: Consumer Service Lloyd G Schermer, CEO	Rev: Assets: Emp:	252 308 3	
LeFrak Organization 9777 Queens Blvd Rego Park, NY 11374 718-459-9021	Real estate development & management company. Type: Private Ind: Real Estate/Bldg Grp: Business Service Samuel J LeFrak, CEO	Rev: Assets: Emp:	2750 NA 20	
Legg Mason Inc 111 S Calvert Street Baltimore, MD 21023 301-539-3400	Investment firm; retail brokerage services. Type: NYSE-LM Ind: Securities Grp: Financial Raymond Mason, CEO	Rev: Assets: Emp:	300 150 3	
Leggett & Platt Inc One Leggett Road Carthage, MO 64836 417-358-8131	Manufacturer of components for bedding/furniture industries. Type: NYSE Ind: Manufacturing Grp: Manufacturing Harry M Cornell, CEO Felix E Wright, Pres Duane Potter, VCh Michael A Glauber, CFO Don La Ferla, IS Robert Jeffries, VP Richard Fanning, VP Roger Gladden, VP C Richard Gamble, VP J Richard Calhoon, IR Lance Deshore, PR	Rev: Assets: Emp:	810 476 11	
Lennar Corp 700 NW 107th Avenue Miami, FL 33172 305-559-4000	Residential builder & developer; homes, subdivisions. Type: NYSE-LEN Ind: Real Estate/Bldg Grp: Business Service Leonard Miller, CEO	Rev: Assets: Emp:	350 150 1	
Lennox International Corp PO Box 809000 Dallas, TX 75380 214-980-6000	Manufacturer of climate control equipment. Type: Private Ind: Instruments Grp: High Tech John W Norris, CEO	Rev: Assets: Emp:	750 NA 5	

Organizations Listed Alphabetically

Organization / Address / Phone	Descriptive Information	Revenue / ($ mil)	Assets / ($ mil)	Emp (thous)
Lerner Stores Inc 460 W 33rd Street New York, NY 10001 212-736-1222	Operator of retail stores; womens apparel. Type: Private-Sub Par: Limited Inc Ind: Retail/Merch Grp: Retail Robert Grayson, CEO	Rev: Assets: Emp:	NA NA NA	
Les Cooperants Ltd 600 Maison Avenue Blvd W Montreal, PQ H3A3A9 Can 514-287-6600	Life insurance company. Type: Private-Mutual Ind: Insurance Grp: Insurance Paul Dolan, CEO	Rev: Assets: Emp:	170 680 1	
Leslie Fay Inc 1400 Broadway New York, NY 10018 212-221-4000	Manufacturer of women's clothing. Type: NYSE-LES Ind: Apparel/Textiles Grp: Consumer Prd John J Pomerantz, CEO Alan Golub, Pres Joel H Newman, VCh Daniel Falkowitz, Tres Paul F Polishan, CFO Donald Kenia, VP Roger Murray, VP Herman Gordon, VP Tony Manning, PR	Rev: Assets: Emp:	683 363 6	
Leventhal, Kenneth Inc 2049 Century Park E Los Angeles, CA 90067 213-277-0880	Nationwide accounting firm. Type: Private Ind: Accounting Grp: Business Service J Rosen, CEO	Rev: Assets: Emp:	400 NA 5	
Lever Brothers Co Inc 390 Park Avenue New York, NY 10022 212-688-6000	Producer of packaged consumer products; US headquarters. Type: Private-Sub-For Ind: Food Processing Grp: Food Processing Morris Tabakoblat, CEO Stuart M Blinder, CFO Ronald C Smith, IS Frank H Healey, R&D A Clive Butler, Sls David F Webb, Mkt Kenneth R Lightcap, IR Burt Hochman, PR	Rev: Assets: Emp:	2750 800 13	
Levesque Beaubien Inc 1155 Metcalfe Street Montreal, PQ H3B4S9 Can 514-879-2222	Investment company; brokerage. Type: Private Ind: Securities Grp: Financial Pierre Brunet, CEO	Rev: Assets: Emp:	170 85 1	
Levi Strauss & Co Inc 1155 Battery Street San Francisco, CA 94111 415-544-6000	Manufacturer of apparel; jeans, pants, sports clothing. Type: Private Ind: Apparel/Textiles Grp: Consumer Prd Robert D Haas, CEO	Rev: Assets: Emp:	3000 NA 30	
Levitz Furniture Corp 6111 Broken Sound Drive Boca Raton, FL 33431 305-994-6006	Furniture retailer. Type: Private Ind: Retail/Merch Grp: Retail Robert M Elliott, CEO	Rev: Assets: Emp:	1000 NA 8	
Lewis Homes Corp 1156 N Mountain Avenue Upland, CA 91786 714-985-0971	Developer of residential property. Type: Private Ind: Real Estate/Bldg Grp: Business Service Randell Lewis, CEO	Rev: Assets: Emp:	500 NA 1	
Lexington, City of City Hall 200 E Main Street Lexington, KY 40507 606-258-3110	City government. Type: City Govt Ind: Local Govt Grp: Govt & Non-Prof Scotty Baesler, CEO	Rev: Assets: Emp:	250 NM 2	
Liberty Life Insurance Co Hampton Blvd PO Box 789 Greenville, SC 29602 803-268-8111	Insurance & broadcasting company. Type: NYSE-LC Ind: Insurance Grp: Insurance Francis M Hipp, CEO	Rev: Assets: Emp:	401 1382 2	
Liberty Mutual Insurance Co 175 Berkeley Street Boston, MA 02117 617-285-7000	Property & casualty insurance company. Type: Private-Mutual Ind: Insurance Grp: Insurance Gary L Countryman, CEO William Commack, VCh Robert H Gruhl, CFO William Commack, R&D John Conners, Sls Robert Hytha, Mkt Therese Maloney, VP Maryann Burke, VP Bruce Davis, VP	Rev: Assets: Emp:	8268 15749 26	

Organizations Listed Alphabetically

Organization / Address / Phone	Descriptive Information	Revenue / Assets / Emp ($ mil) ($ mil) (thous)		

Liberty National Life Insurance Co
PO Box 2612
Birmingham, AL 35202
205-325-2722

Life insurance company.
Type: OTC
Ind: Insurance   Grp: Insurance
John S P Samford, CEO

Rev: 541
Assets: 2607
Emp: 2

Life Insurance Co of Virginia Inc
6610 W Broad Street
Richmond, VA 23230
804-281-6000

Life insurance company.
Type: OTC
Ind: Insurance   Grp: Insurance
Patrick G Ryan, CEO

Rev: 1080
Assets: 2794
Emp: 3

Life Investors Insurance Co of America
4333 Edgewood Road NE
Ceder Rapids, IA 52499
319-398-5811

Life insurance company.
Type: NASDAQ-LINV
Ind: Insurance   Grp: Insurance
Thomas M Collins, CEO

Rev: 1400
Assets: 3500
Emp: 2

Lifetime Corp
99 Summer Street
Boston, MA 02110
617-330-5080

Personnel service for health care industry, home care.
Type: ASE-LFT
Ind: Health Care   Grp: Consumer Service
Anthony H Reeves, CEO

Rev: 377
Assets: 200
Emp: 6

Liggett Group Inc
300 N Duke Street
Durham, NC 27702
919-683-9000

Manufacturer of consumer goods, cigarettes.
Type: NYSE
Ind: Tobacco   Grp: Food Processing
K V Dey, CEO

Rev: 2000
Assets: 1500
Emp: 15

Lilly, Eli & Co
Lilly Corporate Center
Indianapolis, IN 46285
317-261-2000

Worldwide pharmaceutical company.
Type: NYSE-LLY
Ind: Drugs   Grp: Consumer Service
Richard Wood, CEO   Richard D Wood, Chr   Vaughn D Bryson, Pres
James Cornelius, CFO   Dale Kann, IS   Earl Herr, R&D
Eurelio M Cavalier, Sls   E Walter Lange, Mkt   Mark Miles, IR
Brian Dunnivant, PR

Rev: 4070
Assets: 5263
Emp: 31

Limited Inc
Two Limited Towers PO Box 16000
Columbus, OH 43216
614-475-4000

Operator of retail apparel stores.
Type: NYSE-LTD
Ind: Retail/Merch   Grp: Retail
Leslie H Wexner, CEO   Margaret Monaco, Tres   Kenneth B Gilman, CFO
Thomas G Hopkins, R&D   Bella Wexner, VP   Alfred S Dietzel, PR

Rev: 4071
Assets: 2145
Emp: 17

Lin Broadcasting Corp
1370 Avenue of the Americas
New York, NY 10019
212-765-1902

Operator of radio broadcasting stations.
Type: OTC
Ind: Publishing/Com   Grp: Consumer Service
Donald A Pels, CEO

Rev: 226
Assets: 582
Emp: 2

Lincoln Electric Co Inc
22801 St Clair Avenue
Cleveland, OH 44117
216-481-8100

Manufacturer of electrical motors & equipment.
Type: Private
Ind: Manufacturing   Grp: Manufacturing
George Willis, CEO

Rev: 550
Assets: NA
Emp: 5

Lincoln National Corp
1300 S Clinton Street
Fort Wayne, IN 46801
219-427-2000

Life insurance company.
Type: NYSE-LNC
Ind: Insurance   Grp: Insurance
Ian M Rolland, CEO   Richard S Robertson, CFO   David A Allen, IS
Lawrence Edris, R&D   Harlan K Holly, Mkt   John Carr, VP
Reed Miller, VP   Suzanne Womack, VP   Cheryl Brooks, PR

Rev: 7312
Assets: 20964
Emp: 15

Lincoln Property Co
500 N Akard
Dallas, TX 75201
214-740-3300

Real estate development & management company.
Type: Private
Ind: Real Estate/Bldg   Grp: Business Service
A Mack Pogue, CEO

Rev: 1500
Assets: NA
Emp: 5

Lincoln Savings (Cal) & Loan Assn Inc
18200 Von Darman
Irvine, CA 92714
714-553-0200

Thrift institution.
Type: OTC
Ind: Savings & Loan   Grp: Financial
Robin S Symes, CEO

Rev: 425
Assets: 4000
Emp: 1

Organizations Listed Alphabetically

Organization / Address / Phone	Descriptive Information	Revenue ($ mil)	Assets ($ mil)	Emp (thous)
Lincoln-Mercury Div American Road Dearborn, MI 48121 313-322-3000	Automobile manufacturer. Type: Private-Sub Par: Ford Motor Co Ind: Automotive Grp: Manufacturing Ross Roberts, CEO	Rev: NA Assets: NA Emp: NA		
Lionel Corp 441 Lexington Avenue New York, NY 10017 212-818-0630	Toy train manufacturer; retail toy stores. Type: ASE-LIO Ind: Leisure Time Grp: Consumer Service Michael J Vastola, CEO	Rev: 412 Assets: 400 Emp: 3		
Lipton, Thomas J Inc 800 Sylvan Avenue Englewood Cliffs, NJ 07632 201-567-8000	Manufacturer of packaged food products; US headquarters. Type: Private-Sub-For Ind: Food Processing Grp: Food Processing Blaine Hess, CEO Hubert M Tibbetts, Chr John Byrne, Pres Christopher B Fuller, CFO John A Fischer, IS Dr Henry J Izzo, R&D Robert E Livingston, Sls James W Benson, Mkt Edmund Ladendorff, PR	Rev: 1430 Assets: 1000 Emp: 7		
Liquid Air Corp 2121 N California Blvd Walnut Creek, CA 94556 415-977-6500	Manufacturer of liquid gases. Type: NASDAQ-LANA Ind: Chemicals Grp: Basic Industries Jean Henri Delorue, CEO Thomas E Slattery, Chr Thaddeus Pylko, CFO Patrick Maloney, IS Leonard Sis, Sls	Rev: 600 Assets: 800 Emp: 4		
Little, Arthur D & Co Inc 25 Acorn Park Cambridge, MA 02140 617-864-5770	Nationwide consulting company. Type: Private Ind: Consulting Grp: Business Service Charles Limamtia, CEO	Rev: 400 Assets: NA Emp: 3		
Little, Brown & Co Inc 34 Beacon Street Boston, MA 02108 617-227-0730	Publishing company. Type: Private-Sub Par: Time Inc Ind: Publishing/Com Grp: Consumer Service Kevin Dolan, CEO	Rev: NA Assets: NA Emp: NA		
Litton Industries Inc 360 N Cresent Drive Beverly Hills, CA 90210 213-859-5000	Manufacturer of electronic equipment; consumer, defense. Type: NYSE-LIT Ind: Electronics Grp: High Tech Orion L Hoch, CEO Roland O Peterson, Pres Carol A Weisner, Tres Joseph T Casey, CFO Joesph F Caligiuri, VP Alton J Brann, VP M Howard Dingman Jr, VP Richard D Fleck, VP Robert H Lentz, VP Dirk Koerber, PR	Rev: 4864 Assets: 5075 Emp: 55		
Litton Systems Canada Ltd 25 Cityview Drive Toronto, ON M9W5A7 Can 416-249-1231	Manufacturer of aircraft equipment. Type: Private-Sub-for Ind: Electronics Grp: High Tech T McGuigan, CEO	Rev: 383 Assets: 298 Emp: 1		
Live Entertainment Inc 500 N Venture Park Road Newberry Park, CA 91320 805-499-5827	Distributor of recorded music. Type: OTC Ind: Leisure Time Grp: Consumer Service J E Menendez, CEO	Rev: 352 Assets: 131 Emp: 3		
Lloyd's Bank Ltd 199 Water Street New York, NY 10038 212-607-4300	Commercial bank. Type: Private-Sub-For Ind: Banking Grp: Financial David Dreweri, CEO	Rev: 450 Assets: 3500 Emp: 1		
Lloyd's of London Canada Ltd 1155 Rue University Montreal, PQ H3B1S3 Can 514-861-8361	Property & casualty insurance company. Type: Private-Sub-For Ind: Insurance Grp: Insurance E W Tinmouth, CEO	Rev: 417 Assets: 4582 Emp: 2		
Loblaw Companies 22 St Clair Avenue E Toronto, ON M4T2S7 Can 416-922-8500	Operator of retail supermarkets. Type: Private-Sub Par: Weston, George Ltd Ind: Retail/Food Grp: Retail Galen Weston, CEO	Rev: 7336 Assets: 1881 Emp: 33		

Organization / Address / Phone	Descriptive Information	Revenue / ($ mil)	Assets / ($ mil)	Emp (thous)
Lockheed Aeronautical Systems Co 2555 N Hollywood Way Burbank, CA 91520 818-847-6121	Manufacturer of aeronautical equipment. Type: Private-Sub Par: Lockheed Corp Ind: Instruments Grp: High Tech John Brizendine, CEO	Rev: NA	Assets: NA	Emp: NA
Lockheed Corp 4500 Park Granada Blvd Calabasas, CA 91399 818-847-6121	Aerospace manufacturer of defense equipment. Type: NYSE-LK Ind: Aerospace Grp: High Tech Daniel M Tellep, CEO Robert A Fuhrman, Pres Anthony Van Schaick, Tres Vincent N Marafino, CFO Dean O Allen, IS Walter LaBerge, R&D Charles de Bedts, Mkt Daniel H Daniels, Ops Richard Taylor, VP Val Peline, VP H David Crowther, PR	Rev: 10590	Assets: 6643	Emp: 87
Lockheed Engineering & Sciences Div 2400 Nasa Road Houston, TX 77058 713-333-5411	Engineering & research firm. Type: Private-Sub Par: Lockheed Corp Ind: Consulting Grp: Business Service R Young, CEO	Rev: NA	Assets: NA	Emp: NA
Lockheed Missiles & Space Co Inc 1111 Lockheed Way Sunnyvale, CA 94088 408-742-4321	Manufacturer of missiles & space equipment. Type: Private-Sub Par: Lockheed Corp Ind: Aerospace Grp: High Tech John McMahon, CEO	Rev: NA	Assets: NA	Emp: NA
Loctite Corp Hartford Square N 10 Columbus Blvd Hartford, CT 06106 203-520-5000	Specialty chemical company. Type: NYSE Ind: Chemicals Grp: Basic Industries Kenneth W Butterworth, CEO Theodore Patlovich, VCh Robert L Aller, CFO David Freeman, VP Ethan Galloway, VP Edward Daisy, VP	Rev: 417	Assets: 347	Emp: 3
Loewen Ondaatje McCutcheon Inc 40 King Street W Toronto, ON M5H3Y2 Can 416-869-7211	Investment company; brokerage. Type: Private Ind: Non-Bank Fin Grp: Financial Charles Loewen, CEO	Rev: 85	Assets: 85	Emp: 1
Loews Corp 667 Madison Avenue New York, NY 10021 212-545-2000	Insurance services, cigarette manufacturing company. Type: NYSE Ind: Food/Lodging Grp: Consumer Service Laurence A Tisch, CEO Preston R Tisch, Pres Charles B Sposato, Tres Roy E Posner, CFO Carl Rosen, IS Herbert Hofmann, R&D Jonathan M Tisch, VP James S Tisch, VP Andrew H Tisch, VP Barry Hirsch, VP Gary Garson, VP Stuart Opotowsky, VP Michelle Oaklan, PR	Rev: 10865	Assets: 25829	Emp: 22
Loews Hotel Corp 667 Madison Avenue New York, NY 10021 212-545-2000	Owners & operators of hotels. Type: Private-Sub Par: Loews Corp Ind: Food/Lodging Grp: Consumer Service Robert Hausman, CEO	Rev: NA	Assets: NA	Emp: NA
Logicon Inc 3701 Skypark Drive Torrance, CA 90505 213-373-0220	Systems programming company; defense, commercial. Type: NYSE-LGN Ind: Comput/Off Equip Grp: High Tech John R Woodhull, CEO	Rev: 225	Assets: 100	Emp: 3
Lomas & Nettleton Financial Corp 2001 Bryan Tower PO Box 655644 Dallas, TX 75265 214-746-7111	Financial services, mortgage banking. Type: NYSE-LNF Ind: Non-Bank Fin Grp: Financial Ted Enloe, CEO Jess Hay, Chr James Crowson, VCh John F Sexton, CFO Matthew Jacobs, IS Gary White, Mkt Donald Funkhouser, Ops Bradley Buttermore, VP Thomas Clooney, VP Kevin McGarry, PR	Rev: 1235	Assets: 6645	Emp: 5
London Life Insurance Co 255 Dufferin Avenue London, ON N6A4K1 Can 519-432-5281	Life insurance company. Type: Private-mutual Ind: Insurance Grp: Insurance Earl H Orser, CEO R Thomas M Allan, Pres Norman Epp, CFO R Brock Armstrong, R&D Dale Creighton, Mkt L Blake Fewster, VP Charles Kimball, VP Roger G Lillyman, VP William Nursey, VP Allan Edwards, VP	Rev: 1960	Assets: 7932	Emp: 5

Organizations Listed Alphabetically

Organization / Address / Phone	Descriptive Information	Revenue / Assets / Emp ($ mil) ($ mil) (thous)		

Lone Star Gas Co
301 S Harwood Street
Dallas, TX 75201
214-741-3711

Natural gas transmission & sales company.
Type: Private-Sub   Par: Enserch Corp
Ind: Energy   Grp: Basic Industries
David Biegler, CEO

Rev: NA
Assets: NA
Emp: NA

Lone Star Industries Inc
One Greenwich Plaza
Greenwich, CT 06836
203-661-3100

Cement & building materials manufacturing company.
Type: NYSE-LCE
Ind: Building Mat   Grp: Basic Industries
James E Stewart, CEO   William Troutman, Pres   Robert W Hutton, VCh
Jerome Bennett, CFO   James T Cleven, IS   John J Graham, Mkt
Jerome Bennett, VP   Carmine Muratore, VP   James A Powers, PR

Rev: 529
Assets: 1424
Emp: 4

Lone Star Technologies
2200 W Mockingbird Lane
Dallas, TX 75235
214-352-3981

Manufacturer of piping, control systems, pollution control.
Type: NASDAQ-LSST
Ind: Manufacturing   Grp: Manufacturing
Howard Beasly, CEO

Rev: 500
Assets: 350
Emp: 2

Long Beach City College
4901 E Carson Street
Long Beach, CA 90808
213-420-4111

Major educational institution; college.
Type: University
Ind: University   Grp: Govt & Non-Prof
Beverly O'Neil, CEO

Rev: 132
Assets: 132
Emp: 26

Long Beach, City of
City Hall 333 W Ocean Blvd
Long Beach, CA 90802
213-590-6707

City government.
Type: City Govt
Ind: Local Govt   Grp: Govt & Non-Prof
Ernie Kell, CEO

Rev: 623
Assets: NM
Emp: 5

Long Island Lighting Co
175 E Old Country Road
Hicksville, NY 11801
516-933-4590

Electric power utility.
Type: NYSE
Ind: Utility   Grp: Utilities
William J Catacosinos, CEO   Russell C Youngdahl, Pres   Anthony F Earley, VCh
George Sideris, CFO   Arthur N Pietrow, IS   John Weismantle, R&D
Ira L Freilicher, VP   Ralph Brandifino, VP   James E Lois, IR
Joseph W McDonnell, PR

Rev: 2138
Assets: 8326
Emp: 6

Long Island Savings Bank Inc
50 Jackson Avenue
Syosset, NY 11791
516-677-5000

Thrift institution.
Type: Private
Ind: Savings & Loan   Grp: Financial
James J Conway, CEO   Mark Fuster, Tres   Robert R Molinaro, IS
Steven H Larson, R&D   John Talotta, VP   Glenn A MacPherson, VP

Rev: 495
Assets: 5263
Emp: 2

Long Term Credit Bank of Japan Ltd
444 S Flower
Los Angeles, CA 90071
213-629-5777

Commercial bank.
Type: Private-Sub-For
Ind: Banking   Grp: Financial
Hiromi Yokoyama, CEO

Rev: 450
Assets: 3500
Emp: 1

Longs Drug Stores Corp
141 N Civic Drive PO Box 5222
Walnut Creek, CA 94596
415-937-1170

Operator of retail drugstores.
Type: NYSE-LDG
Ind: Retail/Merch   Grp: Retail
J M Long, CEO   R Scott, VCh   W Combs, Tres
D Madsen, CFO   R A Plomgren, R&D   P E Paz, Sls
S D Roath, Mkt

Rev: 1925
Assets: 508
Emp: 11

Longview Fibre Co
PO Box 639
Longview, WA 98632
206-425-1550

Forest products company; lumber, paper, cardboard.
Type: NYSE-LFB
Ind: Paper/Forest Prd   Grp: Basic Industries
Richard P Wollenberg, CEO   George Schwartz, VCh   R G McDermott, CFO
L J Holbrook, IS   D C Stibich, Sls   Robert Wertheimer, Mkt
John Robinson, Ops   Carl Norman, VP   C R Copenhagen, PR

Rev: 657
Assets: 635
Emp: 4

Loral Corp
600 Third Avenue
New York, NY 10016
212-697-1105

Manufacturer of electronics products; defense, radar.
Type: NYSE-LOR
Ind: Electronics   Grp: High Tech
Bernard L Schwartz, CEO   Frank C Lanza, Pres   Michael P DeBlasio, CFO
Rocco R Ruggiero, IS   Lawrence Schwartz, R&D   Elizabeth H Allen, PR

Rev: 1187
Assets: 1200
Emp: 9

Organization / Address / Phone	Descriptive Information	Revenue ($ mil)	Assets ($ mil)	Emp (thous)
Lord & Taylor Inc 424 Fifth Avenue New York, NY 10018 212-391-3344	Operator of retail department stores. Type: Private-Sub Par: May Department Stores Co Ind: Retail/Merch Grp: Retail Marshall Hilsberg, CEO	Rev: NA	Assets: NA	Emp: NA
Lori Corp 384 Old Turnpike Road Southington, CT 06489 203-621-3601	Manufacturing metal products; stampings, dies. Type: ASE Ind: Manufacturing Grp: Manufacturing David Florian, CEO	Rev: 400	Assets: 250	Emp: 3
Lorillard Corp 667 Madison Avenue New York, NY 10021 212-545-2000	Manufacturer of consumer goods, cigarettes. Type: Private-Sub Par: Loews Corp Ind: Tobacco Grp: Food Processing Laurance Tisch, CEO	Rev: 2100	Assets: 1500	Emp: 5
Lorimar Telepictures Inc 475 Park Avenue S New York, NY 10016 212-686-9200	Motion picture & television program production company. Type: ASE-LT Ind: Leisure Time Grp: Consumer Service Merv Adelson, CEO J Anthony Young, CFO Carol J Henry, R&D Barbara S Brogliatti, IR	Rev: 750	Assets: 1400	Emp: 5
Los Angeles County Government 500 W Temple Street Los Angeles, CA 90012 213-974-1411	County government. Type: County Govt Ind: Local Govt Grp: Govt & Non-Prof Edmund Edelman, CEO	Rev: 12100	Assets: NM	Emp: 70
Los Angeles Times Inc Times Mirror Square Los Angeles, CA 90053 213-237-3700	Newspaper publisher. Type: Private-Sub Par: Times Mirror Co Ind: Publishing/Com Grp: Consumer Service Richard Schlosberg, CEO	Rev: NA	Assets: NA	Emp: NA
Los Angeles, City of City Hall 200 N Spring Street Los Angeles, CA 90012 213-485-3311	City government. Type: City Govt Ind: Local Govt Grp: Govt & Non-Prof Tom Bradley, CEO	Rev: 4254	Assets: NM	Emp: 42
Lotus Development Corp 55 Cambridge Parkway Cambridge, MA 02142 617-577-8500	Micro computer software development & publishing. Type: NASDAQ-LOTS Ind: Comput/Off Equip Grp: High Tech Jim Manzi, CEO John W Martin, Tres Robert Schechter, CFO David Roux, IS Edward Belove, R&D William Drummey, Sls Mark Flanagan, Mkt W Frank King, VP Stephen Nill, VP	Rev: 467	Assets: 422	Emp: 4
Louisiana Land & Exploration Co 909 Poydras Street New Orleans, LA 70112 504-566-6500	Oil & natural gas exploration & production company. Type: NYSE-LLX Ind: Energy Grp: Basic Industries H Leighton Steward, CEO E L Williamson, Chr Richard A Bachmann, CFO Rene Fowler, IS Joel Wilkinson, Mkt David E Sibley, VP Suzanne Baer, PR	Rev: 726	Assets: 1429	Emp: 2
Louisiana Pacific Corp 111 SW Fifth Avenue Portland, OR 97204 503-221-0800	Forest products company; lumber, plywood, building materials. Type: NYSE-LPX Ind: Paper/Forest Prd Grp: Basic Industries Harry A Merlo, CEO Lee C Simpson, Pres John C Hart, CFO Mel Boyer, IS William Rooney, Mkt Larry C Campbell, PR	Rev: 1799	Assets: 1796	Emp: 13
Louisiana Power & Light Co 142 Delaronde Street New Orleans, LA 70174 504-366-2345	Electric power utility company. Type: Private-Sub Par: Entergy Corp (Middle South Utilities) Ind: Utility Grp: Utilities James M Cain, CEO	Rev: 1400	Assets: 4500	Emp: 3
Louisiana State University Administrative Bldg Baton Rouge, LA 70803 504-388-1175	Major educational institution; university. Type: University Ind: University Grp: Govt & Non-Prof James H Wharton, CEO	Rev: 153	Assets: 349	Emp: 31

Organizations Listed Alphabetically

Organization / Address / Phone	Descriptive Information	Revenue / Assets / Emp ($ mil) ($ mil) (thous)		

Louisiana, State of
State Capitol
Baton Rouge, LA 70804
504-342-6600

State government.
Type: State Govt
Ind: State/Prov Govt   Grp: Govt & Non-Prof
Charles Roemer, CEO

Rev: 10882
Assets: NM
Emp: 106

Louisville Gas & Electric Co
311 W Chestnut Street
Louisville, KY 40232
502-566-4011

Electric & gas utility.
Type: NYSE
Ind: Utility   Grp: Utilities
Robert L Royer, CEO   William H Hancock, VCh   Lee Fowler, CFO
John Hart, R&D   Fred Wright, Ops   Charles Markel, VP
C Gregory Uligan, VP   Harold Wentworth, VP   William Cummings, VP

Rev: 660
Assets: 1763
Emp: 5

Louisville, City of
City Hall
Louisville, KY 40202
502-587-3061

City government.
Type: City Govt
Ind: Local Govt   Grp: Govt & Non-Prof
Jerry Abramson, CEO

Rev: 250
Assets: NM
Emp: 5

Lowe's Companies Inc
State Highway 268 E
North Wilkesboro, NC 28659
919-651-4000

Operator of retail home improvement & hardware stores.
Type: NYSE-LOW
Ind: Retail/Merch   Grp: Retail
Robert L Strickland, CEO   Leonard Herring, Chr   Harry B Underwood II, CFO
Frank Dooley, IS   Greg Bridgeford, R&D   Wendell R Emerine, Mkt
Robert Schwartz, VP   Jack Shewmaker, VP   Robert Strickland, VP
W Cliff Oxford, PR

Rev: 2517
Assets: 1086
Emp: 15

Loyola University of Chicago
820 N Michigan Avenue
Chicago, IL 60611
312-670-3000

Major educational institution; university.
Type: University
Ind: University   Grp: Govt & Non-Prof
Raymond C Baumhart, CEO

Rev: 194
Assets: 189
Emp: 16

LPL Investment Group
358 Hall Avenue
Wallingford, CT 06492
203-265-8600

Manufacturer of electrical connectors, parts.
Type: NASDAQ-LPLI
Ind: Electronics   Grp: High Tech
L J DeGeorge, CEO

Rev: 600
Assets: 708
Emp: 5

LSB Industries Inc
16 S Pennsylvania Avenue
Oklahoma City, OK 73101
405-235-4546

Manufacturer of chemicals & ball bearings.
Type: ASE
Ind: Chemicals   Grp: Basic Industries
Jack Golsen, CEO

Rev: 250
Assets: 200
Emp: 2

LSI Logic Corp
1551 McCarthy Blvd
Milpitas, CA 95035
408-433-8000

Manufacturer of electronic logic boards, chips.
Type: NASDAQ
Ind: Electronics   Grp: High Tech
Wilfred J Corrigan, CEO   George D Wells, Pres   D Scott Mercer, CFO
James S Koford, IS   Conrad Dell'Oca, R&D   Robert M Skinner, Sls
Robert N Blair, Mkt   Lewis C Wallbridge, VP   Joseph M Zelayeta, VP
Norman Chanoski, VP   Brian Halla, VP

Rev: 379
Assets: 787
Emp: 3

LTV Corp
2001 Ross Avenue
Dallas, TX 75201
214-979-7711

Integrated steel producer & aerospace company.
Type: NYSE
Ind: Steel   Grp: Basic Industries
Raymond A Hay, CEO   David H Hoag, Pres   G Emmett Smith, VCh
K C Caldabaugh, Tres   James F Powers, CFO   Robert Parker, R&D
Billie Smith, Ops   Charles M Palmer, IR   Julian Scheer, PR

Rev: 7325
Assets: 6163
Emp: 39

LTV Steel Co
25 W Prospect Street
Cleveland, OH 44115
216-622-5000

Producer & supplier of steel products
Type: Private-Sub   Par: LTV Corp
Ind: Steel   Grp: Basic Industries
David Hoag, CEO

Rev: 1000
Assets: NA
Emp: 10

Lubrizol Corp
29400 Lakeland Blvd
Wicklife, OH 44092
216-943-4200

Manufacturer of special purpose lubricants.
Type: NYSE-LZ
Ind: Chemicals   Grp: Basic Industries
L E Coleman, CEO   W G Bares, Pres   Phillip Krug, VCh
William T Beargie, CFO   Giorgio Sorani, IS   George R Hill, R&D
William D Manning, Mkt   J I Rue, VP   J F Klemens, PR

Rev: 1126
Assets: 971
Emp: 5

Organizations Listed Alphabetically

Organization / Address / Phone	Descriptive Information	Revenue / ($ mil)	Assets / ($ mil)	Emp (thous)
Luby's Cafeterias Inc 2211 NE Loop 410 San Antonio, TX 78265 512-654-9000	Operator of restaurants & cafeterias. Type: NYSE-LUB Ind: Food/Lodging Grp: Consumer Service John B Lahourcade, CEO	Rev: Assets: Emp:		254 185 5
Lucky Goldstar Group 1050 Wall Street Lindhusrt, NJ 07071 201-460-8010	Manufacturer of consumer electronic equipment; US hdqtrs. Type: Private-Sub-For Ind: Electronics Grp: High Tech Y J Shim, CEO	Rev: Assets: Emp:		1650 NA 2
Lucky Stores Inc 6300 Clark Avenue Dublin, OH 44568 415-833-6000	Retail food supermarkets. Type: NYSE Ind: Retail/Food Grp: Retail John M Lillie, CEO Edgar H Grubb, CFO R Lee Paulson, IS Jack A Hoover, Mkt Leon Roush, VP	Rev: Assets: Emp:		7000 1750 80
Lukens Inc 50 S First Avenue Coatesville, PA 19320 215-383-2000	Manufacturer of steel plates & safety products. Type: NYSE-LUC Ind: Steel Grp: Basic Industries W R Wilson, CEO Frederick Myers, VCh John Bartholdson, CFO James Greenlaw, IS John Bucher, R&D John J King Jr, Sls John Campo, Mkt William Sprague, VP John C Van Roden, VP Charles Hossack, IR Jean Botkin, PR	Rev: Assets: Emp:		605 353 4
Lumbermens Merchandising Inc 137 W Wayne Avenue Wayne, PA 19807 215-293-7000	Operator of retail lumber & home improvement stores. Type: Private Ind: Retail/Merch Grp: Retail Joseph A Hardy, CEO	Rev: Assets: Emp:		1000 NA 4
Lundrigans Group Ltd Riverside Drive Corner Brook, NF A2H6J5 Can 709-637-1200	Engineering & contruction company. Type: Private Ind: Real Estate/Bldg Grp: Business Service A Lundrigan, CEO	Rev: Assets: Emp:		289 118 3
Luria, L & Son Inc 5770 Miami Lakes Drive Hialeah, FL 33014 305-557-9000	Retail catalog store operator. Type: ASE-LUR Ind: Retail/Merch Grp: Retail Leonard Luria, CEO	Rev: Assets: Emp:		250 100 2
Lusk Co 17550 Gillette Irvine, CA 92713 714-261-5999	Real estate development company. Type: Private Ind: Real Estate/Bldg Grp: Business Service John D Lusk, CEO	Rev: Assets: Emp:		400 NA 1
Lutheran Brotherhood 625 Fourth Avenue S Minneapolis, MN 55415 612-340-7000	Life insurance company. Type: Private Ind: Insurance Grp: Insurance Robert P Gandrud, CEO David Larson, VCh Stanley C Townsend, Tres Luther Forde, CFO Edward Lindell, Sls Rolf Bjelland, Mkt Mitchell Felchle, VP Donald Hedding, VP Harlan Hogsven, VP Richard Lund, VP Donald Nelson, VP	Rev: Assets: Emp:		1142 3007 1
LVI Group Inc 345 Hudson Street New York, NY 10014 212-337-6600	General consulting company. Type: NYSE-LVI Ind: Consulting Grp: Business Service Howard Z Lazar, CEO	Rev: Assets: Emp:		474 220 2
Lykes Brothers Inc 215 E Madison Street Tampa, FL 33601 813-223-3981	Food processing, insurance services. Type: Private Ind: Food Processing Grp: Food Processing Charles P Lykes, CEO	Rev: Assets: Emp:		750 NA 5
Lykes Brothers Steamship Co Inc 300 Poydras Street New Orleans, LA 70130 504-523-6611	Operator of water transport; ships, barges. Type: Private Ind: Transport Grp: Business Service W J Amoss, CEO	Rev: Assets: Emp:		550 NA 2

Organizations Listed Alphabetically

Organization / Address / Phone	Descriptive Information	Revenue / Assets / Emp ($ mil) ($ mil) (thous)		

Lyon, William Co Inc
19 Corporated Plaza
Newport Beach, CA 92660
714-833-3600

Home building company.
Type: Private
Ind: Real Estate/Bldg   Grp: Business Service
William Lyon, CEO

Rev: 750
Assets: NA
Emp: 1

Lyondell Petrochemical Corp
1221 McKinney Avenue
Houston, TX 77010
713-652-7200

Manufacturer of petrochemicals.
Type: NYSE-LYO
Ind: Chemicals   Grp: Basic Industries
B G Gower, CEO

Rev: 4696
Assets: 913
Emp: 10

Lyphomed Inc
10401 W Touhy Avenue
Rosemont, IL 60018
312-390-6500

Manufacturer of pharmaceuticals.
Type: NASDAQ-LMED
Ind: Drugs   Grp: Consumer Service
John N Kapoor, CEO

Rev: 128
Assets: 286
Emp: 1

M/A Com Inc
7 New England Executive Park
Burlington, MA 01803
617-272-9600

Manufacturer of microwave components; defense, commercial.
Type: NYSE-MAI
Ind: Telecom   Grp: High Tech
Thomas F Burke, CEO   Richard Hale, Pres   Kenneth Carr, VCh
M Joel Kosheff, CFO   Dr Frank Brand, R&D   James F Bunker, Mkt
Harold C Wells, VP   Donald Stelzer, VP   Michael Ferrantino, VP
Gerald DiPiazza, VP   Joseph C Bothwell Jr, PR

Rev: 424
Assets: 483
Emp: 6

Mabon, Nugent & Co
115 Broadway
New York, NY 10006
212-732-2820

Investment firm; securities trading.
Type: Private
Ind: Securities   Grp: Financial
Steven Erlick, CEO

Rev: 220
Assets: 2200
Emp: 1

MacAndrews & Forbes Inc
36 E 63rd Street
New York, NY 10021
212-688-9000

Manufacturer of personal care products; cosmetics.
Type: Private
Ind: Food Processing   Grp: Food Processing
Ronald O Perelman, CEO

Rev: 2500
Assets: NA
Emp: 25

Mack Trucks Inc
2100 Mack Blvd
Allentown, PA 18103
215-439-3011

Manufacturer of commercial tractor trailers, trucks.
Type: NASDAQ-MACK
Ind: Automotive   Grp: Manufacturing
John Curcio, CEO   Walter C Meck, CFO   William F Mannion, IS
Robert Zalokar, R&D   Paul C Ritter, Sls   Joseph P Rossetti, Mkt
Michael D Tabris, PR

Rev: 2000
Assets: 1400
Emp: 10

MacLean Hunter Ltd
777 Bay Street
Toronto, ON M5W1A7 Can
416-596-5000

Publisher of magazines, business information.
Type: TOR
Ind: Publishing/Com   Grp: Consumer Service
Donald G Campbell, CEO   Ronald Osborne, Chr   Jean R Douville, VCh
J Robert Furse, CFO   Mathew Fyfe, VP   Ernest Cozens, VP
Morris Slemko, VP

Rev: 1107
Assets: 1356
Emp: 11

MacMillan Bloedel Ltd
1075 W Georgia Street
Vancouver, BC V6E3R9 Can
604-661-8000

Forest products company; paper, building materials.
Type: TOR
Ind: Paper/Forest Prd   Grp: Basic Industries
A H Zimmerman, CEO   R V Smith, Chr   C C Knudson, Pres
D L McLauchlin, VCh   G M Fergason, CFO   O L Forgacs, R&D
R Wiewel, Mkt   J St Ross, Ops   J Bauer, VP
R Findlay, VP   J Howard, VP

Rev: 2783
Assets: 2021
Emp: 15

Macmillan Inc
866 Third Avenue
New York, NY 10022
212-702-2000

Publishing company.
Type: Private-Sub-For
Ind: Publishing/Com   Grp: Consumer Service
Edward P Evans, CEO   William F Reilly, Pres   Beverly Shell, VCh
Charles G McCurdy, CFO   Anthony Pizzelanti, IS   William Houghton, VP
Harry A Mcquillen, VP   David R Jackson, PR

Rev: 956
Assets: 937
Emp: 10

Macy, R H & Co Inc
151 W 34th Street
New York, NY 10001
212-560-3600

Operator of retail department stores.
Type: Private
Ind: Retail/Merch   Grp: Retail
Edward S Finkelstein, CEO   Mark S Handler, Pres   Donald Eugene, CFO
Leonard Bellezza, IS   Elias S Gottlieb, R&D   Sandie Treandly, Mkt
Patricia Barry, PR

Rev: 5800
Assets: NA
Emp: 70

Organization / Address / Phone	Descriptive Information	Revenue ($ mil)	Assets ($ mil)	Emp (thous)
Madison Gas & Electric Co 133 S Blair Street Madison, WI 53703 608-252-7000	Electric & gas utility company. Type: NASDAQ-MDSN Ind: Utility Grp: Utilities Donald Helfrecht, CEO	Rev: 250	Assets: 300	Emp: 1
Magic Chef Co 740 King Edward Avenue Cleveland, TN 37311 615-472-3371	Manufacturer of small appliances. Type: Private-Sub Par: Maytag Co Ind: Appliances/Furn Grp: Manufacturing Wayne Cregan, CEO	Rev: NA	Assets: NA	Emp: NA
Magma Copper Co Highway 76 San Manuel, AZ 85631 602-385-3100	Mining & refining company; copper. Type: NASDAQ-MGCP Ind: Metals/Mining Grp: Basic Industries Donald Donahue, CEO	Rev: 500	Assets: 350	Emp: 5
Magna International Inc 36 Apple Creek Blvd Markham, ON L3R 4Y4 Can 416-477-7766	Manufacturer of automotive parts. Type: TOR Ind: Automotive Grp: Manufacturing Frank Stronach, CEO	Rev: 983	Assets: 1091	Emp: 12
Magnetek Inc 11111 Santa Monica Blvd Los Angeles, CA 90025 213-473-6681	Manufacturer of electronic equipment. Type: Private Ind: Manufacturing Grp: Manufacturing Frank Perna, CEO Andrew G Galef, Chr David P Reiland, CFO John R Scherzi, Mkt Robert W Murray, IR	Rev: 1000	Assets: NA	Emp: 10
MAI Basic Four Inc 14101 Myford Road Tustin, CA 92680 714-731-5100	Manufacturer & service company, computers. Type: NYSE-MBF Ind: Comput/Off Equip Grp: High Tech Bennett S LeBow, CEO	Rev: 425	Assets: 375	Emp: 3
Maine, State of State House Augusta, ME 04333 207-289-1110	State government. Type: State Govt Ind: State/Prov Govt Grp: Govt & Non-Prof John R McKernan, CEO	Rev: 2648	Assets: NM	Emp: 25
Malone & Hyde Inc 3030 Poplar Avenue Memphis, TN 38101 901-325-4200	Operator of retail food supermarkets. Type: Private Ind: Retail/Food Grp: Retail J P Jones, CEO	Rev: 4400	Assets: NA	Emp: 21
MAN North America Corp 333 Cedar Avenue Middlesex, NJ 08846 201-469-6600	Manufacturer & importer of industrial machinery; US hdqtrs. Type: Private-Sub-For Ind: Machinery Grp: Manufacturing Ed Padilla, CEO	Rev: 880	Assets: NA	Emp: 3
Management Science America Inc 3445 Peachtree Road Atlanta, GA 30326 404-239-2000	Manufacturer of computer software; mainframe, mini, micro. Type: NASDAQ-MSAI Ind: Comput/Off Equip Grp: High Tech John Imlay, CEO	Rev: 300	Assets: 200	Emp: 3
Manitoba Hydro Electric Board Ltd 820 Taylor Avenue Winnipeg, MB R3C2P4 Can 204-474-3311	Electric power utility company. Type: Prov Govt Ind: Utility Grp: Utilities M Eliesen, CEO	Rev: 485	Assets: 2754	Emp: 4
Manitoba Pool Elevators Ltd 220 Portage Avenue Winnipeg, MB R3C3K7 Can 204-947-1171	Agricultural cooperative; wheat. Type: Govt Corp Ind: Food Processing Grp: Food Processing G S Arason, CEO K J McTaggert, Pres K C Norell, VCh W Sokolowski, CFO B Tuan, IS T D Winters, Sls A Sholudko, Mkt D W Hunter, Ops J Williamson, VP	Rev: 595	Assets: 82	Emp: 1
Manitoba Telephone System Ltd 489 Empress Street Winnipeg, MB R3G2G9 Can 204-947-4111	Telephone utility company. Type: Prov Govt Ind: Telecom Grp: High Tech Jean Edmonds, CEO	Rev: 342	Assets: 837	Emp: 5

Organizations Listed Alphabetically

Organization / Address / Phone	Descriptive Information	Revenue / ($ mil)	Assets / ($ mil)	Emp (thous)

Mannesmann USA Inc
450 Park Avenue
New York, NY 10022
212-702-9420

Manufacturer of industrial machinery.
Type: Private-Sub-For
Ind: Machinery Grp: Manufacturing
Peter Wittgenstein, CEO

Rev: 880
Assets: NA
Emp: 3

Manor Care Inc
10750 Columbia Pike
Silver Spring, MD 20901
301-681-9400

Operator of healthcare nursing centers & hotels.
Type: NYSE-MNR
Ind: Health Care Grp: Consumer Service
Steward Bainum, CEO C Arnold Ronschler, Pres Stewart Bainum, VCh
James A MacCutcheon, CFO Weldon Humphries, VP Raymond G Murphy, VP

Rev: 534
Assets: 797
Emp: 19

Manpower Inc
5301 N Ironwood Place
Milwaukee, WI 53217
608-755-7000

Holding company, personel agency, temporary help.
Type: Private-Sub-For
Ind: Manufacturing Grp: Manufacturing
Mitchell S Fromstein, CEO

Rev: 1500
Assets: 500
Emp: 6

Manufacturers & Traders Trust Co
One M & T Plaza
Buffalo, NY 14240
716-842-4200

Commercial bank.
Type: OTC
Ind: Banking Grp: Financial
R G Wilmers, CEO

Rev: 300
Assets: 3100
Emp: 2

Manufacturers Hanover Corp
270 Park Avenue
New York, NY 10017
212-286-6000

International commercial bank.
Type: NYSE-MHC
Ind: Banking Grp: Financial
John F McGillicuddy, CEO Edward Farley, Pres Edward Miller, VCh
Peter J Tobin, CFO Richard J Matteis, IS Charles H McCabe, Mkt
Martin Zuckerman, VP Denis O'Leary, VP Ernest Stein, VP
Joseph Pollicino, VP Joseph Carroll, VP Thomas Abbate, VP
John J Stefans, PR

Rev: 8545
Assets: 66710
Emp: 30

Manufacturers Life Insurance Co Canada
200 Bloor Street E
Toronto, ON M4W1E5 Can
416-926-0100

Life insurance company.
Type: Private
Ind: Insurance Grp: Insurance
Thomas A DiGiacomo, CEO Donald W Kendall, Tres Robert M Smithen, CFO
Jalynn H Bennett, R&D George E Neal, VP John E Clark, VP
L Elvon Harris, VP Rose M Patten, VP Joseph J Pietroski, VP
Diane M Schwartz, VP

Rev: 5120
Assets: 20305
Emp: 6

Manufacturers National of Detroit Inc
Manufacturers Bank Tower Renaissance Ctr
Detroit, MI 48243
313-222-4000

Commercial bank.
Type: NASDAQ-MNTL
Ind: Banking Grp: Financial
Dean E Richardson, CEO Kenneth Aird, VCh Paul Martzowka, CFO
Alastair Carlyle, IS Robert Cadotte, VP Michael T Monahan, VP
Frank Couzens, VP Paul Hussey, VP Robert Herdoiza, VP
Robert Hughes, VP Michael T Maurer, IR Kathy Pitten, PR

Rev: 924
Assets: 9311
Emp: 6

Manville Corp
Ken Caryl Ranch PO Box 5108
Denver, CO 80217
303-978-2000

Manufacturer of fiber glass & forest products.
Type: NYSE
Ind: Building Mat Grp: Basic Industries
George C Dillon, CEO W Thomas Stephens, Chr John D C Roach, VCh
C Van Draper, Tres S Rollie Heath Jr, CFO Robert Cole, IS
William Sells, R&D William Sherman, Mkt Alfred B Gough, VP
Robert Boardman, VP Donald Fergason, VP Frank McCauley, VP
David Pullen, PR

Rev: 2062
Assets: 2393
Emp: 20

Manville Forest Products Co
1000 Jonesboro Highway
West Monroe, LA 71291
318-362-2000

Manufacturer of forest products.
Type: Private-Sub Par: Manville Corp
Ind: Paper/Forest Prd Grp: Basic Industries
Thomas Stevens, CEO

Rev: NA
Assets: NA
Emp: NA

MAPCO Coal Inc
1717 S Boulder
Tulsa, OK 74101
918-592-7237

Producer & distributor of metallurgical coal.
Type: Private-Sub Par: Mapco Inc
Ind: Metals/Mining Grp: Basic Industries
Joseph Craft, CEO

Rev: NA
Assets: NA
Emp: NA

Organizations Listed Alphabetically

Organization / Address / Phone	Descriptive Information	Revenue / Assets / Emp ($ mil) ($ mil) (thous)		

Mapco Inc
PO Box 645
Tulsa, OK 74101
918-581-1800

Diversified energy company; coal, oil & natural gas.
Type: NYSE
Ind: Energy Grp: Basic Industries
James E Barnes, CEO Robert M Howe, Pres David Bowman, VCh
F S Dickerson III, CFO Philip Baxter, IS Dan Cogman, Ops
Austin Greene, VP James Davis, VP S Fred Issacs, VP
Charles McConnell, VP W Jeffrey Hart, VP Terri Wilson, IR
David S Leslie, PR

Rev: 1802
Assets: 1376
Emp: 5

Maple Leaf Mills Ltd
2300 Yonge Street
Toronto, ON M4P2X5 Can
416-484-7400

Manufacturer of flour, cake mixes.
Type: Private-Sub-For
Ind: Food Processing Grp: Food Processing
Robert DeMone, CEO

Rev: 723
Assets: 340
Emp: 4

Marathon Oil Co
539 S Main Street
Findlay, OH 45840
419-422-2121

Oil exploration, drilling, refining & marketing company.
Type: Private-Sub Par: USX Corp
Ind: Energy Grp: Basic Industries
Victor Beghini, CEO

Rev: NA
Assets: NA
Emp: NA

Marathon Realty Co
123 Fronto Street W
Toronto, ON M5J2M2 Can
416-864-1960

Real estate, development & property management company.
Type: Private-Sub Par: Canadian Pacific Ltd
Ind: Real Estate/Bldg Grp: Business Service
D King, CEO

Rev: 298
Assets: 1700
Emp: 1

Marcade Group Inc
275 Madison Avenue
New York, NY 10016
212-944-0877

Manufacturer of women's apparel.
Type: NYSE-MAR
Ind: Apparel/Textiles Grp: Consumer Prd
Robert Lifton, CEO

Rev: 287
Assets: 200
Emp: 2

Maricopa County Government
111 S Third Avenue
Phoenix, AZ 85003
602-262-3518

County government.
Type: County Govt
Ind: Local Govt Grp: Govt & Non-Prof
Tom Freestone, CEO

Rev: 1300
Assets: NM
Emp: 11

Marine Midland Banks Inc
One Marine Center
Buffalo, NY 14240
716-843-2424

Commercial bank.
Type: NYSE-MM
Ind: Banking Grp: Financial
Northrup Knox, CEO Geoffrey A Thompson, Chr Howard Phanstiel, CFO
Ronald Lawrence, IS Roy Skoba, Mkt Barry Koling, IR
Judith Nolan, PR

Rev: 2500
Assets: 25000
Emp: 15

Marion Labratories Inc
9300 Ward Parkway
Kansas City, MO 64114
816-966-5000

Manufacturer of health care products.
Type: NYSE-MCK
Ind: Drugs Grp: Consumer Service
Ewing M Kauffman, CEO Fred W Lyons Jr, Chr James E McGraw, Pres
Michael E Herman, CFO N Les Clark, IS Lowell Miller, R&D
Harley Tennison, Mkt D Brant Cotterman, Ops Lloyd Hanahan, VP
William Hoskins, VP Larry Wheeler, PR

Rev: 752
Assets: 554
Emp: 4

Maritime Life Assurance Co
2701 Dutch Village Road
Halifax, NS B3J2X5 Can
902-453-4300

Life insurance company.
Type: Private-Sub-For
Ind: Insurance Grp: Insurance
J Dixon Crawford, CEO

Rev: 468
Assets: 1518
Emp: 1

Maritime Telephone & Telegraph Ltd
1505 Barrington Street
Halifax, NS B3J2W3 Can
902-421-4311

Telephone utility company.
Type: TOR-MTT
Ind: Telecom Grp: High Tech
Donald C R Sobey, CEO

Rev: 327
Assets: 785
Emp: 4

Maritz Inc
1375 N Highway Drive
Fenton, MO 63026
314-827-4000

Marketing & business services.
Type: Private
Ind: Retail/Merch Grp: Retail
William E Maritz, CEO

Rev: 1000
Assets: NA
Emp: 5

Mark IV Industries Inc
1 Towne Center 501 J J Audubon Pkwy
Williamsville, NY 14231
716-689-4972

Manufacturer of electronic products; defense, consumer.
Type: NYSE-IV
Ind: Electronics Grp: High Tech
Sal H Alfiero, CEO

Rev: 742
Assets: 800
Emp: 6

Organizations Listed Alphabetically

Organization / Address / Phone	Descriptive Information	Revenue / ($ mil)	Assets / ($ mil)	Emp (thous)
Marley Co Inc 1900 Johnson Drive Mission Woods, KS 66205 913-362-5440	Diversified manufacturing company. Type: Private Ind: Business Service Grp: Business Service Robert J Dineen, CEO	Rev: Assets: Emp:	500 NA 5	
Marmon Group Inc 39 S LaSalle Street Chicago, IL 60603 312-372-9500	Diversified investment company including hotels. Type: Private Ind: Food/Lodging Grp: Consumer Service Robert A Pritzker, CEO	Rev: Assets: Emp:	3500 NA 25	
Marriott Corp Marriott Drive Washington, DC 20058 301-897-9000	Worldwide operator of hotels. Type: NYSE-MHS Ind: Food/Lodging Grp: Consumer Service J W Marriott Jr, CEO Richard E Marriott, VCh William Shaw, CFO James R Yoakum, IS Donald Washburn, R&D Todd Clist, Mkt Daniel Altobello, Ops A Thomas Curren, VP Clifford Ehrlich, VP R Rankin, VP Sterling Colton, VP R A Rankin Jr, PR	Rev: Assets: Emp:	7370 5981 230	
Mars Inc 6885 Elm Street McLean, VA 22101 703-821-4900	Manufacturer of candy products & pet foods. Type: Private Ind: Food Processing Grp: Food Processing Forrest Mars Jr, CEO	Rev: Assets: Emp:	8000 NA 20	
Marsh & McLennan Companies Inc 1221 Avenue of the Americas New York, NY 10020 212-997-2000	Financial services company. Type: NYSE-MMC Ind: Non-Bank Fin Grp: Financial Frank J Tasco, CEO A J C Smith, Pres Robert Newhouse, VCh Frank Borelli, CFO Arthur C Neilson, VP John Regan, VP Robert Haack, VP Edward Cole, VP Gregory Van Gundy, VP	Rev: Assets: Emp:	2272 1830 23	
Marsh Supermarkets Inc 501 Depot Street Yorktown, IN 473961 317-759-8101	Operator of retail food supermarkets. Type: NASDAQ-MARS Ind: Retail/Food Grp: Retail William Givens, CEO	Rev: Assets: Emp:	900 600 9	
Marshall & Isley Corp 770 N Water Street Milwaukee, WI 53202 414-765-7801	Commercial bank. Type: NASDAQ-MRIS Ind: Banking Grp: Financial J A Puelicher, CEO Dennis J Kuester, Chr D J Kuester, Pres J B Wigdale, VCh Gordon Gunnlaugsson, CFO Robert Seidell, IS M J Revanke, VP Hal Reiter, PR	Rev: Assets: Emp:	677 6775 3	
Marshall Industries Inc 9674 Telstar Avenue El Monte, CA 91731 818-459-5500	Manufacturer of semiconductors, tools, electronic parts. Type: NYSE-MI Ind: Electronics Grp: High Tech Gordon Marshall, CEO	Rev: Assets: Emp:	400 200 2	
Marshall's Inc 30 Harvard Mill Square Wakefield, MA 01880 508-721-3300	Operator of retail discount department stores. Type: Private-Sub Par: Melville Corp Ind: Retail/Merch Grp: Retail Frank Arnone, CEO	Rev: Assets: Emp:	NA NA NA	
Martin Marietta Corp 6801 Rockledge Drive Bethesda, MD 20817 301-897-6000	Manufacturer of electronics & aerospace equipment. Type: NYSE-ML Ind: Aerospace Grp: High Tech Norman R Augustine, CEO Caleb B Hurtt, Pres Robert W Powell, Tres Marcus C Bennett, CFO Dan A Peterson, IS David C Dressler, VP Robert J Polutchko, VP Peter B Teets, VP A Thomas Young, VP Richard Adamson, VP William B Harwood, PR	Rev: Assets: Emp:	5727 3319 80	
Martin Marietta Electronics & Missiles PO Box 583 Orlando, FL 32855 305-356-2000	Manufacturer of missiles & electronic systems. Type: Private-Sub Par: Martin Marietta Corp Ind: Aerospace Grp: High Tech Thomas Young, CEO	Rev: Assets: Emp:	NA NA NA	

Organizations Listed Alphabetically

Organization / Address / Phone	Descriptive Information	Revenue / ($ mil)	Assets / ($ mil)	Emp (thous)
Martin Marietta Energy Systems Inc 800 Oak Ridge Turnpike Oak Ridge, TN 37831 615-574-1000	Manufacturer of energy systems. Type: Private-Sub Par: Martin Marietta Corp Ind: Manufacturing Grp: Manufacturing Clyde Hopkins, CEO	Rev: Assets: Emp:	NA NA NA	
Martin Marietta Information Systems Inc 6801 Rockledge Drive Bethesda, MD 20817 301-897-6000	Computer information systems. Type: Private-Sub Par: Martin Marietta Corp Ind: Comput/Off Equip Grp: High Tech Robert Polutchko, CEO	Rev: Assets: Emp:	NA NA NA	
Marubeni Canada Ltd 2 First Canadian Place Toronto, ON M5X1E3 Can 416-368-1171	Grain wholesale & storage company. Type: TOR Ind: Food Processing Grp: Food Processing Y Fukuda, CEO	Rev: Assets: Emp:	1162 425 1	
Marubeni Trading Co USA 200 Park Avenue New York, NY 10166 212-599-3700	International trading company; US headquarters. Type: Private-Sub-For Ind: Manufacturing Grp: Manufacturing not available, CEO	Rev: Assets: Emp:	2750 NA 4	
Maryland, State of State House Annapolis, MD 21404 301-269-6200	State government. Type: State Govt Ind: State/Prov Govt Grp: Govt & Non-Prof William Donald Schaefer, CEO	Rev: Assets: Emp:	11308 NM 94	
Masco Corp 21001 Van Born Road Taylor, MI 48180 313-274-7400	Manufacturer of plumbing hardware. Type: NYSE-MAS Ind: Building Mat Grp: Basic Industries Richard A Manoogian, CEO John F Ullrich, R&D John C Nicholls Jr, PR	Rev: Assets: Emp:	2439 2999 15	
Masco Industries Inc 21001 Van Born Road Taylor, MI 48180 313-274-7405	Manufacturer of plumbing equipment & supplies. Type: NASDAQ-MASX Ind: Automotive Grp: Manufacturing Richard A Manoogian, CEO Irwin H Billig, Pres Timothy Wadhams, Tres James J Sigouin, CFO Lee M Gardner, Mkt Hans R Beisch, VP James W Hook, VP George Manoogian, VP Robert Swope, VP John C Nicholls Jr, PR	Rev: Assets: Emp:	1652 2121 10	
Mason McDuffie Real Estate Inc 25 Orinda Way Orinda, CA 94563 415-254-5640	Operator of retail real estate offices & property managment. Type: Private Ind: Real Estate/Bldg Grp: Business Service Bob Birkell, CEO	Rev: Assets: Emp:	550 NA 1	
Massachusetts Financial Services Inc 500 Boyleston Street Boston, MA 02116 617-954-5000	Investment company; mutual & pension fund management. Type: Private Ind: Non-Bank Fin Grp: Financial Richard Baily, CEO	Rev: Assets: Emp:	550 24200 2	
Massachusetts Inst of Technology 77 Massachusetts Avenue Cambridge, MA 02139 617-253-1000	Major educational institution; university. Type: University Ind: University Grp: Govt & Non-Prof Paul E Gray, CEO	Rev: Assets: Emp:	556 660 12	
Massachusetts Mutual Life Insurance Comp 1295 State Street Springfield, MA 01111 413-788-8411	Life & casualty insurance company. Type: Private Ind: Insurance Grp: Insurance Thomas B Wheeler, CEO James L Wertheimer, CFO John J Pajak, IS James C McKeon PhD, R&D John J Pajak, VP James E Miller, VP Kenneth L Fry, VP Richard Dooley, VP Warren R Wise, VP Paul D Adornato, VP Barry Gottehrer, IR Joseph Mondy, PR	Rev: Assets: Emp:	4632 22589 9	
Massachusetts, State of State House Boston, MA 02133 617-727-2121	State government. Type: State Govt Ind: State/Prov Govt Grp: Govt & Non-Prof Michael S Dukakis, CEO	Rev: Assets: Emp:	15502 NM 94	

Organizations Listed Alphabetically

Organization / Address / Phone	Descriptive Information	Revenue / ($ mil)	Assets / ($ mil)	Emp (thous)
Massey, A T Coal Co Four N Fourth Street Richmond, VA 23219 804-788-1800	Coal mining & processing company. Type: Private-Sub Par: Flour Corp Ind: Metals/Mining Grp: Basic Industries Morgan Massey, CEO	Rev: NA Assets: NA Emp: NA		
Matsushita Electric of Canada Ltd 5770 Ambler Drive Mississauga, ON L4W2T2 Can 416-624-5010	International manufacturer of electronic devices. Type: Private-Sub-For Ind: Electronics Grp: High Tech Allen Higashi, CEO	Rev: 341 Assets: 88 Emp: 1		
Matsushita Electric USA Inc 1 Panasonic Way Secaucus, NJ 07094 201-348-7100	Manufacturer & importer of electronic equipment; US hdqtrs. Type: Private-Sub-For Ind: Electronics Grp: High Tech Akva Imura, CEO	Rev: 1650 Assets: NA Emp: 3		
Mattel Inc 5150 Rosecrans Avenue Hawthorne, CA 90250 213-978-5150	Toy manufacturing company. Type: NYSE Ind: Leisure Time Grp: Consumer Service John W Amerman, CEO Robert Sansone, Pres Lindsey F Williams, VCh James Eskridge, CFO Gary Schwandner, R&D Jill Barad, Mkt Richard W Carslow, Ops Francesca Luzuriago, VP Timothy Reames, VP Michael McCafferty, VP Bill Semos, IR Glenn Bozarth, PR	Rev: 990 Assets: 693 Emp: 20		
Maxicare Health Plans Inc 5200 W Century Blvd Los Angeles, CA 90045 213-568-9000	Heathcare, medical insurance plans. Type: NYSE Ind: Health Care Grp: Consumer Service Fred W Wasserman, CEO Pamela K Anderson, Pres Randall S Anderson, VCh Samuel L Westover, CFO Horace Clark, IS David M Hallis, Mkt Karl Wichser, VP Terry Bayer, VP William Carr, VP David Kibbe, VP David Hallis, VP Stephen Casey, VP	Rev: 1839 Assets: 992 Emp: 15		
Maxtor Corp 211 River Oaks Parkway San Jose, CA 95134 408-942-1700	Manufacturer of magnetic & optical computer data storage. Type: OTC Ind: Comput/Off Equip Grp: High Tech James M McCoy, CEO	Rev: 271 Assets: 277 Emp: 3		
Maxus Energy Corp 717 N Harwood Street Dallas, TX 75201 214-953-2000	Independent producer of oil & natural gas. Type: NYSE-MXS Ind: Energy Grp: Basic Industries Charles L Blackburn, CEO Darrell Black, VCh Don Mielke, CFO Jack Seifrick, IS Dr Martin Schuepbach, R&D Dick Sharples, Mkt Noel Rietman, Ops Donald C Mielke, VP Steven Crowell, VP Ginger Shearburn, PR	Rev: 601 Assets: 1720 Emp: 2		
Maxxam Inc 10880 Wilshire Blvd Los Angeles, CA 90024 213-474-6264	Real estate development & forest products company. Type: ASE-MCO Ind: Real Estate/Bldg Grp: Business Service Charles E Hurwitz, CEO	Rev: 519 Assets: 250 Emp: 1		
May Department Stores Co 611 Olive Street St Louis, MO 63101 314-342-6300	Retail department stores. Type: NYSE-MA Ind: Retail/Merch Grp: Retail David C Farrell, CEO Thomas A Hays, Pres Lawrence Honig, VCh Jerome T Loeb, CFO James Bodemuller, IS Laurence Hellman, R&D Louis Garr, VP R Dean Wolfe, VP James Abrams, IR Frank Williams Jr, PR	Rev: 11525 Assets: 8144 Emp: 80		
Mayer, Oscar Foods Corp 910 Mayer Avenue Madison, WI 53704 608-241-3311	Manufacturer of food products; hot dogs, cold cuts. Type: Private-Sub Par: Philip Morris Companies Inc Ind: Food Processing Grp: Food Processing James McVey, CEO	Rev: NA Assets: NA Emp: NA		
Mayfair Super Markets Inc 681 Newark Avenue Elizabethtown, NJ 07208 201-352-6400	Operator of retail supermarkets. Type: NASDAQ-MYFR Ind: Retail/Food Grp: Retail Stanley Kaufelt, CEO	Rev: 600 Assets: 250 Emp: 5		

Organizations Listed Alphabetically

Organization / Address / Phone	Descriptive Information	Revenue / Assets / Emp

Organization / Address / Phone	Descriptive Information	Revenue ($ mil)	Assets ($ mil)	Emp (thous)
Mayflower Group Inc 9998 N Michigan Road Carmel, IN 46032 317-875-1000	Truck transport, commercial movers. Type: Private Ind: Transport Grp: Business Service John B Smith, CEO John B Smith, Chr Patrick F Carr, CFO Dennis C Norman, IS John Keiffner, Mkt Mr Lynn Smith, PR	Rev: Assets: Emp:		750 NA 2
Maytag Co One Dependability Square Newton, IA 50208 515-792-7000	Manufacturer of kitchen & home appliances. Type: NYSE-MYG Ind: Appliances/Furn Grp: Manufacturing Daniel J Krumm, CEO Edward Hadley, VCh Jerry A Schiller, CFO Dale E Wilke, IS Carleton Zacheis, R&D Frank Vaughn, Sls Janus Cooper, VP William Foust, VP Donald Byers, VP James Bennett, VP Robert Chaplin, VP Janis C Cooper, PR	Rev: Assets: Emp:		1886 1330 5
Mazda Canada Inc 821 Brock Road Soouth Pickering, ON L1W3L6 Can 416-831-4222	Automobile marketing & distribution company. Type: Private-Sub-For Ind: Automotive Grp: Manufacturing K Hayashi, CEO	Rev: Assets: Emp:		441 NA 1
Mazda Motors Corp USA 1 Mazda Drive Flat Rock, MI 48134 313-782-7800	Manufacturer & importer of automobiles; US headquarters. Type: Private-Sub-For Ind: Automotive Grp: Manufacturing Osamu Nobuto, CEO	Rev: Assets: Emp:		1650 NA 11
MBIA Insurance Co 445 Hamilton Avenue White Plains, NY 10602 914-681-1300	Municipal bond insurer. Type: NYSE-MBI Ind: Insurance Grp: Insurance William O Bailey, CEO	Rev: Assets: Emp:		224 1283 2
MCA Inc 100 Universal City Plaza Universal City, CA 91608 818-777-1000	Diversified entertainment & real estate development company. Type: NYSE-MCA Ind: Leisure Time Grp: Consumer Service L R Wasserman, CEO Sidney J Sheinberg, Pres Harold M Haas, CFO George Brenner, IS Irving Azoff, VP Richard E Baker, VP Lawrence P Fraiberg, VP	Rev: Assets: Emp:		3024 4115 16
MCA Records Inc 70 Universal City Plaza Universal City, CA 91608 818-777-4302	Record, tape & music publishing rights & sales company. Type: Private-Sub Par: MCA Inc Ind: Leisure Time Grp: Consumer Service A Teller, CEO	Rev: Assets: Emp:		NA NA NA
McCain Foods Ltd Main Road Florenceville, NB E0J1K0 Can 506-392-5541	Manufacturer of packaged foods. Type: TOR Ind: Food Processing Grp: Food Processing Harrrison McCain, CEO	Rev: Assets: Emp:		1275 6800 10
McCann Erickson Worldwide 485 Lexington Avenue New York, NY 10017 212-697-6000	Advertising & marketing agency. Type: Private-Sub Par: Interpublic Group of Companies Inc Ind: Consulting Grp: Business Service Robert L James, CEO	Rev: Assets: Emp:		250 NA 2
McCarthy Brothers Co 1341 N Rock Hill Road St Louis, MO 63124 314-968-3300	Commercial & institutional construction company. Type: Private Ind: Real Estate/Bldg Grp: Business Service Michael M McCarthy, CEO	Rev: Assets: Emp:		1000 NA 5
McCaw Cellular 5808 Lake Washington NE Kirkland, WA 98033 206-827-4500	Operator of cellular phone systems. Type: Private Ind: Telecom Grp: High Tech Criag McCaw, CEO	Rev: Assets: Emp:		225 300 3
McClatchy Newspapers 2100 Q Street Sacramento, CA 95816 916-321-1000	Newspaper publisher. Type: ASE-MNI Ind: Publishing/Com Grp: Consumer Service C McClatchy, CEO	Rev: Assets: Emp:		400 200 6

Organizations Listed Alphabetically

Organization / Address / Phone	Descriptive Information	Revenue / Assets / Emp ($ mil) ($ mil) (thous)		

McCormack & Dodge Inc
1225 Worcester Road
Natick, MA 01760
508-665-8200

Producer of financial & human-resource application software.
Type: Private-Sub Par: Dun & Bradstreet Corp
Ind: Comput/Off Equip Grp: High Tech
Frank H Dodge, CEO

Rev: NA
Assets: NA
Emp: NA

McCormick & Co Inc
11350 McCormick Road
Hunt Valley, MD 21031
301-771-7301

Food manufacturer.
Type: NASDAQ-MCCRK
Ind: Food Processing Grp: Food Processing
Charles P McCormick, CEO Bailey A Thomas, Pres James J Harrison Jr, CFO
John P Thompson, IS John H Nelson, R&D George Clausen, Ops
John Felton, VP Michael Cipollaro, VP James Hooker, VP
J Donald Jeer, VP John W Felton, PR

Rev: 1184
Assets: 770
Emp: 10

McDermott International Inc
1010 Common Street
New Orleans, LA 70112
504-587-5400

Manufacturer of power generation equipment, marine.
Type: NYSE
Ind: Oil Service Grp: Business Service
J E Cunningham, CEO Robert E Howson, Pres Robert A Jolliff, Tres
Anton Salem, Mkt Edmund A Robidoux, VP Charles F Kraus, VP
Frand C Allen Jr, VP William L Higgins, VP Joe J Stewart, VP
John Pl Eckert, VP Richard E Woolbert, PR

Rev: 2352
Assets: 3825
Emp: 26

McDevitt & Street Co Inc
4824 Parkway Plaza
Charlotte, NC 28217
704-525-8110

General contracting, commercial, institutional.
Type: Private
Ind: Real Estate/Bldg Grp: Business Service
E Robert Street, CEO

Rev: 1000
Assets: NA
Emp: 2

McDonald's Corp
McDonald's Plaza
Oak Brook, IL 60521
312-575-3000

Worldwide operator of fast food restaurants.
Type: NYSE-MCD
Ind: Food/Lodging Grp: Consumer Service
Fred L Turner, CEO Michael R Quinlan, Chr Edward H Rensi, Pres
Jack M Greenberg, CFO Bonnie Kos, IS Paul D Schrage, Mkt
Richard Starmann, VP Delbert Wilson, VP Lynal A Root, VP
Richard G Starmann, PR

Rev: 5566
Assets: 8159
Emp: 175

McDonald's Restaurants of Canada Ltd
McDonald's Place
Don Mills, ON M3C3L4 Can
416-443-1000

Nationwide operator of fast food restaurants.
Type: Private-Sub-For
Ind: Retail/Food Grp: Retail
George A Cohon, CEO

Rev: 987
Assets: 447
Emp: 54

McDonnell Douglas Canada Ltd
Airport Road Toronto Airpoort
Mississauga, ON L5P1B7 Can
416-677-4341

Aerospace & defense systems manufacturing company.
Type: Private-Sub-For
Ind: Aerospace Grp: High Tech
G Ackerson, CEO

Rev: 329
Assets: 238
Emp: 5

McDonnell Douglas Corp
PO Box 516
St Louis, MO 63166
314-232-0232

Manufacturer of aircraft; defense, commercial.
Type: NYSE-MDC
Ind: Aerospace Grp: High Tech
John F McDonnell, CEO Gerald Johnston, Pres Edward C Aldridge, VCh
Jerry G Brown, CFO Jeremy J Causley, IS Ronald Kerber, R&D
William P Brown, Sls Robert H Hood Jr, Mkt John P Capellupo, VP
James MacDonald, VP James T McMillan, VP William Ross, VP
John Yardley, VP Gerald J Meyer, PR

Rev: 15069
Assets: 11885
Emp: 121

McDonnell Douglas Electronic Systems
8201 Greesboro Drive
McLean, VA 22102
703-442-7960

Manufacturer of electronic systems.
Type: Private-Sub Par: McDonnell Douglas Corp
Ind: Electronics Grp: High Tech
Edward Aldridge, CEO

Rev: NA
Assets: NA
Emp: NA

McDonnell Douglas Information Systems
PO Box 516
St Louis, MO 63166
314-232-0232

Operator of computer service company.
Type: Private-Sub Par: McDonnell Douglas Corp
Ind: Comput/Off Equip Grp: High Tech
Jeremy Causley, CEO

Rev: NA
Assets: NA
Emp: NA

McDonnell Douglas Missile Systems Co
PO Box 426
St Charles, MO 63301
314-925-4000

Manufacturer of missiles, military aircraft.
Type: Private-Sub Par: McDonnell Douglas Corp
Ind: Aerospace Grp: High Tech
John Capellupo, CEO

Rev: NA
Assets: NA
Emp: NA

Organizations Listed Alphabetically

Organization / Address / Phone	Descriptive Information	Revenue / Assets / Emp ($ mil) ($ mil) (thous)		

McDonnell Douglas Space Systems Co
5301 Bolsa Avenue
Huntington Beach, CA 92647
714-896-3311

Research & technology for space systems.
Type: Private-Sub Par: McDonnell Douglas Corp
Ind: Aerospace Grp: High Tech
James Dorenbacher, CEO

Rev: NA
Assets: NA
Emp: NA

McGill University
845 Sherbrooke Street W
Montreal, PQ H3A2T5 Can
514-398-4455

Major educational institution; university.
Type: University
Ind: University Grp: Govt & Non-Prof
A J deGranpre, CEO

Rev: 234
Assets: NM
Emp: 21

McGraw Hill Corp
1221 Avenue of the Americas
New York, NY 10020
212-512-2000

Publishing & information services company.
Type: NYSE
Ind: Publishing/Com Grp: Consumer Service
Joseph L Dionne, CEO Richard B Miller, VCh Robert Bahash, CFO
Richard H Shriver, IS David P Forsyth, R&D Kay Knight Clarke, Sls
Thomas J Sullivan, VP Robert Landes, VP Ralph Schulz, VP
Mary A Cooper, IR Donald Rubin, PR

Rev: 1818
Assets: 1758
Emp: 16

McGraw Hill Financial Services Co
25 Broadway
New York, NY 10004
212-208-8000

Provider of electronic publishing; financial services.
Type: Private-Sub Par: McGraw Hill Corp
Ind: Comput/Off Equip Grp: High Tech
Harold McGraw, CEO

Rev: NA
Assets: NA
Emp: NA

MCI Communications Corp
1133 Nineteenth Street NW
Washington, DC 20036
202-872-1600

Long distance telephone company.
Type: NASDAQ-MCIC
Ind: Telecom Grp: High Tech
William G McGowan, CEO Bert C Roberts Jr, Pres W Orville Wright, VCh
Daniel F Akerson, CFO Richard Liebhaber, Mkt H Brian Thompson, Ops
Howard Crane, VP Daniel Crawford, VP Allan Ditchfield, VP
Gerald Kovach, VP Stuart Mencher, VP Howard C Crane, IR
Bernard Goodrich, PR

Rev: 5137
Assets: 5843
Emp: 18

McJunkin Corp
835 Hillcrest Drive
Charleston, WV 25322
304-348-5211

Wholesale equipment dealer, piping, electrical, mining.
Type: Private
Ind: Business Service Grp: Business Service
H B Wehrle, CEO

Rev: 400
Assets: NA
Emp: 1

McKesson Corp
One Post Street
San Francisco, CA 94104
415-983-8300

Prescription drug & health care product company.
Type: NYSE
Ind: Business Service Grp: Business Service
Neil E Harlan, CEO Thomas W Field Jr, Chr Kenneth Hicken, VCh
Alan Seelenfreund, CFO Jack Pfeiffer, IS Rex Malson, Ops
John S Wheaton, VP Ronald Anderson, VP Marvin L Krasnansky, IR
James S Cohune, PR

Rev: 7283
Assets: 2255
Emp: 17

McKinsey & Co Inc
55 E 52nd Street
New York, NY 10022
212-909-8400

Consulting firm.
Type: Private
Ind: Food/Lodging Grp: Consumer Service
Fred Gluck, CEO

Rev: 500
Assets: NA
Emp: 3

McLane Co Inc
3407 S 31st Street
Temple, TX 76502
817-778-7500

Operator of wholesale grocery businesses.
Type: Private
Ind: Retail/Food Grp: Retail
Drayton McLane Jr, CEO

Rev: 2000
Assets: NA
Emp: 3

McLean Industries Inc
660 Madison Avenue Suite 602
New York, NY 10021
212-593-3325

Real estate developers, ocean going vessels.
Type: NYSE-MII
Ind: Transport Grp: Business Service
Hobart Trvesdell, CEO

Rev: 1000
Assets: 1500
Emp: 8

McLouth Steel Products Inc
1650 W Jefferson
Trenton, MI 48183
313-285-1200

Steel producers.
Type: Private
Ind: Steel Grp: Basic Industries
Edward L Sambuchi, CEO

Rev: 500
Assets: NA
Emp: 2

Organizations Listed Alphabetically

Organization / Address / Phone	Descriptive Information	Revenue / ($ mil)	Assets / ($ mil)	Emp (thous)
McMaster University Administrative Bldg Hamilton, ON L8S4L8 Can 416-525-9140	Major educational institution; university. Type: University Ind: University Grp: Govt & Non-Prof J H Panabaker, CEO	Rev: Assets: Emp:	187 NM 16	
MCN (Michigan Consolidated Natgas) Corp 500 Griswold Street Detroit, MI 48226 313-965-2430	Oil & gas pipelines, distribution & storage, gas utility. Type: NYSE-MCN Ind: Utility Grp: Utilities Alfred Glancy, CEO	Rev: Assets: Emp:	1750 2200 4	
MCORP Inc 500 Dallas Bldg Dallas, TX 75201 214-698-5000	Commercial bank. Type: NYSE-M Ind: Banking Grp: Financial Gene H Bishop, CEO Gene H Bishop, Chr John T Cater, Pres Peter B Bartholow, CFO Mark L Bishop, Mkt James M Spellings, VP C Richard Vermillion, VP Charles E McMahen, VP James B Gardner, VP Charles W Dees, VP George A McCane, PR	Rev: Assets: Emp:	1774 20228 8	
McWane Corp 23 Iverness Center Drive Birmingham, AL 35243 205-991-9888	Diversified manufacturing company. Type: Private Ind: Manufacturing Grp: Manufacturing J R McWare, CEO	Rev: Assets: Emp:	500 NA 4	
MDC Holdings Inc 3600 S Yosemite Denver, CO 80237 303-773-1100	Real estate development company. Type: NYSE-MDC Ind: Non-Bank Fin Grp: Financial Larry A Mizel, CEO David Mandarich, Pres Spencer I Browne, VCh Michael Feinstien, CFO David Rest, IS Pete Stofflet, Mkt Charles G Hauber, VP Paul Oberman, VP Paris Reece, VP Pete Stofflet, PR	Rev: Assets: Emp:	841 1993 2	
MDU Resources Group Inc 400 N Fourth Street Bismarck, ND 58501 701-222-7900	Electric power utility company. Type: NYSE-MDU Ind: Utility Grp: Utilities John A Schuchart, CEO Thomas Winter, Tres Harold J Mellen, CFO Sandra Tabor, VP Robert E Wood, VP Lester Loble, VP John Renner, VP Vernon Raile, VP	Rev: Assets: Emp:	344 977 2	
Mead Corp Courthouse Plaza NE Dayton, OH 45463 513-222-6323	Manufacturer of paper & wood products. Type: NYSE-MEA Ind: Paper/Forest Prd Grp: Basic Industries Burnell R Roberts, CEO Steven C Mason, Pres William A Enouen, CFO John Langenbahn, IS Charles Spalding, R&D Wallace O Nugent, Mkt Elias Karter, VP John W Herbert, VP Dudley P Kircher, PR	Rev: Assets: Emp:	4464 2492 21	
Mead Data Central Inc 9393 Springboro Pike Dayton, OH 45401 513-865-6800	Electronic publishing & imaging services. Type: Private-Sub Par: Mead Corp Ind: Comput/Off Equip Grp: High Tech J Simpson, CEO	Rev: Assets: Emp:	NA NA NA	
Mead Pulp Sales Inc Courthouse Plaza Dayton, OH 45463 513-222-6323	Distributor of wood pulp & paper products. Type: Private-Sub Par: Mead Corp Ind: Paper/Forest Prd Grp: Basic Industries J Sasboll, CEO	Rev: Assets: Emp:	NA NA NA	
Meadowdale Foods Inc 8711 Meadowdale Detroit, MI 48228 313-943-3300	Grocery stores, food wholesaling. Type: Private Ind: Retail/Food Grp: Retail David K Page, CEO	Rev: Assets: Emp:	500 NA 2	
Measurex Corp One Results Way Cupertino, CA 95014 408-255-1500	Manufacturer of sensor based control systems. Type: NYSE-MX Ind: Instruments Grp: High Tech David A Bossen, CEO	Rev: Assets: Emp:	265 303 3	

Organizations Listed Alphabetically

Organization / Address / Phone	Descriptive Information	Revenue / ($ mil)	Assets / ($ mil)	Emp (thous)
Medco Containment Services Inc 1900 Pollitt Drive Fair Lawn, NJ 07410 201-794-9010	Medical cost containment service company. Type: NASDAQ-MCCS Ind: Health Care Grp: Consumer Service Martin J Wygod, CEO Ronald Kalish, VCh James V Manning, CFO Per G H Lofberg, R&D Joseph Boiseau, Sls Gary Brozenich, Mkt Paul C Suthern, Ops Terry Latanich, VP James B Duffy, VP	Rev: 502 Assets: 344 Emp: 4		
Media General Inc 333 E Grace Street Richmond, VA 23219 804-649-6000	Communications company; newspapers, TV stations, cable TV. Type: NYSE Ind: Publishing/Com Grp: Consumer Service James S Evans, CEO Alan Donnahoe, VCh J Curtis Barden, CFO Walter Waleski, IS J Stewart Bryan, Sls Andrew Brent, VP	Rev: 756 Assets: 859 Emp: 11		
Media News Group Inc 1101 Pacific Avenue Dallas, TX 75202 214-720-5800	Newspaper publishing. Type: Private Ind: Publishing/Com Grp: Consumer Service W Dean Singleton, CEO	Rev: 750 Assets: NA Emp: 7		
Mediq Inc One Mediq Plaza Pennsauken, NJ 08110 609-665-9300	Medical equipment sales, leasing, rental; ultrasound, x-ray. Type: ASE-MED Ind: Health Care Grp: Consumer Service Bernard Rotco, CEO	Rev: 300 Assets: 200 Emp: 5		
Medtronic Inc 7000 Central Avenue NE Minneapolis, MN 55432 612-574-4000	Manufacturer of healthcare electronic equipment, instruments. Type: NYSE-MDT Ind: Electronics Grp: High Tech Earl E Bakken, CEO Winston R Wallin, Chr Michael J Boris, Tres William Chorske, CFO Thomas Morin, IS Bill Erickson, Sls Daniel E Hopton, VP Richard F Sauter, VP Douglas R Luthringshauser, VP Gerard C Planchon, VP Lowell P Jacobson, VP B Christine Johnson, IR Celia Barnes, PR	Rev: 653 Assets: 641 Emp: 6		
MEI Diversified Inc 90 S 6th Street Minneapolis, MN 55402 612-339-8853	Manufacturer & wholesaler of packaged foods; snack, candy. Type: NYSE-MEI Ind: Food Processing Grp: Food Processing Carl R Pohlad, CEO	Rev: 250 Assets: 150 Emp: 1		
Meijer Inc 2727 Walker Avenue Grand Rapids, MI 49504 616-453-6711	Operator of retail department stores. Type: Private Ind: Retail/Merch Grp: Retail Fred Meijer, CEO	Rev: 2000 Assets: NA Emp: 20		
Mellon Bank Corp Three Mellon Bank Center Pittsburgh, PA 15258 412-234-5000	Commercial bank. Type: NYSE-MEL Ind: Banking Grp: Financial Frank V Cahouet, CEO Anthony P Terracciano, Pres Richard H Daniel, VCh W Keith Smith, CFO George P Dinardo, IS Sandra J McLaughlin, Mkt Frederick Beard, VP Charles L Benjamin, VP Milton E Berglund, VP Robert M Boyles, VP Susan Gallagher, PR	Rev: 3269 Assets: 31153 Emp: 14		
Mellon Stuart Holding Co Inc 1 North Shore Center Pittsburgh, PA 15212 412-323-4600	Commercial construction company. Type: Private Ind: Real Estate/Bldg Grp: Business Service Robert Luffe, CEO	Rev: 750 Assets: NA Emp: 1		
Melville Corp 3000 Westchester Avenue Harrison, NY 10528 914-253-8000	Operator of retail apparel, shoes, drugstores. Type: NYSE-MES Ind: Retail/Merch Grp: Retail Stanley P Goldstein, CEO James A Marcum, Tres Robert D Huth, CFO Francis H Arnone, VP Norman Axelrod, VP Stewart Brown, VP Daniel Katz, VP William Kingsford, VP Ira H Peterman, VP John I Mitchell, IR Mary Yazzetti, PR	Rev: 6780 Assets: 2736 Emp: 97		

Organizations Listed Alphabetically

Organization / Address / Phone	Descriptive Information	Revenue / ($ mil)	Assets / ($ mil)	Emp (thous)
Memorex Telex Corp 6422 E 41st Street Tulsa, OK 74135 918-627-2333	Manufacturer computer equipment. Type: NYSE-TC Ind: Comput/Off Equip Grp: High Tech G Bragg, CEO Giorgio Ronchi, Chr Richard Clarke, CFO Ed Cannon, IS Lyle Wilcox, R&D Jean-Claude Zanolli, Mkt Mr Chris Ing, PR	Rev: Assets: Emp:	850 563 7	
Memotec Data Inc 600 McCaffrey Montreal, PQ H4T1N1 Can 514-738-4781	Manufacturer of communication products. Type: MON Ind: Telecom Grp: High Tech Eric Baker, CEO	Rev: Assets: Emp:	340 765 2	
Memphis Light Gas & Water Inc 220 S Main Street Memphis, TN 38101 901-528-4151	Electric power & water distribution utility company. Type: Private Ind: Utility Grp: Utilities Larry Papasan, CEO	Rev: Assets: Emp:	1100 NA 5	
Memphis State University Administrative Bldg Memphis, TN 38152 901-454-2234	Major educational institution; university. Type: University Ind: University Grp: Govt & Non-Prof Thomas E Carpenter, CEO	Rev: Assets: Emp:	81 125 23	
Memphis, City of City Hall 125 N Mid America Mall Memphis, TN 38103 901-576-6000	City government. Type: City Govt Ind: Local Govt Grp: Govt & Non-Prof Richard C Hackett, CEO	Rev: Assets: Emp:	1439 NM 19	
Mentor Graphics Corp 8500 SW Creekside Beaverton, OR 97005 503-626-7000	Manufacturer of computor equipment & software. Type: NASDAQ-MENT Ind: Business Service Grp: Business Service Thomas H Bruggere, CEO	Rev: Assets: Emp:	301 282 2	
MeraBank Fed Savings Bank Inc 3003 N Central Avenue Phoenix, AZ 85012 602-248-4221	Thrift institution. Type: Private-Sub Par: Pinnacle West Capital Ind: Savings & Loan Grp: Financial Gene E Rice, CEO	Rev: Assets: Emp:	644 8348 2	
Mercantile Bancorp Inc Mercantile Tower St Louis, MO 63166 314-425-2525	Commercial bank. Type: NASDAQ-MTRC Ind: Banking Grp: Financial Donald E Lasater, CEO Neal Farrell, Pres Ralph W Babb Jr, CFO John H Lee, IS John Q Vye, Mkt Richard E McGee, PR	Rev: Assets: Emp:	426 6491 5	
Mercantile Bankshares Corp Two Hopkins Plaza Baltimore, MD 21203 301-237-5900	Commercial bank. Type: NASDAQ Ind: Banking Grp: Financial H Furlong Baldwin, CEO John Mosner, Pres Douglas W Dodge, VCh Charles McGuire, CFO Edward K Dunn, Mkt John A O'Conner, VP Lawrence H Ely, VP	Rev: Assets: Emp:	362 3642 2	
Mercantile Stores Co Inc 1100 N Market Street Wilmington, DE 19801 302-575-1816	Department stores. Type: NYSE Ind: Retail/Merch Grp: Retail Leon F Winbigler, CEO J C Lovell, Pres Harold J Jockers, VCh William Heineman, CFO David R Hunn, Mkt Dennis Murphy, VP William Carr, VP Roger Henry, VP William Heineman, PR	Rev: Assets: Emp:	2266 1452 21	
Mercedes (Daimler Benz) Inc One Mercedes Drive Montvale, NJ 07645 201-573-0600	Manufacturer & importer of automobiles; US headquarters. Type: Private-Sub-For Ind: Automotive Grp: Manufacturing Eric Krampe, CEO	Rev: Assets: Emp:	1540 NA 2	
Mercedes Benz Canada Inc University Place Toronto, ON M4G2L5 Can 416-425-3550	Automotive distribution & marketing company. Type: Private-Sub-For Ind: Automotive Grp: Manufacturing Hans Hinrichs, CEO	Rev: Assets: Emp:	298 128 1	

Organization / Address / Phone	Descriptive Information	Revenue ($ mil)	Assets ($ mil)	Emp (thous)
Mercer, William M Meidinger Inc 1211 Avenue of the Americas New York, NY 10036 212-997-7171	Nationwide consulting company. Type: Private Ind: Consulting Grp: Business Service Peter Coster, CEO	Rev: 300 Assets: NA Emp: 3		
Merchants Distributors Inc 543 12th Street Drive Hickory, NC 28601 704-322-2822	Food wholesalers. Type: Private Ind: Retail/Merch Grp: Retail Boyd George, CEO	Rev: 1000 Assets: NA Emp: 2		
Merchants National Bank & Trust Co One Merchants Plaza Indianapolis, IN 46255 317-267-6100	Commercial bank. Type: NASDAQ-MCHN Ind: Banking Grp: Financial James D Massey, CEO	Rev: 452 Assets: 5256 Emp: 3		
Merck & Co Inc PO Box 2000 Rahway, NJ 07065 201-574-4000	Prescription drug company. Type: NYSE Ind: Drugs Grp: Consumer Service P Roy Vagelos, CEO John E Lyons, Pres Judy C Lewent, Tres Francis H Spiegel Jr, CFO Albert C Cinorre, IS E Scolnick, R&D John E Lyons, Mkt Albert D Angel, IR John Dorley, PR	Rev: 5940 Assets: 6128 Emp: 32		
Mercury Marine Co 6250 W Pioneer Road Fon Du Lac, WI 54936 414-929-5000	Manufacturer of outboard motors. Type: Private-Sub Par: Brunswick Corp Ind: Manufacturing Grp: Manufacturing Thomas R Weigt, CEO	Rev: NA Assets: NA Emp: NA		
Mercy Health Services 34605 12 Mile Road Farmington, MI 48331 313-489-6010	Operator of hospitals, clinics, & rest care. Type: Private Ind: Health Care Grp: Consumer Service Edward Connors, CEO	Rev: 1512 Assets: NA Emp: 19		
Meredith Corp 1716 Locust Street Des Moines, IA 50336 515-284-3000	Diversified media company; magazines, books, television. Type: NYSE-MDP Ind: Publishing/Com Grp: Consumer Service E T Merrdith, CEO Robert A Burnett, Chr Jack D Rehm, Pres James F Stack, CFO Neil Kuehnl, R&D Fred Stines, VP Leo R Armatis, VP Gerald Thornton, VP Allen Sabbag, VP Leo R Armatis, PR	Rev: 678 Assets: 646 Emp: 4		
Meridian Bancorp Inc 35 N Sixth Street Reading, PA 19601 215-320-2000	Commercial bank. Type: NASDAQ Ind: Banking Grp: Financial Samuel A McCullough, CEO Ezekiel S Ketchum, Pres Russell Kunkel, VCh Terry Troupe, CFO Bruce L Ressler, IS Harold L Landis, R&D Richard C Weber, Sls David Sardilli, Ops Robert Williams, VP George E Biechler, IR Doris Piasecki, PR	Rev: 950 Assets: 9523 Emp: 3		
Meridian Minerals Co 5613 DTC Parkway Englewood, CO 80111 303-694-4100	Mineral development & production company. Type: Private-Sub Par: Burlington Resources Ind: Manufacturing Grp: Manufacturing G Thompson, CEO	Rev: NA Assets: NA Emp: NA		
Meridian Oil Inc 2919 Allen Parkway Houston, TX 77091 713-831-1600	Oil exploration & production company. Type: Private-Sub Par: Burlington Resources Ind: Energy Grp: Basic Industries Donald Clayton, CEO	Rev: NA Assets: NA Emp: NA		
Meritor Financial Group Inc 1212 Market Street Philadelphia, PA 19107 215-636-7500	Commercial bank. Type: NASDAQ-MTOR Ind: Banking Grp: Financial Roger S Hillas, CEO Frederick S Hammer, Chr Louis T Cullen, VCh Paul Coppola, Tres Harold L Connell, CFO Larry L Betsinger, IS Joseph R Klinger, VP Harry Hummer, VP Leslie C Voth, PR	Rev: 1646 Assets: 17172 Emp: 9		

Organizations Listed Alphabetically

Organization / Address / Phone	Descriptive Information	Revenue / ($ mil)	Assets / ($ mil)	Emp (thous)

Merrill Lynch & Co Inc
World Financial Center North Tower
New York, NY 10181
212-637-7455

Diversified financial company; brokerage, finance.
Type: NYSE-MER
Ind: Securities   Grp: Financial
William A Schreyer, CEO   Daniel P Tully, Pres   Gerald Crimins, VCh
D Bruce Brunson, Tres   Courtney F Jones, CFO   Duwayne J Peterson, IS
Herbert Allison, VP   Robert Williamson, VP   Arthur Zeikel, VP
Patrick Murphy, VP   Richard Stewart, VP   Paul W Critchlow, PR

Rev: 10547
Assets: 64402
Emp: 42

Merrill Lynch Canada Inc
200 King Street W
Toronto, ON M5H3W3 Can
416-586-6000

Investment company; brokerage.
Type: Private
Ind: Securities   Grp: Financial
Michael O Sanderson, CEO

Rev: 170
Assets: 85
Emp: 1

Merry Go Round Enterprises Inc
1220 Joppa Road
Baltimore, MD 21204
301-828-1000

Operator of retail apparel stores.
Type: NASDAQ-MGRE
Ind: Retail/Merch   Grp: Retail
Harold Goldsmith, CEO

Rev: 299
Assets: 200
Emp: 4

Mervyn's Inc
25001 Industrial Blvd
Hayward, CA 94545
415-785-8800

Operator of retail consumer merchandise stores.
Type: Private-Sub   Par: Dayton Hudson Corp
Ind: Retail/Merch   Grp: Retail
W Rossi, CEO

Rev: NA
Assets: NA
Emp: NA

Mesa Limited Partnership Inc
One Mesa Square
Amarillo, TX 79189
806-378-1000

Oil & gas exploration & development company.
Type: NYSE-MLP
Ind: Energy   Grp: Basic Industries
T Boone Pickens, CEO

Rev: 371
Assets: 3001
Emp: 1

Mesa, City of
City Hall 55 N Center Street
Mesa, AZ 85201
602-834-2388

City government.
Type: City Govt
Ind: Local Govt   Grp: Govt & Non-Prof
Peggy Rubach, CEO

Rev: 250
Assets: NM
Emp: 3

Metal Container Corp
10733 Sunset Office Drive
St Louis, MO 63127
314-577-1700

Manufacturer of containers.
Type: Private-Sub   Par: Anheuser Busch Companies Inc
Ind: Packaging   Grp: Manufacturing
Barry Beracha, CEO

Rev: NA
Assets: NA
Emp: NA

Metallurg Corp
25 E 39th Street
New York, NY 10016
212-686-4010

Metals mining company.
Type: Private
Ind: Metals/Mining   Grp: Basic Industries
Michael A Standen, CEO

Rev: 750
Assets: NA
Emp: 4

Metro Mobile Communications Inc
110 E 59th Street
New York, NY 10022
212-319-7444

Cellular telephone company.
Type: NASDAQ-MCTAC
Ind: Telecom   Grp: High Tech
George L Lendeman, CEO

Rev: 56
Assets: 242
Emp: 1

Metro Richelieu Ltd
9250 Notre Dame E
Montreal, PQ H1L3N4 Can
514-353-5000

Nationwide retailing company.
Type: MON-MTU
Ind: Retail/Food   Grp: Retail
Jacques L Maltais, CEO   Michel Obry, Pres   Rejean Bouchard, VCh
L Serge Gadbois, CFO   Denise Martin, IS   Andre Roy, VP
Charles Roy, VP   Guy Piuze, VP

Rev: 1870
Assets: 484
Emp: 17

Metromail Inc
901 W Bond
Lincoln, NE 68521
402-475-4591

Direct mail & marketing company.
Type: Private-Sub   Par: Donnelley, R R & Sons Co
Ind: Business Service   Grp: Business Service
R Troncone, CEO

Rev: NA
Assets: NA
Emp: NA

Metromedia Inc
1 Harmon Plaza
Secaucus, NJ 07094
201-348-3244

Telecommunications company; paging equipment.
Type: Private-Sub   Par: Southwestern Bell Corp
Ind: Publishing/Com   Grp: Consumer Service
John W Kluge, CEO

Rev: 750
Assets: NA
Emp: 5

Organizations Listed Alphabetically

Organization / Address / Phone	Descriptive Information	Revenue / ($ mil)	Assets / ($ mil)	Emp (thous)
Metropolitan Edison Co 2800 Pottsville Pike Reading, PA 19640 215-929-3601	Electric power utility. Type: Private-Sub Par: General Public Utilities Corp Ind: Utility Grp: Utilities William G Kuhns, CEO Fred Hafer, Pres John L Bachofer, VCh John Graham, CFO Henry Robidoux, R&D Ronald Toole, Sls David S High, Ops	Rev: 656 Assets: 1594 Emp: 2		
Metropolitan Life Insurance Co One Madison Avenue New York, NY 10010 212-578-2211	Life insurance company. Type: Private Ind: Insurance Grp: Insurance John J Creedon, CEO Phillip Briggs, VCh Robert G Schwartz, CFO George B Trotta, Mkt Glen E Coverdale, VP Robert J Crimmins, VP Ted Athanassiades, VP J Pierre Maurer, VP Dorothy Kelly, IR Richard W Keogh, PR	Rev: 30800 Assets: 120400 Emp: 50		
Metropolitan Life Insurance Co of Canada 99 Bank Street Ottawa, ON K1P6B9 Can 613-560-7446	Life insurance company. Type: Private-Mutual Ind: Insurance Grp: Insurance Albert Bates, CEO	Rev: 939 Assets: 3441 Emp: 2		
Meyer, Fred Inc 3800 SE 22nd Avenue Portland, OR 97202 503-232-8844	Operator of retail stores. Type: OTC Ind: Retail/Merch Grp: Retail Fred Stevens, CEO	Rev: 2074 Assets: NA Emp: 21		
MGM United Artists Communications Inc 450 N Roxbury Drive Beverly Hills, CA 90210 213-281-4000	Motion picture & television production company. Type: NYSE Ind: Leisure Time Grp: Consumer Service Jeffery C Barbakow, CEO Sidney Sapsowitz, VCh Trevor Fetter, VP	Rev: 675 Assets: 1365 Emp: 7		
Miami Dade County Community College 11011 SW 104th Street Miami, FL 33176 305-596-1211	Major educational institution; community college. Type: University Ind: University Grp: Govt & Non-Prof Robert H McCabe, CEO	Rev: 165 Assets: 165 Emp: 44		
Miami, City of City Hall 3500 Pan American Drive Miami, FL 33133 305-579-6010	City government. Type: City Govt Ind: Local Govt Grp: Govt & Non-Prof Xavier L Suarez, CEO	Rev: 279 Assets: NM Emp: 4		
Michaels Stores Inc 5931 Campus Circle Drive Irving, TX 75063 214-580-8242	Operator of home products retail stores. Type: ASE-MKE Ind: Retail/Merch Grp: Retail Sam Wyly, CEO	Rev: 250 Assets: 200 Emp: 3		
Michigan Bell Telephone Co 444 Michigan Avenue Detroit, MI 48226 313-223-9900	Telephone utility company. Type: Private-Sub Par: Ameritech (Amer Information Tech Corp) Ind: Telecom Grp: High Tech William Vititoe, CEO	Rev: NA Assets: NA Emp: NA		
Michigan Livestock Co Inc 806 Collidge Road East Lansing, MI 48223 517-337-2856	Agricultural cooperative food products; beef, pork. Type: Private Ind: Food Processing Grp: Food Processing Tom Reed, CEO	Rev: 275 Assets: NA Emp: 1		
Michigan Milk Producers Association Inc 41310 Bridge Street Novi, MI 48050 313-474-6672	Agricultural cooperative food production; dairy products. Type: Private Ind: Food Processing Grp: Food Processing Walter Wosje, CEO	Rev: 550 Assets: 150 Emp: 1		
Michigan National Bankcorp Inc 27777 Inkster Road Farmington Hills, MI 48018 313-473-3000	Commercial bank. Type: OTC Ind: Banking Grp: Financial Robert J Mylod, CEO Eric D Booth, VCh Robert Panizzi, CFO Patrick Crosson, IS Peter Thomsen, Mkt Richard Webb, VP Gisela Gonzalez, VP Lawrence L Gladchun, VP Ariadne Magoulias, PR	Rev: 1040 Assets: 11306 Emp: 7		

Organizations Listed Alphabetically

Organization / Address / Phone	Descriptive Information	Revenue / ($ mil)	Assets / ($ mil)	Emp (thous)
Michigan State University Administrative Bldg East Lansing, MI 48824 517-355-1855	Major educational institution; university. Type: University Ind: University Grp: Govt & Non-Prof John DiBiaggio, CEO	Rev: 471 Assets: 648 Emp: 46		
Michigan Treasurer Employees Rtrmt Sys 425 W Allegan Lansing, MI 48922 517-373-9150	State investment agency; pension management. Type: State Govt Ind: Non-Bank Fin Grp: Financial Dick Grace, CEO	Rev: 440 Assets: 16500 Emp: 2		
Michigan, State of State Capitol Lansing, MI 48909 517-373-1837	State government. Type: State Govt Ind: State/Prov Govt Grp: Govt & Non-Prof James J Blanchard, CEO	Rev: 24491 Assets: NM Emp: 156		
Microage Inc 2308 S 55th Street Temple, AZ 85282 602-968-3168	Operator of retail computer stores. Type: NASDAQ-MICA Ind: Retail/Merch Grp: Retail A Hald, CEO	Rev: 400 Assets: 100 Emp: 4		
Microamerica Inc 33 Boston Post Road West Marlboro, MA 01752 508-480-0780	Operator of retail personal computer stores. Type: NYSE-AGS Ind: Retail/Merch Grp: Retail Lawrence Schoenberg, CEO	Rev: 300 Assets: 150 Emp: 1		
Microdot Inc 20 S Clark Street Chicago, IL 60603 312-899-1925	Manufacturer of metal fasteners; nuts, bolts. Type: Private Ind: Manufacturing Grp: Manufacturing Richard P Strubel, CEO	Rev: 400 Assets: NA Emp: 4		
Micromedex Inc 660 Bannock Street Denver, CO 80204 303-623-8600	Electronic data provider. Type: Private-Sub Par: Mead Corp Ind: Comput/Off Equip Grp: High Tech Bernard Rumack, CEO	Rev: NA Assets: NA Emp: NA		
Micron Technology 2805 E Columbia Road Boise, ID 83706 208-383-4000	Manufacturers of semiconductors, memory boards. Type: NASDAQ-DRAM Ind: Comput/Off Equip Grp: High Tech Richard Strubel, CEO	Rev: 400 Assets: 200 Emp: 5		
Micropolis Corp 21121 Nordhoff Street Chatsworth, CA 91311 818-709-3300	Manufacturer of computer equipment. Type: NASDAQ-MLIS Ind: Comput/Off Equip Grp: High Tech Stuart P Mabon, CEO Ericson Dunstan, Pres Dundas Flaherty, CFO Richard Decker, IS Chester Baffa, Mkt Terrence Ostridge, Ops Eugene Hovanec, VP Barbara Scherer, VP	Rev: 353 Assets: 301 Emp: 3		
Microsoft Corp 16011 NE 36th Way Redmond, WA 98073 206-882-8080	Micro computer software developer & publisher. Type: NASDAQ-MSFT Ind: Comput/Off Equip Grp: High Tech William H Gates, CEO Jon Shirley, Chr Steven Gray, CFO Steven Ballmer, IS Joachim Kempin, Sls Scott Oki, Mkt Jeremy Butler, Ops William Neukon, VP	Rev: 591 Assets: 493 Emp: 3		
Mid America Dairymen Inc 800 W Tampa Street Springfield, MO 65802 417-865-9641	Producer & distributor of dairy products. Type: Private Ind: Food Processing Grp: Food Processing Sam McCroskey, CEO Ivan Strickler, Chr Gary Hanman, Pres Gerald Bos, CFO Larry Claypool, R&D Forrest Bradley, PR	Rev: 1650 Assets: 300 Emp: 4		
Midas International Corp 225 N Michigan Avenue Chicago, IL 60601 312-565-7500	Automotive parts & services company. Type: Private-Sub Par: Whitman Co (IC Industries Inc) Ind: Automotive Grp: Manufacturing John Moore, CEO	Rev: NA Assets: NA Emp: NA		

Organizations Listed Alphabetically

Organization / Address / Phone	Descriptive Information	Revenue / Assets / Emp ($ mil) ($ mil) (thous)		

MidCon Corp
701 E 22nd Street
Lombard, IL 60148
312-691-2500

Natural gas transmission & oil & gas exploration company.
Type: Private-Sub Par: Occidental Petroleum Corp
Ind: Energy   Grp: Basic Industries
Oscar Davis, CEO

Rev: NA
Assets: NA
Emp: NA

Middlesex County Government
40 Thorndike Street
East Cambridge, MA 02141
617-494-4000

County government.
Type: County Govt
Ind: Local Govt   Grp: Govt & Non-Prof
B Grossman, CEO

Rev: 250
Assets: NM
Emp: 1

Midland Affiliated Inc
580 Walnut Street
Cincinnati, OH 45202
513-721-4000

Diversified manufacturing company.
Type: Private
Ind: Manufacturing   Grp: Manufacturing
John Hancock, CEO

Rev: 550
Assets: NA
Emp: 2

Midland Bank PLC
156 W 56th Street
New York, NY 10019
212-969-7000

Commercial bank.
Type: Private-Sub-For
Ind: Banking   Grp: Financial
John Ward, CEO

Rev: 450
Assets: 3500
Emp: 1

Midlantic Banks Inc
Metro Park Plaza
Edison, NJ 08818
201-321-8000

Commercial bank.
Type: NASDAQ
Ind: Banking   Grp: Financial
Robert Van Buren, CEO   Roy T Peraino, Pres   Frank P Garnevicus, CFO
Jeffrey S Griffie, IS   Charles J Ferrero, Mkt   David Sparks, VP
John E Homestead, VP   Richard Rishel, VP   R Ray Lockhart, VP
James J Hartmann, IR   Jim Lacey, PR

Rev: 1847
Assets: 19679
Emp: 10

Midway Airlines Inc
5959 S Cicero Avenue
Chicago, IL 60638
312-838-0001

Domestic airline.
Type: NYSE-MDW
Ind: Airline   Grp: Consumer Service
David Hinson, CEO   Jeffrey H Erickson, Pres   Alfred S Altschul, CFO
Paul H Tate, IS   John P Tague, R&D   Paul C Auger, Sls
Sandra Allen, PR

Rev: 400
Assets: 300
Emp: 4

Midwest Energy Co
401 Douglas Street
Sioux City, IA 51102
712-277-7400

Electric & natural gas utility holding company.
Type: NYSE-MWE
Ind: Utility   Grp: Utilities
Russell E Christiansen, CEO   Richard Engle, Pres   Allan Brink, CFO
Phillip Elm, R&D   Lester Juon, Mkt   Ira Delk, VP
James Coyle, VP   Beverly Wharton, VP   Robert Hutmacher, VP

Rev: 570
Assets: 1092
Emp: 2

Midwest Federal Savings Assn Inc
801 Nicollet Mall
Minneapolis, MN 55402
612-372-6123

Thrift institution.
Type: Private
Ind: Savings & Loan   Grp: Financial
Harold W Greenwood, CEO

Rev: 425
Assets: 3570
Emp: 2

Miles Laboratories Inc
1127 Myrtle Street
Elkhart, IN 46515
219-264-8062

Manufacturer of health care products.
Type: Private-Sub-For
Ind: Drugs   Grp: Consumer Service
D Risse, CEO

Rev: 1650
Assets: NA
Emp: 16

Milk Marketing Inc
8257 Dow Circle
Strongsville, OH 44136
216-826-4730

Producer & distributor of diary products.
Type: Private
Ind: Food Processing   Grp: Food Processing
Gordon Riehl, CEO

Rev: 825
Assets: NA
Emp: 1

Miller Anderson & Sherrerd Inv Mgt Co
2 Bala Cynwyd Plaza
Bala Cynwyd, PA 19004
215-668-0850

Investment firm; pension fund management.
Type: Private
Ind: Non-Bank Fin   Grp: Financial
Paul Miller, CEO

Rev: 300
Assets: 11000
Emp: 1

Miller Brewing Co
3939 W Highland Blvd
Milwaukee, WI 53201
414-931-2000

Beer manufacturing & distribution company.
Type: Private-Sub Par: Philip Morris Companies Inc
Ind: Beverage   Grp: Food Processing
Leonard Goldstein, CEO

Rev: NA
Assets: NA
Emp: NA

Organizations Listed Alphabetically

Organization / Address / Phone	Descriptive Information	Revenue / ($ mil)	Assets / ($ mil)	Emp (thous)
Miller, E A Inc 410 N 200th W Hyrum, UT 84319 801-245-6456	Producer & distributor of food products. Type: Private Ind: Food Processing Grp: Food Processing Mike Bassett, CEO	Rev: Assets: Emp:	1100 NA 4	
Miller, Herman Inc 8500 Byron Road Zeeland, MI 49464 616-772-3300	Manufacturer of office furniture. Type: NASDAQ-MLHR Ind: Manufacturing Grp: Manufacturing Max O DePree, CEO Richard Ruch, Chr Edward R Simon Jr, Pres James Bloem, CFO Wayne Brower, IS Tom Pratt, R&D Arthur Hasse, Sls David L Armstrong, Mkt Gary Miller, VP Robert Harvey, VP Thomas Pratt, VP James Christiansen, VP John Berry, IR Nancy Green, PR	Rev: Assets: Emp:	714 434 6	
Milliken & Co 1045 6th Avenue New York, NY 10018 212-819-4200	Manufacturer of textile products. Type: Private Ind: Apparel/Textiles Grp: Consumer Prd Roger Milliken, CEO	Rev: Assets: Emp:	2400 NA 20	
Million Market Newspaper/Times Mirror 711 Third Avenue New York, NY 10017 212-692-7100	Regional & neighborhood newspaper publisher. Type: Private-Sub Par: Times Mirror Co Ind: Publishing/Com Grp: Consumer Service Kingsley Anthony, CEO	Rev: Assets: Emp:	NA NA NA	
Millipore Corp 80 Ashby Road Bedford, MA 01730 617-275-9200	Manufacturer of filter devices. Type: NYSE-MIL Ind: Instruments Grp: High Tech John A Gilmartin, CEO William L Shippey, Pres Douglas Berthiaume, CFO Gerald C Haley, IS Jack T Johansen, R&D Thomas J Anderson, PR	Rev: Assets: Emp:	622 576 6	
Mills, Olan Inc 4325 Amnicola Highway Chattanooga, TN 37422 615-622-5141	Industrial products supply company. Type: Private Ind: Business Service Grp: Business Service Olan Mills, CEO	Rev: Assets: Emp:	1100 NA 11	
Milton Bradley Co 443 Shaker Road East Longmeadow, MA 01028 413-525-6411	Manufacturer of childrens toys & games. Type: Private-Sub Par: Hasbro Inc Ind: Leisure Time Grp: Consumer Service George Ditomassi, CEO	Rev: Assets: Emp:	250 NA 2	
Milwaukee County Government 901 N 9th Street Milwaukee, WI 53233 414-278-4222	County government. Type: County Govt Ind: Local Govt Grp: Govt & Non-Prof F Thomas Ament, CEO	Rev: Assets: Emp:	1300 NM 12	
Milwaukee, City of City Hall Milwaukee, WI 53202 414-278-2200	City government. Type: City Govt Ind: Local Govt Grp: Govt & Non-Prof John O Norquist, CEO	Rev: Assets: Emp:	592 NM 9	
Miniscribe Corp 1871 Lefthand Circle Longmont, CO 80501 303-651-6000	Manufacturer of computer disk drives. Type: NASDAQ-MINY Ind: Comput/Off Equip Grp: High Tech Q Wiles, CEO	Rev: Assets: Emp:	400 250 7	
Minneapolis, City of City Hall Minneapolis, MN 55415 612-348-2100	City government. Type: City Govt Ind: Local Govt Grp: Govt & Non-Prof Donald M Fraser, CEO	Rev: Assets: Emp:	636 NM 4	
Minnesota Mining & Manufacturing Canada 1840 Oxford Street E London, ON N5A4T1 Can 519-451-2500	Manufacturer of adhesives, tapes & packaging. Type: Private-Sub-For Ind: Chemicals Grp: Basic Industries John Myser, CEO	Rev: Assets: Emp:	425 510 2	

Organizations Listed Alphabetically

Organization / Address / Phone	Descriptive Information	Revenue / ($ mil)	Assets / ($ mil)	Emp (thous)
Minnesota Mining & Manufacturing Co 3M Center St Paul, MN 55144 612-733-1110	Diversified manufacturing; tapes, adhesives, fiber optics. Type: NYSE-MMM Ind: Manufacturing Grp: Manufacturing Allen F Jacobson, CEO Roger W Roberts, CFO Kenneth Schoen, IS Lester C Krogh, R&D Miles A Nelson, IR D H Frenette, PR	Rev: 10581 Assets: 8922 Emp: 83		
Minnesota Mutual Life Ins Co 400 N Robert Street St Paul, MN 55101 612-298-3500	Life insurance company. Type: Private Ind: Insurance Grp: Insurance Coleman Bloomfield, CEO Richard Engen, Pres Robert Hunstad, VCh Joel Mahle, IS David Goers, Mkt Jenean Cordon, Ops George Fremder, VP Milton Hildebrandt, VP James Johnson, VP Mark Hier, PR	Rev: 1394 Assets: 4466 Emp: 4		
Minnesota Power & Light Co 30 W Superior Street Duluth, MN 55802 218-722-2641	Electric power utility company. Type: NYSE-MPL Ind: Utility Grp: Utilities Jack F Rowe, CEO Arend J Sandbulte, Chr David Gartzke, Tres Robert D Edwards, CFO Gerald B Ostroski, IS Stephen Sherner, R&D	Rev: 460 Assets: 1484 Emp: 2		
Minnesota, State of State Capitol St Paul, MN 55155 612-296-6013	State government. Type: State Govt Ind: State/Prov Govt Grp: Govt & Non-Prof Rudy Perpich, CEO	Rev: 13023 Assets: NM Emp: 75		
Minnetonka Corp 104 Peavey Road Chaska, MN 55318 612-448-4181	Manufacturer of cosmetics & gifts. Type: NASDAQ-MINL Ind: Personal Care Grp: Consumer Prd Robert Taylor, CEO	Rev: 210 Assets: 180 Emp: 1		
Minolta Corp 101 Williams Drive Ramsey, NJ 07446 201-825-4000	Manufacturer & importer of electronic equip; US hdqtrs. Type: Private-Sub-For Ind: Electronics Grp: High Tech Sam Kusumoto, CEO	Rev: 825 Assets: NA Emp: 2		
Minstar Inc 100 S Fifth Street Suite 2400 Minneapolis, MN 55402 612-339-7900	Manufacturer of pleasure boats, sporting goods. Type: NASDAQ-MNST Ind: Leisure Time Grp: Consumer Service Irwin Jacobs, CEO Kenneth J Severinson, Pres Kenneth J Severinson, CFO James B Farrell, PR	Rev: 1300 Assets: 1150 Emp: 10		
Minyard Food Stores Inc 777 Freeport Coppel, TX 75109 214-462-8700	Grocery stores. Type: Private Ind: Retail/Food Grp: Retail Liz Minyard, CEO	Rev: 500 Assets: NA Emp: 5		
Mission Viejo Realty Group Inc 24800 Chrisanta Drive Mission Viejo, CA 92691 714-837-6050	Real estate development company. Type: Private-Sub Par: Philip Morris Companies Inc Ind: Real Estate/Bldg Grp: Business Service James Gilleran, CEO	Rev: NA Assets: NA Emp: NA		
Mississippi Power & Light Co 308 E Pearl Street Jackson, MS 39215 601-949-6442	Electric power utility. Type: Private-Sub Par: Entergy Corp (Middle South Utilities) Ind: Utility Grp: Utilities Donald C Lutken, CEO Michael Bemis, Pres James Cofer, Tres George a Goff, CFO Robert Loflin, Sls C Hiram Walters, Mkt Frank Gallaher, Ops	Rev: 684 Assets: 1555 Emp: 2		
Mississippi Power Co 2992 W Beach Street Gulfport, MS 39501 601-864-1211	Electrical power utility company. Type: Private-Sub Par: Southern Co Ind: Utility Grp: Utilities Alan Barton, CEO	Rev: NA Assets: NA Emp: NA		
Mississippi, State of New Capitol Jackson, MS 39201 601-359-3100	State government. Type: State Govt Ind: State/Prov Govt Grp: Govt & Non-Prof Ray Mabus, CEO	Rev: 4929 Assets: NM Emp: 50		

Organizations Listed Alphabetically

Organization / Address / Phone	Descriptive Information	Revenue / Assets / Emp ($ mil) ($ mil) (thous)		

Organization / Address / Phone	Descriptive Information			
Missouri Farmers Association Inc 615 Locust Street Columbia, MO 65201 314-874-5111	Agricultural cooperative food production. Type: Private Ind: Food Processing Grp: Food Processing Bud Frew, CEO	Rev: Assets: Emp:	550 NA 1	
Missouri Kansas Texas Railroad Co 701 Commerce Street Dallas, TX 75202 214-651-6706	Railroad transportation company. Type: NYSE-KT Ind: Railroad Grp: Business Service Reginold N Whitman, CEO Harold L Gastler, Pres K R Ziebarth, CFO Mike P McCasland, IS Harry T Dimmerman, Mkt Reginald N Whitman, IR Jerry M Sheridan, PR	Rev: Assets: Emp:	300 500 3	
Missouri, State of State Capitol Jefferson City, MO 65101 314-751-2151	State government. Type: State Govt Ind: State/Prov Govt Grp: Govt & Non-Prof John D Ashcroft, CEO	Rev: Assets: Emp:	9593 NM 74	
Mitchell Energy & Development Corp 2001 Timberloch Place The Woodlands, TX 77380 713-363-5500	Oil & natural gas exploration & production company. Type: ASE-MND Ind: Energy Grp: Basic Industries George P Mitchell, CEO Philip S Smith, CFO William D Windham, IS F D Covey, R&D Bernard F Clark, Sls Roger L Galatas, VP Thomas P Battle, VP Joseph W Kutchin, PR	Rev: Assets: Emp:	562 2112 2	
Mitchell Hutchins Asset Management Inc 1285 Avenue of the Americas New York, NY 10019 212-713-4000	Investment firm; pension fund management. Type: Private Ind: Non-Bank Fin Grp: Financial Edward Allanson, CEO	Rev: Assets: Emp:	350 13200 1	
Mitel Corp 350 Legget Drive Kanata, ON K2K1X3 Can 613-592-2122	Manufacturer of telecommunications equipment. Type: TOR-MLT Ind: Telecom Grp: High Tech Anthony F Griffiths, CEO John J Jarvis, Pres Dr M Douglas Smeaton, VCh David J Thomas, CFO William G Harris, R&D F Robert Dyer, Mkt Peter Berrie, VP David Hutton, VP Anthony Crisalli, VP Harvey Betsalel, VP	Rev: Assets: Emp:	356 379 4	
Mitre Corp Burlington Road Bedford, MA 01730 617-271-2000	Defense contracting consulting & engineering firm. Type: Private Ind: Business Service Grp: Business Service Charles Zraket, CEO	Rev: Assets: Emp:	550 NA 5	
Mitsubishi Canada Ltd 2181 Commerce Court W Toronto, ON M5L1A5 Can 416-362-6731	Automobile marketing & distribution company. Type: Private-Sub Ind: Conglomerate Grp: Manufacturing Nobuyoshi Hata, CEO	Rev: Assets: Emp:	1275 128 2	
Mitsubishi International USA Inc 520 Madison Avenue New York, NY 10022 212-605-2000	Diversified manufacturing & trading company. Type: Private-Sub-For Ind: Electronics Grp: High Tech Minoru Mikihara, CEO	Rev: Assets: Emp:	3850 NA 8	
Mitsubishi Motors of America Inc 10540 Talbert Fountain Valley, CA 92728 714-963-7677	Distributor & marketer of foriegn built automobiles. Type: Private-Sub-For Ind: Automotive Grp: Manufacturing K Naganuma, CEO	Rev: Assets: Emp:	1500 1000 2	
Mitsui & Co Canada Ltd 3333 Royal Bank Plaza Toronto, ON M5J2J2 Can 416-865-0330	International trading company. Type: Private-Sub-For Ind: Conglomerate Grp: Manufacturing Masahiko Kuji, CEO	Rev: Assets: Emp:	2218 181 1	
Mitsui & Co Trading (USA) 200 Park Avenue Pan American Bldg New York, NY 10166 212-878-4097	Diversified manufacturing & trading company. Type: Private-Sub-For Ind: Manufacturing Grp: Manufacturing Hisao Kondo, CEO	Rev: Assets: Emp:	1100 NA 2	

Organization / Address / Phone	Descriptive Information	Revenue / Assets / Emp ($ mil) ($ mil) (thous)		

Mitsui Manufacturers Bank
515 S Figueroa
Los Angeles, CA 90071
213-485-0331

Commercial bank.
Type: Private-Sub-For
Ind: Banking Grp: Financial
Yutaro Hiyashi, CEO

Rev: 400
Assets: 3300
Emp: 2

MMR Holding Corp
17325 Airline Highway
Baton Rouge, LA 70819
504-293-2701

Contractor, industrial & electical.
Type: NASDAQ-MMRH
Ind: Real Estate/Bldg Grp: Business Service
James Rutland, CEO

Rev: 250
Assets: 200
Emp: 4

MNC (Maryland National Corp) Financial
10 Light Street
Baltimore, MD 21202
301-244-1940

Commercial bank.
Type: OTC-MNCF
Ind: Banking Grp: Financial
Alan Hoblitzell, CEO Daniel J Callahan III, Pres Harry F Right Jr, CFO
Ronald W Davies, IS Daniel G Finney, IR Dee Groff, PR

Rev: 1530
Assets: 17000
Emp: 8

Mobay Corp
Mobay Road
Pittsburgh, PA 15205
412-777-2000

Manufacturer of specialty chemicals; US headquarters.
Type: Private-Sub-For
Ind: Chemicals Grp: Basic Industries
N H Prater, CEO

Rev: 2200
Assets: NA
Emp: 11

Mobil Corp
150 E 42nd Street
New York, NY 10017
212-883-4242

Worldwide oil production & marketing company.
Type: NYSE-MOB
Ind: Energy Grp: Basic Industries
Allen E Murray, CEO R Hartwell Gardner, Tres James Q Riordan, CFO
J F Trautschold, IS J V D'Ambrisi, R&D Richard F Tucker, Sls
Eugene A Renna, Mkt Robert C Musser, VP J Edward Fowler, VP
Dede T Bartlett, VP Robert G Weeks, IR Peter A Spina, PR

Rev: 54361
Assets: 38820
Emp: 69

Mobil Oil Canada Ltd
330 5th Avenue SW
Calgary, AB T2P2J7 Can
403-260-7910

Nationwide exploration, production & marketing company.
Type: Private-Sub-For
Ind: Energy Grp: Basic Industries
John Bauman, CEO

Rev: 1348
Assets: 3123
Emp: 2

Mobile Communications Corp
1800 E Country Line Road
Ridgeland, MS 39157
601-977-0888

Operator of mobile communication network.
Type: NASDAQ
Ind: Telecom Grp: High Tech
John N Palmer, CEO Rainer Sautermeister, VCh Arnold Young, Tres
Richard T Weatherholt, CFO Jai P Bhagat, R&D Paul Kindley, Mkt
Jere T Little, Ops C Victor Raiser, VP Charles Poole, VP
Elizabeth McCullough, VP Ernest Oswalt, VP

Rev: 115
Assets: 344
Emp: 2

Mobile, City of
City Hall
Mobile, AL 36633
205-438-7395

City government.
Type: City Govt
Ind: Local Govt Grp: Govt & Non-Prof
Arthur R Outlaw, CEO

Rev: 250
Assets: NM
Emp: 2

Mocatta Metals Corp
4 World Trade Center
New York, NY 10048
212-912-8400

Metals trading company.
Type: Private
Ind: Securities Grp: Financial
Pete Weller, CEO

Rev: 3300
Assets: 16500
Emp: 1

Modine Manufacturing Co
1500 DeKoven Avenue
Racine, WI 53401
414-636-1200

Manufacturer of heat transfer equipment.
Type: NASDAQ-MODI
Ind: Automotive Grp: Manufacturing
Earl E Richter, CEO Robert M Gunnerson, Tres Alex F Simpson, CFO
Z Philip Saperstein, IS Dean R Zakos, VP R Steven Bullmore, VP
Richard T Savage, VP M Gerald Baker, VP James R Dougall, VP
Victor S Frangopoulas, VP Walter Pavlick, IR

Rev: 424
Assets: 289
Emp: 4

Mohasco Corp
4401 Fair Lakes Court
Fairfax, VA 22033
703-768-8000

Manufacturer of furniture; office, home.
Type: NYSE-MOH
Ind: Building Mat Grp: Basic Industries
Charles M Egan, CEO Herbert J Broner, Chr Robert W Overholtzer, CFO
Max Perlowin, PR

Rev: 409
Assets: 350
Emp: 3

Organizations Listed Alphabetically

Organization / Address / Phone	Descriptive Information	Revenue / Assets / Emp ($ mil) ($ mil) (thous)		

Mohawk Oil Canada Ltd
6400 Robert Street
Burnaby, BC V5G2G2 Can
604-299-7244

Petroleum products company.
Type: TOR
Ind: Energy   Grp: Basic Industries
H Sutherland, CEO

Rev: 343
Assets: 132
Emp: 2

Molex Inc
2222 Wellington Court
Lisle, IL 60532
312-969-4550

Electronic devices, cable, switches, terminals.
Type: NASDAQ-MOLX
Ind: Electronics   Grp: High Tech
John H Krehbiel, CEO   Frederick A Krehbiel, Chr   John Drehbiel, Pres
John Psaltis, CFO   J Joseph King, VP   Werner Fichtner, VP
Ronald Schubel, VP

Rev: 502
Assets: 499
Emp: 6

Molson Companies
2 International Blvd
Toronto, ON M9W1A2 Can
416-675-1786

Nationwide beverage manufacturer; beer.
Type: TOR-MOL
Ind: Food Processing   Grp: Food Processing
J T Black, CEO   M E Erlindson, Tres   S L Hartley, CFO
Sanjib Choudhuri, R&D   E H Molson, VP   J S Lacey, VP
J C Pick, VP   D A Love, VP

Rev: 2070
Assets: 1160
Emp: 11

Monarch Capital Corp
One Financial Plaza
Springfield, MA 01144
413-781-3000

Insurance & brokerage services.
Type: NYSE
Ind: Non-Bank Fin   Grp: Financial
Gordon N Oakes, CEO   George W Sigular, VCh   Ronald Freres, CFO
Nicholas Lyndon, Mkt   Don Skelton, Ops   Raymond Terfera, VP
William Robbie, VP   John Moriarty, VP   James Durham, VP

Rev: 417
Assets: 5805
Emp: 3

Monfort of Colorado Inc
1930 AA Street
Greeley, CO 80632
303-353-2311

Wholesale meats packaging & distribution company.
Type: Private-Sub   Par: Conagra Inc
Ind: Food Processing   Grp: Food Processing
Roland Mapelli, CEO

Rev: 1600
Assets: 250
Emp: 5

Monongahela Power Co
1310 Fairmont Avenue
Fairmont, WV 26554
304-366-3000

Electric power utility company.
Type: Private-Sub   Par: Allegheny Power System Inc
Ind: Utility   Grp: Utilities
Ben Hayes, CEO

Rev: NA
Assets: NA
Emp: NA

Monsanto Canada Inc
2330 Argentia Road
Mississauga, ON L5M2G4 Can
416-826-9222

Diversified chemical company.
Type: Private-Sub-For
Ind: Chemicals   Grp: Basic Industries
H Wyatt, CEO

Rev: 353
Assets: 148
Emp: 1

Monsanto Co
800 N Lindbergh Blvd
St Louis, MO 63167
314-694-1000

Manufacturer of chemical products.
Type: NYSE-MTC
Ind: Chemicals   Grp: Basic Industries
Richard J Mahoney, CEO   Earle H Harbison Jr, Pres   Nicholas Reading, VCh
B Clare Harris, Tres   Francis A Stroble, CFO   Leonard A Cohn, IS
H Schneiderman, R&D   David L Sliney, Mkt   Earl N Brrasfield, VP
Leonard Cohn, VP   Martin Kallen, VP   Thomas Lafferre, VP
Phillip Needleman, VP   Tom Slocum, PR

Rev: 8293
Assets: 8461
Emp: 46

Montana Power & Light Co
40 E Broadway
Butte, MT 59701
406-723-5421

Electric power utility company.
Type: NYSE-MTP
Ind: Utility   Grp: Utilities
W Paul Schmechel, CEO   John Burke, VCh   Frank V Woy, CFO
C Daniel Regan, Mkt   Thomas McElwain, VP   Patricia L duToit, VP
Robert Gannon, VP

Rev: 444
Assets: 1926
Emp: 4

Montana, State of
State Capitol
Helena, MT 59620
406-444-2511

State government.
Type: State Govt
Ind: State/Prov Govt   Grp: Govt & Non-Prof
Stanley Stephens, CEO

Rev: 2282
Assets: NM
Emp: 21

Montgomery Ward & Co Inc
535 W Chicago Avenue
Chicago, IL 60610
312-467-2000

Nationwide retail department store company.
Type: Private
Ind: Retail/Merch   Grp: Retail
Bernard Brennan, CEO   Dominic Mangone, CFO   Richard Bergel, IS
Abram Bluestein, R&D   John A Daynard, Mkt   Charles Holland, IR
Erin Shields, PR

Rev: 4800
Assets: 3000
Emp: 40

Organizations Listed Alphabetically

Organization / Address / Phone	Descriptive Information	Revenue / ($ mil)	Assets / ($ mil)	Emp (thous)
Montgomery Ward Credit Corp 3411 Silverside Road Wilmington, DE 19810 302-478-9240	Financial subsidiary of Montgomery Ward. Type: Private-Sub Par: Montgomery Ward & Co Inc Ind: Non-Bank Fin Grp: Financial R C Carr, CEO	Rev: Assets: Emp:	238 2519 1	
Montreal Trustco Inc 1800 McGill College Avenue Montreal, PQ H3A3K9 Can 514-397-7171	Consumer banking company. Type: Private Ind: Non-Bank Fin Grp: Financial Robert Gratton, CEO	Rev: Assets: Emp:	764 6513 4	
Montreal, Universite de Case Postale 6128 Surrursale A Montreal, PQ H3C3J7 Can 514-343-6111	Major educational institution; university. Type: University Ind: University Grp: Govt & Non-Prof Gilles G Cloutier, CEO	Rev: Assets: Emp:	234 NM 50	
Moog Inc Jamison Road Aurora, NY 14052 716-652-2000	Manufacturer of electronic controls; defense, commercial. Type: ASE-MOG Ind: Electronics Grp: High Tech Richard A Aubrecht, CEO	Rev: Assets: Emp:	350 250 3	
Moore Corp 1 First Canadian Place Toronto, ON M5X1G5 Can 416-364-2600	Manufacturer paper products; computer paper. Type: Private-Sub-For Ind: Comput/Off Equip Grp: High Tech D Barr, CEO	Rev: Assets: Emp:	2571 2142 26	
Moore McCormick Resources Inc One Landmark Square Stamford, CT 06901 203-358-2200	Manufacturer of concrete products. Type: NYSE-MMR Ind: Energy Grp: Basic Industries Paul Tregurtha, CEO	Rev: Assets: Emp:	500 500 5	
Moore Medical Corp 389 John Downey Drive New Britain, CT 06050 203-225-2225	Wholesaler of medical products. Type: ASE-MMD Ind: Health Care Grp: Consumer Service Jerald K Rome, CEO	Rev: Assets: Emp:	250 150 1	
Moorman Manufacturing Co 1000 N 30th Street Quincy, IL 62301 217-222-7100	Producer & distributor of packaged foods. Type: Private Ind: Food Processing Grp: Food Processing Thomas Shade, CEO	Rev: Assets: Emp:	550 NA 5	
Morgan Products Ltd 601 Oregon Street Oshkosh, WI 54903 414-235-7170	Manufacturer of building materials. Type: NYSE-MGN Ind: Building Mat Grp: Basic Industries Arthur L Knight, CEO	Rev: Assets: Emp:	400 350 3	
Morgan Stanley & Co Inc 1251 Avenue of the Americas New York, NY 10020 212-703-4000	Investment banking firm. Type: NYSE-MS Ind: Securities Grp: Financial Parker Gilbert, CEO Richard B Fisher, Pres Richard Greenhill, VCh Bryan J Walsh, CFO Scott G Abbey, IS John Mack, VP Lewis Bernard, VP Anson Beard, VP Peter Roach, PR	Rev: Assets: Emp:	3100 29190 5	
Morgan, J P & Co Inc 23 Wall Street New York, NY 10015 212-344-3000	Commercial bank. Type: NYSE-JPM Ind: Banking Grp: Financial Ellmore C Patterson, CEO Lewis T Preston, Chr Dennis Weatherstone, Pres John R Ruffle, VCh Donald R Brunner, Tres James T Flynn, CFO William Pike, Sls Robert Engel, Mkt A Bruce Brackenridge, VP John T Olds, VP John Morris, PR	Rev: Assets: Emp:	7839 83923 16	
Morgan, J P Securities Inc 23 Wall Street New York, NY 10015 212-483-2323	Investment firm; securities trading. Type: Private Ind: Securities Grp: Financial Louis T Preston, CEO	Rev: Assets: Emp:	350 3300 1	

Organizations Listed Alphabetically

Organization / Address / Phone	Descriptive Information	Revenue / ($ mil)	Assets / ($ mil)	Emp (thous)
MorningStar Foods Inc 5956 Sherry Lane Dallas, TX 75225 214-360-4700	Manufacturer & distributor of dairy products. Type: Private Ind: Food Processing Grp: Food Processing James W Parker, CEO	Rev: Assets: Emp:		1000 NA 5
Morrell, John & Co 250 E Fifth Street Cincinnati, OH 45202 513-852-3500	Consumer food products production & distribution company. Type: Private-Sub Par: United Brands Co Ind: Food Processing Grp: Food Processing Milton Schloss, CEO	Rev: Assets: Emp:		NA NA NA
Morris Affiliated Companies 1650 E Battlefield Springfield, MO 65808 417-887-0333	Real estate development & management company. Type: Private Ind: Real Estate/Bldg Grp: Business Service John L Morris, CEO	Rev: Assets: Emp:		400 NA 2
Morrison Inc 4721 Morrison Drive Mobile, AL 36625 205-344-3000	Engineering & construction company. Type: NASDAQ-MORR Ind: Food/Lodging Grp: Consumer Service E Eugene Bishop, CEO Paul Freeman, Tres James Lambert, CFO Daniel Bettis, R&D John C Metz, VP Joe B Byrum, VP Larry E Davis, VP Robert D McClenagan, VP Richard A McGeoch, IR	Rev: Assets: Emp:		829 299 15
Morrison Knudsen Corp Morrison Knudsen Plaza PO Box 7808 Boise, ID 83707 208-386-5000	Mining & engineering company. Type: NYSE-MRN Ind: Business Service Grp: Business Service William M Agee, CEO W J Deasy, Chr Frank M Adams, VCh Donald Kayser, CFO Denny Gaul, IS R Chastain, Sls M Shirley, Mkt Keith M Price, VP A Morris, VP J Bowden, VP C Staub, VP James B Greene, IR Vern Nelson, PR	Rev: Assets: Emp:		1909 746 15
Morrison Knudsen Eng & Environment One Erieview Plaza Cleveland, OH 44114 216-523-5600	Ship building, ship repair & heavy construction company. Type: Private-Sub Par: Morrison Knudsen Corp Ind: Manufacturing Grp: Manufacturing K Price, CEO	Rev: Assets: Emp:		NA NA NA
Morse Diesel Inc 1515 Broadway New York, NY 10036 212-730-4000	Nationwide advertising agency. Type: Private Ind: Business Service Grp: Business Service Donald Piser, CEO	Rev: Assets: Emp:		825 NA 6
Morse Operations Inc 1240 N Federal Highway Fort Lauderdale, FL 33304 305-563-6331	Operator of automobile dealerships, leasing & renting. Type: Private Ind: Automotive Grp: Manufacturing E J Morse, CEO	Rev: Assets: Emp:		500 NA 1
Morse Shoe Inc 555 Turnpike Street Canton, MA 02021 617-828-9300	Shoe manufacturer. Type: Private Ind: Retail/Merch Grp: Retail Manuel Rosenberg, CEO	Rev: Assets: Emp:		600 NA 6
Mortenson, M A Co Inc 700 Meadow Lane Minneapolis, MN 55422 612-522-2100	General contractors; industrial buildings & warehouses. Type: Private Ind: Real Estate/Bldg Grp: Business Service M A Mortenson Jr, CEO	Rev: Assets: Emp:		500 NA 1
Morton Chemical Co 333 W Wacker Drive Chicago, IL 60606 312-807-3290	Chemical manufacturing company. Type: Private-Sub Par: Morton International Inc Ind: Chemicals Grp: Basic Industries Robert Covalt, CEO	Rev: Assets: Emp:		NA NA NA
Morton International Inc 110 N Wacker Drive Chicago, IL 60606 312-807-2000	Manufacturer of specialty chemicals & salt products. Type: NYSE-MTI Ind: Chemicals Grp: Basic Industries Charles S Locke, CEO S Jay Stewart, Pres Robert Covalt, VCh John R Bowen, CFO Donald L Kidd, IS Thomas S Russel, R&D John F Poe, Sls Raymond L Pierobon, Mkt Hugh Marx, VP Carson B Trenor, IR Richard L Kyrouac, PR	Rev: Assets: Emp:		1407 1100 11

Organization / Address / Phone	Descriptive Information	Revenue / Assets / Emp ($ mil) ($ mil) (thous)	
Morton Salt Co 110 N Wacker Drive Chicago, IL 60606 312-807-2665	Producer & distributor of salt products. Type: Private-Sub Par: Morton International Inc Ind: Food Processing Grp: Food Processing W E Johnston, CEO	Rev: Assets: Emp:	NA NA NA
Motel 6 Lmtd Ptnrship 14651 Dallas Parkway Dallas, TX 75240 214-386-6161	Nationwide operator of motels & restaurants. Type: NASDAQ-SIX Ind: Food/Lodging Grp: Consumer Service Joseph McCarthey, CEO	Rev: Assets: Emp:	450 200 8
Motor Wheel Corp 400 Collins Road Lansing, MI 48910 517-337-5700	Manufacturer of automotive parts; wheels. Type: Private Ind: Automotive Grp: Manufacturing Joseph C Overbeck, CEO	Rev: Assets: Emp:	500 NA 5
Motorola Canada Ltd 3125 Steeles Avenue E Willowdale, ON M2H2H6 Can 416-499-1441	Manufacturer of electrical goods & equipment. Type: Private-Sub-For Ind: Electronics Grp: High Tech Marcel Bernard, CEO	Rev: Assets: Emp:	298 170 3
Motorola Inc 1303 E Algonquin Road Schaumburg, IL 60196 312-397-5000	Manufacturer of electronic equipment; defense, aerospace. Type: NYSE Ind: Electronics Grp: High Tech Robert W Galvin, CEO George M C Fisher, Chr Gary L Tooker, Pres Donald R Jones, CFO Karl J Burgess, IS William V Braun, R&D Larry Friedman, Mkt Albert R Brashear, PR	Rev: Assets: Emp:	8250 6710 102
Motors Insurance (General Motors) Co 3044 W Grand Blvd Detroit, MI 48202 313-556-5000	Property & casualty insurance company. Type: Private-Sub Par: General Motors Corp Ind: Insurance Grp: Insurance Joseph J Pero, CEO	Rev: Assets: Emp:	1075 2453 4
Moyer Packing Co Inc 249 Allentown Road Souderton, PA 18964 215-723-5555	Meatpacking & production. Type: Private Ind: Food Processing Grp: Food Processing Curtis F Moyer, CEO	Rev: Assets: Emp:	500 NA 2
Mrs Paul's Kitchen Inc 5830 Henry Avenue Philadelphia, PA 19128 215-483-4000	Packaged food manufacturer. Type: Private-Sub Par: Campbell Soup Co Ind: Food Processing Grp: Food Processing Steven McNeil, CEO	Rev: Assets: Emp:	NA NA NA
MSA Mine Safety Appliances Co 121 Gamma Drive O'Hara Township, PA 15238 412-967-3000	Manufacturer of safety equipment for use in mines. Type: NASDAQ-MNES Ind: Manufacturing Grp: Manufacturing L N Short, CEO L N Short Jr, Chr D L Zeitler, CFO D E Crean, VP James E Herald, VP W B Miller, VP Frederick Tepper, VP	Rev: Assets: Emp:	406 361 4
MTD Products Inc 5965 Graston Road Valley City, OH 44280 216-225-2600	Diversified manufacturing company. Type: Private Ind: Manufacturing Grp: Manufacturing Curtis E Moll, CEO	Rev: Assets: Emp:	275 NA 3
Multimedia Inc 305 S Main Street Greenville, SC 29601 803-298-4373	Newspapers & television broadcasting company. Type: NASDAQ-MMEDC Ind: Publishing/Com Grp: Consumer Service Walter E Bartlett, CEO	Rev: Assets: Emp:	440 405 6
Munich Reinsurance Co 560 Lexington Avenue New York, NY 10022 212-310-1800	Property & casualty insurance company. Type: Private Ind: Insurance Grp: Insurance Hans Rothrow, CEO	Rev: Assets: Emp:	800 1500 3
Murata North America Inc 5560 Tennyson Plano, TX 75024 214-403-3300	Manufacturer & importer of electronic equip & cameras;US hq. Type: Private-Sub-For Ind: Electronics Grp: High Tech Mike Franz, CEO	Rev: Assets: Emp:	550 NA 2

Organizations Listed Alphabetically

Organization / Address / Phone	Descriptive Information	Revenue / Assets / Emp ($ mil) ($ mil) (thous)		

Murphy Oil Corp
200 Peach Street
El Dorado, AR 71730
501-862-6411

Oil & natural gas production & marketing, & lumber company.
Type: NYSE-MUR
Ind: Energy   Grp: Basic Industries
C H Murphy, CEO   Jack W McNutt, Chr   Claiborne Deming, VCh
B David Richardson, CFO   R Madison Murphy, IS   Jack Brewer, Mkt
Jerry Watkins, VP   W Bayless Rowe, VP   George Brazeal, VP
Melissa Ellis, PR

Rev: 1525
Assets: 2068
Emp: 5

Murray Ohio Manufacturing Co
Franklin Road
Brentwood, TN 37027
615-373-6500

Manufacturer of bicycles.
Type: NYSE-MYO
Ind: Automotive   Grp: Manufacturing
William Hannon, CEO

Rev: 500
Assets: 400
Emp: 4

Musicland Group Inc
7500 Excelsior Blvd
Minneapolis, MN 55426
612-932-7700

Retail stores; audio & video recordings, electronic equip.
Type: Private
Ind: Retail/Merch   Grp: Retail
J W Eugster, CEO

Rev: 500
Assets: NA
Emp: 3

Mutual Benefit Life Insurance Co
520 Broad Street
Newark, NJ 07102
201-481-8000

Life insurance company.
Type: Private
Ind: Insurance   Grp: Insurance
Robert V Van Fossan, CEO   Henry E Kates, Pres   Ted Simmons, VCh
Daniel G Stewart, CFO   Charles C McCaig, IS   Wendell J Bossen, Mkt
Betty Lee Hagerty, IR   Jim Goodness, PR

Rev: 3169
Assets: 10639
Emp: 6

Mutual Life Assurance Co of Canada
227 King Street S
Waterloo, ON N2J4C5 Can
519-888-2235

Life insurance company.
Type: Private
Ind: Insurance   Grp: Insurance
John H Panabaker, CEO   Jack V Masterman, Chr   E Austin Fricker, CFO
William W Yeo, IS   Alison H Watson, R&D   John M Riley, Sls
Lyle G Shapansky, Mkt   Glenn E Beir, VP   David M MacIntosh, VP
Mary F McLaughlin, PR

Rev: 2343
Assets: 9322
Emp: 4

Mutual Life Ins Co of New York (MONY)
1740 Broadway
New York, NY 10019
212-708-2000

Life insurance company.
Type: Private-Mutual
Ind: Insurance   Grp: Insurance
James A Atwood, CEO   James Farley, Pres   Rita K Farrelly, VCh
F Allen Spooner, CFO   Rita K Farrelly, IS   Michael Cohen, Sls
Albert J Schiff, Mkt   Kenneth M Levine, VP   Gorden Perry, VP
Neal Jewell, VP   Lawrence M Clark, PR

Rev: 5235
Assets: 17706
Emp: 8

Mutual of America Life Insurance Co
666 Fifth Avenue
New York, NY 10113
212-399-1600

Life insurance company.
Type: Private-Mutual
Ind: Insurance   Grp: Insurance
William J Flynn, CEO   Dwight Bartlett III, Pres   Manfred Altstadt, CFO
Thomas Roach, IS   Howard Lichtenstein, Mkt   Linda DeHooge, VP
Thomas J Moran, VP   Sarah W Belle, VP   Joseph E King, VP
Kenneth McCaffrey, PR

Rev: 1011
Assets: 4810
Emp: 9

Mutual of Omaha Insurance Co
Mutual of Omaha Plaza
Omaha, NE 68175
402-342-7600

Property & casualty insurance company.
Type: Private-mutual
Ind: Insurance   Grp: Insurance
Thomas J Skutt, CEO

Rev: 2000
Assets: 1997
Emp: 5

Mylan Laboratories Inc
130 Seventh Street 1030 Century Bldg
Pittsburgh, PA 15222
412-232-0100

Pharmaceutical manufacturing company.
Type: NYSE-MYL
Ind: Drugs   Grp: Consumer Service
Roy McKnight, CEO

Rev: 96
Assets: 109
Emp: 1

Nabisco Brands Inc
Nabisco Plaza Campus Drive
Parsippany, NJ 07054
201-503-7100

Food manufacturer, cookies, cereals.
Type: Private-Sub   Par: RJR Nabisco Inc
Ind: Food Processing   Grp: Food Processing
James Welch, CEO

Rev: NA
Assets: NA
Emp: NA

Organizations Listed Alphabetically

Organization / Address / Phone	Descriptive Information	Revenue / ($ mil)	Assets / ($ mil)	Emp (thous)
Nabisco Brands Ltd 1 Dundas Street W Toronto, ON M5G2A9 Can 416-598-2600	Manufacturer of packaged foods. Type: Private-Sub-For Ind: Food Processing Grp: Food Processing John MacDonald, CEO F Ross Johnson, Chr Robert J Carbonell, VCh Edward J Robinson, CFO John H Clarke, R&D Gerald Long, VP Harold Henderson, VP John D Martin, VP Dennis Durden, VP Kenneth D Taylor, VP Dean Posvar, VP	Rev: Assets: Emp:	699 704 4	
NACCO Industries 12800 Shaker Blvd Cleveland, OH 44120 216-752-1000	Coal mining, electrical appliances, & forklift trucks. Type: NYSE Ind: Metals/Mining Grp: Basic Industries Ward Smith, CEO Clifford Miercort, Chr K Donald Grischow, Tres Herschell Cashion, R&D Thomas A Koza, VP H Dean Jocot, VP	Rev: Assets: Emp:	616 837 6	
Nalco Chemical Co One Nalco Center Naperville, IL 60566 312-961-9500	Manufacturer of specialty chemical products. Type: NYSE-NCL Ind: Chemicals Grp: Basic Industries W H Clark, CEO Keith W Davis, Pres Rodney M Bloom, CFO David R Bertran, IS Ronald J Allain, R&D Richard E Myers, Sls John Berthoud, Mkt Donald M Weber, PR	Rev: Assets: Emp:	994 839 5	
Narragansett Electric Co 280 Melrose Street Providence, RI 02901 401-941-1400	Electric power utility company. Type: Private-Sub Par: New England Electric System Inc Ind: Utility Grp: Utilities Robert McCabe, CEO	Rev: Assets: Emp:	NA NA NA	
Nash Finch Co 3381 Gorham Avenue St Louis Park, MN 55426 612-929-0371	Operator of retail sporting goods stores. Type: NASDAQ-NAFC Ind: Retail/Food Grp: Retail Harold Finch, CEO Russell Mammel, Pres Dennis Fairchild, CFO Clarence Walters, IS J Eisenberg, R&D Jerry Barber, Mkt Katherine Borchardt, PR	Rev: Assets: Emp:	1700 500 8	
Nashua Corp 44 Franklin Street Nashua, NH 03061 603-880-2323	Manufacturer of coated products, leasing,photocopy supplies. Type: NYSE-NSH Ind: Manufacturing Grp: Manufacturing Charles E Clough, CEO Daniel Junius, Tres William Luke, CFO Timothy Gallagher, IS John J Montesi, R&D Eric N Birch, VP Joseph Kershaw, VP Paul Buffum, VP Lloyd S Nelson, VP William Wehrle, PR	Rev: Assets: Emp:	989 450 7	
Nashville, City of City Hall Nashville, TN 37201 615-259-6047	City government. Type: City Govt Ind: Local Govt Grp: Govt & Non-Prof Bill Boner, CEO	Rev: Assets: Emp:	1027 NM 16	
Nassau County Government One West Street Mineola, NY 11501 516-535-3000	County government. Type: County Govt Ind: Local Govt Grp: Govt & Non-Prof Thomas S Gulotta, CEO	Rev: Assets: Emp:	3600 NM 20	
National Advanced Systems Corp 750 Central Expressway Santa Clara, CA 95054 408-970-1000	Manufacturer of semiconductor & systems products. Type: Private-Sub Par: National Semiconductor Corp Ind: Electronics Grp: High Tech D Martin, CEO	Rev: Assets: Emp:	NA NA NA	
National Aluminum Corp Two Robinson Plaza Pittsburgh, PA 15205 412-788-0190	Manufacturer of aluminum products. Type: Private-Sub Par: National Steel (Nat'l Intergroup) Corp Ind: Metals/Mining Grp: Basic Industries John McKibbin, CEO	Rev: Assets: Emp:	NA NA NA	
National Amusements Corp 200 Elm Street Dedham, MA 02026 617-461-1600	Movie theaters, broadcast, cable TV. Type: Private Ind: Leisure Time Grp: Consumer Service Sumner M Redstone, CEO	Rev: Assets: Emp:	1250 NA 10	

Organizations Listed Alphabetically

Organization / Address / Phone	Descriptive Information	Revenue / ($ mil)	Assets / ($ mil)	Emp (thous)
National Assn of Letter Carriers 100 Indiana Avenue NW Washington, DC 20001 202-393-4695	National labor union. Type: Membership Org Ind: Membership Org Grp: Govt & Non-Prof Vincent R Sombrotto, CEO	Rev: Assets: Emp:		250 NM 300
National Bank of Canada Ltd 600 De La Gauchetiere W Montreal, PQ H3B4A8 Can 514-394-4000	Commercial bank. Type: TOR Ind: Banking Grp: Financial Michel Belanger, CEO Michael Belanger, Chr Andre Berard, Pres Rene Fortier, VCh Robert Cardinal, CFO Jules Gagne, Mkt	Rev: Assets: Emp:		2633 26285 13
National Bank of Washington Inc 1414 Fourth Avenue Seattle, WA 98111 206-344-2300	Commercial bank. Type: Private Ind: Banking Grp: Financial Gerry Cameron, CEO	Rev: Assets: Emp:		450 4500 3
National Beverage Corp PO Box 13889 Fort Lauderdale, FL 32859 305-857-3300	Soft drink manufacturer. Type: Private Ind: Food Processing Grp: Food Processing Nick A Caporella, CEO	Rev: Assets: Emp:		500 NA 1
National Broadcasting Co 30 Rockefeller Center New York, NY 10020 212-664-4444	Operator of television & radio broadcasting networks. Type: Private-Sub Par: General Electric Co Ind: Publishing/Com Grp: Consumer Service Robert Wright, CEO	Rev: Assets: Emp:		NA NA NA
National Car Rental Inc 7700 France Avenue S Minneapolis, MN 55435 612-830-2121	Automobile rental & leasing company. Type: Private Ind: Consumer Service Grp: Consumer Service Vincent A Wasik, CEO	Rev: Assets: Emp:		750 NA 10
National City Corp 1900 E Nineth Street Cleveland, OH 44114 216-575-2000	Commercial bank. Type: NYSE-NCC Ind: Banking Grp: Financial Edward B Brandon, CEO A Stevens Miles, Pres David A Daberko, VCh William R Robertson, CFO Harold B Todd Jr, IS Morton Boyd, VP Gene F Carpenter, VP Charles W Hall, VP Thomas Richlovsky, IR David Talbott, PR	Rev: Assets: Emp:		2227 21623 11
National Cleaning Contractors Inc 60 Madison Avenue New York, NY 10010 212-689-4050	Industrial cleaning & maintenance company. Type: Private Ind: Business Service Grp: Business Service M Sweig, CEO	Rev: Assets: Emp:		500 NA 10
National Community Bank 113 W Essex Street Maywood, NJ 07607 201-845-1000	Commercial bank. Type: NASDAQ Ind: Banking Grp: Financial Fairleigh S Dickinson, CEO	Rev: Assets: Emp:		321 3614 2
National Computer Systems Inc 11000 Prarie Lakes Drive Hopkins, MN 55344 612-829-3000	Manufacturer of information systems, proprietary software. Type: NASDAQ-NLCS Ind: Comput/Off Equip Grp: High Tech Charles Oswald, CEO	Rev: Assets: Emp:		250 150 3
National Convenience Stores Inc 100 Waugh Drive Houston, TX 77007 713-863-2200	Operator of convenience retail stores. Type: NYSE-NCS Ind: Retail/Food Grp: Retail V H VanHorn, CEO	Rev: Assets: Emp:		1073 600 11
National Coop Refinery Assn Inc 2000 S Main Street McPherson, KS 67460 316-241-2340	Petroleum refining & distribution company. Type: Private Ind: Energy Grp: Basic Industries Larry Williams, CEO Robert G Hull, CFO Kenneth Cummings, IS Ronald Schaumburg, PR	Rev: Assets: Emp:		1100 500 1

Organizations Listed Alphabetically

Organization / Address / Phone	Descriptive Information	Revenue / ($ mil)	Assets / ($ mil)	Emp (thous)
National Credit Union Administration 1776 G Street NW Washington, DC 20456 202-357-1055	Federal government financial agency. Type: Federal Govt Ind: Federal Govt Fin Grp: Financial Roger W Jepsen, CEO	Rev: 500 Assets: NM Emp: 3		
National Data Corp One National Data Plaza Atlanta, GA 30329 404-329-8500	Computerized information services; cash mgt, telemarketing. Type: NASDAQ-NDTA Ind: Comput/Off Equip Grp: High Tech L Whitney, CEO	Rev: 227 Assets: 150 Emp: 3		
National Distillers & Chemicals Corp 99 Park Avenue New York, NY 10016 212-949-5000	Manufacturer of specialty chemicals & liquors. Type: NYSE-CUE Ind: Chemicals Grp: Basic Industries John H Stookey, CEO	Rev: 2922 Assets: 2908 Emp: 12		
National Education Association 1201 Sixteenth Street NW Washington, DC 20036 202-833-4000	National labor union. Type: Membership Org Ind: Membership Org Grp: Govt & Non-Prof Mary H Furtrell, CEO	Rev: 1000 Assets: NM Emp: 1700		
National Education Corp 18400 Von Karman Avenue Irvine, CA 92715 714-474-9400	Training company; industrial, home study. Type: NYSE-NEC Ind: Business Service Grp: Business Service H David Bright, CEO	Rev: 400 Assets: 200 Emp: 4		
National Fuel Gas Co 30 Rockefeller Plaza New York, NY 10112 212-541-7533	Natural gas production & utility holding company. Type: NYSE-NFG Ind: Utility Grp: Utilities Bernard J Kennedy, CEO John M Brown, VCh Joseph Pawlowski, CFO Thomas Burns, VP Richard DiValerio, VP Phillip Ackerman, VP	Rev: 769 Assets: 1177 Emp: 5		
National Geographic Society Inc 1145 17th Street NW Washington, DC 20036 202-857-7000	Publisher of specialty periodicals & magazines. Type: Private Ind: Publishing/Com Grp: Consumer Service Gilbert Grosvnor, CEO	Rev: 550 Assets: NA Emp: 3		
National Gypsum Co 4500 Lincoln Plaza Dallas, TX 75201 214-740-4500	Mining & minerals production. Type: NYSE Ind: Building Mat Grp: Basic Industries John P Hayes, CEO Bernard L Kasriel, Pres Paul T Even, Tres J Michael Conaway, CFO Joseph A Keller, R&D James C Quinly, VP Edward A Porter, VP Allan Cecil, PR	Rev: 1221 Assets: 1610 Emp: 8		
National Health Laboratories Inc 7590 Fay Avenue La Jolla, CA 92037 619-454-3314	Operator of clinical laboratories. Type: NASDAQ-NHLI Ind: Health Care Grp: Consumer Service R O Perelman, CEO	Rev: 314 Assets: 315 Emp: 3		
National Home Life Assurance Co Liberty Park Valley Forge, PA 19493 215-648-5000	Life insurance company. Type: OTC Ind: Insurance Grp: Insurance Donald D Kennedy, CEO	Rev: 1155 Assets: 3118 Emp: 3		
National Life Assurance Co of Canada 522 University Avenue Toronto, ON M5G 1Y7 Can 416-598-2122	Life insurance company. Type: Private Ind: Insurance Grp: Insurance V P Tonna, CEO	Rev: 271 Assets: 917 Emp: 1		
National Life Insurance Co National Life Drive Montpelier, VT 05604 802-229-3333	Life insurance company. Type: Private-Mutual Ind: Insurance Grp: Insurance John H Harding, CEO	Rev: 717 Assets: 3590 Emp: 2		

Organizations Listed Alphabetically

Organization / Address / Phone	Descriptive Information	Revenue / ($ mil)	Assets / ($ mil)	Emp (thous)
National Life of Vermont 1 National Life Drive Montpelier, VT 05604 802-229-3333	Life insurance company. Type: Private-Mutual Ind: Insurance Grp: Insurance Frederic H Bertrand, CEO John H Harding, Pres Richard J Borda, CFO Mark J Levesque, IS William Callnan, R&D James B Antell, Sls Ronald E Bishop, Mkt Brian Vachon, IR Jane Robb, PR	Rev: 850 Assets: 3980 Emp: 2		
National Medical Enterprises Inc 11620 Wilshire Blvd Los Angeles, CA 90025 213-479-5526	Operator of hospitals, clinics & health care centers. Type: NYSE Ind: Health Care Grp: Consumer Service Richard K Eamer, CEO Leonard Cohen, Pres John C Bedrosian, VCh Taylor R Jenson, CFO Peter deWetter, Mkt Bruce Busby, VP Michael Focht, VP Paul J Russell, IR Mary C Stancill, PR	Rev: 3202 Assets: 3507 Emp: 85		
National Patent Development Co 9 W 57th Street New York, NY 10019 212-826-8500	Investment company; medical equipment & products. Type: ASE-NPD Ind: Health Care Grp: Consumer Service Jerome I Feldman, CEO	Rev: 265 Assets: 300 Emp: 1		
National Propane Co 69 Denton Avenue New Hyde Park, NY 11040 516-352-6500	Production & distribution of propane. Type: Private-Sub Par: DWG Corp Ind: Energy Grp: Basic Industries Russell Boyle, CEO	Rev: NA Assets: NA Emp: NA		
National Real Estate Service Ltd 1075 W Georgia Street Vancouver, BC V6E4G8 Can 604-685-3474	Nationwide network of real estate sales offices. Type: Private Ind: Real Estate/Bldg Grp: Business Service Carl Neilsen, CEO	Rev: 170 Assets: NA Emp: 4		
National Sanitary Supply Corp 13217 S Figeroa Street Los Angeles, CA 90061 213-532-4800	Manufacturer of maintenance supply products. Type: NASDAQ-NSSX Ind: Manufacturing Grp: Manufacturing Robert Garber, CEO	Rev: 300 Assets: 200 Emp: 1		
National Sea Products Ltd 1959 Upper Water Street Halifax, NS B3J3B7 Can 902-422-9381	Food products company; seafood. Type: TOR Ind: Food Processing Grp: Food Processing W O Morrow, CEO G E M Cummings, Chr M L Pitman, Tres R A McColloch, CFO R K Joyce, IS F D McGee, Sls C J Gower, Mkt D J Hennigar, VP H E Demone, VP K H Ritcey, VP K L Nelson, VP J P MacDonald, VP I H Langlands, VP	Rev: 477 Assets: 343 Emp: 8		
National Semiconductor Corp 2900 Semiconductor Drive PO Box 58090 Santa Clara, CA 95052 408-721-5000	Manufacturer of integrated circuits. Type: NYSE Ind: Electronics Grp: High Tech Charles E Sporck, CEO James Smaha, VCh Gary P Arnold, CFO David N Martin, IS F Joseph Van Poppelen, Mkt John Webb, VP J Philip Russell, VP Michael Hawkins, VP Clements Pausa, VP Linda Baker, IR Mike Hawkins, PR	Rev: 2470 Assets: 1777 Emp: 38		
National Service Industries Inc 1180 Peachtree Street NE Atlanta, GA 30309 404-892-2400	Manufacturer of lighting equipment, uniform rental. Type: NYSE-NSI Ind: Electronics Grp: High Tech Erwin Zaban, CEO Sidney Kirschner, Chr Don Hubble, VCh Robert H Creviston, CFO Herbert P Bruce, IS James E Brown, Mkt Kenneth Speer, Ops Walter Buce, VP S Booker Carter, VP	Rev: 1414 Assets: 825 Emp: 20		
National Starch & Chemical Corp Finderne Avenue Bridgewater, NJ 08807 201-685-5000	Manufacturer of specialty chemicals; US headquarters. Type: Private-Sub-For Ind: Chemicals Grp: Basic Industries Nicholas Marotta, CEO James A Kennedy, Pres Robert B Albert, CFO Frank V Caccavo, IS Cheater D Szymanski, R&D Henry M Barry, PR	Rev: 1210 Assets: 750 Emp: 8		

Organizations Listed Alphabetically

Organization / Address / Phone	Descriptive Information	Revenue / ($ mil)	Assets / ($ mil)	Emp (thous)
National Steel (Nat'l Intergroup) Corp 20 Stanwix Pittsburgh, PA 15222 412-394-4100	Integrated manufacturer of steel. Type: NYSE Ind: Steel Grp: Basic Industries Howard M Love, CEO James E Haas, Pres Laurence J Farley, CFO Edward J Klein, PR	Rev: 3081	Assets: 2000	Emp: 7
National Victoria & Grey Trustco Ltd 1 Ontario Street Stratford, ON N5A6S9 Can 519-271-2050	Consumer banking company. Type: Private Ind: Non-Bank Fin Grp: Financial Henry N R Jackman, CEO William Somerville, Chr Bryan Mehlenbacher, Pres Christopher Fleming, VCh W John Switzer, CFO T Cavanaugh, Ops J Mould A Schillup, VP J Brethour, VP T Greenough, VP	Rev: 1073	Assets: 10362	Emp: 4
National Westminster Bank of Canada Ltd 2060 Royal Bank Plaza Toronto, ON M5J2J1 Can 416-865-0170	Commercial bank. Type: Private-Sub-For Ind: Banking Grp: Financial Alex S Yankovich, CEO	Rev: 82	Assets: 1461	Emp: 1
National Westminster Bank USA 60 Hempstead Avenue West Hempstead, NY 11552 516-560-7050	Commercial bank. Type: Private-Sub-For Ind: Banking Grp: Financial Robert Wallace, CEO William T Knowles, Chr John A Petts, CFO Robert G Chapman, IS Chris Cameris, IR Tim Connolly, PR	Rev: 1200	Assets: 12000	Emp: 5
Nationale Nederlanden Insurance Co 1050 Connecticut Avenue NW Washington, DC 20036 202-463-7964	Property & casualty insurance company. Type: Private-Sub-For Ind: Insurance Grp: Insurance Ewald Kist, CEO	Rev: 1000	Assets: 1500	Emp: 2
Nationwide Electronics Inc 3003 Wakefield Drive Carpentersville, IL 60110 312-426-5900	Manufacturer & distributor of electronic products. Type: Private Ind: Electronics Grp: High Tech Robert Martin, CEO	Rev: 1100	Assets: NA	Emp: 2
Nationwide Insurance Co One Nationwide Plaza Columbus, OH 43216 614-249-7111	Life insurance company. Type: Private Ind: Insurance Grp: Insurance John E Fisher, CEO John L Marakas, Pres Peter F Frenzer, CFO Danny M Fullerton, IS J Richard Bull, IR Lou Fabro, PR	Rev: 5000	Assets: 12000	Emp: 12
Natural Gas Corp of California 77 Beale Street San Francisco, CA 94106 415-972-7000	Natural gas public utility company. Type: Private-Sub Par: Pacific Gas & Electric Co Ind: Utility Grp: Utilities John Sproul, CEO	Rev: NA	Assets: NA	Emp: NA
Navistar International Corp 401 N Michigan Avenue Chicago, IL 60611 312-836-2000	Manufacturer of trucks; industrial, commercial. Type: NYSE Ind: Automotive Grp: Manufacturing James C Cotting, CEO Neil Springer, Chr Robert Lannert, Tres Robert Morrison, CFO Robert Shaughnessy, Mkt John Sheahin, VP Francis J Gerlis, VP	Rev: 4080	Assets: 2522	Emp: 16
Navistar International Corp of Canada 120 King Street Hamilton, ON L8N3S5 Can 416-528-7700	Manufacturer of trucks & heavy equipment. Type: Private-Sub-For Ind: Automotive Grp: Manufacturing Wayne Krzysiak, CEO	Rev: 935	Assets: 425	Emp: 2
NBD Bancorp (Natl Bank Detroit) Inc 611 Woodward Avenue Detroit, MI 48226 313-225-1000	Commercial bank. Type: NYSE-NBD Ind: Banking Grp: Financial Charles T Fisher, CEO Verne G Istock, VCh D Dean Kaylor, CFO James E Barlett, IS Russell C Browne Jr, Mkt James E Barlett, Ops Jonathan T Walton, VP William E Blevins, VP Thomas Jeffs, VP John T Walton, VP Gerald Hanson, VP Daniel T Lis, VP J Richard Johnson, PR	Rev: 2181	Assets: 24176	Emp: 12

Organizations Listed Alphabetically

Organization / Address / Phone	Descriptive Information	Revenue / ($ mil)	Assets / ($ mil)	Emp (thous)
NBI Inc 3450 Mitchell Lane Boulder, CO 80301 303-444-5710	Operator of retail computer hardware & software stores. Type: NASDAQ-NBI Ind: Retail/Merch Grp: Retail Thomas Kavanaugh, CEO	Rev: Assets: Emp:	400 200 4	
NCH Corp 2727 Chemsearch Blvd PO Box 152170 Irving, TX 75015 214-438-0211	Manufacturer of specialty chemicals. Type: NYSE-NCH Ind: Chemicals Grp: Basic Industries Lester A Levy, CEO	Rev: Assets: Emp:	565 500 4	
NCNB (No Carolina Natl Bank) Corp One NCNB Plaza Charlotte, NC 28255 704-374-5000	Commercial bank. Type: NYSE-NCB Ind: Banking Grp: Financial Hugh L McColl, CEO Francis B Kemp, Pres Timothy P Hartman, CFO O Darwin Smith, IS Brad Iverson, Mkt Joseph B Martin, VP William P Middlemas, VP Kenneth Lewis, VP Fredric Figge, VP James M Berry, VP Rusty J Page, PR	Rev: Assets: Emp:	2829 29848 18	
NCNB Texas National Bank (Republic Bank) 1800 Republic Bank Bldg 326 N St Paul Dallas, TX 75201 214-977-4000	Commercial bank. Type: NYSE-FRB Ind: Banking Grp: Financial Albert V Casey, CEO Albert V Casey, Chr Edward R McPherson, CFO Jerry McElhatton, IS Jeff Johnson, Mkt Joe Bowles, IR Marie Dunn, PR	Rev: Assets: Emp:	2900 33000 15	
NCR Corp 1700 S Patterson Blvd Dayton, OH 45479 513-445-5000	Manufacturer of computers & point of sale equipment. Type: NYSE Ind: Comput/Off Equip Grp: High Tech Charles E Exley, CEO Gilbert P Williamson, Pres William F Buster, VCh D W Russler, CFO James K Hull, IS Tom T Tang, R&D Giuseppe Bassani, VP R Elton White, VP John L Giering, VP S Richard Reece, VP Giuseppe Bassani, IR Gary R Stechmesser, PR	Rev: Assets: Emp:	5990 4717 60	
Nebraska, State of State Capitol Lincoln, NE 68509 402-471-2311	State government. Type: State Govt Ind: State/Prov Govt Grp: Govt & Non-Prof Kay A Orr, CEO	Rev: Assets: Emp:	3721 NM 34	
NEC Nippon Electric Corp USA 8 Old Sod Farm Road Melville, NY 11747 516-753-7000	Manufacturer & importer of electronic equipment; US hdqtrs. Type: Private-Sub-For Ind: Electronics Grp: High Tech Tadashi Suzuki, CEO	Rev: Assets: Emp:	2200 NA 4	
Needham Worldwide Advertising Inc 437 Madison Avenue New York, NY 10022 212-415-2000	Advertising agency. Type: Private Ind: Business Service Grp: Business Service Keith L Rienhard, CEO	Rev: Assets: Emp:	1100 NA 2	
Neiman Marcus Co 27 Boylston Street Chestnut Hill, MA 02167 617-232-0760	Retail department store. Type: Private-Sub Par: General Cimema Corp Ind: Retail/Merch Grp: Retail Richard Smith, CEO	Rev: Assets: Emp:	1200 1300 13	
Nekoosa Papers Inc 100 Wisconsin River Drive Port Edwards, WI 54469 715-887-5111	Manufacturer of paper, paper products. Type: Private-Sub Par: Great Northern Nekoosa Corp Ind: Paper/Forest Prd Grp: Basic Industries Arnold M Nemirow, CEO	Rev: Assets: Emp:	3000 NA 20	
Neoax Inc Four High Ridge Parkway Stamford, CT 06904 203-322-8333	Manufacturer of car & truck parts. Type: NASDAQ-NOAX Ind: Automotive Grp: Manufacturing Wallace B Askins, CEO	Rev: Assets: Emp:	314 250 2	

Organizations Listed Alphabetically

Organization / Address / Phone	Descriptive Information	Revenue / ($ mil)	Assets / ($ mil)	Emp (thous)
NERCO Inc 11 SW Columbia Portland, OR 97201 503-796-6600	Mining company; coal, gold, silver. Type: NYSE-NER Ind: Energy Grp: Basic Industries Gerald K Drummond, CEO Laurence Heiner, Pres Roy R Watts, CFO E P Ingraham, IS Robert L Autrey, R&D Leslie Lehmann, VP Charles Adams, VP William W Lyons, PR	Rev: Assets: Emp:	662 1206 2	
NES Corp 3003 Wakefield Drive Carpentersville, IL 60110 312-426-5900	Manufacturer of industrial instruments. Type: Private Ind: Instruments Grp: High Tech Robert Martin, CEO	Rev: Assets: Emp:	825 NA 3	
Nesbitt Thomson Inc 150 King Street W Toronto, ON M4M1J9 Can 416-586-3600	Investment company; brokerage. Type: Private Ind: Securities Grp: Financial J Brian Aune, CEO	Rev: Assets: Emp:	223 1088 2	
Nestle Enterprises Ltd 1185 Eglinton Avenue E Don Mills, ON M3C3C7 Can 416-429-4411	Manufacturer of packaged goods; food, beverages. Type: Private-Sub-For Ind: Food Processing Grp: Food Processing Ian Murray, CEO	Rev: Assets: Emp:	521 229 2	
Nestle USA Inc 100 Manhattanville Road Purchase, NY 10577 914-251-3000	International producer of packaged foods; US headquarters. Type: Private-Sub-For Ind: Food Processing Grp: Food Processing Allan MacDonald, CEO	Rev: Assets: Emp:	2200 NA 11	
Network Systems Corp 7600 Boone Avenue N Minneapolis, MN 55428 612-424-4888	Manufacturer of data communications equipment. Type: NASDAQ-NSCO Ind: Comput/Off Equip Grp: High Tech James E Thornton, CEO	Rev: Assets: Emp:	131 240 1	
Neuberger & Berman Inc 522 Fifth Avenue New York, NY 10036 212-730-7370	Investment firm; securities trading. Type: Private Ind: Securities Grp: Financial Vince Cavallo, CEO	Rev: Assets: Emp:	220 4400 1	
Neutrogena Corp 5755 W 96th Street Los Angeles, CA 90045 213-642-1150	Cosmetic manufacturer, skin care products, sundries. Type: NASDAQ-NGNA Ind: Personal Care Grp: Consumer Prd Lloyd E Cotsen, CEO	Rev: Assets: Emp:	178 93 1	
Nevada Bell Corp 645 E Plumb Lane Reno, NV 89502 702-789-6000	Telephone public utility company. Type: Private-Sub Par: Pacific Telesis Group Inc Ind: Telecom Grp: High Tech Dennis Malley, CEO	Rev: Assets: Emp:	NA NA NA	
Nevada Power Co 6226 W Sahara Avenue Las Vegas, NV 89102 702-367-5000	Electric power utility. Type: NYSE-NVP Ind: Utility Grp: Utilities Conrad L Ryan, CEO	Rev: Assets: Emp:	409 1014 2	
Nevada, State of State Capitol Carson City, NV 89710 702-885-5000	State government. Type: State Govt Ind: State/Prov Govt Grp: Govt & Non-Prof Richard H Byran, CEO	Rev: Assets: Emp:	2436 NM 16	
New Brunswick Elect Power Comm Ltd 515 King Street Fredericton, NB E3B4X1 Can 506-458-4444	Electric power utility. Type: Govt Authority Ind: Utility Grp: Utilities Rayburn D Doucett, CEO Arthur J O'Conner, Pres Kenneth B Little, CFO Frank H Ryder, R&D Terrence S Thompson, Mkt Richard A Toner, VP G Linwood Titus, VP Peter J Dykeman, VP	Rev: Assets: Emp:	737 2419 3	
New Electric Transmission Corp Four Park Street Concord, NH 03301 603-225-5528	Electric power utility company. Type: Private-Sub Par: New England Electric System Inc Ind: Utility Grp: Utilities Russell Holden, CEO	Rev: Assets: Emp:	NA NA NA	

Organizations Listed Alphabetically

Organization / Address / Phone	Descriptive Information	Revenue / Assets / Emp ($ mil) ($ mil) (thous)		

New England Business Service
500 Main Street
Groton, MA 01450
508-448-6111

Manufacturer of business forms, office supplies & furniture.
Type: NASDAQ
Ind: Comput/Off Equip   Grp: High Tech
Richard H Rhoads, CEO

Rev: 217
Assets: 80
Emp: 2

New England Electric System Inc
25 Research Drive
Westborough, MA 01581
508-366-9011

Electric utility system.
Type: NYSE-NES
Ind: Utility   Grp: Utilities
John W Rowe, CEO   Joan T Bok, Chr   John Kaslow, VCh
Alfred Houston, CFO   George Sasdi, R&D   Robert Bigelow, Sls
Glenn Schleede, Mkt   John Dickson, VP   Robert Smith, VP
Frederic Greenman, VP

Rev: 1461
Assets: 3111
Emp: 5

New England Mutual Life Insurance Co
501 Boylston Street
Boston, MA 02117
617-578-2000

Life insurance company.
Type: Private-Mutual
Ind: Insurance   Grp: Insurance
Edward E Phillips, CEO   John A Fibiger, Pres   F Brooks Cowgill, Tres
Ralph F Verni, CFO   Michael Brown, IS   Keenan F King, VP
Robert Schneider, VP   Edward Berthiame, VP   Michael Brown, VP
Francis Malone, VP   Daniel Logan, IR   Peter Harrington, PR

Rev: 3802
Assets: 14273
Emp: 8

New England Telephone & Telegraph Co
185 Franklin Street
Boston, MA 02107
617-743-9800

Telephone public utility company.
Type: Private-Sub Par: NYNEX Corp
Ind: Telecom   Grp: High Tech
Paul C O'Brian, CEO

Rev: NA
Assets: NA
Emp: NA

New England Tile Corp
183 Columbia Road
Hanover, MA 02339
617-826-5144

Construction & real estate development company.
Type: Private
Ind: Real Estate/Bldg   Grp: Business Service
Earl Opdyke, CEO

Rev: 550
Assets: NA
Emp: 2

New Hampshire, State of
State House
Concord, NH 03301
603-271-1110

State government.
Type: State Govt
Ind: State/Prov Govt   Grp: Govt & Non-Prof
Judd Gregg, CEO

Rev: 1921
Assets: NM
Emp: 21

New Jersey Bell Telephone Co
540 Broad Street
Newark, NJ 07101
201-649-9900

Telephone public utility company.
Type: Private-Sub Par: Bell Atlantic Corp
Ind: Telecom   Grp: High Tech
Anton Campannella, CEO

Rev: NA
Assets: NA
Emp: NA

New Jersey Divison of Investment
349 W State Street
Trenton, NJ 08625
609-292-5106

State investment agency; pension management.
Type: State Govt
Ind: Non-Bank Fin   Grp: Financial
Roland M Machold, CEO

Rev: 1475
Assets: 22433
Emp: 1

New Jersey Manufacturers Insurance Co
Sullivan Way
West Trenton, NJ 08628
609-883-1300

Property & casualty insurance company.
Type: OTC
Ind: Insurance   Grp: Insurance
Vincent E Hoyer, CEO

Rev: 380
Assets: 1394
Emp: 2

New Jersey National Bank
1 W State Street
Trenton, NJ 08650
609-771-5700

Commercial bank.
Type: Private-Sub Par: Corestates Financial Corp
Ind: Banking   Grp: Financial
John H Walther, CEO

Rev: 500
Assets: 3500
Emp: 2

New Jersey, State of
State Capitol
Trenton, NJ 08625
609-292-2121

State government.
Type: State Govt
Ind: State/Prov Govt   Grp: Govt & Non-Prof
Thomas H Kean, CEO

Rev: 20700
Assets: NM
Emp: 105

New Jersy Resources Inc
1415 Wyckoff Road
Wall, NJ 07719
201-938-1480

Natural gas utility.
Type: NYSE-NJR
Ind: Utility   Grp: Utilities
James T Dolan, CEO

Rev: 350
Assets: 700
Emp: 2

Organizations Listed Alphabetically

Organization / Address / Phone	Descriptive Information	Revenue / ($ mil)	Assets / ($ mil)	Emp (thous)
New Mexico, State of State Capitol Sante Fe, NM 87503 505-827-4011	State government. Type: State Govt Ind: State/Prov Govt Grp: Govt & Non-Prof Garrey E Carruthers, CEO	Rev: Assets: Emp:	4168 NM 42	
New Orleans Public Service Co 225 Baronne Street New Orleans, LA 70112 504-595-3100	Electric power utility company. Type: Private-Sub Par: Entergy Corp (Middle South Utilities) Ind: Utility Grp: Utilities James McCain, CEO	Rev: Assets: Emp:	NA NA NA	
New Orleans, City of City Hall New Orleans, LA 70112 504-586-4000	City government. Type: City Govt Ind: Local Govt Grp: Govt & Non-Prof Sidney J Barthelemy, CEO	Rev: Assets: Emp:	645 NM 11	
New Plan Realty Inc 1120 Avenue of the Americas New York, NY 10036 212-869-3000	Real estate investment firm. Type: NYSE-NPR Ind: Real Estate/Bldg Grp: Business Service William Newman, CEO	Rev: Assets: Emp:	245 300 1	
New Process Corp 220 Hickory Street Warren, PA 16366 814-723-3600	Direct mail retailer of apparel & home items. Type: ASE-NOZ Ind: Retail/Merch Grp: Retail Murray K McComas, CEO	Rev: Assets: Emp:	325 200 1	
New World Entertainment 1440 S Sepulveda Blvd Los Angeles, CA 90025 213-444-8100	Distributors of motion pictures, television productions. Type: ASE Ind: Leisure Time Grp: Consumer Service Harry Sloan, CEO	Rev: Assets: Emp:	279 200 1	
New York Life Insurance Co 51 Madison Avenue New York, NY 10010 212-576-7000	Life insurance company. Type: Private Ind: Insurance Grp: Insurance Donald K Ross, CEO George Bundschuh, VCh William E Keiter, CFO Michael McLaughlin, IS William Yelverton, R&D Lee M Gammill Jr, Mkt Malcolm Mackay, VP Richard Hansen, VP Herbert Cheskis, VP Walter Shur, VP John T Bardeleben, VP Harry G Hohn, VP George Trapp, PR	Rev: Assets: Emp:	12374 43417 20	
New York Life Insurance Co of Canada 121 Bloor Street E Toronto, ON M4W3N2 Can 416-960-4500	Life insurance company. Type: Private-Mutual Ind: Insurance Grp: Insurance Barrie Usher, CEO	Rev: Assets: Emp:	209 680 1	
New York Power Authority 1633 Broadway New York, NY 10019 212-468-6000	State electric power generating authority. Type: Govt Authority Ind: Govt Authority Grp: Govt & Non-Prof Richard Flynn, CEO	Rev: Assets: Emp:	1250 5100 10	
New York State Electric & Gas Inc Route 13 Dryden Road PO Box 287 Ithaca, NY 14851 607-347-4131	Electric & gas utility company. Type: NYSE Ind: Utility Grp: Utilities James A Carrigg, CEO Allen E Kintigh, Pres Dolores Hix, VCh Richard A Jacobson, CFO J E Murphy, IS R R Tedesco, R&D Orlin W Darrach, Mkt William McCann, Ops Paul Komar, VP Irene Stillings, VP John Fiala, VP Michael Turkovic, VP Ken B Hooper, PR	Rev: Assets: Emp:	1340 4693 5	
New York State Retirement Fund Inc 10 Corporate Woods Drive Albany, NY 12211 518-447-2741	State investment agency; pension fund management. Type: State Govt Ind: Non-Bank Fin Grp: Financial Harold N Langwitz, CEO	Rev: Assets: Emp:	700 27500 2	
New York State Teachers Investment Fund 10 Corporate Woods Drive Albany, NY 12211 518-447-2741	State investment agency; pension management. Type: State Govt Ind: Non-Bank Fin Grp: Financial Harold N Langwitz, CEO	Rev: Assets: Emp:	450 16500 2	

Organization / Address / Phone	Descriptive Information	Revenue ($ mil)	Assets ($ mil)	Emp (thous)
New York Telephone Co 1095 Avenue of the Americas New York, NY 10036 212-395-2121	Telephone public utility company. Type: Private-Sub Par: NYNEX Corp Ind: Telecom Grp: High Tech Frederic Salerno, CEO	Rev: NA	Assets: NA	Emp: NA
New York Times Co 29 W 43rd Street New York, NY 10036 212-556-1234	Publisher of newspapers. Type: NYSE Ind: Publishing/Com Grp: Consumer Service Arthur Ochs Sulzberger, CEO Walter E Mattson, Pres Richard G Thomas, Tres David L Gorham, CFO Katherine P Darrow, IS Michael E Ryan, R&D Benjamen Handelman, VP Frank R Gatti, VP Nancy Nielsen, IR Marjorie W Longley, PR	Rev: 1701	Assets: 1915	Emp: 11
New York University Washington Square New York, NY 10003 212-598-3127	Major educational institution; university. Type: University Ind: University Grp: Govt & Non-Prof John Brademas, CEO	Rev: 553	Assets: 548	Emp: 40
New York, City of City Hall New York, NY 10007 212-566-1300	City government. Type: City Govt Ind: Local Govt Grp: Govt & Non-Prof Edward I Koch, CEO	Rev: 27197	Assets: NM	Emp: 339
New York, State of State Capitol Albany, NY 12224 518-474-2121	State government. Type: State Govt Ind: State/Prov Govt Grp: Govt & Non-Prof Mario M Cuomo, CEO	Rev: 64568	Assets: NM	Emp: 288
New York-Off Track Betting Inc 1501 Broadway New York, NY 10036 212-704-5000	State agency; operator of horse race gambling parlors. Type: Private Ind: Leisure Time Grp: Consumer Service Howard P Giordano, CEO	Rev: 1100	Assets: NA	Emp: 2
Newark, City of City Hall 920 Broad Street Newark, NJ 07102 201-733-6400	City government. Type: City Govt Ind: Local Govt Grp: Govt & Non-Prof Sharpe James, CEO	Rev: 313	Assets: NM	Emp: 5
Newell Co Newell Center 29 Stephenson Street Freeport, IL 61032 815-235-4171	Manufacturer of hardware & houseware products. Type: NYSE-NWL Ind: Manufacturing Grp: Manufacturing Alton F Doody, CEO Daniel C Ferguson, Chr William P Sovey, Pres Clarence Davenport, Tres William Alldredge, CFO Donald Krause, R&D Robert F Gilbert, Mkt Johannes Tempelaar-Leitz, VP Roland Knecht, VP Thomas Ferguson, VP John Eaton, VP Shirley Martin, VP William Doppstadt, VP Byron H Stebbins, PR	Rev: 988	Assets: 820	Emp: 11
Newfoundland & Labrador Hydro Electric 50 Elizabeth Avenue St Johns, NF A1A2X8 Can 709-737-1400	Electric power utility. Type: Govt Corp Ind: Utility Grp: Utilities Cyril J Abery, CEO	Rev: 282	Assets: 1857	Emp: 1
Newmark & Lewis Inc 595 S Broadway Hicksville, NY 11801 516-681-6900	Operator of retail consumer electronics stores. Type: ASE-NLI Ind: Retail/Merch Grp: Retail Warren G Hyman, CEO	Rev: 250	Assets: 150	Emp: 3
Newmont Gold Corp 1700 Lincoln Street Denver, CO 80203 303-863-7414	Gold mining company. Type: NYSE Ind: Metals/Mining Grp: Basic Industries Gordon R Parker, CEO	Rev: 389	Assets: 598	Emp: 6

Organizations Listed Alphabetically

Organization / Address / Phone	Descriptive Information	Revenue / ($ mil)	Assets / ($ mil)	Emp (thous)
Newmont Mining Corp 1700 Lincoln Street Denver, CO 80203 303-863-7414	Mining company. Type: NYSE-NEM Ind: Metals/Mining Grp: Basic Industries Gordon R Parker, CEO Paul L Maroni, Tres Edward P Fontaine, CFO Thomas Van Riper, IS Paul E Mortimer, R&D Donald McCall, Sls Ronald J Vance, Mkt John H Johnson, VP Graham M Clark, VP Leonard Harris, VP James F Hill, PR	Rev: Assets: Emp:	501 1321 5	
Niagara Frontier Services Inc 60 Dingens Street Buffalo, NY 14206 716-823-3712	Operator of retail food stores. Type: Private Ind: Retail/Food Grp: Retail Seville Nanula, CEO	Rev: Assets: Emp:	825 NA 5	
Niagara Mohawk Power Corp 300 Erie Blvd W Syracuse, NY 13202 315-474-1511	Electric power utility. Type: NYSE-NMK Ind: Utility Grp: Utilities William F Allyn, CEO William J Donlon, Chr John M Endries, Pres John Hennessey, VCh John W Powers, CFO Michael Cullen, IS Andrew Vesey, R&D Michael J Cahill, Mkt Gerald Garcey, VP James Goramn, VP Edward Hoffman, VP Darlene Kerr, VP Richard E A Duffy, PR	Rev: Assets: Emp:	2801 7076 11	
Niagara Share Corp 70 Niagara Street Buffalo, NY 14202 716-856-2600	Investment group. Type: NYSE-NGS Ind: Securities Grp: Financial Paul Schoelkopf, CEO	Rev: Assets: Emp:	250 200 1	
Nichimen Trading Co USA 1185 Avenue of the Americas New York, NY 10036 212-719-1000	International trading company; US headquarters. Type: Private-Sub-For Ind: Manufacturing Grp: Manufacturing K Nomura, CEO	Rev: Assets: Emp:	1650 NA 1	
Nichols, S E Inc 275 7th Avenue New York, NY 10001 212-206-9400	Operator of retail discount stores. Type: ASE-NCL Ind: Retail/Merch Grp: Retail Kennith H Davis, CEO	Rev: Assets: Emp:	350 250 4	
NICOR (Northern Illinois Gas) Corp 1700 W Ferry Road Naperville, IL 60566 312-242-4470	Natural gas exploration, production & local utility company. Type: NYSE-GAS Ind: Utility Grp: Utilities Richard G Cline, CEO Larry Garberding, Pres Donald Lohrentz, Tres John J Lannon, CFO John C Flowers, Sls Kathleen L Halloran, VP	Rev: Assets: Emp:	1509 2100 4	
Nielsen, A C Co Nielsen Plaza Northbrook, IL 60062 312-498-6300	Consumer marketing research service company. Type: Private-Sub Par: Dun & Bradstreet Corp Ind: Comput/Off Equip Grp: High Tech John Holt, CEO	Rev: Assets: Emp:	NA NA NA	
Nike Inc 3900 SW Murray Blvd Beaverton, OR 97005 503-641-6453	Manufacturer, athletic wear & sport shoes. Type: NYSE Ind: Apparel/Textiles Grp: Consumer Prd Philip H Knight, CEO Dale Wahl, Tres George E Porter, CFO Mel Hochhalter, IS Mark Parker, R&D Nick Kartalis, Sls Thomas Clarke, Mkt Lindsay D Stewart, VP Douglas Houser, VP Ronald E Nelson, VP Harry Carsh, VP Kevin R Brown, PR	Rev: Assets: Emp:	1203 709 6	
Nikko Securities Co Intl Inc One World Financial Ctr 200 Liberty St New York, NY 10281 212-416-5400	Investment firm; securities trading. Type: Private Ind: Securities Grp: Financial Toshio Mori, CEO	Rev: Assets: Emp:	330 3300 1	
Nippon Credit Bank Ltd 800 Wilshire Blvd 14th Floor Los Angeles, CA 90017 213-629-5566	Commercial bank. Type: Private-Sub-For Ind: Banking Grp: Financial Nobuyoshi Nagaya, CEO	Rev: Assets: Emp:	450 3500 1	

Organizations Listed Alphabetically

Organization / Address / Phone	Descriptive Information	Revenue / ($ mil)	Assets / ($ mil)	Emp (thous)
NIPSCO Northern Indiana Pub Serv Co 5265 Hohman Avenue Hammond, IN 46320 219-853-5200	Electric & gas utility. Type: NYSE Ind: Utility Grp: Utilities Edmund A Schroer, CEO Jack Stine, VCh Stephen Adik, Tres Jerry M Springer, CFO Joseph L Turner, R&D Patricia Homrich, VP John W Dunn, VP	Rev: 1526	Assets: 3685	Emp: 5
Nissan Automobile Canada Ltd 2233 Argentia Road Mississauga, ON L5M2L5 Can 416-821-9180	Automobile marketing & distribution company. Type: Private-Sub-For Ind: Automotive Grp: Manufacturing R Hoshind, CEO	Rev: 575	Assets: 170	Emp: 1
Nissan Motor Corp USA 18501 S Figueroa Carson, CA 90248 212-532-3111	Manufacturer & importer of automobiles; US headquarters. Type: Private-Sub-For Ind: Automotive Grp: Manufacturing Yutaka Kume, CEO	Rev: 4400	Assets: NA	Emp: 15
Nissho Iwai Canada Ltd 2624 Dunsmuir Street Vancouver, BC V7X1L3 Can 604-684-8351	Manufacturer of iron & steel products. Type: Private Ind: Manufacturing Grp: Manufacturing I Okamoto, CEO	Rev: 340	Assets: 170	Emp: 2
Nissho Iwai Trading Co USA 1211 Avenue of the Americas New York, NY 10036 212-704-6500	International trading company; US headquarters. Type: Private-Sub-For Ind: Manufacturing Grp: Manufacturing M Nishura, CEO	Rev: 1650	Assets: NA	Emp: 2
Nixdorf US Inc 52 Third Avenue Burlington, MA 01803 617-273-0480	Manufacturer & importer of computer equipment; US hdqtrs. Type: Private-Sub-For Ind: Comput/Off Equip Grp: High Tech John Paul, CEO	Rev: 880	Assets: NA	Emp: 8
NL Industries Inc 3000 North Belt Houston, TX 77032 713-987-4000	Manufacturer of lead products & chemicals. Type: NYSE-NL Ind: Oil Service Grp: Business Service Harold C Simmons, CEO J Landis Martin, Chr Susan E Alderton, CFO Claude Stam, IS Edward C Hutcheson, Mkt Robert P Wallace, PR	Rev: 1100	Assets: 1400	Emp: 13
Noble Affiliates Inc 110 W Broadway Ardmore, OK 73402 405-223-4110	Oil & gas exploration & production company. Type: NYSE-NBL Ind: Oil Service Grp: Business Service Sam Noble, CEO	Rev: 192	Assets: 527	Emp: 2
Noland Co 2700 Warwick Blvd Newport News, VA 23607 804-928-9000	Wholesale plumbing, heating, refrigeration supplies. Type: NASDAQ-NOLD Ind: Building Mat Grp: Basic Industries G C Barber, CEO Carl Watson, Chr James E Sikes, Tres John E Gullett, IS Frank L Brewer, Sls A W Granzow, Mkt James F Davenport, VP Charles Gillie, VP William T Overman, VP Dennis E Rawls, VP Rihard L Welborn, VP William T Smith, IR	Rev: 461	Assets: 201	Emp: 2
Noma Industries Ltd 4211 Yonge Street Willowdale, ON M2P2A9 Can 416-222-6662	Manufacturer of electronic components. Type: TOR Ind: Electronics Grp: High Tech H Thomas Beck, CEO	Rev: 448	Assets: 281	Emp: 4
Nomura Securities International Inc 180 Maiden Lane The Continental Center New York, NY 10038 212-208-9300	Investment firm; securities trading. Type: Private Ind: Securities Grp: Financial Katsuya Takanashi, CEO	Rev: 330	Assets: 3300	Emp: 1

Organizations Listed Alphabetically

Organization / Address / Phone	Descriptive Information	Revenue / ($ mil)	Assets / ($ mil)	Emp (thous)
Noranda Forest Inc 55 Yonge Street Toronto, ON M5E1S4 Can 416-365-0710	Forest products company; lumber, paper. Type: Private-Sub Par: Noranda Inc Ind: Paper/Forest Prd Grp: Basic Industries Timothy Kenny, CEO	Rev: Assets: Emp:	3668 3339 16	
Noranda Inc Commerce Court W Toronto, ON M5L1B6 Can 416-982-7111	Mining company. Type: NYSE Ind: Metals/Mining Grp: Basic Industries Alfred Powis, CEO Adam Zimmerman, VCh Bruce Bone, Tres Alan R Thomas, CFO Craig Tedmon, R&D E Courtney Pratt, VP Frank Lederman, VP Gary Corlett, VP	Rev: Assets: Emp:	7529 7961 48	
Norcen Energy Resources Ltd 715 5th Avenue SW Calgary, AB T2P2X7 Can 403-231-0111	Oil & gas exploration & production company. Type: TOR-NCN Ind: Energy Grp: Basic Industries Paul M Marshall, CEO Edward G Battle, Chr J Trevor Eyton, VCh Paul H Palmer, CFO Barry Cochrane, R&D	Rev: Assets: Emp:	622 1968 2	
Norden Inc Norden Plaza Norwalk, CT 06856 203-852-5000	Manufacturer of defense systems. Type: Private-Sub Par: United Technologies Corp Ind: Aerospace Grp: High Tech Edward Decker, CEO	Rev: Assets: Emp:	NA NA NA	
Nordson Corp 28601 Clemens Road Westlake, OH 44145 216-892-1580	Manufacturer of industrial equipment. Type: NASDAQ-NDSN Ind: Equipment Grp: Manufacturing Eric T Nord, CEO	Rev: Assets: Emp:	350 250 2	
Nordstrom Inc 1501 Fifth Avenue Seattle, WA 98101 206-628-2111	Retail family apparel. Type: NASDAQ Ind: Retail/Merch Grp: Retail James F Nordstrom, CEO John A McMillan, Chr John McMillan, Pres Bruce Nordstrom, VCh John Goesling, CFO R Gary Baughn, IS Cynthia Demme, Sls R Gary Baughn, VP Robert Bender, VP Gail Cottle, VP Raymond Johnson, VP R Gary Baughn, IR Chris Bridenbaugh, PR	Rev: Assets: Emp:	2328 1572 33	
Norfolk Southern Corp Three Commerical Place Norfolk, VA 23510 804-629-2600	Railroad, trucking & real estate company. Type: NYSE-NSC Ind: Railroad Grp: Business Service Arnold B McKinnon, CEO John R Turbyfill, CFO Gerald Durand, IS Paul R Rudder, R&D R W Coffey, Sls D Henry Watts, Mkt Kenneth Maxfield, VP Joseph Newkirk, VP D Henry Watts, VP Robert E L deButts, VP William B Bales, VP Robert W Coffey, VP Deborah Noxon, IR Magda A Ratajski, PR	Rev: Assets: Emp:	4462 10159 34	
Norfolk, City of City Hall Norfolk, VA 23501 804-441-2679	City government. Type: City Govt Ind: Local Govt Grp: Govt & Non-Prof Joseph A Leafe, CEO	Rev: Assets: Emp:	405 NM 9	
Norinchukin Bank Inc One World Trade Center New York, NY 10048 212-697-1717	Commercial bank. Type: Private-Sub-For Ind: Banking Grp: Financial Hiroshi Ohno, CEO	Rev: Assets: Emp:	450 3500 1	
Norstar BanCorp 1450 Western Avenue Albany, NY 12203 518-447-4043	Commercial bank. Type: NYSE-FLT Ind: Banking Grp: Financial Richard Cornwall, CEO	Rev: Assets: Emp:	1000 11132 1	
Nortek Inc 50 Kennedy Plaza Providence, RI 02903 401-751-1600	Building materials & equipment company. Type: NYSE-NTK Ind: Manufacturing Grp: Manufacturing Ralph R Papitto, CEO Ralph R Papitto, Chr Richard L Bready, Pres Regina Winkfield, IS Kenneth L Donohue, PR	Rev: Assets: Emp:	1224 1052 9	

Organizations Listed Alphabetically

Organization / Address / Phone	Descriptive Information	Revenue / ($ mil)	Assets / ($ mil)	Emp (thous)
North American Coal Corp 12800 Shaker Blvd Cleveland, OH 44120 216-752-1000	Coal mining company. Type: NYSE-NC Ind: Energy Grp: Basic Industries Otis Bennett, CEO	Rev: Assets: Emp:	600 400 5	
North American Life Assurance Co 5650 Yonge Street Toronto, ON M2M4G4 Can 416-229-4515	Life insurance company. Type: TOR Ind: Insurance Grp: Insurance W E Bradford, CEO K L Kirk, Pres B Moore, CFO J Lynch, IS J Deschenes, R&D W Riddall, Sls K Henry, Mkt M Kelly, Ops C Barbosa, VP	Rev: Assets: Emp:	944 3838 3	
North American Philips Corp 100 E 42nd Street New York, NY 10017 212-697-3600	International manufacturer of electronic products. Type: Private-Sub-For Ind: Electronics Grp: High Tech Gerrit Jeelof, CEO Einar Kloster, Pres Debra McClister, VCh Stanley I Cundey, CFO Charles E Ferguson, IS Dr Larry French, R&D Albert A Ruttner, PR	Rev: Assets: Emp:	5424 3423 52	
North American Van Lines Inc 5001 US Highway 30 W Fort Wayne, IN 46818 219-429-2511	Trucking company, commercial freight, household moves. Type: Private-Sub Par: Norfolk Southern Corp Ind: Transport Grp: Business Service J Ruffolo, CEO	Rev: Assets: Emp:	NA NA NA	
North Carolina Retirement Fund 325 N Salisbury Street Raleigh, NC 27611 919-733-3211	State investment agency; pension funds. Type: State Govt Ind: Non-Bank Fin Grp: Financial Doug Chapel, CEO	Rev: Assets: Emp:	350 11000 1	
North Carolina State University Administrative Bldg Raleigh, NC 27695 919-737-2011	Major educational institution; university. Type: University Ind: University Grp: Govt & Non-Prof Bruce R Poulton, CEO	Rev: Assets: Emp:	210 447 27	
North Carolina, State of State Capitol Raleigh, NC 27611 919-733-1110	State government. Type: State Govt Ind: State/Prov Govt Grp: Govt & Non-Prof James G Martin, CEO	Rev: Assets: Emp:	12205 NM 107	
North Dakota, State of State Capitol Bismarck, ND 58505 701-224-2000	State government. Type: State Govt Ind: State/Prov Govt Grp: Govt & Non-Prof George A Sinner, CEO	Rev: Assets: Emp:	1949 NM 19	
North Pacific Lumber Inc 1505 SE Gideon Portland, OR 97202 503-231-1166	Wholesale forest products, agricultural products. Type: Private Ind: Paper/Forest Prd Grp: Basic Industries Leo T Gibbons, CEO	Rev: Assets: Emp:	600 NA 1	
Northeast Bancorportion Church & Elm Streets New Haven, CT 06502 203-773-0500	Commercial bank. Type: NASDAQ-NBIC Ind: Banking Grp: Financial Frank J Kugler, CEO George Kabureck, Pres Peter V Young, VCh Ernest Verrico, CFO Leo Kleine, R&D David Evans, Mkt Joseph Gozzo, Ops Ann Rutherford, VP Edward Williams, VP Joseph Zajac, VP	Rev: Assets: Emp:	323 3394 3	
Northeast Savings Inc 50 State Street Hartford, CT 06103 203-280-1000	Thrift institution. Type: NYSE-NSB Ind: Savings & Loan Grp: Financial George P Rutland, CEO Kent Dixon, Chr Howard G Carpenter, VCh Gregory Coleman, CFO Donald V Breen, IS Homer Lang, R&D Ross C Fritschler, Mkt Salvatore Grasso, Ops Gregory Kateff, VP Sandra L Stack, IR Donna Berdick, PR	Rev: Assets: Emp:	798 7943 3	

Organizations Listed Alphabetically

Organization / Address / Phone	Descriptive Information	Revenue / Assets / Emp ($ mil) ($ mil) (thous)		

| Northeast Utilities Inc
107 Selden Street
Berlin, CT 06037
203-665-5000 | Electric power utility holding company.
Type: NYSE-NU
Ind: Utility   Grp: Utilities
William B Ellis, CEO   Bernard M Fox, Pres   Robert E Busch, CFO
Tod Dixon, IS   Ray Donovan, Mkt   Robert Aronsen, VP
Walter Torrance, VP   John Cook, PR | Rev:
Assets:
Emp: | 2279
6765
9 |

| Northeastern University
360 Huntington Avenue
Boston, MA 02115
617-437-2000 | Major educational institution; university.
Type: University
Ind: University   Grp: Govt & Non-Prof
Kenneth G Ryder, CEO | Rev:
Assets:
Emp: | 147
139
40 |

| Northern Illinois University
Administrative Bldg
DeKalb, IL 60115
815-753-1271 | Major educational institution; university.
Type: University
Ind: University   Grp: Govt & Non-Prof
John E Latourette, CEO | Rev:
Assets:
Emp: | 136
229
27 |

| Northern Pacific Lumber Co Inc
1505 SE Gideon
Portland, OR 97202
503-231-1166 | Forest products company; lumber, building materials.
Type: Private
Ind: Paper/Forest Prd   Grp: Basic Industries
Tom Tomjack, CEO | Rev:
Assets:
Emp: | 550
NA
2 |

| Northern Plains Natural Gas Co
2223 Dodge Street
Omaha, NE 68102
402-633-5000 | Exploration, production, transport & sale of natural gas.
Type: Private-Sub Par: Enron Corp
Ind: Energy   Grp: Basic Industries
Larry DeRoin, CEO | Rev:
Assets:
Emp: | NA
NA
NA |

| Northern States Power Co
414 Nicollet Mall
Minneapolis, MN 55401
612-330-5500 | Electric power utility.
Type: NYSE-NSP
Ind: Utility   Grp: Utilities
James J Howard, CEO   James Doudiet, CFO   Robert J Miller, IS
James R Tacheny, R&D   Keith H Wietecki, Mkt   Peter Vanderpoel, IR
Joseph Cascalenda, PR | Rev:
Assets:
Emp: | 2007
4496
8 |

| Northern Telecom Ltd
3 Robert Speck Parkway
Mississauga, ON L4Z2G5 Can
416-897-9000 | Manufacturer of telephone communication equipment.
Type: Private-Sub Par: Bell Canada Inc (BCE Inc)
Ind: Telecom   Grp: High Tech
C Millar, CEO | Rev:
Assets:
Emp: | 3613
NA
35 |

| Northern Trust Corp
50 S LaSalle Street
Chicago, IL 60675
312-630-6000 | Commercial bank.
Type: NASDAQ-NTRS
Ind: Banking   Grp: Financial
Weston R Christopherson, CEO   David W Fox, Pres   Robert Reusche', VCh
Gilian Geniesse, R&D   Charles Jessopp, IR   Sue Rageas, PR | Rev:
Assets:
Emp: | 1003
9133
5 |

| Northern Virginia Community College
8333 Little River Turnpike
Annadale, VA 22003
703-323-3381 | Major educational institution; community college.
Type: University
Ind: University   Grp: Govt & Non-Prof
Richard J Ernst, CEO | Rev:
Assets:
Emp: | 59
119
36 |

| Northrop Corp
1840 Century Park E
Los Angeles, CA 90067
213-553-6262 | Manufacturer of defense equipment; aircraft, missiles.
Type: NYSE-NOC
Ind: Aerospace   Grp: High Tech
Thomas V Jones, CEO   Kent Kresa, Pres   Stanley Ebner, VCh
John B Campbell, CFO   W R Howard, IS   C Robert Gates, Mkt
David Ferguson, VP   Joseph Gallagher, VP   Sheila Gibbons, VP
Les Daly, PR | Rev:
Assets:
Emp: | 5797
3139
45 |

| Northwest Pipeline Corp
295 Chipeta Way
Salt Lake City, UT 84108
801-584-7308 | Natural gas & oil pipeline transmission company.
Type: Private-Sub Par: Williams Companies Inc
Ind: Transport   Grp: Business Service
Robert Keener, CEO | Rev:
Assets:
Emp: | NA
NA
NA |

| Northwest Territories Power Corp
7509 51st Avenue
Edmonton, AB T6C4J8 Can
403-465-3377 | Electric utility; federal government operated.
Type: Govt Corp
Ind: Federal Govt   Grp: Govt & Non-Prof
J Robertson, CEO | Rev:
Assets:
Emp: | 1020
NM
5 |

Organizations Listed Alphabetically

Organization / Address / Phone	Descriptive Information	Revenue / ($ mil)	Assets / ($ mil)	Emp (thous)

Northwestern Mutual Life Insurance Co
720 E Wisconsin Avenue
Milwaukee, WI 53202
414-271-1444

Nationwide life insurance company.
Type: Private
Ind: Insurance   Grp: Insurance
Donald J Schuenke, CEO   Robert E Carlson, VCh   Richard W Wright, CFO
Edward A Flitz, IS   Robert Carlson, Mkt   James D Ericson, VP
Madonna M Hotstetter, VP   William C Koenig, VP   Gordon Davidson, VP
Robert O Carboni, IR   Thomas W Towers, PR

Rev: 5737
Assets: 25362
Emp: 9

Northwestern National Life Insurance Co
20 Washington Avenue S
Minneapolis, MN 55440
612-372-5432

Life insurance company.
Type: NASDAQ-NWNL
Ind: Insurance   Grp: Insurance
John E Pearson, CEO   John G Turner, Pres   John H Flittie, CFO
John O Peterson, IS   James R Miller, R&D   R Michael Conley, Sls
James R Brennan, Mkt   David K Cummings, PR

Rev: 2270
Assets: 7594
Emp: 3

Northwestern Steel & Wire Corp
121 Wallace Street
Sterling, IL 61081
815-625-2500

Manufacturer of industrial steel parts.
Type: Private
Ind: Manufacturing   Grp: Manufacturing
Robert M Wilthew, CEO

Rev: 500
Assets: NA
Emp: 3

Northwestern University
633 Clark Street
Evanston, IL 60211
312-492-3741

Major educational institution; university.
Type: University
Ind: University   Grp: Govt & Non-Prof
Arnold R Weber, CEO

Rev: 262
Assets: 361
Emp: 21

Norton Co
120 Front Street
Worcester, MA 01608
508-795-5000

Manufacturer of control devices; chemical industry.
Type: NYSE-NRT
Ind: Manufacturing   Grp: Manufacturing
John M Nelson, CEO   Bernard F Meyer, VCh   Michael F Mee, CFO
John Wilkens, IS   Peter M Bell, R&D   Joseph J Cusimano, VP
Luise Laucirica, VP   Douglas W Gutow, VP   F Alan Frick, VP
Carol B Hillman, IR   Francis J Doherty, PR

Rev: 1410
Assets: 1088
Emp: 16

Norwest Corp
Sixth & Marquette 1200 Peavey Bldg
Minneapolis, MN 55479
612-372-8268

Commercial bank.
Type: NYSE-NOB
Ind: Banking   Grp: Financial
Lloyd P Johnson, CEO   Richard Kovacevich, Pres   Leslie S Biller, VCh
John T Thornton, CFO   Brian Phillips, IS   Alan Johnson, Sls
Jeff Christensen, Mkt   Kenneth Murray, VP   William Queenan, VP
Harold S Webster, IR   Jack Kerr, PR

Rev: 2475
Assets: 20564
Emp: 16

Norwich Easton Pharmaceuticals Co
17 Eaton Avenue
Norwich, NY 13815
607-335-2111

Pharmaceuticals manufacturing company.
Type: Private-Sub   Par: Procter & Gamble Co
Ind: Drugs   Grp: Consumer Service
Harry Tecklenburg, CEO

Rev: NA
Assets: NA
Emp: NA

Nova Corp of Alberta Ltd
801 7th Avenue SW
Calgary, AB T2P2N6 Can
403-290-6000

Energy exploration & development company.
Type: TOR
Ind: Energy   Grp: Basic Industries
S Robert Blair, CEO

Rev: 3350
Assets: 7006
Emp: 8

Nova Scotia Power Corp
1894 Barrington Street
Halifax, NS B3J2W5 Can
902-428-6221

Electric power utility company.
Type: Prov Govt
Ind: Utility   Grp: Utilities
J MacDonald, CEO   S Robert Blair, Chr   James H Butler, Pres
H J Sanders Pearson, VCh   William G Wilson, CFO   Wayne E Nysetvold, IS
Donald J Boommer, VP   Bruce W Simpson, VP   Donald G Olafson, VP
Pierre Choquette, VP

Rev: 411
Assets: 1254
Emp: 2

Novell Inc
1170 N Industrial Park Drive
Orem, UT 84057
801-226-8202

Computer network software manufacturer.
Type: OTC
Ind: Comput/Off Equip   Grp: High Tech
Raymond J Noorda, CEO

Rev: 282
Assets: 227
Emp: 2

Organizations Listed Alphabetically

Organization / Address / Phone	Descriptive Information	Revenue / ($ mil)	Assets / ($ mil)	Emp (thous)
Noverco Inc 1170 Peel Street Montreal, PQ H3B4P2 Can 514-393-2650	Metals & minerals processing company. Type: TOR-NVC Ind: Metals/Mining Grp: Basic Industries Roger Charbonneau, CEO Marcel Dutil, Chr Celine Pelletier, Tres Denis Aubin, CFO Joseph Baladi, R&D Louise Legare, VP Rene Bedard, VP	Rev: Assets: Emp:	879 1207 3	
Noxell Corp 11050 York Road Hunt Valley, MD 21030 301-785-7300	Manufacturer of personal care products. Type: NASDAQ-NOXLB Ind: Personal Care Grp: Consumer Prd George L Bunting, CEO Marvin L Hathaway, Pres Sears W Ingraham, VCh Robert W Pierce, CFO James M Burke, IS Richart N Lenham, R&D Eugene H Levering, Sls Peter M Troup, Mkt Frank Kneller, VP Deborah Alford, PR	Rev: Assets: Emp:	522 330 2	
NPS Group Inc 600 Meadowland Parkway Secaucus, NJ 07094 201-865-6550	Real estate development company. Type: Private Ind: Real Estate/Bldg Grp: Business Service Colin Halpern, CEO	Rev: Assets: Emp:	550 NA 5	
Nucor Corp 4425 Randolph Road Charlotte, NC 28211 704-366-7000	Manufacturer of steel products; industrial, commercial. Type: NYSE-NUE Ind: Steel Grp: Basic Industries F Kenneth Iverson, CEO H David Aycock, Pres Samuel Siegel, CFO James E Campbell, VP John Correnti, VP	Rev: Assets: Emp:	543 426 4	
NUI Corp 1011 Rt 22 W Bridgewater, NJ 08807 201-685-3900	Oil & gas exploration & distribution. Type: NYSE-NUI Ind: Energy Grp: Basic Industries John Kean, CEO	Rev: Assets: Emp:	350 250 2	
Nuveen, John & Co Inc 333 W Wacker Drive Chicago, IL 60606 312-917-7700	Investment management. Type: Private Ind: Securities Grp: Financial Richard Franke, CEO	Rev: Assets: Emp:	450 363 1	
NVF Co Yorklyn Road PO Box 68 Yorklyn, DE 19736 302-239-5281	Manufacturer of basic steel products. Type: OTC Ind: Steel Grp: Basic Industries Victor Posner, CEO	Rev: Assets: Emp:	1200 500 10	
NVR Limited Partnership Inc 7601 Lewinsville Road McLean, VA 22102 703-761-2000	Developer of homes; single family residences. Type: ASE-NVR Ind: Real Estate/Bldg Grp: Business Service Dwight C Schar, CEO	Rev: Assets: Emp:	1000 500 4	
NWA (Northwest Airlines) Inc Minneapolis St Paul Intl Airport St Paul, MN 55111 612-726-2111	International airline. Type: NYSE-NWA Ind: Airline Grp: Consumer Service Steven G Rothmeier, CEO John F Horn, Pres Benjamin G Griggs, VCh John A Edwardson, CFO Walter Pemberton, IS A B McGary, Mkt William D Slattery, Ops Allan K Pray, VP David W Behrends, VP Alan Muncaster, PR	Rev: Assets: Emp:	5650 4372 36	
NYNEX Business Information Systems Inc 65 W Red Oak Lane White Plains, NY 10604 914-683-2398	Operator of retail computer stores. Type: Private-Sub Par: NYNEX Corp Ind: Comput/Off Equip Grp: High Tech Douglas Mello, CEO	Rev: Assets: Emp:	NA NA NA	
NYNEX Corp 335 Madison Avenue New York, NY 10017 212-370-7400	Regional telecommunications company. Type: NYSE-NYN Ind: Telecom Grp: High Tech Delbert C Staley, CEO Grace J Fippinger, Tres William G Burns, CFO C S Skrzypczak, R&D Paul J Goetz, Sls James E Hennessy, Mkt Dwight A Kellogg, VP Robert J Ekenrode, VP William C Fergeson, VP Raymong F Burke, VP Ivan Seidenberg, IR John Bonamo, PR	Rev: Assets: Emp:	12661 25362 97	

Organizations Listed Alphabetically

Organization / Address / Phone	Descriptive Information	Revenue / ($ mil)	Assets / ($ mil)	Emp (thous)
NYNEX Mobile Communications Co One Blue Hill Plaza Pearl River, NY 10965 914-577-5200	Manufacturer & marketer of mobile & cellular phones. Type: Private-Sub Par: NYNEX Corp Ind: Telecom Grp: High Tech Charles Many, CEO	Rev: Assets: Emp:	NA NA NA	
O'Sullivan Corp Valley Avenue Winchester, VA 22601 703-667-6666	Manufacturer rubber & plastic, storage facilities. Type: NASDAQ-OSL Ind: Tire/Rubber Grp: Basic Industries A Bryant, CEO	Rev: Assets: Emp:	250 175 2	
Oakland Community College 2480 Opdyke Road Bloomfield Hills, MI 48013 313-540-1500	Major educational institution; community college. Type: University Ind: University Grp: Govt & Non-Prof R Stephen Nicholson, CEO	Rev: Assets: Emp:	57 113 30	
Oakland County Government 1200 N Telegraph Pontiac, MI 48053 313-858-0480	County government. Type: County Govt Ind: Local Govt Grp: Govt & Non-Prof Roy Rewold, CEO	Rev: Assets: Emp:	725 NM 4	
Oakland, City of City Hall Plaza Oakland, CA 94612 415-273-3141	City government. Type: City Govt Ind: Local Govt Grp: Govt & Non-Prof Lionel J Wilson, CEO	Rev: Assets: Emp:	396 NM 4	
Oakwood Hospital Corp 18101 Oakwood Blvd Detroit, MI 48123 313-593-7000	Operator of a hospital & clinics. Type: Private Ind: Health Care Grp: Consumer Service Gerald Fitzgerald, CEO	Rev: Assets: Emp:	253 NA 3	
Occidental Chemical Corp 1980 Post Oak Road Houston, TX 77056 713-840-7100	Manufacturer of chemical products. Type: Private-Sub Par: Occidental Petroleum Corp Ind: Chemicals Grp: Basic Industries Ray Irani, CEO	Rev: Assets: Emp:	NA NA NA	
Occidental Petroleum Corp 10889 Wilshire Blvd Los Angeles, CA 90024 213-879-1700	International oil & gas production & marketing company. Type: NYSE-OXY Ind: Energy Grp: Basic Industries Armand Hammer, CEO Ray R Irani, Pres O C Davis, VCh John J Dorgan, CFO John Bennett, IS Frank Friedman, R&D Richard Chen, Sls Dale Laurance, Ops Richard Jacobs, VP Michael Hammer, VP Angelo Leparulo, VP William F McSweeny, VP Franklin D Ashley, PR	Rev: Assets: Emp:	19417 20747 45	
Ocean Drilling Exploration Co 1600 Canal Street New Orleans, LA 70161 504-561-2811	Oil & natural gas exploration & production company. Type: Private-Sub Par: Murphy Oil Corp Ind: Oil Service Grp: Business Service Hugh J Kelly, CEO James Kilpatrick, VCh Odie Vaughn, Tres Richard Roberson, CFO Stephen Hurley, R&D Enoch Dawkins, Mkt W J Wilkenson, Ops	Rev: Assets: Emp:	406 1026 4	
Ocean Spray Cranberries Inc 225 Water Street Plymouth, MA 02360 508-747-1000	Manufacturer of cranberry & citrus products. Type: Private-Coop Ind: Food Processing Grp: Food Processing Robert St Jacques, CEO John S Llewellyn, Chr Alexander Turnbull, CFO Thomas Modestino, IS James Tillotson, R&D Patrick McCarthy, Sls Thomas Bullock, Mkt Curtis Collison Jr, IR Christine Masclee, PR	Rev: Assets: Emp:	625 400 3	
Oceanic Properties Inc 650 Iwi Lei Street Honolulu, HI 96817 808-548-4811	Real estate development company. Type: Private-Sub Par: Castle & Cooke Inc Ind: Real Estate/Bldg Grp: Business Service Bill Mills, CEO	Rev: Assets: Emp:	NA NA NA	
OECD European Common Market 2001 L Street NW US Headquarters Washington, DC 20036 202-785-6323	International organization of cooperating countries. Type: Federal Govt Ind: Federal Govt Grp: Govt & Non-Prof Michael Moynihan, CEO	Rev: Assets: Emp:	250 NM 1	

Organizations Listed Alphabetically

Organization / Address / Phone	Descriptive Information	Revenue / ($ mil)	Assets / ($ mil)	Emp (thous)
Office Depot Inc 851 Broken Sound Parkway Boca Raton, FL 33487 407-994-2131	Operator of large volume office supply stores. Type: NASDAQ-ODEP Ind: Retail/Merch Grp: Retail D Fuente, CEO	Rev: Assets: Emp:		300 150 3
Ogden Corp Two Pennsylvania Plaza New York, NY 10121 212-868-6100	Environmental, building management & food service company. Type: NYSE Ind: Conglomerate Grp: Manufacturing Ralph E Ablon, CEO Donald A Krenz, Pres Abraham Zaleznik, VCh Maria P Monet, CFO Donald Krenz, R&D David Sokol, Ops Philip F Ruppel, PR	Rev: Assets: Emp:		1088 2202 35
Ogilvy Group Inc 2 E 48th Street New York, NY 10017 212-907-3400	Advertising agency holding company. Type: NASDAQ-OGIL Ind: Business Service Grp: Business Service William Phillips, CEO	Rev: Assets: Emp:		575 639 2
Ohio Bell Telephone Co 45 Erieview Plaza Cleveland, OH 44114 216-822-9700	Telephone public utility company. Type: Private-Sub Par: Ameritech (Amer Information Tech Corp) Ind: Telecom Grp: High Tech Edward Bell, CEO	Rev: Assets: Emp:		NA NA NA
Ohio Casualty Corp 136 N Third Street Hamilton, OH 45025 513-867-3000	Property & casualty insurance company. Type: OTC Ind: Insurance Grp: Insurance Joseph L Marcum, CEO William L Woodall, Pres Jeffery Lowe, VCh Barry S Porter, Tres C David Mencer, CFO Robert L McMaken, IS Charles Bergmann, R&D Lauren N Patch, Mkt Howard Sloneker, VP Robert L McMaken, PR	Rev: Assets: Emp:		1623 2922 6
Ohio Edison Co 76 S Main Street Akron, OH 44308 216-384-5100	Electric power utility. Type: NYSE-OEC Ind: Utility Grp: Utilities J T Rogers, CEO Douglas W Tschappat, Pres Victor A Owoc, CFO David L Nemeth, IS Chisna H Fleming, R&D Donald L Rearick, Mkt John A Gill, VP Theodore Struck, VP Harvey Wagner, VP Howard Tuber, VP Joanne Martin, VP Frank E Derry, IR Ralph J Dinicola, PR	Rev: Assets: Emp:		2143 7556 8
Ohio Mattress Co 1228 Euclid Avenue Halle Bldg Cleveland, OH 44115 216-522-1310	Manufacturer of bedding products. Type: NYSE-OMT Ind: Building Mat Grp: Basic Industries Ernest M Wuliger, CEO Ronald E Trzcinski, Pres T L Smudz, CFO Richard Alston, IS Robert Wagner, R&D Gary Pleasant, Mkt Ernest M Wuliger, IR Denise Fillip, PR	Rev: Assets: Emp:		600 400 5
Ohio Power Co 301 Cleveland Avenue SW Canton, OH 44702 216-456-8173	Electric power utility. Type: Private-Sub Par: American Electric Power Co Inc Ind: Utility Grp: Utilities W S White, CEO C A Heller, Pres Peter DeMaria, CFO Richard Disbrow, VP John Dolan, VP Lawrence Hoover, VP Gerald Maloney, VP	Rev: Assets: Emp:		1387 3494 8
Ohio Public Employees Retirement Fund 45 N Fourth Street Columbus, OH 43215 614-221-7012	State investment agency; pension management. Type: State Govt Ind: Non-Bank Fin Grp: Financial William McLaughan, CEO	Rev: Assets: Emp:		450 16500 1
Ohio State University Administrative Bldg Columbus, OH 43210 614-422-6446	Major educational institution; university. Type: University Ind: University Grp: Govt & Non-Prof Edward Jennings, CEO	Rev: Assets: Emp:		641 886 59
Ohio Valley Transmission Corp 311 W Chestnut Street Louisville, KY 40202 502-566-4011	Electric & gas utility company. Type: Private-Sub Par: Louisville Gas & Electric Co Ind: Utility Grp: Utilities Robert Royer, CEO	Rev: Assets: Emp:		NA NA NA

Organizations Listed Alphabetically

Organization / Address / Phone	Descriptive Information	Revenue / ($ mil)	Assets / ($ mil)	Emp (thous)
Ohio, State of State Capitol Columbus, OH 43266 614-466-2000	State government. Type: State Govt Ind: State/Prov Govt Grp: Govt & Non-Prof Richard F Celeste, CEO	Rev: Assets: Emp:	24229 NM 151	
Ohio, State Teachers Retirement System 275 E Broad Street Columbus, OH 43215 614-227-4062	State investment agency; pension management. Type: Private Ind: Non-Bank Fin Grp: Financial C James Grothaus, CEO Victor Miller, Pres Stephen Mitchell, VCh J Alan Steele, CFO Cynthia Hvizdos, VP J Richard Zimmerman, VP	Rev: Assets: Emp:	1490 14231 1	
Oklahoma City, City of City Hall Plaza Oklahoma City, OK 73102 405-231-2424	City government. Type: City Govt Ind: Local Govt Grp: Govt & Non-Prof Ron Norick, CEO	Rev: Assets: Emp:	352 NM 4	
Oklahoma Gas & Electric Co 321 N Harvey Avenue Oklahoma City, OK 73102 405-272-3000	Electric power & gas utility company. Type: NYSE-OGE Ind: Utility Grp: Utilities James G Harlow, CEO Al M Stecker, Tres Don L Young, CFO Richard C Day, Mkt Kenneth J Baltes, VP James R Helton, VP Steven E Moore, VP	Rev: Assets: Emp:	1098 2521 4	
Oklahoma Publishing Co Inc 25 NE Fourth Street Oklahoma City, OK 73125 405-232-3311	Publishing, broadcasting, entertainment company. Type: Private Ind: Publishing/Com Grp: Consumer Service Edward L Gaylord, CEO	Rev: Assets: Emp:	750 NA 7	
Oklahoma State University Main Campus Stillwater, OK 74078 405-624-5000	Major educational institution; university. Type: University Ind: University Grp: Govt & Non-Prof John Campbell, CEO	Rev: Assets: Emp:	172 207 24	
Oklahoma, State of State Capitol Oklahoma City, OK 73105 405-521-2011	State government. Type: State Govt Ind: State/Prov Govt Grp: Govt & Non-Prof Henry Bellmon, CEO	Rev: Assets: Emp:	7409 NM 72	
Olco Petroleum Group Ltd 2561 Avenue Georges V Montreal, PQ H1L6J7 Can 514-353-6821	Petroleum products distribution company. Type: MON-OCLA Ind: Energy Grp: Basic Industries Wilfred Kaneb, CEO Mark S Kaneb, Pres Carl E Emond, CFO Frederick Kaneb, VP Kevin Taylor, VP	Rev: Assets: Emp:	304 91 1	
Old Kent Financial Corp One Vandenberg Center Grand Rapids, MI 49503 616-774-5000	Commercial bank. Type: NASDAQ-OKEN Ind: Banking Grp: Financial John C Canepa, CEO Robert Sadler, VCh William Waanders, CFO David Radius, IS Richard M Wright, Mkt Lisa Wilson, PR	Rev: Assets: Emp:	726 7854 3	
Old Republic International Corp 397 N Michigan Avenue Chicago, IL 60601 312-346-8100	Life, casualty & property insurance company. Type: NASDAQ-OLDR Ind: Insurance Grp: Insurance William Stover, CEO A C Zucaro, Pres A C Zucaro, CFO Edward O'Connor, IS Ann Stipisich, PR	Rev: Assets: Emp:	1200 3000 5	
Old Stone Corp 150 S Main Street Providence, RI 02903 401-278-2000	Commercial bank. Type: NASDAQ-OSTN Ind: Banking Grp: Financial Theodore Barnes, CEO Thomas F Hogg, CFO Beverly E Najarian, IS Maria Bessette, R&D Jay G Conway, PR	Rev: Assets: Emp:	350 4500 2	
Oldsmobile Div 920 Townsend Street Lansing, MI 48921 517-377-5000	Manufacturer & distributor of automobiles. Type: Private-Sub Par: General Motors Corp Ind: Automotive Grp: Manufacturing William Lane, CEO	Rev: Assets: Emp:	NA NA NA	

Organizations Listed Alphabetically

Organization / Address / Phone	Descriptive Information	Revenue / Assets / Emp ($ mil) ($ mil) (thous)		

Olin Corp
120 Long Ridge Road
Stamford, CT 06904
203-356-2000

Manufacturer of specialty chemicals; defense, commercial.
Type: NYSE
Ind: Chemicals   Grp: Basic Industries
John W Johnstone, CEO   Richard Berry, VCh   C Robert Tully, CFO
Ross Ahntholz, IS   John P Marano Jr, R&D   John J Margherio, Sls
George H Nusloch, PR

Rev: 2308
Assets: 1940
Emp: 17

Olsten Corp
1 Merrick Avenue
Westbury, NY 11590
516-832-8200

Nationwide personnel agency; temporary help.
Type: ASE-OLS
Ind: Business Service   Grp: Business Service
William Olsten, CEO

Rev: 400
Assets: 150
Emp: 2

Omaha, City of
City Hall 1819 Farnam Street
Omaha, NE 68183
402-444-5000

City government.
Type: City Govt
Ind: Local Govt   Grp: Govt & Non-Prof
Walter M Calinger, CEO

Rev: 250
Assets: NM
Emp: 2

Omnicom Group Inc
437 Madison Avenue
New York, NY 10022
212-415-2000

Advertising agency holding company.
Type: NASDAQ-OMCM
Ind: Business Service   Grp: Business Service
Bruce Crawford, CEO   John Watt, Tres   Fred J Meyer, CFO
Raymond McGovern, VP   Keith Bremer, VP   Barry J Wagner, VP

Rev: 881
Assets: 1135
Emp: 3

Oneida Ltd
Kenwood Avenue
Oneida, NY 13421
315-361-3000

Manufacturer of tableware.
Type: NYSE-OCQ
Ind: Appliances/Furn   Grp: Manufacturing
William D Matthews, CEO

Rev: 400
Assets: 500
Emp: 4

Oneok Inc
100 W Fifth Street
Tulsa, OK 74103
918-588-7000

Natural gas utility company.
Type: NYSE-OKE
Ind: Utility   Grp: Utilities
J D Scott, CEO   J R Mosteller, Pres   B M Van Meter, VCh
P A Wimpey, CFO   N E Duckworth, VP

Rev: 571
Assets: 958
Emp: 2

Onex Corp
Commerce Court W Box 153
Toronto, ON M5L1E7 Can
416-362-7711

Diversified holding company; conglomerate.
Type: TOR-OCX
Ind: Conglomerate   Grp: Manufacturing
Gerald W Schwartz, CEO   Ewout R Heersink, VP   Anthony R Melman, VP
John L Shortly, VP   John Elder, VP

Rev: 1628
Assets: 1593
Emp: 21

Ontario Hydro Corp
700 University Avenue
Toronto, ON M5G1X6 Can
416-592-5111

Electric power utility company.
Type: Prov Govt
Ind: Utility   Grp: Utilities
Milan Nastich, CEO

Rev: 4488
Assets: 27758
Emp: 32

Oppenheimer & Co Inc
Oppenheimer Tower World Financial Center
New York, NY 10281
212-667-7000

Investment firm; securities trading.
Type: Private
Ind: Securities   Grp: Financial
Stephen Robert, CEO

Rev: 750
Assets: 5000
Emp: 2

Oracle Systems Corp
20 Davis Drive
Belmont, CA 94002
415-598-8000

Producer of computer software; datamanagement systems.
Type: NASDAQ-ORCL
Ind: Comput/Off Equip   Grp: High Tech
Robert N Miner, CEO

Rev: 584
Assets: 500
Emp: 5

Oral-B Laboratories Inc
One Lagoon Drive
Redwood, CA 94065
415-598-5000

Manufacturer of dental hygene products.
Type: Private-Sub   Par: Gillette Co
Ind: Health Care   Grp: Consumer Service
Jacques Lagarde, CEO

Rev: NA
Assets: NA
Emp: NA

Orange & Rockland Utilities Corp
1 Blue Hill Plaza
Pearl River, NY 10965
914-352-6000

Electric power utility.
Type: NYSE-ORU
Ind: Utility   Grp: Utilities
James F Smith, CEO   Thomas A Griffin, Pres   Robert J McBennett, Tres
Patrick J Chambers, CFO   Raymond J Richardson, R&D   Linda Winikow, VP
Victor A Roque, VP   Frank Fischer, VP

Rev: 486
Assets: 922
Emp: 2

Organizations Listed Alphabetically

Organization / Address / Phone	Descriptive Information	Revenue / ($ mil)	Assets / ($ mil)	Emp (thous)
Orange County Government Civic Center Plaza Santa Ana, CA 92701 714-834-3100	County government. Type: County Govt Ind: Local Govt Grp: Govt & Non-Prof Harriett M Wieder, CEO	Rev: Assets: Emp:	2800 NM 15	
Ore-Ida Foods Inc 220 W Park Center Blvd Boise, ID 83707 208-383-6100	Manufacturer of frozen food. Type: Private-Sub Par: Heinz, H J Co Ind: Food Processing Grp: Food Processing G Herrick, CEO	Rev: Assets: Emp:	500 NA 2	
Oregon State University Administrative Bldg Corvallis, OR 97331 503-754-0123	Major educational institution; university. Type: University Ind: University Grp: Govt & Non-Prof John V Byrne, CEO	Rev: Assets: Emp:	180 238 21	
Oregon Steel Mills Inc 14400 N Rivergate Blvd Portland, OR 97208 503-286-9651	Manufacturer of electric furnaces, steel works & mills.. Type: NASDAQ-OS Ind: Equipment Grp: Manufacturing Lee Emerson, CEO	Rev: Assets: Emp:	250 150 1	
Oregon, State of State Capitol Salem, OR 97310 503-378-3131	State government. Type: State Govt Ind: State/Prov Govt Grp: Govt & Non-Prof Neil Goldschmidt, CEO	Rev: Assets: Emp:	7165 NM 56	
Orion Capital Insurance Co 780 NW Lejeunne Road Miami, FL 33126 305-445-8333	Property & casualty insurance company. Type: OTC Ind: Insurance Grp: Insurance Paul Fraynd, CEO	Rev: Assets: Emp:	450 100 2	
Orion Pictures Corp 711 Fifth Avenue New York, NY 10022 212-758-5100	Motion picture production & distribution company. Type: NYSE-OPC Ind: Leisure Time Grp: Consumer Service Eric Pleskow, CEO	Rev: Assets: Emp:	469 350 3	
Oryx Energy Co 15 Essex Road Paramus, NJ 07652 201-845-5533	Manufacturer of computer hardware; software research & dev. Type: NASDAQ Ind: Comput/Off Equip Grp: High Tech Perry Laurence, CEO	Rev: Assets: Emp:	1200 800 1	
Oshawa Group Ltd 302 East Mall Islington, ON M9B6B8 Can 416-236-1971	Operator of retail department stores. Type: TOR Ind: Retail/Food Grp: Retail Ray Wolfe, CEO	Rev: Assets: Emp:	3634 572 19	
Oshkosh B'Gosh Inc 112 Otter Avenue Oshkosh, WI 54901 414-231-8800	Childerns clothing manufacturer. Type: NASDAQ-GOSHA Ind: Apparel/Textiles Grp: Consumer Prd C F Hyde, CEO	Rev: Assets: Emp:	253 139 3	
Oshkosh Truck Corp 2307 Oshkosh Street Oshkosh, WI 54903 414-235-9150	Manufacturer of specialty vehicles & trucks. Type: NASDAQ-OTRK Ind: Automotive Grp: Manufacturing John Mosling, CEO	Rev: Assets: Emp:	450 350 2	
Otis Elevator Co 10 Farm Springs Road Farmington, CT 06032 203-674-4000	Manufacturer of elevators. Type: Private-Sub Par: United Technologies Corp Ind: Equipment Grp: Manufacturing Carl Krapek, CEO	Rev: Assets: Emp:	NA NA NA	
Outboard Marine Corp 100 Sea Horse Drive Waukegan, IL 60085 312-689-6200	Manufacturer of leisure time equipment; outboard engines. Type: NYSE-OM Ind: Leisure Time Grp: Consumer Service Charles D Strang, CEO James C Chapman, Pres Clarence Bangert, VCh Samuel J Winett, CFO Harry Adams, IS Edgar Rose, R&D D F Myers, Mkt Edgar Rose, VP Robert Randolph, VP Jerome Stumbas, VP Samuel Winett, VP M J Waninger, IR Ronald Kuykendal, PR	Rev: Assets: Emp:	1605 1141 13	

Organizations Listed Alphabetically

Organization / Address / Phone	Descriptive Information	Revenue / ($ mil)	Assets / ($ mil)	Emp (thous)

Overnite Transportation Co
1000 Semmes Avenue
Richmond, VA 23224
824-231-8000

Nationwide truck transport company.
Type: Private-Sub   Par: Union Pacific Corp
Ind: Transport   Grp: Business Service
J Harwood Cochrane, CEO

Rev: 550
Assets: 450
Emp: 8

Overseas Shipholding Group Inc
1114 Avenue of the Americas
New York, NY 10036
212-869-1222

Ocean transport shipping company.
Type: NYSE-OSG
Ind: Business Service   Grp: Business Service
Morton P Hyman, CEO   Michael Recanati, CFO   Morris Feder, Mkt
Alan Struthers, PR

Rev: 333
Assets: 1318
Emp: 2

Owens & Minor Inc
2727 Enterprise Parkway
Richmond, VA 23229
804-747-9794

Wholesale distributor of medical supplies.
Type: NYSE-OMI
Ind: Drugs   Grp: Consumer Service
G Milmer Minor, CEO   William F Fife, VCh   Richard C Ciofani, CFO
Robert Anderson, VP   Henry Berling, VP

Rev: 732
Assets: 190
Emp: 1

Owens Corning Fiberglas Corp
Fiberglas Tower
Toledo, OH 43659
419-248-8000

Manufacturer of fiberglass products; insulation, bldg mat.
Type: NYSE-OCF
Ind: Building Mat   Grp: Basic Industries
William W Boeschenstein, CEO   Max O Weber, Pres   Harry G Kaminer, Tres
Paul V Daverio, CFO   Dennis R Barber, IS   Robert C Doban, R&D
Joseph J Doherty, Mkt   John E Gates, VP   C Peter Hauck, VP
Gilbert Coors, VP   Lewis W Saxby, VP   Guy O Mabry, VP
William Colville, VP   Bradford C Oleman, PR

Rev: 2831
Assets: 1596
Emp: 18

Owens Illinois Inc
One Sea Gate Plaza
Toledo, OH 43666
419-247-5000

Manufacturer of glass packaging.
Type: Private
Ind: Packaging   Grp: Manufacturing
Robert J Lanigan, CEO   Joseph H Lemieux, Pres   Jerome A Bohland, CFO
Kenneth Lemke, R&D   Charles H Pietsch, Mkt   Sam P Allen, PR

Rev: 3800
Assets: 3500
Emp: 40

Oxbow Corp
333 Elm Street
Dedham, MA 02026
617-461-0550

Natural resource & energy company.
Type: Private
Ind: Energy   Grp: Basic Industries
William Koch, CEO

Rev: 1000
Assets: NA
Emp: 1

Oxford Development Co Inc
7316 Wisconsin Avenue SE
Bethesda, MD 20814
301-654-3100

Real estate development company.
Type: Private
Ind: Real Estate/Bldg   Grp: Business Service
Patrick Fitzpatrick, CEO

Rev: 550
Assets: NA
Emp: 5

Oxford Industries Inc
222 Piedmont Avenue NE
Atlanta, GA 30308
404-659-2424

Manufacturer of brand apparel products.
Type: NYSE-OXM
Ind: Apparel/Textiles   Grp: Consumer Prd
J Hicks Lanier, CEO   Abner Avirett, Tres   R William Lee Jr, CFO
John A Baumgartner, IS   William Mitchell, R&D   Lawrence Menter, Sls
Kontz L Mitchell, Mkt   Jonathan M Fee, VP   Knowlton J O'Reilly, VP
R William Lee Jr, PR

Rev: 591
Assets: 223
Emp: 8

Oxford Paper Co
Rumford Mill
Rumford, ME 04276
207-364-4521

Manufacturer of paper & related products.
Type: Private-Sub   Par: Boise Cascade Corp
Ind: Paper/Forest Prd   Grp: Basic Industries
Peter Norrie, CEO

Rev: NA
Assets: NA
Emp: NA

Paccar Inc
777 106th Avenue NE
Bellevue, WA 98004
206-455-7400

Manufacturer of heavy trucks.
Type: NASDAQ-PCAR
Ind: Automotive   Grp: Manufacturing
Charles M Pigott, CEO   Joseph M Dunn, Pres   David Hovind, VCh
William Bosisvert, CFO   Dean Watkins, IS   John Salathe Jr, R&D
Leonard Haba, VP   Ronald Hollyoak, VP   Jack Quinlin, VP
Jack C McRae, PR

Rev: 3122
Assets: 2832
Emp: 10

Paccar of Canada Ltd
6711 Mississauga Road
Mississauga, ON L5N2W3 Can
416-858-7070

Manufacturer of truck bodies.
Type: Private-Sub-For
Ind: Automotive   Grp: Manufacturing
C Pigott, CEO

Rev: 425
Assets: 213
Emp: 2

Organizations Listed Alphabetically

Organization / Address / Phone	Descriptive Information	Revenue / Assets / Emp ($ mil) ($ mil) (thous)		

Pace Membership Warehouses Inc
3350 Peoria
Aurora, CO 80010
303-364-0700

Operator of retail department stores.
Type: NASDAQ-PMWI
Ind: Retail/Merch   Grp: Retail
Henry Haimsohn, CEO

Rev: 1271
Assets: 750
Emp: 3

Pacific Bell Directory Inc
101 Spear Street
San Francisco, CA 94105
415-995-4400

Telephone directory publishing company.
Type: Private-Sub   Par: Pacific Telesis Group Inc
Ind: Publishing/Com   Grp: Consumer Service
John Gaulding, CEO

Rev: NA
Assets: NA
Emp: NA

Pacific Bell Inc
140 New Montgomery Street
San Francisco, CA 94105
415-542-9000

Telephone public utility company.
Type: Private-Sub   Par: Pacific Telesis Group Inc
Ind: Telecom   Grp: High Tech
Phillup Quigley, CEO

Rev: NA
Assets: NA
Emp: NA

Pacific Energy Co
6055 E Washington Blvd
Commerce, CA 90017
213-725-1139

Oil & gas exploration, production & transmission company.
Type: Private-Sub   Par: Pacific Enterprises Corp
Ind: Energy   Grp: Basic Industries
Daniel Siegel, CEO

Rev: NA
Assets: NA
Emp: NA

Pacific Enterprises Corp
801 S Grand Avenue
Los Angeles, CA 90017
213-895-5000

Natural gas utility company.
Type: NYSE-PET
Ind: Utility   Grp: Utilities
P A Miller, CEO

Rev: 5932
Assets: 6866
Emp: 13

Pacific First Federal Savings Bank Inc
1145 Broadway
Tacoma, WA 98401
206-383-7605

Thrift institution.
Type: NASDAQ
Ind: Savings & Loan   Grp: Financial
Jerry E Pohlman, CEO   William D Pettit, Pres   George Johnson, CFO
Richard Nichols, IS   Barbara McCaffery, Sls   Greg Stitt, Mkt
Michael Rogers, IR   Susan Cassidy, PR

Rev: 524
Assets: 6622
Emp: 2

Pacific Gas & Electric Co
77 Beale Street
San Francisco, CA 94106
415-781-4211

Electric & gas utility.
Type: NYSE-PCG
Ind: Utility   Grp: Utilities
Richard A Clarke, CEO   George Maneatis, Pres   Stanley Skinner, VCh
Mason Willrich, CFO   John C Danielsen, IS   Gregory M Rueger, R&D
John C Keyser, Mkt   Gregory Rueger, VP   Norman Bryan, VP
George Clifton, VP   Russell Cunningham, VP   John Danielson, VP
Grant N Horne, IR   David M Monfried, PR

Rev: 7646
Assets: 21068
Emp: 27

Pacific Gas Transmission Co
160 Spear Street
San Francisco, CA 94105
415-781-0474

Natural gas public utility company.
Type: Private-Sub   Par: Pacific Gas & Electric Co
Ind: Utility   Grp: Utilities
Steven Reynolds, CEO

Rev: NA
Assets: NA
Emp: NA

Pacific Holding Co Inc
10900 Wilshire Suite 1600
Los Angeles, CA 90024
213-208-6055

Operator of hotels & restaurants.
Type: Private
Ind: Food/Lodging   Grp: Consumer Service
David H Murdock, CEO

Rev: 1000
Assets: NA
Emp: 10

Pacific Interstate Co
801 S Grand Avenue
Los Angeles, CA 90017
213-895-5223

Energy company; oil & gas transmission.
Type: Private-Sub   Par: Pacific Enterprises Corp
Ind: Energy   Grp: Basic Industries
Robert Lock, CEO

Rev: NA
Assets: NA
Emp: NA

Pacific Mutual Life Insurance Co
700 Newport Center Drive
Newport Beach, CA 92660
714-640-3011

Life insurance company.
Type: Private-Mutual
Ind: Insurance   Grp: Insurance
Thomas C Sutton, CEO   Harry G Bubb, Chr   Glen S Schafer, CFO
William A Roberts, IS   Lynn C Miller, R&D   Robert G Haskell, PR

Rev: 2540
Assets: 6981
Emp: 3

Pacific Resources Inc
PO Box 3379
Honolulu, HI 96842
808-547-3111

Petroleum refining & marketing company.
Type: NYSE-PRI
Ind: Food Processing   Grp: Food Processing
Robert G Reed, CEO   Robert Loughridge Jr, CFO   Fidencio M Mares, IS
Andrea L Simpson, PR

Rev: 1050
Assets: 700
Emp: 11

Organizations Listed Alphabetically

Organization / Address / Phone	Descriptive Information	Revenue / Assets / Emp ($ mil) ($ mil) (thous)		

Pacific Scene Inc
3900 Harney
San Diego, CA 92110
619-299-5100

Real estate development company.
Type: Private
Ind: Real Estate/Bldg   Grp: Business Service
Ed Peterson, CEO

Rev: 550
Assets: NA
Emp: 1

Pacific Telecom Inc
805 Broadway
Vancouver, WA 98668
206-696-0983

Telecommunications company.
Type: Private-Sub   Par: Pacificorp Corp
Ind: Telecom   Grp: High Tech
Charles E Robinson, CEO   Charles Peterson, VCh   Brian Wirkkala, CFO
James Bulgrin, IS   James P Best, VP   Vern K Dunham, VP

Rev: 552
Assets: 1242
Emp: 4

Pacific Telesis Group Inc
140 New Montgomery Street
San Francisco, CA 94105
415-882-8000

Regional telecommunications company.
Type: NYSE-PAC
Ind: Telecom   Grp: High Tech
Sam Ginn, CEO   Philip Quigley, Pres   C Lee Cox, VCh
John E Hulse, CFO   Arthur Latno Jr, Mkt   H Trevor Jones, Ops
Kendall Murphy, VP   Richard Van Allen, VP   Lydell Christiansen, VP
John M Demgen, IR   Diane Olberg, PR

Rev: 9483
Assets: 21191
Emp: 70

Pacificare Health Systems Inc
5995 Plaza Drive
Cypress, CA 90630
714-952-1121

Operator of HMO clinics.
Type: NASDAQ-PHSY
Ind: Health Care   Grp: Consumer Service
Samuel Tibbitts, CEO

Rev: 250
Assets: 200
Emp: 1

Pacificorp Corp
851 SW Sixth Avenue
Portland, OR 97204
503-464-6000

Electric power utility holding company.
Type: NYSE-PPW
Ind: Utility   Grp: Utilities
Don C Frisbee, CEO   Al Gleason, Pres   Gerard K Drummond, VCh
Gayle L Veber, CFO   David F Bolender, VP   Sara Baker, PR

Rev: 3519
Assets: 11396
Emp: 14

Packerland Packing Co Inc
2580 University Avenue
Green Bay, WI 54301
414-468-4000

Producer & distributor of packaged foods; meats.
Type: Private
Ind: Food Processing   Grp: Food Processing
David Backer, CEO

Rev: 550
Assets: NA
Emp: 2

PacTel Cellular Co
2355 Main Street
Irvine, CA 92714
714-553-6087

Cellular mobile communications services.
Type: Private-Sub   Par: Pacific Telesis Group Inc
Ind: Telecom   Grp: High Tech
Jeffrey Hultman, CEO

Rev: NA
Assets: NA
Emp: NA

Paine Webber Group Inc
1285 Avenue of the Americas
New York, NY 10019
212-713-2000

Full service securites firm.
Type: NYSE-PWJ
Ind: Securities   Grp: Financial
Donald B Marron, CEO   Donald E Nickelson, Pres   Pierce R Smith, Tres
Mark Nussbaum, CFO   Martin Stein, IS   Dorothy Haughty, VP
James Treadway, VP   John S Lampe, PR

Rev: 2512
Assets: 17934
Emp: 13

Pall Corp
30 Sea Cliff Avenue
Glen Cove, NY 11542
516-671-4000

Manufacturer of filter products; aerospace, medical.
Type: ASE
Ind: Machinery   Grp: Manufacturing
David B Pall, CEO

Rev: 429
Assets: 570
Emp: 6

Palm Beach Inc
400 Pike Street
Cincinnati, OH 45202
513-241-4260

Manufacturer of family apparel.
Type: Private
Ind: Apparel/Textiles   Grp: Consumer Prd
Alfred P Fuoco, CEO

Rev: 400
Assets: NA
Emp: 5

Pamida Corp
8800 F Street
Omaha, NE 68127
402-339-2400

Discount department stores.
Type: Private
Ind: Retail/Merch   Grp: Retail
C Clayton Burkstrand, CEO

Rev: 500
Assets: NA
Emp: 5

Pamplin, R B Corp
900 SW Fifth Street
Portland, OR 97204
503-248-1133

Manufacturing, textiles, concrete, asphalt.
Type: Private
Ind: Real Estate/Bldg   Grp: Business Service
R B Pamplin, CEO

Rev: 500
Assets: NA
Emp: 5

Organizations Listed Alphabetically

Organization / Address / Phone	Descriptive Information	Revenue / ($ mil)	Assets / ($ mil)	Emp (thous)
Pan Am Shuttle Inc Marine Terminal Flushing, NY 11371 718-803-6607	Regional commercial airline. Type: Private-Sub Par: Pan American Corp Ind: Airline Grp: Consumer Service Thomas Plaskett, CEO	Rev: NA	Assets: NA	Emp: NA
Pan Am World Services Inc 7315 N Atlantic Avenue Cape Canaveral, FL 32920 305-784-7100	Commercial airplane maintenance service company. Type: Private-Sub Par: Pan American Corp Ind: Business Service Grp: Business Service Russell Barnes, CEO	Rev: NA	Assets: NA	Emp: NA
Pan American Corp Pan Am Bldg 200 Park Avenue New York, NY 10166 212-880-1234	International airline company. Type: NYSE-PN Ind: Airline Grp: Consumer Service Thomas G Plaskett, CEO Laurence K Billett, VCh Richard H Francis, CFO Robert W Mann Jr, IS Peter T McHugh, Mkt Robert L Gould, Ops C J Davies, VP Jeffrey Kriendler, PR	Rev: 3569	Assets: 2149	Emp: 20
Panasonic Matsushita Electric Corp 300 S Grand Avenue Los Angeles, CA 90071 713-895-7200	Manufacturer & importer of electronic equipment; US hdqtrs. Type: Private-Sub-For Ind: Electronics Grp: High Tech Kirk Nakamura, CEO	Rev: 2000	Assets: NA	Emp: 2
PanCanadian Petroleum 150 9th Avenue SW Calgary, AB T2P3H9 Can 403-290-2000	Petroleum exploration & production company. Type: Private-Sub Par: Canadian Pacific Ltd Ind: Energy Grp: Basic Industries Bartlett B Rombough, CEO C Barrie Clark, Pres J Joseph Doolan, CFO Donald Maxwell, IS Kenneth B Cusworth, R&D William Reinwart, Mkt	Rev: 587	Assets: 2273	Emp: 1
Panhandle Eastern Corp 3000 Bissonnet Avenue Houston, TX 77005 713-664-3401	Natural gas exploration, production & pipeline company. Type: NYSE-PEL Ind: Utility Grp: Utilities Robert D Hunsucker, CEO Richard Dixon, VCh Charles Lasseter, CFO James A Hart, Mkt Gregory Gruber, VP Herbert Schultz, VP	Rev: 1262	Assets: 2973	Emp: 3
Pannill Knitting Co 202 Cleveland Avenue Martinsville, VA 24115 703-638-8841	Manufacturer of apparel; casual wear, sweatsuits. Type: NYSE-PKC Ind: Apparel/Textiles Grp: Consumer Prd William G Pannill, CEO	Rev: 275	Assets: 200	Emp: 4
Pansophic Systems Inc 709 Enterprise Drive Oak Brook, IL 60521 312-572-6000	Computer software manufacturer & marketer. Type: NYSE-PNS Ind: Comput/Off Equip Grp: High Tech William G Nelson, CEO	Rev: 250	Assets: 174	Emp: 2
Pantry Inc 1801 Douglas Drive Sanford, NC 27330 919-774-6700	Operator of retail convenience food stores. Type: Private Ind: Retail/Food Grp: Retail Truby Proctor, CEO	Rev: 275	Assets: NA	Emp: 2
Paper Corp of America 1325 Morris Drive Wayne, PA 19087 215-296-4470	Manufacturer & distributor of paper. Type: Private-Sub Par: Alco Industries Inc Ind: Paper/Forest Prd Grp: Basic Industries Edward Patrone, CEO	Rev: NA	Assets: NA	Emp: NA
Paperboard Industries 144 Front Street W Toronto, ON M5J1G2 Can 416-596-7180	Paper products company; packaging, boxes. Type: TOR Ind: Packaging Grp: Manufacturing Ian Ross, CEO	Rev: 340	Assets: 255	Emp: 3
Paradyne Corp 8550 Ulmerton Road Largo, FL 34641 813-530-2000	Manufacturer of data communications equipment. Type: NYSE-PDN Ind: Telecom Grp: High Tech Paul J Ferri, CEO	Rev: 250	Assets: 200	Emp: 3
Paragon Group Inc 7557 Rambler Road Suite 1200 Dallas, TX 75231 214-891-2000	Real estate development & management firm. Type: Private Ind: Real Estate/Bldg Grp: Business Service W R Cooper, CEO	Rev: 750	Assets: NA	Emp: 2

Organizations Listed Alphabetically

Organization / Address / Phone	Descriptive Information	Revenue / ($ mil)	Assets / ($ mil)	Emp (thous)
Paramount Communications Corp One Gulf & Western Plaza New York, NY 10023 212-333-7000	Motion picture, entertainment & publishing company. Type: NYSE-GW Ind: Conglomerate Grp: Manufacturing Martin S Davis, CEO Martin S Davis, Chr Donald Oresman, VCh Ronald L Nelson, CFO Raymond M Novak, IS Michael Hope, Ops Edward T Weaver, VP Jerry Sherman, VP James Parent, VP Peter Butler, VP	Rev: Assets: Emp:	5108 5378 40	
Paramount Pictures Corp 5555 Melrose Avenue Los Angeles, CA 90038 213-468-5000	Motion picture & television producer, distributor. Type: Private-Sub Par: Paramount Communications Corp Ind: Leisure Time Grp: Consumer Service Frank Mancuso, CEO	Rev: Assets: Emp:	1000 NA 8	
Park Communications Inc Terrace Hill Ithaca, NY 14850 607-272-9020	Television broadcasting company. Type: NASDAQ-PARC Ind: Publishing/Com Grp: Consumer Service Roy H Park, CEO	Rev: Assets: Emp:	160 267 2	
Parker Bertea Aerospace Group 18321 Jamboree Blvd Irvine, CA 92715 714-833-3000	Manufacturer of motion control systems for space. Type: Private-Sub Par: Parker Hannifin Corp Ind: Aerospace Grp: High Tech Paul Schloemer, CEO	Rev: Assets: Emp:	NA NA NA	
Parker Hannifin Corp 17325 Euclid Avenue Cleveland, OH 44112 216-531-3000	Manufacturer of metal parts; automotive, industrial, repair. Type: NYSE Ind: Manufacturing Grp: Manufacturing Patrick S Parker, CEO Paul G Schloemer, Chr Duane E Collins, VCh Wallace C Young, Tres Michael J Hiemstra, CFO Paul L Carson, IS William Wilkerson, R&D Joseph Whiteman, VP John Hanson, VP James Mockler, VP Richard G Charlton, PR	Rev: Assets: Emp:	2252 1742 33	
Parsons & Whittemore Corp 666 Third Avenue New York, NY 10017 212-972-2000	Manufacturer of paper products. Type: Private Ind: Paper/Forest Prd Grp: Basic Industries George Landegger, CEO	Rev: Assets: Emp:	550 NA 3	
Parsons Corp 100 W Walnut Street Pasadena, CA 91124 818-440-2000	Engineering & construction company. Type: Private Ind: Business Service Grp: Business Service Willian E Leonard, CEO	Rev: Assets: Emp:	1000 NA 10	
Pathe Communications 8670 Wilshire Blvd Beverly Hills, CA 90211 213-658-2100	Movie production & theatre operations company. Type: NYSE-PCC Ind: Leisure Time Grp: Consumer Service G Parrentti, CEO	Rev: Assets: Emp:	371 798 2	
Pattison, Jim Industries Ltd 1055 W Hastings Street Vancouver, BC V6E2H2 Can 604-688-6764	Air transport holding company. Type: Private Ind: Airline Grp: Consumer Service James Patterson, CEO	Rev: Assets: Emp:	1384 678 8	
Pauley Petroleum Inc 10000 Santa Monica Blvd Los Angeles, CA 90067 213-879-5000	Oil & gas exploration, refining & distribution company. Type: ASE-PP Ind: Energy Grp: Basic Industries William Pagin, CEO	Rev: Assets: Emp:	200 250 1	
Pay Less Drug Stores 9275 SW Peyton Lane Wilsonville, OR 97070 503-682-4100	Drugs, sundries, & toiletry retailer. Type: Private-Sub Par: K Mart Corp Ind: Retail/Merch Grp: Retail Edward Hart, CEO	Rev: Assets: Emp:	1500 NA 15	
Pay N Pak Inc 1209 S Central Kent, WA 98031 206-854-5450	Home improvment retail stores. Type: Private Ind: Retail/Merch Grp: Retail David J Heerensperger, CEO	Rev: Assets: Emp:	500 NA 2	

Organizations Listed Alphabetically

Organization / Address / Phone	Descriptive Information	Revenue / Assets / Emp ($ mil) ($ mil) (thous)		

Payless Cashways Inc
2301 Main PO Box 466
Kansas City, MO 64141
816-234-6000
Operator of retail food supermarkets.
Type: Private
Ind: Retail/Merch   Grp: Retail
David Stanley, CEO   Larry Kunz, Pres   Stephen A Lightstone, CFO
Vince E Heiker, IS   John Freehling, R&D   Dale C Pond, Mkt
Linda Ward, PR
Rev: 1750
Assets: 800
Emp: 13

PCL Construction Group Ltd
5410 99th Street
Edmonton, AB T6E3P4 Can
403-435-9711
Nationwide construction & development company.
Type: Private
Ind: Real Estate/Bldg   Grp: Business Service
R Stollery, CEO
Rev: 1071
Assets: 308
Emp: 4

PCS Inc
9501 E Shea Blvd
Scottsdale, AZ 85260
602-391-4600
Computer services company; processor of medical claims.
Type: Private-Sub   Par: McKesson Corp
Ind: Comput/Off Equip   Grp: High Tech
Don Dahlin, CEO
Rev: NA
Assets: NA
Emp: NA

Peabody Holding Co
301 N Memorial Drive
St Louis, MO 63102
314-342-3400
Coal mining & distributing company.
Type: Private
Ind: Energy   Grp: Basic Industries
Gordon R Parker, CEO   Robert Quenon, Chr   Francis Barkoffske, VCh
Steven Schaab, Tres   Michael Scharf, CFO   Robert Wallace, R&D
Christopher Farrand, VP   William Buck, VP   John Goroncy, VP
Rev: 1758
Assets: 2449
Emp: 6

Peat Marwick Main & Co
345 Park Avenue
New York, NY 10022
212-758-9700
Major accounting firm.
Type: Private
Ind: Accounting   Grp: Business Service
Larry D Horner, CEO
Rev: 4000
Assets: NA
Emp: 30

Peat Marwick Main & Co
Scotia Plaza 40 King Street E
Toronto, ON M5H3Z2 Can
416-863-3300
National accounting firm.
Type: Private
Ind: Accounting   Grp: Business Service
Ross Walker, CEO
Rev: 128
Assets: NM
Emp: 2

Pechiney World Trade Inc
475 Steamboat Road
Greenwich, CT 06830
203-622-8300
Operator of steel & metals service centers.
Type: Private
Ind: Business Service   Grp: Business Service
Michael Messud, CEO
Rev: 1100
Assets: NA
Emp: 1

Peck, C L Contractors Inc
10866 Wilshire Blvd
Los Angeles, CA 90024
213-470-1885
Manufacturer of electronic equipment & components.
Type: Private
Ind: Electronics   Grp: High Tech
Vick Segal, CEO
Rev: 550
Assets: NA
Emp: 1

Pemex (Petroleos Mexicos SA)
3600 S Gessner
Houston, TX 77063
713-978-7974
Petroleum exploration & distribution company; US hdqtrs.
Type: Private-Sub-For
Ind: Energy   Grp: Basic Industries
Ramon Guerrero, CEO
Rev: 12100
Assets: NA
Emp: 142

Penn Central Corp
One E Fourth Street
Cincinnati, OH 45202
513-579-6600
Manufacturer of telecommunications cable.
Type: NYSE-PC
Ind: Manufacturing   Grp: Manufacturing
Carl H Lindner, CEO   Ronald F Walker, Pres   Neil Hahl, VCh
David S Street, CFO   Phillip Hagel, Sls   Robert Olsen, VP
James Schwab, VP   Robert M Burton, PR
Rev: 1547
Assets: 2400
Emp: 14

Penn Mutual Life Insurance Co
Independence Square
Philadelphia, PA 19172
215-625-5000
Life insurance company.
Type: Private-Mutual
Ind: Insurance   Grp: Insurance
John E Tait, CEO   Richard J Pinola, Pres   Thomas E Stiles, CFO
Paul Trainor, IS   Thomas Stoudt, Mkt   Suzanne Young, IR
Judith Eckles, PR
Rev: 1589
Assets: 4984
Emp: 5

Penn Traffic Inc
319 Washington
Johnstown, PA 15901
814-536-4411
Operator of retail food stores.
Type: ASE
Ind: Retail/Food   Grp: Retail
Guido Malconi, CEO
Rev: 1180
Assets: NA
Emp: 10

Organization / Address / Phone	Descriptive Information	Revenue / ($ mil)	Assets / ($ mil)	Emp (thous)

Pennbancorp Inc(Integra Financial)
Four PPG Place
Pittsburgh, PA 15222
814-644-8184

Commercial bank.
Type: NASDAQ-ITGR
Ind: Banking   Grp: Financial
George E Kesel, CEO

Rev: 333
Assets: 3304
Emp: 2

Penney, J C Co
14841 N Dallas Parkway
Dalla, TX 75240
214-591-1000

Nationwide operator of retail department stores.
Type: NYSE-JCP
Ind: Retail/Merch   Grp: Retail
William R Howell, CEO   David F Miller, Pres   Robert B Gill, VCh
Robert E Northam, CFO   David V Evans, IS   Peter G Fenlon, Sls
John A Wells, VP   William R Johnson, PR

Rev: 14833
Assets: 12254
Emp: 180

Pennsylvania Electric Co
1001 Broad Street
Johnstown, PA 15907
814-533-8111

Electric power utility company.
Type: Private-Sub   Par: General Public Utilities Corp
Ind: Utility   Grp: Utilities
William G Kuhns, CEO   Robert L Wise, Chr   John G Graham, CFO
Jack A Poole, Ops

Rev: 761
Assets: 1760
Emp: 4

Pennsylvania Power & Light Co
2 N Ninth Street
Allentown, PA 18101
215-770-5151

Electric power utility.
Type: NYSE-PPL
Ind: Utility   Grp: Utilities
Robert K Campbell, CEO   Merlin Hertzog, VCh   Charles E Russoli, CFO
Clair W Noll, IS   William F Hecht, Mkt   Bruce Kenyon, Ops
John Biggar, VP   Gennaro Caliendo, VP   Thomas Crimmins, VP
John F Klemencic, IR   John Miller, PR

Rev: 2214
Assets: 7525
Emp: 8

Pennsylvania Power Co
One E Washington Street
New Castle, PA 16103
412-652-5331

Electic power utility company.
Type: Private-Sub   Par: Ohio Edison Co
Ind: Utility   Grp: Utilities
Justin Rogers, CEO

Rev: NA
Assets: NA
Emp: NA

Pennsylvania State University
Administrative Bldg
University Park, PA 16802
814-865-4700

Major educational institution; university.
Type: University
Ind: University   Grp: Govt & Non-Prof
Bryce Jordan, CEO

Rev: 383
Assets: 602
Emp: 39

Pennsylvania, State of
State Capitol
Harrisburg, PA 17120
717-787-2121

State government.
Type: State Govt
Ind: State/Prov Govt   Grp: Govt & Non-Prof
Robert P Casey, CEO

Rev: 27163
Assets: NM
Emp: 144

Pennwalt Corp
Three Parkway
Philadelphia, PA 19102
215-587-7000

Manufacturer of specialty chemicals.
Type: NYSE-PSM
Ind: Chemicals   Grp: Basic Industries
Edwin E Tuttle, CEO   Seymour S Preston, Pres   Paul Clark, Tres
Robert M Rubin, IS   William Tuemmler, R&D   Graham Bowen-Ashwin, VP
Emil J Mikity, VP   Peter J McCarthy, PR

Rev: 1024
Assets: 950
Emp: 5

Pennzoil Co
Pennzoil Place
Houston, TX 77252
713-546-4000

Petroleum products company; exploration, production, retail.
Type: NYSE
Ind: Energy   Grp: Basic Industries
Randle B McDonald, CEO   James Malone, VCh   Patrick L Manning, IS
Robert Semrad, VP   Richard Valentine, VP   Terry Hemeyer, PR

Rev: 2274
Assets: 4480
Emp: 8

Penske, Roger Corp
600 Parsippany Road
Parsippany, NJ 07054
201-428-7500

Operator of automotive sales & leasing businesses.
Type: Private
Ind: Business Service   Grp: Business Service
Roger S Penske, CEO

Rev: 2000
Assets: NA
Emp: 10

Pentair Inc
1700 W Highway 36
St Paul, MN 55113
612-636-7920

Manufacturer of forest products.
Type: OTC
Ind: Paper/Forest Prd   Grp: Basic Industries
D Eugene Nugent, CEO   S A Johnson, Pres   David Lentz, VCh
Roy T Rueb, Tres   John H Grunewald, CFO   W F Fuehrer, R&D
Mark T Schroepfer, VP   Barbara Boisen, PR

Rev: 823
Assets: 745
Emp: 9

Organizations Listed Alphabetically

Organization / Address / Phone	Descriptive Information	Revenue / ($ mil)	Assets / ($ mil)	Emp (thous)

People's Bank
899 Main Street
Bridgeport, CT 06604
203-579-7171

Thrift institution.
Type: Private
Ind: Savings & Loan   Grp: Financial
Norwick Goodspeed, CEO

Rev: 600
Assets: 6321
Emp: 2

Peoples Energy Corp
122 S Michigan Avenue
Chicago, IL 60603
312-431-4000

Natural gas utility.
Type: NYSE-PGL
Ind: Utility   Grp: Utilities
Eugene A Tracy, CEO   Richard E Terry, Pres   J Bruce Hasch, VCh
Donald G Holm, CFO   Michael S Reeves, Mkt   James Hinchliff, VP
Patrick Doyle, VP   John Lawrisuk, VP   John Mooney, VP

Rev: 1117
Assets: 1408
Emp: 3

Pep Boys/Manny Moe Jack Inc
3111 W Allegheny
Philadelphia, PA 19132
215-229-9000

Automotive parts retail store operator.
Type: NYSE-PBY
Ind: Retail/Merch   Grp: Retail
Benjamin Strauss, CEO   Mitchell Liebovitz, Pres   Michael Holden, CFO
Robert Goodman, IS   Anne Thompson, Mkt   Phillip Adcock, Ops
Frederick Stampone, VP   Bruce Chidsey, VP   Joseph Cirelli, VP
Donald Denbo, VP   Thomas McSorley, VP

Rev: 656
Assets: 582
Emp: 4

Pepper Companies
643 N Orleans Street
Chicago, IL 60610
312-266-4703

Industrial construction contracting company.
Type: Private
Ind: Real Estate/Bldg   Grp: Business Service
Richard S Pepper, CEO

Rev: 500
Assets: NA
Emp: 1

Pepperidge Farm Inc
595 Westport Avenue
Norwalk, CT 06856
203-846-7000

Packaged food manufacturer.
Type: Private-Sub   Par: Campbell Soup Co
Ind: Food Processing   Grp: Food Processing
Richard Shea, CEO

Rev: NA
Assets: NA
Emp: NA

Pepsi Cola Canada Ltd
1255 Bay Street
Toronto, ON M5R 2G9 Can
416-964-1313

Manufacturer of beverages; softdrinks.
Type: Private
Ind: Food Processing   Grp: Food Processing
Wayne Mailloux, CEO

Rev: 259
Assets: 211
Emp: 2

Pepsico Foods International
400 Frito Lay Tower Exchange Park
Dallas, TX 75235
214-956-3700

Manufacturer & distributor of snack food products.
Type: Private-Sub   Par: PepsiCo Inc
Ind: Food Processing   Grp: Food Processing
John Pingel, CEO

Rev: NA
Assets: NA
Emp: NA

PepsiCo Inc
Anderson Hill Road
Purchase, NY 10577
914-253-2000

Beverage company; restaurants, packaged foods.
Type: NYSE-PEP
Ind: Beverage   Grp: Food Processing
D Wayne Calloway, CEO   Roger Enrico, Pres   Robert G Dettmer, CFO
Allan B Deering, IS   Donovan Carleton, R&D   J Roger King, VP
Edward Lahey, VP   Joseph F McCann, PR

Rev: 13007
Assets: 11135
Emp: 235

Perdue Farms Inc
Old Ocean City Road
Salisbury, MD 21801
301-543-3000

Poulty processing company.
Type: Private
Ind: Food Processing   Grp: Food Processing
Frank Perdue, CEO

Rev: 1500
Assets: NA
Emp: 15

Pergamon Holding Corp
Maxwell House Fairview Park
Elmsford, NY 10523
914-592-9141

Publisher of books.
Type: Private
Ind: Publishing/Com   Grp: Consumer Service
Robert Miranda, CEO

Rev: 825
Assets: NA
Emp: 8

Perimian Partners Ltd
2500 City West Blvd
Houston, TX 77251
713-787-2222

Crude oil trading, storage & transport company.
Type: NYSE-PAA
Ind: Energy   Grp: Basic Industries
H M Love, CEO

Rev: 2289
Assets: 555
Emp: 2

Organizations Listed Alphabetically

Organization / Address / Phone	Descriptive Information	Revenue / ($ mil)	Assets / ($ mil)	Emp (thous)

Perini Corp
73 Mt Wayte Avenue
Framingham, MA 01701
508-875-6171

International construction company.
Type: ASE-PCR
Ind: Real Estate/Bldg   Grp: Business Service
David B Perini, CEO   Joseph Perini, Pres   Robert Band, Tres
James M Markert, CFO   Joseph McGarry, IS   John Chiaverini, Mkt
Warren Pettingell, VP   Patricia Kelly, VP   Robert Higgins, VP
Charles J Patterson, PR

Rev: 849
Assets: 374
Emp: 3

Perkin Elmer Corp
761 Main Avenue
Norwalk, CT 06859
203-762-1000

Manufacturer of analytical electronic instruments.
Type: NYSE-PKN
Ind: Instruments   Grp: High Tech
Horace G McDonell, CEO   Gaynor N Kelley, Pres   C Wendell Bergere, VCh
Rhonda Seegal, Tres   F Gordon Bitter, CFO   William Morlock, IS
William Sawch, VP   Julianne A Grace, VP   Edward Bloch, PR

Rev: 1165
Assets: 1368
Emp: 11

Perpetual American Bank Inc
8200 Greensboro Drive
McLean, VA 22101
703-442-7000

Thrift institution.
Type: NASDAQ-PFCP
Ind: Savings & Loan   Grp: Financial
Thomas J Owen, CEO   Joseph W Barr, Tres   Joe Cicero, CFO
David Taylor, Sls   Judith E McCaffrey, VP   Wendy Sharp, VP
John P Walsh, VP   William T Lynne, VP   Robert A Barton, IR
Stephen Smith, PR

Rev: 561
Assets: 5853
Emp: 2

Perry Drug Stores Inc
5400 Perry Drive
Pontiac, MI 48056
313-334-1300

Regional operator of retail drugstores.
Type: NYSE-PDS
Ind: Retail/Merch   Grp: Retail
Jack A Robinson, CEO

Rev: 600
Assets: 400
Emp: 7

Pet Inc
400 S Fourth Street
St Louis, MO 63102
314-621-5400

Manufacturer of food products, consumer goods
Type: Private-Sub   Par: Whitman Co (IC Industries Inc)
Ind: Food Processing   Grp: Food Processing
Ray Morris, CEO

Rev: NA
Assets: NA
Emp: NA

Peters, J M Co
1601 Dove Street
Newport Beach, CA 92660
714-833-9331

Real estate development company.
Type: ASE-JMP
Ind: Real Estate/Bldg   Grp: Business Service
J Peters, CEO

Rev: 300
Assets: 250
Emp: 1

Petrie Stores Corp
70 Enterprise Avenue
Secaucus, NJ 07094
201-866-3600

Womens retail clothing stores.
Type: NYSE
Ind: Retail/Merch   Grp: Retail
Milton Petrie, CEO   Milton Petrie, Chr   Hilda Kirschbaum Gerstein, VCh
Peter A Left, CFO   Dorothy Fink Stern, Mkt   Jean Roberts, Ops
Bernard Apple, VP   Allan Laufgraben, VP   Nancy Barrett, VP
Edward Citro, VP   Scott Galin, VP

Rev: 1242
Assets: 1134
Emp: 7

Petro Canada
150 6th Avenue SW
Calgary, AB T2P3E3 Can
403-296-5850

Oil & natural gas production & marketing company.
Type: Govt Corp
Ind: Energy   Grp: Basic Industries
W H Hopper, CEO

Rev: 4415
Assets: 7185
Emp: 8

Petroleum Heat & Power Co
Davenport Street
Stamford, CT 06904
203-323-2121

Fuel oil supplier; delivery, furnace burner.
Type: ASE-PHP
Ind: Energy   Grp: Basic Industries
Malvin P Sevin, CEO

Rev: 462
Assets: 350
Emp: 2

Petrolite Corp
100 N Broadway
St Louis, MO 63102
314-241-8370

Manufacturer of specialty chemicals.
Type: OTC-PLIT
Ind: Chemicals   Grp: Basic Industries
Ellis Brown, CEO

Rev: 375
Assets: 250
Emp: 3

Peugeot USA Inc
One Peugeot Plaza
Lindhurst, NJ 07071
201-935-8400

Manufacturer & importer of automobiles; US headquarters.
Type: Private-Sub-For
Ind: Automotive   Grp: Manufacturing
Pascal Henault, CEO

Rev: 825
Assets: NA
Emp: 2

Organizations Listed Alphabetically

Organization / Address / Phone	Descriptive Information	Revenue / ($ mil)	Assets / ($ mil)	Emp (thous)
Pfizer Inc 235 E 42nd Street New York, NY 10017 212-573-2323	International drug company; human, animal, specialty chem. Type: NYSE Ind: Drugs Grp: Consumer Service Edward T Pratt, CEO Gerald D Laubach, Pres Edward Bessey, VCh Jean-Paul Valles, CFO Barry M Bloom, R&D Thomas Connors, VP M Kenneth Bowler, VP C L Clemente, VP Joseph Harmon, VP John Jefferis, VP Robert L Shafer, PR	Rev: Assets: Emp:		5385 7638 41
Pharma Plus Drugmarts Ltd 111 Merton Street Toronto, ON M4T3A9 Can 416-483-4611	Operator of retail drugstores. Type: Private Ind: Retail/Merch Grp: Retail Bill Atkinson, CEO	Rev: Assets: Emp:		319 110 2
Phelps Co Inc PO Box 2440 Greeley, CO 80632 303-353-7000	Commercial construction company. Type: Private Ind: Real Estate/Bldg Grp: Business Service Robert G Tointon, CEO	Rev: Assets: Emp:		600 NA 3
Phelps Dodge Corp 2600 N Central Avenue Phoenix, AZ 85004 602-234-8100	Mining & manufacturing company; copper, wire products. Type: NYSE-PD Ind: Metals/Mining Grp: Basic Industries G Robert Durham, CEO Leonard R Judd, VCh Frank J Longto, CFO Patrick Ryan, R&D Arthur R Miele, Mkt Richard Rice, Ops William Tubman, VP Frank Longto, VP Nicholas Balich, VP Patrick Ryan, VP Nicholas Balich, PR	Rev: Assets: Emp:		2320 2755 11
PHH Group Inc 11333 McCormick Road Hunt Valley, MD 21031 301-771-3600	Leasing company; commercial auto & truck fleets. Type: NYSE-PHH Ind: Business Service Grp: Business Service Jerome W Geckle, CEO Robert D Kunisch, Chr Terry Kridler, Tres Roy A Meierhenry, CFO Michael J Mobley, IS Eugene A Arbaugh, Mkt Samuel Penn, VP Phillip Taft, VP John Conner Jr, VP William Adler, VP Joachim Diedrich, VP Donna C Stortgol, IR S Peter Brinch, PR	Rev: Assets: Emp:		1735 4231 5
Philadelphia Electric Co 2301 Market Street Philadelphia, PA 19101 215-841-4000	Electric power utility company. Type: NYSE Ind: Utility Grp: Utilities Joseph F Paquette, CEO Corbin MacNeil, VCh Richard G Gilmore, CFO Richard G Gilmore, IS A J Weigand, R&D Kenneth G Lawrence, Mkt Dickinson Smith, VP Eugene Bradley, VP Albert Solecki, VP Clifford Brenner, IR Neil McDermott, PR	Rev: Assets: Emp:		3229 11863 11
Philadelphia National Bank Co Broad & Chestnut Streets Philadelphia, PA 19101 215-629-3512	Commercial bank. Type: OTC Ind: Banking Grp: Financial Frederick Heldring, CEO	Rev: Assets: Emp:		1500 12000 6
Philadelphia, City of City Hall Philadelphia, PA 19107 512-686-2181	City government. Type: City Govt Ind: Local Govt Grp: Govt & Non-Prof W Wilson Goode, CEO	Rev: Assets: Emp:		2692 NM 31
Philip Morris Companies Inc 120 Park Avenue New York, NY 10017 212-880-5000	Manufacturer of tobacco, brewing & consumer food products. Type: NYSE-MO Ind: Tobacco Grp: Food Processing Hamish Maxwell, CEO John A Murphy, Pres William Murray, VCh Hans G Storr, CFO F Robert Kurinsky, IS Kenneth Houghton, R&D William I Campbell, Mkt Donald Fried, VP Alexander Holtzmann, VP James T Breedlove, VP Patricia Malzacher, VP George L Knox, PR	Rev: Assets: Emp:		31742 36960 155

Organizations Listed Alphabetically

Organization / Address / Phone	Descriptive Information	Revenue / Assets / Emp ($ mil) ($ mil) (thous)		

Philipp Brothers Chemicals Inc
1 Parker Plaza
Fort Lee, NJ 07024
201-944-6020

Manufacturer of specialty chemicals.
Type: Private
Ind: Chemicals   Grp: Basic Industries
Nathan Bistricher, CEO

Rev: 550
Assets: NA
Emp: 1

Philips Canada Ltd
601 Milner Avenue
Montreal, ON M1B1M8 Can
416-292-5161

Manufacturer of electronics products.
Type: Private-Sub-For
Ind: Electronics   Grp: High Tech
Alfred Nieukerke, CEO

Rev: 468
Assets: NA
Emp: 3

Philips Industries Inc
4801 Springfield Street
Dayton, OH 45401
513-253-7171

Manufacturer of trailer homes, recreational vehicles.
Type: NYSE-PHL
Ind: Manufacturing   Grp: Manufacturing
Jesse Philips, CEO   Robert W Brethen, Chr   Thomas C Haas, Tres
Leonard Reardon, CFO   Art Kern, IS   William McCanna, Ops
David Jeanmougin, VP   George Loving, VP   C Neal Baileys, VP
William H Roberts, PR

Rev: 693
Assets: 353
Emp: 10

Phillips 66 Co
Fouth & Keeler Streets
Bartlesville, OK 74004
918-661-4948

Petroleum refining & marketing company.
Type: Private-Sub   Par: Phillips Petroleum Co
Ind: Energy   Grp: Basic Industries
B Thompson, CEO

Rev: NA
Assets: NA
Emp: NA

Phillips Petroleum Co
Phillips Bldg
Bartlesville, OK 74004
918-661-6600

Petroleum exploration, production & marketing company.
Type: NYSE
Ind: Energy   Grp: Basic Industries
C J Silas, CEO   Glenn A Cox, Pres   L Richards, VCh
R E Bonnell, CFO   P J Gottardi, IS   C F Cook, R&D
Robert G Wallace, Mkt   D Tippeconnie, VP   J Bryan Whitworth, PR

Rev: 11490
Assets: 11968
Emp: 25

Phillips Pipeline Co
370 Adams Bldg
Bartlesville, OK 74004
918-661-6600

Petroleum & natural gas pipeline company.
Type: Private-Sub   Par: Phillips Petroleum Co
Ind: Energy   Grp: Basic Industries
W Shriver, CEO

Rev: NA
Assets: NA
Emp: NA

Phillips Van Heusen Corp
1290 Avenue of the Americas
New York, NY 10104
212-541-5200

Manufacturer of apparel & shoes.
Type: NYSE-PVH
Ind: Apparel/Textiles   Grp: Consumer Prd
Lawrence S Phillips, CEO   Bruce Klatsky, Pres   Irwin W Winter, CFO
Walter Zambrovitz, IS   James J Murphy, Sls   Mark Weber, Mkt
Walter C Zambrovitz, VP   Cynthia L Tarantino, VP   Henry J Justus, PR

Rev: 641
Assets: 323
Emp: 7

PHM (Pulte Home) Corp
6400 Farmington Road
West Bloomfield, MI 48033
313-661-1500

Home building company.
Type: NYSE-PHM
Ind: Real Estate/Bldg   Grp: Business Service
James Grosfeld, CEO   James Grosfeld, Chr   Robert K Burgess, Pres
William Pulte, VCh   Richard C Staky, CFO   Barb Schlatterbeck, IS
Martha Anderson, Mkt   David Elbing, VP   Bryan Noreen, VP
Richard C Staky, PR

Rev: 834
Assets: 590
Emp: 2

Phoenix Continental Ltd
439 University Avenue
Toronto, ON M5G1Y8 Can
416-596-6100

Property & casualty insurance company.
Type: Private-Sub-For
Ind: Insurance   Grp: Insurance
William W Ward, CEO

Rev: 333
Assets: 604
Emp: 1

Phoenix Mutual Life Insurance Co
One American Row
Hartford, CT 06115
203-275-5000

Life insurance company.
Type: Private
Ind: Insurance   Grp: Insurance
John Gummere, CEO   Robert W Fiondella, Pres   David W Searfoss, CFO
Frederick W Sawyer, IS   Philip R McLoughlin, IR   Jo Anne Leventhal, PR

Rev: 1319
Assets: 5678
Emp: 4

Phoenix, City of
City Hall 251 W Washington Street
Phoenix, AZ 85003
602-262-7111

City government.
Type: City Govt
Ind: Local Govt   Grp: Govt & Non-Prof
Terry Goddard, CEO

Rev: 782
Assets: NM
Emp: 9

Organizations Listed Alphabetically

Organization / Address / Phone	Descriptive Information	Revenue / ($ mil)	Assets / ($ mil)	Emp (thous)
Pic N Save Corp 2430 E Del Amo Blvd Dominguez, CA 90220 213-537-9220	Retail discount store operator; closeout merchandise. Type: OTC Ind: Retail/Merch Grp: Retail Lewis B Merrifield, CEO	Rev: Assets: Emp:		402 262 4
Piccadilly Cafeterias Inc 3232 Sherwood Forest Blvd Baton Rouge, LA 70816 504-293-9440	Operator of cafeteria restaurants. Type: NASDAQ-PICC Ind: Food/Lodging Grp: Consumer Service James Malmberg, CEO	Rev: Assets: Emp:		276 150 8
PIE Nationwide Trucking Corp 4250 Kings Road Jacksonville, FL 32209 904-798-2000	Nationwide transportation company; trucking. Type: Private Ind: Transport Grp: Business Service Charles F Rodgers, CEO	Rev: Assets: Emp:		750 NA 7
Piedmont Aviation Inc 4001 N Liberty Street Winston Salem, NC 27105 919-767-5100	Commercial airline Type: Private-Sub Par: US Air Group Inc Ind: Airline Grp: Consumer Service Edwin Colodny, CEO	Rev: Assets: Emp:		3000 1718 20
Piedmont Natural Gas Co 1915 Rexford Road Charlotte, NC 28233 704-364-3120	Natural gas refining & distribution company. Type: NYSE-PNY Ind: Energy Grp: Basic Industries John Maxheim, CEO	Rev: Assets: Emp:		431 700 2
Pier 1 Imports Inc 301 Commerce Street Fort Worth, TX 76102 817-878-8000	Operator of retail home furnishing stores. Type: NYSE-PIR Ind: Retail/Merch Grp: Retail Clark A Johnson, CEO	Rev: Assets: Emp:		415 300 4
Pierce, S S Co 74 Seneca Street Dundee, NY 14837 607-243-7171	Manufacturer of fruit juices. Type: Private-Sub Ind: Food Processing Grp: Food Processing Arthur Wolcotts, CEO	Rev: Assets: Emp:		600 400 7
Piggly Wiggly Southern Inc 100 Brinson Road Vidalia, GA 30474 912-537-9871	Operator of retail food supermarkets. Type: Private Ind: Retail/Food Grp: Retail Paul Garretson, CEO	Rev: Assets: Emp:		825 NA 7
Pilgrams Pride Corp 110 S Texas Street Pittsburg, TX 75686 214-856-7901	Food processing company; chicken. Type: Private Ind: Food Processing Grp: Food Processing Cliff Butler, CEO	Rev: Assets: Emp:		550 NA 5
Pillsbury Co Pillsbury Center 200 S Sixth Street Minneapolis, MN 55402 612-330-4966	Manufacturer of foods, cookies, cake mixes etc. Type: NYSE-PSY Ind: Food Processing Grp: Food Processing William H Spoor, CEO Herbert D Ihle, Tres Roger L Headrick, CFO John M Hammitt, IS James R Behnke, R&D Russell Bragg, VP John W Argent, VP Terry Bowmaster, VP Michael Ellewein, VP Johnny W Thompson, PR	Rev: Assets: Emp:		6191 3840 100
Pima Savings Assn Inc 5151 E Broadway Tuscon, AZ 85732 602-747-8484	Thrift institution. Type: OTC Ind: Savings & Loan Grp: Financial Floyd W Sedlmayr, CEO	Rev: Assets: Emp:		248 3226 1
Pinnacle West Capital 2828 N Central Avenue Phoenix, AZ 85004 602-222-6951	Diversified co, electric utility, banking & development. Type: NYSE-PNW Ind: Utility Grp: Utilities Keith L Turley, CEO Donald Hepperman, Tres Henry B Sargent, CFO Paul Converti, IS Arlyn Larson, R&D Faye Widenmann, Mkt Steve Carr, PR	Rev: Assets: Emp:		0 15054 17

Organizations Listed Alphabetically

Organization / Address / Phone	Descriptive Information	Revenue / ($ mil)	Assets / ($ mil)	Emp (thous)
Pioneer HiBred International Inc 700 Capital Square 400 Locust Des Moines, IA 50309 515-245-3500	Agri business; seeds & growing materials. Type: OTC Ind: Food Processing Grp: Food Processing Thomas N Urban, CEO James Ansorge, CFO John James, IS Donald Duvick, R&D Julie Muckler, IR Steven Daugherty, PR	Rev: Assets: Emp:		400 587 5
Pioneer Standard Electric Inc 4800 E 131st Street Garfield Heights, OH 44105 216-587-3600	Distributor of electronic parts & industrial gases. Type: NASDAQ-PIDS Ind: Electronics Grp: High Tech P Heller, CEO	Rev: Assets: Emp:		300 200 2
Piper Jaffray & Hopwood Inc Piper Jaffray Tower 222 S 9th Street Minneapolis, MN 55440 612-342-6000	Brokerage firm. Type: Private Ind: Securities Grp: Financial Addison L Piper, CEO	Rev: Assets: Emp:		176 392 1
Pitney Bowes Inc World HQ Walter H Wheeler Jr Drive Stamford, CT 06926 203-356-5000	Manufacturer of mailing equipment for business. Type: NYSE-PBI Ind: Comput/Off Equip Grp: High Tech George B Harvey, CEO Carmine F Adimando, CFO Dennis A Jones, IS Carole C St Mark, R&D Daniel J McCarthy, Mkt Carole St Mark, VP Douglas A Riggs, VP John Moody, VP Hiro Hiranandani, VP Henry J Spring Jr, PR	Rev: Assets: Emp:		2650 4788 29
Pitt Des Moines Inc 3400 Grand Avenue Pittsburgh, PA 15225 412-331-3000	Steel fabricator & operator of steel service centers. Type: ASE-PDM Ind: Manufacturing Grp: Manufacturing William Jackson, CEO	Rev: Assets: Emp:		330 250 3
Pittsburgh National Bank Co Fifth Avenue & Wood Street Pittsburgh, PA 15222 412-355-2000	Commercial bank. Type: Private-Sub Par: PNC Financial Corp Ind: Banking Grp: Financial R C Milsom, CEO	Rev: Assets: Emp:		1300 15765 4
Pittsburgh, City of City Hall 414 Grant Street Pittsburgh, PA 15219 412-255-2626	City government. Type: City Govt Ind: Local Govt Grp: Govt & Non-Prof Richard S Caliguiri, CEO	Rev: Assets: Emp:		329 NM 6
Pittston Co One Pickwick Plaza PO Box 8900 Greenwich, CT 06836 203-622-0900	Coal mining, security & delivery services. Type: NYSE Ind: Energy Grp: Basic Industries Paul W Douglas, CEO Paul C Farrell, VCh David L Marshall, CFO Kevin A Quinn, R&D Robert J Murphy, VP William J Byrne Jr, IR Arthur Rocke, PR	Rev: Assets: Emp:		1583 992 17
Pittway Corp 333 Skokie Blvd Northbrook, IL 60065 312-498-1260	Manufacturer of security equipment; alarms, fire detectors. Type: ASE Ind: Electronics Grp: High Tech Nelson Harris, CEO King Harris, Pres Paul R Gauvreau, CFO Leo A Guthart, VP Howard Isenberg, VP	Rev: Assets: Emp:		771 602 6
Pizza Hut Inc 9111 E Douglas Wichita, KS 67201 316-681-9000	Operator of retail restaurants, franchises. Type: Private-Sub Par: PepsiCo Inc Ind: Food/Lodging Grp: Consumer Service Stephen Reinemund, CEO	Rev: Assets: Emp:		NA NA NA
Placer Dome Ltd Toronto Dominion Center Toronto, ON M5K1N3 Can 416-868-6060	Mining & development company. Type: TOR Ind: Metals/Mining Grp: Basic Industries Fraser Fell, CEO	Rev: Assets: Emp:		709 1839 4
Placid Oil Co 3900 Thanksgiving Dallas, TX 75201 214-741-3081	Oil & gas exploration. Type: Private Ind: Energy Grp: Basic Industries C D Brown, CEO	Rev: Assets: Emp:		1000 NA 1

Organization / Address / Phone	Descriptive Information	Revenue / Assets / Emp ($ mil) ($ mil) (thous)		

Organization / Address / Phone	Descriptive Information	Rev:	Assets:	Emp:
Planning Research Corp 1500 Planning Research Drive McLean, VA 22102 703-556-1000	Computer services & consulting company. Type: Private-sub Par: Emhart Corp Ind: Consulting Grp: Business Service Wayne Shelton, CEO	654	547	7
Playskool Inc 1027 Newport Avenue Pawtuckett, RI 02862 401-727-5576	Manufacturer infant & childrens toys, equipment & apparel. Type: Private-Sub Par: Hasbro Inc Ind: Leisure Time Grp: Consumer Service Daniel Owen, CEO	250	NA	2
Playtex Corp 700 Fairfield Avenue Stamford, CT 06904 203-356-8000	Manufacturer of personal care garments & products. Type: Private Ind: Apparel/Textiles Grp: Consumer Prd Joel E Smilow, CEO	750	NA	8
Plough Inc 3030 Jackson Avenue Memphis, TN 38151 901-320-2801	Manufacturer of consumer products; tanning lotion, drugs. Type: Private-Sub Par: Schering Plough Corp Ind: Personal Care Grp: Consumer Prd Lee Jenkins, CEO	NA	NA	NA
Ploysar Ltd 201 Front Street N Sarnia, ON N7T7V1 Can 519-332-1212	Manufacturer of rubber products. Type: TOR Ind: Chemicals Grp: Basic Industries R Dudley, CEO	2103	2015	15
Ply Gem Industries Inc 919 Third Avenue New York, NY 10022 212-832-1550	Plywood & paneling manufacturing company. Type: ASE-PGI Ind: Building Mat Grp: Basic Industries Jeffrey S Silverman, CEO	383	300	3
PMA Reinsurance Corp 925 Chestnut Street Philadelphia, PA 19107 215-629-5000	Property & casualty insurance company. Type: OTC Ind: Insurance Grp: Insurance John W Smithson, CEO	750	250	3
PMC Corp 12243 Branford Street Sun Valley, CA 91352 818-896-1101	Manufacturer of specialty chemicals. Type: Private Ind: Manufacturing Grp: Manufacturing Philip Kamins, CEO	500	NA	5
PNC Financial Corp Fifth Avenue & Wood Street Pittsburgh, PA 15265 412-762-2728	Commercial bank. Type: NYSE-PNC Ind: Banking Grp: Financial Thomas H O'Brien, CEO Robert Chappell, VCh Charles J Thayer, CFO James Dicostanzo, R&D John Alden, Mkt Richard Smoot, Ops Marlyn Carle, VP Edward Junker, VP Oliver Birckhead, VP J David Grissom, VP Pat Yoder, PR	3827	40811	15
Polaroid Corp 549 Technology Square Cambridge, MA 02139 617-577-2000	Manufacturer of cameras & film. Type: NYSE Ind: Leisure Time Grp: Consumer Service William J McCune, CEO I MacAllister Booth, Chr Sheldon Buckler, VCh Owen J Gaffney, CFO Peter O Kliem, R&D Joseph J McLaughlin, Mkt Milton Dietz, VP Robert Delahunt, VP Sam Yanes, IR Palmer Swanson, PR	1863	1957	13
Policy Management Systems Inc One Wilson Road Blythewood, SC 29016 803-735-4000	Manufacturer of computer software. Type: NASDAQ-PMSC Ind: Business Service Grp: Business Service Sterling E Beale, CEO	217	301	2
Polo/Ralph Lauren Corp 40 W 55th Street New York, NY 10019 212-974-6868	Manufacturer of fashion apparel for men, women, children. Type: Private Ind: Apparel/Textiles Grp: Consumer Prd Peter Strom, CEO	1000	NA	2

Organizations Listed Alphabetically

Organization / Address / Phone	Descriptive Information	Revenue / Assets / Emp ($ mil) ($ mil) (thous)		

Polysar Energy & Chemical (Can Dev) Corp
444 Yonge Street
Toronto, ON M5B2H4 Can
416-598-7200

Manufacturer of rubber products.
Type: Private-Sub   Par: Nova Corp of Alberta Ltd
Ind: Chemicals   Grp: Basic Industries
R Dudley, CEO

Rev: 2439
Assets: 4629
Emp: 7

Ponderosa Steak Houses Inc
Terminal Drive Dayton Int'l Airport
Dayton, OH 45377
513-454-2400

Operator of family restaurants.
Type: Private
Ind: Food/Lodging   Grp: Consumer Service
Mike Jenkins, CEO

Rev: 550
Assets: NA
Emp: 11

Pontiac Motors Div
One Pontiac Plaza
Pontiac, MI 48053
313-857-5000

Manufacturer & distributor of automobiles.
Type: Private-Sub   Par: General Motors Corp
Ind: Automotive   Grp: Manufacturing
Michael Losh, CEO

Rev: NA
Assets: NA
Emp: NA

Pope & Talbot Inc
1500 SW First Street
Portland, OR 97201
503-228-9161

Forest products company; lumber, paper.
Type: NYSE-POP
Ind: Paper/Forest Prd   Grp: Basic Industries
Peter T Pope, CEO   R Steven Mason, Pres   Carlos M Lamadrid, CFO
John W Cokins, Mkt   Richard N Moffitt, VP   Malcolm Bellafronto Jr, VP
Michael Flannery, VP   Gary A Nees, VP   Walter E Sinclair, VP

Rev: 515
Assets: 319
Emp: 4

Port Authority of New York & New Jersey
One World Trade Center
New York, NY 10048
212-466-7000

Government authority operating airports, bridges & tunnels.
Type: Govt Authority
Ind: Govt Authority   Grp: Govt & Non-Prof
Philip Kaltendacher, CEO

Rev: 2350
Assets: 5500
Emp: 20

Portland General Electric Co
121 SW Salmon Street
Portland, OR 97204
503-226-8333

Electric power utility.
Type: NYSE
Ind: Utility   Grp: Utilities
Ken L Harrison, CEO   Richard Reiten, Pres   Leonard Girard, VCh
Clifford Morton, CFO   Gregg Anderson, VP   C Hobbs, VP

Rev: 762
Assets: 2511
Emp: 3

Portland, City of
City Hall
Portland, OR 97204
503-248-4120

City government.
Type: City Govt
Ind: Local Govt   Grp: Govt & Non-Prof
John Clark, CEO

Rev: 309
Assets: NM
Emp: 4

Potamkin Co Inc
785 Eleventh Avenue
New York, NY 10019
212-399-4400

Automobile dealerships.
Type: Private
Ind: Automotive   Grp: Manufacturing
Victor Potamkin, CEO

Rev: 1000
Assets: NA
Emp: 4

Potlatch Corp
One Maritime Plaza
San Francisco, CA 94111
415-576-8800

Forest products company; lumber, paper.
Type: NYSE-PCH
Ind: Paper/Forest Prd   Grp: Basic Industries
Richard B Madden, CEO   John M Richards, CFO   Charles L Neuner, R&D
James Fleshman, Mkt   Richard Congreve, VP   George C Cheek, PR

Rev: 1084
Assets: 1272
Emp: 7

Potomac Edison Co
Downsville Pike
Hagerstown, MD 21740
301-790-3400

Electric power utility company.
Type: Private-Sub   Par: Allegheny Power System Inc
Ind: Utility   Grp: Utilities
Elmer Kaelin, CEO

Rev: NA
Assets: NA
Emp: NA

Potomac Electric Power Co
1900 Pennsylvania Avenue NW
Washington, DC 20068
202-872-2456

Electric power utility company.
Type: NYSE-POM
Ind: Utility   Grp: Utilities
W Reid Thompson, CEO   H Lowell Davis, Chr   Edward Caine, Pres
Peter H Benzinger, VCh   B Thomas Haynes, Tres   Paul F Naughton, CFO
James S Culp, IS   Frank J Spingler, VP   Donald K James, VP
John McConomy, VP

Rev: 1350
Assets: 4146
Emp: 5

PPG Canada Inc
50 St Clair Avenue W
Toronto, ON M4V1M9 Can
416-923-5441

Manufacturer of glass; automotive, construction.
Type: Private-Sub-For
Ind: Building Mat   Grp: Basic Industries
J MacMillan, CEO

Rev: 479
Assets: 437
Emp: 3

Organizations Listed Alphabetically

Organization / Address / Phone	Descriptive Information	Revenue / Assets / Emp ($ mil) ($ mil) (thous)		

PPG Industries Inc
One PPG Place
Pittsburgh, PA 15272
412-434-3131

Manufacturer of glass; automobile, building, house.
Type: NYSE-PPG
Ind: Manufacturing   Grp: Manufacturing
Vincent A Sarni, CEO   Edward J Slack, Pres   Robert H Mitchel, CFO
Sally Wellinger, IS   Richard Rompala, R&D   Joseph Rowe, VP
Franklin H Green, VP   David C Green, PR

Rev: 5617
Assets: 5154
Emp: 36

Prairie Farms Dairy Inc
1100 N Broadway
Carlinville, IL 62626
217-854-2547

Producer & distributor of food products; dairy.
Type: Private
Ind: Food Processing   Grp: Food Processing
Lenord Southwell, CEO

Rev: 330
Assets: NA
Emp: 1

Prange, H C Co Inc
2314 Memorial
Sheboygan, WI 53081
414-459-4800

Operator of retail merchandise stores.
Type: Private
Ind: Retail/Merch   Grp: Retail
Henry Prange, CEO

Rev: 275
Assets: NA
Emp: 3

Pratt & Lambert Inc
75 Tonawanda Street
Buffalo, NY 14207
716-873-6000

Manufacturer of paints & specialty chemicals.
Type: ASE-PM
Ind: Chemicals   Grp: Basic Industries
Raymond D Stevens, CEO

Rev: 250
Assets: 200
Emp: 2

Pratt & Whitney Aircraft Inc
400 Main Street
East Hartford, CT 06108
203-565-9500

Manufacturer of aircraft equipment; jet engines.
Type: Private-Sub   Par: United Technologies Corp
Ind: Aerospace   Grp: High Tech
James O'Conner, CEO

Rev: NA
Assets: NA
Emp: NA

Pratt & Whitney Canada Inc
1000 Boul Marie Victorin
Longueuill, PQ J4K4X9 Can
514-677-9411

Manufacturer of aircraft engines, turbines.
Type: Private-Sub-For
Ind: Aerospace   Grp: High Tech
E Smith, CEO

Rev: 839
Assets: 700
Emp: 9

Pratt Hotel Corp
13455 Noel Road
Dallas, TX 75240
214-386-9777

Operator of hotels & a gambling casino.
Type: ASE-PHC
Ind: Food/Lodging   Grp: Consumer Service
Jack E Pratt, CEO

Rev: 250
Assets: 300
Emp: 4

Precision Castparts Inc
4600 SE Harney Drive
Portland, OR 97206
503-777-3881

Manufacturer of specialty castings for aerospace industry.
Type: NASDAQ-PCST
Ind: Steel   Grp: Basic Industries
Edward H Cooley, CEO   William C McCormick, Pres   Roy M Marvin, Tres
William D Larsson, CFO   Peter G Waite, Sls   J William Crawford, Mkt
Corwin G Mathews, VP   G Thompson Allens, VP

Rev: 414
Assets: 298
Emp: 6

Premark International Corp
1717 Deerfield Road
Deerfield, IL 60015
312-405-6000

Manufacturer of plastic products for home use.
Type: NYSE-PMI
Ind: Tire/Rubber   Grp: Basic Industries
Warrem L Batts, CEO   A J English, VCh   David Simon, CFO
Ian J A Scott, IS   Becky Osterberg, Sls   Robert J Fisher, VP
William L Jackson, VP   Ralph Wilson, VP   Wallace J Nicols, VP
Becky Osterberg, PR

Rev: 2397
Assets: 1655
Emp: 24

Premetalco Inc
2860 Commerce Court W
Toronto, ON M5L1C9 Can
416-366-3954

Manufacturer of basic steel products.
Type: TOR
Ind: Steel   Grp: Basic Industries
T Graham Locke, CEO

Rev: 271
Assets: 170
Emp: 1

Premier Bancorp (Louisiana Bancshares)
451 Florida Street
Baton Rouge, LA 70801
504-389-4206

Commercial bank.
Type: NASDAQ-PRBC
Ind: Banking   Grp: Financial
Charles W McCoy, CEO

Rev: 393
Assets: 4078
Emp: 3

Premier Industrial Corp
4500 Euclid Avenue
Cleveland, OH 44103
216-391-8300

Manufacturer of electronic components.
Type: NYSE-PRE
Ind: Business Service   Grp: Business Service
Morton L Mandel, CEO   G Lee Griffin, Chr   R Neil Williams, CFO
David Pou, IS   L Biff Motley, Mkt   L Biff Motley, PR

Rev: 566
Assets: 263
Emp: 4

Organizations Listed Alphabetically

Organization / Address / Phone	Descriptive Information	Revenue / ($ mil)	Assets / ($ mil)	Emp (thous)
Prescott Ball & Turben Inc 1331 Euclid Avenue Cleveland, OH 44115 216-574-7300	Investment firm; securities trading. Type: Private Ind: Securities Grp: Financial Lawrence G Kirsbaum, CEO	Rev: 275 Assets: 2200 Emp: 1		
President of the United States of America Executive Office Bldg Washington, DC 20503 202-395-3080	Executive branch of the United States Federal Government. Type: Federal Govt Ind: Federal Govt Grp: Govt & Non-Prof George H W Bush, CEO	Rev: 12335 Assets: NM Emp: 1		
Preston Corp 151 Easton Blvd Preston, MD 21655 301-673-7151	Transportation company; trucking. Type: NASDAQ-PTRK Ind: Transport Grp: Business Service W David Gaulden, CEO William B Potter, Chr Arvis T Harris, Pres Thomas C Vogt, Tres Sean Callahan, CFO William Johnson, Mkt Carl E Pounders, Ops Ross Whealton, IR Paul Galey, PR	Rev: 594 Assets: 338 Emp: 8		
Price Co 2657 Ariane Drive San Diego, CA 92117 619-581-4600	Wholesale grocery, hardware, appliances. Type: NASDAQ Ind: Retail/Merch Grp: Retail Sol Price, CEO Robert E Price, Chr Richard M Libenson, Pres Richard Lebenson, VCh Giles H Bateman, CFO Theodore Wallace, VP Jaclyn Horton, VP	Rev: 4162 Assets: 993 Emp: 8		
Price Waterhouse & Co Inc 1251 Avenue of the Americas New York, NY 10020 212-489-8900	Nationwide accounting firm. Type: Private Ind: Accounting Grp: Business Service Joseph E Connor, CEO	Rev: 2250 Assets: NA Emp: 25		
Price Waterhouse Ltd One First Canadian Place Toronto, ON M5X1H7 Can 416-863-1133	National accounting firm. Type: Private Ind: Accounting Grp: Business Service Richard Stackhouse, CEO	Rev: 170 Assets: NM Emp: 2		
Price, T Rowe Associates Inc 100 E Pratt Street Baltimore, MD 21202 301-547-2308	Investment firm; mutual funds. Type: Private Ind: Non-Bank Fin Grp: Financial George J Collins, CEO	Rev: 142 Assets: 105 Emp: 2		
Pride Refining Inc 500 Chestnut Abilene, TX 79602 915-677-2223	Petrouleum products refining & distribution company. Type: Private Ind: Energy Grp: Basic Industries Jimmy Morris, CEO	Rev: 550 Assets: NA Emp: 1		
Primark Corp 8251 Greensboro Drive Suite 700 McLean, VA 22102 703-790-7600	Aviation services & leasing company. Type: NYSE Ind: Utility Grp: Utilities Joseph E Kasputys, CEO	Rev: 108 Assets: 259 Emp: 1		
Primary Industries Corp 666 Fifth Avenue New York, NY 10103 212-581-9200	Operator of steel & metals service center. Type: Private Ind: Equipment Grp: Manufacturing Gavin Parfit, CEO	Rev: 550 Assets: NA Emp: 3		
Prime Computer Inc Prime Park Natick, MA 01760 508-655-8000	Manufacturer of mid range computers. Type: NYSE Ind: Comput/Off Equip Grp: High Tech Anthony L Craig, CEO Richard B Goldman, CFO Dwight Muller, IS Richard Snyder, R&D Corneliius McMullan, VP Donald Newman, IR Joe Gavaghan, PR	Rev: 1595 Assets: 1651 Emp: 12		
Prime Motor Inns Inc 700 Route 46 E Fairfield, NJ 07006 201-882-1010	Nationwide operator of hotels & motors inns. Type: NYSE-PDQ Ind: Food/Lodging Grp: Consumer Service Peter E Simon, CEO	Rev: 410 Assets: 904 Emp: 5		

Organizations Listed Alphabetically

Organization / Address / Phone	Descriptive Information	Revenue / Assets / Emp ($ mil) ($ mil) (thous)		

Primerica Corp
American Lane PO Box 3610
Greenwich, CT 06838
203-552-2000

Diversified financial services; insurance, investments.
Type: NYSE-PA
Ind: Packaging   Grp: Manufacturing
Sanford I Weill, CEO   F Gregory Fitz-Gerald, VCh   Thomas Gaughan, IS
John Hsu, R&D   Richard Daddadario, Sls   Joann Heffernen Heisen, IR
Kenneth N Koprowski, PR

Rev: 1004
Assets: 14435
Emp: 18

Princess House Inc
455 Somerset Avenue
North Dighton, MA 02764
617-823-0713

Manufacturer of consumer products.
Type: Private-Sub   Par: Colgate Palmolive Co
Ind: Personal Care   Grp: Consumer Prd
Richard Brown, CEO

Rev: NA
Assets: NA
Emp: NA

Princeton University
Administrative Bldg
Princeton, NJ 08544
609-452-3000

Major educational institution; university.
Type: University
Ind: University   Grp: Govt & Non-Prof
Harold T Shapiro, CEO

Rev: 245
Assets: 471
Emp: 11

Principle Financial Group Inc
711 High Street
Des Moines, IA 50309
515-247-5111

Life insurance company.
Type: Private
Ind: Insurance   Grp: Insurance
John Taylor, CEO   G David Hurd, Pres   David Drury, VCh
David A Kauf, CFO   Donald Carter, IS   Donald Carter, VP
Robert Delaney, VP   Thomas Gaard, VP   Donald Keown, VP
Stephan Jones, VP   Ronald Keller, VP   Donald Carter, IR
Walter Walsh, PR

Rev: 6577
Assets: 23493
Emp: 10

Printing Holding Co
350 Park Avenue
New York, NY 10022
212-735-8800

Printing company.
Type: Private
Ind: Manufacturing   Grp: Manufacturing
Gerald S Armstrong, CEO

Rev: 1000
Assets: NA
Emp: 10

Procter & Gamble Co
One Procter & Gamble Plaza
Cincinnati, OH 45202
513-562-1100

Manufacturer of household products.
Type: NYSE
Ind: Personal Care   Grp: Consumer Prd
John G Smale, CEO   James W Nethercott, CFO   Gordon F Brunner, R&D
Louis A Pritchett, Sls   Gerald S Gendell, PR

Rev: 19491
Assets: 14820
Emp: 75

Procter & Gamble Inc
4711 Yonge Street
Toronto, ON M5W1C5 Can
416-730-4711

Manufacturer of packaged goods; detergents, personal care.
Type: Private-Sub-For
Ind: Food Processing   Grp: Food Processing
R Kendall, CEO   Edwin L Artzt, Chr   John E Pepper, Pres
George M Gibson, Tres   J Richard Andre, R&D   Louis A Pritchett, Sls
Gary E Booth, VP   Edwin H Eaton Jr, VP   Peter Morris, VP
Geoffrey Place, VP   Thomas A Laco, VP   W Wallace Abbott, VP

Rev: 891
Assets: 719
Emp: 3

Progressive Insurance Co
6000 Parkland Blvd
Mayfield Heights, OH 44124
216-464-8000

Property & casualty insurance company.
Type: NYSE-PGR
Ind: Insurance   Grp: Insurance
Peter B Lewis, CEO   Bruce Marlow, Pres   Edward Wiegner, VCh
Norton Rose, CFO   Gregory Buckley, Sls   William P Cadden, VP
Stephen Leaman, VP   Robert L Moore, VP   Jerry Shroat, VP
Rex Wolf, VP

Rev: 1275
Assets: 2307
Emp: 3

Proudfoot, Alexander Inc
1700 Palm Beach Lakes Blvd
West Palm Beach, FL 33401
407-697-9600

Management consulting company.
Type: Private
Ind: Consulting   Grp: Business Service
Tom Hutton, CEO

Rev: 300
Assets: NA
Emp: 3

Provence of Alberta Treasury Branches
9925 109th Street
Edmonton, AB T5J2N6 Can
403-493-7015

Consumer banking provincial agency.
Type: Prov Govt
Ind: Federal Govt Fin   Grp: Financial
A O Bray, CEO

Rev: 445
Assets: 4692
Emp: 3

Organizations Listed Alphabetically

Organization / Address / Phone	Descriptive Information	Revenue / ($ mil)	Assets / ($ mil)	Emp (thous)
Providence Journal Inc 75 Fountain Street Providence, RI 02902 401-277-7000	Newspaper publishing company. Type: Private Ind: Publishing/Com Grp: Consumer Service Steven Hamblett, CEO	Rev: Assets: Emp:		550 NA 5
Provident Life & Accident Ins Co Fountain Square Chattanooga, TN 37402 615-755-1011	Life & casualty insurance company. Type: NASDAQ-PACC Ind: Insurance Grp: Insurance Winston W Walker, CEO Thomas C Hardy, CFO Patrick J Haverty, IS John K Witherspoon, R&D Michael E Bishop, IR Valerie Hamilton, PR	Rev: Assets: Emp:		2050 7468 10
Provident Mutual Life Ins Co of Phil 1600 Market Street Philadelphia, PA 19103 215-636-5000	Life insurance company. Type: Private-Mutual Ind: Insurance Grp: Insurance L J Rowell, CEO	Rev: Assets: Emp:		879 3371 2
Provident National Assurance Co Fountain Square Chattanooga, TN 37402 615-755-1011	Life insurance company. Type: Private-Sub Ind: Insurance Grp: Insurance Carolyn King, CEO Winston W Walker, Chr Carolyn King, Pres Thomas C Hardy, CFO Patrick J Haverty, IS John K Witherspoon, R&D Michael E Bishop, IR Valerie Hamilton, PR	Rev: Assets: Emp:		500 5239 2
Provigo Incorporated 800 Dorchester Blvd W Montreal, PQ H3B1Y2 Can 514-866-9781	Nationwide retailing company. Type: TOR-PGI Ind: Retail/Food Grp: Retail Pierre Lortie, CEO Henri Roy, Pres Jean-Claude Merizzi, VCh Richard Sutton, Tres Germain P Lecours, CFO Paul Birons, IS Claude Leduc, Mkt	Rev: Assets: Emp:		7175 1363 14
Province of Alberta Legislative Bldg Edmonton, AB T5K2B6 Can 403-427-2711	Provincial government. Type: Prov Govt Ind: State/Prov Govt Grp: Govt & Non-Prof Donald Getty, CEO	Rev: Assets: Emp:		12240 NM 71
Province of British Columbia Parliment Bldgs Victoria, BC V8V1X4 Can 604-387-1337	Provincial government. Type: Prov Govt Ind: State/Prov Govt Grp: Govt & Non-Prof William N VanderZalm, CEO	Rev: Assets: Emp:		11220 NM 59
Province of Manitoba Legislative Bldg Winnipeg, MB R3C0V8 Can 204-945-3744	Provincial government. Type: Prov Govt Ind: State/Prov Govt Grp: Govt & Non-Prof Gary Albert Filmon, CEO	Rev: Assets: Emp:		4080 NM 18
Province of New Brunswick Legislative Bldg Fredericton, NB E3B5H1 Can 506-453-2240	Provincial government. Type: Prov Govt Ind: State/Prov Govt Grp: Govt & Non-Prof Frank McKenna, CEO	Rev: Assets: Emp:		2550 NM 32
Province of Newfoundland Confederation Bldg St Johns, NF A1C5T7 Can 709-737-3612	Provincial government. Type: Prov Govt Ind: State/Prov Govt Grp: Govt & Non-Prof A Brian Peckford, CEO	Rev: Assets: Emp:		2244 NM 22
Province of Nova Scotia Province House Halifax, NS B3J2T3 Can 902-424-2700	Provincial government. Type: Prov Govt Ind: State/Prov Govt Grp: Govt & Non-Prof John M Buchanan, CEO	Rev: Assets: Emp:		2958 NM 21
Province of Ontario Parliment Bldgs Toronto, ON M7A1A1 Can 416-965-3535	Provincial government. Type: Prov Govt Ind: State/Prov Govt Grp: Govt & Non-Prof David Peterson, CEO	Rev: Assets: Emp:		26520 NM 123

Organizations Listed Alphabetically

Organization / Address / Phone	Descriptive Information	Revenue / Assets / Emp ($ mil) ($ mil) (thous)		

Province of Prince Edward Island
Province House
Charlotetown, PE C1A7N8 Can
902-892-3428

Provincial government.
Type: Prov Govt
Ind: State/Prov Govt   Grp: Govt & Non-Prof
Joseph A Ghiz, CEO

Rev: 444
Assets: NM
Emp: 4

Province of Quebec
Hotel du Parliment
Quebec City, PQ G1A1A3 Can
418-643-1430

Provincial government.
Type: Prov Govt
Ind: State/Prov Govt   Grp: Govt & Non-Prof
Robert Bourassa, CEO

Rev: 27540
Assets: NM
Emp: 105

Province of Saskatchewan
Legislative Bldg
Regina, SK S4S0B3 Can
306-565-6291

Provincial government.
Type: Prov Govt
Ind: State/Prov Govt   Grp: Govt & Non-Prof
Grant Devine, CEO

Rev: 4080
Assets: NM
Emp: 23

Prudential Assurance Group
101 Frederick Street
Kitchener, ON N2H6R2 Can
519-888-5700

Life insurance company.
Type: Private-Sub-For
Ind: Insurance   Grp: Insurance
Michael Beck, CEO   Garnett L Keith, Chr   Joseph J Melone, Pres
John P Murray, CFO   Malcolm D MacKinnon, IS   George L Ball, VP
Richard G Merrill, VP   Edward D Zinbarg, VP   Robert E Riley, VP
James W Stevens, VP

Rev: 612
Assets: 2282
Emp: 1

Prudential Assurance Group Ltd Canada
195 Dufferin Avenue
Kitchener, ON N6A1K7 Can
519-433-1231

Property & casualty insurance company.
Type: Private-Sub-For
Ind: Insurance   Grp: Insurance
Richard Hughes, CEO

Rev: 299
Assets: 521
Emp: 1

Prudential Bache Securities Inc
One Seaport Plaza 199 Water Street
New York, NY 10292
212-214-1000

Investment firm; securities trading.
Type: Private
Ind: Securities   Grp: Financial
George L Ball, CEO

Rev: 3500
Assets: 33000
Emp: 16

Prudential Ins Co of America, Canada
200 Consilium Place
Scarborough, ON M1H3E6 Can
416-296-0777

Life insurance company.
Type: Private-Mutual
Ind: Insurance   Grp: Insurance
Ronald D Barbaro, CEO

Rev: 559
Assets: 2310
Emp: 3

Prudential Insurance Co of America
Prudential Plaza
Newark, NJ 07101
201-877-6000

Life insurance company.
Type: Private-Mutual
Ind: Insurance   Grp: Insurance
Robert C Winters, CEO   Malcolm MacKinnon, IS   Joseph Vecchione, PR

Rev: 33724
Assets: 153023
Emp: 75

PS Group Inc
4370 La Jolla Village Drive
San Diego, CA 92122
619-546-5001

Petroleum sales & travel agency company.
Type: NYSE-PSG
Ind: Airline   Grp: Consumer Service
Paul C Barkley, CEO

Rev: 216
Assets: 692
Emp: 1

PSI Public Service Co of Indiana
100 E Main Street
Plainfield, IN 46168
317-839-9611

Electric utility holding company.
Type: NYSE
Ind: Utility   Grp: Utilities
James E Rogers, CEO   Darrell V Menscer, Pres   Jon D Noland, VCh
J Wayne Leonard, CFO   Larry E Thomas, Ops   Joseph W Messick, VP
Duejean C Garrett, VP   Harold L Issacs, VP

Rev: 1043
Assets: 2129
Emp: 4

Public Service Co of Colorado
550 15th Street
Denver, CO 80202
303-571-7511

Electric power utility company.
Type: Private-Sub   Par: Central & South West Corp
Ind: Utility   Grp: Utilities
Delwin D Hock, CEO   Clark B Ewald, VCh   Richard Kelly, Tres
James N Bumpus, CFO   R O Williams, R&D   Patrick McCarter, Ops
James R McCotter, VP

Rev: 1685
Assets: 2984
Emp: 7

Public Service Co of New Hampshire
1000 Elm Street
Manchester, NH 03105
603-669-4000

Electric power utility company.
Type: NYSE-PNH
Ind: Utility   Grp: Utilities
John c Duffett, CEO   George Branscombe, Tres   Charles Bayless, CFO
George S Thomas, R&D   Ralph Johnston, Mkt   Ted C Feigenbaum, Ops
Carl Legacy, VP   James Nevins, VP

Rev: 603
Assets: 2704
Emp: 3

Organization / Address / Phone	Descriptive Information	Revenue / ($ mil)	Assets / ($ mil)	Emp (thous)
Public Service Co of New Mexico Alvarado Square Albuquerque, NM 87158 505-848-2700	Electric power utility company. Type: NYSE Ind: Utility Grp: Utilities Jerry D Geist, CEO James Mulcock, VCh Mitchell Marzec, Tres Max Maerki, CFO Billy D Lackey, VP Joellyn Murphy, VP	Rev: 842	Assets: 2393	Emp: 4
Public Service Co of Oklahoma 212 E Sixth Street Tulsa, OK 74119 918-599-2000	Electric power utility holding company Type: NYSE Ind: Utility Grp: Utilities Martin E Fate, CEO	Rev: 604	Assets: 1211	Emp: 2
Public Service Enterprise Group Inc 80 Park Plaza Newark, NJ 07101 201-430-7000	Electric & gas utility. Type: NYSE-PEG Ind: Utility Grp: Utilities E James Ferland, CEO Francis J Riepl, Tres Everett L Morris, CFO Paul H Way, IS Stephen Mallard, R&D Fredrick R Desanti, Mkt Robert S Smith, VP R Edwin Selover, VP Parker C Peterman, VP Robert W Lockwood, IR Robert Kinkead, PR	Rev: 4395	Assets: 11690	Emp: 15
Public Works Canada Sir Charles Tupper Bldg Ottawa, ON K1A0M2 Can 613-998-7724	Federal government agency. Type: Federal Govt Ind: Federal Govt Grp: Govt & Non-Prof R J Giroux, CEO	Rev: 1190	Assets: NM	Emp: 8
Publix Super Markets Inc 1936 George Jenkins Blvd Lakeland, FL 33802 813-688-1188	Operator of retail food supermarkets. Type: Private Ind: Retail/Food Grp: Retail George W Jenkins, CEO Mark C Hollis, Pres John Turner, CFO Danny Risener, IS R William Schroter, Mkt	Rev: 4200	Assets: 1000	Emp: 22
Puerto Rico Telephone Inc General P O Box 998 San Juan, PR 00936 809-782-8282	Operator of telephone communications utility company. Type: Private Ind: Utility Grp: Utilities Favio Garcia, CEO	Rev: 550	Assets: NA	Emp: 5
Puerto Rico, Territory of United States El Capitolio Avinda Munoz Revera San Juan, PR 00904 809-724-2030	Territory of the United States, government headquarters. Type: US Territory Ind: State/Prov Govt Grp: Govt & Non-Prof Rafael Hernandez Colon, CEO	Rev: 5000	Assets: NM	Emp: 90
Puget Sound BanCorp 1119 Pacific Avenue Tacoma, WA 98402 206-593-3600	Commercial bank. Type: NASDAQ-PSNB Ind: Banking Grp: Financial W W Philip, CEO Roy Henderson, Pres Lazarus Politakis, VCh Jonathan Fine, Tres Don Vandenheuvel, CFO W Ray Highsmith, Mkt Gene Amar, Ops James Maxwell, VP Amos Walter, VP Richard B Odlin, VP	Rev: 395	Assets: 3947	Emp: 3
Puget Sound Power & Light Co Puget Power Bldg 411 108th Avenue NE Bellevue, WA 98009 206-454-6363	Electric power company. Type: NYSE Ind: Utility Grp: Utilities J W Ellis, CEO Richard Sonstelie, Pres Melvyn Ryan, VCh Russel Olson, CFO W J Finnegan, R&D Neil McReynolds, Mkt Robert Myers, Ops Wilbur Watson, VP James Eldredge, VP Eugene Andrews, VP Ronald Bailey, VP	Rev: 783	Assets: 2356	Emp: 2
Pulitzer Publishing Co 900 N Tucker Blvd St Louis, MO 63101 314-622-7000	Newspaper publisher, television & radio broadcasting. Type: OTC Ind: Publishing/Com Grp: Consumer Service Joseph Pulitzer, CEO	Rev: 391	Assets: 227	Emp: 4
Pullman Peabody Co 182 Nassau Street Princeton, NJ 08540 609-683-1770	Manufacturer, pumps, aircraft seating, tempeture systems. Type: Private Ind: Automotive Grp: Manufacturing Richard W Vieser, CEO Thomas M Begel, Chr Andrew M Massimilla, Pres Anthony J Garcia, CFO Anthony J Garcia, PR	Rev: 600	Assets: 500	Emp: 8

Organizations Listed Alphabetically

Organization / Address / Phone	Descriptive Information	Revenue / ($ mil)	Assets / ($ mil)	Emp (thous)
Purdel Cooperative Agro Alimentaire 155 St Jean Baptiste Bic, PQ G0L10 Can 418-736-4363	Agricultural cooperative. Type: Private-Coop Ind: Food Processing Grp: Food Processing N Theberge, CEO	Rev: 255 Assets: 85 Emp: 2		
Purdue University Administrative Bldg West Lafayette, IN 47907 317-749-2108	Major educational institution; university. Type: University Ind: University Grp: Govt & Non-Prof Steven C Beering, CEO	Rev: 332 Assets: 537 Emp: 37		
Puritan Bennett Corp 9401 Indian Creek Parkway Overland Park, KS 66225 913-661-0444	Manufacturer of medical equipment & gases. Type: NASDAQ-PBEN Ind: Health Care Grp: Consumer Service B Dole, CEO	Rev: 250 Assets: 100 Emp: 2		
Putnam Management Co Inc One PO Square Boston, MA 02109 617-292-1000	Investment management company. Type: Private Ind: Non-Bank Fin Grp: Financial Lawrence J Lasser, CEO	Rev: 500 Assets: 22000 Emp: 1		
Putnam Publishing Group Inc 200 Madison Avenue New York, NY 10016 212-576-8900	Book publishers. Type: Private-Sub Par: MCA Inc Ind: Publishing/Com Grp: Consumer Service Phyllis Grann, CEO	Rev: NA Assets: NA Emp: NA		
PWA (Canadian Airlines) Corp 700 2nd Street SW Calgary, AB T2P2W2 CAN 403-294-2000	Nationwide airline. Type: TOR Ind: Airline Grp: Consumer Service R T Eyton, CEO	Rev: 1850 Assets: 1806 Emp: 14		
Q & O Paper Co 80 King Street St Catharines, ON L2R 7B2 Can 416-688-5030	Forest products company. Type: TOR Ind: Paper/Forest Prd Grp: Basic Industries J Houghton, CEO	Rev: 478 Assets: 490 Emp: 3		
QIT Fer et Titane Inc 770 Sherbrooke Ouest Montreal, PQ H3A1G1 Can 514-288-8400	Manufacturer of precious metals. Type: MON Ind: Metals/Mining Grp: Basic Industries G Charette, CEO	Rev: 428 Assets: 621 Emp: 2		
QMS Inc One Magnum Pass Mobile, AL 36618 205-633-4300	Manufacturer of laser printers;design & produce graphic sys. Type: NASDAQ-AQM Ind: Comput/Off Equip Grp: High Tech James Busby, CEO	Rev: 250 Assets: 150 Emp: 1		
Quaker Oats Co 321 N Clark Street Chicago, IL 60654 312-222-7111	Manufacturer of packaged goods; cereals, syrup, pet food. Type: NYSE-OAT Ind: Food Processing Grp: Food Processing Michael J Callahan, CEO William D Smithburg, Chr Frank J Morgan, Pres Ronald Brzezinski, IS David R Nogle, R&D John Boynton, VP John Calhoun, VP Terence Duffy, VP James Tindall, VP Deborah E Kelly, IR C Clarkson Hine, PR	Rev: 5330 Assets: 2975 Emp: 31		
Quaker State Oil Refining Co 255 Elm Street Oil City, PA 16301 814-676-7676	Producer of oil products; lubricants, motor oil. Type: NYSE-KSF Ind: Energy Grp: Basic Industries James D Berry, CEO Quentin E Wood, Chr Jack W Corn, Pres Conrad A Conrad, CFO John R Sedalcko, IS Embert H DeLong, R&D William E Marshall, Sls Earl V Swift, Mkt John Sedlacko, VP Robert Rossiter, VP Benton H Faulkner, PR	Rev: 869 Assets: 740 Emp: 6		
Quanex Corp 1900 West Loop S Suite 1500 Houston, TX 77027 713-961-4600	Industrial machinery manufacturer. Type: NYSE-NX Ind: Manufacturing Grp: Manufacturing Carl E Pfeiffer, CEO Robert C Snyder, VCh Wayne M Rose, CFO James Hill, Mkt Robert Kelly, VP Joseph Peery, VP James Parrish, VP	Rev: 463 Assets: 302 Emp: 2		

Organizations Listed Alphabetically

Organization / Address / Phone	Descriptive Information	Revenue / Assets / Emp ($ mil) ($ mil) (thous)		

Quantum Chemical Corp
99 Park Avenue
New York, NY 10016
212-949-5000

Chemical company; polyethylene, propane gas.
Type: NYSE-CUE
Ind: Chemicals   Grp: Basic Industries
John Hoyt Stookey, CEO

Rev: 2922
Assets: 2908
Emp: 14

Quantum Corp
1804 McCarthy Blvd
Milpitas, CA 95035
408-262-1100

Manufacturer of disk drives.
Type: NASDAQ-QNTM
Ind: Comput/Off Equip   Grp: High Tech
S Berkley, CEO

Rev: 400
Assets: 200
Emp: 1

Quebec, Universite du
2875 Boul Laurier
Sainte Foy, PQ G1V2M3 Can
418-657-3551

Major educational institution; university.
Type: University
Ind: University   Grp: Govt & Non-Prof
Gilles Boulet, CEO

Rev: 327
Assets: NM
Emp: 31

Quebecor Inc
225 E Rue Roy
Montreal, PQ H2W2N6 Can
514-282-9600

Communications & publishing company.
Type: ASE
Ind: Publishing/Com   Grp: Consumer Service
Pierre Peladeau, CEO   Jean Neveu, Pres   Jacques Beauchamp, CFO
Jean Guy Duchaine, R&D   Gerard Desmarais, Ops   Louis St Arnaud, VP
Paul Decoste, VP

Rev: 1093
Assets: 1225
Emp: 11

Questar Corp
180 E First South Street
Salt Lake City, UT 84147
801-534-5000

Exploration, production & distribution of natural gas.
Type: NYSE-STR
Ind: Utility   Grp: Utilities
R D Cash, CEO   Stephen E Parks, Tres   William F Edwards, CFO
N R Potter, IS   Michael Benefield, R&D   Gary G Sackett, VP
Clyde M Heiner, VP   Connie C Holbrook, VP   R LaVaun Cox, VP
R Curtis Burnett, PR

Rev: 486
Assets: 1026
Emp: 2

Quiktrip Corp
901 N Mingo Road
Tulsa, OK 74116
918-836-8551

Operator of retail convenience food stores.
Type: Private
Ind: Retail/Food   Grp: Retail
Terry Carter, CEO

Rev: 550
Assets: NA
Emp: 2

Racetrac Petroleum Corp
2625 Cumberland
Atlanta, GA 30339
404-434-0400

Convenience stores, gasoline retailing.
Type: Private
Ind: Retail/Merch   Grp: Retail
Carl Bolch, CEO

Rev: 500
Assets: NA
Emp: 1

Radio Shack Inc
1600 One Tandy Center
Fort Worth, TX 76102
817-390-3011

Manufacturer & retailer of consumer electronics.
Type: Private-Sub   Par: Tandy Corp
Ind: Retail/Merch   Grp: Retail
Bernard Appel, CEO

Rev: NA
Assets: NA
Emp: NA

Rainier Bancorp Inc
1301 Fifth Avenue
Seattle, WA 98101
206-621-4111

Commercial bank.
Type: Private-Sub   Par: Security Pacific Corp
Ind: Banking   Grp: Financial
John D Mangels, CEO   Jon Christoffersen, Pres   Michael J Coie, CFO
C Thomas Cook, IS   Laura Liswood, Mkt   C Bruce Emry, IR
David J Jepsen, PR

Rev: 850
Assets: 9216
Emp: 6

Raleigh, City
City Hall 222 W Hargett Street
Raleigh, NC 27602
919-890-3050

City government.
Type: City Govt
Ind: Local Govt   Grp: Govt & Non-Prof
Avery Upchurch, CEO

Rev: 250
Assets: NM
Emp: 2

Raleys Inc
500 W Capitol
Broderick, CA 95605
916-444-8150

Grocery stores.
Type: Private
Ind: Retail/Food   Grp: Retail
Thomas P Raley, CEO

Rev: 1000
Assets: NA
Emp: 6

Ralston Purina Co
Checkerboard Square
St Louis, MO 63164
314-982-1000

Manufacturer of packaged foods; pet foods, tuna, bread.
Type: NYSE-RAL
Ind: Food Processing   Grp: Food Processing
William P Stiritz, CEO   Jay Brown, VCh   Ronald D Winney, Tres
James R Elsesser, CFO   Franklin Cornwell, R&D   Elmer D Richars, PR

Rev: 5876
Assets: 4044
Emp: 57

Organizations Listed Alphabetically

Organization / Address / Phone	Descriptive Information	Revenue / ($ mil)	Assets / ($ mil)	Emp (thous)
Ramada Inc 3838 E Van Buren Street Phoenix, AZ 85008 602-273-4000	Nationwide operator of hotels, gambling casinos, restaurants. Type: NYSE-RAM Ind: Food/Lodging Grp: Consumer Service Richard Snell, CEO Wilfried Grau, VCh Robert Haddock, CFO Darrell D Waite, IS Gus Boss, R&D John Davis-Slade, Mkt Tim Maland, VP Tom North, VP Joseph Cole, IR Kathy Hernandez, PR	Rev: Assets: Emp:	477 705 15	
Rand Corp 1700 Main Street Santa Monica, CA 90406 213-393-0411	Non-profit special interest group. Type: Federal Govt Ind: Membership Org Grp: Govt & Non-Prof Donald B Rice, CEO	Rev: Assets: Emp:	500 NM 2	
Randalls Food Markets Inc 16000 Barkers Point Lane Suite 200 Houston, TX 77079 713-497-8191	Grocery stores. Type: Private Ind: Retail/Food Grp: Retail Robert R Onstead, CEO	Rev: Assets: Emp:	1000 NA 10	
Rapid American Corp Trump Tower 725 Fifth Avenue New York, NY 10022 212-621-4500	Operator of retail stores; US headquarters. Type: Private-Sub-For Ind: Retail/Merch Grp: Retail Michellam Riklas, CEO	Rev: Assets: Emp:	2200 1500 42	
Raychem Corp 300 Constitution Drive Menlo Park, CA 94025 415-361-3333	Manufacturer of components for power generating systems. Type: NYSE Ind: Manufacturing Grp: Manufacturing Paul M Cook, CEO Robert M Halperin, Pres Michael Everett, VCh Raymond J Sims, CFO Edward Keible, R&D William Mitchell, Sls William Berry, VP Gerald Delaney, VP Frederick Grattan, VP Thomas Huseby, VP Frederick M Hoar, IR	Rev: Assets: Emp:	1095 1149 9	
Raymond International Inc 2801 Post Oaks Blvd Houston, TX 77056 713-623-1500	Real estate development & management company. Type: Private Ind: Real Estate/Bldg Grp: Business Service William Conway, CEO	Rev: Assets: Emp:	1100 NA 2	
Raytheon Co 141 Spring Street Lexington, MA 02173 617-862-6600	Manufacturer of electronic systems & subsystems. Type: NYSE Ind: Electronics Grp: High Tech Thomas L Phillips, CEO R Gene Shilley, Pres Herbert Deitcher, Tres Sheldon Rutstein, CFO Robert B Almeida, IS Hermann Statz, R&D Philip A Phalon, Mkt Colman Mockler, VP Barbara Hauptfuhrer, VP Walter H Palmer, PR	Rev: Assets: Emp:	8192 4740 76	
Re Max Ltd 7101 Cyntex Drive Mississauga, ON L5N6H5 Can 416-542-2400	Nationwide network of real estate sales offices. Type: Private Ind: Real Estate/Bldg Grp: Business Service Frank Polzler, CEO	Rev: Assets: Emp:	425 NA 7	
Readers Digest Assn Inc Bedford Road Pleasantville, NY 10570 914-769-7000	Publishing company. Type: Private Ind: Publishing/Com Grp: Consumer Service George V Grune, CEO	Rev: Assets: Emp:	1500 NA 6	
Recarey Enterprises Inc 2332 Birkell Avenue Miami, FL 33129 305-854-4000	Operator of hospitals & clinics. Type: Private Ind: Health Care Grp: Consumer Service Alex Campus, CEO	Rev: Assets: Emp:	550 NA 4	
Recognition Equipment Inc 2701 E Grauwyler Road Irving, TX 75061 214-579-6000	Manufacturer of computerized optical scanning equipment. Type: NYSE-REC Ind: Comput/Off Equip Grp: High Tech William G Moore, CEO	Rev: Assets: Emp:	275 200 3	
Red Apple Companies Inc 265 W 87th Street New York, NY 10024 212-580-6800	Retail supermarkets. Type: Private Ind: Retail/Food Grp: Retail John A Catsimatidis, CEO	Rev: Assets: Emp:	750 NA 7	

Organizations Listed Alphabetically

Organization / Address / Phone	Descriptive Information	Revenue / ($ mil)	Assets / ($ mil)	Emp (thous)
Red Owl Holdings Inc 215 E Excelsior Hopkins, MN 55343 612-932-2132	Food wholesaling Type: Private Ind: Retail/Food Grp: Retail C Patrick Schulke, CEO	Rev: Assets: Emp:	750 NA 3	
Redman Industries Inc 2550 Walnut Hill Lane Redman Plaza E Dallas, TX 75229 214-353-3600	Manufacturer of aluminum doors & windows. Type: NYSE-RE Ind: Building Mat Grp: Basic Industries James Redman, CEO	Rev: Assets: Emp:	357 142 3	
Redpath Industries Ltd 2100 Royal Bank Plaza Toronto, ON M5J2J2 Can 416-865-0400	Mining company. Type: TOR-RIN Ind: Food Processing Grp: Food Processing L R Wilsom, CEO W Darcy McKeough, Pres Neil M Shaw, VCh Paul Murray, CFO John Swan, VP	Rev: Assets: Emp:	600 416 4	
Reebok International Ltd 150 Royall Street Canton, MA 02021 617-580-1600	Manufacturer of recreational footwear. Type: NYSE-RBK Ind: Apparel/Textiles Grp: Consumer Prd Paul B Fireman, CEO C Joseph Labonte, Pres Paul Duncan, CFO Thomas Sheridan, IS Robert E Meers, Sls Frank J O'Connell, VP John H Duerden, VP Angel Martinez, VP Rihcard L Bryant, VP Frank J O'Connell, IR Sharon Cohen, PR	Rev: Assets: Emp:	1791 1063 13	
Reed Inc 207 Queens Way W Toronto, ON M5J1A7 Can 416-862-5000	Manufacturer of wood products, pulp timber. Type: TOR Ind: Paper/Forest Prd Grp: Basic Industries D Wilkins, CEO	Rev: Assets: Emp:	350 352 2	
Reeves Brothers Inc 1271 Avenue of the Americas 3rd Floor New York, NY 10020 212-315-2323	Manufacturer of apparel products. Type: Private Ind: Apparel/Textiles Grp: Consumer Prd James Hart, CEO	Rev: Assets: Emp:	550 NA 5	
Regis Corp 5000 Normandale Road Minneapolis, MN 55436 612-929-6776	Operator of personal care shops & beauty parlors. Type: Private Ind: Business Service Grp: Business Service Myron Kunin, CEO	Rev: Assets: Emp:	550 NA 5	
Reichhold Chemicals Inc 525 N Broadway White Plains, NY 10603 914-682-5700	Manufacturer of synthetics, specialty chemicals. Type: NASDAQ-RCI Ind: Chemicals Grp: Basic Industries Thomas Mitchell, CEO	Rev: Assets: Emp:	801 500 6	
Reitman's Canada Ltd 250 O Sauve Montreal, PQ H3L1Z2 Can 514-384-1140	Manufacturer of apparel products. Type: TOR Ind: Apparel/Textiles Grp: Consumer Prd Jack Reitman, CEO	Rev: Assets: Emp:	300 149 5	
Reliance Electric Corp PO Box 99502 Cleveland, OH 44122 216-266-7000	Manufacturer, electric motors, controls, power transmission. Type: Private Ind: Electronics Grp: High Tech John C Morley, CEO K C Moore Jr, CFO James Conroy, IS Peter Tsivitse, R&D W Michael Corkran, PR	Rev: Assets: Emp:	1500 NA 15	
Reliance Group Holdings Inc 55 E 52nd Street New York, NY 10055 212-909-1100	Diversified insurance, investment & consulting company. Type: OTC Ind: Non-Bank Fin Grp: Financial S P Steinberg, CEO Robert M Steinberg, Pres Lowell C Freiberg, CFO Joan Arena, IS Henry Lambert, R&D Brian Martin, IR Colleen Jenks, PR	Rev: Assets: Emp:	3400 6079 10	
Renault America Corp 4000 Chownunt Center Southfield, MI 48075 313-358-8800	Manufacturer & importer of motor vehicles; US headquarters. Type: Private-Sub-For Ind: Automotive Grp: Manufacturing Bernard Vernoux, CEO	Rev: Assets: Emp:	550 NA 1	

Organizations Listed Alphabetically

Organization / Address / Phone	Descriptive Information	Revenue ($ mil)	Assets ($ mil)	Emp (thous)
Rent-a-Center Inc 9920 E Harry Street Wichita, KS 67207 316-689-4100	Rent & wholesale household appliances. Type: Private-Sub-For Ind: Business Service Grp: Business Service Walter E Gates, CEO	Rev: 250 Assets: 200 Emp: 2		
Repap Enterprises Corp 1150 Peel Street Suite 3200 Montreal, PQ H3B3V2 Can 514-879-1316	Integrated forest products company. Type: TOR-RPP Ind: Paper/Forest Prd Grp: Basic Industries George S Petty, CEO James N Bowersock, Pres Joseph Kass, VCh Ronald H Summer, CFO Joseph Simone, Sls J Patrick Maley, Mkt Harry R Papushka, Ops Georges Farah, VP Terry McBride, VP	Rev: 795 Assets: 1925 Emp: 5		
Republic Bank of New York Inc 452 Fifth Avenue New York, NY 10018 212-525-5000	Commercial bank. Type: NYSE Ind: Banking Grp: Financial Walter H Weiner, CEO Jeff Keil, Pres Cyril Dwek, VCh Thomas Robards, CFO William Segal, Mkt Ernest Ginsberg, VP Dow Schlein, VP John Kaberle, VP Edmond Safra, VP Sharon Connor, IR Linda Rosenfeld, PR	Rev: 2106 Assets: 24519 Emp: 9		
Republic Health Services Inc 14951 Dallas Parkway Dallas, TX 75240 214-851-3100	Own & operate hospitals. Type: Private Ind: Health Care Grp: Consumer Service Bryan P Marsal, CEO	Rev: 500 Assets: NA Emp: 5		
Republican National Committee 310 First Street SE Eisenhower Center Washington, DC 20003 202-863-8500	Political party, national organization. Type: Federal Govt Ind: Membership Org Grp: Govt & Non-Prof Lee Atwater, CEO	Rev: 1000 Assets: NM Emp: 5		
Research Cottrell Inc Route 22 W PO Box 1500 Somerville, NJ 08876 201-685-4000	Nationwide consulting company. Type: Private Ind: Consulting Grp: Business Service Benjamin Rawls, CEO	Rev: 500 Assets: NA Emp: 2		
Resorts International Inc 915 NE 125th Street North Miami, FL 33161 305-891-2500	Hotels & casinos, owners & operators. Type: ASE Ind: Leisure Time Grp: Consumer Service Merv Griffin, CEO	Rev: 456 Assets: 1035 Emp: 9		
Restaurant Enterprises Group Inc 2701 Alton Avenue Irvine, CA 92714 714-863-6300	Operator of restaurants. Type: Private Ind: Food/Lodging Grp: Consumer Service Norman Habermann, CEO	Rev: 1250 Assets: NA Emp: 30		
Retail, Wholesale & Dept Store Union 30 E 29th Street New York, NY 10016 212-684-5300	National labor union. Type: Membership Org Ind: Membership Org Grp: Govt & Non-Prof Lenore Miller, CEO	Rev: 250 Assets: NM Emp: 200		
Reuters Inc 1700 Broadway 5th Floor New York, NY 10019 212-603-3300	Electronic publishing & distribution company; US hdqtrs. Type: Private-Sub-For Ind: Comput/Off Equip Grp: High Tech Andre Villeneuve, CEO	Rev: 825 Assets: NA Emp: 8		
Revco Drug Stores Inc 1925 Enterprise Drive Twinsburg, OH 44087 216-425-9811	Operator of retail drugstores. Type: Private Ind: Retail/Merch Grp: Retail Boake A Sells, CEO William B Holmes, CFO William P Seltzer, IS Carl A Bellini, R&D James Adamson, Mkt Kathleen Obert, PR	Rev: 2500 Assets: 1000 Emp: 25		
Revenue Canada, Customs & Excise Connaught Bldg Mackenzie Avenue Ottawa, ON K1A0L5 Can 613-957-0275	Federal government agency. Type: Federal Govt Ind: Federal Govt Grp: Govt & Non-Prof R Hubbard, CEO	Rev: 2040 Assets: NM Emp: 10		

Organizations Listed Alphabetically

Organization / Address / Phone	Descriptive Information	Revenue / Assets / Emp ($ mil) ($ mil) (thous)		

Revenue Canada, Taxation
875 Heron Road
Ottawa, ON K1A0L8 Can
613-957-0275

Federal government agency.
Type: Federal Govt
Ind: Federal Govt   Grp: Govt & Non-Prof
Pierre Gravelle, CEO

Rev: 2550
Assets: NM
Emp: 17

Revere Copper & Brass Inc
High Ridge Park PO Box 10327
Stamford, CT 06904
203-358-5300

Manufacturer of copper, brass & aluminum products.
Type: OTC
Ind: Manufacturing   Grp: Manufacturing
William Erbey, CEO

Rev: 600
Assets: 400
Emp: 4

Revlon Group Inc
625 Madison Avenue
New York, NY 10022
212-572-5000

Manufacturer of personal care products; cosmetics.
Type: Private
Ind: Personal Care   Grp: Consumer Prd
Ronald Perelman, CEO   Bruce Slovin, Pres   Fred L Tepperman, CFO
Robin Cohn, PR

Rev: 1815
Assets: 1000
Emp: 16

Rexene Corportation
126 E 56th Street
New York, NY 10022
212-644-8200

Manufacturer of thermo plastic & petrochemical products.
Type: NYSE-RXN
Ind: Chemicals   Grp: Basic Industries
A J Smith, CEO

Rev: 553
Assets: 511
Emp: 5

Reynolds & Reynolds Corp
800 Germantown Street
Dayton, OH 45407
513-443-2000

Manufacturer of manual systems & business forms.
Type: NASDAQ-REYNA
Ind: Business Service   Grp: Business Service
Terry D Carder, CEO   David R Holmes, Pres   Robert C Nevins, VCh
Dale Medford, CFO   Joseph Bausman, IS   Adam Lutynski, VP
Michael Gapinski, VP   Jack Martin, IR   Paul Guthrie, PR

Rev: 600
Assets: 399
Emp: 5

Reynolds Metals Co
6601 Broad Street Road
Richmond, VA 23261
804-281-2000

Integrated producer of aluminum products.
Type: NYSE-RLM
Ind: Metals/Mining   Grp: Basic Industries
William O Bourke, CEO   Richard G Holder, Pres   Yale Brandt, VCh
R Bern Crowl, CFO   James T Matsey, IS   Rodney Hanneman, R&D
John Lowrie, Mkt   Rodney Hanneman, Ops   John McGill, VP
John Noonan, VP   Richard Peters, VP   Randolph Reynolds, VP
Joseph F Awad, PR

Rev: 5619
Assets: 5032
Emp: 29

Reynolds, R J Tobacco Co
401 N Main Street
Winston-Salem, NC 27102
919-741-5000

Consumer tobacco products company.
Type: Private-Sub   Par: RJR Nabisco Inc
Ind: Tobacco   Grp: Food Processing
Edward Horrigan, CEO

Rev: NA
Assets: NA
Emp: NA

Rhode Island Hospital Trust Natl Bank
One Hospital Trust Plaza
Providence, RI 02903
401-278-8000

Commercial bank.
Type: Private-Sub   Par: Bank of Boston Corp
Ind: Banking   Grp: Financial
A M Anderson, CEO

Rev: 300
Assets: 3061
Emp: 2

Rhode Island, State of
State House
Providence, RI 02903
401-277-2000

State government.
Type: State Govt
Ind: State/Prov Govt   Grp: Govt & Non-Prof
Edward D DiPrete, CEO

Rev: 2569
Assets: NM
Emp: 25

Riceland Foods Inc
2120 Park Avenue
Stuttgart, AR 72160
501-673-5500

Producer & distributor of packaged foods.
Type: Private
Ind: Food Processing   Grp: Food Processing
Richard Bell, CEO   Charles A Gunnell, CFO   Ben Shelton, IS
Don McCaskill, R&D   Carl Brothers, Mkt   Bill Reed, PR

Rev: 825
Assets: 250
Emp: 3

Rich Products Corp
1150 Niagara Street
Buffalo, NY 14213
716-878-8000

Frozen foods, pro sports, broadcasting company.
Type: Private
Ind: Food Processing   Grp: Food Processing
Robert E Rich Jr, CEO

Rev: 750
Assets: NA
Emp: 5

Richardson Vicks Inc
10 Westprot Road
Wilton, CT 06897
203-834-5000

Manufacturer personal care products.
Type: Private-Sub   Par: Procter & Gamble Co
Ind: Personal Care   Grp: Consumer Prd
William Bergman, CEO

Rev: NA
Assets: NA
Emp: NA

Organizations Listed Alphabetically

Organization / Address / Phone	Descriptive Information	Revenue / ($ mil)	Assets / ($ mil)	Emp (thous)
Richardson, James & Sons Ltd One Lombard Plaza Winnipeg, MB R3B0Y1 Can 204-934-5811	Securities investment firm. Type: Private Ind: Securities Grp: Financial G Richardson, CEO	Rev: Assets: Emp:	1068 1165 3	
Richfood Inc 2000 Richfood Road Mechanicsville, VA 23111 804-746-6000	Operator of retail supermarkets. Type: Private Ind: Retail/Food Grp: Retail W C Tallaferro, CEO	Rev: Assets: Emp:	1100 NA 2	
Richmond, City of City Hall Richmond, VA 23219 804-780-7977	City government. Type: City Govt Ind: Local Govt Grp: Govt & Non-Prof Geline Williams, CEO	Rev: Assets: Emp:	250 NM 2	
Riggs National Corp 1503 Pennsylvania Avenue NW Washington, DC 20005 202-835-6000	Commercial bank. Type: NASDAQ-RIGS Ind: Banking Grp: Financial Timothy A Lex, CEO Joe L Allbritton, Chr Thomas Wren, Pres Jackson Gilbert, VCh James E O'Neill, CFO Walter Howell, IS David Palombi, Mkt Frank Langhammer, VP Timothy Coughlin, VP David Brown, VP Donald Doyle, VP Henry Dudley, VP David Palombi, PR	Rev: Assets: Emp:	562 7002 2	
Righa Corp 2 Davol Square Providence, RI 02903 401-421-4410	Insurance company. Type: Private Ind: Insurance Grp: Insurance Bruce Bradley, CEO	Rev: Assets: Emp:	550 3000 1	
Riklis Corp 725 5th Avenue New York, NY 10022 212-735-9500	Operator of retail stores. Type: Private Ind: Retail/Merch Grp: Retail Meshulam Riklis, CEO	Rev: Assets: Emp:	3000 NA 50	
Rinker Materials Corp 1501 Belvedere Road West Palm Beach, FL 33406 407-833-5555	Building material products company. Type: Private Ind: Building Mat Grp: Basic Industries David Clark, CEO	Rev: Assets: Emp:	275 NA 3	
Rio Algom Ltd 120 Adelaide Street W Toronto, ON M5H1W5 Can 416-367-4000	Mining company. Type: ASE Ind: Metals/Mining Grp: Basic Industries George Albino, CEO	Rev: Assets: Emp:	1682 1785 8	
Riser Foods Inc 5300 Richmond Road Bedford Heights, OH 44146 216-292-7000	Operator of retail supermarkets. Type: ASE-RSR Ind: Retail/Food Grp: Retail M L Berstein, CEO	Rev: Assets: Emp:	1057 228 10	
Rite Aid Corp Trindle Road & Railroad Avenue Harrisburg, PA 17105 717-761-2633	Operator of retail drug, auto parts & book stores. Type: NYSE-RAD Ind: Retail/Merch Grp: Retail Alex Grass, CEO Martin Grass, Pres Robert F Brown, Tres Frank Bergonzi, CFO Joseph Groelly, IS Gerald Cardinale, Mkt Suzanne Mead, IR Jennifer Dewalt, PR	Rev: Assets: Emp:	2486 1224 28	
Riverside, City of City Hall 3900 Main Street Riverside, CA 92522 714-782-5551	City government. Type: City Govt Ind: Local Govt Grp: Govt & Non-Prof Albert C Brown, CEO	Rev: Assets: Emp:	250 NM 2	
RJR Nabisco Inc 300 Galleria Parkway Atlanta, GA 30339 404-770-6000	Worldwide consumer products company. Type: NYSE Ind: Tobacco Grp: Food Processing F Ross Johnson, CEO Edward J Robinson, CFO Dr Robert Carbonell, R&D William J Liss, PR	Rev: Assets: Emp:	15766 16861 120	

Organizations Listed Alphabetically

Organization / Address / Phone	Descriptive Information	Revenue / ($ mil)	Assets / ($ mil)	Emp (thous)
RKO General Inc 1440 Broadway New York, NY 10018 212-764-7000	Operator of television & radio broadcasting. Type: Private-Sub Par: GenCorp Inc Ind: Publishing/Com Grp: Consumer Service Pat Servodidio, CEO	Rev: Assets: Emp:	NA NA NA	
RLC Corp One Rollins Plaza PO Box 1791 Wilmington, DE 19899 302-429-2700	Leasing company; truck fleets. Type: NYSE-RLC Ind: Transport Grp: Business Service John W Rollins, CEO	Rev: Assets: Emp:	450 400 3	
Roadway Services Inc 1077 Gorge Blvd Akron, OH 44309 216-384-8184	Nationwide truck transport company. Type: NASDAQ-ROAD Ind: Transport Grp: Business Service William W Blodgett, CEO Joseph M Clapp, Chr Michael Newton, Tres Douglas Wilson, CFO A C Snelson, IS William Klug, Ops A C Snelson, VP Timothy Lynch, VP Douglas Wilson, IR Barbara Hasenstab, PR	Rev: Assets: Emp:	2185 1193 27	
Robertshaw Controls Co 1701 Byrd Avenue Richmond, VA 23261 804-281-0700	Manufacturer of air conditioning & refrigeration units. Type: OTC Ind: Manufacturing Grp: Manufacturing E Barry Stephens, CEO	Rev: Assets: Emp:	500 500 7	
Robertson, H H Co 2 Gateway Center Pittsburgh, PA 15222 412-281-3200	International construction company. Type: NYSE-RHH Ind: Manufacturing Grp: Manufacturing Jack Hatcher, CEO William Panazzi, Tres John W Viehman, CFO Robert G Lindner, R&D Frank Roland, Mkt James Douglas, VP John W Viehman, PR	Rev: Assets: Emp:	414 296 5	
Robin Hood Multifoods Inc 243 Consumers Road Willowdale, ON M2J4W8 Can 416-496-1515	Manufacturer of food products; flour. Type: TOR Ind: Food Processing Grp: Food Processing Logan Brown, CEO	Rev: Assets: Emp:	366 129 2	
Robins, A H Co Inc 1407 Cummings Drive PO Box 26609 Richmond, VA 23220 804-257-2000	Manufacturer of pharmaceuticals. Type: NYSE Ind: Drugs Grp: Consumer Service E Claiborne Robins, CEO Robert G Watts, VCh G E R Stiles, CFO Thomas R Ransom, IS C D Lunsford, R&D Charles E Hart, Mkt John Gordon, VP John D Taylor, PR	Rev: Assets: Emp:	934 1075 8	
Robinson Humphrey Co Inc 3333 Peachtree Road NE Atlanta, GA 30326 404-266-6000	Investment firm; securities trading. Type: Private Ind: Securities Grp: Financial Justus C Martin, CEO	Rev: Assets: Emp:	220 2200 1	
Rochester & Pittsburgh Coal Corp 655 Church Street Indiana, PA 15701 412-349-5800	Coal mining company. Type: Private Ind: Metals/Mining Grp: Basic Industries William Kegel, CEO	Rev: Assets: Emp:	500 250 5	
Rochester Community Savings Bank 40 Franklin Street Roschester, NY 14604 716-262-5800	Thrift institution. Type: NASDAQ-RCSB Ind: Savings & Loan Grp: Financial Leonard Simon, CEO Joe Hammele, Pres Edward Pettinella, CFO Larry Mulligan, IS Robert Eberle, R&D Charis Copin, Mkt Robert Eberle, PR	Rev: Assets: Emp:	350 4000 2	
Rochester Gas & Electric Corp 89 E Avenue Rochester, NY 14649 716-546-2700	Electric & gas utility. Type: NYSE-RGS Ind: Utility Grp: Utilities Harry G Saddock, CEO Roger Kober, Pres John Oberlies, VCh Robert Henderson, CFO John Arthur, IS David Laniak, R&D Daniel Baier, VP John Kuebel, VP Alan Lohrmann, VP David Heligman, VP	Rev: Assets: Emp:	774 1823 3	

Organizations Listed Alphabetically

Organization / Address / Phone	Descriptive Information	Revenue / ($ mil)	Assets / ($ mil)	Emp (thous)
Rochester Telephone Corp 180 S Clinton Avenue Rochester, NY 14646 716-777-1000	Telephone utility. Type: NYSE-RTC Ind: Telecom Grp: High Tech Alan C Hasselwander, CEO Ronald Bittner, VCh Frederick Pestorius, CFO John K Purcell, R&D Richard Sayers, Mkt Louis Massaro, Ops Barbara Osterman, VP Josephine Trubek, VP	Rev: Assets: Emp:	479 885 3	
Rochester, City of City Hall 30 Church Street Rochester, NY 14614 716-428-7045	City government. Type: City Govt Ind: Local Govt Grp: Govt & Non-Prof Thomas P Ryan, CEO	Rev: Assets: Emp:	413 NM 7	
Rock Island Refining Co 5000 W 86th Street Indianapolis, IN 46268 317-872-3200	Petroleum refining. Type: Private Ind: Energy Grp: Basic Industries William E Huff, CEO	Rev: Assets: Emp:	800 NA 2	
Rock Tenn Corp 504 Thrasher Street Norcross, GA 30071 404-448-2193	Packaging company, manufacuturer of cartons & boxes. Type: Private Ind: Packaging Grp: Manufacturing A Worley Brown, CEO	Rev: Assets: Emp:	500 NA 5	
Rockefeller Group Inc 1230 Avenue of the Americas New York, NY 10020 212-698-8676	Real estate, telecomm, entertainment company. Type: Private Ind: Real Estate/Bldg Grp: Business Service Richard A Voell, CEO	Rev: Assets: Emp:	1000 NA 5	
Rockwell International Corp 600 Grant Street Pittsburgh, PA 15219 412-565-2000	Manufacturer of aerospace, defense & industrial equipment. Type: NYSE-ROK Ind: Conglomerate Grp: Manufacturing Donald R Beall, CEO George Jeffs, VCh Lee Cramer, Tres Robert A dePalma, CFO Sue Araki, IS Robert L Cattoi, R&D Kent Black, Ops Sam Iacobellis, VP Richard R Mau, IR M Jeffrey Charney, PR	Rev: Assets: Emp:	11046 4925 112	
Rockwell International of Canada Ltd 150 Bartley Drive Toronto, ON M4A1C7 Can 416-757-1101	Manufacturer of aerospace equipment & systems. Type: Private-Sub-For Ind: Aerospace Grp: High Tech R Kingston, CEO	Rev: Assets: Emp:	437 296 2	
Rogers Communications Inc Commercial Union Tower Toronto, ON M5K1J5 Can 416-864-2373	Operator of cable television systems. Type: TOR-RCLA Ind: Publishing/Com Grp: Consumer Service Ronald D Besse, CEO	Rev: Assets: Emp:	304 946 4	
Rohm & Hass Co Independence Mall W Philadelphia, PA 19105 215-592-3000	Chemical & plastics manufacturing company. Type: NYSE Ind: Chemicals Grp: Basic Industries J Lawrence Wilson, CEO John P Mulroney, Pres John Doyle, VCh Fred W Shaffer, CFO William Groetzinger, IS Robert E Naylor, R&D Robert Naylor, VP Donald Garaventi, VP John McKeogh, IR Laura Hadden, PR	Rev: Assets: Emp:	2535 2242 13	
Rohr Industries Inc Foot of H Street Chula Vista, CA 92012 619-691-4111	Component manufacturer for aerospace & defense industries. Type: NYSE-RHR Ind: Aerospace Grp: High Tech H W Todd, CEO Ronald Miller, Tres David J Ruggles, CFO Graydon A Wetzler, IS Peter Colston, R&D Donald Purdy, Mkt William Billingslea, VP David Ruggles, VP Robert H Goldsmith, VP John Sandford, VP Richard Madsen, VP Gerald Broening, PR	Rev: Assets: Emp:	907 883 11	
Rolland Inc 2000 Avenue McGill Montreal, PQ H3A3H3 Can 514-289-1779	Forest products company; paper, building materials. Type: TOR Ind: Paper/Forest Prd Grp: Basic Industries Lucien G Rolland, CEO	Rev: Assets: Emp:	378 142 2	

Organizations Listed Alphabetically

Organization / Address / Phone	Descriptive Information	Revenue / ($ mil)	Assets / ($ mil)	Emp (thous)
Rollins Environmental Services Inc One Rollins Plaza Wilmington, DE 19803 302-429-2700	Hazardous waste management company. Type: NYSE-REN Ind: Business Service Grp: Business Service John W Rollins, CEO	Rev: Assets: Emp:		206 214 2
Rollins Inc 2170 Piedmont Road NE Atlanta, GA 30324 404-888-2000	Provider of home services; lawn care, pest control,security. Type: NYSE-ROL Ind: Business Service Grp: Business Service O Wayne Rollins, CEO	Rev: Assets: Emp:		380 147 5
Rolls Royce Industries Canada Inc 100 Alexis Nihon Blvd Ville St Laurent, PQ H4M2P5 Can 514-747-7742	Manufacturer of aerospace equipment; jet engines. Type: Private-Sub-For Ind: Aerospace Grp: High Tech T G Parker, CEO	Rev: Assets: Emp:		213 149 2
Roper Corp 931 Broad Street Augusta, GA 30901 404-724-0822	Kitchen appliance manufacturer. Type: NYSE-ROP Ind: Manufacturing Grp: Manufacturing Harold G Bernthal, CEO Robert E Cook, Chr Dennis D Shrewsbury, CFO Ron Burns, IS Dan Nielsen, R&D Jerry D Cope, Mkt Robert L Wood, PR	Rev: Assets: Emp:		703 251 6
Rorer Group Inc 500 Virginia Drive Fort Washington, PA 19034 215-628-6000	Worldwide manufacturer of pharmaceutical products. Type: TOR-NYSE Ind: Drugs Grp: Consumer Service Robert E Cawthorn, CEO Richard Storm, Pres Ralph Thurman, VCh Daniel J Paracka, CFO Paul Krautheim, IS James R Tretter, R&D Susan E Atkins, PR	Rev: Assets: Emp:		1042 1388 8
Rose's Stores Inc 218 Garnett Street Henderson, NC 27536 919-492-8111	Regional operator of discount stores. Type: NASDAQ-RSTO Ind: Retail/Merch Grp: Retail Lucius H Harvin, CEO Jack E Bush, Pres David C Rose, CFO Len Priode, IS John McElroy, Mkt Donald G Hunt, Ops	Rev: Assets: Emp:		1439 436 17
Roseburg Forest Products Inc Highway 99 S Dillard, OR 97432 503-679-3311	Forest products company. Type: Private Ind: Paper/Forest Prd Grp: Basic Industries John Stephens, CEO	Rev: Assets: Emp:		600 NA 6
Rosenthal Companies Inc 3400 Columbia Parkway Arlington, VA 22204 703-920-8700	Auto dealerships. Type: Private Ind: Automotive Grp: Manufacturing Robert M Rosenthal, CEO	Rev: Assets: Emp:		500 NA 1
Ross Stores Inc 8333 Central Avenue Newark, CA 94560 415-790-4400	Operator of retail merchandise stores. Type: OTC Ind: Retail/Merch Grp: Retail Norman Ferber, CEO	Rev: Assets: Emp:		626 NA 5
Rothmans Inc 1500 Don Mills Road Don Mills, ON M3B3L1 Can 416-449-5525	Tobacco products company; cigarettes. Type: TOR-ROC Ind: Tobacco Grp: Food Processing P J Fennell, CEO	Rev: Assets: Emp:		352 338 3
Rothschild, L F, Unterberg, Towbin Inc 222 Broadway New York, NY 10038 212-238-2000	Investment firm; securities trading. Type: Private Ind: Securities Grp: Financial Gary Lieberman, CEO	Rev: Assets: Emp:		825 7700 2
Rouge Steel Co American Road Dearborn, MI 48122 313-322-3000	Basic steel manufacturing company. Type: Private-Sub Par: Ford Motor Co Ind: Steel Grp: Basic Industries John Betti, CEO	Rev: Assets: Emp:		NA NA NA

Organizations Listed Alphabetically

Organization / Address / Phone	Descriptive Information	Revenue / ($ mil)	Assets / ($ mil)	Emp (thous)
Roundy's Inc 23000 Roundy Drive Pewaukee, WI 53072 414-547-7999	Operator of retail grocery stores. Type: OTC Ind: Retail/Food Grp: Retail John Dickson, CEO Terry Kapron, Pres Robert D Ranus, CFO Gary Weckwerth, IS Carol Ziebell, PR	Rev: 2000 Assets: 500 Emp: 5		
Rouse Co Rouse Company Bldg Columbia, MD 21044 301-992-6000	Developer of commercial real estate. Type: OTC Ind: Manufacturing Grp: Manufacturing Mathias J Devito, CEO Michael D Spear, Pres R W Harwood, VCh Jeffrey Donahue, Tres Anthony W Deering, CFO Marlys Easstt, Mkt Ronald L Bergman, VP Phillip T Duffy, VP	Rev: 461 Assets: 2080 Emp: 5		
Rover Group Inc 4390 Parlimanent Place Laham, MD 20706 301-731-9040	Manufacturer of utility motor vehicles; US headquarters. Type: Private-Sub-For Ind: Automotive Grp: Manufacturing Charles Hughes, CEO	Rev: 550 Assets: NA Emp: 1		
Rowan Corp 5051 Westheimer Houston, TX 77056 713-621-7800	Oil & gas exploration company. Type: Private Ind: Energy Grp: Basic Industries C R Palmer, CEO	Rev: 250 Assets: 150 Emp: 2		
Royal Bank of Canada Ltd 1 Place Ville Marie 35th Floor Montreal, PQ H3C3A9 Can 514-874-2110	Commercial bank. Type: TOR Ind: Banking Grp: Financial Allan R Taylor, CEO John Cleghorne, Pres A H Michel, VCh M J Regan, CFO B V Kelly, VP M C S Baptista, VP R Bodt, VP D L Robertson, VP	Rev: 9006 Assets: 93546 Emp: 46		
Royal Canadian Mint Ltd 355 River Road Ottawa, ON K1S0G8 Can 613-992-2348	Federal government agency Type: Federal Govt Ind: Federal Govt Grp: Govt & Non-Prof Maurice Lafontaine, CEO	Rev: 878 Assets: 108 Emp: 1		
Royal Insurance Co 10 Wellington Street E Toronto, ON M5E1L5 Can 416-366-7511	Property & casualty insurance company. Type: Private-Sub-For Ind: Insurance Grp: Insurance Roy Elms, CEO	Rev: 638 Assets: 1150 Emp: 2		
Royal Insurance Co of America 10 S Riverside Plaza Chicago, IL 60606 312-522-2000	Property & casualty insurance company. Type: OTC Ind: Insurance Grp: Insurance George W Ansbro, CEO	Rev: 1200 Assets: 1600 Emp: 6		
Royal LePage Real Estate Ltd 33 Yonge Street Toronto, ON M5E1G4 Can 416-862-0611	Nationwide network of real estate sales offices. Type: TOR-RLG Ind: Real Estate/Bldg Grp: Business Service Gordon C Gray, CEO George J Cormack, Pres Gino Romanese, VCh W Peter Rollason, CFO M Wayne Mondville, Sls Oswald Jurock, Ops Fred W Sheldon, VP Glenn Quarrington, VP P Douglas Scanlan, VP George Soteroff, VP	Rev: 554 Assets: 405 Emp: 8		
RPM Corp 2628 Pearl Road Medina, OH 44258 216-225-3192	Manufacturer of chemical products. Type: NASDAQ-RPOW Ind: Chemicals Grp: Basic Industries Thomas Sullivan, CEO	Rev: 350 Assets: 300 Emp: 2		
Rubbermaid Inc 1147 Adron Road Wooster, OH 44691 216-264-6464	Manufacturer of rubber & plastic home products. Type: NYSE Ind: Manufacturing Grp: Manufacturing Stanley C Gault, CEO Walter W Williams, Pres Wolfgang Schmidt, VCh Joseph G Meehan, CFO Joseph W Balnave, IS Kenneth Morris, R&D Richard S Thomas, Mkt Carl Bowers, VP Richard D Gates, IR Patricia Sacha, PR	Rev: 1194 Assets: 782 Emp: 8		

Organizations Listed Alphabetically

Organization / Address / Phone	Descriptive Information	Revenue / ($ mil)	Assets / ($ mil)	Emp (thous)
Ruddick Corp 2000 First Union Plaza Charlotte, NC 28282 704-372-5404	Operator of retail grocery stores. Type: NASDAQ-RDK Ind: Retail/Food Grp: Retail R Dickson, CEO	Rev: Assets: Emp:		1400 700 11
Ruffin Corp 1522 S Florence Wichita, KS 67209 316-942-7940	Operator of retail merchandise stores. Type: Private Ind: Retail/Merch Grp: Retail Phil G Ruffin, CEO	Rev: Assets: Emp:		750 NA 1
Rugby Darby Group Inc 100 Banks Avenue Rockville Center, NY 11570 516-536-3000	Manufacturer healthcare & pharmecueticals. Type: Private Ind: Drugs Grp: Consumer Service Michael Ashkin, CEO	Rev: Assets: Emp:		400 NA 2
Russ Togs Inc 1411 Broadway New York, NY 10018 212-642-8500	Manufacturer of apparel products. Type: NYSE-RTS Ind: Apparel/Textiles Grp: Consumer Prd Eli L Rousso, CEO	Rev: Assets: Emp:		260 150 3
Russell Corp Lee Street PO Box 272 Alexander City, AL 35010 205-234-4251	Manufacturer of apparel products. Type: NYSE-RML Ind: Apparel/Textiles Grp: Consumer Prd Eugene C Gwaltney, CEO Dwight L Carlisle Jr, Chr James D Nabors, CFO James D Peoples, IS Fletcher D Adamson, R&D Marvin Seals III, Mkt William T Dixon Jr, IR Nancy Goldsmith, PR	Rev: Assets: Emp:		531 561 13
Russell, Frank Co 909 A Street Tacoma, WA 98402 206-572-9500	Investment management consulting company. Type: Private Ind: Consulting Grp: Business Service George Russell, CEO	Rev: Assets: Emp:		165 NA 1
Rutgers University Administrative Bldg New Brunswick, NJ 08903 201-932-1766	Major educational institution; university. Type: University Ind: University Grp: Govt & Non-Prof Walter K Gordon, CEO	Rev: Assets: Emp:		351 605 42
Ryan Homes Inc 100 Ryan Court Pittsburgh, PA 15205 412-276-8000	Builder of residential homes. Type: Private-Sub Par: NVR Limited Partnership Inc Ind: Real Estate/Bldg Grp: Business Service Dwight Schar, CEO	Rev: Assets: Emp:		750 NA 1
Ryan's Family Steak Houses Inc 405 Lancaster Avenue Greer, SC 29651 803-879-1000	Operator of restaurants. Type: NASDAQ-RYAN Ind: Food/Lodging Grp: Consumer Service Alvin A McCall, CEO	Rev: Assets: Emp:		234 142 5
Ryder System Inc 3600 NW 82nd Avenue Miami, FL 33166 305-593-3726	Leasing company; trucks fleets, individual rentals. Type: NYSE-E Ind: Business Service Grp: Business Service M Anthony Burns, CEO David R Parker, Pres Charles F Wilson, Tres Edwin A Huston, CFO Anthony G Tegnelia, IS Russell Pfaff, R&D Jordan J Bingham, Mkt Ronald H Dunbar, VP Wendell Beard, VP Joshua High, VP	Rev: Assets: Emp:		5030 6039 45
Rykoff Sexton Inc 761 Terminal Street Los Angeles, CA 90021 213-622-4131	Manufacturer of food products. Type: NYSE-RYK Ind: Retail/Food Grp: Retail Roger W Coleman, CEO Keith McCann, Tres Victor B Chavez, CFO Thomas O Brant, IS Neil Sell, VP Richard Martin, VP Lewis Chertkow, IR	Rev: Assets: Emp:		1143 326 5

Organizations Listed Alphabetically

Organization / Address / Phone	Descriptive Information	Revenue / ($ mil)	Assets / ($ mil)	Emp (thous)
Ryland Group Inc 10221 Wincopin Circle Columbia, MD 21044 301-730-7222	Home construction company. Type: NYSE-RYL Ind: Real Estate/Bldg Grp: Business Service Charles E Peck, CEO James F McEneaney, VCh Thurman W Bretz, CFO Frederick Condit, IS George L Tresnak, R&D Thurman Bretz, Mkt Robert Paul, VP Phillip Creek, VP Nancy L Smith, IR Catherine Barham, PR	Rev: Assets: Emp:	881 458 3	
Rymer Foods Inc 300 W Washington Blvd Chicago, IL 60606 312-419-0060	Food processing company; frozen foods. Type: NYSE-RYR Ind: Food Processing Grp: Food Processing Barry Rymer, CEO	Rev: Assets: Emp:	350 250 3	
SAAB Scandia America Inc Saab Drive Orange, CT 06477 203-795-5671	Manufacturer of motor vehicles; US headquarters. Type: Private-Sub-For Ind: Electronics Grp: High Tech Robert J Sinclair, CEO	Rev: Assets: Emp:	1100 NA 2	
Saatchi, Saatchi Co 405 Lexington Avenue New York, NY 10017 212-661-0800	International advertising & consulting company. Type: Private Ind: Business Service Grp: Business Service Edward L Wax, CEO	Rev: Assets: Emp:	1500 NA 2	
Sacramento, City of City Hall Sacramento, CA 95814 916-449-5407	City government. Type: City Govt Ind: Local Govt Grp: Govt & Non-Prof Anne Rudin, CEO	Rev: Assets: Emp:	250 NM 3	
Safecard Services Inc 6400 NW 6th Way Fort Lauderdale, FL 33309 305-491-2111	Marketing & mail order service company. Type: NASDAQ-SFCD Ind: Business Service Grp: Business Service Peter Halmos, CEO	Rev: Assets: Emp:	125 222 2	
SAFECO Corp SAFECO Plaza Seattle, WA 98185 206-545-5000	Insurance company. Type: NYSE Ind: Insurance Grp: Insurance Bruce Maines, CEO Roland M Trafton, Pres James Cannon, VCh Boh A Vickey, CFO Dennis Carlson, IS Robert Swegle, Mkt Lynn Huff, VP Karl Papenfus, VP Wayne Brown, VP Gordon Hamilton, IR Lynn Bonneau, PR	Rev: Assets: Emp:	3018 7732 9	
Safeguard Scientific Corp 630 Park Avenue King of Prussia, PA 19406 215-265-4000	Manufacturer of communications & transmission equipment. Type: NYSE-SFE Ind: Telecom Grp: High Tech Warrem Musser, CEO	Rev: Assets: Emp:	284 250 1	
Safety Kleen Corp 777 Big Timber Road Elgin, IL 60120 312-697-8460	Manufacturer of products for hazardous waste removal. Type: NYSE-SK Ind: Business Service Grp: Business Service Russell A Gwillim, CEO Donald W Brinckman, Chr Laurence M Rudnick, Tres Robert W Willmschen, CFO Wallace K Louder, IS Joseph Knott, R&D David Dattilo, Sls Michael H Carney, Mkt Scott Fore, VP Kenneth Gordon, VP James Isanhart, VP Dale Vrannik, VP Joseph Hamlet, VP	Rev: Assets: Emp:	417 399 4	
Safeway Stores Inc Fourth & Jackson Streets Oakland, CA 94660 415-891-3000	Retail food supermarkets. Type: Private Ind: Retail/Food Grp: Retail Peter A Magowan, CEO James A Rowland, Pres Harry D Sunderland, CFO R W Davis, IS Donald J Smith, Mkt Robert E Bradford, PR	Rev: Assets: Emp:	13612 4372 100	
Safeway Texas Corp 4301 Windfern Houston, TX 77041 713-460-5000	Operator of retail grocery markets. Type: Private Ind: Retail/Food Grp: Retail Dean Gantt, CEO	Rev: Assets: Emp:	750 NA 3	

Organizations Listed Alphabetically

Organization / Address / Phone	Descriptive Information	Revenue ($ mil)	Assets ($ mil)	Emp (thous)
Salant Corp (Manhattan Inds) 1155 Avenue of the Americas New York, NY 10036 212-221-7500	Clothing manufacturer, supplier of department stores. Type: NYSE-SLT Ind: Apparel/Textiles Grp: Consumer Prd Ray W Williams, CEO	Rev: 370	Assets: 184	Emp: 4
Salem Carpet Mills Corp NCNB Plaza Winston-Salem, NC 27101 919-727-1200	Manufacturer of carpeting. Type: NASDAQ-SLCR Ind: Tire/Rubber Grp: Basic Industries Douglas Foster, CEO	Rev: 300	Assets: 250	Emp: 3
Salomon Inc 1221 Avenue of the Americas New York, NY 10020 212-764-3700	Worldwide investment banking firm. Type: NYSE-SB Ind: Securities Grp: Financial John H Gutfreund, CEO Thomas Strauss, VCh Gedale Horowitz, VP James Massey, VP Walter Baker, VP Richard DiDonna, VP Gerald Nagy, VP Robert Salomon, PR	Rev: 6146	Assets: 85256	Emp: 7
Salt Lake City, City of City Hall 324 S State Street Salt Lake City, UT 84111 801-535-7704	City government. Type: City Govt Ind: Local Govt Grp: Govt & Non-Prof James W Davis, CEO	Rev: 250	Assets: NM	Emp: 2
Salt River Project Inc 1521 Project Drive Phoenix, AZ 85251 602-236-5900	Electric power utility company. Type: Private Ind: Utility Grp: Utilities John Lassen, CEO	Rev: 1100	Assets: NA	Emp: 5
Sammons Enterprises Inc 403 S Akard Dallas, TX 75202 214-670-9790	Insurance, cable TV, manufacturer of industrial equipment. Type: Private Ind: Telecom Grp: High Tech Robert W Korba, CEO	Rev: 1500	Assets: NA	Emp: 5
Samsung Electronics USA Inc 1 Excecutive Drive Fort Lee, NJ 07024 201-592-7900	Manufacturer of consumer electronic equipment; US hdqtrs. Type: Private-Sub-For Ind: Electronics Grp: High Tech O B Chae, CEO	Rev: 1100	Assets: NA	Emp: 1
San Antonio Savings Assn Inc 601 NW Loop 410 San Antonio, TX 78296 512-340-7272	Thrift institution. Type: Private Ind: Savings & Loan Grp: Financial W W McAllister, CEO	Rev: 300	Assets: 3000	Emp: 1
San Antonio, City of City Hall San Antonio, TX 78285 512-299-7060	City government. Type: City Govt Ind: Local Govt Grp: Govt & Non-Prof Henry Cisneros, CEO	Rev: 1202	Assets: NM	Emp: 12
San Bernadino County Government 385 N Arrowhead San Bernadino, CA 92415 714-387-2020	County government. Type: County Govt Ind: Local Govt Grp: Govt & Non-Prof John Joyner, CEO	Rev: 1650	Assets: NM	Emp: 10
San Diego County Government 1600 Pacific Highway San Diego, CA 92101 619-531-5700	County government. Type: County Govt Ind: Local Govt Grp: Govt & Non-Prof Leon L Williams, CEO	Rev: 2550	Assets: NM	Emp: 15
San Diego Gas & Electric Co 101 Ash Street San Diego, CA 92110 619-696-2000	Electric power & natural gas utility company. Type: NYSE-SDO Ind: Utility Grp: Utilities Thomas A Page, CEO Jack Thomas, Pres Stephen Baum, VCh R Lee Haney, CFO James Holcombe, R&D Donald Felsinger, Mkt Gary Cotton, Ops Margot Kyd, VP Richard Manning, VP George Weida, VP Frank Ault, VP Delroy Richardson, VP	Rev: 2076	Assets: 3533	Emp: 4

Organizations Listed Alphabetically

Organization / Address / Phone	Descriptive Information	Revenue / ($ mil)	Assets / ($ mil)	Emp (thous)
San Diego State University Administrative Bldg San Diego, CA 92182 714-265-5200	Major educational institution; university. Type: University Ind: University Grp: Govt & Non-Prof Thomas B Day, CEO	Rev: Assets: Emp:		171 145 39
San Diego, City of City Hall 202 C Street San Diego, CA 92101 619-236-6330	City government. Type: City Govt Ind: Local Govt Grp: Govt & Non-Prof Maureen O'Conner, CEO	Rev: Assets: Emp:		766 NM 8
San Francisco State University 1600 Holloway Avenue San Francisco, CA 94132 415-469-2141	Major educational institution; university. Type: University Ind: University Grp: Govt & Non-Prof Thomas Spencer, CEO	Rev: Assets: Emp:		117 106 28
San Francisco, City of City Hall San Francisco, CA 94102 415-554-3456	City government. Type: City Govt Ind: Local Govt Grp: Govt & Non-Prof Art Agnos, CEO	Rev: Assets: Emp:		2079 NM 25
San Jacinto Savings Assn Inc 6800 West Loop S Houston, TX 77235 713-661-7000	Thrift institution. Type: Private Ind: Savings & Loan Grp: Financial Dennis R Lane, CEO	Rev: Assets: Emp:		436 4594 2
San Jose State University Administrative Bldg San Jose, CA 95192 408-277-2000	Major educational institution; university. Type: University Ind: University Grp: Govt & Non-Prof Gail Fullerton, CEO	Rev: Assets: Emp:		134 145 28
San Jose, City of City Hall 801 N First Street San Jose, CA 95110 408-277-4237	City government. Type: City Govt Ind: Local Govt Grp: Govt & Non-Prof Thomas McEnery, CEO	Rev: Assets: Emp:		518 NM 4
San Juan Basin Royalty Trust Inc PO Box 2604 Fort Worth, TX 76113 817-338-8607	Gas production company. Type: NYSE-SJT Ind: Non-Bank Fin Grp: Financial Lee Ann Anderson, CEO	Rev: Assets: Emp:		34 5 1
Sanders Associates Inc Daniel Webster Highway South Nashua, NH 03061 603-885-4321	Manufacturer of electronic systems for defense & commercial. Type: Private-Sub Par: Lockheed Corp Ind: Electronics Grp: High Tech John Krieck, CEO	Rev: Assets: Emp:		1000 NA 10
Sandoz USA Inc 608 Fifth Avenue New York, NY 10020 212-307-1122	Manufacturer of pharmaceutical products; US headquarters. Type: Private-Sub-For Ind: Drugs Grp: Consumer Service Daniel C Wagniere, CEO	Rev: Assets: Emp:		1650 NA 13
Santa Ana, City of City Hall Civic Center Plaza Santa Ana, CA 92702 714-647-6910	City government. Type: City Govt Ind: Local Govt Grp: Govt & Non-Prof Daniel Young, CEO	Rev: Assets: Emp:		250 NM 3
Santa Barbara Savings Assn Inc 3908 State Street Santa Barbara, CA 93102 805-682-5000	Thrift institution. Type: Private Ind: Savings & Loan Grp: Financial Philip R Brinkerhoff, CEO	Rev: Assets: Emp:		450 4500 2
Santa Clara County Government 70 Hedding Street San Jose, CA 95110 408-299-2323	County government. Type: County Govt Ind: Local Govt Grp: Govt & Non-Prof Zoe Loferen, CEO	Rev: Assets: Emp:		1825 NM 11

Organization / Address / Phone	Descriptive Information	Revenue / ($ mil)	Assets / ($ mil)	Emp (thous)
Santa Fe Energy Corp 1616 S Voss Road Houston, TX 77057 713-783-2401	Natural resource & energy production company. Type: Private-Sub Par: Santa Fe Southern Pacific Corp Ind: Utility Grp: Utilities James Payne, CEO	Rev: Assets: Emp:	NA NA NA	
Santa Fe Pacific Minerals Corp 6209 Uptown NE Albuquerque, NM 87125 505-881-3050	Producer of minerals; mining, metals refining. Type: Private-Sub Par: Santa Fe Southern Pacific Corp Ind: Metals/Mining Grp: Basic Industries Richard Zitting, CEO	Rev: Assets: Emp:	NA NA NA	
Santa Fe Pacific Pipelines Inc 888 S Figureroa Los Angeles, CA 90017 213-614-1095	Oil & natural gas pipeline transportation company. Type: Private-Sub Par: Santa Fe Southern Pacific Corp Ind: Transport Grp: Business Service John DesBarres, CEO	Rev: Assets: Emp:	NA NA NA	
Santa Fe Southern Pacific Corp 224 S Michigan Avenue Chicago, IL 60604 312-786-6000	Railroad, pipeline, & real estate company. Type: NYSE-SFX Ind: Railroad Grp: Business Service Robert D Krebs, CEO W John Swartz, VCh Orval M Adam, CFO Jerome Kever, Mkt Daniel Westerbeck, VP Elaine Conley Pierce, VP Jerome F Donohoe, VP Dennie Springer, VP Robert E Gehrt, PR	Rev: Assets: Emp:	3144 6824 26	
Sanwa Bank of California 444 Market Street San Francisco, CA 94111 415-765-9500	Commercial bank. Type: Private-Sub-For Ind: Banking Grp: Financial M Yoda, CEO	Rev: Assets: Emp:	800 7000 4	
Sanyo Manufacturing Corp 3333 Sanyo Road Forest City, AR 72335 501-633-5030	Manufacturer & importer of consumer electronics; US hdqtrs. Type: Private-Sub-For Ind: Electronics Grp: High Tech T Sujiwara, CEO	Rev: Assets: Emp:	1100 NA 4	
Sara Lee Corp Three First National Plaza Chicago, IL 60602 312-726-2600	Manufacturer of food products, pastry and cakes. Type: NYSE-SLE Ind: Food Processing Grp: Food Processing John H Bryan, CEO John H Bryan Jr, Chr Michael E Murphy, CFO Vincent Swoyer, IS Robert Lauer, PR	Rev: Assets: Emp:	11206 5663 105	
Sara Lee Corp of Canada Commerce Court Toronto, ON M5L1E7 Can 416-860-0048	Manufacturer of food products; pastry, food foods. Type: Private-Sub-For Ind: Food Processing Grp: Food Processing John Cardwell, CEO	Rev: Assets: Emp:	255 213 3	
Sargent & Lundy Inc 55 E Monroe Street Chicago, IL 60603 312-269-2000	Architectural engineering & consulting company. Type: Private Ind: Consulting Grp: Business Service William Chittenden, CEO	Rev: Assets: Emp:	550 NA 5	
Sarofim, Fayez Investment Mgt Co 2 Houston Center Houston, TX 77010 713-654-4484	Investment firm. Type: Private Ind: Non-Bank Fin Grp: Financial Fayez Sarofim, CEO	Rev: Assets: Emp:	300 11000 1	
Saskatchewan Power Corp 2025 Victoria Avenue Regina, SK S4P0S1 Can 306-566-2121	Electric power utility. Type: Govt Corp Ind: Utility Grp: Utilities George D Hill, CEO George D Hill, Chr Fred Bates, VCh Harvey Jim, CFO Bob Lawrence, Ops Lawrie Portigal, VP	Rev: Assets: Emp:	774 2733 3	
Saskatchewan Telecommunications Ltd 2121 Saskatchewan Drive Regina, SK S4P3Y2 Can 306-347-2200	Telephone utility company. Type: Govt Corp Ind: Telecom Grp: High Tech James A Coombs, CEO Roger E Bason, CFO B William Lambert, R&D David R Carlin, Ops Christopher J Elmer, VP John Meldrum, VP George Spencer, VP William Bruce, VP	Rev: Assets: Emp:	436 896 5	

Organizations Listed Alphabetically

Organization / Address / Phone	Descriptive Information	Revenue / Assets / Emp ($ mil) ($ mil) (thous)		

Saskatchewan Wheat Pool Ltd
2625 Victoria Avenue
Regina, SK S4T7T9 Can
306-569-4411

Agricultural cooperative; wheat.
Type: Govt Corp
Ind: Food Processing   Grp: Food Processing
J Milt Fair, CEO   C Ron Kasha, CFO   Harold A White, Ops
Alvin J Gallinger, VP   Don Loewen, VP   Dona Allewell, VP
Jim MacDonald, VP

Rev: 1508
Assets: 680
Emp: 4

Saskatchewan, University of
Administrative Bldg
Saskatoon, SK S7N0W0 Can
306-244-4343

Major educational institution; university.
Type: University
Ind: University   Grp: Govt & Non-Prof
L F Kristjanson, CEO

Rev: 187
Assets: NM
Emp: 18

Saturn Corp
1400 Stephenson Highway
Troy, MI 48007
313-524-5721

Manufacturer & distributor of automobiles.
Type: Private-Sub   Par: General Motors Corp
Ind: Automotive   Grp: Manufacturing
Richard LeFauve, CEO

Rev: NA
Assets: NA
Emp: NA

Savannah Electric & Power Inc
600 E Bay Street
Savannah, GA 31401
912-238-2251

Electric power utility company
Type: Private-Sub   Par: Southern Co
Ind: Utility   Grp: Utilities
A Gignilliat, CEO

Rev: NA
Assets: NA
Emp: NA

Savannah Foods & Industries Inc
PO Box 339
Savannah, GA 31402
912-234-1261

Sugar production company.
Type: NASDAQ-SVAN
Ind: Food Processing   Grp: Food Processing
William W Sprague, CEO   William R Steinhauer, CFO   O Blanco, IS
James M Taylor, R&D   Charles R Donnelly, Sls   Edward H Hill, Mkt
George Fawcett, Ops   Benjamin Oxnard, VP   Odilo Blanco, IR
Edward H Hill, PR

Rev: 917
Assets: 395
Emp: 2

Save Mart Supermarkets Inc
1800 Standford
Modesto, CA 93350
209-577-1600

Operator of retail supermarkets.
Type: Private
Ind: Retail/Food   Grp: Retail
Robert Piccinini, CEO

Rev: 500
Assets: NA
Emp: 3

Savin Corp
9 W Broad Street
Stamford, CT 06904
203-967-5000

Manufacturer of office copy machines.
Type: NYSE-SVB
Ind: Comput/Off Equip   Grp: High Tech
David G Sadler, CEO

Rev: 361
Assets: 300
Emp: 2

SCANA (So Carolina Elec & Gas) Corp
1426 Main Street
Columbia, SC 29201
803-748-3000

Electric & gas utility company.
Type: NYSE-SCG
Ind: Utility   Grp: Utilities
John A Warren, CEO   L Gressette, Pres   W Timmerman, CFO
R Cohen, R&D   C McFadden, Sls   Barbara Blair, VP
Harriett Gardner, VP   E Roberts, VP   E Frick, VP

Rev: 1083
Assets: 2887
Emp: 4

SCECORP Southern California Edison Co
2244 Walnut Grove Avenue
Rosemead, CA 91770
818-302-1297

Public utility holding company; electric power.
Type: NYSE-SCE
Ind: Utility   Grp: Utilities
Howard P Allen, CEO   David Fogarty, VCh   Michael Noel, Tres
John E Bryson, CFO   Glenn J Bjorklund, R&D   Jennifer Moran, VP
John Bury, VP   Michael Peevy, VP   David Barry, VP
Lewis M Phelps, IR   Thomas Micheletti, PR

Rev: 6253
Assets: 14866
Emp: 17

Schapiro, M A & Co
One Chase Manhattan Plaza
New York, NY 10005
212-980-5353

Investment firm; securities trading.
Type: Private
Ind: Securities   Grp: Financial
Ashter Schapiro, CEO

Rev: 275
Assets: 2200
Emp: 1

Scherer, R P Corp
2075 W Big Beaver Road
Troy, MI 480077
313-649-0900

Manufacurer of gelatin capsules & seals, dental supplies.
Type: NASDAQ-SCHC
Ind: Health Care   Grp: Consumer Service
Wilbur Mack, CEO

Rev: 350
Assets: 300
Emp: 5

Organization / Address / Phone	Descriptive Information	Revenue / ($ mil)	Assets / ($ mil)	Emp (thous)
Schering Corp Galloping Hill Road Kenilworth, NJ 07033 201-822-7450	Manufacturer of consumer products. Type: Private-Sub Par: Schering Plough Corp Ind: Personal Care Grp: Consumer Prd Richard Jogan, CEO	Rev: Assets: Emp:	NA NA NA	
Schering Plough Corp One Giralda Farms Madison, NJ 07940 201-822-7000	Manufacturer of pharmaceutical & consumer products. Type: NYSE Ind: Drugs Grp: Consumer Service Robert P Luciano, CEO Richard J Kogan, Pres Harold R Hiser Jr, CFO James E Harwood, IS Alexander Lane, R&D Linn Weiss, IR Allan S Kushen, PR	Rev: Assets: Emp:	2969 3426 22	
Schlott, Richard Realty Inc 1550 Route 23 N Wayne, NJ 07470 201-633-5000	Real estate development & management company. Type: Private Ind: Real Estate/Bldg Grp: Business Service Richard Schlott, CEO	Rev: Assets: Emp:	3300 NA 4	
Schlumberger Ltd 277 Park Avenue New York, NY 10172 212-350-9400	Oilfield services & measurement systems. Type: NYSE-SBL Ind: Oil Service Grp: Business Service Euan Baird, CEO Roland Genin, VCh Arthur Lindenauer, CFO Michel Gouillard, IS Rene Mitieus, R&D David Browning, VP Jimmy Callson, VP John Ingram, VP Andre' Misk, VP	Rev: Assets: Emp:	4925 5600 48	
Schneider Corp 321 Courtland Avenue Kitchener, ON N2G3X8 Can 519-885-8100	Diversified manufacturer of parts; automotive, industrial. Type: TOR Ind: Manufacturing Grp: Manufacturing F Schneider, CEO	Rev: Assets: Emp:	581 170 4	
Schneider Inc 1370 Washington Pike Bridgeville, PA 15017 412-257-6000	Construction & commercial development company. Type: Private Ind: Real Estate/Bldg Grp: Business Service Lex Tsadgaris, CEO	Rev: Assets: Emp:	550 NA 11	
Schneider National Inc 2777 Southridge Road Green Bay, WI 54304 414-497-2201	Trucking company. Type: Private Ind: Transport Grp: Business Service Donald J Schneider, CEO	Rev: Assets: Emp:	500 NA 5	
Schnuck Markets Inc 12921 Enterprise Bridgeton, MO 63044 314-344-9600	Grocery stores. Type: Private Ind: Retail/Food Grp: Retail Donald O Schnuck, CEO	Rev: Assets: Emp:	1000 NA 10	
Schottenstein Stores Inc 1800 Moler Road Columbus, OH 43207 614-221-9200	Department stores & furniture. Type: Private Ind: Retail/Merch Grp: Retail Jerome Schottenstein, CEO	Rev: Assets: Emp:	500 NA 5	
Schreiber Foods Inc 425 Pine Street Green Bay, WI 54307 414-437-7601	Grocery stores. Type: Private Ind: Food Processing Grp: Food Processing Robert G Bush, CEO	Rev: Assets: Emp:	1000 NA 5	
Schroder, IBJ Bank & Trust Co One State Street New York, NY 10004 212-858-2000	Commercial bank. Type: Private-Sub-For Ind: Banking Grp: Financial Peter Handy, CEO	Rev: Assets: Emp:	350 2500 2	
Schulman, A Inc 3550 W Market Street Akron, OH 44313 216-666-3751	Manufacturer of plastics. Type: NASDAQ-SHLM Ind: Chemicals Grp: Basic Industries William Zekan, CEO Paul C Barkley, Chr George M Shortley, Pres Lawrence A Guske, CFO	Rev: Assets: Emp:	598 240 2	

Organizations Listed Alphabetically

Organization / Address / Phone	Descriptive Information	Revenue / ($ mil)	Assets / ($ mil)	Emp (thous)
Schulman, A Inc 3550 W Market Street Akron, OH 44313 216-666-3751	Manufacturer of plastics. Type: NASDAQ-SHLM Ind: Chemicals Grp: Basic Industries William Zekan, CEO Paul C Barkley, Chr George M Shortley, Pres Lawrence A Guske, CFO	Rev: Assets: Emp:	598 240 2	
Schwab, Charles & Co 101 Montgomery Street The Schwab Bldg San Francisco, CA 94104 415-627-7000	National securities brokerage firm. Type: NYSE-SCH Ind: Securities Grp: Financial Charles R Schwab, CEO Lawrence J Stupski, Pres David Pottruck, VCh A John Gambs, CFO Mark B Armann, IS James Wiggett, VP Hugo Quackenbush, VP Barbara Wolfe, VP	Rev: Assets: Emp:	770 4235 5	
Schwans Sale Enterprises Inc 115 W College Marshall, MN 56258 507-532-3274	Manufacturer of frozen food. Type: Private Ind: Food Processing Grp: Food Processing Marvin Schwan, CEO	Rev: Assets: Emp:	600 NA 6	
Schwegmann Giant Super Markets Inc PO Box 26099 New Orleans, LA 70186 504-947-9921	Grocery stores. Type: Private Ind: Retail/Food Grp: Retail John F Schwegmann, CEO	Rev: Assets: Emp:	500 NA 5	
SCI Systems Inc 5000 Technology Drive Huntsville, AL 35805 205-882-4800	Computer products. Type: NASDAQ-SCIS Ind: Comput/Off Equip Grp: High Tech Olin B King, CEO A Eugene Sapp Jr, Pres Ronald Borelli, VCh James R Daniel, CFO Richard Holloway, R&D Donald Andres, VP Robert Behlman, VP James Chiavetta, VP James R Daniel, PR	Rev: Assets: Emp:	774 485 9	
Science Applications Intl Inc 1200 Prospect Street La Jolla, CA 92037 619-454-3811	System integration products. Type: Private Ind: Consulting Grp: Business Service J R Beyster, CEO	Rev: Assets: Emp:	750 NA 8	
Scientific Atlanta Inc One Technology Parkway PO Box 105600 Atlanta, GA 30348 404-441-4000	Manufacturer of electronic telecommunications equipment. Type: NYSE-SFA Ind: Telecom Grp: High Tech Sidney Topol, CEO William E Johnson, Chr John H Levergood, Pres Raymond M Hartnett, CFO Sezer M Soylemez, IS Allen H Ecker, R&D Laurence Bradner, VP Robert F Murphy, PR	Rev: Assets: Emp:	509 316 4	
SCOA Industries Inc 15 Dan Road Canton, MA 02021 617-821-1000	Operator of retail department stores. Type: NYSE-HDS Ind: Retail/Merch Grp: Retail Stephen A Goldberger, CEO	Rev: Assets: Emp:	1671 899 16	
ScotiaMcLeod Ltd Commercial Union Tower Toronto, ON M5K1M2 Can 416-863-7411	Investment company; brokerage. Type: Private Ind: Securities Grp: Financial Austin Taylor, CEO	Rev: Assets: Emp:	213 170 2	
Scott Paper Co Scott Plaza Philadelphia, PA 19113 215-522-5000	World's leading manufacturer of sanitary paper products. Type: NYSE-SPP Ind: Paper/Forest Prd Grp: Basic Industries Philip E Lippincott, CEO Robert E McAvoy, VCh Ashok N Bakhru, CFO Darwin A John, IS Drexel D Jones, R&D Lee B Griffith, Mkt J Lawrence Shane, VP Norman W Begun, PR	Rev: Assets: Emp:	4726 5156 27	
Scott's Hospitality Inc 89 Chestnut Street Toronto, ON M5G1R1 Can 416-977-6001	Hotel, food service & truck transport company. Type: TOR Ind: Food/Lodging Grp: Consumer Service George R Gardiner, CEO	Rev: Assets: Emp:	906 728 24	
Scotty's Inc Recker Highway Winter Haven, FL 33882 813-299-1111	Operator of retail home improvement stores. Type: NYSE-SHB Ind: Retail/Food Grp: Retail P S Linder, CEO	Rev: Assets: Emp:	551 315 6	

Organizations Listed Alphabetically

Organization / Address / Phone	Descriptive Information	Revenue / ($ mil)	Assets / ($ mil)	Emp (thous)
Scoular Corp 9110 W Dodge Road Omaha, NE 68114 402-390-3030	Grain storage & trading company. Type: Private Ind: Food Processing Grp: Food Processing Marshall E Faith, CEO	Rev: Assets: Emp:	1500 NA 1	
Scripps Howard Inc 1100 Central Trust Tower Cincinnati, OH 45202 513-977-3000	Communications, radio & television Type: NASDAQ-SCRP Ind: Publishing/Com Grp: Consumer Service Jack Howard, CEO	Rev: Assets: Emp:	1000 546 10	
Scripps, E W Corp 1409 Foulk Road Wilmington, DE 19803 302-478-4141	Diversified media company; newspapers, TV & radio stations. Type: NASDAQ-EWSCA Ind: Publishing/Com Grp: Consumer Service Charles E Scripps, CEO Lawrence A Lesser, Chr E John Wolfzorn, Tres Daniel J Castellini, CFO Gilles R Champagne, R&D William Burleigh, Sls Robert J O'Connell, Mkt Michael Callaghan, VP Frank H Shepherd, VP	Rev: Assets: Emp:	1215 1556 8	
Scudder Stevens & Clark 160 Federal Street Boston, MA 02110 617-439-4640	Investment firm. Type: Private Ind: Non-Bank Fin Grp: Financial George Johnson, CEO	Rev: Assets: Emp:	850 33000 3	
Sea Land Corp 10 Parsonage Road Edison, NJ 08837 201-632-2000	Containerized freight transportation company. Type: OTC Ind: Transport Grp: Business Service Robert Hintz, CEO	Rev: Assets: Emp:	2000 NA 10	
Sea Ray Corp 2600 Sea Ray Blvd Knoxville, TN 37914 615-522-4181	Manufacturer of pleasure boats. Type: Private-Sub Par: Brunswick Corp Ind: Leisure Time Grp: Consumer Service John Hedburg, CEO	Rev: Assets: Emp:	NA NA NA	
Seaboard Corp 200 Boylston Street Boston, MA 02167 617-332-8492	Agricultural products & services company. Type: ASE-SEB Ind: Food Processing Grp: Food Processing H H Bresky, CEO	Rev: Assets: Emp:	448 400 2	
Seaboard Lumber Sales Co 1066 W Hastings Vancouver, BC V6E3W9 Can 604-684-3171	Operator of retail building materials stores. Type: TOR Ind: Retail/Merch Grp: Retail T Buell, CEO	Rev: Assets: Emp:	428 88 1	
Seagate Technology Inc 920 Disc Drive Scotts Valley, CA 95066 408-438-6550	Manufacturer, computer disk drives. Type: OTC-SGAT Ind: Comput/Off Equip Grp: High Tech Alan F Shugart, CEO David T Mitchell, Pres Donald L Waite, CFO Douglas K Mahon, R&D Gary L Allison, Mkt Gary Allison, VP Robert Dunlop, VP Ronald Brown, VP Joe Chen, VP Thomas Dillon, VP Donald L Waite, IR	Rev: Assets: Emp:	1266 1094 7	
Seagram Co Ltd 1430 Rue Peel Montreal, PQ H3A1S9 Can 514-849-5271	Producer of distilled spirits, wines & juices. Type: NYSE-VO Ind: Food Processing Grp: Food Processing Edgar M Bronfman, CEO David G Sacks, Pres Jeananne K Hauswald, Tres Richard Karl Goeltz, CFO Stephen E Herbits, VP Edward F McDonnell, VP Ronald P Carzoli, VP Gabor Jellinek, VP	Rev: Assets: Emp:	4298 8242 19	
Seagrams, Joseph E & Sons Inc 375 Park Avenue New York, NY 10022 212-572-7000	Manufacturer & distributor of liquor. Type: Private-Sub-For Ind: Beverage Grp: Food Processing Edgar M Bronfman, CEO Jeaneann Hauswald, CFO Thomas Trainer, IS Leslie Bluhm, R&D Jerome S Mann, Sls Thomas K McInerney, Mkt Richard P Swigart, PR	Rev: Assets: Emp:	3000 6000 10	
Sealed Air Corp Park 80 Plaza E Saddle Brook, NJ 07662 201-791-7600	Manufacturer of packaging materials. Type: NYSE-SEE Ind: Packaging Grp: Manufacturing T J Dermot Dunphy, CEO	Rev: Assets: Emp:	346 256 3	

Organizations Listed Alphabetically

Organization / Address / Phone	Descriptive Information	Revenue / ($ mil)	Assets / ($ mil)	Emp (thous)

Seamen's Bank for Savings Inc
30 Wall Street
New York, NY 10005
212-428-4500

Thrift institution.
Type: ASE-SMN
Ind: Savings & Loan   Grp: Financial
Robert Tedd Enloe, CEO   Michael K Shaughnessy, Tres   Myrna V Anolin, CFO
Patrick Schiavo, IS   Barbara Laughlin, Mkt   Robert K Utley, VP
Edward Polito, VP   Patrick L Sheehan, VP   Stephen A Swartz, VP
Lucy T Tinker, VP   Robert S Bennett, VP   Stephen S Swartz, IR
Thomas Farley, PR

Rev: 436
Assets: 4708
Emp: 2

Searle, G D & Co
5200 Old Orchard Road
Skokie, IL 60077
312-982-7000

Manufacturer & distributor of pharmaceutical products.
Type: Private-Sub   Par: Monsanto Co
Ind: Drugs   Grp: Consumer Service
Sheldon Gilgore, CEO

Rev: NA
Assets: NA
Emp: NA

Sears Acceptance Co Canada Ltd
222 Jarvis Street
Toronto, ON M5B2B8 Can
416-362-1711

Financial subsidiary of Sears Roebuck.
Type: Private-Sub-For
Ind: Non-Bank Fin   Grp: Financial
Ray Bird, CEO   Albert James, Pres   Michael Phillups, VCh
Nancy Houghton, Tres   George Slook, CFO   Joseph Rychalsky, R&D

Rev: 204
Assets: 1034
Emp: 1

Sears Canada Ltd
222 Jarvis Street
Toronto, ON M5B2B8 Can
416-362-1711

Nationwide operator of retail department stores, catalogs.
Type: Private-Sub-For
Ind: Retail/Merch   Grp: Retail
C R Sharpe, CEO

Rev: 3430
Assets: 2229
Emp: 50

Sears Roebuck & Co
Sears Tower
Chicago, IL 60684
312-875-2500

Department store, insurance & investment company.
Type: NYSE
Ind: Retail/Merch   Grp: Retail
Edward A Brennan, CEO   Allan B Stewart, VCh   Edward J Condon, Tres
James M Denny, CFO   Charles F Moran, IS   Charles Carlson, R&D
Charles Ruder, Sls   Warren F Cooper, VP   John S Vivian, VP
Randolf Aires, VP   David Norum, VP   David Shute, VP

Rev: 50252
Assets: 77952
Emp: 400

Sears Roebuck Acceptance Corp
3711 Kennett Pike
Greenville, DE 19807
302-652-3666

Financial subsidiary of Sears Roebuck Company.
Type: Private-Sub   Par: Sears Roebuck & Co
Ind: Non-Bank Fin   Grp: Financial
Robert F Gurnee, CEO   Edward A Brennan, Chr   Richard M Jones, Pres
James M Denny, CFO   Charles F Moran, IS   Charles J Ruder, PR

Rev: 1008
Assets: 12085
Emp: 3

Sears Savings Bank Inc
701 N Brand Blvd
Glendale, CA 91203
818-956-1800

Thrift institution.
Type: Private-Sub   Par: Sears Roebuck & Co
Ind: Savings & Loan   Grp: Financial
Ronald F Danner, CEO

Rev: 500
Assets: 5207
Emp: 1

Seattle First National Bank Co
701 Fifth Avenue
Seattle, WA 98104
206-358-7800

Commercial bank.
Type: OTC
Ind: Banking   Grp: Financial
Richard P Cooley, CEO

Rev: 1800
Assets: 15000
Emp: 7

Seattle, City of
City Hall Municipal Bldg
Seattle, WA 98104
206-625-4000

City government.
Type: City Govt
Ind: Local Govt   Grp: Govt & Non-Prof
Charles Royer, CEO

Rev: 721
Assets: NM
Emp: 8

Securities & Exchange Commission
450 Fifth Street NW
Washington, DC 20549
202-272-3100

Federal government agency.
Type: Federal Govt
Ind: Federal Govt Fin   Grp: Financial
David S Ruder, CEO

Rev: 250
Assets: NM
Emp: 2

Security Capital/Sentinal R E Corp
1290 Avenue of the Americas
New York, NY 10104
212-408-2900

Investment firm.
Type: Private
Ind: Non-Bank Fin   Grp: Financial
John Striker, CEO   Thomas J Gochberg, Chr   William T Bozar, CFO
Shevaun Sloan, PR

Rev: 550
Assets: 2200
Emp: 1

Organizations Listed Alphabetically

Organization / Address / Phone	Descriptive Information	Revenue / ($ mil)	Assets / ($ mil)	Emp (thous)
Security Pacific Corp 333 S Hope Street Los Angeles, CA 90071 213-345-6211	Commercial bank. Type: NYSE Ind: Banking Grp: Financial Richard J Flamson, CEO George F Moody, Pres Ronald C Gilbert, Tres John F Kooken, CFO Robert F Smith, IS John P Singleton, Mkt Kathleen B Cooper, VP Richard A Warner, VP William A Capps, VP George L Capps, VP David Lovejoy, VP Jay S Gould, IR	Rev: Assets: Emp:	8546 77870 33	
Selective Insurance Co 40 Wantage Avenue Branchville, NJ 07890 201-948-3000	Property & casualty insurance company. Type: NASDAQ-SIGI Ind: Insurance Grp: Insurance Frederick H Jarvis, CEO Walter H Hallowell, VCh Charles L Tice, Tres Dominic Addesso, CFO	Rev: Assets: Emp:	480 962 2	
Selig Chemical Industries Inc 840 Selig Drive SW Atlanta, GA 30316 404-691-9220	Manufacturer of specialty chemicals. Type: Private-Sub Par: National Service Industries Inc Ind: Chemicals Grp: Basic Industries L Joels, CEO	Rev: Assets: Emp:	NA NA NA	
Seligman Marketing Inc One Bankers Trust Plaza New York, NY 10006 800-221-2450	Investment firm. Type: Private Ind: Non-Bank Fin Grp: Financial David B Cornstein, CEO	Rev: Assets: Emp:	500 NA 5	
Seneca Foods Corp 1162 Pittford-Victor Road Pittsford, NY 14534 716-385-9500	Manufacturer of canned & bottled fruits, vegetables etc. Type: NASDAQ-SENE Ind: Food Processing Grp: Food Processing Arthur Wolcott, CEO	Rev: Assets: Emp:	800 600 8	
Sentry Insurance Co 1800 N Point Drive Stevens Point, WI 54481 715-346-6000	Property & casualty insurance company. Type: Private-Mutual Ind: Insurance Grp: Insurance Larry C Ballard, CEO David R Miller, Pres Bernard Hlavac, CFO	Rev: Assets: Emp:	1422 3197 4	
Sequa Corp 200 Park Avenue New York, NY 10166 212-986-5500	Manufacturer of precision metal components. Type: NYSE-SQA Ind: Metals/Mining Grp: Basic Industries Norman E Alexander, CEO	Rev: Assets: Emp:	1713 1959 16	
Service America Corp 88 Gatehouse Road Stamford, CT 06902 203-964-5000	Operator of vending machines & cafeterias. Type: Private Ind: Food/Lodging Grp: Consumer Service Carr Newcomer, CEO	Rev: Assets: Emp:	1000 NA 10	
Service Corp International 1929 Allen Parkway Houston, TX 77019 713-522-5141	Funeral service company. Type: NYSE-SRV Ind: Business Service Grp: Business Service Robert L Waltrip, CEO B D Hunter, VCh Ben B Dees, CFO Donald R Campbell, Ops	Rev: Assets: Emp:	616 1667 7	
Service Employees International Union 1313 L Street NW Washington, DC 20005 202-898-3200	National labor union. Type: Membership Org Ind: Membership Org Grp: Govt & Non-Prof John J Sweeney, CEO	Rev: Assets: Emp:	500 NM 850	
Service Master Industries Inc 2300 Warrenville Road Downers Grove, IL 60515 312-964-1300	Personnel service company to the health care industry. Type: NYSE Ind: Business Service Grp: Business Service Kenneth T Wessner, CEO C William Pollard, Chr Carlos Cantu, VCh Robert D Erickson, CFO Doug Neis, IS William Bond, R&D Charles W Stair, Sls David Baseler, Mkt Vernon T Squires, VP Roger Ervin, PR	Rev: Assets: Emp:	1531 484 17	

Organizations Listed Alphabetically

Organization / Address / Phone	Descriptive Information	Revenue / ($ mil)	Assets / ($ mil)	Emp (thous)

Service Merchandise Co Inc
2968 Foster Creighton Drive
Nashville, TN 37202
615-251-6666

Operator of retail catalog stores.
Type: NYSE-SME
Ind: Retail/Merch Grp: Retail
Glen A Bodzy, CEO Raymond Zimmerman, Chr Howard Levy, VCh
S P Braud, CFO Roger Lancina, IS Frank Bisceglia, Sls
Robert Islinger, Mkt S P Braud, PR

Rev: 3093
Assets: 1711
Emp: 27

Service Star Corp
Marie Street
East Butler, PA 16029
412-283-4567

Operator of retail merchandise stores.
Type: Private
Ind: Retail/Merch Grp: Retail
Larry Zehfuss, CEO

Rev: 880
Assets: 250
Emp: 2

Services Group of America
2030 Airport Way S
Seattle, WA 98134
206-623-5023

Food distributing, insurance company.
Type: Private
Ind: Retail/Food Grp: Retail
Thomas J Stewart, CEO

Rev: 1500
Assets: NA
Emp: 5

Servistar Corp
Grant Avenue
East Butler, PA 16029
412-283-4567

Retail operator of hardware & home improvement stores.
Type: Private
Ind: Retail/Merch Grp: Retail
Lawrence T Zekfuss, CEO Al Mielcuszny, CFO Al Mielcuszny, IS
Donald C Belt, Sls Donald C Belt, Mkt Paul E Pentz, PR

Rev: 1000
Assets: 500
Emp: 1

SFFED Corp
88 Kearny Street
San Francisco, CA 94108
415-955-5800

Thrift institution.
Type: NASDAQ-SFFD
Ind: Savings & Loan Grp: Financial
Patrick H Price, CEO

Rev: 400
Assets: 4499
Emp: 2

SFN Companies Inc
1900 E Lake Avenue
Glenview, IL 60025
312-657-3900

Publisher of books.
Type: Private
Ind: Publishing/Com Grp: Consumer Service
George Artandi, CEO

Rev: 440
Assets: NA
Emp: 4

Shaklee Corp
444 Market Street
San Francisco, CA 94111
415-954-3000

Direct mail retail firm; health foods, personal care.
Type: OTC
Ind: Drugs Grp: Consumer Service
David M Chamberlain, CEO Edward Beck, VCh Robert A Gunst, CFO
Rakesh K Kaul, R&D Nevin Anderson, VP Stephen Locke, VP
Ann Heller, VP Allen Simon, VP

Rev: 628
Assets: 435
Emp: 3

Shared Medical Systems Corp
51 Valley Stream Parkway
Malvern, PA 19355
215-296-6300

Manufacturer of computer software; medical accounting & mgt.
Type: NASDAQ-SMED
Ind: Comput/Off Equip Grp: High Tech
R James Macaleer, CEO

Rev: 379
Assets: 285
Emp: 4

Sharp Electronics USA Inc
Sharp Plaza
Mahwah, NJ 07430
201-529-8200

Manufacturer & importer of electronic equipment; US hdqtrs.
Type: Private-Sub-For
Ind: Electronics Grp: High Tech
S Hirooka, CEO

Rev: 1100
Assets: NA
Emp: 2

Shaw Industries Inc
616 E Walnut Avenue
Dalton, GA 30722
404-278-3812

Carpet manufacturing company.
Type: NYSE-SHX
Ind: Apparel/Textiles Grp: Consumer Prd
J C Shaw, CEO Robert E Shaw, Chr W Norris Little, Pres
William C Lusk Jr, CFO C R Quinn, IS J D Miller, R&D
Vance D Bell, Mkt W Norris Little, Ops Douglas Hoskins, VP
Bennie Laughter, VP Warren M Sims Jr, PR

Rev: 958
Assets: 546
Emp: 5

Shawmut Corp
One Federal Street
Boston, MA 02211
617-292-2000

Commercial bank.
Type: NYSE-SNC
Ind: Banking Grp: Financial
Joel B Alvord, CEO Gunnar Overstrom, Pres John P Hammill, VCh
Frederick Pleva, VP Raymond Guenta, VP John Gould, PR

Rev: 2811
Assets: 26475
Emp: 17

Shaws Supermarkets Inc
140 Laurel Street
East Bridgewater, MA 02333
508-378-7211

Operator of retail food supermarkets.
Type: Private
Ind: Retail/Food Grp: Retail
David Jenkins, CEO

Rev: 1100
Assets: NA
Emp: 11

Organizations Listed Alphabetically

Organization / Address / Phone	Descriptive Information	Revenue / ($ mil)	Assets / ($ mil)	Emp (thous)

Shearson Lehman Hutton Inc
American Express Tower World Trade Center
New York, NY 10285
212-298-2000

Worldwide full-line securites firm.
Type: NYSE-SLH
Ind: Securities   Grp: Financial
Peter A Cohen, CEO   Jeffrey B Lane, Pres   Herbert S Freiman, VCh
Robert Druskin, CFO   Joseph J Plumeri, VP   Sherman Lewis, VP
Albert C Bellas, VP   Peter J DaPuzzo, VP   Richard H Darsky, VP
Eliot M Fried, VP

Rev: 10529
Assets: 84840
Emp: 28

Shell Canada Ltd
400 4th Avenue SW
Calgary, AB T2P0J4 Can
403-232-3111

Petroleum exploration, production & marketing company.
Type: TOR-SHE
Ind: Energy   Grp: Basic Industries
John M MacLead, CEO   J E Czaja, VCh   E F J Marschall, Tres
G B Darou, CFO   D G Stoneman, Mkt   Donald Taylor, VP
R A MacDonell, VP   H W Lemieux, VP   G L Peterson, VP

Rev: 4301
Assets: 4773
Emp: 7

Shell Oil Co
One Shell Plaza
Houston, TX 77002
713-241-6161

Petroleum exploration, production & distribution company.
Type: Private
Ind: Energy   Grp: Basic Industries
Frank H Richardson, CEO   J C Jacobsen, CFO   Leroy Drury, IS
James R Street, R&D   S L Miller, Mkt   R G Dillard, PR

Rev: 21000
Assets: 30000
Emp: 41

Sheller Globe Corp
1505 Jefferson Avenue
Toledo, OH 43624
419-255-8840

Manufacturer of automobile parts & components.
Type: ASE
Ind: Automotive   Grp: Manufacturing
Alfred H Grava, CEO   Robert Plew, Pres   Joseph Hayes, VCh
Mark Tanner, CFO   Darrell Sallee, IS   Richard Rytel, Sls
Stephen Hood, Mkt   Roger L Burtaw, Ops   Jay Nowak, VP
Calvin Gray, VP

Rev: 840
Assets: 904
Emp: 10

Shelter Insurance Co
1817 W Broadway
Columbia, MO 65218
314-445-8441

Property & casualty insurance company.
Type: Private-Mutual
Ind: Insurance   Grp: Insurance
Gustav J Lehr, CEO

Rev: 350
Assets: 600
Emp: 2

Sherritt Gordon Mines Ltd
2800 Commerce Court W
Toronto, ON M5L1B1 Can
416-363-9241

Mining company.
Type: TOR-SE
Ind: Metals/Mining   Grp: Basic Industries
E L Donegan, CEO   A R Latham, Chr   P A Bonyun, Tres
K J Harvey, CFO   D R Weir, IS   R R Topp, R&D
R M Garvey, VP   B W Kushnir, VP   D G Maschmeyer, VP
F I Piper, VP   P S Bleach, VP   D M Kossey, VP

Rev: 463
Assets: 546
Emp: 3

Sherwin Williams Co
101 Prospect Avenue NW
Cleveland, OH 44115
216-566-2000

Manufacturer of paints & coatings.
Type: NYSE-SHW
Ind: Building Mat   Grp: Basic Industries
John G Breen, CEO   Thomas A Commes, Pres   Thomas R Miklich, CFO
F Thomas Krotine, R&D   Thomas Kroeger, VP   Larry Pitorak, VP
Leonard Ward, VP   Francis Piccirillo, VP   Dianne B McCormick, PR

Rev: 1950
Assets: 1259
Emp: 17

Sherwood Medical Co
1831 Olive Street
St Louis, MO 63103
314-241-1673

Manufacturer of medical supplies.
Type: Private-Sub   Par: American Home Products Corp
Ind: Health Care   Grp: Consumer Service
David Low, CEO

Rev: NA
Assets: NA
Emp: NA

SHL Systemhouse Inc
99 Bank Street
Vancouver, BC V6C1T2 Can
604-236-9734

Computer consulting company.
Type: TOR
Ind: Comput/Off Equip   Grp: High Tech
Roderick Bryden, CEO

Rev: 425
Assets: 170
Emp: 1

Shoko Chukin Bank Ltd
2 Wall Street
New York, NY 10005
212-693-1660

Commercial bank.
Type: Private-Sub-For
Ind: Banking   Grp: Financial
Kazuo Yamakawa, CEO

Rev: 450
Assets: 3500
Emp: 1

Organizations Listed Alphabetically

Organization / Address / Phone	Descriptive Information	Revenue / ($ mil)	Assets / ($ mil)	Emp (thous)
Shoney's Inc 1727 Elm Hill Pike Nashville, TN 37201 615-361-5201	Family restaurants. Type: NASDAQ-SHONC Ind: Food/Lodging Grp: Consumer Service R L Danner, CEO J Mitchell Boyd, Chr Gary Spoleta, Pres W Craig Barber, Tres Taylor H Henry, CFO Kevin Henderson, R&D Vearl Starnes, Sls Steve Sanders, Ops John Clark, VP David Dobbs, VP T J Evans, VP Bill Long, VP Ronald Walker, VP	Rev: Assets: Emp:		782 404 12
ShopKo Stores Inc 700 Pilgrim Way Green Bay, WI 54304 414-497-2211	Operator of retail food & sundrie stores. Type: Private-Sub Par: Super Valu Stores Inc Ind: Retail/Merch Grp: Retail William Tyrell, CEO	Rev: Assets: Emp:		NA NA NA
Showboat Inc 2800 E Fremont Las Vegas, NV 89104 702-385-9123	Operator of gambling casinos & hotels. Type: NYSE-SBO Ind: Leisure Time Grp: Consumer Service Joseph Kelley, CEO	Rev: Assets: Emp:		295 250 3
Shreveport, City of City Hall Shreveport, LA 71130 318-226-6250	City government. Type: City Govt Ind: Local Govt Grp: Govt & Non-Prof John Hussey, CEO	Rev: Assets: Emp:		250 NM 2
Shulton Inc 697 Route 46 Clifton, NJ 07015 201-340-6000	Manufacturer of consumer products. Type: Private-Sub Par: American Cyanamid Co Ind: Personal Care Grp: Consumer Prd Robert Hiatt, CEO	Rev: Assets: Emp:		NA NA NA
Shurfine Central Corp 2100 N Mannheim Northlake, IL 60164 312-681-2000	Construction & commercial building company. Type: Private Ind: Real Estate/Bldg Grp: Business Service Brian Bihke, CEO	Rev: Assets: Emp:		825 NA 2
Sidbec Ltd 300 Leo Parizeau Montreal, PQ H2W2S7 Can 514-286-8600	Manufacturer of steel products. Type: TOR Ind: Steel Grp: Basic Industries Pierre Laurin, CEO John LeBoutillier, Chr Paul E Landry, CFO J Pierre Picard, Mkt Pierre Lacroix, VP Georges H Laferriere, VP J P Richard Leblanc, VP Dominique Poulin-Gouin, VP Serge Wagner, PR	Rev: Assets: Emp:		549 435 3
Siemens Corp 186 Wood Avenue S Iselin, NJ 08830 201-321-3400	International manufacturer of electronic equip; US hdqtrs. Type: Private-Sub-For Ind: Electronics Grp: High Tech Robert McKinnon, CEO	Rev: Assets: Emp:		2530 NM 26
Sierra Pacific Resources Co 6100 Neil Road Reno, NV 89520 702-689-3600	Electric power utility company. Type: NYSE-SRP Ind: Utility Grp: Utilities Joe L Gremban, CEO	Rev: Assets: Emp:		408 1244 2
Sigma Aldrich Corp 3050 Spruce Street St Louis, MO 63103 314-771-5765	Manufacturer of organic chemicals used in research. Type: NASDAQ-SIAL Ind: Drugs Grp: Consumer Service Alfred Bader, CEO	Rev: Assets: Emp:		300 226 2
Signet Banking Corp 7 N Eighth Street Richmond, VA 23260 804-747-2000	Commercial bank. Type: NYSE-SBK Ind: Banking Grp: Financial Frederick Deane, CEO Robert M Freeman, Pres Malcolm McDonald, VCh W B Millner III, CFO John A Patterson, IS Malcolm S McDonald, Mkt Alexander Berry, VP Malcolm S McDonald, IR Mary Nelson, PR	Rev: Assets: Emp:		1286 11002 6
Signode Corp 3610 W Lake Avenue Glenview, IL 60025 312-724-6100	Manufacturer of electronic parts, industrial components. Type: Private-Sub Par: Illinois Tool Works Inc Ind: Manufacturing Grp: Manufacturing John Powers, CEO	Rev: Assets: Emp:		935 NA 8

Organization / Address / Phone	Descriptive Information	Revenue / ($ mil)	Assets / ($ mil)	Emp (thous)
Sikorsky Inc 6900 Main Street Stamford, CT 06601 203-386-4000	Military & commercial helicopter manufacturer. Type: Private-Sub Par: United Technologies Corp Ind: Aerospace Grp: High Tech Eugene Buckley, CEO	Rev: Assets: Emp:	NA NA NA	
Silcorp Ltd 6205 Airport Road Mississauga, ON L4V1E1 Can 416-678-9700	Nationwide retail company. Type: TOR-SIL Ind: Retail/Merch Grp: Retail Eric F Findlay, CEO Larry Hurst, Tres Dale Pettit, CFO Clifford Denny, R&D Vladimir Romanchych, Sls Betty Ann Lipke, VP Robert Ferguson, VP R Gary Miller, VP	Rev: Assets: Emp:	614 200 2	
Silicon Graphics Inc 2011 N Shoreline Blvd Mountain View, CA 94043 415-960-1980	Manufacturer of computer graphic terminals. Type: NASDAQ-SGIC Ind: Comput/Off Equip Grp: High Tech James Clark, CEO	Rev: Assets: Emp:	264 175 1	
Simon & Schuster Inc 1230 Avenue of the Americas New York, NY 10020 212-698-7000	Publisher of books. Type: Private-Sub Par: Paramount Communications Corp Ind: Publishing/Com Grp: Consumer Service Richard Snyder, CEO	Rev: Assets: Emp:	500 NA 3	
Simplex Wire & Cable Co 2073 Woodberry Avenue Portsmouth, NH 03801 603-436-6100	Manufacturer of communication cables. Type: Private-Sub Par: Tyco Laboratories Inc Ind: Electronics Grp: High Tech John McIntyre, CEO	Rev: Assets: Emp:	NA NA NA	
Simplot, J R Co 999 Main Street Boise, ID 83701 208-336-2110	Manufacturer of packaged food products. Type: Private Ind: Food Processing Grp: Food Processing Gordon Smith, CEO	Rev: Assets: Emp:	1500 NA 10	
Simpson Investment Co Inc 1201 Third Avenue Seattle, WA 98101 206-292-5000	Forest products company. Type: Private Ind: Paper/Forest Prd Grp: Basic Industries Furman Mosely, CEO	Rev: Assets: Emp:	550 NA 5	
Simpson Timber Corp 900 4th Avenue Seattle, WA 98164 206-292-5000	Lumber & plywood doors, building board. Type: Private Ind: Paper/Forest Prd Grp: Basic Industries Thomas R Ingham, CEO	Rev: Assets: Emp:	1000 NA 2	
Simpsons Ltd 401 Bay Street Toronto, ON M5H3K2 Can 416-861-9111	Operator of department stores. Type: Private-Sub Par: Hudson's Bay Co Ind: Retail/Merch Grp: Retail G Kosich, CEO	Rev: Assets: Emp:	553 383 6	
Sinclair Marketing Inc 3401 Fairbanks Kansas City, KS 66106 913-321-3700	Refiner & distributor of petroleum products. Type: Private Ind: Energy Grp: Basic Industries Earl Holding, CEO	Rev: Assets: Emp:	550 NA 1	
SIPCO (Swift Independent Corp) 1401 Elm Street Dallas, TX 75202 214-573-2333	Meat packing company. Type: ASE-SFT Ind: Food Processing Grp: Food Processing Kenneth Monfort, CEO Don Mueller, CFO Jerry Turnwall, IS Rod Bowling, R&D Doug Carey, Sls Joe Meilinger, Mkt Gene Meakins, PR	Rev: Assets: Emp:	3000 300 10	
Sizzler Restaurants International Inc 5400 Alla Road Los Angeles, CA 90066 213-827-2300	Operator & franchiser of fast food restaurants. Type: NASDAQ-SIZZ Ind: Food/Lodging Grp: Consumer Service James Collins, CEO	Rev: Assets: Emp:	311 86 5	
Skyline Corp 2520 By-Pass Road PO Box 743 Elkhart, IN 46515 219-294-6521	Manufacturer of trailer homes, recreational vehicles. Type: NYSE-SKY Ind: Manufacturing Grp: Manufacturing Arthur J Decio, CEO	Rev: Assets: Emp:	384 163 3	

Organizations Listed Alphabetically

Organization / Address / Phone	Descriptive Information	Revenue / Assets / Emp ($ mil) ($ mil) (thous)		

Slater Industries Inc
1120 King Street W
Toronto, ON L8P3C8 Can
416-529-5422

Manufacturer of basic steel products.
Type: TOR
Ind: Steel   Grp: Basic Industries
J Fingold, CEO

Rev: 298
Assets: 213
Emp: 2

Slattery Group Inc
1044 Northern Blvd
Roslyn, NY 11576
516-484-5858

Construction company; highways, bridges.
Type: NYSE-SGI
Ind: Real Estate/Bldg   Grp: Business Service
Milton Cooper, CEO

Rev: 240
Assets: 200
Emp: 2

Smith Barney Harris Upham & Co
1345 Avenue of the Americas
New York, NY 10105
212-698-6000

Investment firm; retail brokerage.
Type: Private
Ind: Securities   Grp: Financial
Frank Zarb, CEO

Rev: 1100
Assets: 11000
Emp: 6

Smith International Inc
17640 Hardy Street
Houston, TX 77205
713-443-3370

Oil field drilling equipment manufacturer.
Type: NYSE-SII
Ind: Transport   Grp: Business Service
Douglas L Rock, CEO

Rev: 250
Assets: 200
Emp: 2

Smith Management Corp
1550 S Redwood
Salt Lake City, UT 84104
801-974-1400

Operator of retail food stores.
Type: Private
Ind: Retail/Food   Grp: Retail
Jeff Smith, CEO

Rev: 1100
Assets: NA
Emp: 5

Smith, A O Corp
11270 W Park Place
Milwaukee, WI 53223
414-359-4000

Manufacturer of automotive & construction parts.
Type: ASE-SMCA
Ind: Automotive   Grp: Manufacturing
Thomas I Dolan, CEO   Robert J O'Toole, Pres   Donald Dunaway, VCh
Glen R Bomberger, CFO   Eugene R Kleinberg, IS   Charles J Bishop, R&D
Rod LeMense, Mkt   Edward O'Conner, VP   Curtis Laetz, VP
Edward J O'Connor, PR

Rev: 1015
Assets: 808
Emp: 10

Smithfield Foods Inc
501 N Church Street
Smithfield, VA 23430
703-357-4321

Grocery wholesaler.
Type: NASDAQ-SFDS
Ind: Food Processing   Grp: Food Processing
Joseph W Luter, CEO   Alan Anderson, Pres   C Larry Pope, Tres
Aaron Trub, CFO   Carl J Wood, R&D   Robert Manly, VP
J Sam Sawyer, VP   John C Schroder, VP   Elaine Abicht, VP
William Hellman, VP

Rev: 916
Assets: 131
Emp: 4

SmithKline Beckman Animal Health Product
1600 Paoli Pike
West Chester, PA 19380
215-251-7400

Manufacturer of animal health products.
Type: Private-Sub   Par: Smithkline Beckman Corp
Ind: Drugs   Grp: Consumer Service
Norman Blanchard, CEO

Rev: NA
Assets: NA
Emp: NA

Smithkline Beckman Corp
One Franklin Plaza
Philadelphia, PA 19101
215-751-4000

Manufacturer of prescription drugs for people & livestock.
Type: NYSE-SKB
Ind: Drugs   Grp: Consumer Service
Henry Wendt, CEO   George W Ebright, Pres   Gavin S Herbert, VCh
Duncan Cocroft, Tres   Kenneth N Kermes, CFO   John Blood, IS
Stanley T Crooke, R&D   Thomas M Collins, PR

Rev: 4749
Assets: 5017
Emp: 42

Smoot Grain Co
4666 Faries Parkway
Decatur, IL 62525
913-827-8734

Animal feed company.
Type: Private-Sub   Par: Archer Daniels Midland Co
Ind: Food Processing   Grp: Food Processing
David Warrington, CEO

Rev: NA
Assets: NA
Emp: NA

SMP Inc
29501 Clayton Blvd
Wickliffe, OH 44092
216-585-3100

Manufacturer of high technology products.
Type: Private-Sub   Par: TRW Inc
Ind: Aerospace   Grp: High Tech
J Cripe, CEO

Rev: NA
Assets: NA
Emp: NA

Smucker, J M Co
Strawberry Lane
Orrville, OH 44667
216-682-0015

Producer of packaged foods; jams, jellies.
Type: NYSE-SJM
Ind: Food Processing   Grp: Food Processing
Paul H Smucker, CEO

Rev: 353
Assets: 188
Emp: 3

Organizations Listed Alphabetically

Organization / Address / Phone	Descriptive Information	Revenue / ($ mil)	Assets / ($ mil)	Emp (thous)
Snacks & International Consumer Products 180 E Broad Street Columbus, OH 43215 614-225-4000	Manufacturer of consumer food products. Type: Private-Sub Par: Borden Inc Ind: Food Processing Grp: Food Processing George Waydo, CEO	Rev: Assets: Emp:	NA NA NA	
Snap-on Tools Corp 2801 80th Street Kenosha, WI 53141 414-656-5200	Manufacturer of tools for professional mechanics. Type: NYSE-SNA Ind: Manufacturing Grp: Manufacturing Marion R Gregory, CEO Michael Montemurro, Tres Lowell L Larson, CFO Cliff McRae, IS Jay W Schultz, R&D Daniel J Riordan, Sls Earl B Reed, Mkt Clarence Niemi, PR	Rev: Assets: Emp:	855 668 7	
SNC Group Inc 2 Place Felix Martin Montreal, PQ H2Z1Z3 Can 514-866-1000	Manufacturer of compression engines for industrial use. Type: MON Ind: Business Service Grp: Business Service C A Dagenais, CEO	Rev: Assets: Emp:	375 305 4	
Snyder General Corp 2001 Ross Avenue Dallas, TX 75201 214-979-3100	Climate conrol equipment. Type: Private Ind: Manufacturing Grp: Manufacturing Richard W Snyder, CEO	Rev: Assets: Emp:	500 NA 5	
Sobeys Inc 115 King Street Stellarton, NS B0K1S0 Can 902-752-8371	Operator of retail grocery stores. Type: Private-Sub Par: Empire Co Ind: Retail/Food Grp: Retail David Sobey, CEO	Rev: Assets: Emp:	893 213 9	
Societe Generale Financement du Quebec 155 University Montreal, PQ H3B3A7 Can 514-875-0330	Provincial government financing agency. Type: Prov Govt Ind: Federal Govt Fin Grp: Financial Bernard Caussignac, CEO	Rev: Assets: Emp:	425 1020 5	
Society Bank Corp 800 Superior Avenue Cleveland, OH 44114 216-689-3000	Commercial bank. Type: NASDAQ-SOCI Ind: Banking Grp: Financial James S Reid, CEO Robert W Gillespie, Chr Roger Noall, Pres Robert M Patrick, CFO Mary Holbert, R&D James Smith, Mkt Carl Heintel, VP Anthony Heyworth, VP D Allen McDaniel, VP Bruce C Murray, VP Robert G Nemer, VP F Scott O'Donnell, VP John Fuller, PR	Rev: Assets: Emp:	972 10009 6	
Society for Savings 31 Pratt Street Hartford, CT 06103 203-727-5000	Commercial bank. Type: NASDAQ-SOCS Ind: Banking Grp: Financial Elliott Miller, CEO Albert Fiacre, CFO Karen Antion, IS Frank Litwin, Mkt Robert Beggs, PR	Rev: Assets: Emp:	400 4000 1	
Softsel Computer Products Inc 546 N Oak Street Inglewood, CA 90302 213-412-1700	Wholesaler of computer software. Type: NASDAQ-SOFT Ind: Comput/Off Equip Grp: High Tech Bob Leff, CEO	Rev: Assets: Emp:	550 200 2	
Sonat Exploration Co PO Box 1513 Houston, TX 77251 713-940-4000	Oil & gas exploration, production, transmission & marketing. Type: Private-Sub Par: Sonat Inc Ind: Energy Grp: Basic Industries Donald Russell, CEO	Rev: Assets: Emp:	NA NA NA	
Sonat Inc Southern National Bldg Birmingham, AL 35203 205-325-3800	Production & distribution of natural gas. Type: NYSE-SNT Ind: Utility Grp: Utilities Ronald L Kuehn, CEO J Robert Doody, VCh Thomas Barker, CFO Duane Kerper, IS James Yardley, R&D William Smith, Sls Donald Russell, Mkt Ralph Spinnier, VP Dan Langford, VP	Rev: Assets: Emp:	1392 3139 7	

Organizations Listed Alphabetically

Organization / Address / Phone	Descriptive Information	Revenue / ($ mil)	Assets / ($ mil)	Emp (thous)
Sonoco Products Co N Second Street Hartsville, SC 29550 803-383-7000	Manufacturer of paperboard & plastic containers. Type: NASDAQ-SONO Ind: Paper/Forest Prd Grp: Basic Industries Charles W Coker, CEO Thomas C Coxe, Pres F Trent Hill, CFO H D Tomer, IS J G Caudle, R&D J R Tinnell, Ops Peter Coggeshall, VP F Bennett Williams, VP H E DeLoach Jr, PR	Rev: 1599	Assets: 977	Emp: 14
Sony Corp of America Sony Drive Park Ridge, NJ 07656 201-930-1000	Manufacturer of consumer electronic equipment; US hdqtrs. Type: Private-Sub-For Ind: Electronics Grp: High Tech Neil Vanderdussen, CEO	Rev: 3300	Assets: NA	Emp: 4
Soo Line Corp Soo Line Bldg Fifth & Marquette Minneapolis, MN 55440 612-347-8000	Railroad transportation & real estate company. Type: NYSE-SOO Ind: Transport Grp: Business Service Dennis M Cavanaugh, CEO James A Mogen, Tres James Lee, CFO Michael Fox, IS Peter McNamee, Mkt John C Miller, VP Fern B Albers, VP Wayne C Serkland, VP John Bergene, PR	Rev: 570	Assets: 905	Emp: 5
Sotheby's Holdings Inc 1334 York Avenue New York, NY 10021 212-606-7000	Art auctioneer, world's largest. Type: ASE-BID Ind: Retail/Merch Grp: Retail A Alfred Taubman, CEO	Rev: 349	Assets: 503	Emp: 1
South Carolina National Corp 1426 Main Street Columbia, SC 29226 803-765-3000	Commercial bank. Type: NASDAQ-SCNC Ind: Banking Grp: Financial Thomas N Bagnal, CEO James G Lindley, Chr Robert S McCoy, Pres Arthur Bjontegard, VCh Gary M Duncan, CFO Carl M Manheim Jr, IS James Bostics, Sls W D King, Mkt James B Murphy, VP T Stephen Lynch, VP William Murphy, VP Robert S McCoy, IR Charles T Cole Jr, PR	Rev: 551	Assets: 5655	Emp: 4
South Carolina, State of State House Columbus, SC 29211 803-734-1000	State government. Type: State Govt Ind: State/Prov Govt Grp: Govt & Non-Prof Carroll A Campbell, CEO	Rev: 6425	Assets: NM	Emp: 74
South Central Bell Telephone Co 600 N 19th Street Birmingham, AL 35203 205-321-1000	Telephone utility company. Type: Private-Sub Par: BellSouth Corp Ind: Telecom Grp: High Tech Karl Bailey, CEO	Rev: NA	Assets: NA	Emp: NA
South Dakota, State of State Capitol Pierre, SD 57501 605-773-3011	State government. Type: State Govt Ind: State/Prov Govt Grp: Govt & Non-Prof George Mickelson, CEO	Rev: 1535	Assets: NM	Emp: 17
Southam Inc 150 Bloor Street W Toronto, ON M5S2Y8 Can 416-927-1877	Communications & publishing company. Type: TOR-STM Ind: Publishing/Com Grp: Consumer Service Hugh G Hallward, CEO John P Fisher, Chr William J Mann, VCh Brian Gibbings, Tres John G Craig, CFO L John Rothwell, IS Paddy Sherman, Ops Paul Renaud, VP Margeret Marwood, VP	Rev: 1406	Assets: 1057	Emp: 16
Southdown Inc 1200 Smith Street Suite 2200 Houston, TX 77002 713-658-8921	Manufacturer of cement & concrete building materials. Type: NYSE-SDW Ind: Building Mat Grp: Basic Industries G Walter Loewenbaum, CEO Clarence C Comer, Chr Edgar J Marston, VCh Kenneth D Cohn, Tres James L Persky, CFO Dennis M Thies, R&D John F Platt, Sls Allan b Korsakov, Mkt	Rev: 605	Assets: 1211	Emp: 4
Southeast Banking Corp One SE Financial Center Miami, FL 33131 305-375-7500	Commercial bank. Type: NYSE-STB Ind: Banking Grp: Financial Charles Zwick, CEO John E Porta, Pres Kristen M Hudak, CFO Thomas M Blodgett, IS Scott A Bailey, R&D Beverly P Chambers, Mkt Ida L Roberts, IR	Rev: 1066	Assets: 12469	Emp: 7

Organizations Listed Alphabetically

Organization / Address / Phone	Descriptive Information	Revenue ($ mil)	Assets ($ mil)	Emp (thous)
Southeastern Michigan Gas Corp 2915 Lapeer Road Port Huron, MI 48060 313-987-7900	Natural gas utility company. Type: NASDAQ-SMGS Ind: Utility Grp: Utilities James Shaw, CEO	Rev: 300 Assets: 500 Emp: 1		
Southern Bell Telephone & Telegraph Co 675 W Peachtree Street Atlanta, GA 30375 404-529-8611	Telephone utility company. Type: Private-Sub Par: BellSouth Corp Ind: Telecom Grp: High Tech Frank Skinner, CEO	Rev: NA Assets: NA Emp: NA		
Southern California Gas Co 810 S Flower Street Los Angeles, CA 90017 213-689-2345	Natural gas utility company. Type: Private-Sub Par: Pacific Enterprises Corp Ind: Utility Grp: Utilities Paul A Miller, CEO James R Ukropina, Pres Willis B Wood, VCh Lloyd A Levitin, CFO James T Pollard, IS J Foster Hames, VP Charles Weiss, VP William Cole, VP Paul Williams, VP J Patrick Garner, VP Mickey Foster, IR	Rev: 5339 Assets: 5027 Emp: 28		
Southern Co 64 Perimeter Center E Atlanta, GA 30346 404-393-0650	Electric utility holding company. Type: NYSE-SO Ind: Utility Grp: Utilities Edward L Addison, CEO Tommy Chishom, Tres W L Westbrook, CFO Euel M Wade Jr, IS Charles Goodman, R&D James S Kirley, Mkt Alan R Barton, VP Arthur Gigniliat, VP Douglas L McCrary, VP Gale E Klappa, PR	Rev: 7235 Assets: 19729 Emp: 31		
Southern Farm Bureau Insurance Co 1401 Livingston Lane Jackson, MS 39205 601-982-7777	Property & casualty insurance company. Type: OTC Ind: Insurance Grp: Insurance James D Graugnard, CEO	Rev: 700 Assets: 600 Emp: 3		
Southern Illinois University Administrative Bldg Carbondale, IL 62901 618-453-2121	Major educational institution; university. Type: University Ind: University Grp: Govt & Non-Prof John C Guyon, CEO	Rev: 196 Assets: 146 Emp: 25		
Southern Indiana Gas & Electric Co 20 NW Fourth Street Evansville, IN 47741 812-424-6411	Electric & natural gas utility company. Type: NYSE-SIG Ind: Utility Grp: Utilities Norman Wagner, CEO	Rev: 290 Assets: 450 Emp: 1		
Southern Natural Gas Co 1900 5th Avenue N Birmingham, AL 35202 205-325-7410	Electric power utility company. Type: Private-Sub Par: Sonat Inc Ind: Utility Grp: Utilities William E Matthews, CEO	Rev: 1400 Assets: 1700 Emp: 2		
Southern New England Telephone Inc 227 Church Street New Haven, CT 06510 203-771-5200	Telephone utility. Type: NYSE Ind: Telecom Grp: High Tech Walter H Monteith, CEO Daniel Miglio, CFO Charles Harrison, IS Richard Donofrio, Mkt Robert E Neal, Ops A Kelly, VP Jean Handley, VP	Rev: 1583 Assets: 3067 Emp: 14		
Southern Pacific Transport Corp 1 Market Plaza San Francisco, CA 94105 415-541-1000	Railroad & trucking transportation company. Type: NYSE-SFX Ind: Transport Grp: Business Service D McNear, CEO	Rev: 2412 Assets: 4709 Emp: 23		
Southern Peru Copper Co Inc 180 Maiden Lane New York, NY 10038 212-510-2000	Mining & minerals processing company. Type: Private Ind: Metals/Mining Grp: Basic Industries Richard Osborne, CEO	Rev: 275 Assets: NA Emp: 3		

Organizations Listed Alphabetically

Organization / Address / Phone	Descriptive Information	Revenue / Assets / Emp ($ mil) ($ mil) (thous)		

Southern States Cooperative Inc
6606 W Broad Street
Richmond, VA 23260
804-281-1000

Retail petroleum products.
Type: Private
Ind: Food Processing   Grp: Food Processing
Gene A Jones, CEO   Jonathan A Hawkins, Tres   C A Miller,III, IS
W M Smith, Mkt   Robert W Taylor, VP   George Winstead, VP
George R Duncan, VP   N Hopper Ancarrow, VP   M T Ragsdale, VP

Rev: 967
Assets: 382
Emp: 3

Southern Union Co
Renaissance Tower
Dallas, TX 75270
214-748-8511

Oil & gas production company.
Type: NYSE-SUG
Ind: Utility   Grp: Utilities
Frank W Denius, CEO

Rev: 191
Assets: 370
Emp: 1

Southland Canada Inc
3185 Willingdon Green
Burnaby, BC V5G4P3 Can
604-299-0700

Operator of retail convenience stores.
Type: Private-Sub-For
Ind: Retail/Food   Grp: Retail
John Thompson, CEO

Rev: 448
Assets: 145
Emp: 6

Southland Corp
2828 N Haskell Avenue
Dallas, TX 75204
214-828-7011

Operator of convenience stores.
Type: Private
Ind: Retail/Food   Grp: Retail
John P Thompson, CEO   Jere W Thompson, Chr   Clark J Matthews II, CFO
David Karney, IS   Kenneth Slauth, R&D   John F Antioco, Mkt
Henry T Stanley Jr, PR

Rev: 9000
Assets: NA
Emp: 50

Southland Financial Corp
5215 N O'Connor Blvd
Irving, TX 75039
214-828-7011

Financial services, real estate, contracting,
Type: NASDAQ-SFIN
Ind: Non-Bank Fin   Grp: Financial
Ben Carpenter, CEO

Rev: 250
Assets: 1500
Emp: 1

Southmark Corp
1601 LBJ Freeway
Dallas, TX 75234
214-241-8787

Real estate development & financial services company.
Type: NYSE-SM
Ind: Real Estate/Bldg   Grp: Business Service
Gene E Phillips, CEO   William S Friedman, VCh   Donald W Hair, CFO
Jim C Hunt, IS   Thomas Walker, R&D   James R Gilley, VP
D Vinson Marley, VP   Thomas C Walker, IR   Susan Childs, PR

Rev: 2838
Assets: 9161
Emp: 33

SouthTrust Corp
420 N 20th Street
Birmingham, AL 35203
205-254-5523

Commercial bank.
Type: NASDAQ-SOTR
Ind: Banking   Grp: Financial
Wallace D Malone, CEO   Roy W Gilbert, Pres   James W Rainier, VCh
Aubrey D Barnard, CFO   Charles Murrell, IS   James R Buell Jr, Mkt
James R Buell Jr, IR   Betty Snoddy, PR

Rev: 627
Assets: 6645
Emp: 4

Southwest Airlines Co
PO Box 37611
Love Field, TX 75235
214-353-6100

Regional airline.
Type: NYSE-LUV
Ind: Airline   Grp: Consumer Service
Herbert D Kelleher, CEO   Robert W Lawless, Pres   Gary Barron, VCh
John G Denison, CFO   Dan Hay, IS   Camille Keith, Sls
Donald G Valentine, Mkt   Paul Sterbenz, Ops   John Owen, VP
Gary Kelly, VP   James Wimberly, VP   David L Brown, PR

Rev: 860
Assets: 1308
Emp: 6

Southwest Gas Corp
5241 Spring Mountain
Las Vegas, NV 89102
702-876-7011

Natural gas utility & financial services company.
Type: NASDAQ
Ind: Utility   Grp: Utilities
Kenny C Guinn, CEO   Michael Maffie, Pres   Marvin Shaw, VCh
David Sloan, CFO   William Morrison, IS   Frederick Joels, R&D
John Mayo, Ops   Thomas Trimble, VP   Adolph Dubuc, VP
Thomas Olson, VP   Joy Ray, VP   Faye Ringler, VP

Rev: 558
Assets: 3679
Emp: 2

Southwest Texas State University
Administrative Bldg
San Marcos, TX 78666
512-245-2111

Major educational institution; university.
Type: University
Ind: University   Grp: Govt & Non-Prof
Michael L Abbott, CEO

Rev: 62
Assets: 114
Emp: 21

Organizations Listed Alphabetically

Organization / Address / Phone	Descriptive Information	Revenue / ($ mil)	Assets / ($ mil)	Emp (thous)
Southwestern Bell Corp One Bell Center St Louis, MO 63101 314-235-9800	Holding company for telephone & communication companies. Type: NYSE-SBC Ind: Telecom Grp: High Tech Zane E Barnes, CEO Edward Whitacre, Pres William Dreyer, VP Rogert Glaser, VP Ann Goddard, VP Richard Harris, VP Gray Kerrick, VP Gerald Blatherwick, PR	Rev: 8473 Assets: 20985 Emp: 75		
Southwestern Bell Mobile Systems Inc 17330 Preston Road Dallas, TX 75252 214-733-2000	Manufacturer & marketer of cellular mobile communications. Type: Private-Sub Par: Southwestern Bell Corp Ind: Telecom Grp: High Tech John Stupka, CEO	Rev: NA Assets: NA Emp: NA		
Southwestern Bell Publishing Inc 12800 Publications Drive St Louis, MO 63131 314-957-2261	Publisher of printed directories. Type: Private-Sub Par: Southwestern Bell Corp Ind: Publishing/Com Grp: Consumer Service William Dreyer, CEO	Rev: NA Assets: NA Emp: NA		
Southwestern Electric Power 428 Travis Street Shreveport, LA 71156 318-222-2141	Electric power utility. Type: Private-Sub Par: Central & South West Corp Ind: Utility Grp: Utilities John W Turk, CEO Henry D Mattison, Chr W H Snow, CFO Leslie E Dillahunty, Ops W J Googe, VP Paul Hellinghausen, VP	Rev: 742 Assets: 1889 Emp: 2		
Southwestern Life Insurance Co PO Box 2699 Dallas, TX 75221 214-954-7111	Life insurance company. Type: OTC Ind: Insurance Grp: Insurance John W Gardiner, CEO Robert Shaw, Chr Douglas Ward, CFO George Priest, IS Steven R Johnson, Mkt	Rev: 1601 Assets: 5799 Emp: 5		
Southwestern Public Service Co Tyler & Sixth Streets Amarillo, TX 79101 806-378-2121	Electric power utility. Type: NYSE Ind: Utility Grp: Utilities Bert Ballengee, CEO W R Esler, Pres Robert Dickerson, Tres Coyt Webb, CFO Sam Hunter, R&D Gary L Gibson, Mkt Carl E Jeans, VP Albert Smith, VP Lorene Lacer, VP Mary Pullam, VP Bill D Helton, VP Henry Hamilton, VP	Rev: 794 Assets: 1667 Emp: 2		
Southwire Co Inc 140 Fertilla Street Carrolton, GA 30119 404-832-4242	Metal fabricating, wire cable manufacturing. Type: Private Ind: Metals/Mining Grp: Basic Industries Roy Richards, CEO	Rev: 750 Assets: NA Emp: 3		
Sovereign Bank Corp One Commerce Place Nashville, TN 37219 615-749-3333	Commercial bank. Type: OTC Ind: Banking Grp: Financial Owen G Shell, CEO	Rev: 400 Assets: 4000 Emp: 2		
Sovran Financial Corp One Commercial Place Norfolk, VA 23510 804-441-4000	Commercial bank. Type: NYSE-SOV Ind: Banking Grp: Financial C Coleman McGehee, CEO C A Cutchins III, Chr Dennis C Bottorff, Pres Albert B Gornto Jr, CFO John Brewington, IS W Kelly Scott, R&D W Kelly Scott, Mkt W Kelly Scott, IR Josephine West, PR	Rev: 2302 Assets: 21349 Emp: 10		
Spalding & Evenflow Corp 5750 N Hoover Tampa, FL 33630 813-887-5200	Diversified manufacturer of industrial products. Type: Private Ind: Manufacturing Grp: Manufacturing Riccardo Cisneros, CEO	Rev: 330 Assets: NA Emp: 3		
Spanos, A G Construction Inc 1341 W Robin Hood Stockton, CA 95207 209-478-7954	Heavy construction & commercial building company. Type: Private Ind: Real Estate/Bldg Grp: Business Service Alex Spanos, CEO	Rev: 715 Assets: NA Emp: 2		
Spartan Food Systems Inc Interstate 85 & Frontage Road Spartanburg, SC 29304 803-579-1220	Food vending machines & institutional food services. Type: Private-Sub Par: TW Service Inc Ind: Food/Lodging Grp: Consumer Service E Packing, CEO	Rev: NA Assets: NA Emp: NA		

Organizations Listed Alphabetically

Organization / Address / Phone	Descriptive Information	Revenue / Assets / Emp ($ mil) ($ mil) (thous)		

Spartan Stores Inc
850 76th Street SW
Grand Rapids, MI 49518
616-878-2000

Operator of retail discount department stores.
Type: Private
Ind: Retail/Food   Grp: Retail
Patrick Quinn, CEO

Rev: 1650
Assets: NA
Emp: 4

Spear, Leeds & Kellogg Inc
115 Broadway
New York, NY 10006
212-587-8800

Investment firm; securities trading.
Type: Private
Ind: Securities   Grp: Financial
Peter Kellogg, CEO

Rev: 450
Assets: 4400
Emp: 1

Spiegel Corp
1515 W 22nd Street
Oak Brook, IL 60522
312-986-8800

Catalog merchandise retailer.
Type: NASDAQ-SPGL
Ind: Retail/Merch   Grp: Retail
Michael Otto, CEO

Rev: 1100
Assets: 900
Emp: 6

Sprague Technologies Inc
4 Stamford Forum
Stamford, CT 06901
203-964-8600

Manufacturer of electronic parts.
Type: Private
Ind: Electronics   Grp: High Tech
Edward Kosnik, CEO   Charles D Park, CFO   Robert Heise, IS
Janet Crane, PR

Rev: 450
Assets: 400
Emp: 7

Springs Industries Inc
205 N White Street
Fort Mill, SC 29715
803-547-2901

Manufacturer of apparel products.
Type: NYSE-SMI
Ind: Apparel/Textiles   Grp: Consumer Prd
Walter Y Elisha, CEO   W Paul Tippett, Pres   Murphy Fontenot, VCh
A Ward Peacock, CFO   Robert M Bruton, IS   James E Hendrix, R&D
Bruce Roberts, Mkt   Julius Lasnick, VP   John Cauthen, VP
J Spratt White, VP   Robert Thompson Jr, IR   Robert E Slough, PR

Rev: 1825
Assets: 1118
Emp: 19

SPS Technologies Inc
Route 332
Newtown, PA 18940
215-860-3000

Manufacturer of metal products, fasteners.
Type: NYSE-ST
Ind: Manufacturing   Grp: Manufacturing
John R Selby, CEO

Rev: 350
Assets: 250
Emp: 3

SPX Sealed Power Corp
100 Terrace Plaza
Muskegon, MI 49443
616-724-5000

Manufacturer of automobile parts & components.
Type: NYSE-SPW
Ind: Automotive   Grp: Manufacturing
Robert D Tuttle, CEO   Dale A Johnson, Pres   David Reynolds, VCh
Donald Johnson, Tres   R Budd Werner, CFO   Richard Cochrane, IS
R Hoffmeister, R&D   Charles N Hough, VP   Bjorn Iwarson, VP
Peter Turner, VP   Roland Gerber, VP   John D Tyson, IR
Hal W Maertz, PR

Rev: 877
Assets: 702
Emp: 8

Square D Co
Executive Plaza 1415 S Roselle
Palatine, IL 60067
312-397-2600

Manufacturer of electronic control devices.
Type: NYSE-SQD
Ind: Electronics   Grp: High Tech
C E Ashley, CEO   Dalton L Knauss, Chr   Jerre Stead, Pres
T L Bindley, CFO   Simon Yin, R&D   Clive Thompson, Sls
Richard A Hegeman, Mkt   J K Glore, VP   D S Free, VP
C W Denny, VP   T H Brown, VP   C L Hite, VP
W W Kurczewski, VP   Robert P Fiorani, IR   C M Michalski, PR

Rev: 1657
Assets: 1336
Emp: 21

Squibb Corp
PO Box 4000
Princeton, NJ 08540
609-921-4000

International pharmeceutical & health care company.
Type: NYSE-SQB
Ind: Drugs   Grp: Consumer Service
Richard M Furland, CEO   Jan Leschly, Pres   Charles A Sanders, VCh
Anthony W Ruggiero, CFO   John Parker Jr, IS   Dr C A Sanders, R&D
Joseph Scolari, VP   Joseph T Stewart Jr, PR

Rev: 2586
Assets: 3083
Emp: 18

SRI International Inc
333 Ravenswood Avenue
Menlo Park, CA 94025
415-326-6200

Nationwide consulting company.
Type: Private
Ind: Consulting   Grp: Business Service
William F Miller, CEO

Rev: 300
Assets: NA
Emp: 3

Organizations Listed Alphabetically

Organization / Address / Phone	Descriptive Information	Revenue ($ mil)	Assets ($ mil)	Emp (thous)
SSMC Inc (Singer Co) 8 Stamford Forum Stamford, CT 06904 203-356-4200	Manufacturer of consumer & industrial sewing machines. Type: Private Ind: Electronics Grp: High Tech W F Smied, CEO Paul A Bilzerian, Chr Joseph J Campanella, Pres David Smith, IS Thomas Elliott, PR	Rev: 1750	Assets: 1000	Emp: 15
SSQ Mutuelle d'Assurance Ltd 2525 Laurier Blvd Sainte Foy, PQ G1V4H6 Can 418-651-7000	Life insurance company. Type: Private Ind: Insurance Grp: Insurance Leopold Marquis, CEO	Rev: 210	Assets: 490	Emp: 1
St Joe Paper Co 803 Edward Ball Bldg Jacksonville, FL 32201 904-356-8311	Forest products company; paper, paperboard, packaging. Type: OTC Ind: Paper/Forest Prd Grp: Basic Industries Jake C Belin, CEO	Rev: 650	Assets: 450	Emp: 5
St John Health Corp 22101 Moross Detroit, MI 48236 313-343-4000	Operator of hospitals & clinics. Type: Private Ind: Health Care Grp: Consumer Service Gleen Wesselmann, CEO	Rev: 318	Assets: NA	Emp: 3
St John's University Grand Central & Utopia Parkways Jamaica, NY 11439 516-990-6161	Major educational institution; university. Type: University Ind: University Grp: Govt & Non-Prof Joseph T Cahill, CEO	Rev: 330	Assets: 330	Emp: 21
St Lawrence Cement Inc 1945 Graham Blvd Montreal, PQ H3R1H1 Can 514-340-1881	Cement manufacturing company. Type: TOR-STA Ind: Building Mat Grp: Basic Industries Erwin Machler, CEO Walter Penny, Chr Frank DeWitt, VCh Guy Turgeon, CFO Yves Delagrave, Mkt Pierre Viger, VP Edward Bailey, VP	Rev: 623	Assets: 552	Emp: 3
St Louis County Government 41 S Central Clayton, MO 63105 314-889-2000	County government. Type: County Govt Ind: Local Govt Grp: Govt & Non-Prof Gene McNary, CEO	Rev: 650	Assets: NM	Emp: 4
St Louis, City of City Hall St Louis, MO 63103 314-622-3201	City government. Type: City Govt Ind: Local Govt Grp: Govt & Non-Prof Vincent Schoemehl, CEO	Rev: 532	Assets: NM	Emp: 8
St Paul Companies Inc 385 Washington Street St Paul, MN 55102 612-221-7911	Insurance & financial services. Type: NASDAQ-STPL Ind: Insurance Grp: Insurance Robert J Haugh, CEO Douglas W Leatherdale, Pres James Duffy, VCh Gary P Hanson, IS John C Field, Mkt William Hay, VP Frederick Knox, VP Howard Daltron, VP Mark Pabst, VP A Kent Shamblin, IR Irma Kamperschroer, PR	Rev: 3631	Assets: 10382	Emp: 10
St Paul, City of City Hall St Paul, MN 55102 612-298-4323	City government. Type: City Govt Ind: Local Govt Grp: Govt & Non-Prof George Latimer, CEO	Rev: 296	Assets: NM	Emp: 3
St Petersburg, City of City Hall St Petersburg, FL 33731 813-893-7117	City government. Type: City Govt Ind: Local Govt Grp: Govt & Non-Prof Robert L Ulrich, CEO	Rev: 250	Assets: NM	Emp: 3
Staley Continental Incorported One Continental Towers 1701 Golf Road Rolling Meadows, IL 60008 312-981-1696	Operator of grain elevators, feed processors. Type: NYSE-STA Ind: Food Processing Grp: Food Processing Donald Nordlund, CEO	Rev: 3100	Assets: 1745	Emp: 10

Organizations Listed Alphabetically

Organization / Address / Phone	Descriptive Information	Revenue / ($ mil)	Assets / ($ mil)	Emp (thous)
Stanadyne Inc 100 Deerfield Road Windsor, CT 06095 203-525-0821	Manufacturer of machine parts. Type: Private Ind: Manufacturing Grp: Manufacturing George Michel, CEO George J Michel, CFO Richard Trondsen, IS Edwin L Russell, R&D Mark Jurras, IR Jules Boissonneault, PR	Rev: Assets: Emp:		500 500 5
Standard Brands Paint Co 4300 W 190th Street Torrance, CA 90509 213-214-2411	Retailer of home decorating products. Type: NYSE-SBP Ind: Building Mat Grp: Basic Industries Stuart D Buchalter, CEO Ery W Kehaya, Chr Marvin Coghill, Pres Guy Ross, Tres J Alec Murray, CFO Anthony A D Arrowsmith, Mkt Krishnamurthy Rangarajan, VP Graham D Evans, VP	Rev: Assets: Emp:		304 243 4
Standard Commerical Tobacco Co 2201 Miller Road PO Box 450 Wilson, NC 27893 919-291-5507	Tobacco products; cigarettes, cigars, pipe tobacco. Type: NYSE-STW Ind: Tobacco Grp: Food Processing E W Kehaya, CEO	Rev: Assets: Emp:		935 559 5
Standard Federal Bank Inc 2401 W Big Beaver Troy, MI 48084 313-643-9600	Thrift institution. Type: NYSE-SFB Ind: Savings & Loan Grp: Financial Thomas R Ricketts, CEO Garry Carley, VCh Jack A Wood, Tres Joseph Krul, CFO William Yaw, VP Ronald Palmer, VP Raymond Smith, VP Clyde J B Dougherty, VP Robert Bonkowski, VP	Rev: Assets: Emp:		867 9573 2
Standard Life Assurance Co 1245 Sherbrooke W Montreal, PQ H3G 1G3 Can 514-284-6711	Life insurance company. Type: Private-Mutual Ind: Insurance Grp: Insurance Alestair Fernie, CEO	Rev: Assets: Emp:		842 3964 1
Standard Motor Products Inc 37-18 Northern Blvd Long Island City, NY 11101 718-392-0200	Manufacturer of automotive parts; brakes, air conditioners. Type: NYSE-SMP Ind: Automotive Grp: Manufacturing Bernard Fife, CEO	Rev: Assets: Emp:		398 350 3
Standard Pacific Corp 1565 W MacArthur Blvd Costa Mesa, CA 92626 714-546-1161	Construction company. Type: NASDAQ-SPF Ind: Real Estate/Bldg Grp: Business Service B Dickson, CEO	Rev: Assets: Emp:		450 200 1
Standard Products Co 2130 W 110th Street Cleveland, OH 44102 216-281-8300	Manufacturer of parts for the automotive industry. Type: NYSE-SPD Ind: Automotive Grp: Manufacturing James S Reid, CEO Robert Stevens, VCh Joseph A Robinson, CFO John Clegg, IS Joel H Nussbaum, R&D John Woodland, VP Thomas Stecz, VP John Drinko, VP Joseph A Robinson, PR	Rev: Assets: Emp:		508 255 5
Standard Register Co 600 Albany Street Dayton, OH 45401 513-443-1000	Manufacturer of commercial cash registers. Type: NASDAQ-SREG Ind: Comput/Off Equip Grp: High Tech Craig J Brown, CEO John K Darragh, Chr Colm O'Hara, VCh E L Lehman, IS Frank V Parenti, R&D J J Parente, Sls Gerard B Chadwick, Mkt Otto Stock, VP Norman Young, VP J David Hackworth, IR Douglas Lunne, PR	Rev: Assets: Emp:		675 444 6
Standard Shares Inc 333 Skokie Blvd Northbrook, IL 60065 312-498-1260	Manufacturer of security equipment, alarms. Type: ASE-SWD Ind: Electronics Grp: High Tech Nelson Harris, CEO	Rev: Assets: Emp:		795 600 6
Standex International Corp 6 Manor Parkway Salem, NH 03079 603-893-9701	Manufacturer of office equipment, printing, publishing. Type: NYSE-SXI Ind: Electronics Grp: High Tech Daniel E Hogan, CEO	Rev: Assets: Emp:		430 276 6

Organization / Address / Phone	Descriptive Information	Revenue / ($ mil)	Assets / ($ mil)	Emp (thous)
Stanford University 210 Encina Hall Stanford, CA 94305 415-497-2300	Major educational institution; university. Type: University Ind: University Grp: Govt & Non-Prof Donald Kennedy, CEO	Rev: Assets: Emp:		649 598 21
Stanhome Inc 333 Western Avenue Westfield, MA 01085 413-562-3631	Retail marketer of home wares, personal care products. Type: NYSE-STH Ind: Manufacturing Grp: Manufacturing H L Tower, CEO Alejandro Diaz Vargas, Pres Eugene Friedman, VCh Allan Keirstead, CFO Thomas Evangelista, R&D Gary R LaFountain, Sls J Robert Ward-Burns, VP Ronald Jalbert, VP Bruce H Wyatt, VP	Rev: Assets: Emp:		433 244 4
Stanley Works Inc 1000 Stanley Drive PO Box 7000 New Britain, CT 06050 203-225-5111	Manufacturer of hand tools. Type: NYSE-SWK Ind: Manufacturing Grp: Manufacturing Richard H Ayers, CEO R Alan Hunter, CFO James B Gufstafson, IS Francis E Hummell, Mkt Paul Marier, VP Lloyd Wallis, VP Peter J Kilduff, IR Ronald F Gilrain, PR	Rev: Assets: Emp:		1909 1405 19
Staplecont Inc 210 W Market Street Greenwood, MS 38930 601-453-6231	Producer & manufacturer of packaged food products. Type: Private Ind: Food Processing Grp: Food Processing Woods Eastland, CEO	Rev: Assets: Emp:		550 NA 1
Star Kist Seafood Co 180 E Ocean Blvd Long Beach, CA 90802 213-590-3605	Manufacturer & canner of seafood. Type: Private-Sub Par: Heinz, H J Co Ind: Food Processing Grp: Food Processing Keith Hauge, CEO	Rev: Assets: Emp:		500 NA 2
Star Market Co 625 Mt Auburn Street Cambridge, MA 02138 617-661-2200	Operator of retail food supermarkets. Type: Private-Sub Par: American Stores Co Ind: Retail/Merch Grp: Retail Martin Scholtens, CEO	Rev: Assets: Emp:		NA NA NA
State Auto Mutual Insurance Co 518 E Broad Street Columbus, OH 43216 614-464-5000	Property & casualty insurance company. Type: Private-Mutual Ind: Insurance Grp: Insurance Robert L Bailey, CEO	Rev: Assets: Emp:		400 500 2
State Farm Group Ltd Canada 1801 Brimley Road Scarborough, ON M1P3H3 Can 416-321-4000	Property & casualty insurance company. Type: Private-Sub-For Ind: Insurance Grp: Insurance Earl Sheeler, CEO	Rev: Assets: Emp:		324 559 1
State Farm Insurance Co One State Farm Plaza Bloomington, IL 61710 309-766-2311	Life insurance company. Type: NYSE Ind: Insurance Grp: Insurance Edward B Rust, CEO Marvin D Bower, Pres Rex J Bates, CFO John R Stuckey, IS Wayne Sorenson, R&D Don D Rood, Mkt Ron Arnold, PR	Rev: Assets: Emp:		2358 8453 6
State Mutual Life Assurance Co of Amer 440 Lincoln Street Worcester, MA 01605 508-852-1000	Life insurance company. Type: Private-Mutual Ind: Insurance Grp: Insurance Frederick Fedeli, CEO Albert J Long, IS John M Quinlan, Mkt David Portney, PR	Rev: Assets: Emp:		1718 4376 4
State Savings Bank Inc 20 E Broad Street Columbus, OH 43215 614-460-6100	Thrift institution. Type: Private Ind: Savings & Loan Grp: Financial Donald B Shackelford, CEO	Rev: Assets: Emp:		139 1520 1

Organizations Listed Alphabetically

Organization / Address / Phone	Descriptive Information	Revenue / Assets / Emp ($ mil) ($ mil) (thous)		

State Street Bank Inc 225 Franklin Street Boston, MA 02101 617-786-3000	Commercial bank. Type: NASDAQ-STBK Ind: Banking Grp: Financial William S Edgerly, CEO Peter E Madden, Pres Howard Fairweather, VCh David A Spina, CFO Ronald Golz, VP George Fesus, VP Norton Q Sloan, VP Charles Kelly, VP David Sexton, VP Bradford Tripp, VP E D Coxe, PR	Rev: Assets: Emp:	897 7246 4
State Univ of New York Capen Hall Buffalo, NY 14260 716-831-2000	Major educational institution; university. Type: University Ind: University Grp: Govt & Non-Prof Richard A Wiesen, CEO	Rev: Assets: Emp:	230 846 29
Statesman Group Life Insurance Co 1400 Des Moines Bldg Des Moines, IA 50309 515-284-7500	Life insurance company. Type: NASDAQ-STTG Ind: Insurance Grp: Insurance David Noble, CEO	Rev: Assets: Emp:	678 2402 1
Statistics Canada R H Coats Bldg Tunney's Pasture Ottawa, ON K1A0T6 Can 613-990-8116	Federal government agency. Type: Federal Govt Ind: Federal Govt Grp: Govt & Non-Prof Ivan P Fellegi, CEO	Rev: Assets: Emp:	765 NM 5
Steego Corp 319 Clematis Street West Palm Beach, FL 33401 407-655-9700	Manufacturer & retailer of automotive parts. Type: NYSE-STG Ind: Automotive Grp: Manufacturing J Russell Duncan, CEO	Rev: Assets: Emp:	235 250 2
Steelcase Inc 901 44th Street Grand Rapids, MI 49501 616-247-2710	Manufacturer of office furniture. Type: Private Ind: Appliances/Furn Grp: Manufacturing Robert C Pew, CEO	Rev: Assets: Emp:	1800 NA 13
Stein Roe & Farnham Inc 1 S Wacker Drive PO Box 1162 Chicago, IL 60690 312-368-7800	Investment firm. Type: Private Ind: Non-Bank Fin Grp: Financial Gary Countryman, CEO	Rev: Assets: Emp:	400 13200 1
Steinberg Inc 3500 De Maisonneuve W 2 Place Alexis Nihon Montreal, PQ H3Z1Y3 Can 514-931-9131	Operator of retail food supermarkets. Type: TOR Ind: Retail/Food Grp: Retail Pierre Brodeur, CEO Irving Ludmer, Chr H Arnold Steinberg, VCh Laurier Carpentier, CFO Marcel Croux, IS Harold G Geraghty, R&D Alain Bilodeau, VP Ronald M Kirshner, VP	Rev: Assets: Emp:	3897 1296 36
Stelco Inc Toronto Dominion Centre IBM Tower Toronto, ON M5K1J4 Can 416-362-2161	Integrated steel manufacturer. Type: TOR Ind: Steel Grp: Basic Industries J D Allan, CEO J E Hood, VCh P D Mathews, CFO L C McLean, R&D R E Henealt, Mkt F Telmer, VP L Killaly, VP T Meadowcraft, VP M Tuvikene, VP	Rev: Assets: Emp:	2305 2029 16
Stepan Co Edens & Winnetka Roads Winnetka, IL 60093 312-446-7500	Manufacturer of specialty chemicals. Type: ASE-SCL Ind: Chemicals Grp: Basic Industries F Quinn Stepan, CEO	Rev: Assets: Emp:	300 250 1
Stephens Inc 114 E Capitol Avenue PO Box 3507 Little Rock, AR 72203 501-374-4361	Investment firm; securities trading. Type: Private Ind: Securities Grp: Financial Warren Stephens, CEO	Rev: Assets: Emp:	300 2200 1
Sterling Chemical Corp 333 Clay Street Houston, TX 77002 713-650-3700	Manufacturer of chemical products. Type: NYSE Ind: Chemicals Grp: Basic Industries Gordon Cain, CEO	Rev: Assets: Emp:	600 400 2

Organization / Address / Phone	Descriptive Information	Revenue / Assets / Emp ($ mil) ($ mil) (thous)		

Sterling Drug Inc
90 Park Avenue
New York, NY 10016
212-907-2000

Manufacturer of chemicals & drugs.
Type: NYSE-STY
Ind: Drugs   Grp: Consumer Service
John Pietruski, CEO   James G Andress, Pres   Gary D Penisten, CFO
Lawrence Chakrin, R&D   Terry G Kelley, PR

Rev: 2300
Assets: 1724
Emp: 21

Sterling Electronics Corp
4201 SW Freeway
Houston, TX 77001
713-623-6600

Manufacturer of electronic parts & plastic products.
Type: ASE-SEC
Ind: Electronics   Grp: High Tech
Michael Spolane, CEO

Rev: 225
Assets: 150
Emp: 2

Steuart Investment Co Inc
4646 40th Street NW
Washington, DC 20016
202-537-8940

Real estate development company.
Type: Private
Ind: Real Estate/Bldg   Grp: Business Service
John C Johnson, CEO

Rev: 550
Assets: NA
Emp: 1

Stevens, J P & Co Inc
Stevens Tower 1185 Avenue of the Americas
New York, NY 10036
212-930-2000

Manufacturer of home furnishings & cotton fabrics.
Type: NYSE-STN
Ind: Apparel/Textiles   Grp: Consumer Prd
Whitney Stevens, CEO   Ward Burns, Pres   Marshall N Morton, CFO
David M Tracy, Mkt   James R Franklin, PR

Rev: 1660
Assets: 941
Emp: 27

Stewart & Stevenson Services Inc
2707 North Loop W
Houston, TX 77008
713-868-7700

Assembler of diesel engines & manufacturer of generators.
Type: NASDAQ-SSSS
Ind: Manufacturing   Grp: Manufacturing
Thomas Langham, CEO

Rev: 474
Assets: 400
Emp: 3

Stingray Pipeline Co
3000 Bissonnet
Houston, TX 77251
713-627-5400

Oil & gas pipelines transmission company.
Type: Private-Sub   Par: Panhandle Eastern Corp
Ind: Transport   Grp: Business Service
Conrad Lawson, CEO

Rev: NA
Assets: NA
Emp: NA

Stolt Tankers & Terminals Inc
8 Sound Drive
Greenwich, CT 06807
203-625-9400

Warehouse storage & deep sea transportation company.
Type: OTC
Ind: Transport   Grp: Business Service
J Stolt-Nielson, Jr, CEO

Rev: 400
Assets: 500
Emp: 1

Stone & Webster Inc
One Penn Plaza 250 W 34th Street
New York, NY 10119
212-290-7500

Construction engineering company.
Type: NYSE
Ind: Consulting   Grp: Business Service
William F Allen, CEO   Walter Sullivan, Pres   William Egan, VCh
Robert Gallagher, CFO   Joel Skidmore, VP   Bruce Coles, VP

Rev: 324
Assets: 565
Emp: 4

Stone Container Corp
150 Michigan Avenue
Chicago, IL 60601
312-346-6600

Packaging & wood fibre products.
Type: NYSE-STO
Ind: Paper/Forest Prd   Grp: Basic Industries
Roger W Stone, CEO   Roger W Stone, Chr   James Doughan, VCh
Arnold F Brookstone, CFO   Thomas Cutilletta, IS   Harold E Gregg, R&D
William Klaisle, Mkt   Morty Rosenkranz, VP   Covington Shackelford, VP
Alan Stone, VP   John Bence, VP   William Klaisle, PR

Rev: 3742
Assets: 2395
Emp: 21

Stop & Shop (SSC Holdings) Inc
1776 Heritage Drive PO Box 369
North Quincy, MA 02171
617-770-8000

Operator of retail food supermarkets.
Type: Private
Ind: Retail/Merch   Grp: Retail
Avram J Goldberg, CEO   Carol R Goldberg, Pres   Joseph McGlinchey, CFO
Aileen Gorman, IR   Andrea White, PR

Rev: 4400
Assets: NA
Emp: 45

Storage Technology Corp
2270 S 88th Street
Louisville, CO 80028
303-673-5020

Computer disk drive manufacturer.
Type: NYSE-STK
Ind: Comput/Off Equip   Grp: High Tech
Ryal R Poppa, CEO   James MacGuire, Pres   Carl Vertuca, Tres
William R Mansfield, CFO   Donald Manuell, IS   Sewell I Sleek, R&D
Richard R Douglas, Mkt   Sewell Sleek, VP   Harry Pforzheimer, PR

Rev: 874
Assets: 847
Emp: 8

Storer Communications Inc
12000 Biscayne Blvd
Miami, FL 33181
305-899-1000

Operator of radio & TV broadcasting stations.
Type: Private
Ind: Publishing/Com   Grp: Consumer Service
Mike Tallent, CEO

Rev: 825
Assets: NA
Emp: 5

Organizations Listed Alphabetically

Organization / Address / Phone	Descriptive Information	Revenue / ($ mil)	Assets / ($ mil)	Emp (thous)
Strategic Planning Associates Inc 2300 N Street NW Washington, DC 20037 202-778-7000	Nationwide consulting company. Type: Private Ind: Consulting Grp: Business Service Walker Lewis, CEO	Rev: Assets: Emp:	28 26 1	
Stratus Computer Inc 55 Fairbanks Blvd Marlborough, MA 01752 617-460-2000	Manufacturer of fault tolerant computers. Type: NASDAQ-STRA Ind: Comput/Off Equip Grp: High Tech William E Foster, CEO	Rev: Assets: Emp:	265 200 2	
Strawbridge & Clothier Inc 801 Market Street Philadelphia, PA 19107 215-629-6000	Operator of retail department stores. Type: NASDAQ-STRW Ind: Retail/Merch Grp: Retail Peter Strawbridge, CEO	Rev: Assets: Emp:	904 650 5	
Stride Rite Corp 5 Cambridge Center Cambridge, MA 02142 617-491-8800	Manufacturer of shoes. Type: NYSE-SRR Ind: Apparel/Textiles Grp: Consumer Prd Arnold Hiatt, CEO	Rev: Assets: Emp:	379 243 3	
Stroh Brewery Co 100 River Place Detroit, MI 48207 313-446-2000	Manufacturer of beverage products; beer. Type: Private Ind: Beverage Grp: Food Processing Peter W Stroh, CEO	Rev: Assets: Emp:	2000 NA 10	
Student Loan Marketing Assn Inc 1050 Thomas Jefferson Street NW Washington, DC 20007 202-333-8000	Financial intermediary to the education finance market. Type: NASDAQ Ind: Non-Bank Fin Grp: Financial Edward A Fox, CEO Ronald Hunt, VCh Albert L Lord, CFO Lawrence A Hough, Mkt Suzanne J Peck, Ops Gerald Cohen, VP Michael A Wyatt, VP Mitchell Johnson, VP Daniel Boehmer, VP Richard Boyle, VP Beth Van Houten, IR Nancy Grund, PR	Rev: Assets: Emp:	1729 28627 7	
Subaru America Corp Subaru Plaza 2235 Route 70 W Cherry Hill, NJ 08002 609-488-8500	Manufacturer & importer of motor vehicles; US headquarters. Type: NASDAQ-SBRU Ind: Automotive Grp: Manufacturing Harvey H Lamm, CEO Thomas R Gibson, Pres Marvin Riesenbach, CFO Donald M Finello, IS Charles D Mahin, Sls David L Sippel, Mkt Henry Greenwald, VP William Stanton, VP John Pinti, VP John Coyle, VP Thomas Braun, VP David L Sippel, IR Fred Heiler, PR	Rev: Assets: Emp:	1673 727 1	
Sudbury Inc 3733 Park Drive E Cleveland, OH 44122 216-464-7026	Automobile parts manufacturer. Type: OTC Ind: Automotive Grp: Manufacturing Tinkham Veale, CEO	Rev: Assets: Emp:	600 400 5	
Suffolk County Government County Bldg Veterans Memorial Highway Hauppauge, NY 11788 516-360-4000	County government. Type: County Govt Ind: Local Govt Grp: Govt & Non-Prof Patrick G Halpin, CEO	Rev: Assets: Emp:	2050 NM 12	
Sumitomo Canada Ltd 701 W Georgia Street Vancouver, BC V7Y 1E9 Can 604-682-2256	Importer & wholesaler of steel pipe & tube. Type: Private-Sub-For Ind: Manufacturing Grp: Manufacturing T Ucmyama, CEO	Rev: Assets: Emp:	1063 NA 1	
Sumitomo Trading Co USA 345 Park Avenue New York, NY 10154 212-207-0700	International trading company; US headquarters. Type: Private-Sub-For Ind: Manufacturing Grp: Manufacturing E Miyoshi, CEO	Rev: Assets: Emp:	1650 NA 4	
Sumitomo Trust & Banking Co 527 Madison Avenue New York, NY 10022 212-326-0500	Commercial bank. Type: Private Ind: Banking Grp: Financial Hidehiko Asai, CEO	Rev: Assets: Emp:	600 5500 4	

Organizations Listed Alphabetically

Organization / Address / Phone	Descriptive Information	Revenue / ($ mil)	Assets / ($ mil)	Emp (thous)
Summa Corp 3800 Howard Hughes Parkway Las Vegas, NV 89109 702-791-4000	Operator of hotels & gambling casinos. Type: Private Ind: Leisure Time Grp: Consumer Service John Goolsby, CEO	Rev: Assets: Emp:	550 NA 5	
Summit Bancorp 367 Springfield Avenue Summit, NJ 07901 201-522-8400	Commercial bank Type: NASDAQ-SUBN Ind: Banking Grp: Financial Thomas D Sayles, CEO	Rev: Assets: Emp:	500 5000 2	
Summit Health Ltd 1800 Avenue of the Stars Los Angeles, CA 90067 213-201-4000	Operator of hospitals, nursing homes, medical offices. Type: NASDAQ-SUMH Ind: Health Care Grp: Consumer Service Don Freeberg, CEO	Rev: Assets: Emp:	400 250 7	
Sun Carriers Inc 1400 N Providence Road Media, PA 19063 215-891-7100	Nationwide trucking company. Type: Private Ind: Transport Grp: Business Service Albert Labinger, CEO Donald E Mayoras, Pres H A Trucksess III, CFO Peter C Monti, IS Donald E Mayoras, IR Marilyn Yelton, PR	Rev: Assets: Emp:	750 600 9	
Sun Co Inc 100 Matsonford Road Radnor, PA 19087 215-293-6000	Manufacturer of high performance workstations. Type: NYSE-SUN Ind: Energy Grp: Basic Industries Robert T Clements, CEO Robert P Hauptfuhrer, Pres D P Cooke, IS Robert A Baillie, R&D Robert H Campbell, Mkt Patrick Coggins, VP R Jackman, PR	Rev: Assets: Emp:	9744 8616 21	
Sun Diamond Growers of California Inc 5568 Gibraltar Drive Pleasanton, CA 94566 415-463-8200	Agricultural cooperative food productions; raisins, fruit. Type: Private Ind: Food Processing Grp: Food Processing Larry Busboom, CEO Richard Miller, Chr Larry D Busboom, CFO Richard Douglas, PR	Rev: Assets: Emp:	660 250 1	
Sun Distributors Inc One Logan Square Philadelphia, PA 19103 215-665-3650	Wholesaler of power equipment, automotive machinery. Type: NYSE Ind: Equipment Grp: Manufacturing Donald J Marshall, CEO	Rev: Assets: Emp:	425 400 4	
Sun Electric Corp One Sun Parkway Crystal Lake, IL 60014 815-459-7700	Manufacturer of electronic automotive test equipment. Type: NYSE-SE Ind: Electronics Grp: High Tech D Barry Davis, CEO	Rev: Assets: Emp:	225 250 3	
Sun Energy Partners LP Inc 5656 Blackwell Dallas, TX 75231 214-890-6207	Oil & natural gas exploration & production company. Type: NYSE-SLP Ind: Energy Grp: Basic Industries James McCormick, CEO	Rev: Assets: Emp:	1570 2000 2	
Sun Exploration Corp 5656 Blackwell Dallas, TX 75231 214-890-6000	Gas & oil exploration. Type: Private-Sub Par: Sun Co Inc Ind: Energy Grp: Basic Industries J McCormick, CEO	Rev: Assets: Emp:	3000 2000 1	
Sun Life Assurance Co of Canada 200 University Avenue Toronto, ON M5H3C7 Can 416-595-7500	Life insurance company. Type: TOR Ind: Insurance Grp: Insurance John D McNeil, CEO John Gardner, Pres Donald L Harrison, VCh Michael Hasley, CFO Donald Stewart, IS Robert Mifflin, R&D Cameron Leamy, Mkt Warwick Jamieson, VP Gregory W Gee, VP Lance W Kemp, VP Stephen Browne, VP	Rev: Assets: Emp:	4215 19711 5	
Sun Life Assurance Co of Canada US One Sun Life Executive Park Wellesley, MA 02181 617-237-6030	Life insurance company. Type: Private-Sub-For Ind: Insurance Grp: Insurance John D McNeil, CEO	Rev: Assets: Emp:	449 3505 2	

Organizations Listed Alphabetically

Organization / Address / Phone	Descriptive Information	Revenue / Assets / Emp ($ mil) ($ mil) (thous)		

Sun Microsystems Inc
2550 Garcia Avenue
Mountain View, CA 94043
415-960-1300

Manufacturer of work station computers.
Type: OTC-SUNW
Ind: Comput/Off Equip   Grp: High Tech
Scott McNeally, CEO   Bernard Lacroute, VCh   Joseph A Graziano, CFO
Michael A Graves, IS   William N Joy, R&D   Joseph P Roebuck, Sls
Robert Garrows, Ops   Laurence Garlick, VP   Austin Wing Mayer, IR

Rev: 1052
Assets: 757
Emp: 7

Sun Refining & Marketing Div
1801 Market Street
Philadelphia, PA 19103
215-977-3332

Oil refining & marketing company.
Type: Private-Sub   Par: Sun Co Inc
Ind: Energy   Grp: Basic Industries
David Knoll, CEO

Rev: NA
Assets: NA
Emp: NA

Sunbelt Savings Assn Inc
4901 LBJ Freeway
Dallas, TX 75234
214-980-4441

Thrift institution.
Type: Private
Ind: Savings & Loan   Grp: Financial
Thomas J Wageman, CEO

Rev: 400
Assets: 4000
Emp: 1

Sunbuy Inc
4445 Garand
Montreal, PQ H4R 2H9 Can
514-335-0260

Merchandising company.
Type: Private-Sub   Par: Cantrex Group Inc
Ind: Retail/Merch   Grp: Retail
Mark Bureau, CEO

Rev: 298
Assets: 85
Emp: 1

Suncor Inc
36 York Mills Road
North York, ON M2P2C5 Can
416-733-7300

Producer & distributor of petroleum products.
Type: TOR
Ind: Energy   Grp: Basic Industries
Michael M Koerner, CEO   Thomas Thomson, Chr   Douglas MacKenzie, VCh
Peter C Harris, CFO   Michael W O'Brien, R&D   Michael Supple, VP
Robert Writz, VP   Peter Spelliscy, VP   William Turner, VP
Grant Allan, VP   George Eynon, VP

Rev: 1143
Assets: 1720
Emp: 4

Sundstrand Corp
4949 Harrison Avenue
Rockford, IL 61125
815-226-6000

Manufacturer of industrial equipment.
Type: NYSE-SNS
Ind: Machinery   Grp: Manufacturing
Evans W Erikson, CEO   Harry C Stonecipher, Chr   Phillip Polgreen, VCh
Paul Donavan, CFO   John B Martocci Jr, IS   Robert Smuland, R&D
Bernard Weiss, VP   Stanley Moeschl, VP   DeWayne Fellows, VP
Claude Vernam, IR   Philip W Polgreen, PR

Rev: 1477
Assets: 1567
Emp: 14

Sunkist Growers Inc
14130 Riverside Drive
Sherman Oaks, CA 91423
818-986-4800

Agricultural products producer & distributor; citrus, fruit.
Type: Private
Ind: Food Processing   Grp: Food Processing
Russell Hanlon, CEO   Robert R Campbell, IS   Maurice V Johnson, R&D
David P Bernstein, Mkt   Curtis W Anderson, PR

Rev: 1100
Assets: 250
Emp: 2

Suntrust Banks Corp
25 Park Place NE
Atlanta, GA 30303
404-588-7455

Commercial bank.
Type: NYSE-STI
Ind: Banking   Grp: Financial
Robert Strickland, CEO   Joel R Wells Jr, Pres   James B Williams, VCh
John W Speigel, CFO   George A Snelling, IS   Donald Senterfitt, VP
Jesse S Hall, VP   Anthony Gray, VP   Charles Lybrook, VP
Bertt Madden, VP   Willis Johnson, PR

Rev: 2889
Assets: 29177
Emp: 20

Super Food Services Inc
3185 Elbee Road
Dayton, OH 45439
513-294-1731

Wholesale food & personal health care company.
Type: ASE-SFS
Ind: Retail/Food   Grp: Retail
Jack Twyman, CEO   Samuel L Robinson, Pres   John Demos, VCh
Robert Frank, Tres   Robert F Koogler, CFO   Larry G Dear, IS
Al Burshtan, Mkt   James Potter, Ops   Vaughn Lewis, VP
Jerry Presnell, VP   John Demos, IR   Al Burshtan, PR

Rev: 1573
Assets: 224
Emp: 2

Super Rite Foods Inc
3900 Industrial Road
Harrisburg, PA 17110
717-232-6821

Operator of wholesale food distribution warehouses.
Type: NASDAQ-SRFI
Ind: Retail/Food   Grp: Retail
Alexander Grass, CEO

Rev: 757
Assets: 450
Emp: 3

Organizations Listed Alphabetically

Organization / Address / Phone	Descriptive Information	Revenue / ($ mil)	Assets / ($ mil)	Emp (thous)
Super Valu Stores Inc 11840 Valley View Road Eden Prairie, MN 55344 612-828-4000	Retail food supermarket operator. Type: NYSE-SVU Ind: Retail/Food Grp: Retail Michael W Wright, CEO Sumner H Goldman, VCh David Cairns, Tres John B Ferris, CFO H S Smith III, IS Gordon W Hippen, R&D Thomas L Dekko, Sls Jeffrey Noddle, Mkt Phillip A Dabill, VP Laurence L Anderson, VP Ronald C Tortelli, VP William Tyrrell, VP Michael Mulligan, IR Valerie Koutnik, PR	Rev: 10296 Assets: 2305 Emp: 41		
Superior Industries International Inc 7800 Woodley Avenue Van Nuys, CA 91406 818-781-4973	Manufacturer of motor vehicle steering parts, accessories. Type: NASDAQ-SUP Ind: Automotive Grp: Manufacturing Louis Borick, CEO	Rev: 300 Assets: 150 Emp: 2		
Superior Water, Light & Power Co 1230 Tower Avenue Superior, WI 54880 715-394-5511	Electric & water utility company. Type: Private-Sub Par: Minnesota Power & Light Co Ind: Utility Grp: Utilities Gene McGillis, CEO	Rev: NA Assets: NA Emp: NA		
Superiors Brand Meats Inc 1888 Southway SE Massillon, OH 44648 216-832-7491	Producer & distributor of packaged foods; meats. Type: Private Ind: Food Processing Grp: Food Processing Neil Genshst, CEO	Rev: 550 Assets: NA Emp: 5		
Supermarkets General Corp 301 Blair Road Woodbridge, NJ 07095 201-499-3000	Operator of retail food markets & home improvement stores. Type: Private Ind: Retail/Food Grp: Retail Kenneth Peskin, CEO	Rev: 6000 Assets: NA Emp: 30		
Supply & Services Canada 11 Laurier St Place du Portage Phase III Hull, PQ K1A0S5 Can 819-997-6363	Federal government agency. Type: Federal Govt Ind: Federal Govt Grp: Govt & Non-Prof Georgina Wyman, CEO	Rev: 2040 Assets: NM Emp: 10		
Suzuki Motor Corp USA Inc 3251 E Imperial Highway Brea, CA 92621 714-996-7040	Manufacturer & importer of motor vehicles; US headquarters. Type: Private-Sub-For Ind: Automotive Grp: Manufacturing T Arai, CEO	Rev: 1100 Assets: NA Emp: 1		
Sverdrup Corp 801 N 11th Street St Louis, MO 63101 314-436-7600	Engineering, architect, construct, real estate. Type: Private Ind: Real Estate/Bldg Grp: Business Service Brice R Smith, CEO	Rev: 400 Assets: NA Emp: 4		
Sweet Life Foods Inc PO Box 385 Suffield, CT 06096 203-623-1681	Producer & distributor of packaged food products. Type: Private Ind: Food Processing Grp: Food Processing Julian Leavitt, CEO	Rev: 1000 Assets: NA Emp: 3		
Swinerton & Walberg Inc 580 California Avenue San Francisco, CA 94111 415-421-2980	Construction & real estate development company. Type: Private Ind: Real Estate/Bldg Grp: Business Service Dave Grubb, CEO	Rev: 550 Assets: NA Emp: 5		
Swiss Bank Corp Four World Trade Center New York, NY 10048 212-938-3500	Commercial bank. Type: Private-Sub-For Ind: Banking Grp: Financial Willi Wittzler, CEO	Rev: 450 Assets: 3500 Emp: 1		
Swiss Reinsurance Co 237 Park Avenue New York, NY 10017 212-907-8000	Property & casualty insurance company. Type: Private-Sub-For Ind: Insurance Grp: Insurance N David Thompson, CEO	Rev: 900 Assets: 1200 Emp: 3		
Sybron Corp 411 E Wisconson Milwaukee, WI 53202 414-274-6600	Diversified manufacturing company; US headquarters. Type: Private-Sub-For Ind: Manufacturing Grp: Manufacturing Kenneth Yontz, CEO	Rev: 825 Assets: NA Emp: 7		

Organizations Listed Alphabetically

Organization / Address / Phone	Descriptive Information	Revenue / ($ mil)	Assets / ($ mil)	Emp (thous)
Syms Corp Syms Way Secuacus, NJ 07094 201-902-9600	Operator of discount retail apparel stores. Type: NYSE-SYM Ind: Retail/Merch Grp: Retail Sy Syms Merns, CEO	Rev: 283	Assets: 200	Emp: 2
Syntex Corp 3401 Hillview Drive Palo Alto, CA 94304 415-885-5050	Pharmaceutical & health care products manufacturing company. Type: NYSE-SYN Ind: Drugs Grp: Consumer Service Albert Bowers, CEO Paul E Freiman, Pres Alan Stevenson, Tres Richard P Powers, CFO John H Fried, R&D Hans A Wolf, Mkt Burton Rogers, VP William Gomez, VP Thomas L Gutshall, VP Kathleen N Gary, PR	Rev: 1272	Assets: 1444	Emp: 9
Syracuse University Administrative Bldg Syracuse, NY 13244 315-423-1870	Major educational institution; university. Type: University Ind: University Grp: Govt & Non-Prof Melvin A Eggers, CEO	Rev: 187	Assets: 341	Emp: 23
SYSCO Corp 1390 Enclave Parkway Houston, TX 77077 713-877-1122	Wholesaler of food & supplies to restaurants & institutions. Type: NYSE-SYY Ind: Business Service Grp: Business Service John F Baugh, CEO John F Woodhouse, Chr Bill M Lindig, Pres E James Lowrey, CFO John B Smart Jr, IS David Smallwood, Sls Robert Planck, Mkt Bill Delaney, PR	Rev: 4385	Assets: 1021	Emp: 13
Syscon Corp 1000 Thomas Jefferson Street Washington, DC 20007 202-342-4000	Manufacturer of computer systems. Type: Private-Sub Par: Harnischfeger Corp Ind: Comput/Off Equip Grp: High Tech Joe Yglesias, CEO	Rev: NA	Assets: NA	Emp: NA
Taco Bell Inc 17901 Von Karman Avenue Irvine, CA 92714 714-863-4501	Operator of retail fast food restaurants, franchises. Type: Private-Sub Par: PepsiCo Inc Ind: Food/Lodging Grp: Consumer Service John Martin, CEO	Rev: NA	Assets: NA	Emp: NA
TAD Technical Services Inc 639 Massachusetts Avenue Cambridge, MA 02139 617-868-1650	Nationwide consulting company. Type: Private Ind: Consulting Grp: Business Service David McGrath, CEO	Rev: 350	Assets: NA	Emp: 3
Taiyo Kobe Bank Ltd 444 S Flower Street Los Angeles, CA 90071 213-629-3939	Commercial bank. Type: Private-Sub-For Ind: Banking Grp: Financial Akita Amaka, CEO	Rev: 450	Assets: 3500	Emp: 1
Talley Industries Inc 2702 N 44th Street Phoenix, AZ 85008 602-957-7711	Manufacturer of electronic components. Type: NYSE-TAL Ind: Manufacturing Grp: Manufacturing William H Mallender, CEO	Rev: 360	Assets: 533	Emp: 4
Talman Home Fed Savings & Loan Inc 30 W Monroe Street Chicago, IL 60603 312-726-8915	Thrift institution. Type: NASDAQ-TLMN Ind: Savings & Loan Grp: Financial Theodore H Roberts, CEO William H Tyda, Pres Jerome P Croke, VCh Robert H Jones, CFO Jay T Fitts, Sls William Long, VP Wade Parker, VP	Rev: 543	Assets: 6337	Emp: 2
Tambrands Inc One Marcus Avenue Lake Success, NY 11042 516-437-8800	Manufacturer of personal care products. Type: NYSE-TMB Ind: Personal Care Grp: Consumer Prd E Russell Sprague, CEO Douglas J Hansen, Tres William J Liipfert, IS Kenneth Merrill, R&D Harry W Rowe, Sls Pablo P Zamora, VP John F H White, VP William Witt, VP Harry E Raber, VP Michael F Speed, VP Paul E Konney, PR	Rev: 563	Assets: 465	Emp: 4

Organizations Listed Alphabetically

Organization / Address / Phone	Descriptive Information	Revenue / Assets / Emp ($ mil) ($ mil) (thous)		

Tampa, City of
City Hall 306 E Jackson Street
Tampa, FL 33602
813-223-8251

City government.
Type: City Govt
Ind: Local Govt   Grp: Govt & Non-Prof
Sandra Freedman, CEO

Rev: 300
Assets: NM
Emp: 4

Tandem Computers Inc
19333 Vallco Parkway
Cupertino, CA 95014
408-725-6000

Manufacturer of mid range critical application computers.
Type: NYSE-TDM
Ind: Comput/Off Equip   Grp: High Tech
James G Treybig, CEO   Robert C Marshall, Pres   Gerd Stoecker, Tres
David J Rynne, CFO   Alois J Strnad, IS   Donald E Fowler, R&D
Lawrence W McGraw, Sls   Gerald L Peterson, Mkt   Ralph Ungermann, VP
Stephen Schmidt, VP   Jeri E Flinn, PR

Rev: 1315
Assets: 1318
Emp: 9

Tandon Corp
301 Science Drive
Moorpark, CA 93201
805-523-0340

Manufacturer of personal computers & workstations.
Type: NASDAQ-TCOR
Ind: Comput/Off Equip   Grp: High Tech
S Tandon, CEO

Rev: 309
Assets: 250
Emp: 4

Tandy Corp
1800 One Tandy Center
Fort Worth, TX 76102
817-390-3700

Manufacturer electronic products via retail stores.
Type: NYSE-TAN
Ind: Comput/Off Equip   Grp: High Tech
John V Roach, CEO   Paul L Hill, Tres   Phil Bradtmiller, CFO
Carroll Lou, IS   John Patterson, R&D   Bob Myers, Mkt
Jim Sheets, VP   John Burman, VP   Ronald L Parrish, VP
Jana Freundlich, VP   Louann Blaylock, IR   Emily Blackely, PR

Rev: 3794
Assets: 2530
Emp: 30

Tandy Electronics Manufacturing Inc
918 One Tandy Center
Fort Worth, TX 76102
817-390-3689

Manufacturer of consumer electronic products.
Type: Private-Sub   Par: Tandy Corp
Ind: Electronics   Grp: High Tech
Robert McClure, CEO

Rev: NA
Assets: NA
Emp: NA

Tang Industries Inc
1965 Pratt Blvd
Elk Grove, IL 60007
312-981-8200

Metal fabricating & distribution.
Type: Private
Ind: Steel   Grp: Basic Industries
Cyrus Tang, CEO

Rev: 750
Assets: NA
Emp: 7

Target Stores Inc
33 S Sixth Street
Minneapolis, MN 55440
612-370-6073

Operator of retail department stores.
Type: Private-Sub   Par: Dayton Hudson Corp
Ind: Retail/Merch   Grp: Retail
Robert Ulrich, CEO

Rev: NA
Assets: NA
Emp: NA

Tarrant County Government
100 E Weatherford
Ft Worth, TX 76196
817-334-1441

County government.
Type: County Govt
Ind: Local Govt   Grp: Govt & Non-Prof
Roy English, CEO

Rev: 300
Assets: NM
Emp: 3

Tasty Baking Co
2801 W Hunting Park Avenue
Philadelphia, PA 19129
215-221-8500

Food products manufacturing company; bread, baked goods.
Type: ASE
Ind: Food/Lodging   Grp: Consumer Service
Philip J Baur, CEO

Rev: 250
Assets: 200
Emp: 2

Tauber Oil Co
55 Waugh Drive
Houston, TX 77210
713-869-8700

Petroleum & petrochemical products.
Type: Private
Ind: Energy   Grp: Basic Industries
O J Tauber, CEO

Rev: 1000
Assets: NA
Emp: 1

Taubman Co Inc
PO Box 200
Bloomfield Hills, MI 48303
313-258-6800

Owner & operator of shopping centers.
Type: Private
Ind: Real Estate/Bldg   Grp: Business Service
A Alfred Taubman, CEO

Rev: 3000
Assets: NA
Emp: 1

Taubman Investment Co
200 Long Lake Road
Bloomfield Hills, MI 48013
313-258-7600

Department stores & restaurants.
Type: Private
Ind: Real Estate/Bldg   Grp: Business Service
A Alfred Taubman, CEO

Rev: 1000
Assets: NA
Emp: 10

Organizations Listed Alphabetically

Organization / Address / Phone	Descriptive Information	Revenue / Assets / Emp ($ mil) ($ mil) (thous)	

TBC Corp
4770 Hickory Hill Road
Memphis, TN 38181
901-363-8030

Operator of retail automotive parts & tires stores.
Type: NASDAQ-TBCC
Ind: Retail/Merch   Grp: Retail
Iriving Krantzman, CEO

Rev: 450
Assets: 200
Emp: 3

TBWA Advertising Inc
292 Madison Avenue
New York, NY 10017
212-725-1150

Advertising agency.
Type: Private
Ind: Business Service   Grp: Business Service
William Tragos, CEO

Rev: 550
Assets: NA
Emp: 1

TCBY Enterprises Inc
113300 Rodney Parham
Little Rock, AR 72212
501-225-0349

Operator of fast food retail stores; frozen yogurt.
Type: NASDAQ-TCBY
Ind: Food/Lodging   Grp: Consumer Service
F Hickingbotham, CEO

Rev: 200
Assets: 150
Emp: 1

TCC Beverages Ltd(Coca Cola Sys Canada)
42 46 Overlea Blvd
Toronto, ON M4H 1B8 Can
416-424-6000

Regional bottler of soft drinks.
Type: TOR
Ind: Food Processing   Grp: Food Processing
Ira C Herbert, CEO

Rev: 745
Assets: 539
Emp: 5

TCF Banking & Savings Inc
801 Marquette Avenue
Minneapolis, MN 55402
612-370-7000

Thrift institution.
Type: NASDAQ-TCF
Ind: Savings & Loan   Grp: Financial
William A Cooper, CEO   Thomas Cusick, Pres   Joseph Clifford, VCh
Lynn Nagorske, CFO   Earl Stratton, IS   Gregory Czerwinski, Mkt
Neil Whitehouse, VP   Gregory Pulles, VP   Cynthia Wind, PR

Rev: 581
Assets: 5259
Emp: 2

TDC Development Corp
3100 E 29th Street
Long Beach, CA 90801
213-433-9931

Real estate development & management company.
Type: Private-Sub
Ind: Real Estate/Bldg   Grp: Business Service
not available, CEO

Rev: 1100
Assets: NA
Emp: 2

Team Inc
1019 S Hood
Alvin, TX 77511
713-331-6154

Manufacturer of machinery, trucking, communications.
Type: NASDAQ-TMI
Ind: Machinery   Grp: Manufacturing
Wesley Hall, CEO

Rev: 250
Assets: 125
Emp: 1

Tech Data Corp
5777 Myerlake Circle
Clearwater, FL 33518
813-539-7429

Operator of retail stores; personal computers.
Type: NASDAQ-TECD
Ind: Retail/Merch   Grp: Retail
Edward Raymund, CEO

Rev: 275
Assets: 150
Emp: 1

TECO Energy (Tampa Elec) Inc
702 N Franklin Street
Tampa, FL 33602
813-228-4111

Electric power utility company.
Type: NYSE
Ind: Utility   Grp: Utilities
H L Culbreath, CEO   Timothy L Guzzle, Pres   Girard Anderson, VCh
Alan Oak, CFO   Gregory Ehlers, IS   Royston Eustace, VP
Keith Surgenor, VP   James H Woodroffe, VP

Rev: 1034
Assets: 2315
Emp: 4

Tecumseh Products Co
100 E Patterson
Tecumseh, MI 49286
517-423-8411

Manufacturer of automotive parts.
Type: OTC
Ind: Manufacturing   Grp: Manufacturing
Kenneth G Herrick, CEO   Todd W Herrick, Chr   Harry L Hans, VCh
John Foss, CFO   Dennis Salo, IS   Ottel Rieger, R&D
Jack Duncan, Mkt   L D Thomson, VP   S O Kruger, VP
E B Rapin, VP   F D Randall, VP   Kenneth F Goldmann, PR

Rev: 1094
Assets: 900
Emp: 10

Tejas Gas Corp
333 Clay Street
Houston, TX 77002
713-658-0509

Production & transmission of natural gas.
Type: NASDAQ-HAML
Ind: Energy   Grp: Basic Industries
F Hamilton, CEO

Rev: 250
Assets: 125
Emp: 1

Tejon Ranch Corp
4436 Lebec Road
Lebec, CA 93243
805-248-6774

Real estate development company.
Type: ASE-TRC
Ind: Food Processing   Grp: Food Processing
Jack Hunt, CEO

Rev: 14
Assets: 42
Emp: 1

Organizations Listed Alphabetically

Organization / Address / Phone	Descriptive Information	Revenue / ($ mil)	Assets / ($ mil)	Emp (thous)
Tektronix Inc 14150 SW Karl Braun Drive Beaverton, OR 97077 503-627-7111	Manufacturer of electronic products & systems. Type: NYSE-TEK Ind: Instruments Grp: High Tech David P Friedley, CEO Larry N Choruby, CFO Richard Knight, IS Kevin Considine, R&D Lawrence Kaplin, VP Frederick Hanson, VP John Landis, VP Allan Leedy, VP Fletcher Chamberlin, IR Jan Ohman, PR	Rev: 1412 Assets: 1024 Emp: 16		
Telco Oilfield Services Inc 105 Pondview Drive Meriden, CT 06450 203-237-9655	Oil field service company. Type: Private-Sub Par: Sonat Inc Ind: Oil Service Grp: Business Service Ralph Spinnier, CEO	Rev: NA Assets: NA Emp: NA		
Telecom USA Inc 61 Perimeter Park NE Atlanta, GA 30341 404-458-4927	Telecommunications company; cellular telephones. Type: Private Ind: Telecom Grp: High Tech Gene Gabbard, CEO	Rev: 200 Assets: 150 Emp: 2		
Telecomm Plus International Inc 8000 N Federal Highway Boca Raton, FL 33431 407-997-9999	Nationwide consulting company. Type: Private Ind: Consulting Grp: Business Service Has Schromm, CEO	Rev: 300 Assets: NA Emp: 3		
Telecommunications Inc 4643 S Ulster Street Denver, CO 80237 303-721-5500	Cable television, programming & investment company. Type: NASDAQ-TCOMA Ind: Publishing/Com Grp: Consumer Service Bob Magness, CEO John Malone, Pres	Rev: 1709 Assets: 6296 Emp: 8		
Teledyne Aerospace Systems Div 1007 E 10th Street Fairmont, MN 56031 507-235-3355	Manufacturer of industrial aviation, electronic parts. Type: Private-Sub Par: Teledyne Inc Ind: Aerospace Grp: High Tech Alton Reinke, CEO	Rev: NA Assets: NA Emp: NA		
Teledyne Continental Motors Inc 76 Getty Street Muskegon, MI 49442 616-724-2151	Manufacturer of industrial machinery parts. Type: Private-Sub Par: Teledyne Inc Ind: Machinery Grp: Manufacturing Thomas Keenan, CEO	Rev: NA Assets: NA Emp: NA		
Teledyne Controls Div 12333 W Olympic Blvd West Los Angeles, CA 90064 213-820-4616	Manufacturer of electronic control equipment. Type: Private-Sub Par: Teledyne Inc Ind: Electronics Grp: High Tech J Rodrequez, CEO	Rev: NA Assets: NA Emp: NA		
Teledyne Inc 1901 Avenue of the Stars Los Angeles, CA 90067 213-277-3311	Manufacturer of aircraft engines & aerospace equipment. Type: NYSE Ind: Conglomerate Grp: Manufacturing Henry E Singleton, CEO George A Roberts, Chr Hudson Drake, VCh Gordon Bean, CFO William Rutledge, Mkt Judith Nelson, VP Leo Killen, VP	Rev: 4598 Assets: 5125 Emp: 60		
Teledyne Republic Div 15655 Brookpark Road Cleveland, OH 44142 216-267-2700	Manufacturer of electronic equipment. Type: Private-Sub Par: Teledyne Inc Ind: Electronics Grp: High Tech Richard Finley, CEO	Rev: NA Assets: NA Emp: NA		
Teledyne Ryan Electronics Div 8650 Balboa Avenue San Diego, CA 92123 619-560-6400	Electronics manufacturer. Type: Private-Sub Par: Teledyne Inc Ind: Electronics Grp: High Tech Robert Steenburge, CEO	Rev: NA Assets: NA Emp: NA		
Teleflex Corp 155 S Limerick Road Limerick, PA 19468 215-948-5100	Manufacturer of aerospace equipment. Type: ASE-TFX Ind: Aerospace Grp: High Tech Lennox K Black, CEO	Rev: 350 Assets: 300 Emp: 2		

Organization / Address / Phone	Descriptive Information	Revenue / Assets / Emp ($ mil) ($ mil) (thous)		

Teleglobe Canada Ltd
600 McCaffrey Street
Montreal, PQ H3T1N1 Can
514-289-7272

Telecommucation services company.
Type: TOR
Ind: Telecom   Grp: High Tech
Jean Claude Delorme, CEO

Rev: 314
Assets: 769
Emp: 2

Telephone & Data Corp
79 W Monroe Street
Chicago, IL 60603
312-630-1900

Telephone systems & cellular phones; local utiltiy.
Type: ASE-TDS
Ind: Telecom   Grp: High Tech
Leroy Carlson, CEO

Rev: 250
Assets: 200
Emp: 3

Telerate Inc
One World Trade Center
New York, NY 10048
212-938-5200

Electronic communication of investment information.
Type: NYSE
Ind: Comput/Off Equip   Grp: High Tech
Neil S Hirsch, CEO   John P Terranova, Pres   John D Jessop, VCh
Alan L Zimmerman, CFO

Rev: 440
Assets: 543
Emp: 3

Temple Inland Inc
303 S Temple Drive
Diboll, TX 75941
409-829-1313

Forest products company; lumber, plywood, packaging.
Type: NYSE-TIN
Ind: Paper/Forest Prd   Grp: Basic Industries
Arthur Temple, CEO   Clifford Grum, Chr   W Wayne McDonald, CFO
Ben Lancashire, VP   David Dolben, VP   Joseph Tomlinson, VP
James Wash, VP   Chester Winter, VP   Richard Warner, VP
Joseph M Areddy, PR

Rev: 1774
Assets: 1982
Emp: 13

Temple University
Broad St & Montgomery Avenue
Philadelphia, PA 19122
215-787-7000

Major educational institution; university.
Type: University
Ind: University   Grp: Govt & Non-Prof
Peter J Liacouras, CEO

Rev: 350
Assets: 376
Emp: 36

Temple, Barker & Sloane Inc
33 Hayden Avenue
Lexington, MA 02173
617-861-7580

Nationwide consulting company.
Type: Private
Ind: Consulting   Grp: Business Service
Carl Sloane, CEO

Rev: 275
Assets: NA
Emp: 3

Tenneco Inc
Tenneco Bldg PO Box 2511
Houston, TX 77002
713-757-2131

Natural gas pipeline & automotive parts company.
Type: NYSE-TGT
Ind: Conglomerate   Grp: Manufacturing
J L Ketelsen, CEO   John P Diesel, Pres   Allen McInness, VCh
Robert T Blakely, CFO   Kenneth Otto, Mkt   Walter Sapp, Ops
Kenneth Allen, VP   Edward Bernacki, VP   Herbert Lanese, VP
Peter Menikoff, VP   Joseph Macrum, PR

Rev: 13591
Assets: 13857
Emp: 94

Tennesse Valley Authority Inc
400 W Summit Street
Knoxville, TN 37902
615-632-2101

Federally owned power utility.
Type: Govt Corp
Ind: Utility   Grp: Utilities
Marvin Runyon, CEO   Marvin Runyon, Chr   John B Waters, Pres
William F Willis, VCh   William Malec, CFO   Louis Grande, IS
William Bivens, R&D   Jimmy L Cross, Ops   Craven Crowell, VP
Oliver Kinglsey, VP   Joseph Bynum, VP

Rev: 5322
Assets: 25823
Emp: 12

Tennessee, State of
State Capitol
Nashville, TN 37219
615-741-2001

State government.
Type: State Govt
Ind: State/Prov Govt   Grp: Govt & Non-Prof
Ned Ray McWherter, CEO

Rev: 8799
Assets: NM
Emp: 79

Teradyne Inc
321 Harrison Avenue
Boston, MA 02118
617-482-2700

Manufacturer of electronic test equipment.
Type: NYSE
Ind: Instruments   Grp: High Tech
Alexander V d'Arbeloff, CEO   Loren G Eaton, VCh   Owen W Robbins, CFO
Frederick T Van Veen, VP   Richard Testa, VP   Stuart Osattin, VP

Rev: 463
Assets: 434
Emp: 5

Terex Corp
201 W Walnut Street
Green Bay, WI 54303
414-453-5322

Manufacturer of industrial & mining equipment.
Type: NASDAQ-TERX
Ind: Manufacturing   Grp: Manufacturing
R Lenz, CEO

Rev: 500
Assets: 350
Emp: 4

Organizations Listed Alphabetically

Organization / Address / Phone	Descriptive Information	Revenue / ($ mil)	Assets / ($ mil)	Emp (thous)
Tesoro Petroleum Corp 8700 Tesoro Drive PO Box 17536 San Antonio, TX 78286 512-828-8484	Oil & gas exploration, production & marketing company. Type: NYSE Ind: Energy Grp: Basic Industries Dennis F Juren, CEO Donald Bonacci, VCh James R Hyslop, CFO Jack Watson, IS William W Cromey, Mkt Peter Woofter, VP W Reed Williams, VP John Tidmarsh, VP Jerry Casparis, VP Kathryn W Moser, PR	Rev: 1172 Assets: 490 Emp: 3		
Texaco Canada Ltd 90 Wynford Drive Don Mills, ON M3C1K5 Can 416-441-7811	Petroleum production & marketing company. Type: TOR Ind: Energy Grp: Basic Industries Robert B Peterson, CEO P Bijur, Chr G H Agnew, Pres S J Walker, VCh C C Wild, CFO A J Galipeault, VP	Rev: 2263 Assets: 3482 Emp: 3		
Texaco Chemical Co 4800 Fournace Place Bellaire, TX 77401 713-666-8000	Chemical manufacturer. Type: Private-Sub Par: Texaco Inc Ind: Chemicals Grp: Basic Industries W Reals, CEO	Rev: NA Assets: NA Emp: NA		
Texaco Inc 2000 Westchester Avenue White Plains, NY 10650 914-253-4000	International petroleum production & distribution company. Type: NYSE Ind: Energy Grp: Basic Industries Alfred C DeCrane, CEO James W Kinnear, Chr James L Dunlap, Pres R G Brinkman, CFO J L Hodges, IS Dale F Pollart, R&D Gerald Rome, VP L Paul Teague, VP Joseph Butera, VP Floyd Ferguson, VP Mauricio Salazar, VP William K Tell Jr, IR Peter J Dowd, PR	Rev: 35138 Assets: 26337 Emp: 50		
Texaco Refining & Marketing Inc 1111 Rusk Avenue Houston, TX 77002 713-650-4000	Refine & market petroleum & natural gas products. Type: Private-Sub Par: Texaco Inc Ind: Energy Grp: Basic Industries Glen Tilton, CEO	Rev: NA Assets: NA Emp: NA		
Texaco USA Inc 1111 Rusk Avenue Houston, TX 77002 713-650-4000	Petroleum products distribution division. Type: Private-Sub Par: Texaco Inc Ind: Retail/Merch Grp: Retail James Dunlap, CEO	Rev: NA Assets: NA Emp: NA		
Texas A & M University Administrative Bldg College Station, TX 77843 713-845-3211	Major educational institution; university. Type: University Ind: University Grp: Govt & Non-Prof William H Moblem, CEO	Rev: 392 Assets: 396 Emp: 40		
Texas Air Corp (Continental Airlines) 333 Clay Street Suite 4040 Houston, TX 77002 713-658-9588	International airline. Type: ASE-TEX Ind: Airline Grp: Consumer Service Francisco A Lorenzo, CEO James Arpey, VCh Robert D Snedeker, CFO Robert Ferguson, R&D John B Adams, Mkt Charles Goolsbee, VP Cynthia Creager, VP Clark Onstad, VP Janice Bryant, VP Arthur Kent, VP Bruce Hicks, PR	Rev: 8752 Assets: 8199 Emp: 63		
Texas American Bancshares Inc 500 Throckmorton Street Fort Worth, TX 76102 817-884-4040	Commercial bank. Type: NYSE-TXA Ind: Banking Grp: Financial Joseph M Grant, CEO L O Brightbill III, Pres J C Brown, VCh Gary Cage, CFO Fred L Jones, IS Ann Quinn, Mkt Weldon Whiteside, VP Gretchen F Smith, VP Bruce Petty, VP Michael Morrison, VP Paul Isham, VP Jack L Gregory, VP Gail Cooksey, PR	Rev: 445 Assets: 4383 Emp: 4		
Texas Commerce Bancshares Inc 600 Travis Street Houston, TX 77002 713-236-4865	Commercial bank. Type: Private-Sub Par: Chemical New York Corp Ind: Banking Grp: Financial Ben Love, CEO	Rev: 1600 Assets: 19000 Emp: 8		

Organizations Listed Alphabetically

Organization / Address / Phone	Descriptive Information	Revenue / ($ mil)	Assets / ($ mil)	Emp (thous)
Texas Eastern Corp 1221 McKinney Street Houston, TX 77252 713-759-3131	Natural gas pipeline company. Type: NYSE-TET Ind: Utility Grp: Utilities I David Bufkin, CEO Dennis R Hendrix, Chr Henry A King, VCh Paul Fergeson, Tres H L Rush Jr, IS E E Hickam, VP Derrell Cody, VP G L Mazenec, VP Fred Wichlep, IR James R Young, PR	Rev: 3481 Assets: 5444 Emp: 8		
Texas Industries Inc 8100 Carpenter Freeway Dallas, TX 75247 214-637-3100	Producer of steel products for construction/manufacturing. Type: NYSE Ind: Building Mat Grp: Basic Industries Robert D Rogers, CEO Gordon E Forward, Chr Larry Clark, Tres Richard M Fowler, CFO Richard Harlow, IS Libor F Rostik, R&D Dennis E Beach, VP Ronald Lincoln, VP Lloyd Schmelzle, VP Jeffry Werner, VP Peter Wright, VP Robert C Moore, VP D Randall Jones, PR	Rev: 635 Assets: 662 Emp: 6		
Texas Instruments Inc 13500 N Central Expressway Dallas, TX 75265 214-995-2011	Manufacturer of electronic/electrical equipment. Type: NYSE Ind: Electronics Grp: High Tech Jerry Junkins, CEO William I George, Pres William A Aylesworth, CFO George H Heilmeier, R&D Liston M Rice Jr, Mkt Norman Neureiter, PR	Rev: 6295 Assets: 4428 Emp: 83		
Texas Oil & Gas Corp 1700 Pacific Avenue Dallas, TX 75201 214-954-2000	Oil & gas exploration & production company. Type: Private-Sub Par: USX Corp Ind: Energy Grp: Basic Industries Michael Talbert, CEO	Rev: NA Assets: NA Emp: NA		
Texas Teachers Retirement Fund 1001 Trinity Street Austin, TX 78701 512-397-6460	State investment agency; pension management. Type: State Govt Ind: Non-Bank Fin Grp: Financial Bruce Hineman, CEO	Rev: 450 Assets: 16500 Emp: 1		
Texas Tech University Administrative Bldg Lubbock, TX 79409 806-742-2011	Major educational institution; university. Type: University Ind: University Grp: Govt & Non-Prof Lauro G Cavazos, CEO	Rev: 143 Assets: 342 Emp: 26		
Texas Utilities Co 2001 Bryan Tower Dallas, TX 75201 214-653-4600	Electric power utility. Type: NYSE-TXU Ind: Utility Grp: Utilities Jerry Farrington, CEO Erle Nye, Pres W H Goodenough, CFO H B Keating, IS H Jarrell Gobbs, Mkt Peter Tinkham, VP T Baker, VP T R Griffin, PR	Rev: 4154 Assets: 16058 Emp: 16		
Texas Utilities Electric Co 2001 Bryan Tower Dallas, TX 75201 214-812-1200	Electric power utility company. Type: Private-Sub Par: Texas Utilities Co Ind: Utility Grp: Utilities Max Tanner, CEO	Rev: NA Assets: NA Emp: NA		
Texas Utilities Mining Co 400 N Olive Street Dallas, TX 75201 214-812-5600	Operator of fuel production facilities. Type: Private-Sub Par: Texas Utilities Co Ind: Metals/Mining Grp: Basic Industries John Janek, CEO	Rev: NA Assets: NA Emp: NA		
Texas, State of State Capitol Austin, TX 78711 512-463-4630	State government. Type: State Govt Ind: State/Prov Govt Grp: Govt & Non-Prof William P Clements, CEO	Rev: 35579 Assets: NM Emp: 229		
Textron Aircraft Engine Components Div 549 Cedar Street Newington, CT 06111 203-666-4601	Manufacturer of aircraft components. Type: Private-Sub Par: Textron Inc Ind: Aerospace Grp: High Tech Arthur Weigel, CEO	Rev: NA Assets: NA Emp: NA		

Organizations Listed Alphabetically

Organization / Address / Phone	Descriptive Information	Revenue / ($ mil)	Assets / ($ mil)	Emp (thous)
Textron Defense Systems Div 201 Lowell Street Wilmington, MA 01887 508-657-5111	Manufacturer of aerospace technology & parts. Type: Private-Sub Par: Textron Inc Ind: Aerospace Grp: High Tech Harold McCard, CEO	Rev: NA Assets: NA Emp: NA		
Textron Inc 40 Westminster Street Providence, RI 02903 401-421-2800	Manufacturer of aerospace equipment, financial services. Type: NYSE-TXT Ind: Conglomerate Grp: Manufacturing B F Dolan, CEO William Ledbetter, Pres Thomas D Soutter, VCh Dennis G Little, CFO Cecil W Labhart, IS William Anders, Ops Donald Farrar, VP Quentin Achuff, VP William Wayland, VP Raymond W Caine Jr, PR	Rev: 7286 Assets: 12554 Emp: 60		
Textron Marine Systems Div 6800 Plaza Drive Lowell, MA 01851 508-452-8961	Manufacturer of commercial products. Type: Private-Sub Par: Textron Inc Ind: Manufacturing Grp: Manufacturing J Kelly, CEO	Rev: NA Assets: NA Emp: NA		
TGI Friday's Inc 14665 Midway Road Dallas, TX 75380 214-450-5400	Operator of restaurants. Type: NYSE-TGI Ind: Food/Lodging Grp: Consumer Service Curtis L Carlson, CEO	Rev: 340 Assets: 400 Emp: 4		
Thermo Electron Corp 45 First Street Waltham, MA 02154 617-890-8700	Manufacturer of industrial process equipment. Type: NYSE-TMO Ind: Electronics Grp: High Tech George N Hatsopoulos, CEO Theo Melas-Kyriazi, Tres John N Hatsopoulos, CFO Robert Howard, Sls Peter Pantazelos, Mkt Arvin H Smith, VP John P Appleton, VP Marshall Armstrong, VP Jerry P Davis, VP William Rainville, VP	Rev: 501 Assets: 490 Emp: 4		
Thiokol Aerospace Group Inc 2475 Washington Blvd Ogden, UT 84401 801-625-4801	Developer of high technology propulsion systems. Type: Private-Sub Par: Thiokol Corp Ind: Aerospace Grp: High Tech E Garrison, CEO	Rev: NA Assets: NA Emp: NA		
Thiokol Corp 110 N Wacker Drive Chicago, IL 60606 312-807-2000	Manufacturer of aerospace products; propulsion systems. Type: NYSE-TKC Ind: Aerospace Grp: High Tech Charles S Locke, CEO	Rev: 1168 Assets: 900 Emp: 9		
Third National Bank Co 201 Fourth Avenue N Nashville, TN 37219 615-748-4000	Commercial bank. Type: OTC Ind: Banking Grp: Financial J Eugene Southwood, CEO	Rev: 500 Assets: 4000 Emp: 2		
Thomas & Betts Corp 920 Route 202 Raritan, NJ 08869 201-685-1600	International manufacturer of electronic components. Type: NYSE-TNB Ind: Electronics Grp: High Tech J David Parkinson, CEO T Kevin Dunnigan, Chr James Hay, VCh Ronald Babcock, CFO Charles Havers, IS James Oberlender, Mkt Janice Way, VP Reijo Salo, VP Dominic Pileggi, VP David Hunihan, VP Robert Berry, VP	Rev: 515 Assets: 493 Emp: 5		
Thomas Industries Inc 4360 Brownsboro Road Louisville, KY 40232 502-893-4600	Manufacturer of lighting equipment. Type: NYSE-TII Ind: Building Mat Grp: Basic Industries Thomas R Fuller, CEO Timothy Brown, VCh Phillip Stuecker, Tres C Barr Schuler, CFO Allan E Eggers, Mkt John S Kahler, Ops Floyd Worley, VP	Rev: 348 Assets: 208 Emp: 3		
Thompson, J Walter Group Inc 466 Lexington Avenue New York, NY 10017 212-210-7000	Nationwide advertising agency. Type: Private-sub-for Ind: Business Service Grp: Business Service Burt Manning, CEO	Rev: 500 Assets: NA Emp: 5		

Organizations Listed Alphabetically

Organization / Address / Phone	Descriptive Information	Revenue / Assets / Emp ($ mil) ($ mil) (thous)		

Thomson McKinnon Securities Inc
One New York Plaza
New York, NY 10004
212-482-7000

Investment firm; securities trading.
Type: Private
Ind: Securities   Grp: Financial
J Ronald Morgan, CEO

Rev: 750
Assets: 7000
Emp: 5

Thomson Newspapers Ltd
65 Queen Street W
Toronto, ON M5H2M8 Can
416-864-1710

Publisher of newspapers.
Type: TOR
Ind: Publishing/Com   Grp: Consumer Service
K R Thompson, CEO   Peter T Bogart, CFO   John A Tory, VP
Michael W Johnston, VP   Ronald B Mitchell, VP   Michael R Doody, VP

Rev: 1027
Assets: 1708
Emp: 13

Thorn Apple Valley
18700 W Ten Mile
Southfield, MI 48075
313-552-0700

Producer of packaged food products.
Type: Private
Ind: Food Processing   Grp: Food Processing
Henry S Dorfman, CEO   Joel Dorfman, Chr   Issac Gold, VCh
Louis Glazier, CFO   Doug Schultz, IS   Keith Jahnke, Sls
Joseph McCloskey, Mkt   George Weiss, VP   Michael Farley, PR

Rev: 593
Assets: 103
Emp: 4

Thorne Ernst & Whinney Ltd
Commerce Court W
Toronto, ON M5L1C6 Can
416-864-9520

National accounting firm.
Type: Private
Ind: Accounting   Grp: Business Service
Robert T Trunbull, CEO

Rev: 213
Assets: NM
Emp: 4

Three Beall Brothers Inc
1237 E Rusk Street
Jacksonville, TX 75766
214-586-9823

Operator of retail merchandise stores.
Type: Private
Ind: Retail/Merch   Grp: Retail
Frank Fietz, CEO

Rev: 550
Assets: NA
Emp: 5

ThreeCom (3Com) Corp
3165 Kifer Road
Santa Clara, CA 95052
408-562-6400

Computer networking company.
Type: OTC
Ind: Comput/Off Equip   Grp: High Tech
Bill Crouse, CEO

Rev: 400
Assets: 350
Emp: 4

Thrifty Corp
3424 Wilshire Blvd
Los Angeles, CA 90010
213-251-6000

Operator of retail drugstores.
Type: Private-Sub   Par: Pacific Enterprises Corp
Ind: Retail/Merch   Grp: Retail
Leonard Strauss, CEO

Rev: NA
Assets: NA
Emp: NA

Thrifty Oil Co
10000 Lakewood Blvd
Downey, CA 90240
213-923-9876

Distributor of petroleum products.
Type: Private
Ind: Retail/Merch   Grp: Retail
Ted Orden, CEO

Rev: 1000
Assets: NA
Emp: 1

Thums Long Beach Co Inc
300 Oceangate
Long Beach, CA 90802
213-436-9211

Petroleum products distribution company.
Type: Private
Ind: Energy   Grp: Basic Industries
Tom Klaric, CEO

Rev: 550
Assets: NA
Emp: 2

Thyssen USA Corp
1114 Avenue of the Americas
New York, NY 10036
212-512-9700

Manufacturer of steel products, auto bodies; US hdqtrs.
Type: Private-Sub-For
Ind: Steel   Grp: Basic Industries
Gunther Drechsler, CEO

Rev: 2200
Assets: NA
Emp: 1

TIAA CREF Inc
730 Third Avenue
New York, NY 10017
212-490-9000

Investment firm; pension fund management.
Type: Private
Ind: Non-Bank Fin   Grp: Financial
Clifton R Wharton, CEO   Walter E Ehlers, Pres   Richard J Adamski, Tres
Thomas G Walsh, CFO   James A Wolf, IS   Linda Lamel, R&D
Torrey D Dodson Jr, Mkt   John McCormack, VP   Russell Bone, VP
Susan P Young, VP   Robert Perrin, IR   Claire M Sheahan, PR

Rev: 8409
Assets: 30768
Emp: 3

TIC United Corp
4645 N Central
Dallas, TX 75205
214-559-0580

Truck transport company.
Type: Private
Ind: Transport   Grp: Business Service
Brian Parker, CEO

Rev: 275
Assets: NA
Emp: 2

Organizations Listed Alphabetically

Organization / Address / Phone	Descriptive Information	Revenue / ($ mil)	Assets / ($ mil)	Emp (thous)
Ticor Corp 6300 Wilshire Blvd Los Angeles, CA 90048 213-852-6000	Title insurance & real estate tax services. Type: Private Ind: Insurance Grp: Insurance Winston V Morrow, CEO	Rev: Assets: Emp:		750 2000 7
TIE Communications Inc 12 Commerce Drive Shelton, CT 06484 203-926-2000	Manufacturer of telephone products. Type: ASE-TIE Ind: Telecom Grp: High Tech Thomas L Kelly, CEO	Rev: Assets: Emp:		255 254 3
Tiffany Corp 727 Fifth Avenue New York, NY 10022 212-755-8000	Operator of jewelry stores. Type: NYSE-TIF Ind: Retail/Merch Grp: Retail William R Chaney, CEO	Rev: Assets: Emp:		290 250 1
Tiger International Inc 1888 Century Park E Los Angeles, CA 90067 213-522-6300	Air freight & trucking company. Type: Private-Sub Par: Federal Express Corp Ind: Business Service Grp: Business Service James A Cronin, CEO Larry G Morris, CFO Richard L Smith, IS Jack T Kane, Sls Ned H Wallace, Mkt Joseph K McDonnell, IR	Rev: Assets: Emp:		1300 1100 8
Time Inc Rockefeller Center New York, NY 10020 212-586-1212	Media & entertainment company; magazines, cable TV, books. Type: NYSE-TL Ind: Publishing/Com Grp: Consumer Service J Richard Munro, CEO N J Nicholas Jr, Pres Gerald Levin, VCh Glenn A Britt, CFO Philip Lochner, Sls Louis Slovinsky, PR	Rev: Assets: Emp:		4507 4913 20
Times Mirror Co Times Mirror Square Los Angeles, CA 90053 213-972-3700	Newspaper & magazine publishing, TV broadcasting & cable. Type: NYSE Ind: Publishing/Com Grp: Consumer Service Robert F Erburu, CEO David A Laventhol, Pres W Thomas Johnson, VCh Charles R Redmond, CFO Martin C Glassman, IS Edward E Johnson, R&D Phillip Williams, Mkt Charles R Redmond, Ops Donald Wright, VP Patrick Butler, VP Daniel Curry, VP Edward Johnson, VP Mark L Schwanbeck, IR Donald S Kellermann, PR	Rev: Assets: Emp:		3333 3476 28
Timex Group Inc Parkswood Extension Waterbury, CT 06722 203-573-5000	Manufacturer of consumer products; watches, clocks. Type: Private Ind: Instruments Grp: High Tech James W Binns, CEO	Rev: Assets: Emp:		825 NA 2
Timken Co 1835 Dueber Avenue SW Canton, OH 44706 216-438-3000	Manufacturer of bearings. Type: NYSE-TKR Ind: Machinery Grp: Manufacturing W R Timken, CEO Joseph F Toot Jr, Pres Peter T Ashton, VCh J Kevin Ramsey, CFO P J Kost, IS R Leibensperger, R&D P J Ashton, Mkt Donald L Hart, VP Robert Leibensperger, VP Thomas M Cline, IR James P Mulder, PR	Rev: Assets: Emp:		1554 1593 18
Tishman Realty Corp 520 Madison Avenue New York, NY 10022 212-957-5400	Real estate development & investment company. Type: Private Ind: Real Estate/Bldg Grp: Business Service Robert Tishman, CEO	Rev: Assets: Emp:		750 NA 1
TJ International Inc 9777 W Chinden Blvd Boise, ID 83714 208-375-4450	Manufacturer of building products, doors, frames. Type: NASDAQ-TJCO Ind: Building Mat Grp: Basic Industries H E Thomas, CEO	Rev: Assets: Emp:		400 200 3
TJX Corp One Mercer Road Natick, MA 01760 508-651-6000	Operator of discounted retail family apparel stores. Type: Private-Sub Par: Zayre Corp Ind: Retail/Merch Grp: Retail Bernard Cammarata, CEO	Rev: Assets: Emp:		1921 1000 22
TLC Beatrice Internatl Holding Co 99 Wall Street New York, NY 10005 212-269-4544	Food processing. Type: Private Ind: Conglomerate Grp: Manufacturing Reginald F Lewis, CEO	Rev: Assets: Emp:		1500 NA 10

Organizations Listed Alphabetically

Organization / Address / Phone	Descriptive Information	Revenue / ($ mil)	Assets / ($ mil)	Emp (thous)
TMK United Corp 3001 Third Avenue S Birmingham, AL 35233 205-325-4200	Insurance company. Type: Private Ind: Non-Bank Fin Grp: Financial John W Rotenstreich, CEO	Rev: Assets: Emp:	250 450 2	
TNP Texas New Mexico Power Co 4100 International Plaza Fort Worth, TX 76113 817-731-0099	Electric power utility company. Type: NYSE Ind: Utility Grp: Utilities R D Woofter, CEO	Rev: Assets: Emp:	366 435 1	
Todd Shipyards Corp 1102 SW Massachusetts Seattle, WA 98134 206-223-1560	Shipbuilding & repair company. Type: NYSE Ind: Manufacturing Grp: Manufacturing L David Black, CEO	Rev: Assets: Emp:	351 394 4	
Tokai Bank Ltd 534 W Sixth Street Los Angeles, CA 90014 213-972-0200	Commercial bank. Type: Private-Sub-For Ind: Banking Grp: Financial A Hasegawa, CEO	Rev: Assets: Emp:	800 7000 3	
Toledo Edison Co 300 Madison Avenue Toledo, OH 43652 419-249-5000	Electrical utility company. Type: Private-Sub Par: Centerior Energy Corp Ind: Utility Grp: Utilities Robert J Farling, CEO Murray R Edelman, Pres Paul Smart, VCh Donald Saunders, CFO Thomas Quinn, Mkt David Monseau, Ops Richard Crouse, VP E Lyle Pepin, VP Donald Shelton, VP	Rev: Assets: Emp:	628 4135 3	
Toledo, City of City Hall 1 Government Center Toledo, OH 43604 419-245-1001	City government. Type: City Govt Ind: Local Govt Grp: Govt & Non-Prof Donna Owens, CEO	Rev: Assets: Emp:	250 NM 2	
Toll Brothers Corp 101 Witmer Road Horsham, PA 19044 215-441-4400	Builders & developers, one family homes. Type: NYSE-TOL Ind: Real Estate/Bldg Grp: Business Service Robert I Toll, CEO	Rev: Assets: Emp:	200 256 2	
Tonka Corp 6000 Clearwater Drive Minnetonka, MN 55343 612-936-3300	Toy manufacturing company. Type: Private Ind: Manufacturing Grp: Manufacturing Steven G Shank, CEO	Rev: Assets: Emp:	550 500 5	
Topco Associates Inc 7711 Gross Pointe Road Skokie, IL 60077 312-676-3030	Operator of retail food supermarkets. Type: Private Ind: Retail/Food Grp: Retail Marcell Lussier, CEO	Rev: Assets: Emp:	2200 NA 1	
Tops Markets Inc 60 Dingens Street Buffalo, NY 14206 716-823-3712	Grocery & convenience store. Type: Private Ind: Retail/Food Grp: Retail Savino P Nanula, CEO	Rev: Assets: Emp:	1000 NA 4	
Torchmark Corp 2001 Third Avenue S Birmingham, AL 35233 205-325-4200	Property & casualty insurance company. Type: NYSE-TMK Ind: Non-Bank Fin Grp: Financial R K Richey, CEO Jon W Rotenstreich, Pres William Graves, VCh Terry White, CFO Michael Fagin, Mkt Samuel Upchurch, Ops	Rev: Assets: Emp:	1670 4428 9	
Toro Co 8111 Lyndale Avenue S Bloomington, MN 55420 612-888-8801	Consumer lawn & home maintenance equipment. Type: NYSE-TTC Ind: Equipment Grp: Manufacturing Stephen F Keating, CEO Kendrick B Melrose, Chr David Morris, Pres Robert A Peterson, CFO Steve Gammon, IS Rich Mueller, Sls David Recker, Mkt J David McIntosh, VP Mary Elliott, PR	Rev: Assets: Emp:	609 268 3	

Organizations Listed Alphabetically

Organization / Address / Phone	Descriptive Information	Revenue / Assets / Emp ($ mil) ($ mil) (thous)		

Toronto Dominion Bank Ltd
Toronto Dominion Centre
Toronto, ON M5K1J4 Can
416-982-8222

Commercial bank.
Type: TOR
Ind: Banking   Grp: Financial
Robert M Thomson, CEO

Rev: 4370
Assets: 46346
Emp: 22

Toronto Hydro Ltd
14 Carlton Street
Toronto, ON M5B1K5 Can
416-595-6400

Electric power utility company.
Type: TOR
Ind: Utility   Grp: Utilities
Richard Hopkins, CEO

Rev: 394
Assets: 293
Emp: 1

Toronto Stock Exchange Ltd
Exchange Tower 2 First Canadian Place
Toronto, ON M5X1J2 Can
416-947-4700

Investment company; brokerage.
Type: Private
Ind: Non-Bank Fin   Grp: Financial
J Pearce Bunting, CEO

Rev: 213
Assets: 2125
Emp: 1

Toronto, University of
Administrative Bldg
Toronto, ON M5S1A1 Can
416-978-2011

Major educational institution; university.
Type: University
Ind: University   Grp: Govt & Non-Prof
John B Aird, CEO

Rev: 561
Assets: NM
Emp: 54

Torstar Corp
1 Yonge Street
Toronto, ON M5E1P9 Can
416-367-2000

Publisher of newspapers.
Type: TOR
Ind: Publishing/Com   Grp: Consumer Service
Beland H Honderich, CEO   David A Galloway, Pres   D Todd Smith, Tres
Robert J Steacy, CFO   Warren D Bingham, R&D   Thomas L Murtha, Sls
J Blair Mackenzie, VP   Diane Kesler-Corneil, VP   David R Jolley, VP
John F Baxter, VP

Rev: 813
Assets: 702
Emp: 5

Tosco Corp
2401 Colorado Avenue
Santa Monica, CA 90406
213-207-6000

Independent petroleum refiner.
Type: NYSE
Ind: Energy   Grp: Basic Industries
Clarence G Frame, CEO   John G Drosdick, Pres   Eric Schwartz, CFO
S Denny Smith, IS   William A Floyd, Mkt   Robert E Sears, IR
James E Simmons, PR

Rev: 1142
Assets: 556
Emp: 1

Toshiba America Electric Corp
9740 Irvine Blvd
Irvine, CA 92718
714-583-3000

Manufacturer & importer of electronic equipment; US hdqtrs.
Type: Private-Sub-For
Ind: Electronics   Grp: High Tech
Kiichi Hataya, CEO

Rev: 825
Assets: NA
Emp: 2

Total Petroleum North America Ltd
639 5th Avenue SW
Calgary, AB T2P0M9 Can
403-267-3000

Oil & gas production & marketing company.
Type: ASE-TPN
Ind: Energy   Grp: Basic Industries
Philippe Dunoyer, CEO

Rev: 1969
Assets: 1120
Emp: 5

Total System Services Corp
1000 Fifth Avenue
Columbus, GA 31901
404-649-2204

Bankcard processors.
Type: NASDAQ-TSTS
Ind: Business Service   Grp: Business Service
James H Blanchard, CEO   Richard Ussery, Chr   H Lynn Page, VCh
James P Lipham, CFO   Philip Tomlinson, Mkt   Kenneth E Evans, Ops
William Blizard, VP   William Pruett, VP   Kenneth Tye, VP
D John Boyd, VP

Rev: 56
Assets: 45
Emp: 1

Touche Ross & Co
1633 Broadway
New York, NY 10019
212-489-1600

Nationwide accounting firm.
Type: Private
Ind: Accounting   Grp: Business Service
Edward A Kangas, CEO

Rev: 1750
Assets: NA
Emp: 20

Touche Ross Ltd
150 King Street W
Toronto, ON M5H1J9 Can
416-599-5399

National accounting firm.
Type: Private
Ind: Accounting   Grp: Business Service
Allan Dilworth, CEO

Rev: 170
Assets: NM
Emp: 3

Towers, Perrin, Forster & Crosby Inc
245 Park Avenue
New York, NY 10167
212-309-3400

Nationwide consulting company.
Type: Private
Ind: Consulting   Grp: Business Service
James E Kielley, CEO

Rev: 500
Assets: NA
Emp: 5

Organization / Address / Phone	Descriptive Information	Revenue / ($ mil)	Assets / ($ mil)	Emp (thous)
Town & Country Corp 25 Union Street Chelsea, MA 02150 617-884-8500	Manufacturer & marketer of fine jewelrey. Type: ASE-TNC Ind: Manufacturing Grp: Manufacturing C Carey, CEO	Rev: Assets: Emp:	450 200 2	
Toyo Menka Trading Co USA One World Trade Center New York, NY 10048 212-466-4600	International trading company; US headquarters. Type: Private-Sub-For Ind: Manufacturing Grp: Manufacturing Hideo Hirata, CEO	Rev: Assets: Emp:	1100 NA 3	
Toyo Trust Ltd 444 S Flower Los Angeles, CA 90071 213-624-2424	Commercial bank. Type: Private-Sub-For Ind: Banking Grp: Financial Masaoki Takamura, CEO	Rev: Assets: Emp:	450 3500 1	
Toyota Canada Inc 1291 Bellamy Road N Scarborough, ON M1H 1H9 Can 416-438-6320	Automotive distributing & marketing company. Type: Private-Sub-For Ind: Automotive Grp: Manufacturing Oshio Kunii, CEO	Rev: Assets: Emp:	983 170 2	
Toyota Motor Sales USA 19000 S Western Street Torrance, CA 90509 213-618-4000	Manufacturer & importer of motor vehicles; US headquarters. Type: Private-Sub-For Ind: Automotive Grp: Manufacturing Yukiyasu Naimoli, CEO	Rev: Assets: Emp:	8800 NA 21	
Toys R Us Inc 395 W Passaic Street Rochelle Park, NJ 07662 201-845-5033	Retail stores; toys, childrens clothing. Type: NYSE-TOY Ind: Retail/Merch Grp: Retail Charles Lazarus, CEO Norman Ricken, Pres Robert C Nakasone, VCh Michael Goldstein, CFO Dennis Healey, IS Thomas Reinebach, R&D Van H Butler, Mkt E Kent Kinard, Ops Angela Bourdon, PR	Rev: Assets: Emp:	4001 2555 28	
Tracor Inc 6500 Tracor Lane Austin, TX 78725 512-926-2800	Manufacturer electronic equipment. Type: Private Ind: Electronics Grp: High Tech Donald N Smith, CEO	Rev: Assets: Emp:	750 500 9	
Trailer Train Corp 101 N Wacker Drive Chicago, IL 60606 312-853-3223	Automotive transport company. Type: Private Ind: Transport Grp: Business Service Raymond Burton, CEO	Rev: Assets: Emp:	515 1268 1	
Trailways Inc 901 Main Street Dallas, TX 75201 214-744-6500	Nationwide operator of consumer bus transportation system. Type: Private-Sub Ind: Transport Grp: Business Service Fred Currey, CEO	Rev: Assets: Emp:	275 NA 3	
Trammell Crow Corp 3500 LTV Center 2001 Ross Avenue Dallas, TX 75201 214-742-2000	Real estate development & management company. Type: Private Ind: Real Estate/Bldg Grp: Business Service J McDonald Williams, CEO	Rev: Assets: Emp:	1500 NA 6	
Trans Alta Utilities Corp 110 12th Avenue SW Calgary, AB T2P2M1 Can 403-267-7110	Utility holding company. Type: TOR-TAU Ind: Utility Grp: Utilities M M Williams, CEO K F McCready, Pres H G Schaeffer, VCh W A Veres, Tres W L Fraser, VP W Neiboer, VP W Saponja, VP	Rev: Assets: Emp:	818 3134 3	
Trans Canada Pipelines Ltd 530 8th Avenue SW Calgary, AB T2P2M7 Can 403-269-5611	Natural gas pipeline transportation company. Type: TOR-TRP Ind: Utility Grp: Utilities Gordon P Osler, CEO	Rev: Assets: Emp:	2779 4270 2	

Organizations Listed Alphabetically

Organization / Address / Phone	Descriptive Information	Revenue / Assets / Emp ($ mil) ($ mil) (thous)		

Trans World Airlines Inc
605 Third Avenue
New York, NY 10158
212-692-3000

Airline transportation company.
Type: NYSE-TWA
Ind: Airline Grp: Consumer Service
Carl C Icahn, CEO D Joseph Coor, Pres Mark Mulvaney, CFO
Jerry Doherty, IS Mort Ehrlich, Mkt Donald Morrison, PR

Rev: 4000
Assets: 3500
Emp: 29

Trans World Music Inc
38 Corporate Circle
Albany, NY 12203
518-452-1242

Operator of retail stores; video, audio cassetes & tapes.
Type: NASDAQ-TWMC
Ind: Retail/Merch Grp: Retail
Robert Higgins, CEO

Rev: 268
Assets: 225
Emp: 3

Transamerica Corp
600 Montgomery Street
San Francisco, CA 94111
415-983-4000

Diversified financial company; insurance, investment.
Type: NYSE-TA
Ind: Insurance Grp: Insurance
James R Harvey, CEO Frank C Herringer, Pres Gary L Depolo, CFO
Peter J Dawson, IS Lawrence W Briscoe, R&D Richard J Olsen, Mkt
William H McClave Jr, IR Greg G Wilcox, PR

Rev: 7879
Assets: 26759
Emp: 17

Transamerica Life Insurance Co
1150 S Olive Street
Los Angeles, CA 90015
213-742-3111

Life insurance company.
Type: Private-Sub Par: Transamerica Corp
Ind: Insurance Grp: Insurance
Richard J Eskoff, CEO Charles E LeDoyen, CFO

Rev: 2073
Assets: 5533
Emp: 1

Transamerica Occidental Life Ins Co
Hill & Olive at 12th Street
Los Angeles, CA 90015
213-742-2111

Life insurance company.
Type: Private-Sub Par: Transamerica Corp
Ind: Insurance Grp: Insurance
David Carpenter, CEO William A Simpson, Pres Charles E LeDoyen, CFO

Rev: 1700
Assets: 6000
Emp: 4

Transammonia Inc
350 Park Avenue
New York, NY 10022
212-223-3200

Trading fertilizers & petroleum products.
Type: Private
Ind: Chemicals Grp: Basic Industries
Ronald P Stanton, CEO

Rev: 1250
Assets: NA
Emp: 1

TransCapital Financial Corp(Ohio Sav Bk)
1100 Superior Avenue
Cleveland, OH 44114
216-621-9600

Thrift institution.
Type: NYSE-TFC
Ind: Savings & Loan Grp: Financial
Jack D Burstein, CEO

Rev: 619
Assets: 6361
Emp: 2

Transco Coal Co
2800 Post Oak Blvd
Houston, TX 77056
713-439-2000

Coal mining & processing company.
Type: Private-Sub Par: Transco Energy Co
Ind: Metals/Mining Grp: Basic Industries
James Wise, CEO

Rev: NA
Assets: NA
Emp: NA

Transco Energy Co
2800 Post Oak Blvd
Houston, TX 77056
713-439-2000

Natural gas transportation company.
Type: NYSE-E
Ind: Utility Grp: Utilities
George S Slocum, CEO John U Clark, Tres Jim P Wise, CFO
Susan K Chism, IS Jay P Lukens, R&D William H Heil, Mkt
Jay Elston, VP Larry Wolfe, VP Lee Mcduff, VP
Beverly Freeman, IR Gretchen Weis, PR

Rev: 2774
Assets: 3527
Emp: 5

Transcon Inc
625 The City Drive S
Orange, CA 92668
714-385-1591

Regional trucking company.
Type: NYSE-TCL
Ind: Transport Grp: Business Service
Orin S Neiman, CEO James R Chisholm, CFO Larry R Corn, Mkt

Rev: 322
Assets: 114
Emp: 4

Transcontinental Gas Pipeline Corp
2800 Post Oak Blvd
Houston, TX 77056
713-439-2000

Natural gas pipeline transmission company.
Type: Private-Sub Par: Transco Energy Co
Ind: Energy Grp: Basic Industries
George Slocum, CEO

Rev: NA
Assets: NA
Emp: NA

Transnational Motors Inc
618 Kenmore SE
Grand Rapids, MI 49506
616-949-7570

Manufacturer of automotive parts & components.
Type: Private
Ind: Automotive Grp: Manufacturing
Robert L Hooker, CEO

Rev: 500
Assets: NA
Emp: 3

Organizations Listed Alphabetically

Organization / Address / Phone	Descriptive Information	Revenue / ($ mil)	Assets / ($ mil)	Emp (thous)
Transok Inc 600 Main Street Tulsa, OK 74101 918-583-1121	Electric power utility company. Type: Private-Sub Par: Central & South West Corp Ind: Utility Grp: Utilities E Brooks, CEO	Rev: NA	Assets: NA	Emp: NA
Transport Canada 330 Sparks Street Place de Ville Tower Ottawa, ON K1A0N5 Can 613-996-5861	Federal government agency. Type: Federal Govt Ind: Federal Govt Grp: Govt & Non-Prof Glen Shortliffe, CEO Gerald Maier, Chr James M Cameron, Pres Mitchell T G Graye, CFO Charles Fischer, VP George Hugh, VP C Kennedy Orr, VP Raymond Sim, VP Robert Hodgins, VP Brian Hill, VP	Rev: 5610	Assets: NM	Emp: 21
Transtechnology Corp 15233 Ventura Blvd Van Nuys, CA 91403 213-990-5920	Manufacturer of electronic parts & connectors. Type: NYSE-TT Ind: Electronics Grp: High Tech Arch C Scurlock, CEO	Rev: 225	Assets: 200	Emp: 3
Travelers Co of Canada Ltd 400 University Avenue Toronto, ON M5G1S7 Can 416-586-3000	Life insurance company. Type: Private-Sub-For Ind: Insurance Grp: Insurance Daniel Damov, CEO	Rev: 303	Assets: 406	Emp: 1
Travelers Insurance Corp One Tower Square Hartford, CT 06183 203-277-0111	Life, property & casualty insurance company. Type: NYSE-TIC Ind: Insurance Grp: Insurance Edward H Budd, CEO Richard Shima, VCh Thomas O Thorsen, CFO Lawrence Bacon, IS Charles Wardell, Mkt Thomas Messmore, VP F Peter Libassi, PR	Rev: 18986	Assets: 53332	Emp: 29
Treasure Chest Advertising Inc 511 W Citrus Edge Glendora, CA 91470 818-914-3981	Marketing communications company. Type: Private Ind: Publishing/Com Grp: Consumer Service Sandy Scheller, CEO	Rev: 550	Assets: NA	Emp: 5
Tredegar Industries Inc 5020 Castlewood Road Richmond, VA 23234 804-275-9211	Manufacturer of railroad spikes & joints. Type: NYSE Ind: Manufacturing Grp: Manufacturing Frank Williams, CEO	Rev: 650	Assets: 350	Emp: 1
Tri Valley Growers Inc 1255 Battery Street Haas Bldg San Francisco, CA 94111 415-445-1600	Agricultural products packager & distributor. Type: Private Ind: Food Processing Grp: Food Processing James Saras, CEO	Rev: 550	Assets: NA	Emp: 1
Triangle Industries Inc 900 Third Avenue New York, NY 10022 212-230-3000	Manufacturer of coin counting equipment, vending machines. Type: NASDAQ-CJII Ind: Equipment Grp: Manufacturing Nelson Peltz, CEO Peter W May, Pres Joseph A Levato, CFO Henry J Leingang, IS Jerry Hostetter, PR	Rev: 2668	Assets: 1585	Emp: 15
Triangle Publications Inc 4 Radnor Center Radnor, PA 19087 215-293-8500	Publisher of magazines & periodicals. Type: Private Ind: Publishing/Com Grp: Consumer Service Joe Cele, CEO	Rev: 1100	Assets: NA	Emp: 3
Tribune Broadcasting Co 435 Michigan Avenue Chicago, IL 60611 312-222-3939	Television broadcasting cable TV & networks. Type: Private-Sub Par: Tribune Co Ind: Publishing/Com Grp: Consumer Service James C Dowdle, CEO	Rev: NA	Assets: NA	Emp: NA

Organizations Listed Alphabetically

Organization / Address / Phone	Descriptive Information	Revenue / ($ mil)	Assets / ($ mil)	Emp (thous)
Tribune Co 435 N Michigan Avenue Chicago, IL 60611 312-222-9100	Newspaper publishing company; TV broadcasting. Type: NYSE-TRB Ind: Publishing/Com Grp: Consumer Service Stanton R Cook, CEO Charles Brumback, Pres David Granat, Tres Scott C Smith, CFO R Mark Malloy, R&D Joseph Hays, Mkt Roy Bell, Ops Geoffrey Anderson, VP Vincent Casanova, VP Lisa Featherer, VP Dennis Homerin, VP Joyce Hutchinson, VP Robert Bousau, IR Joseph Andrew Hays, PR	Rev: Assets: Emp:		2335 2942 17
Tridel Enterprises Inc 4800 Dufferin Street Downsview, ON M3H5S9 Can 416-661-9290	Construction company. Type: Private-Sub Ind: Real Estate/Bldg Grp: Business Service Levio Delzotto, CEO	Rev: Assets: Emp:		340 595 2
Trilon Financial Corp Toronto Dominion Centre Royal Trust Tower Toronto, ON M5K1G8 Can 416-363-0061	Diversified financial company. Type: TOR-TFC Ind: Non-Bank Fin Grp: Financial Allen T Lambert, CEO Melvin M Hawkrigg, Chr Gordon Cunningham, Pres Frank N C Lochan, CFO J William Bartlett, R&D R Thomas Allen, VP Douglas S Alexander, VP Hartland MacDougall, VP Eric Daly, VP Derek Shanks, VP	Rev: Assets: Emp:		3301 27051 23
Trimac Ltd 800 5th Avenue SW Calgary, AB T2P2P9 Can 403-298-5100	Diversified transportation company. Type: TOR Ind: Transport Grp: Business Service John McCaig, CEO	Rev: Assets: Emp:		288 NA 3
Trinity Industries Inc 2525 Stemmons Freeway Dallas, TX 75207 214-631-4420	Rail car manufacturer. Type: NYSE-TRN Ind: Manufacturing Grp: Manufacturing W Ray Wallace, CEO Neil O Shoop, Tres K W Lewis, CFO John Sanford, IS R A Martin, Sls Ralph A Banks, VP Richard Brown, VP Lee McElroy, VP Jack Cunningham, VP F Dean Phillips, VP Dean Phelps, PR	Rev: Assets: Emp:		1001 878 6
Trinova Corp 1705 Indianwood Circle Maumee, OH 43537 419-891-2200	Manufacturer of control systems. Type: NYSE-TNV Ind: Machinery Grp: Manufacturing Darryl F Allen, CEO Stephen W Nagy, CFO Ralph F Lehman Jr, IS Charles A Lupien, R&D John P Nichols, VP James Kline, VP J Rodney Glansdorp, VP Howard Selland, VP Warren N Bimblick, IR Thomas Ainsworth, PR	Rev: Assets: Emp:		1919 1432 30
TriStar Pictures Inc 711 Fifth Avenue New York, NY 10022 212-751-4400	Motion pictures, televison & entertainment company. Type: Private Ind: Leisure Time Grp: Consumer Service Victor Kaufman, CEO	Rev: Assets: Emp:		350 750 2
Trizec Corp 700 2nd Street SW Calgary, AB T2P2W2 Can 403-269-8241	Diversified real estate development company. Type: TOR Ind: Real Estate/Bldg Grp: Business Service Harold P Milavsky, CEO Kevin E Benson, Pres Ron D Ghitter, VCh Joseph F Killi, CFO Robert J French, VP William G Chidley, VP	Rev: Assets: Emp:		1014 7325 6
Trump Organization Inc 725 Fifth Avenue New York, NY 10022 212-832-2000	Hotels, casinos & real estate development. Type: Private Ind: Real Estate/Bldg Grp: Business Service Vincent A Wasik, CEO	Rev: Assets: Emp:		1000 NA 10
Trust Co of the West Inc 400 S Hope Street Los Angeles, CA 90067 213-683-4000	Investment firm. Type: Private Ind: Non-Bank Fin Grp: Financial Tom E Larkin, CEO	Rev: Assets: Emp:		275 11000 2

Organization / Address / Phone	Descriptive Information	Revenue / Assets / Emp ($ mil) ($ mil) (thous)		

Trustcorp Inc
Three SeaGate
Toledo, OH 43603
419-259-8950

Commercial bank.
Type: NASDAQ-TTCO
Ind: Banking   Grp: Financial
Chester Devenow, CEO   John Joslin, Pres   Worth Wilson, VCh
Marege Cherri, IS   Thomas Cox, Mkt   J Lennard Barker, VP
Parker Freeman, VP   Robert Jacob, VP   Jeffery E Smith, VP
Kathy Rotte, IR   Peggy Bergeman, PR

Rev: 563
Assets: 5947
Emp: 3

TRW Electronic Products Inc
3650 N Nevada Avenue
Colorado Springs, CO 80907
303-475-0660

High technology services corporation.
Type: Private-Sub   Par: TRW Inc
Ind: Business Service   Grp: Business Service
Richard Godfrey, CEO

Rev: NA
Assets: NA
Emp: NA

TRW Inc
1900 Richmond Road
Cleveland, OH 44124
216-291-7000

Diversified, multinational, technology oriented company.
Type: NYSE-TRW
Ind: Electronics   Grp: High Tech
Joseph T Gorman, CEO   Ruben F Mettler, Chr   J R Burnett, VCh
Richard Whilden, IS   Melvin A Shader, R&D   Martin Coyle, VP
William Evans, VP   Chester Macey, VP   Charles Miller, VP
Robert D Lundy, PR

Rev: 6982
Assets: 4442
Emp: 73

TRW Pressure Systems Inc
2017 Camfield Avenue
Los Angeles, CA 90040
213-685-4520

Manufacturer of pressure control systems.
Type: Private-Sub   Par: TRW Inc
Ind: Manufacturing   Grp: Manufacturing
Michael Hersh, CEO

Rev: NA
Assets: NA
Emp: NA

Tucson Electric Power Co
220 W Sixth Street
Tucson, AZ 85702
602-622-6661

Electric power utility.
Type: NYSE-TEP
Ind: Utility   Grp: Utilities
Einar Greve, CEO   Joe G Coykendall, CFO   George Breen, R&D
Frederic N Finney, Ops   Joseph Wilcox, VP   Gary Ellerd, VP
Ira Adler, VP   Thomas Delawder, VP

Rev: 543
Assets: 2840
Emp: 2

Tucson Realty & Trust Inc
18990 E River Road
Tucson, AZ 85718
602-577-7000

Real estate development company.
Type: Private
Ind: Real Estate/Bldg   Grp: Business Service
Martin C O'Shea, CEO

Rev: 550
Assets: NA
Emp: 1

Tucson, City of
City Hall
Tucson, AZ 85726
602-791-4201

City government.
Type: City Govt
Ind: Local Govt   Grp: Govt & Non-Prof
Thomas J Volgy, CEO

Rev: 327
Assets: NM
Emp: 4

Tulane University
6823 St Charles Avenue
New Orleans, LA 70118
504-865-5000

Major educational institution; university.
Type: University
Ind: University   Grp: Govt & Non-Prof
Eamon A Kelly, CEO

Rev: 158
Assets: 198
Emp: 13

Tulsa, City of
City Hall 200 Civic Center
Tulsa, OK 74103
918-596-7777

City government.
Type: City Govt
Ind: Local Govt   Grp: Govt & Non-Prof
Rodger Randle, CEO

Rev: 250
Assets: NM
Emp: 3

Tultex Corportation
22 E Church Street
Martinsville, VA 24115
703-632-2961

Manufacturer of textile products; yarns, apparel.
Type: NYSE-TTX
Ind: Apparel/Textiles   Grp: Consumer Prd
W F Franck, CEO

Rev: 350
Assets: 300
Emp: 8

Tupperware Worldwide Inc
3175 N Orange Blossom Trail
Kissimmee, FL 32741
407-826-5050

Manufacturer & distributors of consumer products.
Type: Private-Sub   Par: Premark International Corp
Ind: Manufacturing   Grp: Manufacturing
William Jackson, CEO

Rev: NA
Assets: NA
Emp: NA

Turbo Resources Ltd
815 8th Avenue SW
Calgary, AB T2P3P2 Can
403-294-6400

Petroleum exploration & production company.
Type: TOR
Ind: Energy   Grp: Basic Industries
Robert G Brodie, CEO   Paul Core, VCh   Robert McClinton, CFO
Bruce Millar, Mkt   J Gerald Sioui, VP

Rev: 474
Assets: 306
Emp: 2

Organizations Listed Alphabetically

Organization / Address / Phone	Descriptive Information	Revenue / ($ mil)	Assets / ($ mil)	Emp (thous)

Turner Broadcasting System Inc
1050 Techwood Drive NW
Atlanta, GA 30318
404-827-1700

Cable & over the air television networks & stations.
Type: ASE-TBS
Ind: Publishing/Com   Grp: Consumer Service
R E Turner, CEO   Randolph Booth, Tres   Henry Gillespie, Sls
Burton Reinhardt, Ops   Robert Wussler, VP   Eugene Wright, VP
Gerald Hogan, VP   William Ghegan, VP

Rev: 652
Assets: 1838
Emp: 6

Turner Corp
633 Third Avenue
New York, NY 10017
212-878-0400

Nation's largest builder of commercial property.
Type: NYSE-TUR
Ind: Real Estate/Bldg   Grp: Business Service
Alfred T McNeill, CEO   Herbert D Conant, Chr   Allen H Wahlberg, CFO
Richard A Schell, IS   Frank Thomas, R&D   Thomas B Gerlach, Mkt
Anthony Breu, VP   Leslie Shute, VP   Ralph Johnson, VP
Jim Brown, PR

Rev: 3196
Assets: 920
Emp: 10

Turner Development Corp
4014 Gunn Highway
Tampa, FL 33624
813-963-0786

Real estate development company.
Type: Private-Sub   Par: Turner Corp
Ind: Real Estate/Bldg   Grp: Business Service
Y Roth, CEO

Rev: NA
Assets: NA
Emp: NA

TW Service Inc
S 61 Paramus Road
Paramus, NJ 07652
201-712-0500

Food service company; vending machines, restaurants.
Type: NYSE-TW
Ind: Food/Lodging   Grp: Consumer Service
Frank L Salizzoni, CEO

Rev: 3574
Assets: 2106
Emp: 120

Twentieth (20th) Century Industries Inc
6301 Owensmouth
Woodland Hills, CA 91367
818-704-3700

Property & casualty insurance company.
Type: NASDAQ-TWEN
Ind: Non-Bank Fin   Grp: Financial
Louis W Foster, CEO   Neil Ashley, Pres   Joseph J Urist, CFO
William Dailey, IS   William Crain, Mkt   William Mellick, Ops
Richard Andre, VP   Richard Dinon, VP   Margaret Chang, VP
A Kobayashi, VP

Rev: 622
Assets: 857
Emp: 2

Twin County Grocers Inc
145 Talmadge Road
Edison, NJ 08818
201-287-4600

Operator of retail food stores.
Type: Private
Ind: Retail/Food   Grp: Retail
James Burke, CEO

Rev: 1100
Assets: NA
Emp: 2

Tyco Laboratories Inc
One Tyco Park
Exeter, NH 03833
603-778-9700

Diversified manufacturer of control equipment,circuit boards
Type: NYSE-TYC
Ind: Manufacturing   Grp: Manufacturing
John F Fort, CEO   John Armacost, VCh   Richard D Power, CFO
Richard Dunn, VP   Irving Gutin, VP   Joshua Berman, VP
Katheryn H Carter, PR

Rev: 1575
Assets: 9419
Emp: 10

Tyler Corp
3200 San Jacinto Tower
Dallas, TX 75201
214-754-7800

Manufacturer of specialty chemicals; explosives.
Type: NYSE-TYL
Ind: Steel   Grp: Basic Industries
Joseph E McKinney, CEO   Charles Fisher, VCh   David L Smart, Tres
Richard Margerison, CFO   Thomas Landry, VP   Neil J O'Brien, VP
John Warner, VP   Lucy B LeBeau, PR

Rev: 665
Assets: 348
Emp: 6

Tyson Foods Inc
2210 W Oaklawn
Springdale, AR 72764
501-756-4000

Producer of packaged food products.
Type: NASDAQ-TYSNA
Ind: Food Processing   Grp: Food Processing
Don Tyson, CEO   Leland E Tollett, Pres   Wayne Britt, Tres
Gerald Johnston, CFO   Dan Snyder, IS   James Whitmore, R&D
Robert Womack, Sls   Donald E Wray, Mkt   Bob Justus, PR

Rev: 1936
Assets: 889
Emp: 16

UAL Inc (United Airlines)
1200 Algonquin Road
Elk Grove Townshp, IL 60666
312-952-4000

International airline.
Type: NYSE
Ind: Airline   Grp: Consumer Service
Stephen M Wolf, CEO   James Guyette, VCh   John C Pope, CFO
J Donald Karmazin, IS   John R Zeeman, Mkt   Hart A Langer, Ops
Marlys N Clark, VP   George J Aste, VP   Joseph T Kane, VP
Russell R Mack Jr, PR

Rev: 8982
Assets: 6701
Emp: 66

Organizations Listed Alphabetically

Organization / Address / Phone	Descriptive Information	Revenue / ($ mil)	Assets / ($ mil)	Emp (thous)
UAP Inc 1 Valleybrook Drive Montreal, PQ H3B2S8 Can 514-256-5031	Manufacturer of automotive parts. Type: MON Ind: Automotive Grp: Manufacturing Claude Ducharme, CEO	Rev: Assets: Emp:	298 170 2	
UBS Securities Inc 299 Park Avenue 4th Floor New York, NY 10171 212-230-4000	Investment firm; securities trading. Type: Private Ind: Securities Grp: Financial Alfred R Nangrard, CEO	Rev: Assets: Emp:	250 4400 1	
UDC Universal Development Corp 205 N Michigan Avenue Chicago, IL 60601 312-726-1885	Real estate developers, mortgage services, contracting. Type: NYSE-UDC Ind: Real Estate/Bldg Grp: Business Service J Mensk, CEO	Rev: Assets: Emp:	400 200 1	
UGI Corp 460 N Gulf Road King of Prussia, PA 19406 215-337-1000	Electric & gas utility company. Type: NYSE-UGI Ind: Utility Grp: Utilities James Sutton, CEO	Rev: Assets: Emp:	425 350 2	
UIS Inc 600 Fifth Avenue New York, NY 10020 212-581-7660	Auto parts manufacturer Type: Private Ind: Automotive Grp: Manufacturing Harry Lebensfeld, CEO	Rev: Assets: Emp:	500 NA 5	
Ultramar Canada Inc 2020 University Montreal, PQ H3A2L4 Can 514-499-6111	Oil & gas exploration & production company. Type: MON Ind: Energy Grp: Basic Industries Jean Gaulin, CEO	Rev: Assets: Emp:	1238 952 2	
UNC Inc 175 Admiral Cochrane Drive Annapolis, MD 21401 301-266-7333	Aerospace & aviation manufacturing. Type: NYSE-UNC Ind: Instruments Grp: High Tech Dan A Colussy, CEO Robert Pevenstein, CFO Marc R Jartman, Mkt Bruce R Robinson, VP Nicholas Kaufman, VP Vernon Hux, VP Rihcard Lange, VP	Rev: Assets: Emp:	401 408 3	
Unicorp American Corp 156 E 46th Street New York, NY 10017 212-972-6100	Real estate & investment service company. Type: ASE-UAC Ind: Real Estate/Bldg Grp: Business Service Wayne Stemmer, CEO	Rev: Assets: Emp:	266 250 1	
Unicorp Canada Corp (Union Enterprises) 21 St Clair Avenue E Toronto, ON M4T2T7 Can 416-961-1200	Diversified manufacturing company. Type: TOR Ind: Manufacturing Grp: Manufacturing George S Mann, CEO James Leech, Pres Michael R Kordyback, VCh Christopher Jamison, CFO Gordon Widdes, IS Mart Hommik, R&D Stephen Bellringer, Ops Deborah Stewart, VP Frederick Godard, VP	Rev: Assets: Emp:	1721 5041 4	
Unifi Inc 7201 W Friendly Avenue Greensboro, NC 27410 919-294-4410	Manufacturer of synthetic fibers. Type: NASDAQ-UNFI Ind: Manufacturing Grp: Manufacturing G Mebane, CEO	Rev: Assets: Emp:	400 200 2	
Unilever (United States) Inc 10 E 53rd Street New York, NY 10022 212-888-1260	Manufacturer of packaged goods; foods, detergents. Type: Private-Sub-For Ind: Food Processing Grp: Food Processing G Stevens, CEO	Rev: Assets: Emp:	5400 4500 41	
Unilever Canada Ltd 160 Bloor Street E Toronto, ON M4W3R2 Can 416-964-1857	Manufacturer of consumer packaged goods. Type: Private-Sub-For Ind: Food Processing Grp: Food Processing Lawrence Strong, CEO	Rev: Assets: Emp:	774 394 6	
Union Bank of Switzerland 299 Park Avenue New York, NY 10171 212-715-3000	Commercial bank. Type: Private-Sub-For Ind: Banking Grp: Financial Pierre deWeck, CEO	Rev: Assets: Emp:	450 3500 1	

Organizations Listed Alphabetically

Organization / Address / Phone	Descriptive Information	Revenue / ($ mil)	Assets / ($ mil)	Emp (thous)

Union Camp Corp
1600 Valley Road
Wayne, NJ 07470
201-628-2000

Packaging & chemical companies.
Type: NYSE
Ind: Paper/Forest Prd   Grp: Basic Industries
Raymond E Cartledge, CEO   James Piette, VCh   Donald Barney, Tres
J M Reed, CFO   J F Ineson, IS   W H Trice, R&D
C S Howell, Mkt   Russell Boekenheide, VP   William Howes, VP
James O Crisp, VP   Alexander Calder III, PR

Rev: 2661
Assets: 3094
Emp: 19

Union Carbide Canada Ltd
123 Eglinton Avenue E
Toronto, ON M4P1J3 Can
416-488-1444

Diversified manufacturer of chemical products.
Type: TOR
Ind: Chemicals   Grp: Basic Industries
W Norman Kissick, CEO   W Norman Kissick, Chr   Allan S Cole, Tres
Gilbert E Playford, CFO   Dennis C Champ, VP   Gilbert E Playford, VP
Steven J Roschuk, VP   Neil F Weaver, VP   Jan Gerhardt, VP

Rev: 483
Assets: 682
Emp: 5

Union Carbide Corp
39 Old Ridgbury Road
Danbury, CT 06817
203-794-2000

International chemical corporation.
Type: NYSE-UK
Ind: Chemicals   Grp: Basic Industries
Robert D Kennedy, CEO   J C Stephenson, CFO   L M Baker, R&D
Ronald S Wishart, PR

Rev: 8324
Assets: 8441
Emp: 44

Union Central Life Insurance Co
4850 Street Road
Trevose, PA 19049
215-322-3000

Life insurance company.
Type: Private-Mutual
Ind: Insurance   Grp: Insurance
Charles C Hinckley, CEO

Rev: 847
Assets: 2547
Emp: 2

Union Electric Co
1901 Chouteau Avenue PO Box 149
St Louis, MO 63166
314-621-3222

Electric power utility company.
Type: NYSE-UEP
Ind: Utility   Grp: Utilities
William E Cornelius, CEO   Earl K Dille, Pres   Donald Brandt, CFO
Harry G Meyer, IS   G James Haven, R&D   George Wagner, Mkt
Ronald Zdellar, VP   Michael Montana, VP   Harry Wuertenbacher, PR

Rev: 2029
Assets: 5827
Emp: 9

Union Enterprises Ltd
21 St Clair Avenue E
Toronto, ON M4T2T7 Can
416-964-6300

Utility holding company.
Type: Private-Sub   Par: Unicorp Canada Corp (Union Enterprises)
Ind: Utility   Grp: Utilities
George Mann, CEO

Rev: 1131
Assets: 1275
Emp: 6

Union Equity Cooperative Exchange Inc
2300 N 10th Street
Enid, OK 73701
405-233-5100

Oil refining & distribution cooperative.
Type: Private
Ind: Food Processing   Grp: Food Processing
William Allen, CEO

Rev: 550
Assets: NA
Emp: 1

Union Gas Holdings Corp
122 W Myrtle
Independence, KS 67301
316-331-4500

Producer & distributor of natural gas.
Type: Private
Ind: Energy   Grp: Basic Industries
Anthony L Geller, CEO

Rev: 1500
Assets: NA
Emp: 3

Union Gas Ltd
50 Kell Drive N
Chatham, ON N7M5M1 Can
519-352-3100

Natural gas utility company.
Type: Private-Sub   Par: Unicorp Canada Corp (Union Enterprises)
Ind: Utility   Grp: Utilities
W Darcy Mckeough, CEO

Rev: 1148
Assets: 1190
Emp: 3

Union Pacific Corp
345 Park Avenue
New York, NY 10154
212-418-7800

Railroad, trucking, natural resource & real estate company
Type: NYSE
Ind: Railroad   Grp: Business Service
Michael H Walsh, CEO   Drew Lewis, Chr   Gary Stewart, Tres
L White Matthews III, CFO   John P Halen, VP   John Dowling, VP
Edmund Hawley, VP   Carl Von Bernuth, VP   Charles Olsen, VP
Gary F Schuster, IR   Harvey Turner, PR

Rev: 7000
Assets: 11000
Emp: 30

Union Pacific Railroad Corp
1416 Dodge Street
Omaha, NE 68179
402-271-5000

Railroad transportation company.
Type: Private-Sub   Par: Union Pacific Corp
Ind: Railroad   Grp: Business Service
Michael Walsh, CEO

Rev: NA
Assets: NA
Emp: NA

Organizations Listed Alphabetically

Organization / Address / Phone	Descriptive Information	Revenue / Assets / Emp ($ mil) ($ mil) (thous)		

Union Texas Petroleum Inc
1330 Post Oak Blvd
Houston, TX 77056
713-623-6544

Petroleum products, development & exploration.
Type: NYSE-UTH
Ind: Energy   Grp: Basic Industries
William J Cepica, CEO   William Kripps, VCh   R L Ryan, CFO
Albert Berman, VP   William Brabham, VP   Sanford Lobliner, VP
T Keith Wiggins, VP   W L Brabham, PR

Rev: 1152
Assets: 1717
Emp: 2

Union Trust Co
300 Main Street
Stamford, CT 06904
203-348-6211

Commercial bank.
Type: Private-Sub   Par: Northeast Bancorportion
Ind: Banking   Grp: Financial
Frank J Kugler, CEO

Rev: 500
Assets: 4000
Emp: 2

Uniroyal Goodrich Canada Inc
409 Weber Street
Kitchener, ON N2G4J5 Can
519-749-8473

Manufacturer of automotive tires & rubber products.
Type: TOR
Ind: Tire/Rubber   Grp: Basic Industries
William Davis, CEO

Rev: 307
Assets: 206
Emp: 3

Unisys Canada Inc
2001 Sheppard Avenue E
North York, ON M2J4Z7 Can
416-495-0515

Manufacturer of a full range of computers.
Type: Private-Sub-For
Ind: Comput/Off Equip   Grp: High Tech
Kenneth Calmenson, CEO

Rev: 623
Assets: 436
Emp: 3

Unisys Corp
Township Line & Union Meeting Rd
Blue Bell, PA 19422
215-542-4011

Worldwide manufacturer of computers & related products.
Type: NYSE-UIS
Ind: Comput/Off Equip   Grp: High Tech
W Michael Blumenthal, CEO   Leon J Level, Tres   Curt Hessler, CFO
Alan G Jones, IS   Hollis L Caswell, R&D   Jeanette Lerman, IR
Jack McHale, PR

Rev: 9902
Assets: 11535
Emp: 90

United Artists Corp
2930 E Third Avenue
Denver, CO 80206
303-321-4242

Motion picture & cable television company.
Type: NYSE
Ind: Leisure Time   Grp: Consumer Service
Stewart D Blair, CEO

Rev: 842
Assets: 1904
Emp: 3

United Assn of Plumbing & Pipe Fitting
901 Massachusetts Avenue
Washington, DC 20001
202-628-5823

National labor union.
Type: Membership Org
Ind: Membership Org   Grp: Govt & Non-Prof
Marvin J Boede, CEO

Rev: 250
Assets: NM
Emp: 325

United Auto Workers
800 E Jefferson Avenue
Detroit, MI 48214
313-926-5000

National labor union.
Type: Membership Org
Ind: Membership Org   Grp: Govt & Non-Prof
Owen Bieber, CEO

Rev: 1000
Assets: NM
Emp: 1200

United Banks of Colorado Inc
1700 Lincoln Street
Denver, CO 80274
303-861-4700

Commercial bank.
Type: NASDAQ-UBKS
Ind: Banking   Grp: Financial
N Berne Hart, CEO   Charles R Hazelrigg, Pres   Dennis D Erickson, CFO
Richard Watt, IS   Candice W Rogers, Mkt   Peg McKechnie, IR
Mark L Swanson, PR

Rev: 438
Assets: 5540
Emp: 3

United Brands Co
One E Fourth Street
Cincinnati, OH 45202
513-579-2115

Food products company; Chiquita bananas, Morrell meats.
Type: NYSE-UB
Ind: Food Processing   Grp: Food Processing
Carl H Linder, CEO   Ronald F Walker, Pres   Keith Lindner, VCh
Fred J Runk, CFO   C Richard Keener, IS   Peter Shea, R&D
Robert Dearth, Ops   Robert Crowe, VP   Thomas Mitchell, VP
William Tsacalis, VP   Sandra Heinman, PR

Rev: 3503
Assets: 1436
Emp: 40

United Brotherhood of Carpenters America
101 Constitution Avenue NW
Washington, DC 20001
202-546-6206

National labor union.
Type: Membership Org
Ind: Membership Org   Grp: Govt & Non-Prof
Sigurd Lucassen, CEO

Rev: 500
Assets: NM
Emp: 600

United Cable Television Inc
4700 S Syracuse Parkway
Denver, CO 80237
303-779-5999

Operator of cable television systems.
Type: NYSE
Ind: Publishing/Com   Grp: Consumer Service
Gene W Schneider, CEO

Rev: 261
Assets: 697
Emp: 2

Organizations Listed Alphabetically

Organization / Address / Phone	Descriptive Information	Revenue / ($ mil)	Assets / ($ mil)	Emp (thous)
United Co Glenway Avenue Bristol, VA 24201 703-466-3322	Oil, gas, real estate, financial services. Type: Private Ind: Aerospace Grp: High Tech James W McGlochlin, CEO	Rev: Assets: Emp:		500 NA 2
United Cooperatives of Ontario Ltd 5600 Cantross Court Mississauga, ON L5A3A4 Can 416-890-8500	Agricultural cooperative. Type: Private-Coop Ind: Food Processing Grp: Food Processing Robert Bethune, CEO	Rev: Assets: Emp:		416 153 1
United Engineers & Construction Inc 30 S 17th Street Philadelphia, PA 19101 215-422-3000	Manufacturer of construction equipment. Type: Private-Sub Par: Raytheon Co Ind: Equipment Grp: Manufacturing Gunnar Sarsten, CEO	Rev: Assets: Emp:		NA NA NA
United Food & Commercial Workers Union 1775 K Street NW Washington, DC 20006 202-223-3111	National labor union. Type: Membership Org Ind: Membership Org Grp: Govt & Non-Prof William H Wynn, CEO	Rev: Assets: Emp:		1000 NM 1400
United Grain Growers Ltd 433 Main Street Winnipeg, MB R3C3A7 Can 204-944-5411	Agricultural cooperative. Type: Private Ind: Food Processing Grp: Food Processing L F J Hehn, CEO D R Cusitar, VP T M Allen, VP W G Morken, VP G W Moore, VP R W McGowan, VP M Sherman, VP	Rev: Assets: Emp:		748 277 2
United Grocers Inc 6433 SE Lake Road Milwalkee, OR 97222 503-653-6330	Operator of retail food stores. Type: Private Ind: Retail/Food Grp: Retail Allan Jones, CEO	Rev: Assets: Emp:		825 NA 3
United Healthcare Corp 300 Opus Center 9900 Bren Road E Minnetonka, MN 55343 612-936-1300	Operator of managed healthcare delivery systems, HMO'S. Type: NASDAQ-UNIH Ind: Health Care Grp: Consumer Service K L Simmons, CEO	Rev: Assets: Emp:		435 210 5
United Illuminating Co 80 Temple Street New Haven, CT 06506 203-787-7200	Electric power utility company. Type: NYSE Ind: Utility Grp: Utilities Richard J Grossi, CEO William Elder, Tres Robert Fiscus, CFO Charles Cook, R&D James Crowe, Mkt David Hoskinson, Ops Harold Moore, VP Stephen Goldschmidt, VP E Jon Majkowski, VP Robert Hyde, VP	Rev: Assets: Emp:		519 2365 2
United Industrial Corp 18 E 48th Street New York, NY 10017 212-752-8787	Manufacturer of industrial heat treating equipment. Type: NYSE-UIC Ind: Equipment Grp: Manufacturing Bernard Fein, CEO	Rev: Assets: Emp:		300 300 4
United Investors Inc 2001 Third Avenue S Birmingham, AL 35233 205-325-4200	Managers of investments via United Mutual Funds. Type: Private Ind: Non-Bank Fin Grp: Financial J P Bryan, CEO	Rev: Assets: Emp:		282 8003 2
United Jersey Banks Inc 301 Carnegie Center Princeton, NJ 08543 609-987-3200	Commercial bank. Type: NYSE-UJB Ind: Banking Grp: Financial T Joseph Stemrod, CEO John G Collins, Pres John Howell, VCh Jack Haggerty, CFO Alan Posencheg, IS Lenore Smith, Mkt Edmund Weiss, VP Lenore Smith, VP Donald Lewis, VP William Cosgrove, VP John Battaglia, VP Sandra Sosinski, IR Jim Adamczyk, PR	Rev: Assets: Emp:		1032 10311 3

Organizations Listed Alphabetically

Organization / Address / Phone	Descriptive Information	Revenue / ($ mil)	Assets / ($ mil)	Emp (thous)
United Merchants & Manufacturers Inc 1407 Broadway New York, NY 10018 212-930-3900	Manufacturer of apparel products. Type: NYSE Ind: Apparel/Textiles Grp: Consumer Prd Martin J Schwab, CEO Uzi Ruskin, Chr Sidney Margolis, VCh Judith A Nadzick, CFO William Carroll, IS Arthur Charwat, Mkt Harold Hoke, Ops Norman Forman, VP Michael Harris, VP Natalie Buchanan, PR	Rev: Assets: Emp:	646 412 10	
United Mine Workers of America 900 15th Street NW Washington, DC 20005 202-842-7200	National labor union. Type: Membership Org Ind: Membership Org Grp: Govt & Non-Prof Richard Trumka, CEO	Rev: Assets: Emp:	250 NM 200	
United Missouri Bancshares 1010 Grand Avenue Kansas City, MO 644141 816-556-7000	Commercial bank. Type: NASDAQ-UMSB Ind: Banking Grp: Financial Rufus Kemper, CEO Malcolm M Aslin, Pres William Teiwes, CFO Dan Spencer, IS J Lyle Wells, Sls Margie Hurley, Mkt Melinda Moss, PR	Rev: Assets: Emp:	600 6000 3	
United Nations First Avenue New York, NY 10017 212-963-1234	International organization of world governments. Type: Federal Govt Ind: Federal Govt Grp: Govt & Non-Prof Javier Perez de Cuellar, CEO	Rev: Assets: Emp:	2000 NM 4	
United of Omaha Life Insurance Co Mutual of Omaha Plaza Omaha, NE 68175 402-342-7600	Life insurance company. Type: OTC Ind: Insurance Grp: Insurance William J Hetzler, CEO	Rev: Assets: Emp:	882 3211 3	
United Paperworkers Intl Union 3340 Perimeter Hill Drive Nashville, TN 37202 615-834-8590	National labor union. Type: Membership Org Ind: Membership Org Grp: Govt & Non-Prof Wayne E Glenn, CEO	Rev: Assets: Emp:	250 NM 250	
United Parcel Service Inc 51 Weaver Street Greenwich, CT 06830 203-622-6000	Small package delivery company. Type: Private Ind: Business Service Grp: Business Service John Rogers, CEO Edwin A Jacoby, CFO Frank Erbrick, IS Robert Logan, R&D John W Alden, Mkt Robert E Smith, IR Robert Kenney, PR	Rev: Assets: Emp:	10000 NA 175	
United Refining Corp 15 Bradley Street Warren, PA 16365 814-723-1500	Petroleum refinery company. Type: Private Ind: Energy Grp: Basic Industries John A Catsimatidis, CEO	Rev: Assets: Emp:	750 NA 3	
United States Agency for Intl Develpmnt 320 Twenty-first Street NW Washington, DC 20523 202-647-1850	Federal government agency. Type: Federal Govt Ind: Federal Govt Grp: Govt & Non-Prof M Alan Woods, CEO	Rev: Assets: Emp:	750 NM 5	
United States AMTRAK Natl Rail Passenger 400 N Capitol Street NW Washington, DC 20001 202-383-3000	Federal government agency. Type: Federal Govt Ind: Federal Govt Grp: Govt & Non-Prof W Graham Clayton, CEO	Rev: Assets: Emp:	1000 NM 10	
United States Central Intelligence Agncy Office of Logistics Washington, DC 20505 703-351-1100	Federal government agency. Type: Federal Govt Ind: Federal Govt Grp: Govt & Non-Prof William H Webster, CEO	Rev: Assets: Emp:	2000 NM 10	
United States Commodity Credit Corp Dept of Ag Fourteenth St & Independence Washington, DC 20250 202-447-5237	Federal government agency. Type: Federal Govt Ind: Federal Govt Fin Grp: Financial Milton J Hertz, CEO	Rev: Assets: Emp:	2000 NM 3	

Organizations Listed Alphabetically

Organization / Address / Phone	Descriptive Information	Revenue / Assets / Emp ($ mil) ($ mil) (thous)		

United States Courts
Supreme Court Bldg 1 First Street NE
Washington, DC 20543
202-479-3000

Judicial branch of the United States Federal Government.
Type: Federal Govt
Ind: Federal Govt   Grp: Govt & Non-Prof
William H Rehnquist, CEO

Rev: 1541
Assets: NM
Emp: 9

United States Dept Health & Human Serv
200 Independence Avenue SW
Washington, DC 20201
202-245-6296

Federal government agency.
Type: Federal Govt
Ind: Federal Govt   Grp: Govt & Non-Prof
Louis W Sullivan, CEO

Rev: 11000
Assets: NM
Emp: 43

United States Dept Housing & Urban Dev
451 Seventh Street SW
Washington, DC 20410
202-655-4000

Federal government agency.
Type: Federal Govt
Ind: Federal Govt   Grp: Govt & Non-Prof
Jack F Kemp, CEO

Rev: 3261
Assets: NM
Emp: 13

United States Dept of Agriculture
Fourteenth St & Independence Ave
Washington, DC 20250
202-447-2791

Federal government agency.
Type: Federal Govt
Ind: Federal Govt   Grp: Govt & Non-Prof
Clayton K Yeutter, CEO

Rev: 50842
Assets: NM
Emp: 104

United States Dept of Commerce
Fourteenth St & Constitution Ave
Washington, DC 20230
202-377-2000

Federal government agency.
Type: Federal Govt
Ind: Federal Govt   Grp: Govt & Non-Prof
Robert A Mosbacher, CEO

Rev: 3152
Assets: NM
Emp: 86

United States Dept of Defense
The Pentagon
Washington, DC 20301
202-545-6700

Federal government agency.
Type: Federal Govt
Ind: Federal Govt   Grp: Govt & Non-Prof
Richard Cheney, CEO

Rev: 3000
Assets: NM
Emp: 28

United States Dept of Education
400 Maryland Avenue SW
Washington, DC 20202
202-245-3192

Federal government agency.
Type: Federal Govt
Ind: Federal Govt   Grp: Govt & Non-Prof
Lauro F Cavazos, CEO

Rev: 25886
Assets: NM
Emp: 5

United States Dept of Energy
1000 Independence Avenue SW
Washington, DC 20585
202-586-5000

Federal government agency.
Type: Federal Govt
Ind: Federal Govt   Grp: Govt & Non-Prof
James D Watkins, CEO

Rev: 12404
Assets: NM
Emp: 16

United States Dept of Justice
Constitution Avenue & Tenth St NW
Washington, DC 20530
202-633-2000

Federal government agency.
Type: Federal Govt
Ind: Federal Govt   Grp: Govt & Non-Prof
Dick Thornburgh, CEO

Rev: 6882
Assets: NM
Emp: 80

United States Dept of Labor
200 Constitution Avenue NW
Washington, DC 20210
202-523-8165

Federal government agency.
Type: Federal Govt
Ind: Federal Govt   Grp: Govt & Non-Prof
Elizabeth H Dole, CEO

Rev: 31379
Assets: NM
Emp: 18

United States Dept of State
2201 C Street NW
Washington, DC 20520
202-647-4000

Federal government agency.
Type: Federal Govt
Ind: Federal Govt   Grp: Govt & Non-Prof
James A Baker, CEO

Rev: 4437
Assets: NM
Emp: 26

United States Dept of the Air Force
The Pentagon
Washington, DC 20330
202-545-6700

Federal government agency, Department of Defense.
Type: Federal Govt
Ind: Federal Govt   Grp: Govt & Non-Prof
Edward C Aldridge, CEO

Rev: 107800
Assets: NM
Emp: 931

United States Dept of the Army
The Pentagon
Washington, DC 20310
202-545-6700

Federal government agency, Department of Defense.
Type: Federal Govt
Ind: Federal Govt   Grp: Govt & Non-Prof
John O Marsh, CEO

Rev: 85700
Assets: NM
Emp: 1110

Organizations Listed Alphabetically

Organization / Address / Phone	Descriptive Information	Revenue / Assets / Emp ($ mil) ($ mil) (thous)		

Organization / Address / Phone	Descriptive Information	Rev	Assets	Emp
United States Dept of the Interior 1800 C Street NW Washington, DC 20240 202-343-3171	Federal government agency. Type: Federal Govt Ind: Federal Govt Grp: Govt & Non-Prof Manuel Lujan, CEO	2953	NM	9
United States Dept of the Navy The Pentagon Washington, DC 20350 202-545-6700	Federal government agency, Department of Defense. Type: Federal Govt Ind: Federal Govt Grp: Govt & Non-Prof William L Ball, CEO	109500	NM	1113
United States Dept of the Treasury 1500 Pennsylvania Avenue NW Washington, DC 20220 202-566-2000	Federal government agency. Type: Federal Govt Ind: Federal Govt Grp: Govt & Non-Prof Nicholas F Brady, CEO	13000	NM	156
United States Dept of Transportation 400 Seventh Street SW Washington, DC 20590 202-366-4000	Federal government agency. Type: Federal Govt Ind: Federal Govt Grp: Govt & Non-Prof Samuel K Skinner, CEO	27772	NM	64
United States Environmental Protect Agcy 401 M Street SW Washington, DC 20460 202-382-2090	Federal government agency. Type: Federal Govt Ind: Federal Govt Grp: Govt & Non-Prof William K Reilly, CEO	4787	NM	15
United States Export-Import Bank 811 Vermont Avenue NW Washington, DC 20571 202-566-8990	Federal government agency. Type: Federal Govt Ind: Federal Govt Fin Grp: Financial John A Bohn, CEO	1500	22000	3
United States Farmers Home Admim Dept of Ag Fourteenth St & Independence Washington, DC 20250 202-447-4323	Federal government agency. Type: Federal Govt Ind: Federal Govt Fin Grp: Financial Vance Clark, CEO	1000	NM	2
United States General Services Admin Eighteenth & F Streets NW Washington, DC 20405 202-655-4000	Federal government agency. Type: Federal Govt Ind: Federal Govt Grp: Govt & Non-Prof John E Alderson, CEO	3360	NM	19
United States Information Agency 301 Fourth Street SW Washington, DC 20547 202-655-4000	Federal government agency. Type: Federal Govt Ind: Federal Govt Grp: Govt & Non-Prof Bruce S Gelb, CEO	1400	NM	9
United States Internal Revenue Service Dept of the Treasury 1111 Constitution NW Washington, DC 20224 202-566-5000	Federal government agency. Type: Federal Govt Ind: Federal Govt Grp: Govt & Non-Prof Lawrence B Gibbs, CEO	11101	NM	67
United States Leasing International Inc 733 Front Street San Francisco, CA 94111 415-627-9000	Car, truck, equipment rental & leasing. Type: Private-Sub Par: Ford Motor Co Ind: Non-Bank Fin Grp: Financial D E Mundell, CEO Lynn K Ducken, CFO John L Whipple, IS Ernest J Haycox, PR	548	2218	2
United States Natl Aerospace & Space Adm 600 Independence Avenue NW Washington, DC 20546 202-453-1000	Federal government agency. Type: Federal Govt Ind: Federal Govt Grp: Govt & Non-Prof James C Fletcher, CEO	13148	NM	24
United States Nuclear Regulatory Comm 1717 H Street NW Washington, DC 20555 301-492-7000	Federal government agency. Type: Federal Govt Ind: Federal Govt Grp: Govt & Non-Prof Lando W Zech, CEO	500	NM	3

Organizations Listed Alphabetically

Organization / Address / Phone	Descriptive Information	Revenue / ($ mil)	Assets / ($ mil)	Emp (thous)
United States Office of Personnel Mgt 1900 E Street NW Washington, DC 20415 202-632-5491	Federal government agency. Type: Federal Govt Ind: Federal Govt Grp: Govt & Non-Prof Constance Berry Newman, CEO	Rev: Assets: Emp:		850 NM 5
United States Panama Canal Commission 2000 L Street NW Washington, DC 20036 202-634-6441	Federal government agency. Type: Federal Govt Ind: Federal Govt Grp: Govt & Non-Prof Dennis P McAuliffe, CEO	Rev: Assets: Emp:		1400 NM 9
United States Postal Service 475 L'Enfant Plaza SW Washington, DC 20260 202-268-2000	Postal service for the United States. Type: Federal Govt Ind: Federal Govt Grp: Govt & Non-Prof John N Griesemer, CEO	Rev: Assets: Emp:		36000 NM 802
United States Small Business Admin Imperial Bldg 1441 L Street NW Washington, DC 20416 202-653-6554	Federal government agency. Type: Federal Govt Ind: Federal Govt Grp: Govt & Non-Prof Susan S Engeleiter, CEO	Rev: Assets: Emp:		437 NM 4
United States Social Security Admin Dept Health/Human Serv 6401 Security Blvd Baltimore, MD 21235 301-594-1234	Federal government agency. Type: Federal Govt Ind: Federal Govt Grp: Govt & Non-Prof Dorcas R Hardy, CEO	Rev: Assets: Emp:		15000 NM 71
United States Veterans Administration 810 Vermont Avenue NW Washington, DC 20420 202-233-2300	Federal government agency. Type: Federal Govt Ind: Federal Govt Grp: Govt & Non-Prof Edward J Derwinski, CEO	Rev: Assets: Emp:		29963 NM 206
United Stationers Inc 2200 E Golf Road Des Plaines, IL 60016 312-699-5000	Stationery, office supply & furniture company. Type: NASDAQ-USTR Ind: Comput/Off Equip Grp: High Tech Joel Spungin, CEO Frank A Ehmann, Pres Marshall A Gardner, CFO Patrick L Murray, IS Arnold W Johnsen, Sls Joseph R Templet, Mkt Jerold Hecktman, PR	Rev: Assets: Emp:	1000 500 3	
United Steelworkers of America 815 Sixteenth Street NW Washington, DC 20006 202-638-6929	National labor union. Type: Membership Org Ind: Membership Org Grp: Govt & Non-Prof Lynn Williams, CEO	Rev: Assets: Emp:		500 NM 900
United Technologies Corp United Technologies Bldg Hartford, CT 06101 203-728-7000	Jet engines, helicopters, missiles, elevators, air cond. Type: NYSE-UTX Ind: Aerospace Grp: High Tech Robert F Daniell, CEO Franklyn A Caine, Tres Mark S Coran, CFO John M Hammitt, IS Robert J Hermann, R&D Franklin J Parisi, PR	Rev: Assets: Emp:	18518 12748 185	
United Technologies Space Systems Div United Technologies Bldg Hartford, CT 06101 203-728-7000	Engineer & design space systems. Type: Private-Sub Par: United Technologies Corp Ind: Aerospace Grp: High Tech William Evans, CEO	Rev: Assets: Emp:	NA NA NA	
United Telecommunications Inc 2330 Shawnee Mission Parkway Westwood, KS 66205 913-676-3000	Nationwide telephone utility holding company. Type: NYSE-UT Ind: Telecom Grp: High Tech Paul H Henson, CEO William T Esrey, Chr John F Dodd, VCh C W Battey, CFO John A Mihalovich, IS Dan J Evanoff, Mkt Don Jensen, VP Gene Betts, VP Dan Evanoff, VP Donald Forsythe, VP Jay Keithley, VP Donald G Forsythe, PR	Rev: Assets: Emp:	6493 9817 42	
United Telephone Co of Florida 555 Lake Border Drive Altamonte Springs, FL 32715 407-889-6000	Telephone utility company. Type: Private-Sub Par: United Telecommunications Inc Ind: Telecom Grp: High Tech Troy Todd, CEO	Rev: Assets: Emp:	NA NA NA	

Organizations Listed Alphabetically

Organization / Address / Phone	Descriptive Information	Revenue / ($ mil)	Assets / ($ mil)	Emp (thous)
United Telephone Co of Indiana 3570 E US 30 Warsaw, IN 46580 219-267-6161	Telephone utility company. Type: Private-Sub Par: United Telecommunications Inc Ind: Telecom Grp: High Tech George White, CEO	Rev: Assets: Emp:	NA NA NA	
United Telephone of Ohio 665 Lexington Avenue Mansfield, OH 44907 419-755-8011	Telephone utility company. Type: Private-Sub Par: United Telecommunications Inc Ind: Telecom Grp: High Tech D Kelly, CEO	Rev: Assets: Emp:	NA NA NA	
United Van Lines (Unigroup) Inc 1 United Drive Fenton, MO 63026 314-326-3100	Moving company. Type: Private Ind: Transport Grp: Business Service Robert J Baer, CEO Maurice Greenblatt, Chr James R Kendrick, CFO Charles R Childers, IS James Wilson, Mkt Cliff Saxton, IR Barb Schaumburg, PR	Rev: Assets: Emp:	750 250 3	
United Westburne Inc 6333 Boul Decarie Montreal, PQ H3W3E1 Can 514-342-5181	Manufacturer of plumbing fixtures. Type: Private-Sub-For Ind: Manufacturing Grp: Manufacturing Sam Abramavitvch, CEO	Rev: Assets: Emp:	1469 674 12	
Univar Corp 1600 Norton Bldg 801 Second Avenue Seattle, WA 98104 206-447-5911	Manufacturer of specialty chemicals. Type: NYSE-UVX Ind: Chemicals Grp: Basic Industries James H Wiborg, CEO James W Bernard, Chr Gary Pruitt, Tres N Stewart Rogers, CFO Barry C Maulding, VP Robert A Steinseifer, VP Guenter Zimmer, VP Albert McNeight, VP David C Gentry, VP	Rev: Assets: Emp:	1117 395 5	
Universal City Studios Inc 100 Universal City Studios Drive Universal City, CA 91608 818-777-1000	Distribution of motion pictures, television, radio. Type: Private-Sub Par: MCA Inc Ind: Leisure Time Grp: Consumer Service S J Stein, CEO	Rev: Assets: Emp:	NA NA NA	
Universal Coop Inc 7801 Metro Parkway Minneapolis, MN 55420 612-854-0800	Diversified manufacturer of automotive parts & components. Type: Private Ind: Automotive Grp: Manufacturing Patrick Finley, CEO	Rev: Assets: Emp:	275 NA 1	
Universal Foods Corp 433 E Michigan Street Milwaukee, WI 53202 414-271-6755	Food processor; cheeses, food ingredients. Type: NYSE-UFC Ind: Food Processing Grp: Food Processing John L Murray, CEO David B Essner, CFO Don Bardonner, IS Gary W Sanderson, R&D Harry J Smith, Sls Leigh Brinkeroff, Mkt Gary Sanderson, VP James Palo, VP F Preston Mottram, VP Paula C Norton, PR	Rev: Assets: Emp:	721 404 5	
Universal Furniture Industries Inc 2622 Uwharrie Road High Point, NC 27263 919-884-4322	Furniture manufacturer. Type: OTC Ind: Appliances/Furn Grp: Manufacturing Carter Fox, CEO	Rev: Assets: Emp:	400 200 4	
Universal Health Services Inc 367 S Gulph Road King of Prussia, PA 19406 215-768-3300	Operator of acute care & psychiatric hospitals. Type: NASDAQ-UHSIB Ind: Health Care Grp: Consumer Service Alan B Miller, CEO Sidney Miller, VCh Kirk Gorman, CFO Robert Fleming, R&D Steven Volla, Ops Thomas Bender, VP Richard Wright, VP Bruce Gilbert, VP Joyce Lunney, VP Marian Simpson, VP Steve Filton, VP	Rev: Assets: Emp:	860 543 14	
Universal Leaf Tobacco Co Inc 1501 N Hamilton Street Richmond, VA 23230 804-359-9311	Tobacco brokerage & service company; insurance services. Type: NYSE-UVV Ind: Tobacco Grp: Food Processing Gordon L Crenshaw, CEO Henry Harrell, Pres O Kemp Dozier, CFO James Poulson, IS Nancy Powell, IR Debra Outlaw, PR	Rev: Assets: Emp:	2104 943 14	

Organizations Listed Alphabetically

Organization / Address / Phone	Descriptive Information	Revenue / Assets / Emp ($ mil) ($ mil) (thous)		
University of Akron Administrative Bldg Akron, OH 44325 216-375-7111	Major educational institution; university. Type: University Ind: University Grp: Govt & Non-Prof William V Muse, CEO	Rev: Assets: Emp:	95 196 29	
University of Arizona Administrative Bldg Tucson, AZ 85721 602-626-4824	Major educational institution; university. Type: University Ind: University Grp: Govt & Non-Prof Henry Koffler, CEO	Rev: Assets: Emp:	374 484 34	
University of Cal San Diego Administrative Bldg La Jolla, CA 92092 714-452-2230	Major educational institution; university. Type: University Ind: University Grp: Govt & Non-Prof Richard C Atkinson, CEO	Rev: Assets: Emp:	415 411 14	
University of Cal San Francisco Administrative Bldg San Francisco, CA 94143 415-669-9000	Major educational institution; university. Type: University Ind: University Grp: Govt & Non-Prof Julius R Krevans, CEO	Rev: Assets: Emp:	395 371 5	
University of California Berkeley Administrative Bldg Berkeley, CA 94720 415-642-6000	Major educational institution; university. Type: University Ind: University Grp: Govt & Non-Prof Ira Michael Heyman, CEO	Rev: Assets: Emp:	428 751 38	
University of California Davis Administrative Bldg Davis, CA 95616 916-752-1011	Major educational institution; university. Type: University Ind: University Grp: Govt & Non-Prof Theodore L Hullar, CEO	Rev: Assets: Emp:	428 516 22	
University of California Los Angeles 405 Hilgard Avenue Los Angeles, CA 90024 213-825-4321	Major educational institution; university. Type: University Ind: University Grp: Govt & Non-Prof Charles E Young, CEO	Rev: Assets: Emp:	799 583 40	
University of Chicago 5801 S Ellis Chicago, IL 60637 312-753-1234	Major educational institution; university. Type: University Ind: University Grp: Govt & Non-Prof Hanna Holborn Gray, CEO	Rev: Assets: Emp:	435 356 16	
University of Cincinnati Clifton Avenue Cincinnati, OH 45221 513-475-8000	Major educational institution; university. Type: University Ind: University Grp: Govt & Non-Prof Joseph A Steger, CEO	Rev: Assets: Emp:	381 431 40	
University of Colorado Administrative Bldg Boulder, CO 80309 303-492-0111	Major educational institution; university. Type: University Ind: University Grp: Govt & Non-Prof James N Corbridge, CEO	Rev: Assets: Emp:	189 255 25	
University of Connecticut Administrative Bldg Storrs, CT 06268 203-486-2337	Major educational institution; university. Type: University Ind: University Grp: Govt & Non-Prof John T Casteen, CEO	Rev: Assets: Emp:	176 325 26	
University of Florida Administrative Bldg Gainesville, FL 32611 904-392-3261	Major educational institution; university. Type: University Ind: University Grp: Govt & Non-Prof Marshall M Criser, CEO	Rev: Assets: Emp:	440 573 41	
University of Georgia Administrative Bldg Athens, GA 30602 404-542-3030	Major educational institution; university. Type: University Ind: University Grp: Govt & Non-Prof Charles B Knapp, CEO	Rev: Assets: Emp:	266 352 29	

Organizations Listed Alphabetically

Organization / Address / Phone	Descriptive Information	Revenue / Assets / Emp ($ mil) ($ mil) (thous)		

University of Hawaii
2500 Campus Road
Honolulu, HI 96822
808-948-8111

Major educational institution; university.
Type: University
Ind: University   Grp: Govt & Non-Prof
Albert J Simone, CEO

Rev: 204
Assets: 361
Emp: 23

University of Houston
4800 Calhoun Blvd
Houston, TX 77004
713-749-1011

Major educational institution; university.
Type: University
Ind: University   Grp: Govt & Non-Prof
Richard L VanHorn, CEO

Rev: 211
Assets: 356
Emp: 34

University of Illinois
Administrative Bldg
Champaign, IL 61801
217-333-1000

Major educational institution; university.
Type: University
Ind: University   Grp: Govt & Non-Prof
Morton W Weir, CEO

Rev: 460
Assets: 777
Emp: 40

University of Illinois at Chicago
1737 W Polk
Chicago, IL 60680
312-996-3000

Major educational institution; university.
Type: University
Ind: University   Grp: Govt & Non-Prof
Donald N Langenberg, CEO

Rev: 396
Assets: 660
Emp: 27

University of Iowa
Administrative Bldg
Iowa City, IA 52242
319-353-2121

Major educational institution; university.
Type: University
Ind: University   Grp: Govt & Non-Prof
Hunter R Rawling, CEO

Rev: 415
Assets: 631
Emp: 34

University of Kansas
Administrative Bldg
Lawrence, KS 66045
913-864-2700

Major educational institution; university.
Type: University
Ind: University   Grp: Govt & Non-Prof
Gene A Budig, CEO

Rev: 151
Assets: 416
Emp: 27

University of Kentucky
Administrative Bldg
Lexington, KY 40506
606-258-9000

Major educational institution; university.
Type: University
Ind: University   Grp: Govt & Non-Prof
David P Roselle, CEO

Rev: 334
Assets: 326
Emp: 24

University of Louisville
Administrative Bldg
Louisville, KY 40292
502-588-5555

Major educational institution; university.
Type: University
Ind: University   Grp: Govt & Non-Prof
Donald C Swain, CEO

Rev: 194
Assets: 298
Emp: 22

University of Maryland
Administrative Bldg
College Park, MD 20742
301-454-0100

Major educational institution; university.
Type: University
Ind: University   Grp: Govt & Non-Prof
Michael K Hooker, CEO

Rev: 279
Assets: 354
Emp: 41

University of Massachusetts
Administrative Bldg
Amherst, MA 01003
413-545-0111

Major educational institution; university.
Type: University
Ind: University   Grp: Govt & Non-Prof
Joseph Duffey, CEO

Rev: 264
Assets: 264
Emp: 30

University of Miami
Administrative Bldg
Coral Gables, FL 33124
305-284-2211

Major educational institution; university.
Type: University
Ind: University   Grp: Govt & Non-Prof
Edward T Foote, CEO

Rev: 263
Assets: 260
Emp: 21

University of Michigan
Administrative Bldg
Ann Arbor, MI 48109
313-764-1817

Major educational institution; university.
Type: University
Ind: University   Grp: Govt & Non-Prof
James J Duderstadt, CEO

Rev: 818
Assets: 971
Emp: 39

University of Michigan Hospitals Inc
1500 E Medical Center
Ann Arbor, MI 48109
313-936-4000

Operator of hospitals & clinics.
Type: Private
Ind: Health Care   Grp: Consumer Service
John Forsyth, CEO

Rev: 511
Assets: NA
Emp: 6

Organizations Listed Alphabetically

Organization / Address / Phone	Descriptive Information	Revenue ($ mil)	Assets ($ mil)	Emp (thous)
University of Minnesota 100 Church Street Minneapolis, MN 55455 612-373-2851	Major educational institution; university. Type: University Ind: University Grp: Govt & Non-Prof Richard J Sauer, CEO	Rev: 748	Assets: 991	Emp: 52
University of Missouri 105 Jesse Hall Columbia, MO 65211 314-882-3387	Major educational institution; university. Type: University Ind: University Grp: Govt & Non-Prof Haskell Monroe, CEO	Rev: 303	Assets: 249	Emp: 25
University of Nebraska 14th & R Streets Lincoln, NE 68588 402-472-7211	Major educational institution; university. Type: University Ind: University Grp: Govt & Non-Prof Martin A Massengale, CEO	Rev: 359	Assets: 451	Emp: 25
University of New Mexico Administrative Bldg Albuquerque, NM 87131 505-277-0111	Major educational institution; university. Type: University Ind: University Grp: Govt & Non-Prof Gerald May, CEO	Rev: 144	Assets: 245	Emp: 27
University of North Carolina Administrative Bldg Chapel Hill, NC 27514 919-962-2338	Major educational institution; university. Type: University Ind: University Grp: Govt & Non-Prof Paul Harden, CEO	Rev: 389	Assets: 427	Emp: 25
University of North Texas Administrative Bldg Denton, TX 76203 817-565-2000	Major educational institution; university. Type: University Ind: University Grp: Govt & Non-Prof Alfred F Hurley, CEO	Rev: 94	Assets: 118	Emp: 23
University of Oklahoma 660 Parrington Oval Norman, OK 73019 405-624-5000	Major educational institution; university. Type: University Ind: University Grp: Govt & Non-Prof David Swank, CEO	Rev: 167	Assets: 216	Emp: 22
University of Pennsylvania Administrative Bldg Philadelphia, PA 19104 215-898-5000	Major educational institution; university. Type: University Ind: University Grp: Govt & Non-Prof E Sheldon Hackney, CEO	Rev: 580	Assets: 1201	Emp: 26
University of Pittsburgh 4200 Fifth Avenue Pittsburgh, PA 15260 412-624-4141	Major educational institution; university. Type: University Ind: University Grp: Govt & Non-Prof Wesley W Posvar, CEO	Rev: 308	Assets: 422	Emp: 33
University of South Carolina Administrative Bldg Columbia, SC 29208 803-777-0411	Major educational institution; university. Type: University Ind: University Grp: Govt & Non-Prof James B Holderman, CEO	Rev: 166	Assets: 521	Emp: 23
University of South Florida 4202 Flagler Avenue Tampa, FL 33620 813-974-2011	Major educational institution; university. Type: University Ind: University Grp: Govt & Non-Prof Francis T Borkowski, CEO	Rev: 130	Assets: 187	Emp: 31
University of Southern California University Park Los Angeles, CA 90089 213-743-2311	Major educational institution; university. Type: University Ind: University Grp: Govt & Non-Prof James H Zumberge, CEO	Rev: 381	Assets: 395	Emp: 33
University of Tennessee Cumberland Avenue Knoxville, TN 37996 615-974-2591	Major educational institution; university. Type: University Ind: University Grp: Govt & Non-Prof Jack E Reese, CEO	Rev: 194	Assets: 661	Emp: 26

Organizations Listed Alphabetically

Organization / Address / Phone	Descriptive Information	Revenue / ($ mil)	Assets / ($ mil)	Emp (thous)
University of Texas University Station Austin, TX 78712 512-741-3434	Major educational institution; university. Type: University Ind: University Grp: Govt & Non-Prof William Cunningham, CEO	Rev: 431	Assets: 814	Emp: 52
University of Texas at Arlington 800 S Cooper Street Arlington, TX 76019 817-273-2011	Major educational institution; university. Type: University Ind: University Grp: Govt & Non-Prof Wendell H Nedderman, CEO	Rev: 86	Assets: 140	Emp: 25
University of Toledo 2801 W Bancroft Street Toledo, OH 43606 419-537-4242	Major educational institution; university. Type: University Ind: University Grp: Govt & Non-Prof John Stoepler, CEO	Rev: 79	Assets: 121	Emp: 23
University of Utah Administrative Bldg Salt Lake City, UT 84112 801-581-7200	Major educational institution; university. Type: University Ind: University Grp: Govt & Non-Prof Chase N Peterson, CEO	Rev: 285	Assets: 310	Emp: 29
University of Virginia Administrative Bldg Charlottesville, VA 22903 804-924-0311	Major educational institution; university. Type: University Ind: University Grp: Govt & Non-Prof Robert M O'Neil, CEO	Rev: 338	Assets: 343	Emp: 21
University of Washington Administrative Bldg Seattle, WA 98195 206-543-2100	Major educational institution; university. Type: University Ind: University Grp: Govt & Non-Prof William P Gerberding, CEO	Rev: 530	Assets: 689	Emp: 39
University of Wisconsin 500 Lincoln Drive Madison, WI 53706 608-262-1234	Major educational institution; university. Type: University Ind: University Grp: Govt & Non-Prof Donna E Shacala, CEO	Rev: 607	Assets: 849	Emp: 50
University of Wisconsin Milwaukee Administrative Bldg PO Box 413 Milwaukee, WI 53201 414-963-4444	Major educational institution; university. Type: University Ind: University Grp: Govt & Non-Prof Clifford V Smith, CEO	Rev: 128	Assets: 282	Emp: 29
University Savings Assn Inc 1160 Dairy Ashford Houston, TX 77096 713-596-1000	Thrift institution. Type: Private Ind: Savings & Loan Grp: Financial Richard Collier, CEO	Rev: 450	Assets: 4500	Emp: 2
Unocal Corp 1201 W Fifth Street Los Angeles, CA 90017 213-977-7600	Petroleum production & marketing company. Type: NYSE-UCL Ind: Energy Grp: Basic Industries Richard J Stegemeier, CEO Fred L Hartley, Chr Claude S Brinegar, CFO Neal Schmale, R&D Roger C Beach, Mkt Cloyd Reeg, VP Karen A Sikkema, VP Gary Sproule, VP Thomas Sleeman, VP John Imle, VP Sam A Snyder, VP Karen Sikkema, IR	Rev: 10085	Assets: 9508	Emp: 18
UNR Industries Inc 332 S Michigan Avenue Chicago, IL 60604 312-341-1234	Manufacturer of industrial steel products. Type: OTC-UNR Ind: Manufacturing Grp: Manufacturing Robert Penn, CEO	Rev: 392	Assets: 250	Emp: 2
UNUM Union Mutual Life Insurance Co 2211 Congress Street Portland, ME 04122 207-770-2211	Insurance company. Type: NYSE-UNM Ind: Insurance Grp: Insurance James F Orr, CEO Richard Dalbeck, VCh Frank R Noonan, CFO John Alexander Jr, IS Francis Guthrie Jr, Mkt David Tourangeau, VP Elaine Rosen, VP David Hughes, VP Stephen Center, VP Francis Guthrie Jr, IR Susie L Gribbel, PR	Rev: 2199	Assets: 8127	Emp: 4

Organizations Listed Alphabetically

Organization / Address / Phone	Descriptive Information	Revenue / ($ mil)	Assets / ($ mil)	Emp (thous)

Upjohn Co
7000 Portage Road
Kalamazoo, MI 49001
616-323-4000

Prescription drug company.
Type: NYSE-UPJ
Ind: Drugs   Grp: Consumer Service
Theodore Cooper, CEO   Lawrence C Hoff, Pres   Robert C Salisbury, CFO
Donald R Parfet, IS   Jacob Stucki, R&D   Harold E Chappelear, Mkt
John D Martin, PR

Rev: 2746
Assets: 3139
Emp: 21

URM Stores Inc
7511 N Freya Avenue
Seattle, WA 99207
509-467-2620

Operator of retail food supermarkets.
Type: Private
Ind: Retail/Food   Grp: Retail
Dick King, CEO

Rev: 550
Assets: NA
Emp: 3

US Air Group Inc
2345 Crystal Drive
Arlington, VA 22227
703-892-7000

Airline company.
Type: NYSE-U
Ind: Airline   Grp: Consumer Service
Edwin I Colodny, CEO   Juliette C Heintz, Tres   P Jackson Bell, CFO
John Long, IS   Brian M Dwyer, Sls   Randall Malin, Mkt
Seth E Shofield, VP   John P Frestel, VP   Gordon Linkon, VP
John W Funkhouser, VP   Patricia A Goldman, IR   Cheryl Buckley, PR

Rev: 5707
Assets: 5345
Emp: 24

US Bancorp Inc
111 SW Fifth Avenue
Portland, OR 97208
503-275-6111

Commercial bank.
Type: NASDAQ-USBC
Ind: Banking   Grp: Financial
Roger L Breezley, CEO   Roger L Breezley, Chr   Edmund P Jensen, Pres
Paul M Devore, CFO   William R Ulrich, IS   Richard Weissman, R&D
Thomas J Herburger, Mkt   N Stewart Rogers, VP   Andrew Smith, VP
Robert Ridgley, VP   Joshua Green, VP   Donald F Bowler, IR
Thomas J Herburger, PR

Rev: 1381
Assets: 14383
Emp: 9

US Healthcare Inc
980 Jolly Road
Blue Bell, PA 19422
215-628-4800

Medical insurance company.
Type: NASDAQ-USHC
Ind: Health Care   Grp: Consumer Service
Leonard Abramson, CEO   Leonard Abramson, Pres   David C Smyk, Tres
Robert L Smith, CFO   Thomas A Masci Jr, VP   Alan R Letofsky, VP
Marshall V Rozzi, VP   Samuel A Hoffman, VP   Michael J Cardillo, VP
Richard Cornell MD, VP

Rev: 739
Assets: 271
Emp: 10

US Home Corp
1800 West Loop S
Houston, TX 77027
713-877-2311

Developer & builder of homes.
Type: NYSE-UH
Ind: Real Estate/Bldg   Grp: Business Service
Isaac Heimbinder, CEO

Rev: 736
Assets: 943
Emp: 2

US Industrial Chemicals Co
11500 Northlake Drive
Cincinnati, OH 45249
513-530-6510

Manufacturer of chemicals.
Type: Private-Sub   Par: Quantum Chemical Corp
Ind: Chemicals   Grp: Basic Industries
James Schorr, CEO

Rev: NA
Assets: NA
Emp: NA

US Life Insurance Corp
125 Maiden Lane
New York, NY 10038
212-709-6000

Life insurance company.
Type: NYSE-USH
Ind: Insurance   Grp: Insurance
Gordeon E Crosby, CEO   John Gavrity, Pres   Wesley Forte, VCh
Greer Henderson, CFO   Paul Clarkson, R&D   James Pack, Sls
Edward Goodstone, Mkt   George McQueen, Ops   James F Devarso, VP
J Dewbre, VP   Henry Furlong, VP   Timothy J Sullivan, VP

Rev: 1279
Assets: 4145
Emp: 3

US Marine & Bayline Co
17825 59th Avenue
Arlington, WA 98223
206-435-5540

Manufacturer of outboard motors.
Type: Private-Sub   Par: Brunswick Corp
Ind: Leisure Time   Grp: Consumer Service
Dave Livingston, CEO

Rev: NA
Assets: NA
Emp: NA

US Plywood Corp
133 Peachtree NE
Atlanta, GA 30348
404-521-4000

Manufacturer & distributor of plywood products.
Type: Private
Ind: Building Mat   Grp: Basic Industries
T Marshall Hahn, CEO

Rev: 1650
Assets: NA
Emp: 2

Organizations Listed Alphabetically

Organization / Address / Phone	Descriptive Information	Revenue / ($ mil)	Assets / ($ mil)	Emp (thous)
US Shoe Corp One Eastwood Drive Cincinnati, OH 45227 513-527-7000	Consumer goods company with footwear manufacturing, retail. Type: NYSE-USR Ind: Retail/Merch Grp: Retail Philip G Barach, CEO Philip G Barach, Chr Howard Platt, VCh Edward J Klee, CFO Carol Biemel, IS Henry Billeter, Mkt Martin Sherman, VP Edwin Gerth, VP James Crowe, VP Gail Wright, PR	Rev: 2343 Assets: 1111 Emp: 46		
US Sprint Inc 8140 Ward Parkway Kansas City, MO 64131 816-941-5000	Nationwide long distance telephone service company. Type: Private-Sub Par: United Telecommunications Inc Ind: Telecom Grp: High Tech William Esery, CEO	Rev: 2420 Assets: NA Emp: 14		
US Steel/Carnegie Pension Fund Inc 45 Wall Street New York, NY 10005 212-806-4500	Investment company; pension fund management. Type: Private Ind: Non-Bank Fin Grp: Financial Daniel Davidson, CEO	Rev: 300 Assets: 11000 Emp: 1		
US Surgical Corp 150 Glover Avenue Norwalk, CT 06856 203-866-5050	Manufacturer & develop surgical equipment. Type: NYSE-USS Ind: Health Care Grp: Consumer Service Leon Hirsch, CEO	Rev: 300 Assets: 250 Emp: 3		
US Trust Corp 45 Wall Street New York, NY 10005 212-806-4500	Commercial bank. Type: OTC Ind: Banking Grp: Financial Daniel P Davison, CEO H Marshall Schwartz, Pres Briscoe R Smith, VCh Norbert Strickland, CFO Edmond Drewsen, IS Laird Grant, R&D Robert Hogan, Sls Jeffrey Maurer, Mkt David F Davis, VP Thomas Doran, VP Richard Mullan, VP Thomas Strong, VP Robert A Miller, VP Joesph Baratta, VP	Rev: 362 Assets: 2516 Emp: 2		
US West Communications Inc 1801 California Denver, CO 80202 303-624-2424	Telephone public utility company. Type: Private-Sub Par: US West Inc Ind: Telecom Grp: High Tech Gary Ames, CEO	Rev: NA Assets: NA Emp: NA		
US West Communications-Omaha 1301 DOTM Omaha, NE 68102 402-422-2000	Telephone utility company; regional headquarters. Type: Private-Sub Par: US West Inc Ind: Telecom Grp: High Tech Janice Stoney, CEO	Rev: NA Assets: NA Emp: NA		
US West Communications-Seattle 1600 Bell Plaza Seattle, WA 98191 206-346-5000	Telephone utility company; regional headquarters. Type: Private-Sub Par: US West Inc Ind: Telecom Grp: High Tech Bruce Samson, CEO	Rev: NA Assets: NA Emp: NA		
US West Inc 7800 E Orchard Road Englewood, CO 80111 303-793-6500	Regional telecommunications company. Type: NYSE-USW Ind: Telecom Grp: High Tech Jack A MacAllister, CEO Richard D Mccormick, Pres Howard P Doerr, CFO Richard Callahan, IS Bruce R Bond, R&D Charles M Lillis, Mkt Judith A Servoss, PR	Rev: 9211 Assets: 22416 Emp: 70		
USA Petroleum Corp 2701 Ocean Park Blvd Santa Monica, CA 90405 213-452-6200	Distributor & retailer of gasoline. Type: Private Ind: Retail/Merch Grp: Retail John Moller, CEO	Rev: 2200 Assets: NA Emp: 1		
USA Today Inc 535 Madison Avenue New York, NY 10022 212-715-2100	Publisher of national newspaper. Type: Private-Sub Par: Gannett Co Inc Ind: Publishing/Com Grp: Consumer Service Ramon Gaulke, CEO	Rev: NA Assets: NA Emp: NA		
USAA Financial Services Inc 9800 Fredericksburg Road USAA Bldg San Antonio, TX 78288 512-498-7290	Property & casualty insurance company. Type: OTC Ind: Insurance Grp: Insurance Thomas E Carpenter, CEO	Rev: 398 Assets: 625 Emp: 2		

Organizations Listed Alphabetically

Organization / Address / Phone	Descriptive Information	Revenue / Assets / Emp ($ mil) ($ mil) (thous)		

USF & G Corp
100 Light Street
Baltimore, MD 21202
301-547-3000

Property & casualty insurance company.
Type: NYSE-FG
Ind: Insurance   Grp: Insurance
Jack Moseley, CEO   James A Flick, Pres   James M Raley, VCh
Stephen B Cook, CFO   David Meehan, IS   W Minor Carter, Mkt
Paul Scheel, VP   Francis X Bossle, VP   John MacColl, VP
Kathleen Wycoff, VP   Paul Schlough, VP   W Minor Carter, IR
James Harrington, PR

Rev: 5582
Assets: 12361
Emp: 10

USG Corp
101 S Wacker Drive
Chicago, IL 60606
312-321-4000

Manufacturer of gypsum products.
Type: NYSE-USG
Ind: Building Mat   Grp: Basic Industries
Robert J Day, CEO   Ralph C Joynes, Pres   Anthony Falvo, VCh
William Hogan, Tres   Eugene Miller, CFO   John Malone, IS
Brian Burroughs, R&D   Edwin Wade, VP   Harold Pendexter, VP
Eugene Miller, PR

Rev: 2248
Assets: 1821
Emp: 15

UST United States Tobacco Co
100 W Putnam Avenue
Greenwich, CT 06830
203-661-1100

Manufacturer of tobacco products; cigarettes, cigars, pipe.
Type: NYSE-UST
Ind: Tobacco   Grp: Food Processing
Louis F Bantle, CEO   Nicholas A Buoniconti, Pres   Vincent A Gierer Jr, CFO
Harry W Peter III, PR

Rev: 565
Assets: 549
Emp: 3

USX Corp
600 Grant Street
Pittsburgh, PA 15219
412-433-1121

Oil, gas & steel company.
Type: NYSE-X
Ind: Steel   Grp: Basic Industries
David M Roderick, CEO   Charles Corry, Pres   Thomas Graham, VCh
W Bruce Thomas, CFO   R G Clements, IS   William E Swales, R&D
J Bruce Johnson, VP   Victor Beghini, VP   Richard Hays, VP
Earl W Mallick, PR

Rev: 16877
Assets: 19474
Emp: 80

UT Automotive Co
5200 AutoClub Drive
Dearborn, MI 48126
313-593-9000

Manufacturer of automotive parts.
Type: Private-Sub   Par: United Technologies Corp
Ind: Automotive   Grp: Manufacturing
Edward Irving, CEO

Rev: NA
Assets: NA
Emp: NA

Utah Power & Light Co
1407 W North Temple
Salt Lake City, UT 84110
801-535-2000

Electric power production company; electric utility.
Type: Private-Sub   Par: Pacificorp Corp
Ind: Utility   Grp: Utilities
Frank Davis, CEO

Rev: 100
Assets: 3125
Emp: 5

Utah, State of
State Capitol
Salt Lake City, UT 84114
801-533-4000

State government.
Type: State Govt
Ind: State/Prov Govt   Grp: Govt & Non-Prof
Norman H Bangerter, CEO

Rev: 4240
Assets: NM
Emp: 37

Utica National Insurance Co
180 Genesee Street
Utica, NY 13413
315-735-3321

Property & casualty insurance company.
Type: Private-Mutual
Ind: Insurance   Grp: Insurance
W Craig, CEO

Rev: 400
Assets: 1000
Emp: 2

Utilicorp United Inc
911 Main Street
Kansas City, MO 64199
816-421-6600

Utility holding company; electric & gas.
Type: NYSE-UCU
Ind: Utility   Grp: Utilities
Richard Green, CEO

Rev: 600
Assets: 1200
Emp: 3

Utility Fuels Co
611 Walker Street
Houston, TX 77002
713-629-3001

Utility support company; coal supplier.
Type: Private-Sub   Par: Houston Industries Inc
Ind: Metals/Mining   Grp: Basic Industries
Ken Smith, CEO

Rev: 1000
Assets: NA
Emp: 4

Valcom Inc
10810 Farnam Street
Omaha, NE 68154
402-392-3900

Retail chain franchisor; computer & software stores.
Type: OTC
Ind: Retail/Merch   Grp: Retail
Bill Fairfield, CEO

Rev: 400
Assets: 200
Emp: 1

Organizations Listed Alphabetically

Organization / Address / Phone	Descriptive Information	Revenue / Assets / Emp ($ mil) ($ mil) (thous)		

Valero Energy Corp
530 McCullough Avenue PO Box 500
San Antonio, TX 78215
512-246-2000

Petroleum refining company.
Type: NYSE-VLO
Ind: Energy   Grp: Basic Industries
William E Greehey, CEO   Palmer L Moe, Pres   Bruce A Smith, Tres
Edward C Benninger, CFO   Jimmy James, IS   Luis De La Garca, PR

Rev: 629
Assets: 965
Emp: 2

Valhi Corp
5430 LBJ Freeway
Dallas, TX 75240
214-386-4110

Food products company; sugar.
Type: NYSE-VHI
Ind: Food Processing   Grp: Food Processing
Harold C Simmons, CEO

Rev: 1000
Assets: 800
Emp: 8

Valley Federal Savings Assn Inc
6842 Van Nuys Blvd
Van Nuys, CA 91405
818-904-3000

Thrift institution.
Type: OTC-VFED
Ind: Savings & Loan   Grp: Financial
Dan E Nelms, CEO   Jack R Allewaert, Pres   Jack R Allewaert, CFO
Linda M Martin, IS   John R Marquis, Mkt   Gregory K Hughes, IR

Rev: 350
Assets: 3324
Emp: 1

Valley National Corp
241 N Central Avenue
Phoenix, AZ 85004
602-261-2900

Commercial bank.
Type: OTC-VNCP
Ind: Banking   Grp: Financial
James P Simons, CEO   Richard Lehmann, Pres   Richard M Greenwood, CFO
Richard Picard, IS   Wendy Huck, R&D   N W Pope, Mkt
Meegan Silvern, IR   Steve Roman, PR

Rev: 1100
Assets: 11300
Emp: 7

Valmont Industries Inc
Highway 272
Valley, NE 68064
402-359-2201

Retailer of farm equipment & machinery.
Type: NASDAQ-VALM
Ind: Equipment   Grp: Manufacturing
William Welsh, CEO

Rev: 700
Assets: 500
Emp: 4

Valspar Corp
1101 Third Street S
Minneapolis, MN 55415
612-332-7371

Manufacturer of paints & coatings.
Type: ASE
Ind: Building Mat   Grp: Basic Industries
C A Wurtele, CEO   R Pajor, Pres   B Eppel, Tres
Paul Reyelts, CFO   P Fritzke, Sls   H S True, VP
G Meyer, VP   O Huggard, VP   V Greci, VP
J Seiberlich, VP

Rev: 480
Assets: 233
Emp: 5

Value Line Inc
711 Third Avenue
New York, NY 10017
800-223-0818

Investment information & mutual fund management company.
Type: NASDAQ-VALU
Ind: Non-Bank Fin   Grp: Financial
Jean Bernhard Buttner, CEO

Rev: 75
Assets: 96
Emp: 1

Van Dorn Co
2700 E 79th Street
Cleveland, OH 44104
216-361-5234

Manufacturer of specialty containers.
Type: NYSE-VDC
Ind: Packaging   Grp: Manufacturing
Lawrence C Jones, CEO

Rev: 334
Assets: 250
Emp: 2

Van Kampen Merritt Inc
1001 Warrenville Road
Lisle, IL 60532
312-719-6000

Investment firm; bond trading.
Type: Private-Sub   Par: Xerox Corp
Ind: Securities   Grp: Financial
John Merritt, CEO

Rev: 440
Assets: 4400
Emp: 1

Van Munching & Co Inc
1270 Avenue of the Americas
New York, NY 10020
212-265-2685

Producer & distributor of packaged foods.
Type: Private
Ind: Food Processing   Grp: Food Processing
Leo VanMunching, CEO

Rev: 550
Assets: NA
Emp: 1

Vanguard Energy Corp
1111 North Loop W
Houston, TX 77008
713-880-8750

Natural resource development & energy company.
Type: Private
Ind: Energy   Grp: Basic Industries
Tom Garner, CEO

Rev: 825
Assets: NA
Emp: 1

Vanguard Group Mutual Funds Inc
PO Box 2600
Valley Forge, PA 19482
215-648-6000

Mutual fund investment company.
Type: Private
Ind: Non-Bank Fin   Grp: Financial
John Bogel, CEO

Rev: 550
Assets: 22000
Emp: 1

Organizations Listed Alphabetically

Organization / Address / Phone	Descriptive Information	Revenue / ($ mil)	Assets / ($ mil)	Emp (thous)
Vanity Fair Inc 640 Fifth Avenue New York, NY 10019 212-582-6767	Manufacturer of apparel; womens nightwear, lingerie. Type: Private-Sub Par: VF Corp Ind: Apparel/Textiles Grp: Consumer Prd Peter Velardi, CEO	Rev: Assets: Emp:	NA NA NA	
Vantage Companies Inc 2777 Stemmons Freeway Dallas, TX 75207 214-631-0600	Commercial real estate sales & management company. Type: Private Ind: Real Estate/Bldg Grp: Business Service Easton Bell, CEO	Rev: Assets: Emp:	550 NA 2	
Variable Annuity Life Insurance Co 2929 Allen Parkway Houston, TX 77019 713-526-5251	Life insurance company. Type: Private Ind: Insurance Grp: Insurance Stephen D Bickel, CEO Mark W Shartle, CFO Walter B Colvin, IS Joe C Osborne, Mkt William A Wilson, PR	Rev: Assets: Emp:	1880 7771 2	
Varian Associates Inc 611 Hansen Way Palo Alto, CA 94303 415-493-4000	Manufacturer of electronic components. Type: NYSE-VAR Ind: Electronics Grp: High Tech Thomas D Sege, CEO Norman H Pond, Pres Vincent Battaglia, VCh Robert A Lemos, CFO Alan J Bennett, R&D James Taylor, VP Wayne Somrak, VP William Moore, VP Gary E Simpson, IR Allen Jones, PR	Rev: Assets: Emp:	983 830 12	
Varity Corp 595 Bay Street Toronto, ON M5G2C3 Can 416-593-3811	Manufacturer of farm equipment. Type: TOR-VAT Ind: Equipment Grp: Manufacturing Victor Rice, CEO Vincent D Laurenzo, Pres Neil D Arnold, VCh James Vance, CFO F Chapman, VP	Rev: Assets: Emp:	1942 1384 15	
Verbatim Corp 1200 W T Harris Blvd Charlotte, NC 28213 704-547-6500	Manufacturer of floppy disks. Type: Private-Sub Par: Eastman Kodak Co Ind: Comput/Off Equip Grp: High Tech Richard Bourns, CEO	Rev: Assets: Emp:	NA NA NA	
Vermont American Corp 100 E Liberty Street Louisville, KY 40202 502-587-6851	Manufacturer of home tools & lawn mowers. Type: ASE-VAC Ind: Appliances/Furn Grp: Manufacturing Lee B Thomas, CEO	Rev: Assets: Emp:	400 300 3	
Vermont, State of State House Montpelier, VT 05602 802-828-1110	State government. Type: State Govt Ind: State/Prov Govt Grp: Govt & Non-Prof Madeleine M Kunin, CEO	Rev: Assets: Emp:	1351 NM 13	
Versatec Inc 2710 Walsh Avenue Santa Clara, CA 95051 408-988-2800	Manufacturer of computer systems. Type: Private-Sub Par: Xerox Corp Ind: Comput/Off Equip Grp: High Tech Charles Askands, CEO	Rev: Assets: Emp:	NA NA NA	
Vestron Inc 60 Long Ridge Road Stamford, CT 06905 203-968-0000	Manufacturer of pre-recorded video cassettes. Type: NYSE Ind: Leisure Time Grp: Consumer Service Jon Pesinger, CEO	Rev: Assets: Emp:	275 200 1	
VF Corp 1047 N Park Road Wyomissing, PA 19610 215-378-1151	Manufacturer of apparel products. Type: NYSE-VFC Ind: Apparel/Textiles Grp: Consumer Prd Lawrence R Pugh, CEO Robert E Gregory Jr, Pres Gerald Johnson, CFO Robert Stec, Mkt Prakash Bhatt, Ops Harold McKemy, VP Janet Peters, VP Gary Dunham, VP Laurie M Tarnoski, PR	Rev: Assets: Emp:	2516 1760 30	
Via Rail Canada Inc 2 Place Ville Marie Montreal, PQ H3C3N3 Can 514-286-2311	Nationwide government owned passenger railroad company. Type: Govt Corp Ind: Railroad Grp: Business Service Denis de Belleval, CEO Lawrence Hanigan, Pres Roy Arnold, VCh Nicole Beaudoin-Sauve, CFO Rejean Bechamp, R&D Murray Jackson, Mkt Carole Mackaay, VP James Roche, VP Jean-Roch Boivin, VP	Rev: Assets: Emp:	670 910 7	

Organizations Listed Alphabetically

Organization / Address / Phone	Descriptive Information	Revenue / ($ mil)	Assets / ($ mil)	Emp (thous)
Viacom International Inc 200 Elm Street Dedham, MA 02026 617-461-1600	Diversified entertainment & communications company. Type: ASE Ind: Publishing/Com Grp: Consumer Service Sumner M Redstone, CEO Frank J Biondi Jr, Chr Raymond Boyce, VCh George S Smith Jr, CFO Neil Braun, R&D William Roskin, VP Kevin Lawan, VP Ira Korff, VP Thomas Dooley, VP Neil Braun, VP Harry Schleiff, VP Raymond A Boyce, IR Hilary Condit, PR	Rev: Assets: Emp:		1258 3980 4
Vicorp Restaurants Corp 400 W 48th Street Denver, CO 80216 303-296-2121	Operator of restaurants. Type: NASDAQ-VRES Ind: Food/Lodging Grp: Consumer Service Charles Fredrickson, CEO	Rev: Assets: Emp:		315 250 13
Victor Technologies Corp 395 Phoenixville Pike Malvern, PA 19355 215-251-5000	Manufacturer & importer of electronic equipment; US hdqtrs. Type: Private-Sub-For Ind: Electronics Grp: High Tech Joe Federman, CEO	Rev: Assets: Emp:		550 NA 2
Village Super Markets Inc 733 Mountain Avenue Springfield, NJ 07801 201-467-2200	Operator of retail super markets. Type: NASDAQ-VLGE Ind: Retail/Food Grp: Retail Nicholas Sumas, CEO	Rev: Assets: Emp:		600 300 4
Virginia Beach, City of City Hall Municipal Center Virginia Beach, VA 23456 804-427-4111	City government. Type: City Govt Ind: Local Govt Grp: Govt & Non-Prof Robert Jones, CEO	Rev: Assets: Emp:		378 NM 10
Virginia Commonwealth University 910 W Franklin Street Richmond, VA 23284 804-257-0100	Major educational institution; university. Type: University Ind: University Grp: Govt & Non-Prof Edmund F Ackell, CEO	Rev: Assets: Emp:		301 240 23
Virginia Electric & Power Co 701 E Byrd Street Richmond, VA 23261 804-771-3193	Electric power utility company. Type: Private-Sub Par: Dominion Resources Inc Ind: Utility Grp: Utilities William Berry, CEO	Rev: Assets: Emp:		NA NA NA
Virginia Polytechnic Institute Administrative Bldg Blacksburg, VA 24061 703-961-6000	Major educational institution; university. Type: University Ind: University Grp: Govt & Non-Prof James D McComas, CEO	Rev: Assets: Emp:		226 397 25
Virginia, State of State Capitol Richmond, VA 23219 804-786-0000	State government. Type: State Govt Ind: State/Prov Govt Grp: Govt & Non-Prof Gerald L Baliles, CEO	Rev: Assets: Emp:		12101 NM 119
Vishay Intertechnology Corp 63 Lincoln Highway Malvern, PA 19355 919-365-3800	Manufacturer of electronics components, semiconductors. Type: NYSE-VSH Ind: Electronics Grp: High Tech Felix Zandman, CEO	Rev: Assets: Emp:		250 200 3
Vista Chemical Corp 15990 N Barker's Landing Road Houston, TX 77079 713-531-3200	Manufacturer of industrial cleaning chemicals. Type: NYSE-VC Ind: Chemicals Grp: Basic Industries John D Burns, CEO Robert E Lehmkuhl, VCh John J Weidner, CFO Larry D Gallmore, IS Charles M Starks, R&D B E A Larsen, Mkt W Jan B Vogel, VP Ralph Ferrell, VP Gary Draper, VP Roberrt Dale, VP Elliot A Vogelfanger, IR Michael Reynolds, PR	Rev: Assets: Emp:		781 521 2
Vitt Media International Inc 1114 Avenue of the Americas New York, NY 10036 212-921-0500	Advertising services company. Type: Private Ind: Business Service Grp: Business Service Sam Vitt, CEO	Rev: Assets: Emp:		250 NA 1

Organization / Address / Phone	Descriptive Information	Revenue / ($ mil)	Assets / ($ mil)	Emp (thous)
Vlassic Foods Inc 33200 W 14 Mile Road West Bloomfield, MI 48033 313-851-9400	Producer & distributor of packaged foods; pickles, peppers. Type: Private-Sub Par: Campbell Soup Co Ind: Food Processing Grp: Food Processing John Dorrance, CEO	Rev: Assets: Emp:	NA NA NA	
VLSI Technology Inc 1101 McKay Drive San Jose, CA 95131 408-924-1810	Semiconductor manufacturer. Type: NASDAQ-VLSI Ind: Electronics Grp: High Tech Alfred Stein, CEO	Rev: Assets: Emp:	300 150 2	
Volkswagen America Inc 888 W Big Beaver Troy, MI 48007 313-362-6000	Manufacturer & importer of automobiles; US headquarters. Type: Private-Sub-For Ind: Automotive Grp: Manufacturing Hanz Hungerhard, CEO	Rev: Assets: Emp:	1100 NA 11	
Volkswagen Canada Ltd 1940 Eglinton Avenue E Scarborough, ON M1L2M2 Can 416-288-3000	Automobile marketing & distribution company. Type: Private-Sub-For Ind: Automotive Grp: Manufacturing Noel Phillips, CEO	Rev: Assets: Emp:	654 287 1	
Volt Information Sciences Corp 101 Park Avenue New York, NY 10178 212-309-0200	Manufacturer of computerized typesetting & telecom equip. Type: NASDAQ-VOLT Ind: Comput/Off Equip Grp: High Tech William Shaw, CEO	Rev: Assets: Emp:	450 300 18	
Volvo Canada Ltd 175 Gordon Baker Road North York, ON M1L2M2 Can 416-493-3700	Automotive distribution & marketing company. Type: Private-Sub-For Ind: Automotive Grp: Manufacturing Bjorn Ahlstrom, CEO	Rev: Assets: Emp:	298 170 1	
Volvo North America Corp Rockleigh Industrial Way Rockleigh, NJ 07647 201-768-7300	Manufacturer & importer of automobiles; US headquarters. Type: Private-Sub-For Ind: Automotive Grp: Manufacturing Bjorn Ahlstrem, CEO	Rev: Assets: Emp:	1100 NA 3	
Vons Companies Inc 10150 Lower Azusa El Mone, CA 91731 818-579-1400	Operator of retail food supermarkets. Type: Private Ind: Retail/Food Grp: Retail Roger Stenglen, CEO	Rev: Assets: Emp:	3300 NA 19	
VS Services Ltd Islington & Evans Avenue Toronto, ON M8Z5Y7 Can 416-255-1331	Operator of vending machines, food services. Type: Private-Sub-For Ind: Food Processing Grp: Food Processing D Chant, CEO	Rev: Assets: Emp:	298 85 5	
Vulcan Materials Co One Metroplex Drive Birmingham, AL 35209 205-877-3000	Manufacturer of industrial chemicals. Type: NYSE-VMC Ind: Manufacturing Grp: Manufacturing Herbert A Sklenar, CEO William J Grayson, VCh Peter J Clemens III, CFO Harry L Nelson, IS C A Machemehl, R&D Robert W Lee, Ops E Starke Sydnor, PR	Rev: Assets: Emp:	1053 958 6	
Waban Inc One Mercer Road Natick, MA 01760 508-651-6500	Operator of club retail stores; food & home improvement. Type: NYSE-WBN Ind: Retail/Merch Grp: Retail S L Feldberg, CEO	Rev: Assets: Emp:	2000 750 15	
Wackenhut Corp 1500 San Remo Avenue Coral Gables, FL 33146 305-666-5656	Security service company. Type: NYSE-WAK Ind: Business Service Grp: Business Service George R Wackenhut, CEO Richard Wackenhut, Pres C Calving Harris, CFO Robert C Kneip, R&D Alan Bernstein, Ops Ruth Wackenhut, VP	Rev: Assets: Emp:	401 150 7	
Wajax Ltd 770 Sherbrooke Street Montreal, PQ H3A1Z1 Can 514-238-7291	Building & construction materials wholesaler. Type: TOR Ind: Building Mat Grp: Basic Industries R Chorlton, CEO	Rev: Assets: Emp:	298 170 2	

Organizations Listed Alphabetically

Organization / Address / Phone	Descriptive Information	Revenue / Assets / Emp ($ mil) ($ mil) (thous)		

Wakefern Food Corp
600 York Street
Elizabeth, NJ 07207
201-527-3300

Manufacturer & distributor of food products.
Type: Private
Ind: Food Processing   Grp: Food Processing
Jerome Yaguda, CEO

Rev: 3300
Assets: NA
Emp: 4

Wal Mart Stores Inc
702 SW Eighth Street
Bentonville, AR 72716
501-273-4000

National retail discount store operator.
Type: NYSE-WMT
Ind: Retail/Merch   Grp: Retail
Sam M Walton, CEO   David O Glass, Chr   Donald G Soderquist, Pres
Bobby Martin, IS   William Fields, Sls   Dean L Sanders, VP
Mac Gammon, VP   A L Miles, VP   John E Tate, VP
Nick White, VP   Don Shinkle, PR

Rev: 20649
Assets: 5132
Emp: 200

Walbridge, Aldinger & Co Inc
38099 Schoolcraft Road
Livonia, MI 48150
313-591-6000

General contractors & construction management.
Type: Private
Ind: Real Estate/Bldg   Grp: Business Service
John Rakolta, CEO

Rev: 500
Assets: NA
Emp: 1

Waldbaum Inc
Hemlock Street
Central Islap, NY 11722
516-582-9300

Operator of retail supermarkets & drugstores.
Type: Private-Sub   Par: Great Atlantic & Pacific Tea Co
Ind: Retail/Food   Grp: Retail
Aaron Malinsky, CEO

Rev: 1800
Assets: 1000
Emp: 14

Walden Book Co Inc
201 High Ridge Road
Stamford, CT 06904
203-356-7500

Operator or retail book stores.
Type: Private-Sub   Par: K Mart Corp
Ind: Retail/Merch   Grp: Retail
Henry Hoffman, CEO

Rev: 500
Assets: NA
Emp: 5

Walgreen Co
200 Wilmot Road
Deerfield, IL 60015
312-940-2500

Operator of retail drugstores.
Type: NYSE-WAG
Ind: Retail/Merch   Grp: Retail
Charles R Walgreen, CEO   Fred F Canning, Pres   L Daniel Jorndt, Tres
Charles D Hunter, CFO   William A Shiel, IS   John A Rubino, R&D
V A Brunner, Mkt   John R Brown, VP   Glenn S Kraiss, VP
Robert Atlas, VP   Jerome B Karlen, VP   William O Shank, VP
Thomas L Mammoser, IR   Henry Cade, PR

Rev: 4884
Assets: 1512
Emp: 35

Wallace Computer Services Inc
4600 W Roosevelt Road
Hillside, IL 60162
312-626-2000

Manufacturer of computer paper products.
Type: NYSE-WCS
Ind: Comput/Off Equip   Grp: High Tech
Theodore Dimitriou, CEO

Rev: 383
Assets: 292
Emp: 3

Walton Monroe Textiles Inc
PO Box 1046
Monroe, GA 30655
404-267-9411

Manufacturer of textiles.
Type: Private
Ind: Apparel/Textiles   Grp: Consumer Prd
G Stephen Felker, CEO

Rev: 500
Assets: NA
Emp: 5

Wang Laboratories Inc
One Industrial Avenue
Lowell, MA 01851
508-459-5000

Manufacturer of mid range computers.
Type: ASE
Ind: Comput/Off Equip   Grp: High Tech
An Wang, CEO   Frederick A Wang, Pres   Timothy C Cronin, IS
Horace Tsiang, R&D   Ian Diery, Sls   Kenneth A Olisa, Mkt
Ian Diery, VP   Harold P Ano, VP   Peter McElroy, PR

Rev: 3068
Assets: 2838
Emp: 31

Warburg, S G Securities Inc
787 7th Avenue
New York, NY 10019
212-459-7000

Investment firm; securities trading.
Type: Private
Ind: Securities   Grp: Financial
David Scoley, CEO

Rev: 220
Assets: 2200
Emp: 1

Ward Marlette Ltd
20 Queen Street W
Toronto, ON M5H3R3 Can
416-340-8390

National accounting firm.
Type: Private
Ind: Accounting   Grp: Business Service
Keith McNair, CEO

Rev: 106
Assets: NM
Emp: 2

Wardair International Ltd
3111 Convair Drive
Mississauga, ON L5P1C2 Can
416-671-3100

Nationwide airline.
Type: TOR
Ind: Airline   Grp: Consumer Service
Maxwell Ward, CEO

Rev: 441
Assets: 673
Emp: 3

Organizations Listed Alphabetically

Organization / Address / Phone	Descriptive Information	Revenue / ($ mil)	Assets / ($ mil)	Emp (thous)

Warnaco Inc
350 Lafayette Street
Bridgeport, CT 06601
203-579-8272

Family apparel.
Type: Private
Ind: Apparel/Textiles   Grp: Consumer Prd
Linda J Wachner, CEO   Roger Williams, CFO   Albert Curcio, IS
Dr William Aldrich, R&D   Carol Leslie, PR

Rev: 750
Assets: NA
Emp: 10

Warner Brothers Inc
4000 Warner Blvd
Burbank, CA 91522
818-954-6000

Producers of motion pictures, television, entertainment.
Type: Private-Sub   Par: Warner Communications Inc
Ind: Publishing/Com   Grp: Consumer Service
Robert Daly, CEO

Rev: NA
Assets: NA
Emp: NA

Warner Communications Inc
75 Rockefeller Plaza
New York, NY 10019
212-484-8000

Motion picture, recording & publishing company.
Type: NYSE-WCI
Ind: Leisure Time   Grp: Consumer Service
Steven J Ross, CEO   Martin D Payson, Pres   Deane Johnson, VCh
Bert Wasserman, CFO   Don Winski, IS   Edwin Hamowy, R&D
Geoffrey W Holmes, Sls   David R Hass, Mkt   Robert Morgado, VP
Warren Christie, VP   R Michael Hayes, VP   Spencer R Hays, VP
John Thomas, VP   Geoffrey W Holmes, PR

Rev: 4206
Assets: 4598
Emp: 31

Warner Lambert Co
201 Tabor Road
Morris Plains, NJ 07950
201-540-2000

Ethical pharmaceutical company.
Type: NYSE
Ind: Drugs   Grp: Consumer Service
Joseph D Williams, CEO   Melvin R Goodes, Pres   Donald O'Neill, VCh
Robert R Dircks, CFO   Thomas Hippe, IS   Ronald Cresswell, R&D
Elias Hebeka, Ops   Rae Paltiel, VP   Ronald Zier, PR

Rev: 3908
Assets: 2703
Emp: 33

Warner Publishing Inc
666 Fifth Avenue
New York, NY 10019
212-484-2900

Publisher of books, comics, consumer products.
Type: Private-Sub   Par: Warner Communications Inc
Ind: Publishing/Com   Grp: Consumer Service
William Sarnoff, CEO

Rev: NA
Assets: NA
Emp: NA

Warren Equities Inc
10 E 53rd Street
New York, NY 10022
212-751-8100

Operator of retail stores & real estate investment company.
Type: Private
Ind: Retail/Merch   Grp: Retail
Warren Alpert, CEO

Rev: 500
Assets: NA
Emp: 1

Warren, George E Co Inc
50 Milk Street
Boston, MA 02109
617-451-2300

Petroleum trading company.
Type: Private
Ind: Energy   Grp: Basic Industries
Thomas L Corr, CEO

Rev: 1750
Assets: NA
Emp: 1

Washington Energy Co
815 Mercer Street
Seattle, WA 98109
206-622-6767

Electric power utility.
Type: NASDAQ-WECO
Ind: Utility   Grp: Utilities
James A Thorpe, CEO   Robert Golliver, Pres   Charles Petek, CFO

Rev: 345
Assets: 589
Emp: 1

Washington Gas Co
1100 H Street NW
Washington, DC 20080
703-750-4440

Natural gas utility company.
Type: NYSE-WGL
Ind: Utility   Grp: Utilities
Patrick E Clarke, CEO   Donald Heim, Chr   Patrick Maher, Pres
Thomas Duckenfield, VCh   Reginald G Fuller, CFO   Jerimiah Hughitt, R&D
James Freeeman, Mkt   Roy Kahn, Ops   John Keane, VP
Patricia Woolsey, VP   Frederic Kline, VP   Douglas Pope, VP
Lewis Unkle, VP

Rev: 698
Assets: 923
Emp: 3

Washington Mutual Savings Inc
1101 Second Avenue
Seattle, WA 98101
206-464-4400

Thrift institution.
Type: NASDAQ-WMSB
Ind: Savings & Loan   Grp: Financial
Louis H Pepper, CEO   William A Longbrake, Pres   Kerry Killinger, CFO
Robert J Mathison, IS   Lindy Friedlander, R&D   Kerry Killinger, Mkt
Melinda McCorkle, IR   Deloria Jones, PR

Rev: 584
Assets: 6364
Emp: 2

Organizations Listed Alphabetically

Organization / Address / Phone	Descriptive Information	Revenue / ($ mil)	Assets / ($ mil)	Emp (thous)
Washington Post Co 1150 Fifteenth Street NW Washington, DC 20071 202-334-6600	Newspaper, television stations & cable television. Type: ASE-WPOB Ind: Publishing/Com Grp: Consumer Service Katharine Graham, CEO Richard D Simmons, Pres Diana Daniels, VCh Martin Cohen, CFO Edward Van Gombos, IS Ross F Hamachek, R&D Howard E Wall, VP Guyon Knight, VP Beverly Keil, VP Leonade Jones, VP Guyon Knight, IR Virginia Rodriguez, PR	Rev: 1368 Assets: 1422 Emp: 7		
Washington State University Administrative Bldg Pullman, WA 99164 509-335-3564	Major educational institution; university. Type: University Ind: University Grp: Govt & Non-Prof Samuel H Smith, CEO	Rev: 212 Assets: 821 Emp: 21		
Washington Water Power Co East 1411 Mission Avenue Spokane, WA 99202 509-489-0500	Electric power & natural gas utility company. Type: NYSE-WWP Ind: Utility Grp: Utilities Paul A Redmond, CEO James R Harvey, Pres W Lester Bryan, VCh Jon Eliassen, CFO David Damiano, R&D Gary Ely, Mkt Robert Fikai, Ops Robert McLendan, VP Joseph Piedmont, VP Ronald Davis, VP Terry Syms, VP	Rev: 543 Assets: 1378 Emp: 1		
Washington, District of Columbia District Bldg 1350 Pennsylvania Avenue Washington, DC 20004 202-727-1000	Government of the District of Columbia. Type: Fed District Ind: State/Prov Govt Grp: Govt & Non-Prof Marion S Barry, CEO	Rev: 3238 Assets: NM Emp: 52		
Washington, State of Legislative Bldg Olympia, WA 98504 206-753-5000	State government. Type: State Govt Ind: State/Prov Govt Grp: Govt & Non-Prof Booth Gardner, CEO	Rev: 11219 Assets: NM Emp: 97		
Waste Management Inc 3003 Butterfield Road Oak Brook, IL 60521 312-654-8800	Disposal company for industrial & home waste. Type: NYSE-WMX Ind: Business Service Grp: Business Service Dean L Buntrock, CEO Phillip B Rooney, Pres James E Koenig, Tres Donald F Flynn, CFO Ned Heinbach, IS Harold Gershowitz, VP Jerry E Dempsey, VP William Hulligan, VP Francis B Moore, VP Joseph L Pokorny, PR	Rev: 3566 Assets: 4879 Emp: 35		
Waterloo, University of Administrative Bldg Waterloo, ON N2L3G1 Can 519-885-1211	Major educational institution; university. Type: University Ind: University Grp: Govt & Non-Prof J P R Wadsworth, CEO	Rev: 187 Assets: NM Emp: 27		
Watkins Johnson Co 3333 Hillview Avenue Palo Alto, CA 94304 415-493-4141	Manufacturer of electronic defense subsystems. Type: NYSE-WJ Ind: Electronics Grp: High Tech Dean A Watkins, CEO	Rev: 275 Assets: 250 Emp: 3		
Watts Industries Inc 815 Chestnut Street North Andover, MA 01845 508-688-1811	Manufacturer of liquid control products; valves. Type: NASDAQ-WATT Ind: Manufacturing Grp: Manufacturing Charles Grigg, CEO	Rev: 250 Assets: 200 Emp: 2		
Wausau Paper Mills Co One Clarks Island Wausau, WI 54401 715-845-5266	Manufacturer of fine stationery. Type: NASDAQ-WSAU Ind: Paper/Forest Prd Grp: Basic Industries Richard Radt, CEO	Rev: 300 Assets: 200 Emp: 2		
Wawa Inc Baltimore Pike Wawa, PA 19063 215-358-8000	Operator of retail merchandise stores. Type: Private Ind: Retail/Merch Grp: Retail Richard D Wood, CEO	Rev: 400 Assets: NA Emp: 4		
Wawanesa Mutual Insurance Co 191 Broadway Winnipeg, MB R3C3P1 Can 204-985-3811	Property & casualty insurance company. Type: Private-Mutual Ind: Insurance Grp: Insurance I M Montgomery, CEO	Rev: 408 Assets: 632 Emp: 1		

Organizations Listed Alphabetically

Organization / Address / Phone	Descriptive Information	Revenue / ($ mil)	Assets / ($ mil)	Emp (thous)
Waxman Industries Inc 24460 Aurora Road Cleveland, OH 44146 216-439-1830	Wholesale, retail plumbing/electrical prts, hardware stores. Type: NYSE-WAXM Ind: Retail/Merch Grp: Retail M Waxman, CEO	Rev: Assets: Emp:	250 125 1	
Wayne County Government City County Bldg Detroit, MI 48226 313-224-0286	County government. Type: County Govt Ind: Local Govt Grp: Govt & Non-Prof Arthur M Carter, CEO	Rev: Assets: Emp:	825 NM 5	
Wayne State University 5050 Cass Avenue Detroit, MI 48202 313-577-2424	Major educational institution; university. Type: University Ind: University Grp: Govt & Non-Prof David Adamany, CEO	Rev: Assets: Emp:	265 376 31	
Webb, Del E Corp 2331 E Camelback Phoenix, AZ 85016 602-468-6800	Developer of planned residential communities. Type: NYSE-WBB Ind: Real Estate/Bldg Grp: Business Service Philip J Dion, CEO	Rev: Assets: Emp:	350 300 4	
Webb, Jervis B Co Inc 1 Webb Drive Farmington Hills, MI 48018 313-553-1000	Manufacturer of industrial process handling equipment. Type: Private Ind: Equipment Grp: Manufacturing George Webb, CEO	Rev: Assets: Emp:	550 NA 3	
Wegmans Food Markets Inc 1500 Brooks Avenue Rochester, NY 14692 716-328-2550	Operator of retail food supermarkets. Type: Private Ind: Retail/Food Grp: Retail Robert B Wegman, CEO	Rev: Assets: Emp:	1000 NA 5	
Weight Watchers International 500 N Broadway Jericho, NY 11753 516-939-0400	Franchiser of weight loss organizations; food manufacturer. Type: Private-Sub Par: Heinz, H J Co Ind: Food Processing Grp: Food Processing Charles Berger, CEO	Rev: Assets: Emp:	500 NA 2	
Weirton Steel Corp 400 Three Springs Drive Weirton, WV 26062 304-797-2000	Integrated steel manufacturer. Type: Private Ind: Steel Grp: Basic Industries Herbert Elish, CEO Warren E Bartel, Pres Thomas W Evans, IS W T Saunders, R&D D M Gould, Sls James B Bruhn, Mkt W C Brenneisen, VP Charles R Cronin, PR	Rev: Assets: Emp:	1384 687 8	
Weis Markets Inc 1000 S Second Street Sunbury, PA 17801 717-286-4571	Operator of retail supermarkets. Type: NYSE Ind: Retail/Food Grp: Retail Segfried Weis, CEO Robert F Weis, CFO Alan Barrick, IS Richard Madison, Sls Norman S Rich, Ops Walter Bruce, VP Richard Wetzel, VP George Michalak, VP	Rev: Assets: Emp:	1189 596 15	
Weisman, Frederick Co Inc 6710 Baymeadow Drive Glen Burnie, MD 21061 301-760-1500	Auto importing & insurance company. Type: Private Ind: Automotive Grp: Manufacturing Frederick Weisman, CEO	Rev: Assets: Emp:	1250 NA 1	
Weldwood of Canada Ltd 1055 W Hastings Street Vancouver, BC V6B3V8 Can 604-687-7366	Forest products company; paper, building materials. Type: Private-Sub Ind: Paper/Forest Prd Grp: Basic Industries Thomas A Buell, CEO Graham I Bender, Pres Colin Warner, CFO Rick Franko, Sls Harry Karasiuk, Ops George R Richards, VP Leon Pond, VP	Rev: Assets: Emp:	761 601 4	
Wellington Management/TDPL Inc 75 State Street Boston, MA 02109 617-951-5000	Mutual fund & pension fund investment firm. Type: Private Ind: Non-Bank Fin Grp: Financial Robert Doran, CEO	Rev: Assets: Emp:	700 27500 1	

Organizations Listed Alphabetically

Organization / Address / Phone	Descriptive Information	Revenue / ($ mil)	Assets / ($ mil)	Emp (thous)
Wellman Corp 1040 Broad street Shrewsbury, NJ 07702 201-388-0120	Manufacturer of polyester & wool products & home furnishings. Type: Private Ind: Tire/Rubber Grp: Basic Industries Thomas Duff, CEO	Rev: 260	Assets: 200	Emp: 2
Wells Fargo & Co 420 Montgomery Street San Francisco, CA 94163 415-477-1000	Commercial bank. Type: NYSE-WFC Ind: Banking Grp: Financial Carl E Reichardt, CEO Paul Hazen, Pres William Adlinger, VCh Alan J Pabst, Tres Clyde W Ostler, CFO Leslie Altick, R&D Jeff Kopec, Mkt John F Grundhofer, VP Robert L Joss, VP David M Petrone, VP William F Zuendt, VP Leslie L Altick, PR	Rev: 4853	Assets: 46617	Emp: 20
Wells Rich Greene Inc 9 W 57th Street New York, NY 10019 212-303-5000	Nationwide advertising agency. Type: Private Ind: Business Service Grp: Business Service Mary Wells Lawrence, CEO	Rev: 550	Assets: NA	Emp: 2
Wendy's International Inc 4288 W Dublin Granville Road Dublin, OH 43017 614-764-3100	Operator of fast food restaurants. Type: NYSE-WEN Ind: Food/Lodging Grp: Consumer Service Edward L Austin, CEO James W Near, Chr Robert L Barney, VCh John F Brownley, Tres John K Casey, CFO James W Near, VP Robert L Barney, VP Emil Brolick, VP Donald Calhoon, VP Dennis Campbell, VP	Rev: 2902	Assets: 777	Emp: 42
Wertheim Schroder & Co Inc 787 Seventh Avenue New York, NY 10089 212-492-6000	Investment firm; securities trading. Type: Private Ind: Securities Grp: Financial James Harmon, CEO	Rev: 330	Assets: 3300	Emp: 1
West Co W Bridge Street Phoenixville, PA 19460 215-935-4500	Manufacturer of medical supplies. Type: NYSE-WST Ind: Health Care Grp: Consumer Service William S West, CEO	Rev: 250	Assets: 200	Emp: 3
West Fraser Timber Co 1100 Melville Street Vancouver, BC V6E4A6 Can 604-681-8282	Forest products company. Type: TOR Ind: Paper/Forest Prd Grp: Basic Industries Henry H Ketcham, CEO Henry Ketcham, Pres Russell C Linton, VCh Martti Solin, CFO Erest Thony, Sls Gary Townsend, Ops C Paul Daniels, VP Noordin Nanji, VP	Rev: 394	Assets: 447	Emp: 3
West One Bank Corp PO Box 8247 Boise, ID 83733 208-388-7791	Commercial bank. Type: NASDAQ-WEST Ind: Banking Grp: Financial Daniel R Nelson, CEO	Rev: 349	Assets: 3538	Emp: 3
West Point-Pepperell Inc 400 W 10th Street West Point, GA 31833 404-645-4000	Manufacturer of textiles for the apparel industry. Type: NYSE-WPM Ind: Apparel/Textiles Grp: Consumer Prd Joseph L Lanier, CEO	Rev: 1740	Assets: 1850	Emp: 31
West Texas Utilities Co 301 Cypress Street Abilene, TX 79601 915-674-7000	Electric power utility company. Type: Private-Sub Par: Central & South West Corp Ind: Utility Grp: Utilities Glen D Churchill, CEO	Rev: 302	Assets: 737	Emp: 2
West Virginia, State of State Capitol Charleston, WV 25305 304-348-3456	State government. Type: State Govt Ind: State/Prov Govt Grp: Govt & Non-Prof Gaston Caperton, CEO	Rev: 4006	Assets: NM	Emp: 43
Westar Group Ltd (BC Resources Invst) 1900-1176 W Georgia Street Vancouver, BC V6E4B9 Can 604-687-2600	Forest products company; paper, building materials. Type: TOR Ind: Paper/Forest Prd Grp: Basic Industries Edwin C Phillips, CEO	Rev: 288	Assets: 401	Emp: 4

Organizations Listed Alphabetically

Organization / Address / Phone	Descriptive Information	Revenue / ($ mil)	Assets / ($ mil)	Emp (thous)
Westburne International Industries Ltd 1700 633 6th Avenue SW Calgary, AB T2P2Y5 Can 403-292-0200	Oil exploration & production company. Type: TOR Ind: Energy Grp: Basic Industries Terry Dale, CEO	Rev: Assets: Emp:		1216 595 20
Westcoast Energy Inc 1333 W Georgia Street Vancouver, BC V6E3K9 Can 604-664-5500	Natural gas distribution & utility company. Type: NYSE-WE Ind: Energy Grp: Basic Industries Michael E J Phelps, CEO Wilbert Hopper, Chr Arthur Willms, VCh Graham Wilson, CFO John Kavanaugh, R&D Ronald Maas, Mkt William Caswell, Ops Allan Edgeworth, VP Murray Birch, VP Harvey Permack, VP John Podmore, VP Joachim Castelsky, VP	Rev: Assets: Emp:		712 1839 1
Westdeutsche Landesbank AG 450 Park Avenue New York, NY 10022 212-754-9600	Commercial bank. Type: Private-Sub-For Ind: Banking Grp: Financial Horst Senff, CEO	Rev: Assets: Emp:		450 3500 1
Western & Southern Life Ins Co 400 Broadway Cincinnati, OH 45202 513-629-1800	Life insurance company. Type: Private Ind: Insurance Grp: Insurance William J Williams, CEO John Barrett, CFO Kenneth Palmer, IS J J Miller, Mkt Robert Starnes, PR	Rev: Assets: Emp:		970 5028 6
Western Atlas International Inc 10001 Richmond Avenue Houston, TX 77042 713-266-5700	Oil field service company. Type: Private-Sub Par: Litton Industries Inc Ind: Oil Service Grp: Business Service Howard Dingman, CEO	Rev: Assets: Emp:		NA NA NA
Western Capital Investment Corp 700 Seventeenth Street Denver, CO 80202 303-370-1212	Thrift institution. Type: NASDAQ-WECA Ind: Savings & Loan Grp: Financial Junius F Baxter, CEO	Rev: Assets: Emp:		358 3664 2
Western Co of North America 6000 Western Place Fort Worth, TX 76107 817-731-5100	Oil field service company. Type: NYSE-WSN Ind: Energy Grp: Basic Industries Sheldon R Erikson, CEO	Rev: Assets: Emp:		209 534 2
Western Digital Corp 2445 McCabe Way Irvine, CA 92714 714-863-0102	Manufacturer of large-scale integrated circuits, chips. Type: ASE Ind: Electronics Grp: High Tech Roger W Johnson, CEO Edward L Marinaro, Pres John Markovich, Tres A J Moyer, CFO John J Peterson, R&D Alan J Mattal, Sls John Pleso, Mkt John R Mackay, Ops C William Frank, VP John Markovich, IR Mike Pollock, PR	Rev: Assets: Emp:		768 551 7
Western Massachusetts Electric Co 174 Brush Hill Avenue West Springfield, MA 01085 413-785-5871	Electric power utility company. Type: Private-Sub Par: Northeast Utilities Inc Ind: Utility Grp: Utilities R Abair, CEO	Rev: Assets: Emp:		NA NA NA
Western Michigan University Administrative Bldg Kalamazoo, MI 49008 606-383-1600	Major educational institution; university. Type: University Ind: University Grp: Govt & Non-Prof Diether H Haenicke, CEO	Rev: Assets: Emp:		127 187 23
Western Ontario, University of Administrative Bldg London, ON N6A3K7 Can 519-679-2111	Major educational institution; university. Type: University Ind: University Grp: Govt & Non-Prof D B Weldon, CEO	Rev: Assets: Emp:		281 NM 27

Organizations Listed Alphabetically

Organization / Address / Phone	Descriptive Information	Revenue / ($ mil)	Assets / ($ mil)	Emp (thous)
Western Publishing Group Inc 444 Madison Avenue New York, NY 10022 212-688-4500	Publisher of consumer products; books, games, party items. Type: NASDAQ-WPGI Ind: Publishing/Com Grp: Consumer Service Richard Bernstein, CEO	Rev: 551 Assets: 450 Emp: 3		
Western Savings & Loan Assn Inc 6001 N 24th Street Phoenix, AZ 85016 602-248-4600	Thrift institution. Type: Private Ind: Savings & Loan Grp: Financial Robert W Stallings, CEO Gary Driggs, Chr John Driggs, Pres Clark Cederlof, VCh Fred O Stutenroth, CFO Covel D Allen, IS John C Meadows, Mkt Robert Seddon, VP Ed Moomijian, VP John C Meadows, PR	Rev: 498 Assets: 5599 Emp: 2		
Western Union Corp One Lake Street Upper Saddle Rvr, NJ 07458 201-818-5000	Telecommunications company. Type: NYSE-WU Ind: Telecom Grp: High Tech Bennett S LeBow, CEO Robert Amman, Chr William Weksel, VCh Stewart J Paperin, CFO Thomas Murawski, Mkt John C Walters, VP Peter Anderson, VP Edward Fuhrman, VP Carl L Suiter, VP Jonathan Stern, VP	Rev: 879 Assets: 661 Emp: 6		
Westfair Foods Ltd Addington Street Winnipeg, MB R3E2T4 Can 204-786-7941	Operator of retail food supermarkets. Type: Private-Sub Par: Weston, George Ltd Ind: Retail/Food Grp: Retail Mervyn Booty, CEO	Rev: 1233 Assets: 340 Emp: 2		
Westfield Companies One Park Circle Westfield Center, OH 44251 216-887-0101	Property & casualty insurance company. Type: OTC Ind: Insurance Grp: Insurance Dale W Smucker, CEO	Rev: 450 Assets: 800 Emp: 2		
Westinghouse Broadcasting Co 888 Seventh Avenue New York, NY 10106 212-307-3000	Operator of radio & television broadcasting stations. Type: Private-Sub Par: Westinghouse Electric Corp Ind: Publishing/Com Grp: Consumer Service B Staniar, CEO	Rev: NA Assets: NA Emp: NA		
Westinghouse Canada Inc 120 King Street W Hamilton, ON L8N3K2 Can 416-528-8811	Manufacturer of industrial & commercial electrical equipment Type: Private-Sub-For Ind: Aerospace Grp: High Tech E B Priestner, CEO	Rev: 677 Assets: NA Emp: 6		
Westinghouse Credit Corp One Oxford Center Pittsburgh, PA 15219 412-393-3000	Nationwide business finance & leasing company. Type: Private-Sub Par: Westinghouse Electric Corp Ind: Non-Bank Fin Grp: Financial William A Powe, CEO Robert T Barbour, VCh Laurence A Chapman, CFO Robert C Jacobs, Mkt James J Guidotti, Ops James R Murray, VP	Rev: 810 Assets: 7143 Emp: 1		
Westinghouse Electric Corp Gateway Center 11 Stanwix St Pittsburgh, PA 15222 412-244-2000	Manufacturer of power equipment, aircraft engines. Type: NYSE-WX Ind: Electronics Grp: High Tech John C Marous, CEO Paul E Lego, Pres Harry F Murray, CFO William A Coates, IS Isaac R Barpal, R&D Roy V Gavert Jr, Mkt Maurice Sardi, VP Theodore Stern, VP William A Powell, VP Eileen Massaro, IR Charles Carroll, PR	Rev: 12500 Assets: 16937 Emp: 120		
Westmoreland Coal Co 2500 Fidelity Bldg Philadelphia, PA 19109 215-545-2500	Coal mining company. Type: NASDAQ-WMOR Ind: Energy Grp: Basic Industries Pemberton Hutchinson, CEO E B Leisenring Jr, Chr Larry Zalkin, CFO Howard A Jones, IS Charles Brinley, R&D John V Bickford, Sls Joyce A Forte, Mkt Stephen N Anderson, PR	Rev: 620 Assets: 500 Emp: 3		

Organization / Address / Phone	Descriptive Information	Revenue / ($ mil)	Assets / ($ mil)	Emp (thous)
Weston, George Ltd 22 St Clair Avenue E Toronto, ON M4T2S7 Can 416-922-2500	Packaged foods manufacturing company. Type: TOR-WN Ind: Retail/Food Grp: Retail Robert H Kidd, CEO W Galen Weston, Chr Terrence H Wardrop, VCh Michael Lambert, R&D John Laurie, Sls Ivan R Franklin, VP	Rev: 9206	Assets: 2955	Emp: 55
Westpoint Pepperell Inc 400 W Tenth Street West Point, GA 31833 404-645-4000	Textile manufacturers. Type: NYSE Ind: Apparel/Textiles Grp: Consumer Prd Joseph L Lanier, CEO Donald J Keller, Pres Robert Allen, VCh Clayton H Sauers, CFO Marshall N Morton, IS Charles Crowderr, Mkt D Michael Roark, VP Barry Shea, VP Scott Batson, VP Harry Goodrich, VP Donald J Downs, PR	Rev: 2151	Assets: 2454	Emp: 41
Westvaco Corp 299 Park Avenue New York, NY 10171 212-688-5000	Forest products company; paper, industrial packaging. Type: NYSE-W Ind: Paper/Forest Prd Grp: Basic Industries David L Luke, CEO John A Luke, Pres George E Cruser, CFO James E Stoveken Jr, IS John W Glomb, R&D John A Luke Jr, Mkt John C Callihan, IR David Swirengen, PR	Rev: 2187	Assets: 2634	Emp: 15
Wetterau Inc 8920 Pershall Road Hazelwood, MO 63042 314-524-5000	Wholesale grocer to independent markets. Type: OTC-WETT Ind: Business Service Grp: Business Service Ted C Wetterau, CEO Robert K Crutsinger, Pres John D Ryan, VCh Kurt D Blumenthal, CFO Roger D Beard, IS Andrew Levy, R&D Robert E Mohrmann, Mkt Ronald S Humiston, PR	Rev: 4156	Assets: 799	Emp: 14
Weyerhaeuser Co 33663 32nd Avenue S Tacoma, WA 98003 206-924-2345	Forest products company; lumber, plywood, newsprint. Type: NYSE Ind: Paper/Forest Prd Grp: Basic Industries George H Weyerhaeuser, CEO John Creighton, Pres Charles Bingham, VCh Robert Schuyler, CFO Frank Guthrie, IS N E Johnson, R&D Bill Oliver, PR	Rev: 10004	Assets: 15387	Emp: 47
Wheaton Industries Inc 1101 Wheaton Avenue Millville, NJ 08332 609-825-1400	Packaging company. Type: Private Ind: Manufacturing Grp: Manufacturing Frank H Wheaton Jr, CEO	Rev: 500	Assets: NA	Emp: 5
Wheelabrator Technologies Inc 55 Ferncroft Road Danvers, MA 01923 508-777-2207	Waste to energy management company. Type: NASDAQ-WHGP Ind: Business Service Grp: Business Service Paul M Montrone, CEO Rodney Gilbert, Pres David Summers, VCh Donald F Flynn, CFO Robert Barone, VP Ronald Broglio, VP Harold Buirkle, VP Clifford T Dirkes, VP	Rev: 1205	Assets: 1221	Emp: 10
Wheeler Group Inc Greenwoods Industrial Park Route 219 Hartford, CT 06057 203-379-9911	Manufacturer of business supplies, office products, cards. Type: Private-Sub Par: Pitney Bowes Inc Ind: Comput/Off Equip Grp: High Tech Carol St Mark, CEO	Rev: NA	Assets: NA	Emp: NA
Wheeling Pittsburgh Steel Corp 1134 Market Street Wheeling, WV 26003 304-234-2400	Integrated steel manufacturing company. Type: NYSE Ind: Steel Grp: Basic Industries Lloyd C Lubensky, CEO W J Scharffenberger, Chr Richard E Stoll, Pres John P Innes, VCh John Testa, Tres Frederick G Chbosky, CFO Patrick J Meneely, IS Dr William R Samples, R&D Robert F Good, Sls David E Parrish, Mkt John D Hesse, VP James Raymond, VP C Leslie Davies, VP Charlotte A Palmer, IR Raymond A Johnson, PR	Rev: 1001	Assets: 1002	Emp: 8

Organizations Listed Alphabetically

Organization / Address / Phone	Descriptive Information	Revenue / Assets / Emp ($ mil) ($ mil) (thous)		

Whirlpool Corp
2000 US 33 N
Benton Harbor, MI 49022
616-926-5000

Manufacturer of home & kitchen applicances.
Type: NYSE-WHR
Ind: Appliances/Furn   Grp: Manufacturing
David R Whitwam, CEO   Albert E Suter, Pres   Charles D Putnam, VCh
James R Samartini, CFO   William Tibbitts, IS   Stephen Holmes, R&D
Robert W Paul, Sls   Hank Bowman, Mkt   Samuel Bateman, VP
James K Doran, VP   Robert Frey, VP   Ralph F Hake, VP
Andrew J Takacs, PR

Rev: 4421
Assets: 3410
Emp: 29

White Consolidated Industries Inc
11770 Berea Road
Cleveland, OH 44111
216-252-3700

Manufacturer of kitchen appliances, air conditioners.
Type: Private
Ind: Appliances/Furn   Grp: Manufacturing
Andres Scharp, CEO

Rev: 2000
Assets: NA
Emp: 20

White Swan Co
2700 Handley-Ederville Road
Fort Worth, TX 76101
817-284-4844

Operator of retail & wholesale grocery operations.
Type: Private-Sub   Par: Fleming Companies Inc
Ind: Retail/Food   Grp: Retail
Ronald E Elmquist, CEO

Rev: 500
Assets: NA
Emp: 3

Whitman Co (IC Industries Inc)
111 E Wacker Drive
Chicago, IL 60601
312-565-3000

Food processing & beverage bottling company.
Type: NYSE-WH
Ind: Conglomerate   Grp: Manufacturing
Karl D Bays, CEO   Bruce Chelburg, VCh   John P Fagan, CFO
S Ed Kridakorn, IS   J Robert Topper, R&D   Wendell Larson, VP
Ralph Switzer, VP   Charles H Connolly, PR

Rev: 3583
Assets: 3489
Emp: 25

Whittaker Corp
10880 Wilshire Blvd
Los Angeles, CA 90024
213-475-9411

Manufacturer of specialty chemicals.
Type: NYSE-WKR
Ind: Manufacturing   Grp: Manufacturing
Joseph F Alibrandi, CEO

Rev: 201
Assets: 391
Emp: 2

Wholesale Club Inc
7260 Shadeland Station
Indianapolis, IN 46250
317-842-0351

Retailer of consumer goods via warehouse stores.
Type: NASDAQ-WHLS
Ind: Retail/Merch   Grp: Retail
James Berk, CEO

Rev: 402
Assets: 250
Emp: 2

Wichita, City of
City Hall
Wichita, KS 67202
316-268-4331

City government.
Type: City Govt
Ind: Local Govt   Grp: Govt & Non-Prof
S Kamen, CEO

Rev: 292
Assets: NM
Emp: 3

Wickes Companies Inc
3340 Ocean Park Blvd
Santa Monica, CA 90405
213-452-0161

Furniture retailers, lumber, home improvement supplies.
Type: NYSE-WIX
Ind: Retail/Merch   Grp: Retail
Stanford Sigeloff, CEO   Wilhelm Mallory, CFO   Michael Sitrick, IR
Ann Julsen, PR

Rev: 4777
Assets: 4417
Emp: 62

Wickes Lumber Co
706 Deerpath Drive
Vernon Hills, IL 60061
312-367-6540

Retailer of lumber & building products.
Type: Private
Ind: Retail/Merch   Grp: Retail
Joeseph Rosen, CEO

Rev: 1000
Assets: NA
Emp: 5

Wicor Inc
777 E Wisconsin Avenue
Milwaukee, WI 53201
414-291-7026

Natural gas utility holding company.
Type: NYSE-WIC
Ind: Utility   Grp: Utilities
Stuart W Tisdale, CEO

Rev: 850
Assets: 650
Emp: 6

Wilbur Ellis & Co Inc
320 California Street
San Francisco, CA 94101
415-772-4000

Farm supply distributor.
Type: Private
Ind: Food Processing   Grp: Food Processing
Carter P Thacher, CEO

Rev: 750
Assets: NA
Emp: 5

Wiley, John & Sons Inc
605 Third Avenue
New York, NY 10158
211-285-0600

Publisher of educational & reference books.
Type: NASDAQ-WILL
Ind: Publishing/Com   Grp: Consumer Service
Andrew Neilly, CEO

Rev: 258
Assets: 20
Emp: 2

Organizations Listed Alphabetically

Organization / Address / Phone	Descriptive Information	Revenue / ($ mil)	Assets / ($ mil)	Emp (thous)
Willamette Industries Inc 3800 First Interstate Tower Portland, OR 97201 503-227-5581	Manufacturer of forest products. Type: NASDAQ-WMTT Ind: Paper/Forest Prd Grp: Basic Industries William Swindells, CEO Kenneth Hopkins, VCh C W Knodell, CFO Richard M Clark, IS William M Sheilds, VP Steven Rogel, VP David Morthland, VP Catherine Baldwin, IR C W Knodell, PR	Rev: 1716	Assets: 1430	Emp: 9
Willcox & Gibbs Inc 1440 Broadway New York, NY 10036 212-869-1800	Manufacturer of equipment for the textile & apparel ind. Type: NYSE-WG Ind: Equipment Grp: Manufacturing John D Ziegler, CEO	Rev: 300	Assets: 150	Emp: 2
William Beaumont Hospital Inc 3601 W 13 Mile Road Royal Oak, MI 48072 313-551-5000	Operator of hospitals & clinics. Type: Private Ind: Health Care Grp: Consumer Service Kenneth Myers, CEO	Rev: 545	Assets: NA	Emp: 7
Williams Companies Inc One Williams Center Tulsa, OK 74172 918-588-2000	Natural gas pipeline transport company. Type: NYSE-WMB Ind: Utility Grp: Utilities Joseph H Williams, CEO Vernon T Jones, Pres Jack McCarthy, Tres Keith Bailey, CFO John T Miller, IS John Bumgarner, R&D Harold Miller, Ops John Fischer, VP Barry Roth, VP William Collingsworth, VP	Rev: 1673	Assets: 3567	Emp: 8
Williams, A L Corp 3100 Breckinridge Blvd Duluth, GA 30199 404-381-1674	Insurance, brokerage services. Type: NYSE-ALW Ind: Non-Bank Fin Grp: Financial John Treacy Beyer, CEO William Keane, Pres D Richard Williams, CFO William Schnar, R&D James Carey, Mkt G Kirk Ellis, VP Michael Snider, VP Louis Supic, VP David W Ross, VP	Rev: 402	Assets: 1655	Emp: 2
Williams, Roger Foods Inc 2700 Plainfield Pike Cranston, RI 02920 401-942-4000	Producer & distributor of packaged food products. Type: Private Ind: Food Processing Grp: Food Processing Jerry Trutiano, CEO	Rev: 550	Assets: NA	Emp: 1
Wilmington Trust Corp Rodney Square N Wilmington, DE 19890 302-651-1000	Commercial bank. Type: NASDAQ-WILM Ind: Banking Grp: Financial Bernard J Taylor, CEO	Rev: 313	Assets: 2982	Emp: 2
Wilson Foods Corp 4545 Lincoln Blvd Oklahoma City, OK 73105 405-525-4545	Fresh & frozen food products, retail sales & manufacturing. Type: Private-Sub Par: Doskocil Companies Inc Ind: Food Processing Grp: Food Processing David S Smoak, CEO	Rev: 1324	Assets: 219	Emp: 7
Wimpey, George Canada Ltd 80 N Queen Street Toronto, ON M8Z5Z6 Can 416-233-5811	Construction company. Type: Private-Sub-For Ind: Real Estate/Bldg Grp: Business Service David Heppell, CEO	Rev: 340	Assets: 213	Emp: 1
Winkelman Stores Inc 45000 Helm Street Plymouth, MI 48170 313-451-5353	Operator of retail stores; women's apparel. Type: Private-Sub Par: Petrie Stores Corp Ind: Retail/Merch Grp: Retail Ronald Leonetti, CEO	Rev: NA	Assets: NA	Emp: NA
Winn Dixie Stores Inc 5050 Edgewood Court Jacksonville, FL 32203 904-783-5000	Food supermarkets. Type: NYSE-WIN Ind: Retail/Food Grp: Retail A Dano Davis, CEO James Kufeldt, Pres D H Bragin, Tres Richard P McCook, CFO C R Raulerson, IS C L Cotton, VP J H Childers, VP J Shepard Bryan, VP W F Brim, VP F W Hammond, VP T H Moss, VP G E Clerc, PR	Rev: 9008	Assets: 1514	Emp: 40

Organizations Listed Alphabetically

Organization / Address / Phone	Descriptive Information	Revenue / ($ mil)	Assets / ($ mil)	Emp (thous)
Winn Enterprises Inc 231 E 23rd Street Los Angeles, CA 90011 714-637-2730	Manufacturer of dairy products. Type: NASDAQ-WNN Ind: Food Processing Grp: Food Processing Daniel Montano, CEO	Rev: 1000	Assets: 500	Emp: 10
Winnebago Industries Inc Highway 9 & Highway 69 PO Box 152 Forest City, IA 50436 515-582-3535	Manufacturer of mobile homes. Type: NYSE-WGO Ind: Automotive Grp: Manufacturing John K Hanson, CEO Jerome Clouse, Tres Richard Carlson, R&D Bryan Hays, Mkt Sharon Hansen, VP Raymond Beebe, VP Frank Rotta, PR	Rev: 425	Assets: 237	Emp: 4
Winterthur Swiss Insurance Co One World Trade Center New York, NY 10048 212-466-0777	Property & casualty insurance company. Type: OTC Ind: Insurance Grp: Insurance Robert T Guyer, CEO	Rev: 700	Assets: 1200	Emp: 3
Wisconsin Bell Telephone Co 722 N Broadway Milwaukee, WI 53202 414-549-7300	Telephone utility company. Type: Private-Sub Par: Ameritech (Amer Information Tech Corp) Ind: Utility Grp: Utilities Louis Rutigliano, CEO	Rev: NA	Assets: NA	Emp: NA
Wisconsin Dairies Cooperative Inc Route 3 & Highway 12 W Baraboo, WI 53913 608-356-8316	Agricultural cooperative food production; dairy products. Type: Private Ind: Food Processing Grp: Food Processing Don Storhoff, CEO	Rev: 550	Assets: 150	Emp: 1
Wisconsin Energy Co 231 W Michigan Street Milwaukee, WI 53201 414-277-2345	Electric power utility. Type: NYSE-WEC Ind: Utility Grp: Utilities Charles S McNeer, CEO Russell W Britt, Pres Jerry G Remmell, CFO John H Goetsch, VP Richard A Abdoo, VP John W Fleissner, VP	Rev: 1541	Assets: 2849	Emp: 6
Wisconsin Gas Co Inc 626 E Wisconsin Milwaukee, WI 53202 414-291-7000	Natural gas distribution utility company. Type: Private Ind: Utility Grp: Utilities Thomas F Schrader, CEO	Rev: 825	Assets: NA	Emp: 3
Wisconsin Investment Board 121 E Wilson Street Madison, WI 53702 608-266-2381	State employees retirement fund. Type: State Govt Ind: Non-Bank Fin Grp: Financial Marshall Burkes, CEO	Rev: 1560	Assets: 12881	Emp: 1
Wisconsin Public Service Corp 700 N Adams Street Green Bay, WI 54307 414-433-1598	Electric & gas utility. Type: NYSE-WPS Ind: Utility Grp: Utilities Paul D Ziemer, CEO Linus M Stoll, Chr John V Henderson, VCh James Leithen, CFO Paul Reinhart, Sls J Gus Swoboda, Mkt Daniel Bollom, Ops Donald Hintz, VP Parick Schrickel, VP Robert Knuth, VP	Rev: 604	Assets: 843	Emp: 3
Wisconsin, State of State Capitol Madison, WI 53702 608-266-2111	State government. Type: State Govt Ind: State/Prov Govt Grp: Govt & Non-Prof Tommy G Thompson, CEO	Rev: 12463	Assets: NM	Emp: 76
Witco Corp 520 Madison Avenue New York, NY 10022 212-605-3800	Manufacturer of specialty chemicals. Type: NYSE Ind: Chemicals Grp: Basic Industries William Wishnick, CEO Thomas J Bickett, Pres Denis Andreuzzi, VCh William R Toller, CFO Eric Davies, IS Dr Howard Bryant, R&D William Toller, VP William Setzler, VP Alan Abrams, VP Harvey Golubock, VP Carl Soderlind, IR Sandy Lynn Levy, PR	Rev: 1586	Assets: 1115	Emp: 11
WLR Foods Inc PO Box 228 Hilton, VA 22831 703-867-9221	Food products company; chicken, turkey. Type: NASDAQ-WLRF Ind: Food Processing Grp: Food Processing C W Wompler, CEO	Rev: 371	Assets: 300	Emp: 3

Organizations Listed Alphabetically

Organization / Address / Phone	Descriptive Information	Revenue / ($ mil)	Assets / ($ mil)	Emp (thous)
Wolohan Lumber Corp 1740 Midland Road Saginaw, MI 48605 517-793-4532	Operator of retail lumber & building supplies stores. Type: NASDAQ-WLHN Ind: Retail/Merch Grp: Retail David Wallace, CEO	Rev: 300	Assets: 150	Emp: 1
Wolverine World Wide Inc 9341 Courtland Drive Rockland, MI 49351 616-866-5500	Manufacturer of casual shoe products. Type: NYSE Ind: Apparel/Textiles Grp: Consumer Prd George A Andrews, CEO Thomas D Gleason, Chr Geoffrey B Bloom, Pres Jerome F Hoffman, Tres Robert S Wolff, VP Timothy J O'Donovan, VP Lawrence C Paulson, VP	Rev: 324	Assets: 184	Emp: 5
Wood Gundy Inc Royal Trust Tower Toronto, ON M5K1M7 Can 416-869-8100	Investment company; brokerage. Type: Private Ind: Securities Grp: Financial G E King, CEO	Rev: 255	Assets: 213	Emp: 2
Woodside Management Inc 141 Tremont Street Boston, MA 02111 617-426-7661	Nationwide travel services company. Type: Private Ind: Business Service Grp: Business Service Robert C Warner, CEO	Rev: 250	Assets: NA	Emp: 3
Woodward & Lothrop Inc 11th Street & F Street Washington, DC 20013 202-347-5300	Operator of retail department stores. Type: Private Ind: Retail/Merch Grp: Retail Arnold Aronson, CEO	Rev: 550	Assets: NA	Emp: 5
Woodward's Ltd 101 W Hastings Street Vancouver, BC V6B4G1 Can 604-684-5231	Operator of retail department stores. Type: TOR Ind: Retail/Merch Grp: Retail Charles N W Woodward, CEO	Rev: 577	Assets: 238	Emp: 4
Woolworth, F W Canada Ltd 33 Adelaide Street W Toronto, ON M5H1P5 Can 416-361-2111	Nationwide retail discount store operator. Type: Private-Sub-For Ind: Retail/Merch Grp: Retail R Whithell, CEO Frank Allan Robertson, Chr Willliam John Douglas Woodward, VCh Phillip Charles McComb, Ops Gregory John Duncan McKinstry, VP Leonard Edward Laycock, VP	Rev: 1722	Assets: 566	Emp: 27
Woolworth, F W Co 233 Broadway New York, NY 10279 212-553-2000	Worldwide retailer; discount stores. Type: NYSE-Z Ind: Retail/Merch Grp: Retail Harold E Sells, CEO Frederick E Hennig, Pres William K Lavin, CFO Charles T Young, IS C Jackson Gray, R&D Joseph Carroll, Mkt Arnold Anderson, VP Henry Miner, VP Thomas Page, VP William Forcht, VP Joseph F Carroll, PR	Rev: 8088	Assets: 3535	Emp: 65
World Bank 1818 H Street NW Washington, DC 20433 202-477-1234	International financial agency. Type: Federal Govt Ind: Federal Govt Fin Grp: Financial Barber Conaele, CEO	Rev: 2000	Assets: NM	Emp: 4
World Carpets Inc 1 World Plaza Dalton, GA 30720 404-278-8000	Manufacturer of carpeting. Type: Private Ind: Apparel/Textiles Grp: Consumer Prd Martha McCorkle, CEO	Rev: 275	Assets: NA	Emp: 2
World Oil Co Inc 9302 S Garfield South Gate, CA 90280 213-560-8801	Petroleum products distribution company. Type: Private Ind: Energy Grp: Basic Industries Robert Ross, CEO	Rev: 550	Assets: NA	Emp: 1
Worldmark Corp 1208 US Highway 1 North Palm Beach, FL 33408 305-626-3116	Building materials, intermediate aluminum products. Type: Private Ind: Building Mat Grp: Basic Industries Dean Rhoads, CEO	Rev: 500	Assets: NA	Emp: 1

Organizations Listed Alphabetically

Organization / Address / Phone	Descriptive Information	Revenue / ($ mil)	Assets / ($ mil)	Emp (thous)
Worlds of Wonder Inc 4209 Technology Drive Fremont, CA 94538 415-659-4300	Manufacturer & distributor of childrens toys. Type: NASDAQ-WOW Ind: Leisure Time Grp: Consumer Service Donald Kingsbourough, CEO	Rev: Assets: Emp:	300 214 2	
Worldwide Volkswagen Inc Greenbush Road Orangeburg, NY 10962 914-578-5000	Auto distributing. Type: Private Ind: Automotive Grp: Manufacturing Victor Elmaleh, CEO	Rev: Assets: Emp:	750 NA 1	
Worthington Industries Inc 1205 Dearborn Drive Columbus, OH 43085 614-438-3210	Manufacturer, close tolerance steel, cylinders, plastics. Type: NASDAQ-WTHG Ind: Steel Grp: Basic Industries John H McConnell, CEO Donal H Malenick, Pres Joseph H Stegmayer, CFO Dale Eager, IS Greg McLean, R&D Edward A Ferkany, Sls Robert J Klein, Mkt Charles D Minor, VP Charles R Carson, VP Robert B McCurry, VP Bruce Ruhl, PR	Rev: Assets: Emp:	904 507 7	
WPL Holdings (Wisconsin Power Co) 222 W Washington Avenue Madison, WI 53703 608-252-3311	Electric power utility. Type: NYSE-WPH Ind: Utility Grp: Utilities James R Underkofler, CEO Erroll B Davis, Chr Thomas Landgraf, VCh Edward Gleason, CFO Luann Killeen, IS David Ellstad, R&D A Nino Amato, Mkt William Keepers, Ops	Rev: Assets: Emp:	601 1026 3	
Wright Shuchart Inc 425 Pompius Avenue N Seattle, WA 98109 206-447-7654	Natural resource development & energy company. Type: Private Ind: Energy Grp: Basic Industries Bruce Conner, CEO	Rev: Assets: Emp:	550 NA 2	
Wrigley, William Jr Co 410 N Michigan Avenue Chicago, IL 60611 312-644-2121	Consumer food products company; chewing gum. Type: NYSE-WWY Ind: Food Processing Grp: Food Processing William Wrigley, CEO R Darrell Ewers, VCh Edmund R Meyer, CFO Herb Zugel, IS Dr P Schnell, R&D Anthony Cipollina, Sls Ronald O Cox, Mkt Alfons Jakob, VP Graham Morgan, VP Edgar Swanson, VP H J Kin, VP Joan Weber, PR	Rev: Assets: Emp:	891 440 6	
WTD Industries Inc 10300 SW Greeburg Portland, OR 97228 503-246-3440	Diversified manufacturing company. Type: NASDAQ-WTDI Ind: Manufacturing Grp: Manufacturing Bruce Engel, CEO	Rev: Assets: Emp:	500 250 2	
WWF Paper Corp 2 Bala Plaza Bala Cynwyd, PA 19004 215-667-9210	Fine paper distributor. Type: Private Ind: Paper/Forest Prd Grp: Basic Industries Edward V Furlong, CEO	Rev: Assets: Emp:	600 NA 3	
Wyatt Inc 900 Chapel Street New Haven, CT 06507 203-787-2175	Petroleum wholesaling. Type: Private Ind: Energy Grp: Basic Industries Kirk F Blanchard, CEO	Rev: Assets: Emp:	600 NA 1	
Wyeth-Ayerst Laboratories Inc 31 Morehall Road Frazer, PA 19355 215-644-8000	Manufacturer of prescription drugs. Type: Private-Sub Par: American Home Products Corp Ind: Drugs Grp: Consumer Service Fred Hassan, CEO	Rev: Assets: Emp:	NA NA NA	
Wyle Laboratories Inc 128 Maryland Street El Segundo, CA 90245 213-322-1763	Manufacturer of micro computer components, electronics. Type: NYSE-WYL Ind: Comput/Off Equip Grp: High Tech Stanley A Wainer, CEO	Rev: Assets: Emp:	411 400 2	
Wyman Gordon Co 105 Madison Street Worcester, MA 01613 508-756-5111	Mining & metals processing company. Type: NASDAQ Ind: Metals/Mining Grp: Basic Industries Joseph R Carter, CEO	Rev: Assets: Emp:	272 352 3	

Organization / Address / Phone	Descriptive Information	Revenue / ($ mil)	Assets / ($ mil)	Emp (thous)
Wynn's International Inc 2600 E Nutwood Avenue Fullerton, CA 92621 714-992-2000	Manufacturer of automotive lubricants & parts. Type: NYSE-WN Ind: Automotive Grp: Manufacturing Wesley E Bellwood, CEO	Rev: Assets: Emp:	300 250 2	
Wyoming, State of State Capitol Cheyenne, WY 82002 307-777-7220	State government. Type: State Govt Ind: State/Prov Govt Grp: Govt & Non-Prof Mike J Sullivan, CEO	Rev: Assets: Emp:	2684 NM 13	
Wyse Technology Inc 3571 N First Street San Jose, CA 95134 408-433-1000	Manufacturer of micro computers. Type: NYSE-WYS Ind: Comput/Off Equip Grp: High Tech Bernard K Tse, CEO	Rev: Assets: Emp:	275 200 2	
Xcan Grain Ltd 360 Main Winnipeg, MB R3C3Z3 Can 204-949-1388	Agricultural cooperative; grains, wheat. Type: Private-Coop Ind: Food Processing Grp: Food Processing Bill Strath, CEO	Rev: Assets: Emp:	383 85 1	
Xerox Canada Ltd 5650 Yonge Street North York, ON M2M4G7 Can 416-229-3769	Manufacturer of document processing equipment. Type: TOR-XXC Ind: Comput/Off Equip Grp: High Tech David R McCamus, CEO Peter Brophey, Pres Daryl Walker, CFO Robert Marchessault, R&D Dennis Finnegan, Sls A Kevin Francis, Mkt H Allan Murray, Ops Kenneth Shepherd, VP Thomas Watson, VP Allan D Lin, VP Douglas Harper, VP	Rev: Assets: Emp:	958 1591 7	
Xerox Corp 800 Long Ridge Road PO Box 1600 Stamford, CT 06904 203-968-3000	Manufacturer of document processing equip & fin services. Type: NYSE-XRX Ind: Comput/Off Equip Grp: High Tech David T Kearns, CEO Paul Allaire, Pres William Glavin, VCh Stuart B Ross, CFO Patricia C Barron, IS William Spencer, R&D Dwight F Ryan, Sls E Barry Rand, Mkt Robert Kammerer, Ops L Lyndon Haddon, VP Eunice Filter, VP Douglas M Reid, VP Wayland Hicks, VP Robert J Kammerer, IR Peter Hawes, PR	Rev: Assets: Emp:	16441 26441 113	
Xidex Corp 525 University Avenue Palo Alto, CA 94301 408-988-3472	Manufacturer of data storage products. Type: NASDAQ-XIDX Ind: Comput/Off Equip Grp: High Tech Bert Zaccaria, CEO Craig Gentner, CFO Christine Allen, Mkt Jerri Buzzell, PR	Rev: Assets: Emp:	570 770 6	
XL/Datacomp Inc 908 N Elm Street Hinsdale, IL 60521 312-323-1200	Reseller of major computer systems. Type: NASDAQ-XLDC Ind: Comput/Off Equip Grp: High Tech R J Passaneau, CEO	Rev: Assets: Emp:	231 193 2	
XTRA Corp 60 State Street Boston, MA 02109 617-367-5000	Leasing company; trucks, trailers, shipping containers. Type: NYSE-XTR Ind: Transport Grp: Business Service Charles F Kaye, CEO	Rev: Assets: Emp:	250 300 2	
Yale University Administrative Bldg New Haven, CT 06520 203-436-0300	Major educational institution; university. Type: University Ind: University Grp: Govt & Non-Prof Benno C Schmidt, CEO	Rev: Assets: Emp:	350 660 13	
Yasuda Trust & Banking Co One World Trade Center New York, NY 10048 212-432-2300	Commercial bank. Type: Private-Sub-For Ind: Banking Grp: Financial Minoru Yamada, CEO	Rev: Assets: Emp:	450 3500 1	

Organizations Listed Alphabetically

Organization / Address / Phone	Descriptive Information	Revenue / ($ mil)	Assets / ($ mil)	Emp (thous)

Yellow Freight System Inc
10990 Roe Avenue
Overland Park, KS 66207
913-345-1020

Nationwide trucking company.
Type: NASDAQ-YELL
Ind: Transport   Grp: Business Service
George E Powell, CEO   George E Powell III, Pres   David E Loeffler, CFO
Robert Callaghan, IS   Carl Ruder, R&D   Douglas Fisher, Mkt
Robert Bostick, Ops   William Martin, VP   Gail Parris, VP
Daniel Hornbeck, VP   Michael Haughton, IR   James Felkner, PR

Rev: 2016
Assets: 1021
Emp: 28

York International Corp
1750 Toronita Street
York, PA 17402
717-846-1988

Manufacturer of air conditioning & refrigeration.
Type: NYSE-YRK
Ind: Manufacturing   Grp: Manufacturing
Stanley Hiller, CEO   Michael R Young, Pres   Dean T Ducray, CFO
Orville Trimbly, IS   Patrick M Early, PR

Rev: 900
Assets: 500
Emp: 7

Young & Rubicam Inc
285 Madison Avenue
New York, NY 10017
212-210-3000

Advertising firm.
Type: Private
Ind: Business Service   Grp: Business Service
Alexander Kroll, CEO

Rev: 750
Assets: NA
Emp: 10

Young's Markets Inc
500 S Central Avenue
Los Angeles, CA 90013
213-629-5571

Operator of retail food supermarkets.
Type: Private
Ind: Retail/Food   Grp: Retail
Vernon Underwood, CEO

Rev: 600
Assets: NA
Emp: 3

Zachry, H B Co Inc
527 Logwood
San Antonio, TX 78221
512-922-1213

General contracting company.
Type: Private
Ind: Real Estate/Bldg   Grp: Business Service
H Bartell Zachry Jr, CEO

Rev: 500
Assets: NA
Emp: 5

Zale Corp
901 W Walnut Hill Lane
Irving, TX 75038
214-580-4670

Specialty retail; fine jewelry & giftware.
Type: Private
Ind: Retail/Merch   Grp: Retail
Irving R Gerstein, CEO   Charles Altman, Pres   Merrill Wertheimer, CFO
Nicholas White, Mkt   Jerry Daws, Ops   H R Lively, VP

Rev: 909
Assets: 1126
Emp: 10

Zapata Corp
Zapata Tower PO Box 4240
Houston, TX 77210
713-226-6000

Oil & gas exploration & production company.
Type: NYSE-ZOS
Ind: Energy   Grp: Basic Industries
Ronald C Lassiter, CEO

Rev: 194
Assets: 771
Emp: 1

Zayre Corp
770 Cochituate Road
Framingham, MA 01701
508-390-1000

Operator of apparel retail stores.
Type: NYSE-ZY
Ind: Retail/Merch   Grp: Retail
Sumner L Feldberg, CEO   Richard Lesser, VCh   Steven Wishner, Tres
Donald G Campbell, CFO   Robert Hernandez, IS   David Snell, Mkt
Stanley Oldfield, VP   Armand Correia, VP   Paul Butka, VP
Alfred Appel, VP   Irving Ritz, VP   Stanley Berkovitz, PR

Rev: 1921
Assets: 1462
Emp: 19

Zeller's Inc
5100 De Maisonneuve
Montreal, PQ H4A1Y6 Can
514-483-7600

Operator of department stores.
Type: Private-Sub   Par: Hudson's Bay Co
Ind: Retail/Merch   Grp: Retail
John Levy, CEO

Rev: 1573
Assets: 595
Emp: 12

Zenith Data Systems Corp
1661 Feehanville Drive
Mount Prospect, IL 60056
312-699-4800

Manufacturers of personal computers & electronic products.
Type: Private-Sub   Par: Zenith Electronics Corp
Ind: Comput/Off Equip   Grp: High Tech
John Frank, CEO

Rev: NA
Assets: NA
Emp: NA

Zenith Electronics Corp
1000 Milwaukee Avenue
Glenview, IL 60025
312-391-7000

Manufacturer of industrial & home electronic equipment.
Type: NYSE-ZE
Ind: Electronics   Grp: High Tech
Jerry K Pearlman, CEO   Jerry K Pearlman, Chr   David S Levin, Tres
Kell B Benson, CFO   John I Taylor, IR   David W Denton, PR

Rev: 2686
Assets: 1428
Emp: 36

Zenith Insurance Co
15760 Venture Blvd
Encino, CA 91436
818-990-9300

Property & casualty insurance company.
Type: OTC
Ind: Insurance   Grp: Insurance
Stanley R Zax, CEO

Rev: 300
Assets: 600
Emp: 2

Organizations Listed Alphabetically

Organization / Address / Phone	Descriptive Information	Revenue / Assets / Emp ($ mil) ($ mil) (thous)		

Organization / Address / Phone	Descriptive Information	Revenue ($ mil)	Assets ($ mil)	Emp (thous)
Zenith National Insurance Co 15760 Ventura Blvd Encino, CA 91436 819-990-9300	Insurance company. Type: Private-Sub Ind: Insurance Grp: Insurance Stanley R Zax, CEO Fredricka Taubitz, CFO James P Ross, VP Westley M Heyward, VP Arlington C Ansbro, VP John E Broderick, VP James L Cinney, VP	Rev: Assets: Emp:		472 791 2
Zurich Insurance Co 231 N Martingale Road Schaumburg, IL 60196 312-843-6000	Property & casualty insurance company. Type: Private-Sub-For Ind: Insurance Grp: Insurance William H Bolinder, CEO	Rev: Assets: Emp:		688 1921 4
Zurich Insurance Co Canada Ltd 375 University Avenue Toronto, ON M5G2J7 Can 416-593-4444	Property & casualty insurance company. Type: Private-Sub-For Ind: Insurance Grp: Insurance Paul D McGarry, CEO	Rev: Assets: Emp:		389 672 1
Zurn Industries Inc One Zurn Place Erie, PA 16514 814-452-2111	Waste to energy management & water control company. Type: NYSE-ZRN Ind: Instruments Grp: High Tech George H Schofield, CEO George Schofield, Chr Joseph Sharbaugh, Tres William Freeman, CFO Gerry Trichel, IS F Cole Stearns, R&D Charles L Hedrick, Sls Donald F Fessier, Mkt James A Zurn, VP Edward Donn, VP Richard Nanula, VP David L Lund, VP John E Rutzler, VP	Rev: Assets: Emp:		485 360 4

Section 2

Organizations Listed by Revenue

Organizations Listed by Revenue

Rank	Organization	Phone	City / State or Province	Revenue ($ mil)	Assets ($ mil)	Emp (thous)
1	General Motors Corp	313-556-5000	Detroit, MI	123641	90571	766
2	United States Dept of the Navy	202-545-6700	Washington, DC	109500	NM	1113
3	United States Dept of the Air Force	202-545-6700	Washington, DC	107800	NM	931
4	Ford Motor Co	313-322-3000	Dearborn, MI	92446	143367	185
5	Exxon Corp	212-333-1000	New York, NY	88563	74293	101
6	United States Dept of the Army	202-545-6700	Washington, DC	85700	NM	1110
7	California, State of	916-322-9900	Sacramento, CA	73542	NM	328
8	New York, State of	518-474-2121	Albany, NY	64568	NM	288
9	IBM (Intl Business Mach) Corp	914-765-1900	Armonk, NY	59681	73037	387
10	Mobil Corp	212-883-4242	New York, NY	54361	38820	69
11	United States Dept of Agriculture	202-447-2791	Washington, DC	50842	NM	104
12	Sears Roebuck & Co	312-875-2500	Chicago, IL	50252	77952	400
13	General Electric Co	203-373-2431	Fairfield, CT	50089	110865	298
14	Cargill Inc	612-475-7575	Minnetonka, MN	40000	NA	45
15	United States Postal Service	202-268-2000	Washington, DC	36000	NM	802
16	Texas, State of	512-463-4630	Austin, TX	35579	NM	229
17	Chrysler Corp	313-956-5741	Highland Park, MI	35472	48567	130
18	American Telephone & Telegraph Co	212-605-5500	New York, NY	35210	35152	304
19	Texaco Inc	914-253-4000	White Plains, NY	35138	26337	50
20	Prudential Insurance Co of America	201-877-6000	Newark, NJ	33724	153023	75
21	DuPont, E I DeNemours & Co	302-774-1000	Wilmington, DE	32917	30719	141
22	Citicorp Inc	212-559-1000	New York, NY	32024	207666	89
23	Philip Morris Companies Inc	212-880-5000	New York, NY	31742	36960	155
24	United States Dept of Labor	202-523-8165	Washington, DC	31379	NM	18
25	Metropolitan Life Insurance Co	212-578-2211	New York, NY	30800	120400	50
26	United States Veterans Administration	202-233-2300	Washington, DC	29963	NM	206
27	United States Dept of Transportation	202-366-4000	Washington, DC	27772	NM	64
28	Chevron Corp	415-894-7700	San Francisco, CA	27722	33968	54
29	Province of Quebec	418-643-1430	Quebec City, PQ Can	27540	NM	105
30	Illinois, State of	217-782-2099	Springfield, IL	27399	NM	155
31	K Mart Corp	313-643-1000	Troy, MI	27301	12126	200
32	New York, City of	212-566-1300	New York, NY	27197	NM	339
33	Pennsylvania, State of	717-787-2121	Harrisburg, PA	27163	NM	144
34	Province of Ontario	416-965-3535	Toronto, ON Can	26520	NM	123
35	United States Dept of Education	202-245-3192	Washington, DC	25886	NM	5
36	Michigan, State of	517-373-1837	Lansing, MI	24491	NM	156
37	Aetna Life & Casualty Co	203-273-0123	Hartford, CT	24296	81415	42
38	Ohio, State of	614-466-2000	Columbus, OH	24229	NM	151
39	Florida, State of	904-488-1234	Tallahassee, FL	23940	NM	139
40	Amoco Corp	312-856-6111	Chicago, IL	23919	29919	53
41	American Express Co	212-640-2000	New York, NY	22934	142704	100
42	Shell Oil Co	713-241-6161	Houston, TX	21000	30000	41
43	New Jersey, State of	609-292-2121	Trenton, NJ	20700	NM	105
44	Wal Mart Stores Inc	501-273-4000	Bentonville, AR	20649	5132	200
45	Canadian Department of Defense	613-995-2534	Ottawa, ON Can	20298	NM	120
46	Federal Reserve System Headquarters	202-452-3000	Washington, DC	19526	293674	24
47	Procter & Gamble Co	513-562-1100	Cincinnati, OH	19491	14820	75
48	Occidental Petroleum Corp	213-879-1700	Los Angeles, CA	19417	20747	45
49	ITT Corp	212-752-6000	New York, NY	19355	41941	117
50	Kroger Co	513-762-4000	Cincinnati, OH	19100	4200	150

Organizations Listed by Revenue

Rank	Organization	Phone	City / State or Province	Revenue ($ mil)	Assets ($ mil)	Emp (thous)
51	Travelers Insurance Corp	203-277-0111	Hartford, CT	18986	53332	29
52	Atlantic Richfield Co	213-486-3511	Los Angeles, CA	18868	21514	27
53	United Technologies Corp	203-728-7000	Hartford, CT	18518	12748	185
54	American Stores Co	801-539-0112	Salt Lake City, UT	18478	7010	165
55	CIGNA Corp	215-557-5000	Philadelphia, PA	17889	55825	49
56	Boeing Corp	206-655-2121	Seattle, WA	17340	12608	153
57	Eastman Kodak Co	716-724-4000	Rochester, NY	17034	22964	145
58	USX Corp	412-433-1121	Pittsburgh, PA	16877	19474	80
59	Dow Chemical Co	517-636-1000	Midland, MI	16682	16239	56
60	GTE Corp	203-965-2000	Stamford, CT	16460	31104	200
61	Xerox Corp	203-968-3000	Stamford, CT	16441	26441	113
62	General Motors of Canada Ltd	416-644-5000	Oshawa, ON Can	16414	1448	44
63	RJR Nabisco Inc	404-770-6000	Atlanta, GA	15766	16861	120
64	Massachusetts, State of	617-727-2121	Boston, MA	15502	NM	94
65	McDonnell Douglas Corp	314-232-0232	St Louis, MO	15069	11885	121
66	Koch Industries Inc	316-832-5500	Wichita, KS	15000	NA	8
67	United States Social Security Admin	301-594-1234	Baltimore, MD	15000	NM	71
68	Penney, J C Co	214-591-1000	Dalla, TX	14833	12254	180
69	BellSouth Corp	404-249-2000	Atlanta, GA	13687	28472	101
70	American International Group Inc	212-770-7000	New York, NY	13613	37409	38
71	Safeway Stores Inc	415-891-3000	Oakland, CA	13612	4372	100
72	Tenneco Inc	713-757-2131	Houston, TX	13591	13857	94
73	Ford Motor Canada Ltd	416-845-2511	Oakville, ON Can	13552	3067	27
74	Georgia, State of	404-656-2000	Atlanta, GA	13455	NM	98
75	United States Natl Aerospace & Space Adm	202-453-1000	Washington, DC	13148	NM	24
76	Minnesota, State of	612-296-6013	St Paul, MN	13023	NM	75
77	PepsiCo Inc	914-253-2000	Purchase, NY	13007	11135	235
78	Continental Grain Co	212-207-5100	New York, NY	13000	NA	12
79	United States Dept of the Treasury	202-566-2000	Washington, DC	13000	NM	156
80	NYNEX Corp	212-370-7400	New York, NY	12661	25362	97
81	Westinghouse Electric Corp	412-244-2000	Pittsburgh, PA	12500	16937	120
82	Wisconsin, State of	608-266-2111	Madison, WI	12463	NM	76
83	United States Dept of Energy	202-586-5000	Washington, DC	12404	NM	16
84	Chase Manhattan Bank Inc	212-552-2222	New York, NY	12375	97455	42
85	New York Life Insurance Co	212-576-7000	New York, NY	12374	43417	20
86	President of the United States of Amer	202-395-3080	Washington, DC	12335	NM	1
87	Province of Alberta	403-427-2711	Edmonton, AB Can	12240	NM	71
88	North Carolina, State of	919-733-1110	Raleigh, NC	12205	NM	107
89	Dayton Hudson Corp	612-370-6948	Minneapolis, MN	12204	6523	150
90	Virginia, State of	804-786-0000	Richmond, VA	12101	NM	119
91	Los Angeles County Government	213-974-1411	Los Angeles, CA	12100	NM	70
92	Pemex (Petroleos Mexicos SA)	713-978-7974	Houston, TX	12100	NA	142
93	American Brands Inc	203-698-5000	Old Greenwich, CT	11980	12201	85
94	Allied Signal Inc	713-224-6611	Morristown, NJ	11909	10005	110
95	May Department Stores Co	314-342-6300	St Louis, MO	11525	8144	80
96	Phillips Petroleum Co	918-661-6600	Bartlesville, OK	11490	11968	25
97	Digital Equipment Corp	617-493-5111	Maynard, MA	11475	10112	122
98	Maryland, State of	301-269-6200	Annapolis, MD	11308	NM	94
99	Indiana, State of	317-232-4000	Indianapolis, IN	11256	NM	59
100	Province of British Columbia	604-387-1337	Victoria, BC Can	11220	NM	59

Organizations Listed by Revenue

Rank	Organization	Phone	City / State or Province	Revenue ($ mil)	Assets ($ mil)	Emp (thous)
101	Washington, State of	206-753-5000	Olympia, WA	11219	NM	97
102	Sara Lee Corp	312-726-2600	Chicago, IL	11206	5663	105
103	Federated Department Stores Inc	513-579-7000	Cincinnati, OH	11118	6009	64
104	United States Internal Revenue Service	202-566-5000	Washington, DC	11101	NM	67
105	Rockwell International Corp	412-565-2000	Pittsburgh, PA	11046	4925	112
106	British Petroleum America	216-586-4141	Cleveland, OH	11000	24000	47
107	United States Dept Health & Human Serv	202-245-6296	Washington, DC	11000	NM	43
108	Louisiana, State of	504-342-6600	Baton Rouge, LA	10882	NM	106
109	Bell Atlantic Corp	215-963-6000	Philadelphia, PA	10880	24729	81
110	Loews Corp	212-545-2000	New York, NY	10865	25829	22
111	Goodyear Tire & Rubber Co	216-796-2121	Akron, OH	10810	8618	114
112	General Electric Credit Corp	212-751-5315	New York, NY	10655	74645	10
113	General Motors Acceptance Corp	313-556-5000	Detroit, MI	10645	99041	10
114	Lockheed Corp	818-847-6121	Calabasas, CA	10590	6643	87
115	Minnesota Mining & Manufacturing Co	612-733-1110	St Paul, MN	10581	8922	83
116	Merrill Lynch & Co Inc	212-637-7455	New York, NY	10547	64402	42
117	Shearson Lehman Hutton Inc	212-298-2000	New York, NY	10529	84840	28
118	Fleming Companies Inc	405-840-7200	Oklahoma City, OK	10467	2559	25
119	Caterpillar Inc	309-675-1000	Peoria, IL	10435	9686	58
120	Super Valu Stores Inc	612-828-4000	Eden Prairie, MN	10296	2305	41
121	Federal National Mortgage Corp	202-537-7000	Washington, DC	10266	112258	5
122	Canadian Pacific Ltd	514-395-5151	Montreal, PQ Can	10214	15003	76
123	BankAmerica Corp	415-622-3456	San Francisco, CA	10182	94647	54
124	Unocal Corp	213-977-7600	Los Angeles, CA	10085	9508	18
125	Hewlett Parkard Co	415-857-1501	Palo Alto, CA	10070	7497	87
126	Great Atlantic & Pacific Tea Co	201-573-9700	Montvale, NJ	10068	2640	92
127	Weyerhaeuser Co	206-924-2345	Tacoma, WA	10004	15387	47
128	Kraft Inc	312-498-4000	Glenview, IL	10000	6000	45
129	United Parcel Service Inc	203-622-6000	Greenwich, CT	10000	NA	175
130	Ameritech (Amer Information Tech Corp)	312-750-5000	Chicago, IL	9903	19163	77
131	Unisys Corp	215-542-4011	Blue Bell, PA	9902	11535	90
132	BHP Australia (Broken Hill) Inc	415-981-1515	San Francisco, CA	9900	NA	42
133	Aluminum Co of America	412-553-4545	Pittsburgh, PA	9795	10538	59
134	Sun Co Inc	215-293-6000	Radnor, PA	9744	8616	21
135	Anheuser Busch Companies Inc	314-577-2000	St Louis, MO	9705	7110	40
136	Missouri, State of	314-751-2151	Jefferson City, MO	9593	NM	74
137	General Dynamics Corp	314-889-8200	St Louis, MO	9551	6118	103
138	International Paper Co	914-397-1500	Purchase, NY	9533	9462	55
139	Georgia Pacific Corp	404-521-4000	Atlanta, GA	9509	7115	44
140	Pacific Telesis Group Inc	415-882-8000	San Francisco, CA	9483	21191	70
141	Conagra Inc	402-978-4000	Omaha, NE	9475	3043	43
142	US West Inc	303-793-6500	Englewood, CO	9211	22416	70
143	Weston, George Ltd	416-922-2500	Toronto, ON Can	9206	2955	55
144	ALCAN Aluminum Co of Canada Ltd	514-848-8000	Montreal, PQ Can	9165	9153	67
145	IBP Corp	402-494-2061	Dakota City, NE	9068	1154	18
146	Winn Dixie Stores Inc	904-783-5000	Jacksonville, FL	9008	1514	40
147	Royal Bank of Canada Ltd	514-874-2110	Montreal, PQ Can	9006	93546	46
148	Johnson & Johnson Corp	201-524-0400	New Brunswick, NJ	9001	7119	81
149	Southland Corp	214-828-7011	Dallas, TX	9000	NA	50
150	UAL Inc (United Airlines)	312-952-4000	Elk Grove Townshp, IL	8982	6701	66

Organizations Listed by Revenue

Rank	Organization	Phone	City / State or Province	Revenue ($ mil)	Assets ($ mil)	Emp (thous)
151	Equitable Life Assurance Society Inc	212-554-1234	New York, NY	8898	49288	25
152	AMR (American Airlines) Corp	817-355-1234	Ft Worth, TX	8824	9722	68
153	Toyota Motor Sales USA	213-618-4000	Torrance, CA	8800	NA	21
154	Tennessee, State of	615-741-2001	Nashville, TN	8799	NM	79
155	Texas Air Corp (Continental Airlines)	713-658-9588	Houston, TX	8752	8199	63
156	Connecticut, State of	203-240-0555	Hartford, CT	8599	NM	62
157	Security Pacific Corp	213-345-6211	Los Angeles, CA	8546	77870	33
158	Manufacturers Hanover Corp	212-286-6000	New York, NY	8545	66710	30
159	Southwestern Bell Corp	314-235-9800	St Louis, MO	8473	20985	75
160	TIAA CREF Inc	212-490-9000	New York, NY	8409	30768	3
161	Coca Cola Corp	404-676-2121	Atlanta, GA	8338	7450	40
162	Union Carbide Corp	203-794-2000	Danbury, CT	8324	8441	44
163	Monsanto Co	314-694-1000	St Louis, MO	8293	8461	46
164	Liberty Mutual Insurance Co	617-285-7000	Boston, MA	8268	15749	26
165	Motorola Inc	312-397-5000	Schaumburg, IL	8250	6710	102
166	CNA Financial Corp	312-822-5000	Chicago, IL	8204	22941	17
167	Colorado, State of	303-866-5000	Denver, CO	8200	NM	62
168	Ashland Oil Inc	606-329-3333	Russell, KY	8196	4254	30
169	Raytheon Co	617-862-6600	Lexington, MA	8192	4740	76
170	Coastal Corp	713-877-1400	Houston, TX	8187	7865	16
171	Woolworth, F W Co	212-553-2000	New York, NY	8088	3535	65
172	Alabama, State of	205-261-2500	Montgomery, AL	8068	NM	80
173	Mars Inc	703-821-4900	McLean, VA	8000	NA	20
174	Hancock, John Mutual Life Insurance Co	617-421-6000	Boston, MA	7926	10067	25
175	Transamerica Corp	415-983-4000	San Francisco, CA	7879	26759	17
176	Canadian Imperial Bank of Commerce Ltd	416-980-2211	Toronto, ON Can	7854	80485	36
177	Morgan, J P & Co Inc	212-344-3000	New York, NY	7839	83923	16
178	Pacific Gas & Electric Co	415-781-4211	San Francisco, CA	7646	21068	27
179	Chemical New York Corp	212-310-6161	New York, NY	7644	67349	20
180	CSX Corp	804-782-1400	Richmond, VA	7592	13026	54
181	Noranda Inc	416-982-7111	Toronto, ON Can	7529	7961	48
182	Beatrice Foods (BCI Holdings Inc)	312-782-3820	Chicago, IL	7500	5000	42
183	Brascan Ltd	416-363-9491	Toronto, ON Can	7491	4126	1
184	Oklahoma, State of	405-521-2011	Oklahoma City, OK	7409	NM	72
185	Marriott Corp	301-897-9000	Washington, DC	7370	5981	230
186	Campeau Corp	416-868-6460	Toronto, ON Can	7368	12151	110
187	Chrysler Canada Ltd	519-973-2000	Windsor, ON Can	7368	2656	12
188	Loblaw Companies	416-922-8500	Toronto, ON Can	7336	1881	33
189	LTV Corp	214-979-7711	Dallas, TX	7325	6163	39
190	Arizona, State of	602-255-4900	Phoenix, AZ	7324	NM	53
191	Lincoln National Corp	219-427-2000	Fort Wayne, IN	7312	20964	15
192	Kentucky, State of	502-465-2500	Frankfort, KY	7295	NM	71
193	Textron Inc	401-421-2800	Providence, RI	7286	12554	60
194	McKesson Corp	415-983-8300	San Francisco, CA	7283	2255	17
195	Borden Inc	212-573-4000	New York, NY	7244	4440	33
196	Southern Co	404-393-0650	Atlanta, GA	7235	19729	31
197	Provigo Incorporated	514-866-9781	Montreal, PQ Can	7175	1363	14
198	Oregon, State of	503-378-3131	Salem, OR	7165	NM	56
199	Honeywell Inc	612-870-5200	Minneapolis, MN	7148	5089	62
200	Lucky Stores Inc	415-833-6000	Dublin, OH	7000	1750	80

Organizations Listed by Revenue

Rank	Organization	Phone	City / State or Province	Revenue ($ mil)	Assets ($ mil)	Emp (thous)
201	Union Pacific Corp	212-418-7800	New York, NY	7000	11000	30
202	TRW Inc	216-291-7000	Cleveland, OH	6982	4442	73
203	Delta Air Lines Inc	404-765-2600	Atlanta, GA	6915	5748	38
204	United States Dept of Justice	202-633-2000	Washington, DC	6882	NM	80
205	Baxter Travenol Laboratories Inc	312-948-2000	Deerfield, IL	6861	8550	64
206	Ford Credit Corp	313-322-3000	Dearborn, MI	6819	56276	9
207	Bank of Montreal	514-877-7110	Montreal, PQ Can	6816	67073	34
208	Archer Daniels Midland Co	217-424-5200	Decatur, IL	6798	4398	9
209	Melville Corp	914-253-8000	Harrison, NY	6780	2736	97
210	Albertson's Inc	208-385-6200	Boise, ID	6773	1591	50
211	Alaska, State of	907-465-2111	Juneau, AK	6726	NM	26
212	Emerson Electric Co	314-553-2000	St Louis, MO	6652	5027	71
213	Iowa, State of	515-281-5011	Des Moines, IA	6603	NM	59
214	Principle Financial Group Inc	515-247-5111	Des Moines, IA	6577	23493	10
215	United Telecommunications Inc	913-676-3000	Westwood, KS	6493	9817	42
216	South Carolina, State of	803-734-1000	Columbus, SC	6425	NM	74
217	Federal Reserve Bank of New York Inc	212-720-5000	New York, NY	6381	99785	4
218	Texas Instruments Inc	214-995-2011	Dallas, TX	6295	4428	83
219	SCECORP Southern California Edison Co	818-302-1297	Rosemead, CA	6253	14866	17
220	Pillsbury Co	612-330-4966	Minneapolis, MN	6191	3840	100
221	Salomon Inc	212-764-3700	New York, NY	6146	85256	7
222	Imperial Oil Ltd	416-968-4111	Toronto, ON Can	6124	7461	13
223	Supermarkets General Corp	201-499-3000	Woodbridge, NJ	6000	NA	30
224	NCR Corp	513-445-5000	Dayton, OH	5990	4717	60
225	Bristol Meyers Co	212-546-4000	New York, NY	5973	5190	35
226	Merck & Co Inc	201-574-4000	Rahway, NJ	5940	6128	32
227	First Interstate BanCorp Inc	213-614-6001	Los Angeles, CA	5932	63703	38
228	Pacific Enterprises Corp	213-895-5000	Los Angeles, CA	5932	6866	13
229	Continental International Corp	212-440-3980	New York, NY	5878	13302	17
230	Ralston Purina Co	314-982-1000	St Louis, MO	5876	4044	57
231	Kansas, State of	913-296-0111	Topeka, KS	5872	NM	54
232	FPL (Florida Power & Light) Group Inc	407-694-6300	North Palm Beach, FL	5854	11793	19
233	Bankers Trust New York Corp	212-250-2500	New York, NY	5851	57942	13
234	Macy, R H & Co Inc	212-560-3600	New York, NY	5800	NA	70
235	Northrop Corp	213-553-6262	Los Angeles, CA	5797	3139	45
236	Grace, W R & Co	212-819-5500	New York, NY	5786	5310	46
237	Northwestern Mutual Life Insurance Co	414-271-1444	Milwaukee, WI	5737	25362	9
238	Martin Marietta Corp	301-897-6000	Bethesda, MD	5727	3319	80
239	Enron Corp	713-853-6161	Houston, TX	5708	8695	8
240	US Air Group Inc	703-892-7000	Arlington, VA	5707	5345	24
241	NWA (Northwest Airlines) Inc	612-726-2111	St Paul, MN	5650	4372	36
242	Reynolds Metals Co	804-281-2000	Richmond, VA	5619	5032	29
243	PPG Industries Inc	412-434-3131	Pittsburgh, PA	5617	5154	36
244	Commonwealth Edison Co	312-294-4321	Chicago, IL	5613	17822	18
245	Transport Canada	613-996-5861	Ottawa, ON Can	5610	NM	21
246	Kaiser Permanente Medical	415-428-5000	Oakland, CA	5584	4161	50
247	USF & G Corp	301-547-3000	Baltimore, MD	5582	12361	10
248	McDonald's Corp	312-575-3000	Oak Brook, IL	5566	8159	175
249	American Home Products Corp	212-878-5000	New York, NY	5501	4611	45
250	BAT US Inc	502-581-8000	Louisville, KY	5500	NA	16

Organizations Listed by Revenue

Rank	Organization	Phone	City / State or Province	Revenue ($ mil)	Assets ($ mil)	Emp (thous)
251	Bunge Corp	212-943-6600	New York, NY	5500	NA	3
252	Honda of America Corp	513-642-5000	Marysville, OH	5500	NA	16
253	Bethlehem Steel Corp	215-694-2424	Bethlehem, PA	5489	4449	45
254	Bank of Nova Scotia Ltd	416-866-6161	Toronto, ON Can	5437	60716	26
255	North American Philips Corp	212-697-3600	New York, NY	5424	3423	52
256	Bell Canada Inc (BCE Inc)	514-870-1511	Montreal, PQ Can	5421	11482	110
257	Unilever (United States) Inc	212-888-1260	New York, NY	5400	4500	41
258	Kimberly Clark Corp	214-830-1200	Dallas, TX	5394	4268	47
259	Pfizer Inc	212-573-2323	New York, NY	5385	7638	41
260	Deere & Co	309-765-8000	Moline, IL	5365	5245	38
261	Southern California Gas Co	213-689-2345	Los Angeles, CA	5339	5027	28
262	Quaker Oats Co	312-222-7111	Chicago, IL	5330	2975	31
263	Tennesse Valley Authority Inc	615-632-2101	Knoxville, TN	5322	25823	12
264	Bank of Boston Corp	617-434-2200	Boston, MA	5296	36060	20
265	Heinz, H J Co	412-456-5700	Pittsburgh, PA	5244	3605	39
266	Mutual Life Ins Co of New York (MONY)	212-708-2000	New York, NY	5235	17706	8
267	General Mills Inc	612-540-2311	Minneapolis, MN	5179	2672	74
268	MCI Communications Corp	202-872-1600	Washington, DC	5137	5843	18
269	Flour Corp	714-975-2000	Irvine, CA	5132	2073	18
270	Champion International Corp	203-358-7000	Stamford, CT	5129	6700	30
271	Manufacturers Life Insurance Co Canada	416-926-0100	Toronto, ON Can	5120	20305	6
272	Consolidated Edison New York Inc	212-460-4600	New York, NY	5109	9552	19
273	Paramount Communications Corp	212-333-7000	New York, NY	5108	5378	40
274	Imasco Ltd	514-937-9111	Montreal, PQ Can	5101	4514	60
275	James River Corp	804-644-5411	Richmond, VA	5098	5006	34
276	Ryder System Inc	305-593-3726	Miami, FL	5030	6039	45
277	Federal Aviation Administration	202-366-4000	Washington, DC	5000	NM	15
278	Federal Deposit Insurance Corp	202-393-8400	Washington, DC	5000	NM	4
279	Nationwide Insurance Co	614-249-7111	Columbus, OH	5000	12000	12
280	Puerto Rico, Territory of United States	809-724-2030	San Juan, PR	5000	NM	90
281	Blue Cross Blue Shield of Michigan Inc	313-225-8000	Detroit, MI	4950	12852	9
282	Abbott Laboratories Inc	312-937-6100	Abbott Park, IL	4937	4825	39
283	Dana Corp	419-535-4500	Toledo, OH	4936	4786	40
284	Mississippi, State of	601-359-3100	Jackson, MS	4929	NM	50
285	Schlumberger Ltd	212-350-9400	New York, NY	4925	5600	48
286	Walgreen Co	312-940-2500	Deerfield, IL	4884	1512	35
287	Campbell Soup Co	609-342-4800	Camden, NJ	4869	3610	48
288	Litton Industries Inc	213-859-5000	Beverly Hills, CA	4864	5075	55
289	Wells Fargo & Co	415-477-1000	San Francisco, CA	4853	46617	20
290	Electronic Data Systems Corp	214-661-6000	Dallas, TX	4844	3416	45
291	American Electric Power Co Inc	614-223-1000	Columbus, OH	4841	2762	23
292	Halliburton Co	214-978-2600	Dallas, TX	4839	4722	28
293	First Chicago Corp	312-732-4000	Chicago, IL	4815	44432	16
294	Kiewit, Peter & Sons Inc	402-342-2052	Omaha, NE	4800	NA	30
295	Montgomery Ward & Co Inc	312-467-2000	Chicago, IL	4800	3000	40
296	United States Environmental Protect Agcy	202-382-2090	Washington, DC	4787	NM	15
297	Wickes Companies Inc	213-452-0161	Santa Monica, CA	4777	4417	62
298	Capital Cities--Amer Broadcasting Co Inc	212-456-7777	New York, NY	4773	6089	20
299	Smithkline Beckman Corp	215-751-4000	Philadelphia, PA	4749	5017	42
300	Colgate Palmolive Co	212-310-2000	New York, NY	4734	3218	25

Organizations Listed by Revenue

Rank	Organization	Phone	City / State or Province	Revenue ($ mil)	Assets ($ mil)	Emp (thous)
301	Scott Paper Co	215-522-5000	Philadelphia, PA	4726	5156	27
302	Bayer USA	412-394-5500	Pittsburgh, PA	4719	3627	26
303	Burlington Northern Inc	817-878-2000	Fort Worth, TX	4701	6330	39
304	CPC International Inc	201-894-4000	Englewood Cliffs, NJ	4701	3342	39
305	Lyondell Petrochemical Corp	713-652-7200	Houston, TX	4696	913	10
306	Connecticut General Life Ins Co	203-726-6000	Bloomfield, CT	4692	26786	12
307	Massachusetts Mutual Life Insurance Comp	413-788-8411	Springfield, MA	4632	22589	9
308	Teledyne Inc	213-277-3311	Los Angeles, CA	4598	5125	60
309	American Cyanamid Co	201-831-2000	Wayne, NJ	4592	4593	36
310	Hydro Quebec Ltd	514-289-2211	Montreal, PQ Can	4510	26998	19
311	Time Inc	212-586-1212	New York, NY	4507	4913	20
312	Bechtel Group Inc	415-768-1234	San Francisco, CA	4500	NA	20
313	Ontario Hydro Corp	416-592-5111	Toronto, ON Can	4488	27758	32
314	Mead Corp	513-222-6323	Dayton, OH	4464	2492	21
315	Norfolk Southern Corp	804-629-2600	Norfolk, VA	4462	10159	34
316	United States Dept of State	202-647-4000	Washington, DC	4437	NM	26
317	Whirlpool Corp	616-926-5000	Benton Harbor, MI	4421	3410	29
318	Petro Canada	403-296-5850	Calgary, AB Can	4415	7185	8
319	Eastern Airlines Inc	305-873-2211	Miami, FL	4402	3673	37
320	Farmland Industries Inc	816-459-6000	Kansas City, MO	4400	1000	6
321	Malone & Hyde Inc	901-325-4200	Memphis, TN	4400	NA	21
322	Nissan Motor Corp USA	212-532-3111	Carson, CA	4400	NA	15
323	Stop & Shop (SSC Holdings) Inc	617-770-8000	North Quincy, MA	4400	NA	45
324	Public Service Enterprise Group Inc	201-430-7000	Newark, NJ	4395	11690	15
325	SYSCO Corp	713-877-1122	Houston, TX	4385	1021	13
326	Toronto Dominion Bank Ltd	416-982-8222	Toronto, ON Can	4370	46346	22
327	Kellogg Co	616-966-2000	Battle Creek, MI	4349	3298	23
328	Labatt, John Ltd	519-673-5050	London, ON Can	4341	2157	18
329	Shell Canada Ltd	403-232-3111	Calgary, AB Can	4301	4773	7
330	Seagram Co Ltd	514-849-5271	Montreal, PQ Can	4298	8242	19
331	Dun & Bradstreet Corp	212-593-6800	New York, NY	4267	5024	90
332	Amerada Hess Corp	212-997-8500	New York, NY	4264	5372	8
333	Cooper Industries Inc	713-739-5400	Houston, TX	4258	4384	46
334	Los Angeles, City of	213-485-3311	Los Angeles, CA	4254	NM	42
335	Utah, State of	801-533-4000	Salt Lake City, UT	4240	NM	37
336	Great West Life Assurance Co	204-946-1190	Winnipeg, MB Can	4221	14669	5
337	Arkansas, State of	501-371-3000	Little Rock, AR	4219	NM	44
338	Sun Life Assurance Co of Canada	416-595-7500	Toronto, ON Can	4215	19711	5
339	Warner Communications Inc	212-484-8000	New York, NY	4206	4598	31
340	Publix Super Markets Inc	813-688-1188	Lakeland, FL	4200	1000	22
341	Hanson Industries (Hanson Trust) Inc	201-549-7050	Iselin, NJ	4180	3200	37
342	New Mexico, State of	505-827-4011	Sante Fe, NM	4168	NM	42
343	Price Co	619-581-4600	San Diego, CA	4162	993	8
344	Wetterau Inc	314-524-5000	Hazelwood, MO	4156	799	14
345	Texas Utilities Co	214-653-4600	Dallas, TX	4154	16058	16
346	Hospital Corp of America	615-327-9551	Nashville, TN	4111	5388	86
347	Boise Cascade Corp	208-384-6161	Boise, ID	4095	3610	20
348	Navistar International Corp	312-836-2000	Chicago, IL	4080	2522	16
349	Employment & Immigration Canada	819-994-6313	Hull, PQ Can	4080	NM	24
350	Province of Manitoba	204-945-3744	Winnipeg, MB Can	4080	NM	18

Organizations Listed by Revenue

Rank	Organization	Phone	City / State or Province	Revenue ($ mil)	Assets ($ mil)	Emp (thous)
351	Province of Saskatchewan	306-565-6291	Regina, SK Can	4080	NM	23
352	Apple Computer Inc	408-996-1010	Cupertino, CA	4071	2082	7
353	Limited Inc	614-475-4000	Columbus, OH	4071	2145	17
354	BASF Corp	201-397-2700	Parsippany, NJ	4070	2200	21
355	Lilly, Eli & Co	317-261-2000	Indianapolis, IN	4070	5263	31
356	Inland Steel Industries Inc	312-346-0300	Chicago, IL	4068	2925	21
357	West Virginia, State of	304-348-3456	Charleston, WV	4006	NM	43
358	Toys R Us Inc	201-845-5033	Rochelle Park, NJ	4001	2555	28
359	Allied Stores Corp	212-764-2000	New York, NY	4000	5000	25
360	ARA Holding Co	215-238-3000	Philadelphia, PA	4000	1500	110
361	Carlson Companies Inc	612-540-5000	Minneapolis, MN	4000	NA	50
362	Goldman, Sachs & Co	212-902-1000	New York, NY	4000	51301	7
363	Peat Marwick Main & Co	212-758-9700	New York, NY	4000	NA	30
364	Trans World Airlines Inc	212-692-3000	New York, NY	4000	3500	29
365	International Thomson Organisation Ltd	416-977-8700	Toronto, ON Can	3987	3776	23
366	Chubb Corp	201-580-2000	Warren, NJ	3980	9741	12
367	Canadian National Railway	514-399-5430	Montreal, PQ Can	3975	5870	44
368	Hudson's Bay Co	416-861-6112	Toronto, ON Can	3971	2966	40
369	AMAX Inc	212-856-4200	New York, NY	3944	4076	20
370	Dresser Industries Inc	214-740-6000	Dallas, TX	3942	2899	31
371	Warner Lambert Co	201-540-2000	Morris Plains, NJ	3908	2703	33
372	Cook County Government	312-443-5500	Chicago, IL	3900	NM	23
373	Steinberg Inc	514-931-9131	Montreal, PQ Can	3897	1296	36
374	Federal Express Corp	901-369-3600	Memphis, TN	3883	3009	49
375	Coca Cola Enterprises Inc	404-676-2100	Atlanta, GA	3874	4669	11
376	Kemper Corp	312-540-2000	Long Grove, IL	3861	12078	16
377	Clark Oil & Refining Co	314-889-9600	St Louis, MO	3850	NA	3
378	Elf Aquitaine Inc	203-358-5000	Stamford, CT	3850	NA	8
379	Mitsubishi International USA Inc	212-605-2000	New York, NY	3850	NA	8
380	PNC Financial Corp	412-762-2728	Pittsburgh, PA	3827	40811	15
381	American General Corp	713-522-1111	Houston, TX	3823	30422	18
382	California Public Emp Retirement System	916-445-7700	Sacramento, CA	3821	41249	2
383	Alco Standard Corp	215-296-8000	Valley Forge, PA	3817	1399	16
384	Food Lion Inc	704-633-8250	Salisbury, NC	3815	1089	36
385	New England Mutual Life Insurance Co	617-578-2000	Boston, MA	3802	14273	8
386	Borg Warner Corp	312-322-8500	Chicago, IL	3800	3000	60
387	Owens Illinois Inc	419-247-5000	Toledo, OH	3800	3500	40
388	Tandy Corp	817-390-3700	Fort Worth, TX	3794	2530	30
389	Stone Container Corp	312-346-6600	Chicago, IL	3742	2395	21
390	Nebraska, State of	402-471-2311	Lincoln, NE	3721	NM	34
391	Fireman's Fund Inc	415-899-2000	Novato, CA	3704	11190	10
392	Noranda Forest Inc	416-365-0710	Toronto, ON Can	3668	3339	16
393	Great Western Financial Corp	213-852-3411	Beverly Hills, CA	3665	32815	13
394	Grumman Corp	516-575-0574	Bethpage, NY	3649	2566	30
395	Houston Industries Inc	713-228-2474	Houston, TX	3649	10219	10
396	Oshawa Group Ltd	416-236-1971	Islington, ON Can	3634	572	19
397	St Paul Companies Inc	612-221-7911	St Paul, MN	3631	10382	10
398	Control Data Corp	612-853-8100	Minneapolis, MN	3628	2534	34
399	Duke Power Co	704-373-4011	Charlotte, NC	3627	8891	21
400	Northern Telecom Ltd	416-897-9000	Mississauga, ON Can	3613	NA	35

Organizations Listed by Revenue

Rank	Organization	Phone	City / State or Province	Revenue ($ mil)	Assets ($ mil)	Emp (thous)
401	Nassau County Government	516-535-3000	Mineola, NY	3600	NM	20
402	Great Northern Nekoosa Corp	203-359-4000	Stamford, CT	3588	3821	20
403	Whitman Co (IC Industries Inc)	312-565-3000	Chicago, IL	3583	3489	25
404	Gillette Co	617-421-7000	Boston, MA	3581	2868	29
405	TW Service Inc	201-712-0500	Paramus, NJ	3574	2106	120
406	Pan American Corp	212-880-1234	New York, NY	3569	2149	20
407	Waste Management Inc	312-654-8800	Oak Brook, IL	3566	4879	35
408	Entergy Corp (Middle South Utilities)	504-529-5262	New Orleans, LA	3565	15942	15
409	Pacificorp Corp	503-464-6000	Portland, OR	3519	11396	14
410	United Brands Co	513-579-2115	Cincinnati, OH	3503	1436	40
411	American Standard Inc	212-703-5100	New York, NY	3500	2200	40
412	Dean Witter Reynolds Inc	212-392-2222	New York, NY	3500	33000	19
413	Marmon Group Inc	312-372-9500	Chicago, IL	3500	NA	25
414	Prudential Bache Securities Inc	212-214-1000	New York, NY	3500	33000	16
415	Bergen Brunswig Corp	714-385-4000	Orange, CA	3486	889	6
416	Combustion Engineering Inc	203-329-8771	Stamford, CT	3484	2546	29
417	Texas Eastern Corp	713-759-3131	Houston, TX	3481	5444	8
418	Eaton Corp	216-523-5000	Cleveland, OH	3469	3034	43
419	Disney, Walt Co	818-840-1000	Burbank, CA	3438	5109	39
420	Humana Inc	502-580-1000	Louisville, KY	3435	3422	49
421	Sears Canada Ltd	416-362-1711	Toronto, ON Can	3430	2229	50
422	Chesebrough Ponds Inc	203-222-3000	Greenwich, CT	3400	1500	25
423	Reliance Group Holdings Inc	212-909-1100	New York, NY	3400	6079	10
424	Ames Department Stores Inc	203-563-8234	Rocky Hill, CT	3363	1700	21
425	United States General Services Admin	202-655-4000	Washington, DC	3360	NM	19
426	Allstate Life Insurance Co	312-291-5000	Northbrook, IL	3354	5972	3
427	Nova Corp of Alberta Ltd	403-290-6000	Calgary, AB Can	3350	7006	8
428	Dominion Resources Inc	804-755-5700	Richmond, VA	3344	9495	15
429	Times Mirror Co	213-972-3700	Los Angeles, CA	3333	3476	28
430	Ahmanson, H F & Co (Home Savings of Am)	213-487-4277	Los Angeles, CA	3315	40258	9
431	Gannett Co Inc	703-284-6000	Arlington, VA	3314	3793	30
432	Cummins Engine Co Inc	812-377-5000	Columbus, IN	3310	2064	26
433	Greyhound Corp	602-248-4000	Phoenix, AZ	3305	5034	37
434	Trilon Financial Corp	416-363-0061	Toronto, ON Can	3301	27051	23
435	Associated Milk Producers Inc	512-340-9100	San Antonio, TX	3300	500	3
436	Ciba Geigy USA Corp	914-478-3131	Ardsley, NY	3300	NA	16
437	Drexel Burnham Lambert Inc	212-480-6000	New York, NY	3300	NA	10
438	Harvest States Cooperatives Inc	612-646-9433	St Paul, MN	3300	NA	2
439	Kanematsu Gosho USA Inc	212-704-9400	New York, NY	3300	NA	8
440	Mocatta Metals Corp	212-912-8400	New York, NY	3300	16500	1
441	Schlott, Richard Realty Inc	201-633-5000	Wayne, NJ	3300	NA	4
442	Sony Corp of America	201-930-1000	Park Ridge, NJ	3300	NA	4
443	Vons Companies Inc	818-579-1400	El Mone, CA	3300	NA	19
444	Wakefern Food Corp	201-527-3300	Elizabeth, NJ	3300	NA	4
445	Canada Safeway Ltd	403-260-8600	Calgary, AB Can	3291	821	22
446	FMC Corp	312-861-6000	Chicago, IL	3287	2749	24
447	Brunswick Corp	312-470-4700	Skokie, IL	3282	2092	29
448	Mellon Bank Corp	412-234-5000	Pittsburgh, PA	3269	31153	14
449	United States Dept Housing & Urban Dev	202-655-4000	Washington, DC	3261	NM	13
450	Financial Corp of America	714-553-6900	Irvine, CA	3250	22000	6

Organizations Listed by Revenue

Rank	Organization	Phone	City / State or Province	Revenue ($ mil)	Assets ($ mil)	Emp (thous)
451	Bank of New England Corp	617-742-4000	Boston, MA	3247	30110	18
452	Washington, District of Columbia	202-727-1000	Washington, DC	3238	NM	52
453	Philadelphia Electric Co	215-841-4000	Philadelphia, PA	3229	11863	11
454	Armco Inc	201-316-5200	Parsippany, NJ	3227	2788	16
455	National Medical Enterprises Inc	213-479-5526	Los Angeles, CA	3202	3507	85
456	Turner Corp	212-878-0400	New York, NY	3196	920	10
457	Celanese Corp (Hoechst)	201-231-2000	Somerville, NJ	3190	2400	21
458	Canada Life Assurance Co	416-597-1456	Toronto, ON Can	3170	9661	3
459	Mutual Benefit Life Insurance Co	201-481-8000	Newark, NJ	3169	10639	6
460	United States Dept of Commerce	202-377-2000	Washington, DC	3152	NM	86
461	Santa Fe Southern Pacific Corp	312-786-6000	Chicago, IL	3144	6824	26
462	Columbia Gas System Inc	302-429-5000	Wilmington, DE	3128	5641	11
463	Paccar Inc	206-455-7400	Bellevue, WA	3122	2832	10
464	AMI American Medical International Inc	213-278-6200	Beverly Hills, CA	3111	832	46
465	Detroit Edison Co	313-237-8000	Detroit, MI	3102	10060	10
466	Grand Union Co	201-890-6000	Wayne, NJ	3100	750	25
467	Johnson Controls Inc	414-228-1200	Milwaukee, WI	3100	2013	29
468	Morgan Stanley & Co Inc	212-703-4000	New York, NY	3100	29190	5
469	Staley Continental Incorporated	312-981-1696	Rolling Meadows, IL	3100	1745	10
470	Service Merchandise Co Inc	615-251-6666	Nashville, TN	3093	1711	27
471	National Steel (Nat'l Intergroup) Corp	412-394-4100	Pittsburgh, PA	3081	2000	7
472	Wang Laboratories Inc	508-459-5000	Lowell, MA	3068	2838	31
473	Avon Products Inc	212-546-6015	New York, NY	3063	2460	28
474	Continental Bank Corp	312-828-2345	Chicago, IL	3061	30578	8
475	Fleet/Norstar Financial Corp	401-278-5800	Providence, RI	3051	29052	15
476	First Executive Corp	213-312-1000	Los Angeles, CA	3049	18225	1
477	MCA Inc	818-777-1000	Universal City, CA	3024	4115	16
478	Ingersoll-Rand Corp	201-573-0123	Woodcliff Lake, NJ	3021	2483	30
479	SAFECO Corp	206-545-5000	Seattle, WA	3018	7732	9
480	American Financial Corp	513-579-2121	Cincinnati, OH	3000	8000	10
481	Apex Oil Co	314-889-9600	St Louis, MO	3000	NA	8
482	Arthur, Andersen & Co Inc	312-580-0069	Chicago, IL	3000	NA	30
483	Burlington Industries Inc	919-379-2000	Greensboro, NC	3000	2300	25
484	Crum & Foster Inc	201-285-7000	Morristown, NJ	3000	7500	8
485	Eckerd, Jack Corp	813-397-7461	Largo, FL	3000	NA	30
486	Hutton, E F Group Inc	212-742-5000	New York, NY	3000	25000	15
487	Levi Strauss & Co Inc	415-544-6000	San Francisco, CA	3000	NA	30
488	Piedmont Aviation Inc	919-767-5100	Winston Salem, NC	3000	1718	20
489	Riklis Corp	212-735-9500	New York, NY	3000	NA	50
490	Seagrams, Joseph E & Sons Inc	212-572-7000	New York, NY	3000	6000	10
491	SIPCO (Swift Independent Corp)	214-573-2333	Dallas, TX	3000	300	10
492	Sun Exploration Corp	214-890-6000	Dallas, TX	3000	2000	1
493	Taubman Co Inc	313-258-6800	Bloomfield Hills, MI	3000	NA	1
494	United States Dept of Defense	202-545-6700	Washington, DC	3000	NM	28
495	Nekoosa Papers Inc	715-887-5111	Port Edwards, WI	3000	NA	20
496	Giant Food Inc	301-341-4100	Landover, MD	2987	983	25
497	AmBase Corp (Home Group Inc)	212-530-6800	New York, NY	2978	13302	8
498	Schering Plough Corp	201-822-7000	Madison, NJ	2969	3426	22
499	Contel Corp	404-391-8000	Atlanta, GA	2964	5865	23
500	Province of Nova Scotia	902-424-2700	Halifax, NS Can	2958	NM	21

Organizations Listed by Revenue

Rank	Organization	Phone	City / State or Province	Revenue ($ mil)	Assets ($ mil)	Emp (thous)
501	United States Dept of the Interior	202-343-3171	Washington, DC	2953	NM	9
502	Crown Life Insurance Co	416-928-4500	Toronto, ON Can	2944	7419	4
503	CMS Energy-Consumers Power Co	313-436-9261	Dearborn, MI	2943	8305	11
504	Genuine Parts Co	404-953-1700	Atlanta, GA	2942	1141	15
505	National Distillers & Chemicals Corp	212-949-5000	New York, NY	2922	2908	12
506	Quantum Chemical Corp	212-949-5000	New York, NY	2922	2908	14
507	Confederation Life Insurance Co	416-323-8111	Toronto, ON Can	2919	9173	5
508	Air Canada Ltd	514-879-7000	Montreal, PQ Can	2912	2921	24
509	Chrysler Financial Corp	313-244-3060	Troy, MI	2908	25277	6
510	Wendy's International Inc	614-764-3100	Dublin, OH	2902	777	42
511	NCNB Texas National Bank (Republic Bank)	214-977-4000	Dallas, TX	2900	33000	15
512	First Union National Bank Corp	704-374-6565	Charlotte, NC	2898	28978	16
513	Agway Inc	315-477-7061	Syracuse, NY	2894	1497	9
514	Suntrust Banks Corp	404-588-7455	Atlanta, GA	2889	29177	20
515	ICH Corp	502-897-1861	Louisville, KY	2885	9294	7
516	Donnelley, R R & Sons Co	312-326-8000	Chicago, IL	2878	2346	21
517	Guardian Life Insurance Co of America	212-598-8000	New York, NY	2876	4168	5
518	Intel Corp	408-987-8080	Santa Clara, CA	2875	3550	30
519	Southmark Corp	214-241-8787	Dallas, TX	2838	9161	33
520	General Public Utilities Corp	201-263-6500	Parsippany, NJ	2834	6415	4
521	Owens Corning Fiberglas Corp	419-248-8000	Toledo, OH	2831	1596	18
522	NCNB (No Carolina Natl Bank) Corp	704-374-5000	Charlotte, NC	2829	29848	18
523	Hawaii, State of	808-548-2211	Honolulu, HI	2818	NM	48
524	California Federal S & L Assn Inc	213-932-4321	Los Angeles, CA	2816	27482	6
525	Shawmut Corp	617-292-2000	Boston, MA	2811	26475	17
526	Abitibi Price Ltd	416-369-6700	Toronto, ON Can	2809	2236	24
527	First Fidelity BanCorp Inc	201-565-3200	Newark, NJ	2806	29777	15
528	Hercules Inc	302-594-5000	Wilmington, DE	2802	3325	23
529	Niagara Mohawk Power Corp	315-474-1511	Syracuse, NY	2801	7076	11
530	Orange County Government	714-834-3100	Santa Ana, CA	2800	NM	15
531	MacMillan Bloedel Ltd	604-661-8000	Vancouver, BC Can	2783	2021	15
532	Trans Canada Pipelines Ltd	403-269-5611	Calgary, AB Can	2779	4270	2
533	CBS Inc	212-975-4321	New York, NY	2778	4407	20
534	Transco Energy Co	713-439-2000	Houston, TX	2774	3527	5
535	Emhart Corp	203-678-3000	Farmington, CT	2763	2427	33
536	American Grain Inc	515-223-3700	Des Moines, IA	2750	NM	1
537	Blue Cross Blue Shield of Massachusetts	617-956-2000	Boston, MA	2750	7140	7
538	Cavenham (USA) Inc	203-655-6211	Darien, CT	2750	500	21
539	Certified Grocers of America Inc	213-726-2601	Los Angeles, CA	2750	NA	3
540	D'Arcy Masius Benton & Bowles Inc	212-758-6200	New York, NY	2750	NA	7
541	LeFrak Organization	718-459-9021	Rego Park, NY	2750	NA	20
542	Lever Brothers Co Inc	212-688-6000	New York, NY	2750	800	13
543	Marubeni Trading Co USA	212-599-3700	New York, NY	2750	NA	4
544	Upjohn Co	616-323-4000	Kalamazoo, MI	2746	3139	21
545	Enserch Corp	214-651-8700	Dallas, TX	2739	2970	19
546	Canada Packers Inc	416-869-6049	Toronto, ON Can	2739	711	12
547	General Re Corp	203-328-5000	Stamford, CT	2736	9394	3
548	Banc One Corp	614-463-5944	Columbus, OH	2734	25274	17
549	Aon Corp (Combined Int'l)	312-701-3000	Chicago, IL	2732	8266	7
550	Philadelphia, City of	512-686-2181	Philadelphia, PA	2692	NM	31

Organizations Listed by Revenue

Rank	Organization	Phone	City / State or Province	Revenue ($ mil)	Assets ($ mil)	Emp (thous)
551	Consolidated Freightways Inc	415-494-2900	Palo Alto, CA	2689	1536	29
552	Consolidated Rail Corp (CONRAIL)	215-977-4000	Philadelphia, PA	2689	1711	30
553	Kerr McGee Corp	405-270-1313	Oklahoma City, OK	2689	3123	10
554	Zenith Electronics Corp	312-391-7000	Glenview, IL	2686	1428	36
555	Wyoming, State of	307-777-7220	Cheyenne, WY	2684	NM	13
556	Armstrong World Industries Inc	717-397-0611	Lancaster, PA	2680	2098	28
557	AMP Inc	717-564-0100	Harrisburg, PA	2670	2376	24
558	Triangle Industries Inc	212-230-3000	New York, NY	2668	1585	15
559	Union Camp Corp	201-628-2000	Wayne, NJ	2661	3094	19
560	Circle K Corp	602-253-9600	Phoenix, AZ	2657	1536	25
561	Pitney Bowes Inc	203-356-5000	Stamford, CT	2650	4788	29
562	Maine, State of	207-289-1110	Augusta, ME	2648	NM	25
563	IBM (Intl Business Mach) Canada Ltd	416-474-2111	Markham, ON Can	2638	2023	12
564	American Petrofina Inc	214-750-2400	Dallas, TX	2635	2356	4
565	National Bank of Canada Ltd	514-394-4000	Montreal, PQ Can	2633	26285	13
566	Bank of New York Co	212-495-1784	New York, NY	2620	47388	18
567	Carter Hawley Hale Stores Inc	213-620-0150	Los Angeles, CA	2617	1672	33
568	Squibb Corp	609-921-4000	Princeton, NJ	2586	3083	18
569	Chicago, City of	312-744-3300	Chicago, IL	2581	NM	43
570	Moore Corp	416-364-2600	Toronto, ON Can	2571	2142	26
571	Rhode Island, State of	401-277-2000	Providence, RI	2569	NM	25
572	Glendale Federal Savings & Loan Assn	818-500-2000	Glendale, CA	2562	23711	8
573	Dillard Department Stores Inc	501-376-5200	Little Rock, AR	2558	2068	23
574	Canadian Pacific Forest Products Ltd	807-475-2110	Thunder Bay, ON Can	2555	2358	17
575	San Diego County Government	619-531-5700	San Diego, CA	2550	NM	15
576	Province of New Brunswick	506-453-2240	Fredericton, NB Can	2550	NM	32
577	Revenue Canada, Taxation	613-957-0275	Ottawa, ON Can	2550	NM	17
578	Barnett Banks Inc	904-791-7720	Jacksonville, FL	2546	25748	15
579	Pacific Mutual Life Insurance Co	714-640-3011	Newport Beach, CA	2540	6981	3
580	Rohm & Hass Co	215-592-3000	Philadelphia, PA	2535	2242	13
581	Dofasco Inc	416-544-3761	Hamilton, ON Can	2535	5069	23
582	Siemens Corp	201-321-3400	Iselin, NJ	2530	NM	26
583	First Nationwide Bank Inc	415-772-1400	San Francisco, CA	2527	34810	4
584	Canada Post Corp	613-952-1524	Ottawa, ON Can	2525	2235	61
585	Lowe's Companies Inc	919-651-4000	North Wilkesboro, NC	2517	1086	15
586	VF Corp	215-378-1151	Wyomissing, PA	2516	1760	30
587	Central & South West Corp	214-754-1000	Dallas, TX	2512	8110	10
588	Paine Webber Group Inc	212-713-2000	New York, NY	2512	17934	13
589	Advance Publications	718-981-1234	Staten Island, NY	2500	NA	20
590	ARCO Chemical Co	215-359-2000	Newtown Square, PA	2500	2500	3
591	Astroline Corp	508-942-1600	Reading, MA	2500	NA	1
592	Coopers & Lybrand Inc	212-536-2000	New York, NY	2500	NA	30
593	Hillsborough Holdings (Walter, Jim Corp)	813-871-4811	Tampa, FL	2500	3000	20
594	Hyatt Corp	312-750-1234	Chicago, IL	2500	NA	40
595	Irving Bank Corp	212-635-1111	New York, NY	2500	25000	11
596	Johnson, S C & Son Inc	414-631-2000	Racine, WI	2500	NA	12
597	Kidde Inc	201-368-9000	Saddlebrook, NJ	2500	1750	35
598	MacAndrews & Forbes Inc	212-688-9000	New York, NY	2500	NA	25
599	Marine Midland Banks Inc	716-843-2424	Buffalo, NY	2500	25000	15
600	Revco Drug Stores Inc	216-425-9811	Twinsburg, OH	2500	1000	25

Organizations Listed by Revenue

Rank	Organization	Phone	City / State or Province	Revenue ($ mil)	Assets ($ mil)	Emp (thous)
601	Federal Reserve Bank of San Francisco	415-974-2000	San Francisco, CA	2493	34502	3
602	Rite Aid Corp	717-761-2633	Harrisburg, PA	2486	1224	28
603	Crownx Inc	416-928-7722	Toronto, ON Can	2480	7641	30
604	Norwest Corp	612-372-8268	Minneapolis, MN	2475	20564	16
605	National Semiconductor Corp	408-721-5000	Santa Clara, CA	2470	1777	38
606	Castle & Cooke Inc	213-824-1500	Los Angeles, CA	2469	1922	42
607	Federal Reserve Bank of Chicago Inc	312-322-5111	Chicago, IL	2469	34695	3
608	Consolidated Natural Gas Co	412-227-1000	Pittsburgh, PA	2468	4109	8
609	Canada Trust Financial Services Co	416-869-6100	Toronto, ON Can	2468	21707	11
610	La Confederation Desjardins Du Quebec	514-281-8666	Montreal, PQ Can	2445	25139	24
611	First Bank System Inc	612-370-5100	Minneapolis, MN	2441	24248	12
612	Masco Corp	313-274-7400	Taylor, MI	2439	2999	15
613	Polysar Energy & Chemical (Can Dev) Corp	416-598-7200	Toronto, ON Can	2439	4629	7
614	Nevada, State of	702-885-5000	Carson City, NV	2436	NM	16
615	Air Products & Chemicals Inc	215-481-4911	Allentown, PA	2432	2999	22
616	Dairymen Inc	502-426-6455	Louisville, KY	2420	250	4
617	Executive Life Insurance Co	213-312-1000	Inglewood, CA	2420	11400	2
618	US Sprint Inc	816-941-5000	Kansas City, MO	2420	NA	14
619	Goodrich, B F Co	216-374-3985	Arkon, OH	2417	2073	12
620	Southern Pacific Transport Corp	415-541-1000	San Francisco, CA	2412	4709	23
621	Milliken & Co	212-819-4200	New York, NY	2400	NA	20
622	Premark International Corp	312-405-6000	Deerfield, IL	2397	1655	24
623	State Farm Insurance Co	309-766-2311	Bloomington, IL	2358	8453	6
624	Household International Inc	312-564-3663	Prospect Heights, IL	2352	21032	30
625	McDermott International Inc	504-587-5400	New Orleans, LA	2352	3825	26
626	Englehard Corp	201-632-6000	Edison, NJ	2351	1413	8
627	Port Authority of New York & New Jersey	212-466-7000	New York, NY	2350	5500	20
628	US Shoe Corp	513-527-7000	Cincinnati, OH	2343	1111	46
629	Mutual Life Assurance Co of Canada	519-888-2235	Waterloo, ON Can	2343	9322	4
630	Tribune Co	312-222-9100	Chicago, IL	2335	2942	17
631	Berkshire Hathaway Inc	402-346-1400	Omaha, NE	2333	6817	25
632	Nordstrom Inc	206-628-2111	Seattle, WA	2328	1572	33
633	IDS Finacial Services Inc	612-372-3131	Minneapolis, MN	2326	8963	6
634	American Family Corp	404-323-3431	Columbus, GA	2325	6074	3
635	General Cimema Corp	617-232-8200	Chestnut Hill, MA	2324	1898	26
636	Continental Assurance Co	312-822-5000	Chicago, IL	2323	6138	6
637	Phelps Dodge Corp	602-234-8100	Phoenix, AZ	2320	2755	11
638	Baker Hughes Co	713-439-8600	Houston, TX	2316	2118	21
639	Olin Corp	203-356-2000	Stamford, CT	2308	1940	17
640	Stelco Inc	416-362-2161	Toronto, ON Can	2305	2029	16
641	Sovran Financial Corp	804-441-4000	Norfolk, VA	2302	21349	10
642	Dade County Government	305-375-4176	Miami, FL	2300	NM	22
643	Sterling Drug Inc	212-907-2000	New York, NY	2300	1724	21
644	Domtar Inc	514-848-5400	Montreal, PQ Can	2298	2708	16
645	Hormel, George A & Co	507-437-5611	Austin, MN	2293	707	7
646	Perimian Partners Ltd	713-787-2222	Houston, TX	2289	555	2
647	Montana, State of	406-444-2511	Helena, MT	2282	NM	21
648	Black & Decker Corp	301-583-3900	Towson, MD	2281	1825	23
649	Northeast Utilities Inc	203-665-5000	Berlin, CT	2279	6765	9
650	Pennzoil Co	713-546-4000	Houston, TX	2274	4480	8

Organizations Listed by Revenue

Rank	Organization	Phone	City / State or Province	Revenue ($ mil)	Assets ($ mil)	Emp (thous)
651	Carolina Power & Light Co	919-836-6111	Raleigh, NC	2273	7504	10
652	Marsh & McLennan Companies Inc	212-997-2000	New York, NY	2272	1830	23
653	Northwestern National Life Insurance Co	612-372-5432	Minneapolis, MN	2270	7594	3
654	Mercantile Stores Co Inc	302-575-1816	Wilmington, DE	2266	1452	21
655	Texaco Canada Ltd	416-441-7811	Don Mills, ON Can	2263	3482	3
656	Caisse de Depot du Quebec Ltd	514-842-3261	Montreal, PQ Can	2253	25550	3
657	Parker Hannifin Corp	216-531-3000	Cleveland, OH	2252	1742	33
658	Anschutz Corp	303-298-1000	Denver, CO	2250	NA	20
659	Butt, H E Grocery Co	512-270-8000	San Antonio, TX	2250	NA	15
660	Gateway Foods Corp	608-785-1330	LaCrosse, WI	2250	NA	6
661	Hallmark Cards Inc	816-274-5111	Kansas City, MO	2250	NA	20
662	Price Waterhouse & Co Inc	212-489-8900	New York, NY	2250	NA	25
663	USG Corp	312-321-4000	Chicago, IL	2248	1821	15
664	Canadian Tire Co	416-480-3000	Toronto, ON Can	2245	1301	6
665	Province of Newfoundland	709-737-3612	St Johns, NF Can	2244	NM	22
666	National City Corp	216-575-2000	Cleveland, OH	2227	21623	11
667	Kaiser Technology Corp	415-271-3300	Oakland, CA	2219	2404	11
668	Mitsui & Co Canada Ltd	416-865-0330	Toronto, ON Can	2218	181	1
669	Pennsylvania Power & Light Co	215-770-5151	Allentown, PA	2214	7525	8
670	Alumax Inc	415-348-3400	San Mateo, CA	2200	1800	11
671	Amfac Inc	415-772-3400	San Francisco, CA	2200	1400	19
672	Burnett, Leo Co Inc	312-565-5959	Chicago, IL	2200	NA	4
673	Canon USA Inc	516-488-6700	Lake Success, NY	2200	NA	4
674	Cotter & Co	312-975-2700	Chicago, IL	2200	NA	3
675	Cumberland Farms Corp	617-828-4900	Canton, MA	2200	NA	12
676	Donaldson, Lufkin & Jenrette Inc	212-504-3000	New York, NY	2200	20900	3
677	Gold Kist Inc	404-393-5000	Atlanta, GA	2200	650	11
678	Grand Met USA Inc	201-573-4000	Montvale, NJ	2200	NA	21
679	Growmark Inc	309-557-6000	Bloomington, IL	2200	NA	1
680	Hyundai USA Inc	714-890-6000	Garden Grove, CA	2200	NA	4
681	Mobay Corp	412-777-2000	Pittsburgh, PA	2200	NA	11
682	NEC Nippon Electric Corp USA	516-753-7000	Melville, NY	2200	NA	4
683	Nestle USA Inc	914-251-3000	Purchase, NY	2200	NA	11
684	Rapid American Corp	212-621-4500	New York, NY	2200	1500	42
685	Thyssen USA Corp	212-512-9700	New York, NY	2200	NA	1
686	Topco Associates Inc	312-676-3030	Skokie, IL	2200	NA	1
687	USA Petroleum Corp	213-452-6200	Santa Monica, CA	2200	NA	1
688	UNUM Union Mutual Life Insurance Co	207-770-2211	Portland, ME	2199	8127	4
689	Westvaco Corp	212-688-5000	New York, NY	2187	2634	15
690	Roadway Services Inc	216-384-8184	Akron, OH	2185	1193	27
691	NBD Bancorp (Natl Bank Detroit) Inc	313-225-1000	Detroit, MI	2181	24176	12
692	Land O'Lakes Inc	612-481-2222	North Arden Hills, MN	2180	750	6
693	Allegheny Power System Inc	212-752-2121	New York, NY	2171	1031	6
694	Hershey Foods Corp	717-534-4000	Hershey, PA	2168	1765	12
695	Westpoint Pepperell Inc	404-645-4000	West Point, GA	2151	2454	41
696	Ohio Edison Co	216-384-5100	Akron, OH	2143	7556	8
697	Congress of the United States of America	202-224-3121	Washington, DC	2139	NM	17
698	Long Island Lighting Co	516-933-4590	Hicksville, NY	2138	8326	6
699	American President Companies Ltd	415-272-8000	Oakland, CA	2131	1711	5
700	Corning Glass Works Inc	607-974-9000	Corning, NY	2122	2898	25

Organizations Listed by Revenue

Rank	Organization	Phone	City / State or Province	Revenue ($ mil)	Assets ($ mil)	Emp (thous)
701	Republic Bank of New York Inc	212-525-5000	New York, NY	2106	24519	9
702	Universal Leaf Tobacco Co Inc	804-359-9311	Richmond, VA	2104	943	14
703	Ploysar Ltd	519-332-1212	Sarnia, ON Can	2103	2015	15
704	Lorillard Corp	212-545-2000	New York, NY	2100	1500	5
705	Harris Corp	305-727-9100	Melbourne, FL	2099	1644	23
706	Fruehauf Corp	313-267-1000	Detroit, MI	2094	1584	15
707	First Wachovia Corp	919-770-5000	Winston-Salem, NC	2091	21815	14
708	Citizens & Southern Co	404-581-2121	Atlanta, GA	2090	21098	14
709	Electrolux US Inc	404-933-1000	Marietta, GA	2090	NA	21
710	Knight Ridder Inc	305-376-3800	Miami, FL	2083	2357	20
711	San Francisco, City of	415-554-3456	San Francisco, CA	2079	NM	25
712	San Diego Gas & Electric Co	619-696-2000	San Diego, CA	2076	3533	4
713	Meyer, Fred Inc	503-232-8844	Portland, OR	2074	NA	21
714	Transamerica Life Insurance Co	213-742-3111	Los Angeles, CA	2073	5533	1
715	Molson Companies	416-675-1786	Toronto, ON Can	2070	1160	11
716	Browning Ferris Industries Inc	713-870-8100	Houston, TX	2067	1872	20
717	Compaq Computer Corp	713-370-0670	Houston, TX	2066	1590	12
718	Manville Corp	303-978-2000	Denver, CO	2062	2393	20
719	Bonneville Power Administration	503-230-5000	Portland, OR	2050	NM	5
720	Provident Life & Accident Ins Co	615-755-1011	Chattanooga, TN	2050	7468	10
721	Suffolk County Government	516-360-4000	Hauppauge, NY	2050	NM	12
722	Capital Holding Co	502-560-2000	Louisville, KY	2046	12963	8
723	Agriculture Canada	613-995-8963	Ottawa, ON Can	2040	NM	11
724	Bank of Canada	613-563-8111	Ottawa, ON Can	2040	NM	2
725	Health & Welfare Canada	613-957-2991	Ottawa, ON Can	2040	NM	9
726	Revenue Canada, Customs & Excise	613-957-0275	Ottawa, ON Can	2040	NM	10
727	Supply & Services Canada	819-997-6363	Hull, PQ Can	2040	NM	10
728	Connecticut Mutual Life Insurance Co	203-727-6500	Hartford, CT	2039	11230	20
729	Centerior Energy Corp	216-622-9800	Cleveland, OH	2038	11573	9
730	Core Mark International Inc	604-273-7721	Richmond, BC Can	2032	431	3
731	Union Electric Co	314-621-3222	St Louis, MO	2029	5827	9
732	Beverly Enterprises Inc	818-793-2911	Pasadena, CA	2025	1845	106
733	Inco Ltd	416-361-7511	Toronto, ON Can	2017	3307	19
734	Yellow Freight System Inc	913-345-1020	Overland Park, KS	2016	1021	28
735	Consolidated Bathurst Inc	514-875-2160	Montreal, PQ Can	2016	1936	15
736	Interco Inc	314-863-1100	St Louis, MO	2012	1775	38
737	Ethyl Corp	804-788-5000	Richmond, VA	2011	5251	10
738	Northern States Power Co	612-330-5500	Minneapolis, MN	2007	4496	8
739	Florida Progress Corp	813-895-1700	St Petersburg, FL	2002	4304	8
740	Arthur, Young & Co Inc	212-407-1500	New York, NY	2000	NA	25
741	Bell Laboratories of AT&T	201-582-3000	Murray Hill, NJ	2000	NA	20
742	Best Products Co Inc	804-261-2000	Richmond, VA	2000	1000	15
743	Costco Wholesale	206-828-8100	Kirkland, WA	2000	1200	5
744	Deloitte, Haskins & Sells Inc	212-790-0500	New York, NY	2000	NA	25
745	Dominicks Finer Foods Inc	312-562-1000	Northlake, IL	2000	NA	10
746	Ernst & Whinney Inc	216-861-5000	Cleveland, OH	2000	NA	30
747	Farley Industries Inc	312-876-1724	Chicago, IL	2000	NA	25
748	Federal Home Loan Bank Board	202-377-6000	Washington, DC	2000	NM	10
749	Finevest Services	203-629-8750	Greenwich, CT	2000	NA	12
750	Graybar Electric Co Inc	314-727-3900	St Louis, MO	2000	NA	5

Organizations Listed by Revenue

Rank	Organization	Phone	City / State or Province	Revenue ($ mil)	Assets ($ mil)	Emp (thous)
751	Hearst Corp	212-262-5700	New York, NY	2000	NA	15
752	Hertz Corp	201-307-2000	Park Ridge, NJ	2000	3400	15
753	International Monitary Fund	202-623-7000	Washington, DC	2000	NM	4
754	Liggett Group Inc	919-683-9000	Durham, NC	2000	1500	15
755	Mack Trucks Inc	215-439-3011	Allentown, PA	2000	1400	10
756	McLane Co Inc	817-778-7500	Temple, TX	2000	NA	3
757	Meijer Inc	616-453-6711	Grand Rapids, MI	2000	NA	20
758	Mutual of Omaha Insurance Co	402-342-7600	Omaha, NE	2000	1997	5
759	Panasonic Matsushita Electric Corp	713-895-7200	Los Angeles, CA	2000	NA	2
760	Penske, Roger Corp	201-428-7500	Parsippany, NJ	2000	NA	10
761	Roundy's Inc	414-547-7999	Pewaukee, WI	2000	500	5
762	Sea Land Corp	201-632-2000	Edison, NJ	2000	NA	10
763	Stroh Brewery Co	313-446-2000	Detroit, MI	2000	NA	10
764	United Nations	212-963-1234	New York, NY	2000	NM	4
765	United States Central Intelligence Agncy	703-351-1100	Washington, DC	2000	NM	10
766	United States Commodity Credit Corp	202-447-5237	Washington, DC	2000	NM	3
767	Waban Inc	508-651-6500	Natick, MA	2000	750	15
768	White Consolidated Industries Inc	216-252-3700	Cleveland, OH	2000	NA	20
769	World Bank	202-477-1234	Washington, DC	2000	NM	4
770	Dillon Co	316-663-6801	Hutchinson, KS	2000	NA	20
771	ITT Automotive Inc	313-540-9666	Bloomfield Hills, MI	2000	NA	15
772	Home Depot Inc	404-433-8211	Atlanta, GA	1999	699	9
773	Arkla Inc	318-226-2700	Shreveport, LA	1996	3249	6
774	Asarco Inc	212-510-2000	New York, NY	1988	2223	9
775	Bruno's Inc	205-940-9400	Birmingham, AL	1982	592	6
776	Total Petroleum North America Ltd	403-267-3000	Calgary, AB Can	1969	1120	5
777	London Life Insurance Co	519-432-5281	London, ON Can	1960	7932	5
778	Dover Corp	212-826-7160	New York, NY	1956	1366	20
779	Sherwin Williams Co	216-566-2000	Cleveland, OH	1950	1259	17
780	North Dakota, State of	701-224-2000	Bismarck, ND	1949	NM	19
781	Freeport McMoran Inc	504-582-4000	New Orleans, LA	1945	3730	6
782	Varity Corp	416-593-3811	Toronto, ON Can	1942	1384	15
783	Bally Manufacturing Corp	312-399-1300	Chicago, IL	1941	2867	17
784	Tyson Foods Inc	501-756-4000	Springdale, AR	1936	889	16
785	Illinois Tool Works Inc	312-693-3040	Chicago, IL	1930	1380	14
786	Longs Drug Stores Corp	415-937-1170	Walnut Creek, CA	1925	508	11
787	New Hampshire, State of	603-271-1110	Concord, NH	1921	NM	21
788	TJX Corp	508-651-6000	Natick, MA	1921	1000	22
789	Zayre Corp	508-390-1000	Framingham, MA	1921	1462	19
790	Trinova Corp	419-891-2200	Maumee, OH	1919	1432	30
791	Idaho, State of	208-334-2411	Boise, ID	1915	NM	19
792	Morrison Knudsen Corp	208-386-5000	Boise, ID	1909	746	15
793	Stanley Works Inc	203-225-5111	New Britain, CT	1909	1405	19
794	Delaware, State of	302-736-4000	Dover, DE	1907	NM	21
795	Ivaco Inc	514-288-4545	Montreal, PQ Can	1902	827	13
796	GenCorp Inc	216-869-4200	Akron, OH	1891	1230	16
797	Bear Stearns Companies Inc	212-272-2000	New York, NY	1888	32171	4
798	Maytag Co	515-792-7000	Newton, IA	1886	1330	5
799	Variable Annuity Life Insurance Co	713-526-5251	Houston, TX	1880	7771	2
800	International Multifoods Corp	612-340-3300	Minneapolis, MN	1874	716	9

Organizations Listed by Revenue

Rank	Organization	Phone	City / State or Province	Revenue ($ mil)	Assets ($ mil)	Emp (thous)
801	Associated Wholesale Grocers Inc	913-321-1313	Kansas City, KS	1870	NA	2
802	Metro Richelieu Ltd	514-353-5000	Montreal, PQ Can	1870	484	17
803	Baltimore Gas & Electric Co	301-234-5000	Baltimore, MD	1864	5126	9
804	Polaroid Corp	617-577-2000	Cambridge, MA	1863	1957	13
805	PWA (Canadian Airlines) Corp	403-294-2000	Calgary, AB CAN	1850	1806	14
806	Midlantic Banks Inc	201-321-8000	Edison, NJ	1847	19679	10
807	Maxicare Health Plans Inc	213-568-9000	Los Angeles, CA	1839	992	15
808	Crown Cork & Seal Co	215-698-5100	Philadelphia, PA	1834	1073	13
809	Santa Clara County Government	408-299-2323	San Jose, CA	1825	NM	11
810	Springs Industries Inc	803-547-2901	Fort Mill, SC	1825	1118	19
811	General American Life Insurance Co	314-231-1700	St Louis, MO	1824	4369	4
812	McGraw Hill Corp	212-512-2000	New York, NY	1818	1758	16
813	Avnet Inc	516-466-7000	Great Neck, NY	1817	1153	11
814	Hoechst American Corp	201-231-2000	Somerville, NJ	1815	1300	11
815	Revlon Group Inc	212-572-5000	New York, NY	1815	1000	16
816	Diamond Shamrock R & M Corp	512-641-6800	San Antonio, TX	1804	843	4
817	Amdahl Corp	408-746-6000	Sunnyvale, CA	1802	1931	11
818	Mapco Inc	918-581-1800	Tulsa, OK	1802	1376	5
819	Equitable Variable Life	212-554-4035	New York, NY	1800	8000	3
820	Helmsley Spear Co	212-687-6400	New York, NY	1800	NA	12
821	Hy Vee Food Stores Inc	515-774-2121	Chariton, IA	1800	NA	10
822	Seattle First National Bank Co	206-358-7800	Seattle, WA	1800	15000	7
823	Steelcase Inc	616-247-2710	Grand Rapids, MI	1800	NA	13
824	Waldbaum Inc	516-582-9300	Central Islap, NY	1800	1000	14
825	Louisiana Pacific Corp	503-221-0800	Portland, OR	1799	1796	13
826	Reebok International Ltd	617-580-1600	Canton, MA	1791	1063	13
827	Kelly, Douglas & Co	604-661-1200	Vancouver, BC Can	1785	404	15
828	Harcourt Brace Jovanovich Inc	305-345-2000	Orlando, FL	1782	3233	14
829	MCORP Inc	214-698-5000	Dallas, TX	1774	20228	8
830	Temple Inland Inc	409-829-1313	Diboll, TX	1774	1982	13
831	Detroit, City of	313-224-3400	Detroit, MI	1763	NM	19
832	General Signal Corp	203-357-8800	Stamford, CT	1760	1397	21
833	Peabody Holding Co	314-342-3400	St Louis, MO	1758	2449	6
834	Belk Store Services Inc	704-372-8900	Charlotte, NC	1750	NA	30
835	Citicorp Savings Inc	212-559-1000	New York, NY	1750	17500	4
836	Colt Industries Inc	212-940-0400	New York, NY	1750	1400	18
837	Cox Enterprises Inc	404-843-5000	Atlanta, GA	1750	NA	14
838	Fort Howard Paper Co	414-435-8821	Green Bay, WI	1750	2000	16
839	Goldome Federal Savings Bank Inc	716-847-5800	Buffalo, NY	1750	17500	5
840	MCN (Michigan Consolidated Natgas) Corp	313-965-2430	Detroit, MI	1750	2200	4
841	Payless Cashways Inc	816-234-6000	Kansas City, MO	1750	800	13
842	SSMC Inc (Singer Co)	203-356-4200	Stamford, CT	1750	1000	15
843	Touche Ross & Co	212-489-1600	New York, NY	1750	NA	20
844	Warren, George E Co Inc	617-451-2300	Boston, MA	1750	NA	1
845	Canadian Wheat Board	204-983-0239	Winnipeg, MB Can	1750	3488	1
846	West Point-Pepperell Inc	404-645-4000	West Point, GA	1740	1850	31
847	PHH Group Inc	301-771-3600	Hunt Valley, MD	1735	4231	5
848	Associates Corp of America Inc	214-659-4000	Dallas, TX	1733	15000	7
849	Alco Industries Inc	215-666-0930	Valley Forge, PA	1732	468	6
850	Student Loan Marketing Assn Inc	202-333-8000	Washington, DC	1729	28627	7

Organizations Listed by Revenue

Rank	Organization	Phone	City / State or Province	Revenue ($ mil)	Assets ($ mil)	Emp (thous)
851	Woolworth, F W Canada Ltd	416-361-2111	Toronto, ON Can	1722	566	27
852	Circuit City Stores Inc	804-257-4292	Richmond, VA	1721	587	10
853	Unicorp Canada Corp (Union Enterprises)	416-961-1200	Toronto, ON Can	1721	5041	4
854	State Mutual Life Assurance Co of Amer	508-852-1000	Worcester, MA	1718	4376	4
855	Willamette Industries Inc	503-227-5581	Portland, OR	1716	1430	9
856	Sequa Corp	212-986-5500	New York, NY	1713	1959	16
857	Becton, Dickinson & Co	201-848-6800	Franklin Lakes, NJ	1709	2067	21
858	Telecommunications Inc	303-721-5500	Denver, CO	1709	6296	8
859	Brown Group Inc	314-854-4000	St Louis, MO	1707	728	30
860	New York Times Co	212-556-1234	New York, NY	1701	1915	11
861	Nash Finch Co	612-929-0371	St Louis Park, MN	1700	500	8
862	Transamerica Occidental Life Ins Co	213-742-2111	Los Angeles, CA	1700	6000	4
863	Groupe des Epiciers unis, Metro Richelieu	514-643-1000	Montreal, PQ Can	1700	850	3
864	Dylex Ltd	416-586-7000	Toronto, ON Can	1697	595	18
865	British Col Hydro & Power Authority Ltd	604-663-2212	Vancouver, BC Can	1689	8332	6
866	Public Service Co of Colorado	303-571-7511	Denver, CO	1685	2984	7
867	Rio Algom Ltd	416-367-4000	Toronto, ON Can	1682	1785	8
868	Anglo Canadian Telephone Co	514-341-6321	Saint Laurent, PQ Can	1676	3169	22
869	Subaru America Corp	609-488-8500	Cherry Hill, NJ	1673	727	1
870	Williams Companies Inc	918-588-2000	Tulsa, OK	1673	3567	8
871	Hill's Department Stores Inc	617-821-1000	Canton, MA	1671	1000	14
872	SCOA Industries Inc	617-821-1000	Canton, MA	1671	899	16
873	Torchmark Corp	205-325-4200	Birmingham, AL	1670	4428	9
874	Stevens, J P & Co Inc	212-930-2000	New York, NY	1660	941	27
875	Square D Co	312-397-2600	Palatine, IL	1657	1336	21
876	Masco Industries Inc	313-274-7405	Taylor, MI	1652	2121	10
877	Aero Mexico SA	305-591-1494	Miami, FL	1650	NA	16
878	Bozell Jacobs Kenyon Inc	212-727-5000	New York, NY	1650	NA	4
879	Central Soya Co	219-425-5100	Fort Wayne, IN	1650	500	3
880	Denny's Inc	714-739-8100	La Mirada, CA	1650	NA	63
881	Excello Corp	313-624-7800	Walled Lake, MI	1650	NA	18
882	First National Supermarkets Inc	216-587-7100	Maple Heights, OH	1650	NA	16
883	GFI Knoll International Holdings Inc	201-843-0900	Saddlebrook, NJ	1650	NA	11
884	ICI (Imperial Chemical) America Inc	302-886-3000	Wilmington, DE	1650	NA	11
885	Isuzu Motors USA Inc	213-949-0611	Whitter, CA	1650	NA	2
886	Kidder, Peabody & Co Inc	212-510-3000	New York, NY	1650	16500	7
887	Lucky Goldstar Group	201-460-8010	Lindhusrt, NJ	1650	NA	2
888	Matsushita Electric USA Inc	201-348-7100	Secaucus, NJ	1650	NA	3
889	Mazda Motors Corp USA	313-782-7800	Flat Rock, MI	1650	NA	11
890	Mid America Dairymen Inc	417-865-9641	Springfield, MO	1650	300	4
891	Miles Laboratories Inc	219-264-8062	Elkhart, IN	1650	NA	16
892	Nichimen Trading Co USA	212-719-1000	New York, NY	1650	NA	1
893	Nissho Iwai Trading Co USA	212-704-6500	New York, NY	1650	NA	2
894	San Bernadino County Government	714-387-2020	San Bernadino, CA	1650	NM	10
895	Sandoz USA Inc	212-307-1122	New York, NY	1650	NA	13
896	Spartan Stores Inc	616-878-2000	Grand Rapids, MI	1650	NA	4
897	Sumitomo Trading Co USA	212-207-0700	New York, NY	1650	NA	4
898	US Plywood Corp	404-521-4000	Atlanta, GA	1650	NA	2
899	Meritor Financial Group Inc	215-636-7500	Philadelphia, PA	1646	17172	9
900	Itel Corp	312-902-1515	Chicago, IL	1644	4001	9

Organizations Listed by Revenue

Rank	Organization	Phone	City / State or Province	Revenue ($ mil)	Assets ($ mil)	Emp (thous)
901	CIP Inc	514-878-4811	Montreal, PQ Can	1637	1573	8
902	Imperial Tobacco Ltd	514-932-6161	Montreal, PQ Can	1637	NA	7
903	Corestates Financial Corp	215-629-3869	Philadelphia, PA	1630	16430	8
904	Onex Corp	416-362-7711	Toronto, ON Can	1628	1593	21
905	Jackson National Life Ins Co	517-394-3400	Lansing, MI	1626	3643	4
906	Ohio Casualty Corp	513-867-3000	Hamilton, OH	1623	2922	6
907	Federal Industries Ltd	204-942-8161	Winnipeg, MB Can	1623	808	15
908	Aid Association for Lutherans Inc	414-734-5721	Appleton, WI	1618	6246	1
909	Columbia Pictures	212-751-4400	New York, NY	1616	3565	10
910	Outboard Marine Corp	312-689-6200	Waukegan, IL	1605	1141	13
911	Dow Jones & Co	212-416-2000	New York, NY	1603	2112	11
912	Great American (CA) First Savings Bank	619-231-1885	San Diego, CA	1601	16084	3
913	Southwestern Life Insurance Co	214-954-7111	Dallas, TX	1601	5799	5
914	Baker International Corp	714-634-2333	Orange, CA	1600	1500	20
915	Koppers Co Inc	412-227-2000	Pittsburg, PA	1600	1200	12
916	Monfort of Colorado Inc	303-353-2311	Greeley, CO	1600	250	5
917	Texas Commerce Bancshares Inc	713-236-4865	Houston, TX	1600	19000	8
918	Sonoco Products Co	803-383-7000	Hartsville, SC	1599	977	14
919	Holiday (Inn) Corp	901-762-8600	Memphis, TN	1597	2139	45
920	Prime Computer Inc	508-655-8000	Natick, MA	1595	1651	12
921	Penn Mutual Life Insurance Co	215-625-5000	Philadelphia, PA	1589	4984	5
922	Witco Corp	212-605-3800	New York, NY	1586	1115	11
923	Holly Farms Corp	901-761-3610	Memphis, TN	1583	757	15
924	Pittston Co	203-622-0900	Greenwich, CT	1583	992	17
925	Southern New England Telephone Inc	203-771-5200	New Haven, CT	1583	3067	14
926	Avery International Corp	818-304-2000	Pasadena, CA	1582	1119	12
927	Hanover Insurance Co	508-853-7200	Worcester, MA	1581	2649	6
928	Home Federal Savings & Loan Assn Inc	619-699-8000	San Diego, CA	1578	17009	5
929	Tyco Laboratories Inc	603-778-9700	Exeter, NH	1575	9419	10
930	Super Food Services Inc	513-294-1731	Dayton, OH	1573	224	2
931	Zeller's Inc	514-483-7600	Montreal, PQ Can	1573	595	12
932	Sun Energy Partners LP Inc	214-890-6207	Dallas, TX	1570	2000	2
933	Wisconsin Investment Board	608-266-2381	Madison, WI	1560	12881	1
934	GEICO Corp	301-986-3000	Washington, DC	1557	3061	5
935	Timken Co	216-438-3000	Canton, OH	1554	1593	18
936	Dean Foods Co	312-678-1680	Franklin Park, IL	1552	499	7
937	Automatic Data Processing Inc	201-994-5000	Roseland, NJ	1549	1653	23
938	Penn Central Corp	513-579-6600	Cincinnati, OH	1547	2400	14
939	United States Courts	202-479-3000	Washington, DC	1541	NM	9
940	Wisconsin Energy Co	414-277-2345	Milwaukee, WI	1541	2849	6
941	Mercedes (Daimler Benz) Inc	201-573-0600	Montvale, NJ	1540	NA	2
942	Grainger, W W Inc	312-982-9000	Skokie, IL	1535	936	7
943	South Dakota, State of	605-773-3011	Pierre, SD	1535	NM	17
944	Service Master Industries Inc	312-964-1300	Downers Grove, IL	1531	484	17
945	MNC (Maryland National Corp) Financial	301-244-1940	Baltimore, MD	1530	17000	8
946	Correctional Service of Canada	613-993-7501	Ottawa, ON Can	1530	NM	11
947	Environment Canada	819-997-2800	Hull, PQ Can	1530	NM	9
948	NIPSCO Northern Indiana Pub Serv Co	219-853-5200	Hammond, IN	1526	3685	5
949	Murphy Oil Corp	501-862-6411	El Dorado, AR	1525	2068	5
950	Coors, Aldolph Co	303-279-6565	Golden, CO	1522	1571	10

Organizations Listed by Revenue

Rank	Organization	Phone	City / State or Province	Revenue ($ mil)	Assets ($ mil)	Emp (thous)
951	Federal Reserve Bank of Richmond Inc	804-643-1250	Richmond, VA	1513	24861	2
952	Mercy Health Services	313-489-6010	Farmington, MI	1512	NA	19
953	NICOR (Northern Illinois Gas) Corp	312-242-4470	Naperville, IL	1509	2100	4
954	Saskatchewan Wheat Pool Ltd	306-569-4411	Regina, SK Can	1508	680	4
955	Alden, John Financial Corp	305-470-3100	Miami, FL	1500	NA	3
956	Amoskeag Co	617-262-4000	Boston, MA	1500	1000	25
957	Amway Corp	606-676-6000	Ada, MI	1500	NA	10
958	Boston Safe Deposit & Trust Co	617-722-7000	Boston, MA	1500	12000	3
959	Burlington Resources	206-467-3838	Seattle, WA	1500	NA	15
960	Cabot Corp	617-890-0200	Waltham, MA	1500	1800	9
961	Connecticut Bank & Trust Co NA	203-244-5000	Hartford, CT	1500	1200	7
962	Connell Ltd (Avondale Foods) Ptr Inc	617-567-2600	East Boston, MA	1500	NA	5
963	Delaware North Companies	716-881-6500	Buffalo, NY	1500	NA	35
964	DHL Airways/Worldwide Express Inc	415-593-7474	Redwood City, CA	1500	NA	15
965	Dillingham Corp	415-362-1501	San Francisco, CA	1500	NA	5
966	Dow Corning Corp	517-496-4000	Auburn, MI	1500	1500	6
967	Dunavant Enterprises Inc	901-369-1500	Memphis, TN	1500	NA	2
968	Duracell Corp	203-796-4000	Bethel, CT	1500	NA	10
969	Giant Eagle Inc	412-963-6200	Pittsburgh, PA	1500	NA	14
970	Global Petroleum Corp	617-894-8800	Waltham, MA	1500	NA	1
971	Guardsman Products Inc	616-957-2600	Grand Rapids, MI	1500	500	10
972	Gulf States Toyota Corp	713-744-3300	Houston, TX	1500	NA	3
973	HealthTrust Corp	615-383-4444	Nashville, TN	1500	NA	20
974	Heileman, G Brewing Co Inc	608-785-1000	LaCrosse, WI	1500	1200	7
975	IU International Corp	302-571-5000	Philadelphia, PA	1500	900	15
976	JMB Institutional Realty	312-440-4800	Chicago, IL	1500	15000	5
977	Knoll International Holdings	212-826-2400	New York, NY	1500	NA	20
978	Leaseway Transportation Corp	216-464-3300	Beachwood, OH	1500	1100	20
979	Lincoln Property Co	214-740-3300	Dallas, TX	1500	NA	5
980	Manpower Inc	608-755-7000	Milwaukee, WI	1500	500	6
981	Mitsubishi Motors of America Inc	714-963-7677	Fountain Valley, CA	1500	1000	2
982	Perdue Farms Inc	301-543-3000	Salisbury, MD	1500	NA	15
983	Philadelphia National Bank Co	215-629-3512	Philadelphia, PA	1500	12000	6
984	Readers Digest Assn Inc	914-769-7000	Pleasantville, NY	1500	NA	6
985	Reliance Electric Corp	216-266-7000	Cleveland, OH	1500	NA	15
986	Saatchi, Saatchi Co	212-661-0800	New York, NY	1500	NA	2
987	Sammons Enterprises Inc	214-670-9790	Dallas, TX	1500	NA	5
988	Scoular Corp	402-390-3030	Omaha, NE	1500	NA	1
989	Services Group of America	206-623-5023	Seattle, WA	1500	NA	5
990	Simplot, J R Co	208-336-2110	Boise, ID	1500	NA	10
991	TLC Beatrice Internatl Holding Co	212-269-4544	New York, NY	1500	NA	10
992	Trammell Crow Corp	214-742-2000	Dallas, TX	1500	NA	6
993	Union Gas Holdings Corp	316-331-4500	Independence, KS	1500	NA	3
994	United States Export-Import Bank	202-566-8990	Washington, DC	1500	22000	3
995	ITT Defense Technology Corp	703-276-8300	Arlington, VA	1500	NA	10
996	Kelly Springfield Tire Co	301-777-6000	Cumberland, MD	1500	NA	10
997	Pay Less Drug Stores	503-682-4100	Wilsonville, OR	1500	NA	15
998	Central Capital Corp	902-420-2000	Halifax, NS Can	1494	13622	4
999	Ohio, State Teachers Retirement System	614-227-4062	Columbus, OH	1490	14231	1
1000	Lauder, Estee Cosmetics Ltd	416-292-1111	Scarborough, ON Can	1488	595	5

Organizations Listed by Revenue

Rank	Organization	Phone	City / State or Province	Revenue ($ mil)	Assets ($ mil)	Emp (thous)
1001	Industrial Alliance Life Insurance Co	418-463-5784	Sillery, PQ Can	1487	4389	2
1002	Sundstrand Corp	815-226-6000	Rockford, IL	1477	1567	14
1003	Imperial Life Assurance Co	416-926-2600	Toronto, ON Can	1477	5180	4
1004	New Jersey Divison of Investment	609-292-5106	Trenton, NJ	1475	22433	1
1005	International Minerals & Chemical Corp	312-564-8600	Northbrook, IL	1471	1794	10
1006	General Accident Insurance Co	215-625-1000	Philadelphia, PA	1470	4168	4
1007	United Westburne Inc	514-342-5181	Montreal, PQ Can	1469	674	12
1008	Baltimore, City of	301-396-4892	Baltimore, MD	1464	NM	29
1009	ITT Financial Corportion	314-821-6060	St Louis, MO	1462	8999	7
1010	New England Electric System Inc	508-366-9011	Westborough, MA	1461	3111	5
1011	Centex Corp	214-559-6500	Dallas, TX	1460	1039	5
1012	El Paso Natural Gas Co	915-541-2600	El Paso, TX	1447	3279	3
1013	E-Systems Inc	214-661-1000	Dallas, TX	1443	758	17
1014	Arizona Public Service Co	602-250-1000	Phoenix, AZ	1442	5991	9
1015	Memphis, City of	901-576-6000	Memphis, TN	1439	NM	19
1016	Rose's Stores Inc	919-492-8111	Henderson, NC	1439	436	17
1017	Inspiration Resources Corp	212-503-3100	New York, NY	1436	842	6
1018	General Electric Canada Co	416-858-5100	Mississauga, ON Can	1436	876	10
1019	Houston, City of	713-222-3141	Houston, TX	1434	NM	21
1020	Lipton, Thomas J Inc	201-567-8000	Englewood Cliffs, NJ	1430	1000	7
1021	Employers Reinsurance Co	913-676-5200	Overland Park, KS	1425	4293	4
1022	Home Life Insurance Co	212-428-2000	New York, NY	1423	3542	3
1023	Sentry Insurance Co	715-346-6000	Stevens Point, WI	1422	3197	4
1024	Inter City Gas Corp	204-944-9920	Winnepeg, MB Can	1421	1687	6
1025	Beneficial Corp	302-798-0800	Wilmington, DE	1418	7544	7
1026	Cominco Ltd	604-682-0611	Vancouver, BC Can	1418	1798	9
1027	Consumers Gas Ltd	416-864-3399	Toronto, ON Can	1417	1726	8
1028	Gulf States Utilities Co	409-838-6631	Beaumont, TX	1415	6858	5
1029	National Service Industries Inc	404-892-2400	Atlanta, GA	1414	825	20
1030	Tektronix Inc	503-627-7111	Beaverton, OR	1412	1024	16
1031	Laurentian Group Corp	418-647-5151	Quebec, PQ Can	1411	8244	7
1032	Bowater Inc	203-656-7200	Darien, CT	1410	1881	5
1033	Golden West Financial Corp	415-446-6000	Oakland, CA	1410	16721	2
1034	Norton Co	508-795-5000	Worcester, MA	1410	1088	16
1035	Morton International Inc	312-807-2000	Chicago, IL	1407	1100	11
1036	EG & G Inc	617-237-5100	Wellesley, MA	1406	539	22
1037	Fleetwood Enterprises Inc	714-351-3500	Riverside, CA	1406	514	11
1038	Southam Inc	416-927-1877	Toronto, ON Can	1406	1057	16
1039	Esselte Corp	516-741-1477	Garden City, NY	1401	1073	3
1040	Chicago Pacific Corp	312-435-7300	Chicago, IL	1400	1128	20
1041	Hennepin County Government	612-348-3000	Minneapolis, MN	1400	NM	9
1042	Hook SupeRX Stores Inc	317-353-1451	Indianapolis, IN	1400	NA	14
1043	Life Investors Insurance Co of America	319-398-5811	Ceder Rapids, IA	1400	3500	2
1044	Louisiana Power & Light Co	504-366-2345	New Orleans, LA	1400	4500	3
1045	Ruddick Corp	704-372-5404	Charlotte, NC	1400	700	11
1046	Southern Natural Gas Co	205-325-7410	Birmingham, AL	1400	1700	2
1047	United States Information Agency	202-655-4000	Washington, DC	1400	NM	9
1048	United States Panama Canal Commission	202-634-6441	Washington, DC	1400	NM	9
1049	Keycorp Inc	518-486-8500	Albany, NY	1394	14646	8
1050	Minnesota Mutual Life Ins Co	612-298-3500	St Paul, MN	1394	4466	4

Organizations Listed by Revenue

Rank	Organization	Phone	City / State or Province	Revenue ($ mil)	Assets ($ mil)	Emp (thous)
1051	Sonat Inc	205-325-3800	Birmingham, AL	1392	3139	7
1052	Ohio Power Co	216-456-8173	Canton, OH	1387	3494	8
1053	Cincinnati Gas & Electric Co	513-381-2000	Cincinnati, OH	1386	3361	5
1054	Weirton Steel Corp	304-797-2000	Weirton, WV	1384	687	8
1055	Pattison, Jim Industries Ltd	604-688-6764	Vancouver, BC Can	1384	678	8
1056	US Bancorp Inc	503-275-6111	Portland, OR	1381	14383	9
1057	CBI Industries Inc	312-572-7000	Oak Brook, IL	1376	1343	15
1058	Fischbach Corp	212-986-4100	New York, NY	1375	500	16
1059	Crossland Savings Fed Savings Bank Inc	718-780-0400	Brooklyn, NY	1374	15144	4
1060	Washington Post Co	202-334-6600	Washington, DC	1368	1422	7
1061	Data General Corp	508-366-8911	Westboro, MA	1365	1078	15
1062	Hasbro Inc	401-727-5000	Pawtucket, RI	1358	1112	8
1063	Arkansas Power & Light Co	501-371-4000	Little Rock, AR	1357	3928	5
1064	Brown Forman Inc	502-585-1100	Louisville, KY	1355	932	9
1065	Vermont, State of	802-828-1110	Montpelier, VT	1351	NM	13
1066	Potomac Electric Power Co	202-872-2456	Washington, DC	1350	4146	5
1067	Mobil Oil Canada Ltd	403-260-7910	Calgary, AB Can	1348	3123	2
1068	New York State Electric & Gas Inc	607-347-4131	Ithaca, NY	1340	4693	5
1069	Fieldcrest Cannon Inc	919-627-3000	Eden, NC	1338	812	22
1070	British Columbia Telephone Ltd	604-432-2151	Burnaby, BC Can	1332	2723	15
1071	Cyprus Minerals Co	303-643-5000	Englewood, CO	1327	1651	7
1072	Wilson Foods Corp	405-525-4545	Oklahoma City, OK	1324	219	7
1073	First Boston Inc	212-909-2000	New York, NY	1323	36148	6
1074	Blue Cross Blue Shield of Illinois Inc	312-938-7500	Chicago, IL	1320	3428	4
1075	Blue Cross Blue Shield of Pennsylvania	215-448-5000	Philadelphia, PA	1320	3103	2
1076	Indiana Farm Bureau Coop Assn Inc	317-631-8361	Indianapolis, IN	1320	250	1
1077	Phoenix Mutual Life Insurance Co	203-275-5000	Hartford, CT	1319	5678	4
1078	Tandem Computers Inc	408-725-6000	Cupertino, CA	1315	1318	9
1079	Arvin Industries Inc	812-379-3000	Columbus, IN	1313	1058	17
1080	Crane Co	212-415-7300	New York, NY	1313	682	10
1081	Comdisco Inc	312-698-3000	Rosemont, IL	1309	3488	2
1082	Gibraltar Savings (CA) Inc	213-278-8720	Beverly Hills, CA	1309	15011	3
1083	Lafarge Corp	703-264-3600	Reston, VA	1309	1199	8
1084	Hiram Walker Gooderham Worts Ltd	519-254-5171	Windsor, ON Can	1309	NA	6
1085	General Instrument Corp	212-207-6200	New York, NY	1305	1309	29
1086	Gibraltar Savings (Texas) Assn Inc	713-872-3100	Houston, TX	1301	12724	3
1087	Fidelcor Inc	215-985-6000	Philadelphia, PA	1300	13000	6
1088	Maricopa County Government	602-262-3518	Phoenix, AZ	1300	NM	11
1089	Milwaukee County Government	414-278-4222	Milwaukee, WI	1300	NM	12
1090	Minstar Inc	612-339-7900	Minneapolis, MN	1300	1150	10
1091	Pittsburgh National Bank Co	412-355-2000	Pittsburgh, PA	1300	15765	4
1092	Tiger International Inc	213-522-6300	Los Angeles, CA	1300	1100	8
1093	Echlin Inc	203-481-5751	Branford, CT	1294	1087	15
1094	Signet Banking Corp	804-747-2000	Richmond, VA	1286	11002	6
1095	Illinois Power Co	217-424-6600	Decatur, IL	1285	6053	5
1096	Amoco Canada Petroleum Co	403-233-1313	Calgary, AB Can	1285	1833	2
1097	Ford, Henry Health Care Corp	313-876-2600	Detroit, MI	1280	NA	15
1098	Harsco Corp	717-763-7064	Wormleysburg, PA	1279	893	12
1099	US Life Insurance Corp	212-709-6000	New York, NY	1279	4145	3
1100	Clark Equipment Corp	219-239-0100	South Bend, IN	1278	951	9

Organizations Listed by Revenue

Rank	Organization	Phone	City / State or Province	Revenue ($ mil)	Assets ($ mil)	Emp (thous)
1101	K Mart Canada Ltd	416-792-4400	Brampton, ON Can	1278	530	33
1102	American Greetings Corp	216-252-7300	Cleveland, OH	1275	1088	21
1103	Bindley Western Industries	317-298-9900	Indianapolis, IN	1275	264	2
1104	Progressive Insurance Co	216-464-8000	Mayfield Heights, OH	1275	2307	3
1105	Dow Chemical Canada Ltd	519-339-3131	Sarnia, ON Can	1275	NA	4
1106	McCain Foods Ltd	506-392-5541	Florenceville, NB Can	1275	6800	10
1107	Mitsubishi Canada Ltd	416-362-6731	Toronto, ON Can	1275	128	2
1108	Syntex Corp	415-885-5050	Palo Alto, CA	1272	1444	9
1109	Pace Membership Warehouses Inc	303-364-0700	Aurora, CO	1271	750	3
1110	Kelly Services Corp	313-362-4444	Troy, MI	1269	326	5
1111	Certainteed Corp	215-341-7000	Valley Forge, PA	1267	1108	8
1112	Seagate Technology Inc	408-438-6550	Scotts Valley, CA	1266	1094	7
1113	Dome Petroleum Ltd	403-231-3000	Calgary, AB Can	1266	3529	4
1114	Panhandle Eastern Corp	713-664-3401	Houston, TX	1262	2973	3
1115	Clorox Co	415-271-7000	Oakland, CA	1260	1156	6
1116	Federal Reserve Bank of Dallas Inc	214-651-6111	Dallas, TX	1258	15185	2
1117	Viacom International Inc	617-461-1600	Dedham, MA	1258	3980	4
1118	Jefferson Smurfit Corp	314-746-1100	St Louis, MO	1255	817	8
1119	GAP Stores Inc	415-952-4400	San Bruno, CA	1252	481	14
1120	Amstar Corp	212-489-9000	New York, NY	1250	1500	5
1121	Cole National Corp	216-449-4100	Cleveland, OH	1250	NA	11
1122	Cuyahoga County Government	216-443-7000	Cleveland, OH	1250	NM	8
1123	Furrs Inc	806-763-1931	Lubbock, TX	1250	NA	10
1124	Gates Corp	303-744-1911	Denver, CO	1250	NA	12
1125	Gillett Group Inc	615-292-0045	Nashville, TN	1250	NA	5
1126	Hartz Mountain Corp	201-481-4800	Harrison, NJ	1250	NA	5
1127	Hillman Industries Inc	412-281-2620	Pittsburgh, PA	1250	NA	5
1128	Ingram Industries Inc	615-793-5000	Nashville, TN	1250	NA	7
1129	LaSalle Energy Corp	214-871-5333	Dallas, TX	1250	NA	2
1130	National Amusements Corp	617-461-1600	Dedham, MA	1250	NA	10
1131	New York Power Authority	212-468-6000	New York, NY	1250	5100	10
1132	Restaurant Enterprises Group Inc	714-863-6300	Irvine, CA	1250	NA	30
1133	Transammonia Inc	212-223-3200	New York, NY	1250	NA	1
1134	Weisman, Frederick Co Inc	301-760-1500	Glen Burnie, MD	1250	NA	1
1135	Fletcher Challenge Canada Ltd	604-665-3821	Vancouver, BC Can	1250	1415	7
1136	Columbia Savings (CA) Savings Assn Inc	213-657-6123	Beverly Hills, CA	1249	12744	3
1137	Petrie Stores Corp	201-866-3600	Secaucus, NJ	1242	1134	7
1138	Ultramar Canada Inc	514-499-6111	Montreal, PQ Can	1238	952	2
1139	Lomas & Nettleton Financial Corp	214-746-7111	Dallas, TX	1235	6645	5
1140	Westfair Foods Ltd	204-786-7941	Winnipeg, MB Can	1233	340	2
1141	Alexander & Alexander Service Inc	212-840-8500	New York, NY	1228	2635	16
1142	Atco Ltd	403-292-7500	Calgary, AB Can	1227	2737	5
1143	American Express Credit Corp	302-594-3350	Wilmington, DE	1224	9800	2
1144	Nortek Inc	401-751-1600	Providence, RI	1224	1052	9
1145	Emery Air Freight Corp	203-762-8601	Wilton, CT	1223	733	17
1146	Jefferson Pilot Corp	919-378-2011	Greensboro, NC	1223	4174	8
1147	National Gypsum Co	214-740-4500	Dallas, TX	1221	1610	8
1148	Westburne International Industries Ltd	403-292-0200	Calgary, AB Can	1216	595	20
1149	Scripps, E W Corp	302-478-4141	Wilmington, DE	1215	1556	8
1150	Federated Cooperatives Ltd	306-244-3311	Saskatoon, SK Can	1214	451	2

Organizations Listed by Revenue

Rank	Organization	Phone	City / State or Province	Revenue ($ mil)	Assets ($ mil)	Emp (thous)
1151	Ecolab (Economics Laboratory) Inc	612-293-2233	St Paul, MN	1212	943	12
1152	National Starch & Chemical Corp	201-685-5000	Bridgewater, NJ	1210	750	8
1153	APL Corp	305-866-7771	Miami, FL	1209	584	12
1154	Wheelabrator Technologies Inc	508-777-2207	Danvers, MA	1205	1221	10
1155	Boston Edison Co	617-424-2000	Boston, MA	1203	2817	4
1156	Nike Inc	503-641-6453	Beaverton, OR	1203	709	6
1157	San Antonio, City of	512-299-7060	San Antonio, TX	1202	NM	12
1158	Figgie International Holding Inc	804-264-5600	Richmond, VA	1201	1022	17
1159	Armtek Corp	203-784-2200	New Haven, CT	1200	1000	12
1160	Charter Medical Corp	912-742-1161	Macon, GA	1200	NA	12
1161	Collins & Aikman Corp	212-578-1200	New York, NY	1200	750	13
1162	Commercial Credit Corp	301-332-3000	Baltimore, MD	1200	4900	5
1163	DWG Corp	305-866-7771	Miami, FL	1200	1000	15
1164	Harris County Government	713-221-5000	Houston, TX	1200	NM	10
1165	IMC Fertilizer Corp	312-564-8600	Northbrook, IL	1200	1000	6
1166	Laidlaw Industries Inc	312-439-6686	Hinsdale, IL	1200	600	5
1167	National Westminster Bank USA	516-560-7050	West Hempstead, NY	1200	12000	5
1168	Neiman Marcus Co	617-232-0760	Chestnut Hill, MA	1200	1300	13
1169	NVF Co	302-239-5281	Yorklyn, DE	1200	500	10
1170	Old Republic International Corp	312-346-8100	Chicago, IL	1200	3000	5
1171	Oryx Energy Co	201-845-5533	Paramus, NJ	1200	800	1
1172	Royal Insurance Co of America	312-522-2000	Chicago, IL	1200	1600	6
1173	Deluxe Check Printers Inc	612-483-7111	St Paul, MN	1196	786	17
1174	Rubbermaid Inc	216-264-6464	Wooster, OH	1194	782	8
1175	Empire Co	902-755-4440	Stellarton, NS Can	1193	880	4
1176	Interpublic Group of Companies Inc	212-399-8000	New York, NY	1192	1601	14
1177	Chevron Canada Resources Ltd	403-234-5000	Calgary, AB Can	1190	850	2
1178	Public Works Canada	613-998-7724	Ottawa, ON Can	1190	NM	8
1179	Hartford Life Insurance Co	203-547-5000	Hartford, CT	1189	3495	4
1180	Weis Markets Inc	717-286-4571	Sunbury, PA	1189	596	15
1181	Harnischfeger Corp	414-671-4000	Brookfield, WI	1187	1195	7
1182	Loral Corp	212-697-1105	New York, NY	1187	1200	9
1183	Bombardier Inc	514-861-9481	Montreal, PQ Can	1187	740	10
1184	Claiborne, Liz Co Inc	212-354-4900	New York, NY	1184	629	10
1185	McCormick & Co Inc	301-771-7301	Hunt Valley, MD	1184	770	10
1186	Algoma Steel Ltd	705-945-2788	Sault Ste Marie, ON Ca	1183	1231	11
1187	Penn Traffic Inc	814-536-4411	Johnstown, PA	1180	NA	10
1188	Boston, City of	617-725-4500	Boston, MA	1179	NM	21
1189	Federal Mogul Corp	313-354-7700	Southfield, MI	1177	811	16
1190	Hartmarx Corp	312-372-6300	Chicago, IL	1174	734	16
1191	Tesoro Petroleum Corp	512-828-8484	San Antonio, TX	1172	490	3
1192	DuPont Canada Ltd	416-821-3300	Mississauga, ON Can	1171	649	4
1193	Thiokol Corp	312-807-2000	Chicago, IL	1168	900	9
1194	Kansas Power & Light Co	913-296-6300	Topeka, KS	1166	1777	5
1195	Harris Trust & Savings Bank	312-461-2121	Chicago, IL	1165	11276	4
1196	Perkin Elmer Corp	203-762-1000	Norwalk, CT	1165	1368	11
1197	Marubeni Canada Ltd	416-368-1171	Toronto, ON Can	1162	425	1
1198	Federal Reserve Bank of Boston Inc	617-973-3000	Boston, MA	1156	17450	2
1199	National Home Life Assurance Co	215-648-5000	Valley Forge, PA	1155	3118	3
1200	Computer Sciences Corp	213-615-0311	El Segundo, CA	1152	661	13

Organizations Listed by Revenue

Rank	Organization	Phone	City / State or Province	Revenue ($ mil)	Assets ($ mil)	Emp (thous)
1201	Union Texas Petroleum Inc	713-623-6544	Houston, TX	1152	1717	2
1202	Ensite Ltd	519-257-4412	Windsor, ON Can	1150	631	3
1203	Crown Central Petroleum Corp	301-539-7400	Baltimore, MD	1149	443	6
1204	Union Gas Ltd	519-352-3100	Chatham, ON Can	1148	1190	3
1205	Rykoff Sexton Inc	213-622-4131	Los Angeles, CA	1143	326	5
1206	Suncor Inc	416-733-7300	North York, ON Can	1143	1720	4
1207	Lutheran Brotherhood	612-340-7000	Minneapolis, MN	1142	3007	1
1208	Tosco Corp	213-207-6000	Santa Monica, CA	1142	556	1
1209	CIL Inc	416-229-7000	North York, ON Can	1139	989	6
1210	Falconbridge Ltd	416-863-7000	Toronto, ON Can	1139	2244	9
1211	Commercial Metals Co	214-689-4300	Dallas, TX	1137	337	4
1212	Farmers Union Central Exchange Inc	612-451-1772	South St Paul, MN	1135	500	3
1213	Blount Inc	205-244-4000	Montgomery, AL	1134	665	6
1214	Farmers Group Insurance Inc	213-932-3200	Los Angeles, CA	1133	1528	16
1215	Union Enterprises Ltd	416-964-6300	Toronto, ON Can	1131	1275	6
1216	Lubrizol Corp	216-943-4200	Wicklife, OH	1126	971	5
1217	Advanced Micro Devices Inc	408-732-2400	Sunnyvale, CA	1122	919	19
1218	Federal Paper Board Co Inc	201-391-1776	Montvale, NJ	1117	1335	5
1219	Peoples Energy Corp	312-431-4000	Chicago, IL	1117	1408	3
1220	Univar Corp	206-447-5911	Seattle, WA	1117	395	5
1221	Federal Reserve Bank of Cleveland Inc	216-579-2000	Cleveland, OH	1114	16294	2
1222	Integrated Resources	212-353-7000	New York, NY	1111	6252	3
1223	Coast Savings & Loan Assc Inc	213-688-2000	Los Angeles, CA	1110	12647	3
1224	MacLean Hunter Ltd	416-596-5000	Toronto, ON Can	1107	1356	11
1225	Consumers Distributing Co	416-245-4900	Rexdale, ON Can	1105	425	11
1226	Ace Hardware Corp	312-990-6600	Oak Brook, IL	1100	250	2
1227	Affiliated Foods Inc	817-281-4417	Keller, TX	1100	NA	1
1228	Allegheny Ludlum Steel Corp	412-394-2800	Pittsburgh, PA	1100	NA	5
1229	Asahi Chemical Industries	212-695-6720	New York, NY	1100	NA	1
1230	Associated Grocers Inc	206-762-2100	Seattle, WA	1100	NA	2
1231	Ayer, N W Inc	212-708-5000	New York, NY	1100	NA	2
1232	Best Western International Assn Inc	602-957-4200	Phoenix, AZ	1100	NA	1
1233	Blue Bell Inc	919-373-3400	Greensboro, NC	1100	NA	5
1234	Blue Cross Blue Shield of Alabama Inc	205-988-2100	Birmingham, AL	1100	2856	5
1235	Blue Cross Blue Shield of Virginia Inc	804-359-7000	Richmond, VA	1100	2856	2
1236	Bridgestone Tire USA Inc	213-320-6031	Torrance, CA	1100	NA	2
1237	Cain Chemical Corp	713-622-2246	Houston, TX	1100	NA	3
1238	Calcot Ltd Inc	805-327-5961	Bakersfield, CA	1100	NA	2
1239	Cenex Corp	612-451-5151	Inver Grove Heights, M	1100	NA	2
1240	Centerre Trust Co	314-231-9300	St Louis, MO	1100	11000	4
1241	Certified Grocers Midwest Inc	312-585-7000	Chicago, IL	1100	NA	2
1242	CF Industries Inc	312-438-9500	Long Grove, IL	1100	1000	2
1243	City Public Service Inc	512-227-3211	San Antonio, TX	1100	NA	5
1244	Connell Rice & Sugar Inc	201-233-0700	Westfield, NJ	1100	NA	2
1245	CountryMark Inc	614-548-8200	Delaware, OH	1100	250	1
1246	Daewoo Group	201-896-2824	Carlstadt, NJ	1100	NA	2
1247	Eighty Four Lumber Co	412-228-8820	Eighty Four, PA	1100	NA	5
1248	Erbamont Inc	203-967-4882	Stamford, CT	1100	NA	11
1249	Fuji Industries Inc	212-943-4435	New York, NY	1100	NA	2
1250	Fujitsu Inc	213-327-2151	Torrance, CA	1100	NA	2

Organizations Listed by Revenue

Rank	Organization	Phone	City / State or Province	Revenue ($ mil)	Assets ($ mil)	Emp (thous)
1251	Fuller, George A Co Inc	212-355-2700	New York, NY	1100	NA	2
1252	Grossmans Inc	617-848-0100	Braintree, MA	1100	NA	11
1253	Hartford National Corp	203-728-2000	Hartford, CT	1100	12000	5
1254	Hitachi Sales Corp of America	213-537-8383	Compton, CA	1100	NA	2
1255	Huffington, Roy M Inc	713-651-1600	Houston, TX	1100	NA	2
1256	Itoh, C Trading Co USA	212-818-8000	New York, NY	1100	NA	3
1257	Katz Communications Inc	212-572-5500	New York, NY	1100	NA	2
1258	Memphis Light Gas & Water Inc	901-528-4151	Memphis, TN	1100	NA	5
1259	Miller, E A Inc	801-245-6456	Hyrum, UT	1100	NA	4
1260	Mills, Olan Inc	615-622-5141	Chattanooga, TN	1100	NA	11
1261	Mitsui & Co Trading (USA)	212-878-4097	New York, NY	1100	NA	2
1262	National Coop Refinery Assn Inc	316-241-2340	McPherson, KS	1100	500	1
1263	Nationwide Electronics Inc	312-426-5900	Carpentersville, IL	1100	NA	2
1264	Needham Worldwide Advertising Inc	212-415-2000	New York, NY	1100	NA	2
1265	New York-Off Track Betting Inc	212-704-5000	New York, NY	1100	NA	2
1266	NL Industries Inc	713-987-4000	Houston, TX	1100	1400	13
1267	Pechiney World Trade Inc	203-622-8300	Greenwich, CT	1100	NA	1
1268	Raymond International Inc	713-623-1500	Houston, TX	1100	NA	2
1269	Richfood Inc	804-746-6000	Mechanicsville, VA	1100	NA	2
1270	SAAB Scandia America Inc	203-795-5671	Orange, CT	1100	NA	2
1271	Salt River Project Inc	602-236-5900	Phoenix, AZ	1100	NA	5
1272	Samsung Electronics USA Inc	201-592-7900	Fort Lee, NJ	1100	NA	1
1273	Sanyo Manufacturing Corp	501-633-5030	Forest City, AR	1100	NA	4
1274	Sharp Electronics USA Inc	201-529-8200	Mahwah, NJ	1100	NA	2
1275	Shaws Supermarkets Inc	508-378-7211	East Bridgewater, MA	1100	NA	11
1276	Smith Barney Harris Upham & Co	212-698-6000	New York, NY	1100	11000	6
1277	Smith Management Corp	801-974-1400	Salt Lake City, UT	1100	NA	5
1278	Spiegel Corp	312-986-8800	Oak Brook, IL	1100	900	6
1279	Sunkist Growers Inc	818-986-4800	Sherman Oaks, CA	1100	250	2
1280	Suzuki Motor Corp USA Inc	714-996-7040	Brea, CA	1100	NA	1
1281	TDC Development Corp	213-433-9931	Long Beach, CA	1100	NA	2
1282	Toyo Menka Trading Co USA	212-466-4600	New York, NY	1100	NA	3
1283	Triangle Publications Inc	215-293-8500	Radnor, PA	1100	NA	3
1284	Twin County Grocers Inc	201-287-4600	Edison, NJ	1100	NA	2
1285	Valley National Corp	602-261-2900	Phoenix, AZ	1100	11300	7
1286	Volkswagen America Inc	313-362-6000	Troy, MI	1100	NA	11
1287	Volvo North America Corp	201-768-7300	Rockleigh, NJ	1100	NA	3
1288	Oklahoma Gas & Electric Co	405-272-3000	Oklahoma City, OK	1098	2521	4
1289	California State Auto Association	415-565-2012	San Francisco, CA	1096	1932	3
1290	First Federal of Michigan Inc	313-965-1400	Detroit, MI	1096	11942	3
1291	Centel Corp	312-399-2500	Chicago, IL	1095	3753	13
1292	Raychem Corp	415-361-3333	Menlo Park, CA	1095	1149	9
1293	Tecumseh Products Co	517-423-8411	Tecumseh, MI	1094	900	10
1294	Quebecor Inc	514-282-9600	Montreal, PQ Can	1093	1225	11
1295	Empire of America Fed Savings Bank Inc	716-845-7101	Buffalo, NY	1090	11281	3
1296	Foster Wheeler Corp	201-730-4000	Clinton, NJ	1090	1109	18
1297	Ogden Corp	212-868-6100	New York, NY	1088	2202	35
1298	Potlatch Corp	415-576-8800	San Francisco, CA	1084	1272	7
1299	Franklin Life Insurance Co	217-528-2011	Springfield, IL	1083	11642	4
1300	SCANA (So Carolina Elec & Gas) Corp	803-748-3000	Columbia, SC	1083	2887	4

Organizations Listed by Revenue

Rank	Organization	Phone	City / State or Province	Revenue ($ mil)	Assets ($ mil)	Emp (thous)
1301	Life Insurance Co of Virginia Inc	804-281-6000	Richmond, VA	1080	2794	3
1302	Motors Insurance (General Motors) Co	313-556-5000	Detroit, MI	1075	2453	4
1303	Ball Corp	317-747-6100	Muncie, IN	1073	877	7
1304	National Convenience Stores Inc	713-863-2200	Houston, TX	1073	600	11
1305	National Victoria & Grey Trustco Ltd	519-271-2050	Stratford, ON Can	1073	10362	4
1306	PCL Construction Group Ltd	403-435-9711	Edmonton, AB Can	1071	308	4
1307	Bemis Co Inc	612-340-6000	Minneapolis, MN	1069	595	8
1308	Alltel Corp	216-650-7000	Hudson, OH	1068	2153	8
1309	Gerber Products Co	616-928-2000	Fremont, MI	1068	697	15
1310	Richardson, James & Sons Ltd	204-934-5811	Winnipeg, MB Can	1068	1165	3
1311	Boatmen's Bancshares Inc	314-425-7525	St Louis, MO	1066	14676	5
1312	Southeast Banking Corp	305-375-7500	Miami, FL	1066	12469	7
1313	Duquesne Light Co Inc	412-393-6000	Pittsburgh, PA	1063	3877	4
1314	Sumitomo Canada Ltd	604-682-2256	Vancouver, BC Can	1063	NA	1
1315	Franklin Savings Assn Inc	913-242-6300	Ottawa, KS	1059	13419	2
1316	Riser Foods Inc	216-292-7000	Bedford Heights, OH	1057	228	10
1317	Co-operative Federee de Quebec Ltd	514-383-6450	Montreal, PQ Can	1057	235	5
1318	Vulcan Materials Co	205-877-3000	Birmingham, AL	1053	958	6
1319	Ameritrust Corp	216-737-5000	Cleveland, OH	1052	10738	4
1320	Sun Microsystems Inc	415-960-1300	Mountain View, CA	1052	757	7
1321	Dime Savings Bank of New York Inc	516-227-6030	Garden City, NY	1051	12007	6
1322	Borman's Inc	313-270-1000	Detroit, MI	1050	600	11
1323	Pacific Resources Inc	808-547-3111	Honolulu, HI	1050	700	11
1324	AVCO Financial Services Inc	714-553-1200	Irvine, CA	1047	4173	7
1325	City Fed Financial Corp	201-658-4100	Bedminster, NJ	1046	10585	5
1326	DiGiorgio Corp	415-765-0100	San Francisco, CA	1046	226	5
1327	DPL (Dayton Power & Light) Corp	513-224-6000	Dayton, OH	1044	2338	4
1328	Comerica Inc	313-222-3300	Detroit, MI	1043	11145	7
1329	PSI Public Service Co of Indiana	317-839-9611	Plainfield, IN	1043	2129	4
1330	Balfour Maclaine Corp(former Kay Corp)	212-269-0800	New York, NY	1042	500	1
1331	CIT Group Financial Corp	201-740-5000	Livingston, NJ	1042	9337	4
1332	Keystone Provident Life Insurance Co	617-338-3500	Boston, MA	1042	3836	2
1333	Rorer Group Inc	215-628-6000	Fort Washington, PA	1042	1388	8
1334	Getty Petroleum Corp	516-338-6000	Jericho, NY	1041	1500	7
1335	Michigan National Bankcorp Inc	313-473-3000	Farmington Hills, MI	1040	11306	7
1336	Baybanks Inc	617-482-1040	Boston, MA	1037	8678	6
1337	Henley Group Inc	603-926-5911	Hampton, NH	1036	4503	2
1338	TECO Energy (Tampa Elec) Inc	813-228-4111	Tampa, FL	1034	2315	4
1339	Dominion Textile Inc	514-989-6000	Montreal, PQ Can	1034	1228	14
1340	Honda Canada Inc	416-284-8110	Scarborough, ON Can	1034	850	1
1341	United Jersey Banks Inc	609-987-3200	Princeton, NJ	1032	10311	3
1342	Computer Associates International Inc	516-333-6700	Jericho, NY	1030	NA	9
1343	Nashville, City of	615-259-6047	Nashville, TN	1027	NM	16
1344	Thomson Newspapers Ltd	416-864-1710	Toronto, ON Can	1027	1708	13
1345	Collins Foods International Inc	213-827-2300	Los Angeles, CA	1024	394	13
1346	Pennwalt Corp	215-587-7000	Philadelphia, PA	1024	950	5
1347	Carson, Pirie, Scott & Co	312-641-7000	Chicago, IL	1023	666	18
1348	Energy, Mines & Resources Canada	613-995-4510	Ottawa, ON Can	1020	NM	5
1349	External Affairs Canada	613-996-9134	Ottawa, ON Can	1020	NM	4
1350	Fisheries & Oceans Canada	613-993-0600	Ottawa, ON Can	1020	NM	6

Organizations Listed by Revenue

Rank	Organization	Phone	City / State or Province	Revenue ($ mil)	Assets ($ mil)	Emp (thous)
1351	Great Atlantic & Pacific Co of Canada	416-239-7171	Toronto, ON Can	1020	425	20
1352	Indian & Northern Affairs Canada	819-997-0380	Hull, PQ Can	1020	NM	5
1353	Northwest Territories Power Corp	403-465-3377	Edmonton, AB Can	1020	NM	5
1354	Hechinger Co	301-341-1000	Landover, MD	1019	681	6
1355	Crestar Financial Corp (United VA)	804-782-5000	Richmond, VA	1016	10408	6
1356	Smith, A O Corp	414-359-4000	Milwaukee, WI	1015	808	10
1357	Trizec Corp	403-269-8241	Calgary, AB Can	1014	7325	6
1358	Mutual of America Life Insurance Co	212-399-1600	New York, NY	1011	4810	9
1359	Ferro Corp	216-641-8580	Cleveland, OH	1009	588	8
1360	Sears Roebuck Acceptance Corp	302-652-3666	Greenville, DE	1008	12085	3
1361	Allegheny Corp	212-752-1356	New York, NY	1006	1630	9
1362	Arrow Electronics Inc	516-391-1300	Melville, NY	1006	530	5
1363	Laidlaw Transportation Ltd	416-336-1800	Burlington, ON Can	1006	1391	15
1364	Fruit of the Loom Inc	312-876-1724	Chicago, IL	1005	1830	15
1365	Primerica Corp	203-552-2000	Greenwich, CT	1004	14435	18
1366	Emco Ltd	519-451-1250	London, ON Can	1004	572	9
1367	Jacksonville, City of	904-630-1776	Jacksonville, FL	1003	NM	8
1368	Northern Trust Corp	312-630-6000	Chicago, IL	1003	9133	5
1369	Trinity Industries Inc	214-631-4420	Dallas, TX	1001	878	6
1370	Wheeling Pittsburgh Steel Corp	304-234-2400	Wheeling, WV	1001	1002	8
1371	A Mark Financial Corp	213-319-0200	Santa Monica, CA	1000	NA	1
1372	AFL-CIO American Federation of Labor	202-637-5000	Washington, DC	1000	NM	5000
1373	Alleco Inc	301-341-6000	Hyattsville, MD	1000	600	4
1374	Amsted Industries Inc	312-645-1700	Chicago, IL	1000	NA	10
1375	Andersen Corp	612-439-5150	Bayport, MN	1000	NA	6
1376	Aristech Chemical Corp	412-433-2747	Pittsburgh, PA	1000	NA	6
1377	Avis Corp	516-222-3000	Garden City, NY	1000	NA	13
1378	Beef America Inc	402-397-2000	Omaha, NE	1000	NA	2
1379	Chilewich Sons Inc	212-344-3400	New York, NY	1000	NA	1
1380	Cityfed Financial Corp	407-655-5919	Palm Beach, FL	1000	10585	5
1381	Clark Construction Enterprises Inc	301-657-7100	Bethesda, MD	1000	NA	4
1382	Crowley Maritime Corp	415-546-2500	San Francisco, CA	1000	NA	5
1383	Cullum Companies	214-661-9700	Dallas, TX	1000	NA	10
1384	DeBartolo, Edward J Co Inc	216-758-7292	Youngstown, OH	1000	NA	10
1385	Democratic National Committee	202-863-8000	Washington, DC	1000	NM	5
1386	DeMoulas Super Markets Inc	508-851-7381	Tewksbury, MA	1000	NA	9
1387	Domino's Pizza Inc	313-668-4000	Ann Arbor, MI	1000	NA	15
1388	Dravo Corp	412-566-3000	Pittsburgh, PA	1000	500	5
1389	Dyson Kissner Moran Corp	212-661-4600	New York, NY	1000	NA	5
1390	Eagle Food Center Corp	309-787-7700	Milan, IL	1000	NA	10
1391	Edison Brothers Stores Inc	314-331-6000	St Louis, MO	1000	500	22
1392	Epic Healthcare Group Inc	214-869-0707	Irving, TX	1000	NA	10
1393	Esprit de Corp Inc	415-648-6900	San Francisco, CA	1000	NA	2
1394	Fidelity Investments Corp	617-523-1919	Boston, MA	1000	85000	6
1395	First Brands Corp	203-790-2900	Danbury, CT	1000	NA	5
1396	First Interstate Bank of Texas	713-224-6611	Houston, TX	1000	10000	4
1397	Flying J Inc	801-734-9416	West Brigham, UT	1000	NA	2
1398	Gallo, Ernest & Julio Winery Inc	209-579-3111	Modesto, CA	1000	NA	5
1399	Gelco Corp	612-828-1000	Eden Prairie, MN	1000	2500	7
1400	Gilbane Building Co	401-456-5800	Providence, RI	1000	NA	1

Organizations Listed by Revenue

Rank	Organization	Phone	City / State or Province	Revenue ($ mil)	Assets ($ mil)	Emp (thous)
1401	Golden State Foods Corp	818-793-3135	Pasadena, CA	1000	NA	4
1402	Golub Corp	518-355-5000	Schenectady, NY	1000	NA	10
1403	Gould Inc	312-640-4000	Rolling Meadows, IL	1000	1400	11
1404	Grocers Supply Co Inc	713-747-5000	Houston, TX	1000	NA	2
1405	Hanna, M A Corp	216-589-4000	Cleveland, OH	1000	300	8
1406	Hannaford Brothers	207-883-2911	Scarborough, ME	1000	500	10
1407	Harris Wholesale Corp	919-977-1054	Solon, NC	1000	NA	1
1408	Holiday Companies Inc	612-830-8700	Minneapolis, MN	1000	NA	5
1409	Household Manufacturing Corp	312-564-3910	Prospect Heights, IL	1000	500	10
1410	Hughes Markets Inc	213-227-8211	Los Angeles, CA	1000	NA	5
1411	Hunt Consolidated Oil Co	214-744-7911	Dallas, TX	1000	NA	2
1412	Hunt Corp	317-241-6301	Indianapolis, IN	1000	NA	3
1413	Idle Wild Foods Inc	617-757-7761	Worcester, MA	1000	NA	4
1414	International Controls Inc	305-997-7400	Boca Raton, FL	1000	500	8
1415	International Brotherhood of Teamsters	202-624-6800	Washington, DC	1000	NM	2000
1416	Johnson, Axel & Co Inc	212-758-3200	New York, NY	1000	NA	1
1417	Kash n Karry Food Stores Inc	813-621-0200	Tampa, FL	1000	NA	5
1418	Kohler Co	414-457-4441	Kohler, WI	1000	NA	10
1419	Lazard Freres & Co	212-489-6600	New York, NY	1000	10000	1
1420	Lear Siegler Seating Corp	313-746-1500	Southfield, MI	1000	NA	5
1421	Levitz Furniture Corp	305-994-6006	Boca Raton, FL	1000	NA	8
1422	Lumbermens Merchandising Inc	215-293-7000	Wayne, PA	1000	NA	4
1423	Magnetek Inc	213-473-6681	Los Angeles, CA	1000	NA	10
1424	Maritz Inc	314-827-4000	Fenton, MO	1000	NA	5
1425	McCarthy Brothers Co	314-968-3300	St Louis, MO	1000	NA	5
1426	McDevitt & Street Co Inc	704-525-8110	Charlotte, NC	1000	NA	2
1427	McLean Industries Inc	212-593-3325	New York, NY	1000	1500	8
1428	Merchants Distributors Inc	704-322-2822	Hickory, NC	1000	NA	2
1429	MorningStar Foods Inc	214-360-4700	Dallas, TX	1000	NA	5
1430	National Education Association	202-833-4000	Washington, DC	1000	NM	1700
1431	Nationale Nederlanden Insurance Co	202-463-7964	Washington, DC	1000	1500	2
1432	Norstar BanCorp	518-447-4043	Albany, NY	1000	11132	1
1433	NVR Limited Partnership Inc	703-761-2000	McLean, VA	1000	500	4
1434	Oxbow Corp	617-461-0550	Dedham, MA	1000	NA	1
1435	Pacific Holding Co Inc	213-208-6055	Los Angeles, CA	1000	NA	10
1436	Parsons Corp	818-440-2000	Pasadena, CA	1000	NA	10
1437	Placid Oil Co	214-741-3081	Dallas, TX	1000	NA	1
1438	Polo/Ralph Lauren Corp	212-974-6868	New York, NY	1000	NA	2
1439	Potamkin Co Inc	212-399-4400	New York, NY	1000	NA	4
1440	Printing Holding Co	212-735-8800	New York, NY	1000	NA	10
1441	Raleys Inc	916-444-8150	Broderick, CA	1000	NA	6
1442	Randalls Food Markets Inc	713-497-8191	Houston, TX	1000	NA	10
1443	Republican National Committee	202-863-8500	Washington, DC	1000	NM	5
1444	Rockefeller Group Inc	212-698-8676	New York, NY	1000	NA	5
1445	Sanders Associates Inc	603-885-4321	South Nashua, NH	1000	NA	10
1446	Schnuck Markets Inc	314-344-9600	Bridgeton, MO	1000	NA	10
1447	Schreiber Foods Inc	414-437-7601	Green Bay, WI	1000	NA	5
1448	Scripps Howard Inc	513-977-3000	Cincinnati, OH	1000	546	10
1449	Service America Corp	203-964-5000	Stamford, CT	1000	NA	10
1450	Servistar Corp	412-283-4567	East Butler, PA	1000	500	1

Organizations Listed by Revenue

Rank	Organization	Phone	City / State or Province	Revenue ($ mil)	Assets ($ mil)	Emp (thous)
1451	Simpson Timber Corp	206-292-5000	Seattle, WA	1000	NA	2
1452	Sweet Life Foods Inc	203-623-1681	Suffield, CT	1000	NA	3
1453	Tauber Oil Co	713-869-8700	Houston, TX	1000	NA	1
1454	Taubman Investment Co	313-258-7600	Bloomfield Hills, MI	1000	NA	10
1455	Thrifty Oil Co	213-923-9876	Downey, CA	1000	NA	1
1456	Tops Markets Inc	716-823-3712	Buffalo, NY	1000	NA	4
1457	Trump Organization Inc	212-832-2000	New York, NY	1000	NA	10
1458	United Auto Workers	313-926-5000	Detroit, MI	1000	NM	1200
1459	United Food & Commercial Workers Union	202-223-3111	Washington, DC	1000	NM	1400
1460	United States AMTRAK Natl Rail Passenger	202-383-3000	Washington, DC	1000	NM	10
1461	United States Farmers Home Admim	202-447-4323	Washington, DC	1000	NM	2
1462	United Stationers Inc	312-699-5000	Des Plaines, IL	1000	500	3
1463	Valhi Corp	214-386-4110	Dallas, TX	1000	800	8
1464	Wegmans Food Markets Inc	716-328-2550	Rochester, NY	1000	NA	5
1465	Wickes Lumber Co	312-367-6540	Vernon Hills, IL	1000	NA	5
1466	Winn Enterprises Inc	714-637-2730	Los Angeles, CA	1000	500	10
1467	Celeron Corp	713-750-4552	Houston, TX	1000	NA	4
1468	Food Emporium	212-579-3400	Bronx, NY	1000	NA	10
1469	Kohl's Food Stores	414-771-8000	Milwaukee, WI	1000	NA	10
1470	LTV Steel Co	216-622-5000	Cleveland, OH	1000	NA	10
1471	Paramount Pictures Corp	213-468-5000	Los Angeles, CA	1000	NA	8
1472	Utility Fuels Co	713-629-3001	Houston, TX	1000	NA	4
1473	CNW Corp	312-559-7000	Chicago, IL	995	1727	10
1474	Auto Owners Group Insurance Co	517-323-1200	Lansing, MI	994	1724	3
1475	Nalco Chemical Co	312-961-9500	Naperville, IL	994	839	5
1476	Bradlees Stores Inc	617-770-8000	Braintree, MA	990	NA	13
1477	Doubleday & Co Inc	212-984-7561	New York, NY	990	NA	9
1478	Mattel Inc	213-978-5150	Hawthorne, CA	990	693	20
1479	Detroit Medical Center Inc	313-745-5192	Detroit, MI	989	NA	12
1480	Nashua Corp	603-880-2323	Nashua, NH	989	450	7
1481	Newell Co	815-235-4171	Freeport, IL	988	820	11
1482	McDonald's Restaurants of Canada Ltd	416-443-1000	Don Mills, ON Can	987	447	54
1483	Indiana Michigan Power Co	219-425-2111	Fort Wayne, IN	983	3993	4
1484	Varian Associates Inc	415-493-4000	Palo Alto, CA	983	830	12
1485	Magna International Inc	416-477-7766	Markham, ON Can	983	1091	12
1486	Toyota Canada Inc	416-438-6320	Scarborough, ON Can	983	170	2
1487	Anchor Glass Container	813-884-0000	Tampa, FL	978	773	8
1488	Bausch & Lomb Inc	716-338-6000	Rochester, NY	978	1211	10
1489	Canadian Utilities Ltd	403-420-7121	Edmonton, AB Can	978	2231	1
1490	Atlanta Gas Light Co	404-584-4000	Atlanta, GA	976	1221	4
1491	Imperial Savings Assn Inc	619-292-3000	San Diego, CA	972	10800	4
1492	Society Bank Corp	216-689-3000	Cleveland, OH	972	10009	6
1493	Western & Southern Life Ins Co	513-629-1800	Cincinnati, OH	970	5028	6
1494	Allegheny International Inc	412-562-4000	Pittsburgh, PA	968	841	12
1495	Southern States Cooperative Inc	804-281-1000	Richmond, VA	967	382	3
1496	Shaw Industries Inc	404-278-3812	Dalton, GA	958	546	5
1497	Xerox Canada Ltd	416-229-3769	North York, ON Can	958	1591	7
1498	Fisher Scientific Group Inc	619-457-3565	La Jolla, CA	957	579	6
1499	Macmillan Inc	212-702-2000	New York, NY	956	937	10
1500	Hilton Hotels Corp	213-278-4321	Beverly Hills, CA	954	1893	18

Organizations Listed by Revenue

Rank	Organization	Phone	City / State or Province	Revenue ($ mil)	Assets ($ mil)	Emp (thous)
1501	Alameda County	415-272-6691	Oakland, CA	950	NM	6
1502	Meridian Bancorp Inc	215-320-2000	Reading, PA	950	9523	3
1503	Cargill Ltd	204-947-0141	Winnipeg, MB Can	947	274	1
1504	North American Life Assurance Co	416-229-4515	Toronto, ON Can	944	3838	3
1505	Culbro Corp	212-561-8700	New York, NY	942	396	5
1506	Metropolitan Life Insurance Co of Canada	613-560-7446	Ottawa, ON Can	939	3441	2
1507	Itoh, C & Co Canada Ltd	604-683-5764	Vancouver, BC Can	937	425	1
1508	Kinder Care Centers Inc	205-277-5090	Montgomery, AL	936	6087	15
1509	Fox & Lazo Inc	609-424-2800	Haddonfield, NJ	935	NA	2
1510	Signode Corp	312-724-6100	Glenview, IL	935	NA	8
1511	Standard Commerical Tobacco Co	919-291-5507	Wilson, NC	935	559	5
1512	Navistar International Corp of Canada	416-528-7700	Hamilton, ON Can	935	425	2
1513	American National Insurance Co	409-763-4461	Galveston, TX	934	4303	2
1514	Federal Reserve Bank of Atlanta Inc	404-521-8500	Atlanta, GA	934	14294	2
1515	Fuqua Industries Inc	404-658-9000	Atlanta, GA	934	1146	16
1516	Robins, A H Co Inc	804-257-2000	Richmond, VA	934	1075	8
1517	Alberta & Southern Gas Co	403-260-9911	Calgary, AB Can	932	473	1
1518	Allegheny County Government	412-355-6940	Pittsburgh, PA	925	NM	8
1519	Indal Ltd	416-743-1400	Weston, ON Can	925	530	9
1520	Manufacturers National of Detroit Inc	313-222-4000	Detroit, MI	924	9311	6
1521	Canfor Corp	604-661-5241	Vancouver, BC Can	921	986	4
1522	Atkinson, Guy F Co of California	415-876-1000	S San Francisco, CA	920	305	8
1523	Central Louisiana Electric Co	318-484-7400	Pineville, LA	920	NA	5
1524	Savannah Foods & Industries Inc	912-234-1261	Savannah, GA	917	395	2
1525	Smithfield Foods Inc	703-357-4321	Smithfield, VA	916	131	4
1526	Briggs & Stratton Corp	414-259-5333	Wauwatosa, WI	914	511	10
1527	Highland Superstores Corp	313-451-3200	Plymouth, MI	911	700	5
1528	Alberta Government Telephone Co	403-425-2110	Edmonton, AB Can	911	2006	11
1529	Cincinnati Financial Corp	513-870-2000	Fairfield, OH	910	2117	2
1530	Zale Corp	214-580-4670	Irving, TX	909	1126	10
1531	Rohr Industries Inc	619-691-4111	Chula Vista, CA	907	883	11
1532	Scott's Hospitality Inc	416-977-6001	Toronto, ON Can	906	728	24
1533	Strawbridge & Clothier Inc	215-629-6000	Philadelphia, PA	904	650	5
1534	Worthington Industries Inc	614-438-3210	Columbus, OH	904	507	7
1535	Kaufman & Broad Inc	213-312-5000	Los Angeles, CA	903	603	3
1536	Caesars World Inc	213-552-2711	Los Angeles, CA	902	831	11
1537	Huntington Bancshares Inc	614-476-8300	Columbus, OH	901	9506	6
1538	Armstrong Rubber Co	203-784-2200	New Haven, CT	900	600	8
1539	Bell & Howell Co	312-470-7100	Skokie, IL	900	800	10
1540	Big Bear Inc	614-464-6500	Columbus, OH	900	500	9
1541	Carnival Cruise Lines Inc	305-599-2600	Miami, FL	900	NA	10
1542	Cyclops Industries Inc	412-343-4000	Pittsburgh, PA	900	NA	7
1543	Ebasco Services Inc	212-839-1000	New York, NY	900	NA	5
1544	First American Bankshares Inc	202-383-1400	Washington, DC	900	8000	6
1545	Heritage Communications Inc	515-246-1440	Des Moines, IA	900	700	2
1546	Marsh Supermarkets Inc	317-759-8101	Yorktown, IN	900	600	9
1547	Swiss Reinsurance Co	212-907-8000	New York, NY	900	1200	3
1548	York International Corp	717-846-1988	York, PA	900	500	7
1549	Brooklyn Union Gas Co	718-403-2000	Brooklyn, NY	899	1257	4
1550	Dominion Bankshares Inc	703-563-7749	Roanoke, VA	898	9204	6

Organizations Listed by Revenue

Rank	Organization	Phone	City / State or Province	Revenue ($ mil)	Assets ($ mil)	Emp (thous)
1551	Consolidated Papers Inc	715-422-3111	Wisconsin Rapids, WI	897	935	5
1552	State Street Bank Inc	617-786-3000	Boston, MA	897	7246	4
1553	AMCA (Amer Can of Canada) Intl Ltd	416-432-2151	Rexdale, ON Can	893	NA	10
1554	Sobeys Inc	902-752-8371	Stellarton, NS Can	893	213	9
1555	Interlake Corp	312-986-6600	Oak Brook, IL	892	660	11
1556	Wrigley, William Jr Co	312-644-2121	Chicago, IL	891	440	6
1557	Procter & Gamble Inc	416-730-4711	Toronto, ON Can	891	719	3
1558	First of America Bank Corp	616-383-9000	Kalamazoo, MI	885	9769	5
1559	Hillenbrand Industries Inc	812-934-7000	Batesville, IN	884	735	8
1560	United of Omaha Life Insurance Co	402-342-7600	Omaha, NE	882	3211	3
1561	Foremost Insurance Co	616-942-3000	Grand Rapids, MI	881	814	2
1562	Omnicom Group Inc	212-415-2000	New York, NY	881	1135	3
1563	Ryland Group Inc	301-730-7222	Columbia, MD	881	458	3
1564	Crown Henry & Co Inc	312-236-6300	Chicago, IL	880	NA	4
1565	Dubuque Packing Co Inc	402-397-2000	Omaha, NE	880	NA	3
1566	Durwood Inc	816-221-4000	Kansas City, MO	880	NA	8
1567	MAN North America Corp	201-469-6600	Middlesex, NJ	880	NA	3
1568	Mannesmann USA Inc	212-702-9420	New York, NY	880	NA	3
1569	Nixdorf US Inc	617-273-0480	Burlington, MA	880	NA	8
1570	Service Star Corp	412-283-4567	East Butler, PA	880	250	2
1571	Lawson Mardon Group Ltd	416-821-9711	Mississauga, ON Can	880	707	7
1572	Provident Mutual Life Ins Co of Phil	215-636-5000	Philadelphia, PA	879	3371	2
1573	Western Union Corp	201-818-5000	Upper Saddle Rvr, NJ	879	661	6
1574	Noverco Inc	514-393-2650	Montreal, PQ Can	879	1207	3
1575	Royal Canadian Mint Ltd	613-992-2348	Ottawa, ON Can	878	108	1
1576	SPX Sealed Power Corp	616-724-5000	Muskegon, MI	877	702	8
1577	Crown Forest Industries Ltd	604-668-4242	Vancouver, BC Can	876	717	5
1578	Storage Technology Corp	303-673-5020	Louisville, CO	874	847	8
1579	Lavalin Inc	514-288-1740	Montreal, PQ Can	870	451	6
1580	Quaker State Oil Refining Co	814-676-7676	Oil City, PA	869	740	6
1581	Standard Federal Bank Inc	313-643-9600	Troy, MI	867	9573	2
1582	First City Bancorp of Texas Inc	713-658-6873	Houston, TX	865	12195	7
1583	Southwest Airlines Co	214-353-6100	Love Field, TX	860	1308	6
1584	Universal Health Services Inc	215-768-3300	King of Prussia, PA	860	543	14
1585	Dallas, City of	214-670-4054	Dallas, TX	859	NM	14
1586	Cincinnati Milacron Inc	513-841-8100	Cincinnati, OH	857	721	8
1587	American United Life Insurance Co	317-263-1877	Indianapolis, IN	856	3361	3
1588	IBC Holdings (Interstate Bakeries Corp)	816-561-6600	Kansas City, MO	855	646	10
1589	Snap-on Tools Corp	414-656-5200	Kenosha, WI	855	668	7
1590	Federated Investment Corp	412-288-1900	Pittsburgh, PA	850	44000	3
1591	Firstar (First Wisconsin Corp)	414-765-4321	Milwaukee, WI	850	7193	5
1592	Memorex Telex Corp	918-627-2333	Tulsa, OK	850	563	7
1593	National Life of Vermont	802-229-3333	Montpelier, VT	850	3980	2
1594	Rainier Bancorp Inc	206-621-4111	Seattle, WA	850	9216	6
1595	Scudder Stevens & Clark	617-439-4640	Boston, MA	850	33000	3
1596	United States Office of Personnel Mgt	202-632-5491	Washington, DC	850	NM	5
1597	Wicor Inc	414-291-7026	Milwaukee, WI	850	650	6
1598	Central Guaranty Trust Ltd	416-345-4000	Toronto, ON Can	850	5100	3
1599	Perini Corp	508-875-6171	Framingham, MA	849	374	3
1600	Union Central Life Insurance Co	215-322-3000	Trevose, PA	847	2547	2

Organizations Listed by Revenue

Rank	Organization	Phone	City / State or Province	Revenue ($ mil)	Assets ($ mil)	Emp (thous)
1601	Public Service Co of New Mexico	505-848-2700	Albuquerque, NM	842	2393	4
1602	United Artists Corp	303-321-4242	Denver, CO	842	1904	3
1603	Standard Life Assurance Co	514-284-6711	Montreal, PQ Can	842	3964	1
1604	MDC Holdings Inc	303-773-1100	Denver, CO	841	1993	2
1605	International Flavors & Fragrances Inc	212-765-5500	New York, NY	840	882	4
1606	Sheller Globe Corp	419-255-8840	Toledo, OH	840	904	10
1607	Pratt & Whitney Canada Inc	514-677-9411	Longueuill, PQ Can	839	700	9
1608	Canada Cement Lafarge Ltd	514-861-1411	Montreal, PQ Can	838	638	6
1609	GAF Corp	201-628-3000	Wayne, NJ	837	1298	5
1610	PHM (Pulte Home) Corp	313-661-1500	West Bloomfield, MI	834	590	2
1611	Morrison Inc	205-344-3000	Mobile, AL	829	299	15
1612	Dexter Corp	203-627-9051	Windsor Locks, CT	827	626	6
1613	AG Processing Inc	402-334-8010	Omaha, NE	825	250	1
1614	Blue Cross Blue Shield of Oregon Inc	503-225-5221	Portland, OR	825	2142	2
1615	California & Hawaiian Sugar Inc	415-356-6000	Concord, CA	825	250	3
1616	Clajon Production Corp	915-683-4181	Midland, TX	825	NA	1
1617	Consolidated Coal Corp	412-831-4000	Pittsburgh, PA	825	NA	7
1618	Darigold Inc	206-284-7220	Seattle, WA	825	NA	3
1619	Elrick & Lavidge Inc	312-726-0666	Chicago, IL	825	NA	8
1620	FDL Foods Inc	319-588-5400	Dubuque, IA	825	NA	4
1621	Fedco Inc	213-946-2511	Santa Fe Springs, CA	825	NA	11
1622	Foodmaker (Jack in the Box) Inc	619-571-2121	San Diego, CA	825	NA	26
1623	Granada Corp	713-783-1310	Houston, TX	825	NA	2
1624	Hardware Wholesalers Inc	219-749-8531	Fort Wayne, IN	825	250	1
1625	Intelsat Corp	202-944-6800	Washington, DC	825	NA	2
1626	Jordache Enterprises Inc	212-279-7343	New York, NY	825	NA	3
1627	Kawasaki Industries USA Inc	714-770-0400	Irvine, CA	825	NA	5
1628	King County Government	206-344-4100	Seattle, WA	825	NM	5
1629	Milk Marketing Inc	216-826-4730	Strongsville, OH	825	NA	1
1630	Minolta Corp	201-825-4000	Ramsey, NJ	825	NA	2
1631	Morse Diesel Inc	212-730-4000	New York, NY	825	NA	6
1632	NES Corp	312-426-5900	Carpentersville, IL	825	NA	3
1633	Niagara Frontier Services Inc	716-823-3712	Buffalo, NY	825	NA	5
1634	Pergamon Holding Corp	914-592-9141	Elmsford, NY	825	NA	8
1635	Peugeot USA Inc	201-935-8400	Lindhurst, NJ	825	NA	2
1636	Piggly Wiggly Southern Inc	912-537-9871	Vidalia, GA	825	NA	7
1637	Reuters Inc	212-603-3300	New York, NY	825	NA	8
1638	Riceland Foods Inc	501-673-5500	Stuttgart, AR	825	250	3
1639	Rothschild, L F, Unterberg, Towbin Inc	212-238-2000	New York, NY	825	7700	2
1640	Shurfine Central Corp	312-681-2000	Northlake, IL	825	NA	2
1641	Storer Communications Inc	305-899-1000	Miami, FL	825	NA	5
1642	Sybron Corp	414-274-6600	Milwaukee, WI	825	NA	7
1643	Timex Group Inc	203-573-5000	Waterbury, CT	825	NA	2
1644	Toshiba America Electric Corp	714-583-3000	Irvine, CA	825	NA	2
1645	United Grocers Inc	503-653-6330	Milwalkee, OR	825	NA	3
1646	Vanguard Energy Corp	713-880-8750	Houston, TX	825	NA	1
1647	Wayne County Government	313-224-0286	Detroit, MI	825	NM	5
1648	Wisconsin Gas Co Inc	414-291-7000	Milwaukee, WI	825	NA	3
1649	Pentair Inc	612-636-7920	St Paul, MN	823	745	9
1650	AM International Inc	312-558-1966	Chicago, IL	821	777	8

Organizations Listed by Revenue

Rank	Organization	Phone	City / State or Province	Revenue ($ mil)	Assets ($ mil)	Emp (thous)
1651	University of Michigan	313-764-1817	Ann Arbor, MI	818	971	39
1652	Trans Alta Utilities Corp	403-267-7110	Calgary, AB Can	818	3134	3
1653	Alaska Air Group Inc	206-433-3200	Seattle, WA	814	730	6
1654	Torstar Corp	416-367-2000	Toronto, ON Can	813	702	5
1655	Central Power & Light Co	512-881-5300	Corpus Christi, TX	812	3000	3
1656	Leggett & Platt Inc	417-358-8131	Carthage, MO	810	476	11
1657	Westinghouse Credit Corp	412-393-3000	Pittsburgh, PA	810	7143	1
1658	Denver, City of	303-575-2721	Denver, CO	808	NM	11
1659	Gaz Metropolitain Inc	514-598-3444	Montreal, PQ Can	808	1020	2
1660	Child World Inc	617-588-7300	Avon, MA	807	400	4
1661	Inter Exchange Auto Club of Southern Cal	213-741-3111	Los Angeles, CA	802	1424	3
1662	Intergraph Corp	205-772-2000	Huntsville, AL	801	831	6
1663	Reichhold Chemicals Inc	914-682-5700	White Plains, NY	801	500	6
1664	American Continental Corp	602-957-7170	Phoenix, AZ	800	5000	3
1665	American Security Bank NA	202-624-4000	Washington, DC	800	6500	2
1666	American Television & Communications Inc	203-328-0600	Stamford, CT	800	600	2
1667	Arizona Bank Corp	602-262-2000	Phoenix, AZ	800	6500	2
1668	Bank of Tokyo Trust	212-766-3472	New York, NY	800	7000	1
1669	Beckman Instruments Inc	714-871-4848	Fullerton, CA	800	500	7
1670	Borg Warner Acceptance Corp	312-329-6500	Chicago, IL	800	7000	3
1671	Delchamps Inc	205-433-0431	Mobile, AL	800	350	6
1672	Employers of Texas Insurance Co	214-760-6100	Dallas, TX	800	800	3
1673	Erie Insurance Exchange Inc	814-870-2000	Erie, PA	800	1500	3
1674	Fine Homes International L P Inc	203-356-1400	Stamford, CT	800	730	6
1675	Israel Discount Bank	212-551-8500	New York, NY	800	6000	4
1676	Jacobs Engineering Group Inc	818-449-2171	Pasadena, CA	800	600	6
1677	Munich Reinsurance Co	212-310-1800	New York, NY	800	1500	3
1678	Rock Island Refining Co	317-872-3200	Indianapolis, IN	800	NA	2
1679	Sanwa Bank of California	415-765-9500	San Francisco, CA	800	7000	4
1680	Seneca Foods Corp	716-385-9500	Pittsford, NY	800	600	8
1681	Tokai Bank Ltd	213-972-0200	Los Angeles, CA	800	7000	3
1682	University of California Los Angeles	213-825-4321	Los Angeles, CA	799	583	40
1683	Northeast Savings Inc	203-280-1000	Hartford, CT	798	7943	3
1684	Amsouth Bancorp Inc	205-320-7151	Birmingham, AL	797	8313	4
1685	Austin, City of	512-499-2250	Austin, TX	795	NM	9
1686	Standard Shares Inc	312-498-1260	Northbrook, IL	795	600	6
1687	Repap Enterprises Corp	514-879-1316	Montreal, PQ Can	795	1925	5
1688	Block, H & R Inc	816-753-6900	Kansas City, MO	794	677	4
1689	Southwestern Public Service Co	806-378-2121	Amarillo, TX	794	1667	2
1690	Anchorage, City of	907-264-4431	Anchorage, AK	790	NM	4
1691	Alberta Wheat Pool Ltd	403-290-4910	Calgary, AB Can	788	1497	2
1692	Jamesway Corp	201-330-6000	Secaucus, NJ	783	400	8
1693	Puget Sound Power & Light Co	206-454-6363	Bellevue, WA	783	2356	2
1694	Phoenix, City of	602-262-7111	Phoenix, AZ	782	NM	9
1695	Shoney's Inc	615-361-5201	Nashville, TN	782	404	12
1696	Vista Chemical Corp	713-531-3200	Houston, TX	781	521	2
1697	Columbus Southern Power Co	614-223-1000	Columbus, OH	778	2067	3
1698	First Colony Life Insurance Co	804-845-0911	Lynchburg, VA	777	2549	2
1699	Chevron Canada Ltd	604-668-5300	Vancouver, BC Can	777	830	1
1700	Rochester Gas & Electric Corp	716-546-2700	Rochester, NY	774	1823	3

Organizations Listed by Revenue

Rank	Organization	Phone	City / State or Province	Revenue ($ mil)	Assets ($ mil)	Emp (thous)
1701	SCI Systems Inc	205-882-4800	Huntsville, AL	774	485	9
1702	Saskatchewan Power Corp	306-566-2121	Regina, SK Can	774	2733	3
1703	Unilever Canada Ltd	416-964-1857	Toronto, ON Can	774	394	6
1704	Pittway Corp	312-498-1260	Northbrook, IL	771	602	6
1705	Eagle Picher Industries Inc	513-721-7010	Cincinnati, OH	770	583	9
1706	Schwab, Charles & Co	415-627-7000	San Francisco, CA	770	4235	5
1707	National Fuel Gas Co	212-541-7533	New York, NY	769	1177	5
1708	Airborne Freight Corp	206-285-4600	Seattle, WA	768	329	7
1709	Delmarva Power & Light Co	302-429-3011	Wilmington, DE	768	1915	3
1710	Kaman Corp	203-243-8311	Bloomfield, CT	768	420	6
1711	Western Digital Corp	714-863-0102	Irvine, CA	768	551	7
1712	San Diego, City of	619-236-6330	San Diego, CA	766	NM	8
1713	Statistics Canada	613-990-8116	Ottawa, ON Can	765	NM	5
1714	Atlantic Financial Federal Inc	215-668-6600	Bala Cynwyd, PA	764	7799	2
1715	Diversified Energies Inc	612-372-4664	Minneapolis, MN	764	819	5
1716	Montreal Trustco Inc	514-397-7171	Montreal, PQ Can	764	6513	4
1717	Portland General Electric Co	503-226-8333	Portland, OR	762	2511	3
1718	Pennsylvania Electric Co	814-533-8111	Johnstown, PA	761	1760	4
1719	Weldwood of Canada Ltd	604-687-7366	Vancouver, BC Can	761	601	4
1720	Bard, C R Inc	201-277-8000	Murray Hill, NJ	758	531	8
1721	Canada Mortgage & Housing Corp	613-748-2000	Ottawa, ON CAN	758	8109	3
1722	Super Rite Foods Inc	717-232-6821	Harrisburg, PA	757	450	3
1723	Cray Research Inc	612-333-5889	Minneapolis, MN	756	991	5
1724	Media General Inc	804-649-6000	Richmond, VA	756	859	11
1725	Kellwood Co	314-576-3100	Chesterfield, MO	754	447	15
1726	Marion Labratories Inc	816-966-5000	Kansas City, MO	752	554	4
1727	Farm House Foods Corp	414-271-5050	Milwaukee, WI	751	195	8
1728	Federal Reserve Bank of Kansas City Inc	816-881-2000	Kansas City, MO	751	12690	2
1729	Amerco (U-Haul) Inc	602-263-6011	Phoenix, AZ	750	NA	15
1730	American Breco Inc	213-553-1009	Los Angeles, CA	750	NA	5
1731	American Protection Industries Inc	213-442-5700	Los Angeles, CA	750	NA	5
1732	Anchor Hocking Corp	614-687-2111	Lancaster, OH	750	500	10
1733	Arcata Corp	415-781-4200	San Francisco, CA	750	NA	10
1734	Arkansas Best Corp	501-785-6000	Fort Smith, AR	750	400	8
1735	Associated Metals & Minerals Inc	914-251-5400	White Plains, NY	750	NA	1
1736	Bacardi Import Corp	809-795-1560	San Juan, PR	750	NA	2
1737	Bath Iron Works Inc	207-443-3311	Bath, ME	750	NA	7
1738	Blair, John & Co	212-603-5000	New York, NY	750	NA	7
1739	Braman Enterprises Inc	305-576-6900	Miami, FL	750	NA	1
1740	Brookshire Grocery Co	214-534-3000	Tyler, TX	750	NA	5
1741	Businessland Inc	408-437-4156	San Jose, CA	750	NA	9
1742	Centrust Savings Bank Inc	305-376-5000	Miami, FL	750	7500	2
1743	Channel Home Centers Inc	201-887-7000	Whippany, NJ	750	NA	10
1744	Cone Mills Corp	919-379-6510	Greensboro, NC	750	NA	10
1745	Continental Bancorp Inc	215-564-7000	Philadelphia, PA	750	6000	3
1746	Crown American Corp	814-536-4441	Johnstown, PA	750	NA	10
1747	Dallas County Government	214-749-8011	Dallas, TX	750	NM	5
1748	Drummond Coal Corp	205-945-6500	Birmingham, AL	750	NA	3
1749	Duchossois Industries Inc	312-279-3600	Elmhurst, IL	750	NA	8
1750	Dynalectron Corp	703-264-0330	McLean, VA	750	250	15

Organizations Listed by Revenue

Rank	Organization	Phone	City / State or Province	Revenue ($ mil)	Assets ($ mil)	Emp (thous)
1751	DynCorp Inc	703-356-0480	McLean, VA	750	NA	10
1752	Eby Brown Companies	312-242-1919	Aurora, IL	750	NA	1
1753	Essex Group Inc	219-461-4000	Fort Wayne, IN	750	NA	5
1754	Farm Fresh Inc	405-765-6656	Norfolk, VA	750	NA	5
1755	Farmstead Foods Corp	507-377-4200	Albert Lea, MN	750	NA	3
1756	Ferrell Companies Inc	816-792-1600	Liberty, MO	750	NA	3
1757	First City Industries Inc	213-852-0499	Beverly Hills, CA	750	1100	10
1758	First Texas Financial Corp	214-960-4500	Dallas, TX	750	6000	4
1759	Guardian Industries Corp	313-349-6700	Northville, MI	750	NA	7
1760	HCB Contractors Inc	214-747-8541	Dallas, TX	750	NA	1
1761	Holman Enterprises Inc	609-663-5200	Pennsauken, NJ	750	NA	2
1762	Honeywell Bull (Cie des Machines Bull)	617-895-6000	Waltham, MA	750	NA	7
1763	Horsehead Industries Inc	212-972-2100	New York, NY	750	NA	3
1764	Hyster Co Inc	503-280-7000	Portland, OR	750	NA	5
1765	Illinois Central Gulf Railroad Co	312-565-1600	Chicago, IL	750	1500	5
1766	Insilco Corp	203-634-2000	Meridan, CT	750	700	10
1767	J & L Specialty Products Inc	412-338-1600	Pittsburgh, PA	750	NA	2
1768	Johnson & Higgins Inc	212-574-7000	New York, NY	750	2000	7
1769	Johnson Coca Cola Bottling Inc	615-899-3449	Chattanooga, TN	750	NA	5
1770	Jordan Co	212-460-1920	New York, NY	750	NA	7
1771	JPS Textile Group Inc	803-271-9919	Greenville, SC	750	NA	10
1772	Kendall Co	617-574-7000	Boston, MA	750	NA	10
1773	Lennox International Corp	214-980-6000	Dallas, TX	750	NA	5
1774	Lorimar Telepictures Inc	212-686-9200	New York, NY	750	1400	5
1775	Lykes Brothers Inc	813-223-3981	Tampa, FL	750	NA	5
1776	Lyon, William Co Inc	714-833-3600	Newport Beach, CA	750	NA	1
1777	Mayflower Group Inc	317-875-1000	Carmel, IN	750	NA	2
1778	Media News Group Inc	214-720-5800	Dallas, TX	750	NA	7
1779	Mellon Stuart Holding Co Inc	412-323-4600	Pittsburgh, PA	750	NA	1
1780	Metallurg Corp	212-686-4010	New York, NY	750	NA	4
1781	Metromedia Inc	201-348-3244	Secaucus, NJ	750	NA	5
1782	National Car Rental Inc	612-830-2121	Minneapolis, MN	750	NA	10
1783	Oklahoma Publishing Co Inc	405-232-3311	Oklahoma City, OK	750	NA	7
1784	Oppenheimer & Co Inc	212-667-7000	New York, NY	750	5000	2
1785	Paragon Group Inc	214-891-2000	Dallas, TX	750	NA	2
1786	PIE Nationwide Trucking Corp	904-798-2000	Jacksonville, FL	750	NA	7
1787	Playtex Corp	203-356-8000	Stamford, CT	750	NA	8
1788	PMA Reinsurance Corp	215-629-5000	Philadelphia, PA	750	250	3
1789	Red Apple Companies Inc	212-580-6800	New York, NY	750	NA	7
1790	Red Owl Holdings Inc	612-932-2132	Hopkins, MN	750	NA	3
1791	Rich Products Corp	716-878-8000	Buffalo, NY	750	NA	5
1792	Ruffin Corp	316-942-7940	Wichita, KS	750	NA	1
1793	Ryan Homes Inc	412-276-8000	Pittsburgh, PA	750	NA	1
1794	Safeway Texas Corp	713-460-5000	Houston, TX	750	NA	3
1795	Science Applications Intl Inc	619-454-3811	La Jolla, CA	750	NA	8
1796	Southwire Co Inc	404-832-4242	Carrolton, GA	750	NA	3
1797	Sun Carriers Inc	215-891-7100	Media, PA	750	600	9
1798	Tang Industries Inc	312-981-8200	Elk Grove, IL	750	NA	7
1799	Thomson McKinnon Securities Inc	212-482-7000	New York, NY	750	7000	5
1800	Ticor Corp	213-852-6000	Los Angeles, CA	750	2000	7

Organizations Listed by Revenue

Rank	Organization	Phone	City / State or Province	Revenue ($ mil)	Assets ($ mil)	Emp (thous)
1801	Tishman Realty Corp	212-957-5400	New York, NY	750	NA	1
1802	Tracor Inc	512-926-2800	Austin, TX	750	500	9
1803	United Refining Corp	814-723-1500	Warren, PA	750	NA	3
1804	United States Agency for Intl Develpmnt	202-647-1850	Washington, DC	750	NM	5
1805	United Van Lines (Unigroup) Inc	314-326-3100	Fenton, MO	750	250	3
1806	Warnaco Inc	203-579-8272	Bridgeport, CT	750	NA	10
1807	Wilbur Ellis & Co Inc	415-772-4000	San Francisco, CA	750	NA	5
1808	Worldwide Volkswagen Inc	914-578-5000	Orangeburg, NY	750	NA	1
1809	Young & Rubicam Inc	212-210-3000	New York, NY	750	NA	10
1810	Builders Square Inc	512-731-0500	San Antonio, TX	750	NA	7
1811	Florida National Banks	904-359-5020	Jacksonville, FL	749	7828	5
1812	Cooper Tire & Rubber Co	419-423-1321	Findley, OH	748	443	8
1813	University of Minnesota	612-373-2851	Minneapolis, MN	748	991	52
1814	United Grain Growers Ltd	204-944-5411	Winnipeg, MB Can	748	277	2
1815	Harken Energy Corp	817-354-9944	Bedford, TX	747	500	1
1816	TCC Beverages Ltd(Coca Cola Sys Canada)	416-424-6000	Toronto, ON Can	745	539	5
1817	America West Airlines Inc	602-894-0800	Phoenix, AZ	743	639	5
1818	Equifax Inc	404-885-8000	Atlanta, GA	743	421	10
1819	Mark IV Industries Inc	716-689-4972	Williamsville, NY	742	800	6
1820	Southwestern Electric Power	318-222-2141	Shreveport, LA	742	1889	2
1821	American General Life & Accident Co	615-749-1000	Nashville, TN	741	3472	2
1822	Gulf Canada Ltd	403-233-4000	Calgary, AB Can	740	3159	18
1823	US Healthcare Inc	215-628-4800	Blue Bell, PA	739	271	10
1824	Champion Spark Plug Co	419-247-1600	Toledo, OH	738	576	13
1825	Cincinnati Bell Inc	513-397-9900	Cincinnati, OH	738	1253	10
1826	Flowers Industries Inc	912-226-9110	Thomasville, GA	737	434	9
1827	Kansas City Power & Light Co	816-556-2200	Kansas City, MO	737	2647	3
1828	New Brunswick Elect Power Comm Ltd	506-458-4444	Fredericton, NB Can	737	2419	3
1829	US Home Corp	713-877-2311	Houston, TX	736	943	2
1830	CDI Corp	215-561-1750	Philadelphia, PA	734	NA	8
1831	Auto Club of Michigan Inc	313-336-1234	Dearborn, MI	733	1171	3
1832	Hawaiian Electric Industries Inc	808-543-5662	Honolulu, HI	732	2683	4
1833	Owens & Minor Inc	804-747-9794	Richmond, VA	732	190	1
1834	Home Shopping Inc	813-572-8585	St Petersburg, FL	730	540	6
1835	BCE Development Ltd	416-369-2300	Toronto, ON Can	730	2290	5
1836	Emerson Radio Corp	201-854-6600	North Bergen, NJ	729	255	3
1837	Interhome Energy Inc (Interprov Pipe)	403-232-5500	Calgary, AB Can	729	2509	2
1838	Louisiana Land & Exploration Co	504-566-6500	New Orleans, LA	726	1429	2
1839	Old Kent Financial Corp	616-774-5000	Grand Rapids, MI	726	7854	3
1840	Charming Shoppes Inc	215-245-9100	Bensalem, PA	725	407	6
1841	Oakland County Government	313-858-0480	Pontiac, MI	725	NM	4
1842	Maple Leaf Mills Ltd	416-484-7400	Toronto, ON Can	723	340	4
1843	Dennison Manufacturing Co	508-879-0511	Framingham, MA	722	516	8
1844	Intermark Inc	619-459-3841	La Jolla, CA	721	400	7
1845	Seattle, City of	206-625-4000	Seattle, WA	721	NM	8
1846	Universal Foods Corp	414-271-6755	Milwaukee, WI	721	404	5
1847	CCL Industries Ltd	416-756-8500	Willowdale, ON Can	720	496	6
1848	Dairy Mart Convenience Stores Inc	203-741-3611	Enfield, CT	717	400	6
1849	National Life Insurance Co	802-229-3333	Montpelier, VT	717	3590	2
1850	Danaher Corp	202-333-1805	Washington, DC	716	576	5

Organizations Listed by Revenue

Rank	Organization	Phone	City / State or Province	Revenue ($ mil)	Assets ($ mil)	Emp (thous)
1851	Spanos, A G Construction Inc	209-478-7954	Stockton, CA	715	NA	2
1852	Miller, Herman Inc	616-772-3300	Zeeland, MI	714	434	6
1853	Henleys Group Ltd	514-397-7640	Montreal, PQ Can	714	NA	1
1854	CAE Industries Ltd	416-865-0070	Toronto, ON Can	712	986	7
1855	Westcoast Energy Inc	604-664-5500	Vancouver, BC Can	712	1839	1
1856	Chesapeake Corp	804-697-1000	Richmond, VA	711	662	7
1857	Placer Dome Ltd	416-868-6060	Toronto, ON Can	709	1839	4
1858	Anchor Savings Bank Inc	516-295-0400	Northport, NY	703	7946	2
1859	Roper Corp	404-724-0822	Augusta, GA	703	251	6
1860	General Motors Acceptance Corp Canada	416-234-6616	Toronto, ON Can	703	6097	1
1861	Alexander & Baldwin Inc	808-525-6611	Honolulu, HI	702	1070	3
1862	Alexander's Inc	212-869-0368	New York, NY	700	NA	9
1863	Battelle Memorial Institute Inc	614-424-6424	Columbus, OH	700	NA	10
1864	Bowery Savings Bank Inc	212-953-8400	New York, NY	700	7000	2
1865	Brenlin Corp	216-762-2420	Akron, OH	700	NA	3
1866	Carteret Savings Bank Corporated	201-326-1000	Morristown, NJ	700	6000	2
1867	Chemical Waste Corp	312-572-8800	Oak Brook, IL	700	876	6
1868	Citizens Fidelity Corp	502-581-2100	Louisville, KY	700	5000	3
1869	CVN Companies Inc	612-559-8000	Minneapolis, MN	700	300	4
1870	New York State Retirement Fund Inc	518-447-2741	Albany, NY	700	27500	2
1871	Southern Farm Bureau Insurance Co	601-982-7777	Jackson, MS	700	600	3
1872	Valmont Industries Inc	402-359-2201	Valley, NE	700	500	4
1873	Wellington Management/TDPL Inc	617-951-5000	Boston, MA	700	27500	1
1874	Winterthur Swiss Insurance Co	212-466-0777	New York, NY	700	1200	3
1875	Kraft Ltd	514-341-5000	Montreal, PQ Can	700	372	3
1876	First American Corp	615-748-2100	Nashville, TN	699	7204	4
1877	Nabisco Brands Ltd	416-598-2600	Toronto, ON Can	699	704	4
1878	Washington Gas Co	703-750-4440	Washington, DC	698	923	3
1879	Curtice Burns Inc	716-325-1020	Rochester, NY	695	377	6
1880	Agropur Coop Agro Alimentaire Ltd	514-332-2220	Montreal, PQ Can	695	198	2
1881	Co Steel Inc	416-686-2500	Whitby, ON Can	694	550	3
1882	Philips Industries Inc	513-253-7171	Dayton, OH	693	353	10
1883	Zurich Insurance Co	312-843-6000	Schaumburg, IL	688	1921	4
1884	Dibrell Brothers	804-792-7511	Danville, VA	685	500	5
1885	Fuller, H B Co	612-645-3401	St Paul, MN	685	434	5
1886	Bramalea Ltd	416-487-3861	Toronto, ON Can	685	3506	3
1887	Mississippi Power & Light Co	601-949-6442	Jackson, MS	684	1555	2
1888	Leslie Fay Inc	212-221-4000	New York, NY	683	363	6
1889	Burns Food Ltd	403-265-8140	Calgary, AB Can	680	NA	3
1890	Digital Equipment of Canada Ltd	613-592-5111	Kanata, ON Can	680	255	3
1891	GW Utilities Ltd	416-363-3300	Toronto, ON Can	680	1020	4
1892	Meredith Corp	515-284-3000	Des Moines, IA	678	646	4
1893	Statesman Group Life Insurance Co	515-284-7500	Des Moines, IA	678	2402	1
1894	Marshall & Isley Corp	414-765-7801	Milwaukee, WI	677	6775	3
1895	Westinghouse Canada Inc	416-528-8811	Hamilton, ON Can	677	NA	6
1896	Atlantic Energy Co	609-645-4100	Pleasantville, NJ	676	1660	2
1897	Broward County Government	305-357-7000	Fort Lauderdale, FL	675	NM	5
1898	MGM United Artists Communications Inc	213-281-4000	Beverly Hills, CA	675	1365	7
1899	Standard Register Co	513-443-1000	Dayton, OH	675	444	6
1900	Eastern Enterprises Inc	617-647-2300	Weston, MA	672	1087	4

Organizations Listed by Revenue

Rank	Organization	Phone	City / State or Province	Revenue ($ mil)	Assets ($ mil)	Emp (thous)
1901	Alliance Ro-Na Home Inc	519-664-2252	St Jacobs, ON Can	672	170	8
1902	Cooperators General Insurance Co	519-824-4400	Guelph, ON Can	670	951	3
1903	Via Rail Canada Inc	514-286-2311	Montreal, PQ Can	670	910	7
1904	Family Dollar Stores Inc	704-847-6961	Charlotte, NC	669	291	6
1905	Tyler Corp	214-754-7800	Dallas, TX	665	348	6
1906	Goodyear Canada Inc	416-626-4611	Islington, ON Can	664	419	6
1907	NERCO Inc	503-796-6600	Portland, OR	662	1206	2
1908	Calmat Co	213-258-2777	Los Angeles, CA	661	765	3
1909	Associated Food Stores Inc	801-973-4400	Salt Lake City, UT	660	NA	3
1910	California State University System	213-590-5731	Long Beach, CA	660	660	210
1911	Commonwealth Energy System	617-225-4000	Cambridge, MA	660	600	3
1912	El Paso Products Co Inc	915-333-7200	Dallas, TX	660	NA	2
1913	First Maryland BanCorp Inc	301-244-4000	Baltimore, MD	660	5881	3
1914	FL Industries Inc	201-535-9522	Livingston, NJ	660	NA	6
1915	Louisville Gas & Electric Co	502-566-4011	Louisville, KY	660	1763	5
1916	Sun Diamond Growers of California Inc	415-463-8200	Pleasanton, CA	660	250	1
1917	BCE PubliTech Inc	416-964-1374	Toronto, ON Can	659	510	6
1918	Canadian Commerical Corp	613-996-0034	Ottawa, ON Can	659	420	1
1919	Commerical Union Insurance Co	617-725-6000	Boston, MA	658	1167	4
1920	Handy & Harman Inc	212-752-3400	New York, NY	658	466	4
1921	Longview Fibre Co	206-425-1550	Longview, WA	657	635	4
1922	Metropolitan Edison Co	215-929-3601	Reading, PA	656	1594	2
1923	Pep Boys/Manny Moe Jack Inc	215-229-9000	Philadelphia, PA	656	582	4
1924	Apollo Computer Inc	508-256-6600	Chelmsford, MA	654	497	4
1925	Central Maine Power Inc	207-623-3521	Augusta, ME	654	1211	3
1926	Planning Research Corp	703-556-1000	McLean, VA	654	547	7
1927	Volkswagen Canada Ltd	416-288-3000	Scarborough, ON Can	654	287	1
1928	Medtronic Inc	612-574-4000	Minneapolis, MN	653	641	6
1929	Atlantic Mutual Insurance Co	212-943-1800	New York, NY	652	1191	2
1930	Turner Broadcasting System Inc	404-827-1700	Atlanta, GA	652	1838	6
1931	Carolina Freight Corp	704-435-6811	Cherryville, NC	651	347	10
1932	Anixter Brothers Inc	312-677-2600	Skokie, IL	650	600	3
1933	Ausimont NV Inc	617-899-3000	Waltham, MA	650	500	2
1934	Bartlett Agricultural Enterprises Inc	816-753-6300	Kansas City, MO	650	NA	2
1935	Big Three Industries Inc	713-868-0333	Houston, TX	650	1000	5
1936	IMO Industries	609-896-7600	Lawrenceville, NJ	650	550	4
1937	Industrial Bank of Japan Trust Co	212-557-3500	New York, NY	650	5500	3
1938	Joy Manufacturing Co	412-562-4500	Pittsburgh, PA	650	500	5
1939	St Joe Paper Co	904-356-8311	Jacksonville, FL	650	450	5
1940	St Louis County Government	314-889-2000	Clayton, MO	650	NM	4
1941	Tredegar Industries Inc	804-275-9211	Richmond, VA	650	350	1
1942	Stanford University	415-497-2300	Stanford, CA	649	598	21
1943	Amica Mutual Insurance Co	401-521-9100	Providence, RI	646	1142	2
1944	Butler Manufacturing Co	816-968-3000	Kansas City, MO	646	266	4
1945	United Merchants & Manufacturers Inc	212-930-3900	New York, NY	646	412	10
1946	New Orleans, City of	504-586-4000	New Orleans, LA	645	NM	11
1947	MeraBank Fed Savings Bank Inc	602-248-4221	Phoenix, AZ	644	8348	2
1948	Ellis Don Ltd	519-455-6770	London, ON Can	643	196	3
1949	General Foods Ltd	416-441-5000	Don Mills, ON Can	643	392	4
1950	Ohio State University	614-422-6446	Columbus, OH	641	886	59

Organizations Listed by Revenue

Rank	Organization	Phone	City / State or Province	Revenue ($ mil)	Assets ($ mil)	Emp (thous)
1951	Phillips Van Heusen Corp	212-541-5200	New York, NY	641	323	7
1952	El Paso Electric Co Inc	915-543-5711	El Paso, TX	639	1975	3
1953	Great Lakes Forest Products Ltd	807-475-2110	Thunder Bay, ON Can	638	723	5
1954	Husky Oil Ltd	403-298-6111	Calgary, AB Can	638	1700	2
1955	Royal Insurance Co	416-366-7511	Toronto, ON Can	638	1150	2
1956	Minneapolis, City of	612-348-2100	Minneapolis, MN	636	NM	4
1957	Jerrico (Long John Silvers Res) Inc	606-263-6000	Lexington, KY	635	428	18
1958	Texas Industries Inc	214-637-3100	Dallas, TX	635	662	6
1959	Bancorp Hawaii Inc	808-537-8111	Honolulu, HI	630	6635	3
1960	Helene Curtis Industries Inc	312-292-2121	Chicago, IL	629	325	4
1961	Valero Energy Corp	512-246-2000	San Antonio, TX	629	965	2
1962	Canadian Occidental Petroleum Ltd	403-234-6700	Calgary, AB Can	629	1153	1
1963	Shaklee Corp	415-954-3000	San Francisco, CA	628	435	3
1964	Toledo Edison Co	419-249-5000	Toledo, OH	628	4135	3
1965	SouthTrust Corp	205-254-5523	Birmingham, AL	627	6645	4
1966	Ross Stores Inc	415-790-4400	Newark, CA	626	NA	5
1967	Commerce Clearing House Inc	312-940-4600	Riverwoods, IL	625	355	7
1968	Ocean Spray Cranberries Inc	508-747-1000	Plymouth, MA	625	400	3
1969	First City Financial Corp	604-685-2489	Vancouver, BC Can	625	4225	7
1970	First Pennsylvania Corp	215-786-5000	Philadelphia, PA	623	6407	4
1971	Long Beach, City of	213-590-6707	Long Beach, CA	623	NM	5
1972	St Lawrence Cement Inc	514-340-1881	Montreal, PQ Can	623	552	3
1973	Unisys Canada Inc	416-495-0515	North York, ON Can	623	436	3
1974	Millipore Corp	617-275-9200	Bedford, MA	622	576	6
1975	Twentieth (20th) Century Industries Inc	818-704-3700	Woodland Hills, CA	622	857	2
1976	Norcen Energy Resources Ltd	403-231-0111	Calgary, AB Can	622	1968	2
1977	First Tennessee National Corp	901-523-5630	Memphis, TN	621	5800	4
1978	Westmoreland Coal Co	215-545-2500	Philadelphia, PA	620	500	3
1979	TransCapital Financial Corp(Ohio Sav Bk)	216-621-9600	Cleveland, OH	619	6361	2
1980	Edgcomb Corp	212-246-1000	New York, NY	617	450	2
1981	Central Illinois Public Service Co	217-523-3600	Springfield, IL	616	1678	3
1982	Great Lakes Chemical Corp	317-463-2511	West Lafayette, IN	616	664	4
1983	NACCO Industries	216-752-1000	Cleveland, OH	616	837	6
1984	Service Corp International	713-522-5141	Houston, TX	616	1667	7
1985	Hubbell Inc	203-789-1100	Orange, CT	614	523	5
1986	Silcorp Ltd	416-678-9700	Mississauga, ON Can	614	200	2
1987	Prudential Assurance Group	519-888-5700	Kitchener, ON Can	612	2282	1
1988	Ipalco Enterprises Inc	317-261-8261	Indianapolis, IN	609	1752	2
1989	Toro Co	612-888-8801	Bloomington, MN	609	268	3
1990	University of Wisconsin	608-262-1234	Madison, WI	607	849	50
1991	Alberto Culver Co	312-450-3000	Melrose Park, IL	605	303	5
1992	Lukens Inc	215-383-2000	Coatesville, PA	605	353	4
1993	Southdown Inc	713-658-8921	Houston, TX	605	1211	4
1994	Public Service Co of Oklahoma	918-599-2000	Tulsa, OK	604	1211	2
1995	Wisconsin Public Service Corp	414-433-1598	Green Bay, WI	604	843	3
1996	Public Service Co of New Hampshire	603-669-4000	Manchester, NH	603	2704	3
1997	Consolidated Stores Corp	614-224-1297	Columbus, OH	601	286	5
1998	Maxus Energy Corp	214-953-2000	Dallas, TX	601	1720	2
1999	WPL Holdings (Wisconsin Power Co)	608-252-3311	Madison, WI	601	1026	3
2000	ADT Inc	215-558-1100	New York, NY	600	500	8

Organizations Listed by Revenue

Rank	Organization	Phone	City / State or Province	Revenue ($ mil)	Assets ($ mil)	Emp (thous)
2001	Allied Van Lines Inc	312-681-8000	Broadview, IL	600	200	5
2002	Ampex Corp	212-759-6301	New York, NY	600	NA	5
2003	Andersons Inc	419-893-5050	Maumee, OH	600	NA	1
2004	Big V Supermarkets Inc	914-651-4411	Florida, NY	600	NA	3
2005	C & S Wholesale Grocery Inc	802-257-4371	Brattleboro, VT	600	NA	1
2006	California First Bank Inc	415-445-0200	San Francisco, CA	600	6000	4
2007	Chemed	513-762-6900	Cincinnati, OH	600	NA	6
2008	Continental Cablevision Corp	617-742-9500	Boston, MA	600	NA	5
2009	Dixie Yarns	615-698-2501	Chattanooga, TN	600	250	10
2010	Encyclopedia Britannica Inc	312-347-7000	Chicago, IL	600	NA	2
2011	Equimark Corp	412-288-5000	Pittsburgh, PA	600	6000	2
2012	Exide Corp	215-674-9500	Horsham, PA	600	NA	6
2013	Faberge Inc	212-307-8000	New York, NY	600	300	4
2014	Federated Mutual Insurance Co	507-455-5200	Owatonna, MN	600	1025	2
2015	Fuji Bank & Trust	212-839-5600	New York, NY	600	5000	3
2016	Green, B & Co Inc	301-247-8300	Baltimore, MD	600	NA	1
2017	Harte Hanks Communications Inc	512-344-8000	San Antonio, TX	600	1000	7
2018	Harvard Industries Inc	314-382-5590	St Louis, MO	600	400	4
2019	Himont Inc	302-594-5500	Wilmington, DE	600	400	1
2020	Intelligent Electronics Inc	215-524-1800	Exton, PA	600	300	1
2021	Intertan Corp	817-332-7181	Fort Worth, TX	600	400	6
2022	Iowa Public Service Co	712-277-7500	Sioux City, IA	600	1100	2
2023	Irvine Corp	714-720-2000	Newport Beach, CA	600	NA	1
2024	Jepson Corp	312-834-3710	Elmhurst, IL	600	400	6
2025	JM Petroleum Corp	214-953-0330	Dallas, TX	600	NA	1
2026	King Kullen Grocery Inc	516-333-7100	Westbury, NY	600	NA	6
2027	Lear Petroleum Corp	214-363-6085	Dallas, TX	600	400	1
2028	Liquid Air Corp	415-977-6500	Walnut Creek, CA	600	800	4
2029	LPL Investment Group	203-265-8600	Wallingford, CT	600	708	5
2030	Mayfair Super Markets Inc	201-352-6400	Elizabethtown, NJ	600	250	5
2031	Morse Shoe Inc	617-828-9300	Canton, MA	600	NA	6
2032	North American Coal Corp	216-752-1000	Cleveland, OH	600	400	5
2033	North Pacific Lumber Inc	503-231-1166	Portland, OR	600	NA	1
2034	Ohio Mattress Co	216-522-1310	Cleveland, OH	600	400	5
2035	People's Bank	203-579-7171	Bridgeport, CT	600	6321	2
2036	Perry Drug Stores Inc	313-334-1300	Pontiac, MI	600	400	7
2037	Phelps Co Inc	303-353-7000	Greeley, CO	600	NA	3
2038	Pierce, S S Co	607-243-7171	Dundee, NY	600	400	7
2039	Pullman Peabody Co	609-683-1770	Princeton, NJ	600	500	8
2040	Revere Copper & Brass Inc	203-358-5300	Stamford, CT	600	400	4
2041	Reynolds & Reynolds Corp	513-443-2000	Dayton, OH	600	399	5
2042	Roseburg Forest Products Inc	503-679-3311	Dillard, OR	600	NA	6
2043	Schwans Sale Enterprises Inc	507-532-3274	Marshall, MN	600	NA	6
2044	Sterling Chemical Corp	713-650-3700	Houston, TX	600	400	2
2045	Sudbury Inc	216-464-7026	Cleveland, OH	600	400	5
2046	Sumitomo Trust & Banking Co	212-326-0500	New York, NY	600	5500	4
2047	United Missouri Bancshares	816-556-7000	Kansas City, MO	600	6000	3
2048	Utilicorp United Inc	816-421-6600	Kansas City, MO	600	1200	3
2049	Village Super Markets Inc	201-467-2200	Springfield, NJ	600	300	4
2050	WWF Paper Corp	215-667-9210	Bala Cynwyd, PA	600	NA	3

Organizations Listed by Revenue

Rank	Organization	Phone	City / State or Province	Revenue ($ mil)	Assets ($ mil)	Emp (thous)
2051	Wyatt Inc	203-787-2175	New Haven, CT	600	NA	1
2052	Young's Markets Inc	213-629-5571	Los Angeles, CA	600	NA	3
2053	Redpath Industries Ltd	416-865-0400	Toronto, ON Can	600	416	4
2054	Schulman, A Inc	216-666-3751	Akron, OH	598	240	2
2055	Atlanta, City of	404-658-6100	Atlanta, GA	596	NM	7
2056	Finning Ltd	604-872-4444	Vancouver, BC Can	595	558	3
2057	Manitoba Pool Elevators Ltd	204-947-1171	Winnipeg, MB Can	595	82	1
2058	Preston Corp	301-673-7151	Preston, MD	594	338	8
2059	Thorn Apple Valley	313-552-0700	Southfield, MI	593	103	4
2060	Milwaukee, City of	414-278-2200	Milwaukee, WI	592	NM	9
2061	Cineplex Odeon Corp	416-596-2200	Toronto, ON Can	592	485	3
2062	Microsoft Corp	206-882-8080	Redmond, WA	591	493	3
2063	Oxford Industries Inc	404-659-2424	Atlanta, GA	591	223	8
2064	Dollar General Corp	502-237-5444	Scottsville, KY	590	300	7
2065	Durr Fillauer Medical Inc	205-241-8800	Montgomery, AL	588	178	2
2066	GATX Corp	312-621-6200	Chicago, IL	587	2605	2
2067	Hollinger Inc	416-363-8721	Toronto, ON Can	587	850	5
2068	PanCanadian Petroleum	403-290-2000	Calgary, AB Can	587	2273	1
2069	Oracle Systems Corp	415-598-8000	Belmont, CA	584	500	5
2070	Washington Mutual Savings Inc	206-464-4400	Seattle, WA	584	6364	2
2071	Bank of California (Mitsubishi Bank)	213-621-1200	Los Angeles, CA	583	6887	1
2072	American Building Maintenance Ind Inc	415-864-5150	San Francisco, CA	582	172	32
2073	TCF Banking & Savings Inc	612-370-7000	Minneapolis, MN	581	5259	2
2074	Schneider Corp	519-885-8100	Kitchener, ON Can	581	170	4
2075	University of Pennsylvania	215-898-5000	Philadelphia, PA	580	1201	26
2076	Cadillac Fairview Corp	416-598-8200	Toronto, ON Can	579	3521	4
2077	Allied Products Corp	312-454-1020	Chicago, IL	578	441	5
2078	Woodward's Ltd	604-684-5231	Vancouver, BC Can	577	238	4
2079	Ogilvy Group Inc	212-907-3400	New York, NY	575	639	2
2080	Gendis Inc	204-474-5200	Winnipeg, MB Can	575	262	7
2081	Nissan Automobile Canada Ltd	416-821-9180	Mississauga, ON Can	575	170	1
2082	Federal Reserve Bank of St Louis	314-444-8444	St Louis, MO	574	9329	1
2083	Federal Reserve Bank of Philadelphia Inc	215-574-6000	Philadelphia, PA	572	9116	1
2084	Oneok Inc	918-588-7000	Tulsa, OK	571	958	2
2085	Commercial Federal Savings Assn Inc	402-554-9200	Omaha, NE	570	6655	2
2086	Midwest Energy Co	712-277-7400	Sioux City, IA	570	1092	2
2087	Soo Line Corp	612-347-8000	Minneapolis, MN	570	905	5
2088	Xidex Corp	408-988-3472	Palo Alto, CA	570	770	6
2089	Glatfelter, P H Co	717-225-4711	Spring Grove, PA	569	663	3
2090	Premier Industrial Corp	216-391-8300	Cleveland, OH	566	263	4
2091	NCH Corp	214-438-0211	Irving, TX	565	500	4
2092	UST United States Tobacco Co	203-661-1100	Greenwich, CT	565	549	3
2093	Allied Signal Canada Inc	416-967-7211	Mississauga, ON Can	565	425	5
2094	Export Development Corp	613-598-2500	Ottawa, ON Can	565	5893	1
2095	Tambrands Inc	516-437-8800	Lake Success, NY	563	465	4
2096	Trustcorp Inc	419-259-8950	Toledo, OH	563	5947	3
2097	Mitchell Energy & Development Corp	713-363-5500	The Woodlands, TX	562	2112	2
2098	Riggs National Corp	202-835-6000	Washington, DC	562	7002	2
2099	Perpetual American Bank Inc	703-442-7000	McLean, VA	561	5853	2
2100	Toronto, University of	416-978-2011	Toronto, ON Can	561	NM	54

Organizations Listed by Revenue

Rank	Organization	Phone	City / State or Province	Revenue ($ mil)	Assets ($ mil)	Emp (thous)
2101	Jostens Inc	612-830-3336	Minneapolis, MN	560	407	7
2102	Kentucky Utilities Co	606-255-1461	Lexington, KY	560	1108	2
2103	Prudential Ins Co of America, Canada	416-296-0777	Scarborough, ON Can	559	2310	3
2104	Southwest Gas Corp	702-876-7011	Las Vegas, NV	558	3679	2
2105	Indianapolis, City of	317-236-3600	Indianapolis, IN	557	NM	11
2106	Carpenter Technology Corp	215-371-2000	Reading, PA	556	635	4
2107	Massachusetts Inst of Technology	617-253-1000	Cambridge, MA	556	660	12
2108	Royal LePage Real Estate Ltd	416-862-0611	Toronto, ON Can	554	405	8
2109	La-Z-Boy Chair Co	313-242-1444	Monroe, MI	553	400	4
2110	New York University	212-598-3127	New York, NY	553	548	40
2111	Rexene Corportation	212-644-8200	New York, NY	553	511	5
2112	Simpsons Ltd	416-861-9111	Toronto, ON Can	553	383	6
2113	Pacific Telecom Inc	206-696-0983	Vancouver, WA	552	1242	4
2114	Scotty's Inc	813-299-1111	Winter Haven, FL	551	315	6
2115	South Carolina National Corp	803-765-3000	Columbia, SC	551	5655	4
2116	Western Publishing Group Inc	212-688-4500	New York, NY	551	450	3
2117	Donohue Inc	418-522-6471	Quebec, PQ Can	551	771	4
2118	Amcena Inc	212-391-4141	New York, NY	550	NA	5
2119	American Crystal Sugar Co	218-236-4400	Moorhead, MN	550	NA	2
2120	American Seaway Foods Inc	216-663-5500	Edford Heights, OH	550	NA	2
2121	Ask Mr Foster Travel Inc	818-988-0181	Van Nuys, CA	550	NA	2
2122	Associated Electric Co-op Inc	417-881-1204	Springfield, MO	550	NA	2
2123	Associated Grocers of Colorado Inc	303-297-9121	Wheatridge, CO	550	NA	1
2124	Aurora Eby Brown Co Inc	312-897-8674	Aurora, IL	550	NA	1
2125	Austin Co Inc	615-638-4124	Greeneville, TN	550	NA	1
2126	Avondale Industries Inc	504-436-2121	New Orleans, LA	550	NA	5
2127	Baird & Warner Inc	312-368-1855	Chicago, IL	550	NA	2
2128	Banco Nacional de Mexico	212-838-8300	New York, NY	550	4000	2
2129	Barclays American Corp	212-412-4000	New York, NY	550	4500	3
2130	Baroid Corp	713-987-4000	Houston, TX	550	600	3
2131	Basic American Foods Inc	415-981-5590	San Francisco, CA	550	NA	5
2132	Bayless, A J Markets Inc	602-731-6800	Tempe, AZ	550	NA	3
2133	Bayliner Marine Corp	206-435-5571	Arlington, WA	550	NA	4
2134	Beazley, William Co Inc	203-562-9801	New Haven, CT	550	NA	5
2135	Bergner, P A & Co Inc	414-347-4141	Milwaukee, WI	550	NA	5
2136	Binswanger Co Inc	215-448-6000	Philadelphia, PA	550	NA	1
2137	Boys Market Inc	213-258-8080	Los Angeles, CA	550	NA	4
2138	Bright Banc Savings Assn Inc	214-638-9500	Dallas, TX	550	5500	2
2139	Cablec Corp	914-634-0100	New City, NY	550	NA	5
2140	California Almond Growers Inc	916-442-0771	Sacramento, CA	550	NA	3
2141	Capital Group Inc	213-486-9200	Los Angeles, CA	550	27500	2
2142	Cardinal Industries Inc	614-861-3211	Columbus, OH	550	NA	5
2143	Colonial Oil Industries Inc	912-236-1331	Savannah, GA	550	NA	1
2144	Colonial Pipeline Co Inc	404-261-1470	Atlanta, GA	550	NA	1
2145	Consolidated Grain & Barge Co Inc	314-658-9200	St Louis, MO	550	NA	1
2146	Coopervision Inc	415-856-5000	Palo Alto, CA	550	1000	5
2147	Dai Ichi Kangyo Bank Ltd	212-466-5200	New York, NY	550	5000	2
2148	Diamandis Communications Corp	212-719-6000	New York, NY	550	NA	1
2149	Diamond Bathurst Corp	813-884-0000	Tampa, FL	550	250	5
2150	Dillon Reed & Co Inc	212-906-7000	New York, NY	550	5500	1

Organizations Listed by Revenue

Rank	Organization	Phone	City / State or Province	Revenue ($ mil)	Assets ($ mil)	Emp (thous)
2151	E-Z Serve Inc	817-267-1777	Bedford, TX	550	239	5
2152	Econocom USA Inc	901-762-9200	Memphis, TN	550	NA	1
2153	Emigrant Savings Bank Inc	212-883-5800	New York, NY	550	5500	2
2154	First Federal Savings & Loan Assn Inc	716-238-2100	Rochester, NY	550	5500	2
2155	Franklin Mint Corp	215-459-6000	Media, PA	550	NA	5
2156	Geneva Management Inc	703-522-2300	Arlington, VA	550	NA	1
2157	Georgia Gulf Corp	404-395-4500	Atlanta, GA	550	250	5
2158	Georgia Kraft Corp	404-232-0851	Rome, GA	550	500	5
2159	Gitano Orit Imports Inc	212-819-0707	New York, NY	550	NA	1
2160	Grocery Supply Co Inc	214-885-7621	Sulphur Springs, TX	550	NA	2
2161	Groves, S J & Sons Co Inc	612-546-6943	Minneapolis, MN	550	NA	5
2162	Guilford Mills Inc	919-292-7550	Greensboro, NC	550	300	6
2163	Harley Davidson Inc	414-342-4680	Milwaukee, WI	550	400	4
2164	Hongkong & Shanghai Banking Corp	212-839-5000	New York, NY	550	4500	1
2165	Huntsman Chemical & Oil Corp	801-532-5200	Salt Lake City, UT	550	NA	1
2166	Ingersoll International Inc	815-987-6000	Rockford, IL	550	NA	5
2167	Ingles Markets Inc	704-669-2941	Black Mountain, NC	550	NA	5
2168	Intercontinental Hotels Corportion	201-307-3300	Montvale, NJ	550	NA	8
2169	Interstate Milk Producers Inc	215-322-0200	Southampton, PA	550	NA	2
2170	Jaguar Cars Inc	201-592-5200	Leonia, NJ	550	NA	1
2171	JP Industries Inc	313-663-6749	Ann Arbor, MI	550	400	3
2172	K & B Inc	504-586-1234	New Orleans, LA	550	NA	5
2173	Kaiser Engineers Inc	415-268-6000	Oakland, CA	550	NA	2
2174	Keith, Ben E Co	817-332-9171	Fort Worth, TX	550	NA	1
2175	Kendavis Holding Co Inc	817-335-5101	Fort Worth, TX	550	NA	5
2176	Ketchum Communications Inc	412-456-3500	Pittsburgh, PA	550	NA	1
2177	Kobe Steel Corp USA	212-751-9400	New York, NY	550	NA	1
2178	Koenig & Strey Inc	312-729-6610	Glenview, IL	550	NA	1
2179	Lamb Technicon Inc	313-497-6652	Warren, MI	550	NA	2
2180	Lincoln Electric Co Inc	216-481-8100	Cleveland, OH	550	NA	5
2181	Lykes Brothers Steamship Co Inc	504-523-6611	New Orleans, LA	550	NA	2
2182	Mason McDuffie Real Estate Inc	415-254-5640	Orinda, CA	550	NA	1
2183	Massachusetts Financial Services Inc	617-954-5000	Boston, MA	550	24200	2
2184	Michigan Milk Producers Association Inc	313-474-6672	Novi, MI	550	150	1
2185	Midland Affiliated Inc	513-721-4000	Cincinnati, OH	550	NA	2
2186	Missouri Farmers Association Inc	314-874-5111	Columbia, MO	550	NA	1
2187	Mitre Corp	617-271-2000	Bedford, MA	550	NA	5
2188	Moorman Manufacturing Co	217-222-7100	Quincy, IL	550	NA	5
2189	Murata North America Inc	214-403-3300	Plano, TX	550	NA	2
2190	National Geographic Society Inc	202-857-7000	Washington, DC	550	NA	3
2191	New England Tile Corp	617-826-5144	Hanover, MA	550	NA	2
2192	Northern Pacific Lumber Co Inc	503-231-1166	Portland, OR	550	NA	2
2193	NPS Group Inc	201-865-6550	Secaucus, NJ	550	NA	5
2194	Overnite Transportation Co	824-231-8000	Richmond, VA	550	450	8
2195	Oxford Development Co Inc	301-654-3100	Bethesda, MD	550	NA	5
2196	Pacific Scene Inc	619-299-5100	San Diego, CA	550	NA	1
2197	Packerland Packing Co Inc	414-468-4000	Green Bay, WI	550	NA	2
2198	Parsons & Whittemore Corp	212-972-2000	New York, NY	550	NA	3
2199	Peck, C L Contractors Inc	213-470-1885	Los Angeles, CA	550	NA	1
2200	Philipp Brothers Chemicals Inc	201-944-6020	Fort Lee, NJ	550	NA	1

Organizations Listed by Revenue

Rank	Organization	Phone	City / State or Province	Revenue ($ mil)	Assets ($ mil)	Emp (thous)
2201	Pilgrams Pride Corp	214-856-7901	Pittsburg, TX	550	NA	5
2202	Ponderosa Steak Houses Inc	513-454-2400	Dayton, OH	550	NA	11
2203	Pride Refining Inc	915-677-2223	Abilene, TX	550	NA	1
2204	Primary Industries Corp	212-581-9200	New York, NY	550	NA	3
2205	Providence Journal Inc	401-277-7000	Providence, RI	550	NA	5
2206	Puerto Rico Telephone Inc	809-782-8282	San Juan, PR	550	NA	5
2207	Quiktrip Corp	918-836-8551	Tulsa, OK	550	NA	2
2208	Recarey Enterprises Inc	305-854-4000	Miami, FL	550	NA	4
2209	Reeves Brothers Inc	212-315-2323	New York, NY	550	NA	5
2210	Regis Corp	612-929-6776	Minneapolis, MN	550	NA	5
2211	Renault America Corp	313-358-8800	Southfield, MI	550	NA	1
2212	Righa Corp	401-421-4410	Providence, RI	550	3000	1
2213	Rover Group Inc	301-731-9040	Laham, MD	550	NA	1
2214	Sargent & Lundy Inc	312-269-2000	Chicago, IL	550	NA	5
2215	Schneider Inc	412-257-6000	Bridgeville, PA	550	NA	11
2216	Security Capital/Sentinal R E Corp	212-408-2900	New York, NY	550	2200	1
2217	Simpson Investment Co Inc	206-292-5000	Seattle, WA	550	NA	5
2218	Sinclair Marketing Inc	913-321-3700	Kansas City, KS	550	NA	1
2219	Softsel Computer Products Inc	213-412-1700	Inglewood, CA	550	200	2
2220	Staplecont Inc	601-453-6231	Greenwood, MS	550	NA	1
2221	Steuart Investment Co Inc	202-537-8940	Washington, DC	550	NA	1
2222	Summa Corp	702-791-4000	Las Vegas, NV	550	NA	5
2223	Superiors Brand Meats Inc	216-832-7491	Massillon, OH	550	NA	5
2224	Swinerton & Walberg Inc	415-421-2980	San Francisco, CA	550	NA	5
2225	TBWA Advertising Inc	212-725-1150	New York, NY	550	NA	1
2226	Three Beall Brothers Inc	214-586-9823	Jacksonville, TX	550	NA	5
2227	Thums Long Beach Co Inc	213-436-9211	Long Beach, CA	550	NA	2
2228	Tonka Corp	612-936-3300	Minnetonka, MN	550	500	5
2229	Treasure Chest Advertising Inc	818-914-3981	Glendora, CA	550	NA	5
2230	Tri Valley Growers Inc	415-445-1600	San Francisco, CA	550	NA	1
2231	Tucson Realty & Trust Inc	602-577-7000	Tucson, AZ	550	NA	1
2232	Union Equity Cooperative Exchange Inc	405-233-5100	Enid, OK	550	NA	1
2233	URM Stores Inc	509-467-2620	Seattle, WA	550	NA	3
2234	Van Munching & Co Inc	212-265-2685	New York, NY	550	NA	1
2235	Vanguard Group Mutual Funds Inc	215-648-6000	Valley Forge, PA	550	22000	1
2236	Vantage Companies Inc	214-631-0600	Dallas, TX	550	NA	2
2237	Victor Technologies Corp	215-251-5000	Malvern, PA	550	NA	2
2238	Webb, Jervis B Co Inc	313-553-1000	Farmington Hills, MI	550	NA	3
2239	Wells Rich Greene Inc	212-303-5000	New York, NY	550	NA	2
2240	Williams, Roger Foods Inc	401-942-4000	Cranston, RI	550	NA	1
2241	Wisconsin Dairies Cooperative Inc	608-356-8316	Baraboo, WI	550	150	1
2242	Woodward & Lothrop Inc	202-347-5300	Washington, DC	550	NA	5
2243	World Oil Co Inc	213-560-8801	South Gate, CA	550	NA	1
2244	Wright Shuchart Inc	206-447-7654	Seattle, WA	550	NA	2
2245	Aetna Life Insurance Co	416-864-8000	Toronto, ON Can	550	1636	1
2246	Sidbec Ltd	514-286-8600	Montreal, PQ Can	549	435	3
2247	American Maize Products Co	203-356-9000	Stamford, CT	548	420	3
2248	United States Leasing International Inc	415-627-9000	San Francisco, CA	548	2218	2
2249	Canam Manac Group Inc	418-228-8031	Ville St Georges, PQ C	547	562	5
2250	Hibernia Corp	504-586-5552	New Orleans, LA	546	5313	3

Organizations Listed by Revenue

Rank	Organization	Phone	City / State or Province	Revenue ($ mil)	Assets ($ mil)	Emp (thous)
2251	Indiana National Corp	317-266-6000	Indianapolis, IN	545	5927	3
2252	William Beaumont Hospital Inc	313-551-5000	Royal Oak, MI	545	NA	7
2253	Constar International	615-267-2973	Chattanooga, TN	544	230	4
2254	Banco Popular de Puerto Rico Inc	212-928-8600	New York, NY	543	5707	7
2255	Bearings Inc	216-881-2838	Cleveland, OH	543	223	4
2256	Nucor Corp	704-366-7000	Charlotte, NC	543	426	4
2257	Talman Home Fed Savings & Loan Inc	312-726-8915	Chicago, IL	543	6337	2
2258	Tucson Electric Power Co	602-622-6661	Tucson, AZ	543	2840	2
2259	Washington Water Power Co	509-489-0500	Spokane, WA	543	1378	1
2260	Grafton Group Ltd	416-461-9411	Toronto, ON Can	543	275	4
2261	Liberty National Life Insurance Co	205-325-2722	Birmingham, AL	541	2607	2
2262	European American Bancorp	516-296-5000	Uniondale, NY	540	5335	3
2263	Foxboro Co	617-543-8750	Foxboro, MA	540	472	7
2264	Fairchild Industries Inc	703-478-5800	Chantilly, VA	539	441	5
2265	First Empire State Corp	716-842-4200	Buffalo, NY	537	5908	3
2266	Affiliated Publications Inc	617-929-2000	Boston, MA	534	425	4
2267	Berkley, W R Insurance Co	203-629-2880	Greenwich, CT	534	1232	2
2268	Manor Care Inc	301-681-9400	Silver Spring, MD	534	797	19
2269	Handleman Co	313-362-4400	Troy, MI	532	284	3
2270	Hon Industries Inc	319-264-7400	Muscatine, IA	532	276	5
2271	St Louis, City of	314-622-3201	St Louis, MO	532	NM	8
2272	Cleveland, City of	216-664-2220	Cleveland, OH	531	NM	10
2273	First National Cincinnati Corp	513-632-4000	Cincinnati, OH	531	5214	3
2274	Russell Corp	205-234-4251	Alexander City, AL	531	561	13
2275	Kimball International Inc	812-482-1600	Jasper, IN	530	320	8
2276	University of Washington	206-543-2100	Seattle, WA	530	689	39
2277	Lone Star Industries Inc	203-661-3100	Greenwich, CT	529	1424	4
2278	Fay's Drug Co	315-451-8000	Liverpool, NY	527	300	6
2279	Kansas Gas & Electric Co	316-261-6611	Wichita, KS	526	2443	3
2280	Pacific First Federal Savings Bank Inc	206-383-7605	Tacoma, WA	524	6622	2
2281	Credithrift Financial Inc	812-424-8031	Evansville, IN	523	2772	4
2282	First Security Corp	801-350-5325	Salt Lake City, UT	522	5159	3
2283	Noxell Corp	301-785-7300	Hunt Valley, MD	522	330	2
2284	Nestle Enterprises Ltd	416-429-4411	Don Mills, ON Can	521	229	2
2285	Ametek Inc	212-935-8640	New York, NY	520	448	5
2286	Foote, Cone & Belding Inc	312-751-7000	Chicago, IL	520	350	4
2287	Harvard University	617-495-1000	Cambridge, MA	520	5100	19
2288	Maxxam Inc	213-474-6264	Los Angeles, CA	519	250	1
2289	United Illuminating Co	203-787-7200	New Haven, CT	519	2365	2
2290	San Jose, City of	408-277-4237	San Jose, CA	518	NM	4
2291	Pope & Talbot Inc	503-228-9161	Portland, OR	515	319	4
2292	Thomas & Betts Corp	201-685-1600	Raritan, NJ	515	493	5
2293	Trailer Train Corp	312-853-3223	Chicago, IL	515	1268	1
2294	Carter Wallace Inc	212-758-4500	New York, NY	514	400	3
2295	EL Financial Corp	416-868-1880	Toronto, ON Can	513	1312	1
2296	Four Seasons Hotels Ltd	416-449-1750	Toronto, ON Can	513	167	10
2297	American Water Works Co Inc	609-346-8200	Voorhees, NJ	512	1737	4
2298	Budget Rent-a-Car Inc	312-580-5000	Chicago, IL	512	500	5
2299	Circus Circus Enterprises Inc	702-734-0410	Las Vegas, NV	512	524	9
2300	University of Michigan Hospitals Inc	313-936-4000	Ann Arbor, MI	511	NA	6

Organizations Listed by Revenue

Rank	Organization	Phone	City / State or Province	Revenue ($ mil)	Assets ($ mil)	Emp (thous)
2301	Buffalo, City of	716-855-4841	Buffalo, NY	510	NM	10
2302	Department of Justice Canada	613-995-2569	Ottawa, ON Can	510	NM	1
2303	ICG Utilities Ltd	416-491-1880	Toronto, ON Can	510	638	1
2304	Kidd Creek Mines Ltd	416-863-7000	Toronto, ON Can	510	1020	3
2305	Kruger Inc	514-737-1131	Montreal, PQ CAN	510	765	6
2306	Scientific Atlanta Inc	404-441-4000	Atlanta, GA	509	316	4
2307	Standard Products Co	216-281-8300	Cleveland, OH	508	255	5
2308	Kansas City Southern Industries Inc	816-556-0303	Kansas City, MO	507	979	5
2309	Fifth Third BanCorp Inc	513-579-5300	Cincinnati, OH	506	5246	3
2310	Honolulu, City of	808-523-4111	Honolulu, HI	506	NM	8
2311	FHP International Corp	714-963-7233	Fountain Valley, CA	504	182	1
2312	Franklin, Benj Federal Savings Assn Inc	503-275-1201	Portland, OR	504	5469	2
2313	Kansas City, City of	816-274-2595	Kansas City, MO	503	NM	7
2314	Cameron Iron Works Inc	713-939-2211	Houston, TX	502	757	7
2315	Hughes Supply Inc	305-841-4710	Orlando, FL	502	224	4
2316	Medco Containment Services Inc	201-794-9010	Fair Lawn, NJ	502	344	4
2317	Molex Inc	312-969-4550	Lisle, IL	502	499	6
2318	Edwards, A G & Sons Inc	314-289-3000	St Louis, MO	501	1063	7
2319	Newmont Mining Corp	303-863-7414	Denver, CO	501	1321	5
2320	Thermo Electron Corp	617-890-8700	Waltham, MA	501	490	4
2321	Cascades Inc	819-363-2245	Kingsey Falls, PQ Can	501	458	3
2322	Aarque Companies Inc	716-664-6014	Jamestown, NY	500	NA	3
2323	ACI Holdings Inc	714-752-8576	Newport Beach, CA	500	250	3
2324	Advo System Inc	203-285-6100	Windsor, CT	500	300	6
2325	AFG Industries Inc	714-553-9026	Irvine, CA	500	500	3
2326	Air Express International	203-655-7900	Darien, CT	500	200	3
2327	Alberici, J S Construction Co Inc	314-261-2611	St Louis, MO	500	NA	2
2328	Alcatel Business Systems Inc	800-556-1234	Milpitas, CA	500	NA	5
2329	Almac's Corp	401-438-2700	East Providence, RI	500	NA	2
2330	American Enterprise Institute	202-862-5800	Washington, DC	500	NM	2
2331	American Fed of State, Cnty & Muni Emp	202-429-1130	Washington, DC	500	NM	1100
2332	American Federation of Teachers	202-879-4400	Washington, DC	500	NM	700
2333	American Restaurant Group Inc	714-721-8000	Newport Beach, CA	500	NA	15
2334	American Savings & Loan Assn Inc	209-948-1116	Stockton, CA	500	4000	2
2335	American Savings Bank (NY) Inc	212-575-7600	New York, NY	500	4500	2
2336	AmeriFirst Federal Savings Miami Inc	305-577-1600	Miami, FL	500	4500	2
2337	Amerisure Companies	313-965-8600	Detroit, MI	500	300	2
2338	Anthony, C R Co Inc	405-235-3711	Oklahoma City, OK	500	NA	5
2339	Apache Corp	303-837-5000	Denver, CO	500	350	2
2340	Asplundh Tree Experts Inc	215-784-4200	Willow Grove, PA	500	NA	6
2341	ATCOR Inc	312-339-1610	Harvey, IL	500	250	4
2342	Austin Industries Inc	214-630-5100	Dallas, TX	500	NA	5
2343	Auto Zone Corp	901-325-4600	Memphis, TN	500	NA	5
2344	Barton Malow Co	313-351-4000	Southfield, MI	500	NA	3
2345	Blair Corp	814-723-3600	Warren, PA	500	159	4
2346	Booz, Allen & Hamilton Inc	212-697-1900	New York, NY	500	NA	4
2347	Brookings Institution	202-797-6000	Washington, DC	500	NM	2
2348	Builder Marts of America Inc	803-297-6101	Greenville, SC	500	NA	4
2349	Carlisle Companies Inc	513-241-2500	Cincinnati, OH	500	NA	5
2350	Carpenter, E R Corp	804-359-0800	Richmond, VA	500	NA	5

Organizations Listed by Revenue

Rank	Organization	Phone	City / State or Province	Revenue ($ mil)	Assets ($ mil)	Emp (thous)
2351	CC Industries Inc	312-236-6300	Chicago, IL	500	NA	5
2352	Ceco Corp	312-789-1400	Oak Brook, IL	500	NA	5
2353	Central Bancorp Inc	513-651-8000	Cincinnati, OH	500	5000	3
2354	Central Newspapers Inc	317-633-9027	Indianapolis, IN	500	NA	5
2355	Chase Enterprises Inc	203-549-1674	Hartford, CT	500	NA	5
2356	Chemcentral Corp	312-594-7000	Chicago, IL	500	NA	1
2357	Citibank Arizona	602-248-2200	Phoenix, AZ	500	5000	3
2358	Clarendon America Insurance Co	302-656-0142	Wilmington, DE	500	500	1
2359	Club Corp of America	214-243-6191	Dallas, TX	500	NA	6
2360	Coca Cola Bottling Co of New York	203-625-4000	Greenwich, CT	500	NA	2
2361	Coca Cola Bottling of Chicago Inc	312-775-0900	Chicago, IL	500	NA	2
2362	Coleman Co	316-261-3211	Wichita, KS	500	500	5
2363	Communications Workers of America	202-728-2300	Washington, DC	500	NM	700
2364	Community Fed Savings (MO) Assn Inc	314-822-5000	St Louis, MO	500	5000	2
2365	Computervision Corp	617-275-1800	Bedford, MA	500	431	5
2366	Consolidated Beef Industries Inc	414-437-4311	Green Bay, WI	500	NA	1
2367	Continental Companies Inc	305-445-2493	Maimi, FL	500	NA	8
2368	Cooke, Jack Kent Corp	703-687-4000	Middleburg, VA	500	NA	1
2369	Coulter Electronics Corp	305-885-0131	Hialeah, FL	500	NA	5
2370	Curry Corp	914-725-3500	Scarsdale, NY	500	NA	1
2371	Dan River Inc	804-799-7000	Danville, VA	500	NA	5
2372	Dauphin Deposit Corp	717-255-2121	Harrisburg, PA	500	5000	2
2373	Day & Zimmermann Inc	215-299-8000	Philadelphia, PA	500	NA	6
2374	Delta Woodside Industries Inc	803-232-8300	Greenville, SC	500	500	4
2375	Dobbs Houses Inc	901-766-3600	Memphis, TN	500	NA	2
2376	Dr Pepper/Seven Up Inc	214-824-0331	Dallas, TX	500	NA	1
2377	First Jersey National Corp	201-547-7000	Jersey City, NJ	500	5000	3
2378	First Kentucky National Corp	502-581-4498	Louisville, KY	500	5500	5
2379	Foodarama Supermarket Corp	201-462-4700	Freehold, NJ	500	300	7
2380	Ford Motor Insurance Co	313-322-9045	Dearborn, MI	500	1000	2
2381	Gates Learjet Corp	602-745-5100	Tucson, AZ	500	NA	2
2382	General Development Corp	305-350-1200	Miami, FL	500	600	2
2383	Georgia Crown Distributing Corp	404-568-4580	Columbus, GA	500	NA	1
2384	Gifford Hill & Co Inc	214-258-7000	Irving, TX	500	NA	3
2385	Gordon Food Service Corp	616-530-7000	Grand Rapids, MI	500	NA	3
2386	Gore, W L & Associates Inc	302-738-4880	Newark, DE	500	NA	5
2387	Griffin Corp	212-753-1230	New York, NY	500	NA	5
2388	GSC Enterprises Inc	214-885-7621	Sulphur Springs, TX	500	NA	1
2389	Hallmark Electronics Corp	214-343-5000	Dallas, TX	500	NA	2
2390	Hamilton Bank Corp	717-569-8731	Lancaster, PA	500	4500	2
2391	Harbert Corp	205-987-5500	Birmingham, AL	500	NA	1
2392	Heard, Bill Enterprises Inc	404-561-6213	Columbus, GA	500	NA	1
2393	Hendrick Management Corp	704-529-0578	Charlotte, NC	500	NA	1
2394	Huber, J M Corp	201-549-8600	Edison, NJ	500	NA	3
2395	ICC Industries Inc	212-903-1700	New York, NY	500	NA	2
2396	Imperial Eastman Corp	312-967-4500	Niles, IL	500	500	5
2397	IMS International Inc	212-371-2310	New York, NY	500	400	6
2398	Inland Real Estate Corp	312-218-8000	Oak Brook, IL	500	NA	2
2399	International Assn of Machinists	202-857-5200	Washington, DC	500	NM	800
2400	International Brotherhood Electrical Wkr	202-833-7000	Washington, DC	500	NM	1000

Organizations Listed by Revenue

Rank	Organization	Phone	City / State or Province	Revenue ($ mil)	Assets ($ mil)	Emp (thous)
2401	Investors Management Corp	919-781-9310	Raleigh, NC	500	NA	10
2402	Jitney Jungle Stores Inc	601-948-0361	Jackson, MS	500	NA	5
2403	Kane Miller Corp	914-631-6900	Tarrytown, NY	500	NA	3
2404	Koll Co Inc	714-833-3030	Newport Beach, CA	500	NA	1
2405	Bean, L L Corp	207-865-4761	Freeport, ME	500	NA	3
2406	Landmark Land Co Inc	408-625-4060	Carmel, CA	500	2500	2
2407	Lewis Homes Corp	714-985-0971	Upland, CA	500	NA	1
2408	Lone Star Technologies	214-352-3981	Dallas, TX	500	350	2
2409	Magma Copper Co	602-385-3100	San Manuel, AZ	500	350	5
2410	Marley Co Inc	913-362-5440	Mission Woods, KS	500	NA	5
2411	McKinsey & Co Inc	212-909-8400	New York, NY	500	NA	3
2412	McLouth Steel Products Inc	313-285-1200	Trenton, MI	500	NA	2
2413	McWane Corp	205-991-9888	Birmingham, AL	500	NA	4
2414	Meadowdale Foods Inc	313-943-3300	Detroit, MI	500	NA	2
2415	Minyard Food Stores Inc	214-462-8700	Coppel, TX	500	NA	5
2416	Moore McCormick Resources Inc	203-358-2200	Stamford, CT	500	500	5
2417	Morse Operations Inc	305-563-6331	Fort Lauderdale, FL	500	NA	1
2418	Mortenson, M A Co Inc	612-522-2100	Minneapolis, MN	500	NA	1
2419	Motor Wheel Corp	517-337-5700	Lansing, MI	500	NA	5
2420	Moyer Packing Co Inc	215-723-5555	Souderton, PA	500	NA	2
2421	Murray Ohio Manufacturing Co	615-373-6500	Brentwood, TN	500	400	4
2422	Musicland Group Inc	612-932-7700	Minneapolis, MN	500	NA	3
2423	National Beverage Corp	305-857-3300	Fort Lauderdale, FL	500	NA	1
2424	National Cleaning Contractors Inc	212-689-4050	New York, NY	500	NA	10
2425	National Credit Union Administration	202-357-1055	Washington, DC	500	NM	3
2426	New Jersey National Bank	609-771-5700	Trenton, NJ	500	3500	2
2427	Northwestern Steel & Wire Corp	815-625-2500	Sterling, IL	500	NA	3
2428	Pamida Corp	402-339-2400	Omaha, NE	500	NA	5
2429	Pamplin, R B Corp	503-248-1133	Portland, OR	500	NA	5
2430	Pay N Pak Inc	206-854-5450	Kent, WA	500	NA	2
2431	Pepper Companies	312-266-4703	Chicago, IL	500	NA	1
2432	PMC Corp	818-896-1101	Sun Valley, CA	500	NA	5
2433	Provident National Assurance Co	615-755-1011	Chattanooga, TN	500	5239	2
2434	Putnam Management Co Inc	617-292-1000	Boston, MA	500	22000	1
2435	Racetrac Petroleum Corp	404-434-0400	Atlanta, GA	500	NA	1
2436	Rand Corp	213-393-0411	Santa Monica, CA	500	NM	2
2437	Republic Health Services Inc	214-851-3100	Dallas, TX	500	NA	5
2438	Research Cottrell Inc	201-685-4000	Somerville, NJ	500	NA	2
2439	Robertshaw Controls Co	804-281-0700	Richmond, VA	500	500	7
2440	Rochester & Pittsburgh Coal Corp	412-349-5800	Indiana, PA	500	250	5
2441	Rock Tenn Corp	404-448-2193	Norcross, GA	500	NA	5
2442	Rosenthal Companies Inc	703-920-8700	Arlington, VA	500	NA	1
2443	Save Mart Supermarkets Inc	209-577-1600	Modesto, CA	500	NA	3
2444	Schneider National Inc	414-497-2201	Green Bay, WI	500	NA	5
2445	Schottenstein Stores Inc	614-221-9200	Columbus, OH	500	NA	5
2446	Schwegmann Giant Super Markets Inc	504-947-9921	New Orleans, LA	500	NA	5
2447	Sears Savings Bank Inc	818-956-1800	Glendale, CA	500	5207	1
2448	Seligman Marketing Inc	800-221-2450	New York, NY	500	NA	5
2449	Service Employees International Union	202-898-3200	Washington, DC	500	NM	850
2450	Snyder General Corp	214-979-3100	Dallas, TX	500	NA	5

Organizations Listed by Revenue

Rank	Organization	Phone	City / State or Province	Revenue ($ mil)	Assets ($ mil)	Emp (thous)
2451	Stanadyne Inc	203-525-0821	Windsor, CT	500	500	5
2452	Summit Bancorp	201-522-8400	Summit, NJ	500	5000	2
2453	Terex Corp	414-453-5322	Green Bay, WI	500	350	4
2454	Third National Bank Co	615-748-4000	Nashville, TN	500	4000	2
2455	Thompson, J Walter Group Inc	212-210-7000	New York, NY	500	NA	5
2456	Towers, Perrin, Forster & Crosby Inc	212-309-3400	New York, NY	500	NA	5
2457	Transnational Motors Inc	616-949-7570	Grand Rapids, MI	500	NA	3
2458	UIS Inc	212-581-7660	New York, NY	500	NA	5
2459	Union Trust Co	203-348-6211	Stamford, CT	500	4000	2
2460	United Brotherhood of Carpenters America	202-546-6206	Washington, DC	500	NM	600
2461	United Co	703-466-3322	Bristol, VA	500	NA	2
2462	United States Nuclear Regulatory Comm	301-492-7000	Washington, DC	500	NM	3
2463	United Steelworkers of America	202-638-6929	Washington, DC	500	NM	900
2464	Walbridge, Aldinger & Co Inc	313-591-6000	Livonia, MI	500	NA	1
2465	Walton Monroe Textiles Inc	404-267-9411	Monroe, GA	500	NA	5
2466	Warren Equities Inc	212-751-8100	New York, NY	500	NA	1
2467	Wheaton Industries Inc	609-825-1400	Millville, NJ	500	NA	5
2468	White Swan Co	817-284-4844	Fort Worth, TX	500	NA	3
2469	Worldmark Corp	305-626-3116	North Palm Beach, FL	500	NA	1
2470	WTD Industries Inc	503-246-3440	Portland, OR	500	250	2
2471	Zachry, H B Co Inc	512-922-1213	San Antonio, TX	500	NA	5
2472	Brown & Root Inc	713-676-3011	Houston, TX	500	NA	2
2473	Houston Lighting & Power Co	713-229-7267	Houston, TX	500	NA	2
2474	ITT Fluid Technology Corp	201-444-6030	Midland Park, NJ	500	NA	4
2475	Ore-Ida Foods Inc	208-383-6100	Boise, ID	500	NA	2
2476	Simon & Schuster Inc	212-698-7000	New York, NY	500	NA	3
2477	Star Kist Seafood Co	213-590-3605	Long Beach, CA	500	NA	2
2478	Walden Book Co Inc	203-356-7500	Stamford, CT	500	NA	5
2479	Weight Watchers International	516-939-0400	Jericho, NY	500	NA	2
2480	Horn & Hardart Co	702-369-9500	Las Vegas, NV	499	400	6
2481	Bandag Inc	319-262-1400	Muscatine, IA	498	315	2
2482	Western Savings & Loan Assn Inc	602-248-4600	Phoenix, AZ	498	5599	2
2483	Homestead Savings Fed Savings Assn Inc	415-387-4300	San Francisco, CA	497	5751	2
2484	General Trustco of Canada Ltd	416-867-3200	Toronto, ON Can	497	4204	2
2485	Barnes Group Inc	203-583-7070	Bristol, CT	496	312	5
2486	Iowa Illinois Gas & Electric Inc	319-326-7111	Davenport, IA	496	1242	2
2487	Long Island Savings Bank Inc	516-677-5000	Syosset, NY	495	5263	2
2488	Cablevision Systems Inc	516-364-8450	Woodbury, NY	493	1171	2
2489	Colonial Penn Insurance Co	215-988-8000	Philadelphia, PA	486	873	2
2490	Orange & Rockland Utilities Corp	914-352-6000	Pearl River, NY	486	922	2
2491	Questar Corp	801-534-5000	Salt Lake City, UT	486	1026	2
2492	Zurn Industries Inc	814-452-2111	Erie, PA	485	360	4
2493	Hayes Dana Inc	416-687-4200	St Catharines, ON Can	485	192	3
2494	Manitoba Hydro Electric Board Ltd	204-474-3311	Winnipeg, MB Can	485	2754	4
2495	Cornell University	607-256-1000	Ithaca, NY	484	608	24
2496	Union Carbide Canada Ltd	416-488-1444	Toronto, ON Can	483	682	5
2497	First Virginia Banks Inc	703-241-4000	Falls Church, VA	482	4796	4
2498	Howard Savings Bank Inc	201-533-7400	Livingston, NJ	481	5221	2
2499	Charter Co	513-579-2482	Cincinnati, OH	480	295	2
2500	Selective Insurance Co	201-948-3000	Branchville, NJ	480	962	2

Organizations Listed by Revenue

Rank	Organization	Phone	City / State or Province	Revenue ($ mil)	Assets ($ mil)	Emp (thous)
2501	Valspar Corp	612-332-7371	Minneapolis, MN	480	233	5
2502	Commerce Bancshares Inc	816-234-2000	Kansas City, MO	479	5444	4
2503	First Florida Banks Inc	813-224-1111	Tampa, FL	479	5132	4
2504	Rochester Telephone Corp	716-777-1000	Rochester, NY	479	885	3
2505	PPG Canada Inc	416-923-5441	Toronto, ON Can	479	437	3
2506	CRS Sirrine Inc	713-552-2000	Houston, TX	478	186	3
2507	INA Life Insurance Co	215-241-4000	Philadelphia, PA	478	2521	2
2508	Q & O Paper Co	416-688-5030	St Catharines, ON Can	478	490	3
2509	Ramada Inc	602-273-4000	Phoenix, AZ	477	705	15
2510	National Sea Products Ltd	902-422-9381	Halifax, NS Can	477	343	8
2511	American Carriers Inc	913-451-2811	Overland Park, KS	475	250	5
2512	Envirodyne Industries	312-649-0600	Chicago, IL	475	400	5
2513	Florida Rock Industries Inc	904-355-1781	Jacksonville, FL	475	300	4
2514	First Alabama Bancshares	205-832-8490	Montgomery, AL	474	5174	3
2515	LVI Group Inc	212-337-6600	New York, NY	474	220	2
2516	Stewart & Stevenson Services Inc	713-868-7700	Houston, TX	474	400	3
2517	Turbo Resources Ltd	403-294-6400	Calgary, AB Can	474	306	2
2518	Florida Federal Savings & Loan Inc	813-893-1131	St Petersburg, FL	472	5157	2
2519	Zenith National Insurance Co	819-990-9300	Encino, CA	472	791	2
2520	American Healthcare Management	214-387-9181	Dallas, TX	471	NA	8
2521	Cilcorp Inc	309-672-5271	Peoria, IL	471	1096	2
2522	Michigan State University	517-355-1855	East Lansing, MI	471	648	46
2523	Orion Pictures Corp	212-758-5100	New York, NY	469	350	3
2524	Bow Valley Industries Ltd	403-261-6100	Calgary, AB Can	468	935	2
2525	Camco Inc	416-629-3000	Mississauga, ON Can	468	213	5
2526	Cara Operations Ltd	416-962-4571	Toronto, ON Can	468	298	6
2527	Carling O'Keefe Breweries Canada Ltd	416-675-3960	Rexdale, ON Can	468	425	4
2528	Deere, John Ltd	416-734-4501	Welland, ON Can	468	425	2
2529	Maritime Life Assurance Co	902-453-4300	Halifax, NS Can	468	1518	1
2530	Philips Canada Ltd	416-292-5161	Montreal, ON Can	468	NA	3
2531	General Host Corp	203-357-9900	Stamford, CT	467	533	6
2532	Lotus Development Corp	617-577-8500	Cambridge, MA	467	422	4
2533	Genesco Inc	615-367-7000	Nashville, TN	463	265	6
2534	Quanex Corp	713-961-4600	Houston, TX	463	302	2
2535	Teradyne Inc	617-482-2700	Boston, MA	463	434	5
2536	Sherritt Gordon Mines Ltd	416-363-9241	Toronto, ON Can	463	546	3
2537	Petroleum Heat & Power Co	203-323-2121	Stamford, CT	462	350	2
2538	Noland Co	804-928-9000	Newport News, VA	461	201	2
2539	Rouse Co	301-992-6000	Columbia, MD	461	2080	5
2540	Minnesota Power & Light Co	218-722-2641	Duluth, MN	460	1484	2
2541	University of Illinois	217-333-1000	Champaign, IL	460	777	40
2542	Colorado Springs, City of	303-578-6600	Colorado Springs, CO	458	NM	4
2543	AST Research Inc	714-863-1333	Irvine, CA	456	200	2
2544	Lands End Inc	608-935-9341	Dodgeville, WI	456	151	2
2545	Resorts International Inc	305-891-2500	North Miami, FL	456	1035	9
2546	Goulds Pumps Inc	315-568-2811	Seneca Falls, NY	454	366	4
2547	Lancaster Colony Corp	614-224-7141	Columbus, OH	453	286	5
2548	Atari Corp	408-745-2000	Sunnyvale, CA	452	NA	4
2549	Merchants National Bank & Trust Co	317-267-6100	Indianapolis, IN	452	5256	3
2550	Diebold Inc	216-489-4000	Canton, OH	451	455	5

Organizations Listed by Revenue

Rank	Organization	Phone	City / State or Province	Revenue ($ mil)	Assets ($ mil)	Emp (thous)
2551	Inacomp Computer Centers Inc	317-844-9666	Indianapolis, IN	451	963	4
2552	Banque National de Paris	212-980-5185	New York, NY	450	3500	1
2553	Bates, Ted Worldwide Inc	212-297-7000	New York, NY	450	NA	5
2554	Bayerische Vereinsbank AG	212-210-0300	New York, NY	450	3500	1
2555	Bell Industries Inc	213-826-6778	Los Angeles, CA	450	NA	4
2556	CML Group Inc	508-264-4155	Acton, MA	450	150	3
2557	Commerzbank AG	212-208-6200	New York, NY	450	3500	1
2558	Commtron Corp	515-226-3000	Des Moines, IA	450	150	1
2559	Credit Agricole Mutuel Paris	212-418-2200	New York, NY	450	3500	1
2560	Credit Lyonnais France	212-344-0500	New York, NY	450	3500	1
2561	Daiwa Bank & Trust Co	212-399-2710	New York, NY	450	3500	2
2562	Deutsche Bank AG	212-940-8000	New York, NY	450	3500	1
2563	Dresdner Bank AG	212-425-4640	New York, NY	450	3500	1
2564	Farwest Financial Corp	213-277-3055	Los Angeles, CA	450	4760	2
2565	Generale Banque (Societe Generale)	212-418-8700	New York, NY	450	3500	1
2566	Genlyte Group Inc	201-864-3000	Secaucus, NJ	450	350	4
2567	Grey Advertising Inc	212-546-2000	New York, NY	450	150	3
2568	Hadson Corp	405-235-9500	Oklahoma City, OK	450	300	2
2569	Harleysville Insurance Co	215-256-5000	Harleysville, PA	450	850	2
2570	Hudson Foods Inc	501-636-1100	Rogers, AR	450	250	5
2571	Kyowa Bank Ltd	212-432-6400	New York, NY	450	3500	1
2572	LA Gear Inc	213-822-1995	Los Angeles, CA	450	300	4
2573	Laclede Gas Co	314-342-0500	St Louis, MO	450	800	2
2574	Lavoro Banca Roma Ltd	212-581-0710	New York, NY	450	3500	1
2575	Lloyd's Bank Ltd	212-607-4300	New York, NY	450	3500	1
2576	Long Term Credit Bank of Japan Ltd	213-629-5777	Los Angeles, CA	450	3500	1
2577	Midland Bank PLC	212-969-7000	New York, NY	450	3500	1
2578	Motel 6 Lmtd Ptnrship	214-386-6161	Dallas, TX	450	200	8
2579	National Bank of Washington Inc	206-344-2300	Seattle, WA	450	4500	3
2580	New York State Teachers Investment Fund	518-447-2741	Albany, NY	450	16500	2
2581	Nippon Credit Bank Ltd	213-629-5566	Los Angeles, CA	450	3500	1
2582	Norinchukin Bank Inc	212-697-1717	New York, NY	450	3500	1
2583	Nuveen, John & Co Inc	312-917-7700	Chicago, IL	450	363	1
2584	Ohio Public Employees Retirement Fund	614-221-7012	Columbus, OH	450	16500	1
2585	Orion Capital Insurance Co	305-445-8333	Miami, FL	450	100	2
2586	Oshkosh Truck Corp	414-235-9150	Oshkosh, WI	450	350	2
2587	RLC Corp	302-429-2700	Wilmington, DE	450	400	3
2588	Santa Barbara Savings Assn Inc	805-682-5000	Santa Barbara, CA	450	4500	2
2589	Shoko Chukin Bank Ltd	212-693-1660	New York, NY	450	3500	1
2590	Spear, Leeds & Kellogg Inc	212-587-8800	New York, NY	450	4400	1
2591	Sprague Technologies Inc	203-964-8600	Stamford, CT	450	400	7
2592	Standard Pacific Corp	714-546-1161	Costa Mesa, CA	450	200	1
2593	Swiss Bank Corp	212-938-3500	New York, NY	450	3500	1
2594	Taiyo Kobe Bank Ltd	213-629-3939	Los Angeles, CA	450	3500	1
2595	TBC Corp	901-363-8030	Memphis, TN	450	200	3
2596	Texas Teachers Retirement Fund	512-397-6460	Austin, TX	450	16500	1
2597	Town & Country Corp	617-884-8500	Chelsea, MA	450	200	2
2598	Toyo Trust Ltd	213-624-2424	Los Angeles, CA	450	3500	1
2599	Union Bank of Switzerland	212-715-3000	New York, NY	450	3500	1
2600	University Savings Assn Inc	713-596-1000	Houston, TX	450	4500	2

Organizations Listed by Revenue

Rank	Organization	Phone	City / State or Province	Revenue ($ mil)	Assets ($ mil)	Emp (thous)
2601	Volt Information Sciences Corp	212-309-0200	New York, NY	450	300	18
2602	Westdeutsche Landesbank AG	212-754-9600	New York, NY	450	3500	1
2603	Westfield Companies	216-887-0101	Westfield Center, OH	450	800	2
2604	Yasuda Trust & Banking Co	212-432-2300	New York, NY	450	3500	1
2605	Comcast Corp	215-665-1700	Philadelphia, PA	449	2371	3
2606	Sun Life Assurance Co of Canada US	617-237-6030	Wellesley, MA	449	3505	2
2607	Canron Ltd	416-364-6600	Toronto, ON Can	449	215	4
2608	Betz Laboratories Inc	215-355-3300	Trevose, PA	448	319	3
2609	Seaboard Corp	617-332-8492	Boston, MA	448	400	2
2610	Noma Industries Ltd	416-222-6662	Willowdale, ON Can	448	281	4
2611	Southland Canada Inc	604-299-0700	Burnaby, BC Can	448	145	6
2612	Hartford Steam Boiler Inspection Inc	203-722-1866	Hartford, CT	447	730	4
2613	Central Fidelity Banks Inc	804-782-4000	Richmond, VA	446	4731	3
2614	Karcher, Carl Enterprises Inc	714-774-5796	Anaheim, CA	446	300	12
2615	Texas American Bancshares Inc	817-884-4040	Fort Worth, TX	445	4383	4
2616	Provence of Alberta Treasury Branches	403-493-7015	Edmonton, AB Can	445	4692	3
2617	Healthco International Inc	617-423-6045	Boston, MA	444	300	3
2618	Montana Power & Light Co	406-723-5421	Butte, MT	444	1926	4
2619	Province of Prince Edward Island	902-892-3428	Charlotetown, PE Can	444	NM	4
2620	Georgia Federal Bank Inc	404-330-2440	Atlanta, GA	443	4365	2
2621	Culinar Inc	514-288-3101	Montreal, PQ Can	441	189	5
2622	Mazda Canada Inc	416-831-4222	Pickering, ON Can	441	NA	1
2623	Wardair International Ltd	416-671-3100	Mississauga, ON Can	441	673	3
2624	Amalgamated Sugar Co	801-399-3431	Ogden, UT	440	750	5
2625	Associated Madison Asset Management Inc	212-351-2600	New York, NY	440	16500	1
2626	Banca Serfin	212-635-2300	New York, NY	440	3500	2
2627	Friona Industries Inc	806-247-3991	Friona, TX	440	NA	1
2628	GNB Inc	612-681-5000	Mendota Heights, MN	440	NA	4
2629	Michigan Treasurer Employees Rtrmt Sys	517-373-9150	Lansing, MI	440	16500	2
2630	Multimedia Inc	803-298-4373	Greenville, SC	440	405	6
2631	SFN Companies Inc	312-657-3900	Glenview, IL	440	NA	4
2632	Telerate Inc	212-938-5200	New York, NY	440	543	3
2633	University of Florida	904-392-3261	Gainesville, FL	440	573	41
2634	Van Kampen Merritt Inc	312-719-6000	Lisle, IL	440	4400	1
2635	Analog Devices Inc	617-329-4700	Norwood, MA	439	449	5
2636	American National Bank & Trust Co	312-661-5000	Chicago, IL	438	4567	3
2637	Central Hudson Gas & Electric Co	914-452-2000	Poughkeepsie, NY	438	1046	2
2638	United Banks of Colorado Inc	303-861-4700	Denver, CO	438	5540	3
2639	United States Small Business Admin	202-653-6554	Washington, DC	437	NM	4
2640	Rockwell International of Canada Ltd	416-757-1101	Toronto, ON Can	437	296	2
2641	San Jacinto Savings Assn Inc	713-661-7000	Houston, TX	436	4594	2
2642	Seamen's Bank for Savings Inc	212-428-4500	New York, NY	436	4708	2
2643	Saskatchewan Telecommunications Ltd	306-347-2200	Regina, SK Can	436	896	5
2644	United Healthcare Corp	612-936-1300	Minnetonka, MN	435	210	5
2645	University of Chicago	312-753-1234	Chicago, IL	435	356	16
2646	Central Illinois Light Co	309-672-5271	Peoria, IL	434	924	2
2647	Homestake Mining Co	415-981-8150	San Francisco, CA	433	984	2
2648	Stanhome Inc	413-562-3631	Westfield, MA	433	244	4
2649	Formica Corp	201-890-9400	Wayne, NJ	432	250	4
2650	Cincinnati, City of	513-352-3250	Cincinnati, OH	431	NM	6

Organizations Listed by Revenue

Rank	Organization	Phone	City / State or Province	Revenue ($ mil)	Assets ($ mil)	Emp (thous)
2651	Columbia University	212-280-1754	New York, NY	431	409	21
2652	Piedmont Natural Gas Co	704-364-3120	Charlotte, NC	431	700	2
2653	University of Texas	512-741-3434	Austin, TX	431	814	52
2654	Standex International Corp	603-893-9701	Salem, NH	430	276	6
2655	Eljer Industries Inc	214-881-7177	Plano, TX	429	197	4
2656	Pall Corp	516-671-4000	Glen Cove, NY	429	570	6
2657	Cross & Trecker Corp	313-644-4343	Bloomfield Hills, MI	428	381	4
2658	University of California Berkeley	415-642-6000	Berkeley, CA	428	751	38
2659	University of California Davis	916-752-1011	Davis, CA	428	516	22
2660	QIT Fer et Titane Inc	514-288-8400	Montreal, PQ Can	428	621	2
2661	Seaboard Lumber Sales Co	604-684-3171	Vancouver, BC Can	428	88	1
2662	Mercantile Bancorp Inc	314-425-2525	St Louis, MO	426	6491	5
2663	Corroon & Black Corp	212-363-4100	New York, NY	425	957	4
2664	Lincoln Savings (Cal) & Loan Assn Inc	714-553-0200	Irvine, CA	425	4000	1
2665	MAI Basic Four Inc	714-731-5100	Tustin, CA	425	375	3
2666	Midwest Federal Savings Assn Inc	612-372-6123	Minneapolis, MN	425	3570	2
2667	Sun Distributors Inc	215-665-3650	Philadelphia, PA	425	400	4
2668	UGI Corp	215-337-1000	King of Prussia, PA	425	350	2
2669	Winnebago Industries Inc	515-582-3535	Forest City, IA	425	237	4
2670	Bathurst Paper Ltd	514-875-2160	Montreal, PQ Can	425	468	3
2671	Cantrex Group Inc	514-335-0260	Montreal, PQ Can	425	213	2
2672	CB Pak Inc	516-875-2160	Montreal, PQ Can	425	425	6
2673	Groupe Ro-na Inc	514-599-5100	Boucherville, PQ Can	425	213	2
2674	Minnesota Mining & Manufacturing Canada	519-451-2500	London, ON Can	425	510	2
2675	Paccar of Canada Ltd	416-858-7070	Mississauga, ON Can	425	213	2
2676	Re Max Ltd	416-542-2400	Mississauga, ON Can	425	NA	7
2677	SHL Systemhouse Inc	604-236-9734	Vancouver, BC Can	425	170	1
2678	Societe Generale Financement du Quebec	514-875-0330	Montreal, PQ Can	425	1020	5
2679	M/A Com Inc	617-272-9600	Burlington, MA	424	483	6
2680	Modine Manufacturing Co	414-636-1200	Racine, WI	424	289	4
2681	Commercial Union Assurance Group Ltd	416-361-2500	Toronto, ON Can	421	774	1
2682	Church's Fried Chicken Inc	512-735-9392	San Antonio, TX	420	301	13
2683	Columbus, City of	614-222-7671	Columbus, OH	420	NM	6
2684	Kay Jewelers Corp	703-683-3800	Alexandria, VA	420	275	5
2685	Kennametal Inc	412-539-5000	Latrobe, PA	420	359	5
2686	Casey's General Stores Inc	515-263-3700	Des Moines, IA	419	200	4
2687	Loctite Corp	203-520-5000	Hartford, CT	417	347	3
2688	Monarch Capital Corp	413-781-3000	Springfield, MA	417	5805	3
2689	Safety Kleen Corp	312-697-8460	Elgin, IL	417	399	4
2690	Lloyd's of London Canada Ltd	514-861-8361	Montreal, PQ Can	417	4582	2
2691	Bank Laurentienne du Canada	514-284-3931	Montreal, PQ Can	416	4117	2
2692	United Cooperatives of Ontario Ltd	416-890-8500	Mississauga, ON Can	416	153	1
2693	Pier 1 Imports Inc	817-878-8000	Fort Worth, TX	415	300	4
2694	University of Cal San Diego	714-452-2230	La Jolla, CA	415	411	14
2695	University of Iowa	319-353-2121	Iowa City, IA	415	631	34
2696	Precision Castparts Inc	503-777-3881	Portland, OR	414	298	6
2697	Robertson, H H Co	412-281-3200	Pittsburgh, PA	414	296	5
2698	Rochester, City of	716-428-7045	Rochester, NY	413	NM	7
2699	Le Groupe Ro Na Inc	514-599-5100	Boucherville, PQ Can	413	115	1
2700	Greif Brothers Corp	614-363-1271	Delaware, OH	412	267	4

Organizations Listed by Revenue

Rank	Organization	Phone	City / State or Province	Revenue ($ mil)	Assets ($ mil)	Emp (thous)
2701	Idaho Power Co	208-383-2200	Boise, ID	412	1609	2
2702	Lionel Corp	212-818-0630	New York, NY	412	400	3
2703	Wyle Laboratories Inc	213-322-1763	El Segundo, CA	411	400	2
2704	Farm Credit Corp	613-996-6606	Ottawa, ON Can	411	4177	1
2705	Nova Scotia Power Corp	902-428-6221	Halifax, NS Can	411	1254	2
2706	Prime Motor Inns Inc	201-882-1010	Fairfield, NJ	410	904	5
2707	Bank South Corp	404-529-4521	Atlanta, GA	409	4881	2
2708	Mohasco Corp	703-768-8000	Fairfax, VA	409	350	3
2709	Nevada Power Co	702-367-5000	Las Vegas, NV	409	1014	2
2710	Alberta Energy Co	403-423-8333	Edmonton, AB Can	409	1641	1
2711	Fremont General Corp	213-483-0991	Santa Monica, CA	408	1240	2
2712	Lance Inc	704-554-1421	Charlotte, NC	408	256	3
2713	Sierra Pacific Resources Co	702-689-3600	Reno, NV	408	1244	2
2714	Wawanesa Mutual Insurance Co	204-985-3811	Winnipeg, MB Can	408	632	1
2715	Dart Group Corp	301-731-1200	Landover, MD	406	250	5
2716	Equitable Resources Co Inc	412-261-3000	Pittsburgh, PA	406	1069	2
2717	MSA Mine Safety Appliances Co	412-967-3000	O'Hara Township, PA	406	361	4
2718	Ocean Drilling Exploration Co	504-561-2811	New Orleans, LA	406	1026	4
2719	Norfolk, City of	804-441-2679	Norfolk, VA	405	NM	9
2720	Fiberglas Canada Inc	416-733-1600	Willowdale, ON Can	405	205	3
2721	Duke University	919-684-8111	Durham, NC	404	405	13
2722	Gibson Greetings Inc	513-841-6600	Cincinnati, OH	404	326	4
2723	DeSoto Inc	312-391-9000	Des Plaines, IL	403	219	2
2724	Economical Group Ltd	519-888-8200	Kitchener, ON Can	403	741	1
2725	Pic N Save Corp	213-537-9220	Dominguez, CA	402	262	4
2726	Wholesale Club Inc	317-842-0351	Indianapolis, IN	402	250	2
2727	Williams, A L Corp	404-381-1674	Duluth, GA	402	1655	2
2728	Allis Chalmers Corp	414-475-2000	West Allis, WI	401	10	1
2729	Central Bancshares Inc	205-933-3000	Birmingham, AL	401	4109	3
2730	Liberty Life Insurance Co	803-268-8111	Greenville, SC	401	1382	2
2731	UNC Inc	301-266-7333	Annapolis, MD	401	408	3
2732	Wackenhut Corp	305-666-5656	Coral Gables, FL	401	150	7
2733	Adia Services Inc	415-324-0696	Menlo Park, CA	400	200	3
2734	Alamo Rent-a-Car Inc	305-522-0000	Fort Lauderdale, FL	400	NA	4
2735	American Mutual Liability	508-245-6000	Wakefield, MA	400	800	2
2736	Applied Materials Inc	408-727-5555	Santa Clara, CA	400	200	2
2737	Bain & Co	617-572-2000	Boston, MA	400	NA	3
2738	Banc One Wisconsin	414-765-3000	Milwaukee, WI	400	4000	2
2739	Bassett Furniture Industries Inc	703-629-7511	Bassett, VA	400	250	6
2740	Becor Western Inc	414-768-4000	South Milwaukee, WI	400	NA	4
2741	Best Buy Co	612-831-4552	Minneapolis, MN	400	300	2
2742	Birmingham Steel Corp	205-985-9290	Birmingham, AL	400	NA	3
2743	Borden Chemicals & Plastics Inc	504-673-6121	Geismar, LA	400	NA	4
2744	Brown Brothers Harriman & Co	212-483-1818	New York, NY	400	2200	1
2745	Catalyst Energy Development Inc	212-949-0040	New York, NY	400	1200	1
2746	Chaparral Steel	214-775-8241	Midlothian, TX	400	300	1
2747	Church & Dwight Co	609-683-5900	Princeton, NJ	400	150	1
2748	Coachmen Industries Inc	219-262-0123	Elkhart, IN	400	NA	4
2749	Commercial Intertech	216-746-8011	Youngstown, OH	400	250	4
2750	Convergent Technologies Inc	408-434-2848	San Jose, CA	400	295	15

Organizations Listed by Revenue

Rank	Organization	Phone	City / State or Province	Revenue ($ mil)	Assets ($ mil)	Emp (thous)
2751	Cooper Companies	415-856-5000	Palo Alto, CA	400	NA	4
2752	Country Companies	309-557-2111	Bloomington, IL	400	800	2
2753	Crystal Brands Inc	203-254-6200	Southport, CT	400	300	3
2754	Datapoint Corp	512-699-7000	San Antonio, TX	400	NA	4
2755	Dataproducts Corp	818-887-8000	Woodland Hills, CA	400	NA	3
2756	Delaware Management Investment Advisors	215-988-1333	Philadelphia, PA	400	15400	1
2757	DeTomaso Industries	201-842-7200	Red Bank, NJ	400	250	2
2758	Everex Systems Inc	415-498-1111	Fremont, CA	400	300	2
2759	Far West Savings Assn Inc	714-833-8383	Newport Beach, CA	400	4000	1
2760	Federal Signal Corp	312-954-2000	Oak Brook, IL	400	300	3
2761	Fiduciary Trust Co	212-466-4100	New York, NY	400	15400	1
2762	Financial Corp of Santa Barbara	805-682-2300	Santa Barbara, CA	400	5000	1
2763	First Federal Savings of Pittsburgh Inc	412-392-5500	Pittsburgh, PA	400	4000	1
2764	First Financial Management Corp	404-321-0120	Atlanta, GA	400	200	3
2765	First Minnesota Savings Bank Inc	612-371-3700	Minneapolis, MN	400	4000	1
2766	First Mississippi Corp	601-948-7550	Jackson, MS	400	500	2
2767	Flint Ink Corp	313-538-6800	Detroit, MI	400	NA	4
2768	Freedom Newspapers Inc	714-542-4415	Irvine, CA	400	NA	5
2769	General Felt Industries Inc	201-843-0900	Saddle Brook, NJ	400	NA	4
2770	Gordon Jewelry Corp	713-222-8080	Houston, TX	400	NA	5
2771	Grand Trunk Corp	313-962-2260	Detroit, MI	400	500	4
2772	Great American (AZ) First Savings Bank	602-279-3456	Phoenix, AZ	400	4000	1
2773	Haworth Corp	616-392-5961	Holland, MI	400	NA	4
2774	Healthcare International Inc	512-346-4300	Austin, TX	400	400	4
2775	Hexcel Corp	415-828-4200	San Francisco, CA	400	300	3
2776	Home Interiors & Gifts Inc	214-386-1000	Dallas, TX	400	NA	2
2777	Home Owners Federal S & L Assn	617-482-0630	Boston, MA	400	4218	2
2778	Horizon Bancorp Inc	201-539-7700	Morristown, NJ	400	4000	3
2779	Humiston Keeling Corp	312-943-6066	Chicago, IL	400	NA	1
2780	International Data Corp	508-875-5000	Framingham, MA	400	NA	4
2781	Jersey City, City of	201-547-5202	Jersey City, NJ	400	NM	3
2782	Jorgensen, Earle M Corp	213-567-1122	Lynwood, CA	400	400	4
2783	Journal Communications Co Inc	414-224-2000	Milwaukee, WI	400	NA	4
2784	Kohls Department Stores	414-784-4480	Brookfield, WI	400	NA	4
2785	Krueger, W A Co	602-948-5650	Scottsdale, AZ	400	300	3
2786	Lamson & Sessions Co	216-464-3400	Cleveland, OH	400	250	3
2787	Leventhal, Kenneth Inc	213-277-0880	Los Angeles, CA	400	NA	5
2788	Little, Arthur D & Co Inc	617-864-5770	Cambridge, MA	400	NA	3
2789	Lori Corp	203-621-3601	Southington, CT	400	250	3
2790	Lusk Co	714-261-5999	Irvine, CA	400	NA	1
2791	Marshall Industries Inc	818-459-5500	El Monte, CA	400	200	2
2792	McClatchy Newspapers	916-321-1000	Sacramento, CA	400	200	6
2793	McJunkin Corp	304-348-5211	Charleston, WV	400	NA	1
2794	Microage Inc	602-968-3168	Temple, AZ	400	100	4
2795	Microdot Inc	312-899-1925	Chicago, IL	400	NA	4
2796	Micron Technology	208-383-4000	Boise, ID	400	200	5
2797	Midway Airlines Inc	312-838-0001	Chicago, IL	400	300	4
2798	Miniscribe Corp	303-651-6000	Longmont, CO	400	250	7
2799	Mitsui Manufacturers Bank	213-485-0331	Los Angeles, CA	400	3300	2
2800	Morgan Products Ltd	414-235-7170	Oshkosh, WI	400	350	3

Organizations Listed by Revenue

Rank	Organization	Phone	City / State or Province	Revenue ($ mil)	Assets ($ mil)	Emp (thous)
2801	Morris Affiliated Companies	417-887-0333	Springfield, MO	400	NA	2
2802	National Education Corp	714-474-9400	Irvine, CA	400	200	4
2803	NBI Inc	303-444-5710	Boulder, CO	400	200	4
2804	Olsten Corp	516-832-8200	Westbury, NY	400	150	2
2805	Oneida Ltd	315-361-3000	Oneida, NY	400	500	4
2806	Palm Beach Inc	513-241-4260	Cincinnati, OH	400	NA	5
2807	Pioneer HiBred International Inc	515-245-3500	Des Moines, IA	400	587	5
2808	Quantum Corp	408-262-1100	Milpitas, CA	400	200	1
2809	Rugby Darby Group Inc	516-536-3000	Rockville Center, NY	400	NA	2
2810	SFFED Corp	415-955-5800	San Francisco, CA	400	4499	2
2811	Society for Savings	203-727-5000	Hartford, CT	400	4000	1
2812	Sovereign Bank Corp	615-749-3333	Nashville, TN	400	4000	2
2813	State Auto Mutual Insurance Co	614-464-5000	Columbus, OH	400	500	2
2814	Stein Roe & Farnham Inc	312-368-7800	Chicago, IL	400	13200	1
2815	Stolt Tankers & Terminals Inc	203-625-9400	Greenwich, CT	400	500	1
2816	Summit Health Ltd	213-201-4000	Los Angeles, CA	400	250	7
2817	Sunbelt Savings Assn Inc	214-980-4441	Dallas, TX	400	4000	1
2818	Sverdrup Corp	314-436-7600	St Louis, MO	400	NA	4
2819	ThreeCom (3Com) Corp	408-562-6400	Santa Clara, CA	400	350	4
2820	TJ International Inc	208-375-4450	Boise, ID	400	200	3
2821	UDC Universal Development Corp	312-726-1885	Chicago, IL	400	200	1
2822	Unifi Inc	919-294-4410	Greensboro, NC	400	200	2
2823	Universal Furniture Industries Inc	919-884-4322	High Point, NC	400	200	4
2824	Utica National Insurance Co	315-735-3321	Utica, NY	400	1000	2
2825	Valcom Inc	402-392-3900	Omaha, NE	400	200	1
2826	Vermont American Corp	502-587-6851	Louisville, KY	400	300	3
2827	Wawa Inc	215-358-8000	Wawa, PA	400	NA	4
2828	Standard Motor Products Inc	718-392-0200	Long Island City, NY	398	350	3
2829	USAA Financial Services Inc	512-498-7290	San Antonio, TX	398	625	2
2830	Interface Corporation	404-882-1891	LaGrange, GA	397	493	4
2831	Entree Corp	414-271-2768	Milwaukee, WI	396	200	5
2832	First Hawaiian Inc	808-525-7000	Honolulu, HI	396	4239	2
2833	Oakland, City of	415-273-3141	Oakland, CA	396	NM	4
2834	University of Illinois at Chicago	312-996-3000	Chicago, IL	396	660	27
2835	Evans, Bob Farms Inc	614-491-2225	Columbus, OH	395	219	12
2836	Puget Sound BanCorp	206-593-3600	Tacoma, WA	395	3947	3
2837	University of Cal San Francisco	415-669-9000	San Francisco, CA	395	371	5
2838	Toronto Hydro Ltd	416-595-6400	Toronto, ON Can	394	293	1
2839	West Fraser Timber Co	604-681-8282	Vancouver, BC Can	394	447	3
2840	Hunt, J B Transportion Services Inc	501-659-8800	Lowell, AR	393	301	3
2841	Premier Bancorp (Louisiana Bancshares)	504-389-4206	Baton Rouge, LA	393	4078	3
2842	Texas A & M University	713-845-3211	College Station, TX	392	396	40
2843	UNR Industries Inc	312-341-1234	Chicago, IL	392	250	2
2844	Pulitzer Publishing Co	314-622-7000	St Louis, MO	391	227	4
2845	Newmont Gold Corp	303-863-7414	Denver, CO	389	598	6
2846	University of North Carolina	919-962-2338	Chapel Hill, NC	389	427	25
2847	Zurich Insurance Co Canada Ltd	416-593-4444	Toronto, ON Can	389	672	1
2848	Holly Corp	214-979-0210	Dallas, TX	386	153	1
2849	Belo, A H Corp	214-745-8730	Dallas, TX	385	720	2
2850	AAR	312-439-3939	Elk Grove, IL	384	329	4

Organizations Listed by Revenue

Rank	Organization	Phone	City / State or Province	Revenue ($ mil)	Assets ($ mil)	Emp (thous)
2851	Citadel Holding Corp(Fidelity Fed Svng)	213-956-7100	Glendale, CA	384	4642	1
2852	Skyline Corp	219-294-6521	Elkhart, IN	384	163	3
2853	Grow Group Inc	212-599-4400	New York, NY	383	223	4
2854	Pennsylvania State University	814-865-4700	University Park, PA	383	602	39
2855	Ply Gem Industries Inc	212-832-1550	New York, NY	383	300	3
2856	Wallace Computer Services Inc	312-626-2000	Hillside, IL	383	292	3
2857	Canadian Pacific Express Ltd	416-498-8850	Toronto, ON Can	383	213	3
2858	Canterra Energy Ltd	403-267-9111	Calgary, AB Can	383	2550	2
2859	Coronet Carpets Inc	514-293-3155	Farnham, PQ Can	383	170	2
2860	Litton Systems Canada Ltd	416-249-1231	Toronto, ON Can	383	298	1
2861	Xcan Grain Ltd	204-949-1388	Winnipeg, MB Can	383	85	1
2862	Albuquerque, City of	505-768-3000	Albuquerque, NM	382	NM	5
2863	Great American Commmunications Co	513-579-2177	Cincinnati, OH	382	1965	3
2864	Calgary Cooperative Assn Ltd	403-253-0345	Calgary, AB Can	382	86	3
2865	University of Southern California	213-743-2311	Los Angeles, CA	381	395	33
2866	University of Cincinnati	513-475-8000	Cincinnati, OH	381	431	40
2867	Gaylord Container	312-405-5500	Deerfield, IL	380	200	3
2868	Ladd Furniture Inc	919-889-0333	High Point, NC	380	173	6
2869	New Jersey Manufacturers Insurance Co	609-883-1300	West Trenton, NJ	380	1394	2
2870	Rollins Inc	404-888-2000	Atlanta, GA	380	147	5
2871	LSI Logic Corp	408-433-8000	Milpitas, CA	379	787	3
2872	Shared Medical Systems Corp	215-296-6300	Malvern, PA	379	285	4
2873	Stride Rite Corp	617-491-8800	Cambridge, MA	379	243	3
2874	Virginia Beach, City of	804-427-4111	Virginia Beach, VA	378	NM	10
2875	Rolland Inc	514-289-1779	Montreal, PQ Can	378	142	2
2876	Lifetime Corp	617-330-5080	Boston, MA	377	200	6
2877	Hyundai Auto Canada Inc	416-477-0202	Markham, ON Can	377	184	1
2878	Castle, A M & Co	312-455-7111	Franklin Park, IL	375	300	2
2879	Equitable BanCorp Inc	301-547-4000	Baltimore, MD	375	5186	3
2880	Lane Co Inc	804-369-5641	Altavista, VA	375	250	4
2881	Petrolite Corp	314-241-8370	St Louis, MO	375	250	3
2882	SNC Group Inc	514-866-1000	Montreal, PQ Can	375	305	4
2883	Banner Industries Inc	216-464-3650	Beachwood, OH	374	1066	5
2884	Eastern Utilities Associates Inc	617-357-9590	Boston, MA	374	1203	1
2885	University of Arizona	602-626-4824	Tucson, AZ	374	484	34
2886	Drug Trading Co	416-288-1100	Scarborough, ON Can	373	213	1
2887	City National Corp	213-550-5400	Beverly Hills, CA	371	4296	2
2888	Mesa Limited Partnership Inc	806-378-1000	Amarillo, TX	371	3001	1
2889	Pathe Communications	213-658-2100	Beverly Hills, CA	371	798	2
2890	WLR Foods Inc	703-867-9221	Hilton, VA	371	300	3
2891	Salant Corp (Manhattan Inds)	212-221-7500	New York, NY	370	184	4
2892	Block Drug Co Inc	201-434-3000	Jersey City, NJ	369	356	3
2893	Ford Credit Canada Ltd	416-845-2511	Oakville, ON Can	369	3367	1
2894	Comstock Group Inc	203-792-9800	Danbury, CT	368	NA	5
2895	Dynatech Corp	617-272-3304	Burlington, MA	368	254	3
2896	Houghton Mifflin Co	617-725-5000	Boston, MA	368	262	2
2897	Kinney Shoes of Canada Ltd	416-742-3590	Weston, ON Can	367	156	5
2898	Genovese Drug Stores Inc	516-420-1900	Melville, NY	366	200	4
2899	TNP Texas New Mexico Power Co	817-731-0099	Fort Worth, TX	366	435	1
2900	General Accident Assurnace Co of Canada	416-368-4733	Toronto, ON Can	366	581	1

Organizations Listed by Revenue

Rank	Organization	Phone	City / State or Province	Revenue ($ mil)	Assets ($ mil)	Emp (thous)
2901	Robin Hood Multifoods Inc	416-496-1515	Willowdale, ON Can	366	129	2
2902	Ameron Inc	213-268-4111	Monterey Park, CA	364	312	4
2903	Mercantile Bankshares Corp	301-237-5900	Baltimore, MD	362	3642	2
2904	US Trust Corp	212-806-4500	New York, NY	362	2516	2
2905	Heinz, H J Co of Canada	416-226-5757	Willowdale, ON Can	362	207	2
2906	General Nutrition Inc	412-288-4600	Pittsburgh, PA	361	136	6
2907	Savin Corp	203-967-5000	Stamford, CT	361	300	2
2908	Talley Industries Inc	602-957-7711	Phoenix, AZ	360	533	4
2909	Citibank Canada Ltd	416-947-5500	Toronto, ON Can	360	4167	1
2910	Denison Mines Ltd	416-865-1991	Toronto, ON Can	360	1003	5
2911	Inglis Ltd	416-821-6400	Mississauga, ON Can	360	149	3
2912	COMSAT Communications Satellite Inc	202-863-6000	Washington, DC	359	1163	3
2913	University of Nebraska	402-472-7211	Lincoln, NE	359	451	25
2914	American Business Products Inc	404-953-8300	Atlanta, GA	358	152	4
2915	Western Capital Investment Corp	303-370-1212	Denver, CO	358	3664	2
2916	Jacobson Stores Inc	517-764-6400	Jackson, MI	357	250	5
2917	Redman Industries Inc	214-353-3600	Dallas, TX	357	142	3
2918	Group Olympia Ltd	514-771-0400	St Simon de Bagot, PQ	357	170	1
2919	Mitel Corp	613-592-2122	Kanata, ON Can	356	379	4
2920	HAL (Hawaiian Air) Inc	808-525-5511	Honolulu, HI	354	167	3
2921	Micropolis Corp	818-709-3300	Chatsworth, CA	353	301	3
2922	Smucker, J M Co	216-682-0015	Orrville, OH	353	188	3
2923	Acklands Ltd	204-956-0880	Winnipeg, MB Can	353	196	3
2924	Monsanto Canada Inc	416-826-9222	Mississauga, ON Can	353	148	1
2925	Heilig Meyers Co	804-359-9171	Richmond, VA	352	150	3
2926	Live Entertainment Inc	805-499-5827	Newberry Park, CA	352	131	3
2927	Oklahoma City, City of	405-231-2424	Oklahoma City, OK	352	NM	4
2928	Rothmans Inc	416-449-5525	Don Mills, ON Can	352	338	3
2929	Arden Group Inc	213-638-2842	Compton, CA	351	250	3
2930	Rutgers University	201-932-1766	New Brunswick, NJ	351	605	42
2931	Todd Shipyards Corp	206-223-1560	Seattle, WA	351	394	4
2932	Ford Electronics Manufacturing Corp	416-475-8510	Markham, ON Can	351	170	2
2933	ACF Industries Inc	314-344-4500	Earth City, MO	350	500	3
2934	Acme Steel Co	312-849-2500	Chicago, IL	350	250	3
2935	Alling & Cory Corp	716-454-1880	Rochester, NY	350	NA	1
2936	American Savings (UT) Assn Inc	801-483-5800	Salt Lake City, UT	350	3100	1
2937	American Savings Assn of Florida Inc	305-653-5353	Miami, FL	350	3500	1
2938	Argonaut Insurance Co	415-326-0900	Menlo Park, CA	350	1500	2
2939	Arix Corp	408-432-1200	San Jose, CA	350	200	1
2940	Bay State Gas Co	617-828-8650	Canton, MA	350	NA	2
2941	Capitol Federal Savings (Kansas) Inc	913-235-1341	Topeka, KS	350	3000	1
2942	CF & I Steel Corp	303-561-6000	Pueblo, CO	350	200	2
2943	Champion Enterprises Inc	313-796-2145	Dryden, MI	350	NA	3
2944	Chevy Chase Savings Bank Inc	301-986-7000	Chevy Chase, MD	350	3500	1
2945	Clabir Corp	813-577-5007	St Petersburg, FL	350	300	3
2946	Cleveland Cliffs Inc	216-694-5700	Cleveland, OH	350	NA	3
2947	Columbia Savings (CO) Assn Inc	303-773-3444	Englewood, CO	350	3500	1
2948	Crompton & Knowles Inc	203-353-5400	Stamford, CT	350	NA	3
2949	Cubic Corp	619-277-6780	San Diego, CA	350	300	3
2950	Dayco Corp	513-226-7000	Dayton, OH	350	250	4

Organizations Listed by Revenue

Rank	Organization	Phone	City / State or Province	Revenue ($ mil)	Assets ($ mil)	Emp (thous)
2951	Diasonics Inc	415-872-2722	San Francisco, CA	350	200	2
2952	Energen Corp	205-326-2700	Birmingham, AL	350	300	1
2953	Epstein, A & Sons International Inc	312-454-9100	Chicago, IL	350	NA	1
2954	Farah Inc	915-593-4444	El Paso, TX	350	250	4
2955	Hill Financial Savings Assn Inc	215-679-9506	Red Hill, PA	350	3500	1
2956	Horizon Industries Inc	404-629-7721	Calhoun, GA	350	200	3
2957	Huffy Corp	513-866-6251	Miamisburg, OH	350	300	3
2958	Instrument Systems Inc	516-938-5544	Jericho, NY	350	300	3
2959	Inter Regional Financial Corp	612-371-7750	Minneapolis, MN	350	3500	3
2960	JWP Corp	914-935-4000	Purchase, NY	350	250	3
2961	KDI Corp	513-272-1421	Cincinnati, OH	350	300	4
2962	Kerr Glass Manufacturing Corp	213-556-2200	Los Angeles, CA	350	200	3
2963	Laclede Steel Co	314-425-1400	St Louis, MO	350	200	3
2964	Landmark Communications Inc	804-446-2000	Norfolk, VA	350	300	4
2965	Lazare Kaplan International Inc	212-972-9700	New York, NY	350	100	2
2966	Lennar Corp	305-559-4000	Miami, FL	350	150	1
2967	Mitchell Hutchins Asset Management Inc	212-713-4000	New York, NY	350	13200	1
2968	Moog Inc	716-652-2000	Aurora, NY	350	250	3
2969	Morgan, J P Securities Inc	212-483-2323	New York, NY	350	3300	1
2970	New Jersy Resources Inc	201-938-1480	Wall, NJ	350	700	2
2971	Nichols, S E Inc	212-206-9400	New York, NY	350	250	4
2972	Nordson Corp	216-892-1580	Westlake, OH	350	250	2
2973	North Carolina Retirement Fund	919-733-3211	Raleigh, NC	350	11000	1
2974	NUI Corp	201-685-3900	Bridgewater, NJ	350	250	2
2975	Old Stone Corp	401-278-2000	Providence, RI	350	4500	2
2976	Rochester Community Savings Bank	716-262-5800	Roschester, NY	350	4000	2
2977	RPM Corp	216-225-3192	Medina, OH	350	300	2
2978	Rymer Foods Inc	312-419-0060	Chicago, IL	350	250	3
2979	Scherer, R P Corp	313-649-0900	Troy, MI	350	300	5
2980	Schroder, IBJ Bank & Trust Co	212-858-2000	New York, NY	350	2500	2
2981	Shelter Insurance Co	314-445-8441	Columbia, MO	350	600	2
2982	SPS Technologies Inc	215-860-3000	Newtown, PA	350	250	3
2983	TAD Technical Services Inc	617-868-1650	Cambridge, MA	350	NA	3
2984	Teleflex Corp	215-948-5100	Limerick, PA	350	300	2
2985	Temple University	215-787-7000	Philadelphia, PA	350	376	36
2986	TriStar Pictures Inc	212-751-4400	New York, NY	350	750	2
2987	Tultex Corportation	703-632-2961	Martinsville, VA	350	300	8
2988	Valley Federal Savings Assn Inc	818-904-3000	Van Nuys, CA	350	3324	1
2989	Webb, Del E Corp	602-468-6800	Phoenix, AZ	350	300	4
2990	Yale University	203-436-0300	New Haven, CT	350	660	13
2991	Boise Cascade Canada Ltd	416-231-3010	Toronto, ON Can	350	425	2
2992	Reed Inc	416-862-5000	Toronto, ON Can	350	352	2
2993	Sotheby's Holdings Inc	212-606-7000	New York, NY	349	503	1
2994	West One Bank Corp	208-388-7791	Boise, ID	349	3538	3
2995	CSL Group Inc	514-288-0221	Montreal, PQ Can	349	207	5
2996	Honeywell Ltd	416-499-6111	Willowdale, ON Can	349	205	4
2997	Thomas Industries Inc	502-893-4600	Louisville, KY	348	208	3
2998	Community Psychiatric Centers Inc	415-397-6151	San Francisco, CA	347	478	4
2999	Brush Wellman Inc	216-443-1000	Cleveland, OH	346	358	3
3000	Keystone International Inc	713-466-1176	Houston, TX	346	340	3

Organizations Listed by Revenue

Rank	Organization	Phone	City / State or Province	Revenue ($ mil)	Assets ($ mil)	Emp (thous)
3001	Sealed Air Corp	201-791-7600	Saddle Brook, NJ	346	256	3
3002	Kollmorgen Corp	203-327-7222	Stamford, CT	345	224	4
3003	Washington Energy Co	206-622-6767	Seattle, WA	345	589	1
3004	Allen Group Inc	516-293-5500	Melville, NY	344	328	5
3005	Iowa Resources (Iowa Power & Light) Inc	515-281-2900	Des Moines, IA	344	1168	2
3006	MDU Resources Group Inc	701-222-7900	Bismarck, ND	344	977	2
3007	Caesars New Jersey	609-348-4411	Atlantic City, NJ	343	300	3
3008	Mohawk Oil Canada Ltd	604-299-7244	Burnaby, BC Can	343	132	2
3009	Manitoba Telephone System Ltd	204-947-4111	Winnipeg, MB Can	342	837	5
3010	Matsushita Electric of Canada Ltd	416-624-5010	Mississauga, ON Can	341	88	1
3011	DSC Communications Corp	214-519-3000	Plano, TX	340	429	3
3012	TGI Friday's Inc	214-450-5400	Dallas, TX	340	400	4
3013	Alberta Power Ltd	403-420-5035	Edmonton, AB Can	340	1275	2
3014	Atlantic Packaging Products Ltd	416-298-8101	Scarborough, ON Can	340	170	2
3015	Becker Milk Co	416-698-2591	Scarborough, ON Can	340	170	3
3016	BID Building Materials Canada	416-661-5950	Downsview, ON Can	340	170	4
3017	Bruncor Inc	506-694-6330	St John, NB Can	340	808	3
3018	Derlan Industries Inc	416-364-5852	Toronto, ON Can	340	213	5
3019	Doman Industries Ltd	604-748-3711	Duncan, BC Can	340	170	1
3020	Enfield Corp	416-445-7438	Toronto, ON Can	340	510	3
3021	Fednav Ltd	514-878-6500	Montreal, PQ Can	340	595	1
3022	General Chemical Canada Ltd	416-896-9595	Mississauga, ON Can	340	213	3
3023	IPSCO Inc	306-949-3530	Regina, SK Can	340	340	2
3024	Laurentian Bank of Canada	514-284-7967	Montreal, PQ CAN	340	3400	2
3025	Memotec Data Inc	514-738-4781	Montreal, PQ Can	340	765	2
3026	Nissho Iwai Canada Ltd	604-684-8351	Vancouver, BC Can	340	170	2
3027	Paperboard Industries	416-596-7180	Toronto, ON Can	340	255	3
3028	Tridel Enterprises Inc	416-661-9290	Downsview, ON Can	340	595	2
3029	Wimpey, George Canada Ltd	416-233-5811	Toronto, ON Can	340	213	1
3030	Anaheim, City of	714-999-5166	Anaheim, CA	339	NM	2
3031	Hall, Frank B & Co Inc	914-769-9200	Briarcliff Manor, NY	339	1237	4
3032	Fort Worth, City of	817-870-6117	Fort Worth, TX	338	NM	5
3033	House of Fabrics Inc	818-995-7000	Sherman Oaks, CA	338	200	3
3034	University of Virginia	804-924-0311	Charlottesville, VA	338	343	21
3035	KN Energy Inc	303-989-1740	Lakewood, CO	335	650	3
3036	Deere, John Capital Corp	702-786-5527	Reno, NV	334	2958	1
3037	Great Lakes Bancorp Inc	313-769-8300	Ann Arbor, MI	334	3638	1
3038	University of Kentucky	606-258-9000	Lexington, KY	334	326	24
3039	Van Dorn Co	216-361-5234	Cleveland, OH	334	250	2
3040	Anadarko Petroleum Corp	713-875-1101	Houston, TX	333	1490	1
3041	Harland, John H Co Inc	404-981-9460	Decatur, GA	333	295	6
3042	Overseas Shipholding Group Inc	212-869-1222	New York, NY	333	1318	2
3043	Pennbancorp Inc(Integra Financial)	814-644-8184	Pittsburgh, PA	333	3304	2
3044	Consumers Packaging Inc	416-232-3283	Etobicoke, ON Can	333	286	3
3045	Phoenix Continental Ltd	416-596-6100	Toronto, ON Can	333	604	1
3046	Purdue University	317-749-2108	West Lafayette, IN	332	537	37
3047	Downey Savings & Loan Assn Inc	714-549-8811	Costa Mesa, CA	331	4333	1
3048	Hawker Siddeley Canada Inc	416-362-2941	Toronto, ON Can	331	208	3
3049	Bexar County Government	512-220-2496	San Antonio, TX	330	NM	3
3050	Brigham Young University	801-378-4418	Provo, UT	330	396	29

Organizations Listed by Revenue

Rank	Organization	Phone	City / State or Province	Revenue ($ mil)	Assets ($ mil)	Emp (thous)
3051	Carroll McEntee & McGinley Inc	212-825-6780	New York, NY	330	3300	1
3052	Cowen & Co	212-495-6000	New York, NY	330	3300	1
3053	Daiwa Securities America Inc	212-945-0100	New York, NY	330	3300	1
3054	First Options of Chicago Inc	312-786-3000	Chicago, IL	330	3300	1
3055	Heritage Today Corp	704-542-6000	Charlotte, NC	330	NA	3
3056	Nikko Securities Co Intl Inc	212-416-5400	New York, NY	330	3300	1
3057	Nomura Securities International Inc	212-208-9300	New York, NY	330	3300	1
3058	Pitt Des Moines Inc	412-331-3000	Pittsburgh, PA	330	250	3
3059	Prairie Farms Dairy Inc	217-854-2547	Carlinville, IL	330	NA	1
3060	Spalding & Evenflow Corp	813-887-5200	Tampa, FL	330	NA	3
3061	St John's University	516-990-6161	Jamaica, NY	330	330	21
3062	Wertheim Schroder & Co Inc	212-492-6000	New York, NY	330	3300	1
3063	Fairfield Communities Inc	501-664-6000	Little Rock, AR	329	644	2
3064	Pittsburgh, City of	412-255-2626	Pittsburgh, PA	329	NM	6
3065	Assurance vie Desjardins Ltd	418-835-2323	Levis, PQ Can	329	1057	1
3066	McDonnell Douglas Canada Ltd	416-677-4341	Mississauga, ON Can	329	238	5
3067	Angelica Corp	314-991-2934	St Louis, MO	328	NA	3
3068	Coca Cola Consolidated	704-551-4400	Charlotte, NC	328	150	2
3069	CPI Inc	314-231-1575	St Louis, MO	328	250	5
3070	Tucson, City of	602-791-4201	Tucson, AZ	327	NM	4
3071	British Columbia, The University of	604-228-2211	Vancouver, BC Can	327	NM	28
3072	Maritime Telephone & Telegraph Ltd	902-421-4311	Halifax, NS Can	327	785	4
3073	Quebec, Universite du	418-657-3551	Sainte Foy, PQ Can	327	NM	31
3074	International Forest Products (Whonnock)	604-681-3221	Vancouver, BC Can	326	261	2
3075	CTS Corp	219-293-7511	Elkhart, IN	325	300	2
3076	New Process Corp	814-723-3600	Warren, PA	325	200	1
3077	Stone & Webster Inc	212-290-7500	New York, NY	324	565	4
3078	Wolverine World Wide Inc	616-866-5500	Rockland, MI	324	184	5
3079	Canpotex Ltd	306-931-2200	Saskatoon, SK Can	324	73	1
3080	State Farm Group Ltd Canada	416-321-4000	Scarborough, ON Can	324	559	1
3081	Atmos Energy Corp	214-934-9227	Dallas, TX	323	600	2
3082	Dallas Corp	214-233-6611	Dallas, TX	323	NA	2
3083	Northeast Bancorportion	203-773-0500	New Haven, CT	323	3394	3
3084	Transcon Inc	714-385-1591	Orange, CA	322	114	4
3085	Augat Inc	617-543-4300	Mansfield, MA	321	278	4
3086	National Community Bank	201-845-1000	Maywood, NJ	321	3614	2
3087	Allstate Insurance Co Canada	416-477-6900	Markham, ON Can	320	565	2
3088	First Citizens Bank & Trust Co	919-755-7215	Raleigh, NC	319	3218	3
3089	Pharma Plus Drugmarts Ltd	416-483-4611	Toronto, ON Can	319	110	2
3090	AMC Entertainment Inc	816-221-4000	Kansas City, MO	318	300	6
3091	St John Health Corp	313-343-4000	Detroit, MI	318	NA	3
3092	Gainers Ltd	403-471-0611	Edmonton, AB Can	318	170	2
3093	Iowa State University	515-294-4111	Ames, IA	316	332	30
3094	Indiana University	812-332-0211	Bloomington, IN	315	572	34
3095	Vicorp Restaurants Corp	303-296-2121	Denver, CO	315	250	13
3096	Groupe Pharmaceutique Focus Inc	514-254-4937	Montreal, PQ Can	315	95	1
3097	National Health Laboratories Inc	619-454-3314	La Jolla, CA	314	315	3
3098	Neoax Inc	203-322-8333	Stamford, CT	314	250	2
3099	Birks, Henry & Sons Ltd	613-236-3641	Ottawa, ON Can	314	234	5
3100	Teleglobe Canada Ltd	514-289-7272	Montreal, PQ Can	314	769	2

Organizations Listed by Revenue

Rank	Organization	Phone	City / State or Province	Revenue ($ mil)	Assets ($ mil)	Emp (thous)
3101	Newark, City of	201-733-6400	Newark, NJ	313	NM	5
3102	Wilmington Trust Corp	302-651-1000	Wilmington, DE	313	2982	2
3103	Farm & Home Savings Assn Inc	417-667-3333	Nevada, MO	312	3548	1
3104	Federal Reserve Bank of Minneapolis Inc	612-340-2345	Minneapolis, MN	312	5473	1
3105	Firestone Tire & Rubber Co	216-379-7000	Akron, OH	312	730	55
3106	FPI Fishery Products International Ltd	709-570-0000	St Johns, NF Can	312	263	9
3107	Sizzler Restaurants International Inc	213-827-2300	Los Angeles, CA	311	86	5
3108	Banister Continental Corp	403-462-9430	Edmonton, AB Can	311	213	1
3109	Portland, City of	503-248-4120	Portland, OR	309	NM	4
3110	Tandon Corp	805-523-0340	Moorpark, CA	309	250	4
3111	Firestone Canada Inc	416-521-1111	Hamilton, ON Can	309	256	3
3112	University of Pittsburgh	412-624-4141	Pittsburgh, PA	308	422	33
3113	Ashton Tate Inc	213-329-8000	Torrance, CA	307	305	3
3114	Uniroyal Goodrich Canada Inc	519-749-8473	Kitchener, ON Can	307	206	3
3115	Bohemia Inc	503-342-6262	Eugene, OR	306	250	2
3116	Asamera Inc	403-269-5521	Calgary, AB Can	306	293	1
3117	Bolt Beranek & Newman Inc	617-873-2000	Cambridge, MA	305	264	3
3118	Standard Brands Paint Co	213-214-2411	Torrance, CA	304	243	4
3119	Olco Petroleum Group Ltd	514-353-6821	Montreal, PQ Can	304	91	1
3120	Rogers Communications Inc	416-864-2373	Toronto, ON Can	304	946	4
3121	University of Missouri	314-882-3387	Columbia, MO	303	249	25
3122	Travelers Co of Canada Ltd	416-586-3000	Toronto, ON Can	303	406	1
3123	Citizens Utilities Co	203-427-8953	Stamford, CT	302	1033	2
3124	West Texas Utilities Co	915-674-7000	Abilene, TX	302	737	2
3125	Campbell Soup Co Canada	416-251-1131	Toronto, ON Can	302	147	2
3126	Citizens Savings Assn Inc	305-577-0400	Miami, FL	301	2998	2
3127	Hovnanian Enterprises Inc	201-747-7800	Red Bank, NJ	301	318	2
3128	Mentor Graphics Corp	503-626-7000	Beaverton, OR	301	282	2
3129	Virginia Commonwealth University	804-257-0100	Richmond, VA	301	240	23
3130	Caterpillar of Canada Ltd	416-846-3222	Mississauga, ON Can	301	113	1
3131	Alliance Mutual Funds Inc	800-221-5672	New York, NY	300	11000	1
3132	Anacomp Inc	317-844-9666	Indianapolis, IN	300	250	2
3133	Andrew Corp	312-349-3300	Orland Park, IL	300	200	3
3134	Applied Magnetics Corp	805-967-8227	Goleta, CA	300	NA	3
3135	Arbor Drugs Inc	313-643-9420	Troy, MI	300	150	4
3136	Ashland Coal Inc	304-526-3333	Huntington, VA	300	250	2
3137	Astoria Federal Savings Assn Inc	718-545-4400	Long Island City, NY	300	3084	1
3138	Banta, George Corp	414-722-7777	Menasha, WI	300	200	3
3139	Blockbuster Entertainment Inc	214-341-7700	Dallas, TX	300	100	1
3140	Boston Companies Inc	800-225-5267	Boston, MA	300	11000	1
3141	Boston Consulting Group Inc	617-973-1200	Boston, MA	300	NA	3
3142	Brand Companies Inc	312-298-1200	Park Ridge, IL	300	150	1
3143	Brintec Systems Corp	203-456-8000	Willimantic, CT	300	300	4
3144	Copperweld Corp	412-263-3200	Pittsburgh, PA	300	NA	3
3145	Crawford & Co	404-256-0830	Atlanta, GA	300	200	5
3146	Dionex Corp	408-737-0700	Sunnyvale, CA	300	200	1
3147	Douglas & Lomason Co	313-478-7800	Framingham, MI	300	200	4
3148	Duriron Co	513-226-4000	Dayton, OH	300	200	3
3149	Fedders Corp	201-234-2100	Peapack, NJ	300	200	1
3150	First American Bank of Virginia Co	703-821-7777	McLean, VA	300	3200	2

Organizations Listed by Revenue

Rank	Organization	Phone	City / State or Province	Revenue ($ mil)	Assets ($ mil)	Emp (thous)
3151	First Commerce Corp	504-561-1371	New Orleans, LA	300	3000	2
3152	Fischer Francis Trees & Watts Inc	212-350-8000	New York, NY	300	11000	1
3153	Forest City Enterprises Inc	216-267-1200	Cleveland, OH	300	200	3
3154	Furr's/Bishop's Cafeterias Inc	806-792-7151	Lubbock, TX	300	200	10
3155	General Binding Corp	312-272-3700	Northbrook, IL	300	200	4
3156	Genicom Corp	703-949-1000	Waaynesboro, VA	300	150	4
3157	Guardian Savings (Texas) Assn Inc	713-784-4413	Houston, TX	300	3000	1
3158	Hancock Fabrics Inc	601-842-2834	Tupelo, MS	300	200	3
3159	Hay Group Inc	215-875-2300	Philadelphia, PA	300	NA	3
3160	Heck's Inc	304-755-8331	Nitro, WV	300	200	5
3161	Heekin Can Inc	513-489-3200	Cinncinnati, OH	300	200	2
3162	International Shipholding Corp	504-529-5461	New Orleans, LA	300	200	1
3163	International Union Operating Engineers	202-429-9100	Washington, DC	300	NM	375
3164	Johnson Worldwide Associates Inc	414-631-2000	Racine, WI	300	200	2
3165	Justin Industries Inc	817-336-5125	Fort Worth, TX	300	150	4
3166	Kearney, A T Inc	312-648-0111	Chicago, IL	300	NA	3
3167	Ketchum & Co	201-815-2800	Clark, NJ	300	150	1
3168	Legg Mason Inc	301-539-3400	Baltimore, MD	300	150	3
3169	Management Science America Inc	404-239-2000	Atlanta, GA	300	200	3
3170	Manufacturers & Traders Trust Co	716-842-4200	Buffalo, NY	300	3100	2
3171	Mediq Inc	609-665-9300	Pennsauken, NJ	300	200	5
3172	Mercer, William M Meidinger Inc	212-997-7171	New York, NY	300	NA	3
3173	Microamerica Inc	508-480-0780	West Marlboro, MA	300	150	1
3174	Miller Anderson & Sherrerd Inv Mgt Co	215-668-0850	Bala Cynwyd, PA	300	11000	1
3175	Missouri Kansas Texas Railroad Co	214-651-6706	Dallas, TX	300	500	3
3176	National Sanitary Supply Corp	213-532-4800	Los Angeles, CA	300	200	1
3177	Office Depot Inc	407-994-2131	Boca Raton, FL	300	150	3
3178	Peters, J M Co	714-833-9331	Newport Beach, CA	300	250	1
3179	Pioneer Standard Electric Inc	216-587-3600	Garfield Heights, OH	300	200	2
3180	Proudfoot, Alexander Inc	407-697-9600	West Palm Beach, FL	300	NA	3
3181	Rhode Island Hospital Trust Natl Bank	401-278-8000	Providence, RI	300	3061	2
3182	Salem Carpet Mills Corp	919-727-1200	Winston-Salem, NC	300	250	3
3183	San Antonio Savings Assn Inc	512-340-7272	San Antonio, TX	300	3000	1
3184	Sarofim, Fayez Investment Mgt Co	713-654-4484	Houston, TX	300	11000	1
3185	Sigma Aldrich Corp	314-771-5765	St Louis, MO	300	226	2
3186	Southeastern Michigan Gas Corp	313-987-7900	Port Huron, MI	300	500	1
3187	SRI International Inc	415-326-6200	Menlo Park, CA	300	NA	3
3188	Stepan Co	312-446-7500	Winnetka, IL	300	250	1
3189	Stephens Inc	501-374-4361	Little Rock, AR	300	2200	1
3190	Superior Industries International Inc	818-781-4973	Van Nuys, CA	300	150	2
3191	Tampa, City of	813-223-8251	Tampa, FL	300	NM	4
3192	Tarrant County Government	817-334-1441	Ft Worth, TX	300	NM	3
3193	Telecomm Plus International Inc	407-997-9999	Boca Raton, FL	300	NA	3
3194	United Industrial Corp	212-752-8787	New York, NY	300	300	4
3195	US Steel/Carnegie Pension Fund Inc	212-806-4500	New York, NY	300	11000	1
3196	US Surgical Corp	203-866-5050	Norwalk, CT	300	250	3
3197	VLSI Technology Inc	408-924-1810	San Jose, CA	300	150	2
3198	Wausau Paper Mills Co	715-845-5266	Wausau, WI	300	200	2
3199	Willcox & Gibbs Inc	212-869-1800	New York, NY	300	150	2
3200	Wolohan Lumber Corp	517-793-4532	Saginaw, MI	300	150	1

Organizations Listed by Revenue

Rank	Organization	Phone	City / State or Province	Revenue ($ mil)	Assets ($ mil)	Emp (thous)
3201	Worlds of Wonder Inc	415-659-4300	Fremont, CA	300	214	2
3202	Wynn's International Inc	714-992-2000	Fullerton, CA	300	250	2
3203	Zenith Insurance Co	818-990-9300	Encino, CA	300	600	2
3204	Reitman's Canada Ltd	514-384-1140	Montreal, PQ Can	300	149	5
3205	Gerber Scientific Co	203-644-1551	South Windsor, CT	299	245	2
3206	Merry Go Round Enterprises Inc	301-828-1000	Baltimore, MD	299	200	4
3207	Prudential Assurance Group Ltd Canada	519-433-1231	Kitchener, ON Can	299	521	1
3208	Baton Rouge, City of	504-389-3100	Baton Rouge, LA	298	NM	5
3209	Alberta Natural Gas Co	403-260-9911	Calgary, AB Can	298	340	2
3210	BASF Canada Inc	416-675-3611	Toronto, ON Can	298	128	1
3211	Bristol Meyers Canada Inc	416-362-4281	Toronto, ON Can	298	213	2
3212	British Columbia Railway Co	604-986-2012	Vancouver, BC Can	298	1190	3
3213	Celanese Canada Inc	514-871-5511	Montreal, PQ Can	298	219	2
3214	Co-op Atlantic Ltd	506-858-6000	Moncton, NB Can	298	85	1
3215	Computer Innovations Distribution Inc	416-793-9000	Mississauga, ON Can	298	170	1
3216	Consumers Co-op Refineries Ltd	306-244-3311	Saskatoon, SK Can	298	85	1
3217	Cyanamid Canada Inc	416-470-3600	Willowdale, ON Can	298	170	2
3218	Dominion Securities Inc	416-864-4000	Toronto, ON Can	298	255	2
3219	Eldorado Nuclear Ltd	613-238-5222	Ottawa, ON Can	298	765	1
3220	Groupe Videotron Ltee	514-281-1212	Montreal, PQ Can	298	213	1
3221	Harlequin Enterprises Ltd	416-445-5860	Don Mills, ON Can	298	NA	2
3222	Hewlett Packard Canada Ltd	416-678-9430	Mississauga, ON Can	298	298	1
3223	Hudson Bay Mining & Smelting Co	416-362-2192	Toronto, ON Can	298	255	2
3224	ITT Canada Ltd	416-863-9666	Toronto, ON Can	298	383	3
3225	Lake Ontario Cement Ltd	416-977-0611	Toronto, ON Can	298	255	1
3226	Marathon Realty Co	416-864-1960	Toronto, ON Can	298	1700	1
3227	Mercedes Benz Canada Inc	416-425-3550	Toronto, ON Can	298	128	1
3228	Motorola Canada Ltd	416-499-1441	Willowdale, ON Can	298	170	3
3229	Slater Industries Inc	416-529-5422	Toronto, ON Can	298	213	2
3230	Sunbuy Inc	514-335-0260	Montreal, PQ Can	298	85	1
3231	UAP Inc	514-256-5031	Montreal, PQ Can	298	170	2
3232	Volvo Canada Ltd	416-493-3700	North York, ON Can	298	170	1
3233	VS Services Ltd	416-255-1331	Toronto, ON Can	298	85	5
3234	Wajax Ltd	514-238-7291	Montreal, PQ Can	298	170	2
3235	Gearhart Industries Inc	817-293-1300	Fort Worth, TX	297	355	4
3236	St Paul, City of	612-298-4323	St Paul, MN	296	NM	3
3237	BIC Corp	203-783-2000	Milford, CT	295	243	2
3238	Showboat Inc	702-385-9123	Las Vegas, NV	295	250	3
3239	Wichita, City of	316-268-4331	Wichita, KS	292	NM	3
3240	Cansulex Ltd	604-688-1501	Vancouver, BC Can	292	170	1
3241	Fabri Centers of America Inc	216-464-2500	Beachwood, OH	291	200	3
3242	Coscan Development Corp	416-369-8200	Toronto, ON Can	291	656	1
3243	Dominion of Canada General Insurance Co	416-362-7231	Toronto, ON Can	291	491	1
3244	Southern Indiana Gas & Electric Co	812-424-6411	Evansville, IN	290	450	1
3245	Tiffany Corp	212-755-8000	New York, NY	290	250	1
3246	Lundrigans Group Ltd	709-637-1200	Corner Brook, NF Can	289	118	3
3247	Trimac Ltd	403-298-5100	Calgary, AB Can	288	NA	3
3248	Westar Group Ltd (BC Resources Invst)	604-687-2600	Vancouver, BC Can	288	401	4
3249	Marcade Group Inc	212-944-0877	New York, NY	287	200	2
3250	Chili's Inc	214-980-9917	Dallas, TX	285	200	10

Organizations Listed by Revenue

Rank	Organization	Phone	City / State or Province	Revenue ($ mil)	Assets ($ mil)	Emp (thous)
3251	University of Utah	801-581-7200	Salt Lake City, UT	285	310	29
3252	Basic American Medical Corp	317-783-5461	Indianapolis, IN	284	300	4
3253	Safeguard Scientific Corp	215-265-4000	King of Prussia, PA	284	250	1
3254	Harper Group Inc	415-978-0600	San Francisco, CA	283	250	2
3255	Syms Corp	201-902-9600	Secuacus, NJ	283	200	2
3256	Burlington Coat Factory Inc	609-387-7800	Burlington, NJ	282	NA	3
3257	Novell Inc	801-226-8202	Orem, UT	282	227	2
3258	United Investors Inc	205-325-4200	Birmingham, AL	282	8003	2
3259	BP Petroleum Canada Ltd	403-237-1234	Calgary, AB Can	282	747	2
3260	Newfoundland & Labrador Hydro Electric	709-737-1400	St Johns, NF Can	282	1857	1
3261	Enron Canada Ltd	403-298-2690	Calgary, AB Can	281	85	1
3262	Laval, Universite	418-656-2131	Quebec, PQ Can	281	NM	31
3263	Western Ontario, University of	519-679-2111	London, ON Can	281	NM	27
3264	Bernard, Chaus Inc	212-354-1280	New York, NY	280	150	3
3265	Citytrust Bank Corp	203-384-5212	Bridgeport, CT	280	2601	2
3266	King World Productions Inc	201-522-0100	Short Hills, NJ	280	117	2
3267	Miami, City of	305-579-6010	Miami, FL	279	NM	4
3268	New World Entertainment	213-444-8100	Los Angeles, CA	279	200	1
3269	University of Maryland	301-454-0100	College Park, MD	279	354	41
3270	Berrie, Russ & Co Inc	201-891-7500	Oakland, NJ	278	212	3
3271	Concurrent Computer Corp	201-946-8883	Holmdel, NJ	278	200	3
3272	Indiana University at Indianapolis	317-635-8661	Indianapolis, IN	278	290	26
3273	Bank Leumi Trust Co	212-382-4000	New York, NY	276	3140	3
3274	Piccadilly Cafeterias Inc	504-293-9440	Baton Rouge, LA	276	150	8
3275	Laurentian General Insurance Co	514-842-6212	Montreal, PQ Can	276	969	1
3276	Albany International Corp	518-445-2200	Menands, NY	275	NA	3
3277	Albrecht, Fred W Grocery Co Inc	216-733-2861	Akron, OH	275	NA	3
3278	Allen & Co Inc	212-832-8000	New York, NY	275	2200	1
3279	American Cast Iron Pipe Inc	205-325-7701	Birmingham, AL	275	NA	2
3280	Arch Mineral Corp	314-231-1010	St Louis, MO	275	NA	2
3281	Audiovox Corp	516-231-7750	Hauppauge, NY	275	150	1
3282	Audits & Surveys Inc	212-627-9700	New York, NY	275	NA	4
3283	Avtex Fibers Inc	215-251-7700	Berwyn Park, PA	275	NA	3
3284	Baddaur Inc	901-365-8880	Memphis, TN	275	NA	2
3285	BDM International Inc	703-821-5000	McLean, VA	275	NA	4
3286	Black & Veatch Inc	913-339-2000	Kansas City, MO	275	NA	3
3287	Brooks Fashion Stores Inc	212-714-8600	New York, NY	275	NA	2
3288	Cajun Electric Power Cooperative Inc	504-291-3060	Baton Rouge, LA	275	NA	1
3289	Computer Factory Inc	914-347-5000	Elmsford, NY	275	NA	3
3290	Deutsche Bank Capital Corp	212-612-0600	New York, NY	275	3300	1
3291	Doskocil Companies Inc	316-663-1000	Hutchinson, KS	275	250	1
3292	Electric Power Research Institute Inc	415-855-2000	Palo Alto, CA	275	NA	2
3293	Fidelity Brokerage Services Inc	617-570-7000	Boston, MA	275	2200	1
3294	Galaxy Carpet Mills Inc	312-593-0555	Elk Grove Village, IL	275	150	3
3295	Glickenhaus & Co	212-953-7800	New York, NY	275	2200	1
3296	Gruntal & Co Inc	212-267-8800	New York, NY	275	2200	1
3297	HBE Corp	314-567-9000	St Louis, MO	275	NA	2
3298	Health Tex Inc	203-661-2000	Greenwich, CT	275	NA	3
3299	Hyplains Dressed Beef Inc	316-227-7135	Dodge City, KS	275	NA	1
3300	K & E Holding Inc	212-880-2000	New York, NY	275	NA	3

Organizations Listed by Revenue

Rank	Organization	Phone	City / State or Province	Revenue ($ mil)	Assets ($ mil)	Emp (thous)
3301	Leaf Inc	312-940-7500	Bannockburn, IL	275	NA	3
3302	Michigan Livestock Co Inc	517-337-2856	East Lansing, MI	275	NA	1
3303	MTD Products Inc	216-225-2600	Valley City, OH	275	NA	3
3304	Pannill Knitting Co	703-638-8841	Martinsville, VA	275	200	4
3305	Pantry Inc	919-774-6700	Sanford, NC	275	NA	2
3306	Prange, H C Co Inc	414-459-4800	Sheboygan, WI	275	NA	3
3307	Prescott Ball & Turben Inc	216-574-7300	Cleveland, OH	275	2200	1
3308	Recognition Equipment Inc	214-579-6000	Irving, TX	275	200	3
3309	Rinker Materials Corp	407-833-5555	West Palm Beach, FL	275	NA	3
3310	Schapiro, M A & Co	212-980-5353	New York, NY	275	2200	1
3311	Southern Peru Copper Co Inc	212-510-2000	New York, NY	275	NA	3
3312	Tech Data Corp	813-539-7429	Clearwater, FL	275	150	1
3313	Temple, Barker & Sloane Inc	617-861-7580	Lexington, MA	275	NA	3
3314	TIC United Corp	214-559-0580	Dallas, TX	275	NA	2
3315	Trailways Inc	214-744-6500	Dallas, TX	275	NA	3
3316	Trust Co of the West Inc	213-683-4000	Los Angeles, CA	275	11000	2
3317	Universal Coop Inc	612-854-0800	Minneapolis, MN	275	NA	1
3318	Vestron Inc	203-968-0000	Stamford, CT	275	200	1
3319	Watkins Johnson Co	415-493-4141	Palo Alto, CA	275	250	3
3320	World Carpets Inc	404-278-8000	Dalton, GA	275	NA	2
3321	Wyse Technology Inc	408-433-1000	San Jose, CA	275	200	2
3322	Dresser Canada Inc	416-826-8411	Mississauga, ON Can	275	196	2
3323	Altus Bank	205-473-0500	Mobile, AL	274	2774	2
3324	Interstate Power Co	319-582-5421	Dubuque, IA	274	540	2
3325	Wyman Gordon Co	508-756-5111	Worcester, MA	272	352	3
3326	AVX Corp	516-829-8500	Great Neck, NY	271	200	2
3327	Big B Inc	205-424-3421	Bessemer, AL	271	150	2
3328	Maxtor Corp	408-942-1700	San Jose, CA	271	277	3
3329	National Life Assurance Co of Canada	416-598-2122	Toronto, ON Can	271	917	1
3330	Premetalco Inc	416-366-3954	Toronto, ON Can	271	170	1
3331	Graphic Industries Inc	404-874-3327	Atlanta, GA	270	200	2
3332	LDI Corp	216-687-0100	Cleveland, OH	270	125	2
3333	Dreyfus Corp	212-715-6000	New York, NY	268	763	2
3334	Trans World Music Inc	518-452-1242	Albany, NY	268	225	3
3335	Greenman Brothers Inc	516-293-5300	Farmingdale, NY	267	150	2
3336	Jannock Ltd	416-364-8586	Toronto, ON Can	267	337	4
3337	Unicorp American Corp	212-972-6100	New York, NY	266	250	1
3338	University of Georgia	404-542-3030	Athens, GA	266	352	29
3339	Gilbert Associates Inc	215-775-2600	Reading, PA	265	200	4
3340	International Dairy Queen	612-830-0200	Bloomington, MN	265	150	5
3341	International Technology Corp	213-378-9933	Torrance, CA	265	300	2
3342	Measurex Corp	408-255-1500	Cupertino, CA	265	303	3
3343	National Patent Development Co	212-826-8500	New York, NY	265	300	1
3344	Stratus Computer Inc	617-460-2000	Marlborough, MA	265	200	2
3345	Wayne State University	313-577-2424	Detroit, MI	265	376	31
3346	Amcast Industrial Corp	513-298-5251	Dayton, OH	264	200	2
3347	Silicon Graphics Inc	415-960-1980	Mountain View, CA	264	175	1
3348	University of Massachusetts	413-545-0111	Amherst, MA	264	264	30
3349	General Homes Corp	713-270-4177	Houston, TX	263	438	2
3350	University of Miami	305-284-2211	Coral Gables, FL	263	260	21

Organizations Listed by Revenue

Rank	Organization	Phone	City / State or Province	Revenue ($ mil)	Assets ($ mil)	Emp (thous)
3351	Burns Fry Ltd	416-365-4000	Toronto, ON Can	263	1616	2
3352	Financial Trustco Capital Ltd	416-366-8990	Toronto, ON Can	263	1831	1
3353	Foster, L B Co	201-533-1100	Pittsburgh, PA	262	107	1
3354	Genetech Corp	415-952-1000	S San Francisco, CA	262	669	2
3355	Northwestern University	312-492-3741	Evanston, IL	262	361	21
3356	Brendle's Inc	919-835-3400	Elkin, NC	261	150	3
3357	United Cable Television Inc	303-779-5999	Denver, CO	261	697	2
3358	Laurentian Mutual Insurance Co	418-647-5255	Quebec, PQ Can	261	804	1
3359	ACCO World Corp	312-480-9700	Northbrook, IL	260	220	3
3360	Donaldson Co	612-887-3131	Minneapolis, MN	260	200	2
3361	Esterline Corp	206-453-6000	Bellevue, WA	260	190	2
3362	Russ Togs Inc	212-642-8500	New York, NY	260	150	3
3363	Wellman Corp	201-388-0120	Shrewsbury, NJ	260	200	2
3364	Pepsi Cola Canada Ltd	416-964-1313	Toronto, ON Can	259	211	2
3365	AMDURA Corp(American Hoist & Derrick)	612-293-4567	St Paul, MN	258	205	2
3366	Dell Computer Corp	512-338-4400	Austin, TX	258	150	2
3367	Kentucky Power Co	606-327-1111	Ashland, KY	258	600	1
3368	Wiley, John & Sons Inc	211-285-0600	New York, NY	258	20	2
3369	Boston University	617-353-2000	Boston, MA	257	211	31
3370	Connecticut Natural Gas Co	203-727-3000	Hartford, CT	255	300	7
3371	TIE Communications Inc	203-926-2000	Shelton, CT	255	254	3
3372	Barbecon Inc	416-488-3344	Toronto, ON Can	255	128	1
3373	Brunswick Mining & Smelting Corp	506-522-2100	Toronto, ON Can	255	340	3
3374	Canadian Marconi Co	514-341-7630	Montreal, PQ Can	255	170	2
3375	Canadian Western Natural Gas Co	403-245-7110	Calgary, AB Can	255	340	1
3376	Carlson Marketing Group Ltd	416-236-1991	Toronto, ON Can	255	85	1
3377	Century 21 Canada Ltd	604-273-2721	Richmond, BC Can	255	NA	6
3378	Commonwealth Holiday Inns Ltd	416-675-2030	Rexdale, ON Can	255	255	10
3379	Gordon Capital Corp	416-364-9393	Toronto, ON Can	255	170	1
3380	Inland Natural Gas Co	604-684-0484	Vancouver, BC Can	255	383	1
3381	Purdel Cooperative Agro Alimentaire	418-736-4363	Bic, PQ Can	255	85	2
3382	Sara Lee Corp of Canada	416-860-0048	Toronto, ON Can	255	213	3
3383	Wood Gundy Inc	416-869-8100	Toronto, ON Can	255	213	2
3384	Luby's Cafeterias Inc	512-654-9000	San Antonio, TX	254	185	5
3385	Georgetown University	202-625-0100	Washington, DC	253	255	16
3386	Oakwood Hospital Corp	313-593-7000	Detroit, MI	253	NA	3
3387	Oshkosh B'Gosh Inc	414-231-8800	Oshkosh, WI	253	139	3
3388	Lee Enterprises Inc	319-383-2202	Davenport, IA	252	308	3
3389	Investors Group Inc	204-943-0361	Winnipeg, MB Can	252	1604	1
3390	Ampco Pittsburgh Corp	412-456-4400	Pittsburgh, PA	251	295	3
3391	CB & T Bancshares Inc	404-649-2387	Columbus, GA	251	1957	2
3392	Chris-Craft Industries Inc	212-421-0200	New York, NY	251	909	1
3393	AL Laboratories Inc	201-947-7774	Fort Lee, NJ	250	200	1
3394	Aaron Rents Inc	404-231-0011	Atlanta, GA	250	250	2
3395	Addington Resources Inc	606-928-3433	Ashland, KY	250	289	2
3396	Akron, City of	216-375-2345	Akron, OH	250	NM	3
3397	Allegheny & Western Energy	304-343-4327	Charleston, WV	250	250	1
3398	Amalgamated Clothing & Textile Workers	212-242-0700	New York, NY	250	NM	350
3399	American Fed of Musicians of US & Canada	212-867-1330	New York, NY	250	NM	250
3400	American Federation of Government Emp	202-737-8700	Washington, DC	250	NM	250

Organizations Listed by Revenue

Rank	Organization	Phone	City / State or Province	Revenue ($ mil)	Assets ($ mil)	Emp (thous)
3401	American Management Corp	703-841-6000	Arlington, VA	250	150	3
3402	American Postal Workers Union	202-842-4200	Washington, DC	250	NM	350
3403	Anthem Electronics Inc	408-295-4200	San Jose, CA	250	200	3
3404	Anthony Industries Inc	213-724-2800	Los Angeles, CA	250	NA	2
3405	Arlington, City of	817-459-6121	Arlington, TX	250	NM	3
3406	Associated Actors & Artistes of America	212-869-0358	New York, NY	250	NM	220
3407	Astec Industries Inc	615-867-4210	Chattanooga, TN	250	150	2
3408	Baker, J Inc	617-364-3000	Boston, MA	250	200	3
3409	Braniff Airline Corp	214-358-6011	Dallas, TX	250	100	2
3410	Cato Corp	704-554-8510	Charlotte, NC	250	150	22
3411	Century Telephone Enterprises Inc	318-388-9000	Monroe, LA	250	400	3
3412	Charlotte, City of	704-336-2244	Charlotte, NC	250	NM	4
3413	Chemical Leaman Corp	215-363-4200	Exton, PA	250	150	2
3414	Cobe Laboratories Inc	303-232-6800	Denver, CO	250	200	2
3415	Commodore International	215-431-9100	West Chester, PA	250	200	3
3416	Corpus Christi, City of	512-880-3100	Corpus Christi, TX	250	NM	3
3417	Des Moines, City of	515-283-4944	Des Moines, IA	250	NM	2
3418	Diversified Industries Inc	314-862-8200	St Louis, MO	250	200	3
3419	Duplex Products Inc	815-895-2100	Sycamore, IL	250	200	2
3420	El Paso, City of	915-541-4766	El Paso, TX	250	NM	2
3421	Entertainment Marketing Inc	713-995-4433	Houston, TX	250	200	1
3422	Erie County Government	716-846-8500	Buffalo, NY	250	NM	2
3423	Excel Industries Inc	219-264-2131	Elkhart, IN	250	200	2
3424	FGIC Inc	212-607-3000	New York, NY	250	958	1
3425	First Capital Holding Corp	213-551-1000	Los Angeles, CA	250	750	1
3426	Flow General Inc	703-893-5915	McLean, VA	250	200	2
3427	Fluorocarbon Co	714-831-5350	South Laguna, CA	250	200	2
3428	Fraternal Order of Police	502-452-2828	Louisville, KY	250	NM	200
3429	Fresno, City of	209-488-1561	Fresno, CA	250	NM	2
3430	Gleason Corp	716-272-6000	Rochester, NY	250	300	3
3431	Grand Rapids, City of	616-456-3160	Grand Rapids, MI	250	NM	2
3432	Grant Thornton Inc	312-856-0001	Chicago, IL	250	NA	3
3433	Graphic Communications Intl Union	202-461-1400	Washington, DC	250	NM	200
3434	Greenwood Mills Corp	803-229-2571	Greenwood, SC	250	NA	3
3435	Grubb & Ellis Co	415-956-1990	San Francisco, CA	250	300	3
3436	Hotel & Restrauant Employees Intl Union	202-393-4373	Washington, DC	250	NM	330
3437	Howell Corp	713-658-4000	Houston, TX	250	300	1
3438	Ideal Basic Industries Corp	303-623-5661	Denver, CO	250	250	2
3439	Idex Corp	312-498-7070	Northbrook, IL	250	200	3
3440	IE Industries Inc	319-398-4411	Cedar Rapids, IA	250	640	2
3441	Imperial Holly Corp	713-491-9181	Sugar Land, TX	250	200	2
3442	Indiana Energy Inc	317-926-3351	Indianapolis, IN	250	600	2
3443	International Aluminum Co	213-264-1670	Monterey Park, CA	250	150	2
3444	International Telecharge Corp	214-744-0240	Dallas, TX	250	200	3
3445	International Union Electronic & Elec	202-296-1200	Washington, DC	250	NM	200
3446	ISS International Service Corp	212-382-9800	New York, NY	250	150	4
3447	Jackson, City of	601-630-1776	Jackson, MS	250	NM	2
3448	Keystone Consolidated Industries Inc	214-458-0028	Dallas, TX	250	200	2
3449	Laborers' Intl Union of North America	202-737-8320	Washington, DC	250	NM	450
3450	Lamar Life Insurance Corp	601-949-3100	Jackson, MI	250	1200	1

Organizations Listed by Revenue

Rank	Organization	Phone	City / State or Province	Revenue ($ mil)	Assets ($ mil)	Emp (thous)
3451	Las Vegas, City of	702-386-6241	Las Vegas, NV	250	NM	3
3452	Lexington, City of	606-258-3110	Lexington, KY	250	NM	2
3453	Louisville, City of	502-587-3061	Louisville, KY	250	NM	5
3454	LSB Industries Inc	405-235-4546	Oklahoma City, OK	250	200	2
3455	Luria, L & Son Inc	305-557-9000	Hialeah, FL	250	100	2
3456	Madison Gas & Electric Co	608-252-7000	Madison, WI	250	300	1
3457	MEI Diversified Inc	612-339-8853	Minneapolis, MN	250	150	1
3458	Mesa, City of	602-834-2388	Mesa, AZ	250	NM	3
3459	Michaels Stores Inc	214-580-8242	Irving, TX	250	200	3
3460	Middlesex County Government	617-494-4000	East Cambridge, MA	250	NM	1
3461	MMR Holding Corp	504-293-2701	Baton Rouge, LA	250	200	4
3462	Mobile, City of	205-438-7395	Mobile, AL	250	NM	2
3463	Moore Medical Corp	203-225-2225	New Britain, CT	250	150	1
3464	National Assn of Letter Carriers	202-393-4695	Washington, DC	250	NM	300
3465	National Computer Systems Inc	612-829-3000	Hopkins, MN	250	150	3
3466	Newmark & Lewis Inc	516-681-6900	Hicksville, NY	250	150	3
3467	Niagara Share Corp	716-856-2600	Buffalo, NY	250	200	1
3468	O'Sullivan Corp	703-667-6666	Winchester, VA	250	175	2
3469	OECD European Common Market	202-785-6323	Washington, DC	250	NM	1
3470	Omaha, City of	402-444-5000	Omaha, NE	250	NM	2
3471	Oregon Steel Mills Inc	503-286-9651	Portland, OR	250	150	1
3472	Pacificare Health Systems Inc	714-952-1121	Cypress, CA	250	200	1
3473	Pansophic Systems Inc	312-572-6000	Oak Brook, IL	250	174	2
3474	Paradyne Corp	813-530-2000	Largo, FL	250	200	3
3475	Pratt & Lambert Inc	716-873-6000	Buffalo, NY	250	200	2
3476	Pratt Hotel Corp	214-386-9777	Dallas, TX	250	300	4
3477	Puritan Bennett Corp	913-661-0444	Overland Park, KS	250	100	2
3478	QMS Inc	205-633-4300	Mobile, AL	250	150	1
3479	Raleigh, City	919-890-3050	Raleigh, NC	250	NM	2
3480	Rent-a-Center Inc	316-689-4100	Wichita, KS	250	200	2
3481	Retail, Wholesale & Dept Store Union	212-684-5300	New York, NY	250	NM	200
3482	Richmond, City of	804-780-7977	Richmond, VA	250	NM	2
3483	Riverside, City of	714-782-5551	Riverside, CA	250	NM	2
3484	Rowan Corp	713-621-7800	Houston, TX	250	150	2
3485	Sacramento, City of	916-449-5407	Sacramento, CA	250	NM	3
3486	Salt Lake City, City of	801-535-7704	Salt Lake City, UT	250	NM	2
3487	Santa Ana, City of	714-647-6910	Santa Ana, CA	250	NM	3
3488	Securities & Exchange Commission	202-272-3100	Washington, DC	250	NM	2
3489	Shreveport, City of	318-226-6250	Shreveport, LA	250	NM	2
3490	Smith International Inc	713-443-3370	Houston, TX	250	200	2
3491	Southland Financial Corp	214-828-7011	Irving, TX	250	1500	1
3492	St Petersburg, City of	813-893-7117	St Petersburg, FL	250	NM	3
3493	Tasty Baking Co	215-221-8500	Philadelphia, PA	250	200	2
3494	Team Inc	713-331-6154	Alvin, TX	250	125	1
3495	Tejas Gas Corp	713-658-0509	Houston, TX	250	125	1
3496	Telephone & Data Corp	312-630-1900	Chicago, IL	250	200	3
3497	TMK United Corp	205-325-4200	Birmingham, AL	250	450	2
3498	Toledo, City of	419-245-1001	Toledo, OH	250	NM	2
3499	Tulsa, City of	918-596-7777	Tulsa, OK	250	NM	3
3500	UBS Securities Inc	212-230-4000	New York, NY	250	4400	1

Organizations Listed by Revenue

Rank	Organization	Phone	City / State or Province	Revenue ($ mil)	Assets ($ mil)	Emp (thous)
3501	United Assn of Plumbing & Pipe Fitting	202-628-5823	Washington, DC	250	NM	325
3502	United Mine Workers of America	202-842-7200	Washington, DC	250	NM	200
3503	United Paperworkers Intl Union	615-834-8590	Nashville, TN	250	NM	250
3504	Vishay Intertechnology Corp	919-365-3800	Malvern, PA	250	200	3
3505	Vitt Media International Inc	212-921-0500	New York, NY	250	NA	1
3506	Watts Industries Inc	508-688-1811	North Andover, MA	250	200	2
3507	Waxman Industries Inc	216-439-1830	Cleveland, OH	250	125	1
3508	West Co	215-935-4500	Phoenixville, PA	250	200	3
3509	Woodside Management Inc	617-426-7661	Boston, MA	250	NA	3
3510	XTRA Corp	617-367-5000	Boston, MA	250	300	2
3511	Hongkong Bank of Canada	604-685-1000	Vancouver, BC Can	250	3045	2
3512	Butler Paper Co	303-790-8343	Englewood, CO	250	NA	2
3513	Dayton Industries Inc	414-241-6200	Mequon, WI	250	NA	2
3514	Ethan Allen Inc	203-743-8000	Danbury, CT	250	NA	2
3515	McCann Erickson Worldwide	212-697-6000	New York, NY	250	NA	2
3516	Milton Bradley Co	413-525-6411	East Longmeadow, MA	250	NA	2
3517	Playskool Inc	401-727-5576	Pawtuckett, RI	250	NA	2
3518	Pima Savings Assn Inc	602-747-8484	Tuscon, AZ	248	3226	1
3519	Alberta Mortgage & Housing Corp	403-468-3535	Edmonton, AB Can	248	3346	1
3520	George Washington University	202-676-6000	Washington, DC	245	256	21
3521	New Plan Realty Inc	212-869-3000	New York, NY	245	300	1
3522	Princeton University	609-452-3000	Princeton, NJ	245	471	11
3523	Brown, Alex & Sons Inc	301-727-1700	Baltimore, MD	244	861	1
3524	General Datacomm Industries Inc	203-574-1118	Middlebury, CT	240	290	3
3525	Graco Inc	612-623-6000	Minneapolis, MN	240	200	2
3526	Slattery Group Inc	516-484-5858	Roslyn, NY	240	200	2
3527	Montgomery Ward Credit Corp	302-478-9240	Wilmington, DE	238	2519	1
3528	Birmingham, City of	205-254-2277	Birmingham, AL	237	NM	3
3529	Steego Corp	407-655-9700	West Palm Beach, FL	235	250	2
3530	Ryan's Family Steak Houses Inc	803-879-1000	Greer, SC	234	142	5
3531	Alberta, The University of	403-432-3111	Edmonton, AB Can	234	NM	29
3532	Calgary, The University of	403-220-5110	Calgary, AB Can	234	NM	21
3533	McGill University	514-398-4455	Montreal, PQ Can	234	NM	21
3534	Montreal, Universite de	514-343-6111	Montreal, PQ Can	234	NM	50
3535	Cross, A T Co	401-333-1200	Lincoln, RI	232	176	2
3536	XL/Datacomp Inc	312-323-1200	Hinsdale, IL	231	193	2
3537	DeKalb Corp	815-758-3461	DeKalb, IL	230	203	5
3538	State Univ of New York	716-831-2000	Buffalo, NY	230	846	29
3539	Hees Internationaal Corp	416-865-0430	Toronto, ON Can	230	3249	1
3540	Bairnco Corp	212-490-8722	New York, NY	228	297	2
3541	Digital Communications Inc	404-442-4000	Alpharetta, GA	228	252	2
3542	Agency Rent-A-Car Inc	216-349-1000	Solon, OH	227	351	3
3543	National Data Corp	404-329-8500	Atlanta, GA	227	150	3
3544	Lin Broadcasting Corp	212-765-1902	New York, NY	226	582	2
3545	Virginia Polytechnic Institute	703-961-6000	Blacksburg, VA	226	397	25
3546	Fluke, John Manufacturing Co	206-347-6100	Everett, WA	225	200	2
3547	Harman International Industries Inc	202-955-6130	Washington, DC	225	200	3
3548	IPCO Corp	914-682-4500	White Plains, NY	225	150	3
3549	Logicon Inc	213-373-0220	Torrance, CA	225	100	3
3550	McCaw Cellular	206-827-4500	Kirkland, WA	225	300	3

Organizations Listed by Revenue

Rank	Organization	Phone	City / State or Province	Revenue ($ mil)	Assets ($ mil)	Emp (thous)
3551	Sterling Electronics Corp	713-623-6600	Houston, TX	225	150	2
3552	Sun Electric Corp	815-459-7700	Crystal Lake, IL	225	250	3
3553	Transtechnology Corp	213-990-5920	Van Nuys, CA	225	200	3
3554	MBIA Insurance Co	914-681-1300	White Plains, NY	224	1283	2
3555	Nesbitt Thomson Inc	416-586-3600	Toronto, ON Can	223	1088	2
3556	Bateman Eichler Hill Richards Inc	213-683-3500	Los Angeles, CA	220	2200	1
3557	Blunt Ellis & Loewi Inc	414-347-3400	Milwaukee, WI	220	2200	1
3558	Bradford, J C & Co	615-748-9000	Nashville, TN	220	2200	1
3559	Dain Bosworth Inc	612-371-2711	Minneapolis, MN	220	2200	1
3560	Interstate Johnson Lane Corp	704-379-9000	Charlotte, NC	220	2200	1
3561	Janney Montgomery Scott Inc	215-665-6000	Philadelphia, PA	220	2200	1
3562	Jones, Edward D & Co	314-851-2000	St Louis, MO	220	2200	1
3563	Keefe, Bruyette & Woods Inc	212-323-8300	New York, NY	220	80	1
3564	Mabon, Nugent & Co	212-732-2820	New York, NY	220	2200	1
3565	Neuberger & Berman Inc	212-730-7370	New York, NY	220	4400	1
3566	Robinson Humphrey Co Inc	404-266-6000	Atlanta, GA	220	2200	1
3567	Warburg, S G Securities Inc	212-459-7000	New York, NY	220	2200	1
3568	Chips & Technologies Inc	408-434-0600	San Jose, CA	218	100	2
3569	New England Business Service	508-448-6111	Groton, MA	217	80	2
3570	Policy Management Systems Inc	803-735-4000	Blythewood, SC	217	301	2
3571	PS Group Inc	619-546-5001	San Diego, CA	216	692	1
3572	International Lease Finance Corp	213-658-7871	Beverly Hills, CA	213	1765	1
3573	Canada Trust Realtors Ltd	416-361-8657	Toronto, ON Can	213	NA	4
3574	Federal Business Development Bank Ltd	514-283-5904	Montreal, PQ Can	213	1530	1
3575	Rolls Royce Industries Canada Inc	514-747-7742	Ville St Laurent, PQ C	213	149	2
3576	ScotiaMcLeod Ltd	416-863-7411	Toronto, ON Can	213	170	2
3577	Thorne Ernst & Whinney Ltd	416-864-9520	Toronto, ON Can	213	NM	4
3578	Toronto Stock Exchange Ltd	416-947-4700	Toronto, ON Can	213	2125	1
3579	Washington State University	509-335-3564	Pullman, WA	212	821	21
3580	University of Houston	713-749-1011	Houston, TX	211	356	34
3581	General Refractories Co	215-667-7900	Bala Cynwyd, PA	210	250	1
3582	Minnetonka Corp	612-448-4181	Chaska, MN	210	180	1
3583	North Carolina State University	919-737-2011	Raleigh, NC	210	447	27
3584	SSQ Mutuelle d'Assurance Ltd	418-651-7000	Sainte Foy, PQ Can	210	490	1
3585	Western Co of North America	817-731-5100	Fort Worth, TX	209	534	2
3586	New York Life Insurance Co of Canada	416-960-4500	Toronto, ON Can	209	680	1
3587	Rollins Environmental Services Inc	302-429-2700	Wilmington, DE	206	214	2
3588	Advest Inc	203-525-1421	Hartford, CT	205	895	2
3589	Cintas Corp	513-489-4000	Cincinnati, OH	205	180	3
3590	Artra Group Inc	312-441-6650	Winnetka, IL	204	150	2
3591	University of Hawaii	808-948-8111	Honolulu, HI	204	361	23
3592	Sears Acceptance Co Canada Ltd	416-362-1711	Toronto, ON Can	204	1034	1
3593	Franklin Resources Group Inc	415-570-3000	San Mateo, CA	202	177	2
3594	Whittaker Corp	213-475-9411	Los Angeles, CA	201	391	2
3595	Alpha Industries Inc	617-935-5150	Woburn, MA	200	150	2
3596	Audio/Video Affiliates Inc	513-274-3737	Dayton, OH	200	150	2
3597	Baker Fentress & Co	312-236-9190	Chicago, IL	200	150	1
3598	Baldor Electric Co	501-646-4711	Fort Smith, AR	200	200	2
3599	Calgon Carbon	412-787-6700	Robinson Twnshp, PA	200	200	1
3600	Caremark Inc	714-851-2311	Newport Beach, CA	200	150	1

Organizations Listed by Revenue

Rank	Organization	Phone	City / State or Province	Revenue ($ mil)	Assets ($ mil)	Emp (thous)
3601	Charter Power Systems	215-828-9000	Plymouth Meeting, PA	200	250	2
3602	Chock-Full-O-Nuts Corp	212-532-0300	New York, NY	200	200	3
3603	Conner Peripherals Corp	408-433-3340	San Jose, CA	200	100	1
3604	Dress Barn Inc	203-327-4242	Stamford, CT	200	100	3
3605	Flextronics Inc	415-792-4177	Newark, CA	200	100	3
3606	JPM Industries Inc	312-598-1300	Bridgeview, IL	200	200	1
3607	Pauley Petroleum Inc	213-879-5000	Los Angeles, CA	200	250	1
3608	TCBY Enterprises Inc	501-225-0349	Little Rock, AR	200	150	1
3609	Telecom USA Inc	404-458-4927	Atlanta, GA	200	150	2
3610	Toll Brothers Corp	215-441-4400	Horsham, PA	200	256	2
3611	Arizona State University	602-965-9011	Tempe, AZ	196	318	45
3612	Southern Illinois University	618-453-2121	Carbondale, IL	196	146	25
3613	Hamilton Oil Corp	303-863-3000	Denver, CO	195	838	1
3614	Loyola University of Chicago	312-670-3000	Chicago, IL	194	189	16
3615	University of Louisville	502-588-5555	Louisville, KY	194	298	22
3616	University of Tennessee	615-974-2591	Knoxville, TN	194	661	26
3617	Zapata Corp	713-226-6000	Houston, TX	194	771	1
3618	Katy Industries Inc	312-697-8900	Elgin, IL	192	298	2
3619	Noble Affiliates Inc	405-223-4110	Ardmore, OK	192	527	2
3620	Southern Union Co	214-748-8511	Dallas, TX	191	370	1
3621	Clarkson Gordon Ltd	416-864-1234	Toronto, ON Can	191	NM	3
3622	Banks of Mid-America Inc	405-231-6000	Oklahoma City, OK	190	2269	2
3623	University of Colorado	303-492-0111	Boulder, CO	189	255	25
3624	Syracuse University	315-423-1870	Syracuse, NY	187	341	23
3625	McMaster University	416-525-9140	Hamilton, ON Can	187	NM	16
3626	Saskatchewan, University of	306-244-4343	Saskatoon, SK Can	187	NM	18
3627	Waterloo, University of	519-885-1211	Waterloo, ON Can	187	NM	27
3628	Coleco Industries Inc	203-725-6000	West Hartford, CT	185	NA	2
3629	Flightsafety International Inc	718-565-4100	Flushing, NY	183	451	2
3630	Oregon State University	503-754-0123	Corvallis, OR	180	238	21
3631	DCNY Discount Corp of New York Inc	212-248-8900	New York, NY	178	2386	1
3632	Imperial Bank Corp	213-417-5600	Los Angeles, CA	178	2428	2
3633	Neutrogena Corp	213-642-1150	Los Angeles, CA	178	93	1
3634	Piper Jaffray & Hopwood Inc	612-342-6000	Minneapolis, MN	176	392	1
3635	University of Connecticut	203-486-2337	Storrs, CT	176	325	26
3636	Athlone Industries Inc	201-887-9100	Parsippany, NJ	175	NA	2
3637	Golden Nugget Inc	702-385-7111	Las Vegas, NV	175	1038	2
3638	Oklahoma State University	405-624-5000	Stillwater, OK	172	207	24
3639	Auburn University	205-826-4000	Auburn University, AL	171	330	21
3640	San Diego State University	714-265-5200	San Diego, CA	171	145	39
3641	Coopers & Lybrand Ltd	416-869-1130	Toronto, ON Can	170	NM	3
3642	Deloitte Haskins & Sells Ltd	416-861-9700	Toronto, ON Can	170	NM	3
3643	Les Cooperants Ltd	514-287-6600	Montreal, PQ Can	170	680	1
3644	Levesque Beaubien Inc	514-879-2222	Montreal, PQ Can	170	85	1
3645	Merrill Lynch Canada Inc	416-586-6000	Toronto, ON Can	170	85	1
3646	National Real Estate Service Ltd	604-685-3474	Vancouver, BC Can	170	NA	4
3647	Price Waterhouse Ltd	416-863-1133	Toronto, ON Can	170	NM	2
3648	Touche Ross Ltd	416-599-5399	Toronto, ON Can	170	NM	3
3649	Acuson Corp	415-969-9112	Mountain View, CA	169	91	1
3650	University of Oklahoma	405-624-5000	Norman, OK	167	216	22

Organizations Listed by Revenue

Rank	Organization	Phone	City / State or Province	Revenue ($ mil)	Assets ($ mil)	Emp (thous)
3651	La Sauvegarde Assurance sur la vie Ltd	514-285-7700	Montreal, PQ Can	167	677	1
3652	ICN Pharmaceuticals Inc	714-545-0100	Costa Mesa, CA	166	465	2
3653	University of South Carolina	803-777-0411	Columbia, SC	166	521	23
3654	Miami Dade County Community College	305-596-1211	Miami, FL	165	165	44
3655	Russell, Frank Co	206-572-9500	Tacoma, WA	165	NA	1
3656	Armor All Products Corp	714-533-1003	Irvine, CA	163	150	1
3657	Helmerich & Payne Inc	918-742-5531	Tulsa, OK	160	576	1
3658	Park Communications Inc	607-272-9020	Ithaca, NY	160	267	2
3659	Applied Biosystems Inc	415-570-6667	Foster City, CA	158	151	1
3660	Tulane University	504-865-5000	New Orleans, LA	158	198	13
3661	Florida State University	904-644-2525	Tallahassee, FL	156	253	23
3662	Louisiana State University	504-388-1175	Baton Rouge, LA	153	349	31
3663	Florida East Coast Industries Inc	904-829-3421	St Augustine, FL	151	561	2
3664	University of Kansas	913-864-2700	Lawrence, KS	151	416	27
3665	Century Communications Inc	203-966-8746	New Canaan, CT	150	300	1
3666	Crown Crafts Inc	404-629-7941	Calhoun, GA	150	100	2
3667	Ducommun Inc	213-612-4200	Cypress, CA	150	100	3
3668	Northeastern University	617-437-2000	Boston, MA	147	139	40
3669	University of New Mexico	505-277-0111	Albuquerque, NM	144	245	27
3670	Coldwell Banker & Co	213-402-5022	Los Angeles, CA	144	NA	NA
3671	Texas Tech University	806-742-2011	Lubbock, TX	143	342	26
3672	Price, T Rowe Associates Inc	301-547-2308	Baltimore, MD	142	105	2
3673	Battle Mountain Corp	713-227-6330	Houston, TX	141	206	1
3674	Global Marine Inc	713-596-5100	Houston, TX	141	696	1
3675	Barclays Bank of Canada Ltd	416-862-0594	Toronto, ON Can	140	1872	1
3676	California State Univ Long Beach	213-498-4158	Long Beach, CA	139	271	36
3677	Cypress Semiconductor Inc	408-943-2600	San Jose, CA	139	245	2
3678	DST Systems Inc	816-221-5545	Kansas City, MO	139	184	1
3679	State Savings Bank Inc	614-460-6100	Columbus, OH	139	1520	1
3680	Northern Illinois University	815-753-1271	DeKalb, IL	136	229	27
3681	Green Tree Acceptance Corp	612-293-3400	St Paul, MN	134	645	2
3682	San Jose State University	408-277-2000	San Jose, CA	134	145	28
3683	Long Beach City College	213-420-4111	Long Beach, CA	132	132	26
3684	Network Systems Corp	612-424-4888	Minneapolis, MN	131	240	1
3685	University of South Florida	813-974-2011	Tampa, FL	130	187	31
3686	Information Resources Inc	312-726-1221	Chicago, IL	129	151	2
3687	Lyphomed Inc	312-390-6500	Rosemont, IL	128	286	1
3688	University of Wisconsin Milwaukee	414-963-4444	Milwaukee, WI	128	282	29
3689	Doane Raymond Associates Ltd	902-421-1734	Halifax, NS Can	128	NM	2
3690	Peat Marwick Main & Co	416-863-3300	Toronto, ON Can	128	NM	2
3691	Western Michigan University	606-383-1600	Kalamazoo, MI	127	187	23
3692	Safecard Services Inc	305-491-2111	Fort Lauderdale, FL	125	222	2
3693	California State Univ Northridge	213-885-1200	Northridge, CA	120	86	30
3694	EMP Employers Mutual Casualty Ins Co	515-280-2511	Des Moines, IA	118	298	1
3695	Autodesk Corp	415-332-2344	Sausalito, CA	117	170	2
3696	San Francisco State University	415-469-2141	San Francisco, CA	117	106	28
3697	Mobile Communications Corp	601-977-0888	Ridgeland, MS	115	344	2
3698	Kent State University	216-672-2121	Kent, OH	114	167	22
3699	KLA Instruments Corp	408-988-6100	Santa Clara, CA	113	135	1
3700	Illinois State University	309-438-2111	Normal, IL	112	270	24

Organizations Listed by Revenue

Rank	Organization	Phone	City / State or Province	Revenue ($ mil)	Assets ($ mil)	Emp (thous)
3701	California State Univ Fullerton	714-773-2011	Fullerton, CA	110	84	26
3702	California State Univ Sacramento	916-454-6011	Sacramento, CA	110	106	26
3703	Commonwealth Life Ins Co	502-587-7371	Louisville, KY	110	2890	2
3704	California State Univ Los Angeles	213-224-0111	Los Angeles, CA	108	132	23
3705	Primark Corp	703-790-7600	McLean, VA	108	259	1
3706	Freeport McMoran Gold Inc	504-582-4000	New Orleans, LA	106	169	1
3707	Ward Marlette Ltd	416-340-8390	Toronto, ON Can	106	NM	2
3708	Hecla Mining Co	208-769-4107	Coeur D'Alene, ID	105	189	1
3709	Forest Laboratories Inc	212-421-7850	New York, NY	101	194	1
3710	Utah Power & Light Co	801-535-2000	Salt Lake City, UT	100	3125	5
3711	American Capital Corp	713-993-0500	Houston, TX	99	71	1
3712	Mylan Laboratories Inc	412-232-0100	Pittsburgh, PA	96	109	1
3713	University of Akron	216-375-7111	Akron, OH	95	196	29
3714	University of North Texas	817-565-2000	Denton, TX	94	118	23
3715	Eastern Michigan University	313-487-1849	Ypsilanti, MI	91	128	22
3716	University of Texas at Arlington	817-273-2011	Arlington, TX	86	140	25
3717	Collins, Barrow, Maheu, Noiseux Ltd	403-298-1500	Calgary, AB Can	85	NM	1
3718	Loewen Ondaatje McCutcheon Inc	416-869-7211	Toronto, ON Can	85	85	1
3719	Alza Corp	415-494-5222	Palo Alto, CA	84	262	1
3720	National Westminster Bank of Canada Ltd	416-865-0170	Toronto, ON Can	82	1461	1
3721	Memphis State University	901-454-2234	Memphis, TN	81	125	23
3722	Georgia State Unversity	404-658-2000	Atlanta, GA	80	110	24
3723	University of Toledo	419-537-4242	Toledo, OH	79	121	23
3724	Amgen Corp	805-499-5725	Thousand Oaks, CA	78	207	1
3725	Value Line Inc	800-223-0818	New York, NY	75	96	1
3726	Colonial Group Inc	617-426-3750	Boston, MA	74	82	1
3727	First Union Real Estate Inc	216-781-4030	Cleveland, OH	74	439	1
3728	Houston Community College	713-868-0700	Houston, TX	72	110	28
3729	Southwest Texas State University	512-245-2111	San Marcos, TX	62	114	21
3730	Centocor Inc	215-296-4488	Malvern, PA	60	153	1
3731	Northern Virginia Community College	703-323-3381	Annadale, VA	59	119	36
3732	Oakland Community College	313-540-1500	Bloomfield Hills, MI	57	113	30
3733	Metro Mobile Communications Inc	212-319-7444	New York, NY	56	242	1
3734	Total System Services Corp	404-649-2204	Columbus, GA	56	45	1
3735	Cetus Corp	415-420-3300	Emeryville, CA	45	274	1
3736	Criterion Investment Management Inc	713-751-2400	Houston, TX	42	11586	1
3737	San Juan Basin Royalty Trust Inc	817-338-8607	Fort Worth, TX	34	5	1
3738	Genetics Institute Inc	617-876-1170	Cambridge, MA	30	197	1
3739	Strategic Planning Associates Inc	202-778-7000	Washington, DC	28	26	1
3740	Batterymarch Financial Management Inc	617-973-9300	Boston, MA	20	8600	1
3741	Tejon Ranch Corp	805-248-6774	Lebec, CA	14	42	1

Revenue information not available for 371 organizations.

Section 3

Organizations Listed Geographically

Organizations Listed Geographically

Revenue ($ mil)	Organization/ Industry	Address	City / Phone	State/ Zip	Province/ Postcode

State / Province: Alabama

Revenue	Organization/Industry	Address	City / Phone	State/Zip
531	Russell Corp / Apparel/Textiles	Lee Street / PO Box 272	Alexander City / 205-234-4251	AL 35010
271	Big B Inc / Retail/Merch	2600 Morgan Road SE	Bessemer / 205-424-3421	AL 35023
400	Birmingham Steel Corp / Steel	3000 Riverchase Galleria	Birmingham / 205-985-9290	AL 35201
500	Harbert Corp / Real Estate/Bldg	1 Riverchase Parkway	Birmingham / 205-987-5500	AL 35201
275	American Cast Iron Pipe Inc / Manufacturing	2930 16th Street N	Birmingham / 205-325-7701	AL 35202
541	Liberty National Life Insurance Co / Insurance	PO Box 2612	Birmingham / 205-325-2722	AL 35202
1400	Southern Natural Gas Co / Utility	1900 5th Avenue N	Birmingham / 205-325-7410	AL 35202
797	Amsouth Bancorp Inc / Banking	1900 Fifth Ave N / First Southern Bldg	Birmingham / 205-320-7151	AL 35203
237	Birmingham, City of / Local Govt	City Hall / 710 N 20th Street	Birmingham / 205-254-2277	AL 35203
350	Energen Corp / Energy	2101 Sixth Avenue N	Birmingham / 205-326-2700	AL 35203
1392	Sonat Inc / Utility	Southern National Bldg	Birmingham / 205-325-3800	AL 35203
NA	South Central Bell Telephone Co / Telecom	600 N 19th Street	Birmingham / 205-321-1000	AL 35203
627	SouthTrust Corp / Banking	420 N 20th Street	Birmingham / 205-254-5523	AL 35203
750	Drummond Coal Corp / Energy	530 Beacon Parkway	Birmingham / 205-945-6500	AL 35209
1053	Vulcan Materials Co / Manufacturing	One Metroplex Drive	Birmingham / 205-877-3000	AL 35209
1982	Bruno's Inc / Retail/Food	300 Research Parkway	Birmingham / 205-940-9400	AL 35211
401	Central Bancshares Inc / Banking	701 S 20th Street	Birmingham / 205-933-3000	AL 35233
250	TMK United Corp / Non-Bank Fin	3001 Third Avenue S	Birmingham / 205-325-4200	AL 35233
1670	Torchmark Corp / Non-Bank Fin	2001 Third Avenue S	Birmingham / 205-325-4200	AL 35233
282	United Investors Inc / Non-Bank Fin	2001 Third Avenue S	Birmingham / 205-325-4200	AL 35233
NA	BellSouth Services Inc / Telecom	3535 Colonade Parkway	Birmingham / 205-321-1000	AL 35243
500	McWane Corp / Manufacturing	23 Iverness Center Drive	Birmingham / 205-991-9888	AL 35243
NA	Alabama Power Co / Utility	600 N 18th Street	Birmingham / 205-250-1000	AL 35291
1100	Blue Cross Blue Shield of Alabama Inc / Insurance	450 Riverchase Parkway E	Birmingham / 205-988-2100	AL 35298
774	SCI Systems Inc / Comput/Off Equip	5000 Technology Drive	Huntsville / 205-882-4800	AL 35805
801	Intergraph Corp / Comput/Off Equip	One Madison Industrial Park	Huntsville / 205-772-2000	AL 35807
474	First Alabama Bancshares / Banking	PO Box 1448	Montgomery / 205-832-8490	AL 36102
588	Durr Fillauer Medical Inc / Instruments	218 Commerce Street / PO Box 951	Montgomery / 205-241-8800	AL 36104
1134	Blount Inc / Building Mat	4520 Executive Park Drive	Montgomery / 205-244-4000	AL 36116
936	Kinder Care Centers Inc / Business Service	2400 Presidents Drive	Montgomery / 205-277-5090	AL 36116
8068	Alabama, State of / State/Prov Govt	State Capitol	Montgomery / 205-261-2500	AL 36136

State / Province: Alabama

Organizations Listed Geographically

Revenue ($ mil)	Organization/ Industry	Address	City / Phone	State/ Zip	Province/ Postcode
800	Delchamps Inc Retail/Food	305 Delchamp Drive	Mobile 205-433-0431	AL 36602	
274	Altus Bank Savings & Loan	851 S Beltline Highway	Mobile 205-473-0500	AL 36606	
250	QMS Inc Comput/Off Equip	One Magnum Pass	Mobile 205-633-4300	AL 36618	
829	Morrison Inc Food/Lodging	4721 Morrison Drive	Mobile 205-344-3000	AL 36625	
250	Mobile, City of Local Govt	City Hall	Mobile 205-438-7395	AL 36633	
171	Auburn University University	Administrative Bldg	Auburn University 205-826-4000	AL 36849	

State / Province: Alaska

Revenue ($ mil)	Organization/ Industry	Address	City / Phone	State/ Zip	Province/ Postcode
790	Anchorage, City of Local Govt	City Hall	Anchorage 907-264-4431	AK 99519	
6726	Alaska, State of State/Prov Govt	State Capitol	Juneau 907-465-2111	AK 99811	

State / Province: Arizona

Revenue ($ mil)	Organization/ Industry	Address	City / Phone	State/ Zip	Province/ Postcode
800	Arizona Bank Corp Banking	101 N First Avenue	Phoenix 602-262-2000	AZ 85002	
1300	Maricopa County Government Local Govt	111 S Third Avenue	Phoenix 602-262-3518	AZ 85003	
782	Phoenix, City of Local Govt	City Hall 251 W Washington Street	Phoenix 602-262-7111	AZ 85003	
2320	Phelps Dodge Corp Metals/Mining	2600 N Central Avenue	Phoenix 602-234-8100	AZ 85004	
0	Pinnacle West Capital Utility	2828 N Central Avenue	Phoenix 602-222-6951	AZ 85004	
1100	Valley National Corp Banking	241 N Central Avenue	Phoenix 602-261-2900	AZ 85004	
2657	Circle K Corp Retail/Food	1601 N Seventh Street	Phoenix 602-253-9600	AZ 85006	
7324	Arizona, State of State/Prov Govt	State Capitol	Phoenix 602-255-4900	AZ 85007	
477	Ramada Inc Food/Lodging	3838 E Van Buren Street	Phoenix 602-273-4000	AZ 85008	
360	Talley Industries Inc Manufacturing	2702 N 44th Street	Phoenix 602-957-7711	AZ 85008	
500	Citibank Arizona Banking	3300 N Central Street	Phoenix 602-248-2200	AZ 85012	
400	Great American (AZ) First Savings Bank Savings & Loan	3200 N Central Avenue	Phoenix 602-279-3456	AZ 85012	
644	MeraBank Fed Savings Bank Inc Savings & Loan	3003 N Central Avenue	Phoenix 602-248-4221	AZ 85012	
1100	Best Western International Assn Inc Food/Lodging	6201 N 24th Parkway	Phoenix 602-957-4200	AZ 85016	
350	Webb, Del E Corp Real Estate/Bldg	2331 E Camelback	Phoenix 602-468-6800	AZ 85016	
498	Western Savings & Loan Assn Inc Savings & Loan	6001 N 24th Street	Phoenix 602-248-4600	AZ 85016	
743	America West Airlines Inc Airline	4000 E Sky Harbor Blvd	Phoenix 602-894-0800	AZ 85034	
750	Amerco (U-Haul) Inc Business Service	2727 N Central Avenue	Phoenix 602-263-6011	AZ 85036	
1442	Arizona Public Service Co Utility	411 N Central Avenue	Phoenix 602-250-1000	AZ 85072	
3305	Greyhound Corp Business Service	Greyhound Tower	Phoenix 602-248-4000	AZ 85077	
800	American Continental Corp Savings & Loan	2735 E Camelback Road	Phoenix 602-957-7170	AZ 85106	
250	Mesa, City of Local Govt	City Hall 55 N Center Street	Mesa 602-834-2388	AZ 85201	

Organizations Listed Geographically

Revenue ($ mil)	Organization/ Industry	Address	City / Phone	State/ Zip	Province/ Postcode
1100	Salt River Project Inc Utility	1521 Project Drive	Phoenix 602-236-5900	AZ 85251	
400	Krueger, W A Co Business Service	7301 E Helm Drive	Scottsdale 602-948-5650	AZ 85260	
NA	PCS Inc Comput/Off Equip	9501 E Shea Blvd	Scottsdale 602-391-4600	AZ 85260	
550	Bayless, A J Markets Inc Retail/Food	2720 S Hardy Drive # 4	Tempe 602-731-6800	AZ 85282	
400	Microage Inc Retail/Merch	2308 S 55th Street	Temple 602-968-3168	AZ 85282	
196	Arizona State University University	Administrative Bldg	Tempe 602-965-9011	AZ 85287	
500	Magma Copper Co Metals/Mining	Highway 76	San Manuel 602-385-3100	AZ 85631	
543	Tucson Electric Power Co Utility	220 W Sixth Street	Tucson 602-622-6661	AZ 85702	
500	Gates Learjet Corp Aerospace	1255 E Aero Park Blvd	Tucson 602-745-5100	AZ 85706	
550	Tucson Realty & Trust Inc Real Estate/Bldg	18990 E River Road	Tucson 602-577-7000	AZ 85718	
374	University of Arizona University	Administrative Bldg	Tucson 602-626-4824	AZ 85721	
327	Tucson, City of Local Govt	City Hall	Tucson 602-791-4201	AZ 85726	
248	Pima Savings Assn Inc Savings & Loan	5151 E Broadway	Tuscon 602-747-8484	AZ 85732	

State / Province: Arkansas

Revenue ($ mil)	Organization/ Industry	Address	City / Phone	State/ Zip	Province/ Postcode
NA	Deltic Farm & Lumber Co Paper/Forest Prd	200 Peach Street	El Dorado 501-878-5194	AR 71730	
1525	Murphy Oil Corp Energy	200 Peach Street	El Dorado 501-862-6411	AR 71730	
825	Riceland Foods Inc Food Processing	2120 Park Avenue	Stuttgart 501-673-5500	AR 72160	
4219	Arkansas, State of State/Prov Govt	State Capitol	Little Rock 501-371-3000	AR 72201	
2558	Dillard Department Stores Inc Retail/Merch	900 W Capitol Avenue	Little Rock 501-376-5200	AR 72201	
329	Fairfield Communities Inc Real Estate/Bldg	2800 Cantrell Road PO Box 3375	Little Rock 501-664-6000	AR 72202	
1357	Arkansas Power & Light Co Utility	First Commercial Bldg 425 W Capitol	Little Rock 501-371-4000	AR 72203	
300	Stephens Inc Securities	114 E Capitol Avenue PO Box 3507	Little Rock 501-374-4361	AR 72203	
200	TCBY Enterprises Inc Food/Lodging	113300 Rodney Parham	Little Rock 501-225-0349	AR 72212	
1100	Sanyo Manufacturing Corp Electronics	3333 Sanyo Road	Forest City 501-633-5030	AR 72335	
20649	Wal Mart Stores Inc Retail/Merch	702 SW Eighth Street	Bentonville 501-273-4000	AR 72716	
393	Hunt, J B Transportion Services Inc Transport	Highway 71 N	Lowell 501-659-8800	AR 72745	
450	Hudson Foods Inc Food Processing	13th Street & Hudson Road	Rogers 501-636-1100	AR 72756	
1936	Tyson Foods Inc Food Processing	2210 W Oaklawn	Springdale 501-756-4000	AR 72764	
750	Arkansas Best Corp Transport	1000 S 21st Street	Fort Smith 501-785-6000	AR 72901	
200	Baldor Electric Co Electronics	5711 S 7th Street	Fort Smith 501-646-4711	AR 72902	

State / Province: California

Revenue ($ mil)	Organization/ Industry	Address	City / Phone	State/ Zip	Province/ Postcode
802	Inter Exchange Auto Club of Southern Cal Insurance	2601 S Figueroa Street	Los Angeles 213-741-3111	CA 90007	

State / Province: California

Organizations Listed Geographically

Revenue ($ mil)	Organization/ Industry	Address	City / Phone	State/ Zip	Province/ Postcode
178	Imperial Bank Corp Banking	Century Blvd	Los Angeles 213-417-5600	CA 90009	
3315	Ahmanson, H F & Co (Home Savings of Am) Savings & Loan	3731 Wilshire Blvd	Los Angeles 213-487-4277	CA 90010	
1133	Farmers Group Insurance Inc Insurance	4680 Wilshire Blvd	Los Angeles 213-932-3200	CA 90010	
NA	Thrifty Corp Retail/Merch	3424 Wilshire Blvd	Los Angeles 213-251-6000	CA 90010	
1000	Winn Enterprises Inc Food Processing	231 E 23rd Street	Los Angeles 714-637-2730	CA 90011	
12100	Los Angeles County Government Local Govt	500 W Temple Street	Los Angeles 213-974-1411	CA 90012	
4254	Los Angeles, City of Local Govt	City Hall 200 N Spring Street	Los Angeles 213-485-3311	CA 90012	
600	Young's Markets Inc Retail/Food	500 S Central Avenue	Los Angeles 213-629-5571	CA 90013	
800	Tokai Bank Ltd Banking	534 W Sixth Street	Los Angeles 213-972-0200	CA 90014	
2073	Transamerica Life Insurance Co Insurance	1150 S Olive Street PO Box 54178 Terminal Annex	Los Angeles 213-742-3111	CA 90015	
1700	Transamerica Occidental Life Ins Co Insurance	Hill & Olive at 12th Street	Los Angeles 213-742-2111	CA 90015	
583	Bank of California (Mitsubishi Bank) Banking	800 Wilshire Blvd	Los Angeles 213-621-1200	CA 90017	
220	Bateman Eichler Hill Richards Inc Securities	700 S Flower Street	Los Angeles 213-683-3500	CA 90017	
1110	Coast Savings & Loan Assc Inc Savings & Loan	1000 Wilshire Blvd	Los Angeles 213-688-2000	CA 90017	
450	Nippon Credit Bank Ltd Banking	800 Wilshire Blvd 14th Floor	Los Angeles 213-629-5566	CA 90017	
NA	Pacific Energy Co Energy	6055 E Washington Blvd	Commerce 213-725-1139	CA 90017	
5932	Pacific Enterprises Corp Utility	801 S Grand Avenue	Los Angeles 213-895-5000	CA 90017	
NA	Pacific Interstate Co Energy	801 S Grand Avenue	Los Angeles 213-895-5223	CA 90017	
NA	Santa Fe Pacific Pipelines Inc Transport	888 S Figureroa	Los Angeles 213-614-1095	CA 90017	
5339	Southern California Gas Co Utility	810 S Flower Street	Los Angeles 213-689-2345	CA 90017	
10085	Unocal Corp Energy	1201 W Fifth Street	Los Angeles 213-977-7600	CA 90017	
1143	Rykoff Sexton Inc Retail/Food	761 Terminal Street	Los Angeles 213-622-4131	CA 90021	
519	Maxxam Inc Real Estate/Bldg	10880 Wilshire Blvd	Los Angeles 213-474-6264	CA 90024	
19417	Occidental Petroleum Corp Energy	10889 Wilshire Blvd	Los Angeles 213-879-1700	CA 90024	
1000	Pacific Holding Co Inc Food/Lodging	10900 Wilshire Suite 1600	Los Angeles 213-208-6055	CA 90024	
550	Peck, C L Contractors Inc Electronics	10866 Wilshire Blvd	Los Angeles 213-470-1885	CA 90024	
799	University of California Los Angeles University	405 Hilgard Avenue	Los Angeles 213-825-4321	CA 90024	
201	Whittaker Corp Manufacturing	10880 Wilshire Blvd	Los Angeles 213-475-9411	CA 90024	
903	Kaufman & Broad Inc Real Estate/Bldg	11601 Wilshire Blvd	Los Angeles 213-312-5000	CA 90025	
1000	Magnetek Inc Manufacturing	11111 Santa Monica Blvd	Los Angeles 213-473-6681	CA 90025	
3202	National Medical Enterprises Inc Health Care	11620 Wilshire Blvd	Los Angeles 213-479-5526	CA 90025	
279	New World Entertainment Leisure Time	1440 S Sepulveda Blvd	Los Angeles 213-444-8100	CA 90025	
108	California State Univ Los Angeles University	5151 State University Drive	Los Angeles 213-224-0111	CA 90032	

State / Province: California

Organizations Listed Geographically

Revenue ($ mil)	Organization/ Industry	Address	City / Phone	State/ Zip	Province/ Postcode
2816	California Federal S & L Assn Inc Savings & Loan	5670 Wilshire Blvd	Los Angeles 213-932-4321	CA 90036	
1000	Paramount Pictures Corp Leisure Time	5555 Melrose Avenue	Los Angeles 213-468-5000	CA 90038	
250	Anthony Industries Inc Leisure Time	4900 S Eastern Avenue	Los Angeles 213-724-2800	CA 90040	
2750	Certified Grocers of America Inc Retail/Food	2601 S Eastern Avenue	Los Angeles 213-726-2601	CA 90040	
NA	TRW Pressure Systems Inc Manufacturing	2017 Camfield Avenue	Los Angeles 213-685-4520	CA 90040	
550	Boys Market Inc Retail/Food	5531 Monte Vista	Los Angeles 213-258-8080	CA 90042	
NA	Hughes Aircraft Co Aerospace	PO Box 45006	Los Angeles 213-568-6321	CA 90045	
1839	Maxicare Health Plans Inc Health Care	5200 W Century Blvd	Los Angeles 213-568-9000	CA 90045	
178	Neutrogena Corp Personal Care	5755 W 96th Street	Los Angeles 213-642-1150	CA 90045	
750	Ticor Corp Insurance	6300 Wilshire Blvd	Los Angeles 213-852-6000	CA 90048	
450	Bell Industries Inc Electronics	11812 San Vicente Blvd	Los Angeles 213-826-6778	CA 90049	
NA	Los Angeles Times Inc Publishing/Com	Times Mirror Square	Los Angeles 213-237-3700	CA 90053	
3333	Times Mirror Co Publishing/Com	Times Mirror Square	Los Angeles 213-972-3700	CA 90053	
5932	First Interstate BanCorp Inc Banking	707 Wilshire Blvd	Los Angeles 213-614-6001	CA 90054	
300	National Sanitary Supply Corp Manufacturing	13217 S Figeroa Street	Los Angeles 213-532-4800	CA 90061	
750	American Protection Industries Inc Consumer Service	12223 W Olympic Blvd	Los Angeles 213-442-5700	CA 90064	
3049	First Executive Corp Non-Bank Fin	11444 W Olympic Blvd	Los Angeles 213-312-1000	CA 90064	
NA	Teledyne Controls Div Electronics	12333 W Olympic Blvd	West Los Angeles 213-820-4616	CA 90064	
661	Calmat Co Building Mat	3200 San Fernando Road	Los Angeles 213-258-2777	CA 90065	
1000	Hughes Markets Inc Retail/Food	2716 San Fernando	Los Angeles 213-227-8211	CA 90065	
1024	Collins Foods International Inc Food/Lodging	12655 W Jefferson Blvd	Los Angeles 213-827-2300	CA 90066	
450	LA Gear Inc Apparel/Textiles	4221 Redwood Avenue	Los Angeles 213-822-1995	CA 90066	
311	Sizzler Restaurants International Inc Food/Lodging	5400 Alla Road	Los Angeles 213-827-2300	CA 90066	
750	American Breco Inc Real Estate/Bldg	1875 Century Park E	Los Angeles 213-553-1009	CA 90067	
902	Caesars World Inc Leisure Time	1801 Century Park E Suite 2600	Los Angeles 213-552-2711	CA 90067	
450	Farwest Financial Corp Savings & Loan	1800 Avenue of the Stars	Los Angeles 213-277-3055	CA 90067	
250	First Capital Holding Corp Non-Bank Fin	1900 Avenue of the Stars	Los Angeles 213-551-1000	CA 90067	
350	Kerr Glass Manufacturing Corp Packaging	1840 Century Park E	Los Angeles 213-556-2200	CA 90067	
400	Leventhal, Kenneth Inc Accounting	2049 Century Park E	Los Angeles 213-277-0880	CA 90067	
5797	Northrop Corp Aerospace	1840 Century Park E	Los Angeles 213-553-6262	CA 90067	
200	Pauley Petroleum Inc Energy	10000 Santa Monica Blvd	Los Angeles 213-879-5000	CA 90067	
400	Summit Health Ltd Health Care	1800 Avenue of the Stars	Los Angeles 213-201-4000	CA 90067	
4598	Teledyne Inc Conglomerate	1901 Avenue of the Stars	Los Angeles 213-277-3311	CA 90067	

State / Province: California

Organizations Listed Geographically

Revenue ($ mil)	Organization/ Industry	Address	City / Phone	State/ Zip	Province/ Postcode
1300	Tiger International Inc Business Service	1888 Century Park E	Los Angeles 213-522-6300	CA 90067	
275	Trust Co of the West Inc Non-Bank Fin	400 S Hope Street	Los Angeles 213-683-4000	CA 90067	
18868	Atlantic Richfield Co Energy	515 S Flower Street	Los Angeles 213-486-3511	CA 90071	
550	Capital Group Inc Non-Bank Fin	333 S Hope Street	Los Angeles 213-486-9200	CA 90071	
2617	Carter Hawley Hale Stores Inc Retail/Merch	550 S Flower Street	Los Angeles 213-620-0150	CA 90071	
2469	Castle & Cooke Inc Food Processing	10900 Wilshire Blvd	Los Angeles 213-824-1500	CA 90071	
144	Coldwell Banker & Co Real Estate/Bldg	533 Fremont Avenue	Los Angeles 213-402-5022	CA 90071	
450	Long Term Credit Bank of Japan Ltd Banking	444 S Flower	Los Angeles 213-629-5777	CA 90071	
400	Mitsui Manufacturers Bank Banking	515 S Figueroa	Los Angeles 213-485-0331	CA 90071	
2000	Panasonic Matsushita Electric Corp Electronics	300 S Grand Avenue	Los Angeles 713-895-7200	CA 90071	
8546	Security Pacific Corp Banking	333 S Hope Street	Los Angeles 213-345-6211	CA 90071	
450	Taiyo Kobe Bank Ltd Banking	444 S Flower Street	Los Angeles 213-629-3939	CA 90071	
450	Toyo Trust Ltd Banking	444 S Flower	Los Angeles 213-624-2424	CA 90071	
381	University of Southern California University	University Park	Los Angeles 213-743-2311	CA 90089	
954	Hilton Hotels Corp Food/Lodging	9336 Civic Center Drive	Beverly Hills 213-278-4321	CA 90209	
3111	AMI American Medical International Inc Business Service	414 N Camden Drive	Beverly Hills 213-278-6200	CA 90210	
371	City National Corp Banking	400 N Roxbury Drive	Beverly Hills 213-550-5400	CA 90210	
1309	Gibraltar Savings (CA) Inc Savings & Loan	9111 Wilshire Blvd	Beverly Hills 213-278-8720	CA 90210	
4864	Litton Industries Inc Electronics	360 N Cresent Drive	Beverly Hills 213-859-5000	CA 90210	
675	MGM United Artists Communications Inc Leisure Time	450 N Roxbury Drive	Beverly Hills 213-281-4000	CA 90210	
1249	Columbia Savings (CA) Savings Assn Inc Savings & Loan	8840 Wilshire Blvd	Beverly Hills 213-657-6123	CA 90211	
750	First City Industries Inc Manufacturing	8383 Wilshire Blvd Suite 800	Beverly Hills 213-852-0499	CA 90211	
3665	Great Western Financial Corp Savings & Loan	8484 Wilshire Blvd	Beverly Hills 213-852-3411	CA 90211	
213	International Lease Finance Corp Business Service	8484 Wilshire Blvd	Beverly Hills 213-658-7871	CA 90211	
371	Pathe Communications Leisure Time	8670 Wilshire Blvd	Beverly Hills 213-658-2100	CA 90211	
351	Arden Group Inc Retail/Food	2020 S Central Avenue	Compton 213-638-2842	CA 90220	
1100	Hitachi Sales Corp of America Electronics	401 W Artesia Blvd	Compton 213-537-8383	CA 90220	
402	Pic N Save Corp Retail/Merch	2430 E Del Amo Blvd	Dominguez 213-537-9220	CA 90220	
1000	Thrifty Oil Co Retail/Merch	10000 Lakewood Blvd	Downey 213-923-9876	CA 90240	
1152	Computer Sciences Corp Comput/Off Equip	2100 E Grand Avenue	El Segundo 213-615-0311	CA 90245	
411	Wyle Laboratories Inc Comput/Off Equip	128 Maryland Street	El Segundo 213-322-1763	CA 90245	
4400	Nissan Motor Corp USA Automotive	18501 S Figueroa	Carson 212-532-3111	CA 90248	
990	Mattel Inc Leisure Time	5150 Rosecrans Avenue	Hawthorne 213-978-5150	CA 90250	

State / Province: California

Organizations Listed Geographically

Revenue ($ mil)	Organization/ Industry	Address	City / Phone	State/ Zip	Province/ Postcode
400	Jorgensen, Earle M Corp Manufacturing	10700 Alameda Street	Lynwood 213-567-1122	CA 90262	
550	World Oil Co Inc Energy	9302 S Garfield	South Gate 213-560-8801	CA 90280	
550	Softsel Computer Products Inc Comput/Off Equip	546 N Oak Street	Inglewood 213-412-1700	CA 90302	
2420	Executive Life Insurance Co Insurance	PO Box 6090	Inglewood 213-312-1000	CA 90312	
1000	A Mark Financial Corp Non-Bank Fin	100 Wilshire Blvd	Santa Monica 213-319-0200	CA 90401	
408	Fremont General Corp Insurance	1633 26th Street Suite 300	Santa Monica 213-483-0991	CA 90404	
2200	USA Petroleum Corp Retail/Merch	2701 Ocean Park Blvd	Santa Monica 213-452-6200	CA 90405	
4777	Wickes Companies Inc Retail/Merch	3340 Ocean Park Blvd	Santa Monica 213-452-0161	CA 90405	
500	Rand Corp Membership Org	1700 Main Street	Santa Monica 213-393-0411	CA 90406	
1142	Tosco Corp Energy	2401 Colorado Avenue	Santa Monica 213-207-6000	CA 90406	
307	Ashton Tate Inc Comput/Off Equip	20101 Hamilton Avenue	Torrance 213-329-8000	CA 90502	
1100	Fujitsu Inc Electronics	19600 S Vermont	Torrance 213-327-2151	CA 90502	
265	International Technology Corp Business Service	23456 Hawthorne Blvd	Torrance 213-378-9933	CA 90505	
225	Logicon Inc Comput/Off Equip	3701 Skypark Drive	Torrance 213-373-0220	CA 90505	
1100	Bridgestone Tire USA Inc Tire/Rubber	2000 W 190th Street	Torrance 213-320-6031	CA 90509	
304	Standard Brands Paint Co Building Mat	4300 W 190th Street	Torrance 213-214-2411	CA 90509	
8800	Toyota Motor Sales USA Automotive	19000 S Western Street	Torrance 213-618-4000	CA 90509	
1650	Isuzu Motors USA Inc Automotive	300 Pellesseir Place	Whitter 213-949-0611	CA 90601	
150	Ducommun Inc Manufacturing	10824 Hope Street	Cypress 213-612-4200	CA 90630	
250	Pacificare Health Systems Inc Health Care	5995 Plaza Drive	Cypress 714-952-1121	CA 90630	
NA	Alpha Beta Co Retail/Food	777 S Harbor Blvd	La Habra 714-738-2000	CA 90631	
1650	Denny's Inc Food/Lodging	16700 Valley View Avenue	La Mirada 714-739-8100	CA 90637	
825	Fedco Inc Retail/Merch	9300 Santa Fe Street	Santa Fe Springs 213-946-2511	CA 90670	
1100	TDC Development Corp Real Estate/Bldg	3100 E 29th Street	Long Beach 213-433-9931	CA 90801	
660	California State University System University	400 Golden Shore	Long Beach 213-590-5731	CA 90802	
623	Long Beach, City of Local Govt	City Hall 333 W Ocean Blvd	Long Beach 213-590-6707	CA 90802	
500	Star Kist Seafood Co Food Processing	180 E Ocean Blvd	Long Beach 213-590-3605	CA 90802	
550	Thums Long Beach Co Inc Energy	300 Oceangate	Long Beach 213-436-9211	CA 90802	
132	Long Beach City College University	4901 E Carson Street	Long Beach 213-420-4111	CA 90808	
139	California State Univ Long Beach University	1250 Bellflower Blvd	Long Beach 213-498-4158	CA 90840	
NA	Douglas Aircraft Co Aerospace	3855 Lakewood Blvd	Long Beach 213-593-5511	CA 90846	
2025	Beverly Enterprises Inc Business Service	99 S Oakland Avenue	Pasadena 818-793-2911	CA 91101	
1000	Golden State Foods Corp Food Processing	234 E Colorado	Pasadena 818-793-3135	CA 91101	

State / Province: California

Organizations Listed Geographically

Revenue ($ mil)	Organization/ Industry	Address	City / Phone	State/ Zip	Province/ Postcode
800	Jacobs Engineering Group Inc Real Estate/Bldg	251 S Lake Avenue	Pasadena 818-449-2171	CA 91101	
1582	Avery International Corp Manufacturing	150 N Orange Grove Blvd	Pasadena 818-304-2000	CA 91103	
1000	Parsons Corp Business Service	100 W Walnut Street	Pasadena 818-440-2000	CA 91124	
2562	Glendale Federal Savings & Loan Assn Savings & Loan	700 N Brand Blvd	Glendale 818-500-2000	CA 91203	
500	Sears Savings Bank Inc Savings & Loan	701 N Brand Blvd	Glendale 818-956-1800	CA 91203	
384	Citadel Holding Corp(Fidelity Fed Svng) Savings & Loan	600 N Brand Blvd	Glendale 213-956-7100	CA 91209	
353	Micropolis Corp Comput/Off Equip	21121 Nordhoff Street	Chatsworth 818-709-3300	CA 91311	
78	Amgen Corp Business Service	1900 Oak Terrace Lane	Thousand Oaks 805-499-5725	CA 91320	
352	Live Entertainment Inc Leisure Time	500 N Venture Park Road	Newberry Park 805-499-5827	CA 91320	
120	California State Univ Northridge University	1811 Nordhoff Street	Northridge 213-885-1200	CA 91330	
500	PMC Corp Manufacturing	12243 Branford Street	Sun Valley 818-896-1101	CA 91352	
NA	HR Textron Inc Non-Bank Fin	25200 W Rye Canyon Road	Valencia 805-259-4030	CA 91355	
NA	Jafra Cosmetics Inc Personal Care	2451 Townsgate	Westlake Village 805-496-1911	CA 91361	
400	Dataproducts Corp Comput/Off Equip	6200 Canoga Avenue	Woodland Hills 818-887-8000	CA 91365	
NA	Guidance & Control Systems Div Aerospace	5500 Canoga Avenue	Woodland Hills 818-715-4040	CA 91367	
622	Twentieth (20th) Century Industries Inc Non-Bank Fin	6301 Owensmouth	Woodland Hills 818-704-3700	CA 91367	
10590	Lockheed Corp Aerospace	4500 Park Granada Blvd	Calabasas 818-847-6121	CA 91399	
225	Transtechnology Corp Electronics	15233 Ventura Blvd	Van Nuys 213-990-5920	CA 91403	
350	Valley Federal Savings Assn Inc Savings & Loan	6842 Van Nuys Blvd	Van Nuys 818-904-3000	CA 91405	
550	Ask Mr Foster Travel Inc Business Service	7833 Haskell Avenue	Van Nuys 818-988-0181	CA 91406	
300	Superior Industries International Inc Automotive	7800 Woodley Avenue	Van Nuys 818-781-4973	CA 91406	
338	House of Fabrics Inc Retail/Merch	13400 Riverside Drive	Sherman Oaks 818-995-7000	CA 91423	
1100	Sunkist Growers Inc Food Processing	14130 Riverside Drive	Sherman Oaks 818-986-4800	CA 91423	
300	Zenith Insurance Co Insurance	15760 Venture Blvd	Encino 818-990-9300	CA 91436	
472	Zenith National Insurance Co Insurance	15760 Ventura Blvd	Encino 819-990-9300	CA 91436	
550	Treasure Chest Advertising Inc Publishing/Com	511 W Citrus Edge	Glendora 818-914-3981	CA 91470	
NA	Lockheed Aeronautical Systems Co Instruments	2555 N Hollywood Way	Burbank 818-847-6121	CA 91520	
NA	Buena Vista International Inc Leisure Time	350 S Buena Vista Street	Burbank 818-560-1000	CA 91521	
NA	Buena Vista Pictures Distribution Inc Leisure Time	350 S Buena Vista Street	Burbank 818-560-5000	CA 91521	
3438	Disney, Walt Co Leisure Time	500 Buena Vista Street	Burbank 818-840-1000	CA 91521	
NA	Warner Brothers Inc Publishing/Com	4000 Warner Blvd	Burbank 818-954-6000	CA 91522	
3024	MCA Inc Leisure Time	100 Universal City Plaza	Universal City 818-777-1000	CA 91608	
NA	MCA Records Inc Leisure Time	70 Universal City Plaza	Universal City 818-777-4302	CA 91608	

State / Province: California

Organizations Listed Geographically

Revenue ($ mil)	Organization/ Industry	Address	City / Phone	State/ Zip	Province/ Postcode
NA	Universal City Studios Inc Leisure Time	100 Universal City Studios Drive	Universal City 818-777-1000	CA	91608
400	Marshall Industries Inc Electronics	9674 Telstar Avenue	El Monte 818-459-5500	CA	91731
3300	Vons Companies Inc Retail/Food	10150 Lower Azusa	El Mone 818-579-1400	CA	91731
364	Ameron Inc Building Mat	4700 Romona Blvd	Monterey Park 213-268-4111	CA	91754
250	International Aluminum Co Building Mat	767 Monterey Pass Road	Monterey Park 213-264-1670	CA	91754
6253	SCECORP Southern California Edison Co Utility	2244 Walnut Grove Avenue	Rosemead 818-302-1297	CA	91770
500	Lewis Homes Corp Real Estate/Bldg	1156 N Mountain Avenue	Upland 714-985-0971	CA	91786
907	Rohr Industries Inc Aerospace	Foot of H Street	Chula Vista 619-691-4111	CA	92012
NA	Aerojet Inc Aerospace	10300 N Torrey Pines Road	La Jolla 619-455-8500	CA	92037
957	Fisher Scientific Group Inc Instruments	11255 N Torrey Pines Road	La Jolla 619-457-3565	CA	92037
314	National Health Laboratories Inc Health Care	7590 Fay Avenue	La Jolla 619-454-3314	CA	92037
750	Science Applications Intl Inc Consulting	1200 Prospect Street	La Jolla 619-454-3811	CA	92037
721	Intermark Inc Retail/Merch	1020 Prospect Street	La Jolla 619-459-3841	CA	92038
415	University of Cal San Diego University	Administrative Bldg	La Jolla 714-452-2230	CA	92092
1578	Home Federal Savings & Loan Assn Inc Savings & Loan	625 Broadway	San Diego 619-699-8000	CA	92101
2550	San Diego County Government Local Govt	1600 Pacific Highway	San Diego 619-531-5700	CA	92101
766	San Diego, City of Local Govt	City Hall 202 C Street	San Diego 619-236-6330	CA	92101
550	Pacific Scene Inc Real Estate/Bldg	3900 Harney	San Diego 619-299-5100	CA	92110
2076	San Diego Gas & Electric Co Utility	101 Ash Street	San Diego 619-696-2000	CA	92110
825	Foodmaker (Jack in the Box) Inc Food/Lodging	9330 Balboa Avenue	San Diego 619-571-2121	CA	92112
4162	Price Co Retail/Merch	2657 Ariane Drive	San Diego 619-581-4600	CA	92117
216	PS Group Inc Airline	4370 La Jolla Village Drive	San Diego 619-546-5001	CA	92122
350	Cubic Corp Electronics	9333 Balboa Avenue	San Diego 619-277-6780	CA	92123
NA	General Dynamics Space Systems Div Aerospace	5001 Kearny Villa Road	San Diego 619-573-8000	CA	92123
972	Imperial Savings Assn Inc Savings & Loan	9275 Sky Park Court	San Diego 619-292-3000	CA	92123
NA	Teledyne Ryan Electronics Div Electronics	8650 Balboa Avenue	San Diego 619-560-6400	CA	92123
171	San Diego State University University	Administrative Bldg	San Diego 714-265-5200	CA	92182
1601	Great American (CA) First Savings Bank Savings & Loan	600 B Street	San Diego 619-231-1885	CA	92183
1650	San Bernadino County Government Local Govt	385 N Arrowhead	San Bernadino 714-387-2020	CA	92415
250	Riverside, City of Local Govt	City Hall 3900 Main Street	Riverside 714-782-5551	CA	92522
1406	Fleetwood Enterprises Inc Leisure Time	3125 Myers Street	Riverside 714-351-3500	CA	92523
1100	Suzuki Motor Corp USA Inc Automotive	3251 E Imperial Highway	Brea 714-996-7040	CA	92621
300	Wynn's International Inc Automotive	2600 E Nutwood Avenue	Fullerton 714-992-2000	CA	92621

State / Province: California

Organizations Listed Geographically

Revenue ($ mil)	Organization/ Industry	Address	City / Phone	State/ Zip	Province/ Postcode
331	Downey Savings & Loan Assn Inc Savings & Loan	3200 Bristol Street	Costa Mesa 714-549-8811	CA 92626	
166	ICN Pharmaceuticals Inc Drugs	3300 Hyland Avenue	Costa Mesa 714-545-0100	CA 92626	
450	Standard Pacific Corp Real Estate/Bldg	1565 W MacArthur Blvd	Costa Mesa 714-546-1161	CA 92626	
110	California State Univ Fullerton University	800 N State College Blvd	Fullerton 714-773-2011	CA 92634	
800	Beckman Instruments Inc Comput/Off Equip	2500 Harbor Blvd	Fullerton 714-871-4848	CA 92635	
2200	Hyundai USA Inc Automotive	7373 Hunt Avenue	Garden Grove 714-890-6000	CA 92642	
NA	McDonnell Douglas Space Systems Co Aerospace	5301 Bolsa Avenue	Huntington Beach 714-896-3311	CA 92647	
500	ACI Holdings Inc Transport	1811 Quail Second	Newport Beach 714-752-8576	CA 92660	
500	American Restaurant Group Inc Food/Lodging	450 Newport Centre Drive	Newport Beach 714-721-8000	CA 92660	
200	Caremark Inc Retail/Merch	4340 Von Karman	Newport Beach 714-851-2311	CA 92660	
400	Far West Savings Assn Inc Savings & Loan	4001 MacArthur Blvd	Newport Beach 714-833-8383	CA 92660	
600	Irvine Corp Real Estate/Bldg	550 Newport Center	Newport Beach 714-720-2000	CA 92660	
500	Koll Co Inc Real Estate/Bldg	4343 Von Karment	Newport Beach 714-833-3030	CA 92660	
750	Lyon, William Co Inc Real Estate/Bldg	19 Corporated Plaza	Newport Beach 714-833-3600	CA 92660	
2540	Pacific Mutual Life Insurance Co Insurance	700 Newport Center Drive	Newport Beach 714-640-3011	CA 92660	
300	Peters, J M Co Real Estate/Bldg	1601 Dove Street	Newport Beach 714-833-9331	CA 92660	
1600	Baker International Corp Oil Service	500 City Parkway W	Orange 714-634-2333	CA 92668	
3486	Bergen Brunswig Corp Drugs	4000 Metropolitan Drive	Orange 714-385-4000	CA 92668	
322	Transcon Inc Transport	625 The City Drive S	Orange 714-385-1591	CA 92668	
250	Fluorocarbon Co Manufacturing	27611 La Paz Road	South Laguna 714-831-5350	CA 92677	
425	MAI Basic Four Inc Comput/Off Equip	14101 Myford Road	Tustin 714-731-5100	CA 92680	
NA	Mission Viejo Realty Group Inc Real Estate/Bldg	24800 Chrisanta Drive	Mission Viejo 714-837-6050	CA 92691	
2800	Orange County Government Local Govt	Civic Center Plaza	Santa Ana 714-834-3100	CA 92701	
250	Santa Ana, City of Local Govt	City Hall Civic Center Plaza	Santa Ana 714-647-6910	CA 92702	
456	AST Research Inc Comput/Off Equip	2121 Alton Avenue	Irvine 714-863-1333	CA 92713	
400	Lusk Co Real Estate/Bldg	17550 Gillette	Irvine 714-261-5999	CA 92713	
163	Armor All Products Corp Business Service	22 Corporate Park Drive	Irvine 714-533-1003	CA 92714	
400	Freedom Newspapers Inc Publishing/Com	17666 Fitch	Irvine 714-542-4415	CA 92714	
425	Lincoln Savings (Cal) & Loan Assn Inc Savings & Loan	18200 Von Darman	Irvine 714-553-0200	CA 92714	
NA	PacTel Cellular Co Telecom	2355 Main Street	Irvine 714-553-6087	CA 92714	
1250	Restaurant Enterprises Group Inc Food/Lodging	2701 Alton Avenue	Irvine 714-863-6300	CA 92714	
NA	Taco Bell Inc Food/Lodging	17901 Von Karman Avenue	Irvine 714-863-4501	CA 92714	
768	Western Digital Corp Electronics	2445 McCabe Way	Irvine 714-863-0102	CA 92714	

State / Province: California

Organizations Listed Geographically

Revenue ($ mil)	Organization/ Industry	Address	City / Phone	State/ Zip	Province/ Postcode
500	AFG Industries Inc — Manufacturing	18200 Von Karman Avenue Suite700	Irvine 714-553-9026	CA	92715
NA	Allergan Inc — Drugs	2525 Dupont Drive	Irvine 714-752-4500	CA	92715
1047	AVCO Financial Services Inc — Non-Bank Fin	3349 Michelson	Irvine 714-553-1200	CA	92715
3250	Financial Corp of America — Savings & Loan	18401 Von Karman Avenue	Irvine 714-553-6900	CA	92715
400	National Education Corp — Business Service	18400 Von Karman Avenue	Irvine 714-474-9400	CA	92715
NA	Parker Bertea Aerospace Group — Aerospace	18321 Jamboree Blvd	Irvine 714-833-3000	CA	92715
825	Kawasaki Industries USA Inc — Manufacturing	9950 Jermino Road	Irvine 714-770-0400	CA	92718
825	Toshiba America Electric Corp — Electronics	9740 Irvine Blvd	Irvine 714-583-3000	CA	92718
504	FHP International Corp — Health Care	9900 Talbot Avenue	Fountain Valley 714-963-7233	CA	92728
1500	Mitsubishi Motors of America Inc — Automotive	10540 Talbert	Fountain Valley 714-963-7677	CA	92728
5132	Flour Corp — Real Estate/Bldg	3333 Michelson Drive	Irvine 714-975-2000	CA	92730
NA	Disneyland Inc — Leisure Time	1313 Harbor Blvd	Anaheim 714-824-4024	CA	92802
339	Anaheim, City of — Local Govt	City Hall	Anaheim 714-999-5166	CA	92803
446	Karcher, Carl Enterprises Inc — Food/Lodging	1200 N Harbor Blvd	Anaheim 714-774-5796	CA	92803
NA	Aero Products Inc — Electronics	6101 Condor Drive	Moorpark 805-864-5600	CA	93021
400	Financial Corp of Santa Barbara — Savings & Loan	3908 State Street	Santa Barbara 805-682-2300	CA	93102
450	Santa Barbara Savings Assn Inc — Savings & Loan	3908 State Street	Santa Barbara 805-682-5000	CA	93102
300	Applied Magnetics Corp — Comput/Off Equip	75 Robin Hill Road	Goleta 805-967-8227	CA	93177
309	Tandon Corp — Comput/Off Equip	301 Science Drive	Moorpark 805-523-0340	CA	93201
14	Tejon Ranch Corp — Food Processing	4436 Lebec Road	Lebec 805-248-6774	CA	93243
1100	Calcot Ltd Inc — Food Processing	1601 Brundage Lane	Bakersfield 805-327-5961	CA	93307
500	Save Mart Supermarkets Inc — Retail/Food	1800 Standford	Modesto 209-577-1600	CA	93350
250	Fresno, City of — Local Govt	City Hall 2326 Fresno Street	Fresno 209-488-1561	CA	93721
500	Landmark Land Co Inc — Real Estate/Bldg	100 Clock Tower Place	Carmel 408-625-4060	CA	93923
584	Oracle Systems Corp — Comput/Off Equip	20 Davis Drive	Belmont 415-598-8000	CA	94002
400	Adia Services Inc — Business Service	64 Willow Place	Menlo Park 415-324-0696	CA	94025
350	Argonaut Insurance Co — Insurance	250 Middlefield Road	Menlo Park 415-326-0900	CA	94025
1095	Raychem Corp — Manufacturing	300 Constitution Drive	Menlo Park 415-361-3333	CA	94025
300	SRI International Inc — Consulting	333 Ravenswood Avenue	Menlo Park 415-326-6200	CA	94025
169	Acuson Corp — Instruments	1220 Charleston	Mountain View 415-969-9112	CA	94043
264	Silicon Graphics Inc — Comput/Off Equip	2011 N Shoreline Blvd	Mountain View 415-960-1980	CA	94043
1052	Sun Microsystems Inc — Comput/Off Equip	2550 Garcia Avenue	Mountain View 415-960-1300	CA	94043
1500	DHL Airways/Worldwide Express Inc — Transport	333 Twin Dolphin Drive	Redwood City 415-593-7474	CA	94065

State / Province: California

Organizations Listed Geographically

Revenue ($ mil)	Organization/ Industry	Address	City / Phone	State/ Zip	Province/ Postcode
NA	Oral-B Laboratories Inc Health Care	One Lagoon Drive	Redwood 415-598-5000	CA 94065	
1252	GAP Stores Inc Retail/Merch	900 Cherry Avenue	San Bruno 415-952-4400	CA 94066	
920	Atkinson, Guy F Co of California Real Estate/Bldg	10 W Orange Avenue	S San Francisco 415-876-1000	CA 94080	
350	Diasonics Inc Health Care	230 Utah Avenue	San Francisco 415-872-2722	CA 94080	
262	Genetech Corp Business Service	460 Point San Bruno	S San Francisco 415-952-1000	CA 94080	
452	Atari Corp Comput/Off Equip	1196 Borregas Avenue	Sunnyvale 408-745-2000	CA 94086	
1122	Advanced Micro Devices Inc Electronics	901 Thompson Place PO Box 3453	Sunnyvale 408-732-2400	CA 94088	
1802	Amdahl Corp Comput/Off Equip	1250 E Arques Avenue	Sunnyvale 408-746-6000	CA 94088	
NA	ESL Inc Publishing/Com	495 Java Drive	Sunnyvale 408-738-2888	CA 94088	
NA	Lockheed Missiles & Space Co Inc Aerospace	1111 Lockheed Way	Sunnyvale 408-742-4321	CA 94088	
750	Wilbur Ellis & Co Inc Food Processing	320 California Street	San Francisco 415-772-4000	CA 94101	
582	American Building Maintenance Ind Inc Business Service	333 Fell Street	San Francisco 415-864-5150	CA 94102	
1096	California State Auto Association Insurance	100 Van Ness Avenue	San Francisco 415-565-2012	CA 94102	
2527	First Nationwide Bank Inc Savings & Loan	700 Market Street	San Francisco 415-772-1400	CA 94102	
2079	San Francisco, City of Local Govt	City Hall	San Francisco 415-554-3456	CA 94102	
10182	BankAmerica Corp Banking	Bank of America Center	San Francisco 415-622-3456	CA 94104	
9900	BHP Australia (Broken Hill) Inc Metals/Mining	550 California Street	San Francisco 415-981-1515	CA 94104	
600	California First Bank Inc Banking	350 California Street	San Francisco 415-445-0200	CA 94104	
27722	Chevron Corp Energy	225 Bush Street	San Francisco 415-894-7700	CA 94104	
250	Grubb & Ellis Co Real Estate/Bldg	1 Montgomery Street	San Francisco 415-956-1990	CA 94104	
7283	McKesson Corp Business Service	One Post Street	San Francisco 415-983-8300	CA 94104	
770	Schwab, Charles & Co Securities	101 Montgomery Street The Schwab Bldg	San Francisco 415-627-7000	CA 94104	
4500	Bechtel Group Inc Real Estate/Bldg	50 Beale Street	San Francisco 415-768-1234	CA 94105	
NA	Chevron USA Inc Retail/Merch	575 Market Street	San Francisco 415-894-7700	CA 94105	
2493	Federal Reserve Bank of San Francisco Federal Govt Fin	101 Market Street	San Francisco 415-974-2000	CA 94105	
NA	Pacific Bell Directory Inc Publishing/Com	101 Spear Street	San Francisco 415-995-4400	CA 94105	
NA	Pacific Bell Inc Telecom	140 New Montgomery Street	San Francisco 415-542-9000	CA 94105	
NA	Pacific Gas Transmission Co Utility	160 Spear Street	San Francisco 415-781-0474	CA 94105	
9483	Pacific Telesis Group Inc Telecom	140 New Montgomery Street	San Francisco 415-882-8000	CA 94105	
2412	Southern Pacific Transport Corp Transport	1 Market Plaza	San Francisco 415-541-1000	CA 94105	
NA	Natural Gas Corp of California Utility	77 Beale Street	San Francisco 415-972-7000	CA 94106	
7646	Pacific Gas & Electric Co Utility	77 Beale Street	San Francisco 415-781-4211	CA 94106	
1000	Esprit de Corp Inc Apparel/Textiles	900 Minnesota Street	San Francisco 415-648-6900	CA 94107	

State / Province: California

Organizations Listed Geographically

Revenue ($ mil)	Organization/ Industry	Address	City / Phone	State/ Zip	Province/ Postcode
283	Harper Group Inc Transport	260 Townsend Road	San Francisco 415-978-0600	CA	94107
750	Arcata Corp Publishing/Com	601 California	San Francisco 415-781-4200	CA	94108
550	Basic American Foods Inc Food Processing	550 Kearny	San Francisco 415-981-5590	CA	94108
400	Hexcel Corp Chemicals	650 California Street	San Francisco 415-828-4200	CA	94108
433	Homestake Mining Co Metals/Mining	650 California Street	San Francisco 415-981-8150	CA	94108
400	SFFED Corp Savings & Loan	88 Kearny Street	San Francisco 415-955-5800	CA	94108
825	California & Hawaiian Sugar Inc Food Processing	1390 Willow Pass Road	Concord 415-356-6000	CA	94111
347	Community Psychiatric Centers Inc Health Care	517 Washington Street	San Francisco 415-397-6151	CA	94111
1000	Crowley Maritime Corp Transport	101 California Street	San Francisco 415-546-2500	CA	94111
1046	DiGiorgio Corp Food Processing	One Maritime Plaza	San Francisco 415-765-0100	CA	94111
1500	Dillingham Corp Real Estate/Bldg	2 Embarcadero Drive	San Francisco 415-362-1501	CA	94111
NA	Dole Packaged Foods Inc Food Processing	50 California Street	San Francisco 415-986-3000	CA	94111
3000	Levi Strauss & Co Inc Apparel/Textiles	1155 Battery Street	San Francisco 415-544-6000	CA	94111
1084	Potlatch Corp Paper/Forest Prd	One Maritime Plaza	San Francisco 415-576-8800	CA	94111
800	Sanwa Bank of California Banking	444 Market Street	San Francisco 415-765-9500	CA	94111
628	Shaklee Corp Drugs	444 Market Street	San Francisco 415-954-3000	CA	94111
550	Swinerton & Walberg Inc Real Estate/Bldg	580 California Avenue	San Francisco 415-421-2980	CA	94111
7879	Transamerica Corp Insurance	600 Montgomery Street	San Francisco 415-983-4000	CA	94111
550	Tri Valley Growers Inc Food Processing	1255 Battery Street Haas Bldg	San Francisco 415-445-1600	CA	94111
548	United States Leasing International Inc Non-Bank Fin	733 Front Street	San Francisco 415-627-9000	CA	94111
2200	Amfac Inc Business Service	44 Montgomery Street PO Box 7813	San Francisco 415-772-3400	CA	94120
497	Homestead Savings Fed Savings Assn Inc Savings & Loan	5757 Geary Blvd	San Francisco 415-387-4300	CA	94121
117	San Francisco State University University	1600 Holloway Avenue	San Francisco 415-469-2141	CA	94132
395	University of Cal San Francisco University	Administrative Bldg	San Francisco 415-669-9000	CA	94143
4853	Wells Fargo & Co Banking	420 Montgomery Street	San Francisco 415-477-1000	CA	94163
570	Xidex Corp Comput/Off Equip	525 University Avenue	Palo Alto 408-988-3472	CA	94301
84	Alza Corp Business Service	950 Page Mill Road	Palo Alto 415-494-5222	CA	94303
NA	CF AirFreight Inc Transport	3350 W Bayshore Road	Palo Alto 415-855-9100	CA	94303
2689	Consolidated Freightways Inc Transport	3240 Hillview Avenue	Palo Alto 415-494-2900	CA	94303
983	Varian Associates Inc Electronics	611 Hansen Way	Palo Alto 415-493-4000	CA	94303
400	Cooper Companies Electronics	3145 Porter Drive	Palo Alto 415-856-5000	CA	94304
550	Coopervision Inc Instruments	3145 Porter Drive	Palo Alto 415-856-5000	CA	94304
275	Electric Power Research Institute Inc Membership Org	3412 Hillview Avenue	Palo Alto 415-855-2000	CA	94304

State / Province: California

Organizations Listed Geographically

Revenue ($ mil)	Organization/ Industry	Address	City / Phone	State/ Zip	Province/ Postcode
10070	Hewlett Parkard Co Comput/Off Equip	3000 Hanover Street	Palo Alto 415-857-1501	CA 94304	
1272	Syntex Corp Drugs	3401 Hillview Drive	Palo Alto 415-885-5050	CA 94304	
275	Watkins Johnson Co Electronics	3333 Hillview Avenue	Palo Alto 415-493-4141	CA 94304	
649	Stanford University University	210 Encina Hall	Stanford 415-497-2300	CA 94305	
2200	Alumax Inc Metals/Mining	400 S El Camino	San Mateo 415-348-3400	CA 94402	
158	Applied Biosystems Inc Instruments	850 Lincoln Centre Drive	Foster City 415-570-6667	CA 94404	
202	Franklin Resources Group Inc Non-Bank Fin	777 Mariners Island Blvd	San Mateo 415-570-3000	CA 94404	
400	Everex Systems Inc Comput/Off Equip	48431 Milmont Drive	Fremont 415-498-1111	CA 94538	
300	Worlds of Wonder Inc Leisure Time	4209 Technology Drive	Fremont 415-659-4300	CA 94538	
NA	Mervyn's Inc Retail/Merch	25001 Industrial Blvd	Hayward 415-785-8800	CA 94545	
600	Liquid Air Corp Chemicals	2121 N California Blvd	Walnut Creek 415-977-6500	CA 94556	
200	Flextronics Inc Electronics	35325 Fircrest	Newark 415-792-4177	CA 94560	
626	Ross Stores Inc Retail/Merch	8333 Central Avenue	Newark 415-790-4400	CA 94560	
550	Mason McDuffie Real Estate Inc Real Estate/Bldg	25 Orinda Way	Orinda 415-254-5640	CA 94563	
660	Sun Diamond Growers of California Inc Food Processing	5568 Gibraltar Drive	Pleasanton 415-463-8200	CA 94566	
NA	Chevron Chemical Co Chemicals	6001 Bollinger Canyon Road	San Ramon 415-842-1000	CA 94583	
NA	Chevron Overseas Petroleum Co Energy	6001 Bollinger Canyon Road	San Ramon 415-842-1000	CA 94583	
1925	Longs Drug Stores Corp Retail/Merch	141 N Civic Drive PO Box 5222	Walnut Creek 415-937-1170	CA 94596	
45	Cetus Corp Business Service	1400 53rd Street	Emeryville 415-420-3300	CA 94608	
950	Alameda County Local Govt	1221 Oak Street	Oakland 415-272-6691	CA 94612	
2131	American President Companies Ltd Transport	1800 Harrison Street	Oakland 415-272-8000	CA 94612	
NA	American President Trucking Co Transport	1800 Harrison Street	Oakland 415-272-8000	CA 94612	
1260	Clorox Co Personal Care	1221 Broadway	Oakland 415-271-7000	CA 94612	
1410	Golden West Financial Corp Savings & Loan	1901 Harrison Street	Oakland 415-446-6000	CA 94612	
5584	Kaiser Permanente Medical Health Care	One Kaiser Plaza	Oakland 415-428-5000	CA 94612	
396	Oakland, City of Local Govt	City Hall Plaza	Oakland 415-273-3141	CA 94612	
550	Kaiser Engineers Inc Real Estate/Bldg	1800 Harrison Street	Oakland 415-268-6000	CA 94623	
2219	Kaiser Technology Corp Metals/Mining	300 Lakeside Drive	Oakland 415-271-3300	CA 94643	
13612	Safeway Stores Inc Retail/Food	Fourth & Jackson Streets	Oakland 415-891-3000	CA 94660	
428	University of California Berkeley University	Administrative Bldg	Berkeley 415-642-6000	CA 94720	
117	Autodesk Corp Comput/Off Equip	2320 Marinship Way	Sausalito 415-332-2344	CA 94965	
300	Dionex Corp Instruments	1228 Titan Way	Sunnyvale 408-737-0700	CA 94986	
3704	Fireman's Fund Inc Insurance	777 San Marin Drive	Novato 415-899-2000	CA 94998	

State / Province: California

Organizations Listed Geographically

Revenue ($ mil)	Organization/ Industry	Address	City / Phone	State/ Zip	Province/ Postcode
4071	Apple Computer Inc Comput/Off Equip	20525 Mariani Avenue	Cupertino 408-996-1010	CA 95014	
265	Measurex Corp Instruments	One Results Way	Cupertino 408-255-1500	CA 95014	
1315	Tandem Computers Inc Comput/Off Equip	19333 Vallco Parkway	Cupertino 408-725-6000	CA 95014	
500	Alcatel Business Systems Inc Comput/Off Equip	1623 Buckeye Drive	Milpitas 800-556-1234	CA 95035	
218	Chips & Technologies Inc Electronics	3050 Zanker Road	San Jose 408-434-0600	CA 95035	
379	LSI Logic Corp Electronics	1551 McCarthy Blvd	Milpitas 408-433-8000	CA 95035	
400	Quantum Corp Comput/Off Equip	1804 McCarthy Blvd	Milpitas 408-262-1100	CA 95035	
NA	Versatec Inc Comput/Off Equip	2710 Walsh Avenue	Santa Clara 408-988-2800	CA 95051	
2875	Intel Corp Electronics	3065 Bowers Avenue	Santa Clara 408-987-8080	CA 95052	
113	KLA Instruments Corp Instruments	2051 Mission College	Santa Clara 408-988-6100	CA 95052	
2470	National Semiconductor Corp Electronics	2900 Semiconductor Drive PO Box 58090	Santa Clara 408-721-5000	CA 95052	
400	ThreeCom (3Com) Corp Comput/Off Equip	3165 Kifer Road	Santa Clara 408-562-6400	CA 95052	
400	Applied Materials Inc Electronics	3050 Bowers Avenue	Santa Clara 408-727-5555	CA 95054	
NA	National Advanced Systems Corp Electronics	750 Central Expressway	Santa Clara 408-970-1000	CA 95054	
1266	Seagate Technology Inc Comput/Off Equip	920 Disc Drive	Scotts Valley 408-438-6550	CA 95066	
518	San Jose, City of Local Govt	City Hall 801 N First Street	San Jose 408-277-4237	CA 95110	
1825	Santa Clara County Government Local Govt	70 Hedding Street	San Jose 408-299-2323	CA 95110	
350	Arix Corp Comput/Off Equip	821 Fox Lane	San Jose 408-432-1200	CA 95131	
750	Businessland Inc Retail/Merch	1001 Ridder Park Drive	San Jose 408-437-4156	CA 95131	
200	Conner Peripherals Corp Comput/Off Equip	2221 Old Oakland Road	San Jose 408-433-3340	CA 95131	
300	VLSI Technology Inc Electronics	1101 McKay Drive	San Jose 408-924-1810	CA 95131	
139	Cypress Semiconductor Inc Electronics	3901 N First Street	San Jose 408-943-2600	CA 95134	
271	Maxtor Corp Comput/Off Equip	211 River Oaks Parkway	San Jose 408-942-1700	CA 95134	
275	Wyse Technology Inc Comput/Off Equip	3571 N First Street	San Jose 408-433-1000	CA 95134	
400	Convergent Technologies Inc Comput/Off Equip	2700 N First Street	San Jose 408-434-2848	CA 95150	
NA	Chemical Systems Inc Chemicals	PO Box 49028	San Jose 408-224-7796	CA 95161	
134	San Jose State University University	Administrative Bldg	San Jose 408-277-2000	CA 95192	
500	American Savings & Loan Assn Inc Savings & Loan	222 N El Dorado Street	Stockton 209-948-1116	CA 95202	
715	Spanos, A G Construction Inc Real Estate/Bldg	1341 W Robin Hood	Stockton 209-478-7954	CA 95207	
1000	Gallo, Ernest & Julio Winery Inc Food Processing	600 Yosemite Blvd	Modesto 209-579-3111	CA 95354	
250	Anthem Electronics Inc Electronics	1040 E Brokaw Road	San Jose 408-295-4200	CA 95431	
1000	Raleys Inc Retail/Food	500 W Capitol	Broderick 916-444-8150	CA 95605	
428	University of California Davis University	Administrative Bldg	Davis 916-752-1011	CA 95616	

State / Province: California

Organizations Listed Geographically

Revenue ($ mil)	Organization/ Industry	Address	City / Phone	State/ Zip	Province/ Postcode
550	California Almond Growers Inc Food Processing	1802 C Street	Sacramento 916-442-0771	CA 95814	
3821	California Public Emp Retirement System Non-Bank Fin	400 P Street	Sacramento 916-445-7700	CA 95814	
73542	California, State of State/Prov Govt	State Capitol	Sacramento 916-322-9900	CA 95814	
250	Sacramento, City of Local Govt	City Hall	Sacramento 916-449-5407	CA 95814	
400	McClatchy Newspapers Publishing/Com	2100 Q Street	Sacramento 916-321-1000	CA 95816	
110	California State Univ Sacramento University	6000 J Street	Sacramento 916-454-6011	CA 95819	

State / Province: Colorado

Revenue ($ mil)	Organization/ Industry	Address	City / Phone	State/ Zip	Province/ Postcode
1271	Pace Membership Warehouses Inc Retail/Merch	3350 Peoria	Aurora 303-364-0700	CO 80010	
874	Storage Technology Corp Comput/Off Equip	2270 S 88th Street	Louisville 303-673-5020	CO 80028	
550	Associated Grocers of Colorado Inc Retail/Food	4891 Independence Suite 201	Wheatridge 303-297-9121	CO 80033	
350	Columbia Savings (CO) Assn Inc Savings & Loan	5850 S Ulster Circle E	Englewood 303-773-3444	CO 80111	
NA	Meridian Minerals Co Manufacturing	5613 DTC Parkway	Englewood 303-694-4100	CO 80111	
9211	US West Inc Telecom	7800 E Orchard Road	Englewood 303-793-6500	CO 80111	
250	Butler Paper Co Paper/Forest Prd	23 Inverness Way E	Englewood 303-790-8343	CO 80155	
1327	Cyprus Minerals Co Energy	9100 E Mineral Circle	Englewood 303-643-5000	CO 80155	
2250	Anschutz Corp Energy	555 17th Street	Denver 303-298-1000	CO 80202	
808	Denver, City of Local Govt	City & County Bldg	Denver 303-575-2721	CO 80202	
195	Hamilton Oil Corp Energy	1560 Broadway	Denver 303-863-3000	CO 80202	
250	Ideal Basic Industries Corp Building Mat	950 17th Street	Denver 303-623-5661	CO 80202	
NA	Ladd Petroleum Inc Energy	830 Denver Club Bldg 518 17th Street	Denver 303-620-0100	CO 80202	
1685	Public Service Co of Colorado Utility	550 15th Street	Denver 303-571-7511	CO 80202	
NA	US West Communications Inc Telecom	1801 California	Denver 303-624-2424	CO 80202	
358	Western Capital Investment Corp Savings & Loan	700 Seventeenth Street	Denver 303-370-1212	CO 80202	
500	Apache Corp Energy	1700 Lincoln Street	Denver 303-837-5000	CO 80203	
8200	Colorado, State of State/Prov Govt	State Capitol	Denver 303-866-5000	CO 80203	
389	Newmont Gold Corp Metals/Mining	1700 Lincoln Street	Denver 303-863-7414	CO 80203	
501	Newmont Mining Corp Metals/Mining	1700 Lincoln Street	Denver 303-863-7414	CO 80203	
NA	Micromedex Inc Comput/Off Equip	660 Bannock Street	Denver 303-623-8600	CO 80204	
842	United Artists Corp Leisure Time	2930 E Third Avenue	Denver 303-321-4242	CO 80206	
1250	Gates Corp Tire/Rubber	900 S Broadway	Denver 303-744-1911	CO 80209	
250	Cobe Laboratories Inc Health Care	1185 Oak Street	Denver 303-232-6800	CO 80215	
335	KN Energy Inc Energy	12055 W Second Place	Lakewood 303-989-1740	CO 80215	

State / Province: Colorado

Organizations Listed Geographically

Revenue ($ mil)	Organization/ Industry	Address	City / Phone	State/ Zip	Province/ Postcode
315	Vicorp Restaurants Corp Food/Lodging	400 W 48th Street	Denver 303-296-2121	CO 80216	
2062	Manville Corp Building Mat	Ken Caryl Ranch PO Box 5108	Denver 303-978-2000	CO 80217	
841	MDC Holdings Inc Non-Bank Fin	3600 S Yosemite	Denver 303-773-1100	CO 80237	
1709	Telecommunications Inc Publishing/Com	4643 S Ulster Street	Denver 303-721-5500	CO 80237	
261	United Cable Television Inc Publishing/Com	4700 S Syracuse Parkway	Denver 303-779-5999	CO 80237	
438	United Banks of Colorado Inc Banking	1700 Lincoln Street	Denver 303-861-4700	CO 80274	
400	NBI Inc Retail/Merch	3450 Mitchell Lane	Boulder 303-444-5710	CO 80301	
189	University of Colorado University	Administrative Bldg	Boulder 303-492-0111	CO 80309	
NA	Angus Petroleum Corp Energy	350 Indiana Street	Golden 303-278-4300	CO 80401	
1522	Coors, Aldolph Co Beverage	600 9th Street	Golden 303-279-6565	CO 80401	
400	Miniscribe Corp Comput/Off Equip	1871 Lefthand Circle	Longmont 303-651-6000	CO 80501	
1600	Monfort of Colorado Inc Food Processing	1930 AA Street	Greeley 303-353-2311	CO 80632	
600	Phelps Co Inc Real Estate/Bldg	PO Box 2440	Greeley 303-353-7000	CO 80632	
458	Colorado Springs, City of Local Govt	City Hall	Colorado Springs 303-578-6600	CO 80901	
NA	TRW Electronic Products Inc Business Service	3650 N Nevada Avenue	Colorado Springs 303-475-0660	CO 80907	
350	CF & I Steel Corp Manufacturing	225 Canal Street	Pueblo 303-561-6000	CO 81002	

State / Province: Connecticut

Revenue ($ mil)	Organization/ Industry	Address	City / Phone	State/ Zip	Province/ Postcode
768	Kaman Corp Conglomerate	1332 Blue Hills Avenue PO Box 1	Bloomfield 203-243-8311	CT 06002	
496	Barnes Group Inc Manufacturing	123 Main Street	Bristol 203-583-7070	CT 06010	
2763	Emhart Corp Manufacturing	426 Colt Highway	Farmington 203-678-3000	CT 06032	
NA	Otis Elevator Co Equipment	10 Farm Springs Road	Farmington 203-674-4000	CT 06032	
NA	Connecticut Light & Power Co Utility	Selden Street	Belden 203-665-5123	CT 06037	
2279	Northeast Utilities Inc Utility	107 Selden Street	Berlin 203-665-5000	CT 06037	
250	Moore Medical Corp Health Care	389 John Downey Drive	New Britain 203-225-2225	CT 06050	
1909	Stanley Works Inc Manufacturing	1000 Stanley Drive PO Box 7000	New Britain 203-225-5111	CT 06050	
NA	Wheeler Group Inc Comput/Off Equip	Greenwoods Industrial Park Route 219	Hartford 203-379-9911	CT 06057	
3363	Ames Department Stores Inc Retail/Merch	2418 Main Street	Rocky Hill 203-563-8234	CT 06067	
299	Gerber Scientific Co Instruments	83 Gerber Road W	South Windsor 203-644-1551	CT 06074	
717	Dairy Mart Convenience Stores Inc Retail/Merch	240 South Road	Enfield 203-741-3611	CT 06082	
500	Advo System Inc Business Service	One Univac Lane	Windsor 203-285-6100	CT 06095	
500	Stanadyne Inc Manufacturing	100 Deerfield Road	Windsor 203-525-0821	CT 06095	

State / Province: Connecticut

Organizations Listed Geographically

Revenue ($ mil)	Organization/ Industry	Address	City / Phone	State/ Zip	Province/ Postcode
827	Dexter Corp Chemicals	One Elm Street	Windsor Locks 203-627-9051	CT 06096	
NA	Hamilton Standard Inc Aerospace	One Hamilton Road	Windsor 203-654-6000	CT 06096	
1000	Sweet Life Foods Inc Food Processing	PO Box 385	Suffield 203-623-1681	CT 06096	
18518	United Technologies Corp Aerospace	United Technologies Bldg	Hartford 203-728-7000	CT 06101	
NA	United Technologies Space Systems Div Aerospace	United Technologies Bldg	Hartford 203-728-7000	CT 06101	
447	Hartford Steam Boiler Inspection Inc Manufacturing	One State Street	Hartford 203-722-1866	CT 06102	
205	Advest Inc Securities	280 Turnbull Street	Hartford 203-525-1421	CT 06103	
500	Chase Enterprises Inc Real Estate/Bldg	One Commercial Plaza	Hartford 203-549-1674	CT 06103	
798	Northeast Savings Inc Savings & Loan	50 State Street	Hartford 203-280-1000	CT 06103	
400	Society for Savings Banking	31 Pratt Street	Hartford 203-727-5000	CT 06103	
8599	Connecticut, State of State/Prov Govt	State Capitol	Hartford 203-240-0555	CT 06106	
417	Loctite Corp Chemicals	Hartford Square N 10 Columbus Blvd	Hartford 203-520-5000	CT 06106	
NA	Pratt & Whitney Aircraft Inc Aerospace	400 Main Street	East Hartford 203-565-9500	CT 06108	
185	Coleco Industries Inc Manufacturing	999 Quaker Lane S	West Hartford 203-725-6000	CT 06110	
NA	Textron Aircraft Engine Components Div Aerospace	549 Cedar Street	Newington 203-666-4601	CT 06111	
1500	Connecticut Bank & Trust Co NA Banking	1 Constitution	Hartford 203-244-5000	CT 06115	
NA	Fox, G Co Retail/Merch	960 Main Street	Hartford 203-522-1920	CT 06115	
1189	Hartford Life Insurance Co Insurance	Hartford Plaza	Hartford 203-547-5000	CT 06115	
1100	Hartford National Corp Banking	777 Main Street	Hartford 203-728-2000	CT 06115	
1319	Phoenix Mutual Life Insurance Co Insurance	One American Row	Hartford 203-275-5000	CT 06115	
255	Connecticut Natural Gas Co Utility	100 Columbus Blvd	Hartford 203-727-3000	CT 06144	
4692	Connecticut General Life Ins Co Insurance	900 Cottage Grove	Bloomfield 203-726-6000	CT 06152	
2039	Connecticut Mutual Life Insurance Co Insurance	140 Garden Street	Hartford 203-727-6500	CT 06154	
24296	Aetna Life & Casualty Co Insurance	151 Farmington Avenue	Hartford 203-273-0123	CT 06156	
18986	Travelers Insurance Corp Insurance	One Tower Square	Hartford 203-277-0111	CT 06183	
300	Brintec Systems Corp Telecom	1600 W Main Street	Willimantic 203-456-8000	CT 06226	
176	University of Connecticut University	Administrative Bldg	Storrs 203-486-2337	CT 06268	
NA	Electric Boat Div Manufacturing	75 Eastern Point Road	Groton 203-441-1000	CT 06340	
1294	Echlin Inc Automotive	100 Double Beach Road	Branford 203-481-5751	CT 06405	
50089	General Electric Co Electronics	3135 Easton Turnpike	Fairfield 203-373-2431	CT 06431	
750	Insilco Corp Manufacturing	1000 Research Parkway	Meridan 203-634-2000	CT 06450	
NA	Telco Oilfield Services Inc Oil Service	105 Pondview Drive	Meriden 203-237-9655	CT 06450	
295	BIC Corp Manufacturing	Wiley Street	Milford 203-783-2000	CT 06460	

State / Province: Connecticut

Organizations Listed Geographically

Revenue ($ mil)	Organization/ Industry	Address	City / Phone	State/ Zip	Province/ Postcode
614	Hubbell Inc Electronics	584 Derby Milford Road	Orange 203-789-1100	CT 06477	
1100	SAAB Scandia America Inc Electronics	Saab Drive	Orange 203-795-5671	CT 06477	
255	TIE Communications Inc Telecom	12 Commerce Drive	Shelton 203-926-2000	CT 06484	
400	Lori Corp Manufacturing	384 Old Turnpike Road	Southington 203-621-3601	CT 06489	
400	Crystal Brands Inc Apparel/Textiles	Crystal Brands Road	Southport 203-254-6200	CT 06490	
600	LPL Investment Group Electronics	358 Hall Avenue	Wallingford 203-265-8600	CT 06492	
NA	Dictaphone Corp Comput/Off Equip	3191 Broadbridge Avenue	Stratford 203-381-7000	CT 06497	
323	Northeast Bancorportion Banking	Church & Elm Streets	New Haven 203-773-0500	CT 06502	
519	United Illuminating Co Utility	80 Temple Street	New Haven 203-787-7200	CT 06506	
600	Wyatt Inc Energy	900 Chapel Street	New Haven 203-787-2175	CT 06507	
550	Beazley, William Co Inc Real Estate/Bldg	97 Whitney Avenue	New Haven 203-562-9801	CT 06510	
1583	Southern New England Telephone Inc Telecom	227 Church Street	New Haven 203-771-5200	CT 06510	
1200	Armtek Corp Manufacturing	500 Sargent Drive	New Haven 203-784-2200	CT 06511	
350	Yale University University	Administrative Bldg	New Haven 203-436-0300	CT 06520	
900	Armstrong Rubber Co Tire/Rubber	500 Sargent Drive	New Haven 203-784-2200	CT 06536	
280	Citytrust Bank Corp Banking	961 Main Street	Bridgeport 203-384-5212	CT 06601	
NA	Sikorsky Inc Aerospace	6900 Main Street	Stamford 203-386-4000	CT 06601	
750	Warnaco Inc Apparel/Textiles	350 Lafayette Street	Bridgeport 203-579-8272	CT 06601	
600	People's Bank Savings & Loan	899 Main Street	Bridgeport 203-579-7171	CT 06604	
825	Timex Group Inc Instruments	Parkswood Extension	Waterbury 203-573-5000	CT 06722	
240	General Datacomm Industries Inc Telecom	1579 Straits Turnpike	Middlebury 203-574-1118	CT 06762	
1500	Duracell Corp Electronics	Berkshire Industrial Park	Bethel 203-796-4000	CT 06801	
400	Stolt Tankers & Terminals Inc Transport	8 Sound Drive	Greenwich 203-625-9400	CT 06807	
368	Comstock Group Inc Real Estate/Bldg	38 Old Ridgebury Road	Danbury 203-792-9800	CT 06810	
250	Ethan Allen Inc Appliances/Furn	Ethan Allen Drive	Danbury 203-743-8000	CT 06810	
1000	First Brands Corp Personal Care	39 Old Ridgebury Road	Danbury 203-790-2900	CT 06817	
8324	Union Carbide Corp Chemicals	39 Old Ridgbury Road	Danbury 203-794-2000	CT 06817	
500	Air Express International Transport	120 Tokeneke Road	Darien 203-655-7900	CT 06820	
1410	Bowater Inc Paper/Forest Prd	One Parklands Drive PO Box 401	Darien 203-656-7200	CT 06820	
NA	Brink's Inc Transport	Thorndal Circle	Darien 203-655-8781	CT 06820	
2750	Cavenham (USA) Inc Retail/Merch	25 Old Kings Highway N	Darien 203-655-6211	CT 06820	
3400	Chesebrough Ponds Inc Personal Care	33 Benedict Place	Greenwich 203-222-3000	CT 06830	
500	Coca Cola Bottling Co of New York Food Processing	20 Horseneck Lane	Greenwich 203-625-4000	CT 06830	

State / Province: Connecticut

Organizations Listed Geographically

Revenue ($ mil)	Organization/ Industry	Address	City / Phone	State/ Zip	Province/ Postcode
2000	Finevest Services Food Processing	191 Mason Street	Greenwich 203-629-8750	CT 06830	
275	Health Tex Inc Apparel/Textiles	33 Benedict Plaza	Greenwich 203-661-2000	CT 06830	
1100	Pechiney World Trade Inc Business Service	475 Steamboat Road	Greenwich 203-622-8300	CT 06830	
10000	United Parcel Service Inc Business Service	51 Weaver Street	Greenwich 203-622-6000	CT 06830	
565	UST United States Tobacco Co Tobacco	100 W Putnam Avenue	Greenwich 203-661-1100	CT 06830	
534	Berkley, W R Insurance Co Insurance	165 Mason Street	Greenwich 203-629-2880	CT 06836	
NA	Climax Metals Co Metals/Mining	Amax Center	Greenwich 203-629-6000	CT 06836	
529	Lone Star Industries Inc Building Mat	One Greenwich Plaza	Greenwich 203-661-3100	CT 06836	
1583	Pittston Co Energy	One Pickwick Plaza PO Box 8900	Greenwich 203-622-0900	CT 06836	
1004	Primerica Corp Packaging	American Lane PO Box 3610	Greenwich 203-552-2000	CT 06838	
150	Century Communications Inc Publishing/Com	65 Locust Avenue	New Canaan 203-966-8746	CT 06840	
NA	Caldor Inc Retail/Merch	20 Glover Avenue	Norwalk 203-846-1641	CT 06850	
NA	Norden Inc Aerospace	Norden Plaza	Norwalk 203-852-5000	CT 06856	
NA	Pepperidge Farm Inc Food Processing	595 Westport Avenue	Norwalk 203-846-7000	CT 06856	
300	US Surgical Corp Health Care	150 Glover Avenue	Norwalk 203-866-5050	CT 06856	
1165	Perkin Elmer Corp Instruments	761 Main Avenue	Norwalk 203-762-1000	CT 06859	
11980	American Brands Inc Tobacco	1700 E Putnam Avenue PO Box 811	Old Greenwich 203-698-5000	CT 06870	
1223	Emery Air Freight Corp Transport	Old Danbury Road	Wilton 203-762-8601	CT 06897	
NA	Richardson Vicks Inc Personal Care	10 Westprot Road	Wilton 203-834-5000	CT 06897	
800	Fine Homes International L P Inc Real Estate/Bldg	10 Stamford Plaza	Stamford 203-356-1400	CT 06901	
500	Moore McCormick Resources Inc Energy	One Landmark Square	Stamford 203-358-2200	CT 06901	
450	Sprague Technologies Inc Electronics	4 Stamford Forum	Stamford 203-964-8600	CT 06901	
800	American Television & Communications Inc Publishing/Com	300 First Stamford Place	Stamford 203-328-0600	CT 06902	
350	Crompton & Knowles Inc Chemicals	One Station Place	Stamford 203-353-5400	CT 06902	
1100	Erbamont Inc Drugs	1266 Main Street Soundview Plaza	Stamford 203-967-4882	CT 06902	
345	Kollmorgen Corp Electronics	66 Gate House Road	Stamford 203-327-7222	CT 06902	
1000	Service America Corp Food/Lodging	88 Gatehouse Road	Stamford 203-964-5000	CT 06902	
548	American Maize Products Co Food Processing	41 Harbor Drive	Stamford 203-356-9000	CT 06904	
NA	American Tobacco Co Tobacco	Six Stamford Forum	Stamford 203-325-4900	CT 06904	
3484	Combustion Engineering Inc Electronics	900 Long Ridge Road PO Box 9308	Stamford 203-329-8771	CT 06904	
200	Dress Barn Inc Retail/Merch	88 Hamilton Avenue	Stamford 203-327-4242	CT 06904	
3850	Elf Aquitaine Inc Energy	High Ridge Road	Stamford 203-358-5000	CT 06904	
467	General Host Corp Retail/Food	22 Gate House Road PO Box 10045	Stamford 203-357-9900	CT 06904	

State / Province: Connecticut

Organizations Listed Geographically

Revenue ($ mil)	Organization/ Industry	Address	City / Phone	State/ Zip	Province/ Postcode
2736	General Re Corp Insurance	Financial Centre PO Box 10351	Stamford 203-328-5000	CT 06904	
1760	General Signal Corp Instruments	High Ridge Park	Stamford 203-357-8800	CT 06904	
3588	Great Northern Nekoosa Corp Paper/Forest Prd	75 Prospect Street	Stamford 203-359-4000	CT 06904	
16460	GTE Corp Telecom	One Stamford Forum	Stamford 203-965-2000	CT 06904	
314	Neoax Inc Automotive	Four High Ridge Parkway	Stamford 203-322-8333	CT 06904	
2308	Olin Corp Chemicals	120 Long Ridge Road	Stamford 203-356-2000	CT 06904	
462	Petroleum Heat & Power Co Energy	Davenport Street	Stamford 203-323-2121	CT 06904	
750	Playtex Corp Apparel/Textiles	700 Fairfield Avenue	Stamford 203-356-8000	CT 06904	
600	Revere Copper & Brass Inc Manufacturing	High Ridge Park PO Box 10327	Stamford 203-358-5300	CT 06904	
361	Savin Corp Comput/Off Equip	9 W Broad Street	Stamford 203-967-5000	CT 06904	
1750	SSMC Inc (Singer Co) Electronics	8 Stamford Forum	Stamford 203-356-4200	CT 06904	
500	Union Trust Co Banking	300 Main Street	Stamford 203-348-6211	CT 06904	
500	Walden Book Co Inc Retail/Merch	201 High Ridge Road	Stamford 203-356-7500	CT 06904	
16441	Xerox Corp Comput/Off Equip	800 Long Ridge Road PO Box 1600	Stamford 203-968-3000	CT 06904	
302	Citizens Utilities Co Utility	High Ridge Park	Stamford 203-427-8953	CT 06905	
275	Vestron Inc Leisure Time	60 Long Ridge Road	Stamford 203-968-0000	CT 06905	
5129	Champion International Corp Paper/Forest Prd	One Champion Plaza	Stamford 203-358-7000	CT 06921	
NA	Clairol Inc Personal Care	One Blachley Road	Stamford 203-632-1500	CT 06922	
2650	Pitney Bowes Inc Comput/Off Equip	World Headquarters Walter H Wheeler Jr Drive	Stamford 203-356-5000	CT 06926	

State / Province: Delaware

Revenue ($ mil)	Organization/ Industry	Address	City / Phone	State/ Zip	Province/ Postcode
500	Gore, W L & Associates Inc Apparel/Textiles	555 Paper Mill Road	Newark 302-738-4880	DE 19711	
1200	NVF Co Steel	Yorklyn Road PO Box 68	Yorklyn 302-239-5281	DE 19736	
1224	American Express Credit Corp Non-Bank Fin	One Rodney Square	Wilmington 302-594-3350	DE 19801	
500	Clarendon America Insurance Co Insurance	1100 N Market Street Wilmington Trust Center	Wilmington 302-656-0142	DE 19801	
2266	Mercantile Stores Co Inc Retail/Merch	1100 N Market Street	Wilmington 302-575-1816	DE 19801	
206	Rollins Environmental Services Inc Business Service	One Rollins Plaza	Wilmington 302-429-2700	DE 19803	
1215	Scripps, E W Corp Publishing/Com	1409 Foulk Road	Wilmington 302-478-4141	DE 19803	
3128	Columbia Gas System Inc Utility	20 Montchanin Road	Wilmington 302-429-5000	DE 19807	
1008	Sears Roebuck Acceptance Corp Non-Bank Fin	3711 Kennett Pike	Greenville 302-652-3666	DE 19807	
238	Montgomery Ward Credit Corp Non-Bank Fin	3411 Silverside Road	Wilmington 302-478-9240	DE 19810	
313	Wilmington Trust Corp Banking	Rodney Square N	Wilmington 302-651-1000	DE 19890	
2802	Hercules Inc Chemicals	Hercules Plaza 1313 N Market Street	Wilmington 302-594-5000	DE 19894	

State / Province: Delaware

Organizations Listed Geographically

Revenue ($ mil)	Organization/ Industry	Address	City / Phone	State/ Zip	Province/ Postcode
600	Himont Inc Chemicals	1313 N Market Street	Wilmington 302-594-5500		DE 19894
1650	ICI (Imperial Chemical) America Inc Chemicals	New Murphy Road & Concord Pike	Wilmington 302-886-3000		DE 19897
NA	Conoco Inc Energy	1007 Market Street	Wilmington 302-774-1000		DE 19898
NA	Consolidated Coal Co Metals/Mining	1007 Market Street	Wilmington 302-774-1000		DE 19898
32917	DuPont, E I DeNemours & Co Chemicals	1007 Market Street	Wilmington 302-774-1000		DE 19898
1418	Beneficial Corp Non-Bank Fin	1100 Carr Road	Wilmington 302-798-0800		DE 19899
768	Delmarva Power & Light Co Utility	800 King Street	Wilmington 302-429-3011		DE 19899
450	RLC Corp Transport	One Rollins Plaza PO Box 1791	Wilmington 302-429-2700		DE 19899
1907	Delaware, State of State/Prov Govt	Legislative Hall	Dover 302-736-4000		DE 19901

State / Province: District of Columbia

Revenue ($ mil)	Organization/ Industry	Address	City / Phone	State/ Zip	Province/ Postcode
250	American Federation of Government Emp Membership Org	80 F Street NW	Washington 202-737-8700		DC 20001
500	American Federation of Teachers Membership Org	555 New Jersey Avenue NW	Washington 202-879-4400		DC 20001
1000	International Brotherhood of Teamsters Membership Org	25 Louisiana Street NW	Washington 202-624-6800		DC 20001
250	National Assn of Letter Carriers Membership Org	100 Indiana Avenue NW	Washington 202-393-4695		DC 20001
250	United Assn of Plumbing & Pipe Fitting Membership Org	901 Massachusetts Avenue	Washington 202-628-5823		DC 20001
500	United Brotherhood of Carpenters America Membership Org	101 Constitution Avenue NW	Washington 202-546-6206		DC 20001
1000	United States AMTRAK Natl Rail Passenger Federal Govt	400 N Capitol Street NW	Washington 202-383-3000		DC 20001
1000	Democratic National Committee Membership Org	430 S Capitol Street SE	Washington 202-863-8000		DC 20003
1000	Republican National Committee Membership Org	310 First Street SE Eisenhower Center	Washington 202-863-8500		DC 20003
3238	Washington, District of Columbia State/Prov Govt	District Bldg 1350 Pennsylvania Avenue	Washington 202-727-1000		DC 20004
250	American Postal Workers Union Membership Org	817 Fourteenth Street NW	Washington 202-842-4200		DC 20005
900	First American Bankshares Inc Banking	First American Bank Bldg	Washington 202-383-1400		DC 20005
500	International Brotherhood Electrical Workers Membership Org	1125 Fifteenth Street NW	Washington 202-833-7000		DC 20005
562	Riggs National Corp Banking	1503 Pennsylvania Avenue NW	Washington 202-835-6000		DC 20005
500	Service Employees International Union Membership Org	1313 L Street NW	Washington 202-898-3200		DC 20005
250	United Mine Workers of America Membership Org	900 15th Street NW	Washington 202-842-7200		DC 20005
1000	AFL-CIO American Federation of Labor Membership Org	815 Sixteenth Street NW	Washington 202-637-5000		DC 20006
NA	Chesapeake & Potomac Telephone Co Telecom	1710 H Street NW	Washington 202-887-0565		DC 20006
500	Communications Workers of America Membership Org	1925 K Street NW	Washington 202-728-2300		DC 20006
250	Laborers' Intl Union of North America Membership Org	905 Sixteenth Street NW	Washington 202-737-8320		DC 20006
1000	United Food & Commercial Workers Union Membership Org	1775 K Street NW	Washington 202-223-3111		DC 20006
500	United Steelworkers of America Membership Org	815 Sixteenth Street NW	Washington 202-638-6929		DC 20006

State / Province: District of Columbia

Organizations Listed Geographically

Revenue ($ mil)	Organization/ Industry	Address	City / Phone	State/ Zip	Province/ Postcode
716	Danaher Corp Manufacturing	3524 Water Street N	Washington 202-333-1805	DC 20007	
250	Hotel & Restrauant Employees Intl Union Membership Org	1219 28th Street NW	Washington 202-393-4373	DC 20007	
1729	Student Loan Marketing Assn Inc Non-Bank Fin	1050 Thomas Jefferson Street NW	Washington 202-333-8000	DC 20007	
NA	Syscon Corp Comput/Off Equip	1000 Thomas Jefferson Street	Washington 202-342-4000	DC 20007	
825	Intelsat Corp Telecom	3400 International Drive NW	Washington 202-944-6800	DC 20008	
800	American Security Bank NA Banking	1501 Pennsylvania Avenue	Washington 202-624-4000	DC 20013	
550	Woodward & Lothrop Inc Retail/Merch	11th Street & F Street	Washington 202-347-5300	DC 20013	
10266	Federal National Mortgage Corp Non-Bank Fin	3900 Wisconsin Avenue NW	Washington 202-537-7000	DC 20016	
550	Steuart Investment Co Inc Real Estate/Bldg	4646 40th Street NW	Washington 202-537-8940	DC 20016	
359	COMSAT Communications Satellite Inc Telecom	950 L'Enfant Plaza SW	Washington 202-863-6000	DC 20024	
500	American Enterprise Institute Membership Org	1150 Seventeenth Street NW	Washington 202-862-5800	DC 20036	
500	American Fed of State, Cnty & Muni Emp Membership Org	1625 L Street NW	Washington 202-429-1130	DC 20036	
500	Brookings Institution Membership Org	1775 Massachusetts Avenue NW	Washington 202-797-6000	DC 20036	
250	Graphic Communications Intl Union Membership Org	1900 L Street NW	Washington 202-461-1400	DC 20036	
225	Harman International Industries Inc Electronics	1155 Connecticut Avenue	Washington 202-955-6130	DC 20036	
500	International Assn of Machinists/Aerospace Membership Org	1300 Connecticut Avenue NW	Washington 202-857-5200	DC 20036	
250	International Union of Electronic & Elec Membership Org	1126 16th Street NW	Washington 202-296-1200	DC 20036	
300	International Union of Operating Engineers Membership Org	1125 17th Street NW	Washington 202-429-9100	DC 20036	
5137	MCI Communications Corp Telecom	1133 Nineteenth Street NW	Washington 202-872-1600	DC 20036	
1000	National Education Association Membership Org	1201 Sixteenth Street NW	Washington 202-833-4000	DC 20036	
550	National Geographic Society Inc Publishing/Com	1145 17th Street NW	Washington 202-857-7000	DC 20036	
1000	Nationale Nederlanden Insurance Co Insurance	1050 Connecticut Avenue NW	Washington 202-463-7964	DC 20036	
250	OECD European Common Market, US HQ Federal Govt	2001 L Street NW	Washington 202-785-6323	DC 20036	
1400	United States Panama Canal Commission Federal Govt	2000 L Street NW	Washington 202-634-6441	DC 20036	
28	Strategic Planning Associates Inc Consulting	2300 N Street NW	Washington 202-778-7000	DC 20037	
2000	Federal Home Loan Bank Board Federal Govt Fin	1700 G Street NW	Washington 202-377-6000	DC 20052	
245	George Washington University University	Administrative Bldg	Washington 202-676-6000	DC 20052	
253	Georgetown University University	37th Street & O Street	Washington 202-625-0100	DC 20057	
7370	Marriott Corp Food/Lodging	Marriott Drive	Washington 301-897-9000	DC 20058	
1350	Potomac Electric Power Co Utility	1900 Pennsylvania Avenue NW	Washington 202-872-2456	DC 20068	
1368	Washington Post Co Publishing/Com	1150 Fifteenth Street NW	Washington 202-334-6600	DC 20071	
1557	GEICO Corp Insurance	Geico Plaza 5260 Western Avenue NW	Washington 301-986-3000	DC 20076	
698	Washington Gas Co Utility	1100 H Street NW	Washington 703-750-4440	DC 20080	

State / Province: District of Columbia

Organizations Listed Geographically

Revenue ($ mil)	Organization/ Industry	Address	City / Phone	State/ Zip	Province/ Postcode
11000	United States Dept Health & Human Serv Federal Govt	200 Independence Avenue SW	Washington 202-245-6296	DC	20201
25886	United States Dept of Education Federal Govt	400 Maryland Avenue SW	Washington 202-245-3192	DC	20202
31379	United States Dept of Labor Federal Govt	200 Constitution Avenue NW	Washington 202-523-8165	DC	20210
13000	United States Dept of the Treasury Federal Govt	1500 Pennsylvania Avenue NW	Washington 202-566-2000	DC	20220
11101	United States Internal Revenue Service Federal Govt	Dept of the Treasury 1111 Constitution Avenue NW	Washington 202-566-5000	DC	20224
3152	United States Dept of Commerce Federal Govt	Fourteenth St & Constitution Ave	Washington 202-377-2000	DC	20230
2953	United States Dept of the Interior Federal Govt	1800 C Street NW	Washington 202-343-3171	DC	20240
2000	United States Commodity Credit Corp Federal Govt Fin	Dept of Agriculture Fourteenth St & Independence	Washington 202-447-5237	DC	20250
50842	United States Dept of Agriculture Federal Govt	Fourteenth St & Independence Ave	Washington 202-447-2791	DC	20250
1000	United States Farmers Home Admim Federal Govt Fin	Dept of Agriculture Fourteenth St & Independence	Washington 202-447-4323	DC	20250
36000	United States Postal Service Federal Govt	475 L'Enfant Plaza SW	Washington 202-268-2000	DC	20260
3000	United States Dept of Defense Federal Govt	The Pentagon	Washington 202-545-6700	DC	20301
85700	United States Dept of the Army Federal Govt	The Pentagon	Washington 202-545-6700	DC	20310
107800	United States Dept of the Air Force Federal Govt	The Pentagon	Washington 202-545-6700	DC	20330
109500	United States Dept of the Navy Federal Govt	The Pentagon	Washington 202-545-6700	DC	20350
3360	United States General Services Admin Federal Govt	Eighteenth & F Streets NW	Washington 202-655-4000	DC	20405
3261	United States Dept Housing & Urban Dev Federal Govt	451 Seventh Street SW	Washington 202-655-4000	DC	20410
850	United States Office of Personnel Mgt Federal Govt	1900 E Street NW	Washington 202-632-5491	DC	20415
437	United States Small Business Admin Federal Govt	Imperial Bldg 1441 L Street NW	Washington 202-653-6554	DC	20416
29963	United States Veterans Administration Federal Govt	810 Vermont Avenue NW	Washington 202-233-2300	DC	20420
5000	Federal Deposit Insurance Corp Federal Govt Fin	550 Seventeenth Street NW	Washington 202-393-8400	DC	20429
2000	International Monitary Fund Federal Govt Fin	700 Nineteenth Street NW	Washington 202-623-7000	DC	20431
2000	World Bank Federal Govt Fin	1818 H Street NW	Washington 202-477-1234	DC	20433
500	National Credit Union Administration Federal Govt Fin	1776 G Street NW	Washington 202-357-1055	DC	20456
4787	United States Environmental Protect Agcy Federal Govt	401 M Street SW	Washington 202-382-2090	DC	20460
12335	President of the United States of Amer Federal Govt	Executive Office Bldg	Washington 202-395-3080	DC	20503
2000	United States Central Intelligence Agncy Federal Govt	Office of Logistics	Washington 703-351-1100	DC	20505
2139	Congress of the United States of America Federal Govt	The Capitol	Washington 202-224-3121	DC	20515
4437	United States Dept of State Federal Govt	2201 C Street NW	Washington 202-647-4000	DC	20520
750	United States Agency for Intl Develpmnt Federal Govt	320 Twenty-first Street NW	Washington 202-647-1850	DC	20523
6882	United States Dept of Justice Federal Govt	Constitution Avenue & Tenth St NW	Washington 202-633-2000	DC	20530
1541	United States Courts Federal Govt	United States Supreme Court Bldg 1 First Street NE	Washington 202-479-3000	DC	20543
13148	United States Natl Aerospace & Space Adm Federal Govt	600 Independence Avenue NW	Washington 202-453-1000	DC	20546

State / Province: District of Columbia

Organizations Listed Geographically

Revenue ($ mil)	Organization/ Industry	Address	City / Phone	State/ Zip	Province/ Postcode
1400	United States Information Agency Federal Govt	301 Fourth Street SW	Washington 202-655-4000	DC 20547	
250	Securities & Exchange Commission Federal Govt Fin	450 Fifth Street NW	Washington 202-272-3100	DC 20549	
19526	Federal Reserve System Headquarters Federal Govt Fin	20th & Constitution Ave NW	Washington 202-452-3000	DC 20551	
500	United States Nuclear Regulatory Comm Federal Govt	1717 H Street NW	Washington 301-492-7000	DC 20555	
1500	United States Export-Import Bank Federal Govt Fin	811 Vermont Avenue NW	Washington 202-566-8990	DC 20571	
12404	United States Dept of Energy Federal Govt	1000 Independence Avenue SW	Washington 202-586-5000	DC 20585	
27772	United States Dept of Transportation Federal Govt	400 Seventh Street SW	Washington 202-366-4000	DC 20590	
5000	Federal Aviation Administration Federal Govt	800 Independence Avenue SW	Washington 202-366-4000	DC 20591	

State / Province: Florida

Revenue ($ mil)	Organization/ Industry	Address	City / Phone	State/ Zip	Province/ Postcode
151	Florida East Coast Industries Inc Railroad	One Malaga Street	St Augustine 904-829-3421	FL 32084	
749	Florida National Banks Banking	225 Water Street	Jacksonville 904-359-5020	FL 32201	
650	St Joe Paper Co Paper/Forest Prd	803 Edward Ball Bldg	Jacksonville 904-356-8311	FL 32201	
2546	Barnett Banks Inc Banking	100 Laura Street	Jacksonville 904-791-7720	FL 32202	
1003	Jacksonville, City of Local Govt	City Hall 220 E Bay Street	Jacksonville 904-630-1776	FL 32202	
NA	Jacksonville Shipyards Inc Manufacturing	750 E Bay Street	Jacksonville 904-355-1711	FL 32203	
9008	Winn Dixie Stores Inc Retail/Food	5050 Edgewood Court	Jacksonville 904-783-5000	FL 32203	
475	Florida Rock Industries Inc Building Mat	155 E 21st Street	Jacksonville 904-355-1781	FL 32206	
750	PIE Nationwide Trucking Corp Transport	4250 Kings Road	Jacksonville 904-798-2000	FL 32209	
23940	Florida, State of State/Prov Govt	State Capitol	Tallahassee 904-488-1234	FL 32301	
156	Florida State University University	Administrative Bldg	Tallahassee 904-644-2525	FL 32306	
NA	Gulf Power Co Utility	75 N Pace Blvd	Pensacola 904-444-6381	FL 32520	
440	University of Florida University	Administrative Bldg	Gainesville 904-392-3261	FL 32611	
NA	United Telephone Co of Florida Telecom	555 Lake Border Drive	Altamonte Springs 407-889-6000	FL 32715	
NA	Tupperware Worldwide Inc Manufacturing	3175 N Orange Blossom Trail	Kissimmee 407-826-5050	FL 32741	
502	Hughes Supply Inc Appliances/Furn	521 W Central Blvd PO Box 2273	Orlando 305-841-4710	FL 32802	
NA	Federal Home Life Insurance Co Insurance	6277 Sea Harbor Drive	Orlando 407-345-3020	FL 32821	
1782	Harcourt Brace Jovanovich Inc Publishing/Com	6277 Sea Harbor Drive	Orlando 305-345-2000	FL 32821	
NA	Disney, Walt World Inc Leisure Time	Lake Buena Vista	Buena Vista 407-824-4024	FL 32830	
NA	Martin Marietta Electronics & Missiles Aerospace	PO Box 583	Orlando 305-356-2000	FL 32855	
500	National Beverage Corp Food Processing	PO Box 13889	Fort Lauderdale 305-857-3300	FL 32859	
2099	Harris Corp Electronics	1025 W NASA Blvd	Melbourne 305-727-9100	FL 32919	
NA	Pan Am World Services Inc Business Service	7315 N Atlantic Avenue	Cape Canaveral 305-784-7100	FL 32920	

State / Province: Florida

Organizations Listed Geographically

Revenue ($ mil)	Organization/ Industry	Address	City / Phone	State/ Zip	Province/ Postcode
500	Coulter Electronics Corp Electronics	600 W 20th Street	Hialeah 305-885-0131	FL 33010	
250	Luria, L & Son Inc Retail/Merch	5770 Miami Lakes Drive	Hialeah 305-557-9000	FL 33014	
263	University of Miami University	Administrative Bldg	Coral Gables 305-284-2211	FL 33124	
1500	Alden, John Financial Corp Insurance	7300 Corporate Center	Miami 305-470-3100	FL 33126	
450	Orion Capital Insurance Co Insurance	780 NW Lejeunne Road	Miami 305-445-8333	FL 33126	
2300	Dade County Government Local Govt	111 NW First Street	Miami 305-375-4176	FL 33128	
550	Recarey Enterprises Inc Health Care	2332 Birkell Avenue	Miami 305-854-4000	FL 33129	
500	AmeriFirst Federal Savings Miami Inc Savings & Loan	One SE Third Avenue	Miami 305-577-1600	FL 33131	
750	Centrust Savings Bank Inc Savings & Loan	101 E Flagler Street	Miami 305-376-5000	FL 33131	
301	Citizens Savings Assn Inc Savings & Loan	999 Brickell Avenue	Miami 305-577-0400	FL 33131	
500	General Development Corp Real Estate/Bldg	1111 S Bayshore Drive	Miami 305-350-1200	FL 33131	
1066	Southeast Banking Corp Banking	One SE Financial Center	Miami 305-375-7500	FL 33131	
2083	Knight Ridder Inc Publishing/Com	One Herald Plaza	Miami 305-376-3800	FL 33132	
500	Continental Companies Inc Food/Lodging	3250 Mary Street	Maimi 305-445-2493	FL 33133	
279	Miami, City of Local Govt	City Hall 3500 Pan American Drive	Miami 305-579-6010	FL 33133	
NA	Del Monte Foods Corp Food Processing	201 Alhambra Circle	Coral Gables 305-520-1000	FL 33134	
750	Braman Enterprises Inc Consumer Service	2044 Biscayne Blvd	Miami 305-576-6900	FL 33137	
900	Carnival Cruise Lines Inc Leisure Time	3915 Biscayne Blvd	Miami 305-599-2600	FL 33137	
1209	APL Corp Manufacturing	6917 Collins Avenue	Miami 305-866-7771	FL 33141	
1200	DWG Corp Energy	6917 Collins Avenue	Miami 305-866-7771	FL 33141	
401	Wackenhut Corp Business Service	1500 San Remo Avenue	Coral Gables 305-666-5656	FL 33146	
4402	Eastern Airlines Inc Airline	Miami International Airport	Miami 305-873-2211	FL 33148	
456	Resorts International Inc Leisure Time	915 NE 125th Street	North Miami 305-891-2500	FL 33161	
1650	Aero Mexico SA Airline	8390 NW 53rd Street	Miami 305-591-1494	FL 33166	
5030	Ryder System Inc Business Service	3600 NW 82nd Avenue	Miami 305-593-3726	FL 33166	
350	American Savings Assn of Florida Inc Savings & Loan	17801 NW 2nd Avenue	Miami 305-653-5353	FL 33169	
350	Lennar Corp Real Estate/Bldg	700 NW 107th Avenue	Miami 305-559-4000	FL 33172	
NA	Belcher Oil Co Energy	8700 W Flagler Street	Miami 305-551-5220	FL 33174	
NA	Florida Power & Light Co Utility	92 Flaglin Street	Miami 305-552-3552	FL 33174	
165	Miami Dade County Community College University	11011 SW 104th Street	Miami 305-596-1211	FL 33176	
825	Storer Communications Inc Publishing/Com	12000 Biscayne Blvd	Miami 305-899-1000	FL 33181	
400	Alamo Rent-a-Car Inc Consumer Service	110 SE Sixth Street	Fort Lauderdale 305-522-0000	FL 33301	
675	Broward County Government Local Govt	115 S Andrews Avenue	Fort Lauderdale 305-357-7000	FL 33301	

State / Province: Florida

Organizations Listed Geographically

Revenue ($ mil)	Organization/ Industry	Address	City / Phone	State/ Zip	Province/ Postcode
500	Morse Operations Inc Automotive	1240 N Federal Highway	Fort Lauderdale 305-563-6331	FL 33304	
125	Safecard Services Inc Business Service	6400 NW 6th Way	Fort Lauderdale 305-491-2111	FL 33309	
300	Proudfoot, Alexander Inc Consulting	1700 Palm Beach Lakes Blvd	West Palm Beach 407-697-9600	FL 33401	
235	Steego Corp Automotive	319 Clematis Street	West Palm Beach 407-655-9700	FL 33401	
NA	ESI Energy Services Inc Energy	100 Australian Avenue	West Palm Beach 407-683-6996	FL 33406	
275	Rinker Materials Corp Building Mat	1501 Belvedere Road	West Palm Beach 407-833-5555	FL 33406	
5854	FPL (Florida Power & Light) Group Inc Utility	Golden Bear Plaza	North Palm Beach 407-694-6300	FL 33408	
500	Worldmark Corp Building Mat	1208 US Highway 1	North Palm Beach 305-626-3116	FL 33408	
1000	International Controls Inc Automotive	5499 N Federal	Boca Raton 305-997-7400	FL 33431	
1000	Levitz Furniture Corp Retail/Merch	6111 Broken Sound Drive	Boca Raton 305-994-6006	FL 33431	
300	Telecomm Plus International Inc Consulting	8000 N Federal Highway	Boca Raton 407-997-9999	FL 33431	
1000	Cityfed Financial Corp Savings & Loan	293 S County Road	Palm Beach 407-655-5919	FL 33480	
300	Office Depot Inc Retail/Merch	851 Broken Sound Parkway	Boca Raton 407-994-2131	FL 33487	
275	Tech Data Corp Retail/Merch	5777 Myerlake Circle	Clearwater 813-539-7429	FL 33518	
3000	Eckerd, Jack Corp Retail/Merch	8333 Bryan Dairy Road	Largo 813-397-7461	FL 33543	
750	Lykes Brothers Inc Food Processing	215 E Madison Street	Tampa 813-223-3981	FL 33601	
479	First Florida Banks Inc Banking	111 Madison Street	Tampa 813-224-1111	FL 33602	
300	Tampa, City of Local Govt	City Hall 306 E Jackson Street	Tampa 813-223-8251	FL 33602	
1034	TECO Energy (Tampa Elec) Inc Utility	702 N Franklin Street	Tampa 813-228-4111	FL 33602	
978	Anchor Glass Container Packaging	1100 Anchor Street	Tampa 813-884-0000	FL 33607	
2500	Hillsborough Holdings (Walter, Jim Corp) Real Estate/Bldg	1500 N Dale Mabry Highway	Tampa 813-871-4811	FL 33607	
1000	Kash n Karry Food Stores Inc Retail/Food	6422 Harney Road	Tampa 813-621-0200	FL 33610	
130	University of South Florida University	4202 Flagler Avenue	Tampa 813-974-2011	FL 33620	
NA	Turner Development Corp Real Estate/Bldg	4014 Gunn Highway	Tampa 813-963-0786	FL 33624	
330	Spalding & Evenflow Corp Manufacturing	5750 N Hoover	Tampa 813-887-5200	FL 33630	
550	Diamond Bathurst Corp Manufacturing	4343 Anchor Place Parkway	Tampa 813-884-0000	FL 33634	
2002	Florida Progress Corp Utility	270 First Avenue S	St Petersburg 813-895-1700	FL 33701	
350	Clabir Corp Manufacturing	10101 9th Street N	St Petersburg 813-577-5007	FL 33716	
730	Home Shopping Inc Retail/Merch	12000 25th Court N	St Petersburg 813-572-8585	FL 33716	
472	Florida Federal Savings & Loan Inc Savings & Loan	360 Central Avenue	St Petersburg 813-893-1131	FL 33731	
250	St Petersburg, City of Local Govt	City Hall	St Petersburg 813-893-7117	FL 33731	
4200	Publix Super Markets Inc Retail/Food	1936 George Jenkins Blvd	Lakeland 813-688-1188	FL 33802	
551	Scotty's Inc Retail/Food	Recker Highway	Winter Haven 813-299-1111	FL 33882	

State / Province: Florida

Organizations Listed Geographically

Revenue ($ mil)	Organization/ Industry	Address	City / Phone	State/ Zip	Province/ Postcode
250	Paradyne Corp Telecom	8550 Ulmerton Road	Largo 813-530-2000	FL 34641	

State / Province: Georgia

Revenue ($ mil)	Organization/ Industry	Address	City / Phone	State/ Zip	Province/ Postcode
333	Harland, John H Co Inc Business Service	2939 Miller Road	Decatur 404-981-9460	GA 30035	
2090	Electrolux US Inc Appliances/Furn	2300 Windy Ridge Parkway	Marietta 404-933-1000	GA 30067	
500	Rock Tenn Corp Packaging	504 Thrasher Street	Norcross 404-448-2193	GA 30071	
750	Southwire Co Inc Metals/Mining	140 Fertilla Street	Carrolton 404-832-4242	GA 30119	
550	Georgia Kraft Corp Packaging	1700 Redmond Road	Rome 404-232-0851	GA 30161	
402	Williams, A L Corp Non-Bank Fin	3100 Breckinridge Blvd	Duluth 404-381-1674	GA 30199	
228	Digital Communications Inc Comput/Off Equip	1000 Alderman Drive	Alpharetta 404-442-4000	GA 30201	
397	Interface Corporation Tire/Rubber	Overland Hill Road	LaGrange 404-882-1891	GA 30241	
976	Atlanta Gas Light Co Utility	235 Peachtree NE	Atlanta 404-584-4000	GA 30302	
743	Equifax Inc Comput/Off Equip	1600 Peachtree Street	Atlanta 404-885-8000	GA 30302	
409	Bank South Corp Banking	55 Marietta Street	Atlanta 404-529-4521	GA 30303	
2090	Citizens & Southern Co Banking	35 Broad Street NW	Atlanta 404-581-2121	GA 30303	
934	Federal Reserve Bank of Atlanta Inc Federal Govt Fin	104 Marietta Street	Atlanta 404-521-8500	GA 30303	
934	Fuqua Industries Inc Conglomerate	4900 Georgia Pacific Center	Atlanta 404-658-9000	GA 30303	
9509	Georgia Pacific Corp Paper/Forest Prd	133 Peachtree Street NE	Atlanta 404-521-4000	GA 30303	
80	Georgia State Unversity University	University Plaza	Atlanta 404-658-2000	GA 30303	
2889	Suntrust Banks Corp Banking	25 Park Place NE	Atlanta 404-588-7455	GA 30303	
NA	Georgia Power Co Utility	333 Piedmont Avenue	Atlanta 404-526-6000	GA 30308	
591	Oxford Industries Inc Apparel/Textiles	222 Piedmont Avenue NE	Atlanta 404-659-2424	GA 30308	
1414	National Service Industries Inc Electronics	1180 Peachtree Street NE	Atlanta 404-892-2400	GA 30309	
8338	Coca Cola Corp Beverage	310 N Avenue NW One Coca Cola Plaza	Atlanta 404-676-2121	GA 30313	
3874	Coca Cola Enterprises Inc Beverage	One Coca Cola Plaza NW	Atlanta 404-676-2100	GA 30313	
NA	Selig Chemical Industries Inc Chemicals	840 Selig Drive SW	Atlanta 404-691-9220	GA 30316	
652	Turner Broadcasting System Inc Publishing/Com	1050 Techwood Drive NW	Atlanta 404-827-1700	GA 30318	
1750	Cox Enterprises Inc Publishing/Com	1400 Lake Hearn Drive NE	Atlanta 404-843-5000	GA 30319	
6915	Delta Air Lines Inc Airline	Hartsfield Atlanta Intl Airport	Atlanta 404-765-2600	GA 30320	
270	Graphic Industries Inc Business Service	2155 Monroe Drive NE	Atlanta 404-874-3327	GA 30324	
380	Rollins Inc Business Service	2170 Piedmont Road NE	Atlanta 404-888-2000	GA 30324	
550	Colonial Pipeline Co Inc Transport	3390 Peachtree Road	Atlanta 404-261-1470	GA 30326	
300	Management Science America Inc Comput/Off Equip	3445 Peachtree Road	Atlanta 404-239-2000	GA 30326	

State / Province: Georgia

Organizations Listed Geographically

Revenue ($ mil)	Organization/ Industry	Address	City / Phone	State/ Zip	Province/ Postcode
220	Robinson Humphrey Co Inc Securities	Atlanta Financial Center 3333 Peachtree Road NE	Atlanta 404-266-6000	GA 30326	
358	American Business Products Inc Paper/Forest Prd	2100 River Edge Parkway Suite 1200	Atlanta 404-953-8300	GA 30328	
NA	BellSouth Advertising & Publishing Corp Publishing/Com	59 Executive Park S	Atlanta 404-982-7400	GA 30329	
400	First Financial Management Corp Comput/Off Equip	3 Corporate Square	Atlanta 404-321-0120	GA 30329	
227	National Data Corp Comput/Off Equip	One National Data Plaza	Atlanta 404-329-8500	GA 30329	
13455	Georgia, State of State/Prov Govt	State Capitol	Atlanta 404-656-2000	GA 30334	
596	Atlanta, City of Local Govt	City Hall 68 Mitchell Street SW	Atlanta 404-658-6100	GA 30335	
2942	Genuine Parts Co Business Service	2999 Circle 75 Parkway	Atlanta 404-953-1700	GA 30339	
1999	Home Depot Inc Retail/Merch	2727 Paces Ferry Road	Atlanta 404-433-8211	GA 30339	
500	Racetrac Petroleum Corp Retail/Merch	2625 Cumberland	Atlanta 404-434-0400	GA 30339	
15766	RJR Nabisco Inc Tobacco	300 Galleria Parkway	Atlanta 404-770-6000	GA 30339	
200	Telecom USA Inc Telecom	61 Perimeter Park NE	Atlanta 404-458-4927	GA 30341	
300	Crawford & Co Business Service	5620 Glenridge Road	Atlanta 404-256-0830	GA 30342	
NA	BellSouth Financial Services Corp Non-Bank Fin	1800 Century Blvd	Atlanta 404-329-4200	GA 30345	
2964	Contel Corp Telecom	245 Perimeter Center Parkway PO Box 105194	Atlanta 404-391-8000	GA 30346	
550	Georgia Gulf Corp Chemicals	400 Perimeter Terrace	Atlanta 404-395-4500	GA 30346	
2200	Gold Kist Inc Food Processing	244 Perimeter Center Parkway NE	Atlanta 404-393-5000	GA 30346	
7235	Southern Co Utility	64 Perimeter Center E	Atlanta 404-393-0650	GA 30346	
443	Georgia Federal Bank Inc Savings & Loan	20 Marietta Street	Atlanta 404-330-2440	GA 30348	
509	Scientific Atlanta Inc Telecom	One Technology Parkway PO Box 105600	Atlanta 404-441-4000	GA 30348	
1650	US Plywood Corp Building Mat	133 Peachtree NE	Atlanta 404-521-4000	GA 30348	
250	Aaron Rents Inc Appliances/Furn	3001 N Fulton Drive NE	Atlanta 404-231-0011	GA 30363	
13687	BellSouth Corp Telecom	1155 Peachtree Street NE	Atlanta 404-249-2000	GA 30367	
NA	Southern Bell Telephone & Telegraph Co Telecom	675 W Peachtree Street	Atlanta 404-529-8611	GA 30375	
825	Piggly Wiggly Southern Inc Retail/Food	100 Brinson Road	Vidalia 912-537-9871	GA 30474	
266	University of Georgia University	Administrative Bldg	Athens 404-542-3030	GA 30602	
500	Walton Monroe Textiles Inc Apparel/Textiles	PO Box 1046	Monroe 404-267-9411	GA 30655	
150	Crown Crafts Inc Apparel/Textiles	Edmond Street	Calhoun 404-629-7941	GA 30701	
350	Horizon Industries Inc Apparel/Textiles	S Industrial Blvd	Calhoun 404-629-7721	GA 30701	
275	World Carpets Inc Apparel/Textiles	1 World Plaza	Dalton 404-278-8000	GA 30720	
958	Shaw Industries Inc Apparel/Textiles	616 E Walnut Avenue	Dalton 404-278-3812	GA 30722	
703	Roper Corp Manufacturing	931 Broad Street	Augusta 404-724-0822	GA 30901	
1200	Charter Medical Corp Business Service	577 Mulberry Street	Macon 912-742-1161	GA 31298	

State / Province: Georgia

Organizations Listed Geographically

Revenue ($ mil)	Organization/ Industry	Address	City / Phone	State/ Zip	Province/ Postcode
NA	Savannah Electric & Power Inc Utility	600 E Bay Street	Savannah 912-238-2251	GA 31401	
550	Colonial Oil Industries Inc Energy	N Lathrop Avenue	Savannah 912-236-1331	GA 31402	
NA	Gulfstream Aerospace Corp Aerospace	Savannah International Airport	Savannah 912-964-3000	GA 31402	
917	Savannah Foods & Industries Inc Food Processing	PO Box 339	Savannah 912-234-1261	GA 31402	
NA	Branitek Inc Packaging	6555 Ambercorn	Savannah 912-354-4885	GA 31405	
737	Flowers Industries Inc Food Processing	PO Box 1338	Thomasville 912-226-9110	GA 31799	
1740	West Point-Pepperell Inc Apparel/Textiles	400 W 10th Street	West Point 404-645-4000	GA 31833	
2151	Westpoint Pepperell Inc Apparel/Textiles	400 W Tenth Street	West Point 404-645-4000	GA 31833	
251	CB & T Bancshares Inc Banking	1148 Broadway	Columbus 404-649-2387	GA 31901	
56	Total System Services Corp Business Service	1000 Fifth Avenue	Columbus 404-649-2204	GA 31901	
500	Heard, Bill Enterprises Inc Automotive	2600 Cross Country Drive	Columbus 404-561-6213	GA 31907	
500	Georgia Crown Distributing Corp Food Processing	7 Crown Circle	Columbus 404-568-4580	GA 31908	
2325	American Family Corp Non-Bank Fin	1932 Wynnton Road	Columbus 404-323-3431	GA 31909	

State / Province: Hawaii

702	Alexander & Baldwin Inc Business Service	822 Bishop Street	Honolulu 808-525-6611	HI 96801	
630	Bancorp Hawaii Inc Banking	111 S King Street	Honolulu 808-537-8111	HI 96813	
396	First Hawaiian Inc Banking	165 S King Street	Honolulu 808-525-7000	HI 96813	
354	HAL (Hawaiian Air) Inc Transport	1164 Bishop Street	Honolulu 808-525-5511	HI 96813	
2818	Hawaii, State of State/Prov Govt	State Capitol	Honolulu 808-548-2211	HI 96813	
732	Hawaiian Electric Industries Inc Utility	900 Richards Street	Honolulu 808-543-5662	HI 96813	
506	Honolulu, City of Local Govt	City Hall	Honolulu 808-523-4111	HI 96813	
NA	Oceanic Properties Inc Real Estate/Bldg	650 Iwi Lei Street	Honolulu 808-548-4811	HI 96817	
204	University of Hawaii University	2500 Campus Road	Honolulu 808-948-8111	HI 96822	
1050	Pacific Resources Inc Food Processing	PO Box 3379	Honolulu 808-547-3111	HI 96842	

State / Province: Idaho

1500	Simplot, J R Co Food Processing	999 Main Street	Boise 208-336-2110	ID 83701	
400	Micron Technology Comput/Off Equip	2805 E Columbia Road	Boise 208-383-4000	ID 83706	
412	Idaho Power Co Utility	1220 W Idaho Street	Boise 208-383-2200	ID 83707	
1909	Morrison Knudsen Corp Business Service	Morrison Knudsen Plaza PO Box 7808	Boise 208-386-5000	ID 83707	
500	Ore-Ida Foods Inc Food Processing	220 W Park Center Blvd	Boise 208-383-6100	ID 83707	
400	TJ International Inc Building Mat	9777 W Chinden Blvd	Boise 208-375-4450	ID 83714	
1915	Idaho, State of State/Prov Govt	State Capitol	Boise 208-334-2411	ID 83720	

State / Province: Idaho

Organizations Listed Geographically

Revenue ($ mil)	Organization/ Industry	Address	City / Phone	State/ Zip	Province/ Postcode
6773	Albertson's Inc Retail/Food	250 Parkcenter Blvd PO Box 20	Boise 208-385-6200	ID 83726	
4095	Boise Cascade Corp Paper/Forest Prd	One Jefferson Square	Boise 208-384-6161	ID 83728	
349	West One Bank Corp Banking	PO Box 8247	Boise 208-388-7791	ID 83733	
105	Hecla Mining Co Metals/Mining	6500 Mineral Drive	Coeur D'Alene 208-769-4107	ID 83814	

State / Province: Illinois

Revenue ($ mil)	Organization/ Industry	Address	City / Phone	State/ Zip	Province/ Postcode
384	AAR Business Service	1111 Nicholas Blvd	Elk Grove 312-439-3939	IL 60007	
275	Galaxy Carpet Mills Inc Appliances/Furn	850 Arthur Avenue	Elk Grove Village 312-593-0555	IL 60007	
750	Tang Industries Inc Steel	1965 Pratt Blvd	Elk Grove 312-981-8200	IL 60007	
1000	Gould Inc Electronics	10 Gould Center	Rolling Meadows 312-640-4000	IL 60008	
3100	Staley Continental Incorported Food Processing	One Continental Towers 1701 Golf Road	Rolling Meadows 312-981-1696	IL 60008	
225	Sun Electric Corp Electronics	One Sun Parkway	Crystal Lake 815-459-7700	IL 60014	
6861	Baxter Travenol Laboratories Inc Drugs	One Baxter Parkway	Deerfield 312-948-2000	IL 60015	
625	Commerce Clearing House Inc Publishing/Com	2700 Lake Cook Road	Riverwoods 312-940-4600	IL 60015	
380	Gaylord Container Manufacturing	500 Lakecook Road	Deerfield 312-405-5500	IL 60015	
NA	Jim Beam Brands Inc Beverage	510 Lake Cook Road	Deerfeild 312-948-0395	IL 60015	
275	Leaf Inc Food Processing	2355 Waukegan Road	Bannockburn 312-940-7500	IL 60015	
2397	Premark International Corp Tire/Rubber	1717 Deerfield Road	Deerfield 312-405-6000	IL 60015	
4884	Walgreen Co Retail/Merch	200 Wilmot Road	Deerfield 312-940-2500	IL 60015	
1000	United Stationers Inc Comput/Off Equip	2200 E Golf Road	Des Plaines 312-699-5000	IL 60016	
403	DeSoto Inc Building Mat	1700 S Mount Prospect Road	Des Plaines 312-391-9000	IL 60017	
1309	Comdisco Inc Business Service	6111 N River Road	Rosemont 312-698-3000	IL 60018	
128	Lyphomed Inc Drugs	10401 W Touhy Avenue	Rosemont 312-390-6500	IL 60018	
550	Koenig & Strey Inc Real Estate/Bldg	999 Waukegan Road	Glenview 312-729-6610	IL 60025	
440	SFN Companies Inc Publishing/Com	1900 E Lake Avenue	Glenview 312-657-3900	IL 60025	
935	Signode Corp Manufacturing	3610 W Lake Avenue	Glenview 312-724-6100	IL 60025	
2686	Zenith Electronics Corp Electronics	1000 Milwaukee Avenue	Glenview 312-391-7000	IL 60025	
NA	Automotive Aftermarket Co Automotive	707 Skokie Blvd	Northbrook 312-272-9600	IL 60026	
1100	CF Industries Inc Chemicals	Salem Lake Drive	Long Grove 312-438-9500	IL 60047	
3861	Kemper Corp Insurance	Route 22	Long Grove 312-540-2000	IL 60049	
NA	Zenith Data Systems Corp Comput/Off Equip	1661 Feehanville Drive	Mount Prospect 312-699-4800	IL 60056	
1000	Wickes Lumber Co Retail/Merch	706 Deerpath Drive	Vernon Hills 312-367-6540	IL 60061	
3354	Allstate Life Insurance Co Insurance	Allstate Plaza S	Northbrook 312-291-5000	IL 60062	

State / Province: Illinois

Organizations Listed Geographically

Revenue ($ mil)	Organization/ Industry	Address	City / Phone	State/ Zip	Province/ Postcode
300	General Binding Corp Comput/Off Equip	One GBC Plaza	Northbrook 312-272-3700	IL 60062	
250	Idex Corp Manufacturing	630 Dundee Road	Northbrook 312-498-7070	IL 60062	
1200	IMC Fertilizer Corp Chemicals	2315 Sanders Road	Northbrook 312-564-8600	IL 60062	
1471	International Minerals & Chemical Corp Chemicals	2315 Sanders Road	Northbrook 312-564-8600	IL 60062	
10000	Kraft Inc Retail/Food	2211 Sanders Road Kraft Court	Glenview 312-498-4000	IL 60062	
NA	Nielsen, A C Co Comput/Off Equip	Nielsen Plaza	Northbrook 312-498-6300	IL 60062	
4937	Abbott Laboratories Inc Drugs	One Abbott Park Road	Abbott Park 312-937-6100	IL 60064	
260	ACCO World Corp Publishing/Com	22150 Sanders Road	Northbrook 312-480-9700	IL 60065	
771	Pittway Corp Electronics	333 Skokie Blvd	Northbrook 312-498-1260	IL 60065	
795	Standard Shares Inc Electronics	333 Skokie Blvd	Northbrook 312-498-1260	IL 60065	
1657	Square D Co Electronics	Executive Plaza 1415 S Roselle	Palatine 312-397-2600	IL 60067	
300	Brand Companies Inc Equipment	1420 Renaissance Drive	Park Ridge 312-298-1200	IL 60068	
2352	Household International Inc Conglomerate	2700 Sanders Road	Prospect Heights 312-564-3663	IL 60070	
1000	Household Manufacturing Corp Manufacturing	2700 Sanders Road	Prospect Heights 312-564-3910	IL 60070	
650	Anixter Brothers Inc Building Mat	4711 Golf Road	Skokie 312-677-2600	IL 60076	
900	Bell & Howell Co Comput/Off Equip	5215 Old Orchard Road	Skokie 312-470-7100	IL 60077	
3282	Brunswick Corp Leisure Time	One Brunswick Plaza	Skokie 312-470-4700	IL 60077	
1535	Grainger, W W Inc Business Service	5500 W Howard Street	Skokie 312-982-9000	IL 60077	
NA	Searle, G D & Co Drugs	5200 Old Orchard Road	Skokie 312-982-7000	IL 60077	
2200	Topco Associates Inc Retail/Food	7711 Gross Pointe Road	Skokie 312-676-3030	IL 60077	
1605	Outboard Marine Corp Leisure Time	100 Sea Horse Drive	Waukegan 312-689-6200	IL 60085	
204	Artra Group Inc Electronics	500 Central Avenue	Winnetka 312-441-6650	IL 60093	
300	Stepan Co Chemicals	Edens & Winnetka Roads	Winnetka 312-446-7500	IL 60093	
1100	Nationwide Electronics Inc Electronics	3003 Wakefield Drive	Carpentersville 312-426-5900	IL 60110	
825	NES Corp Instruments	3003 Wakefield Drive	Carpentersville 312-426-5900	IL 60110	
230	DeKalb Corp Food Processing	3100 Sycamore Road	DeKalb 815-758-3461	IL 60115	
136	Northern Illinois University University	Administrative Bldg	DeKalb 815-753-1271	IL 60115	
750	Eby Brown Companies Retail/Merch	1313 Timber Drive	Aurora 312-242-1919	IL 60120	
192	Katy Industries Inc Conglomerate	853 Dundee Avenue	Elgin 312-697-8900	IL 60120	
417	Safety Kleen Corp Business Service	777 Big Timber Road	Elgin 312-697-8460	IL 60120	
750	Duchossois Industries Inc Manufacturing	845 Larch Avenue	Elmhurst 312-279-3600	IL 60126	
600	Jepson Corp Appliances/Furn	360 W Butterfield Road	Elmhurst 312-834-3710	IL 60126	
375	Castle, A M & Co Metals/Mining	3400 N Wolf Road	Franklin Park 312-455-7111	IL 60131	

State / Province: Illinois

Organizations Listed Geographically

Revenue ($ mil)	Organization/ Industry	Address	City / Phone	State/ Zip	Province/ Postcode
1552	Dean Foods Co Food Processing	3600 N River Road	Franklin Park 312-678-1680	IL 60131	
NA	Boise Cascade Office Products Corp Business Service	800 Bryn Mawr Avenue	Itasca 312-773-6400	IL 60143	
NA	MidCon Corp Energy	701 E 22nd Street	Lombard 312-691-2500	IL 60148	
600	Allied Van Lines Inc Transport	2120 S 25th Street	Broadview 312-681-8000	IL 60153	
605	Alberto Culver Co Personal Care	2525 Armitage Avenue	Melrose Park 312-450-3000	IL 60160	
NA	Jewel Food Stores Retail/Food	1955 W North Avenue	Melrose Park 312-531-6000	IL 60160	
383	Wallace Computer Services Inc Comput/Off Equip	4600 W Roosevelt Road	Hillside 312-626-2000	IL 60162	
2000	Dominicks Finer Foods Inc Food Processing	555 N Northwest Road	Northlake 312-562-1000	IL 60164	
825	Shurfine Central Corp Real Estate/Bldg	2100 N Mannheim	Northlake 312-681-2000	IL 60164	
250	Duplex Products Inc Paper/Forest Prd	1947 Bethany Road	Sycamore 815-895-2100	IL 60178	
8250	Motorola Inc Electronics	1303 E Algonquin Road	Schaumburg 312-397-5000	IL 60196	
688	Zurich Insurance Co Insurance	231 N Martingale Road	Schaumburg 312-843-6000	IL 60196	
262	Northwestern University University	633 Clark Street	Evanston 312-492-3741	IL 60211	
500	ATCOR Inc Manufacturing	16100 S Lathrop Avenue	Harvey 312-339-1610	IL 60426	
200	JPM Industries Inc Publishing/Com	7421 W 100th Place	Bridgeview 312-598-1300	IL 60455	
300	Andrew Corp Electronics	10500 W 153rd Street	Orland Park 312-349-3300	IL 60462	
550	Aurora Eby Brown Co Inc Food Processing	1001 Sullivan	Aurora 312-897-8674	IL 60505	
1531	Service Master Industries Inc Business Service	2300 Warrenville Road	Downers Grove 312-964-1300	IL 60515	
1100	Ace Hardware Corp Retail/Merch	2200 Kensington Court	Oak Brook 312-990-6600	IL 60521	
NA	American Drug Stores Inc Retail/Food	1818 Swift Avenue	Oak Brook 312-572-5000	IL 60521	
700	Chemical Waste Corp Business Service	3001 Butterfield Road	Oak Brook 312-572-8800	IL 60521	
400	Federal Signal Corp Electronics	1415 W 22nd Street	Oak Brook 312-954-2000	IL 60521	
500	Inland Real Estate Corp Real Estate/Bldg	2901 Butterfield Road	Oak Brook 312-218-8000	IL 60521	
892	Interlake Corp Machinery	701 Harger Road	Oak Brook 312-986-6600	IL 60521	
1200	Laidlaw Industries Inc Business Service	15 Spinning Wheel Road	Hinsdale 312-439-6686	IL 60521	
5566	McDonald's Corp Food/Lodging	McDonald's Plaza	Oak Brook 312-575-3000	IL 60521	
250	Pansophic Systems Inc Comput/Off Equip	709 Enterprise Drive	Oak Brook 312-572-6000	IL 60521	
3566	Waste Management Inc Business Service	3003 Butterfield Road	Oak Brook 312-654-8800	IL 60521	
231	XL/Datacomp Inc Comput/Off Equip	908 N Elm Street	Hinsdale 312-323-1200	IL 60521	
1376	CBI Industries Inc Oil Service	800 Jorie Blvd	Oak Brook 312-572-7000	IL 60522	
500	Ceco Corp Building Mat	1400 Kensington Avenue	Oak Brook 312-789-1400	IL 60522	
1100	Spiegel Corp Retail/Merch	1515 W 22nd Street	Oak Brook 312-986-8800	IL 60522	
502	Molex Inc Electronics	2222 Wellington Court	Lisle 312-969-4550	IL 60532	

State / Province: Illinois

Organizations Listed Geographically

Revenue ($ mil)	Organization/ Industry	Address	City / Phone	State/ Zip	Province/ Postcode
440	Van Kampen Merritt Inc Securities	1001 Warrenville Road	Lisle 312-719-6000	IL 60532	
994	Nalco Chemical Co Chemicals	One Nalco Center	Naperville 312-961-9500	IL 60566	
1509	NICOR (Northern Illinois Gas) Corp Utility	1700 W Ferry Road	Naperville 312-242-4470	IL 60566	
NA	Amoco Chemical Co Energy	200 E Randolph Drive	Chicago 312-856-6111	IL 60601	
23919	Amoco Corp Energy	200 E Randolph Drive	Chicago 312-856-6111	IL 60601	
1000	Amsted Industries Inc Manufacturing	3700 Prudential Plaza	Chicago 312-645-1700	IL 60601	
1320	Blue Cross Blue Shield of Illinois Inc Insurance	233 N Michigan Avenue	Chicago 312-938-7500	IL 60601	
800	Borg Warner Acceptance Corp Non-Bank Fin	225 N Michigan	Chicago 312-329-6500	IL 60601	
512	Budget Rent-a-Car Inc Consumer Service	200 N Michigan Avenue	Chicago 312-580-5000	IL 60601	
2200	Burnett, Leo Co Inc Business Service	35 W Wacker	Chicago 312-565-5959	IL 60601	
NA	Canteen Inc Food/Lodging	222 N LaSalle Street	Chicago 312-701-2000	IL 60601	
3287	FMC Corp Equipment	200 E Randolph Drive	Chicago 312-861-6000	IL 60601	
NA	Freeman United Coal Mining Co Metals/Mining	222 N LaSalle Street	Chicago 312-263-4490	IL 60601	
250	Grant Thornton Inc Accounting	Prudential Plaza	Chicago 312-856-0001	IL 60601	
750	Illinois Central Gulf Railroad Co Transport	233 N Michigan Avenue	Chicago 312-565-1600	IL 60601	
NA	Midas International Corp Automotive	225 N Michigan Avenue	Chicago 312-565-7500	IL 60601	
1200	Old Republic International Corp Insurance	397 N Michigan Avenue	Chicago 312-346-8100	IL 60601	
3742	Stone Container Corp Paper/Forest Prd	150 Michigan Avenue	Chicago 312-346-6600	IL 60601	
400	UDC Universal Development Corp Real Estate/Bldg	205 N Michigan Avenue	Chicago 312-726-1885	IL 60601	
3583	Whitman Co (IC Industries Inc) Conglomerate	111 E Wacker Drive	Chicago 312-565-3000	IL 60601	
3000	Arthur, Andersen & Co Inc Accounting	69 W Washington	Chicago 312-580-0069	IL 60602	
7500	Beatrice Foods (BCI Holdings Inc) Food Processing	Two LaSalle Street	Chicago 312-782-3820	IL 60602	
2581	Chicago, City of Local Govt	City Hall 121 N LaSalle Street	Chicago 312-744-3300	IL 60602	
3900	Cook County Government Local Govt	County Bldg	Chicago 312-443-5500	IL 60602	
11206	Sara Lee Corp Food Processing	Three First National Plaza	Chicago 312-726-2600	IL 60602	
1023	Carson, Pirie, Scott & Co Retail/Merch	One S State Street	Chicago 312-641-7000	IL 60603	
4068	Inland Steel Industries Inc Steel	30 W Monroe Street	Chicago 312-346-0300	IL 60603	
3500	Marmon Group Inc Food/Lodging	39 S LaSalle Street	Chicago 312-372-9500	IL 60603	
400	Microdot Inc Manufacturing	20 S Clark Street	Chicago 312-899-1925	IL 60603	
1117	Peoples Energy Corp Utility	122 S Michigan Avenue	Chicago 312-431-4000	IL 60603	
550	Sargent & Lundy Inc Consulting	55 E Monroe Street	Chicago 312-269-2000	IL 60603	
543	Talman Home Fed Savings & Loan Inc Savings & Loan	30 W Monroe Street	Chicago 312-726-8915	IL 60603	
250	Telephone & Data Corp Telecom	79 W Monroe Street	Chicago 312-630-1900	IL 60603	

State / Province: Illinois

Organizations Listed Geographically

Revenue ($ mil)	Organization/ Industry	Address	City / Phone	State/ Zip	Province/ Postcode
3800	Borg Warner Corp Manufacturing	200 S Michigan Avenue	Chicago 312-322-8500	IL 60604	
1400	Chicago Pacific Corp Appliances/Furn	200 S Michigan Avenue	Chicago 312-435-7300	IL 60604	
600	Encyclopedia Britannica Inc Publishing/Com	310 S Michigan	Chicago 312-347-7000	IL 60604	
3144	Santa Fe Southern Pacific Corp Railroad	224 S Michigan Avenue	Chicago 312-786-6000	IL 60604	
392	UNR Industries Inc Manufacturing	332 S Michigan Avenue	Chicago 312-341-1234	IL 60604	
330	First Options of Chicago Inc Securities	One Financial Place 440 S LaSalle Street	Chicago 312-786-3000	IL 60605	
578	Allied Products Corp Manufacturing	10 S Riverside	Chicago 312-454-1020	IL 60606	
821	AM International Inc Business Service	333 W Wacker Drive Suite 900	Chicago 312-558-1966	IL 60606	
9903	Ameritech (Amer Information Tech Corp) Telecom	30 S Wacker Drive	Chicago 312-750-5000	IL 60606	
NA	Ameritech Communications Inc Telecom	500 W Madison	Chicago 312-906-4199	IL 60606	
2732	Aon Corp (Combined Int'l) Non-Bank Fin	123 N Wacker Drive	Chicago 312-701-3000	IL 60606	
550	Baird & Warner Inc Real Estate/Bldg	200 W Madison	Chicago 312-368-1855	IL 60606	
200	Baker Fentress & Co Securities	200 W Madison Street	Chicago 312-236-9190	IL 60606	
500	CC Industries Inc Real Estate/Bldg	300 W Washington	Chicago 312-236-6300	IL 60606	
995	CNW Corp Railroad	165 N Canal One NW Center	Chicago 312-559-7000	IL 60606	
880	Crown Henry & Co Inc Paper/Forest Prd	300 W Washington	Chicago 312-236-6300	IL 60606	
825	Elrick & Lavidge Inc Business Service	10 S Riverside Plaza	Chicago 312-726-0666	IL 60606	
350	Epstein, A & Sons International Inc Consulting	600 W Fulton	Chicago 312-454-9100	IL 60606	
2000	Farley Industries Inc Manufacturing	6300 Sears Tower 233 S Wacker Drive	Chicago 312-876-1724	IL 60606	
NA	Florsheim Shoe Co Retail/Merch	130 Canal Street	Chicago 312-559-2500	IL 60606	
1005	Fruit of the Loom Inc Apparel/Textiles	233 S Wacker Drive 6300 Sears Tower	Chicago 312-876-1724	IL 60606	
587	GATX Corp Business Service	120 S Riverside Plaza	Chicago 312-621-6200	IL 60606	
1174	Hartmarx Corp Apparel/Textiles	101 N Wacker Drive	Chicago 312-372-6300	IL 60606	
2500	Hyatt Corp Food/Lodging	200 W Madison	Chicago 312-750-1234	IL 60606	
NA	Illinois Bell Telephone Co Telecom	212 W Washington Street	Chicago 312-727-9411	IL 60606	
129	Information Resources Inc Comput/Off Equip	150 N Clinton Street	Chicago 312-726-1221	IL 60606	
1644	Itel Corp Manufacturing	Two N Riverside Plaza	Chicago 312-902-1515	IL 60606	
300	Kearney, A T Inc Consulting	222 S Riverside Plaza	Chicago 312-648-0111	IL 60606	
NA	Morton Chemical Co Chemicals	333 W Wacker Drive	Chicago 312-807-3290	IL 60606	
1407	Morton International Inc Chemicals	110 N Wacker Drive	Chicago 312-807-2000	IL 60606	
NA	Morton Salt Co Food Processing	110 N Wacker Drive	Chicago 312-807-2665	IL 60606	
450	Nuveen, John & Co Inc Securities	333 W Wacker Drive	Chicago 312-917-7700	IL 60606	
1200	Royal Insurance Co of America Insurance	10 S Riverside Plaza	Chicago 312-522-2000	IL 60606	

State / Province: Illinois

Organizations Listed Geographically

Revenue ($ mil)	Organization/ Industry	Address	City / Phone	State/ Zip	Province/ Postcode
350	Rymer Foods Inc Food Processing	300 W Washington Blvd	Chicago 312-419-0060	IL	60606
1168	Thiokol Corp Aerospace	110 N Wacker Drive	Chicago 312-807-2000	IL	60606
515	Trailer Train Corp Transport	101 N Wacker Drive	Chicago 312-853-3223	IL	60606
2248	USG Corp Building Mat	101 S Wacker Drive	Chicago 312-321-4000	IL	60606
629	Helene Curtis Industries Inc Personal Care	325 N Wells Street	Chicago 312-292-2121	IL	60610
4800	Montgomery Ward & Co Inc Retail/Merch	535 W Chicago Avenue	Chicago 312-467-2000	IL	60610
500	Pepper Companies Real Estate/Bldg	643 N Orleans Street	Chicago 312-266-4703	IL	60610
475	Envirodyne Industries Manufacturing	142 E Ontario	Chicago 312-649-0600	IL	60611
520	Foote, Cone & Belding Inc Business Service	101 E Erie Street Foote Cone & Belding Ctr	Chicago 312-751-7000	IL	60611
400	Humiston Keeling Corp Retail/Merch	233 E Erie	Chicago 312-943-6066	IL	60611
1500	JMB Institutional Realty Non-Bank Fin	875 N Michigan Avenue	Chicago 312-440-4800	IL	60611
194	Loyola University of Chicago University	820 N Michigan Avenue	Chicago 312-670-3000	IL	60611
4080	Navistar International Corp Automotive	401 N Michigan Avenue	Chicago 312-836-2000	IL	60611
NA	Tribune Broadcasting Co Publishing/Com	435 Michigan Avenue	Chicago 312-222-3939	IL	60611
2335	Tribune Co Publishing/Com	435 N Michigan Avenue	Chicago 312-222-9100	IL	60611
891	Wrigley, William Jr Co Food Processing	410 N Michigan Avenue	Chicago 312-644-2121	IL	60611
2200	Cotter & Co Retail/Merch	2740 N Clybourn Avenue	Chicago 312-975-2700	IL	60614
2878	Donnelley, R R & Sons Co Business Service	2223 Martin Luther King Drive	Chicago 312-326-8000	IL	60616
350	Acme Steel Co Manufacturing	13500 S Perry Avenue	Chicago 312-849-2500	IL	60627
1941	Bally Manufacturing Corp Leisure Time	8700 W Bryn Mawr Avenue	Chicago 312-399-1300	IL	60631
1095	Centel Corp Telecom	O'Hare Plaza 8725 Higgins Road	Chicago 312-399-2500	IL	60631
1930	Illinois Tool Works Inc Manufacturing	8501 W Higgins Road	Chicago 312-693-3040	IL	60631
435	University of Chicago University	5801 S Ellis	Chicago 312-753-1234	IL	60637
1100	Certified Grocers Midwest Inc Retail/Food	4800 S Central	Chicago 312-585-7000	IL	60638
500	Chemcentral Corp Chemicals	7050 W 71st Street	Chicago 312-594-7000	IL	60638
400	Midway Airlines Inc Airline	5959 S Cicero Avenue	Chicago 312-838-0001	IL	60638
500	Coca Cola Bottling of Chicago Inc Food Processing	7400 N Oak Park Blvd	Chicago 312-775-0900	IL	60648
500	Imperial Eastman Corp Manufacturing	6565 W Howard	Niles 312-967-4500	IL	60648
5330	Quaker Oats Co Food Processing	321 N Clark Street	Chicago 312-222-7111	IL	60654
8982	UAL Inc (United Airlines) Airline	1200 Algonquin Road	Elk Grove Townshp 312-952-4000	IL	60666
4815	First Chicago Corp Banking	One First National Plaza	Chicago 312-732-4000	IL	60670
1003	Northern Trust Corp Banking	50 S LaSalle Street	Chicago 312-630-6000	IL	60675
396	University of Illinois at Chicago University	1737 W Polk	Chicago 312-996-3000	IL	60680

State / Province: Illinois

Organizations Listed Geographically

Revenue ($ mil)	Organization/ Industry	Address	City / Phone	State/ Zip	Province/ Postcode
50252	Sears Roebuck & Co Retail/Merch	Sears Tower	Chicago 312-875-2500	IL 60684	
8204	CNA Financial Corp Insurance	CNA Plaza	Chicago 312-822-5000	IL 60685	
2323	Continental Assurance Co Insurance	CNA Plaza	Chicago 312-822-5000	IL 60685	
438	American National Bank & Trust Co Banking	33 N LaSalle Street	Chicago 312-661-5000	IL 60690	
5613	Commonwealth Edison Co Utility	One First National Plaza	Chicago 312-294-4321	IL 60690	
2469	Federal Reserve Bank of Chicago Inc Federal Govt Fin	230 S LaSalle Street	Chicago 312-322-5111	IL 60690	
1165	Harris Trust & Savings Bank Banking	111 W Monroe Street	Chicago 312-461-2121	IL 60690	
400	Stein Roe & Farnham Inc Non-Bank Fin	1 S Wacker Drive PO Box 1162	Chicago 312-368-7800	IL 60690	
3061	Continental Bank Corp Banking	231 S LaSalle Street	Chicago 312-828-2345	IL 60697	
988	Newell Co Manufacturing	Newell Center 29 Stephenson Street	Freeport 815-235-4171	IL 61032	
500	Northwestern Steel & Wire Corp Manufacturing	121 Wallace Street	Sterling 815-625-2500	IL 61081	
550	Ingersoll International Inc Manufacturing	707 Fulton Avenue	Rockford 815-987-6000	IL 61103	
1477	Sundstrand Corp Machinery	4949 Harrison Avenue	Rockford 815-226-6000	IL 61125	
1000	Eagle Food Center Corp Retail/Food	801 E 1st Street	Milan 309-787-7700	IL 61264	
5365	Deere & Co Equipment	John Deere Road	Moline 309-765-8000	IL 61265	
434	Central Illinois Light Co Utility	300 Liberty Street	Peoria 309-672-5271	IL 61602	
471	Cilcorp Inc Utility	300 Liberty Street	Peoria 309-672-5271	IL 61602	
10435	Caterpillar Inc Equipment	100 NE Adams Street	Peoria 309-675-1000	IL 61629	
400	Country Companies Insurance	1701 Towanda Avenue	Bloomington 309-557-2111	IL 61701	
2200	Growmark Inc Retail/Merch	1701 Towanda Avenue	Bloomington 309-557-6000	IL 61701	
2358	State Farm Insurance Co Insurance	One State Farm Plaza	Bloomington 309-766-2311	IL 61710	
112	Illinois State University University	School & North Streets	Normal 309-438-2111	IL 61761	
460	University of Illinois University	Administrative Bldg	Champaign 217-333-1000	IL 61801	
NA	Industrial Machinery Corp Machinery	1800 Gardner Expressway	Quincy 217-222-5400	IL 62301	
550	Moorman Manufacturing Co Food Processing	1000 N 30th Street	Quincy 217-222-7100	IL 62301	
1285	Illinois Power Co Utility	500 S 27th Street	Decatur 217-424-6600	IL 62525	
NA	Smoot Grain Co Food Processing	4666 Faries Parkway	Decatur 913-827-8734	IL 62525	
6798	Archer Daniels Midland Co Food Processing	4666 Faries Parkway	Decatur 217-424-5200	IL 62626	
330	Prairie Farms Dairy Inc Food Processing	1100 N Broadway	Carlinville 217-854-2547	IL 62626	
27399	Illinois, State of State/Prov Govt	State House	Springfield 217-782-2099	IL 62706	
1083	Franklin Life Insurance Co Insurance	Franklin Square	Springfield 217-528-2011	IL 62713	
616	Central Illinois Public Service Co Utility	607 E Adams Street	Springfield 217-523-3600	IL 62739	
196	Southern Illinois University University	Administrative Bldg	Carbondale 618-453-2121	IL 62901	

State / Province: Illinois

Organizations Listed Geographically

Revenue ($ mil)	Organization/ Industry	Address	City / Phone	State/ Zip	Province/ Postcode

State / Province: Indiana

Revenue ($ mil)	Organization/ Industry	Address	City / Phone	State/Zip
300	Anacomp Inc Comput/Off Equip	11550 N Meridian Street	Indianapolis 317-844-9666	IN 46032
750	Mayflower Group Inc Transport	9998 N Michigan Road	Carmel 317-875-1000	IN 46032
1043	PSI Public Service Co of Indiana Utility	100 E Main Street	Plainfield 317-839-9611	IN 46168
250	Indiana Energy Inc Utility	1630 N Meridian Street	Indianapolis 317-926-3351	IN 46202
278	Indiana University at Indianapolis University	355 N Lansing	Indianapolis 317-635-8661	IN 46202
500	Central Newspapers Inc Publishing/Com	307 N Pennsylvania Street	Indianapolis 317-633-9027	IN 46204
NA	Indiana Bell Telephone Co Telecom	240 N Meridian Street	Indianapolis 317-265-2266	IN 46204
1320	Indiana Farm Bureau Coop Assn Inc Food Processing	120 E Market Street	Indianapolis 317-631-8361	IN 46204
11256	Indiana, State of State/Prov Govt	State Capitol	Indianapolis 317-232-4000	IN 46204
557	Indianapolis, City of Local Govt	City & County Bldg	Indianapolis 317-236-3600	IN 46204
609	Ipalco Enterprises Inc Utility	25 Monument Circle	Indianapolis 317-261-8261	IN 46204
NA	AMAX Coal Industries Inc Metals/Mining	Capital Center 251 N Illinois Street	Indianapolis 317-266-1500	IN 46206
856	American United Life Insurance Co Insurance	One American Square PO Box 368	Indianapolis 317-263-1877	IN 46206
NA	Inland Container Corp Packaging	151 N Delaware	Indianapolis 317-262-0222	IN 46206
1400	Hook SupeRX Stores Inc Retail/Merch	PO Box 26285	Indianapolis 317-353-1451	IN 46226
NA	Jenn-Air Corp Appliances/Furn	3035 Shadeland	Indianapolis 317-545-2271	IN 46226
284	Basic American Medical Corp Health Care	4000 E Southport Road	Indianapolis 317-783-5461	IN 46237
451	Inacomp Computer Centers Inc Comput/Off Equip	11550 N Meridian Street	Indianapolis 317-844-9666	IN 46240
1000	Hunt Corp Real Estate/Bldg	2450 S Tibbs Avenue	Indianapolis 317-241-6301	IN 46241
402	Wholesale Club Inc Retail/Merch	7260 Shadeland Station	Indianapolis 317-842-0351	IN 46250
452	Merchants National Bank & Trust Co Banking	One Merchants Plaza	Indianapolis 317-267-6100	IN 46255
545	Indiana National Corp Banking	One Indiana Square	Indianapolis 317-266-6000	IN 46266
1275	Bindley Western Industries Manufacturing	4212 W 71st Street	Indianapolis 317-298-9900	IN 46268
800	Rock Island Refining Co Energy	5000 W 86th Street	Indianapolis 317-872-3200	IN 46268
4070	Lilly, Eli & Co Drugs	Lilly Corporate Center	Indianapolis 317-261-2000	IN 46285
1526	NIPSCO Northern Indiana Pub Serv Co Utility	5265 Hohman Avenue	Hammond 219-853-5200	IN 46320
325	CTS Corp Electronics	905 N West Blvd	Elkhart 219-293-7511	IN 46514
400	Coachmen Industries Inc Automotive	601 E Beardsley Avenue	Elkhart 219-262-0123	IN 46515
250	Excel Industries Inc Automotive	1120 N Main Street	Elkhart 219-264-2131	IN 46515
1650	Miles Laboratories Inc Drugs	1127 Myrtle Street	Elkhart 219-264-8062	IN 46515
384	Skyline Corp Manufacturing	2520 By-Pass Road PO Box 743	Elkhart 219-294-6521	IN 46515

State / Province: Indiana

Organizations Listed Geographically

Revenue ($ mil)	Organization/ Industry	Address	City / Phone	State/ Zip	Province/ Postcode
NA	United Telephone Co of Indiana Telecom	3570 E US 30	Warsaw 219-267-6161	IN 46580	
1278	Clark Equipment Corp Machinery	100 N Michigan Street	South Bend 219-239-0100	IN 46634	
983	Indiana Michigan Power Co Utility	One Summit Square	Fort Wayne 219-425-2111	IN 46801	
7312	Lincoln National Corp Insurance	1300 S Clinton Street	Fort Wayne 219-427-2000	IN 46801	
1650	Central Soya Co Food Processing	1300 Fort Wayne National Bank Bldg	Fort Wayne 219-425-5100	IN 46802	
750	Essex Group Inc Manufacturing	1601 Wall Street	Fort Wayne 219-461-4000	IN 46802	
825	Hardware Wholesalers Inc Retail/Merch	6502 Nelson Road	Fort Wayne 219-749-8531	IN 46803	
NA	North American Van Lines Inc Transport	5001 US Highway 30 W	Fort Wayne 219-429-2511	IN 46818	
NA	Delco Electronics Co Automotive	700 E Firmin	Kokomo 317-457-8461	IN 46904	
884	Hillenbrand Industries Inc Manufacturing	Highway 46	Batesville 812-934-7000	IN 47006	
1313	Arvin Industries Inc Automotive	1531 Thirteen Street	Columbus 812-379-3000	IN 47201	
3310	Cummins Engine Co Inc Automotive	500 Jackson Street PO Box 3005	Columbus 812-377-5000	IN 47202	
1073	Ball Corp Packaging	345 S High Street	Muncie 317-747-6100	IN 47305	
900	Marsh Supermarkets Inc Retail/Food	501 Depot Street	Yorktown 317-759-8101	IN 473961	
315	Indiana University University	Bryan Hall	Bloomington 812-332-0211	IN 47405	
530	Kimball International Inc Manufacturing	1600 Royal Street	Jasper 812-482-1600	IN 47546	
523	Credithrift Financial Inc Non-Bank Fin	601 NW 2nd Street	Evansville 812-424-8031	IN 47708	
290	Southern Indiana Gas & Electric Co Utility	20 NW Fourth Street	Evansville 812-424-6411	IN 47741	
616	Great Lakes Chemical Corp Chemicals	Highway 52 NW	West Lafayette 317-463-2511	IN 47906	
332	Purdue University University	Administrative Bldg	West Lafayette 317-749-2108	IN 47907	

State / Province: Iowa

Revenue ($ mil)	Organization/ Industry	Address	City / Phone	State/ Zip	Province/ Postcode
316	Iowa State University University	Administrative Bldg	Ames 515-294-4111	IA 50011	
1800	Hy Vee Food Stores Inc Retail/Food	1801 Osceola Avenue	Chariton 515-774-2121	IA 50049	
1886	Maytag Co Appliances/Furn	One Dependability Square	Newton 515-792-7000	IA 50208	
2750	American Grain Inc Food Processing	2829 Westtown Park	Des Moines 515-223-3700	IA 50265	
450	Commtron Corp Retail/Merch	1501 50th Street	Des Moines 515-226-3000	IA 50265	
344	Iowa Resources (Iowa Power & Light) Inc Utility	666 Grand Avenue	Des Moines 515-281-2900	IA 50303	
250	Des Moines, City of Local Govt	City Hall East First & Locust Streets	Des Moines 515-283-4944	IA 50307	
118	EMP Employers Mutual Casualty Ins Co Insurance	717 Mulberry Street	Des Moines 515-280-2511	IA 50309	
400	Pioneer HiBred International Inc Food Processing	700 Capital Square 400 Locust	Des Moines 515-245-3500	IA 50309	
6577	Principle Financial Group Inc Insurance	711 High Street	Des Moines 515-247-5111	IA 50309	
678	Statesman Group Life Insurance Co Insurance	1400 Des Moines Bldg	Des Moines 515-284-7500	IA 50309	

State / Province: Iowa

Organizations Listed Geographically

Revenue ($ mil)	Organization/ Industry	Address	City / Phone	State/ Zip	Province/ Postcode
900	Heritage Communications Inc Publishing/Com	2195 Ingersoll Avenue	Des Moines 515-246-1440	IA 50312	
419	Casey's General Stores Inc Retail/Food	1277 NE Broadway	Des Moines 515-263-3700	IA 50313	
6603	Iowa, State of State/Prov Govt	State Capitol	Des Moines 515-281-5011	IA 50319	
678	Meredith Corp Publishing/Com	1716 Locust Street	Des Moines 515-284-3000	IA 50336	
425	Winnebago Industries Inc Automotive	Highway 9 & Highway 69 PO Box 152	Forest City 515-582-3535	IA 50436	
NA	Fort Dodge Laboratories Inc Drugs	800 Fifth Street NW	Fort Dodge 515-955-4600	IA 50501	
600	Iowa Public Service Co Utility	401 Douglas Street	Sioux City 712-277-7500	IA 51102	
570	Midwest Energy Co Utility	401 Douglas Street	Sioux City 712-277-7400	IA 51102	
825	FDL Foods Inc Food Processing	701 E 16th Street	Dubuque 319-588-5400	IA 52001	
274	Interstate Power Co Utility	1000 Main Street	Dubuque 319-582-5421	IA 52004	
NA	Amana Refrigeration Inc Appliances/Furn	Highway 220	Amana 319-622-5511	IA 52204	
415	University of Iowa University	Administrative Bldg	Iowa City 319-353-2121	IA 52242	
250	IE Industries Inc Utility	200 First Street SE	Cedar Rapids 319-398-4411	IA 52401	
1400	Life Investors Insurance Co of America Insurance	4333 Edgewood Road NE	Ceder Rapids 319-398-5811	IA 52499	
498	Bandag Inc Tire/Rubber	Bandag Center	Muscatine 319-262-1400	IA 52761	
532	Hon Industries Inc Manufacturing	414 E Third Street	Muscatine 319-264-7400	IA 52761	
252	Lee Enterprises Inc Publishing/Com	130 E Second Street	Davenport 319-383-2202	IA 52801	
496	Iowa Illinois Gas & Electric Inc Utility	206 E Second Street	Davenport 319-326-7111	IA 52808	

State / Province: Kansas

151	University of Kansas University	Administrative Bldg	Lawrence 913-864-2700	KS 66045	
1059	Franklin Savings Assn Inc Savings & Loan	One Franklin Plaza	Ottawa 913-242-6300	KS 66067	
1870	Associated Wholesale Grocers Inc Retail/Food	5000 Kansas Avenue	Kansas City 913-321-1313	KS 66106	
550	Sinclair Marketing Inc Energy	3401 Fairbanks	Kansas City 913-321-3700	KS 66106	
1425	Employers Reinsurance Co Insurance	5200 Metcalf Avenue	Overland Park 913-676-5200	KS 66201	
NA	Lee Apparel Inc Apparel/Textiles	9001 W 67th Street	Merriam 913-384-4000	KS 66202	
500	Marley Co Inc Business Service	1900 Johnson Drive	Mission Woods 913-362-5440	KS 66205	
6493	United Telecommunications Inc Telecom	2330 Shawnee Mission Parkway	Westwood 913-676-3000	KS 66205	
NA	ADM Milling Co Food Processing	4550 W 109th Street	Shawnee Mission 913-381-7400	KS 66207	
2016	Yellow Freight System Inc Transport	10990 Roe Avenue	Overland Park 913-345-1020	KS 66207	
475	American Carriers Inc Transport	9393 W 110th Street	Overland Park 913-451-2811	KS 66210	
NA	Directories America Inc Publishing/Com	7015 College Blvd	Overland Park 913-491-7000	KS 66211	
250	Puritan Bennett Corp Health Care	9401 Indian Creek Parkway	Overland Park 913-661-0444	KS 66225	

State / Province: Kansas

Organizations Listed Geographically

Revenue ($ mil)	Organization/Industry	Address	City/Phone	State/Zip	Province/Postcode
NA	Hill's Pet Products Inc Food Processing	400 W Eighth Street	Topeka 913-354-8523	KS 66602	
350	Capitol Federal Savings (Kansas) Inc Savings & Loan	700 Kansas Avenue	Topeka 913-235-1341	KS 66603	
1166	Kansas Power & Light Co Utility	818 Kansas Avenue	Topeka 913-296-6300	KS 66612	
5872	Kansas, State of State/Prov Govt	State Capitol	Topeka 913-296-0111	KS 66612	
NA	Beech Aircraft Corp Aerospace	9709 E Central	Wichita 316-681-7111	KS 67201	
526	Kansas Gas & Electric Co Utility	120 E First	Wichita 316-261-6611	KS 67201	
NA	Pizza Hut Inc Food/Lodging	9111 E Douglas	Wichita 316-681-9000	KS 67201	
500	Coleman Co Manufacturing	250 N St Francis	Wichita 316-261-3211	KS 67202	
292	Wichita, City of Local Govt	City Hall	Wichita 316-268-4331	KS 67202	
250	Rent-a-Center Inc Business Service	9920 E Harry Street	Wichita 316-689-4100	KS 67207	
750	Ruffin Corp Retail/Merch	1522 S Florence	Wichita 316-942-7940	KS 67209	
NA	Cessna Aircraft Corp Aerospace	5800 E Pawnee Road	Wichita 316-685-9111	KS 67218	
15000	Koch Industries Inc Manufacturing	4111 E 37th Street N	Wichita 316-832-5500	KS 67220	
1500	Union Gas Holdings Corp Energy	122 W Myrtle	Independence 316-331-4500	KS 67301	
1100	National Coop Refinery Assn Inc Energy	2000 S Main Street	McPherson 316-241-2340	KS 67460	
2000	Dillon Co Retail/Food	700 E 30th	Hutchinson 316-663-6801	KS 67501	
275	Doskocil Companies Inc Building Mat	321 N Main Street	Hutchinson 316-663-1000	KS 67504	
275	Hyplains Dressed Beef Inc Food Processing	2000 E Trail Street	Dodge City 316-227-7135	KS 67801	

State / Province: Kentucky

5500	BAT US Inc Food Processing	2000 Citizens Plaza	Louisville 502-581-8000	KY 40202	
500	First Kentucky National Corp Banking	101 S Fifth Street	Louisville 502-581-4498	KY 40202	
3435	Humana Inc Health Care	Humana Bldg 500 W Main Street	Louisville 502-580-1000	KY 40202	
250	Louisville, City of Local Govt	City Hall	Louisville 502-587-3061	KY 40202	
NA	Ohio Valley Transmission Corp Utility	311 W Chestnut Street	Louisville 502-566-4011	KY 40202	
400	Vermont American Corp Appliances/Furn	100 E Liberty Street	Louisville 502-587-6851	KY 40202	
250	Fraternal Order of Police Membership Org	2100 Gardiner Lane	Louisville 502-452-2828	KY 40205	
2885	ICH Corp Non-Bank Fin	4211 Norbourne Blvd	Louisville 502-897-1861	KY 40207	
1355	Brown Forman Inc Beverage	850 Dixie Highway	Louisville 502-585-1100	KY 40210	
NA	Kentucky Fried Chicken Inc Food/Lodging	1441 Gardiner Lane	Louisville 502-456-8300	KY 40213	
2420	Dairymen Inc Food Processing	10140 Linn Station Road	Louisville 502-426-6455	KY 40223	
2046	Capital Holding Co Non-Bank Fin	680 Fourth Avenue PO Box 32830	Louisville 502-560-2000	KY 40232	
110	Commonwealth Life Ins Co Insurance	Commonwealth Bldg PO Box 32800	Louisville 502-587-7371	KY 40232	

State / Province: Kentucky

Organizations Listed Geographically

Revenue ($ mil)	Organization/ Industry	Address	City / Phone	State/ Zip	Province/ Postcode
660	Louisville Gas & Electric Co Utility	311 W Chestnut Street	Louisville 502-566-4011	KY 40232	
348	Thomas Industries Inc Building Mat	4360 Brownsboro Road	Louisville 502-893-4600	KY 40232	
194	University of Louisville University	Administrative Bldg	Louisville 502-588-5555	KY 40292	
700	Citizens Fidelity Corp Banking	Citizens Plaza	Louisville 502-581-2100	KY 40296	
NA	Island Creek Corp Metals/Mining	2355 Harrodsburg Road	Lexington 606-223-3636	KY 40504	
334	University of Kentucky University	Administrative Bldg	Lexington 606-258-9000	KY 40506	
560	Kentucky Utilities Co Utility	One Quality Street	Lexington 606-255-1461	KY 40507	
250	Lexington, City of Local Govt	City Hall 200 E Main Street	Lexington 606-258-3110	KY 40507	
635	Jerrico (Long John Silvers Res) Inc Food/Lodging	101 Jerrico Drive	Lexington 606-263-6000	KY 40509	
7295	Kentucky, State of State/Prov Govt	State Capitol	Frankfort 502-465-2500	KY 40601	
NA	Industrial Automation Systems Group Inc Electronics	7300 Turfway Road	Florence 606-283-2202	KY 41042	
250	Addington Resources Inc Metals/Mining	9431 Route 60	Ashland 606-928-3433	KY 41101	
258	Kentucky Power Co Utility	1701 Central Avenue	Ashland 606-327-1111	KY 41101	
8196	Ashland Oil Inc Energy	1000 Ashland Drive	Russell 606-329-3333	KY 41169	
590	Dollar General Corp Retail/Merch	427 Beech Street	Scottsville 502-237-5444	KY 42164	

State / Province: Louisiana

Revenue ($ mil)	Organization/ Industry	Address	City / Phone	State/ Zip	Province/ Postcode
550	Avondale Industries Inc Manufacturing	5100 River Road	New Orleans 504-436-2121	LA 70094	
NA	Babcock & Wilcox Co Manufacturing	1010 Common Street	New Orleans 504-587-5400	LA 70112	
3565	Entergy Corp (Middle South Utilities) Utility	225 Baronne Street	New Orleans 504-529-5262	LA 70112	
300	First Commerce Corp Banking	210 Baronne Street	New Orleans 504-561-1371	LA 70112	
106	Freeport McMoran Gold Inc Metals/Mining	1615 Poydras Street	New Orleans 504-582-4000	LA 70112	
726	Louisiana Land & Exploration Co Energy	909 Poydras Street	New Orleans 504-566-6500	LA 70112	
2352	McDermott International Inc Oil Service	1010 Common Street	New Orleans 504-587-5400	LA 70112	
NA	New Orleans Public Service Co Utility	225 Baronne Street	New Orleans 504-595-3100	LA 70112	
645	New Orleans, City of Local Govt	City Hall	New Orleans 504-586-4000	LA 70112	
158	Tulane University University	6823 St Charles Avenue	New Orleans 504-865-5000	LA 70118	
546	Hibernia Corp Banking	313 Carondelet Street	New Orleans 504-586-5552	LA 70130	
550	K & B Inc Retail/Merch	K & B Plaza 1055 St Charles Avenue	New Orleans 504-586-1234	LA 70130	
550	Lykes Brothers Steamship Co Inc Transport	300 Poydras Street	New Orleans 504-523-6611	LA 70130	
300	International Shipholding Corp Transport	650 Poydras Street	New Orleans 504-529-5461	LA 70153	
1945	Freeport McMoran Inc Chemicals	1615 Poydras Street	New Orleans 504-582-4000	LA 70161	
406	Ocean Drilling Exploration Co Oil Service	1600 Canal Street	New Orleans 504-561-2811	LA 70161	

State / Province: Louisiana

Organizations Listed Geographically

Revenue ($ mil)	Organization/ Industry	Address	City / Phone	State/ Zip	Province/ Postcode
1400	Louisiana Power & Light Co Utility	142 Delaronde Street	New Orleans 504-366-2345	LA	70174
500	Schwegmann Giant Super Markets Inc Retail/Food	PO Box 26099	New Orleans 504-947-9921	LA	70186
400	Borden Chemicals & Plastics Inc Chemicals	Highway 73 & 30	Geismar 504-673-6121	LA	70734
393	Premier Bancorp (Louisiana Bancshares) Banking	451 Florida Street	Baton Rouge 504-389-4206	LA	70801
153	Louisiana State University University	Administrative Bldg	Baton Rouge 504-388-1175	LA	70803
10882	Louisiana, State of State/Prov Govt	State Capitol	Baton Rouge 504-342-6600	LA	70804
276	Piccadilly Cafeterias Inc Food/Lodging	3232 Sherwood Forest Blvd	Baton Rouge 504-293-9440	LA	70816
250	MMR Holding Corp Real Estate/Bldg	17325 Airline Highway	Baton Rouge 504-293-2701	LA	70819
298	Baton Rouge, City of Local Govt	City Hall	Baton Rouge 504-389-3100	LA	70821
275	Cajun Electric Power Cooperative Inc Utility	10719 Airline Highway	Baton Rouge 504-291-3060	LA	70895
1996	Arkla Inc Utility	Arkla Bldg 525 Milam	Shreveport 318-226-2700	LA	71101
250	Shreveport, City of Local Govt	City Hall	Shreveport 318-226-6250	LA	71130
742	Southwestern Electric Power Utility	428 Travis Street	Shreveport 318-222-2141	LA	71156
250	Century Telephone Enterprises Inc Telecom	520 Riverside Drive	Monroe 318-388-9000	LA	71201
NA	Manville Forest Products Co Paper/Forest Prd	1000 Jonesboro Highway	West Monroe 318-362-2000	LA	71291
920	Central Louisiana Electric Co Utility	2030 Donahue Ferry Road	Pineville 318-484-7400	LA	71360

State / Province: Maine

Revenue ($ mil)	Organization/ Industry	Address	City / Phone	State/ Zip	Province/ Postcode
500	Bean, L L Corp Retail/Merch	Casco Street	Freeport 207-865-4761	ME	04033
1000	Hannaford Brothers Retail/Food	145 Pleasant Hill Road	Scarborough 207-883-2911	ME	04074
2199	UNUM Union Mutual Life Insurance Co Insurance	2211 Congress Street	Portland 207-770-2211	ME	04122
NA	Oxford Paper Co Paper/Forest Prd	Rumford Mill	Rumford 207-364-4521	ME	04276
2648	Maine, State of State/Prov Govt	State House	Augusta 207-289-1110	ME	04333
654	Central Maine Power Inc Utility	Edison Drive	Augusta 207-623-3521	ME	04336
750	Bath Iron Works Inc Manufacturing	700 Washington	Bath 207-443-3311	ME	04530

State / Province: Maine

Organizations Listed Geographically

Revenue ($ mil)	Organization/ Industry	Address	City / Phone	State/ Zip	Province/ Postcode

State / Province: Maryland

Revenue ($ mil)	Organization/ Industry	Address	City / Phone	State/Zip
550	Rover Group Inc Automotive	4390 Parlimanent Place	Laham 301-731-9040	MD 20706
279	University of Maryland University	Administrative Bldg	College Park 301-454-0100	MD 20742
1000	Alleco Inc Beverage	Allegheny Circle	Hyattsville 301-341-6000	MD 20781
406	Dart Group Corp Retail/Merch	3300 75th Avenue	Landover 301-731-1200	MD 20785
2987	Giant Food Inc Retail/Food	6300 Sheriff Road	Landover 301-341-4100	MD 20785
1019	Hechinger Co Retail/Merch	3500 Pennsy Drive	Landover 301-341-1000	MD 20785
1000	Clark Construction Enterprises Inc Real Estate/Bldg	7500 Old Georgetown Road	Bethesda 301-657-7100	MD 20814
550	Oxford Development Co Inc Real Estate/Bldg	7316 Wisconsin Avenue SE	Bethesda 301-654-3100	MD 20814
350	Chevy Chase Savings Bank Inc Savings & Loan	8401 Connecticut Avenue	Chevy Chase 301-986-7000	MD 20815
5727	Martin Marietta Corp Aerospace	6801 Rockledge Drive	Bethesda 301-897-6000	MD 20817
NA	Martin Marietta Information Systems Inc Comput/Off Equip	6801 Rockledge Drive	Bethesda 301-897-6000	MD 20817
534	Manor Care Inc Health Care	10750 Columbia Pike	Silver Spring 301-681-9400	MD 20901
300	Legg Mason Inc Securities	111 S Calvert Street	Baltimore 301-539-3400	MD 21023
522	Noxell Corp Personal Care	11050 York Road	Hunt Valley 301-785-7300	MD 21030
1184	McCormick & Co Inc Food Processing	11350 McCormick Road	Hunt Valley 301-771-7301	MD 21031
1735	PHH Group Inc Business Service	11333 McCormick Road	Hunt Valley 301-771-3600	MD 21031
461	Rouse Co Manufacturing	Rouse Company Bldg	Columbia 301-992-6000	MD 21044
881	Ryland Group Inc Real Estate/Bldg	10221 Wincopin Circle	Columbia 301-730-7222	MD 21044
1250	Weisman, Frederick Co Inc Automotive	6710 Baymeadow Drive	Glen Burnie 301-760-1500	MD 21061
NA	Constellation Operating Services Inc Utility	250 W Pratt Street	Baltimore 301-783-2827	MD 21201
1149	Crown Central Petroleum Corp Energy	One N Charles	Baltimore 301-539-7400	MD 21201
375	Equitable BanCorp Inc Banking	100 S Charles Street	Baltimore 301-547-4000	MD 21201
660	First Maryland BanCorp Inc Banking	25 S Charles Street	Baltimore 301-244-4000	MD 21201
1464	Baltimore, City of Local Govt	City Hall	Baltimore 301-396-4892	MD 21202
244	Brown, Alex & Sons Inc Securities	135 E Baltimore Street	Baltimore 301-727-1700	MD 21202
1200	Commercial Credit Corp Non-Bank Fin	300 St Paul Place	Baltimore 301-332-3000	MD 21202
1530	MNC (Maryland National Corp) Financial Banking	10 Light Street	Baltimore 301-244-1940	MD 21202
142	Price, T Rowe Associates Inc Non-Bank Fin	100 E Pratt Street	Baltimore 301-547-2308	MD 21202
5582	USF & G Corp Insurance	100 Light Street	Baltimore 301-547-3000	MD 21202
1864	Baltimore Gas & Electric Co Utility	Gas & Electric Bldg Charles Center	Baltimore 301-234-5000	MD 21203

State / Province: Maryland

Organizations Listed Geographically

Revenue ($ mil)	Organization/ Industry	Address	City / Phone	State/ Zip	Province/ Postcode
362	Mercantile Bankshares Corp Banking	Two Hopkins Plaza	Baltimore 301-237-5900	MD 21203	
2281	Black & Decker Corp Manufacturing	701 E Joppa Road	Towson 301-583-3900	MD 21204	
299	Merry Go Round Enterprises Inc Retail/Merch	1220 Joppa Road	Baltimore 301-828-1000	MD 21204	
600	Green, B & Co Inc Retail/Food	3601 Washington Street	Baltimore 301-247-8300	MD 21227	
15000	United States Social Security Admin Federal Govt	Dept of Health & Human Services 6401 Security Blvd	Baltimore 301-594-1234	MD 21235	
401	UNC Inc Instruments	175 Admiral Cochrane Drive	Annapolis 301-266-7333	MD 21401	
11308	Maryland, State of State/Prov Govt	State House	Annapolis 301-269-6200	MD 21404	
1500	Kelly Springfield Tire Co Tire/Rubber	800 Kelly Road	Cumberland 301-777-6000	MD 21502	
594	Preston Corp Transport	151 Easton Blvd	Preston 301-673-7151	MD 21655	
NA	Potomac Edison Co Utility	Downsville Pike	Hagerstown 301-790-3400	MD 21740	
1500	Perdue Farms Inc Food Processing	Old Ocean City Road	Salisbury 301-543-3000	MD 21801	

State / Province: Massachusetts

Revenue ($ mil)	Organization/ Industry	Address	City / Phone	State/ Zip	Province/ Postcode
264	University of Massachusetts University	Administrative Bldg	Amherst 413-545-0111	MA 01003	
250	Milton Bradley Co Leisure Time	443 Shaker Road	East Longmeadow 413-525-6411	MA 01028	
433	Stanhome Inc Manufacturing	333 Western Avenue	Westfield 413-562-3631	MA 01085	
NA	Western Massachusetts Electric Co Utility	174 Brush Hill Avenue	West Springfield 413-785-5871	MA 01085	
4632	Massachusetts Mutual Life Insurance Comp Insurance	1295 State Street	Springfield 413-788-8411	MA 01111	
417	Monarch Capital Corp Non-Bank Fin	One Financial Plaza	Springfield 413-781-3000	MA 01144	
NA	KayBee Toys Inc Retail/Merch	100 West Street	Pittsfield 413-499-0086	MA 01201	
217	New England Business Service Comput/Off Equip	500 Main Street	Groton 508-448-6111	MA 01450	
1365	Data General Corp Comput/Off Equip	4400 Computer Drive	Westboro 508-366-8911	MA 01580	
1461	New England Electric System Inc Utility	25 Research Drive	Westborough 508-366-9011	MA 01581	
1000	Idle Wild Foods Inc Food Processing	256 Franklin Street	Worcester 617-757-7761	MA 01604	
1581	Hanover Insurance Co Insurance	100 North Parkway	Worcester 508-853-7200	MA 01605	
1718	State Mutual Life Assurance Co of Amer Insurance	440 Lincoln Street	Worcester 508-852-1000	MA 01605	
1410	Norton Co Manufacturing	120 Front Street	Worcester 508-795-5000	MA 01608	
272	Wyman Gordon Co Metals/Mining	105 Madison Street	Worcester 508-756-5111	MA 01613	
722	Dennison Manufacturing Co Manufacturing	300 Howard Street	Framingham 508-879-0511	MA 01701	
400	International Data Corp Publishing/Com	5 Speen Street	Framingham 508-875-5000	MA 01701	
849	Perini Corp Real Estate/Bldg	73 Mt Wayte Avenue	Framingham 508-875-6171	MA 01701	
1921	Zayre Corp Retail/Merch	770 Cochituate Road	Framingham 508-390-1000	MA 01701	
450	CML Group Inc Retail/Merch	524 Main Street	Acton 508-264-4155	MA 01720	

State / Province: Massachusetts

Organizations Listed Geographically

Revenue ($ mil)	Organization/ Industry	Address	City / Phone	State/ Zip	Province/ Postcode
500	Computervision Corp Comput/Off Equip	100 Crosby Drive	Bedford 617-275-1800	MA 01730	
622	Millipore Corp Instruments	80 Ashby Road	Bedford 617-275-9200	MA 01730	
550	Mitre Corp Business Service	Burlington Road	Bedford 617-271-2000	MA 01730	
NA	CSA Press Inc Publishing/Com	555 Main Street	Hudson 508-568-0301	MA 01749	
300	Microamerica Inc Retail/Merch	33 Boston Post Road	West Marlboro 508-480-0780	MA 01752	
265	Stratus Computer Inc Comput/Off Equip	55 Fairbanks Blvd	Marlborough 617-460-2000	MA 01752	
11475	Digital Equipment Corp Comput/Off Equip	146 Main Street	Maynard 617-493-5111	MA 01754	
NA	McCormack & Dodge Inc Comput/Off Equip	1225 Worcester Road	Natick 508-665-8200	MA 01760	
1595	Prime Computer Inc Comput/Off Equip	Prime Park	Natick 508-655-8000	MA 01760	
1921	TJX Corp Retail/Merch	One Mercer Road	Natick 508-651-6000	MA 01760	
2000	Waban Inc Retail/Merch	One Mercer Road	Natick 508-651-6500	MA 01760	
200	Alpha Industries Inc Electronics	20 Sylvan Road	Woburn 617-935-5150	MA 01801	
NA	Lechmere Inc Retail/Merch	275 Wildwood Street	Woburn 617-935-8320	MA 01801	
368	Dynatech Corp Comput/Off Equip	3 Executive Park	Burlington 617-272-3304	MA 01803	
424	M/A Com Inc Telecom	7 New England Executive Park	Burlington 617-272-9600	MA 01803	
880	Nixdorf US Inc Comput/Off Equip	52 Third Avenue	Burlington 617-273-0480	MA 01803	
654	Apollo Computer Inc Comput/Off Equip	330 Billerica Road	Chelmsford 508-256-6600	MA 01824	
250	Watts Industries Inc Manufacturing	815 Chestnut Street	North Andover 508-688-1811	MA 01845	
NA	Textron Marine Systems Div Manufacturing	6800 Plaza Drive	Lowell 508-452-8961	MA 01851	
3068	Wang Laboratories Inc Comput/Off Equip	One Industrial Avenue	Lowell 508-459-5000	MA 01851	
2500	Astroline Corp Energy	95 Walkers Brook Drive	Reading 508-942-1600	MA 01867	
1000	DeMoulas Super Markets Inc Retail/Food	875 East Street	Tewksbury 508-851-7381	MA 01876	
400	American Mutual Liability Insurance	Quannapowitt Parkway	Wakefield 508-245-6000	MA 01880	
NA	Marshall's Inc Retail/Merch	30 Harvard Mill Square	Wakefield 508-721-3300	MA 01880	
NA	Textron Defense Systems Div Aerospace	201 Lowell Street	Wilmington 508-657-5111	MA 01887	
1205	Wheelabrator Technologies Inc Business Service	55 Ferncroft Road	Danvers 508-777-2207	MA 01923	
350	Bay State Gas Co Utility	120 Royall Street	Canton 617-828-8650	MA 02021	
2200	Cumberland Farms Corp Retail/Food	777 Dedham Street	Canton 617-828-4900	MA 02021	
1671	Hill's Department Stores Inc Retail/Merch	15 Dan Road	Canton 617-821-1000	MA 02021	
600	Morse Shoe Inc Retail/Merch	555 Turnpike Street	Canton 617-828-9300	MA 02021	
1791	Reebok International Ltd Apparel/Textiles	150 Royall Street	Canton 617-580-1600	MA 02021	
1671	SCOA Industries Inc Retail/Merch	15 Dan Road	Canton 617-821-1000	MA 02021	
1250	National Amusements Corp Leisure Time	200 Elm Street	Dedham 617-461-1600	MA 02026	

State / Province: Massachusetts

Organizations Listed Geographically

Revenue ($ mil)	Organization/ Industry	Address	City / Phone	State/ Zip	Province/ Postcode
1000	Oxbow Corp Energy	333 Elm Street	Dedham 617-461-0550	MA	02026
1258	Viacom International Inc Publishing/Com	200 Elm Street	Dedham 617-461-1600	MA	02026
540	Foxboro Co Instruments	Bristol Park	Foxboro 617-543-8750	MA	02035
321	Augat Inc Electronics	89 Forbes Blvd	Mansfield 617-543-4300	MA	02048
439	Analog Devices Inc Electronics	One Technology Way	Norwood 617-329-4700	MA	02062
NA	Filene's Inc Retail/Merch	426 Washington Street	Boston 617-357-2978	MA	02101
897	State Street Bank Inc Banking	225 Franklin Street	Boston 617-786-3000	MA	02101
1500	Boston Safe Deposit & Trust Co Banking	One Boston Place	Boston 617-722-7000	MA	02106
1156	Federal Reserve Bank of Boston Inc Federal Govt Fin	600 Atlantic Avenue	Boston 617-973-3000	MA	02106
534	Affiliated Publications Inc Publishing/Com	135 Morrissey Blvd	Boston 617-929-2000	MA	02107
NA	New England Telephone & Telegraph Co Telecom	185 Franklin Street	Boston 617-743-9800	MA	02107
300	Boston Companies Inc Non-Bank Fin	One Boston Place	Boston 800-225-5267	MA	02108
658	Commerical Union Insurance Co Insurance	One Beacon Street	Boston 617-725-6000	MA	02108
368	Houghton Mifflin Co Publishing/Com	One Beacon Street	Boston 617-725-5000	MA	02108
NA	Little, Brown & Co Inc Publishing/Com	34 Beacon Street	Boston 617-227-0730	MA	02108
3247	Bank of New England Corp Banking	28 State Street	Boston 617-742-4000	MA	02109
300	Boston Consulting Group Inc Consulting	Exchange Place	Boston 617-973-1200	MA	02109
374	Eastern Utilities Associates Inc Utility	One Liberty Square	Boston 617-357-9590	MA	02109
1000	Fidelity Investments Corp Non-Bank Fin	82 Devonshire Street	Boston 617-523-1919	MA	02109
400	Home Owners Federal S & L Assn Savings & Loan	21 Milk Street	Boston 617-482-0630	MA	02109
500	Putnam Management Co Inc Non-Bank Fin	One PO Square	Boston 617-292-1000	MA	02109
1750	Warren, George E Co Inc Energy	50 Milk Street	Boston 617-451-2300	MA	02109
700	Wellington Management/TDPL Inc Non-Bank Fin	75 State Street	Boston 617-951-5000	MA	02109
250	XTRA Corp Transport	60 State Street	Boston 617-367-5000	MA	02109
5296	Bank of Boston Corp Banking	100 Federal Street	Boston 617-434-2200	MA	02110
1037	Baybanks Inc Banking	175 Federal Street	Boston 617-482-1040	MA	02110
2750	Blue Cross Blue Shield of Massachusetts Insurance	100 Summer Street	Boston 617-956-2000	MA	02110
600	Continental Cablevision Corp Publishing/Com	The Pilot House	Boston 617-742-9500	MA	02110
275	Fidelity Brokerage Services Inc Securities	161 Devonshire Street	Boston 617-570-7000	MA	02110
750	Kendall Co Health Care	One Federal Street	Boston 617-574-7000	MA	02110
1042	Keystone Provident Life Insurance Co Insurance	99 High Street	Boston 617-338-3500	MA	02110
377	Lifetime Corp Health Care	99 Summer Street	Boston 617-330-5080	MA	02110
850	Scudder Stevens & Clark Non-Bank Fin	160 Federal Street	Boston 617-439-4640	MA	02110

State / Province: Massachusetts

Organizations Listed Geographically

Revenue ($ mil)	Organization/ Industry	Address	City / Phone	State/ Zip	Province/ Postcode
74	Colonial Group Inc Non-Bank Fin	One Financial Center	Boston 617-426-3750	MA 02111	
250	Woodside Management Inc Business Service	141 Tremont Street	Boston 617-426-7661	MA 02111	
147	Northeastern University University	360 Huntington Avenue	Boston 617-437-2000	MA 02115	
400	Bain & Co Consulting	2 Copley Place	Boston 617-572-2000	MA 02116	
444	Healthco International Inc Health Care	1125 Stuart Street	Boston 617-423-6045	MA 02116	
550	Massachusetts Financial Services Inc Non-Bank Fin	500 Boyleston Street	Boston 617-954-5000	MA 02116	
7926	Hancock, John Mutual Life Insurance Co Insurance	200 Clarendon Street	Boston 617-421-6000	MA 02117	
8268	Liberty Mutual Insurance Co Insurance	175 Berkeley Street	Boston 617-285-7000	MA 02117	
3802	New England Mutual Life Insurance Co Insurance	501 Boylston Street	Boston 617-578-2000	MA 02117	
463	Teradyne Inc Instruments	321 Harrison Avenue	Boston 617-482-2700	MA 02118	
1500	Connell Ltd (Avondale Foods) Ptr Inc Food Processing	1 Mass Tech Center	East Boston 617-567-2600	MA 02128	
660	Commonwealth Energy System Energy	One Main Street	Cambridge 617-225-4000	MA 02129	
15502	Massachusetts, State of State/Prov Govt	State House	Boston 617-727-2121	MA 02133	
1100	Grossmans Inc Retail/Merch	200 Union Street	Braintree 617-848-0100	MA 02134	
250	Baker, J Inc Retail/Merch	65 Sprague Street	Boston 617-364-3000	MA 02137	
520	Harvard University University	Administrative Bldg	Cambridge 617-495-1000	MA 02138	
NA	Star Market Co Retail/Merch	625 Mt Auburn Street	Cambridge 617-661-2200	MA 02138	
556	Massachusetts Inst of Technology University	77 Massachusetts Avenue	Cambridge 617-253-1000	MA 02139	
1863	Polaroid Corp Leisure Time	549 Technology Square	Cambridge 617-577-2000	MA 02139	
350	TAD Technical Services Inc Consulting	639 Massachusetts Avenue	Cambridge 617-868-1650	MA 02139	
30	Genetics Institute Inc Business Service	87 Cambridge Park Drive	Cambridge 617-876-1170	MA 02140	
400	Little, Arthur D & Co Inc Consulting	25 Acorn Park	Cambridge 617-864-5770	MA 02140	
250	Middlesex County Government Local Govt	40 Thorndike Street	East Cambridge 617-494-4000	MA 02141	
467	Lotus Development Corp Comput/Off Equip	55 Cambridge Parkway	Cambridge 617-577-8500	MA 02142	
379	Stride Rite Corp Apparel/Textiles	5 Cambridge Center	Cambridge 617-491-8800	MA 02142	
450	Town & Country Corp Manufacturing	25 Union Street	Chelsea 617-884-8500	MA 02150	
650	Ausimont NV Inc Chemicals	128 Technology Drive	Waltham 617-899-3000	MA 02154	
1500	Cabot Corp Energy	950 Winter Street	Waltham 617-890-0200	MA 02154	
1500	Global Petroleum Corp Energy	800 South Street	Waltham 617-894-8800	MA 02154	
750	Honeywell Bull (Cie des Machines Bull) Comput/Off Equip	200 Smith Street	Waltham 617-895-6000	MA 02154	
501	Thermo Electron Corp Electronics	45 First Street	Waltham 617-890-8700	MA 02154	
2324	General Cimema Corp Beverage	27 Boylston Street	Chestnut Hill 617-232-8200	MA 02167	
NA	General Cinema Beverages Inc Beverage	1300 Boylston Strett	Chestnut Hill 617-739-2950	MA 02167	

State / Province: Massachusetts

Organizations Listed Geographically

Revenue ($ mil)	Organization/ Industry	Address	City / Phone	State/ Zip	Province/ Postcode
1200	Neiman Marcus Co Retail/Merch	27 Boylston Street	Chestnut Hill 617-232-0760	MA 02167	
448	Seaboard Corp Food Processing	200 Boylston Street	Boston 617-332-8492	MA 02167	
NA	American Overseas Marine Corp Manufacturing	116 E Howard Street	Quincy 617-786-8300	MA 02169	
4400	Stop & Shop (SSC Holdings) Inc Retail/Merch	1776 Heritage Drive PO Box 369	North Quincy 617-770-8000	MA 02171	
NA	Algonquin Gas Transmission Co Energy	1284 Soldiers Field Road	Boston 617-254-4050	MA 02173	
8192	Raytheon Co Electronics	141 Spring Street	Lexington 617-862-6600	MA 02173	
275	Temple, Barker & Sloane Inc Consulting	33 Hayden Avenue	Lexington 617-861-7580	MA 02173	
1406	EG & G Inc Electronics	45 William Street	Wellesley 617-237-5100	MA 02181	
449	Sun Life Assurance Co of Canada US Insurance	One Sun Life Executive Park	Wellesley 617-237-6030	MA 02181	
990	Bradlees Stores Inc Retail/Merch	1 Bradley Circle	Braintree 617-770-8000	MA 02184	
672	Eastern Enterprises Inc Utility	9 Riverside Road	Weston 617-647-2300	MA 02193	
1500	Amoskeag Co Apparel/Textiles	Prudential Center	Boston 617-262-4000	MA 02199	
1203	Boston Edison Co Utility	800 Boylston Street Prudential Center	Boston 617-424-2000	MA 02199	
3581	Gillette Co Personal Care	Prudential Tower Bldg	Boston 617-421-7000	MA 02199	
1179	Boston, City of Local Govt	City Hall	Boston 617-725-4500	MA 02201	
20	Batterymarch Financial Management Inc Non-Bank Fin	600 Atlantic Avenue	Boston 617-973-9300	MA 02210	
2811	Shawmut Corp Banking	One Federal Street	Boston 617-292-2000	MA 02211	
257	Boston University University	Commonwealth Avenue	Boston 617-353-2000	MA 02215	
305	Bolt Beranek & Newman Inc Comput/Off Equip	10 Fawcett Street	Cambridge 617-873-2000	MA 02238	
807	Child World Inc Retail/Merch	25 Littlefield Street	Avon 617-588-7300	MA 02322	
1100	Shaws Supermarkets Inc Retail/Food	140 Laurel Street	East Bridgewater 508-378-7211	MA 02333	
550	New England Tile Corp Real Estate/Bldg	183 Columbia Road	Hanover 617-826-5144	MA 02339	
625	Ocean Spray Cranberries Inc Food Processing	225 Water Street	Plymouth 508-747-1000	MA 02360	
NA	Princess House Inc Personal Care	455 Somerset Avenue	North Dighton 617-823-0713	MA 02764	

State / Province: Michigan

Revenue ($ mil)	Organization/ Industry	Address	City / Phone	State/ Zip	Province/ Postcode
NA	Saturn Corp Automotive	1400 Stephenson Highway	Troy 313-524-5721	MI 48007	
1100	Volkswagen America Inc Automotive	888 W Big Beaver	Troy 313-362-6000	MI 48007	
350	Scherer, R P Corp Health Care	2075 W Big Beaver Road	Troy 313-649-0900	MI 480077	
428	Cross & Trecker Corp Equipment	505 N Woodward Avenue	Bloomfield Hills 313-644-4343	MI 48013	
2000	ITT Automotive Inc Automotive	505 N Woodward Avenue	Bloomfield Hills 313-540-9666	MI 48013	
57	Oakland Community College University	2480 Opdyke Road	Bloomfield Hills 313-540-1500	MI 48013	
1000	Taubman Investment Co Real Estate/Bldg	200 Long Lake Road	Bloomfield Hills 313-258-7600	MI 48013	

State / Province: Michigan

Organizations Listed Geographically

Revenue ($ mil)	Organization/ Industry	Address	City / Phone	State/ Zip	Province/ Postcode
300	Douglas & Lomason Co Automotive	24600 Hallwood Court	Framingham 313-478-7800	MI 48018	
1040	Michigan National Bankcorp Inc Banking	27777 Inkster Road	Farmington Hills 313-473-3000	MI 48018	
550	Webb, Jervis B Co Inc Equipment	1 Webb Drive	Farmington Hills 313-553-1000	MI 48018	
834	PHM (Pulte Home) Corp Real Estate/Bldg	6400 Farmington Road	West Bloomfield 313-661-1500	MI 48033	
NA	Vlassic Foods Inc Food Processing	33200 W 14 Mile Road	West Bloomfield 313-851-9400	MI 48033	
500	Barton Malow Co Real Estate/Bldg	27777 Franklin Road American Ctr Bldg	Southfield 313-351-4000	MI 48034	
1177	Federal Mogul Corp Automotive	26555 Northwestern Highway	Southfield 313-354-7700	MI 48034	
1000	Lear Siegler Seating Corp Automotive	21557 Telegraph	Southfield 313-746-1500	MI 48034	
550	Michigan Milk Producers Association Inc Food Processing	41310 Bridge Street	Novi 313-474-6672	MI 48050	
725	Oakland County Government Local Govt	1200 N Telegraph	Pontiac 313-858-0480	MI 48053	
NA	Pontiac Motors Div Automotive	One Pontiac Plaza	Pontiac 313-857-5000	MI 48053	
600	Perry Drug Stores Inc Retail/Merch	5400 Perry Drive	Pontiac 313-334-1300	MI 48056	
300	Southeastern Michigan Gas Corp Utility	2915 Lapeer Road	Port Huron 313-987-7900	MI 48060	
545	William Beaumont Hospital Inc Health Care	3601 W 13 Mile Road	Royal Oak 313-551-5000	MI 48072	
550	Renault America Corp Automotive	4000 Chownunt Center	Southfield 313-358-8800	MI 48075	
593	Thorn Apple Valley Food Processing	18700 W Ten Mile	Southfield 313-552-0700	MI 48075	
NA	Ameritech Publishing Co Publishing/Com	100 E Big Beaver Road	Troy 313-524-7300	MI 48083	
300	Arbor Drugs Inc Retail/Merch	1818 Maplelawn Drive	Troy 313-643-9420	MI 48084	
2908	Chrysler Financial Corp Non-Bank Fin	901 Wilshire Drive	Troy 313-244-3060	MI 48084	
532	Handleman Co Business Service	500 Kirts Blvd	Troy 313-362-4400	MI 48084	
27301	K Mart Corp Retail/Merch	3100 W Big Beaver Road	Troy 313-643-1000	MI 48084	
1269	Kelly Services Corp Business Service	999 W Big Beaver Road	Troy 313-362-4444	MI 48084	
867	Standard Federal Bank Inc Savings & Loan	2401 W Big Beaver	Troy 313-643-9600	MI 48084	
NA	Allied Signal Automotive Div Automotive	20650 Civic Center	Southfield 313-827-5000	MI 48086	
1650	Excello Corp Manufacturing	850 Ladd Road	Walled Lake 313-624-7800	MI 48088	
NA	Chevrolet Motor Division Automotive	30007 Van Dyke Avenue	Warren 313-556-5000	MI 48090	
550	Lamb Technicon Inc Manufacturing	5663 E Nine Mile Road	Warren 313-497-6652	MI 48091	
334	Great Lakes Bancorp Inc Savings & Loan	One Great Lakes Plaza	Ann Arbor 313-769-8300	MI 48104	
1000	Domino's Pizza Inc Food/Lodging	30 Frank Lloyd Wright Drive	Ann Arbor 313-668-4000	MI 48105	
550	JP Industries Inc Building Mat	325 E Eisenhower Parkway	Ann Arbor 313-663-6749	MI 48108	
818	University of Michigan University	Administrative Bldg	Ann Arbor 313-764-1817	MI 48109	
511	University of Michigan Hospitals Inc Health Care	1500 E Medical Center	Ann Arbor 313-936-4000	MI 48109	
6819	Ford Credit Corp Non-Bank Fin	The American Road	Dearborn 313-322-3000	MI 48121	

State / Province: Michigan

Organizations Listed Geographically

Revenue. ($ mil)	Organization/ Industry	Address	City / Phone	State/ Zip	Province/ Postcode
NA	Ford Div Automotive	American Road	Dearborn 313-322-3000	MI 48121	
92446	Ford Motor Co Automotive	The American Road	Dearborn 313-322-3000	MI 48121	
500	Ford Motor Insurance Co Insurance	The American Road	Dearborn 313-322-9045	MI 48121	
NA	Ford Motor Land Development Corp Real Estate/Bldg	American Road	Dearborn 313-322-3000	MI 48121	
NA	Lincoln-Mercury Div Automotive	American Road	Dearborn 313-322-3000	MI 48121	
NA	Rouge Steel Co Steel	American Road	Dearborn 313-322-3000	MI 48122	
253	Oakwood Hospital Corp Health Care	18101 Oakwood Blvd	Detroit 313-593-7000	MI 48123	
733	Auto Club of Michigan Inc Insurance	17000 Executive Plaza Drive	Dearborn 313-336-1234	MI 48126	
2943	CMS Energy-Consumers Power Co Utility	Fairlane Plaza S 300 Town Center Drive	Dearborn 313-436-9261	MI 48126	
NA	UT Automotive Co Automotive	5200 AutoClub Drive	Dearborn 313-593-9000	MI 48126	
1650	Mazda Motors Corp USA Automotive	1 Mazda Drive	Flat Rock 313-782-7800	MI 48134	
500	Walbridge, Aldinger & Co Inc Real Estate/Bldg	38099 Schoolcraft Road	Livonia 313-591-6000	MI 48150	
553	La-Z-Boy Chair Co Appliances/Furn	1284 N Telegraph Road	Monroe 313-242-1444	MI 48161	
750	Guardian Industries Corp Automotive	43043 W Nine Mile Road	Northville 313-349-6700	MI 48167	
911	Highland Superstores Corp Retail/Merch	909 N Sheldon Road	Plymouth 313-451-3200	MI 48170	
NA	Winkelman Stores Inc Retail/Merch	45000 Helm Street	Plymouth 313-451-5353	MI 48170	
NA	Kelsey Hayes Co Automotive	38481 Huron River Drive	Romulus 313-941-2000	MI 48174	
2439	Masco Corp Building Mat	21001 Van Born Road	Taylor 313-274-7400	MI 48180	
1652	Masco Industries Inc Automotive	21001 Van Born Road	Taylor 313-274-7405	MI 48180	
500	McLouth Steel Products Inc Steel	1650 W Jefferson	Trenton 313-285-1200	MI 48183	
91	Eastern Michigan University University	Administrative Bldg	Ypsilanti 313-487-1849	MI 48197	
989	Detroit Medical Center Inc Health Care	4201 St Antoine	Detroit 313-745-5192	MI 48201	
1280	Ford, Henry Health Care Corp Health Care	2799 W Grand Blvd	Detroit 313-876-2600	MI 48202	
10645	General Motors Acceptance Corp Non-Bank Fin	3044 W Grand Blvd	Detroit 313-556-5000	MI 48202	
123641	General Motors Corp Automotive	3044 W Grand Blvd	Detroit 313-556-5000	MI 48202	
1075	Motors Insurance (General Motors) Co Insurance	3044 W Grand Blvd	Detroit 313-556-5000	MI 48202	
265	Wayne State University University	5050 Cass Avenue	Detroit 313-577-2424	MI 48202	
35472	Chrysler Corp Automotive	12000 Chrysler Drive	Highland Park 313-956-5741	MI 48203	
2000	Stroh Brewery Co Beverage	100 River Place	Detroit 313-446-2000	MI 48207	
2094	Fruehauf Corp Automotive	10900 Harper Avenue	Detroit 313-267-1000	MI 48213	
1000	United Auto Workers Membership Org	800 E Jefferson Avenue	Detroit 313-926-5000	MI 48214	
275	Michigan Livestock Co Inc Food Processing	806 Collidge Road	East Lansing 517-337-2856	MI 48223	
500	Amerisure Companies Insurance	28 W Adams Avenue	Detroit 313-965-8600	MI 48226	

State / Province: Michigan

Organizations Listed Geographically

Revenue ($ mil)	Organization/ Industry	Address	City / Phone	State/ Zip	Province/ Postcode
4950	Blue Cross Blue Shield of Michigan Inc Insurance	600 E Lafayette	Detroit 313-225-8000	MI	48226
1043	Comerica Inc Banking	211 W Fort Street	Detroit 313-222-3300	MI	48226
3102	Detroit Edison Co Utility	2000 Second Avenue	Detroit 313-237-8000	MI	48226
1763	Detroit, City of Local Govt	City & County Bldg 2 Woodward Ave	Detroit 313-224-3400	MI	48226
1096	First Federal of Michigan Inc Savings & Loan	1001 Woodward Avenue	Detroit 313-965-1400	MI	48226
400	Grand Trunk Corp Railroad	131 W Lafayette	Detroit 313-962-2260	MI	48226
1750	MCN (Michigan Consolidated Natgas) Corp Utility	500 Griswold Street	Detroit 313-965-2430	MI	48226
NA	Michigan Bell Telephone Co Telecom	444 Michigan Avenue	Detroit 313-223-9900	MI	48226
2181	NBD Bancorp (Natl Bank Detroit) Inc Banking	611 Woodward Avenue	Detroit 313-225-1000	MI	48226
825	Wayne County Government Local Govt	City County Bldg	Detroit 313-224-0286	MI	48226
500	Meadowdale Foods Inc Retail/Food	8711 Meadowdale	Detroit 313-943-3300	MI	48228
1050	Borman's Inc Retail/Food	18718 Borman Avenue	Detroit 313-270-1000	MI	48232
NA	Cadillac Motor Car Division Automotive	2860 Clark Avenue	Detroit 313-554-6112	MI	48232
318	St John Health Corp Health Care	22101 Moross	Detroit 313-343-4000	MI	48236
400	Flint Ink Corp Manufacturing	25111 Glendale Avenue	Detroit 313-538-6800	MI	48239
NA	ANR Pipeline Co Energy	500 Renaissance Center	Detroit 313-496-7075	MI	48243
924	Manufacturers National of Detroit Inc Banking	Manufacturers Bank Tower Renaissance Center	Detroit 313-222-4000	MI	48243
NA	Chrysler/Plymouth Div Automotive	12000 Chrysler Drive	Highland Park 313-956-5741	MI	48288
NA	Dodge Car & Truck Div Automotive	12000 Chrysler Drive	Highland Park 313-956-5741	MI	48288
NA	Jeep/Eagle Corp Automotive	12000 Chrysler Drive	Highland Park 313-956-5741	MI	48288
NA	Automotive Carrier Div Transport	4111 E Andover Road	Bloomfield Hills 313-258-2000	MI	48303
3000	Taubman Co Inc Real Estate/Bldg	PO Box 200	Bloomfield Hills 313-258-6800	MI	48303
NA	Land Systems Div Equipment	38500 Mound Road	Sterling Heights 313-825-4000	MI	48310
1512	Mercy Health Services Health Care	34605 12 Mile Road	Farmington 313-489-6010	MI	48331
350	Champion Enterprises Inc Automotive	5573 North Street	Dryden 313-796-2145	MI	48428
NA	Buick Motor Division Automotive	902 E Hamilton Avenue	Flint 313-236-0444	MI	48550
300	Wolohan Lumber Corp Retail/Merch	1740 Midland Road	Saginaw 517-793-4532	MI	48605
1500	Dow Corning Corp Manufacturing	2200 W Salzburg Road	Auburn 517-496-4000	MI	48611
16682	Dow Chemical Co Chemicals	2030 Willard H Dow Center	Midland 517-636-1000	MI	48674
471	Michigan State University University	Administrative Bldg	East Lansing 517-355-1855	MI	48824
24491	Michigan, State of State/Prov Govt	State Capitol	Lansing 517-373-1837	MI	48909
500	Motor Wheel Corp Automotive	400 Collins Road	Lansing 517-337-5700	MI	48910
1626	Jackson National Life Ins Co Insurance	5901 Executive Drive	Lansing 517-394-3400	MI	48911

State / Province: Michigan

Organizations Listed Geographically

Revenue ($ mil)	Organization/ Industry	Address	City / Phone	State/ Zip	Province/ Postcode
994	Auto Owners Group Insurance Co Insurance	6101 Anacapri Blvd	Lansing 517-323-1200	MI 48917	
NA	Oldsmobile Div Automotive	920 Townsend Street	Lansing 517-377-5000	MI 48921	
440	Michigan Treasurer Employees Rtrmt Sys Non-Bank Fin	425 W Allegan	Lansing 517-373-9150	MI 48922	
2746	Upjohn Co Drugs	7000 Portage Road	Kalamazoo 616-323-4000	MI 49001	
885	First of America Bank Corp Banking	108 E Michigan Avenue	Kalamazoo 616-383-9000	MI 49007	
127	Western Michigan University University	Administrative Bldg	Kalamazoo 606-383-1600	MI 49008	
4349	Kellogg Co Food Processing	235 Porter Street One Kellogg Square	Battle Creek 616-966-2000	MI 49016	
4421	Whirlpool Corp Appliances/Furn	2000 US 33 N	Benton Harbor 616-926-5000	MI 49022	
NA	KitchenAid Inc Appliances/Furn	701 Main Street	St Joseph 616-982-4500	MI 49085	
250	Lamar Life Insurance Corp Insurance	317 E Capitol Street	Jackson 601-949-3100	MI 49201	
357	Jacobson Stores Inc Retail/Merch	1200 N West Avenue	Jackson 517-764-6400	MI 49202	
1094	Tecumseh Products Co Manufacturing	100 E Patterson	Tecumseh 517-423-8411	MI 49286	
1500	Amway Corp Retail/Merch	7575 E Fulton	Ada 606-676-6000	MI 49301	
324	Wolverine World Wide Inc Apparel/Textiles	9341 Courtland Drive	Rockland 616-866-5500	MI 49351	
1068	Gerber Products Co Food Processing	445 State Street	Fremont 616-928-2000	MI 49412	
400	Haworth Corp Appliances/Furn	One Haworth Center	Holland 616-392-5961	MI 49423	
NA	Teledyne Continental Motors Inc Machinery	76 Getty Street	Muskegon 616-724-2151	MI 49442	
877	SPX Sealed Power Corp Automotive	100 Terrace Plaza	Muskegon 616-724-5000	MI 49443	
714	Miller, Herman Inc Manufacturing	8500 Byron Road	Zeeland 616-772-3300	MI 49464	
500	Gordon Food Service Corp Retail/Merch	333 50th Street SW	Grand Rapids 616-530-7000	MI 49501	
1500	Guardsman Products Inc Chemicals	2960 Lucerne Drive SE	Grand Rapids 616-957-2600	MI 49501	
1800	Steelcase Inc Appliances/Furn	901 44th Street	Grand Rapids 616-247-2710	MI 49501	
250	Grand Rapids, City of Local Govt	City Hall 300 Monroe Street	Grand Rapids 616-456-3160	MI 49503	
726	Old Kent Financial Corp Banking	One Vandenberg Center	Grand Rapids 616-774-5000	MI 49503	
2000	Meijer Inc Retail/Merch	2727 Walker Avenue	Grand Rapids 616-453-6711	MI 49504	
881	Foremost Insurance Co Insurance	5800 Foremost Drive	Grand Rapids 616-942-3000	MI 49506	
500	Transnational Motors Inc Automotive	618 Kenmore SE	Grand Rapids 616-949-7570	MI 49506	
1650	Spartan Stores Inc Retail/Food	850 76th Street SW	Grand Rapids 616-878-2000	MI 49518	

State / Province: Minnesota

Revenue ($ mil)	Organization/ Industry	Address	City / Phone	State/ Zip	Province/ Postcode
1000	Andersen Corp Building Mat	Foot of 5th Avenue	Bayport 612-439-5150	MN 55003	
600	Federated Mutual Insurance Co Insurance	121 E Park Square	Owatonna 507-455-5200	MN 55060	
1100	Cenex Corp Retail/Food	5500 Cenex Drive	Inver Grove Height 612-451-5151	MN 55075	

State / Province: Minnesota

Organizations Listed Geographically

Revenue ($ mil)	Organization/ Industry	Address	City / Phone	State/ Zip	Province/ Postcode
1135	Farmers Union Central Exchange Inc Energy	1180 N Concord	South St Paul 612-451-1772	MN 55075	
1394	Minnesota Mutual Life Ins Co Insurance	400 N Robert Street Minnesota Mutual Life Center	St Paul 612-298-3500	MN 55101	
258	AMDURA Corp(American Hoist & Derrick) Manufacturing	1800 Amhoist Tower 345 St Peter Street	St Paul 612-293-4567	MN 55102	
1212	Ecolab (Economics Laboratory) Inc Chemicals	Osborn Bldg	St Paul 612-293-2233	MN 55102	
134	Green Tree Acceptance Corp Non-Bank Fin	345 St Peter Street	St Paul 612-293-3400	MN 55102	
3631	St Paul Companies Inc Insurance	385 Washington Street	St Paul 612-221-7911	MN 55102	
296	St Paul, City of Local Govt	City Hall	St Paul 612-298-4323	MN 55102	
685	Fuller, H B Co Manufacturing	2400 Energy Park Drive	St Paul 612-645-3401	MN 55108	
5650	NWA (Northwest Airlines) Inc Airline	Minneapolis St Paul Intl Airport	St Paul 612-726-2111	MN 55111	
823	Pentair Inc Paper/Forest Prd	1700 W Highway 36	St Paul 612-636-7920	MN 55113	
440	GNB Inc Electronics	1110 Highway 110	Mendota Heights 612-681-5000	MN 55118	
1196	Deluxe Check Printers Inc Business Service	1080 W County Road F	St Paul 612-483-7111	MN 55126	
2180	Land O'Lakes Inc Food Processing	4001 Lexington Avenue	North Arden Hills 612-481-2222	MN 55126	
10581	Minnesota Mining & Manufacturing Co Manufacturing	3M Center	St Paul 612-733-1110	MN 55144	
13023	Minnesota, State of State/Prov Govt	State Capitol	St Paul 612-296-6013	MN 55155	
210	Minnetonka Corp Personal Care	104 Peavey Road	Chaska 612-448-4181	MN 55318	
750	Red Owl Holdings Inc Retail/Food	215 E Excelsior	Hopkins 612-932-2132	MN 55343	
550	Tonka Corp Manufacturing	6000 Clearwater Drive	Minnetonka 612-936-3300	MN 55343	
435	United Healthcare Corp Health Care	300 Opus Center 9900 Bren Road E	Minnetonka 612-936-1300	MN 55343	
1000	Gelco Corp Business Service	One Gelco Drive	Eden Prairie 612-828-1000	MN 55344	
250	National Computer Systems Inc Comput/Off Equip	11000 Prarie Lakes Drive	Hopkins 612-829-3000	MN 55344	
10296	Super Valu Stores Inc Retail/Food	11840 Valley View Road	Eden Prairie 612-828-4000	MN 55344	
40000	Cargill Inc Food Processing	15407 McGinty Road W	Minnetonka 612-475-7575	MN 55345	
2007	Northern States Power Co Utility	414 Nicollet Mall	Minneapolis 612-330-5500	MN 55401	
1069	Bemis Co Inc Manufacturing	800 Northstar Center	Minneapolis 612-340-6000	MN 55402	
756	Cray Research Inc Comput/Off Equip	608 Second Avenue S	Minneapolis 612-333-5889	MN 55402	
220	Dain Bosworth Inc Securities	100 Dain Tower	Minneapolis 612-371-2711	MN 55402	
12204	Dayton Hudson Corp Retail/Merch	777 Nicollet Mall	Minneapolis 612-370-6948	MN 55402	
764	Diversified Energies Inc Utility	201 S 7th Street	Minneapolis 612-372-4664	MN 55402	
2441	First Bank System Inc Banking	1200 First Bank Place E	Minneapolis 612-370-5100	MN 55402	
400	First Minnesota Savings Bank Inc Savings & Loan	77 S 7th Street	Minneapolis 612-371-3700	MN 55402	
350	Inter Regional Financial Corp Non-Bank Fin	100 Dain Tower	Minneapolis 612-371-7750	MN 55402	
1874	International Multifoods Corp Food Processing	Multifoods Tower PO Box 2942	Minneapolis 612-340-3300	MN 55402	

State / Province: Minnesota

Organizations Listed Geographically

Revenue ($ mil)	Organization/ Industry	Address	City / Phone	State/ Zip	Province/ Postcode
250	MEI Diversified Inc Food Processing	90 S 6th Street	Minneapolis 612-339-8853	MN 55402	
425	Midwest Federal Savings Assn Inc Savings & Loan	801 Nicollet Mall	Minneapolis 612-372-6123	MN 55402	
1300	Minstar Inc Leisure Time	100 S Fifth Street Suite 2400	Minneapolis 612-339-7900	MN 55402	
6191	Pillsbury Co Food Processing	Pillsbury Center 200 S Sixth Street	Minneapolis 612-330-4966	MN 55402	
581	TCF Banking & Savings Inc Savings & Loan	801 Marquette Avenue	Minneapolis 612-370-7000	MN 55402	
3300	Harvest States Cooperatives Inc Food Processing	1667 Snelling Avenue N	St Paul 612-646-9433	MN 55408	
7148	Honeywell Inc Comput/Off Equip	Honeywell Plaza	Minneapolis 612-870-5200	MN 55408	
1142	Lutheran Brotherhood Insurance	625 Fourth Avenue S	Minneapolis 612-340-7000	MN 55415	
636	Minneapolis, City of Local Govt	City Hall	Minneapolis 612-348-2100	MN 55415	
480	Valspar Corp Building Mat	1101 Third Street S	Minneapolis 612-332-7371	MN 55415	
609	Toro Co Equipment	8111 Lyndale Avenue S	Bloomington 612-888-8801	MN 55420	
275	Universal Coop Inc Automotive	7801 Metro Parkway	Minneapolis 612-854-0800	MN 55420	
500	Mortenson, M A Co Inc Real Estate/Bldg	700 Meadow Lane	Minneapolis 612-522-2100	MN 55422	
500	Musicland Group Inc Retail/Merch	7500 Excelsior Blvd	Minneapolis 612-932-7700	MN 55426	
1700	Nash Finch Co Retail/Food	3381 Gorham Avenue	St Louis Park 612-929-0371	MN 55426	
131	Network Systems Corp Comput/Off Equip	7600 Boone Avenue N	Minneapolis 612-424-4888	MN 55428	
260	Donaldson Co Manufacturing	1400 W 94th Street	Minneapolis 612-887-3131	MN 55431	
653	Medtronic Inc Electronics	7000 Central Avenue NE	Minneapolis 612-574-4000	MN 55432	
400	Best Buy Co Retail/Merch	4400 W 78th Street	Minneapolis 612-831-4552	MN 55435	
750	National Car Rental Inc Consumer Service	7700 France Avenue S	Minneapolis 612-830-2121	MN 55435	
550	Regis Corp Business Service	5000 Normandale Road	Minneapolis 612-929-6776	MN 55436	
265	International Dairy Queen Food/Lodging	5701 Green Valley	Bloomington 612-830-0200	MN 55437	
560	Jostens Inc Manufacturing	5501 Norman Center Drive	Minneapolis 612-830-3336	MN 55437	
3628	Control Data Corp Comput/Off Equip	8100 34th Street S	Minneapolis 612-853-8100	MN 55440	
5179	General Mills Inc Food Processing	9200 Wayzata Blvd	Minneapolis 612-540-2311	MN 55440	
1000	Holiday Companies Inc Retail/Merch	4567 W 80th Street	Minneapolis 612-830-8700	MN 55440	
2326	IDS Finaical Services Inc Insurance	IDS Tower 10	Minneapolis 612-372-3131	MN 55440	
2270	Northwestern National Life Insurance Co Insurance	20 Washington Avenue S	Minneapolis 612-372-5432	MN 55440	
176	Piper Jaffray & Hopwood Inc Securities	Piper Jaffray Tower 222 S 9th Street	Minneapolis 612-342-6000	MN 55440	
570	Soo Line Corp Transport	Soo Line Bldg Fifth & Marquette	Minneapolis 612-347-8000	MN 55440	
NA	Target Stores Inc Retail/Merch	33 S Sixth Street	Minneapolis 612-370-6073	MN 55440	
4000	Carlson Companies Inc Food Processing	12755 Highway 55	Minneapolis 612-540-5000	MN 55441	
700	CVN Companies Inc Retail/Merch	1405 N Xenium Lane	Minneapolis 612-559-8000	MN 55441	

State / Province: Minnesota

Organizations Listed Geographically

Revenue ($ mil)	Organization/ Industry	Address	City / Phone	State/ Zip	Province/ Postcode
550	Groves, S J & Sons Co Inc Retail/Merch	10000 Highway 55 W	Minneapolis 612-546-6943	MN 55441	
240	Graco Inc Manufacturing	4050 Olson Memorial Highway	Minneapolis 612-623-6000	MN 55442	
748	University of Minnesota University	100 Church Street	Minneapolis 612-373-2851	MN 55455	
2475	Norwest Corp Banking	Sixth & Marquette 1200 Peavey Bldg	Minneapolis 612-372-8268	MN 55479	
312	Federal Reserve Bank of Minneapolis Inc Federal Govt Fin	250 Marquette Avenue	Minneapolis 612-340-2345	MN 55480	
1400	Hennepin County Government Local Govt	Government Center	Minneapolis 612-348-3000	MN 55487	
460	Minnesota Power & Light Co Utility	30 W Superior Street	Duluth 218-722-2641	MN 55802	
2293	Hormel, George A & Co Food Processing	501 Sixteenth Avenue NE	Austin 507-437-5611	MN 55912	
750	Farmstead Foods Corp Food Processing	East Main Street	Albert Lea 507-377-4200	MN 56007	
NA	Teledyne Aerospace Systems Div Aerospace	1007 E 10th Street	Fairmont 507-235-3355	MN 56031	
600	Schwans Sale Enterprises Inc Food Processing	115 W College	Marshall 507-532-3274	MN 56258	
550	American Crystal Sugar Co Food Processing	101 N Third Street	Moorhead 218-236-4400	MN 56560	

State / Province: Mississippi

300	Hancock Fabrics Inc Retail/Merch	3406 W Main Street	Tupelo 601-842-2834	MS 38801	
550	Staplecont Inc Food Processing	210 W Market Street	Greenwood 601-453-6231	MS 38930	
115	Mobile Communications Corp Telecom	1800 E Country Line Road	Ridgeland 601-977-0888	MS 39157	
NA	American Cellular Communications Inc Telecom	1344 Capital Towers	Jackson 601-353-1300	MS 39201	
4929	Mississippi, State of State/Prov Govt	New Capitol	Jackson 601-359-3100	MS 39201	
400	First Mississippi Corp Metals/Mining	70 North Street	Jackson 601-948-7550	MS 39202	
250	Jackson, City of Local Govt	City Hall	Jackson 601-630-1776	MS 39202	
700	Southern Farm Bureau Insurance Co Insurance	1401 Livingston Lane	Jackson 601-982-7777	MS 39205	
500	Jitney Jungle Stores Inc Retail/Merch	451 N Mill Street	Jackson 601-948-0361	MS 39207	
684	Mississippi Power & Light Co Utility	308 E Pearl Street	Jackson 601-949-6442	MS 39215	
NA	Mississippi Power Co Utility	2992 W Beach Street	Gulfport 601-864-1211	MS 39501	

State / Province: Missouri

1000	Maritz Inc Retail/Merch	1375 N Highway Drive	Fenton 314-827-4000	MO 63026	
750	United Van Lines (Unigroup) Inc Transport	1 United Drive	Fenton 314-326-3100	MO 63026	
4156	Wetterau Inc Business Service	8920 Pershall Road	Hazelwood 314-524-5000	MO 63042	
220	Jones, Edward D & Co Securities	201 Progress Parkway	St Louis 314-851-2000	MO 63043	
1000	Schnuck Markets Inc Retail/Food	12921 Enterprise	Bridgeton 314-344-9600	MO 63044	
350	ACF Industries Inc Railroad	3301 Rider Trail S	Earth City 314-344-4500	MO 63045	
1066	Boatmen's Bancshares Inc Banking	One Boatmen's Plaza 800 Market Street	St Louis 314-425-7525	MO 63101	

State / Province: Missouri

Organizations Listed Geographically

Revenue ($ mil)	Organization/ Industry	Address	City / Phone	State/ Zip	Province/ Postcode
1100	Centerre Trust Co Banking	One Boatmans Plaza 800 Market Street	St Louis 314-231-9300	MO 63101	
450	Laclede Gas Co Utility	720 Olive Street	St Louis 314-342-0500	MO 63101	
11525	May Department Stores Co Retail/Merch	611 Olive Street	St Louis 314-342-6300	MO 63101	
391	Pulitzer Publishing Co Publishing/Com	900 N Tucker Blvd	St Louis 314-622-7000	MO 63101	
8473	Southwestern Bell Corp Telecom	One Bell Center	St Louis 314-235-9800	MO 63101	
400	Sverdrup Corp Real Estate/Bldg	801 N 11th Street	St Louis 314-436-7600	MO 63101	
275	Arch Mineral Corp Metals/Mining	200 N Broadway	St Louis 314-231-1010	MO 63102	
574	Federal Reserve Bank of St Louis Federal Govt Fin	411 Locust	St Louis 314-444-8444	MO 63102	
2012	Interco Inc Apparel/Textiles	101 S Hanley Road	St Louis 314-863-1100	MO 63102	
350	Laclede Steel Co Steel	Equitable Bldg 10 Broadway	St Louis 314-425-1400	MO 63102	
1758	Peabody Holding Co Energy	301 N Memorial Drive	St Louis 314-342-3400	MO 63102	
NA	Pet Inc Food Processing	400 S Fourth Street	St Louis 314-621-5400	MO 63102	
375	Petrolite Corp Chemicals	100 N Broadway	St Louis 314-241-8370	MO 63102	
328	CPI Inc Leisure Time	1706 Washington Avenue	St Louis 314-231-1575	MO 63103	
501	Edwards, A G & Sons Inc Securities	One N Jefferson Avenue	St Louis 314-289-3000	MO 63103	
NA	Sherwood Medical Co Health Care	1831 Olive Street	St Louis 314-241-1673	MO 63103	
300	Sigma Aldrich Corp Drugs	3050 Spruce Street	St Louis 314-771-5765	MO 63103	
532	St Louis, City of Local Govt	City Hall	St Louis 314-622-3201	MO 63103	
3000	Apex Oil Co Energy	8182 Maryland Avenue	St Louis 314-889-9600	MO 63105	
1707	Brown Group Inc Apparel/Textiles	8400 Maryland Avenue	St Louis 314-854-4000	MO 63105	
3850	Clark Oil & Refining Co Energy	8182 Maryland	St Louis 314-889-9600	MO 63105	
250	Diversified Industries Inc Metals/Mining	101 S Hanley Road	St Louis 314-862-8200	MO 63105	
NA	Fisher Controls International Inc Manufacturing	8000 Maryland Avenue	Clayton 314-694-9900	MO 63105	
9551	General Dynamics Corp Aerospace	Pierre Laclede Center	St Louis 314-889-8200	MO 63105	
1255	Jefferson Smurfit Corp Paper/Forest Prd	8182 Maryland Jefferson Smurfit Centre	St Louis 314-746-1100	MO 63105	
650	St Louis County Government Local Govt	41 S Central	Clayton 314-889-2000	MO 63105	
550	Consolidated Grain & Barge Co Inc Food Processing	5100 Oakland Avenue	St Louis 314-658-9200	MO 63110	
9705	Anheuser Busch Companies Inc Beverage	One Busch Place	St Louis 314-577-2000	MO 63118	
600	Harvard Industries Inc Manufacturing	4321 Semple Avenue	St Louis 314-382-5590	MO 63120	
500	Alberici, J S Construction Co Inc Real Estate/Bldg	2150 Kienlen Avenue	St Louis 314-261-2611	MO 63121	
NA	Hercules Construction Co Real Estate/Bldg	8220 Delmar Blvd	St Louis 314-991-3730	MO 63124	
1000	McCarthy Brothers Co Real Estate/Bldg	1341 N Rock Hill Road	St Louis 314-968-3300	MO 63124	
NA	Metal Container Corp Packaging	10733 Sunset Office Drive	St Louis 314-577-1700	MO 63127	

State / Province: Missouri

Revenue ($ mil)	Organization/ Industry	Address	City / Phone	State/ Zip	Province/ Postcode
NA	Busch Agricultural Resources Inc Food Processing	12855 Flushing Meadow Drive	St Louis 314-822-6565	MO	63131
500	Community Fed Savings (MO) Assn Inc Savings & Loan	1 Community Federal Center	St Louis 314-822-5000	MO	63131
1462	ITT Financial Corportion Non-Bank Fin	700 Community	St Louis 314-821-6060	MO	63131
NA	Southwestern Bell Publishing Inc Publishing/Com	12800 Publications Drive	St Louis 314-957-2261	MO	63131
328	Angelica Corp Apparel/Textiles	10178 Corporate Square Road	St Louis 314-991-2934	MO	63132
6652	Emerson Electric Co Electronics	8000 W Florissant Avenue	St Louis 314-553-2000	MO	63136
NA	General Dynamics Services Corp Electronics	12101 Woodcrest Executive Drive	St Louis 314-851-4050	MO	63141
275	HBE Corp Real Estate/Bldg	11330 Olive Street	St Louis 314-567-9000	MO	63141
NA	Doe Run Co Metals/Mining	11885 Lackland Road	St Louis 314-991-7140	MO	63146
NA	Continental Baking Co Food Processing	Checkerboard Square	St Louis 314-982-1000	MO	63164
NA	Everready Battery Corp Electronics	Checkerboard Square	St Louis 314-982-1000	MO	63164
5876	Ralston Purina Co Food Processing	Checkerboard Square	St Louis 314-982-1000	MO	63164
1824	General American Life Insurance Co Insurance	700 Market Street PO Box 396	St Louis 314-231-1700	MO	63166
15069	McDonnell Douglas Corp Aerospace	PO Box 516	St Louis 314-232-0232	MO	63166
NA	McDonnell Douglas Information Systems Comput/Off Equip	PO Box 516	St Louis 314-232-0232	MO	63166
426	Mercantile Bancorp Inc Banking	Mercantile Tower	St Louis 314-425-2525	MO	63166
2029	Union Electric Co Utility	1901 Chouteau Avenue PO Box 149	St Louis 314-621-3222	MO	63166
8293	Monsanto Co Chemicals	800 N Lindbergh Blvd	St Louis 314-694-1000	MO	63167
2000	Graybar Electric Co Inc Electronics	34 N Meramec Avenue	St Louis 314-727-3900	MO	63177
1000	Edison Brothers Stores Inc Retail/Merch	501 N Broadway	St Louis 314-331-6000	MO	63178
754	Kellwood Co Apparel/Textiles	600 Kellwood Parkway	Chesterfield 314-576-3100	MO	63178
NA	McDonnell Douglas Missile Systems Co Aerospace	PO Box 426	St Charles 314-925-4000	MO	63301
318	AMC Entertainment Inc Leisure Time	106 W 14th Street	Kansas City 816-221-4000	MO	64105
139	DST Systems Inc Telecom	1004 Baltimore Avenue	Kansas City 816-221-5545	MO	64105
880	Durwood Inc Real Estate/Bldg	106 W 14th Street	Kansas City 816-221-4000	MO	64105
737	Kansas City Power & Light Co Utility	1330 Baltimore Avenue	Kansas City 816-556-2200	MO	64105
507	Kansas City Southern Industries Inc Railroad	114 W Eleventh Street	Kansas City 816-556-0303	MO	64105
503	Kansas City, City of Local Govt	City Hall	Kansas City 816-274-2595	MO	64106
2250	Hallmark Cards Inc Retail/Merch	2501 McGee Street	Kansas City 816-274-5111	MO	64108
794	Block, H & R Inc Business Service	4410 Main Street	Kansas City 816-753-6900	MO	64111
855	IBC Holdings (Interstate Bakeries Corp) Food Processing	12 E Armour Blvd	Kansas City 816-561-6600	MO	64111
650	Bartlett Agricultural Enterprises Inc Food Processing	4800 Main Street	Kansas City 816-753-6300	MO	64112
275	Black & Veatch Inc Consulting	1500 Meadow Lake Drive	Kansas City 913-339-2000	MO	64114

State / Province: Missouri

Organizations Listed Geographically

Revenue ($ mil)	Organization/ Industry	Address	City / Phone	State/ Zip	Province/ Postcode
752	Marion Labratories Inc Drugs	9300 Ward Parkway	Kansas City 816-966-5000	MO	64114
4400	Farmland Industries Inc Energy	3315 N Oak Traffic Way	Kansas City 816-459-6000	MO	64116
2420	US Sprint Inc Telecom	8140 Ward Parkway	Kansas City 816-941-5000	MO	64131
646	Butler Manufacturing Co Manufacturing	BMA Tower	Kansas City 816-968-3000	MO	64141
1750	Payless Cashways Inc Retail/Merch	2301 Main PO Box 466	Kansas City 816-234-6000	MO	64141
751	Federal Reserve Bank of Kansas City Inc Federal Govt Fin	925 Grand Avenue	Kansas City 816-881-2000	MO	64198
479	Commerce Bancshares Inc Banking	1000 Walnut	Kansas City 816-234-2000	MO	64199
600	Utilicorp United Inc Utility	911 Main Street	Kansas City 816-421-6600	MO	64199
750	Ferrell Companies Inc Energy	One Liberty Plaza	Liberty 816-792-1600	MO	64268
600	United Missouri Bancshares Banking	1010 Grand Avenue	Kansas City 816-556-7000	MO	644141
312	Farm & Home Savings Assn Inc Savings & Loan	221 W Cherry Street	Nevada 417-667-3333	MO	64772
810	Leggett & Platt Inc Manufacturing	One Leggett Road	Carthage 417-358-8131	MO	64836
9593	Missouri, State of State/Prov Govt	State Capitol	Jefferson City 314-751-2151	MO	65101
550	Missouri Farmers Association Inc Food Processing	615 Locust Street	Columbia 314-874-5111	MO	65201
303	University of Missouri University	105 Jesse Hall	Columbia 314-882-3387	MO	65211
350	Shelter Insurance Co Insurance	1817 W Broadway	Columbia 314-445-8441	MO	65218
550	Associated Electric Co-op Inc Utility	2814 S Golden	Springfield 417-881-1204	MO	65801
1650	Mid America Dairymen Inc Food Processing	800 W Tampa Street	Springfield 417-865-9641	MO	65802
400	Morris Affiliated Companies Real Estate/Bldg	1650 E Battlefield	Springfield 417-887-0333	MO	65808

State / Province: Montana

Revenue ($ mil)	Organization/ Industry	Address	City / Phone	State/ Zip	Province/ Postcode
2282	Montana, State of State/Prov Govt	State Capitol	Helena 406-444-2511	MT	59620
444	Montana Power & Light Co Utility	40 E Broadway	Butte 406-723-5421	MT	59701

State / Province: Nebraska

Revenue ($ mil)	Organization/ Industry	Address	City / Phone	State/ Zip	Province/ Postcode
700	Valmont Industries Inc Equipment	Highway 272	Valley 402-359-2201	NE	68064
NA	Armour Food Co Food Processing	ConAgra Center One Central Park Plaza	Omaha 402-978-4000	NE	68102
9475	Conagra Inc Food Processing	Conagra Center One Central Park Plaza	Omaha 402-978-4000	NE	68102
NA	Northern Plains Natural Gas Co Energy	2223 Dodge Street	Omaha 402-633-5000	NE	68102
NA	US West Communications-Omaha Telecom	1301 DOTM	Omaha 402-422-2000	NE	68102
1000	Beef America Inc Food Processing	7171 Mercy Road	Omaha 402-397-2000	NE	68106
880	Dubuque Packing Co Inc Food Processing	7171 Mercy Road	Omaha 402-397-2000	NE	68106
1500	Scoular Corp Food Processing	9110 W Dodge Road	Omaha 402-390-3030	NE	68114
570	Commercial Federal Savings Assn Inc Savings & Loan	2120 S 72nd Street	Omaha 402-554-9200	NE	68124

State / Province: Nebraska

Organizations Listed Geographically

Revenue ($ mil)	Organization/ Industry	Address	City / Phone	State/ Zip	Province/ Postcode
500	Pamida Corp Retail/Merch	8800 F Street	Omaha 402-339-2400	NE 68127	
2333	Berkshire Hathaway Inc Insurance	1440 Kiewit Plaza	Omaha 402-346-1400	NE 68131	
4800	Kiewit, Peter & Sons Inc Real Estate/Bldg	1000 Kiewit Plaza	Omaha 402-342-2052	NE 68131	
825	AG Processing Inc Food Processing	11235 Davenport Street	Omaha 402-334-8010	NE 68154	
400	Valcom Inc Retail/Merch	10810 Farnam Street	Omaha 402-392-3900	NE 68154	
2000	Mutual of Omaha Insurance Co Insurance	Mutual of Omaha Plaza	Omaha 402-342-7600	NE 68175	
882	United of Omaha Life Insurance Co Insurance	Mutual of Omaha Plaza	Omaha 402-342-7600	NE 68175	
NA	Union Pacific Railroad Corp Railroad	1416 Dodge Street	Omaha 402-271-5000	NE 68179	
250	Omaha, City of Local Govt	City Hall 1819 Farnam Street	Omaha 402-444-5000	NE 68183	
3721	Nebraska, State of State/Prov Govt	State Capitol	Lincoln 402-471-2311	NE 68509	
NA	Metromail Inc Business Service	901 W Bond	Lincoln 402-475-4591	NE 68521	
359	University of Nebraska University	14th & R Streets	Lincoln 402-472-7211	NE 68588	
9068	IBP Corp Food Processing	IBP Avenue	Dakota City 402-494-2061	NE 68731	

State / Province: Nevada

Revenue ($ mil)	Organization/ Industry	Address	City / Phone	State/ Zip	Province/ Postcode
175	Golden Nugget Inc Leisure Time	129 Fremont Street	Las Vegas 702-385-7111	NV 89101	
250	Las Vegas, City of Local Govt	City Hall East Stewart Avenue	Las Vegas 702-386-6241	NV 89101	
409	Nevada Power Co Utility	6226 W Sahara Avenue	Las Vegas 702-367-5000	NV 89102	
558	Southwest Gas Corp Utility	5241 Spring Mountain	Las Vegas 702-876-7011	NV 89102	
295	Showboat Inc Leisure Time	2800 E Fremont	Las Vegas 702-385-9123	NV 89104	
512	Circus Circus Enterprises Inc Leisure Time	2880 Las Vegas Blvd	Las Vegas 702-734-0410	NV 89109	
499	Horn & Hardart Co Food/Lodging	101 Convention Drive	Las Vegas 702-369-9500	NV 89109	
550	Summa Corp Leisure Time	3800 Howard Hughes Parkway	Las Vegas 702-791-4000	NV 89109	
334	Deere, John Capital Corp Non-Bank Fin	1 E First Street	Reno 702-786-5527	NV 89501	
NA	Nevada Bell Corp Telecom	645 E Plumb Lane	Reno 702-789-6000	NV 89502	
408	Sierra Pacific Resources Co Utility	6100 Neil Road	Reno 702-689-3600	NV 89520	
2436	Nevada, State of State/Prov Govt	State Capitol	Carson City 702-885-5000	NV 89710	

State / Province: New Hampshire

Revenue ($ mil)	Organization/ Industry	Address	City / Phone	State/ Zip	Province/ Postcode
989	Nashua Corp Manufacturing	44 Franklin Street	Nashua 603-880-2323	NH 03061	
1000	Sanders Associates Inc Electronics	Daniel Webster Highway	South Nashua 603-885-4321	NH 03061	
430	Standex International Corp Electronics	6 Manor Parkway	Salem 603-893-9701	NH 03079	
603	Public Service Co of New Hampshire Utility	1000 Elm Street	Manchester 603-669-4000	NH 03105	
NA	New Electric Transmission Corp Utility	Four Park Street	Concord 603-225-5528	NH 03301	

State / Province: New Hampshire

Organizations Listed Geographically

Revenue ($ mil)	Organization/ Industry	Address	City / Phone	State/ Zip	Province/ Postcode
1921	New Hampshire, State of State/Prov Govt	State House	Concord 603-271-1110	NH 03301	
NA	Simplex Wire & Cable Co Electronics	2073 Woodberry Avenue	Portsmouth 603-436-6100	NH 03801	
NA	Grinnell Corp Electronics	Three Tyco Park	Exeter 603-778-9200	NH 03833	
1575	Tyco Laboratories Inc Manufacturing	One Tyco Park	Exeter 603-778-9700	NH 03833	
1036	Henley Group Inc Business Service	Liberty Lane	Hampton 603-926-5911	NH 03842	

State / Province: New Jersey

Revenue ($ mil)	Organization/ Industry	Address	City / Phone	State/ Zip	Province/ Postcode
NA	Best Foods Baking Group Inc Food Processing	Greenbrook Corporate Ctr 100 Passaic Ave	Fairfield 201-808-3000	NJ 07006	
410	Prime Motor Inns Inc Food/Lodging	700 Route 46 E	Fairfield 201-882-1010	NJ 07006	
NA	Shulton Inc Personal Care	697 Route 46	Clifton 201-340-6000	NJ 07015	
250	AL Laboratories Inc Drugs	One Executive Drive	Fort Lee 201-947-7774	NJ 07024	
550	Philipp Brothers Chemicals Inc Chemicals	1 Parker Plaza	Fort Lee 201-944-6020	NJ 07024	
1100	Samsung Electronics USA Inc Electronics	1 Excecutive Drive	Fort Lee 201-592-7900	NJ 07024	
1250	Hartz Mountain Corp Food Processing	700 S Fourth Street	Harrison 201-481-4800	NJ 07029	
NA	Key Pharmaceuticals Inc Drugs	Galloping Hill Road	Kenilworth 201-298-4000	NJ 07033	
NA	Schering Corp Personal Care	Galloping Hill Road	Kenilworth 201-822-7450	NJ 07033	
1042	CIT Group Financial Corp Non-Bank Fin	650 CIT Drive	Livingston 201-740-5000	NJ 07039	
660	FL Industries Inc Manufacturing	220 S Orange Avenue	Livingston 201-535-9522	NJ 07039	
481	Howard Savings Bank Inc Savings & Loan	200 S Orange Avenue	Livingston 201-533-7400	NJ 07039	
729	Emerson Radio Corp Electronics	One Emerson Lane	North Bergen 201-854-6600	NJ 07047	
3227	Armco Inc Steel	300 Interpace Parkway	Parsippany 201-316-5200	NJ 07054	
4070	BASF Corp Chemicals	Nine Campus Drive	Parsippany 201-397-2700	NJ 07054	
2834	General Public Utilities Corp Utility	100 Interpace Parkway	Parsippany 201-263-6500	NJ 07054	
NA	Nabisco Brands Inc Food Processing	Nabisco Plaza Campus Drive	Parsippany 201-503-7100	NJ 07054	
2000	Penske, Roger Corp Business Service	600 Parsippany Road	Parsippany 201-428-7500	NJ 07054	
3980	Chubb Corp Food/Lodging	15 Mountain View Road	Warren 201-580-2000	NJ 07060	
5940	Merck & Co Inc Drugs	PO Box 2000	Rahway 201-574-4000	NJ 07065	
300	Ketchum & Co Retail/Merch	77 Brant Avenue	Clark 201-815-2800	NJ 07066	
1549	Automatic Data Processing Inc Comput/Off Equip	One ADP Blvd.	Roseland 201-994-5000	NJ 07068	
1650	Lucky Goldstar Group Electronics	1050 Wall Street	Lindhusrt 201-460-8010	NJ 07071	
825	Peugeot USA Inc Automotive	One Peugeot Plaza	Lindhurst 201-935-8400	NJ 07071	
1100	Daewoo Group Manufacturing	100 Daewoo Place	Carlstadt 201-896-2824	NJ 07072	
280	King World Productions Inc Leisure Time	430 Morris Turnpike	Short Hills 201-522-0100	NJ 07078	

State / Province: New Jersey

Organizations Listed Geographically

Revenue ($ mil)	Organization/ Industry	Address	City / Phone	State/ Zip	Province/ Postcode
1100	Connell Rice & Sugar Inc Food Processing	45 Cardinal Drive	Westfield 201-233-0700	NJ	07092
450	Genlyte Group Inc Manufacturing	100 Lighting Way	Secaucus 201-864-3000	NJ	07094
783	Jamesway Corp Retail/Merch	40 Hartz Way	Secaucus 201-330-6000	NJ	07094
1650	Matsushita Electric USA Inc Electronics	1 Panasonic Way	Secaucus 201-348-7100	NJ	07094
750	Metromedia Inc Publishing/Com	1 Harmon Plaza	Secaucus 201-348-3244	NJ	07094
550	NPS Group Inc Real Estate/Bldg	600 Meadowland Parkway	Secaucus 201-865-6550	NJ	07094
1242	Petrie Stores Corp Retail/Merch	70 Enterprise Avenue	Secaucus 201-866-3600	NJ	07094
283	Syms Corp Retail/Merch	Syms Way	Secuacus 201-902-9600	NJ	07094
6000	Supermarkets General Corp Retail/Food	301 Blair Road	Woodbridge 201-499-3000	NJ	07095
NA	New Jersey Bell Telephone Co Telecom	540 Broad Street	Newark 201-649-9900	NJ	07101
33724	Prudential Insurance Co of America Insurance	Prudential Plaza	Newark 201-877-6000	NJ	07101
4395	Public Service Enterprise Group Inc Utility	80 Park Plaza	Newark 201-430-7000	NJ	07101
3169	Mutual Benefit Life Insurance Co Insurance	520 Broad Street	Newark 201-481-8000	NJ	07102
313	Newark, City of Local Govt	City Hall 920 Broad Street	Newark 201-733-6400	NJ	07102
2806	First Fidelity BanCorp Inc Banking	550 Broad Street	Newark 201-565-3200	NJ	07192
3300	Wakefern Food Corp Food Processing	600 York Street	Elizabeth 201-527-3300	NJ	07207
600	Mayfair Super Markets Inc Retail/Food	681 Newark Avenue	Elizabethtown 201-352-6400	NJ	07208
369	Block Drug Co Inc Personal Care	257 Cornelison Avenue	Jersey City 201-434-3000	NJ	07302
500	First Jersey National Corp Banking	2 Montgomery Street	Jersey City 201-547-7000	NJ	07302
400	Jersey City, City of Local Govt	City Hall	Jersey City 201-547-5202	NJ	07302
502	Medco Containment Services Inc Health Care	1900 Pollitt Drive	Fair Lawn 201-794-9010	NJ	07410
1709	Becton, Dickinson & Co Drugs	One Becton Drive	Franklin Lakes 201-848-6800	NJ	07417
1100	Sharp Electronics USA Inc Electronics	Sharp Plaza	Mahwah 201-529-8200	NJ	07430
500	ITT Fluid Technology Corp Manufacturing	444 Godwin Avenue	Midland Park 201-444-6030	NJ	07432
278	Berrie, Russ & Co Inc Leisure Time	111 Bauer Drive	Oakland 201-891-7500	NJ	07436
825	Minolta Corp Electronics	101 Williams Drive	Ramsey 201-825-4000	NJ	07446
879	Western Union Corp Telecom	One Lake Street	Upper Saddle Rvr 201-818-5000	NJ	07458
4592	American Cyanamid Co Chemicals	One Cyanamid Plaza	Wayne 201-831-2000	NJ	07470
432	Formica Corp Chemicals	155 Rt 46 W	Wayne 201-890-9400	NJ	07470
837	GAF Corp Building Mat	1361 Alps Road	Wayne 201-628-3000	NJ	07470
3100	Grand Union Co Retail/Food	201 Willowbrook Blvd	Wayne 201-890-6000	NJ	07470
3300	Schlott, Richard Realty Inc Real Estate/Bldg	1550 Route 23 N	Wayne 201-633-5000	NJ	07470
2661	Union Camp Corp Paper/Forest Prd	1600 Valley Road	Wayne 201-628-2000	NJ	07470

State / Province: New Jersey

Organizations Listed Geographically

Revenue ($ mil)	Organization/ Industry	Address	City / Phone	State/ Zip	Province/ Postcode
175	Athlone Industries Inc Steel	200 Webro Road	Parsippany 201-887-9100	NJ 07540	
550	Jaguar Cars Inc Automotive	600 Willow Tree Road	Leonia 201-592-5200	NJ 07605	
321	National Community Bank Banking	113 W Essex Street	Maywood 201-845-1000	NJ 07607	
4701	CPC International Inc Food Processing	International Plaza	Englewood Cliffs 201-894-4000	NJ 07632	
1430	Lipton, Thomas J Inc Food Processing	800 Sylvan Avenue	Englewood Cliffs 201-567-8000	NJ 07632	
1117	Federal Paper Board Co Inc Paper/Forest Prd	75 Chestnut Ridge Road	Montvale 201-391-1776	NJ 07645	
2200	Grand Met USA Inc Tobacco	100 Paragon Drive	Montvale 201-573-4000	NJ 07645	
10068	Great Atlantic & Pacific Tea Co Retail/Food	2 Paragon Drive PO Box 418	Montvale 201-573-9700	NJ 07645	
550	Intercontinental Hotels Corportion Food/Lodging	100 Paragon Drive	Montvale 201-307-3300	NJ 07645	
1540	Mercedes (Daimler Benz) Inc Automotive	One Mercedes Drive	Montvale 201-573-0600	NJ 07645	
1100	Volvo North America Corp Automotive	Rockleigh Industrial Way	Rockleigh 201-768-7300	NJ 07647	
1200	Oryx Energy Co Comput/Off Equip	15 Essex Road	Paramus 201-845-5533	NJ 07652	
3574	TW Service Inc Food/Lodging	S 61 Paramus Road	Paramus 201-712-0500	NJ 07652	
2000	Hertz Corp Consumer Service	225 Brae Blvd	Park Ridge 201-307-2000	NJ 07656	
3300	Sony Corp of America Electronics	Sony Drive	Park Ridge 201-930-1000	NJ 07656	
400	General Felt Industries Inc Apparel/Textiles	Park 80 Plaza W	Saddle Brook 201-843-0900	NJ 07662	
1650	GFI Knoll International Holdings Inc Apparel/Textiles	Park 80 Plaza W	Saddlebrook 201-843-0900	NJ 07662	
2500	Kidde Inc Conglomerate	Park 80 W Plaza Two	Saddlebrook 201-368-9000	NJ 07662	
346	Sealed Air Corp Packaging	Park 80 Plaza E	Saddle Brook 201-791-7600	NJ 07662	
4001	Toys R Us Inc Retail/Merch	395 W Passaic Street	Rochelle Park 201-845-5033	NJ 07662	
NA	CPL Industries Inc Personal Care	101 N Summit Street	Tenafly 201-568-2303	NJ 07670	
3021	Ingersoll-Rand Corp Machinery	200 Chestnut Ridge	Woodcliff Lake 201-573-0123	NJ 07675	
400	DeTomaso Industries Automotive	107 Monmouth Street	Red Bank 201-842-7200	NJ 07701	
301	Hovnanian Enterprises Inc Real Estate/Bldg	10 Route 35	Red Bank 201-747-7800	NJ 07701	
260	Wellman Corp Tire/Rubber	1040 Broad street	Shrewsbury 201-388-0120	NJ 07702	
350	New Jersy Resources Inc Utility	1415 Wyckoff Road	Wall 201-938-1480	NJ 07719	
500	Foodarama Supermarket Corp Retail/Food	303 W Main Street	Freehold 201-462-4700	NJ 07728	
278	Concurrent Computer Corp Comput/Off Equip	15 Main Street	Holmdel 201-946-8883	NJ 07733	
600	Village Super Markets Inc Retail/Food	733 Mountain Avenue	Springfield 201-467-2200	NJ 07801	
480	Selective Insurance Co Insurance	40 Wantage Avenue	Branchville 201-948-3000	NJ 07890	
500	Summit Bancorp Banking	367 Springfield Avenue	Summit 201-522-8400	NJ 07901	
1046	City Fed Financial Corp Savings & Loan	Route 202-206 Bedminster One	Bedminster 201-658-4100	NJ 07921	
2969	Schering Plough Corp Drugs	One Giralda Farms	Madison 201-822-7000	NJ 07940	

State / Province: New Jersey

Organizations Listed Geographically

Revenue ($ mil)	Organization/ Industry	Address	City / Phone	State/ Zip	Province/ Postcode
3908	Warner Lambert Co Drugs	201 Tabor Road	Morris Plains 201-540-2000	NJ 07950	
11909	Allied Signal Inc Aerospace	PO Box 4000R	Morristown 713-224-6611	NJ 07960	
700	Carteret Savings Bank Corporated Savings & Loan	200 South Street	Morristown 201-326-1000	NJ 07960	
3000	Crum & Foster Inc Insurance	305 Madison Avenue	Morristown 201-285-7000	NJ 07960	
400	Horizon Bancorp Inc Banking	225 South Street	Morristown 201-539-7700	NJ 07960	
NA	Jersey Central Power & Light Co Utility	Madison Avenue	Morristown 201-455-8200	NJ 07960	
758	Bard, C R Inc Drugs	730 Central Avenue	Murray Hill 201-277-8000	NJ 07974	
2000	Bell Laboratories of AT&T Consulting	600 Mountain Avenue	Murray Hill 201-582-3000	NJ 07974	
NA	Dun & Bradstreet Credit Services Co Comput/Off Equip	One Diamond Hill Road	Murray Hill 201-665-6660	NJ 07974	
300	Fedders Corp Appliances/Furn	158 Highway 206 N	Peapack 201-234-2100	NJ 07977	
750	Channel Home Centers Inc Retail/Merch	945 Route 10	Whippany 201-887-7000	NJ 07981	
1673	Subaru America Corp Automotive	Subaru Plaza 2235 Route 70 W	Cherry Hill 609-488-8500	NJ 08002	
282	Burlington Coat Factory Inc Apparel/Textiles	Route 130	Burlington 609-387-7800	NJ 08016	
935	Fox & Lazo Inc Real Estate/Bldg	30 Washington Avenue	Haddonfield 609-424-2800	NJ 08033	
512	American Water Works Co Inc Business Service	1025 Laurel Oak Road	Voorhees 609-346-8200	NJ 08043	
4869	Campbell Soup Co Food Processing	Campbell Place	Camden 609-342-4800	NJ 08103	
750	Holman Enterprises Inc Automotive	7411 Maple Avenue	Pennsauken 609-663-5200	NJ 08109	
300	Mediq Inc Health Care	One Mediq Plaza	Pennsauken 609-665-9300	NJ 08110	
676	Atlantic Energy Co Utility	1199 Black Horse Pike	Pleasantville 609-645-4100	NJ 08232	
500	Wheaton Industries Inc Manufacturing	1101 Wheaton Avenue	Millville 609-825-1400	NJ 08332	
343	Caesars New Jersey Leisure Time	2100 Pacific Avenue	Atlantic City 609-348-4411	NJ 08401	
400	Church & Dwight Co Personal Care	469 N Harrison	Princeton 609-683-5900	NJ 08540	
600	Pullman Peabody Co Automotive	82 Nassau Street	Princeton 609-683-1770	NJ 08540	
2586	Squibb Corp Drugs	PO Box 4000	Princeton 609-921-4000	NJ 08540	
1032	United Jersey Banks Inc Banking	301 Carnegie Center	Princeton 609-987-3200	NJ 08543	
245	Princeton University University	Administrative Bldg	Princeton 609-452-3000	NJ 08544	
1475	New Jersey Divison of Investment Non-Bank Fin	349 W State Street	Trenton 609-292-5106	NJ 08625	
20700	New Jersey, State of State/Prov Govt	State Capitol	Trenton 609-292-2121	NJ 08625	
380	New Jersey Manufacturers Insurance Co Insurance	Sullivan Way	West Trenton 609-883-1300	NJ 08628	
650	IMO Industries Electronics	3450 Princeton Pike	Lawrenceville 609-896-7600	NJ 08648	
500	New Jersey National Bank Banking	1 W State Street	Trenton 609-771-5700	NJ 08650	
1210	National Starch & Chemical Corp Chemicals	Finderne Avenue	Bridgewater 201-685-5000	NJ 08807	
350	NUI Corp Energy	1011 Rt 22 W	Bridgewater 201-685-3900	NJ 08807	

State / Province: New Jersey

Organizations Listed Geographically

Revenue ($ mil)	Organization/ Industry	Address	City / Phone	State/ Zip	Province/ Postcode
1090	Foster Wheeler Corp Real Estate/Bldg	Perryville Corporate Park	Clinton 201-730-4000	NJ 08809	
2351	Englehard Corp Chemicals	Menlo Park	Edison 201-632-6000	NJ 08818	
500	Huber, J M Corp Chemicals	333 Thornall Street	Edison 201-549-8600	NJ 08818	
1847	Midlantic Banks Inc Banking	Metro Park Plaza	Edison 201-321-8000	NJ 08818	
1100	Twin County Grocers Inc Retail/Food	145 Talmadge Road	Edison 201-287-4600	NJ 08818	
4180	Hanson Industries (Hanson Trust) Inc Manufacturing	100 Wood Avenue S	Iselin 201-549-7050	NJ 08830	
2530	Siemens Corp Electronics	186 Wood Avenue S	Iselin 201-321-3400	NJ 08830	
2000	Sea Land Corp Transport	10 Parsonage Road	Edison 201-632-2000	NJ 08837	
880	MAN North America Corp Machinery	333 Cedar Avenue	Middlesex 201-469-6600	NJ 08846	
515	Thomas & Betts Corp Electronics	920 Route 202	Raritan 201-685-1600	NJ 08869	
3190	Celanese Corp (Hoechst) Chemicals	Route 202-206 N	Somerville 201-231-2000	NJ 08876	
1815	Hoechst American Corp Chemicals	1041 Route 202-206 N PO Box 2500	Somerville 201-231-2000	NJ 08876	
500	Research Cottrell Inc Consulting	Route 22 W PO Box 1500	Somerville 201-685-4000	NJ 08876	
351	Rutgers University University	Administrative Bldg	New Brunswick 201-932-1766	NJ 08903	
9001	Johnson & Johnson Corp Drugs	One Johnson & Johnson Plaza	New Brunswick 201-524-0400	NJ 08933	

State / Province: New Mexico

Revenue ($ mil)	Organization/ Industry	Address	City / Phone	State/ Zip	Province/ Postcode
382	Albuquerque, City of Local Govt	City Hall	Albuquerque 505-768-3000	NM 87103	
NA	Santa Fe Pacific Minerals Corp Metals/Mining	6209 Uptown NE	Albuquerque 505-881-3050	NM 87125	
144	University of New Mexico University	Administrative Bldg	Albuquerque 505-277-0111	NM 87131	
842	Public Service Co of New Mexico Utility	Alvarado Square	Albuquerque 505-848-2700	NM 87158	
4168	New Mexico, State of State/Prov Govt	State Capitol	Sante Fe 505-827-4011	NM 87503	

State / Province: New York

Revenue ($ mil)	Organization/ Industry	Address	City / Phone	State/ Zip	Province/ Postcode
275	Brooks Fashion Stores Inc Retail/Merch	370 Seventh Avenue	New York 212-714-8600	NY 10001	
NA	Lerner Stores Inc Retail/Merch	460 W 33rd Street	New York 212-736-1222	NY 10001	
5800	Macy, R H & Co Inc Retail/Merch	151 W 34th Street	New York 212-560-3600	NY 10001	
350	Nichols, S E Inc Retail/Merch	275 7th Avenue	New York 212-206-9400	NY 10001	
250	Amalgamated Clothing & Textile Workers Membership Org	15 Union Square	New York 212-242-0700	NY 10003	
5109	Consolidated Edison New York Inc Utility	4 Irving Place	New York 212-460-4600	NY 10003	
2876	Guardian Life Insurance Co of America Insurance	201 Park Avenue S	New York 212-598-8000	NY 10003	
1111	Integrated Resources Non-Bank Fin	10 Union Square E	New York 212-353-7000	NY 10003	
553	New York University University	Washington Square	New York 212-598-3127	NY 10003	
450	Commerzbank AG Banking	55 Broadway	New York 212-208-6200	NY 10004	

State / Province: New York

Organizations Listed Geographically

Revenue ($ mil)	Organization/ Industry	Address	City / Phone	State/ Zip	Province/ Postcode
450	Dresdner Bank AG Banking	60 Broad Street	New York 212-425-4640	NY 10004	
3300	Drexel Burnham Lambert Inc Securities	60 Broad Street	New York 212-480-6000	NY 10004	
4000	Goldman, Sachs & Co Securities	85 Broad Street	New York 212-902-1000	NY 10004	
3000	Hutton, E F Group Inc Securities	One Battery Park Plaza	New York 212-742-5000	NY 10004	
750	Johnson & Higgins Inc Insurance	125 Broad Street	New York 212-574-7000	NY 10004	
NA	McGraw Hill Financial Services Co Comput/Off Equip	25 Broadway	New York 212-208-8000	NY 10004	
350	Schroder, IBJ Bank & Trust Co Banking	One State Street	New York 212-858-2000	NY 10004	
750	Thomson McKinnon Securities Inc Securities	One New York Plaza	New York 212-482-7000	NY 10004	
300	Alliance Mutual Funds Inc Non-Bank Fin	140 Broadway	New York 800-221-5672	NY 10005	
652	Atlantic Mutual Insurance Co Insurance	45 Wall Street	New York 212-943-1800	NY 10005	
1042	Balfour Maclaine Corp(former Kay Corp) Securities	Wall Street Plaza	New York 212-269-0800	NY 10005	
440	Banca Serfin Banking	88 Pine Street 24th Floor	New York 212-635-2300	NY 10005	
400	Brown Brothers Harriman & Co Securities	59 Wall Street	New York 212-483-1818	NY 10005	
5500	Bunge Corp Food Processing	1 Chase Manhattan Plaza	New York 212-943-6600	NY 10005	
330	Carroll McEntee & McGinley Inc Securities	40 Wall Street	New York 212-825-6780	NY 10005	
1000	Chilewich Sons Inc Food Processing	120 Wall Street	New York 212-344-3400	NY 10005	
425	Corroon & Black Corp Non-Bank Fin	Wall Street Plaza	New York 212-363-4100	NY 10005	
330	Cowen & Co Securities	Financial Square	New York 212-495-6000	NY 10005	
450	Credit Lyonnais France Banking	95 Wall Street	New York 212-344-0500	NY 10005	
178	DCNY Discount Corp of New York Inc Securities	58 Pine Street	New York 212-248-8900	NY 10005	
275	Deutsche Bank Capital Corp Securities	40 Wall Street	New York 212-612-0600	NY 10005	
2200	Donaldson, Lufkin & Jenrette Inc Securities	140 Broadway	New York 212-504-3000	NY 10005	
275	Gruntal & Co Inc Securities	14 Wall Street	New York 212-267-8800	NY 10005	
1423	Home Life Insurance Co Insurance	75 Wall Street	New York 212-428-2000	NY 10005	
2500	Irving Bank Corp Banking	One Wall Street	New York 212-635-1111	NY 10005	
1650	Kidder, Peabody & Co Inc Securities	10 Hanover Square	New York 212-510-3000	NY 10005	
275	Schapiro, M A & Co Securities	One Chase Manhattan Plaza	New York 212-980-5353	NY 10005	
436	Seamen's Bank for Savings Inc Savings & Loan	30 Wall Street	New York 212-428-4500	NY 10005	
450	Shoko Chukin Bank Ltd Banking	2 Wall Street	New York 212-693-1660	NY 10005	
1500	TLC Beatrice Internatl Holding Co Conglomerate	99 Wall Street	New York 212-269-4544	NY 10005	
300	US Steel/Carnegie Pension Fund Inc Non-Bank Fin	45 Wall Street	New York 212-806-4500	NY 10005	
362	US Trust Corp Banking	45 Wall Street	New York 212-806-4500	NY 10005	
3500	Dean Witter Reynolds Inc Securities	2 World Trade Center 66th Floor	New York 212-392-2222	NY 10006	

State / Province: New York

Organizations Listed Geographically

Revenue ($ mil)	Organization/ Industry	Address	City / Phone	State/ Zip	Province/ Postcode
220	Mabon, Nugent & Co Securities	115 Broadway	New York 212-732-2820	NY 10006	
500	Seligman Marketing Inc Non-Bank Fin	One Bankers Trust Plaza	New York 800-221-2450	NY 10006	
450	Spear, Leeds & Kellogg Inc Securities	115 Broadway	New York 212-587-8800	NY 10006	
27197	New York, City of Local Govt	City Hall	New York 212-566-1300	NY 10007	
1650	Bozell Jacobs Kenyon Inc Business Service	40 W 23rd Street	New York 212-727-5000	NY 10010	
750	Jordan Co Retail/Merch	315 Park Avenue S	New York 212-460-1920	NY 10010	
30800	Metropolitan Life Insurance Co Insurance	One Madison Avenue	New York 212-578-2211	NY 10010	
500	National Cleaning Contractors Inc Business Service	60 Madison Avenue	New York 212-689-4050	NY 10010	
12374	New York Life Insurance Co Insurance	51 Madison Avenue	New York 212-576-7000	NY 10010	
275	Audits & Surveys Inc Business Service	650 Avenue of the Americas	New York 212-627-9700	NY 10011	
474	LVI Group Inc Consulting	345 Hudson Street	New York 212-337-6600	NY 10014	
7839	Morgan, J P & Co Inc Banking	23 Wall Street	New York 212-344-3000	NY 10015	
350	Morgan, J P Securities Inc Securities	23 Wall Street	New York 212-483-2323	NY 10015	
1200	Collins & Aikman Corp Manufacturing	210 Madison Avenue	New York 212-578-1200	NY 10016	
942	Culbro Corp Food Processing	387 Park Avenue S	New York 212-561-8700	NY 10016	
1100	Fuji Industries Inc Leisure Time	600 Third Avenue	New York 212-943-4435	NY 10016	
750	Horsehead Industries Inc Business Service	204 E 39th Street	New York 212-972-2100	NY 10016	
1187	Loral Corp Electronics	600 Third Avenue	New York 212-697-1105	NY 10016	
750	Lorimar Telepictures Inc Leisure Time	475 Park Avenue S	New York 212-686-9200	NY 10016	
287	Marcade Group Inc Apparel/Textiles	275 Madison Avenue	New York 212-944-0877	NY 10016	
750	Metallurg Corp Metals/Mining	25 E 39th Street	New York 212-686-4010	NY 10016	
2922	National Distillers & Chemicals Corp Chemicals	99 Park Avenue	New York 212-949-5000	NY 10016	
NA	Putnam Publishing Group Inc Publishing/Com	200 Madison Avenue	New York 212-576-8900	NY 10016	
2922	Quantum Chemical Corp Chemicals	99 Park Avenue	New York 212-949-5000	NY 10016	
250	Retail, Wholesale & Dept Store Union Membership Org	30 E 29th Street	New York 212-684-5300	NY 10016	
2300	Sterling Drug Inc Drugs	90 Park Avenue	New York 212-907-2000	NY 10016	
5501	American Home Products Corp Drugs	685 Third Avenue	New York 212-878-5000	NY 10017	
276	Bank Leumi Trust Co Banking	579 Fifth Avenue	New York 212-382-4000	NY 10017	
800	Bank of Tokyo Trust Banking	360 Madison Avenue	New York 212-766-3472	NY 10017	
5851	Bankers Trust New York Corp Banking	280 Park Avenue	New York 212-250-2500	NY 10017	
450	Bayerische Vereinsbank AG Banking	335 Madison Avenue	New York 212-210-0300	NY 10017	
700	Bowery Savings Bank Inc Savings & Loan	100 E 42nd Street	New York 212-953-8400	NY 10017	
200	Chock-Full-O-Nuts Corp Food Processing	370 Lexington Avenue	New York 212-532-0300	NY 10017	

State / Province: New York

Organizations Listed Geographically

Revenue ($ mil)	Organization/ Industry	Address	City / Phone	State/ Zip	Province/ Postcode
1313	Crane Co Manufacturing	757 Third Avenue	New York 212-415-7300	NY 10017	
550	Emigrant Savings Bank Inc Savings & Loan	5 E 42nd Street	New York 212-883-5800	NY 10017	
1375	Fischbach Corp Real Estate/Bldg	485 Lexington Avenue	New York 212-986-4100	NY 10017	
450	Generale Banque (Societe Generale) Banking	12 E 49th Street	New York 212-418-8700	NY 10017	
275	Glickenhaus & Co Securities	6 E 43rd Street	New York 212-953-7800	NY 10017	
450	Grey Advertising Inc Consulting	777 3rd Avenue	New York 212-546-2000	NY 10017	
500	Griffin Corp Leisure Time	780 Third Avenue	New York 212-753-1230	NY 10017	
800	Israel Discount Bank Banking	511 Fifth Avenue	New York 212-551-8500	NY 10017	
1100	Itoh, C Trading Co USA Manufacturing	335 Madison Avenue	New York 212-818-8000	NY 10017	
275	K & E Holding Inc Business Service	200 Park Avenue	New York 212-880-2000	NY 10017	
1100	Katz Communications Inc Publishing/Com	1 Dag Hammarshield Plaza	New York 212-572-5500	NY 10017	
350	Lazare Kaplan International Inc Retail/Merch	529 Fifth Avenue	New York 212-972-9700	NY 10017	
412	Lionel Corp Leisure Time	441 Lexington Avenue	New York 212-818-0630	NY 10017	
8545	Manufacturers Hanover Corp Banking	270 Park Avenue	New York 212-286-6000	NY 10017	
250	McCann Erickson Worldwide Consulting	485 Lexington Avenue	New York 212-697-6000	NY 10017	
NA	Million Market Newspaper/Times Mirror Publishing/Com	711 Third Avenue	New York 212-692-7100	NY 10017	
54361	Mobil Corp Energy	150 E 42nd Street	New York 212-883-4242	NY 10017	
5424	North American Philips Corp Electronics	100 E 42nd Street	New York 212-697-3600	NY 10017	
12661	NYNEX Corp Telecom	335 Madison Avenue	New York 212-370-7400	NY 10017	
575	Ogilvy Group Inc Business Service	2 E 48th Street	New York 212-907-3400	NY 10017	
550	Parsons & Whittemore Corp Paper/Forest Prd	666 Third Avenue	New York 212-972-2000	NY 10017	
5385	Pfizer Inc Drugs	235 E 42nd Street	New York 212-573-2323	NY 10017	
31742	Philip Morris Companies Inc Tobacco	120 Park Avenue	New York 212-880-5000	NY 10017	
1500	Saatchi, Saatchi Co Business Service	405 Lexington Avenue	New York 212-661-0800	NY 10017	
900	Swiss Reinsurance Co Insurance	237 Park Avenue	New York 212-907-8000	NY 10017	
550	TBWA Advertising Inc Business Service	292 Madison Avenue	New York 212-725-1150	NY 10017	
500	Thompson, J Walter Group Inc Business Service	466 Lexington Avenue	New York 212-210-7000	NY 10017	
8409	TIAA CREF Inc Non-Bank Fin	730 Third Avenue	New York 212-490-9000	NY 10017	
3196	Turner Corp Real Estate/Bldg	633 Third Avenue	New York 212-878-0400	NY 10017	
266	Unicorp American Corp Real Estate/Bldg	156 E 46th Street	New York 212-972-6100	NY 10017	
300	United Industrial Corp Equipment	18 E 48th Street	New York 212-752-8787	NY 10017	
2000	United Nations Federal Govt	First Avenue	New York 212-963-1234	NY 10017	
75	Value Line Inc Non-Bank Fin	711 Third Avenue	New York 800-223-0818	NY 10017	

State / Province: New York

Organizations Listed Geographically

Revenue ($ mil)	Organization/ Industry	Address	City / Phone	State/ Zip	Province/ Postcode
750	Young & Rubicam Inc Business Service	285 Madison Avenue	New York 212-210-3000	NY 10017	
700	Alexander's Inc Retail/Merch	500 Seventh Avenue	New York 212-869-0368	NY 10018	
3500	American Standard Inc Manufacturing	40 W 40th Street	New York 212-703-5100	NY 10018	
280	Bernard, Chaus Inc Apparel/Textiles	1410 Broadway	New York 212-354-1280	NY 10018	
1184	Claiborne, Liz Co Inc Apparel/Textiles	1441 Broadway	New York 212-354-4900	NY 10018	
NA	G&G Shops Inc Retail/Merch	520 Eighth Avenue	New York 212-279-4961	NY 10018	
550	Gitano Orit Imports Inc Apparel/Textiles	1411 Broadway	New York 212-819-0707	NY 10018	
250	ISS International Service Corp Business Service	1430 Broadway	New York 212-382-9800	NY 10018	
825	Jordache Enterprises Inc Apparel/Textiles	498 Seventh Avenue	New York 212-279-7343	NY 10018	
683	Leslie Fay Inc Apparel/Textiles	1400 Broadway	New York 212-221-4000	NY 10018	
NA	Lord & Taylor Inc Retail/Merch	424 Fifth Avenue	New York 212-391-3344	NY 10018	
2400	Milliken & Co Apparel/Textiles	1045 6th Avenue	New York 212-819-4200	NY 10018	
2106	Republic Bank of New York Inc Banking	452 Fifth Avenue	New York 212-525-5000	NY 10018	
NA	RKO General Inc Publishing/Com	1440 Broadway	New York 212-764-7000	NY 10018	
260	Russ Togs Inc Apparel/Textiles	1411 Broadway	New York 212-642-8500	NY 10018	
646	United Merchants & Manufacturers Inc Apparel/Textiles	1407 Broadway	New York 212-930-3900	NY 10018	
3063	Avon Products Inc Personal Care	9 W 57th Street	New York 212-546-6015	NY 10019	
2778	CBS Inc Publishing/Com	51 W 52nd Street	New York 212-975-4321	NY 10019	
450	Daiwa Bank & Trust Co Banking	75 Rockefeller Plaza	New York 212-399-2710	NY 10019	
450	Deutsche Bank AG Banking	9 W 57th Street	New York 212-940-8000	NY 10019	
1800	Equitable Variable Life Insurance	787 7th Avenue	New York 212-554-4035	NY 10019	
2000	Hearst Corp Publishing/Com	959 8th Avenue	New York 212-262-5700	NY 10019	
500	ICC Industries Inc Chemicals	720 Fifth Avenue	New York 212-903-1700	NY 10019	
840	International Flavors & Fragrances Inc Personal Care	521 W 57th Street	New York 212-765-5500	NY 10019	
450	Lavoro Banca Roma Ltd Banking	25 W 51st Street	New York 212-581-0710	NY 10019	
226	Lin Broadcasting Corp Publishing/Com	1370 Avenue of the Americas	New York 212-765-1902	NY 10019	
450	Midland Bank PLC Banking	156 W 56th Street	New York 212-969-7000	NY 10019	
350	Mitchell Hutchins Asset Management Inc Non-Bank Fin	1285 Avenue of the Americas	New York 212-713-4000	NY 10019	
5235	Mutual Life Ins Co of New York (MONY) Insurance	1740 Broadway	New York 212-708-2000	NY 10019	
265	National Patent Development Co Health Care	9 W 57th Street	New York 212-826-8500	NY 10019	
1250	New York Power Authority Govt Authority	1633 Broadway	New York 212-468-6000	NY 10019	
2512	Paine Webber Group Inc Securities	1285 Avenue of the Americas	New York 212-713-2000	NY 10019	
1000	Polo/Ralph Lauren Corp Apparel/Textiles	40 W 55th Street	New York 212-974-6868	NY 10019	

State / Province: New York

Organizations Listed Geographically

Revenue ($ mil)	Organization/ Industry	Address	City / Phone	State/ Zip	Province/ Postcode
1000	Potamkin Co Inc Automotive	785 Eleventh Avenue	New York 212-399-4400	NY 10019	
825	Reuters Inc Comput/Off Equip	1700 Broadway 5th Floor	New York 212-603-3300	NY 10019	
1750	Touche Ross & Co Accounting	1633 Broadway	New York 212-489-1600	NY 10019	
NA	Vanity Fair Inc Apparel/Textiles	640 Fifth Avenue	New York 212-582-6767	NY 10019	
220	Warburg, S G Securities Inc Securities	787 7th Avenue	New York 212-459-7000	NY 10019	
4206	Warner Communications Inc Leisure Time	75 Rockefeller Plaza	New York 212-484-8000	NY 10019	
NA	Warner Publishing Inc Publishing/Com	666 Fifth Avenue	New York 212-484-2900	NY 10019	
550	Wells Rich Greene Inc Business Service	9 W 57th Street	New York 212-303-5000	NY 10019	
1250	Amstar Corp Food Processing	1251 Avenue of the Americas	New York 212-489-9000	NY 10020	
2500	Coopers & Lybrand Inc Accounting	1251 Avenue of the Americas	New York 212-536-2000	NY 10020	
88563	Exxon Corp Energy	1251 Avenue of the Americas	New York 212-333-1000	NY 10020	
600	Faberge Inc Personal Care	725 5th Avenue	New York 212-307-8000	NY 10020	
1192	Interpublic Group of Companies Inc Business Service	1271 Avenue of the Americas	New York 212-399-8000	NY 10020	
1000	Lazard Freres & Co Securities	1 Rockefeller Plaza	New York 212-489-6600	NY 10020	
2272	Marsh & McLennan Companies Inc Non-Bank Fin	1221 Avenue of the Americas	New York 212-997-2000	NY 10020	
1818	McGraw Hill Corp Publishing/Com	1221 Avenue of the Americas	New York 212-512-2000	NY 10020	
3100	Morgan Stanley & Co Inc Securities	1251 Avenue of the Americas	New York 212-703-4000	NY 10020	
NA	National Broadcasting Co Publishing/Com	30 Rockefeller Center	New York 212-664-4444	NY 10020	
2250	Price Waterhouse & Co Inc Accounting	1251 Avenue of the Americas	New York 212-489-8900	NY 10020	
550	Reeves Brothers Inc Apparel/Textiles	1271 Avenue of the Americas 3rd Floor	New York 212-315-2323	NY 10020	
1000	Rockefeller Group Inc Real Estate/Bldg	1230 Avenue of the Americas	New York 212-698-8676	NY 10020	
6146	Salomon Inc Securities	1221 Avenue of the Americas	New York 212-764-3700	NY 10020	
1650	Sandoz USA Inc Drugs	608 Fifth Avenue	New York 212-307-1122	NY 10020	
500	Simon & Schuster Inc Publishing/Com	1230 Avenue of the Americas	New York 212-698-7000	NY 10020	
4507	Time Inc Publishing/Com	Rockefeller Center	New York 212-586-1212	NY 10020	
500	UIS Inc Automotive	600 Fifth Avenue	New York 212-581-7660	NY 10020	
550	Van Munching & Co Inc Food Processing	1270 Avenue of the Americas	New York 212-265-2685	NY 10020	
1500	Knoll International Holdings Automotive	655 Madison Avenue	New York 212-826-2400	NY 10021	
10865	Loews Corp Food/Lodging	667 Madison Avenue	New York 212-545-2000	NY 10021	
NA	Loews Hotel Corp Food/Lodging	667 Madison Avenue	New York 212-545-2000	NY 10021	
2100	Lorillard Corp Tobacco	667 Madison Avenue	New York 212-545-2000	NY 10021	
2500	MacAndrews & Forbes Inc Food Processing	36 E 63rd Street	New York 212-688-9000	NY 10021	
1000	McLean Industries Inc Transport	660 Madison Avenue Suite 602	New York 212-593-3325	NY 10021	

State / Province: New York

Organizations Listed Geographically

Revenue ($ mil)	Organization/ Industry	Address	City / Phone	State/ Zip	Province/ Postcode
349	Sotheby's Holdings Inc Retail/Merch	1334 York Avenue	New York 212-606-7000	NY 10021	
2171	Allegheny Power System Inc Utility	320 Park Avenue	New York 212-752-2121	NY 10022	
275	Allen & Co Inc Securities	711 Fifth Avenue	New York 212-832-8000	NY 10022	
35210	American Telephone & Telegraph Co Telecom	550 Madison Avenue	New York 212-605-5500	NY 10022	
520	Ametek Inc Electronics	410 Park Avenue 21st Floor	New York 212-935-8640	NY 10022	
600	Ampex Corp Publishing/Com	405 Park Avenue	New York 212-759-6301	NY 10022	
550	Banco Nacional de Mexico Banking	375 Park Avenue	New York 212-838-8300	NY 10022	
450	Banque National de Paris Banking	499 Park Avenue	New York 212-980-5185	NY 10022	
251	Chris-Craft Industries Inc Publishing/Com	600 Madison Avenue	New York 212-421-0200	NY 10022	
4734	Colgate Palmolive Co Personal Care	300 Park Avenue	New York 212-310-2000	NY 10022	
1750	Colt Industries Inc Conglomerate	430 Park Avenue	New York 212-940-0400	NY 10022	
1616	Columbia Pictures Leisure Time	711 Fifth Avenue	New York 212-751-4400	NY 10022	
450	Credit Agricole Mutuel Paris Banking	520 Madison Avenue	New York 212-418-2200	NY 10022	
2750	D'Arcy Masius Benton & Bowles Inc Business Service	909 Third Avenue	New York 212-758-6200	NY 10022	
550	Dillon Reed & Co Inc Securities	535 Madison Avenue	New York 212-906-7000	NY 10022	
300	Fischer Francis Trees & Watts Inc Non-Bank Fin	717 Fifth Avenue	New York 212-350-8000	NY 10022	
1100	Fuller, George A Co Inc Real Estate/Bldg	919 Third Avenue	New York 212-355-2700	NY 10022	
10655	General Electric Credit Corp Non-Bank Fin	570 Lexington Avenue	New York 212-751-5315	NY 10022	
NA	Godiva Chocolatier Inc Food Processing	450 Park Avenue	New York 212-486-8750	NY 10022	
NA	GTG Entertainment Co Leisure Time	150 E 52nd Street	New York 212-888-7830	NY 10022	
658	Handy & Harman Inc Metals/Mining	850 Third Avenue	New York 212-752-3400	NY 10022	
500	IMS International Inc Business Service	800 Third Avenue	New York 212-371-2310	NY 10022	
19355	ITT Corp Conglomerate	320 Park Avenue	New York 212-752-6000	NY 10022	
1000	Johnson, Axel & Co Inc Energy	110 E 59th Street	New York 212-758-3200	NY 10022	
550	Kobe Steel Corp USA Steel	535 Madison Avenue	New York 212-751-9400	NY 10022	
2750	Lever Brothers Co Inc Food Processing	390 Park Avenue	New York 212-688-6000	NY 10022	
956	Macmillan Inc Publishing/Com	866 Third Avenue	New York 212-702-2000	NY 10022	
880	Mannesmann USA Inc Machinery	450 Park Avenue	New York 212-702-9420	NY 10022	
500	McKinsey & Co Inc Food/Lodging	55 E 52nd Street	New York 212-909-8400	NY 10022	
56	Metro Mobile Communications Inc Telecom	110 E 59th Street	New York 212-319-7444	NY 10022	
3850	Mitsubishi International USA Inc Electronics	520 Madison Avenue	New York 212-605-2000	NY 10022	
800	Munich Reinsurance Co Insurance	560 Lexington Avenue	New York 212-310-1800	NY 10022	
1100	Needham Worldwide Advertising Inc Business Service	437 Madison Avenue	New York 212-415-2000	NY 10022	

State / Province: New York

Organizations Listed Geographically

Revenue ($ mil)	Organization/ Industry	Address	City / Phone	State/ Zip	Province/ Postcode
881	Omnicom Group Inc Business Service	437 Madison Avenue	New York 212-415-2000	NY 10022	
469	Orion Pictures Corp Leisure Time	711 Fifth Avenue	New York 212-758-5100	NY 10022	
4000	Peat Marwick Main & Co Accounting	345 Park Avenue	New York 212-758-9700	NY 10022	
383	Ply Gem Industries Inc Building Mat	919 Third Avenue	New York 212-832-1550	NY 10022	
1000	Printing Holding Co Manufacturing	350 Park Avenue	New York 212-735-8800	NY 10022	
2200	Rapid American Corp Retail/Merch	Trump Tower 725 Fifth Avenue	New York 212-621-4500	NY 10022	
1815	Revlon Group Inc Personal Care	625 Madison Avenue	New York 212-572-5000	NY 10022	
553	Rexene Corportation Chemicals	126 E 56th Street	New York 212-644-8200	NY 10022	
3000	Riklis Corp Retail/Merch	725 5th Avenue	New York 212-735-9500	NY 10022	
3000	Seagrams, Joseph E & Sons Inc Beverage	375 Park Avenue	New York 212-572-7000	NY 10022	
600	Sumitomo Trust & Banking Co Banking	527 Madison Avenue	New York 212-326-0500	NY 10022	
290	Tiffany Corp Retail/Merch	727 Fifth Avenue	New York 212-755-8000	NY 10022	
750	Tishman Realty Corp Real Estate/Bldg	520 Madison Avenue	New York 212-957-5400	NY 10022	
1250	Transammonia Inc Chemicals	350 Park Avenue	New York 212-223-3200	NY 10022	
2668	Triangle Industries Inc Equipment	900 Third Avenue	New York 212-230-3000	NY 10022	
350	TriStar Pictures Inc Leisure Time	711 Fifth Avenue	New York 212-751-4400	NY 10022	
1000	Trump Organization Inc Real Estate/Bldg	725 Fifth Avenue	New York 212-832-2000	NY 10022	
5400	Unilever (United States) Inc Food Processing	10 E 53rd Street	New York 212-888-1260	NY 10022	
NA	USA Today Inc Publishing/Com	535 Madison Avenue	New York 212-715-2100	NY 10022	
500	Warren Equities Inc Retail/Merch	10 E 53rd Street	New York 212-751-8100	NY 10022	
450	Westdeutsche Landesbank AG Banking	450 Park Avenue	New York 212-754-9600	NY 10022	
551	Western Publishing Group Inc Publishing/Com	444 Madison Avenue	New York 212-688-4500	NY 10022	
1586	Witco Corp Chemicals	520 Madison Avenue	New York 212-605-3800	NY 10022	
NA	ABC Television Network Group Div Publishing/Com	77 W 66th Street	New York 212-456-7777	NY 10023	
4773	Capital Cities--Amer Broadcasting Co Inc Publishing/Com	77 W 66th Street	New York 212-456-7777	NY 10023	
5108	Paramount Communications Corp Conglomerate	One Gulf & Western Plaza	New York 212-333-7000	NY 10023	
750	Red Apple Companies Inc Retail/Food	265 W 87th Street	New York 212-580-6800	NY 10024	
431	Columbia University University	116th Street & Broadway	New York 212-280-1754	NY 10027	
543	Banco Popular de Puerto Rico Inc Banking	4043 Broadway	New York 212-928-8600	NY 10032	
1228	Alexander & Alexander Service Inc Non-Bank Fin	1211 Avenue of the Americas	New York 212-840-8500	NY 10036	
4000	Allied Stores Corp Retail/Merch	1114 Avenue of the Americas	New York 212-764-2000	NY 10036	
550	Amcena Inc Retail/Merch	1114 Avenue of the Americas	New York 212-391-4141	NY 10036	
4264	Amerada Hess Corp Energy	1185 Avenue of the Americas	New York 212-997-8500	NY 10036	

State / Province: New York

Organizations Listed Geographically

Revenue ($ mil)	Organization/ Industry	Address	City / Phone	State/ Zip	Province/ Postcode
250	American Fed of Musicians of US & Canada Membership Org	1501 Broadway	New York 212-867-1330	NY	10036
500	American Savings Bank (NY) Inc Savings & Loan	1133 Avenue of the Americas	New York 212-575-7600	NY	10036
250	Associated Actors & Artistes of America Membership Org	165 W 46th Street	New York 212-869-0358	NY	10036
2000	Deloitte, Haskins & Sells Inc Accounting	1114 Avenue of the Americas	New York 212-790-0500	NY	10036
550	Diamandis Communications Corp Publishing/Com	1515 Broadway	New York 212-719-6000	NY	10036
5786	Grace, W R & Co Chemicals	1114 Avenue of the Americas	New York 212-819-5500	NY	10036
NA	Home Box Office Inc Publishing/Com	1100 Avenue of the Amercias	New York 212-522-1212	NY	10036
3300	Kanematsu Gosho USA Inc Manufacturing	1133 Avenue of the Americas	New York 212-704-9400	NY	10036
NA	Lane Bryant Inc Retail/Merch	11 W 42nd Street	New York 212-930-9482	NY	10036
300	Mercer, William M Meidinger Inc Consulting	1211 Avenue of the Americas	New York 212-997-7171	NY	10036
825	Morse Diesel Inc Business Service	1515 Broadway	New York 212-730-4000	NY	10036
220	Neuberger & Berman Inc Securities	522 Fifth Avenue	New York 212-730-7370	NY	10036
245	New Plan Realty Inc Real Estate/Bldg	1120 Avenue of the Americas	New York 212-869-3000	NY	10036
NA	New York Telephone Co Telecom	1095 Avenue of the Americas	New York 212-395-2121	NY	10036
1701	New York Times Co Publishing/Com	29 W 43rd Street	New York 212-556-1234	NY	10036
1100	New York-Off Track Betting Inc Leisure Time	1501 Broadway	New York 212-704-5000	NY	10036
1650	Nichimen Trading Co USA Manufacturing	1185 Avenue of the Americas	New York 212-719-1000	NY	10036
1650	Nissho Iwai Trading Co USA Manufacturing	1211 Avenue of the Americas	New York 212-704-6500	NY	10036
333	Overseas Shipholding Group Inc Business Service	1114 Avenue of the Americas	New York 212-869-1222	NY	10036
370	Salant Corp (Manhattan Inds) Apparel/Textiles	1155 Avenue of the Americas	New York 212-221-7500	NY	10036
1660	Stevens, J P & Co Inc Apparel/Textiles	Stevens Tower 1185 Avenue of the Americas	New York 212-930-2000	NY	10036
2200	Thyssen USA Corp Steel	1114 Avenue of the Americas	New York 212-512-9700	NY	10036
250	Vitt Media International Inc Business Service	1114 Avenue of the Americas	New York 212-921-0500	NY	10036
300	Willcox & Gibbs Inc Equipment	1440 Broadway	New York 212-869-1800	NY	10036
2978	AmBase Corp (Home Group Inc) Insurance	59 Maiden Lane	New York 212-530-6800	NY	10038
1988	Asarco Inc Metals/Mining	180 Maiden Lane	New York 212-510-2000	NY	10038
5878	Continental International Corp Non-Bank Fin	180 Maiden Lane	New York 212-440-3980	NY	10038
250	FGIC Inc Insurance	175 Water Street	New York 212-607-3000	NY	10038
450	Lloyd's Bank Ltd Banking	199 Water Street	New York 212-607-4300	NY	10038
330	Nomura Securities International Inc Securities	180 Maiden Lane The Continental Center	New York 212-208-9300	NY	10038
825	Rothschild, L F, Unterberg, Towbin Inc Securities	222 Broadway	New York 212-238-2000	NY	10038
275	Southern Peru Copper Co Inc Metals/Mining	180 Maiden Lane	New York 212-510-2000	NY	10038
1279	US Life Insurance Corp Insurance	125 Maiden Lane	New York 212-709-6000	NY	10038

State / Province: New York

Organizations Listed Geographically

Revenue ($ mil)	Organization/ Industry	Address	City / Phone	State/ Zip	Province/ Postcode
32024	Citicorp Inc Banking	399 Park Avenue	New York 212-559-1000	NY 10043	
1750	Citicorp Savings Inc Savings & Loan	399 Park Avenue	New York 212-559-1000	NY 10043	
6381	Federal Reserve Bank of New York Inc Federal Govt Fin	33 Liberty Street	New York 212-720-5000	NY 10045	
600	ADT Inc Electronics	One World Trade Center	New York 215-558-1100	NY 10048	
550	Dai Ichi Kangyo Bank Ltd Banking	One World Trade Center	New York 212-466-5200	NY 10048	
900	Ebasco Services Inc Consulting	Two World Trade Center	New York 212-839-1000	NY 10048	
400	Fiduciary Trust Co Non-Bank Fin	2 World Trade Center	New York 212-466-4100	NY 10048	
600	Fuji Bank & Trust Banking	One World Trade Center	New York 212-839-5600	NY 10048	
550	Hongkong & Shanghai Banking Corp Banking	Five World Trade Center	New York 212-839-5000	NY 10048	
220	Keefe, Bruyette & Woods Inc Securities	Two World Trade Center Suite 8566	New York 212-323-8300	NY 10048	
450	Kyowa Bank Ltd Banking	One World Trade Center	New York 212-432-6400	NY 10048	
3300	Mocatta Metals Corp Securities	4 World Trade Center	New York 212-912-8400	NY 10048	
450	Norinchukin Bank Inc Banking	One World Trade Center	New York 212-697-1717	NY 10048	
2350	Port Authority of New York & New Jersey Govt Authority	One World Trade Center	New York 212-466-7000	NY 10048	
450	Swiss Bank Corp Banking	Four World Trade Center	New York 212-938-3500	NY 10048	
440	Telerate Inc Comput/Off Equip	One World Trade Center	New York 212-938-5200	NY 10048	
1100	Toyo Menka Trading Co USA Manufacturing	One World Trade Center	New York 212-466-4600	NY 10048	
700	Winterthur Swiss Insurance Co Insurance	One World Trade Center	New York 212-466-0777	NY 10048	
450	Yasuda Trust & Banking Co Banking	One World Trade Center	New York 212-432-2300	NY 10048	
1006	Allegheny Corp Non-Bank Fin	Park Avenue Plaza	New York 212-752-1356	NY 10055	
1323	First Boston Inc Securities	Park Avenue Plaza	New York 212-909-2000	NY 10055	
3400	Reliance Group Holdings Inc Non-Bank Fin	55 E 52nd Street	New York 212-909-1100	NY 10055	
650	Industrial Bank of Japan Trust Co Banking	245 Park Avenue	New York 212-557-3500	NY 10067	
12375	Chase Manhattan Bank Inc Banking	One Chase Manhattan Plaza	New York 212-552-2222	NY 10081	
330	Wertheim Schroder & Co Inc Securities	787 Seventh Avenue	New York 212-492-6000	NY 10089	
550	Primary Industries Corp Equipment	666 Fifth Avenue	New York 212-581-9200	NY 10103	
750	Blair, John & Co Business Service	1290 Avenue of the Americas	New York 212-603-5000	NY 10104	
641	Phillips Van Heusen Corp Apparel/Textiles	1290 Avenue of the Americas	New York 212-541-5200	NY 10104	
550	Security Capital/Sentinal R E Corp Non-Bank Fin	1290 Avenue of the Americas	New York 212-408-2900	NY 10104	
1100	Ayer, N W Inc Business Service	1345 Avenue of the Americas	New York 212-708-5000	NY 10105	
1100	Smith Barney Harris Upham & Co Securities	1345 Avenue of the Americas	New York 212-698-6000	NY 10105	
NA	Westinghouse Broadcasting Co Publishing/Com	888 Seventh Avenue	New York 212-307-3000	NY 10106	
617	Edgcomb Corp Manufacturing	30 Rockefeller Plaza	New York 212-246-1000	NY 10112	

State / Province: New York

Organizations Listed Geographically

Revenue ($ mil)	Organization/ Industry	Address	City / Phone	State/ Zip	Province/ Postcode
769	National Fuel Gas Co Utility	30 Rockefeller Plaza	New York 212-541-7533	NY 10112	
1011	Mutual of America Life Insurance Co Insurance	666 Fifth Avenue	New York 212-399-1600	NY 10113	
1100	Asahi Chemical Industries Chemicals	350 Fifth Avenue	New York 212-695-6720	NY 10118	
8898	Equitable Life Assurance Society Inc Insurance	1285 Avenue of the Americas	New York 212-554-1234	NY 10119	
324	Stone & Webster Inc Consulting	One Penn Plaza 250 W 34th Street	New York 212-290-7500	NY 10119	
1088	Ogden Corp Conglomerate	Two Pennsylvania Plaza	New York 212-868-6100	NY 10121	
514	Carter Wallace Inc Drugs	767 Fifth Avenue	New York 212-758-4500	NY 10153	
268	Dreyfus Corp Non-Bank Fin	767 Fifth Avenue	New York 212-715-6000	NY 10153	
1305	General Instrument Corp Electronics	767 Fifth Avenue	New York 212-207-6200	NY 10153	
5973	Bristol Meyers Co Drugs	345 Park Avenue	New York 212-546-4000	NY 10154	
1650	Sumitomo Trading Co USA Manufacturing	345 Park Avenue	New York 212-207-0700	NY 10154	
7000	Union Pacific Corp Railroad	345 Park Avenue	New York 212-418-7800	NY 10154	
101	Forest Laboratories Inc Drugs	150 E 58th Street	New York 212-421-7850	NY 10155	
4000	Trans World Airlines Inc Airline	605 Third Avenue	New York 212-692-3000	NY 10158	
258	Wiley, John & Sons Inc Publishing/Com	605 Third Avenue	New York 211-285-0600	NY 10158	
1800	Helmsley Spear Co Real Estate/Bldg	60 E 42nd Street	New York 212-687-6400	NY 10165	
3944	AMAX Inc Metals/Mining	200 Park Avenue	New York 212-856-4200	NY 10166	
440	Associated Madison Asset Management Inc Non-Bank Fin	200 Park Avenue	New York 212-351-2600	NY 10166	
228	Bairnco Corp Electronics	200 Park Avenue	New York 212-490-8722	NY 10166	
383	Grow Group Inc Building Mat	200 Park Avenue	New York 212-599-4400	NY 10166	
2750	Marubeni Trading Co USA Manufacturing	200 Park Avenue	New York 212-599-3700	NY 10166	
1100	Mitsui & Co Trading (USA) Manufacturing	200 Park Avenue Pan American Bldg	New York 212-878-4097	NY 10166	
3569	Pan American Corp Airline	Pan Am Bldg 200 Park Avenue	New York 212-880-1234	NY 10166	
1713	Sequa Corp Metals/Mining	200 Park Avenue	New York 212-986-5500	NY 10166	
1888	Bear Stearns Companies Inc Securities	245 Park Avenue	New York 212-272-2000	NY 10167	
400	Catalyst Energy Development Inc Utility	245 Park Avenue	New York 212-949-0040	NY 10167	
990	Doubleday & Co Inc Publishing/Com	245 Park Avenue	New York 212-984-7561	NY 10167	
500	Towers, Perrin, Forster & Crosby Inc Consulting	245 Park Avenue	New York 212-309-3400	NY 10167	
1000	Dyson Kissner Moran Corp Manufacturing	230 Park Avenue	New York 212-661-4600	NY 10169	
NA	Furman-Selz Inc Comput/Off Equip	230 Park Avenue	New York 212-309-8200	NY 10169	
4267	Dun & Bradstreet Corp Publishing/Com	299 Park Avenue	New York 212-593-6800	NY 10171	
250	UBS Securities Inc Securities	299 Park Avenue 4th Floor	New York 212-230-4000	NY 10171	
450	Union Bank of Switzerland Banking	299 Park Avenue	New York 212-715-3000	NY 10171	

State / Province: New York

Organizations Listed Geographically

Revenue ($ mil)	Organization/ Industry	Address	City / Phone	State/ Zip	Province/ Postcode
2187	Westvaco Corp Paper/Forest Prd	299 Park Avenue	New York 212-688-5000	NY 10171	
2000	Arthur, Young & Co Inc Accounting	277 Park Avenue	New York 212-407-1500	NY 10172	
7244	Borden Inc Food Processing	277 Park Avenue	New York 212-573-4000	NY 10172	
7644	Chemical New York Corp Banking	277 Park Avenue	New York 212-310-6161	NY 10172	
13000	Continental Grain Co Food Processing	277 Park Avenue	New York 212-207-5100	NY 10172	
1956	Dover Corp Equipment	277 Park Avenue	New York 212-826-7160	NY 10172	
4925	Schlumberger Ltd Oil Service	277 Park Avenue	New York 212-350-9400	NY 10172	
450	Bates, Ted Worldwide Inc Business Service	405 Lexington	New York 212-297-7000	NY 10174	
1436	Inspiration Resources Corp Business Service	250 Park Avenue	New York 212-503-3100	NY 10177	
500	Booz, Allen & Hamilton Inc Consulting	101 Park Avenue	New York 212-697-1900	NY 10178	
450	Volt Information Sciences Corp Comput/Off Equip	101 Park Avenue	New York 212-309-0200	NY 10178	
10547	Merrill Lynch & Co Inc Securities	World Financial Center North Tower	New York 212-637-7455	NY 10181	
550	Barclays American Corp Banking	75 Wall Street	New York 212-412-4000	NY 10265	
13613	American International Group Inc Insurance	70 Pine Street	New York 212-770-7000	NY 10270	
NA	Kinney Shoe Corp Retail/Merch	233 Broadway	New York 212-553-2000	NY 10279	
8088	Woolworth, F W Co Retail/Merch	233 Broadway	New York 212-553-2000	NY 10279	
330	Daiwa Securities America Inc Securities	One World Fin Ctr 200 Liberty St Tower A	New York 212-945-0100	NY 10281	
1603	Dow Jones & Co Publishing/Com	200 Liberty Street World Financial Center	New York 212-416-2000	NY 10281	
330	Nikko Securities Co Intl Inc Securities	One World Financial Center 200 Liberty Street	New York 212-416-5400	NY 10281	
750	Oppenheimer & Co Inc Securities	Oppenheimer Tower World Financial Center	New York 212-667-7000	NY 10281	
22934	American Express Co Non-Bank Fin	American Express Tower World Financial Ctr	New York 212-640-2000	NY 10285	
10529	Shearson Lehman Hutton Inc Securities	American Express Tower World Trade Center	New York 212-298-2000	NY 10285	
2620	Bank of New York Co Banking	48 Wall Street	New York 212-495-1784	NY 10286	
3500	Prudential Bache Securities Inc Securities	One Seaport Plaza 199 Water Street	New York 212-214-1000	NY 10292	
2500	Advance Publications Publishing/Com	950 Fingerboard Road	Staten Island 718-981-1234	NY 10305	
1000	Food Emporium Retail/Food	400 Walnut Avenue	Bronx 212-579-3400	NY 10454	
3300	Ciba Geigy USA Corp Drugs	444 Saw Mill River Parkway	Ardsley 914-478-3131	NY 10502	
59681	IBM (Intl Business Mach) Corp Comput/Off Equip	Old Orchard Road	Armonk 914-765-1900	NY 10504	
339	Hall, Frank B & Co Inc Insurance	549 Pleasantville Road	Briarcliff Manor 914-769-9200	NY 10510	
275	Computer Factory Inc Retail/Merch	399 Executive Blvd	Elmsford 914-347-5000	NY 10523	
825	Pergamon Holding Corp Publishing/Com	Maxwell House Fairview Park	Elmsford 914-592-9141	NY 10523	
6780	Melville Corp Retail/Merch	3000 Westchester Avenue	Harrison 914-253-8000	NY 10528	
1500	Readers Digest Assn Inc Publishing/Com	Bedford Road	Pleasantville 914-769-7000	NY 10570	

State / Province: New York

Revenue ($ mil)	Organization/ Industry	Address	City / Phone	State/ Zip	Province/ Postcode
NA	Donnelly Directory Corp Publishing/Com	287 Bowman Avenue	Purchase 914-933-6400	NY	10577
9533	International Paper Co Paper/Forest Prd	Two Manhattanville Road	Purchase 914-397-1500	NY	10577
350	JWP Corp Business Service	2975 Westchester Avenue	Purchase 914-935-4000	NY	10577
2200	Nestle USA Inc Food Processing	100 Manhattanville Road	Purchase 914-251-3000	NY	10577
13007	PepsiCo Inc Beverage	Anderson Hill Road	Purchase 914-253-2000	NY	10577
500	Curry Corp Consumer Service	727 Central Avenue	Scarsdale 914-725-3500	NY	10583
500	Kane Miller Corp Food Processing	555 White Plains Road	Tarrytown 914-631-6900	NY	10591
224	MBIA Insurance Co Insurance	445 Hamilton Avenue	White Plains 914-681-1300	NY	10602
801	Reichhold Chemicals Inc Chemicals	525 N Broadway	White Plains 914-682-5700	NY	10603
750	Associated Metals & Minerals Inc Metals/Mining	3 N Corporate Park Drive	White Plains 914-251-5400	NY	10604
225	IPCO Corp Health Care	1025 Westchester Avenue	White Plains 914-682-4500	NY	10604
NA	NYNEX Business Information Systems Inc Comput/Off Equip	65 W Red Oak Lane	White Plains 914-683-2398	NY	10604
NA	General Foods Corp Food Processing	250 North Street	White Plains 914-335-2500	NY	10625
35138	Texaco Inc Energy	2000 Westchester Avenue	White Plains 914-253-4000	NY	10650
600	Big V Supermarkets Inc Retail/Food	176 N Main Street	Florida 914-651-4411	NY	10921
550	Cablec Corp Steel	17 Squadron Blvd	New City 914-634-0100	NY	10956
750	Worldwide Volkswagen Inc Automotive	Greenbush Road	Orangeburg 914-578-5000	NY	10962
NA	NYNEX Mobile Communications Co Telecom	One Blue Hill Plaza	Pearl River 914-577-5200	NY	10965
486	Orange & Rockland Utilities Corp Utility	1 Blue Hill Plaza	Pearl River 914-352-6000	NY	10965
1817	Avnet Inc Business Service	80 Cutter Mill Road	Great Neck 516-466-7000	NY	11021
271	AVX Corp Electronics	60 Cuttermill Road	Great Neck 516-829-8500	NY	11021
NA	National Propane Co Energy	69 Denton Avenue	New Hyde Park 516-352-6500	NY	11040
2200	Canon USA Inc Comput/Off Equip	One Cannon Plaza	Lake Success 516-488-6700	NY	11042
563	Tambrands Inc Personal Care	One Marcus Avenue	Lake Success 516-437-8800	NY	11042
398	Standard Motor Products Inc Automotive	37-18 Northern Blvd	Long Island City 718-392-0200	NY	11101
300	Astoria Federal Savings Assn Inc Savings & Loan	3716 30th Avenue	Long Island City 718-545-4400	NY	11103
899	Brooklyn Union Gas Co Utility	195 Montague Street	Brooklyn 718-403-2000	NY	11201
1374	Crossland Savings Fed Savings Bank Inc Savings & Loan	211 Montague Steet	Brooklyn 718-780-0400	NY	11201
183	Flightsafety International Inc Business Service	LaGuardia Airport Marine Air Terminal	Flushing 718-565-4100	NY	11371
NA	Pan Am Shuttle Inc Airline	Marine Terminal	Flushing 718-803-6607	NY	11371
2750	LeFrak Organization Real Estate/Bldg	9777 Queens Blvd	Rego Park 718-459-9021	NY	11374
NA	Bulova Watch Co Inc Manufacturing	One Bulova Avenue	Woodside 718-204-3300	NY	11377
330	St John's University University	Grand Central & Utopia Parkways	Jamaica 516-990-6161	NY	11439

State / Province: New York

Organizations Listed Geographically

Revenue ($ mil)	Organization/ Industry	Address	City / Phone	State/ Zip	Province/ Postcode
3600	Nassau County Government Local Govt	One West Street	Mineola 516-535-3000	NY	11501
1000	Avis Corp Consumer Service	900 Old Country Road	Garden City 516-222-3000	NY	11530
1051	Dime Savings Bank of New York Inc Savings & Loan	1225 Franklin Avenue	Garden City 516-227-6030	NY	11530
1401	Esselte Corp Manufacturing	71 Clinton Road	Garden City 516-741-1477	NY	11530
429	Pall Corp Machinery	30 Sea Cliff Avenue	Glen Cove 516-671-4000	NY	11542
1200	National Westminster Bank USA Banking	60 Hempstead Avenue	West Hempstead 516-560-7050	NY	11552
540	European American Bancorp Banking	EAB Plaza	Uniondale 516-296-5000	NY	11555
400	Rugby Darby Group Inc Drugs	100 Banks Avenue	Rockville Center 516-536-3000	NY	11570
240	Slattery Group Inc Real Estate/Bldg	1044 Northern Blvd	Roslyn 516-484-5858	NY	11576
600	King Kullen Grocery Inc Retail/Food	1194 Prospect Street	Westbury 516-333-7100	NY	11590
400	Olsten Corp Business Service	1 Merrick Avenue	Westbury 516-832-8200	NY	11590
3649	Grumman Corp Aerospace	1111 Stewart Avenue	Bethpage 516-575-0574	NY	11714
1800	Waldbaum Inc Retail/Food	Hemlock Street	Central Islap 516-582-9300	NY	11722
267	Greenman Brothers Inc Retail/Merch	105 Price Parkway	Farmingdale 516-293-5300	NY	11735
344	Allen Group Inc Instruments	534 Broad Hollow Road	Melville 516-293-5500	NY	11747
1006	Arrow Electronics Inc Electronics	25 Hubb Drive	Melville 516-391-1300	NY	11747
366	Genovese Drug Stores Inc Retail/Merch	80 Marcus Drive	Melville 516-420-1900	NY	11747
2200	NEC Nippon Electric Corp USA Electronics	8 Old Sod Farm Road	Melville 516-753-7000	NY	11747
1030	Computer Associates International Inc Comput/Off Equip	125 Jericho Turnpike	Jericho 516-333-6700	NY	11753
1041	Getty Petroleum Corp Energy	125 Jericho Turnpike	Jericho 516-338-6000	NY	11753
350	Instrument Systems Inc Electronics	100 Jericho Quadrangle	Jericho 516-938-5544	NY	11753
500	Weight Watchers International Food Processing	500 N Broadway	Jericho 516-939-0400	NY	11753
703	Anchor Savings Bank Inc Savings & Loan	225 Main Street	Northport 516-295-0400	NY	11768
2050	Suffolk County Government Local Govt	County Bldg Veterans Memorial Highway	Hauppauge 516-360-4000	NY	11788
275	Audiovox Corp Retail/Merch	150 Marcus Blvd	Hauppauge 516-231-7750	NY	11789
495	Long Island Savings Bank Inc Savings & Loan	50 Jackson Avenue	Syosset 516-677-5000	NY	11791
493	Cablevision Systems Inc Publishing/Com	One Media Crossways	Woodbury 516-364-8450	NY	11797
2138	Long Island Lighting Co Utility	175 E Old Country Road	Hicksville 516-933-4590	NY	11801
250	Newmark & Lewis Inc Retail/Merch	595 S Broadway	Hicksville 516-681-6900	NY	11801
275	Albany International Corp Apparel/Textiles	1370 Broadway	Menands 518-445-2200	NY	12201
1000	Norstar BanCorp Banking	1450 Western Avenue	Albany 518-447-4043	NY	12203
268	Trans World Music Inc Retail/Merch	38 Corporate Circle	Albany 518-452-1242	NY	12203
1394	Keycorp Inc Banking	60 State Street	Albany 518-486-8500	NY	12207

State / Province: New York

Organizations Listed Geographically

Revenue ($ mil)	Organization/ Industry	Address	City / Phone	State/ Zip	Province/ Postcode
700	New York State Retirement Fund Inc Non-Bank Fin	10 Corporate Woods Drive	Albany 518-447-2741	NY 12211	
450	New York State Teachers Investment Fund Non-Bank Fin	10 Corporate Woods Drive	Albany 518-447-2741	NY 12211	
64568	New York, State of State/Prov Govt	State Capitol	Albany 518-474-2121	NY 12224	
1000	Golub Corp Retail/Food	501 Duanesburg Road	Schenectady 518-355-5000	NY 12306	
438	Central Hudson Gas & Electric Co Utility	284 South Avenue	Poughkeepsie 914-452-2000	NY 12601	
527	Fay's Drug Co Retail/Merch	7245 Henry Clay Blvd	Liverpool 315-451-8000	NY 13088	
454	Goulds Pumps Inc Manufacturing	240 Fall Street	Seneca Falls 315-568-2811	NY 13148	
2801	Niagara Mohawk Power Corp Utility	300 Erie Blvd W	Syracuse 315-474-1511	NY 13202	
2894	Agway Inc Manufacturing	PO Box 4933	Syracuse 315-477-7061	NY 13221	
NA	Carrier Corp Appliances/Furn	6304 Carrier Parkway	Syracuse 315-432-6000	NY 13221	
187	Syracuse University University	Administrative Bldg	Syracuse 315-423-1870	NY 13244	
400	Utica National Insurance Co Insurance	180 Genesee Street	Utica 315-735-3321	NY 13413	
400	Oneida Ltd Appliances/Furn	Kenwood Avenue	Oneida 315-361-3000	NY 13421	
NA	Norwich Easton Pharmaceuticals Co Drugs	17 Eaton Avenue	Norwich 607-335-2111	NY 13815	
NA	Fisher Price Inc Manufacturing	636 Girard Avenue	East Aurora 716-687-3000	NY 14052	
350	Moog Inc Electronics	Jamison Road	Aurora 716-652-2000	NY 14052	
510	Buffalo, City of Local Govt	City Hall	Buffalo 716-855-4841	NY 14202	
1090	Empire of America Fed Savings Bank Inc Savings & Loan	One Main Place	Buffalo 716-845-7101	NY 14202	
250	Erie County Government Local Govt	95 Franklin Street	Buffalo 716-846-8500	NY 14202	
250	Niagara Share Corp Securities	70 Niagara Street	Buffalo 716-856-2600	NY 14202	
1750	Goldome Federal Savings Bank Inc Savings & Loan	1 Fountain Plaza	Buffalo 716-847-5800	NY 14203	
825	Niagara Frontier Services Inc Retail/Food	60 Dingens Street	Buffalo 716-823-3712	NY 14206	
1000	Tops Markets Inc Retail/Food	60 Dingens Street	Buffalo 716-823-3712	NY 14206	
250	Pratt & Lambert Inc Chemicals	75 Tonawanda Street	Buffalo 716-873-6000	NY 14207	
1500	Delaware North Companies Leisure Time	700 Delaware Avenue	Buffalo 716-881-6500	NY 14209	
750	Rich Products Corp Food Processing	1150 Niagara Street	Buffalo 716-878-8000	NY 14213	
742	Mark IV Industries Inc Electronics	1 Towne Center 501 J J Audubon Pkwy	Williamsville 716-689-4972	NY 14231	
537	First Empire State Corp Banking	One M & T Plaza	Buffalo 716-842-4200	NY 14240	
300	Manufacturers & Traders Trust Co Banking	One M & T Plaza	Buffalo 716-842-4200	NY 14240	
2500	Marine Midland Banks Inc Banking	One Marine Center	Buffalo 716-843-2424	NY 14240	
230	State Univ of New York University	Capen Hall	Buffalo 716-831-2000	NY 14260	
800	Seneca Foods Corp Food Processing	1162 Pittford-Victor Road	Pittsford 716-385-9500	NY 14534	
978	Bausch & Lomb Inc Instruments	One Lincoln First Square	Rochester 716-338-6000	NY 14601	

State / Province: New York

Organizations Listed Geographically

Revenue ($ mil)	Organization/ Industry	Address	City / Phone	State/ Zip	Province/ Postcode
695	Curtice Burns Inc Food Processing	One Lincoln First Square	Rochester 716-325-1020	NY 14603	
350	Rochester Community Savings Bank Savings & Loan	40 Franklin Street	Roschester 716-262-5800	NY 14604	
350	Alling & Cory Corp Paper/Forest Prd	25 Verona Street	Rochester 716-454-1880	NY 14608	
550	First Federal Savings & Loan Assn Inc Savings & Loan	One First Federal Plaza	Rochester 716-238-2100	NY 14614	
413	Rochester, City of Local Govt	City Hall 30 Church Street	Rochester 716-428-7045	NY 14614	
479	Rochester Telephone Corp Telecom	180 S Clinton Avenue	Rochester 716-777-1000	NY 14646	
774	Rochester Gas & Electric Corp Utility	89 E Avenue	Rochester 716-546-2700	NY 14649	
17034	Eastman Kodak Co Leisure Time	343 State Street	Rochester 716-724-4000	NY 14650	
250	Gleason Corp Automotive	30 Corporate Woods	Rochester 716-272-6000	NY 14692	
1000	Wegmans Food Markets Inc Retail/Food	1500 Brooks Avenue	Rochester 716-328-2550	NY 14692	
500	Aarque Companies Inc Manufacturing	PO Box 310	Jamestown 716-664-6014	NY 14702	
2122	Corning Glass Works Inc Manufacturing	Houghton Park	Corning 607-974-9000	NY 14831	
600	Pierce, S S Co Food Processing	74 Seneca Street	Dundee 607-243-7171	NY 14837	
160	Park Communications Inc Publishing/Com	Terrace Hill	Ithaca 607-272-9020	NY 14850	
1340	New York State Electric & Gas Inc Utility	Route 13 Dryden Road PO Box 287	Ithaca 607-347-4131	NY 14851	
484	Cornell University University	Administrative Bldg	Ithaca 607-256-1000	NY 14853	

State / Province: North Carolina

2091	First Wachovia Corp Banking	301 N Main Street	Winston-Salem 919-770-5000	NC 27101	
300	Salem Carpet Mills Corp Tire/Rubber	NCNB Plaza	Winston-Salem 919-727-1200	NC 27101	
NA	Hanes Hosiery Inc Apparel/Textiles	401 Hanes Mill Road	Winston-Salem 919-744-2011	NC 27102	
NA	Reynolds, R J Tobacco Co Tobacco	401 N Main Street	Winston-Salem 919-741-5000	NC 27102	
NA	L'eggs Products Inc Apparel/Textiles	5660 University Parkway	Winston-Salem 919-768-9540	NC 27103	
3000	Piedmont Aviation Inc Airline	4001 N Liberty Street	Winston Salem 919-767-5100	NC 27105	
380	Ladd Furniture Inc Manufacturing	One Plaza Center	High Point 919-889-0333	NC 27261	
400	Universal Furniture Industries Inc Appliances/Furn	2622 Uwharrie Road	High Point 919-884-4322	NC 27263	
1338	Fieldcrest Cannon Inc Apparel/Textiles	326 E Stadium Drive	Eden 919-627-3000	NC 27288	
275	Pantry Inc Retail/Food	1801 Douglas Drive	Sanford 919-774-6700	NC 27330	
1100	Blue Bell Inc Apparel/Textiles	335 Church Center	Greensboro 919-373-3400	NC 27401	
1223	Jefferson Pilot Corp Non-Bank Fin	101 N Elm Street	Greensboro 919-378-2011	NC 27401	
750	Cone Mills Corp Apparel/Textiles	1201 Maple Street	Greensboro 919-379-6510	NC 27405	
550	Guilford Mills Inc Apparel/Textiles	4925 W Market Street	Greensboro 919-292-7550	NC 27407	
3000	Burlington Industries Inc Apparel/Textiles	3330 W Friendly Avenue	Greensboro 919-379-2000	NC 27410	

State / Province: North Carolina

Organizations Listed Geographically

Revenue ($ mil)	Organization/ Industry	Address	City / Phone	State/ Zip	Province/ Postcode
400	Unifi Inc Manufacturing	7201 W Friendly Avenue	Greensboro 919-294-4410	NC 27410	
389	University of North Carolina University	Administrative Bldg	Chapel Hill 919-962-2338	NC 27514	
1439	Rose's Stores Inc Retail/Merch	218 Garnett Street	Henderson 919-492-8111	NC 27536	
319	First Citizens Bank & Trust Co Banking	Martin Wilmington Road	Raleigh 919-755-7215	NC 27601	
2273	Carolina Power & Light Co Utility	411 Fayetteville Street Mall	Raleigh 919-836-6111	NC 27602	
250	Raleigh, City Local Govt	City Hall 222 W Hargett Street	Raleigh 919-890-3050	NC 27602	
350	North Carolina Retirement Fund Non-Bank Fin	325 N Salisbury Street	Raleigh 919-733-3211	NC 27611	
12205	North Carolina, State of State/Prov Govt	State Capitol	Raleigh 919-733-1110	NC 27611	
500	Investors Management Corp Food/Lodging	5151 Glenwood Avenue Beta Center	Raleigh 919-781-9310	NC 27612	
210	North Carolina State University University	Administrative Bldg	Raleigh 919-737-2011	NC 27695	
2000	Liggett Group Inc Tobacco	300 N Duke Street	Durham 919-683-9000	NC 27702	
404	Duke University University	Administrative Bldg	Durham 919-684-8111	NC 27706	
1000	Harris Wholesale Corp Retail/Merch	2841 N Church	Solon 919-977-1054	NC 27802	
NA	Carolina Telephone & Telegraph Co Telecom	720 Western Blvd	Tarboro 919-823-9900	NC 27886	
935	Standard Commerical Tobacco Co Tobacco	2201 Miller Road PO Box 450	Wilson 919-291-5507	NC 27893	
651	Carolina Freight Corp Transport	NC Highway 150 E	Cherryville 704-435-6811	NC 28021	
3815	Food Lion Inc Retail/Food	2110 Harrison Road PO Box 1330	Salisbury 704-633-8250	NC 28145	
250	Charlotte, City of Local Govt	City Hall 600 E Trade Street	Charlotte 704-336-2244	NC 28202	
500	Hendrick Management Corp Real Estate/Bldg	3400 South Blvd	Charlotte 704-529-0578	NC 28209	
408	Lance Inc Food Processing	8600 South Blvd	Charlotte 704-554-1421	NC 28210	
543	Nucor Corp Steel	4425 Randolph Road	Charlotte 704-366-7000	NC 28211	
669	Family Dollar Stores Inc Retail/Merch	10401 Old Monroe Road	Charlotte 704-847-6961	NC 28212	
NA	Verbatim Corp Comput/Off Equip	1200 W T Harris Blvd	Charlotte 704-547-6500	NC 28213	
1000	McDevitt & Street Co Inc Real Estate/Bldg	4824 Parkway Plaza	Charlotte 704-525-8110	NC 28217	
1750	Belk Store Services Inc Retail/Merch	308 E Fifth Street	Charlotte 704-372-8900	NC 28231	
328	Coca Cola Consolidated Beverage	1900 Rerford Road	Charlotte 704-551-4400	NC 28231	
431	Piedmont Natural Gas Co Energy	1915 Rexford Road	Charlotte 704-364-3120	NC 28233	
250	Cato Corp Retail/Merch	8100 Denmark Road	Charlotte 704-554-8510	NC 28234	
3627	Duke Power Co Utility	422 S Church Street	Charlotte 704-373-4011	NC 28242	
2829	NCNB (No Carolina Natl Bank) Corp Banking	One NCNB Plaza	Charlotte 704-374-5000	NC 28255	
330	Heritage Today Corp Publishing/Com	7224 Park Road	Charlotte 704-542-6000	NC 28279	
220	Interstate Johnson Lane Corp Securities	2700 NCNB Plaza 101 S Tyron Street	Charlotte 704-379-9000	NC 28280	
1400	Ruddick Corp Retail/Food	2000 First Union Plaza	Charlotte 704-372-5404	NC 28282	

State / Province: North Carolina

Organizations Listed Geographically

Revenue ($ mil)	Organization/ Industry	Address	City / Phone	State/ Zip	Province/ Postcode
2898	First Union National Bank Corp Banking	Two First Union Plaza	Charlotte 704-374-6565	NC 28288	
1000	Merchants Distributors Inc Retail/Merch	543 12th Street Drive	Hickory 704-322-2822	NC 28601	
261	Brendle's Inc Retail/Merch	1919 N Bridges Street	Elkin 919-835-3400	NC 28621	
2517	Lowe's Companies Inc Retail/Merch	State Highway 268 E	North Wilkesboro 919-651-4000	NC 28659	
550	Ingles Markets Inc Retail/Food	Highway 70 E	Black Mountain 704-669-2941	NC 28711	

State / Province: North Dakota

Revenue ($ mil)	Organization/ Industry	Address	City / Phone	State/ Zip	Province/ Postcode
344	MDU Resources Group Inc Utility	400 N Fourth Street	Bismarck 701-222-7900	ND 58501	
1949	North Dakota, State of State/Prov Govt	State Capitol	Bismarck 701-224-2000	ND 58505	

State / Province: Ohio

Revenue ($ mil)	Organization/ Industry	Address	City / Phone	State/ Zip	Province/ Postcode
412	Greif Brothers Corp Packaging	621 Pennsylvania Avenue	Delaware 614-363-1271	OH 43015	
2902	Wendy's International Inc Food/Lodging	4288 W Dublin Granville Road	Dublin 614-764-3100	OH 43017	
5500	Honda of America Corp Automotive	Honda Parkway	Marysville 513-642-5000	OH 43040	
NA	Energy Services Co Electronics	N Sandursky Street	Mt Vernon 614-393-8200	OH 43050	
904	Worthington Industries Inc Steel	1205 Dearborn Drive	Columbus 614-438-3210	OH 43085	
1100	CountryMark Inc Chemicals	4565 Columbus Price	Delaware 614-548-8200	OH 43105	
750	Anchor Hocking Corp Manufacturing	109 N Broad Street	Lancaster 614-687-2111	OH 43132	
700	Battelle Memorial Institute Inc Consulting	505 King Avenue	Columbus 614-424-6424	OH 43201	
601	Consolidated Stores Corp Retail/Merch	2020 Convair Avenue	Columbus 614-224-1297	OH 43207	
395	Evans, Bob Farms Inc Food/Lodging	3776 S High Street	Columbus 614-491-2225	OH 43207	
500	Schottenstein Stores Inc Retail/Merch	1800 Moler Road	Columbus 614-221-9200	OH 43207	
641	Ohio State University University	Administrative Bldg	Columbus 614-422-6446	OH 43210	
900	Big Bear Inc Retail/Food	770 Goodale Blvd	Columbus 614-464-6500	OH 43212	
4841	American Electric Power Co Inc Utility	1 Riverside Plaza	Columbus 614-223-1000	OH 43215	
778	Columbus Southern Power Co Utility	215 N Front Street	Columbus 614-223-1000	OH 43215	
420	Columbus, City of Local Govt	City Hall	Columbus 614-222-7671	OH 43215	
453	Lancaster Colony Corp Manufacturing	37 W Broad Street	Columbus 614-224-7141	OH 43215	
450	Ohio Public Employees Retirement Fund Non-Bank Fin	45 N Fourth Street	Columbus 614-221-7012	OH 43215	
1490	Ohio, State Teachers Retirement System Non-Bank Fin	275 E Broad Street	Columbus 614-227-4062	OH 43215	
NA	Snacks & International Consumer Products Food Processing	180 E Broad Street	Columbus 614-225-4000	OH 43215	
139	State Savings Bank Inc Savings & Loan	20 E Broad Street	Columbus 614-460-6100	OH 43215	
4071	Limited Inc Retail/Merch	Two Limited Towers PO Box 16000	Columbus 614-475-4000	OH 43216	
5000	Nationwide Insurance Co Insurance	One Nationwide Plaza	Columbus 614-249-7111	OH 43216	

State / Province: Ohio

Organizations Listed Geographically

Revenue ($ mil)	Organization/ Industry	Address	City / Phone	State/ Zip	Province/ Postcode
400	State Auto Mutual Insurance Co Insurance	518 E Broad Street	Columbus 614-464-5000	OH	43216
NA	CompuServe Inc Comput/Off Equip	5000 Arlington Center Blvd	Columbus 614-457-8600	OH	43220
NA	Abercrombie & Fitch Inc Retail/Merch	One Limited Parkway	Columbus 614-479-6500	OH	43230
550	Cardinal Industries Inc Real Estate/Bldg	2040 S Hamilton	Columbus 614-861-3211	OH	43232
901	Huntington Bancshares Inc Banking	41 S High Street	Columbus 614-476-8300	OH	43260
24229	Ohio, State of State/Prov Govt	State Capitol	Columbus 614-466-2000	OH	43266
2734	Banc One Corp Banking	100 E Broad Street	Columbus 614-463-5944	OH	43271
600	Andersons Inc Food Processing	1200 Dussel Drive	Maumee 419-893-5050	OH	43537
1919	Trinova Corp Machinery	1705 Indianwood Circle	Maumee 419-891-2200	OH	43537
563	Trustcorp Inc Banking	Three SeaGate	Toledo 419-259-8950	OH	43603
738	Champion Spark Plug Co Electronics	One Seagate	Toledo 419-247-1600	OH	43604
250	Toledo, City of Local Govt	City Hall 1 Government Center	Toledo 419-245-1001	OH	43604
79	University of Toledo University	2801 W Bancroft Street	Toledo 419-537-4242	OH	43606
840	Sheller Globe Corp Automotive	1505 Jefferson Avenue	Toledo 419-255-8840	OH	43624
628	Toledo Edison Co Utility	300 Madison Avenue	Toledo 419-249-5000	OH	43652
2831	Owens Corning Fiberglas Corp Building Mat	Fiberglas Tower	Toledo 419-248-8000	OH	43659
3800	Owens Illinois Inc Packaging	One Sea Gate Plaza	Toledo 419-247-5000	OH	43666
4936	Dana Corp Automotive	4500 Dorr Street PO Box 1000	Toledo 419-535-4500	OH	43697
2500	Revco Drug Stores Inc Retail/Merch	1925 Enterprise Drive	Twinsburg 216-425-9811	OH	44087
1126	Lubrizol Corp Chemicals	29400 Lakeland Blvd	Wicklife 216-943-4200	OH	44092
NA	SMP Inc Aerospace	29501 Clayton Blvd	Wickliffe 216-585-3100	OH	44092
1052	Ameritrust Corp Banking	900 Euclid Avenue	Cleveland 216-737-5000	OH	44101
2038	Centerior Energy Corp Utility	55 Public Square	Cleveland 216-622-9800	OH	44101
508	Standard Products Co Automotive	2130 W 110th Street	Cleveland 216-281-8300	OH	44102
566	Premier Industrial Corp Business Service	4500 Euclid Avenue	Cleveland 216-391-8300	OH	44103
334	Van Dorn Co Packaging	2700 E 79th Street	Cleveland 216-361-5234	OH	44104
300	Pioneer Standard Electric Inc Electronics	4800 E 131st Street	Garfield Heights 216-587-3600	OH	44105
2000	White Consolidated Industries Inc Appliances/Furn	11770 Berea Road	Cleveland 216-252-3700	OH	44111
2252	Parker Hannifin Corp Manufacturing	17325 Euclid Avenue	Cleveland 216-531-3000	OH	44112
NA	Cleveland Electric Illuminating Co Utility	Illuminating Bldg	Cleveland 216-447-3103	OH	44113
1250	Cuyahoga County Government Local Govt	1219 Ontario Street	Cleveland 216-443-7000	OH	44113
74	First Union Real Estate Inc Real Estate/Bldg	55 Public Square	Cleveland 216-781-4030	OH	44113
11000	British Petroleum America Energy	200 Public Square	Cleveland 216-586-4141	OH	44114

State / Province: Ohio

Organizations Listed Geographically

Revenue ($ mil)	Organization/ Industry	Address	City / Phone	State/ Zip	Province/ Postcode
350	Cleveland Cliffs Inc Metals/Mining	1100 Superior Avenue	Cleveland 216-694-5700	OH	44114
531	Cleveland, City of Local Govt	City Hall 601 Lakeside	Cleveland 216-664-2220	OH	44114
3469	Eaton Corp Conglomerate	Eaton Center 1111 Superior Avenue	Cleveland 216-523-5000	OH	44114
2000	Ernst & Whinney Inc Accounting	2000 National City Bldg	Cleveland 216-861-5000	OH	44114
1009	Ferro Corp Chemicals	1000 Lakeside Avenue	Cleveland 216-641-8580	OH	44114
1000	Hanna, M A Corp Tire/Rubber	1301 E Ninth Street	Cleveland 216-589-4000	OH	44114
270	LDI Corp Comput/Off Equip	1375 E 9th Street	Cleveland 216-687-0100	OH	44114
NA	Morrison Knudsen Eng & Environment Manufacturing	One Erieview Plaza	Cleveland 216-523-5600	OH	44114
2227	National City Corp Banking	1900 E Nineth Street	Cleveland 216-575-2000	OH	44114
NA	Ohio Bell Telephone Co Telecom	45 Erieview Plaza	Cleveland 216-822-9700	OH	44114
972	Society Bank Corp Banking	800 Superior Avenue	Cleveland 216-689-3000	OH	44114
619	TransCapital Financial Corp(Ohio Sav Bk) Savings & Loan	1100 Superior Avenue	Cleveland 216-621-9600	OH	44114
1114	Federal Reserve Bank of Cleveland Inc Federal Govt Fin	East 6th Street & Superior	Cleveland 216-579-2000	OH	441141
543	Bearings Inc Business Service	3600 Euclid Avenue PO Box 6925	Cleveland 216-881-2838	OH	44115
346	Brush Wellman Inc Metals/Mining	1200 Hanna Bldg	Cleveland 216-443-1000	OH	44115
1000	LTV Steel Co Steel	25 W Prospect Street	Cleveland 216-622-5000	OH	44115
600	Ohio Mattress Co Building Mat	1228 Euclid Avenue Halle Bldg	Cleveland 216-522-1310	OH	44115
275	Prescott Ball & Turben Inc Securities	1331 Euclid Avenue	Cleveland 216-574-7300	OH	44115
1950	Sherwin Williams Co Building Mat	101 Prospect Avenue NW	Cleveland 216-566-2000	OH	44115
550	Lincoln Electric Co Inc Manufacturing	22801 St Clair Avenue	Cleveland 216-481-8100	OH	44117
616	NACCO Industries Metals/Mining	12800 Shaker Blvd	Cleveland 216-752-1000	OH	44120
600	North American Coal Corp Energy	12800 Shaker Blvd	Cleveland 216-752-1000	OH	44120
374	Banner Industries Inc Automotive	25700 Science Park Drive	Beachwood 216-464-3650	OH	44122
291	Fabri Centers of America Inc Retail/Merch	23550 Commerce Park Road	Beachwood 216-464-2500	OH	44122
400	Lamson & Sessions Co Manufacturing	25701 Science Park Drive	Cleveland 216-464-3400	OH	44122
1500	Leaseway Transportation Corp Transport	3700 Park East Drive	Beachwood 216-464-3300	OH	44122
1500	Reliance Electric Corp Electronics	PO Box 99502	Cleveland 216-266-7000	OH	44122
600	Sudbury Inc Automotive	3733 Park Drive E	Cleveland 216-464-7026	OH	44122
1250	Cole National Corp Retail/Merch	29001 Cedar Road	Cleveland 216-449-4100	OH	44124
1275	Progressive Insurance Co Insurance	6000 Parkland Blvd	Mayfield Heights 216-464-8000	OH	44124
6982	TRW Inc Electronics	1900 Richmond Road	Cleveland 216-291-7000	OH	44124
300	Forest City Enterprises Inc Real Estate/Bldg	10800 Brookpark Road	Cleveland 216-267-1200	OH	44130
825	Milk Marketing Inc Food Processing	8257 Dow Circle	Strongsville 216-826-4730	OH	44136

State / Province: Ohio

Organizations Listed Geographically

Revenue ($ mil)	Organization/ Industry	Address	City / Phone	State/ Zip	Province/ Postcode
1650	First National Supermarkets Inc Retail/Food	17000 Rockside	Maple Heights 216-587-7100	OH	44137
227	Agency Rent-A-Car Inc Business Service	30000 Aurora Road	Solon 216-349-1000	OH	44139
NA	Teledyne Republic Div Electronics	15655 Brookpark Road	Cleveland 216-267-2700	OH	44142
1275	American Greetings Corp Leisure Time	10500 American Road	Cleveland 216-252-7300	OH	44144
350	Nordson Corp Equipment	28601 Clemens Road	Westlake 216-892-1580	OH	44145
550	American Seaway Foods Inc Retail/Food	22801 Aurora Road	Edford Heights 216-663-5500	OH	44146
1057	Riser Foods Inc Retail/Food	5300 Richmond Road	Bedford Heights 216-292-7000	OH	44146
250	Waxman Industries Inc Retail/Merch	24460 Aurora Road	Cleveland 216-439-1830	OH	44146
1068	Alltel Corp Telecom	100 Executive Parkway	Hudson 216-650-7000	OH	44236
114	Kent State University University	Administrative Bldg	Kent 216-672-2121	OH	44242
450	Westfield Companies Insurance	One Park Circle	Westfield Center 216-887-0101	OH	44251
350	RPM Corp Chemicals	2628 Pearl Road	Medina 216-225-3192	OH	44258
275	MTD Products Inc Manufacturing	5965 Graston Road	Valley City 216-225-2600	OH	44280
275	Albrecht, Fred W Grocery Co Inc Retail/Food	2700 Gilchrist	Akron 216-733-2861	OH	44305
250	Akron, City of Local Govt	City Hall 166 S High Street	Akron 216-375-2345	OH	44308
700	Brenlin Corp Steel	705 Akron Center	Akron 216-762-2420	OH	44308
2143	Ohio Edison Co Utility	76 S Main Street	Akron 216-384-5100	OH	44308
2185	Roadway Services Inc Transport	1077 Gorge Blvd	Akron 216-384-8184	OH	44309
1891	GenCorp Inc Tire/Rubber	175 Ghent Road	Akron 216-869-4200	OH	44313
598	Schulman, A Inc Chemicals	3550 W Market Street	Akron 216-666-3751	OH	44313
10810	Goodyear Tire & Rubber Co Tire/Rubber	1144 E Market Street	Akron 216-796-2121	OH	44316
312	Firestone Tire & Rubber Co Tire/Rubber	1200 Firestone Parkway	Akron 216-379-7000	OH	44317
2417	Goodrich, B F Co Tire/Rubber	500 S Main Street	Arkon 216-374-3985	OH	44318
95	University of Akron University	Administrative Bldg	Akron 216-375-7111	OH	44325
400	Commercial Intertech Machinery	1775 Logan Avenue	Youngstown 216-746-8011	OH	44501
1000	DeBartolo, Edward J Co Inc Retail/Food	7620 Market Street	Youngstown 216-758-7292	OH	44512
7000	Lucky Stores Inc Retail/Food	6300 Clark Avenue	Dublin 415-833-6000	OH	44568
550	Superiors Brand Meats Inc Food Processing	1888 Southway SE	Massillon 216-832-7491	OH	44648
353	Smucker, J M Co Food Processing	Strawberry Lane	Orrville 216-682-0015	OH	44667
1194	Rubbermaid Inc Manufacturing	1147 Adron Road	Wooster 216-264-6464	OH	44691
1387	Ohio Power Co Utility	301 Cleveland Avenue SW	Canton 216-456-8173	OH	44702
1554	Timken Co Machinery	1835 Dueber Avenue SW	Canton 216-438-3000	OH	44706
451	Diebold Inc Comput/Off Equip	818 Mulberry Road SE	Canton 216-489-4000	OH	44711

State / Province: Ohio

Organizations Listed Geographically

Revenue ($ mil)	Organization/ Industry	Address	City / Phone	State/ Zip	Province/ Postcode
NA	United Telephone of Ohio Telecom	665 Lexington Avenue	Mansfield 419-755-8011	OH	44907
910	Cincinnati Financial Corp Non-Bank Fin	6200 S Gilmore Road	Fairfield 513-870-2000	OH	45014
1623	Ohio Casualty Corp Insurance	136 N Third Street	Hamilton 513-867-3000	OH	45025
19100	Kroger Co Retail/Food	1014 Vine Street	Cincinnati 513-762-4000	OH	45201
3000	American Financial Corp Insurance	One E Fourth Street	Cincinnati 513-579-2121	OH	45202
500	Carlisle Companies Inc Tire/Rubber	250 E Fifth Street	Cincinnati 513-241-2500	OH	45202
500	Central Bancorp Inc Banking	Fifth & Main Streets	Cincinnati 513-651-8000	OH	45202
480	Charter Co Energy	One E Fourth Street	Cincinnati 513-579-2482	OH	45202
600	Chemed Chemicals	1200 Dubois Tower	Cincinnati 513-762-6900	OH	45202
NA	Chiquita Brands Inc Food Processing	250 E Fifth Street	Cincinnati 513-784-8000	OH	45202
738	Cincinnati Bell Inc Telecom	201 E Fourth Street	Cincinnati 513-397-9900	OH	45202
1386	Cincinnati Gas & Electric Co Utility	139 E Fourth Street	Cincinnati 513-381-2000	OH	45202
431	Cincinnati, City of Local Govt	City Hall 801 Plum Street	Cincinnati 513-352-3250	OH	45202
NA	Citrus Hill Manufacturing Co Food Processing	One Proctor & Gamble Plaza	Cincinnati 513-983-1100	OH	45202
770	Eagle Picher Industries Inc Equipment	580 Walnut Street	Cincinnati 513-721-7010	OH	45202
11118	Federated Department Stores Inc Retail/Merch	Seven W Seventh Street	Cincinnati 513-579-7000	OH	45202
531	First National Cincinnati Corp Banking	425 Walnut Street	Cincinnati 513-632-4000	OH	45202
NA	Folger's Coffee Co Food Processing	One Proctor & Gambel Plaza	Cincinnati 513-983-1100	OH	45202
382	Great American Commmunications Co Publishing/Com	One E Fourth Street	Cincinnati 513-579-2177	OH	45202
550	Midland Affiliated Inc Manufacturing	580 Walnut Street	Cincinnati 513-721-4000	OH	45202
NA	Morrell, John & Co Food Processing	250 E Fifth Street	Cincinnati 513-852-3500	OH	45202
400	Palm Beach Inc Apparel/Textiles	400 Pike Street	Cincinnati 513-241-4260	OH	45202
1547	Penn Central Corp Manufacturing	One E Fourth Street	Cincinnati 513-579-6600	OH	45202
19491	Procter & Gamble Co Personal Care	One Proctor & Gamble Plaza	Cincinnati 513-562-1100	OH	45202
1000	Scripps Howard Inc Publishing/Com	1100 Central Trust Tower	Cincinnati 513-977-3000	OH	45202
3503	United Brands Co Food Processing	One E Fourth Street	Cincinnati 513-579-2115	OH	45202
970	Western & Southern Life Ins Co Insurance	400 Broadway	Cincinnati 513-629-1800	OH	45202
857	Cincinnati Milacron Inc Machinery	4701 Marburg Avenue	Cincinnati 513-841-8100	OH	45209
381	University of Cincinnati University	Clifton Avenue	Cincinnati 513-475-8000	OH	45221
NA	Kahn's & Co Food Processing	3241 Spring Grove Avenue	Cincinnati 513-541-4000	OH	45225
350	KDI Corp Electronics	5721 Dragon Way	Cincinnati 513-272-1421	OH	45227
2343	US Shoe Corp Retail/Merch	One Eastwood Drive	Cincinnati 513-527-7000	OH	45227
404	Gibson Greetings Inc Retail/Merch	2100 Section Road	Cincinnati 513-841-6600	OH	45237

State / Province: Ohio

Organizations Listed Geographically

Revenue ($ mil)	Organization/ Industry	Address	City / Phone	State/ Zip	Province/ Postcode
205	Cintas Corp Apparel/Textiles	11255 Reed Hartman Highway	Cincinnati 513-489-4000	OH	45241
300	Heekin Can Inc Packaging	11310 Cornel Park	Cinncinnati 513-489-3200	OH	45242
NA	US Industrial Chemicals Co Chemicals	11500 Northlake Drive	Cincinnati 513-530-6510	OH	45249
506	Fifth Third BanCorp Inc Banking	38 Fountain Square	Cincinnati 513-579-5300	OH	45263
350	Huffy Corp Leisure Time	7701 Byers Road	Miamisburg 513-866-6251	OH	45342
550	Ponderosa Steak Houses Inc Food/Lodging	Terminal Drive Dayton Int'l Airport	Dayton 513-454-2400	OH	45377
300	Duriron Co Manufacturing	425 N Findley Street	Dayton 513-226-4000	OH	45401
NA	Mead Data Central Inc Comput/Off Equip	9393 Springboro Pike	Dayton 513-865-6800	OH	45401
693	Philips Industries Inc Manufacturing	4801 Springfield Street	Dayton 513-253-7171	OH	45401
675	Standard Register Co Comput/Off Equip	600 Albany Street	Dayton 513-443-1000	OH	45401
350	Dayco Corp Manufacturing	33 W First Street	Dayton 513-226-7000	OH	45402
1044	DPL (Dayton Power & Light) Corp Utility	Courthouse Plaza SW	Dayton 513-224-6000	OH	45402
600	Reynolds & Reynolds Corp Business Service	800 Germantown Street	Dayton 513-443-2000	OH	45407
NA	Apex Corp Electronics	762 W Stewart Street	Dayton 513-222-7871	OH	45408
200	Audio/Video Affiliates Inc Retail/Merch	2875 Needmore Road	Dayton 513-274-3737	OH	45414
264	Amcast Industrial Corp Manufacturing	3931 S Dixie Avenue	Dayton 513-298-5251	OH	45439
1573	Super Food Services Inc Retail/Food	3185 Elbee Road	Dayton 513-294-1731	OH	45439
4464	Mead Corp Paper/Forest Prd	Courthouse Plaza NE	Dayton 513-222-6323	OH	45463
NA	Mead Pulp Sales Inc Paper/Forest Prd	Courthouse Plaza	Dayton 513-222-6323	OH	45463
5990	NCR Corp Comput/Off Equip	1700 S Patterson Blvd	Dayton 513-445-5000	OH	45479
748	Cooper Tire & Rubber Co Tire/Rubber	Western & Lima Streets	Findley 419-423-1321	OH	45839
NA	Marathon Oil Co Energy	539 S Main Street	Findlay 419-422-2121	OH	45840

State / Province: Ohio

Organizations Listed Geographically

Revenue ($ mil)	Organization/ Industry	Address	City / Phone	State/ Zip	Province/ Postcode

State / Province: Oklahoma

167	University of Oklahoma University	660 Parrington Oval	Norman 405-624-5000	OK 73019	
250	LSB Industries Inc Chemicals	16 S Pennsylvania Avenue	Oklahoma City 405-235-4546	OK 73101	
500	Anthony, C R Co Inc Retail/Merch	701 N Broadway	Oklahoma City 405-235-3711	OK 73102	
352	Oklahoma City, City of Local Govt	City Hall Plaza	Oklahoma City 405-231-2424	OK 73102	
1098	Oklahoma Gas & Electric Co Utility	321 N Harvey Avenue	Oklahoma City 405-272-3000	OK 73102	
7409	Oklahoma, State of State/Prov Govt	State Capitol	Oklahoma City 405-521-2011	OK 73105	
1324	Wilson Foods Corp Food Processing	4545 Lincoln Blvd	Oklahoma City 405-525-4545	OK 73105	
190	Banks of Mid-America Inc Banking	100 Broadway	Oklahoma City 405-231-6000	OK 73125	
2689	Kerr McGee Corp Energy	Kerr McGee Center PO Box 25861	Oklahoma City 405-270-1313	OK 73125	
750	Oklahoma Publishing Co Inc Publishing/Com	25 NE Fourth Street	Oklahoma City 405-232-3311	OK 73125	
10467	Fleming Companies Inc Business Service	6301 Waterford Blvd	Oklahoma City 405-840-7200	OK 73126	
450	Hadson Corp Energy	101 Park Avenue	Oklahoma City 405-235-9500	OK 73126	
192	Noble Affiliates Inc Oil Service	110 W Broadway	Ardmore 405-223-4110	OK 73402	
550	Union Equity Cooperative Exchange Inc Food Processing	2300 N 10th Street	Enid 405-233-5100	OK 73701	
NA	Phillips 66 Co Energy	Fouth & Keeler Streets	Bartlesville 918-661-4948	OK 74004	
11490	Phillips Petroleum Co Energy	Phillips Bldg	Bartlesville 918-661-6600	OK 74004	
NA	Phillips Pipeline Co Energy	370 Adams Bldg	Bartlesville 918-661-6600	OK 74004	
172	Oklahoma State University University	Main Campus	Stillwater 405-624-5000	OK 74078	
NA	MAPCO Coal Inc Metals/Mining	1717 S Boulder	Tulsa 918-592-7237	OK 74101	
1802	Mapco Inc Energy	PO Box 645	Tulsa 918-581-1800	OK 74101	
NA	Transok Inc Utility	600 Main Street	Tulsa 918-583-1121	OK 74101	
571	Oneok Inc Utility	100 W Fifth Street	Tulsa 918-588-7000	OK 74103	
250	Tulsa, City of Local Govt	City Hall 200 Civic Center	Tulsa 918-596-7777	OK 74103	
160	Helmerich & Payne Inc Oil Service	Utica at 21st Street	Tulsa 918-742-5531	OK 74114	
550	Quiktrip Corp Retail/Food	901 N Mingo Road	Tulsa 918-836-8551	OK 74116	
604	Public Service Co of Oklahoma Utility	212 E Sixth Street	Tulsa 918-599-2000	OK 74119	
850	Memorex Telex Corp Comput/Off Equip	6422 E 41st Street	Tulsa 918-627-2333	OK 74135	
NA	Facet Enterprises Inc Manufacturing	7030 S Yale	Tulsa 918-492-1800	OK 74136	
1673	Williams Companies Inc Utility	One Williams Center	Tulsa 918-588-2000	OK 74172	

State / Province: Oregon

| 301 | Mentor Graphics Corp Business Service | 8500 SW Creekside | Beaverton 503-626-7000 | OR 97005 | |

State / Province: Oregon

Organizations Listed Geographically

Revenue ($ mil)	Organization/ Industry	Address	City / Phone	State/ Zip	Province/ Postcode
1203	Nike Inc Apparel/Textiles	3900 SW Murray Blvd	Beaverton 503-641-6453	OR 97005	
1500	Pay Less Drug Stores Retail/Merch	9275 SW Peyton Lane	Wilsonville 503-682-4100	OR 97070	
1412	Tektronix Inc Instruments	14150 SW Karl Braun Drive Tektronix Industrial Park	Beaverton 503-627-7111	OR 97077	
825	Blue Cross Blue Shield of Oregon Inc Insurance	100 SW Market Street	Portland 503-225-5221	OR 97201	
662	NERCO Inc Energy	11 SW Columbia	Portland 503-796-6600	OR 97201	
515	Pope & Talbot Inc Paper/Forest Prd	1500 SW First Street	Portland 503-228-9161	OR 97201	
1716	Willamette Industries Inc Paper/Forest Prd	3800 First Interstate Tower	Portland 503-227-5581	OR 97201	
2074	Meyer, Fred Inc Retail/Merch	3800 SE 22nd Avenue	Portland 503-232-8844	OR 97202	
600	North Pacific Lumber Inc Paper/Forest Prd	1505 SE Gideon	Portland 503-231-1166	OR 97202	
550	Northern Pacific Lumber Co Inc Paper/Forest Prd	1505 SE Gideon	Portland 503-231-1166	OR 97202	
1799	Louisiana Pacific Corp Paper/Forest Prd	111 SW Fifth Avenue	Portland 503-221-0800	OR 97204	
3519	Pacificorp Corp Utility	851 SW Sixth Avenue	Portland 503-464-6000	OR 97204	
500	Pamplin, R B Corp Real Estate/Bldg	900 SW Fifth Street	Portland 503-248-1133	OR 97204	
762	Portland General Electric Co Utility	121 SW Salmon Street	Portland 503-226-8333	OR 97204	
309	Portland, City of Local Govt	City Hall	Portland 503-248-4120	OR 97204	
414	Precision Castparts Inc Steel	4600 SE Harney Drive	Portland 503-777-3881	OR 97206	
250	Oregon Steel Mills Inc Equipment	14400 N Rivergate Blvd	Portland 503-286-9651	OR 97208	
1381	US Bancorp Inc Banking	111 SW Fifth Avenue	Portland 503-275-6111	OR 97208	
504	Franklin, Benj Federal Savings Assn Inc Savings & Loan	501 SE Hawthorne Blvd	Portland 503-275-1201	OR 97214	
825	United Grocers Inc Retail/Food	6433 SE Lake Road	Milwaukee 503-653-6330	OR 97222	
500	WTD Industries Inc Manufacturing	10300 SW Greeburg	Portland 503-246-3440	OR 97228	
2050	Bonneville Power Administration Govt Authority	905 NE Eleventh	Portland 503-230-5000	OR 97232	
750	Hyster Co Inc Equipment	2902 NE Wasco Street	Portland 503-280-7000	OR 97232	
7165	Oregon, State of State/Prov Govt	State Capitol	Salem 503-378-3131	OR 97310	
180	Oregon State University University	Administrative Bldg	Corvallis 503-754-0123	OR 97331	
306	Bohemia Inc Building Mat	2280 Oakmont	Eugene 503-342-6262	OR 97401	
600	Roseburg Forest Products Inc Paper/Forest Prd	Highway 99 S	Dillard 503-679-3311	OR 97432	

State / Province: Pennsylvania

Revenue ($ mil)	Organization/ Industry	Address	City / Phone	State/ Zip	Province/ Postcode
550	Schneider Inc Real Estate/Bldg	1370 Washington Pike	Bridgeville 412-257-6000	PA 15017	
200	Calgon Carbon Manufacturing	400 Media Drive	Robinson Twnshp 412-787-6700	PA 15205	
2200	Mobay Corp Chemicals	Mobay Road	Pittsburgh 412-777-2000	PA 15205	
NA	National Aluminum Corp Metals/Mining	Two Robinson Plaza	Pittsburgh 412-788-0190	PA 15205	

State / Province: Pennsylvania

Organizations Listed Geographically

Revenue ($ mil)	Organization/ Industry	Address	City / Phone	State/ Zip	Province/ Postcode
750	Ryan Homes Inc Real Estate/Bldg	100 Ryan Court	Pittsburgh 412-276-8000	PA 15205	
750	Mellon Stuart Holding Co Inc Real Estate/Bldg	1 North Shore Center	Pittsburgh 412-323-4600	PA 15212	
925	Allegheny County Government Local Govt	119 Courthouse Street	Pittsburgh 412-355-6940	PA 15219	
9795	Aluminum Co of America Metals/Mining	1501 Alcoa Bldg	Pittsburgh 412-553-4545	PA 15219	
251	Ampco Pittsburgh Corp Manufacturing	700 Porter Bldg 600 Grant Street	Pittsburgh 412-456-4400	PA 15219	
2500	ARCO Chemical Co Chemicals	3801 W Chester	Newtown Square 215-359-2000	PA 15219	
4719	Bayer USA Chemicals	One Mellon Center	Pittsburgh 412-394-5500	PA 15219	
406	Equitable Resources Co Inc Utility	420 Blvd of the Allies	Pittsburgh 412-261-3000	PA 15219	
5244	Heinz, H J Co Food Processing	600 Grant Street	Pittsburgh 412-456-5700	PA 15219	
1250	Hillman Industries Inc Manufacturing	Grant Bldg	Pittsburgh 412-281-2620	PA 15219	
650	Joy Manufacturing Co Equipment	301 Grant Street	Pittsburgh 412-562-4500	PA 15219	
1600	Koppers Co Inc Chemicals	Coppers Bldg	Pittsburg 412-227-2000	PA 15219	
329	Pittsburgh, City of Local Govt	City Hall 414 Grant Street	Pittsburgh 412-255-2626	PA 15219	
11046	Rockwell International Corp Conglomerate	600 Grant Street	Pittsburgh 412-565-2000	PA 15219	
16877	USX Corp Steel	600 Grant Street	Pittsburgh 412-433-1121	PA 15219	
810	Westinghouse Credit Corp Non-Bank Fin	One Oxford Center	Pittsburgh 412-393-3000	PA 15219	
262	Foster, L B Co Business Service	415 Holiday Drive	Pittsburgh 201-533-1100	PA 15220	
1100	Allegheny Ludlum Steel Corp Steel	1000 Six PPG Plaza	Pittsburgh 412-394-2800	PA 15222	
2468	Consolidated Natural Gas Co Utility	Four Gateway Center	Pittsburgh 412-227-1000	PA 15222	
300	Copperweld Corp Metals/Mining	Four Gateway Center	Pittsburgh 412-263-3200	PA 15222	
1000	Dravo Corp Manufacturing	One Oliver Plaza	Pittsburgh 412-566-3000	PA 15222	
600	Equimark Corp Banking	2 Oliver Plaza	Pittsburgh 412-288-5000	PA 15222	
850	Federated Investment Corp Non-Bank Fin	Federated Tower 1001 Liberty Center	Pittsburgh 412-288-1900	PA 15222	
400	First Federal Savings of Pittsburgh Inc Savings & Loan	300 Sixth Avenue	Pittsburgh 412-392-5500	PA 15222	
361	General Nutrition Inc Retail/Food	921 Penn Avenue	Pittsburgh 412-288-4600	PA 15222	
550	Ketchum Communications Inc Publishing/Com	300 Blvd of the Allies 6 PPG Place	Pittsburgh 412-456-3500	PA 15222	
96	Mylan Laboratories Inc Drugs	130 Seventh Street 1030 Century Bldg	Pittsburgh 412-232-0100	PA 15222	
3081	National Steel (Nat'l Intergroup) Corp Steel	20 Stanwix	Pittsburgh 412-394-4100	PA 15222	
333	Pennbancorp Inc(Integra Financial) Banking	Four PPG Place	Pittsburgh 814-644-8184	PA 15222	
1300	Pittsburgh National Bank Co Banking	Fifth Avenue & Wood Street	Pittsburgh 412-355-2000	PA 15222	
414	Robertson, H H Co Manufacturing	2 Gateway Center	Pittsburgh 412-281-3200	PA 15222	
12500	Westinghouse Electric Corp Electronics	Westinghouse Bldg Gateway Center 11 Stanwix St	Pittsburgh 412-244-2000	PA 15222	

State / Province: Pennsylvania

Organizations Listed Geographically

Revenue ($ mil)	Organization/ Industry	Address	City / Phone	State/ Zip	Province/ Postcode
330	Pitt Des Moines Inc Manufacturing	3400 Grand Avenue	Pittsburgh 412-331-3000	PA	15225
900	Cyclops Industries Inc Steel	650 Washington Road	Pittsburgh 412-343-4000	PA	15228
968	Allegheny International Inc Appliances/Furn	Two Oliver Plaza PO Box 456	Pittsburgh 412-562-4000	PA	15230
1000	Aristech Chemical Corp Chemicals	600 Grant Street	Pittsburgh 412-433-2747	PA	15230
750	J & L Specialty Products Inc Steel	1 PPG Plaza	Pittsburgh 412-338-1600	PA	15230
NA	Carnegie Natural Gas Co Energy	800 Regis Avenue	Pittsburgh 412-655-8510	PA	15236
1500	Giant Eagle Inc Retail/Food	101 Cappa Drive	Pittsburgh 412-963-6200	PA	15238
406	MSA Mine Safety Appliances Co Manufacturing	121 Gamma Drive	O'Hara Township 412-967-3000	PA	15238
825	Consolidated Coal Corp Energy	1800 Washington Road	Pittsburgh 412-831-4000	PA	15241
3269	Mellon Bank Corp Banking	Three Mellon Bank Center	Pittsburgh 412-234-5000	PA	15258
308	University of Pittsburgh University	4200 Fifth Avenue	Pittsburgh 412-624-4141	PA	15260
3827	PNC Financial Corp Banking	Fifth Avenue & Wood Street	Pittsburgh 412-762-2728	PA	15265
5617	PPG Industries Inc Manufacturing	One PPG Place	Pittsburgh 412-434-3131	PA	15272
1063	Duquesne Light Co Inc Utility	301 Grant Street	Pittsburgh 412-393-6000	PA	15279
NA	Baker Hughes Mining Equipment Equipment	455 Racetrack Road	Meadowlands 412-225-8016	PA	15347
1100	Eighty Four Lumber Co Retail/Merch	Route 519	Eighty Four 412-228-8820	PA	15384
420	Kennametal Inc Equipment	Route 981 at Westmoreland County Airport	Latrobe 412-539-5000	PA	15650
500	Rochester & Pittsburgh Coal Corp Metals/Mining	655 Church Street	Indiana 412-349-5800	PA	15701
1180	Penn Traffic Inc Retail/Food	319 Washington	Johnstown 814-536-4411	PA	15901
750	Crown American Corp Real Estate/Bldg	131 Market Street	Johnstown 814-536-4441	PA	15907
761	Pennsylvania Electric Co Utility	1001 Broad Street	Johnstown 814-533-8111	PA	15907
880	Service Star Corp Retail/Merch	Marie Street	East Butler 412-283-4567	PA	16029
1000	Servistar Corp Retail/Merch	Grant Avenue	East Butler 412-283-4567	PA	16029
NA	Pennsylvania Power Co Utility	One E Washington Street	New Castle 412-652-5331	PA	16103
869	Quaker State Oil Refining Co Energy	255 Elm Street	Oil City 814-676-7676	PA	16301
750	United Refining Corp Energy	15 Bradley Street	Warren 814-723-1500	PA	16365
500	Blair Corp Retail/Merch	220 Hickory Street	Warren 814-723-3600	PA	16366
325	New Process Corp Retail/Merch	220 Hickory Street	Warren 814-723-3600	PA	16366
485	Zurn Industries Inc Instruments	One Zurn Place	Erie 814-452-2111	PA	16514
800	Erie Insurance Exchange Inc Insurance	100 Erie Insurance Place	Erie 814-870-2000	PA	16530
383	Pennsylvania State University University	Administrative Bldg	University Park 814-865-4700	PA	16802
2168	Hershey Foods Corp Food Processing	100 Mansion Road E	Hershey 717-534-4000	PA	17033
1279	Harsco Corp Manufacturing	350 Poplar Church Road PO Box 8888	Wormleysburg 717-763-7064	PA	17043

State / Province: Pennsylvania

Organizations Listed Geographically

Revenue ($ mil)	Organization/ Industry	Address	City / Phone	State/ Zip	Province/ Postcode
500	Dauphin Deposit Corp Banking	213 Market Street	Harrisburg 717-255-2121	PA 17101	
2486	Rite Aid Corp Retail/Merch	Trindle Road & Railroad Avenue PO Box 3165	Harrisburg 717-761-2633	PA 17105	
2670	AMP Inc Electronics	470 Friendship Road	Harrisburg 717-564-0100	PA 17109	
757	Super Rite Foods Inc Retail/Food	3900 Industrial Road	Harrisburg 717-232-6821	PA 17110	
27163	Pennsylvania, State of State/Prov Govt	State Capitol	Harrisburg 717-787-2121	PA 17120	
569	Glatfelter, P H Co Paper/Forest Prd	228 S Main Street	Spring Grove 717-225-4711	PA 17362	
900	York International Corp Manufacturing	1750 Toronita Street	York 717-846-1988	PA 17402	
500	Hamilton Bank Corp Banking	1097 Commercial Avenue	Lancaster 717-569-8731	PA 17601	
2680	Armstrong World Industries Inc Manufacturing	W Liberty Street PO Box 3001	Lancaster 717-397-0611	PA 17604	
1189	Weis Markets Inc Retail/Food	1000 S Second Street	Sunbury 717-286-4571	PA 17801	
5489	Bethlehem Steel Corp Steel	701 E Third Street	Bethlehem 215-694-2424	PA 18016	
350	Hill Financial Savings Assn Inc Savings & Loan	400 Main Street	Red Hill 215-679-9506	PA 18076	
2214	Pennsylvania Power & Light Co Utility	2 N Ninth Street	Allentown 215-770-5151	PA 18101	
2000	Mack Trucks Inc Automotive	2100 Mack Blvd	Allentown 215-439-3011	PA 18103	
2432	Air Products & Chemicals Inc Chemicals	PO Box 538	Allentown 215-481-4911	PA 18105	
350	SPS Technologies Inc Manufacturing	Route 332	Newtown 215-860-3000	PA 18940	
500	Moyer Packing Co Inc Food Processing	249 Allentown Road	Souderton 215-723-5555	PA 18964	
550	Interstate Milk Producers Inc Food Processing	1225 Industrial Highway	Southampton 215-322-0200	PA 18966	
764	Atlantic Financial Federal Inc Savings & Loan	50 Monument Road	Bala Cynwyd 215-668-6600	PA 19004	
210	General Refractories Co Metals/Mining	225 City Avenue	Bala Cynwyd 215-667-7900	PA 19004	
300	Miller Anderson & Sherrerd Inv Mgt Co Non-Bank Fin	2 Bala Cynwyd Plaza	Bala Cynwyd 215-668-0850	PA 19004	
600	WWF Paper Corp Paper/Forest Prd	2 Bala Plaza	Bala Cynwyd 215-667-9210	PA 19004	
725	Charming Shoppes Inc Retail/Merch	450 Winks Lane	Bensalem 215-245-9100	PA 19020	
1042	Rorer Group Inc Drugs	500 Virginia Drive	Fort Washington 215-628-6000	PA 19034	
600	Exide Corp Manufacturing	101 Gibraltar Road	Horsham 215-674-9500	PA 19044	
200	Toll Brothers Corp Real Estate/Bldg	101 Witmer Road	Horsham 215-441-4400	PA 19044	
448	Betz Laboratories Inc Chemicals	4636 Somerton Road	Trevose 215-355-3300	PA 19047	
847	Union Central Life Insurance Co Insurance	4850 Street Road	Trevose 215-322-3000	PA 19049	
550	Franklin Mint Corp Retail/Merch	Baltimore Pike	Media 215-459-6000	PA 19063	
750	Sun Carriers Inc Transport	1400 N Providence Road	Media 215-891-7100	PA 19063	
400	Wawa Inc Retail/Merch	Baltimore Pike	Wawa 215-358-8000	PA 19063	
3817	Alco Standard Corp Conglomerate	825 Duportail Road PO Box 834	Valley Forge 215-296-8000	PA 19087	
NA	Paper Corp of America Paper/Forest Prd	1325 Morris Drive	Wayne 215-296-4470	PA 19087	

State / Province: Pennsylvania

Organizations Listed Geographically

Revenue ($ mil)	Organization/ Industry	Address	City / Phone	State/ Zip	Province/ Postcode
9744	Sun Co Inc Energy	100 Matsonford Road	Radnor 215-293-6000	PA 19087	
1100	Triangle Publications Inc Publishing/Com	4 Radnor Center	Radnor 215-293-8500	PA 19087	
500	Asplundh Tree Experts Inc Business Service	708 Blair Mill Road	Willow Grove 215-784-4200	PA 19090	
NA	Acme Markets Inc Retail/Food	124 N 15th Street	Philadelphia 215-568-3000	PA 19101	
1630	Corestates Financial Corp Banking	Broad & Chestnut Streets	Philadelphia 215-629-3869	PA 19101	
623	First Pennsylvania Corp Banking	1500 Market Street	Philadelphia 215-786-5000	PA 19101	
478	INA Life Insurance Co Insurance	1600 Arch Street	Philadelphia 215-241-4000	PA 19101	
3229	Philadelphia Electric Co Utility	2301 Market Street	Philadelphia 215-841-4000	PA 19101	
1500	Philadelphia National Bank Co Banking	Broad & Chestnut Streets	Philadelphia 215-629-3512	PA 19101	
4749	Smithkline Beckman Corp Drugs	One Franklin Plaza	Philadelphia 215-751-4000	PA 19101	
NA	United Engineers & Construction Inc Equipment	30 S 17th Street	Philadelphia 215-422-3000	PA 19101	
NA	Bell Telephone of Pennsylvania Telecom	One Parkway	Philadelphia 215-466-9900	PA 19102	
449	Comcast Corp Publishing/Com	1414 S Penn Square	Philadelphia 215-665-1700	PA 19102	
750	Continental Bancorp Inc Banking	1500 Market Street	Philadelphia 215-564-7000	PA 19102	
1500	IU International Corp Business Service	1500 Walnut Street	Philadelphia 302-571-5000	PA 19102	
1024	Pennwalt Corp Chemicals	Three Parkway	Philadelphia 215-587-7000	PA 19102	
10880	Bell Atlantic Corp Telecom	1600 Market Street	Philadelphia 215-963-6000	PA 19103	
NA	Bell Atlantic Enterprises Co Telecom	1880 JFK Blvd	Philadelphia 215-963-6666	PA 19103	
550	Binswanger Co Inc Real Estate/Bldg	1635 Market	Philadelphia 215-448-6000	PA 19103	
734	CDI Corp Business Service	10 Penn Center	Philadelphia 215-561-1750	PA 19103	
17889	CIGNA Corp Insurance	One Logan Square	Philadelphia 215-557-5000	PA 19103	
2689	Consolidated Rail Corp (CONRAIL) Railroad	Six Penn Center	Philadelphia 215-977-4000	PA 19103	
500	Day & Zimmermann Inc Consulting	1818 Market Street	Philadelphia 215-299-8000	PA 19103	
400	Delaware Management Investment Advisors Non-Bank Fin	10 Penn Center Plaza	Philadelphia 215-988-1333	PA 19103	
300	Hay Group Inc Consulting	229 S 18th Street Rittenhouse Square	Philadelphia 215-875-2300	PA 19103	
220	Janney Montgomery Scott Inc Securities	5 Penn Center Plaza	Philadelphia 215-665-6000	PA 19103	
879	Provident Mutual Life Ins Co of Phil Insurance	1600 Market Street	Philadelphia 215-636-5000	PA 19103	
425	Sun Distributors Inc Equipment	One Logan Square	Philadelphia 215-665-3650	PA 19103	
NA	Sun Refining & Marketing Div Energy	1801 Market Street	Philadelphia 215-977-3332	PA 19103	
580	University of Pennsylvania University	Administrative Bldg	Philadelphia 215-898-5000	PA 19104	
572	Federal Reserve Bank of Philadelphia Inc Federal Govt Fin	100 N Sixth Street	Philadelphia 215-574-6000	PA 19105	
1470	General Accident Insurance Co Insurance	436 Walnut Street	Philadelphia 215-625-1000	PA 19105	
2535	Rohm & Hass Co Chemicals	Independence Mall W	Philadelphia 215-592-3000	PA 19105	

State / Province: Pennsylvania

Organizations Listed Geographically

Revenue ($ mil)	Organization/ Industry	Address	City / Phone	State/ Zip	Province/ Postcode
4000	ARA Holding Co Business Service	1101 Market Street	Philadelphia 215-238-3000	PA 19107	
1320	Blue Cross Blue Shield of Pennsylvania Insurance	1333 Chestnut Street	Philadelphia 215-448-5000	PA 19107	
1646	Meritor Financial Group Inc Banking	1212 Market Street	Philadelphia 215-636-7500	PA 19107	
2692	Philadelphia, City of Local Govt	City Hall	Philadelphia 512-686-2181	PA 19107	
750	PMA Reinsurance Corp Insurance	925 Chestnut Street	Philadelphia 215-629-5000	PA 19107	
904	Strawbridge & Clothier Inc Retail/Merch	801 Market Street	Philadelphia 215-629-6000	PA 19107	
1300	Fidelcor Inc Banking	Broad & Walnut Streets	Philadelphia 215-985-6000	PA 19109	
620	Westmoreland Coal Co Energy	2500 Fidelity Bldg	Philadelphia 215-545-2500	PA 19109	
4726	Scott Paper Co Paper/Forest Prd	Scott Plaza	Philadelphia 215-522-5000	PA 19113	
350	Temple University University	Broad St & Montgomery Avenue	Philadelphia 215-787-7000	PA 19122	
NA	Mrs Paul's Kitchen Inc Food Processing	5830 Henry Avenue	Philadelphia 215-483-4000	PA 19128	
250	Tasty Baking Co Food/Lodging	2801 W Hunting Park Avenue	Philadelphia 215-221-8500	PA 19129	
656	Pep Boys/Manny Moe Jack Inc Retail/Merch	3111 W Allegheny	Philadelphia 215-229-9000	PA 19132	
1834	Crown Cork & Seal Co Packaging	9300 Ashton Road	Philadelphia 215-698-5100	PA 19136	
NA	Boeing Helicopters Inc Aerospace	Boeing Center	Philadelphia 215-591-2121	PA 19142	
1589	Penn Mutual Life Insurance Co Insurance	Independence Square	Philadelphia 215-625-5000	PA 19172	
486	Colonial Penn Insurance Co Insurance	19th & Market Streets	Philadelphia 215-988-8000	PA 19181	
275	Avtex Fibers Inc Apparel/Textiles	Cassatt Road Bldg 200	Berwyn Park 215-251-7700	PA 19312	
605	Lukens Inc Steel	50 S First Avenue	Coatesville 215-383-2000	PA 19320	
600	Intelligent Electronics Inc Comput/Off Equip	35 E Uwchian Avenue	Exton 215-524-1800	PA 19341	
250	Chemical Leaman Corp Transport	102 Pickering Way	Exton 215-363-4200	PA 19353	
60	Centocor Inc Business Service	244 Great Valley Parkway	Malvern 215-296-4488	PA 19355	
379	Shared Medical Systems Corp Comput/Off Equip	51 Valley Stream Parkway	Malvern 215-296-6300	PA 19355	
550	Victor Technologies Corp Electronics	395 Phoenixville Pike	Malvern 215-251-5000	PA 19355	
250	Vishay Intertechnology Corp Electronics	63 Lincoln Highway	Malvern 919-365-3800	PA 19355	
NA	Wyeth-Ayerst Laboratories Inc Drugs	31 Morehall Road	Frazer 215-644-8000	PA 19355	
250	Commodore International Comput/Off Equip	1200 Wilson Drive	West Chester 215-431-9100	PA 19380	
NA	SmithKline Beckman Animal Health Product Drugs	1600 Paoli Pike	West Chester 215-251-7400	PA 19380	
284	Safeguard Scientific Corp Telecom	630 Park Avenue	King of Prussia 215-265-4000	PA 19406	
425	UGI Corp Utility	460 N Gulf Road	King of Prussia 215-337-1000	PA 19406	
860	Universal Health Services Inc Health Care	367 S Gulph Road	King of Prussia 215-768-3300	PA 19406	
9902	Unisys Corp Comput/Off Equip	Township Line & Union Meeting Rd	Blue Bell 215-542-4011	PA 19422	
739	US Healthcare Inc Health Care	980 Jolly Road	Blue Bell 215-628-4800	PA 19422	

State / Province: Pennsylvania

Organizations Listed Geographically

Revenue ($ mil)	Organization/ Industry	Address	City / Phone	State/ Zip	Province/ Postcode
450	Harleysville Insurance Co Insurance	355 Maple Avenue	Harleysville 215-256-5000	PA 19438	
250	West Co Health Care	W Bridge Street	Phoenixville 215-935-4500	PA 19460	
200	Charter Power Systems Electronics	3043 Walton Road	Plymouth Meeting 215-828-9000	PA 19462	
350	Teleflex Corp Aerospace	155 S Limerick Road	Limerick 215-948-5100	PA 19468	
1732	Alco Industries Inc Manufacturing	Route 363 & Betzwood Bridge Betzwook Industrial Park	Valley Forge 215-666-0930	PA 19482	
1267	Certainteed Corp Building Mat	750 E Swedesford Road	Valley Forge 215-341-7000	PA 19482	
550	Vanguard Group Mutual Funds Inc Non-Bank Fin	PO Box 2600	Valley Forge 215-648-6000	PA 19482	
1155	National Home Life Assurance Co Insurance	Liberty Park	Valley Forge 215-648-5000	PA 19493	
NA	Coloric Corp Appliances/Furn	Washington & Heffner Streets	Topton 215-682-4211	PA 19562	
950	Meridian Bancorp Inc Banking	35 N Sixth Street	Reading 215-320-2000	PA 19601	
556	Carpenter Technology Corp Manufacturing	101 W Bern Street	Reading 215-371-2000	PA 19603	
265	Gilbert Associates Inc Real Estate/Bldg	Morgantown Road	Reading 215-775-2600	PA 19603	
2516	VF Corp Apparel/Textiles	1047 N Park Road	Wyomissing 215-378-1151	PA 19610	
656	Metropolitan Edison Co Utility	2800 Pottsville Pike	Reading 215-929-3601	PA 19640	
1000	Lumbermens Merchandising Inc Retail/Merch	137 W Wayne Avenue	Wayne 215-293-7000	PA 19807	

State / Province: Puerto Rico

Revenue ($ mil)	Organization/ Industry	Address	City / Phone	State/ Zip	Province/ Postcode
5000	Puerto Rico, Territory of United States State/Prov Govt	El Capitolio Avinda Munoz Revera	San Juan 809-724-2030	PR 00904	
750	Bacardi Import Corp Food Processing	PO Box 3549	San Juan 809-795-1560	PR 00936	
550	Puerto Rico Telephone Inc Utility	General P O Box 998	San Juan 809-782-8282	PR 00936	

State / Province: Rhode Island

Revenue ($ mil)	Organization/ Industry	Address	City / Phone	State/ Zip	Province/ Postcode
1358	Hasbro Inc Leisure Time	1027 Newport Avenue	Pawtucket 401-727-5000	RI 02862	
250	Playskool Inc Leisure Time	1027 Newport Avenue	Pawtuckett 401-727-5576	RI 02862	
232	Cross, A T Co Manufacturing	One Albion Road	Lincoln 401-333-1200	RI 02865	
NA	CVS Inc Retail/Merch	One CVS Drive	Woonsocket 401-765-1500	RI 02895	
NA	Narragansett Electric Co Utility	280 Melrose Street	Providence 401-941-1400	RI 02901	
550	Providence Journal Inc Publishing/Com	75 Fountain Street	Providence 401-277-7000	RI 02902	
3051	Fleet/Norstar Financial Corp Banking	50 Kennedy Plaza	Providence 401-278-5800	RI 02903	
1224	Nortek Inc Manufacturing	50 Kennedy Plaza	Providence 401-751-1600	RI 02903	
350	Old Stone Corp Banking	150 S Main Street	Providence 401-278-2000	RI 02903	
300	Rhode Island Hospital Trust Natl Bank Banking	One Hospital Trust Plaza	Providence 401-278-8000	RI 02903	
2569	Rhode Island, State of State/Prov Govt	State House	Providence 401-277-2000	RI 02903	
550	Righa Corp Insurance	2 Davol Square	Providence 401-421-4410	RI 02903	

State / Province: Rhode Island

Organizations Listed Geographically

Revenue ($ mil)	Organization/ Industry	Address	City / Phone	State/ Zip	Province/ Postcode
7286	Textron Inc Conglomerate	40 Westminster Street	Providence 401-421-2800	RI 02903	
500	Almac's Corp Retail/Food	1 Noyes Street E	East Providence 401-438-2700	RI 02916	
550	Williams, Roger Foods Inc Food Processing	2700 Plainfield Pike	Cranston 401-942-4000	RI 02920	
646	Amica Mutual Insurance Co Insurance	10 Weybosset Street	Providence 401-521-9100	RI 02940	
1000	Gilbane Building Co Real Estate/Bldg	7 Jackson Way	Providence 401-456-5800	RI 02940	

State / Province: South Carolina

Revenue ($ mil)	Organization/ Industry	Address	City / Phone	State/ Zip	Province/ Postcode
217	Policy Management Systems Inc Business Service	One Wilson Road	Blythewood 803-735-4000	SC 29016	
1083	SCANA (So Carolina Elec & Gas) Corp Utility	1426 Main Street	Columbia 803-748-3000	SC 29201	
166	University of South Carolina University	Administrative Bldg	Columbia 803-777-0411	SC 29208	
NA	Chem-Nuclear Systems Inc Business Service	220 Stoneridge Drive	Columbia 803-256-0450	SC 29210	
6425	South Carolina, State of State/Prov Govt	State House	Columbus 803-734-1000	SC 29211	
551	South Carolina National Corp Banking	1426 Main Street	Columbia 803-765-3000	SC 29226	
NA	Spartan Food Systems Inc Food/Lodging	Interstate 85 & Frontage Road	Spartanburg 803-579-1220	SC 29304	
1599	Sonoco Products Co Paper/Forest Prd	N Second Street	Hartsville 803-383-7000	SC 29550	
500	Delta Woodside Industries Inc Apparel/Textiles	233 N Main Street	Greenville 803-232-8300	SC 29601	
440	Multimedia Inc Publishing/Com	305 S Main Street	Greenville 803-298-4373	SC 29601	
401	Liberty Life Insurance Co Insurance	Hampton Blvd PO Box 789	Greenville 803-268-8111	SC 29602	
750	JPS Textile Group Inc Apparel/Textiles	555 N Pleasantberg Drive	Greenville 803-271-9919	SC 29607	
500	Builder Marts of America Inc Retail/Merch	1 Independence Pointe	Greenville 803-297-6101	SC 29615	
250	Greenwood Mills Corp Apparel/Textiles	Greenwood Bldg	Greenwood 803-229-2571	SC 29646	
234	Ryan's Family Steak Houses Inc Food/Lodging	405 Lancaster Avenue	Greer 803-879-1000	SC 29651	
1825	Springs Industries Inc Apparel/Textiles	205 N White Street	Fort Mill 803-547-2901	SC 29715	

State / Province: South Dakota

Revenue ($ mil)	Organization/ Industry	Address	City / Phone	State/ Zip	Province/ Postcode
1535	South Dakota, State of State/Prov Govt	State Capitol	Pierre 605-773-3011	SD 57501	

State / Province: Tennessee

Revenue ($ mil)	Organization/ Industry	Address	City / Phone	State/ Zip	Province/ Postcode
500	Murray Ohio Manufacturing Co Automotive	Franklin Road	Brentwood 615-373-6500	TN 37027	
220	Bradford, J C & Co Securities	330 Commerce Street	Nashville 615-748-9000	TN 37201	
1027	Nashville, City of Local Govt	City Hall	Nashville 615-259-6047	TN 37201	
782	Shoney's Inc Food/Lodging	1727 Elm Hill Pike	Nashville 615-361-5201	TN 37201	
463	Genesco Inc Apparel/Textiles	Genesco Park	Nashville 615-367-7000	TN 37202	
3093	Service Merchandise Co Inc Retail/Merch	2968 Foster Creighton Drive	Nashville 615-251-6666	TN 37202	

State / Province: Tennessee

Organizations Listed Geographically

Revenue ($ mil)	Organization/ Industry	Address	City / Phone	State/ Zip	Province/ Postcode
250	United Paperworkers Intl Union Membership Org	3340 Perimeter Hill Drive	Nashville 615-834-8590	TN	37202
4111	Hospital Corp of America Health Care	One Park Plaza	Nashville 615-327-9551	TN	37203
1250	Gillett Group Inc Food Processing	4400 Harding Road	Nashville 615-292-0045	TN	37205
1500	HealthTrust Corp Health Care	4525 Harding Road	Nashville 615-383-4444	TN	37205
1250	Ingram Industries Inc Personal Care	347 Redwood Drive	Nashville 615-793-5000	TN	37217
400	Sovereign Bank Corp Banking	One Commerce Place	Nashville 615-749-3333	TN	37219
8799	Tennessee, State of State/Prov Govt	State Capitol	Nashville 615-741-2001	TN	37219
500	Third National Bank Co Banking	201 Fourth Avenue N	Nashville 615-748-4000	TN	37219
699	First American Corp Banking	First American Center	Nashville 615-748-2100	TN	37237
741	American General Life & Accident Co Insurance	American General Plaza	Nashville 615-749-1000	TN	37250
NA	Magic Chef Co Appliances/Furn	740 King Edward Avenue	Cleveland 615-472-3371	TN	37311
600	Dixie Yarns Apparel/Textiles	1100 S Watkins Street	Chattanooga 615-698-2501	TN	37401
544	Constar International Manufacturing	835 Georgia Avenue	Chattanooga 615-267-2973	TN	37402
2050	Provident Life & Accident Ins Co Insurance	Fountain Square	Chattanooga 615-755-1011	TN	37402
500	Provident National Assurance Co Insurance	Fountain Square	Chattanooga 615-755-1011	TN	37402
250	Astec Industries Inc Equipment	4101 Jerome Avenue	Chattanooga 615-867-4210	TN	37407
750	Johnson Coca Cola Bottling Inc Beverage	PO Box 530	Chattanooga 615-899-3449	TN	37421
1100	Mills, Olan Inc Business Service	4325 Amnicola Highway	Chattanooga 615-622-5141	TN	37422
550	Austin Co Inc Food Processing	206 Cutler Street Corner Cutler & Hall	Greeneville 615-638-4124	TN	37743
NA	Martin Marietta Energy Systems Inc Manufacturing	800 Oak Ridge Turnpike	Oak Ridge 615-574-1000	TN	37831
5322	Tennessee Valley Authority Inc Utility	400 W Summit Street	Knoxville 615-632-2101	TN	37902
NA	Sea Ray Corp Leisure Time	2600 Sea Ray Blvd	Knoxville 615-522-4181	TN	37914
194	University of Tennessee University	Cumberland Avenue	Knoxville 615-974-2591	TN	37996
500	Auto Zone Corp Retail/Merch	3030 Poplar Avenue	Memphis 901-325-4600	TN	38101
4400	Malone & Hyde Inc Retail/Food	3030 Poplar Avenue	Memphis 901-325-4200	TN	38101
1100	Memphis Light Gas & Water Inc Utility	220 S Main Street	Memphis 901-528-4151	TN	38101
621	First Tennessee National Corp Banking	165 Madison Avenue	Memphis 901-523-5630	TN	38103
1439	Memphis, City of Local Govt	City Hall 125 N Mid America Mall	Memphis 901-576-6000	TN	38103
550	Econocom USA Inc Retail/Merch	4385 Poplar Avenue	Memphis 901-762-9200	TN	38117
1597	Holiday (Inn) Corp Food/Lodging	1023 Cherry Road	Memphis 901-762-8600	TN	38117
275	Baddaur Inc Apparel/Textiles	4300 New Getwell Street	Memphis 901-365-8880	TN	38118
1500	Dunavant Enterprises Inc Apparel/Textiles	3595 New Getwell Road	Memphis 901-369-1500	TN	38118
1583	Holly Farms Corp Retail/Food	1755-D Lynnfield Road	Memphis 901-761-3610	TN	38119

State / Province: Tennessee

Organizations Listed Geographically

Revenue ($ mil)	Organization/ Industry	Address	City / Phone	State/ Zip	Province/ Postcode
3883	Federal Express Corp Business Service	2005 Corporate Avenue	Memphis 901-369-3600	TN 38132	
500	Dobbs Houses Inc Food/Lodging	5100 Poplar Avenue	Memphis 901-766-3600	TN 38137	
NA	Dover Elevator International Inc Equipment	6750 Poplar Avenue	Memphis 601-342-4300	TN 38138	
NA	Plough Inc Personal Care	3030 Jackson Avenue	Memphis 901-320-2801	TN 38151	
81	Memphis State University University	Administrative Bldg	Memphis 901-454-2234	TN 38152	
450	TBC Corp Retail/Merch	4770 Hickory Hill Road	Memphis 901-363-8030	TN 38181	

State / Province: Texas

Revenue ($ mil)	Organization/ Industry	Address	City / Phone	State/ Zip	Province/ Postcode
565	NCH Corp Chemicals	2727 Chemsearch Blvd PO Box 152170	Irving 214-438-0211	TX 75015	
550	Murata North America Inc Electronics	5560 Tennyson	Plano 214-403-3300	TX 75024	
909	Zale Corp Retail/Merch	901 W Walnut Hill Lane	Irving 214-580-4670	TX 75038	
1000	Epic Healthcare Group Inc Health Care	433 E Los Colinas Blvd Waterway Tower	Irving 214-869-0707	TX 75039	
250	Southland Financial Corp Non-Bank Fin	5215 N O'Connor Blvd	Irving 214-828-7011	TX 75039	
275	Recognition Equipment Inc Comput/Off Equip	2701 E Grauwyler Road	Irving 214-579-6000	TX 75061	
500	Gifford Hill & Co Inc Building Mat	300 E John W Carpenter Freeway	Irving 214-258-7000	TX 75062	
250	Michaels Stores Inc Retail/Merch	5931 Campus Circle Drive	Irving 214-580-8242	TX 75063	
429	Eljer Industries Inc Manufacturing	901 10th Street	Plano 214-881-7177	TX 75074	
340	DSC Communications Corp Consulting	1000 Coit Road	Plano 214-519-3000	TX 75075	
NA	Electrospace Systems Inc Electronics	1301 E Collins Blvd	Richardson 214-470-2000	TX 75083	
500	Minyard Food Stores Inc Retail/Food	777 Freeport	Coppel 214-462-8700	TX 75109	
NA	Jetco Chemicals Inc Chemicals	200 N 13th Street	Corsicana 214-872-3011	TX 75110	
2512	Central & South West Corp Utility	2121 San Jacinto Street	Dallas 214-754-1000	TX 75201	
NA	Chaco Energy Co Energy	400 N Olive Street	Dallas 214-812-8200	TX 75201	
859	Dallas, City of Local Govt	City Hall	Dallas 214-670-4054	TX 75201	
3942	Dresser Industries Inc Oil Service	1600 Pacific Avenue	Dallas 214-740-6000	TX 75201	
2739	Enserch Corp Utility	300 S St Paul	Dallas 214-651-8700	TX 75201	
NA	Enserch Exploration Inc Energy	1817 Wood Street	Dallas 214-748-1110	TX 75201	
4839	Halliburton Co Oil Service	3600 Lincoln Plaza 500 N Akard Street	Dallas 214-978-2600	TX 75201	
386	Holly Corp Automotive	717 N Harwood Street	Dallas 214-979-0210	TX 75201	
600	JM Petroleum Corp Energy	2323 Bryan Plaza of Americas	Dallas 214-953-0330	TX 75201	
1250	LaSalle Energy Corp Energy	300 Crescent Court Suite 1320	Dallas 214-871-5333	TX 75201	
1500	Lincoln Property Co Real Estate/Bldg	500 N Akard	Dallas 214-740-3300	TX 75201	
NA	Lone Star Gas Co Energy	301 S Harwood Street	Dallas 214-741-3711	TX 75201	

State / Province: Texas

Organizations Listed Geographically

Revenue ($ mil)	Organization/ Industry	Address	City / Phone	State/ Zip	Province/ Postcode
7325	LTV Corp Steel	2001 Ross Avenue	Dallas 214-979-7711	TX 75201	
601	Maxus Energy Corp Energy	717 N Harwood Street	Dallas 214-953-2000	TX 75201	
1774	MCORP Inc Banking	500 Dallas Bldg	Dallas 214-698-5000	TX 75201	
1221	National Gypsum Co Building Mat	4500 Lincoln Plaza	Dallas 214-740-4500	TX 75201	
2900	NCNB Texas National Bank (Republic Bank) Banking	1800 Republic Bank Bldg 326 N St Paul	Dallas 214-977-4000	TX 75201	
1000	Placid Oil Co Energy	3900 Thanksgiving	Dallas 214-741-3081	TX 75201	
500	Snyder General Corp Manufacturing	2001 Ross Avenue	Dallas 214-979-3100	TX 75201	
NA	Texas Oil & Gas Corp Energy	1700 Pacific Avenue	Dallas 214-954-2000	TX 75201	
4154	Texas Utilities Co Utility	2001 Bryan Tower	Dallas 214-653-4600	TX 75201	
NA	Texas Utilities Electric Co Utility	2001 Bryan Tower	Dallas 214-812-1200	TX 75201	
NA	Texas Utilities Mining Co Metals/Mining	400 N Olive Street	Dallas 214-812-5600	TX 75201	
275	Trailways Inc Transport	901 Main Street	Dallas 214-744-6500	TX 75201	
1500	Trammell Crow Corp Real Estate/Bldg	3500 LTV Center 2001 Ross Avenue	Dallas 214-742-2000	TX 75201	
665	Tyler Corp Steel	3200 San Jacinto Tower	Dallas 214-754-7800	TX 75201	
750	Dallas County Government Local Govt	411 Elm Street	Dallas 214-749-8011	TX 75202	
800	Employers of Texas Insurance Co Insurance	1301 Young Street	Dallas 214-760-6100	TX 75202	
1258	Federal Reserve Bank of Dallas Inc Federal Govt Fin	400 S Akard Street	Dallas 214-651-6111	TX 75202	
750	HCB Contractors Inc Real Estate/Bldg	1401 Elm Street Suite 4600	Dallas 214-747-8541	TX 75202	
1000	Hunt Consolidated Oil Co Energy	1401 Elm Street	Dallas 214-744-7911	TX 75202	
750	Media News Group Inc Publishing/Com	1101 Pacific Avenue	Dallas 214-720-5800	TX 75202	
300	Missouri Kansas Texas Railroad Co Railroad	701 Commerce Street	Dallas 214-651-6706	TX 75202	
1500	Sammons Enterprises Inc Telecom	403 S Akard	Dallas 214-670-9790	TX 75202	
3000	SIPCO (Swift Independent Corp) Food Processing	1401 Elm Street	Dallas 214-573-2333	TX 75202	
9000	Southland Corp Retail/Food	2828 N Haskell Avenue	Dallas 214-828-7011	TX 75204	
275	TIC United Corp Transport	4645 N Central	Dallas 214-559-0580	TX 75205	
2635	American Petrofina Inc Energy	Fina Plaza	Dallas 214-750-2400	TX 75206	
600	Lear Petroleum Corp Energy	6688 N Central Expressway	Dallas 214-363-6085	TX 75206	
550	Bright Banc Savings Assn Inc Savings & Loan	2355 Stemmons Freeway	Dallas 214-638-9500	TX 75207	
1001	Trinity Industries Inc Manufacturing	2525 Stemmons Freeway	Dallas 214-631-4420	TX 75207	
550	Vantage Companies Inc Real Estate/Bldg	2777 Stemmons Freeway	Dallas 214-631-0600	TX 75207	
250	Braniff Airline Corp Airline	7701 Lemmon Avenue	Dallas 214-358-6011	TX 75209	
NA	Campbell Taggert Inc Food Processing	6211 Lemmon Avenue	Dallas 214-358-9211	TX 75209	
1460	Centex Corp Business Service	3333 Lee Parkway	Dallas 214-559-6500	TX 75219	

State / Province: Texas

Organizations Listed Geographically

Revenue ($ mil)	Organization/ Industry	Address	City / Phone	State/ Zip	Province/ Postcode
1601	Southwestern Life Insurance Co Insurance	PO Box 2699	Dallas 214-954-7111	TX 75221	
250	International Telecharge Corp Telecom	108 S Akard	Dallas 214-744-0240	TX 75222	
1000	MorningStar Foods Inc Food Processing	5956 Sherry Lane	Dallas 214-360-4700	TX 75225	
357	Redman Industries Inc Building Mat	2550 Walnut Hill Lane Redman Plaza E	Dallas 214-353-3600	TX 75229	
4844	Electronic Data Systems Corp Comput/Off Equip	7171 Forest Lane	Dallas 214-661-6000	TX 75230	
750	Paragon Group Inc Real Estate/Bldg	7557 Rambler Road Suite 1200	Dallas 214-891-2000	TX 75231	
1570	Sun Energy Partners LP Inc Energy	5656 Blackwell	Dallas 214-890-6207	TX 75231	
3000	Sun Exploration Corp Energy	5656 Blackwell	Dallas 214-890-6000	TX 75231	
500	Club Corp of America Leisure Time	2711 LBJ Freeway Suite 800	Dallas 214-243-6191	TX 75234	
NA	General Aviation Services Co Business Service	2075 Diplomat	Dallas 214-406-2000	TX 75234	
2838	Southmark Corp Real Estate/Bldg	1601 LBJ Freeway	Dallas 214-241-8787	TX 75234	
400	Sunbelt Savings Assn Inc Savings & Loan	4901 LBJ Freeway	Dallas 214-980-4441	TX 75234	
500	Lone Star Technologies Manufacturing	2200 W Mockingbird Lane	Dallas 214-352-3981	TX 75235	
NA	Pepsico Foods International Food Processing	400 Frito Lay Tower Exchange Park	Dallas 214-956-3700	TX 75235	
860	Southwest Airlines Co Airline	PO Box 37611	Love Field 214-353-6100	TX 75235	
300	Blockbuster Entertainment Inc Retail/Merch	10460 Miller Road	Dallas 214-341-7700	TX 75238	
471	American Healthcare Management Health Care	14160 Dallas Parkway	Dallas 214-387-9181	TX 75240	
323	Atmos Energy Corp Utility	5430 LBJ Freeway	Dallas 214-934-9227	TX 75240	
285	Chili's Inc Food/Lodging	6820 LBJ Freeway	Dallas 214-980-9917	TX 75240	
323	Dallas Corp Building Mat	6750 LBJ Freeway	Dallas 214-233-6611	TX 75240	
750	First Texas Financial Corp Savings & Loan	14951 Dallas Parkway	Dallas 214-960-4500	TX 75240	
250	Keystone Consolidated Industries Inc Manufacturing	5430 LBJ Freeway	Dallas 214-458-0028	TX 75240	
450	Motel 6 Lmtd Ptnrship Food/Lodging	14651 Dallas Parkway	Dallas 214-386-6161	TX 75240	
14833	Penney, J C Co Retail/Merch	14841 N Dallas Parkway	Dalla 214-591-1000	TX 75240	
250	Pratt Hotel Corp Food/Lodging	13455 Noel Road	Dallas 214-386-9777	TX 75240	
500	Republic Health Services Inc Health Care	14951 Dallas Parkway	Dallas 214-851-3100	TX 75240	
1000	Valhi Corp Food Processing	5430 LBJ Freeway	Dallas 214-386-4110	TX 75240	
500	Hallmark Electronics Corp Retail/Merch	11333 Pagemille	Dallas 214-343-5000	TX 75243	
1000	Cullum Companies Retail/Food	14303 Inwood Road	Dallas 214-661-9700	TX 75244	
660	El Paso Products Co Inc Food Processing	5005 LBJ Freeway Occidental Tower	Dallas 915-333-7200	TX 75244	
500	Austin Industries Inc Real Estate/Bldg	2949 Stemmons Freeway	Dallas 214-630-5100	TX 75247	
1137	Commercial Metals Co Manufacturing	7800 Stemmons Freeway	Dallas 214-689-4300	TX 75247	
NA	Jimmy Dean Meat Co Food Processing	1341 W Mockingbird Lane	Dallas 214-638-1190	TX 75247	

State / Province: Texas

Organizations Listed Geographically

Revenue ($ mil)	Organization/ Industry	Address	City / Phone	State/ Zip	Province/ Postcode
635	Texas Industries Inc Building Mat	8100 Carpenter Freeway	Dallas 214-637-3100	TX 75247	
NA	Southwestern Bell Mobile Systems Inc Telecom	17330 Preston Road	Dallas 214-733-2000	TX 75252	
5394	Kimberly Clark Corp Paper/Forest Prd	PO Box 619100 DFW Airport Station	Dallas 214-830-1200	TX 75261	
385	Belo, A H Corp Publishing/Com	Communications Center	Dallas 214-745-8730	TX 75265	
500	Dr Pepper/Seven Up Inc Beverage	5523 E Mockingbird Lane	Dallas 214-824-0331	TX 75265	
1235	Lomas & Nettleton Financial Corp Non-Bank Fin	2001 Bryan Tower PO Box 655644	Dallas 214-746-7111	TX 75265	
6295	Texas Instruments Inc Electronics	13500 N Central Expressway	Dallas 214-995-2011	TX 75265	
1733	Associates Corp of America Inc Non-Bank Fin	250 Carpenter Freeway	Dallas 214-659-4000	TX 75266	
1443	E-Systems Inc Electronics	6250 LBJ Freeway	Dallas 214-661-1000	TX 75266	
191	Southern Union Co Utility	Renaissance Tower	Dallas 214-748-8511	TX 75270	
750	Lennox International Corp Instruments	PO Box 809000	Dallas 214-980-6000	TX 75380	
340	TGI Friday's Inc Food/Lodging	14665 Midway Road	Dallas 214-450-5400	TX 75380	
400	Home Interiors & Gifts Inc Retail/Merch	4550 Spring Valley Road	Dallas 214-386-1000	TX 75381	
550	Grocery Supply Co Inc Retail/Food	130 Hillcrest Loop 301	Sulphur Springs 214-885-7621	TX 75482	
500	GSC Enterprises Inc Retail/Food	130 Hillcrest	Sulphur Springs 214-885-7621	TX 75482	
550	Pilgrams Pride Corp Food Processing	110 S Texas Street	Pittsburg 214-856-7901	TX 75686	
750	Brookshire Grocery Co Retail/Food	1600 SW Route 323	Tyler 214-534-3000	TX 75703	
550	Three Beall Brothers Inc Retail/Merch	1237 E Rusk Street	Jacksonville 214-586-9823	TX 75766	
1774	Temple Inland Inc Paper/Forest Prd	303 S Temple Drive	Diboll 409-829-1313	TX 75941	
250	Arlington, City of Local Govt	City Hall	Arlington 817-459-6121	TX 76010	
86	University of Texas at Arlington University	800 S Cooper Street	Arlington 817-273-2011	TX 76019	
550	E-Z Serve Inc Retail/Merch	4001 Airport Freeway	Bedford 817-267-1777	TX 76021	
747	Harken Energy Corp Energy	4001 Airport Freeway	Bedford 817-354-9944	TX 76021	
NA	Bell Helicopter Textron Inc Aerospace	600 E Hearst Blvd	Hearst 817-280-2011	TX 76053	
400	Chaparral Steel Steel	300 Ward Road	Midlothian 214-775-8241	TX 76065	
297	Gearhart Industries Inc Energy	1100 Everman Road PO Box 1936	Fort Worth 817-293-1300	TX 76101	
300	Justin Industries Inc Manufacturing	2821 W 7th Street	Fort Worth 817-336-5125	TX 76101	
500	White Swan Co Retail/Food	2700 Handley-Ederville Road	Fort Worth 817-284-4844	TX 76101	
4701	Burlington Northern Inc Railroad	3800 Continental Plaza	Fort Worth 817-878-2000	TX 76102	
338	Fort Worth, City of Local Govt	City Hall 1000 Throckmorton Street	Fort Worth 817-870-6117	TX 76102	
600	Intertan Corp Retail/Merch	2000 Two Tandy Center	Fort Worth 817-332-7181	TX 76102	
550	Keith, Ben E Co Retail/Food	600 E Nineth Street	Fort Worth 817-332-9171	TX 76102	
550	Kendavis Holding Co Inc Equipment	106 W Sixth Street	Fort Worth 817-335-5101	TX 76102	

State / Province: Texas

Organizations Listed Geographically

Revenue ($ mil)	Organization/ Industry	Address	City / Phone	State/ Zip	Province/ Postcode
415	Pier 1 Imports Inc Retail/Merch	301 Commerce Street	Fort Worth 817-878-8000	TX 76102	
NA	Radio Shack Inc Retail/Merch	1600 One Tandy Center	Fort Worth 817-390-3011	TX 76102	
3794	Tandy Corp Comput/Off Equip	1800 One Tandy Center	Fort Worth 817-390-3700	TX 76102	
NA	Tandy Electronics Manufacturing Inc Electronics	918 One Tandy Center	Fort Worth 817-390-3689	TX 76102	
445	Texas American Bancshares Inc Banking	500 Throckmorton Street	Fort Worth 817-884-4040	TX 76102	
209	Western Co of North America Energy	6000 Western Place	Fort Worth 817-731-5100	TX 76107	
34	San Juan Basin Royalty Trust Inc Non-Bank Fin	PO Box 2604	Fort Worth 817-338-8607	TX 76113	
366	TNP Texas New Mexico Power Co Utility	4100 International Plaza	Fort Worth 817-731-0099	TX 76113	
8824	AMR (American Airlines) Corp Airline	4200 American Blvd	Ft Worth 817-355-1234	TX 76155	
300	Tarrant County Government Local Govt	100 E Weatherford	Ft Worth 817-334-1441	TX 76196	
94	University of North Texas University	Administrative Bldg	Denton 817-565-2000	TX 76203	
1100	Affiliated Foods Inc Retail/Food	100 Matt Gibbs Drive	Keller 817-281-4417	TX 76248	
2000	McLane Co Inc Retail/Food	3407 S 31st Street	Temple 817-778-7500	TX 76502	
225	Sterling Electronics Corp Electronics	4201 SW Freeway	Houston 713-623-6600	TX 77001	
141	Battle Mountain Corp Metals/Mining	333 Clay Street 42nd Floor	Houston 713-227-6330	TX 77002	
4258	Cooper Industries Inc Equipment	First City Tower 1001 Fannin Street	Houston 713-739-5400	TX 77002	
42	Criterion Investment Management Inc Non-Bank Fin	1000 Louisiana Suite 600	Houston 713-751-2400	TX 77002	
5708	Enron Corp Utility	1400 Smith Street	Houston 713-853-6161	TX 77002	
865	First City Bancorp of Texas Inc Banking	400 First City Tower 1001 Fannin Street	Houston 713-658-6873	TX 77002	
1000	First Interstate Bank of Texas Banking	1000 Louisiana Street	Houston 713-224-6611	TX 77002	
400	Gordon Jewelry Corp Retail/Merch	820 Fannin Street	Houston 713-222-8080	TX 77002	
1200	Harris County Government Local Govt	1001 Preston Road	Houston 713-221-5000	TX 77002	
3649	Houston Industries Inc Utility	611 Walker	Houston 713-228-2474	TX 77002	
500	Houston Lighting & Power Co Utility	611 Walker Street	Houston 713-229-7267	TX 77002	
250	Howell Corp Energy	1010 Lamar	Houston 713-658-4000	TX 77002	
21000	Shell Oil Co Energy	One Shell Plaza	Houston 713-241-6161	TX 77002	
605	Southdown Inc Building Mat	1200 Smith Street Suite 2200	Houston 713-658-8921	TX 77002	
600	Sterling Chemical Corp Chemicals	333 Clay Street	Houston 713-650-3700	TX 77002	
250	Tejas Gas Corp Energy	333 Clay Street	Houston 713-658-0509	TX 77002	
13591	Tenneco Inc Conglomerate	Tenneco Bldg PO Box 2511	Houston 713-757-2131	TX 77002	
NA	Texaco Refining & Marketing Inc Energy	1111 Rusk Avenue	Houston 713-650-4000	TX 77002	
NA	Texaco USA Inc Retail/Merch	1111 Rusk Avenue	Houston 713-650-4000	TX 77002	
8752	Texas Air Corp (Continental Airlines) Airline	333 Clay Street Suite 4040	Houston 713-658-9588	TX 77002	

State / Province: Texas

Organizations Listed Geographically

Revenue ($ mil)	Organization/ Industry	Address	City / Phone	State/ Zip	Province/ Postcode
1600	Texas Commerce Bancshares Inc Banking	600 Travis Street	Houston 713-236-4865	TX 77002	
1000	Utility Fuels Co Metals/Mining	611 Walker Street	Houston 713-629-3001	TX 77002	
211	University of Houston University	4800 Calhoun Blvd	Houston 713-749-1011	TX 77004	
1262	Panhandle Eastern Corp Utility	3000 Bissonnet Avenue	Houston 713-664-3401	TX 77005	
1073	National Convenience Stores Inc Retail/Food	100 Waugh Drive	Houston 713-863-2200	TX 77007	
650	Big Three Industries Inc Oil Service	3535 W 12th Street	Houston 713-868-0333	TX 77008	
474	Stewart & Stevenson Services Inc Manufacturing	2707 North Loop W	Houston 713-868-7700	TX 77008	
825	Vanguard Energy Corp Energy	1111 North Loop W	Houston 713-880-8750	TX 77008	
4696	Lyondell Petrochemical Corp Chemicals	1221 McKinney Avenue	Houston 713-652-7200	TX 77010	
300	Sarofim, Fayez Investment Mgt Co Non-Bank Fin	2 Houston Center	Houston 713-654-4484	TX 77010	
3823	American General Corp Insurance	2929 Allen Parkway	Houston 713-522-1111	TX 77019	
NA	Continental Airlines Corp Airline	2929 Allen Parkway	Houston 713-630-5000	TX 77019	
616	Service Corp International Business Service	1929 Allen Parkway	Houston 713-522-5141	TX 77019	
1880	Variable Annuity Life Insurance Co Insurance	2929 Allen Parkway	Houston 713-526-5251	TX 77019	
500	Brown & Root Inc Real Estate/Bldg	4100 Clinton Drive	Houston 713-676-3011	TX 77020	
1000	Grocers Supply Co Inc Retail/Food	3131 E Holcombe	Houston 713-747-5000	TX 77021	
2316	Baker Hughes Co Oil Service	3900 Essex Lane	Houston 713-439-8600	TX 77027	
478	CRS Sirrine Inc Consulting	1177 West Loop S	Houston 713-552-2000	TX 77027	
463	Quanex Corp Manufacturing	1900 West Loop S Suite 1500	Houston 713-961-4600	TX 77027	
736	US Home Corp Real Estate/Bldg	1800 West Loop S	Houston 713-877-2311	TX 77027	
550	Baroid Corp Oil Service	3000 North Belt E	Houston 713-987-4000	TX 77032	
1100	NL Industries Inc Oil Service	3000 North Belt	Houston 713-987-4000	TX 77032	
502	Cameron Iron Works Inc Oil Service	13013 Northwest Freeway	Houston 713-939-2211	TX 77040	
1500	Gulf States Toyota Corp Automotive	7701 Wilshire Place Drive	Houston 713-744-3300	TX 77040	
346	Keystone International Inc Manufacturing	9600 W Gulf Drive	Houston 713-466-1176	TX 77040	
750	Safeway Texas Corp Retail/Food	4301 Windfern	Houston 713-460-5000	TX 77041	
825	Granada Corp Food Processing	10900 Richmond Avenue	Houston 713-783-1310	TX 77042	
NA	Western Atlas International Inc Oil Service	10001 Richmond Avenue	Houston 713-266-5700	TX 77042	
1100	Cain Chemical Corp Chemicals	11 Greenwood Plaza	Houston 713-622-2246	TX 77046	
8187	Coastal Corp Energy	9 Greenway Plaza Coastal Tower	Houston 713-877-1400	TX 77046	
1000	Celeron Corp Chemicals	2400 MCorp Plaza	Houston 713-750-4552	TX 77053	
99	American Capital Corp Non-Bank Fin	2800 Post Oak Blvd	Houston 713-993-0500	TX 77056	
NA	Occidental Chemical Corp Chemicals	1980 Post Oak Road	Houston 713-840-7100	TX 77056	

State / Province: Texas

Organizations Listed Geographically

Revenue ($ mil)	Organization/ Industry	Address	City / Phone	State/ Zip	Province/ Postcode
1100	Raymond International Inc Real Estate/Bldg	2801 Post Oaks Blvd	Houston 713-623-1500	TX 77056	
250	Rowan Corp Energy	5051 Westheimer	Houston 713-621-7800	TX 77056	
NA	Transco Coal Co Metals/Mining	2800 Post Oak Blvd	Houston 713-439-2000	TX 77056	
2774	Transco Energy Co Utility	2800 Post Oak Blvd	Houston 713-439-2000	TX 77056	
NA	Transcontinental Gas Pipeline Corp Energy	2800 Post Oak Blvd	Houston 713-439-2000	TX 77056	
1152	Union Texas Petroleum Inc Energy	1330 Post Oak Blvd	Houston 713-623-6544	TX 77056	
300	Guardian Savings (Texas) Assn Inc Savings & Loan	5847 San Felipe	Houston 713-784-4413	TX 77057	
NA	Santa Fe Energy Corp Utility	1616 S Voss Road	Houston 713-783-2401	TX 77057	
NA	Lockheed Engineering & Sciences Div Consulting	2400 Nasa Road	Houston 713-333-5411	TX 77058	
1301	Gibraltar Savings (Texas) Assn Inc Savings & Loan	13401 North Freeway	Houston 713-872-3100	TX 77060	
12100	Pemex (Petroleos Mexicos SA) Energy	3600 S Gessner	Houston 713-978-7974	TX 77063	
2066	Compaq Computer Corp Comput/Off Equip	20555 FM 149	Houston 713-370-0670	TX 77070	
263	General Homes Corp Real Estate/Bldg	7322 SW Freeway	Houston 713-270-4177	TX 77074	
4385	SYSCO Corp Business Service	1390 Enclave Parkway	Houston 713-877-1122	TX 77077	
141	Global Marine Inc Energy	777 N Eldridge Road	Houston 713-596-5100	TX 77079	
1000	Randalls Food Markets Inc Retail/Food	16000 Barkers Point Lane Suite 200	Houston 713-497-8191	TX 77079	
781	Vista Chemical Corp Chemicals	15990 N Barker's Landing Road	Houston 713-531-3200	TX 77079	
NA	Meridian Oil Inc Energy	2919 Allen Parkway	Houston 713-831-1600	TX 77091	
NA	BJ Titan & BJ Services Inc Oil Service	5500 NW Central Drive	Houston 713-439-8600	TX 77092	
450	University Savings Assn Inc Savings & Loan	1160 Dairy Ashford	Houston 713-596-1000	TX 77096	
250	Smith International Inc Transport	17640 Hardy Street	Houston 713-443-3370	TX 77205	
1100	Huffington, Roy M Inc Energy	1100 Louisiana	Houston 713-651-1600	TX 77210	
1000	Tauber Oil Co Energy	55 Waugh Drive	Houston 713-869-8700	TX 77210	
194	Zapata Corp Energy	Zapata Tower PO Box 4240	Houston 713-226-6000	TX 77210	
436	San Jacinto Savings Assn Inc Savings & Loan	6800 West Loop S	Houston 713-661-7000	TX 77235	
250	Entertainment Marketing Inc Comput/Off Equip	10310 Harwin Drive	Houston 713-995-4433	TX 77242	
333	Anadarko Petroleum Corp Energy	16855 Northchase	Houston 713-875-1101	TX 77251	
NA	Enron Oil & Gas Co Energy	1400 Smith Street	Houston 713-853-6161	TX 77251	
1434	Houston, City of Local Govt	City Hall	Houston 713-222-3141	TX 77251	
2289	Perimian Partners Ltd Energy	2500 City West Blvd	Houston 713-787-2222	TX 77251	
NA	Sonat Exploration Co Energy	PO Box 1513	Houston 713-940-4000	TX 77251	
NA	Stingray Pipeline Co Transport	3000 Bissonnet	Houston 713-627-5400	TX 77251	
2274	Pennzoil Co Energy	Pennzoil Place	Houston 713-546-4000	TX 77252	

State / Province: Texas

Organizations Listed Geographically

Revenue ($ mil)	Organization/ Industry	Address	City / Phone	State/ Zip	Province/ Postcode
3481	Texas Eastern Corp Utility	1221 McKinney Street	Houston 713-759-3131	TX 77252	
2067	Browning Ferris Industries Inc Business Service	757 N Eldridge	Houston 713-870-8100	TX 77253	
72	Houston Community College University	22 Waugh Drive	Houston 713-868-0700	TX 77270	
562	Mitchell Energy & Development Corp Energy	2001 Timberloch Place	The Woodlands 713-363-5500	TX 77380	
NA	Texaco Chemical Co Chemicals	4800 Fournace Place	Bellaire 713-666-8000	TX 77401	
250	Imperial Holly Corp Manufacturing	1 Imperial Square	Sugar Land 713-491-9181	TX 77487	
250	Team Inc Machinery	1019 S Hood	Alvin 713-331-6154	TX 77511	
934	American National Insurance Co Insurance	One Moody Plaza	Galveston 409-763-4461	TX 77550	
1415	Gulf States Utilities Co Utility	350 Pine Street	Beaumont 409-838-6631	TX 77701	
392	Texas A & M University University	Administrative Bldg	College Station 713-845-3211	TX 77843	
750	Builders Square Inc Retail/Merch	100 Crossroads	San Antonio 512-731-0500	TX 78201	
420	Church's Fried Chicken Inc Food/Lodging	355 Spencer Lane	San Antonio 512-735-9392	TX 78201	
2250	Butt, H E Grocery Co Retail/Food	646 S Main Street	San Antonio 512-270-8000	TX 78204	
330	Bexar County Government Local Govt	Bexar County Courthouse	San Antonio 512-220-2496	TX 78205	
629	Valero Energy Corp Energy	530 McCullough Avenue PO Box 500	San Antonio 512-246-2000	TX 78215	
3300	Associated Milk Producers Inc Food Processing	6609 Blanco Road	San Antonio 512-340-9100	TX 78216	
600	Harte Hanks Communications Inc Publishing/Com	Harte Hanks Tower 200 Concord Plaza Drive	San Antonio 512-344-8000	TX 78216	
500	Zachry, H B Co Inc Real Estate/Bldg	527 Logwood	San Antonio 512-922-1213	TX 78221	
1804	Diamond Shamrock R & M Corp Energy	9830 Colonnade Blvd	San Antonio 512-641-6800	TX 78230	
254	Luby's Cafeterias Inc Food/Lodging	2211 NE Loop 410	San Antonio 512-654-9000	TX 78265	
400	Datapoint Corp Comput/Off Equip	9725 Datapoint Drive	San Antonio 512-699-7000	TX 78284	
1202	San Antonio, City of Local Govt	City Hall	San Antonio 512-299-7060	TX 78285	
1172	Tesoro Petroleum Corp Energy	8700 Tesoro Drive PO Box 17536	San Antonio 512-828-8484	TX 78286	
398	USAA Financial Services Inc Insurance	9800 Fredericksburg Road USAA Bldg	San Antonio 512-498-7290	TX 78288	
1100	City Public Service Inc Utility	145 Nevarro Street	San Antonio 512-227-3211	TX 78296	
300	San Antonio Savings Assn Inc Savings & Loan	601 NW Loop 410	San Antonio 512-340-7272	TX 78296	
812	Central Power & Light Co Utility	120 N Chaparral Street	Corpus Christi 512-881-5300	TX 78403	
250	Corpus Christi, City of Local Govt	City Hall	Corpus Christi 512-880-3100	TX 78469	
NA	AMP Packaging Systems Inc Electronics	700 E Jeffrey Way	Round Rock 512-244-5110	TX 78664	
62	Southwest Texas State University University	Administrative Bldg	San Marcos 512-245-2111	TX 78666	
450	Texas Teachers Retirement Fund Non-Bank Fin	1001 Trinity Street	Austin 512-397-6460	TX 78701	
35579	Texas, State of State/Prov Govt	State Capitol	Austin 512-463-4630	TX 78711	
431	University of Texas University	University Station	Austin 512-741-3434	TX 78712	

State / Province: Texas

Organizations Listed Geographically

Revenue ($ mil)	Organization/ Industry	Address	City / Phone	State/ Zip	Province/ Postcode
750	Tracor Inc Electronics	6500 Tracor Lane	Austin 512-926-2800	TX 78725	
258	Dell Computer Corp Comput/Off Equip	9505 Arboretum Blvd	Austin 512-338-4400	TX 78759	
400	Healthcare International Inc Health Care	9737 Great Hills Trail	Austin 512-346-4300	TX 78759	
795	Austin, City of Local Govt	City Hall	Austin 512-499-2250	TX 78767	
440	Friona Industries Inc Food Processing	PO Box 369	Friona 806-247-3991	TX 79035	
794	Southwestern Public Service Co Utility	Tyler & Sixth Streets	Amarillo 806-378-2121	TX 79101	
371	Mesa Limited Partnership Inc Energy	One Mesa Square	Amarillo 806-378-1000	TX 79189	
1250	Furrs Inc Retail/Food	1708 Avenue G	Lubbock 806-763-1931	TX 79408	
143	Texas Tech University University	Administrative Bldg	Lubbock 806-742-2011	TX 79409	
300	Furr's/Bishop's Cafeterias Inc Retail/Food	6901 Quaker Avenue	Lubbock 806-792-7151	TX 79493	
302	West Texas Utilities Co Utility	301 Cypress Street	Abilene 915-674-7000	TX 79601	
550	Pride Refining Inc Energy	500 Chestnut	Abilene 915-677-2223	TX 79602	
825	Clajon Production Corp Energy	23 Desta Drive	Midland 915-683-4181	TX 79705	
639	El Paso Electric Co Inc Utility	303 N Oregon Street	El Paso 915-543-5711	TX 79901	
1447	El Paso Natural Gas Co Utility	One Paul Kayser Center	El Paso 915-541-2600	TX 79901	
350	Farah Inc Apparel/Textiles	8889 Gateway W	El Paso 915-593-4444	TX 79985	
250	El Paso, City of Local Govt	Civic Center Plaza	El Paso 915-541-4766	TX 79999	

State / Province: Utah

Revenue ($ mil)	Organization/ Industry	Address	City / Phone	State/ Zip	Province/ Postcode
282	Novell Inc Comput/Off Equip	1170 N Industrial Park Drive	Orem 801-226-8202	UT 84057	
350	American Savings (UT) Assn Inc Savings & Loan	77 W 200th S	Salt Lake City 801-483-5800	UT 84101	
660	Associated Food Stores Inc Retail/Food	1812 S Empire	Salt Lake City 801-973-4400	UT 84104	
1100	Smith Management Corp Retail/Food	1550 S Redwood	Salt Lake City 801-974-1400	UT 84104	
NA	Northwest Pipeline Corp Transport	295 Chipeta Way	Salt Lake City 801-584-7308	UT 84108	
100	Utah Power & Light Co Utility	1407 W North Temple	Salt Lake City 801-535-2000	UT 84110	
522	First Security Corp Banking	79 S Main Street	Salt Lake City 801-350-5325	UT 84111	
550	Huntsman Chemical & Oil Corp Chemicals	2000 Eaglegate Tower 60 E S Temple	Salt Lake City 801-532-5200	UT 84111	
250	Salt Lake City, City of Local Govt	City Hall 324 S State Street	Salt Lake City 801-535-7704	UT 84111	
285	University of Utah University	Administrative Bldg	Salt Lake City 801-581-7200	UT 84112	
4240	Utah, State of State/Prov Govt	State Capitol	Salt Lake City 801-533-4000	UT 84114	
18478	American Stores Co Retail/Food	5201 Amelia Earhart Drive	Salt Lake City 801-539-0112	UT 84116	
486	Questar Corp Utility	180 E First South Street	Salt Lake City 801-534-5000	UT 84147	
1000	Flying J Inc Energy	990 S 50th W	West Brigham 801-734-9416	UT 84302	

State / Province: Utah

Organizations Listed Geographically

Revenue ($ mil)	Organization/ Industry	Address	City / Phone	State/ Zip	Province/ Postcode
1100	Miller, E A Inc Food Processing	410 N 200th W	Hyrum 801-245-6456	UT 84319	
440	Amalgamated Sugar Co Food Processing	First Security Bank Bldg	Ogden 801-399-3431	UT 84401	
NA	Thiokol Aerospace Group Inc Aerospace	2475 Washington Blvd	Ogden 801-625-4801	UT 84401	
330	Brigham Young University University	Administrative Bldg	Provo 801-378-4418	UT 84602	

State / Province: Vermont

Revenue ($ mil)	Organization/ Industry	Address	City / Phone	State/ Zip	Province/ Postcode
600	C & S Wholesale Grocery Inc Retail/Food	Ferry Road	Brattleboro 802-257-4371	VT 05301	
1351	Vermont, State of State/Prov Govt	State House	Montpelier 802-828-1110	VT 05602	
717	National Life Insurance Co Insurance	National Life Drive	Montpelier 802-229-3333	VT 05604	
850	National Life of Vermont Insurance	1 National Life Drive	Montpelier 802-229-3333	VT 05604	

State / Province: Virginia

Revenue ($ mil)	Organization/ Industry	Address	City / Phone	State/ Zip	Province/ Postcode
59	Northern Virginia Community College University	8333 Little River Turnpike	Annadale 703-323-3381	VA 22003	
539	Fairchild Industries Inc Aerospace	Dulles Airport 300 W Service Road	Chantilly 703-478-5800	VA 22021	
409	Mohasco Corp Building Mat	4401 Fair Lakes Court	Fairfax 703-768-8000	VA 22033	
482	First Virginia Banks Inc Banking	6400 Arlington Blvd	Falls Church 703-241-4000	VA 22046	
1309	Lafarge Corp Building Mat	11130 Sunrise Valley Drive	Reston 703-264-3600	VA 22091	
750	Dynalectron Corp Electronics	1313 Dolley Madison Blvd	McLean 703-264-0330	VA 22101	
750	DynCorp Inc Manufacturing	1313 Dolly Madison Blvd	McLean 703-356-0480	VA 22101	
8000	Mars Inc Food Processing	6885 Elm Street	McLean 703-821-4900	VA 22101	
561	Perpetual American Bank Inc Savings & Loan	8200 Greensboro Drive	McLean 703-442-7000	VA 22101	
275	BDM International Inc Consulting	7915 Jones Branch Drive	McLean 703-821-5000	VA 22102	
300	First American Bank of Virginia Co Banking	1970 Chain Bridge Road	McLean 703-821-7777	VA 22102	
250	Flow General Inc Consulting	7655 Old Springhouse Road	McLean 703-893-5915	VA 22102	
NA	McDonnell Douglas Electronic Systems Electronics	8201 Greesboro Drive	McLean 703-442-7960	VA 22102	
1000	NVR Limited Partnership Inc Real Estate/Bldg	7601 Lewinsville Road	McLean 703-761-2000	VA 22102	
654	Planning Research Corp Consulting	1500 Planning Research Drive	McLean 703-556-1000	VA 22102	
108	Primark Corp Utility	8251 Greensboro Drive Suite 700	McLean 703-790-7600	VA 22102	
500	Cooke, Jack Kent Corp Real Estate/Bldg	Kent Farms	Middleburg 703-687-4000	VA 22117	
NA	Hecht's Inc Retail/Merch	685 N Glebe Road	Arlington 703-558-1200	VA 22203	
500	Rosenthal Companies Inc Automotive	3400 Columbia Parkway	Arlington 703-920-8700	VA 22204	
NA	Allied Signal Aerospace Div Aerospace	1000 Wilson Blvd	Arlington 703-276-2000	VA 22209	
250	American Management Corp Comput/Off Equip	1777 N Kent Street	Arlington 703-841-6000	VA 22209	
3314	Gannett Co Inc Publishing/Com	1100 Wilson Blvd	Arlington 703-284-6000	VA 22209	

State / Province: Virginia

Organizations Listed Geographically

Revenue ($ mil)	Organization/ Industry	Address	City / Phone	State/ Zip	Province/ Postcode
550	Geneva Management Inc Business Service	1550 Wilson Blvd	Arlington 703-522-2300	VA 22209	
1500	ITT Defense Technology Corp Aerospace	1000 Wilson Blvd	Arlington 703-276-8300	VA 22209	
5707	US Air Group Inc Airline	2345 Crystal Drive	Arlington 703-892-7000	VA 22227	
420	Kay Jewelers Corp Retail/Food	320 King Street	Alexandria 703-683-3800	VA 22314	
NA	Time-Life Books Inc Publishing/Com	777 Duke Street	Alexandria 703-838-7000	VA 22314	
250	O'Sullivan Corp Tire/Rubber	Valley Avenue	Winchester 703-667-6666	VA 22601	
371	WLR Foods Inc Food Processing	PO Box 228	Hilton 703-867-9221	VA 22831	
338	University of Virginia University	Administrative Bldg	Charlottesville 804-924-0311	VA 22903	
NA	GE Fanuc Automation Inc Equipment	Routes 29 N & 606	Charlottsville 804-978-5000	VA 22906	
300	Genicom Corp Comput/Off Equip	One Genicom Drive	Waaynesboro 703-949-1000	VA 229801	
1100	Richfood Inc Retail/Food	2000 Richfood Road	Mechanicsville 804-746-6000	VA 23111	
2011	Ethyl Corp Chemicals	330 S Fourth Street	Richmond 804-788-5000	VA 23217	
5098	James River Corp Paper/Forest Prd	Tredegar Street PO Box 2218	Richmond 804-644-5411	VA 23217	
711	Chesapeake Corp Paper/Forest Prd	1021 E Cary Street	Richmond 804-697-1000	VA 23218	
7592	CSX Corp Railroad	One James Center	Richmond 804-782-1400	VA 23219	
3344	Dominion Resources Inc Utility	701 E Byrd Street	Richmond 804-755-5700	VA 23219	
1513	Federal Reserve Bank of Richmond Inc Federal Govt Fin	701 E Byrd Street	Richmond 804-643-1250	VA 23219	
NA	Massey, A T Coal Co Metals/Mining	Four N Fourth Street	Richmond 804-788-1800	VA 23219	
756	Media General Inc Publishing/Com	333 E Grace Street	Richmond 804-649-6000	VA 23219	
250	Richmond, City of Local Govt	City Hall	Richmond 804-780-7977	VA 23219	
12101	Virginia, State of State/Prov Govt	State Capitol	Richmond 804-786-0000	VA 23219	
934	Robins, A H Co Inc Drugs	1407 Cummings Drive PO Box 26609	Richmond 804-257-2000	VA 23220	
550	Overnite Transportation Co Transport	1000 Semmes Avenue	Richmond 824-231-8000	VA 23224	
2000	Best Products Co Inc Retail/Merch	Parham Road at Interstate 95	Richmond 804-261-2000	VA 23227	
732	Owens & Minor Inc Drugs	2727 Enterprise Parkway	Richmond 804-747-9794	VA 23229	
1100	Blue Cross Blue Shield of Virginia Inc Insurance	2015 Staples Mill Road	Richmond 804-359-7000	VA 23230	
500	Carpenter, E R Corp Building Mat	5016 Monument Avenue	Richmond 804-359-0800	VA 23230	
1721	Circuit City Stores Inc Retail/Merch	2040 Thalbro Street	Richmond 804-257-4292	VA 23230	
352	Heilig Meyers Co Retail/Merch	2235 Staples Mill Road	Richmond 804-359-9171	VA 23230	
NA	Lawyers Title Insurance Co Insurance	6630n W Broad Street	Richmond 804-281-6700	Va 23230	
1080	Life Insurance Co of Virginia Inc Insurance	6610 W Broad Street	Richmond 804-281-6000	VA 23230	
2104	Universal Leaf Tobacco Co Inc Tobacco	1501 N Hamilton Street	Richmond 804-359-9311	VA 23230	
650	Tredegar Industries Inc Manufacturing	5020 Castlewood Road	Richmond 804-275-9211	VA 23234	

State / Province: Virginia

Organizations Listed Geographically

Revenue ($ mil)	Organization/ Industry	Address	City / Phone	State/ Zip	Province/ Postcode
1286	Signet Banking Corp Banking	7 N Eighth Street	Richmond 804-747-2000	VA	23260
967	Southern States Cooperative Inc Food Processing	6606 W Broad Street	Richmond 804-281-1000	VA	23260
446	Central Fidelity Banks Inc Banking	Broad at Third Street	Richmond 804-782-4000	VA	23261
1016	Crestar Financial Corp (United VA) Banking	919 E Main Street	Richmond 804-782-5000	VA	23261
5619	Reynolds Metals Co Metals/Mining	6601 Broad Street Road	Richmond 804-281-2000	VA	23261
500	Robertshaw Controls Co Manufacturing	1701 Byrd Avenue	Richmond 804-281-0700	VA	23261
NA	Virginia Electric & Power Co Utility	701 E Byrd Street	Richmond 804-771-3193	VA	23261
301	Virginia Commonwealth University University	910 W Franklin Street	Richmond 804-257-0100	VA	23284
1201	Figgie International Holding Inc Conglomerate	1000 Virginia Center Parkway	Richmond 804-264-5600	VA	23295
916	Smithfield Foods Inc Food Processing	501 N Church Street	Smithfield 703-357-4321	VA	23430
378	Virginia Beach, City of Local Govt	City Hall Municipal Center	Virginia Beach 804-427-4111	VA	23456
350	Landmark Communications Inc Publishing/Com	150 Brambleton Avenue	Norfolk 804-446-2000	VA	23501
405	Norfolk, City of Local Govt	City Hall	Norfolk 804-441-2679	VA	23501
4462	Norfolk Southern Corp Railroad	Three Commerical Place	Norfolk 804-629-2600	VA	23510
2302	Sovran Financial Corp Banking	One Commercial Place	Norfolk 804-441-4000	VA	23510
750	Farm Fresh Inc Food Processing	109 S Palm	Norfolk 405-765-6656	VA	23601
461	Noland Co Building Mat	2700 Warwick Blvd	Newport News 804-928-9000	VA	23607
NA	ANR Coal Co Metals/Mining	Crestar Bank Bldg 310 First Street	Roanoke 703-983-0222	VA	24011
898	Dominion Bankshares Inc Banking	213 S Jefferson Street	Roanoke 703-563-7749	VA	24040
400	Bassett Furniture Industries Inc Manufacturing	PO Box 626	Bassett 703-629-7511	VA	24055
226	Virginia Polytechnic Institute University	Administrative Bldg	Blacksburg 703-961-6000	VA	24061
275	Pannill Knitting Co Apparel/Textiles	202 Cleveland Avenue	Martinsville 703-638-8841	VA	24115
350	Tultex Corportation Apparel/Textiles	22 E Church Street	Martinsville 703-632-2961	VA	24115
500	United Co Aerospace	Glenway Avenue	Bristol 703-466-3322	VA	24201
777	First Colony Life Insurance Co Insurance	PO Box 1280	Lynchburg 804-845-0911	VA	24505
375	Lane Co Inc Manufacturing	East Franklin Avenue	Altavista 804-369-5641	VA	24517
500	Dan River Inc Apparel/Textiles	2216 Memorial Drive	Danville 804-799-7000	VA	24541
685	Dibrell Brothers Manufacturing	512 Bridge Street	Danville 804-792-7511	VA	24541
300	Ashland Coal Inc Metals/Mining	2205 5th Street	Huntington 304-526-3333	VA	25701

State / Province: Washington

Revenue ($ mil)	Organization/ Industry	Address	City / Phone	State/ Zip	Province/ Postcode
10004	Weyerhaeuser Co Paper/Forest Prd	33663 32nd Avenue S	Tacoma 206-924-2345	WA	98003
260	Esterline Corp Equipment	10800 NE 8th Street	Bellevue 206-453-6000	WA	98004

State / Province: Washington

Organizations Listed Geographically

Revenue ($ mil)	Organization/ Industry	Address	City / Phone	State/ Zip	Province/ Postcode
3122	Paccar Inc Automotive	777 106th Avenue NE	Bellevue 206-455-7400	WA	98004
783	Puget Sound Power & Light Co Utility	Puget Power Bldg 411 108th Avenue NE	Bellevue 206-454-6363	WA	98009
NA	Boeing Aerospace Corp Aerospace	20403 68th Street	Kent 206-773-2121	WA	98031
500	Pay N Pak Inc Retail/Merch	1209 S Central	Kent 206-854-5450	WA	98031
2000	Costco Wholesale Retail/Merch	10829 120th Avenue NE	Kirkland 206-828-8100	WA	98033
225	McCaw Cellular Telecom	5808 Lake Washington NE	Kirkland 206-827-4500	WA	98033
591	Microsoft Corp Comput/Off Equip	16011 NE 36th Way	Redmond 206-882-8080	WA	98073
2328	Nordstrom Inc Retail/Merch	1501 Fifth Avenue	Seattle 206-628-2111	WA	98101
850	Rainier Bancorp Inc Banking	1301 Fifth Avenue	Seattle 206-621-4111	WA	98101
550	Simpson Investment Co Inc Paper/Forest Prd	1201 Third Avenue	Seattle 206-292-5000	WA	98101
584	Washington Mutual Savings Inc Savings & Loan	1101 Second Avenue	Seattle 206-464-4400	WA	98101
1500	Burlington Resources Energy	999 Third Avenue	Seattle 206-467-3838	WA	98104
825	King County Government Local Govt	County Courthouse	Seattle 206-344-4100	WA	98104
1800	Seattle First National Bank Co Banking	701 Fifth Avenue	Seattle 206-358-7800	WA	98104
721	Seattle, City of Local Govt	City Hall Municipal Bldg	Seattle 206-625-4000	WA	98104
1117	Univar Corp Chemicals	1600 Norton Bldg 801 Second Avenue	Seattle 206-447-5911	WA	98104
17340	Boeing Corp Aerospace	7755 E Marginal Way S	Seattle 206-655-2121	WA	98108
345	Washington Energy Co Utility	815 Mercer Street	Seattle 206-622-6767	WA	98109
550	Wright Shuchart Inc Energy	425 Pompius Avenue N	Seattle 206-447-7654	WA	98109
450	National Bank of Washington Inc Banking	1414 Fourth Avenue	Seattle 206-344-2300	WA	98111
825	Darigold Inc Food Processing	635 Elliott W	Seattle 206-284-7220	WA	98119
768	Airborne Freight Corp Transport	3101 Western Avenue	Seattle 206-285-4600	WA	98121
1100	Associated Grocers Inc Retail/Food	3301 S Norfolk	Seattle 206-762-2100	WA	98124
NA	Boeing Commercial Airplanes Inc Aerospace	Eighth Street & Logan Avenue N	Renton 206-237-2121	WA	98124
1500	Services Group of America Retail/Food	2030 Airport Way S	Seattle 206-623-5023	WA	98134
351	Todd Shipyards Corp Manufacturing	1102 SW Massachusetts	Seattle 206-223-1560	WA	98134
1000	Simpson Timber Corp Paper/Forest Prd	900 4th Avenue	Seattle 206-292-5000	WA	98164
814	Alaska Air Group Inc Airline	19300 S Pacific PO Box 68947	Seattle 206-433-3200	WA	98168
3018	SAFECO Corp Insurance	SAFECO Plaza	Seattle 206-545-5000	WA	98185
NA	US West Communications-Seattle Telecom	1600 Bell Plaza	Seattle 206-346-5000	WA	98191
530	University of Washington University	Administrative Bldg	Seattle 206-543-2100	WA	98195
225	Fluke, John Manufacturing Co Electronics	6920 Seaway Blvd	Everett 206-347-6100	WA	98203
550	Bayliner Marine Corp Leisure Time	17825 59th Avenue NE	Arlington 206-435-5571	WA	98223

State / Province: Washington

Organizations Listed Geographically

Revenue ($ mil)	Organization/ Industry	Address	City / Phone	State/ Zip	Province/ Postcode
NA	US Marine & Bayline Co Leisure Time	17825 59th Avenue	Arlington 206-435-5540	WA	98223
524	Pacific First Federal Savings Bank Inc Savings & Loan	1145 Broadway	Tacoma 206-383-7605	WA	98401
395	Puget Sound BanCorp Banking	1119 Pacific Avenue	Tacoma 206-593-3600	WA	98402
165	Russell, Frank Co Consulting	909 A Street	Tacoma 206-572-9500	WA	98402
11219	Washington, State of State/Prov Govt	Legislative Bldg	Olympia 206-753-5000	WA	98504
657	Longview Fibre Co Paper/Forest Prd	PO Box 639	Longview 206-425-1550	WA	98632
552	Pacific Telecom Inc Telecom	805 Broadway	Vancouver 206-696-0983	WA	98668
212	Washington State University University	Administrative Bldg	Pullman 509-335-3564	WA	99164
543	Washington Water Power Co Utility	East 1411 Mission Avenue	Spokane 509-489-0500	WA	99202
550	URM Stores Inc Retail/Food	7511 N Freya Avenue	Seattle 509-467-2620	WA	99207

State / Province: West Virginia

Revenue ($ mil)	Organization/ Industry	Address	City / Phone	State/ Zip	Province/ Postcode
300	Heck's Inc Retail/Merch	Hub Industrial Park	Nitro 304-755-8331	WV	25143
250	Allegheny & Western Energy Energy	1600 Kanawha Valley Bldg	Charleston 304-343-4327	WV	25301
4006	West Virginia, State of State/Prov Govt	State Capitol	Charleston 304-348-3456	WV	25305
400	McJunkin Corp Business Service	835 Hillcrest Drive	Charleston 304-348-5211	WV	25322
1001	Wheeling Pittsburgh Steel Corp Steel	1134 Market Street	Wheeling 304-234-2400	WV	26003
1384	Weirton Steel Corp Steel	400 Three Springs Drive	Weirton 304-797-2000	WV	26062
NA	Monongahela Power Co Utility	1310 Fairmont Avenue	Fairmont 304-366-3000	WV	26554

State / Province: Wisconsin

Revenue ($ mil)	Organization/ Industry	Address	City / Phone	State/ Zip	Province/ Postcode
1187	Harnischfeger Corp Building Mat	13400 Bishops Lane	Brookfield 414-671-4000	WI	53005
400	Kohls Department Stores Retail/Merch	2315 N 124th Street	Brookfield 414-784-4480	WI	53005
1000	Kohler Co Manufacturing	Kohler Memorial Drive	Kohler 414-457-4441	WI	53044
2000	Roundy's Inc Retail/Food	23000 Roundy Drive	Pewaukee 414-547-7999	WI	53072
275	Prange, H C Co Inc Retail/Merch	2314 Memorial	Sheboygan 414-459-4800	WI	53081
250	Dayton Industries Inc Manufacturing	11516 N Port Washington Road	Mequon 414-241-6200	WI	53092
855	Snap-on Tools Corp Manufacturing	2801 80th Street	Kenosha 414-656-5200	WI	53141
400	Becor Western Inc Equipment	1100 Milwaukee Avenue	South Milwaukee 414-768-4000	WI	53172
550	Harley Davidson Inc Automotive	3700 W Juneau Avenue	Milwaukee 414-342-4680	WI	53201
3100	Johnson Controls Inc Instruments	5757 N Green Bay Avenue	Milwaukee 414-228-1200	WI	53201
NA	Miller Brewing Co Beverage	3939 W Highland Blvd	Milwaukee 414-931-2000	WI	53201
128	University of Wisconsin Milwaukee University	Administrative Bldg PO Box 413	Milwaukee 414-963-4444	WI	53201
850	Wicor Inc Utility	777 E Wisconsin Avenue	Milwaukee 414-291-7026	WI	53201

State / Province: Wisconsin

Organizations Listed Geographically

Revenue ($ mil)	Organization/ Industry	Address	City / Phone	State/ Zip	Province/ Postcode
1541	Wisconsin Energy Co Utility	231 W Michigan Street	Milwaukee 414-277-2345	WI 53201	
400	Banc One Wisconsin Banking	111 E Wisconsin Avenue	Milwaukee 414-765-3000	WI 53202	
220	Blunt Ellis & Loewi Inc Securities	225 E Mason Street	Milwaukee 414-347-3400	WI 53202	
396	Entree Corp Food Processing	111 E Wisconsin Avenue	Milwaukee 414-271-2768	WI 53202	
751	Farm House Foods Corp Retail/Merch	111 E Wisconsin Avenue Suite 1900	Milwaukee 414-271-5050	WI 53202	
850	Firstar (First Wisconsin Corp) Banking	777 E Wisconsin Avenue	Milwaukee 414-765-4321	WI 53202	
677	Marshall & Isley Corp Banking	770 N Water Street	Milwaukee 414-765-7801	WI 53202	
592	Milwaukee, City of Local Govt	City Hall	Milwaukee 414-278-2200	WI 53202	
5737	Northwestern Mutual Life Insurance Co Insurance	720 E Wisconsin Avenue	Milwaukee 414-271-1444	WI 53202	
825	Sybron Corp Manufacturing	411 E Wisconson	Milwaukee 414-274-6600	WI 53202	
721	Universal Foods Corp Food Processing	433 E Michigan Street	Milwaukee 414-271-6755	WI 53202	
NA	Wisconsin Bell Telephone Co Utility	722 N Broadway	Milwaukee 414-549-7300	WI 53202	
825	Wisconsin Gas Co Inc Utility	626 E Wisconsin	Milwaukee 414-291-7000	WI 53202	
550	Bergner, P A & Co Inc Retail/Merch	331 W Wisconsin	Milwaukee 414-347-4141	WI 53203	
400	Journal Communications Co Inc Publishing/Com	333 W State Street	Milwaukee 414-224-2000	WI 53203	
401	Allis Chalmers Corp Equipment	1205 S 70th Street	West Allis 414-475-2000	WI 53214	
1500	Manpower Inc Manufacturing	5301 N Ironwood Place	Milwaukee 608-755-7000	WI 53217	
NA	Fleishman Kurth Malting Co Food Processing	2100 S 43rd Street	Milwaukee 414-384-7400	WI 53219	
914	Briggs & Stratton Corp Machinery	12301 W Wirth Street	Wauwatosa 414-259-5333	WI 53222	
1000	Kohl's Food Stores Retail/Food	11100 W Burleigh	Milwaukee 414-771-8000	WI 53222	
1015	Smith, A O Corp Automotive	11270 W Park Place	Milwaukee 414-359-4000	WI 53223	
1300	Milwaukee County Government Local Govt	901 N 9th Street	Milwaukee 414-278-4222	WI 53233	
424	Modine Manufacturing Co Automotive	1500 DeKoven Avenue	Racine 414-636-1200	WI 53401	
300	Johnson Worldwide Associates Inc Leisure Time	4041 N Main Street	Racine 414-631-2000	WI 53402	
2500	Johnson, S C & Son Inc Personal Care	1525 Howe Street	Racine 414-631-2000	WI 53403	
NA	Beloit Corp Manufacturing	One St Lawrence Avenue	Beloit 608-365-3311	WI 53511	
456	Lands End Inc Retail/Merch	1 Lands' End Lane	Dodgeville 608-935-9341	WI 53595	
1560	Wisconsin Investment Board Non-Bank Fin	121 E Wilson Street	Madison 608-266-2381	WI 53702	
12463	Wisconsin, State of State/Prov Govt	State Capitol	Madison 608-266-2111	WI 53702	
250	Madison Gas & Electric Co Utility	133 S Blair Street	Madison 608-252-7000	WI 53703	
601	WPL Holdings (Wisconsin Power Co) Utility	222 W Washington Avenue	Madison 608-252-3311	WI 53703	
NA	Mayer, Oscar Foods Corp Food Processing	910 Mayer Avenue	Madison 608-241-3311	WI 53704	
607	University of Wisconsin University	500 Lincoln Drive	Madison 608-262-1234	WI 53706	

State / Province: Wisconsin

Organizations Listed Geographically

Revenue ($ mil)	Organization/ Industry	Address	City / Phone	State/ Zip	Province/ Postcode
550	Wisconsin Dairies Cooperative Inc Food Processing	Route 3 & Highway 12 W	Baraboo 608-356-8316	WI 53913	
550	Packerland Packing Co Inc Food Processing	2580 University Avenue	Green Bay 414-468-4000	WI 54301	
500	Consolidated Beef Industries Inc Food Processing	544 Acme Street	Green Bay 414-437-4311	WI 54302	
500	Terex Corp Manufacturing	201 W Walnut Street	Green Bay 414-453-5322	WI 54303	
500	Schneider National Inc Transport	2777 Southridge Road	Green Bay 414-497-2201	WI 54304	
NA	ShopKo Stores Inc Retail/Merch	700 Pilgrim Way	Green Bay 414-497-2211	WI 54304	
1750	Fort Howard Paper Co Paper/Forest Prd	1919 S Broadway	Green Bay 414-435-8821	WI 54307	
1000	Schreiber Foods Inc Food Processing	425 Pine Street	Green Bay 414-437-7601	WI 54307	
604	Wisconsin Public Service Corp Utility	700 N Adams Street	Green Bay 414-433-1598	WI 54307	
300	Wausau Paper Mills Co Paper/Forest Prd	One Clarks Island	Wausau 715-845-5266	WI 54401	
3000	Nekoosa Papers Inc Paper/Forest Prd	100 Wisconsin River Drive	Port Edwards 715-887-5111	WI 54469	
1422	Sentry Insurance Co Insurance	1800 N Point Drive	Stevens Point 715-346-6000	WI 54481	
897	Consolidated Papers Inc Paper/Forest Prd	231 First Avenue N	Wisconsin Rapids 715-422-3111	WI 54494	
1500	Heileman, G Brewing Co Inc Beverage	100 Harborview Plaza	LaCrosse 608-785-1000	WI 54601	
2250	Gateway Foods Corp Retail/Food	PO Box 1957	LaCrosse 608-785-1330	WI 54602	
NA	Superior Water, Light & Power Co Utility	1230 Tower Avenue	Superior 715-394-5511	WI 54880	
253	Oshkosh B'Gosh Inc Apparel/Textiles	112 Otter Avenue	Oshkosh 414-231-8800	WI 54901	
400	Morgan Products Ltd Building Mat	601 Oregon Street	Oshkosh 414-235-7170	WI 54903	
450	Oshkosh Truck Corp Automotive	2307 Oshkosh Street	Oshkosh 414-235-9150	WI 54903	
1618	Aid Association for Lutherans Inc Insurance	4321 N Ballard Road	Appleton 414-734-5721	WI 54919	
NA	Mercury Marine Co Manufacturing	6250 W Pioneer Road	Fon Du Lac 414-929-5000	WI 54936	
300	Banta, George Corp Business Service	Harbor Place	Menasha 414-722-7777	WI 54952	

State / Province: Wyoming

Revenue ($ mil)	Organization/ Industry	Address	City / Phone	State/ Zip	Province/ Postcode
2684	Wyoming, State of State/Prov Govt	State Capitol	Cheyenne 307-777-7220	WY 82002	

State / Province: Alberta

Revenue ($ mil)	Organization/ Industry	Address	City / Phone	State/ Zip	Province/ Postcode
382	Calgary Cooperative Assn Ltd Retail/Food	8818 Macleod Trail SE	Calgary 403-253-0345	AB T2H0M5	
234	Calgary, The University of University	2500 University Drive NW	Calgary 403-220-5110	AB T2N1N4	
4301	Shell Canada Ltd Energy	400 4th Avenue SW	Calgary 403-232-3111	AB T2P0J4	
1190	Chevron Canada Resources Ltd Energy	500 5th Avenue SW	Calgary 403-234-5000	AB T2P0L7	
1969	Total Petroleum North America Ltd Energy	639 5th Avenue SW	Calgary 403-267-3000	AB T2P0M9	
1285	Amoco Canada Petroleum Co Energy	444 7th Avenue SW	Calgary 403-233-1313	AB T2P0Y2	
740	Gulf Canada Ltd Energy	401 9th Avenue SW	Calgary 403-233-4000	AB T2P2H7	

State / Province: Alberta

Organizations Listed Geographically

Revenue ($ mil)	Organization/ Industry	Address	City / Phone	State/ Zip	Province/ Postcode
1266	Dome Petroleum Ltd Energy	333 7th Avenue SW	Calgary 403-231-3000	AB	T2P2H8
1348	Mobil Oil Canada Ltd Energy	330 5th Avenue SW	Calgary 403-260-7910	AB	T2P2J7
383	Canterra Energy Ltd Energy	505 5th Street SW	Calgary 403-267-9111	AB	T2P2K7
818	Trans Alta Utilities Corp Utility	110 12th Avenue SW	Calgary 403-267-7110	AB	T2P2M1
2779	Trans Canada Pipelines Ltd Utility	530 8th Avenue SW	Calgary 403-269-5611	AB	T2P2M7
3350	Nova Corp of Alberta Ltd Energy	801 7th Avenue SW	Calgary 403-290-6000	AB	T2P2N6
788	Alberta Wheat Pool Ltd Food Processing	505 2nd Street SW	Calgary 403-290-4910	AB	T2P2P5
288	Trimac Ltd Transport	800 5th Avenue SW	Calgary 403-298-5100	AB	T2P2P9
3291	Canada Safeway Ltd Retail/Food	1015 4th Street SW	Calgary 403-260-8600	AB	T2P2S6
1850	PWA (Canadian Airlines) Corp Airline	700 2nd Street SW	Calgary 403-294-2000	AB	T2P2W2
1014	Trizec Corp Real Estate/Bldg	700 2nd Street SW	Calgary 403-269-8241	AB	T2P2W2
622	Norcen Energy Resources Ltd Energy	715 5th Avenue SW	Calgary 403-231-0111	AB	T2P2X7
1216	Westburne International Industries Ltd Energy	1700 633 6th Avenue SW	Calgary 403-292-0200	AB	T2P2Y5
729	Interhome Energy Inc (Interprov Pipe) Energy	324 8th Avenue SW	Calgary 403-232-5500	AB	T2P2Z5
282	BP Petroleum Canada Ltd Energy	333 5th Avenue SW	Calgary 403-237-1234	AB	T2P3B6
4415	Petro Canada Energy	150 6th Avenue SW	Calgary 403-296-5850	AB	T2P3E3
638	Husky Oil Ltd Energy	707 8th Avenue SW	Calgary 403-298-6111	AB	T2P3G7
587	PanCanadian Petroleum Energy	150 9th Avenue SW	Calgary 403-290-2000	AB	T2P3H9
932	Alberta & Southern Gas Co Energy	425 1st Street SW	Calgary 403-260-9911	AB	T2P3L8
298	Alberta Natural Gas Co Energy	425 1st Street SW	Calgary 403-260-9911	AB	T2P3L8
306	Asamera Inc Energy	144 4th Avenue SW	Calgary 403-269-5521	AB	T2P3N4
474	Turbo Resources Ltd Energy	815 8th Avenue SW	Calgary 403-294-6400	AB	T2P3P2
468	Bow Valley Industries Ltd Energy	321 6th Avenue SW	Calgary 403-261-6100	AB	T2P3R2
85	Collins, Barrow, Maheu, Noiseux Ltd Accounting	1400 777 8th Avenue SW	Calgary 403-298-1500	AB	T2P3R5
281	Enron Canada Ltd Energy	1300 700 9th Avenue SW	Calgary 403-298-2690	AB	T2P3V4
680	Burns Food Ltd Retail/Merch	150 6th Avenue SW	Calgary 403-265-8140	AB	T2P3X4
629	Canadian Occidental Petroleum Ltd Energy	1500 635 8th Avenue SW	Calgary 403-234-6700	AB	T2P3Z1
255	Canadian Western Natural Gas Co Utility	909 11 Avenue SW	Calgary 403-245-7110	AB	T2R1L8
1227	Atco Ltd Machinery	909 11th Avenue SW	Calgary 403-292-7500	AB	T2R1N6
911	Alberta Government Telephone Co Telecom	10020 100 Street	Edmonton 403-425-2110	AB	T5J0N5
318	Gainers Ltd Food Processing	12425 66th Street	Edmonton 403-471-0611	AB	T5J2H8
445	Provence of Alberta Treasury Branches Federal Govt Fin	9925 109th Street	Edmonton 403-493-7015	AB	T5J2N6
311	Banister Continental Corp Real Estate/Bldg	9910 39th Avenue	Edmonton 403-462-9430	AB	T5J2R4

State / Province: Alberta

Organizations Listed Geographically

Revenue ($ mil)	Organization/ Industry	Address	City / Phone	State/ Zip	Province/ Postcode
340	Alberta Power Ltd Utility	10035 105th Street	Edmonton 403-420-5035	AB	T5J2V6
978	Canadian Utilities Ltd Utility	10035 105 Street	Edmonton 403-420-7121	AB	T5J2V6
409	Alberta Energy Co Energy	10707 100th Avenue	Edmonton 403-423-8333	AB	T5J3M1
12240	Province of Alberta State/Prov Govt	Legislative Bldg	Edmonton 403-427-2711	AB	T5K2B6
248	Alberta Mortgage & Housing Corp Non-Bank Fin	9405 50th Street	Edmonton 403-468-3535	AB	T6B2T4
1020	Northwest Territories Power Corp Federal Govt	7509 51st Avenue	Edmonton 403-465-3377	AB	T6C4J8
1071	PCL Construction Group Ltd Real Estate/Bldg	5410 99th Street	Edmonton 403-435-9711	AB	T6E3P4
234	Alberta, The University of University	Administrative Bldg	Edmonton 403-432-3111	AB	T6G2E5

State / Province: British Columbia

Revenue ($ mil)	Organization/ Industry	Address	City / Phone	State/ Zip	Province/ Postcode
343	Mohawk Oil Canada Ltd Energy	6400 Robert Street	Burnaby 604-299-7244	BC	V5G2G2
448	Southland Canada Inc Retail/Food	3185 Willingdon Green	Burnaby 604-299-0700	BC	V5G4P3
1332	British Columbia Telephone Ltd Telecom	3777 Kingsway	Burnaby 604-432-2151	BC	V5H3Z7
595	Finning Ltd Equipment	555 Great Northern Way	Vancouver 604-872-4444	BC	V5T1E2
1785	Kelly, Douglas & Co Retail/Food	808 Nelson Street	Vancouver 604-661-1200	BC	V6B3S1
761	Weldwood of Canada Ltd Paper/Forest Prd	1055 W Hastings Street	Vancouver 604-687-7366	BC	V6B3V8
577	Woodward's Ltd Retail/Merch	101 W Hastings Street	Vancouver 604-684-5231	BC	V6B4G1
921	Canfor Corp Paper/Forest Prd	3000 Four Bentall Centre 1055 Dunsmuir Street	Vancouver 604-661-5241	BC	V6C1N5
937	Itoh, C & Co Canada Ltd Retail/Merch	200 Granville Street	Vancouver 604-683-5764	BC	V6C1S4
425	SHL Systemhouse Inc Comput/Off Equip	99 Bank Street	Vancouver 604-236-9734	BC	V6C1T2
1418	Cominco Ltd Metals/Mining	2600 - 200 Granville Street	Vancouver 604-682-0611	BC	V6C2R2
876	Crown Forest Industries Ltd Paper/Forest Prd	815 W Hastings Street	Vancouver 604-668-4242	BC	V6C2Y4
250	Hongkong Bank of Canada Banking	885 W Georgia	Vancouver 604-685-1000	BC	V6C3E9
1384	Pattison, Jim Industries Ltd Airline	1055 W Hastings Street	Vancouver 604-688-6764	BC	V6E2H2
255	Inland Natural Gas Co Utility	1066 W Hastings Street	Vancouver 604-684-0484	BC	V6E3G3
712	Westcoast Energy Inc Energy	1333 W Georgia Street	Vancouver 604-664-5500	BC	V6E3K9
2783	MacMillan Bloedel Ltd Paper/Forest Prd	1075 W Georgia Street	Vancouver 604-661-8000	BC	V6E3R9
777	Chevron Canada Ltd Energy	1050 W Pender Street	Vancouver 604-668-5300	BC	V6E3T4
428	Seaboard Lumber Sales Co Retail/Merch	1066 W Hastings Street	Vancouver 604-684-3171	BC	V6E3W9
292	Cansulex Ltd Chemicals	1066 W Hastings Street	Vancouver 604-688-1501	BC	V6E3X1
394	West Fraser Timber Co Paper/Forest Prd	1100 Melville Street	Vancouver 604-681-8282	BC	V6E4A6
288	Westar Group Ltd (BC Resources Invst) Paper/Forest Prd	1900-1176 W Georgia Street	Vancouver 604-687-2600	BC	V6E4B9
170	National Real Estate Service Ltd Real Estate/Bldg	1075 W Georgia Street	Vancouver 604-685-3474	BC	V6E4G8

State / Province: British Columbia

Organizations Listed Geographically

Revenue ($ mil)	Organization/ Industry	Address	City / Phone	State/ Zip	Province/ Postcode
327	British Columbia, The University of University	2075 Wesbrook Mall	Vancouver 604-228-2211	BC	V6T1W5
2032	Core Mark International Inc Retail/Food	13951 Bridgeport Road	Richmond 604-273-7721	BC	V6V1J6
255	Century 21 Canada Ltd Real Estate/Bldg	135-10551 Shellbridge Way	Richmond 604-273-2721	BC	V6X2W9
625	First City Financial Corp Non-Bank Fin	777 Hornby Street 600	Vancouver 604-685-2489	BC	V6Z1S4
1689	British Col Hydro & Power Authority Ltd Utility	970 Burrard Street	Vancouver 604-663-2212	BC	V6Z1Y3
298	British Columbia Railway Co Railroad	221 W Esplanade	Vancouver 604-986-2012	BC	V7M1A5
326	International Forest Products (Whonnock) Paper/Forest Prd	1055 Dunsmuir Street 34th Floor	Vancouver 604-681-3221	BC	V7X1H7
340	Nissho Iwai Canada Ltd Manufacturing	2624 Dunsmuir Street	Vancouver 604-684-8351	BC	V7X1L3
1063	Sumitomo Canada Ltd Manufacturing	701 W Georgia Street	Vancouver 604-682-2256	BC	V7Y1E9
1250	Fletcher Challenge Canada Ltd Paper/Forest Prd	700 W Georgia Street	Vancouver 604-665-3821	BC	V7Y1J7
11220	Province of British Columbia State/Prov Govt	Parliment Bldgs	Victoria 604-387-1337	BC	V8V1X4
340	Doman Industries Ltd Paper/Forest Prd	435 Trunk Road	Duncan 604-748-3711	BC	V9L9Z9

State / Province: Manitoba

353	Acklands Ltd Automotive	125 Higgins Avenue	Winnipeg 204-956-0880	MB	R3B0B6
1623	Federal Industries Ltd Metals/Mining	One Lombard Place S	Winnipeg 204-942-8161	MB	R3B0X3
1068	Richardson, James & Sons Ltd Securities	One Lombard Plaza	Winnipeg 204-934-5811	MB	R3B0Y1
4080	Province of Manitoba State/Prov Govt	Legislative Bldg	Winnipeg 204-945-3744	MB	R3C0V8
485	Manitoba Hydro Electric Board Ltd Utility	820 Taylor Avenue	Winnipeg 204-474-3311	MB	R3C2P4
1750	Canadian Wheat Board Federal Govt	423 Main Street	Winnipeg 204-983-0239	MB	R3C2P5
4221	Great West Life Assurance Co Insurance	100 Osborne Street N	Winnipeg 204-946-1190	MB	R3C3A5
748	United Grain Growers Ltd Food Processing	433 Main Street	Winnipeg 204-944-5411	MB	R3C3A7
252	Investors Group Inc Non-Bank Fin	One Canada Centre 447 Portage	Winnipeg 204-943-0361	MB	R3C3B6
595	Manitoba Pool Elevators Ltd Food Processing	220 Portage Avenue	Winnipeg 204-947-1171	MB	R3C3K7
408	Wawanesa Mutual Insurance Co Insurance	191 Broadway	Winnipeg 204-985-3811	MB	R3C3P1
1421	Inter City Gas Corp Energy	444 St Mary Avenue	Winnepeg 204-944-9920	MB	R3C3T7
383	Xcan Grain Ltd Food Processing	360 Main	Winnipeg 204-949-1388	MB	R3C3Z3
947	Cargill Ltd Food Processing	240 Graham Avenue	Winnipeg 204-947-0141	MB	R3C4C5
1233	Westfair Foods Ltd Retail/Food	Addington Street	Winnipeg 204-786-7941	MB	R3E2T4
342	Manitoba Telephone System Ltd Telecom	489 Empress Street	Winnipeg 204-947-4111	MB	R3G2G9
575	Gendis Inc Retail/Merch	1370 Sony Place	Winnipeg 204-474-5200	MB	R3T1N5

State / Province: New Brunswick

1275	McCain Foods Ltd Food Processing	Main Road	Florenceville 506-392-5541	NB	E0J1K0

State / Province: New Brunswick

Organizations Listed Geographically

Revenue ($ mil)	Organization/ Industry	Address	City / Phone	State/ Zip	Province/ Postcode
298	Co-op Atlantic Ltd Food Processing	123 Halifax Street	Moncton 506-858-6000	NB	E1C5NB
340	Bruncor Inc Manufacturing	1 Brunswick Square	St John 506-694-6330	NB	E2L4K2
737	New Brunswick Elect Power Comm Ltd Utility	515 King Street	Fredericton 506-458-4444	NB	E3B4X1
2550	Province of New Brunswick State/Prov Govt	Legislative Bldg	Fredericton 506-453-2240	NB	E3B5H1

State / Province: Newfoundland

Revenue ($ mil)	Organization/ Industry	Address	City / Phone	State/ Zip	Province/ Postcode
282	Newfoundland & Labrador Hydro Electric Utility	50 Elizabeth Avenue	St Johns 709-737-1400	NF	A1A2X8
312	FPI Fishery Products International Ltd Food Processing	70 O'Leary Avenue	St Johns 709-570-0000	NF	A1C5L1
2244	Province of Newfoundland State/Prov Govt	Confederation Bldg	St Johns 709-737-3612	NF	A1C5T7
289	Lundrigans Group Ltd Real Estate/Bldg	Riverside Drive	Corner Brook 709-637-1200	NF	A2H6J5

State / Province: Nova Scotia

Revenue ($ mil)	Organization/ Industry	Address	City / Phone	State/ Zip	Province/ Postcode
1193	Empire Co Automotive	115 King Street	Stellarton 902-755-4440	NS	B0K1S0
893	Sobeys Inc Retail/Food	115 King Street	Stellarton 902-752-8371	NS	B0K1S0
128	Doane Raymond Associates Ltd Accounting	2000 Barrington Street	Halifax 902-421-1734	NS	B3J2P8
2958	Province of Nova Scotia State/Prov Govt	Province House	Halifax 902-424-2700	NS	B3J2T3
327	Maritime Telephone & Telegraph Ltd Telecom	1505 Barrington Street	Halifax 902-421-4311	NS	B3J2W3
411	Nova Scotia Power Corp Utility	1894 Barrington Street	Halifax 902-428-6221	NS	B3J2W5
468	Maritime Life Assurance Co Insurance	2701 Dutch Village Road	Halifax 902-453-4300	NS	B3J2X5
477	National Sea Products Ltd Food Processing	1959 Upper Water Street	Halifax 902-422-9381	NS	B3J3B7
1494	Central Capital Corp Non-Bank Fin	1801 Hollis Street	Halifax 902-420-2000	NS	B3J3N4

State / Province: Ontario

Revenue ($ mil)	Organization/ Industry	Address	City / Phone	State/ Zip	Province/ Postcode
2525	Canada Post Corp Federal Govt	Sir Alexander Campbell Bldg	Ottawa 613-952-1524	ON	K1A0B1
2040	Agriculture Canada Federal Govt	Sir John Carling Bldg 930 Carling Avenue	Ottawa 613-995-8963	ON	K1A0C5
1020	Energy, Mines & Resources Canada Federal Govt	580 Booth Street	Ottawa 613-995-4510	ON	K1A0E4
1020	Fisheries & Oceans Canada Federal Govt	200 Kent Street Centennial Towers	Ottawa 613-993-0600	ON	K1A0E6
1020	External Affairs Canada Federal Govt	125 Sussex Drive Lester B Pearson Bldg	Ottawa 613-996-9134	ON	K1A0G2
2040	Bank of Canada Federal Govt Fin	234 Wellington Street	Ottawa 613-563-8111	ON	K1A0G9
510	Department of Justice Canada Federal Govt	239 Wellington Street Justice Bldg	Ottawa 613-995-2569	ON	K1A0H8
20298	Canadian Department of Defense Federal Govt	101 Colonel By Drive	Ottawa 613-995-2534	ON	K1A0K2
2040	Health & Welfare Canada Federal Govt	Brooke Claxton Bldg Tunney's Pasture	Ottawa 613-957-2991	ON	K1A0K9
2040	Revenue Canada, Customs & Excise Federal Govt	Connaught Bldg Mackenzie Avenue	Ottawa 613-957-0275	ON	K1A0L5
2550	Revenue Canada, Taxation Federal Govt	875 Heron Road	Ottawa 613-957-0275	ON	K1A0L8

State / Province: Ontario

Organizations Listed Geographically

Revenue ($ mil)	Organization/ Industry	Address	City / Phone	State/ Zip	Province/ Postcode
1190	Public Works Canada Federal Govt	Sir Charles Tupper Bldg Confederation Heights	Ottawa 613-998-7724	ON	K1A0M2
5610	Transport Canada Federal Govt	330 Sparks Street Place de Ville Tower C	Ottawa 613-996-5861	ON	K1A0N5
758	Canada Mortgage & Housing Corp Federal Govt	682 Montreal Road	Ottawa 613-748-2000	ON	K1A0P7
1530	Correctional Service of Canada Federal Govt	340 Laurier Avenue W Sir Wilfrid Laurier Bldg	Ottawa 613-993-7501	ON	K1A0P9
659	Canadian Commerical Corp Federal Govt Fin	50 O'Conner Street	Ottawa 613-996-0034	ON	K1A0S6
765	Statistics Canada Federal Govt	R H Coats Bldg Tunney's Pasture	Ottawa 613-990-8116	ON	K1A0T6
314	Birks, Henry & Sons Ltd Retail/Merch	50 Rideau Street	Ottawa 613-236-3641	ON	K1N5W9
565	Export Development Corp Federal Govt	151 O'Connor Street	Ottawa 613-598-2500	ON	K1P5T9
298	Eldorado Nuclear Ltd Metals/Mining	255 Albert Street	Ottawa 613-238-5222	ON	K1P6A9
939	Metropolitan Life Insurance Co of Canada Insurance	99 Bank Street	Ottawa 613-560-7446	ON	K1P6B9
411	Farm Credit Corp Federal Govt Fin	434 Queen Street	Ottawa 613-996-6606	ON	K1P6J9
878	Royal Canadian Mint Ltd Federal Govt	355 River Road	Ottawa 613-992-2348	ON	K1S0G8
356	Mitel Corp Telecom	350 Legget Drive	Kanata 613-592-2122	ON	K2K1X3
680	Digital Equipment of Canada Ltd Comput/Off Equip	100 Herzberg Road	Kanata 613-592-5111	ON	K2K2A6
16414	General Motors of Canada Ltd Automotive	215 William Street E	Oshawa 416-644-5000	ON	L1G1K7
694	Co Steel Inc Manufacturing	1601 Hopkins Street	Whitby 416-686-2500	ON	L1N5R6
441	Mazda Canada Inc Automotive	821 Brock Road Soouth	Pickering 416-831-4222	ON	L1W3L6
478	Q & O Paper Co Paper/Forest Prd	80 King Street	St Catharines 416-688-5030	ON	L2R7B2
485	Hayes Dana Inc Automotive	1 St Paul Street	St Catharines 416-687-4200	ON	L2R7K9
468	Deere, John Ltd Equipment	Canal Bank Road	Welland 416-734-4501	ON	L3B3N3
2638	IBM (Intl Business Mach) Canada Ltd Comput/Off Equip	3500 Steeles Avenue E	Markham 416-474-2111	ON	L3R2Z1
983	Magna International Inc Automotive	36 Apple Creek Blvd	Markham 416-477-7766	ON	L3R4Y4
351	Ford Electronics Manufacturing Corp Electronics	7455 Birchmount Road	Markham 416-475-8510	ON	L3R5C2
320	Allstate Insurance Co Canada Insurance	10 Allstate Parkway	Markham 416-477-6900	ON	L3R5P8
377	Hyundai Auto Canada Inc Automotive	75 Frontenac	Markham 416-477-0202	ON	L3R6H2
614	Silcorp Ltd Retail/Merch	6205 Airport Road	Mississauga 416-678-9700	ON	L4V1E1
298	Hewlett Packard Canada Ltd Comput/Off Equip	6877 Goreway Drive	Mississauga 416-678-9430	ON	L4V1M8
298	Computer Innovations Distribution Inc Retail/Merch	3415 American Drive	Mississauga 416-793-9000	ON	L4V1T4
565	Allied Signal Canada Inc Automotive	48 Clair Avenue W	Mississauga 416-967-7211	ON	L4V3A3
341	Matsushita Electric of Canada Ltd Electronics	5770 Ambler Drive	Mississauga 416-624-5010	ON	L4W2T2
468	Camco Inc Appliances/Furn	2645 Skymark Avenue	Mississauga 416-629-3000	ON	L4W4H2
301	Caterpillar of Canada Ltd Equipment	1550 Caterpillar Road	Mississauga 416-846-3222	ON	L4X1E7
3613	Northern Telecom Ltd Telecom	3 Robert Speck Parkway	Mississauga 416-897-9000	ON	L4Z2G5

State / Province: Ontario

Organizations Listed Geographically

Revenue ($ mil)	Organization/ Industry	Address	City / Phone	State/ Zip	Province/ Postcode
416	United Cooperatives of Ontario Ltd Food Processing	5600 Cantross Court	Mississauga 416-890-8500	ON	L5A3A4
340	General Chemical Canada Ltd Chemicals	201 City Center Drive	Mississauga 416-896-9595	ON	L5B3A3
353	Monsanto Canada Inc Chemicals	2330 Argentia Road	Mississauga 416-826-9222	ON	L5M2G4
1171	DuPont Canada Ltd Chemicals	6700 Century Avenue	Mississauga 416-821-3300	ON	L5M2H3
575	Nissan Automobile Canada Ltd Automotive	2233 Argentia Road	Mississauga 416-821-9180	ON	L5M2L5
275	Dresser Canada Inc Energy	6688 Kitimat Road	Mississauga 416-826-8411	ON	L5N1P8
880	Lawson Mardon Group Ltd Packaging	6711 Mississauga Road Suite 401	Mississauga 416-821-9711	ON	L5N2W3
425	Paccar of Canada Ltd Automotive	6711 Mississauga Road	Mississauga 416-858-7070	ON	L5N2W3
360	Inglis Ltd Appliances/Furn	1901 Minnesota Court	Mississauga 416-821-6400	ON	L5N3A7
1436	General Electric Canada Co Manufacturing	2300 Meadowvale Blvd	Mississauga 416-858-5100	ON	L5N5P9
425	Re Max Ltd Real Estate/Bldg	7101 Cyntex Drive	Mississauga 416-542-2400	ON	L5N6H5
329	McDonnell Douglas Canada Ltd Aerospace	Airport Road Toronto Airpoort	Mississauga 416-677-4341	ON	L5P1B7
441	Wardair International Ltd Airline	3111 Convair Drive	Mississauga 416-671-3100	ON	L5P1C2
13552	Ford Motor Canada Ltd Automotive	The Canadian Road	Oakville 416-845-2511	ON	L6J5E4
369	Ford Credit Canada Ltd Non-Bank Fin	The Canadian Road	Oakville 416-845-2511	ON	L6L4S9
1278	K Mart Canada Ltd Retail/Merch	8925 Torbram Road	Brampton 416-792-4400	ON	L6T4G1
1006	Laidlaw Transportation Ltd Transport	3221 N Service Road	Burlington 416-336-1800	ON	L7N3G2
2535	Dofasco Inc Steel	1330 Burlington Street E	Hamilton 416-544-3761	ON	L8N3J5
677	Westinghouse Canada Inc Aerospace	120 King Street W	Hamilton 416-528-8811	ON	L8N3K2
935	Navistar International Corp of Canada Automotive	120 King Street	Hamilton 416-528-7700	ON	L8N3S5
309	Firestone Canada Inc Tire/Rubber	120 King Street W	Hamilton 416-521-1111	ON	L8N4C6
298	Slater Industries Inc Steel	1120 King Street W	Toronto 416-529-5422	ON	L8P3C8
187	McMaster University University	Administrative Bldg	Hamilton 416-525-9140	ON	L8S4L8
468	Philips Canada Ltd Electronics	601 Milner Avenue	Montreal 416-292-5161	ON	M1B1M8
1034	Honda Canada Inc Automotive	715 Milner Avenue	Scarborough 416-284-8110	ON	M1B2K8
983	Toyota Canada Inc Automotive	1291 Bellamy Road N	Scarborough 416-438-6320	ON	M1H1H9
559	Prudential Ins Co of America, Canada Insurance	200 Consilium Place	Scarborough 416-296-0777	ON	M1H3E6
654	Volkswagen Canada Ltd Automotive	1940 Eglinton Avenue E	Scarborough 416-288-3000	ON	M1L2M2
298	Volvo Canada Ltd Automotive	175 Gordon Baker Road	North York 416-493-3700	ON	M1L2M2
373	Drug Trading Co Retail/Merch	1960 Eglington Avenue E	Scarborough 416-288-1100	ON	M1L2M5
340	Becker Milk Co Food Processing	671 Warden Avenue	Scarborough 416-698-2591	ON	M1L3Z7
340	Atlantic Packaging Products Ltd Packaging	111 Progress Avenue	Scarborough 416-298-8101	ON	M1P2Y9
324	State Farm Group Ltd Canada Insurance	1801 Brimley Road	Scarborough 416-321-4000	ON	M1P3H3

State / Province: Ontario

Organizations Listed Geographically

Revenue ($ mil)	Organization/ Industry	Address	City / Phone	State/ Zip	Province/ Postcode
1488	Lauder, Estee Cosmetics Ltd Personal Care	161 Commander Blvd	Scarborough 416-292-1111	ON	M1S3K9
298	Motorola Canada Ltd Electronics	3125 Steeles Avenue E	Willowdale 416-499-1441	ON	M2H2H6
510	ICG Utilities Ltd Utility	245 Yorkland Blvd	Toronto 416-491-1880	ON	M2J1R1
383	Canadian Pacific Express Ltd Transport	2255 Sheppard Avenue E	Toronto 416-498-8850	ON	M2J1W7
366	Robin Hood Multifoods Inc Food Processing	243 Consumers Road	Willowdale 416-496-1515	ON	M2J4W8
298	Cyanamid Canada Inc Chemicals	2255 Sheppard Avenue E	Willowdale 416-470-3600	ON	M2J4Y5
720	CCL Industries Ltd Personal Care	235 Yorkland Blvd	Willowdale 416-756-8500	ON	M2J4Y8
623	Unisys Canada Inc Comput/Off Equip	2001 Sheppard Avenue E	North York 416-495-0515	ON	M2J4Z7
349	Honeywell Ltd Comput/Off Equip	155 Gordon Baker Road	Willowdale 416-499-6111	ON	M2M3N7
362	Heinz, H J Co of Canada Food Processing	5650 Yonge Street	Willowdale 416-226-5757	ON	M2M4G3
944	North American Life Assurance Co Insurance	5650 Yonge Street	Toronto 416-229-4515	ON	M2M4G4
958	Xerox Canada Ltd Comput/Off Equip	5650 Yonge Street	North York 416-229-3769	ON	M2M4G7
1139	CIL Inc Manufacturing	90 Sheppard Avenue E	North York 416-229-7000	ON	M2N6H2
448	Noma Industries Ltd Electronics	4211 Yonge Street	Willowdale 416-222-6662	ON	M2P2A9
405	Fiberglas Canada Inc Building Mat	4100 Yonge Street	Willowdale 416-733-1600	ON	M2P2B6
468	Carling O'Keefe Breweries Canada Ltd Beverage	1 Carling Drive	Rexdale 416-675-3960	ON	M2P2C4
1143	Suncor Inc Energy	36 York Mills Road	North York 416-733-7300	ON	M2P2C5
298	Harlequin Enterprises Ltd Publishing/Com	225 Duncan Mill Road	Don Mills 416-445-5860	ON	M3B3K9
352	Rothmans Inc Tobacco	1500 Don Mills Road	Don Mills 416-449-5525	ON	M3B3L1
340	Enfield Corp Manufacturing	1100 Eglinton Avenue E	Toronto 416-445-7438	ON	M3C1H8
2263	Texaco Canada Ltd Energy	90 Wynford Drive	Don Mills 416-441-7811	ON	M3C1K5
513	Four Seasons Hotels Ltd Food/Lodging	1165 Leslie Street	Toronto 416-449-1750	ON	M3C2K8
521	Nestle Enterprises Ltd Food Processing	1185 Eglinton Avenue E	Don Mills 416-429-4411	ON	M3C3C7
643	General Foods Ltd Food Processing	95 Moatfield Drive	Don Mills 416-441-5000	ON	M3C3J5
987	McDonald's Restaurants of Canada Ltd Retail/Food	McDonald's Place	Don Mills 416-443-1000	ON	M3C3L4
340	Tridel Enterprises Inc Real Estate/Bldg	4800 Dufferin Street	Downsview 416-661-9290	ON	M3H5S9
340	BID Building Materials Canada Building Mat	312 Dolomite Drive	Downsview 416-661-5950	ON	M3J3A2
437	Rockwell International of Canada Ltd Aerospace	150 Bartley Drive	Toronto 416-757-1101	ON	M4A1C7
298	Mercedes Benz Canada Inc Automotive	University Place	Toronto 416-425-3550	ON	M4G2L5
745	TCC Beverages Ltd(Coca Cola Sys Canada) Food Processing	42 46 Overlea Blvd	Toronto 416-424-6000	ON	M4H1B8
223	Nesbitt Thomson Inc Securities	150 King Street W	Toronto 416-586-3600	ON	M4M1J9
680	GW Utilities Ltd Utility	One First Canadian Place	Toronto 416-363-3300	ON	M4M1W7
543	Grafton Group Ltd Retail/Merch	9 Sunlight Park Road	Toronto 416-461-9411	ON	M4M3G1

State / Province: Ontario

Organizations Listed Geographically

Revenue ($ mil)	Organization/ Industry	Address	City / Phone	State/ Zip	Province/ Postcode
483	Union Carbide Canada Ltd / Chemicals	123 Eglinton Avenue E	Toronto / 416-488-1444	ON	M4P1J3
2245	Canadian Tire Co / Retail/Merch	2180 Yonge Street	Toronto / 416-480-3000	ON	M4P2V8
723	Maple Leaf Mills Ltd / Food Processing	2300 Yonge Street	Toronto / 416-484-7400	ON	M4P2X5
255	Barbecon Inc / Paper/Forest Prd	20 Eglinton Avenue W	Toronto / 416-488-3344	ON	M4R3G7
685	Bramalea Ltd / Real Estate/Bldg	1867 Yonge Street	Toronto / 416-487-3861	ON	M4S1Y9
7336	Loblaw Companies / Retail/Food	22 St Clair Avenue E	Toronto / 416-922-8500	ON	M4T2S7
9206	Weston, George Ltd / Retail/Food	22 St Clair Avenue E	Toronto / 416-922-2500	ON	M4T2S7
1721	Unicorp Canada Corp (Union Enterprises) / Manufacturing	21 St Clair Avenue E	Toronto / 416-961-1200	ON	M4T2T7
1131	Union Enterprises Ltd / Utility	21 St Clair Avenue E	Toronto / 416-964-6300	ON	M4T2T7
319	Pharma Plus Drugmarts Ltd / Retail/Merch	111 Merton Street	Toronto / 416-483-4611	ON	M4T3A9
479	PPG Canada Inc / Building Mat	50 St Clair Avenue W	Toronto / 416-923-5441	ON	M4V1M9
1477	Imperial Life Assurance Co / Insurance	95 St Clair Avenue W	Toronto / 416-926-2600	ON	M4V1N7
2739	Canada Packers Inc / Food Processing	30 St Clair Avenue W	Toronto / 416-869-6049	ON	M4V3A2
2944	Crown Life Insurance Co / Insurance	120 Bloor Street E	Toronto / 416-928-4500	ON	M4W1B8
2480	Crownx Inc / Health Care	120 Bloor Street	Toronto / 416-928-7722	ON	M4W1B8
5120	Manufacturers Life Insurance Co Canada / Insurance	200 Bloor Street E	Toronto / 416-926-0100	ON	M4W1E5
2919	Confederation Life Insurance Co / Insurance	321 Bloor Street E	Toronto / 416-323-8111	ON	M4W1H1
209	New York Life Insurance Co of Canada / Insurance	121 Bloor Street E	Toronto / 416-960-4500	ON	M4W3N2
774	Unilever Canada Ltd / Food Processing	160 Bloor Street E	Toronto / 416-964-1857	ON	M4W3R2
298	Lake Ontario Cement Ltd / Building Mat	2 Carlton Street	Toronto / 416-977-0611	ON	M5B1J6
394	Toronto Hydro Ltd / Utility	14 Carlton Street	Toronto / 416-595-6400	ON	M5B1K5
204	Sears Acceptance Co Canada Ltd / Non-Bank Fin	222 Jarvis Street	Toronto / 416-362-1711	ON	M5B2B8
3430	Sears Canada Ltd / Retail/Merch	222 Jarvis Street	Toronto / 416-362-1711	ON	M5B2B8
2439	Polysar Energy & Chemical (Can Dev) Corp / Chemicals	444 Yonge Street	Toronto / 416-598-7200	ON	M5B2H4
331	Hawker Siddeley Canada Inc / Manufacturing	7 King Street E	Toronto / 416-362-2941	ON	M5C1A3
340	Derlan Industries Inc / Manufacturing	95 King Street E	Toronto / 416-364-5852	ON	M5C1G4
587	Hollinger Inc / Manufacturing	10 Toronto Street	Toronto / 416-363-8721	ON	M5C2B7
554	Royal LePage Real Estate Ltd / Real Estate/Bldg	33 Yonge Street	Toronto / 416-862-0611	ON	M5E1G4
638	Royal Insurance Co / Insurance	10 Wellington Street E	Toronto / 416-366-7511	ON	M5E1L5
813	Torstar Corp / Publishing/Com	1 Yonge Street	Toronto / 416-367-2000	ON	M5E1P9
3668	Noranda Forest Inc / Paper/Forest Prd	55 Yonge Street	Toronto / 416-365-0710	ON	M5E1S4
906	Scott's Hospitality Inc / Food/Lodging	89 Chestnut Street	Toronto / 416-977-6001	ON	M5G1R1
3170	Canada Life Assurance Co / Insurance	330 University Avenue	Toronto / 416-597-1456	ON	M5G1R8

State / Province: Ontario

Organizations Listed Geographically

Revenue ($ mil)	Organization/ Industry	Address	City / Phone	State/ Zip	Province/ Postcode
303	Travelers Co of Canada Ltd Insurance	400 University Avenue	Toronto 416-586-3000	ON	M5G1S7
4488	Ontario Hydro Corp Utility	700 University Avenue	Toronto 416-592-5111	ON	M5G1X6
271	National Life Assurance Co of Canada Insurance	522 University Avenue	Toronto 416-598-2122	ON	M5G1Y7
333	Phoenix Continental Ltd Insurance	439 University Avenue	Toronto 416-596-6100	ON	M5G1Y8
699	Nabisco Brands Ltd Food Processing	1 Dundas Street W	Toronto 416-598-2600	ON	M5G2A9
1942	Varity Corp Equipment	595 Bay Street	Toronto 416-593-3811	ON	M5G2C3
389	Zurich Insurance Co Canada Ltd Insurance	375 University Avenue	Toronto 416-593-4444	ON	M5G2J7
5437	Bank of Nova Scotia Ltd Banking	44 King Street W	Toronto 416-866-6161	ON	M5H1H1
170	Touche Ross Ltd Accounting	150 King Street W	Toronto 416-599-5399	ON	M5H1J9
1722	Woolworth, F W Canada Ltd Retail/Merch	33 Adelaide Street W	Toronto 416-361-2111	ON	M5H1P5
170	Coopers & Lybrand Ltd Accounting	145 King Street W	Toronto 416-869-1130	ON	M5H1V8
1682	Rio Algom Ltd Metals/Mining	120 Adelaide Street W	Toronto 416-367-4000	ON	M5H1W5
1027	Thomson Newspapers Ltd Publishing/Com	65 Queen Street W	Toronto 416-864-1710	ON	M5H2M8
2468	Canada Trust Financial Services Co Non-Bank Fin	320 Bay Street	Toronto 416-869-6100	ON	M5H2P6
213	Canada Trust Realtors Ltd Real Estate/Bldg	320 Bay Street	Toronto 416-361-8657	ON	M5H2P6
366	General Accident Assurnace Co of Canada Insurance	2 First Canadian Place	Toronto 416-368-4733	ON	M5H2T5
850	Central Guaranty Trust Ltd Securities	366 Bay Street	Toronto 416-345-4000	ON	M5H2W5
298	Bristol Meyers Canada Inc Food Processing	390 Bay Street	Toronto 416-362-4281	ON	M5H2Y2
3971	Hudson's Bay Co Retail/Merch	401 Bay Street E	Toronto 416-861-6112	ON	M5H2Y4
513	EL Financial Corp Non-Bank Fin	165 University Avenue	Toronto 416-868-1880	ON	M5H3B8
291	Dominion of Canada General Insurance Co Insurance	165 University Avenue	Toronto 416-362-7231	ON	M5H3B9
4215	Sun Life Assurance Co of Canada Insurance	200 University Avenue	Toronto 416-595-7500	ON	M5H3C7
553	Simpsons Ltd Retail/Merch	401 Bay Street	Toronto 416-861-9111	ON	M5H3K2
3987	International Thomson Organisation Ltd Publishing/Com	20 Queen Street W	Toronto 416-977-8700	ON	M5H3R3
106	Ward Marlette Ltd Accounting	20 Queen Street W	Toronto 416-340-8390	ON	M5H3R3
579	Cadillac Fairview Corp Real Estate/Bldg	Cadillac Fairview Tower	Toronto 416-598-8200	ON	M5H3R4
592	Cineplex Odeon Corp Leisure Time	214 King Street W	Toronto 416-596-2200	ON	M5H3S6
550	Aetna Life Insurance Co Insurance	145 King Street W	Toronto 416-864-8000	ON	M5H3T7
263	Financial Trustco Capital Ltd Non-Bank Fin	121 King Street W	Toronto 416-366-8990	ON	M5H3T9
170	Merrill Lynch Canada Inc Securities	200 King Street W	Toronto 416-586-6000	ON	M5H3W3
85	Loewen Ondaatje McCutcheon Inc Non-Bank Fin	40 King Street W	Toronto 416-869-7211	ON	M5H3Y2
497	General Trustco of Canada Ltd Non-Bank Fin	120 Adelaide Street W	Toronto 416-867-3200	ON	M5H3Y3
7368	Campeau Corp Real Estate/Bldg	40 King Street	Toronto 416-868-6460	ON	M5H3Y8

State / Province: Ontario

Organizations Listed Geographically

Revenue ($ mil)	Organization/ Industry	Address	City / Phone	State/ Zip	Province/ Postcode
128	Peat Marwick Main & Co Accounting	Scotia Plaza 40 King Street E	Toronto 416-863-3300	ON	M5H3Z2
350	Reed Inc Paper/Forest Prd	207 Queens Way W	Toronto 416-862-5000	ON	M5J1A7
340	Paperboard Industries Packaging	144 Front Street W	Toronto 416-596-7180	ON	M5J1G2
712	CAE Industries Ltd Manufacturing	3060 Royal Bank Plaza	Toronto 416-865-0070	ON	M5J2J1
82	National Westminster Bank of Canada Ltd Banking	2060 Royal Bank Plaza	Toronto 416-865-0170	ON	M5J2J1
2218	Mitsui & Co Canada Ltd Conglomerate	3333 Royal Bank Plaza	Toronto 416-865-0330	ON	M5J2J2
600	Redpath Industries Ltd Food Processing	2100 Royal Bank Plaza	Toronto 416-865-0400	ON	M5J2J2
360	Denison Mines Ltd Metals/Mining	3900 Royal Bank Plaza	Toronto 416-865-1991	ON	M5J2K2
298	Marathon Realty Co Real Estate/Bldg	123 Fronto Street W	Toronto 416-864-1960	ON	M5J2M2
360	Citibank Canada Ltd Banking	123 Front Street W	Toronto 416-947-5500	ON	M5J2M3
170	Deloitte Haskins & Sells Ltd Accounting	95 Wellington Street W	Toronto 416-861-9700	ON	M5J2P4
730	BCE Development Ltd Real Estate/Bldg	Toronto Dominion Centre TD Tower	Toronto 416-369-2300	ON	M5K1A1
267	Jannock Ltd Manufacturing	55 King Street W	Toronto 416-364-8586	ON	M5K1B7
298	Hudson Bay Mining & Smelting Co Metals/Mining	Toronto Dominion Center	Toronto 416-362-2192	ON	M5K1B8
255	Gordon Capital Corp Non-Bank Fin	5401 Toronto Dominion Center	Toronto 416-364-9393	ON	M5K1E7
3301	Trilon Financial Corp Non-Bank Fin	Toronto Dominion Centre Royal Trust Tower	Toronto 416-363-0061	ON	M5K1G8
298	ITT Canada Ltd Electronics	Toronto Dominion Center	Toronto 416-863-9666	ON	M5K1H1
2305	Stelco Inc Steel	Toronto Dominion Centre IBM Tower	Toronto 416-362-2161	ON	M5K1J4
4370	Toronto Dominion Bank Ltd Banking	Toronto Dominion Centre	Toronto 416-982-8222	ON	M5K1J4
304	Rogers Communications Inc Publishing/Com	Commercial Union Tower	Toronto 416-864-2373	ON	M5K1J5
191	Clarkson Gordon Ltd Accounting	77 King Street W	Toronto 416-864-1234	ON	M5K1J7
421	Commercial Union Assurance Group Ltd Insurance	Commercial Union Tower	Toronto 416-361-2500	ON	M5K1L9
213	ScotiaMcLeod Ltd Securities	Commercial Union Tower	Toronto 416-863-7411	ON	M5K1M2
255	Wood Gundy Inc Securities	Royal Trust Tower	Toronto 416-869-8100	ON	M5K1M7
709	Placer Dome Ltd Metals/Mining	Toronto Dominion Center	Toronto 416-868-6060	ON	M5K1N3
7854	Canadian Imperial Bank of Commerce Ltd Banking	Commerce Court W	Toronto 416-980-2211	ON	M5L1A2
1275	Mitsubishi Canada Ltd Conglomerate	2181 Commerce Court W	Toronto 416-362-6731	ON	M5L1A5
298	Dominion Securities Inc Securities	Commerce Court S	Toronto 416-864-4000	ON	M5L1A7
463	Sherritt Gordon Mines Ltd Metals/Mining	2800 Commerce Court W	Toronto 416-363-9241	ON	M5L1B1
1139	Falconbridge Ltd Metals/Mining	Commerce Court W	Toronto 416-863-7000	ON	M5L1B4
510	Kidd Creek Mines Ltd Metals/Mining	Commerce Court W	Toronto 416-863-7000	ON	M5L1B4
255	Brunswick Mining & Smelting Corp Metals/Mining	Commerce Court W	Toronto 506-522-2100	ON	M5L1B6
7529	Noranda Inc Metals/Mining	Commerce Court W	Toronto 416-982-7111	ON	M5L1B6

State / Province: Ontario

Organizations Listed Geographically

Revenue ($ mil)	Organization/ Industry	Address	City / Phone	State/ Zip	Province/ Postcode
7491	Brascan Ltd Energy	4800 Commerce Court W	Toronto 416-363-9491	ON	M5L1B7
213	Thorne Ernst & Whinney Ltd Accounting	Commerce Court W	Toronto 416-864-9520	ON	M5L1C6
271	Premetalco Inc Steel	2860 Commerce Court W	Toronto 416-366-3954	ON	M5L1C9
1628	Onex Corp Conglomerate	Commerce Court W Box 153	Toronto 416-362-7711	ON	M5L1E7
255	Sara Lee Corp of Canada Food Processing	Commerce Court	Toronto 416-860-0048	ON	M5L1E7
140	Barclays Bank of Canada Ltd Banking	3500 Commerce Court W	Toronto 416-862-0594	ON	M5L1G2
230	Hees Internationaal Corp Non-Bank Fin	4400 Commerce Court W	Toronto 416-865-0430	ON	M5L1K5
259	Pepsi Cola Canada Ltd Food Processing	1255 Bay Street	Toronto 416-964-1313	ON	M5R2G9
561	Toronto, University of University	Administrative Bldg	Toronto 416-978-2011	ON	M5S1A1
468	Cara Operations Ltd Food/Lodging	238 Bloor Street W	Toronto 416-962-4571	ON	M5S1T8
659	BCE PubliTech Inc Publishing/Com	150 Bloor Street W	Toronto 416-964-1374	ON	M5S2X9
1406	Southam Inc Publishing/Com	150 Bloor Street W	Toronto 416-927-1877	ON	M5S2Y8
1697	Dylex Ltd Retail/Merch	637 Lakeshore Blvd W	Toronto 416-586-7000	ON	M5V1A8
1020	Great Atlantic & Pacific Co of Canada Retail/Food	5559 Dundas Street W	Toronto 416-239-7171	ON	M5W1A6
1107	MacLean Hunter Ltd Publishing/Com	777 Bay Street	Toronto 416-596-5000	ON	M5W1A7
891	Procter & Gamble Inc Food Processing	4711 Yonge Street	Toronto 416-730-4711	ON	M5W1C5
6124	Imperial Oil Ltd Energy	111 St Clair Avenue W	Toronto 416-968-4111	ON	M5W1K3
449	Canron Ltd Manufacturing	1 First Canadian Place	Toronto 416-364-6600	ON	M5X1A4
2809	Abitibi Price Ltd Paper/Forest Prd	2 First Canadian Place	Toronto 416-369-6700	ON	M5X1A9
2017	Inco Ltd Metals/Mining	1 First Canadian Place	Toronto 416-361-7511	ON	M5X1C4
1417	Consumers Gas Ltd Energy	1 First Canadian Place	Toronto 416-864-3399	ON	M5X1C5
1162	Marubeni Canada Ltd Food Processing	2 First Canadian Place	Toronto 416-368-1171	ON	M5X1E3
2571	Moore Corp Comput/Off Equip	1 First Canadian Place	Toronto 416-364-2600	ON	M5X1G5
263	Burns Fry Ltd Securities	First Canadian Place	Toronto 416-365-4000	ON	M5X1H3
170	Price Waterhouse Ltd Accounting	One First Canadian Place	Toronto 416-863-1133	ON	M5X1H7
291	Coscan Development Corp Real Estate/Bldg	2 First Canadian Place	Toronto 416-369-8200	ON	M5X1H9
213	Toronto Stock Exchange Ltd Non-Bank Fin	Exchange Tower 2 First Canadian Place	Toronto 416-947-4700	ON	M5X1J2
26520	Province of Ontario State/Prov Govt	Parliment Bldgs	Toronto 416-965-3535	ON	M7A1A1
302	Campbell Soup Co Canada Food Processing	60 Birmingham Street	Toronto 416-251-1131	ON	M8V2B8
350	Boise Cascade Canada Ltd Paper/Forest Prd	3300 Bloor Street W	Toronto 416-231-3010	ON	M8X2X2
703	General Motors Acceptance Corp Canada Non-Bank Fin	3300 Bloor Street W	Toronto 416-234-6616	ON	M8X2X5
298	VS Services Ltd Food Processing	Islington & Evans Avenue	Toronto 416-255-1331	ON	M8Z5Y7
340	Wimpey, George Canada Ltd Real Estate/Bldg	80 N Queen Street	Toronto 416-233-5811	ON	M8Z5Z6

State / Province: Ontario

Organizations Listed Geographically

Revenue ($ mil)	Organization/ Industry	Address	City / Phone	State/ Zip	Province/ Postcode
3634	Oshawa Group Ltd Retail/Food	302 East Mall	Islington 416-236-1971	ON	M9B6B8
664	Goodyear Canada Inc Tire/Rubber	10 Four Seasons Place	Islington 416-626-4611	ON	M9B6G2
255	Carlson Marketing Group Ltd Business Service	5353 Dundas Street W	Toronto 416-236-1991	ON	M9B6H8
333	Consumers Packaging Inc Packaging	401 West Mall	Etobicoke 416-232-3283	ON	M9C5J7
925	Indal Ltd Building Mat	4000 Weston Road	Weston 416-743-1400	ON	M9L2W8
367	Kinney Shoes of Canada Ltd Retail/Merch	100 Mainshep Road	Weston 416-742-3590	ON	M9M1L5
893	AMCA (Amer Can of Canada) Intl Ltd Packaging	1 International Blvd	Rexdale 416-432-2151	ON	M9W1A1
2070	Molson Companies Food Processing	2 International Blvd	Toronto 416-675-1786	ON	M9W1A2
1105	Consumers Distributing Co Retail/Merch	62 Belfield Road	Rexdale 416-245-4900	ON	M9W1G2
255	Commonwealth Holiday Inns Ltd Food/Lodging	31 Sasken Drive	Rexdale 416-675-2030	ON	M9W1K8
383	Litton Systems Canada Ltd Electronics	25 Cityview Drive	Toronto 416-249-1231	ON	M9W5A7
298	BASF Canada Inc Chemicals	345 Carlington Drive	Toronto 416-675-3611	ON	M9W6N9
672	Alliance Ro-Na Home Inc Building Mat	34 Henry Street	St Jacobs 519-664-2252	ON	N0B2N0
670	Cooperators General Insurance Co Insurance	130 MacDonell Street Priority Square	Guelph 519-824-4400	ON	N1H6P8
581	Schneider Corp Manufacturing	321 Courtland Avenue	Kitchener 519-885-8100	ON	N2G3X8
403	Economical Group Ltd Insurance	10 Duke Street	Kitchener 519-888-8200	ON	N2G4C1
307	Uniroyal Goodrich Canada Inc Tire/Rubber	409 Weber Street	Kitchener 519-749-8473	ON	N2G4J5
612	Prudential Assurance Group Insurance	101 Frederick Street	Kitchener 519-888-5700	ON	N2H6R2
2343	Mutual Life Assurance Co of Canada Insurance	227 King Street S	Waterloo 519-888-2235	ON	N2J4C5
187	Waterloo, University of University	Administrative Bldg	Waterloo 519-885-1211	ON	N2L3G1
425	Minnesota Mining & Manufacturing Canada Chemicals	1840 Oxford Street E	London 519-451-2500	ON	N5A4T1
1073	National Victoria & Grey Trustco Ltd Non-Bank Fin	1 Ontario Street	Stratford 519-271-2050	ON	N5A6S9
299	Prudential Assurance Group Ltd Canada Insurance	195 Dufferin Avenue	Kitchener 519-433-1231	ON	N6A1K7
281	Western Ontario, University of University	Administrative Bldg	London 519-679-2111	ON	N6A3K7
1960	London Life Insurance Co Insurance	255 Dufferin Avenue	London 519-432-5281	ON	N6A4K1
643	Ellis Don Ltd Real Estate/Bldg	2045 Oxford Street E	London 519-455-6770	ON	N6A4M6
1004	Emco Ltd Building Mat	1108 Dundas Street E	London 519-451-1250	ON	N6A4N7
4341	Labatt, John Ltd Food Processing	451 Ridout Street N	London 519-673-5050	ON	N6A5L3
1148	Union Gas Ltd Utility	50 Kell Drive N	Chatham 519-352-3100	ON	N7M5M1
1275	Dow Chemical Canada Ltd Chemicals	1086 Modeland Road	Sarnia 519-339-3131	ON	N7T7K7
2103	Ploysar Ltd Chemicals	201 Front Street N	Sarnia 519-332-1212	ON	N7T7V1
1150	Ensite Ltd Automotive	2950 Metcalfe Street	Windsor 519-257-4412	ON	N8Y1W9
1309	Hiram Walker Gooderham Worts Ltd Food Processing	2072 Riverside Road E	Windsor 519-254-5171	ON	N8Y4S5

State / Province: Ontario

Organizations Listed Geographically

Revenue ($ mil)	Organization/ Industry	Address	City / Phone	State/ Zip	Province/ Postcode
7368	Chrysler Canada Ltd Automotive	2450 Chrysler Center	Windsor 519-973-2000	ON	N9A4H6
1183	Algoma Steel Ltd Steel	503 Queen Street	Sault Ste Marie 705-945-2788	ON	P6A5P2
2555	Canadian Pacific Forest Products Ltd Paper/Forest Prd	Neebling Avenue	Thunder Bay 807-475-2110	ON	P7C4W3
638	Great Lakes Forest Products Ltd Paper/Forest Prd	Neebing Avenue	Thunder Bay 807-475-2110	ON	P7C4W3

State / Province: Prince Edward Island

444	Province of Prince Edward Island State/Prov Govt	Province House	Charlotetown 902-892-3428	PE	C1A7N8

State / Province: Quebec

255	Purdel Cooperative Agro Alimentaire Food Processing	155 St Jean Baptiste	Bic 418-736-4363	PQ	G0L10
27540	Province of Quebec State/Prov Govt	Hotel du Parliment	Quebec City 418-643-1430	PQ	G1A1A3
1487	Industrial Alliance Life Insurance Co Insurance	1080 Schemin St Louis	Sillery 418-463-5784	PQ	G1K7M3
281	Laval, Universite University	Cite Universitaire	Quebec 418-656-2131	PQ	G1K7P4
1411	Laurentian Group Corp Non-Bank Fin	500 Grande Allee Est	Quebec 418-647-5151	PQ	G1R2J7
261	Laurentian Mutual Insurance Co Insurance	500 Grande Allee Est	Quebec 418-647-5255	PQ	G1R2J7
551	Donohue Inc Paper/Forest Prd	1150 Claire Fontaine	Quebec 418-522-6471	PQ	G1R5G4
327	Quebec, Universite du University	2875 Boul Laurier	Sainte Foy 418-657-3551	PQ	G1V2M3
210	SSQ Mutuelle d'Assurance Ltd Insurance	2525 Laurier Blvd	Sainte Foy 418-651-7000	PQ	G1V4H6
357	Group Olympia Ltd Food Processing	2200 Avenue Pratte	St Simon de Bagot 514-771-0400	PQ	G2S4B6
547	Canam Manac Group Inc Automotive	11535 lre Avenue Bureau 700	Ville St Georges 418-228-8031	PQ	G5Y2C7
329	Assurance vie Desjardins Ltd Insurance	200 Avenue Des Commandeurs	Levis 418-835-2323	PQ	G6V6R2
1700	Groupe des Epiciers unis,Metro Richelieu Non-Bank Fin	11011 Maurice Duplessis	Montreal 514-643-1000	PQ	H1C1V6
1870	Metro Richelieu Ltd Retail/Food	9250 Notre Dame E	Montreal 514-353-5000	PQ	H1L3N4
304	Olco Petroleum Group Ltd Energy	2561 Avenue Georges V	Montreal 514-353-6821	PQ	H1L6J7
315	Groupe Pharmaceutique Focus Inc Drugs	5750 Boul Metropolitain E	Montreal 514-254-4937	PQ	H1S1A7
808	Gaz Metropolitain Inc Utility	1717 Du Havre	Montreal 514-598-3444	PQ	H2K2X3
298	Groupe Videotron Ltee Retail/Merch	2000 Rue Berri	Montreal 514-281-1212	PQ	H2L4V7
1057	Co-operative Federee de Quebec Ltd Food Processing	1055 Rue Marche Centrale	Montreal 514-383-6450	PQ	H2P2W2
1093	Quebecor Inc Publishing/Com	225 E Rue Roy	Montreal 514-282-9600	PQ	H2W2N6
549	Sidbec Ltd Steel	300 Leo Parizeau	Montreal 514-286-8600	PQ	H2W2S7
6816	Bank of Montreal Banking	129 Rue St Jacques	Montreal 514-877-7110	PQ	H2Y1L6
276	Laurentian General Insurance Co Insurance	507 Place D'Armes	Montreal 514-842-6212	PQ	H2Y2W8
4510	Hydro Quebec Ltd Utility	75 Ouest Boul Rene Levesque	Montreal 514-289-2211	PQ	H2Z1A4
2912	Air Canada Ltd Airline	500 Rene Levesque Blvd	Montreal 514-879-7000	PQ	H2Z1X5

State / Province: Quebec

Organizations Listed Geographically

Revenue ($ mil)	Organization/ Industry	Address	City / Phone	State/ Zip	Province/ Postcode
375	SNC Group Inc Business Service	2 Place Felix Martin	Montreal 514-866-1000	PQ	H2Z1Z3
1902	Ivaco Inc Steel	770 Rue Sherbrooke O	Montreal 514-288-4545	PQ	H3A1G1
428	QIT Fer et Titane Inc Metals/Mining	770 Sherbrooke Ouest	Montreal 514-288-8400	PQ	H3A1G1
4298	Seagram Co Ltd Food Processing	1430 Rue Peel	Montreal 514-849-5271	PQ	H3A1S9
298	Wajax Ltd Building Mat	770 Sherbrooke Street	Montreal 514-238-7291	PQ	H3A1Z1
1238	Ultramar Canada Inc Energy	2020 University	Montreal 514-499-6111	PQ	H3A2L4
870	Lavalin Inc Real Estate/Bldg	1130 O Rue Sherbrooke	Montreal 514-288-1740	PQ	H3A2R5
234	McGill University University	845 Sherbrooke Street W	Montreal 514-398-4455	PQ	H3A2T5
340	Laurentian Bank of Canada Banking	1981 Avenue McGill College	Montreal 514-284-7967	PQ	H3A33a
170	Les Cooperants Ltd Insurance	600 Maison Avenue Blvd W	Montreal 514-287-6600	PQ	H3A3A9
2253	Caisse de Depot du Quebec Ltd Non-Bank Fin	1981 Avenue McGill College	Montreal 514-842-3261	PQ	H3A3C7
9165	ALCAN Aluminum Co of Canada Ltd Metals/Mining	1188 Sherbooke Street W	Montreal 514-848-8000	PQ	H3A3G2
378	Rolland Inc Paper/Forest Prd	2000 Avenue McGill	Montreal 514-289-1779	PQ	H3A3H3
416	Bank Laurentienne du Canada Savings & Loan	1981 McGill College Avenue	Montreal 514-284-3931	PQ	H3A3K3
764	Montreal Trustco Inc Non-Bank Fin	1800 McGill College Avenue	Montreal 514-397-7171	PQ	H3A3K9
838	Canada Cement Lafarge Ltd Building Mat	606 Rue Cathcart	Montreal 514-861-1411	PQ	H3B1L7
417	Lloyd's of London Canada Ltd Insurance	1155 Rue University	Montreal 514-861-8361	PQ	H3B1S3
298	Celanese Canada Inc Chemicals	800 Boul Dorchester 0	Montreal 514-871-5511	PQ	H3B1X9
7175	Provigo Incorporated Retail/Food	800 Dorchester Blvd W	Montreal 514-866-9781	PQ	H3B1Y2
1187	Bombardier Inc Manufacturing	800 Boul Dorchester 1700	Montreal 514-861-9481	PQ	H3B1Y8
2016	Consolidated Bathurst Inc Paper/Forest Prd	800 Rene Levesque Blvd W	Montreal 514-875-2160	PQ	H3B1Y9
298	UAP Inc Automotive	1 Valleybrook Drive	Montreal 514-256-5031	PQ	H3B2S8
425	Societe Generale Financement du Quebec Federal Govt Fin	155 University	Montreal 514-875-0330	PQ	H3B3A7
795	Repap Enterprises Corp Paper/Forest Prd	1150 Peel Street Suite 3200	Montreal 514-879-1316	PQ	H3B3V2
2633	National Bank of Canada Ltd Banking	600 De La Gauchetiere W	Montreal 514-394-4000	PQ	H3B4A8
340	Fednav Ltd Transport	600 De La Gaucheitie 0062	Montreal 514-878-6500	PQ	H3B4M3
879	Noverco Inc Metals/Mining	1170 Peel Street	Montreal 514-393-2650	PQ	H3B4P2
170	Levesque Beaubien Inc Securities	1155 Metcalfe Street	Montreal 514-879-2222	PQ	H3B4S9
425	Bathurst Paper Ltd Paper/Forest Prd	800 O Boul Dorchester	Montreal 514-875-2160	PQ	H3C2R5
425	CB Pak Inc Packaging	800 Boul Dorchester	Montreal 516-875-2160	PQ	H3C2R5
349	CSL Group Inc Transport	759 Victoria Square	Montreal 514-288-0221	PQ	H3C2R7
510	Kruger Inc Paper/Forest Prd	3285 Rue Bedford	Montreal 514-737-1131	PQ	H3C2V2
9006	Royal Bank of Canada Ltd Banking	1 Place Ville Marie 35th Floor	Montreal 514-874-2110	PQ	H3C3A9

State / Province: Quebec

Organizations Listed Geographically

Revenue ($ mil)	Organization/ Industry	Address	City / Phone	State/ Zip	Province/ Postcode
10214	Canadian Pacific Ltd Railroad	910 Reel Street Windsor Station	Montreal 514-395-5151	PQ	H3C3E4
5421	Bell Canada Inc (BCE Inc) Telecom	1050 Beaver Hall Hill	Montreal 514-870-1511	PQ	H3C3G4
700	Kraft Ltd Food Processing	8600 Chermin Devonshire	Montreal 514-341-5000	PQ	H3C3J3
234	Montreal, Universite de University	Case Postale 6128 Surrursale A	Montreal 514-343-6111	PQ	H3C3J7
1034	Dominion Textile Inc Apparel/Textiles	1950 O Rue Sherbrooke	Montreal 514-989-6000	PQ	H3C3L1
2298	Domtar Inc Chemicals	395 Boul de Maisonneuve O	Montreal 514-848-5400	PQ	H3C3M1
670	Via Rail Canada Inc Railroad	2 Place Ville Marie	Montreal 514-286-2311	PQ	H3C3N3
3975	Canadian National Railway Railroad	935 De la Gauchetiere Street W	Montreal 514-399-5430	PQ	H3C3N4
842	Standard Life Assurance Co Insurance	1245 Sherbrooke W	Montreal 514-284-6711	PQ	H3G1G3
300	Reitman's Canada Ltd Apparel/Textiles	250 O Sauve	Montreal 514-384-1140	PQ	H3L1Z2
255	Canadian Marconi Co Electronics	2442 Trenton	Montreal 514-341-7630	PQ	H3P1Y9
623	St Lawrence Cement Inc Building Mat	1945 Graham Blvd	Montreal 514-340-1881	PQ	H3R1H1
314	Teleglobe Canada Ltd Telecom	600 McCaffrey Street	Montreal 514-289-7272	PQ	H3T1N1
1469	United Westburne Inc Manufacturing	6333 Boul Decarie	Montreal 514-342-5181	PQ	H3W3E1
3897	Steinberg Inc Retail/Food	3500 De Maisonneuve W 2 Place Alexis Nihon	Montreal 514-931-9131	PQ	H3Z1Y3
5101	Imasco Ltd Personal Care	4 Westmont Square	Montreal 514-937-9111	PQ	H3Z2S8
1573	Zeller's Inc Retail/Merch	5100 De Maisonneuve	Montreal 514-483-7600	PQ	H4A1Y6
1637	Imperial Tobacco Ltd Tobacco	3810 Rue St Antoine	Montreal 514-932-6161	PQ	H4C1B5
213	Rolls Royce Industries Canada Inc Aerospace	100 Alexis Nihon Blvd	Ville St Laurent 514-747-7742	PQ	H4M2P5
695	Agropur Coop Agro Alimentaire Ltd Real Estate/Bldg	333 Lebeau	Montreal 514-332-2220	PQ	H4N1S3
425	Cantrex Group Inc Business Service	4445 Garend Street	Montreal 514-335-0260	PQ	H4R2H7
298	Sunbuy Inc Retail/Merch	4445 Garand	Montreal 514-335-0260	PQ	H4R2H9
1676	Anglo Canadian Telephone Co Telecom	8750 Cote De Liesse	Saint Laurent 514-341-6321	PQ	H4T1H3
340	Memotec Data Inc Telecom	600 McCaffrey	Montreal 514-738-4781	PQ	H4T1N1
714	Henleys Group Ltd Manufacturing	800 Square Victoria	Montreal 514-397-7640	PQ	H4Z1E9
213	Federal Business Development Bank Ltd Federal Govt Fin	800 Carre Victoria	Montreal 514-283-5904	PQ	H4Z1L4
441	Culinar Inc Food Processing	2 Complexe Desjardins 2700	Montreal 514-288-3101	PQ	H5B1B2
167	La Sauvegarde Assurance sur la vie Ltd Insurance	One Complex Desjardins S Tower 25th Floor	Montreal 514-285-7700	PQ	H5B1E2
2445	La Confederation Desjardins Du Quebec Non-Bank Fin	One Complex Desjardins	Montreal 514-281-8666	PQ	H5B1E7
501	Cascades Inc Packaging	404 Rue Marie Victorin	Kingsey Falls 819-363-2245	PQ	J0A1B0
383	Coronet Carpets Inc Apparel/Textiles	1144 E Boul Magenta	Farnham 514-293-3155	PQ	J2N2R4
425	Groupe Ro-na Inc Manufacturing	1250 Nobel	Boucherville 514-599-5100	PQ	J4B5K1
413	Le Groupe Ro Na Inc Building Mat	1250 Nobel	Boucherville 514-599-5100	PQ	J4B5K1

State / Province: Quebec

Revenue ($ mil)	Organization/ Industry	Address	City / Phone	State/ Zip	Province/ Postcode
839	Pratt & Whitney Canada Inc Aerospace	1000 Boul Marie Victorin	Longueuill 514-677-9411	PQ	J4K4X9
1530	Environment Canada Federal Govt	10 Wellington Street Les Terrasses de la Chaudiere	Hull 819-997-2800	PQ	K1A0H3
1020	Indian & Northern Affairs Canada Federal Govt	10 Wellington Street Les Terrasses de la Chaudiere	Hull 819-997-0380	PQ	K1A0H4
4080	Employment & Immigration Canada Federal Govt	Place du Portage Phase IV	Hull 819-994-6313	PQ	K1A0J9
2040	Supply & Services Canada Federal Govt	11 Laurier Street Place du Portage Phase III	Hull 819-997-6363	PQ	K1A0S5
1637	CIP Inc Publishing/Com	30 Carling Terrace	Montreal 514-878-4811	PQ	N0G2W0

State / Province: Saskatchewan

Revenue ($ mil)	Organization/ Industry	Address	City / Phone	State/ Zip	Province/ Postcode
774	Saskatchewan Power Corp Utility	2025 Victoria Avenue	Regina 306-566-2121	SK	S4P0S1
340	IPSCO Inc Manufacturing	Alberta Street N	Regina 306-949-3530	SK	S4P3C7
436	Saskatchewan Telecommunications Ltd Telecom	2121 Saskatchewan Drive	Regina 306-347-2200	SK	S4P3Y2
4080	Province of Saskatchewan State/Prov Govt	Legislative Bldg	Regina 306-565-6291	SK	S4S0B3
1508	Saskatchewan Wheat Pool Ltd Food Processing	2625 Victoria Avenue	Regina 306-569-4411	SK	S4T7T9
324	Canpotex Ltd Chemicals	111 2nd Avenue S	Saskatoon 306-931-2200	SK	S7K1K6
298	Consumers Co-op Refineries Ltd Energy	401 22nd Street E	Saskatoon 306-244-3311	SK	S7K3M9
1214	Federated Cooperatives Ltd Energy	401 22nd Street E	Saskatoon 306-244-3311	SK	S7K3M9
187	Saskatchewan, University of University	Administrative Bldg	Saskatoon 306-244-4343	SK	S7N0W0

State / Province: Saskatchewan

Section 4

Organizations Listed by Industry

Organizations Listed by Industry

Organization	Phone	City / State or Province	Revenue ($ mil)	Assets ($ mil)	Emp (thous)
Major Group: Financial		**Industry: Banking**			
American National Bank & Trust Co	312-661-5000	Chicago, IL	438	4567	3
American Security Bank NA	202-624-4000	Washington, DC	800	6500	2
Ameritrust Corp	216-737-5000	Cleveland, OH	1052	10738	4
Amsouth Bancorp Inc	205-320-7151	Birmingham, AL	797	8313	4
Arizona Bank Corp	602-262-2000	Phoenix, AZ	800	6500	2
Banc One Corp	614-463-5944	Columbus, OH	2734	25274	17
Banc One Wisconsin	414-765-3000	Milwaukee, WI	400	4000	2
Banca Serfin	212-635-2300	New York, NY	440	3500	2
Banco Nacional de Mexico	212-838-8300	New York, NY	550	4000	2
Banco Popular de Puerto Rico Inc	212-928-8600	New York, NY	543	5707	7
Bancorp Hawaii Inc	808-537-8111	Honolulu, HI	630	6635	3
Bank Leumi Trust Co	212-382-4000	New York, NY	276	3140	3
Bank of Boston Corp	617-434-2200	Boston, MA	5296	36060	20
Bank of California (Mitsubishi Bank)	213-621-1200	Los Angeles, CA	583	6887	1
Bank of Montreal	514-877-7110	Montreal, PQ Can	6816	67073	34
Bank of New England Corp	617-742-4000	Boston, MA	3247	30110	18
Bank of New York Co	212-495-1784	New York, NY	2620	47388	18
Bank of Nova Scotia Ltd	416-866-6161	Toronto, ON Can	5437	60716	26
Bank of Tokyo Trust	212-766-3472	New York, NY	800	7000	1
Bank South Corp	404-529-4521	Atlanta, GA	409	4881	2
BankAmerica Corp	415-622-3456	San Francisco, CA	10182	94647	54
Bankers Trust New York Corp	212-250-2500	New York, NY	5851	57942	13
Banks of Mid-America Inc	405-231-6000	Oklahoma City, OK	190	2269	2
Banque National de Paris	212-980-5185	New York, NY	450	3500	1
Barclays American Corp	212-412-4000	New York, NY	550	4500	3
Barclays Bank of Canada Ltd	416-862-0594	Toronto, ON Can	140	1872	1
Barnett Banks Inc	904-791-7720	Jacksonville, FL	2546	25748	15
Baybanks Inc	617-482-1040	Boston, MA	1037	8678	6
Bayerische Vereinsbank AG	212-210-0300	New York, NY	450	3500	1
Boatmen's Bancshares Inc	314-425-7525	St Louis, MO	1066	14676	5
Boston Safe Deposit & Trust Co	617-722-7000	Boston, MA	1500	12000	3
California First Bank Inc	415-445-0200	San Francisco, CA	600	6000	4
Canadian Imperial Bank of Commerce Ltd	416-980-2211	Toronto, ON Can	7854	80485	36
CB & T Bancshares Inc	404-649-2387	Columbus, GA	251	1957	2
Centerre Trust Co	314-231-9300	St Louis, MO	1100	11000	4
Central Bancorp Inc	513-651-8000	Cincinnati, OH	500	5000	3
Central Bancshares Inc	205-933-3000	Birmingham, AL	401	4109	3
Central Fidelity Banks Inc	804-782-4000	Richmond, VA	446	4731	3
Chase Manhattan Bank Inc	212-552-2222	New York, NY	12375	97455	42
Chemical New York Corp	212-310-6161	New York, NY	7644	67349	20
Citibank Arizona	602-248-2200	Phoenix, AZ	500	5000	3
Citibank Canada Ltd	416-947-5500	Toronto, ON Can	360	4167	1
Citicorp Inc	212-559-1000	New York, NY	32024	207666	89
Citizens & Southern Co	404-581-2121	Atlanta, GA	2090	21098	14
Citizens Fidelity Corp	502-581-2100	Louisville, KY	700	5000	3
City National Corp	213-550-5400	Beverly Hills, CA	371	4296	2
Citytrust Bank Corp	203-384-5212	Bridgeport, CT	280	2601	2
Comerica Inc	313-222-3300	Detroit, MI	1043	11145	7
Commerce Bancshares Inc	816-234-2000	Kansas City, MO	479	5444	4
Commerzbank AG	212-208-6200	New York, NY	450	3500	1
Connecticut Bank & Trust Co NA	203-244-5000	Hartford, CT	1500	1200	7
Continental Bancorp Inc	215-564-7000	Philadelphia, PA	750	6000	3

Major Group: Financial   **Industry: Banking**

Organizations Listed by Industry

Organization	Phone	City / State or Province	Revenue ($ mil)	Assets ($ mil)	Emp (thous)
Continental Bank Corp	312-828-2345	Chicago, IL	3061	30578	8
Corestates Financial Corp	215-629-3869	Philadelphia, PA	1630	16430	8
Credit Agricole Mutuel Paris	212-418-2200	New York, NY	450	3500	1
Credit Lyonnais France	212-344-0500	New York, NY	450	3500	1
Crestar Financial Corp (United VA)	804-782-5000	Richmond, VA	1016	10408	6
Dai Ichi Kangyo Bank Ltd	212-466-5200	New York, NY	550	5000	2
Daiwa Bank & Trust Co	212-399-2710	New York, NY	450	3500	2
Dauphin Deposit Corp	717-255-2121	Harrisburg, PA	500	5000	2
Deutsche Bank AG	212-940-8000	New York, NY	450	3500	1
Dominion Bankshares Inc	703-563-7749	Roanoke, VA	898	9204	6
Dresdner Bank AG	212-425-4640	New York, NY	450	3500	1
Equimark Corp	412-288-5000	Pittsburgh, PA	600	6000	2
Equitable BanCorp Inc	301-547-4000	Baltimore, MD	375	5186	3
European American Bancorp	516-296-5000	Uniondale, NY	540	5335	3
Fidelcor Inc	215-985-6000	Philadelphia, PA	1300	13000	6
Fifth Third BanCorp Inc	513-579-5300	Cincinnati, OH	506	5246	3
First Alabama Bancshares	205-832-8490	Montgomery, AL	474	5174	3
First American Bank of Virginia Co	703-821-7777	McLean, VA	300	3200	2
First American Bankshares Inc	202-383-1400	Washington, DC	900	8000	6
First American Corp	615-748-2100	Nashville, TN	699	7204	4
First Bank System Inc	612-370-5100	Minneapolis, MN	2441	24248	12
First Chicago Corp	312-732-4000	Chicago, IL	4815	44432	16
First Citizens Bank & Trust Co	919-755-7215	Raleigh, NC	319	3218	3
First City Bancorp of Texas Inc	713-658-6873	Houston, TX	865	12195	7
First Commerce Corp	504-561-1371	New Orleans, LA	300	3000	2
First Empire State Corp	716-842-4200	Buffalo, NY	537	5908	3
First Fidelity BanCorp Inc	201-565-3200	Newark, NJ	2806	29777	15
First Florida Banks Inc	813-224-1111	Tampa, FL	479	5132	4
First Hawaiian Inc	808-525-7000	Honolulu, HI	396	4239	2
First Interstate BanCorp Inc	213-614-6001	Los Angeles, CA	5932	63703	38
First Interstate Bank of Texas	713-224-6611	Houston, TX	1000	10000	4
First Jersey National Corp	201-547-7000	Jersey City, NJ	500	5000	3
First Kentucky National Corp	502-581-4498	Louisville, KY	500	5500	5
First Maryland BanCorp Inc	301-244-4000	Baltimore, MD	660	5881	3
First National Cincinnati Corp	513-632-4000	Cincinnati, OH	531	5214	3
First of America Bank Corp	616-383-9000	Kalamazoo, MI	885	9769	5
First Pennsylvania Corp	215-786-5000	Philadelphia, PA	623	6407	4
First Security Corp	801-350-5325	Salt Lake City, UT	522	5159	3
First Tennessee National Corp	901-523-5630	Memphis, TN	621	5800	4
First Union National Bank Corp	704-374-6565	Charlotte, NC	2898	28978	16
First Virginia Banks Inc	703-241-4000	Falls Church, VA	482	4796	4
First Wachovia Corp	919-770-5000	Winston-Salem, NC	2091	21815	14
Firstar (First Wisconsin Corp)	414-765-4321	Milwaukee, WI	850	7193	5
Fleet/Norstar Financial Corp	401-278-5800	Providence, RI	3051	29052	15
Florida National Banks	904-359-5020	Jacksonville, FL	749	7828	5
Fuji Bank & Trust	212-839-5600	New York, NY	600	5000	3
Generale Banque (Societe Generale)	212-418-8700	New York, NY	450	3500	1
Hamilton Bank Corp	717-569-8731	Lancaster, PA	500	4500	2
Harris Trust & Savings Bank	312-461-2121	Chicago, IL	1165	11276	4
Hartford National Corp	203-728-2000	Hartford, CT	1100	12000	5
Hibernia Corp	504-586-5552	New Orleans, LA	546	5313	3
Hongkong & Shanghai Banking Corp	212-839-5000	New York, NY	550	4500	1
Hongkong Bank of Canada	604-685-1000	Vancouver, BC Can	250	3045	2
Horizon Bancorp Inc	201-539-7700	Morristown, NJ	400	4000	3

Major Group: Financial   Industry: Banking

Organizations Listed by Industry

Organization	Phone	City / State or Province	Revenue ($ mil)	Assets ($ mil)	Emp (thous)
Huntington Bancshares Inc	614-476-8300	Columbus, OH	901	9506	6
Imperial Bank Corp	213-417-5600	Los Angeles, CA	178	2428	2
Indiana National Corp	317-266-6000	Indianapolis, IN	545	5927	3
Industrial Bank of Japan Trust Co	212-557-3500	New York, NY	650	5500	3
Irving Bank Corp	212-635-1111	New York, NY	2500	25000	11
Israel Discount Bank	212-551-8500	New York, NY	800	6000	4
Keycorp Inc	518-486-8500	Albany, NY	1394	14646	8
Kyowa Bank Ltd	212-432-6400	New York, NY	450	3500	1
Laurentian Bank of Canada	514-284-7967	Montreal, PQ CAN	340	3400	2
Lavoro Banca Roma Ltd	212-581-0710	New York, NY	450	3500	1
Lloyd's Bank Ltd	212-607-4300	New York, NY	450	3500	1
Long Term Credit Bank of Japan Ltd	213-629-5777	Los Angeles, CA	450	3500	1
Manufacturers & Traders Trust Co	716-842-4200	Buffalo, NY	300	3100	2
Manufacturers Hanover Corp	212-286-6000	New York, NY	8545	66710	30
Manufacturers National of Detroit Inc	313-222-4000	Detroit, MI	924	9311	6
Marine Midland Banks Inc	716-843-2424	Buffalo, NY	2500	25000	15
Marshall & Isley Corp	414-765-7801	Milwaukee, WI	677	6775	3
MCORP Inc	214-698-5000	Dallas, TX	1774	20228	8
Mellon Bank Corp	412-234-5000	Pittsburgh, PA	3269	31153	14
Mercantile Bancorp Inc	314-425-2525	St Louis, MO	426	6491	5
Mercantile Bankshares Corp	301-237-5900	Baltimore, MD	362	3642	2
Merchants National Bank & Trust Co	317-267-6100	Indianapolis, IN	452	5256	3
Meridian Bancorp Inc	215-320-2000	Reading, PA	950	9523	3
Meritor Financial Group Inc	215-636-7500	Philadelphia, PA	1646	17172	9
Michigan National Bankcorp Inc	313-473-3000	Farmington Hills, MI	1040	11306	7
Midland Bank PLC	212-969-7000	New York, NY	450	3500	1
Midlantic Banks Inc	201-321-8000	Edison, NJ	1847	19679	10
Mitsui Manufacturers Bank	213-485-0331	Los Angeles, CA	400	3300	2
MNC (Maryland National Corp) Financial	301-244-1940	Baltimore, MD	1530	17000	8
Morgan, J P & Co Inc	212-344-3000	New York, NY	7839	83923	16
National Bank of Canada Ltd	514-394-4000	Montreal, PQ Can	2633	26285	13
National Bank of Washington Inc	206-344-2300	Seattle, WA	450	4500	3
National City Corp	216-575-2000	Cleveland, OH	2227	21623	11
National Community Bank	201-845-1000	Maywood, NJ	321	3614	2
National Westminster Bank of Canada Ltd	416-865-0170	Toronto, ON Can	82	1461	1
National Westminster Bank USA	516-560-7050	West Hempstead, NY	1200	12000	5
NBD Bancorp (Natl Bank Detroit) Inc	313-225-1000	Detroit, MI	2181	24176	12
NCNB (No Carolina Natl Bank) Corp	704-374-5000	Charlotte, NC	2829	29848	18
NCNB Texas National Bank (Republic Bank)	214-977-4000	Dallas, TX	2900	33000	15
New Jersey National Bank	609-771-5700	Trenton, NJ	500	3500	2
Nippon Credit Bank Ltd	213-629-5566	Los Angeles, CA	450	3500	1
Norinchukin Bank Inc	212-697-1717	New York, NY	450	3500	1
Norstar BanCorp	518-447-4043	Albany, NY	1000	11132	1
Northeast Bancorportion	203-773-0500	New Haven, CT	323	3394	3
Northern Trust Corp	312-630-6000	Chicago, IL	1003	9133	5
Norwest Corp	612-372-8268	Minneapolis, MN	2475	20564	16
Old Kent Financial Corp	616-774-5000	Grand Rapids, MI	726	7854	3
Old Stone Corp	401-278-2000	Providence, RI	350	4500	2
Pennbancorp Inc(Integra Financial)	814-644-8184	Pittsburgh, PA	333	3304	2
Philadelphia National Bank Co	215-629-3512	Philadelphia, PA	1500	12000	6
Pittsburgh National Bank Co	412-355-2000	Pittsburgh, PA	1300	15765	4
PNC Financial Corp	412-762-2728	Pittsburgh, PA	3827	40811	15
Premier Bancorp (Louisiana Bancshares)	504-389-4206	Baton Rouge, LA	393	4078	3
Puget Sound BanCorp	206-593-3600	Tacoma, WA	395	3947	3
Rainier Bancorp Inc	206-621-4111	Seattle, WA	850	9216	6

Major Group: Financial   **Industry: Banking**

Organizations Listed by Industry

Organization	Phone	City / State or Province	Revenue ($ mil)	Assets ($ mil)	Emp (thous)
Republic Bank of New York Inc	212-525-5000	New York, NY	2106	24519	9
Rhode Island Hospital Trust Natl Bank	401-278-8000	Providence, RI	300	3061	2
Riggs National Corp	202-835-6000	Washington, DC	562	7002	2
Royal Bank of Canada Ltd	514-874-2110	Montreal, PQ Can	9006	93546	46
Sanwa Bank of California	415-765-9500	San Francisco, CA	800	7000	4
Schroder, IBJ Bank & Trust Co	212-858-2000	New York, NY	350	2500	2
Seattle First National Bank Co	206-358-7800	Seattle, WA	1800	15000	7
Security Pacific Corp	213-345-6211	Los Angeles, CA	8546	77870	33
Shawmut Corp	617-292-2000	Boston, MA	2811	26475	17
Shoko Chukin Bank Ltd	212-693-1660	New York, NY	450	3500	1
Signet Banking Corp	804-747-2000	Richmond, VA	1286	11002	6
Society Bank Corp	216-689-3000	Cleveland, OH	972	10009	6
Society for Savings	203-727-5000	Hartford, CT	400	4000	1
South Carolina National Corp	803-765-3000	Columbia, SC	551	5655	4
Southeast Banking Corp	305-375-7500	Miami, FL	1066	12469	7
SouthTrust Corp	205-254-5523	Birmingham, AL	627	6645	4
Sovereign Bank Corp	615-749-3333	Nashville, TN	400	4000	2
Sovran Financial Corp	804-441-4000	Norfolk, VA	2302	21349	10
State Street Bank Inc	617-786-3000	Boston, MA	897	7246	4
Sumitomo Trust & Banking Co	212-326-0500	New York, NY	600	5500	4
Summit Bancorp	201-522-8400	Summit, NJ	500	5000	2
Suntrust Banks Corp	404-588-7455	Atlanta, GA	2889	29177	20
Swiss Bank Corp	212-938-3500	New York, NY	450	3500	1
Taiyo Kobe Bank Ltd	213-629-3939	Los Angeles, CA	450	3500	1
Texas American Bancshares Inc	817-884-4040	Fort Worth, TX	445	4383	4
Texas Commerce Bancshares Inc	713-236-4865	Houston, TX	1600	19000	8
Third National Bank Co	615-748-4000	Nashville, TN	500	4000	2
Tokai Bank Ltd	213-972-0200	Los Angeles, CA	800	7000	3
Toronto Dominion Bank Ltd	416-982-8222	Toronto, ON Can	4370	46346	22
Toyo Trust Ltd	213-624-2424	Los Angeles, CA	450	3500	1
Trustcorp Inc	419-259-8950	Toledo, OH	563	5947	3
Union Bank of Switzerland	212-715-3000	New York, NY	450	3500	1
Union Trust Co	203-348-6211	Stamford, CT	500	4000	2
United Banks of Colorado Inc	303-861-4700	Denver, CO	438	5540	3
United Jersey Banks Inc	609-987-3200	Princeton, NJ	1032	10311	3
United Missouri Bancshares	816-556-7000	Kansas City, MO	600	6000	3
US Bancorp Inc	503-275-6111	Portland, OR	1381	14383	9
US Trust Corp	212-806-4500	New York, NY	362	2516	2
Valley National Corp	602-261-2900	Phoenix, AZ	1100	11300	7
Wells Fargo & Co	415-477-1000	San Francisco, CA	4853	46617	20
West One Bank Corp	208-388-7791	Boise, ID	349	3538	3
Westdeutsche Landesbank AG	212-754-9600	New York, NY	450	3500	1
Wilmington Trust Corp	302-651-1000	Wilmington, DE	313	2982	2
Yasuda Trust & Banking Co	212-432-2300	New York, NY	450	3500	1

Industry: Banking   **Number: 206**

Major Group: Financial   **Industry: Non-Bank Fin**

Organization	Phone	City / State or Province	Revenue ($ mil)	Assets ($ mil)	Emp (thous)
A Mark Financial Corp	213-319-0200	Santa Monica, CA	1000	NA	1
Alberta Mortgage & Housing Corp	403-468-3535	Edmonton, AB Can	248	3346	1
Alexander & Alexander Service Inc	212-840-8500	New York, NY	1228	2635	16
Allegheny Corp	212-752-1356	New York, NY	1006	1630	9
Alliance Mutual Funds Inc	800-221-5672	New York, NY	300	11000	1
American Capital Corp	713-993-0500	Houston, TX	99	71	1

Major Group: Financial   Industry: Non-Bank Fin

Organizations Listed by Industry

Organization	Phone	City / State or Province	Revenue ($ mil)	Assets ($ mil)	Emp (thous)
American Express Co	212-640-2000	New York, NY	22934	142704	100
American Express Credit Corp	302-594-3350	Wilmington, DE	1224	9800	2
American Family Corp	404-323-3431	Columbus, GA	2325	6074	3
Aon Corp (Combined Int'l)	312-701-3000	Chicago, IL	2732	8266	7
Associated Madison Asset Management Inc	212-351-2600	New York, NY	440	16500	1
Associates Corp of America Inc	214-659-4000	Dallas, TX	1733	15000	7
AVCO Financial Services Inc	714-553-1200	Irvine, CA	1047	4173	7
Batterymarch Financial Management Inc	617-973-9300	Boston, MA	20	8600	1
BellSouth Financial Services Corp	404-329-4200	Atlanta, GA	NA	NA	NA
Beneficial Corp	302-798-0800	Wilmington, DE	1418	7544	7
Borg Warner Acceptance Corp	312-329-6500	Chicago, IL	800	7000	3
Boston Companies Inc	800-225-5267	Boston, MA	300	11000	1
Caisse de Depot du Quebec Ltd	514-842-3261	Montreal, PQ Can	2253	25550	3
California Public Emp Retirement System	916-445-7700	Sacramento, CA	3821	41249	2
Canada Trust Financial Services Co	416-869-6100	Toronto, ON Can	2468	21707	11
Capital Group Inc	213-486-9200	Los Angeles, CA	550	27500	2
Capital Holding Co	502-560-2000	Louisville, KY	2046	12963	8
Central Capital Corp	902-420-2000	Halifax, NS Can	1494	13622	4
Chrysler Financial Corp	313-244-3060	Troy, MI	2908	25277	6
Cincinnati Financial Corp	513-870-2000	Fairfield, OH	910	2117	2
CIT Group Financial Corp	201-740-5000	Livingston, NJ	1042	9337	4
Colonial Group Inc	617-426-3750	Boston, MA	74	82	1
Commercial Credit Corp	301-332-3000	Baltimore, MD	1200	4900	5
Continental International Corp	212-440-3980	New York, NY	5878	13302	17
Corroon & Black Corp	212-363-4100	New York, NY	425	957	4
Credithrift Financial Inc	812-424-8031	Evansville, IN	523	2772	4
Criterion Investment Management Inc	713-751-2400	Houston, TX	42	11586	1
Deere, John Capital Corp	702-786-5527	Reno, NV	334	2958	1
Delaware Management Investment Advisors	215-988-1333	Philadelphia, PA	400	15400	1
Dreyfus Corp	212-715-6000	New York, NY	268	763	2
EL Financial Corp	416-868-1880	Toronto, ON Can	513	1312	1
Federal National Mortgage Corp	202-537-7000	Washington, DC	10266	112258	5
Federated Investment Corp	412-288-1900	Pittsburgh, PA	850	44000	3
Fidelity Investments Corp	617-523-1919	Boston, MA	1000	85000	6
Fiduciary Trust Co	212-466-4100	New York, NY	400	15400	1
Financial Trustco Capital Ltd	416-366-8990	Toronto, ON Can	263	1831	1
First Capital Holding Corp	213-551-1000	Los Angeles, CA	250	750	1
First City Financial Corp	604-685-2489	Vancouver, BC Can	625	4225	7
First Executive Corp	213-312-1000	Los Angeles, CA	3049	18225	1
Fischer Francis Trees & Watts Inc	212-350-8000	New York, NY	300	11000	1
Ford Credit Canada Ltd	416-845-2511	Oakville, ON Can	369	3367	1
Ford Credit Corp	313-322-3000	Dearborn, MI	6819	56276	9
Franklin Resources Group Inc	415-570-3000	San Mateo, CA	202	177	2
General Electric Credit Corp	212-751-5315	New York, NY	10655	74645	10
General Motors Acceptance Corp	313-556-5000	Detroit, MI	10645	99041	10
General Motors Acceptance Corp Canada	416-234-6616	Toronto, ON Can	703	6097	1
General Trustco of Canada Ltd	416-867-3200	Toronto, ON Can	497	4204	2
Gordon Capital Corp	416-364-9393	Toronto, ON Can	255	170	1
Green Tree Acceptance Corp	612-293-3400	St Paul, MN	134	645	2
Groupe des Epiciers unis,Metro Richelieu	514-643-1000	Montreal, PQ Can	1700	850	3
Hees Internationaal Corp	416-865-0430	Toronto, ON Can	230	3249	1
HR Textron Inc	805-259-4030	Valencia, CA	NA	NA	NA
ICH Corp	502-897-1861	Louisville, KY	2885	9294	7
Integrated Resources	212-353-7000	New York, NY	1111	6252	3
Inter Regional Financial Corp	612-371-7750	Minneapolis, MN	350	3500	3

Major Group: Financial   **Industry: Non-Bank Fin**

Organizations Listed by Industry

Organization	Phone	City / State or Province	Revenue ($ mil)	Assets ($ mil)	Emp (thous)
Investors Group Inc	204-943-0361	Winnipeg, MB Can	252	1604	1
ITT Financial Corportion	314-821-6060	St Louis, MO	1462	8999	7
Jefferson Pilot Corp	919-378-2011	Greensboro, NC	1223	4174	8
JMB Institutional Realty	312-440-4800	Chicago, IL	1500	15000	5
La Confederation Desjardins Du Quebec	514-281-8666	Montreal, PQ Can	2445	25139	24
Laurentian Group Corp	418-647-5151	Quebec, PQ Can	1411	8244	7
Loewen Ondaatje McCutcheon Inc	416-869-7211	Toronto, ON Can	85	85	1
Lomas & Nettleton Financial Corp	214-746-7111	Dallas, TX	1235	6645	5
Marsh & McLennan Companies Inc	212-997-2000	New York, NY	2272	1830	23
Massachusetts Financial Services Inc	617-954-5000	Boston, MA	550	24200	2
MDC Holdings Inc	303-773-1100	Denver, CO	841	1993	2
Michigan Treasurer Employees Rtrmt Sys	517-373-9150	Lansing, MI	440	16500	2
Miller Anderson & Sherrerd Inv Mgt Co	215-668-0850	Bala Cynwyd, PA	300	11000	1
Mitchell Hutchins Asset Management Inc	212-713-4000	New York, NY	350	13200	1
Monarch Capital Corp	413-781-3000	Springfield, MA	417	5805	3
Montgomery Ward Credit Corp	302-478-9240	Wilmington, DE	238	2519	1
Montreal Trustco Inc	514-397-7171	Montreal, PQ Can	764	6513	4
National Victoria & Grey Trustco Ltd	519-271-2050	Stratford, ON Can	1073	10362	4
New Jersey Divison of Investment	609-292-5106	Trenton, NJ	1475	22433	1
New York State Retirement Fund Inc	518-447-2741	Albany, NY	700	27500	2
New York State Teachers Investment Fund	518-447-2741	Albany, NY	450	16500	2
North Carolina Retirement Fund	919-733-3211	Raleigh, NC	350	11000	1
Ohio Public Employees Retirement Fund	614-221-7012	Columbus, OH	450	16500	1
Ohio, State Teachers Retirement System	614-227-4062	Columbus, OH	1490	14231	1
Price, T Rowe Associates Inc	301-547-2308	Baltimore, MD	142	105	2
Putnam Management Co Inc	617-292-1000	Boston, MA	500	22000	1
Reliance Group Holdings Inc	212-909-1100	New York, NY	3400	6079	10
San Juan Basin Royalty Trust Inc	817-338-8607	Fort Worth, TX	34	5	1
Sarofim, Fayez Investment Mgt Co	713-654-4484	Houston, TX	300	11000	1
Scudder Stevens & Clark	617-439-4640	Boston, MA	850	33000	3
Sears Acceptance Co Canada Ltd	416-362-1711	Toronto, ON Can	204	1034	1
Sears Roebuck Acceptance Corp	302-652-3666	Greenville, DE	1008	12085	3
Security Capital/Sentinal R E Corp	212-408-2900	New York, NY	550	2200	1
Seligman Marketing Inc	800-221-2450	New York, NY	500	NA	5
Southland Financial Corp	214-828-7011	Irving, TX	250	1500	1
Stein Roe & Farnham Inc	312-368-7800	Chicago, IL	400	13200	1
Student Loan Marketing Assn Inc	202-333-8000	Washington, DC	1729	28627	7
Texas Teachers Retirement Fund	512-397-6460	Austin, TX	450	16500	1
TIAA CREF Inc	212-490-9000	New York, NY	8409	30768	3
TMK United Corp	205-325-4200	Birmingham, AL	250	450	2
Torchmark Corp	205-325-4200	Birmingham, AL	1670	4428	9
Toronto Stock Exchange Ltd	416-947-4700	Toronto, ON Can	213	2125	1
Trilon Financial Corp	416-363-0061	Toronto, ON Can	3301	27051	23
Trust Co of the West Inc	213-683-4000	Los Angeles, CA	275	11000	2
Twentieth (20th) Century Industries Inc	818-704-3700	Woodland Hills, CA	622	857	2
United Investors Inc	205-325-4200	Birmingham, AL	282	8003	2
United States Leasing International Inc	415-627-9000	San Francisco, CA	548	2218	2
US Steel/Carnegie Pension Fund Inc	212-806-4500	New York, NY	300	11000	1
Value Line Inc	800-223-0818	New York, NY	75	96	1
Vanguard Group Mutual Funds Inc	215-648-6000	Valley Forge, PA	550	22000	1
Wellington Management/TDPL Inc	617-951-5000	Boston, MA	700	27500	1
Westinghouse Credit Corp	412-393-3000	Pittsburgh, PA	810	7143	1
Williams, A L Corp	404-381-1674	Duluth, GA	402	1655	2
Wisconsin Investment Board	608-266-2381	Madison, WI	1560	12881	1

Industry: Non-Bank Fin   Number: 115

Major Group: Financial   Industry: Non-Bank Fin

Organizations Listed by Industry

Organization	Phone	City / State or Province	Revenue ($ mil)	Assets ($ mil)	Emp (thous)
Major Group: Financial		**Industry: Savings & Loan**			
Ahmanson, H F & Co (Home Savings of Am)	213-487-4277	Los Angeles, CA	3315	40258	9
Altus Bank	205-473-0500	Mobile, AL	274	2774	2
American Continental Corp	602-957-7170	Phoenix, AZ	800	5000	3
American Savings & Loan Assn Inc	209-948-1116	Stockton, CA	500	4000	2
American Savings (UT) Assn Inc	801-483-5800	Salt Lake City, UT	350	3100	1
American Savings Assn of Florida Inc	305-653-5353	Miami, FL	350	3500	1
American Savings Bank (NY) Inc	212-575-7600	New York, NY	500	4500	2
AmeriFirst Federal Savings Miami Inc	305-577-1600	Miami, FL	500	4500	2
Anchor Savings Bank Inc	516-295-0400	Northport, NY	703	7946	2
Astoria Federal Savings Assn Inc	718-545-4400	Long Island City, NY	300	3084	1
Atlantic Financial Federal Inc	215-668-6600	Bala Cynwyd, PA	764	7799	2
Bank Laurentienne du Canada	514-284-3931	Montreal, PQ Can	416	4117	2
Bowery Savings Bank Inc	212-953-8400	New York, NY	700	7000	2
Bright Banc Savings Assn Inc	214-638-9500	Dallas, TX	550	5500	2
California Federal S & L Assn Inc	213-932-4321	Los Angeles, CA	2816	27482	6
Capitol Federal Savings (Kansas) Inc	913-235-1341	Topeka, KS	350	3000	1
Carteret Savings Bank Corporated	201-326-1000	Morristown, NJ	700	6000	2
Centrust Savings Bank Inc	305-376-5000	Miami, FL	750	7500	2
Chevy Chase Savings Bank Inc	301-986-7000	Chevy Chase, MD	350	3500	1
Citadel Holding Corp(Fidelity Fed Svng)	213-956-7100	Glendale, CA	384	4642	1
Citicorp Savings Inc	212-559-1000	New York, NY	1750	17500	4
Citizens Savings Assn Inc	305-577-0400	Miami, FL	301	2998	2
City Fed Financial Corp	201-658-4100	Bedminster, NJ	1046	10585	5
Cityfed Financial Corp	407-655-5919	Palm Beach, FL	1000	10585	5
Coast Savings & Loan Assc Inc	213-688-2000	Los Angeles, CA	1110	12647	3
Columbia Savings (CA) Savings Assn Inc	213-657-6123	Beverly Hills, CA	1249	12744	3
Columbia Savings (CO) Assn Inc	303-773-3444	Englewood, CO	350	3500	1
Commercial Federal Savings Assn Inc	402-554-9200	Omaha, NE	570	6655	2
Community Fed Savings (MO) Assn Inc	314-822-5000	St Louis, MO	500	5000	2
Crossland Savings Fed Savings Bank Inc	718-780-0400	Brooklyn, NY	1374	15144	4
Dime Savings Bank of New York Inc	516-227-6030	Garden City, NY	1051	12007	6
Downey Savings & Loan Assn Inc	714-549-8811	Costa Mesa, CA	331	4333	1
Emigrant Savings Bank Inc	212-883-5800	New York, NY	550	5500	2
Empire of America Fed Savings Bank Inc	716-845-7101	Buffalo, NY	1090	11281	3
Far West Savings Assn Inc	714-833-8383	Newport Beach, CA	400	4000	1
Farm & Home Savings Assn Inc	417-667-3333	Nevada, MO	312	3548	1
Farwest Financial Corp	213-277-3055	Los Angeles, CA	450	4760	2
Financial Corp of America	714-553-6900	Irvine, CA	3250	22000	6
Financial Corp of Santa Barbara	805-682-2300	Santa Barbara, CA	400	5000	1
First Federal of Michigan Inc	313-965-1400	Detroit, MI	1096	11942	3
First Federal Savings & Loan Assn Inc	716-238-2100	Rochester, NY	550	5500	2
First Federal Savings of Pittsburgh Inc	412-392-5500	Pittsburgh, PA	400	4000	1
First Minnesota Savings Bank Inc	612-371-3700	Minneapolis, MN	400	4000	1
First Nationwide Bank Inc	415-772-1400	San Francisco, CA	2527	34810	4
First Texas Financial Corp	214-960-4500	Dallas, TX	750	6000	4
Florida Federal Savings & Loan Inc	813-893-1131	St Petersburg, FL	472	5157	2
Franklin Savings Assn Inc	913-242-6300	Ottawa, KS	1059	13419	2
Franklin, Benj Federal Savings Assn Inc	503-275-1201	Portland, OR	504	5469	2
Georgia Federal Bank Inc	404-330-2440	Atlanta, GA	443	4365	2
Gibraltar Savings (CA) Inc	213-278-8720	Beverly Hills, CA	1309	15011	3

Major Group: Financial   **Industry: Savings & Loan**

Organizations Listed by Industry

Organization	Phone	City / State or Province	Revenue ($ mil)	Assets ($ mil)	Emp (thous)
Gibraltar Savings (Texas) Assn Inc	713-872-3100	Houston, TX	1301	12724	3
Glendale Federal Savings & Loan Assn	818-500-2000	Glendale, CA	2562	23711	8
Golden West Financial Corp	415-446-6000	Oakland, CA	1410	16721	2
Goldome Federal Savings Bank Inc	716-847-5800	Buffalo, NY	1750	17500	5
Great American (AZ) First Savings Bank	602-279-3456	Phoenix, AZ	400	4000	1
Great American (CA) First Savings Bank	619-231-1885	San Diego, CA	1601	16084	3
Great Lakes Bancorp Inc	313-769-8300	Ann Arbor, MI	334	3638	1
Great Western Financial Corp	213-852-3411	Beverly Hills, CA	3665	32815	13
Guardian Savings (Texas) Assn Inc	713-784-4413	Houston, TX	300	3000	1
Hill Financial Savings Assn Inc	215-679-9506	Red Hill, PA	350	3500	1
Home Federal Savings & Loan Assn Inc	619-699-8000	San Diego, CA	1578	17009	5
Home Owners Federal S & L Assn	617-482-0630	Boston, MA	400	4218	2
Homestead Savings Fed Savings Assn Inc	415-387-4300	San Francisco, CA	497	5751	2
Howard Savings Bank Inc	201-533-7400	Livingston, NJ	481	5221	2
Imperial Savings Assn Inc	619-292-3000	San Diego, CA	972	10800	4
Lincoln Savings (Cal) & Loan Assn Inc	714-553-0200	Irvine, CA	425	4000	1
Long Island Savings Bank Inc	516-677-5000	Syosset, NY	495	5263	2
MeraBank Fed Savings Bank Inc	602-248-4221	Phoenix, AZ	644	8348	2
Midwest Federal Savings Assn Inc	612-372-6123	Minneapolis, MN	425	3570	2
Northeast Savings Inc	203-280-1000	Hartford, CT	798	7943	3
Pacific First Federal Savings Bank Inc	206-383-7605	Tacoma, WA	524	6622	2
People's Bank	203-579-7171	Bridgeport, CT	600	6321	2
Perpetual American Bank Inc	703-442-7000	McLean, VA	561	5853	2
Pima Savings Assn Inc	602-747-8484	Tuscon, AZ	248	3226	1
Rochester Community Savings Bank	716-262-5800	Roschester, NY	350	4000	2
San Antonio Savings Assn Inc	512-340-7272	San Antonio, TX	300	3000	1
San Jacinto Savings Assn Inc	713-661-7000	Houston, TX	436	4594	2
Santa Barbara Savings Assn Inc	805-682-5000	Santa Barbara, CA	450	4500	2
Seamen's Bank for Savings Inc	212-428-4500	New York, NY	436	4708	2
Sears Savings Bank Inc	818-956-1800	Glendale, CA	500	5207	1
SFFED Corp	415-955-5800	San Francisco, CA	400	4499	2
Standard Federal Bank Inc	313-643-9600	Troy, MI	867	9573	2
State Savings Bank Inc	614-460-6100	Columbus, OH	139	1520	1
Sunbelt Savings Assn Inc	214-980-4441	Dallas, TX	400	4000	1
Talman Home Fed Savings & Loan Inc	312-726-8915	Chicago, IL	543	6337	2
TCF Banking & Savings Inc	612-370-7000	Minneapolis, MN	581	5259	2
TransCapital Financial Corp(Ohio Sav Bk)	216-621-9600	Cleveland, OH	619	6361	2
University Savings Assn Inc	713-596-1000	Houston, TX	450	4500	2
Valley Federal Savings Assn Inc	818-904-3000	Van Nuys, CA	350	3324	1
Washington Mutual Savings Inc	206-464-4400	Seattle, WA	584	6364	2
Western Capital Investment Corp	303-370-1212	Denver, CO	358	3664	2
Western Savings & Loan Assn Inc	602-248-4600	Phoenix, AZ	498	5599	2

Industry: Savings & Loan   Number: 92

Major Group: Financial		**Industry: Securities**			
Advest Inc	203-525-1421	Hartford, CT	205	895	2
Allen & Co Inc	212-832-8000	New York, NY	275	2200	1
Baker Fentress & Co	312-236-9190	Chicago, IL	200	150	1
Balfour Maclaine Corp(former Kay Corp)	212-269-0800	New York, NY	1042	500	1
Bateman Eichler Hill Richards Inc	213-683-3500	Los Angeles, CA	220	2200	1
Bear Stearns Companies Inc	212-272-2000	New York, NY	1888	32171	4
Blunt Ellis & Loewi Inc	414-347-3400	Milwaukee, WI	220	2200	1
Bradford, J C & Co	615-748-9000	Nashville, TN	220	2200	1

Major Group: Financial   Industry: Securities

Organizations Listed by Industry

Organization	Phone	City / State or Province	Revenue ($ mil)	Assets ($ mil)	Emp (thous)
Brown Brothers Harriman & Co	212-483-1818	New York, NY	400	2200	1
Brown, Alex & Sons Inc	301-727-1700	Baltimore, MD	244	861	1
Burns Fry Ltd	416-365-4000	Toronto, ON Can	263	1616	2
Carroll McEntee & McGinley Inc	212-825-6780	New York, NY	330	3300	1
Central Guaranty Trust Ltd	416-345-4000	Toronto, ON Can	850	5100	3
Cowen & Co	212-495-6000	New York, NY	330	3300	1
Dain Bosworth Inc	612-371-2711	Minneapolis, MN	220	2200	1
Daiwa Securities America Inc	212-945-0100	New York, NY	330	3300	1
DCNY Discount Corp of New York Inc	212-248-8900	New York, NY	178	2386	1
Dean Witter Reynolds Inc	212-392-2222	New York, NY	3500	33000	19
Deutsche Bank Capital Corp	212-612-0600	New York, NY	275	3300	1
Dillon Reed & Co Inc	212-906-7000	New York, NY	550	5500	1
Dominion Securities Inc	416-864-4000	Toronto, ON Can	298	255	2
Donaldson, Lufkin & Jenrette Inc	212-504-3000	New York, NY	2200	20900	3
Drexel Burnham Lambert Inc	212-480-6000	New York, NY	3300	NA	10
Edwards, A G & Sons Inc	314-289-3000	St Louis, MO	501	1063	7
Fidelity Brokerage Services Inc	617-570-7000	Boston, MA	275	2200	1
First Boston Inc	212-909-2000	New York, NY	1323	36148	6
First Options of Chicago Inc	312-786-3000	Chicago, IL	330	3300	1
Glickenhaus & Co	212-953-7800	New York, NY	275	2200	1
Goldman, Sachs & Co	212-902-1000	New York, NY	4000	51301	7
Gruntal & Co Inc	212-267-8800	New York, NY	275	2200	1
Hutton, E F Group Inc	212-742-5000	New York, NY	3000	25000	15
Interstate Johnson Lane Corp	704-379-9000	Charlotte, NC	220	2200	1
Janney Montgomery Scott Inc	215-665-6000	Philadelphia, PA	220	2200	1
Jones, Edward D & Co	314-851-2000	St Louis, MO	220	2200	1
Keefe, Bruyette & Woods Inc	212-323-8300	New York, NY	220	80	1
Kidder, Peabody & Co Inc	212-510-3000	New York, NY	1650	16500	7
Lazard Freres & Co	212-489-6600	New York, NY	1000	10000	1
Legg Mason Inc	301-539-3400	Baltimore, MD	300	150	3
Levesque Beaubien Inc	514-879-2222	Montreal, PQ Can	170	85	1
Mabon, Nugent & Co	212-732-2820	New York, NY	220	2200	1
Merrill Lynch & Co Inc	212-637-7455	New York, NY	10547	64402	42
Merrill Lynch Canada Inc	416-586-6000	Toronto, ON Can	170	85	1
Mocatta Metals Corp	212-912-8400	New York, NY	3300	16500	1
Morgan Stanley & Co Inc	212-703-4000	New York, NY	3100	29190	5
Morgan, J P Securities Inc	212-483-2323	New York, NY	350	3300	1
Nesbitt Thomson Inc	416-586-3600	Toronto, ON Can	223	1088	2
Neuberger & Berman Inc	212-730-7370	New York, NY	220	4400	1
Niagara Share Corp	716-856-2600	Buffalo, NY	250	200	1
Nikko Securities Co Intl Inc	212-416-5400	New York, NY	330	3300	1
Nomura Securities International Inc	212-208-9300	New York, NY	330	3300	1
Nuveen, John & Co Inc	312-917-7700	Chicago, IL	450	363	1
Oppenheimer & Co Inc	212-667-7000	New York, NY	750	5000	2
Paine Webber Group Inc	212-713-2000	New York, NY	2512	17934	13
Piper Jaffray & Hopwood Inc	612-342-6000	Minneapolis, MN	176	392	1
Prescott Ball & Turben Inc	216-574-7300	Cleveland, OH	275	2200	1
Prudential Bache Securities Inc	212-214-1000	New York, NY	3500	33000	16
Richardson, James & Sons Ltd	204-934-5811	Winnipeg, MB Can	1068	1165	3
Robinson Humphrey Co Inc	404-266-6000	Atlanta, GA	220	2200	1
Rothschild, L F, Unterberg, Towbin Inc	212-238-2000	New York, NY	825	7700	2
Salomon Inc	212-764-3700	New York, NY	6146	85256	7
Schapiro, M A & Co	212-980-5353	New York, NY	275	2200	1
Schwab, Charles & Co	415-627-7000	San Francisco, CA	770	4235	5
ScotiaMcLeod Ltd	416-863-7411	Toronto, ON Can	213	170	2

Major Group: Financial　　　　**Industry: Securities**

Organizations Listed by Industry

Organization	Phone	City / State or Province	Revenue ($ mil)	Assets ($ mil)	Emp (thous)
Shearson Lehman Hutton Inc	212-298-2000	New York, NY	10529	84840	28
Smith Barney Harris Upham & Co	212-698-6000	New York, NY	1100	11000	6
Spear, Leeds & Kellogg Inc	212-587-8800	New York, NY	450	4400	1
Stephens Inc	501-374-4361	Little Rock, AR	300	2200	1
Thomson McKinnon Securities Inc	212-482-7000	New York, NY	750	7000	5
UBS Securities Inc	212-230-4000	New York, NY	250	4400	1
Van Kampen Merritt Inc	312-719-6000	Lisle, IL	440	4400	1
Warburg, S G Securities Inc	212-459-7000	New York, NY	220	2200	1
Wertheim Schroder & Co Inc	212-492-6000	New York, NY	330	3300	1
Wood Gundy Inc	416-869-8100	Toronto, ON Can	255	213	2

Industry: Securities   Number: 73

Major Group: Financial   Industry: Federal Govt Fin

Organization	Phone	City / State or Province	Revenue ($ mil)	Assets ($ mil)	Emp (thous)
Bank of Canada	613-563-8111	Ottawa, ON Can	2040	NM	2
Canadian Commerical Corp	613-996-0034	Ottawa, ON Can	659	420	1
Farm Credit Corp	613-996-6606	Ottawa, ON Can	411	4177	1
Federal Business Development Bank Ltd	514-283-5904	Montreal, PQ Can	213	1530	1
Federal Deposit Insurance Corp	202-393-8400	Washington, DC	5000	NM	4
Federal Home Loan Bank Board	202-377-6000	Washington, DC	2000	NM	10
Federal Reserve Bank of Atlanta Inc	404-521-8500	Atlanta, GA	934	14294	2
Federal Reserve Bank of Boston Inc	617-973-3000	Boston, MA	1156	17450	2
Federal Reserve Bank of Chicago Inc	312-322-5111	Chicago, IL	2469	34695	3
Federal Reserve Bank of Cleveland Inc	216-579-2000	Cleveland, OH	1114	16294	2
Federal Reserve Bank of Dallas Inc	214-651-6111	Dallas, TX	1258	15185	2
Federal Reserve Bank of Kansas City Inc	816-881-2000	Kansas City, MO	751	12690	2
Federal Reserve Bank of Minneapolis Inc	612-340-2345	Minneapolis, MN	312	5473	1
Federal Reserve Bank of New York Inc	212-720-5000	New York, NY	6381	99785	4
Federal Reserve Bank of Philadelphia Inc	215-574-6000	Philadelphia, PA	572	9116	1
Federal Reserve Bank of Richmond Inc	804-643-1250	Richmond, VA	1513	24861	2
Federal Reserve Bank of San Francisco	415-974-2000	San Francisco, CA	2493	34502	3
Federal Reserve Bank of St Louis	314-444-8444	St Louis, MO	574	9329	1
Federal Reserve System Headquarters	202-452-3000	Washington, DC	19526	293674	24
International Monitary Fund	202-623-7000	Washington, DC	2000	NM	4
National Credit Union Administration	202-357-1055	Washington, DC	500	NM	3
Provence of Alberta Treasury Branches	403-493-7015	Edmonton, AB Can	445	4692	3
Securities & Exchange Commission	202-272-3100	Washington, DC	250	NM	2
Societe Generale Financement du Quebec	514-875-0330	Montreal, PQ Can	425	1020	5
United States Commodity Credit Corp	202-447-5237	Washington, DC	2000	NM	3
United States Export-Import Bank	202-566-8990	Washington, DC	1500	22000	3
United States Farmers Home Admim	202-447-4323	Washington, DC	1000	NM	2
World Bank	202-477-1234	Washington, DC	2000	NM	4

Industry: Federal Govt Fin   Number: 28

Major Group: Insurance   Industry: Insurance

Organization	Phone	City / State or Province	Revenue ($ mil)	Assets ($ mil)	Emp (thous)
Aetna Life & Casualty Co	203-273-0123	Hartford, CT	24296	81415	42
Aetna Life Insurance Co	416-864-8000	Toronto, ON Can	550	1636	1
Aid Association for Lutherans Inc	414-734-5721	Appleton, WI	1618	6246	1
Alden, John Financial Corp	305-470-3100	Miami, FL	1500	NA	3
Allstate Insurance Co Canada	416-477-6900	Markham, ON Can	320	565	2
Allstate Life Insurance Co	312-291-5000	Northbrook, IL	3354	5972	3
AmBase Corp (Home Group Inc)	212-530-6800	New York, NY	2978	13302	8
American Financial Corp	513-579-2121	Cincinnati, OH	3000	8000	10

Major Group: Insurance   Industry: Insurance

Organizations Listed by Industry

Organization	Phone	City / State or Province	Revenue ($ mil)	Assets ($ mil)	Emp (thous)
American General Corp	713-522-1111	Houston, TX	3823	30422	18
American General Life & Accident Co	615-749-1000	Nashville, TN	741	3472	2
American International Group Inc	212-770-7000	New York, NY	13613	37409	38
American Mutual Liability	508-245-6000	Wakefield, MA	400	800	2
American National Insurance Co	409-763-4461	Galveston, TX	934	4303	2
American United Life Insurance Co	317-263-1877	Indianapolis, IN	856	3361	3
Amerisure Companies	313-965-8600	Detroit, MI	500	300	2
Amica Mutual Insurance Co	401-521-9100	Providence, RI	646	1142	2
Argonaut Insurance Co	415-326-0900	Menlo Park, CA	350	1500	2
Assurance vie Desjardins Ltd	418-835-2323	Levis, PQ Can	329	1057	1
Atlantic Mutual Insurance Co	212-943-1800	New York, NY	652	1191	2
Auto Club of Michigan Inc	313-336-1234	Dearborn, MI	733	1171	3
Auto Owners Group Insurance Co	517-323-1200	Lansing, MI	994	1724	3
Berkley, W R Insurance Co	203-629-2880	Greenwich, CT	534	1232	2
Berkshire Hathaway Inc	402-346-1400	Omaha, NE	2333	6817	25
Blue Cross Blue Shield of Alabama Inc	205-988-2100	Birmingham, AL	1100	2856	5
Blue Cross Blue Shield of Illinois Inc	312-938-7500	Chicago, IL	1320	3428	4
Blue Cross Blue Shield of Massachusetts	617-956-2000	Boston, MA	2750	7140	7
Blue Cross Blue Shield of Michigan Inc	313-225-8000	Detroit, MI	4950	12852	9
Blue Cross Blue Shield of Oregon Inc	503-225-5221	Portland, OR	825	2142	2
Blue Cross Blue Shield of Pennsylvania	215-448-5000	Philadelphia, PA	1320	3103	2
Blue Cross Blue Shield of Virginia Inc	804-359-7000	Richmond, VA	1100	2856	2
California State Auto Association	415-565-2012	San Francisco, CA	1096	1932	3
Canada Life Assurance Co	416-597-1456	Toronto, ON Can	3170	9661	3
CIGNA Corp	215-557-5000	Philadelphia, PA	17889	55825	49
Clarendon America Insurance Co	302-656-0142	Wilmington, DE	500	500	1
CNA Financial Corp	312-822-5000	Chicago, IL	8204	22941	17
Colonial Penn Insurance Co	215-988-8000	Philadelphia, PA	486	873	2
Commercial Union Assurance Group Ltd	416-361-2500	Toronto, ON Can	421	774	1
Commerical Union Insurance Co	617-725-6000	Boston, MA	658	1167	4
Commonwealth Life Ins Co	502-587-7371	Louisville, KY	110	2890	2
Confederation Life Insurance Co	416-323-8111	Toronto, ON Can	2919	9173	5
Connecticut General Life Ins Co	203-726-6000	Bloomfield, CT	4692	26786	12
Connecticut Mutual Life Insurance Co	203-727-6500	Hartford, CT	2039	11230	20
Continental Assurance Co	312-822-5000	Chicago, IL	2323	6138	6
Cooperators General Insurance Co	519-824-4400	Guelph, ON Can	670	951	3
Country Companies	309-557-2111	Bloomington, IL	400	800	2
Crown Life Insurance Co	416-928-4500	Toronto, ON Can	2944	7419	4
Crum & Foster Inc	201-285-7000	Morristown, NJ	3000	7500	8
Dominion of Canada General Insurance Co	416-362-7231	Toronto, ON Can	291	491	1
Economical Group Ltd	519-888-8200	Kitchener, ON Can	403	741	1
EMP Employers Mutual Casualty Ins Co	515-280-2511	Des Moines, IA	118	298	1
Employers of Texas Insurance Co	214-760-6100	Dallas, TX	800	800	3
Employers Reinsurance Co	913-676-5200	Overland Park, KS	1425	4293	4
Equitable Life Assurance Society Inc	212-554-1234	New York, NY	8898	49288	25
Equitable Variable Life	212-554-4035	New York, NY	1800	8000	3
Erie Insurance Exchange Inc	814-870-2000	Erie, PA	800	1500	3
Executive Life Insurance Co	213-312-1000	Inglewood, CA	2420	11400	2
Farmers Group Insurance Inc	213-932-3200	Los Angeles, CA	1133	1528	16
Federal Home Life Insurance Co	407-345-3020	Orlando, FL	NA	NA	NA
Federated Mutual Insurance Co	507-455-5200	Owatonna, MN	600	1025	2
FGIC Inc	212-607-3000	New York, NY	250	958	1
Fireman's Fund Inc	415-899-2000	Novato, CA	3704	11190	10
First Colony Life Insurance Co	804-845-0911	Lynchburg, VA	777	2549	2
Ford Motor Insurance Co	313-322-9045	Dearborn, MI	500	1000	2

Major Group: Insurance   **Industry: Insurance**

Organizations Listed by Industry

Organization	Phone	City / State or Province	Revenue ($ mil)	Assets ($ mil)	Emp (thous)
Foremost Insurance Co	616-942-3000	Grand Rapids, MI	881	814	2
Franklin Life Insurance Co	217-528-2011	Springfield, IL	1083	11642	4
Fremont General Corp	213-483-0991	Santa Monica, CA	408	1240	2
GEICO Corp	301-986-3000	Washington, DC	1557	3061	5
General Accident Assurnace Co of Canada	416-368-4733	Toronto, ON Can	366	581	1
General Accident Insurance Co	215-625-1000	Philadelphia, PA	1470	4168	4
General American Life Insurance Co	314-231-1700	St Louis, MO	1824	4369	4
General Re Corp	203-328-5000	Stamford, CT	2736	9394	3
Great West Life Assurance Co	204-946-1190	Winnipeg, MB Can	4221	14669	5
Guardian Life Insurance Co of America	212-598-8000	New York, NY	2876	4168	5
Hall, Frank B & Co Inc	914-769-9200	Briarcliff Manor, NY	339	1237	4
Hancock, John Mutual Life Insurance Co	617-421-6000	Boston, MA	7926	10067	25
Hanover Insurance Co	508-853-7200	Worcester, MA	1581	2649	6
Harleysville Insurance Co	215-256-5000	Harleysville, PA	450	850	2
Hartford Life Insurance Co	203-547-5000	Hartford, CT	1189	3495	4
Home Life Insurance Co	212-428-2000	New York, NY	1423	3542	3
IDS Finacial Services Inc	612-372-3131	Minneapolis, MN	2326	8963	6
Imperial Life Assurance Co	416-926-2600	Toronto, ON Can	1477	5180	4
INA Life Insurance Co	215-241-4000	Philadelphia, PA	478	2521	2
Industrial Alliance Life Insurance Co	418-463-5784	Sillery, PQ Can	1487	4389	2
Inter Exchange Auto Club of Southern Cal	213-741-3111	Los Angeles, CA	802	1424	3
Jackson National Life Ins Co	517-394-3400	Lansing, MI	1626	3643	4
Johnson & Higgins Inc	212-574-7000	New York, NY	750	2000	7
Kemper Corp	312-540-2000	Long Grove, IL	3861	12078	16
Keystone Provident Life Insurance Co	617-338-3500	Boston, MA	1042	3836	2
La Sauvegarde Assurance sur la vie Ltd	514-285-7700	Montreal, PQ Can	167	677	1
Lamar Life Insurance Corp	601-949-3100	Jackson, MI	250	1200	1
Laurentian General Insurance Co	514-842-6212	Montreal, PQ Can	276	969	1
Laurentian Mutual Insurance Co	418-647-5255	Quebec, PQ Can	261	804	1
Lawyers Title Insurance Co	804-281-6700	Richmond, Va	NA	NA	NA
Les Cooperants Ltd	514-287-6600	Montreal, PQ Can	170	680	1
Liberty Life Insurance Co	803-268-8111	Greenville, SC	401	1382	2
Liberty Mutual Insurance Co	617-285-7000	Boston, MA	8268	15749	26
Liberty National Life Insurance Co	205-325-2722	Birmingham, AL	541	2607	2
Life Insurance Co of Virginia Inc	804-281-6000	Richmond, VA	1080	2794	3
Life Investors Insurance Co of America	319-398-5811	Ceder Rapids, IA	1400	3500	2
Lincoln National Corp	219-427-2000	Fort Wayne, IN	7312	20964	15
Lloyd's of London Canada Ltd	514-861-8361	Montreal, PQ Can	417	4582	2
London Life Insurance Co	519-432-5281	London, ON Can	1960	7932	5
Lutheran Brotherhood	612-340-7000	Minneapolis, MN	1142	3007	1
Manufacturers Life Insurance Co Canada	416-926-0100	Toronto, ON Can	5120	20305	6
Maritime Life Assurance Co	902-453-4300	Halifax, NS Can	468	1518	1
Massachusetts Mutual Life Insurance Comp	413-788-8411	Springfield, MA	4632	22589	9
MBIA Insurance Co	914-681-1300	White Plains, NY	224	1283	2
Metropolitan Life Insurance Co	212-578-2211	New York, NY	30800	120400	50
Metropolitan Life Insurance Co of Canada	613-560-7446	Ottawa, ON Can	939	3441	2
Minnesota Mutual Life Ins Co	612-298-3500	St Paul, MN	1394	4466	4
Motors Insurance (General Motors) Co	313-556-5000	Detroit, MI	1075	2453	4
Munich Reinsurance Co	212-310-1800	New York, NY	800	1500	3
Mutual Benefit Life Insurance Co	201-481-8000	Newark, NJ	3169	10639	6
Mutual Life Assurance Co of Canada	519-888-2235	Waterloo, ON Can	2343	9322	4
Mutual Life Ins Co of New York (MONY)	212-708-2000	New York, NY	5235	17706	8
Mutual of America Life Insurance Co	212-399-1600	New York, NY	1011	4810	9
Mutual of Omaha Insurance Co	402-342-7600	Omaha, NE	2000	1997	5
National Home Life Assurance Co	215-648-5000	Valley Forge, PA	1155	3118	3

Major Group: Insurance   Industry: Insurance

Organizations Listed by Industry

Organization	Phone	City / State or Province	Revenue ($ mil)	Assets ($ mil)	Emp (thous)
National Life Assurance Co of Canada	416-598-2122	Toronto, ON Can	271	917	1
National Life Insurance Co	802-229-3333	Montpelier, VT	717	3590	2
National Life of Vermont	802-229-3333	Montpelier, VT	850	3980	2
Nationale Nederlanden Insurance Co	202-463-7964	Washington, DC	1000	1500	2
Nationwide Insurance Co	614-249-7111	Columbus, OH	5000	12000	12
New England Mutual Life Insurance Co	617-578-2000	Boston, MA	3802	14273	8
New Jersey Manufacturers Insurance Co	609-883-1300	West Trenton, NJ	380	1394	2
New York Life Insurance Co	212-576-7000	New York, NY	12374	43417	20
New York Life Insurance Co of Canada	416-960-4500	Toronto, ON Can	209	680	1
North American Life Assurance Co	416-229-4515	Toronto, ON Can	944	3838	3
Northwestern Mutual Life Insurance Co	414-271-1444	Milwaukee, WI	5737	25362	9
Northwestern National Life Insurance Co	612-372-5432	Minneapolis, MN	2270	7594	3
Ohio Casualty Corp	513-867-3000	Hamilton, OH	1623	2922	6
Old Republic International Corp	312-346-8100	Chicago, IL	1200	3000	5
Orion Capital Insurance Co	305-445-8333	Miami, FL	450	100	2
Pacific Mutual Life Insurance Co	714-640-3011	Newport Beach, CA	2540	6981	3
Penn Mutual Life Insurance Co	215-625-5000	Philadelphia, PA	1589	4984	5
Phoenix Continental Ltd	416-596-6100	Toronto, ON Can	333	604	1
Phoenix Mutual Life Insurance Co	203-275-5000	Hartford, CT	1319	5678	4
PMA Reinsurance Corp	215-629-5000	Philadelphia, PA	750	250	3
Principle Financial Group Inc	515-247-5111	Des Moines, IA	6577	23493	10
Progressive Insurance Co	216-464-8000	Mayfield Heights, OH	1275	2307	3
Provident Life & Accident Ins Co	615-755-1011	Chattanooga, TN	2050	7468	10
Provident Mutual Life Ins Co of Phil	215-636-5000	Philadelphia, PA	879	3371	2
Provident National Assurance Co	615-755-1011	Chattanooga, TN	500	5239	2
Prudential Assurance Group	519-888-5700	Kitchener, ON Can	612	2282	1
Prudential Assurance Group Ltd Canada	519-433-1231	Kitchener, ON Can	299	521	1
Prudential Ins Co of America, Canada	416-296-0777	Scarborough, ON Can	559	2310	3
Prudential Insurance Co of America	201-877-6000	Newark, NJ	33724	153023	75
Righa Corp	401-421-4410	Providence, RI	550	3000	1
Royal Insurance Co	416-366-7511	Toronto, ON Can	638	1150	2
Royal Insurance Co of America	312-522-2000	Chicago, IL	1200	1600	6
SAFECO Corp	206-545-5000	Seattle, WA	3018	7732	9
Selective Insurance Co	201-948-3000	Branchville, NJ	480	962	2
Sentry Insurance Co	715-346-6000	Stevens Point, WI	1422	3197	4
Shelter Insurance Co	314-445-8441	Columbia, MO	350	600	2
Southern Farm Bureau Insurance Co	601-982-7777	Jackson, MS	700	600	3
Southwestern Life Insurance Co	214-954-7111	Dallas, TX	1601	5799	5
SSQ Mutuelle d'Assurance Ltd	418-651-7000	Sainte Foy, PQ Can	210	490	1
St Paul Companies Inc	612-221-7911	St Paul, MN	3631	10382	10
Standard Life Assurance Co	514-284-6711	Montreal, PQ Can	842	3964	1
State Auto Mutual Insurance Co	614-464-5000	Columbus, OH	400	500	2
State Farm Group Ltd Canada	416-321-4000	Scarborough, ON Can	324	559	1
State Farm Insurance Co	309-766-2311	Bloomington, IL	2358	8453	6
State Mutual Life Assurance Co of Amer	508-852-1000	Worcester, MA	1718	4376	4
Statesman Group Life Insurance Co	515-284-7500	Des Moines, IA	678	2402	1
Sun Life Assurance Co of Canada	416-595-7500	Toronto, ON Can	4215	19711	5
Sun Life Assurance Co of Canada US	617-237-6030	Wellesley, MA	449	3505	2
Swiss Reinsurance Co	212-907-8000	New York, NY	900	1200	3
Ticor Corp	213-852-6000	Los Angeles, CA	750	2000	7
Transamerica Corp	415-983-4000	San Francisco, CA	7879	26759	17
Transamerica Life Insurance Co	213-742-3111	Los Angeles, CA	2073	5533	1
Transamerica Occidental Life Ins Co	213-742-2111	Los Angeles, CA	1700	6000	4
Travelers Co of Canada Ltd	416-586-3000	Toronto, ON Can	303	406	1
Travelers Insurance Corp	203-277-0111	Hartford, CT	18986	53332	29

Major Group: Insurance   Industry: Insurance

Organizations Listed by Industry

Organization	Phone	City / State or Province	Revenue ($ mil)	Assets ($ mil)	Emp (thous)
Union Central Life Insurance Co	215-322-3000	Trevose, PA	847	2547	2
United of Omaha Life Insurance Co	402-342-7600	Omaha, NE	882	3211	3
UNUM Union Mutual Life Insurance Co	207-770-2211	Portland, ME	2199	8127	4
US Life Insurance Corp	212-709-6000	New York, NY	1279	4145	3
USAA Financial Services Inc	512-498-7290	San Antonio, TX	398	625	2
USF & G Corp	301-547-3000	Baltimore, MD	5582	12361	10
Utica National Insurance Co	315-735-3321	Utica, NY	400	1000	2
Variable Annuity Life Insurance Co	713-526-5251	Houston, TX	1880	7771	2
Wawanesa Mutual Insurance Co	204-985-3811	Winnipeg, MB Can	408	632	1
Western & Southern Life Ins Co	513-629-1800	Cincinnati, OH	970	5028	6
Westfield Companies	216-887-0101	Westfield Center, OH	450	800	2
Winterthur Swiss Insurance Co	212-466-0777	New York, NY	700	1200	3
Zenith Insurance Co	818-990-9300	Encino, CA	300	600	2
Zenith National Insurance Co	819-990-9300	Encino, CA	472	791	2
Zurich Insurance Co	312-843-6000	Schaumburg, IL	688	1921	4
Zurich Insurance Co Canada Ltd	416-593-4444	Toronto, ON Can	389	672	1

Industry: Insurance   Number: 189

Major Group: High Tech   Industry: Aerospace

Organization	Phone	City / State or Province	Revenue ($ mil)	Assets ($ mil)	Emp (thous)
Aerojet Inc	619-455-8500	La Jolla, CA	NA	NA	NA
Aircraft Engine Components Div , Textron	203-666-4601	Newington, CT	NA	NA	NA
Allied Signal Aerospace Div	703-276-2000	Arlington, VA	NA	NA	NA
Allied Signal Inc	713-224-6611	Morristown, NJ	11909	10005	110
Beech Aircraft Corp	316-681-7111	Wichita, KS	NA	NA	NA
Bell Helicopter Textron Inc	817-280-2011	Hearst, TX	NA	NA	NA
Boeing Aerospace Corp	206-773-2121	Kent, WA	NA	NA	NA
Boeing Commercial Airplanes Inc	206-237-2121	Renton, WA	NA	NA	NA
Boeing Corp	206-655-2121	Seattle, WA	17340	12608	153
Boeing Helicopters Inc	215-591-2121	Philadelphia, PA	NA	NA	NA
Cessna Aircraft Corp	316-685-9111	Wichita, KS	NA	NA	NA
Douglas Aircraft Co	213-593-5511	Long Beach, CA	NA	NA	NA
Fairchild Industries Inc	703-478-5800	Chantilly, VA	539	441	5
Gates Learjet Corp	602-745-5100	Tucson, AZ	500	NA	2
General Dynamics Corp	314-889-8200	St Louis, MO	9551	6118	103
General Dynamics Space Systems Div	619-573-8000	San Diego, CA	NA	NA	NA
Grumman Corp	516-575-0574	Bethpage, NY	3649	2566	30
Guidance & Control Systems Div	818-715-4040	Woodland Hills, CA	NA	NA	NA
Gulfstream Aerospace Corp	912-964-3000	Savannah, GA	NA	NA	NA
Hamilton Standard Inc	203-654-6000	Windsor, CT	NA	NA	NA
Hughes Aircraft Co	213-568-6321	Los Angeles, CA	NA	NA	NA
ITT Defense Technology Corp	703-276-8300	Arlington, VA	1500	NA	10
Lockheed Corp	818-847-6121	Calabasas, CA	10590	6643	87
Lockheed Missiles & Space Co Inc	408-742-4321	Sunnyvale, CA	NA	NA	NA
Martin Marietta Corp	301-897-6000	Bethesda, MD	5727	3319	80
Martin Marietta Electronics & Missiles	305-356-2000	Orlando, FL	NA	NA	NA
McDonnell Douglas Canada Ltd	416-677-4341	Mississauga, ON Can	329	238	5
McDonnell Douglas Corp	314-232-0232	St Louis, MO	15069	11885	121
McDonnell Douglas Missile Systems Co	314-925-4000	St Charles, MO	NA	NA	NA
McDonnell Douglas Space Systems Co	714-896-3311	Huntington Beach, CA	NA	NA	NA
Norden Inc	203-852-5000	Norwalk, CT	NA	NA	NA
Northrop Corp	213-553-6262	Los Angeles, CA	5797	3139	45
Parker Bertea Aerospace Group	714-833-3000	Irvine, CA	NA	NA	NA
Pratt & Whitney Aircraft Inc	203-565-9500	East Hartford, CT	NA	NA	NA

Major Group: High Tech   Industry: Aerospace

Organizations Listed by Industry

Organization	Phone	City / State or Province	Revenue ($ mil)	Assets ($ mil)	Emp (thous)
Pratt & Whitney Canada Inc	514-677-9411	Longueuill, PQ Can	839	700	9
Rockwell International of Canada Ltd	416-757-1101	Toronto, ON Can	437	296	2
Rohr Industries Inc	619-691-4111	Chula Vista, CA	907	883	11
Rolls Royce Industries Canada Inc	514-747-7742	Ville St Laurent, PQ Can	213	149	2
Sikorsky Inc	203-386-4000	Stamford, CT	NA	NA	NA
SMP Inc	216-585-3100	Wickliffe, OH	NA	NA	NA
Teledyne Aerospace Systems Div	507-235-3355	Fairmont, MN	NA	NA	NA
Teleflex Corp	215-948-5100	Limerick, PA	350	300	2
Textron Defense Systems Div	508-657-5111	Wilmington, MA	NA	NA	NA
Thiokol Aerospace Group Inc	801-625-4801	Ogden, UT	NA	NA	NA
Thiokol Corp	312-807-2000	Chicago, IL	1168	900	9
United Co	703-466-3322	Bristol, VA	500	NA	2
United Technologies Corp	203-728-7000	Hartford, CT	18518	12748	185
United Technologies Space Systems Div	203-728-7000	Hartford, CT	NA	NA	NA
Westinghouse Canada Inc	416-528-8811	Hamilton, ON Can	677	NA	6

Industry: Aerospace   Number: 49

Major Group: High Tech   Industry: Electronics

Organization	Phone	City / State or Province	Revenue ($ mil)	Assets ($ mil)	Emp (thous)
ADT Inc	215-558-1100	New York, NY	600	500	8
Advanced Micro Devices Inc	408-732-2400	Sunnyvale, CA	1122	919	19
Aero Products Inc	805-864-5600	Moorpark, CA	NA	NA	NA
Alpha Industries Inc	617-935-5150	Woburn, MA	200	150	2
Ametek Inc	212-935-8640	New York, NY	520	448	5
AMP Inc	717-564-0100	Harrisburg, PA	2670	2376	24
AMP Packaging Systems Inc	512-244-5110	Round Rock, TX	NA	NA	NA
Analog Devices Inc	617-329-4700	Norwood, MA	439	449	5
Andrew Corp	312-349-3300	Orland Park, IL	300	200	3
Anthem Electronics Inc	408-295-4200	San Jose, CA	250	200	3
Apex Corp	513-222-7871	Dayton, OH	NA	NA	NA
Applied Materials Inc	408-727-5555	Santa Clara, CA	400	200	2
Arrow Electronics Inc	516-391-1300	Melville, NY	1006	530	5
Artra Group Inc	312-441-6650	Winnetka, IL	204	150	2
Augat Inc	617-543-4300	Mansfield, MA	321	278	4
AVX Corp	516-829-8500	Great Neck, NY	271	200	2
Bairnco Corp	212-490-8722	New York, NY	228	297	2
Baldor Electric Co	501-646-4711	Fort Smith, AR	200	200	2
Bell Industries Inc	213-826-6778	Los Angeles, CA	450	NA	4
Canadian Marconi Co	514-341-7630	Montreal, PQ Can	255	170	2
Champion Spark Plug Co	419-247-1600	Toledo, OH	738	576	13
Charter Power Systems	215-828-9000	Plymouth Meeting, PA	200	250	2
Chips & Technologies Inc	408-434-0600	San Jose, CA	218	100	2
Combustion Engineering Inc	203-329-8771	Stamford, CT	3484	2546	29
Cooper Companies	415-856-5000	Palo Alto, CA	400	NA	4
Coulter Electronics Corp	305-885-0131	Hialeah, FL	500	NA	5
CTS Corp	219-293-7511	Elkhart, IN	325	300	2
Cubic Corp	619-277-6780	San Diego, CA	350	300	3
Cypress Semiconductor Inc	408-943-2600	San Jose, CA	139	245	2
Duracell Corp	203-796-4000	Bethel, CT	1500	NA	10
Dynalectron Corp	703-264-0330	McLean, VA	750	250	15
E-Systems Inc	214-661-1000	Dallas, TX	1443	758	17
EG & G Inc	617-237-5100	Wellesley, MA	1406	539	22
Electrospace Systems Inc	214-470-2000	Richardson, TX	NA	NA	NA
Emerson Electric Co	314-553-2000	St Louis, MO	6652	5027	71

Major Group: High Tech   Industry: Electronics

Organizations Listed by Industry

Organization	Phone	City / State or Province	Revenue ($ mil)	Assets ($ mil)	Emp (thous)
Emerson Radio Corp	201-854-6600	North Bergen, NJ	729	255	3
Energy Services Co	614-393-8200	Mt Vernon, OH	NA	NA	NA
Everready Battery Corp	314-982-1000	St Louis, MO	NA	NA	NA
Federal Signal Corp	312-954-2000	Oak Brook, IL	400	300	3
Flextronics Inc	415-792-4177	Newark, CA	200	100	3
Fluke, John Manufacturing Co	206-347-6100	Everett, WA	225	200	2
Ford Electronics Manufacturing Corp	416-475-8510	Markham, ON Can	351	170	2
Fujitsu Inc	213-327-2151	Torrance, CA	1100	NA	2
General Dynamics Services Corp	314-851-4050	St Louis, MO	NA	NA	NA
General Electric Co	203-373-2431	Fairfield, CT	50089	110865	298
General Instrument Corp	212-207-6200	New York, NY	1305	1309	29
GNB Inc	612-681-5000	Mendota Heights, MN	440	NA	4
Gould Inc	312-640-4000	Rolling Meadows, IL	1000	1400	11
Graybar Electric Co Inc	314-727-3900	St Louis, MO	2000	NA	5
Grinnell Corp	603-778-9200	Exeter, NH	NA	NA	NA
Harman International Industries Inc	202-955-6130	Washington, DC	225	200	3
Harris Corp	305-727-9100	Melbourne, FL	2099	1644	23
Hitachi Sales Corp of America	213-537-8383	Compton, CA	1100	NA	2
Hubbell Inc	203-789-1100	Orange, CT	614	523	5
IMO Industries	609-896-7600	Lawrenceville, NJ	650	550	4
Industrial Automation Systems Group Inc	606-283-2202	Florence, KY	NA	NA	NA
Instrument Systems Inc	516-938-5544	Jericho, NY	350	300	3
Intel Corp	408-987-8080	Santa Clara, CA	2875	3550	30
ITT Canada Ltd	416-863-9666	Toronto, ON Can	298	383	3
KDI Corp	513-272-1421	Cincinnati, OH	350	300	4
Kollmorgen Corp	203-327-7222	Stamford, CT	345	224	4
Litton Industries Inc	213-859-5000	Beverly Hills, CA	4864	5075	55
Litton Systems Canada Ltd	416-249-1231	Toronto, ON Can	383	298	1
Loral Corp	212-697-1105	New York, NY	1187	1200	9
LPL Investment Group	203-265-8600	Wallingford, CT	600	708	5
LSI Logic Corp	408-433-8000	Milpitas, CA	379	787	3
Lucky Goldstar Group	201-460-8010	Lindhusrt, NJ	1650	NA	2
Mark IV Industries Inc	716-689-4972	Williamsville, NY	742	800	6
Marshall Industries Inc	818-459-5500	El Monte, CA	400	200	2
Matsushita Electric of Canada Ltd	416-624-5010	Mississauga, ON Can	341	88	1
Matsushita Electric USA Inc	201-348-7100	Secaucus, NJ	1650	NA	3
McDonnell Douglas Electronic Systems	703-442-7960	McLean, VA	NA	NA	NA
Medtronic Inc	612-574-4000	Minneapolis, MN	653	641	6
Minolta Corp	201-825-4000	Ramsey, NJ	825	NA	2
Mitsubishi International USA Inc	212-605-2000	New York, NY	3850	NA	8
Molex Inc	312-969-4550	Lisle, IL	502	499	6
Moog Inc	716-652-2000	Aurora, NY	350	250	3
Motorola Canada Ltd	416-499-1441	Willowdale, ON Can	298	170	3
Motorola Inc	312-397-5000	Schaumburg, IL	8250	6710	102
Murata North America Inc	214-403-3300	Plano, TX	550	NA	2
National Advanced Systems Corp	408-970-1000	Santa Clara, CA	NA	NA	NA
National Semiconductor Corp	408-721-5000	Santa Clara, CA	2470	1777	38
National Service Industries Inc	404-892-2400	Atlanta, GA	1414	825	20
Nationwide Electronics Inc	312-426-5900	Carpentersville, IL	1100	NA	2
NEC Nippon Electric Corp USA	516-753-7000	Melville, NY	2200	NA	4
Noma Industries Ltd	416-222-6662	Willowdale, ON Can	448	281	4
North American Philips Corp	212-697-3600	New York, NY	5424	3423	52
Panasonic Matsushita Electric Corp	713-895-7200	Los Angeles, CA	2000	NA	2
Peck, C L Contractors Inc	213-470-1885	Los Angeles, CA	550	NA	1
Philips Canada Ltd	416-292-5161	Montreal, ON Can	468	NA	3

Major Group: High Tech   Industry: Electronics

Organizations Listed by Industry

Organization	Phone	City / State or Province	Revenue ($ mil)	Assets ($ mil)	Emp (thous)
Pioneer Standard Electric Inc	216-587-3600	Garfield Heights, OH	300	200	2
Pittway Corp	312-498-1260	Northbrook, IL	771	602	6
Raytheon Co	617-862-6600	Lexington, MA	8192	4740	76
Reliance Electric Corp	216-266-7000	Cleveland, OH	1500	NA	15
SAAB Scandia America Inc	203-795-5671	Orange, CT	1100	NA	2
Samsung Electronics USA Inc	201-592-7900	Fort Lee, NJ	1100	NA	1
Sanders Associates Inc	603-885-4321	South Nashua, NH	1000	NA	10
Sanyo Manufacturing Corp	501-633-5030	Forest City, AR	1100	NA	4
Sharp Electronics USA Inc	201-529-8200	Mahwah, NJ	1100	NA	2
Siemens Corp	201-321-3400	Iselin, NJ	2530	NM	26
Simplex Wire & Cable Co	603-436-6100	Portsmouth, NH	NA	NA	NA
Sony Corp of America	201-930-1000	Park Ridge, NJ	3300	NA	4
Sprague Technologies Inc	203-964-8600	Stamford, CT	450	400	7
Square D Co	312-397-2600	Palatine, IL	1657	1336	21
SSMC Inc (Singer Co)	203-356-4200	Stamford, CT	1750	1000	15
Standard Shares Inc	312-498-1260	Northbrook, IL	795	600	6
Standex International Corp	603-893-9701	Salem, NH	430	276	6
Sterling Electronics Corp	713-623-6600	Houston, TX	225	150	2
Sun Electric Corp	815-459-7700	Crystal Lake, IL	225	250	3
Tandy Electronics Manufacturing Inc	817-390-3689	Fort Worth, TX	NA	NA	NA
Teledyne Controls Div	213-820-4616	West Los Angeles, CA	NA	NA	NA
Teledyne Republic Div	216-267-2700	Cleveland, OH	NA	NA	NA
Teledyne Ryan Electronics Div	619-560-6400	San Diego, CA	NA	NA	NA
Texas Instruments Inc	214-995-2011	Dallas, TX	6295	4428	83
Thermo Electron Corp	617-890-8700	Waltham, MA	501	490	4
Thomas & Betts Corp	201-685-1600	Raritan, NJ	515	493	5
Toshiba America Electric Corp	714-583-3000	Irvine, CA	825	NA	2
Tracor Inc	512-926-2800	Austin, TX	750	500	9
Transtechnology Corp	213-990-5920	Van Nuys, CA	225	200	3
TRW Inc	216-291-7000	Cleveland, OH	6982	4442	73
Varian Associates Inc	415-493-4000	Palo Alto, CA	983	830	12
Victor Technologies Corp	215-251-5000	Malvern, PA	550	NA	2
Vishay Intertechnology Corp	919-365-3800	Malvern, PA	250	200	3
VLSI Technology Inc	408-924-1810	San Jose, CA	300	150	2
Watkins Johnson Co	415-493-4141	Palo Alto, CA	275	250	3
Western Digital Corp	714-863-0102	Irvine, CA	768	551	7
Westinghouse Electric Corp	412-244-2000	Pittsburgh, PA	12500	16937	120
Zenith Electronics Corp	312-391-7000	Glenview, IL	2686	1428	36

Industry: Electronics   **Number: 128**

Major Group: High Tech   **Industry: Instruments**

Organization	Phone	City / State or Province	Revenue ($ mil)	Assets ($ mil)	Emp (thous)
Acuson Corp	415-969-9112	Mountain View, CA	169	91	1
Allen Group Inc	516-293-5500	Melville, NY	344	328	5
Applied Biosystems Inc	415-570-6667	Foster City, CA	158	151	1
Bausch & Lomb Inc	716-338-6000	Rochester, NY	978	1211	10
Coopervision Inc	415-856-5000	Palo Alto, CA	550	1000	5
Dionex Corp	408-737-0700	Sunnyvale, CA	300	200	1
Durr Fillauer Medical Inc	205-241-8800	Montgomery, AL	588	178	2
Fisher Scientific Group Inc	619-457-3565	La Jolla, CA	957	579	6
Foxboro Co	617-543-8750	Foxboro, MA	540	472	7
General Signal Corp	203-357-8800	Stamford, CT	1760	1397	21
Gerber Scientific Co	203-644-1551	South Windsor, CT	299	245	2
Johnson Controls Inc	414-228-1200	Milwaukee, WI	3100	2013	29

Major Group: High Tech   **Industry: Instruments**

Organizations Listed by Industry

Organization	Phone	City / State or Province	Revenue ($ mil)	Assets ($ mil)	Emp (thous)
KLA Instruments Corp	408-988-6100	Santa Clara, CA	113	135	1
Lennox International Corp	214-980-6000	Dallas, TX	750	NA	5
Lockheed Aeronautical Systems Co	818-847-6121	Burbank, CA	NA	NA	NA
Measurex Corp	408-255-1500	Cupertino, CA	265	303	3
Millipore Corp	617-275-9200	Bedford, MA	622	576	6
NES Corp	312-426-5900	Carpentersville, IL	825	NA	3
Perkin Elmer Corp	203-762-1000	Norwalk, CT	1165	1368	11
Tektronix Inc	503-627-7111	Beaverton, OR	1412	1024	16
Teradyne Inc	617-482-2700	Boston, MA	463	434	5
Timex Group Inc	203-573-5000	Waterbury, CT	825	NA	2
UNC Inc	301-266-7333	Annapolis, MD	401	408	3
Zurn Industries Inc	814-452-2111	Erie, PA	485	360	4

Industry: Instruments   **Number: 24**

Major Group: High Tech   **Industry: Comput/Off Equip**

Organization	Phone	City / State or Province	Revenue ($ mil)	Assets ($ mil)	Emp (thous)
Alcatel Business Systems Inc	800-556-1234	Milpitas, CA	500	NA	5
Amdahl Corp	408-746-6000	Sunnyvale, CA	1802	1931	11
American Management Corp	703-841-6000	Arlington, VA	250	150	3
Anacomp Inc	317-844-9666	Indianapolis, IN	300	250	2
Apollo Computer Inc	508-256-6600	Chelmsford, MA	654	497	4
Apple Computer Inc	408-996-1010	Cupertino, CA	4071	2082	7
Applied Magnetics Corp	805-967-8227	Goleta, CA	300	NA	3
Arix Corp	408-432-1200	San Jose, CA	350	200	1
Ashton Tate Inc	213-329-8000	Torrance, CA	307	305	3
AST Research Inc	714-863-1333	Irvine, CA	456	200	2
Atari Corp	408-745-2000	Sunnyvale, CA	452	NA	4
Autodesk Corp	415-332-2344	Sausalito, CA	117	170	2
Automatic Data Processing Inc	201-994-5000	Roseland, NJ	1549	1653	23
Beckman Instruments Inc	714-871-4848	Fullerton, CA	800	500	7
Bell & Howell Co	312-470-7100	Skokie, IL	900	800	10
Bolt Beranek & Newman Inc	617-873-2000	Cambridge, MA	305	264	3
Canon USA Inc	516-488-6700	Lake Success, NY	2200	NA	4
Commodore International	215-431-9100	West Chester, PA	250	200	3
Compaq Computer Corp	713-370-0670	Houston, TX	2066	1590	12
CompuServe Inc	614-457-8600	Columbus, OH	NA	NA	NA
Computer Associates International Inc	516-333-6700	Jericho, NY	1030	NA	9
Computer Sciences Corp	213-615-0311	El Segundo, CA	1152	661	13
Computervision Corp	617-275-1800	Bedford, MA	500	431	5
Concurrent Computer Corp	201-946-8883	Holmdel, NJ	278	200	3
Conner Peripherals Corp	408-433-3340	San Jose, CA	200	100	1
Control Data Corp	612-853-8100	Minneapolis, MN	3628	2534	34
Convergent Technologies Inc	408-434-2848	San Jose, CA	400	295	15
Cray Research Inc	612-333-5889	Minneapolis, MN	756	991	5
Data General Corp	508-366-8911	Westboro, MA	1365	1078	15
Datapoint Corp	512-699-7000	San Antonio, TX	400	NA	4
Dataproducts Corp	818-887-8000	Woodland Hills, CA	400	NA	3
Dell Computer Corp	512-338-4400	Austin, TX	258	150	2
Dictaphone Corp	203-381-7000	Stratford, CT	NA	NA	NA
Diebold Inc	216-489-4000	Canton, OH	451	455	5
Digital Communications Inc	404-442-4000	Alpharetta, GA	228	252	2
Digital Equipment Corp	617-493-5111	Maynard, MA	11475	10112	122
Digital Equipment of Canada Ltd	613-592-5111	Kanata, ON Can	680	255	3
Dun & Bradstreet Credit Services Co	201-665-6660	Murray Hill, NJ	NA	NA	NA

Major Group: High Tech   **Industry: Comput/Off Equip**

Organizations Listed by Industry

Organization	Phone	City / State or Province	Revenue ($ mil)	Assets ($ mil)	Emp (thous)
Dynatech Corp	617-272-3304	Burlington, MA	368	254	3
Electronic Data Systems Corp	214-661-6000	Dallas, TX	4844	3416	45
Entertainment Marketing Inc	713-995-4433	Houston, TX	250	200	1
Equifax Inc	404-885-8000	Atlanta, GA	743	421	10
Everex Systems Inc	415-498-1111	Fremont, CA	400	300	2
First Financial Management Corp	404-321-0120	Atlanta, GA	400	200	3
Furman-Selz Inc	212-309-8200	New York, NY	NA	NA	NA
General Binding Corp	312-272-3700	Northbrook, IL	300	200	4
Genicom Corp	703-949-1000	Waaynesboro, VA	300	150	4
Hewlett Packard Canada Ltd	416-678-9430	Mississauga, ON Can	298	298	1
Hewlett Parkard Co	415-857-1501	Palo Alto, CA	10070	7497	87
Honeywell Bull (Cie des Machines Bull)	617-895-6000	Waltham, MA	750	NA	7
Honeywell Inc	612-870-5200	Minneapolis, MN	7148	5089	62
Honeywell Ltd	416-499-6111	Willowdale, ON Can	349	205	4
IBM (Intl Business Mach) Canada Ltd	416-474-2111	Markham, ON Can	2638	2023	12
IBM (Intl Business Mach) Corp	914-765-1900	Armonk, NY	59681	73037	387
Inacomp Computer Centers Inc	317-844-9666	Indianapolis, IN	451	963	4
Information Resources Inc	312-726-1221	Chicago, IL	129	151	2
Intelligent Electronics Inc	215-524-1800	Exton, PA	600	300	1
Intergraph Corp	205-772-2000	Huntsville, AL	801	831	6
LDI Corp	216-687-0100	Cleveland, OH	270	125	2
Logicon Inc	213-373-0220	Torrance, CA	225	100	3
Lotus Development Corp	617-577-8500	Cambridge, MA	467	422	4
MAI Basic Four Inc	714-731-5100	Tustin, CA	425	375	3
Management Science America Inc	404-239-2000	Atlanta, GA	300	200	3
Martin Marietta Information Systems Inc	301-897-6000	Bethesda, MD	NA	NA	NA
Maxtor Corp	408-942-1700	San Jose, CA	271	277	3
McCormack & Dodge Inc	508-665-8200	Natick, MA	NA	NA	NA
McDonnell Douglas Information Systems	314-232-0232	St Louis, MO	NA	NA	NA
McGraw Hill Financial Services Co	212-208-8800	New York, NY	NA	NA	NA
Mead Data Central Inc	513-865-6800	Dayton, OH	NA	NA	NA
Memorex Telex Corp	918-627-2333	Tulsa, OK	850	563	7
Micromedex Inc	303-623-8600	Denver, CO	NA	NA	NA
Micron Technology	208-383-4000	Boise, ID	400	200	5
Micropolis Corp	818-709-3300	Chatsworth, CA	353	301	3
Microsoft Corp	206-882-8080	Redmond, WA	591	493	3
Miniscribe Corp	303-651-6000	Longmont, CO	400	250	7
Moore Corp	416-364-2600	Toronto, ON Can	2571	2142	26
National Computer Systems Inc	612-829-3000	Hopkins, MN	250	150	3
National Data Corp	404-329-8500	Atlanta, GA	227	150	3
NCR Corp	513-445-5000	Dayton, OH	5990	4717	60
Network Systems Corp	612-424-4888	Minneapolis, MN	131	240	1
New England Business Service	508-448-6111	Groton, MA	217	80	2
Nielsen, A C Co	312-498-6300	Northbrook, IL	NA	NA	NA
Nixdorf US Inc	617-273-0480	Burlington, MA	880	NA	8
Novell Inc	801-226-8202	Orem, UT	282	227	2
NYNEX Business Information Systems Inc	914-683-2398	White Plains, NY	NA	NA	NA
Oracle Systems Corp	415-598-8000	Belmont, CA	584	500	5
Oryx Energy Co	201-845-5533	Paramus, NJ	1200	800	1
Pansophic Systems Inc	312-572-6000	Oak Brook, IL	250	174	2
PCS Inc	602-391-4600	Scottsdale, AZ	NA	NA	NA
Pitney Bowes Inc	203-356-5000	Stamford, CT	2650	4788	29
Prime Computer Inc	508-655-8000	Natick, MA	1595	1651	12
QMS Inc	205-633-4300	Mobile, AL	250	150	1
Quantum Corp	408-262-1100	Milpitas, CA	400	200	1

Major Group: High Tech   **Industry: Comput/Off Equip**

Organizations Listed by Industry

Organization	Phone	City / State or Province	Revenue ($ mil)	Assets ($ mil)	Emp (thous)
Recognition Equipment Inc	214-579-6000	Irving, TX	275	200	3
Reuters Inc	212-603-3300	New York, NY	825	NA	8
Savin Corp	203-967-5000	Stamford, CT	361	300	2
SCI Systems Inc	205-882-4800	Huntsville, AL	774	485	9
Seagate Technology Inc	408-438-6550	Scotts Valley, CA	1266	1094	7
Shared Medical Systems Corp	215-296-6300	Malvern, PA	379	285	4
SHL Systemhouse Inc	604-236-9734	Vancouver, BC Can	425	170	1
Silicon Graphics Inc	415-960-1980	Mountain View, CA	264	175	1
Softsel Computer Products Inc	213-412-1700	Inglewood, CA	550	200	2
Standard Register Co	513-443-1000	Dayton, OH	675	444	6
Storage Technology Corp	303-673-5020	Louisville, CO	874	847	8
Stratus Computer Inc	617-460-2000	Marlborough, MA	265	200	2
Sun Microsystems Inc	415-960-1300	Mountain View, CA	1052	757	7
Syscon Corp	202-342-4000	Washington, DC	NA	NA	NA
Tandem Computers Inc	408-725-6000	Cupertino, CA	1315	1318	9
Tandon Corp	805-523-0340	Moorpark, CA	309	250	4
Tandy Corp	817-390-3700	Fort Worth, TX	3794	2530	30
Telerate Inc	212-938-5200	New York, NY	440	543	3
ThreeCom (3Com) Corp	408-562-6400	Santa Clara, CA	400	350	4
Unisys Canada Inc	416-495-0515	North York, ON Can	623	436	3
Unisys Corp	215-542-4011	Blue Bell, PA	9902	11535	90
United Stationers Inc	312-699-5000	Des Plaines, IL	1000	500	3
Verbatim Corp	704-547-6500	Charlotte, NC	NA	NA	NA
Versatec Inc	408-988-2800	Santa Clara, CA	NA	NA	NA
Volt Information Sciences Corp	212-309-0200	New York, NY	450	300	18
Wallace Computer Services Inc	312-626-2000	Hillside, IL	383	292	3
Wang Laboratories Inc	508-459-5000	Lowell, MA	3068	2838	31
Wheeler Group Inc	203-379-9911	Hartford, CT	NA	NA	NA
Wyle Laboratories Inc	213-322-1763	El Segundo, CA	411	400	2
Wyse Technology Inc	408-433-1000	San Jose, CA	275	200	2
Xerox Canada Ltd	416-229-3769	North York, ON Can	958	1591	7
Xerox Corp	203-968-3000	Stamford, CT	16441	26441	113
Xidex Corp	408-988-3472	Palo Alto, CA	570	770	6
XL/Datacomp Inc	312-323-1200	Hinsdale, IL	231	193	2
Zenith Data Systems Corp	312-699-4800	Mount Prospect, IL	NA	NA	NA

Industry: Comput/Off Equip   Number: 128

Major Group: High Tech   Industry: Telecom

Organization	Phone	City / State or Province	Revenue ($ mil)	Assets ($ mil)	Emp (thous)
Alberta Government Telephone Co	403-425-2110	Edmonton, AB Can	911	2006	11
Alltel Corp	216-650-7000	Hudson, OH	1068	2153	8
American Cellular Communications Inc	601-353-1300	Jackson, MS	NA	NA	NA
American Telephone & Telegraph Co	212-605-5500	New York, NY	35210	35152	304
Ameritech (Amer Information Tech Corp)	312-750-5000	Chicago, IL	9903	19163	77
Ameritech Communications Inc	312-906-4199	Chicago, IL	NA	NA	NA
Anglo Canadian Telephone Co	514-341-6321	Saint Laurent, PQ Can	1676	3169	22
Bell Atlantic Corp	215-963-6000	Philadelphia, PA	10880	24729	81
Bell Atlantic Enterprises Co	215-963-6666	Philadelphia, PA	NA	NA	NA
Bell Canada Inc (BCE Inc)	514-870-1511	Montreal, PQ Can	5421	11482	110
Bell Telephone of Pennsylvania	215-466-9900	Philadelphia, PA	NA	NA	NA
BellSouth Corp	404-249-2000	Atlanta, GA	13687	28472	101
BellSouth Services Inc	205-321-1000	Birmingham, AL	NA	NA	NA
Brintec Systems Corp	203-456-8000	Willimantic, CT	300	300	4
British Columbia Telephone Ltd	604-432-2151	Burnaby, BC Can	1332	2723	15

Major Group: High Tech   Industry: Telecom

Organizations Listed by Industry

Organization	Phone	City / State or Province	Revenue ($ mil)	Assets ($ mil)	Emp (thous)
Carolina Telephone & Telegraph Co	919-823-9900	Tarboro, NC	NA	NA	NA
Centel Corp	312-399-2500	Chicago, IL	1095	3753	13
Century Telephone Enterprises Inc	318-388-9000	Monroe, LA	250	400	3
Chesapeake & Potomac Telephone Co	202-887-0565	Washington, DC	NA	NA	NA
Cincinnati Bell Inc	513-397-9900	Cincinnati, OH	738	1253	10
COMSAT Communications Satellite Inc	202-863-6000	Washington, DC	359	1163	3
Contel Corp	404-391-8000	Atlanta, GA	2964	5865	23
DST Systems Inc	816-221-5545	Kansas City, MO	139	184	1
General Datacomm Industries Inc	203-574-1118	Middlebury, CT	240	290	3
GTE Corp	203-965-2000	Stamford, CT	16460	31104	200
Illinois Bell Telephone Co	312-727-9411	Chicago, IL	NA	NA	NA
Indiana Bell Telephone Co	317-265-2266	Indianapolis, IN	NA	NA	NA
Intelsat Corp	202-944-6800	Washington, DC	825	NA	2
International Telecharge Corp	214-744-0240	Dallas, TX	250	200	3
M/A Com Inc	617-272-9600	Burlington, MA	424	483	6
Manitoba Telephone System Ltd	204-947-4111	Winnipeg, MB Can	342	837	5
Maritime Telephone & Telegraph Ltd	902-421-4311	Halifax, NS Can	327	785	4
McCaw Cellular	206-827-4500	Kirkland, WA	225	300	3
MCI Communications Corp	202-872-1600	Washington, DC	5137	5843	18
Memotec Data Inc	514-738-4781	Montreal, PQ Can	340	765	2
Metro Mobile Communications Inc	212-319-7444	New York, NY	56	242	1
Michigan Bell Telephone Co	313-223-9900	Detroit, MI	NA	NA	NA
Mitel Corp	613-592-2122	Kanata, ON Can	356	379	4
Mobile Communications Corp	601-977-0888	Ridgeland, MS	115	344	2
Nevada Bell Corp	702-789-6000	Reno, NV	NA	NA	NA
New England Telephone & Telegraph Co	617-743-9800	Boston, MA	NA	NA	NA
New Jersey Bell Telephone Co	201-649-9900	Newark, NJ	NA	NA	NA
New York Telephone Co	212-395-2121	New York, NY	NA	NA	NA
Northern Telecom Ltd	416-897-9000	Mississauga, ON Can	3613	NA	35
NYNEX Corp	212-370-7400	New York, NY	12661	25362	97
NYNEX Mobile Communications Co	914-577-5200	Pearl River, NY	NA	NA	NA
Ohio Bell Telephone Co	216-822-9700	Cleveland, OH	NA	NA	NA
Pacific Bell Inc	415-542-9000	San Francisco, CA	NA	NA	NA
Pacific Telecom Inc	206-696-0983	Vancouver, WA	552	1242	4
Pacific Telesis Group Inc	415-882-8000	San Francisco, CA	9483	21191	70
PacTel Cellular Co	714-553-6087	Irvine, CA	NA	NA	NA
Paradyne Corp	813-530-2000	Largo, FL	250	200	3
Rochester Telephone Corp	716-777-1000	Rochester, NY	479	885	3
Safeguard Scientific Corp	215-265-4000	King of Prussia, PA	284	250	1
Sammons Enterprises Inc	214-670-9790	Dallas, TX	1500	NA	5
Saskatchewan Telecommunications Ltd	306-347-2200	Regina, SK Can	436	896	5
Scientific Atlanta Inc	404-441-4000	Atlanta, GA	509	316	4
South Central Bell Telephone Co	205-321-1000	Birmingham, AL	NA	NA	NA
Southern Bell Telephone & Telegraph Co	404-529-8611	Atlanta, GA	NA	NA	NA
Southern New England Telephone Inc	203-771-5200	New Haven, CT	1583	3067	14
Southwestern Bell Corp	314-235-9800	St Louis, MO	8473	20985	75
Southwestern Bell Mobile Systems Inc	214-733-2000	Dallas, TX	NA	NA	NA
Telecom USA Inc	404-458-4927	Atlanta, GA	200	150	2
Teleglobe Canada Ltd	514-289-7272	Montreal, PQ Can	314	769	2
Telephone & Data Corp	312-630-1900	Chicago, IL	250	200	3
TIE Communications Inc	203-926-2000	Shelton, CT	255	254	3
United Telecommunications Inc	913-676-3000	Westwood, KS	6493	9817	42
United Telephone Co of Florida	407-889-6000	Altamonte Springs, FL	NA	NA	NA
United Telephone Co of Indiana	219-267-6161	Warsaw, IN	NA	NA	NA
United Telephone of Ohio	419-755-8011	Mansfield, OH	NA	NA	NA

Major Group: High Tech   Industry: Telecom

Organizations Listed by Industry

Organization	Phone	City / State or Province	Revenue ($ mil)	Assets ($ mil)	Emp (thous)
US Sprint Inc	816-941-5000	Kansas City, MO	2420	NA	14
US West Communications Inc	303-624-2424	Denver, CO	NA	NA	NA
US West Communications-Omaha	402-422-2000	Omaha, NE	NA	NA	NA
US West Communications-Seattle	206-346-5000	Seattle, WA	NA	NA	NA
US West Inc	303-793-6500	Englewood, CO	9211	22416	70
Western Union Corp	201-818-5000	Upper Saddle Rvr, NJ	879	661	6

Industry: Telecom   **Number: 76**

Major Group: Manufacturing   **Industry: Appliances/Furn**

Organization	Phone	City / State or Province	Revenue ($ mil)	Assets ($ mil)	Emp (thous)
Aaron Rents Inc	404-231-0011	Atlanta, GA	250	250	2
Allegheny International Inc	412-562-4000	Pittsburgh, PA	968	841	12
Amana Refrigeration Inc	319-622-5511	Amana, IA	NA	NA	NA
Camco Inc	416-629-3000	Mississauga, ON Can	468	213	5
Carrier Corp	315-432-6000	Syracuse, NY	NA	NA	NA
Chicago Pacific Corp	312-435-7300	Chicago, IL	1400	1128	20
Coloric Corp	215-682-4211	Topton, PA	NA	NA	NA
Electrolux US Inc	404-933-1000	Marietta, GA	2090	NA	21
Ethan Allen Inc	203-743-8000	Danbury, CT	250	NA	2
Fedders Corp	201-234-2100	Peapack, NJ	300	200	1
Galaxy Carpet Mills Inc	312-593-0555	Elk Grove Village, IL	275	150	3
Haworth Corp	616-392-5961	Holland, MI	400	NA	4
Hughes Supply Inc	305-841-4710	Orlando, FL	502	224	4
Inglis Ltd	416-821-6400	Mississauga, ON Can	360	149	3
Jenn-Air Corp	317-545-2271	Indianapolis, IN	NA	NA	NA
Jepson Corp	312-834-3710	Elmhurst, IL	600	400	6
KitchenAid Inc	616-982-4500	St Joseph, MI	NA	NA	NA
La-Z-Boy Chair Co	313-242-1444	Monroe, MI	553	400	4
Magic Chef Co	615-472-3371	Cleveland, TN	NA	NA	NA
Maytag Co	515-792-7000	Newton, IA	1886	1330	5
Oneida Ltd	315-361-3000	Oneida, NY	400	500	4
Steelcase Inc	616-247-2710	Grand Rapids, MI	1800	NA	13
Universal Furniture Industries Inc	919-884-4322	High Point, NC	400	200	4
Vermont American Corp	502-587-6851	Louisville, KY	400	300	3
Whirlpool Corp	616-926-5000	Benton Harbor, MI	4421	3410	29
White Consolidated Industries Inc	216-252-3700	Cleveland, OH	2000	NA	20

Industry: Appliances/Furn   **Number: 26**

Major Group: Manufacturing   **Industry: Automotive**

Organization	Phone	City / State or Province	Revenue ($ mil)	Assets ($ mil)	Emp (thous)
Acklands Ltd	204-956-0880	Winnipeg, MB Can	353	196	3
Allied Signal Automotive Div	313-827-5000	Southfield, MI	NA	NA	NA
Allied Signal Canada Inc	416-967-7211	Mississauga, ON Can	565	425	5
Arvin Industries Inc	812-379-3000	Columbus, IN	1313	1058	17
Automotive Aftermarket Co	312-272-9600	Northbrook, IL	NA	NA	NA
Banner Industries Inc	216-464-3650	Beachwood, OH	374	1066	5
Buick Motor Division	313-236-0444	Flint, MI	NA	NA	NA
Cadillac Motor Car Division	313-554-6112	Detroit, MI	NA	NA	NA
Canam Manac Group Inc	418-228-8031	Ville St Georges, PQ Can	547	562	5
Champion Enterprises Inc	313-796-2145	Dryden, MI	350	NA	3
Chevrolet Motor Division	313-556-5000	Warren, MI	NA	NA	NA
Chrysler Canada Ltd	519-973-2000	Windsor, ON Can	7368	2656	12
Chrysler Corp	313-956-5741	Highland Park, MI	35472	48567	130

Major Group: Manufacturing   **Industry: Automotive**

Organizations Listed by Industry

Organization	Phone	City / State or Province	Revenue ($ mil)	Assets ($ mil)	Emp (thous)
Chrysler/Plymouth Div	313-956-5741	Highland Park, MI	NA	NA	NA
Coachmen Industries Inc	219-262-0123	Elkhart, IN	400	NA	4
Cummins Engine Co Inc	812-377-5000	Columbus, IN	3310	2064	26
Dana Corp	419-535-4500	Toledo, OH	4936	4786	40
Delco Electronics Co	317-457-8461	Kokomo, IN	NA	NA	NA
DeTomaso Industries	201-842-7200	Red Bank, NJ	400	250	2
Dodge Car & Truck Div	313-956-5741	Highland Park, MI	NA	NA	NA
Douglas & Lomason Co	313-478-7800	Framingham, MI	300	200	4
Echlin Inc	203-481-5751	Branford, CT	1294	1087	15
Empire Co	902-755-4440	Stellarton, NS Can	1193	880	4
Ensite Ltd	519-257-4412	Windsor, ON Can	1150	631	3
Excel Industries Inc	219-264-2131	Elkhart, IN	250	200	2
Federal Mogul Corp	313-354-7700	Southfield, MI	1177	811	16
Ford Div	313-322-3000	Dearborn, MI	NA	NA	NA
Ford Motor Canada Ltd	416-845-2511	Oakville, ON Can	13552	3067	27
Ford Motor Co	313-322-3000	Dearborn, MI	92446	143367	185
Fruehauf Corp	313-267-1000	Detroit, MI	2094	1584	15
General Motors Corp	313-556-5000	Detroit, MI	123641	90571	766
General Motors of Canada Ltd	416-644-5000	Oshawa, ON Can	16414	1448	44
Gleason Corp	716-272-6000	Rochester, NY	250	300	3
Guardian Industries Corp	313-349-6700	Northville, MI	750	NA	7
Gulf States Toyota Corp	713-744-3300	Houston, TX	1500	NA	3
Harley Davidson Inc	414-342-4680	Milwaukee, WI	550	400	4
Hayes Dana Inc	416-687-4200	St Catharines, ON Can	485	192	3
Heard, Bill Enterprises Inc	404-561-6213	Columbus, GA	500	NA	1
Holly Corp	214-979-0210	Dallas, TX	386	153	1
Holman Enterprises Inc	609-663-5200	Pennsauken, NJ	750	NA	2
Honda Canada Inc	416-284-8110	Scarborough, ON Can	1034	850	1
Honda of America Corp	513-642-5000	Marysville, OH	5500	NA	16
Hyundai Auto Canada Inc	416-477-0202	Markham, ON Can	377	184	1
Hyundai USA Inc	714-890-6000	Garden Grove, CA	2200	NA	4
International Controls Inc	305-997-7400	Boca Raton, FL	1000	500	8
Isuzu Motors USA Inc	213-949-0611	Whitter, CA	1650	NA	2
ITT Automotive Inc	313-540-9666	Bloomfield Hills, MI	2000	NA	15
Jaguar Cars Inc	201-592-5200	Leonia, NJ	550	NA	1
Jeep/Eagle Corp	313-956-5741	Highland Park, MI	NA	NA	NA
Kelsey Hayes Co	313-941-2000	Romulus, MI	NA	NA	NA
Knoll International Holdings	212-826-2400	New York, NY	1500	NA	20
Lear Siegler Seating Corp	313-746-1500	Southfield, MI	1000	NA	5
Lincoln-Mercury Div	313-322-3000	Dearborn, MI	NA	NA	NA
Mack Trucks Inc	215-439-3011	Allentown, PA	2000	1400	10
Magna International Inc	416-477-7766	Markham, ON Can	983	1091	12
Masco Industries Inc	313-274-7405	Taylor, MI	1652	2121	10
Mazda Canada Inc	416-831-4222	Pickering, ON Can	441	NA	1
Mazda Motors Corp USA	313-782-7800	Flat Rock, MI	1650	NA	11
Mercedes (Daimler Benz) Inc	201-573-0600	Montvale, NJ	1540	NA	2
Mercedes Benz Canada Inc	416-425-3550	Toronto, ON Can	298	128	1
Midas International Corp	312-565-7500	Chicago, IL	NA	NA	NA
Mitsubishi Motors of America Inc	714-963-7677	Fountain Valley, CA	1500	1000	2
Modine Manufacturing Co	414-636-1200	Racine, WI	424	289	4
Morse Operations Inc	305-563-6331	Fort Lauderdale, FL	500	NA	1
Motor Wheel Corp	517-337-5700	Lansing, MI	500	NA	5
Murray Ohio Manufacturing Co	615-373-6500	Brentwood, TN	500	400	4
Navistar International Corp	312-836-2000	Chicago, IL	4080	2522	16
Navistar International Corp of Canada	416-528-7700	Hamilton, ON Can	935	425	2

Major Group: Manufacturing   Industry: Automotive

Organizations Listed by Industry

Organization	Phone	City / State or Province	Revenue ($ mil)	Assets ($ mil)	Emp (thous)
Neoax Inc	203-322-8333	Stamford, CT	314	250	2
Nissan Automobile Canada Ltd	416-821-9180	Mississauga, ON Can	575	170	1
Nissan Motor Corp USA	212-532-3111	Carson, CA	4400	NA	15
Oldsmobile Div	517-377-5000	Lansing, MI	NA	NA	NA
Oshkosh Truck Corp	414-235-9150	Oshkosh, WI	450	350	2
Paccar Inc	206-455-7400	Bellevue, WA	3122	2832	10
Paccar of Canada Ltd	416-858-7070	Mississauga, ON Can	425	213	2
Peugeot USA Inc	201-935-8400	Lindhurst, NJ	825	NA	2
Pontiac Motors Div	313-857-5000	Pontiac, MI	NA	NA	NA
Potamkin Co Inc	212-399-4400	New York, NY	1000	NA	4
Pullman Peabody Co	609-683-1770	Princeton, NJ	600	500	8
Renault America Corp	313-358-8800	Southfield, MI	550	NA	1
Rosenthal Companies Inc	703-920-8700	Arlington, VA	500	NA	1
Rover Group Inc	301-731-9040	Laham, MD	550	NA	1
Saturn Corp	313-524-5721	Troy, MI	NA	NA	NA
Sheller Globe Corp	419-255-8840	Toledo, OH	840	904	10
Smith, A O Corp	414-359-4000	Milwaukee, WI	1015	808	10
SPX Sealed Power Corp	616-724-5000	Muskegon, MI	877	702	8
Standard Motor Products Inc	718-392-0200	Long Island City, NY	398	350	3
Standard Products Co	216-281-8300	Cleveland, OH	508	255	5
Steego Corp	407-655-9700	West Palm Beach, FL	235	250	2
Subaru America Corp	609-488-8500	Cherry Hill, NJ	1673	727	1
Sudbury Inc	216-464-7026	Cleveland, OH	600	400	5
Superior Industries International Inc	818-781-4973	Van Nuys, CA	300	150	2
Suzuki Motor Corp USA Inc	714-996-7040	Brea, CA	1100	NA	1
Toyota Canada Inc	416-438-6320	Scarborough, ON Can	983	170	2
Toyota Motor Sales USA	213-618-4000	Torrance, CA	8800	NA	21
Transnational Motors Inc	616-949-7570	Grand Rapids, MI	500	NA	3
UAP Inc	514-256-5031	Montreal, PQ Can	298	170	2
UIS Inc	212-581-7660	New York, NY	500	NA	5
Universal Coop Inc	612-854-0800	Minneapolis, MN	275	NA	1
UT Automotive Co	313-593-9000	Dearborn, MI	NA	NA	NA
Volkswagen America Inc	313-362-6000	Troy, MI	1100	NA	11
Volkswagen Canada Ltd	416-288-3000	Scarborough, ON Can	654	287	1
Volvo Canada Ltd	416-493-3700	North York, ON Can	298	170	1
Volvo North America Corp	201-768-7300	Rockleigh, NJ	1100	NA	3
Weisman, Frederick Co Inc	301-760-1500	Glen Burnie, MD	1250	NA	1
Winnebago Industries Inc	515-582-3535	Forest City, IA	425	237	4
Worldwide Volkswagen Inc	914-578-5000	Orangeburg, NY	750	NA	1
Wynn's International Inc	714-992-2000	Fullerton, CA	300	250	2

Industry: Automotive   Number: 108

Major Group: Manufacturing   Industry: Conglomerate

Organization	Phone	City / State or Province	Revenue ($ mil)	Assets ($ mil)	Emp (thous)
Alco Standard Corp	215-296-8000	Valley Forge, PA	3817	1399	16
Colt Industries Inc	212-940-0400	New York, NY	1750	1400	18
Eaton Corp	216-523-5000	Cleveland, OH	3469	3034	43
Figgie International Holding Inc	804-264-5600	Richmond, VA	1201	1022	17
Fuqua Industries Inc	404-658-9000	Atlanta, GA	934	1146	16
Household International Inc	312-564-3663	Prospect Heights, IL	2352	21032	30
ITT Corp	212-752-6000	New York, NY	19355	41941	117
Kaman Corp	203-243-8311	Bloomfield, CT	768	420	6
Katy Industries Inc	312-697-8900	Elgin, IL	192	298	2
Kidde Inc	201-368-9000	Saddlebrook, NJ	2500	1750	35

Major Group: Manufacturing   Industry: Conglomerate

Organizations Listed by Industry

Organization	Phone	City / State or Province	Revenue ($ mil)	Assets ($ mil)	Emp (thous)
Mitsubishi Canada Ltd	416-362-6731	Toronto, ON Can	1275	128	2
Mitsui & Co Canada Ltd	416-865-0330	Toronto, ON Can	2218	181	1
Ogden Corp	212-868-6100	New York, NY	1088	2202	35
Onex Corp	416-362-7711	Toronto, ON Can	1628	1593	21
Paramount Communications Corp	212-333-7000	New York, NY	5108	5378	40
Rockwell International Corp	412-565-2000	Pittsburgh, PA	11046	4925	112
Teledyne Inc	213-277-3311	Los Angeles, CA	4598	5125	60
Tenneco Inc	713-757-2131	Houston, TX	13591	13857	94
Textron Inc	401-421-2800	Providence, RI	7286	12554	60
TLC Beatrice Internatl Holding Co	212-269-4544	New York, NY	1500	NA	10
Whitman Co (IC Industries Inc)	312-565-3000	Chicago, IL	3583	3489	25

Industry: Conglomerate   Number: 21

Major Group: Manufacturing   Industry: Packaging

Organization	Phone	City / State or Province	Revenue ($ mil)	Assets ($ mil)	Emp (thous)
AMCA (Amer Can of Canada) Intl Ltd	416-432-2151	Rexdale, ON Can	893	NA	10
Anchor Glass Container	813-884-0000	Tampa, FL	978	773	8
Atlantic Packaging Products Ltd	416-298-8101	Scarborough, ON Can	340	170	2
Ball Corp	317-747-6100	Muncie, IN	1073	877	7
Branitek Inc	912-354-4885	Savannah, GA	NA	NA	NA
Cascades Inc	819-363-2245	Kingsey Falls, PQ Can	501	458	3
CB Pak Inc	516-875-2160	Montreal, PQ Can	425	425	6
Consumers Packaging Inc	416-232-3283	Etobicoke, ON Can	333	286	3
Crown Cork & Seal Co	215-698-5100	Philadelphia, PA	1834	1073	13
Georgia Kraft Corp	404-232-0851	Rome, GA	550	500	5
Greif Brothers Corp	614-363-1271	Delaware, OH	412	267	4
Heekin Can Inc	513-489-3200	Cinncinnati, OH	300	200	2
Inland Container Corp	317-262-0222	Indianapolis, IN	NA	NA	NA
Kerr Glass Manufacturing Corp	213-556-2200	Los Angeles, CA	350	200	3
Lawson Mardon Group Ltd	416-821-9711	Mississauga, ON Can	880	707	7
Metal Container Corp	314-577-1700	St Louis, MO	NA	NA	NA
Owens Illinois Inc	419-247-5000	Toledo, OH	3800	3500	40
Paperboard Industries	416-596-7180	Toronto, ON Can	340	255	3
Primerica Corp	203-552-2000	Greenwich, CT	1004	14435	18
Rock Tenn Corp	404-448-2193	Norcross, GA	500	NA	5
Sealed Air Corp	201-791-7600	Saddle Brook, NJ	346	256	3
Van Dorn Co	216-361-5234	Cleveland, OH	334	250	2

Industry: Packaging   Number: 22

Major Group: Manufacturing   Industry: Machinery

Organization	Phone	City / State or Province	Revenue ($ mil)	Assets ($ mil)	Emp (thous)
Atco Ltd	403-292-7500	Calgary, AB Can	1227	2737	5
Briggs & Stratton Corp	414-259-5333	Wauwatosa, WI	914	511	10
Cincinnati Milacron Inc	513-841-8100	Cincinnati, OH	857	721	8
Clark Equipment Corp	219-239-0100	South Bend, IN	1278	951	9
Commercial Intertech	216-746-8011	Youngstown, OH	400	250	4
Industrial Machinery Corp	217-222-5400	Quincy, IL	NA	NA	NA
Ingersoll-Rand Corp	201-573-0123	Woodcliff Lake, NJ	3021	2483	30
Interlake Corp	312-986-6600	Oak Brook, IL	892	660	11
MAN North America Corp	201-469-6600	Middlesex, NJ	880	NA	3
Mannesmann USA Inc	212-702-9420	New York, NY	880	NA	3
Pall Corp	516-671-4000	Glen Cove, NY	429	570	6
Sundstrand Corp	815-226-6000	Rockford, IL	1477	1567	14

Major Group: Manufacturing   Industry: Machinery

Organizations Listed by Industry

Organization	Phone	City / State or Province	Revenue ($ mil)	Assets ($ mil)	Emp (thous)
Team Inc	713-331-6154	Alvin, TX	250	125	1
Teledyne Continental Motors Inc	616-724-2151	Muskegon, MI	NA	NA	NA
Timken Co	216-438-3000	Canton, OH	1554	1593	18
Trinova Corp	419-891-2200	Maumee, OH	1919	1432	30

Industry: Machinery   Number: 16

Major Group: Manufacturing   Industry: Manufacturing

Organization	Phone	City / State or Province	Revenue ($ mil)	Assets ($ mil)	Emp (thous)
Aarque Companies Inc	716-664-6014	Jamestown, NY	500	NA	3
Acme Steel Co	312-849-2500	Chicago, IL	350	250	3
AFG Industries Inc	714-553-9026	Irvine, CA	500	500	3
Agway Inc	315-477-7061	Syracuse, NY	2894	1497	9
Alco Industries Inc	215-666-0930	Valley Forge, PA	1732	468	6
Allied Products Corp	312-454-1020	Chicago, IL	578	441	5
Amcast Industrial Corp	513-298-5251	Dayton, OH	264	200	2
AMDURA Corp(American Hoist & Derrick)	612-293-4567	St Paul, MN	258	205	2
American Cast Iron Pipe Inc	205-325-7701	Birmingham, AL	275	NA	2
American Overseas Marine Corp	617-786-8300	Quincy, MA	NA	NA	NA
American Standard Inc	212-703-5100	New York, NY	3500	2200	40
Ampco Pittsburgh Corp	412-456-4400	Pittsburgh, PA	251	295	3
Amsted Industries Inc	312-645-1700	Chicago, IL	1000	NA	10
Anchor Hocking Corp	614-687-2111	Lancaster, OH	750	500	10
APL Corp	305-866-7771	Miami, FL	1209	584	12
Armstrong World Industries Inc	717-397-0611	Lancaster, PA	2680	2098	28
Armtek Corp	203-784-2200	New Haven, CT	1200	1000	12
ATCOR Inc	312-339-1610	Harvey, IL	500	250	4
Avery International Corp	818-304-2000	Pasadena, CA	1582	1119	12
Avondale Industries Inc	504-436-2121	New Orleans, LA	550	NA	5
Babcock & Wilcox Co	504-587-5400	New Orleans, LA	NA	NA	NA
Barnes Group Inc	203-583-7070	Bristol, CT	496	312	5
Bassett Furniture Industries Inc	703-629-7511	Bassett, VA	400	250	6
Bath Iron Works Inc	207-443-3311	Bath, ME	750	NA	7
Beloit Corp	608-365-3311	Beloit, WI	NA	NA	NA
Bemis Co Inc	612-340-6000	Minneapolis, MN	1069	595	8
BIC Corp	203-783-2000	Milford, CT	295	243	2
Bindley Western Industries	317-298-9900	Indianapolis, IN	1275	264	2
Black & Decker Corp	301-583-3900	Towson, MD	2281	1825	23
Bombardier Inc	514-861-9481	Montreal, PQ Can	1187	740	10
Borg Warner Corp	312-322-8500	Chicago, IL	3800	3000	60
Bruncor Inc	506-694-6330	St John, NB Can	340	808	3
Bulova Watch Co Inc	718-204-3300	Woodside, NY	NA	NA	NA
Butler Manufacturing Co	816-968-3000	Kansas City, MO	646	266	4
CAE Industries Ltd	416-865-0070	Toronto, ON Can	712	986	7
Calgon Carbon	412-787-6700	Robinson Twnshp, PA	200	200	1
Canron Ltd	416-364-6600	Toronto, ON Can	449	215	4
Carpenter Technology Corp	215-371-2000	Reading, PA	556	635	4
CF & I Steel Corp	303-561-6000	Pueblo, CO	350	200	2
CIL Inc	416-229-7000	North York, ON Can	1139	989	6
Clabir Corp	813-577-5007	St Petersburg, FL	350	300	3
Co Steel Inc	416-686-2500	Whitby, ON Can	694	550	3
Coleco Industries Inc	203-725-6000	West Hartford, CT	185	NA	2
Coleman Co	316-261-3211	Wichita, KS	500	500	5
Collins & Aikman Corp	212-578-1200	New York, NY	1200	750	13
Commercial Metals Co	214-689-4300	Dallas, TX	1137	337	4

Major Group: Manufacturing   Industry: Manufacturing

Organizations Listed by Industry

Organization	Phone	City / State or Province	Revenue ($ mil)	Assets ($ mil)	Emp (thous)
Constar International	615-267-2973	Chattanooga, TN	544	230	4
Corning Glass Works Inc	607-974-9000	Corning, NY	2122	2898	25
Crane Co	212-415-7300	New York, NY	1313	682	10
Cross, A T Co	401-333-1200	Lincoln, RI	232	176	2
Daewoo Group	201-896-2824	Carlstadt, NJ	1100	NA	2
Danaher Corp	202-333-1805	Washington, DC	716	576	5
Dayco Corp	513-226-7000	Dayton, OH	350	250	4
Dayton Industries Inc	414-241-6200	Mequon, WI	250	NA	2
Dennison Manufacturing Co	508-879-0511	Framingham, MA	722	516	8
Derlan Industries Inc	416-364-5852	Toronto, ON Can	340	213	5
Diamond Bathurst Corp	813-884-0000	Tampa, FL	550	250	5
Dibrell Brothers	804-792-7511	Danville, VA	685	500	5
Donaldson Co	612-887-3131	Minneapolis, MN	260	200	2
Dow Corning Corp	517-496-4000	Auburn, MI	1500	1500	6
Dravo Corp	412-566-3000	Pittsburgh, PA	1000	500	5
Duchossois Industries Inc	312-279-3600	Elmhurst, IL	750	NA	8
Ducommun Inc	213-612-4200	Cypress, CA	150	100	3
Duriron Co	513-226-4000	Dayton, OH	300	200	3
DynCorp Inc	703-356-0480	McLean, VA	750	NA	10
Dyson Kissner Moran Corp	212-661-4600	New York, NY	1000	NA	5
Edgcomb Corp	212-246-1000	New York, NY	617	450	2
Electric Boat Div	203-441-1000	Groton, CT	NA	NA	NA
Eljer Industries Inc	214-881-7177	Plano, TX	429	197	4
Emhart Corp	203-678-3000	Farmington, CT	2763	2427	33
Enfield Corp	416-445-7438	Toronto, ON Can	340	510	3
Envirodyne Industries	312-649-0600	Chicago, IL	475	400	5
Esselte Corp	516-741-1477	Garden City, NY	1401	1073	3
Essex Group Inc	219-461-4000	Fort Wayne, IN	750	NA	5
Excello Corp	313-624-7800	Walled Lake, MI	1650	NA	18
Exide Corp	215-674-9500	Horsham, PA	600	NA	6
Facet Enterprises Inc	918-492-1800	Tulsa, OK	NA	NA	NA
Farley Industries Inc	312-876-1724	Chicago, IL	2000	NA	25
First City Industries Inc	213-852-0499	Beverly Hills, CA	750	1100	10
Fisher Controls International Inc	314-694-9900	Clayton, MO	NA	NA	NA
Fisher Price Inc	716-687-3000	East Aurora, NY	NA	NA	NA
FL Industries Inc	201-535-9522	Livingston, NJ	660	NA	6
Flint Ink Corp	313-538-6800	Detroit, MI	400	NA	4
Fluorocarbon Co	714-831-5350	South Laguna, CA	250	200	2
Fuller, H B Co	612-645-3401	St Paul, MN	685	434	5
Gaylord Container	312-405-5500	Deerfield, IL	380	200	3
General Electric Canada Co	416-858-5100	Mississauga, ON Can	1436	876	10
Genlyte Group Inc	201-864-3000	Secaucus, NJ	450	350	4
Goulds Pumps Inc	315-568-2811	Seneca Falls, NY	454	366	4
Graco Inc	612-623-6000	Minneapolis, MN	240	200	2
Groupe Ro-na Inc	514-599-5100	Boucherville, PQ Can	425	213	2
Hanson Industries (Hanson Trust) Inc	201-549-7050	Iselin, NJ	4180	3200	37
Harsco Corp	717-763-7064	Wormleysburg, PA	1279	893	12
Hartford Steam Boiler Inspection Inc	203-722-1866	Hartford, CT	447	730	4
Harvard Industries Inc	314-382-5590	St Louis, MO	600	400	4
Hawker Siddeley Canada Inc	416-362-2941	Toronto, ON Can	331	208	3
Henleys Group Ltd	514-397-7640	Montreal, PQ Can	714	NA	1
Hillenbrand Industries Inc	812-934-7000	Batesville, IN	884	735	8
Hillman Industries Inc	412-281-2620	Pittsburgh, PA	1250	NA	5
Hollinger Inc	416-363-8721	Toronto, ON Can	587	850	5
Hon Industries Inc	319-264-7400	Muscatine, IA	532	276	5

Major Group: Manufacturing   Industry: Manufacturing

Organizations Listed by Industry

Organization	Phone	City / State or Province	Revenue ($ mil)	Assets ($ mil)	Emp (thous)
Household Manufacturing Corp	312-564-3910	Prospect Heights, IL	1000	500	10
Idex Corp	312-498-7070	Northbrook, IL	250	200	3
Illinois Tool Works Inc	312-693-3040	Chicago, IL	1930	1380	14
Imperial Eastman Corp	312-967-4500	Niles, IL	500	500	5
Imperial Holly Corp	713-491-9181	Sugar Land, TX	250	200	2
Ingersoll International Inc	815-987-6000	Rockford, IL	550	NA	5
Insilco Corp	203-634-2000	Meridan, CT	750	700	10
IPSCO Inc	306-949-3530	Regina, SK Can	340	340	2
Itel Corp	312-902-1515	Chicago, IL	1644	4001	9
Itoh, C Trading Co USA	212-818-8000	New York, NY	1100	NA	3
ITT Fluid Technology Corp	201-444-6030	Midland Park, NJ	500	NA	4
Jacksonville Shipyards Inc	904-355-1711	Jacksonville, FL	NA	NA	NA
Jannock Ltd	416-364-8586	Toronto, ON Can	267	337	4
Jorgensen, Earle M Corp	213-567-1122	Lynwood, CA	400	400	4
Jostens Inc	612-830-3336	Minneapolis, MN	560	407	7
Justin Industries Inc	817-336-5125	Fort Worth, TX	300	150	4
Kanematsu Gosho USA Inc	212-704-9400	New York, NY	3300	NA	8
Kawasaki Industries USA Inc	714-770-0400	Irvine, CA	825	NA	5
Keystone Consolidated Industries Inc	214-458-0028	Dallas, TX	250	200	2
Keystone International Inc	713-466-1176	Houston, TX	346	340	3
Kimball International Inc	812-482-1600	Jasper, IN	530	320	8
Koch Industries Inc	316-832-5500	Wichita, KS	15000	NA	8
Kohler Co	414-457-4441	Kohler, WI	1000	NA	10
Ladd Furniture Inc	919-889-0333	High Point, NC	380	173	6
Lamb Technicon Inc	313-497-6652	Warren, MI	550	NA	2
Lamson & Sessions Co	216-464-3400	Cleveland, OH	400	250	3
Lancaster Colony Corp	614-224-7141	Columbus, OH	453	286	5
Lane Co Inc	804-369-5641	Altavista, VA	375	250	4
Leggett & Platt Inc	417-358-8131	Carthage, MO	810	476	11
Lincoln Electric Co Inc	216-481-8100	Cleveland, OH	550	NA	5
Lone Star Technologies	214-352-3981	Dallas, TX	500	350	2
Lori Corp	203-621-3601	Southington, CT	400	250	3
Magnetek Inc	213-473-6681	Los Angeles, CA	1000	NA	10
Manpower Inc	608-755-7000	Milwaukee, WI	1500	500	6
Martin Marietta Energy Systems Inc	615-574-1000	Oak Ridge, TN	NA	NA	NA
Marubeni Trading Co USA	212-599-3700	New York, NY	2750	NA	4
McWane Corp	205-991-9888	Birmingham, AL	500	NA	4
Mercury Marine Co	414-929-5000	Fon Du Lac, WI	NA	NA	NA
Meridian Minerals Co	303-694-4100	Englewood, CO	NA	NA	NA
Microdot Inc	312-899-1925	Chicago, IL	400	NA	4
Midland Affiliated Inc	513-721-4000	Cincinnati, OH	550	NA	2
Miller, Herman Inc	616-772-3300	Zeeland, MI	714	434	6
Minnesota Mining & Manufacturing Co	612-733-1110	St Paul, MN	10581	8922	83
Mitsui & Co Trading (USA)	212-878-4097	New York, NY	1100	NA	2
Morrison Knudsen Eng & Environment	216-523-5600	Cleveland, OH	NA	NA	NA
MSA Mine Safety Appliances Co	412-967-3000	O'Hara Township, PA	406	361	4
MTD Products Inc	216-225-2600	Valley City, OH	275	NA	3
Nashua Corp	603-880-2323	Nashua, NH	989	450	7
National Sanitary Supply Corp	213-532-4800	Los Angeles, CA	300	200	1
Newell Co	815-235-4171	Freeport, IL	988	820	11
Nichimen Trading Co USA	212-719-1000	New York, NY	1650	NA	1
Nissho Iwai Canada Ltd	604-684-8351	Vancouver, BC Can	340	170	2
Nissho Iwai Trading Co USA	212-704-6500	New York, NY	1650	NA	2
Nortek Inc	401-751-1600	Providence, RI	1224	1052	9
Northwestern Steel & Wire Corp	815-625-2500	Sterling, IL	500	NA	3

Major Group: Manufacturing   Industry: Manufacturing

Organizations Listed by Industry

Organization	Phone	City / State or Province	Revenue ($ mil)	Assets ($ mil)	Emp (thous)
Norton Co	508-795-5000	Worcester, MA	1410	1088	16
Parker Hannifin Corp	216-531-3000	Cleveland, OH	2252	1742	33
Penn Central Corp	513-579-6600	Cincinnati, OH	1547	2400	14
Philips Industries Inc	513-253-7171	Dayton, OH	693	353	10
Pitt Des Moines Inc	412-331-3000	Pittsburgh, PA	330	250	3
PMC Corp	818-896-1101	Sun Valley, CA	500	NA	5
PPG Industries Inc	412-434-3131	Pittsburgh, PA	5617	5154	36
Printing Holding Co	212-735-8800	New York, NY	1000	NA	10
Quanex Corp	713-961-4600	Houston, TX	463	302	2
Raychem Corp	415-361-3333	Menlo Park, CA	1095	1149	9
Revere Copper & Brass Inc	203-358-5300	Stamford, CT	600	400	4
Robertshaw Controls Co	804-281-0700	Richmond, VA	500	500	7
Robertson, H H Co	412-281-3200	Pittsburgh, PA	414	296	5
Roper Corp	404-724-0822	Augusta, GA	703	251	6
Rouse Co	301-992-6000	Columbia, MD	461	2080	5
Rubbermaid Inc	216-264-6464	Wooster, OH	1194	782	8
Schneider Corp	519-885-8100	Kitchener, ON Can	581	170	4
Signode Corp	312-724-6100	Glenview, IL	935	NA	8
Skyline Corp	219-294-6521	Elkhart, IN	384	163	3
Snap-on Tools Corp	414-656-5200	Kenosha, WI	855	668	7
Snyder General Corp	214-979-3100	Dallas, TX	500	NA	5
Spalding & Evenflow Corp	813-887-5200	Tampa, FL	330	NA	3
SPS Technologies Inc	215-860-3000	Newtown, PA	350	250	3
Stanadyne Inc	203-525-0821	Windsor, CT	500	500	5
Stanhome Inc	413-562-3631	Westfield, MA	433	244	4
Stanley Works Inc	203-225-5111	New Britain, CT	1909	1405	19
Stewart & Stevenson Services Inc	713-868-7700	Houston, TX	474	400	3
Sumitomo Canada Ltd	604-682-2256	Vancouver, BC Can	1063	NA	1
Sumitomo Trading Co USA	212-207-0700	New York, NY	1650	NA	4
Sybron Corp	414-274-6600	Milwaukee, WI	825	NA	7
Talley Industries Inc	602-957-7711	Phoenix, AZ	360	533	4
Tecumseh Products Co	517-423-8411	Tecumseh, MI	1094	900	10
Terex Corp	414-453-5322	Green Bay, WI	500	350	4
Textron Marine Systems Div	508-452-8961	Lowell, MA	NA	NA	NA
Todd Shipyards Corp	206-223-1560	Seattle, WA	351	394	4
Tonka Corp	612-936-3300	Minnetonka, MN	550	500	5
Town & Country Corp	617-884-8500	Chelsea, MA	450	200	2
Toyo Menka Trading Co USA	212-466-4600	New York, NY	1100	NA	3
Tredegar Industries Inc	804-275-9211	Richmond, VA	650	350	1
Trinity Industries Inc	214-631-4420	Dallas, TX	1001	878	6
TRW Pressure Systems Inc	213-685-4520	Los Angeles, CA	NA	NA	NA
Tupperware Worldwide Inc	407-826-5050	Kissimmee, FL	NA	NA	NA
Tyco Laboratories Inc	603-778-9700	Exeter, NH	1575	9419	10
Unicorp Canada Corp (Union Enterprises)	416-961-1200	Toronto, ON Can	1721	5041	4
Unifi Inc	919-294-4410	Greensboro, NC	400	200	2
United Westburne Inc	514-342-5181	Montreal, PQ Can	1469	674	12
UNR Industries Inc	312-341-1234	Chicago, IL	392	250	2
Vulcan Materials Co	205-877-3000	Birmingham, AL	1053	958	6
Watts Industries Inc	508-688-1811	North Andover, MA	250	200	2
Wheaton Industries Inc	609-825-1400	Millville, NJ	500	NA	5
Whittaker Corp	213-475-9411	Los Angeles, CA	201	391	2
WTD Industries Inc	503-246-3440	Portland, OR	500	250	2
York International Corp	717-846-1988	York, PA	900	500	7

Industry: Manufacturing   **Number: 209**

Major Group: Manufacturing   Industry: Manufacturing

Organizations Listed by Industry

Organization	Phone	City / State or Province	Revenue ($ mil)	Assets ($ mil)	Emp (thous)
Major Group: Manufacturing		**Industry: Equipment**			
Allis Chalmers Corp	414-475-2000	West Allis, WI	401	10	1
Astec Industries Inc	615-867-4210	Chattanooga, TN	250	150	2
Baker Hughes Mining Equipment	412-225-8016	Meadowlands, PA	NA	NA	NA
Becor Western Inc	414-768-4000	South Milwaukee, WI	400	NA	4
Brand Companies Inc	312-298-1200	Park Ridge, IL	300	150	1
Caterpillar Inc	309-675-1000	Peoria, IL	10435	9686	58
Caterpillar of Canada Ltd	416-846-3222	Mississauga, ON Can	301	113	1
Cooper Industries Inc	713-739-5400	Houston, TX	4258	4384	46
Cross & Trecker Corp	313-644-4343	Bloomfield Hills, MI	428	381	4
Deere & Co	309-765-8000	Moline, IL	5365	5245	38
Deere, John Ltd	416-734-4501	Welland, ON Can	468	425	2
Dover Corp	212-826-7160	New York, NY	1956	1366	20
Dover Elevator International Inc	601-342-4300	Memphis, TN	NA	NA	NA
Eagle Picher Industries Inc	513-721-7010	Cincinnati, OH	770	583	9
Esterline Corp	206-453-6000	Bellevue, WA	260	190	2
Finning Ltd	604-872-4444	Vancouver, BC Can	595	558	3
FMC Corp	312-861-6000	Chicago, IL	3287	2749	24
GE Fanuc Automation Inc	804-978-5000	Charlottsville, VA	NA	NA	NA
Hyster Co Inc	503-280-7000	Portland, OR	750	NA	5
Joy Manufacturing Co	412-562-4500	Pittsburgh, PA	650	500	5
Kendavis Holding Co Inc	817-335-5101	Fort Worth, TX	550	NA	5
Kennametal Inc	412-539-5000	Latrobe, PA	420	359	5
Land Systems Div	313-825-4000	Sterling Heights, MI	NA	NA	NA
Nordson Corp	216-892-1580	Westlake, OH	350	250	2
Oregon Steel Mills Inc	503-286-9651	Portland, OR	250	150	1
Otis Elevator Co	203-674-4000	Farmington, CT	NA	NA	NA
Primary Industries Corp	212-581-9200	New York, NY	550	NA	3
Sun Distributors Inc	215-665-3650	Philadelphia, PA	425	400	4
Toro Co	612-888-8801	Bloomington, MN	609	268	3
Triangle Industries Inc	212-230-3000	New York, NY	2668	1585	15
United Engineers & Construction Inc	215-422-3000	Philadelphia, PA	NA	NA	NA
United Industrial Corp	212-752-8787	New York, NY	300	300	4
Valmont Industries Inc	402-359-2201	Valley, NE	700	500	4
Varity Corp	416-593-3811	Toronto, ON Can	1942	1384	15
Webb, Jervis B Co Inc	313-553-1000	Farmington Hills, MI	550	NA	3
Willcox & Gibbs Inc	212-869-1800	New York, NY	300	150	2

Industry: Equipment   **Number: 36**

Organization	Phone	City / State or Province	Revenue ($ mil)	Assets ($ mil)	Emp (thous)
Major Group: Basic Industries		**Industry: Building Mat**			
Alliance Ro-Na Home Inc	519-664-2252	St Jacobs, ON Can	672	170	8
Ameron Inc	213-268-4111	Monterey Park, CA	364	312	4
Andersen Corp	612-439-5150	Bayport, MN	1000	NA	6
Anixter Brothers Inc	312-677-2600	Skokie, IL	650	600	3
BID Building Materials Canada	416-661-5950	Downsview, ON Can	340	170	4
Blount Inc	205-244-4000	Montgomery, AL	1134	665	6
Bohemia Inc	503-342-6262	Eugene, OR	306	250	2
Calmat Co	213-258-2777	Los Angeles, CA	661	765	3
Canada Cement Lafarge Ltd	514-861-1411	Montreal, PQ Can	838	638	6

Major Group: Basic Industries   Industry: Building Mat

Organizations Listed by Industry

Organization	Phone	City / State or Province	Revenue ($ mil)	Assets ($ mil)	Emp (thous)
Carpenter, E R Corp	804-359-0800	Richmond, VA	500	NA	5
Ceco Corp	312-789-1400	Oak Brook, IL	500	NA	5
Certainteed Corp	215-341-7000	Valley Forge, PA	1267	1108	8
Dallas Corp	214-233-6611	Dallas, TX	323	NA	2
DeSoto Inc	312-391-9000	Des Plaines, IL	403	219	2
Doskocil Companies Inc	316-663-1000	Hutchinson, KS	275	250	1
Emco Ltd	519-451-1250	London, ON Can	1004	572	9
Fiberglas Canada Inc	416-733-1600	Willowdale, ON Can	405	205	3
Florida Rock Industries Inc	904-355-1781	Jacksonville, FL	475	300	4
GAF Corp	201-628-3000	Wayne, NJ	837	1298	5
Gifford Hill & Co Inc	214-258-7000	Irving, TX	500	NA	3
Grow Group Inc	212-599-4400	New York, NY	383	223	4
Harnischfeger Corp	414-671-4000	Brookfield, WI	1187	1195	7
Ideal Basic Industries Corp	303-623-5661	Denver, CO	250	250	2
Indal Ltd	416-743-1400	Weston, ON Can	925	530	9
International Aluminum Co	213-264-1670	Monterey Park, CA	250	150	2
JP Industries Inc	313-663-6749	Ann Arbor, MI	550	400	3
Lafarge Corp	703-264-3600	Reston, VA	1309	1199	8
Lake Ontario Cement Ltd	416-977-0611	Toronto, ON Can	298	255	1
Le Groupe Ro Na Inc	514-599-5100	Boucherville, PQ Can	413	115	1
Lone Star Industries Inc	203-661-3100	Greenwich, CT	529	1424	4
Manville Corp	303-978-2000	Denver, CO	2062	2393	20
Masco Corp	313-274-7400	Taylor, MI	2439	2999	15
Mohasco Corp	703-768-8000	Fairfax, VA	409	350	3
Morgan Products Ltd	414-235-7170	Oshkosh, WI	400	350	3
National Gypsum Co	214-740-4500	Dallas, TX	1221	1610	8
Noland Co	804-928-9000	Newport News, VA	461	201	2
Ohio Mattress Co	216-522-1310	Cleveland, OH	600	400	5
Owens Corning Fiberglas Corp	419-248-8000	Toledo, OH	2831	1596	18
Ply Gem Industries Inc	212-832-1550	New York, NY	383	300	3
PPG Canada Inc	416-923-5441	Toronto, ON Can	479	437	3
Redman Industries Inc	214-353-3600	Dallas, TX	357	142	3
Rinker Materials Corp	407-833-5555	West Palm Beach, FL	275	NA	3
Sherwin Williams Co	216-566-2000	Cleveland, OH	1950	1259	17
Southdown Inc	713-658-8921	Houston, TX	605	1211	4
St Lawrence Cement Inc	514-340-1881	Montreal, PQ Can	623	552	3
Standard Brands Paint Co	213-214-2411	Torrance, CA	304	243	4
Texas Industries Inc	214-637-3100	Dallas, TX	635	662	6
Thomas Industries Inc	502-893-4600	Louisville, KY	348	208	3
TJ International Inc	208-375-4450	Boise, ID	400	200	3
US Plywood Corp	404-521-4000	Atlanta, GA	1650	NA	2
USG Corp	312-321-4000	Chicago, IL	2248	1821	15
Valspar Corp	612-332-7371	Minneapolis, MN	480	233	5
Wajax Ltd	514-238-7291	Montreal, PQ Can	298	170	2
Worldmark Corp	305-626-3116	North Palm Beach, FL	500	NA	1

Industry: Building Mat   **Number: 54**

Major Group: Basic Industries   **Industry: Chemicals**

Organization	Phone	City / State or Province	Revenue ($ mil)	Assets ($ mil)	Emp (thous)
Air Products & Chemicals Inc	215-481-4911	Allentown, PA	2432	2999	22
American Cyanamid Co	201-831-2000	Wayne, NJ	4592	4593	36
ARCO Chemical Co	215-359-2000	Newtown Square, PA	2500	2500	3
Aristech Chemical Corp	412-433-2747	Pittsburgh, PA	1000	NA	6
Asahi Chemical Industries	212-695-6720	New York, NY	1100	NA	1

Major Group: Basic Industries   Industry: Chemicals

Organizations Listed by Industry

Organization	Phone	City / State or Province	Revenue ($ mil)	Assets ($ mil)	Emp (thous)
Ausimont NV Inc	617-899-3000	Waltham, MA	650	500	2
BASF Canada Inc	416-675-3611	Toronto, ON Can	298	128	1
BASF Corp	201-397-2700	Parsippany, NJ	4070	2200	21
Bayer USA	412-394-5500	Pittsburgh, PA	4719	3627	26
Betz Laboratories Inc	215-355-3300	Trevose, PA	448	319	3
Borden Chemicals & Plastics Inc	504-673-6121	Geismar, LA	400	NA	4
Cain Chemical Corp	713-622-2246	Houston, TX	1100	NA	3
Canpotex Ltd	306-931-2200	Saskatoon, SK Can	324	73	1
Cansulex Ltd	604-688-1501	Vancouver, BC Can	292	170	1
Celanese Canada Inc	514-871-5511	Montreal, PQ Can	298	219	2
Celanese Corp (Hoechst)	201-231-2000	Somerville, NJ	3190	2400	21
Celeron Corp	713-750-4552	Houston, TX	1000	NA	4
CF Industries Inc	312-438-9500	Long Grove, IL	1100	1000	2
Chemcentral Corp	312-594-7000	Chicago, IL	500	NA	1
Chemed	513-762-6900	Cincinnati, OH	600	NA	6
Chemical Systems Inc	408-224-7796	San Jose, CA	NA	NA	NA
Chevron Chemical Co	415-842-1000	San Ramon, CA	NA	NA	NA
CountryMark Inc	614-548-8200	Delaware, OH	1100	250	1
Crompton & Knowles Inc	203-353-5400	Stamford, CT	350	NA	3
Cyanamid Canada Inc	416-470-3600	Willowdale, ON Can	298	170	2
Dexter Corp	203-627-9051	Windsor Locks, CT	827	626	6
Domtar Inc	514-848-5400	Montreal, PQ Can	2298	2708	16
Dow Chemical Canada Ltd	519-339-3131	Sarnia, ON Can	1275	NA	4
Dow Chemical Co	517-636-1000	Midland, MI	16682	16239	56
DuPont Canada Ltd	416-821-3300	Mississauga, ON Can	1171	649	4
DuPont, E I DeNemours & Co	302-774-1000	Wilmington, DE	32917	30719	141
Ecolab (Economics Laboratory) Inc	612-293-2233	St Paul, MN	1212	943	12
Englehard Corp	201-632-6000	Edison, NJ	2351	1413	8
Ethyl Corp	804-788-5000	Richmond, VA	2011	5251	10
Ferro Corp	216-641-8580	Cleveland, OH	1009	588	8
Formica Corp	201-890-9400	Wayne, NJ	432	250	4
Freeport McMoran Inc	504-582-4000	New Orleans, LA	1945	3730	6
General Chemical Canada Ltd	416-896-9595	Mississauga, ON Can	340	213	3
Georgia Gulf Corp	404-395-4500	Atlanta, GA	550	250	5
Grace, W R & Co	212-819-5500	New York, NY	5786	5310	46
Great Lakes Chemical Corp	317-463-2511	West Lafayette, IN	616	664	4
Guardsman Products Inc	616-957-2600	Grand Rapids, MI	1500	500	10
Hercules Inc	302-594-5000	Wilmington, DE	2802	3325	23
Hexcel Corp	415-828-4200	San Francisco, CA	400	300	3
Himont Inc	302-594-5500	Wilmington, DE	600	400	1
Hoechst American Corp	201-231-2000	Somerville, NJ	1815	1300	11
Huber, J M Corp	201-549-8600	Edison, NJ	500	NA	3
Huntsman Chemical & Oil Corp	801-532-5200	Salt Lake City, UT	550	NA	1
ICC Industries Inc	212-903-1700	New York, NY	500	NA	2
ICI (Imperial Chemical) America Inc	302-886-3000	Wilmington, DE	1650	NA	11
IMC Fertilizer Corp	312-564-8600	Northbrook, IL	1200	1000	6
International Minerals & Chemical Corp	312-564-8600	Northbrook, IL	1471	1794	10
Jetco Chemicals Inc	214-872-3011	Corsicana, TX	NA	NA	NA
Koppers Co Inc	412-227-2000	Pittsburg, PA	1600	1200	12
Liquid Air Corp	415-977-6500	Walnut Creek, CA	600	800	4
Loctite Corp	203-520-5000	Hartford, CT	417	347	3
LSB Industries Inc	405-235-4546	Oklahoma City, OK	250	200	2
Lubrizol Corp	216-943-4200	Wicklife, OH	1126	971	5
Lyondell Petrochemical Corp	713-652-7200	Houston, TX	4696	913	10
Minnesota Mining & Manufacturing Canada	519-451-2500	London, ON Can	425	510	2

Major Group: Basic Industries   **Industry: Chemicals**

Organizations Listed by Industry

Organization	Phone	City / State or Province	Revenue ($ mil)	Assets ($ mil)	Emp (thous)
Mobay Corp	412-777-2000	Pittsburgh, PA	2200	NA	11
Monsanto Canada Inc	416-826-9222	Mississauga, ON Can	353	148	1
Monsanto Co	314-694-1000	St Louis, MO	8293	8461	46
Morton Chemical Co	312-807-3290	Chicago, IL	NA	NA	NA
Morton International Inc	312-807-2000	Chicago, IL	1407	1100	11
Nalco Chemical Co	312-961-9500	Naperville, IL	994	839	5
National Distillers & Chemicals Corp	212-949-5000	New York, NY	2922	2908	12
National Starch & Chemical Corp	201-685-5000	Bridgewater, NJ	1210	750	8
NCH Corp	214-438-0211	Irving, TX	565	500	4
Occidental Chemical Corp	713-840-7100	Houston, TX	NA	NA	NA
Olin Corp	203-356-2000	Stamford, CT	2308	1940	17
Pennwalt Corp	215-587-7000	Philadelphia, PA	1024	950	5
Petrolite Corp	314-241-8370	St Louis, MO	375	250	3
Philipp Brothers Chemicals Inc	201-944-6020	Fort Lee, NJ	550	NA	1
Ploysar Ltd	519-332-1212	Sarnia, ON Can	2103	2015	15
Polysar Energy & Chemical (Can Dev) Corp	416-598-7200	Toronto, ON Can	2439	4629	7
Pratt & Lambert Inc	716-873-6000	Buffalo, NY	250	200	2
Quantum Chemical Corp	212-949-5000	New York, NY	2922	2908	14
Reichhold Chemicals Inc	914-682-5700	White Plains, NY	801	500	6
Rexene Corportation	212-644-8200	New York, NY	553	511	5
Rohm & Hass Co	215-592-3000	Philadelphia, PA	2535	2242	13
RPM Corp	216-225-3192	Medina, OH	350	300	2
Schulman, A Inc	216-666-3751	Akron, OH	598	240	2
Selig Chemical Industries Inc	404-691-9220	Atlanta, GA	NA	NA	NA
Stepan Co	312-446-7500	Winnetka, IL	300	250	1
Sterling Chemical Corp	713-650-3700	Houston, TX	600	400	2
Texaco Chemical Co	713-666-8000	Bellaire, TX	NA	NA	NA
Transammonia Inc	212-223-3200	New York, NY	1250	NA	1
Union Carbide Canada Ltd	416-488-1444	Toronto, ON Can	483	682	5
Union Carbide Corp	203-794-2000	Danbury, CT	8324	8441	44
Univar Corp	206-447-5911	Seattle, WA	1117	395	5
US Industrial Chemicals Co	513-530-6510	Cincinnati, OH	NA	NA	NA
Vista Chemical Corp	713-531-3200	Houston, TX	781	521	2
Witco Corp	212-605-3800	New York, NY	1586	1115	11

Industry: Chemicals   **Number: 94**

Major Group: Basic Industries   **Industry: Metals/Mining**

Addington Resources Inc	606-928-3433	Ashland, KY	250	289	2
ALCAN Aluminum Co of Canada Ltd	514-848-8000	Montreal, PQ Can	9165	9153	67
Alumax Inc	415-348-3400	San Mateo, CA	2200	1800	11
Aluminum Co of America	412-553-4545	Pittsburgh, PA	9795	10538	59
AMAX Coal Industries Inc	317-266-1500	Indianapolis, IN	NA	NA	NA
AMAX Inc	212-856-4200	New York, NY	3944	4076	20
ANR Coal Co	703-983-0222	Roanoke, VA	NA	NA	NA
Arch Mineral Corp	314-231-1010	St Louis, MO	275	NA	2
Asarco Inc	212-510-2000	New York, NY	1988	2223	9
Ashland Coal Inc	304-526-3333	Huntington, VA	300	250	2
Associated Metals & Minerals Inc	914-251-5400	White Plains, NY	750	NA	1
Battle Mountain Corp	713-227-6330	Houston, TX	141	206	1
BHP Australia (Broken Hill) Inc	415-981-1515	San Francisco, CA	9900	NA	42
Brunswick Mining & Smelting Corp	506-522-2100	Toronto, ON Can	255	340	3
Brush Wellman Inc	216-443-1000	Cleveland, OH	346	358	3
Castle, A M & Co	312-455-7111	Franklin Park, IL	375	300	2

Major Group: Basic Industries   **Industry: Metals/Mining**

Organizations Listed by Industry

Organization	Phone	City / State or Province	Revenue ($ mil)	Assets ($ mil)	Emp (thous)
Cleveland Cliffs Inc	216-694-5700	Cleveland, OH	350	NA	3
Climax Metals Co	203-629-6000	Greenwich, CT	NA	NA	NA
Cominco Ltd	604-682-0611	Vancouver, BC Can	1418	1798	9
Consolidated Coal Co	302-774-1000	Wilmington, DE	NA	NA	NA
Copperweld Corp	412-263-3200	Pittsburgh, PA	300	NA	3
Denison Mines Ltd	416-865-1991	Toronto, ON Can	360	1003	5
Diversified Industries Inc	314-862-8200	St Louis, MO	250	200	3
Doe Run Co	314-991-7140	St Louis, MO	NA	NA	NA
Eldorado Nuclear Ltd	613-238-5222	Ottawa, ON Can	298	765	1
Falconbridge Ltd	416-863-7000	Toronto, ON Can	1139	2244	9
Federal Industries Ltd	204-942-8161	Winnipeg, MB Can	1623	808	15
First Mississippi Corp	601-948-7550	Jackson, MS	400	500	2
Freeman United Coal Mining Co	312-263-4490	Chicago, IL	NA	NA	NA
Freeport McMoran Gold Inc	504-582-4000	New Orleans, LA	106	169	1
General Refractories Co	215-667-7900	Bala Cynwyd, PA	210	250	1
Handy & Harman Inc	212-752-3400	New York, NY	658	466	4
Hecla Mining Co	208-769-4107	Coeur D'Alene, ID	105	189	1
Homestake Mining Co	415-981-8150	San Francisco, CA	433	984	2
Hudson Bay Mining & Smelting Co	416-362-2192	Toronto, ON Can	298	255	2
Inco Ltd	416-361-7511	Toronto, ON Can	2017	3307	19
Island Creek Corp	606-223-3636	Lexington, KY	NA	NA	NA
Kaiser Technology Corp	415-271-3300	Oakland, CA	2219	2404	11
Kidd Creek Mines Ltd	416-863-7000	Toronto, ON Can	510	1020	3
Magma Copper Co	602-385-3100	San Manuel, AZ	500	350	5
MAPCO Coal Inc	918-592-7237	Tulsa, OK	NA	NA	NA
Massey, A T Coal Co	804-788-1800	Richmond, VA	NA	NA	NA
Metallurg Corp	212-686-4010	New York, NY	750	NA	4
NACCO Industries	216-752-1000	Cleveland, OH	616	837	6
National Aluminum Corp	412-788-0190	Pittsburgh, PA	NA	NA	NA
Newmont Gold Corp	303-863-7414	Denver, CO	389	598	6
Newmont Mining Corp	303-863-7414	Denver, CO	501	1321	5
Noranda Inc	416-982-7111	Toronto, ON Can	7529	7961	48
Noverco Inc	514-393-2650	Montreal, PQ Can	879	1207	3
Phelps Dodge Corp	602-234-8100	Phoenix, AZ	2320	2755	11
Placer Dome Ltd	416-868-6060	Toronto, ON Can	709	1839	4
QIT Fer et Titane Inc	514-288-8400	Montreal, PQ Can	428	621	2
Reynolds Metals Co	804-281-2000	Richmond, VA	5619	5032	29
Rio Algom Ltd	416-367-4000	Toronto, ON Can	1682	1785	8
Rochester & Pittsburgh Coal Corp	412-349-5800	Indiana, PA	500	250	5
Santa Fe Pacific Minerals Corp	505-881-3050	Albuquerque, NM	NA	NA	NA
Sequa Corp	212-986-5500	New York, NY	1713	1959	16
Sherritt Gordon Mines Ltd	416-363-9241	Toronto, ON Can	463	546	3
Southern Peru Copper Co Inc	212-510-2000	New York, NY	275	NA	3
Southwire Co Inc	404-832-4242	Carrolton, GA	750	NA	3
Texas Utilities Mining Co	214-812-5600	Dallas, TX	NA	NA	NA
Transco Coal Co	713-439-2000	Houston, TX	NA	NA	NA
Utility Fuels Co	713-629-3001	Houston, TX	1000	NA	4
Wyman Gordon Co	508-756-5111	Worcester, MA	272	352	3

Industry: Metals/Mining   Number: 64

Major Group: Basic Industries   Industry: Energy

Alberta & Southern Gas Co	403-260-9911	Calgary, AB Can	932	473	1
Alberta Energy Co	403-423-8333	Edmonton, AB Can	409	1641	1

Major Group: Basic Industries   Industry: Energy

Organizations Listed by Industry

Organization	Phone	City / State or Province	Revenue ($ mil)	Assets ($ mil)	Emp (thous)
Alberta Natural Gas Co	403-260-9911	Calgary, AB Can	298	340	2
Algonquin Gas Transmission Co	617-254-4050	Boston, MA	NA	NA	NA
Allegheny & Western Energy	304-343-4327	Charleston, WV	250	250	1
Amerada Hess Corp	212-997-8500	New York, NY	4264	5372	8
American Petrofina Inc	214-750-2400	Dallas, TX	2635	2356	4
Amoco Canada Petroleum Co	403-233-1313	Calgary, AB Can	1285	1833	2
Amoco Chemical Co	312-856-6111	Chicago, IL	NA	NA	NA
Amoco Corp	312-856-6111	Chicago, IL	23919	29919	53
Anadarko Petroleum Corp	713-875-1101	Houston, TX	333	1490	1
Angus Petroleum Corp	303-278-4300	Golden, CO	NA	NA	NA
ANR Pipeline Co	313-496-7075	Detroit, MI	NA	NA	NA
Anschutz Corp	303-298-1000	Denver, CO	2250	NA	20
Apache Corp	303-837-5000	Denver, CO	500	350	2
Apex Oil Co	314-889-9600	St Louis, MO	3000	NA	8
Asamera Inc	403-269-5521	Calgary, AB Can	306	293	1
Ashland Oil Inc	606-329-3333	Russell, KY	8196	4254	30
Astroline Corp	508-942-1600	Reading, MA	2500	NA	1
Atlantic Richfield Co	213-486-3511	Los Angeles, CA	18868	21514	27
Belcher Oil Co	305-551-5220	Miami, FL	NA	NA	NA
Bow Valley Industries Ltd	403-261-6100	Calgary, AB Can	468	935	2
BP Petroleum Canada Ltd	403-237-1234	Calgary, AB Can	282	747	2
Brascan Ltd	416-363-9491	Toronto, ON Can	7491	4126	1
British Petroleum America	216-586-4141	Cleveland, OH	11000	24000	47
Burlington Resources	206-467-3838	Seattle, WA	1500	NA	15
Cabot Corp	617-890-0200	Waltham, MA	1500	1800	9
Canadian Occidental Petroleum Ltd	403-234-6700	Calgary, AB Can	629	1153	1
Canterra Energy Ltd	403-267-9111	Calgary, AB Can	383	2550	2
Carnegie Natural Gas Co	412-655-8510	Pittsburgh, PA	NA	NA	NA
Chaco Energy Co	214-812-8200	Dallas, TX	NA	NA	NA
Charter Co	513-579-2482	Cincinnati, OH	480	295	2
Chevron Canada Ltd	604-668-5300	Vancouver, BC Can	777	830	1
Chevron Canada Resources Ltd	403-234-5000	Calgary, AB Can	1190	850	2
Chevron Corp	415-894-7700	San Francisco, CA	27722	33968	54
Chevron Overseas Petroleum Co	415-842-1000	San Ramon, CA	NA	NA	NA
Clajon Production Corp	915-683-4181	Midland, TX	825	NA	1
Clark Oil & Refining Co	314-889-9600	St Louis, MO	3850	NA	3
Coastal Corp	713-877-1400	Houston, TX	8187	7865	16
Colonial Oil Industries Inc	912-236-1331	Savannah, GA	550	NA	1
Commonwealth Energy System	617-225-4000	Cambridge, MA	660	600	3
Conoco Inc	302-774-1000	Wilmington, DE	NA	NA	NA
Consolidated Coal Corp	412-831-4000	Pittsburgh, PA	825	NA	7
Consumers Co-op Refineries Ltd	306-244-3311	Saskatoon, SK Can	298	85	1
Consumers Gas Ltd	416-864-3399	Toronto, ON Can	1417	1726	8
Crown Central Petroleum Corp	301-539-7400	Baltimore, MD	1149	443	6
Cyprus Minerals Co	303-643-5000	Englewood, CO	1327	1651	7
Diamond Shamrock R & M Corp	512-641-6800	San Antonio, TX	1804	843	4
Dome Petroleum Ltd	403-231-3000	Calgary, AB Can	1266	3529	4
Dresser Canada Inc	416-826-8411	Mississauga, ON Can	275	196	2
Drummond Coal Corp	205-945-6500	Birmingham, AL	750	NA	3
DWG Corp	305-866-7771	Miami, FL	1200	1000	15
Elf Aquitaine Inc	203-358-5000	Stamford, CT	3850	NA	8
Energen Corp	205-326-2700	Birmingham, AL	350	300	1
Enron Canada Ltd	403-298-2690	Calgary, AB Can	281	85	1
Enron Oil & Gas Co	713-853-6161	Houston, TX	NA	NA	NA
Enserch Exploration Inc	214-748-1110	Dallas, TX	NA	NA	NA

Major Group: Basic Industries   Industry: Energy

Organizations Listed by Industry

Organization	Phone	City / State or Province	Revenue ($ mil)	Assets ($ mil)	Emp (thous)
ESI Energy Services Inc	407-683-6996	West Palm Beach, FL	NA	NA	NA
Exxon Corp	212-333-1000	New York, NY	88563	74293	101
Farmers Union Central Exchange Inc	612-451-1772	South St Paul, MN	1135	500	3
Farmland Industries Inc	816-459-6000	Kansas City, MO	4400	1000	6
Federated Cooperatives Ltd	306-244-3311	Saskatoon, SK Can	1214	451	2
Ferrell Companies Inc	816-792-1600	Liberty, MO	750	NA	3
Flying J Inc	801-734-9416	West Brigham, UT	1000	NA	2
Gearhart Industries Inc	817-293-1300	Fort Worth, TX	297	355	4
Getty Petroleum Corp	516-338-6000	Jericho, NY	1041	1500	7
Global Marine Inc	713-596-5100	Houston, TX	141	696	1
Global Petroleum Corp	617-894-8800	Waltham, MA	1500	NA	1
Gulf Canada Ltd	403-233-4000	Calgary, AB Can	740	3159	18
Hadson Corp	405-235-9500	Oklahoma City, OK	450	300	2
Hamilton Oil Corp	303-863-3000	Denver, CO	195	838	1
Harken Energy Corp	817-354-9944	Bedford, TX	747	500	1
Howell Corp	713-658-4000	Houston, TX	250	300	1
Huffington, Roy M Inc	713-651-1600	Houston, TX	1100	NA	2
Hunt Consolidated Oil Co	214-744-7911	Dallas, TX	1000	NA	2
Husky Oil Ltd	403-298-6111	Calgary, AB Can	638	1700	2
Imperial Oil Ltd	416-968-4111	Toronto, ON Can	6124	7461	13
Inter City Gas Corp	204-944-9920	Winnepeg, MB Can	1421	1687	6
Interhome Energy Inc (Interprov Pipe)	403-232-5500	Calgary, AB Can	729	2509	2
JM Petroleum Corp	214-953-0330	Dallas, TX	600	NA	1
Johnson, Axel & Co Inc	212-758-3200	New York, NY	1000	NA	1
Kerr McGee Corp	405-270-1313	Oklahoma City, OK	2689	3123	10
KN Energy Inc	303-989-1740	Lakewood, CO	335	650	3
Ladd Petroleum Inc	303-620-0100	Denver, CO	NA	NA	NA
LaSalle Energy Corp	214-871-5333	Dallas, TX	1250	NA	2
Lear Petroleum Corp	214-363-6085	Dallas, TX	600	400	1
Lone Star Gas Co	214-741-3711	Dallas, TX	NA	NA	NA
Louisiana Land & Exploration Co	504-566-6500	New Orleans, LA	726	1429	2
Mapco Inc	918-581-1800	Tulsa, OK	1802	1376	5
Marathon Oil Co	419-422-2121	Findlay, OH	NA	NA	NA
Maxus Energy Corp	214-953-2000	Dallas, TX	601	1720	2
Meridian Oil Inc	713-831-1600	Houston, TX	NA	NA	NA
Mesa Limited Partnership Inc	806-378-1000	Amarillo, TX	371	3001	1
MidCon Corp	312-691-2500	Lombard, IL	NA	NA	NA
Mitchell Energy & Development Corp	713-363-5500	The Woodlands, TX	562	2112	2
Mobil Corp	212-883-4242	New York, NY	54361	38820	69
Mobil Oil Canada Ltd	403-260-7910	Calgary, AB Can	1348	3123	2
Mohawk Oil Canada Ltd	604-299-7244	Burnaby, BC Can	343	132	2
Moore McCormick Resources Inc	203-358-2200	Stamford, CT	500	500	5
Murphy Oil Corp	501-862-6411	El Dorado, AR	1525	2068	5
National Coop Refinery Assn Inc	316-241-2340	McPherson, KS	1100	500	1
National Propane Co	516-352-6500	New Hyde Park, NY	NA	NA	NA
NERCO Inc	503-796-6600	Portland, OR	662	1206	2
Norcen Energy Resources Ltd	403-231-0111	Calgary, AB Can	622	1968	2
North American Coal Corp	216-752-1000	Cleveland, OH	600	400	5
Northern Plains Natural Gas Co	402-633-5000	Omaha, NE	NA	NA	NA
Nova Corp of Alberta Ltd	403-290-6000	Calgary, AB Can	3350	7006	8
NUI Corp	201-685-3900	Bridgewater, NJ	350	250	2
Occidental Petroleum Corp	213-879-1700	Los Angeles, CA	19417	20747	45
Olco Petroleum Group Ltd	514-353-6821	Montreal, PQ Can	304	91	1
Oxbow Corp	617-461-0550	Dedham, MA	1000	NA	1
Pacific Energy Co	213-725-1139	Commerce, CA	NA	NA	NA

Major Group: Basic Industries   Industry: Energy

Organizations Listed by Industry

Organization	Phone	City / State or Province	Revenue ($ mil)	Assets ($ mil)	Emp (thous)
Pacific Interstate Co	213-895-5223	Los Angeles, CA	NA	NA	NA
PanCanadian Petroleum	403-290-2000	Calgary, AB Can	587	2273	1
Pauley Petroleum Inc	213-879-5000	Los Angeles, CA	200	250	1
Peabody Holding Co	314-342-3400	St Louis, MO	1758	2449	6
Pemex (Petroleos Mexicos SA)	713-978-7974	Houston, TX	12100	NA	142
Pennzoil Co	713-546-4000	Houston, TX	2274	4480	8
Perimian Partners Ltd	713-787-2222	Houston, TX	2289	555	2
Petro Canada	403-296-5850	Calgary, AB Can	4415	7185	8
Petroleum Heat & Power Co	203-323-2121	Stamford, CT	462	350	2
Phillips 66 Co	918-661-4948	Bartlesville, OK	NA	NA	NA
Phillips Petroleum Co	918-661-6600	Bartlesville, OK	11490	11968	25
Phillips Pipeline Co	918-661-6600	Bartlesville, OK	NA	NA	NA
Piedmont Natural Gas Co	704-364-3120	Charlotte, NC	431	700	2
Pittston Co	203-622-0900	Greenwich, CT	1583	992	17
Placid Oil Co	214-741-3081	Dallas, TX	1000	NA	1
Pride Refining Inc	915-677-2223	Abilene, TX	550	NA	1
Quaker State Oil Refining Co	814-676-7676	Oil City, PA	869	740	6
Rock Island Refining Co	317-872-3200	Indianapolis, IN	800	NA	2
Rowan Corp	713-621-7800	Houston, TX	250	150	2
Shell Canada Ltd	403-232-3111	Calgary, AB Can	4301	4773	7
Shell Oil Co	713-241-6161	Houston, TX	21000	30000	41
Sinclair Marketing Inc	913-321-3700	Kansas City, KS	550	NA	1
Sonat Exploration Co	713-940-4000	Houston, TX	NA	NA	NA
Sun Co Inc	215-293-6000	Radnor, PA	9744	8616	21
Sun Energy Partners LP Inc	214-890-6207	Dallas, TX	1570	2000	2
Sun Exploration Corp	214-890-6000	Dallas, TX	3000	2000	1
Sun Refining & Marketing Div	215-977-3332	Philadelphia, PA	NA	NA	NA
Suncor Inc	416-733-7300	North York, ON Can	1143	1720	4
Tauber Oil Co	713-869-8700	Houston, TX	1000	NA	1
Tejas Gas Corp	713-658-0509	Houston, TX	250	125	1
Tesoro Petroleum Corp	512-828-8484	San Antonio, TX	1172	490	3
Texaco Canada Ltd	416-441-7811	Don Mills, ON Can	2263	3482	3
Texaco Inc	914-253-4000	White Plains, NY	35138	26337	50
Texaco Refining & Marketing Inc	713-650-4000	Houston, TX	NA	NA	NA
Texas Oil & Gas Corp	214-954-2000	Dallas, TX	NA	NA	NA
Thums Long Beach Co Inc	213-436-9211	Long Beach, CA	550	NA	2
Tosco Corp	213-207-6000	Santa Monica, CA	1142	556	1
Total Petroleum North America Ltd	403-267-3000	Calgary, AB Can	1969	1120	5
Transcontinental Gas Pipeline Corp	713-439-2000	Houston, TX	NA	NA	NA
Turbo Resources Ltd	403-294-6400	Calgary, AB Can	474	306	2
Ultramar Canada Inc	514-499-6111	Montreal, PQ Can	1238	952	2
Union Gas Holdings Corp	316-331-4500	Independence, KS	1500	NA	3
Union Texas Petroleum Inc	713-623-6544	Houston, TX	1152	1717	2
United Refining Corp	814-723-1500	Warren, PA	750	NA	3
Unocal Corp	213-977-7600	Los Angeles, CA	10085	9508	18
Valero Energy Corp	512-246-2000	San Antonio, TX	629	965	2
Vanguard Energy Corp	713-880-8750	Houston, TX	825	NA	1
Warren, George E Co Inc	617-451-2300	Boston, MA	1750	NA	1
Westburne International Industries Ltd	403-292-0200	Calgary, AB Can	1216	595	20
Westcoast Energy Inc	604-664-5500	Vancouver, BC Can	712	1839	1
Western Co of North America	817-731-5100	Fort Worth, TX	209	534	2
Westmoreland Coal Co	215-545-2500	Philadelphia, PA	620	500	3
World Oil Co Inc	213-560-8801	South Gate, CA	550	NA	1
Wright Shuchart Inc	206-447-7654	Seattle, WA	550	NA	2
Wyatt Inc	203-787-2175	New Haven, CT	600	NA	1

Major Group: Basic Industries   Industry: Energy

Organizations Listed by Industry

Organization	Phone	City / State or Province	Revenue ($ mil)	Assets ($ mil)	Emp (thous)
Zapata Corp	713-226-6000	Houston, TX	194	771	1

Industry: Energy **Number: 168**

Major Group: Basic Industries **Industry: Paper/Forest Prd**

Abitibi Price Ltd	416-369-6700	Toronto, ON Can	2809	2236	24
Alling & Cory Corp	716-454-1880	Rochester, NY	350	NA	1
American Business Products Inc	404-953-8300	Atlanta, GA	358	152	4
Barbecon Inc	416-488-3344	Toronto, ON Can	255	128	1
Bathurst Paper Ltd	514-875-2160	Montreal, PQ Can	425	468	3
Boise Cascade Canada Ltd	416-231-3010	Toronto, ON Can	350	425	2
Boise Cascade Corp	208-384-6161	Boise, ID	4095	3610	20
Bowater Inc	203-656-7200	Darien, CT	1410	1881	5
Butler Paper Co	303-790-8343	Englewood, CO	250	NA	2
Canadian Pacific Forest Products Ltd	807-475-2110	Thunder Bay, ON Can	2555	2358	17
Canfor Corp	604-661-5241	Vancouver, BC Can	921	986	4
Champion International Corp	203-358-7000	Stamford, CT	5129	6700	30
Chesapeake Corp	804-697-1000	Richmond, VA	711	662	7
Consolidated Bathurst Inc	514-875-2160	Montreal, PQ Can	2016	1936	15
Consolidated Papers Inc	715-422-3111	Wisconsin Rapids, WI	897	935	5
Crown Forest Industries Ltd	604-668-4242	Vancouver, BC Can	876	717	5
Crown Henry & Co Inc	312-236-6300	Chicago, IL	880	NA	4
Deltic Farm & Lumber Co	501-878-5194	El Dorado, AR	NA	NA	NA
Doman Industries Ltd	604-748-3711	Duncan, BC Can	340	170	1
Donohue Inc	418-522-6471	Quebec, PQ Can	551	771	4
Duplex Products Inc	815-895-2100	Sycamore, IL	250	200	2
Federal Paper Board Co Inc	201-391-1776	Montvale, NJ	1117	1335	5
Fletcher Challenge Canada Ltd	604-665-3821	Vancouver, BC Can	1250	1415	7
Fort Howard Paper Co	414-435-8821	Green Bay, WI	1750	2000	16
Georgia Pacific Corp	404-521-4000	Atlanta, GA	9509	7115	44
Glatfelter, P H Co	717-225-4711	Spring Grove, PA	569	663	3
Great Lakes Forest Products Ltd	807-475-2110	Thunder Bay, ON Can	638	723	5
Great Northern Nekoosa Corp	203-359-4000	Stamford, CT	3588	3821	20
International Forest Products (Whonnock)	604-681-3221	Vancouver, BC Can	326	261	2
International Paper Co	914-397-1500	Purchase, NY	9533	9462	55
James River Corp	804-644-5411	Richmond, VA	5098	5006	34
Jefferson Smurfit Corp	314-746-1100	St Louis, MO	1255	817	8
Kimberly Clark Corp	214-830-1200	Dallas, TX	5394	4268	47
Kruger Inc	514-737-1131	Montreal, PQ CAN	510	765	6
Longview Fibre Co	206-425-1550	Longview, WA	657	635	4
Louisiana Pacific Corp	503-221-0800	Portland, OR	1799	1796	13
MacMillan Bloedel Ltd	604-661-8000	Vancouver, BC Can	2783	2021	15
Manville Forest Products Co	318-362-2000	West Monroe, LA	NA	NA	NA
Mead Corp	513-222-6323	Dayton, OH	4464	2492	21
Mead Pulp Sales Inc	513-222-6323	Dayton, OH	NA	NA	NA
Nekoosa Papers Inc	715-887-5111	Port Edwards, WI	3000	NA	20
Noranda Forest Inc	416-365-0710	Toronto, ON Can	3668	3339	16
North Pacific Lumber Inc	503-231-1166	Portland, OR	600	NA	1
Northern Pacific Lumber Co Inc	503-231-1166	Portland, OR	550	NA	2
Oxford Paper Co	207-364-4521	Rumford, ME	NA	NA	NA
Paper Corp of America	215-296-4470	Wayne, PA	NA	NA	NA
Parsons & Whittemore Corp	212-972-2000	New York, NY	550	NA	3
Pentair Inc	612-636-7920	St Paul, MN	823	745	9
Pope & Talbot Inc	503-228-9161	Portland, OR	515	319	4

Major Group: Basic Industries **Industry: Paper/Forest Prd**

Organizations Listed by Industry

Organization	Phone	City / State or Province	Revenue ($ mil)	Assets ($ mil)	Emp (thous)
Potlatch Corp	415-576-8800	San Francisco, CA	1084	1272	7
Q & O Paper Co	416-688-5030	St Catharines, ON Can	478	490	3
Reed Inc	416-862-5000	Toronto, ON Can	350	352	2
Repap Enterprises Corp	514-879-1316	Montreal, PQ Can	795	1925	5
Rolland Inc	514-289-1779	Montreal, PQ Can	378	142	2
Roseburg Forest Products Inc	503-679-3311	Dillard, OR	600	NA	6
Scott Paper Co	215-522-5000	Philadelphia, PA	4726	5156	27
Simpson Investment Co Inc	206-292-5000	Seattle, WA	550	NA	5
Simpson Timber Corp	206-292-5000	Seattle, WA	1000	NA	2
Sonoco Products Co	803-383-7000	Hartsville, SC	1599	977	14
St Joe Paper Co	904-356-8311	Jacksonville, FL	650	450	5
Stone Container Corp	312-346-6600	Chicago, IL	3742	2395	21
Temple Inland Inc	409-829-1313	Diboll, TX	1774	1982	13
Union Camp Corp	201-628-2000	Wayne, NJ	2661	3094	19
Wausau Paper Mills Co	715-845-5266	Wausau, WI	300	200	2
Weldwood of Canada Ltd	604-687-7366	Vancouver, BC Can	761	601	4
West Fraser Timber Co	604-681-8282	Vancouver, BC Can	394	447	3
Westar Group Ltd (BC Resources Invst)	604-687-2600	Vancouver, BC Can	288	401	4
Westvaco Corp	212-688-5000	New York, NY	2187	2634	15
Weyerhaeuser Co	206-924-2345	Tacoma, WA	10004	15387	47
Willamette Industries Inc	503-227-5581	Portland, OR	1716	1430	9
WWF Paper Corp	215-667-9210	Bala Cynwyd, PA	600	NA	3

Industry: Paper/Forest Prd   Number: 71

Major Group: Basic Industries   Industry: Steel

Organization	Phone	City / State or Province	Revenue ($ mil)	Assets ($ mil)	Emp (thous)
Algoma Steel Ltd	705-945-2788	Sault Ste Marie, ON Can	1183	1231	11
Allegheny Ludlum Steel Corp	412-394-2800	Pittsburgh, PA	1100	NA	5
Armco Inc	201-316-5200	Parsippany, NJ	3227	2788	16
Athlone Industries Inc	201-887-9100	Parsippany, NJ	175	NA	2
Bethlehem Steel Corp	215-694-2424	Bethlehem, PA	5489	4449	45
Birmingham Steel Corp	205-985-9290	Birmingham, AL	400	NA	3
Brenlin Corp	216-762-2420	Akron, OH	700	NA	3
Cablec Corp	914-634-0100	New City, NY	550	NA	5
Chaparral Steel	214-775-8241	Midlothian, TX	400	300	1
Cyclops Industries Inc	412-343-4000	Pittsburgh, PA	900	NA	7
Dofasco Inc	416-544-3761	Hamilton, ON Can	2535	5069	23
Inland Steel Industries Inc	312-346-0300	Chicago, IL	4068	2925	21
Ivaco Inc	514-288-4545	Montreal, PQ Can	1902	827	13
J & L Specialty Products Inc	412-338-1600	Pittsburgh, PA	750	NA	2
Kobe Steel Corp USA	212-751-9400	New York, NY	550	NA	1
Laclede Steel Co	314-425-1400	St Louis, MO	350	200	3
LTV Corp	214-979-7711	Dallas, TX	7325	6163	39
LTV Steel Co	216-622-5000	Cleveland, OH	1000	NA	10
Lukens Inc	215-383-2000	Coatesville, PA	605	353	4
McLouth Steel Products Inc	313-285-1200	Trenton, MI	500	NA	2
National Steel (Nat'l Intergroup) Corp	412-394-4100	Pittsburgh, PA	3081	2000	7
Nucor Corp	704-366-7000	Charlotte, NC	543	426	4
NVF Co	302-239-5281	Yorklyn, DE	1200	500	10
Precision Castparts Inc	503-777-3881	Portland, OR	414	298	6
Premetalco Inc	416-366-3954	Toronto, ON Can	271	170	1
Rouge Steel Co	313-322-3000	Dearborn, MI	NA	NA	NA
Sidbec Ltd	514-286-8600	Montreal, PQ Can	549	435	3
Slater Industries Inc	416-529-5422	Toronto, ON Can	298	213	2

Major Group: Basic Industries   Industry: Steel

Organizations Listed by Industry

Organization	Phone	City / State or Province	Revenue ($ mil)	Assets ($ mil)	Emp (thous)
Stelco Inc	416-362-2161	Toronto, ON Can	2305	2029	16
Tang Industries Inc	312-981-8200	Elk Grove, IL	750	NA	7
Thyssen USA Corp	212-512-9700	New York, NY	2200	NA	1
Tyler Corp	214-754-7800	Dallas, TX	665	348	6
USX Corp	412-433-1121	Pittsburgh, PA	16877	19474	80
Weirton Steel Corp	304-797-2000	Weirton, WV	1384	687	8
Wheeling Pittsburgh Steel Corp	304-234-2400	Wheeling, WV	1001	1002	8
Worthington Industries Inc	614-438-3210	Columbus, OH	904	507	7

Industry: Steel   **Number: 36**

Major Group: Basic Industries   **Industry: Tire/Rubber**

Organization	Phone	City / State or Province	Revenue ($ mil)	Assets ($ mil)	Emp (thous)
Armstrong Rubber Co	203-784-2200	New Haven, CT	900	600	8
Bandag Inc	319-262-1400	Muscatine, IA	498	315	2
Bridgestone Tire USA Inc	213-320-6031	Torrance, CA	1100	NA	2
Carlisle Companies Inc	513-241-2500	Cincinnati, OH	500	NA	5
Cooper Tire & Rubber Co	419-423-1321	Findley, OH	748	443	8
Firestone Canada Inc	416-521-1111	Hamilton, ON Can	309	256	3
Firestone Tire & Rubber Co	216-379-7000	Akron, OH	312	730	55
Gates Corp	303-744-1911	Denver, CO	1250	NA	12
GenCorp Inc	216-869-4200	Akron, OH	1891	1230	16
Goodrich, B F Co	216-374-3985	Arkon, OH	2417	2073	12
Goodyear Canada Inc	416-626-4611	Islington, ON Can	664	419	6
Goodyear Tire & Rubber Co	216-796-2121	Akron, OH	10810	8618	114
Hanna, M A Corp	216-589-4000	Cleveland, OH	1000	300	8
Interface Corporation	404-882-1891	LaGrange, GA	397	493	4
Kelly Springfield Tire Co	301-777-6000	Cumberland, MD	1500	NA	10
O'Sullivan Corp	703-667-6666	Winchester, VA	250	175	2
Premark International Corp	312-405-6000	Deerfield, IL	2397	1655	24
Salem Carpet Mills Corp	919-727-1200	Winston-Salem, NC	300	250	3
Uniroyal Goodrich Canada Inc	519-749-8473	Kitchener, ON Can	307	206	3
Wellman Corp	201-388-0120	Shrewsbury, NJ	260	200	2

Industry: Tire/Rubber   **Number: 20**

Organizations Listed by Industry

Organization	Phone	City / State or Province	Revenue ($ mil)	Assets ($ mil)	Emp (thous)
Major Group: Business Service		**Industry: Oil Service**			
Baker Hughes Co	713-439-8600	Houston, TX	2316	2118	21
Baker International Corp	714-634-2333	Orange, CA	1600	1500	20
Baroid Corp	713-987-4000	Houston, TX	550	600	3
Big Three Industries Inc	713-868-0333	Houston, TX	650	1000	5
BJ Titan & BJ Services Inc	713-439-8600	Houston, TX	NA	NA	NA
Cameron Iron Works Inc	713-939-2211	Houston, TX	502	757	7
CBI Industries Inc	312-572-7000	Oak Brook, IL	1376	1343	15
Dresser Industries Inc	214-740-6000	Dallas, TX	3942	2899	31
Halliburton Co	214-978-2600	Dallas, TX	4839	4722	28
Helmerich & Payne Inc	918-742-5531	Tulsa, OK	160	576	1
McDermott International Inc	504-587-5400	New Orleans, LA	2352	3825	26
NL Industries Inc	713-987-4000	Houston, TX	1100	1400	13
Noble Affiliates Inc	405-223-4110	Ardmore, OK	192	527	2
Ocean Drilling Exploration Co	504-561-2811	New Orleans, LA	406	1026	4
Schlumberger Ltd	212-350-9400	New York, NY	4925	5600	48
Telco Oilfield Services Inc	203-237-9655	Meriden, CT	NA	NA	NA
Western Atlas International Inc	713-266-5700	Houston, TX	NA	NA	NA

Industry: Oil Service   **Number: 17**

Major Group: Business Service   **Industry: Railroad**

Organization	Phone	City / State or Province	Revenue ($ mil)	Assets ($ mil)	Emp (thous)
ACF Industries Inc	314-344-4500	Earth City, MO	350	500	3
British Columbia Railway Co	604-986-2012	Vancouver, BC Can	298	1190	3
Burlington Northern Inc	817-878-2000	Fort Worth, TX	4701	6330	39
Canadian National Railway	514-399-5430	Montreal, PQ Can	3975	5870	44
Canadian Pacific Ltd	514-395-5151	Montreal, PQ Can	10214	15003	76
CNW Corp	312-559-7000	Chicago, IL	995	1727	10
Consolidated Rail Corp (CONRAIL)	215-977-4000	Philadelphia, PA	2689	1711	30
CSX Corp	804-782-1400	Richmond, VA	7592	13026	54
Florida East Coast Industries Inc	904-829-3421	St Augustine, FL	151	561	2
Grand Trunk Corp	313-962-2260	Detroit, MI	400	500	4
Kansas City Southern Industries Inc	816-556-0303	Kansas City, MO	507	979	5
Missouri Kansas Texas Railroad Co	214-651-6706	Dallas, TX	300	500	3
Norfolk Southern Corp	804-629-2600	Norfolk, VA	4462	10159	34
Santa Fe Southern Pacific Corp	312-786-6000	Chicago, IL	3144	6824	26
Union Pacific Corp	212-418-7800	New York, NY	7000	11000	30
Union Pacific Railroad Corp	402-271-5000	Omaha, NE	NA	NA	NA
Via Rail Canada Inc	514-286-2311	Montreal, PQ Can	670	910	7

Industry: Railroad   **Number: 17**

Major Group: Business Service   **Industry: Real Estate/Bldg**

Organization	Phone	City / State or Province	Revenue ($ mil)	Assets ($ mil)	Emp (thous)
Agropur Coop Agro Alimentaire Ltd	514-332-2220	Montreal, PQ Can	695	198	2
Alberici, J S Construction Co Inc	314-261-2611	St Louis, MO	500	NA	2
American Breco Inc	213-553-1009	Los Angeles, CA	750	NA	5
Atkinson, Guy F Co of California	415-876-1000	S San Francisco, CA	920	305	8
Austin Industries Inc	214-630-5100	Dallas, TX	500	NA	5
Baird & Warner Inc	312-368-1855	Chicago, IL	550	NA	2
Banister Continental Corp	403-462-9430	Edmonton, AB Can	311	213	1
Barton Malow Co	313-351-4000	Southfield, MI	500	NA	3
BCE Development Ltd	416-369-2300	Toronto, ON Can	730	2290	5

Major Group: Business Service   Industry: Real Estate/Bldg

Organizations Listed by Industry

Organization	Phone	City / State or Province	Revenue ($ mil)	Assets ($ mil)	Emp (thous)
Beazley, William Co Inc	203-562-9801	New Haven, CT	550	NA	5
Bechtel Group Inc	415-768-1234	San Francisco, CA	4500	NA	20
Binswanger Co Inc	215-448-6000	Philadelphia, PA	550	NA	1
Bramalea Ltd	416-487-3861	Toronto, ON Can	685	3506	3
Brown & Root Inc	713-676-3011	Houston, TX	500	NA	2
Cadillac Fairview Corp	416-598-8200	Toronto, ON Can	579	3521	4
Campeau Corp	416-868-6460	Toronto, ON Can	7368	12151	110
Canada Trust Realtors Ltd	416-361-8657	Toronto, ON Can	213	NA	4
Cardinal Industries Inc	614-861-3211	Columbus, OH	550	NA	5
CC Industries Inc	312-236-6300	Chicago, IL	500	NA	5
Century 21 Canada Ltd	604-273-2721	Richmond, BC Can	255	NA	6
Chase Enterprises Inc	203-549-1674	Hartford, CT	500	NA	5
Clark Construction Enterprises Inc	301-657-7100	Bethesda, MD	1000	NA	4
Coldwell Banker & Co	213-402-5022	Los Angeles, CA	144	NA	NA
Comstock Group Inc	203-792-9800	Danbury, CT	368	NA	5
Cooke, Jack Kent Corp	703-687-4000	Middleburg, VA	500	NA	1
Coscan Development Corp	416-369-8200	Toronto, ON Can	291	656	1
Crown American Corp	814-536-4441	Johnstown, PA	750	NA	10
Dillingham Corp	415-362-1501	San Francisco, CA	1500	NA	5
Durwood Inc	816-221-4000	Kansas City, MO	880	NA	8
Ellis Don Ltd	519-455-6770	London, ON Can	643	196	3
Fairfield Communities Inc	501-664-6000	Little Rock, AR	329	644	2
Fine Homes International L P Inc	203-356-1400	Stamford, CT	800	730	6
First Union Real Estate Inc	216-781-4030	Cleveland, OH	74	439	1
Fischbach Corp	212-986-4100	New York, NY	1375	500	16
Flour Corp	714-975-2000	Irvine, CA	5132	2073	18
Ford Motor Land Development Corp	313-322-3000	Dearborn, MI	NA	NA	NA
Forest City Enterprises Inc	216-267-1200	Cleveland, OH	300	200	3
Foster Wheeler Corp	201-730-4000	Clinton, NJ	1090	1109	18
Fox & Lazo Inc	609-424-2800	Haddonfield, NJ	935	NA	2
Fuller, George A Co Inc	212-355-2700	New York, NY	1100	NA	2
General Development Corp	305-350-1200	Miami, FL	500	600	2
General Homes Corp	713-270-4177	Houston, TX	263	438	2
Gilbane Building Co	401-456-5800	Providence, RI	1000	NA	1
Gilbert Associates Inc	215-775-2600	Reading, PA	265	200	4
Grubb & Ellis Co	415-956-1990	San Francisco, CA	250	300	3
Harbert Corp	205-987-5500	Birmingham, AL	500	NA	1
HBE Corp	314-567-9000	St Louis, MO	275	NA	2
HCB Contractors Inc	214-747-8541	Dallas, TX	750	NA	1
Helmsley Spear Co	212-687-6400	New York, NY	1800	NA	12
Hendrick Management Corp	704-529-0578	Charlotte, NC	500	NA	1
Hercules Construction Co	314-991-3730	St Louis, MO	NA	NA	NA
Hillsborough Holdings (Walter, Jim Corp)	813-871-4811	Tampa, FL	2500	3000	20
Hovnanian Enterprises Inc	201-747-7800	Red Bank, NJ	301	318	2
Hunt Corp	317-241-6301	Indianapolis, IN	1000	NA	3
Inland Real Estate Corp	312-218-8000	Oak Brook, IL	500	NA	2
Irvine Corp	714-720-2000	Newport Beach, CA	600	NA	1
Jacobs Engineering Group Inc	818-449-2171	Pasadena, CA	800	600	6
Kaiser Engineers Inc	415-268-6000	Oakland, CA	550	NA	2
Kaufman & Broad Inc	213-312-5000	Los Angeles, CA	903	603	3
Kiewit, Peter & Sons Inc	402-342-2052	Omaha, NE	4800	NA	30
Koenig & Strey Inc	312-729-6610	Glenview, IL	550	NA	1
Koll Co Inc	714-833-3030	Newport Beach, CA	500	NA	1
Landmark Land Co Inc	408-625-4060	Carmel, CA	500	2500	2
Lavalin Inc	514-288-1740	Montreal, PQ Can	870	451	6

Major Group: Business Service　　　　**Industry: Real Estate/Bldg**

Organizations Listed by Industry

Organization	Phone	City / State or Province	Revenue ($ mil)	Assets ($ mil)	Emp (thous)
LeFrak Organization	718-459-9021	Rego Park, NY	2750	NA	20
Lennar Corp	305-559-4000	Miami, FL	350	150	1
Lewis Homes Corp	714-985-0971	Upland, CA	500	NA	1
Lincoln Property Co	214-740-3300	Dallas, TX	1500	NA	5
Lundrigans Group Ltd	709-637-1200	Corner Brook, NF Can	289	118	3
Lusk Co	714-261-5999	Irvine, CA	400	NA	1
Lyon, William Co Inc	714-833-3600	Newport Beach, CA	750	NA	1
Marathon Realty Co	416-864-1960	Toronto, ON Can	298	1700	1
Mason McDuffie Real Estate Inc	415-254-5640	Orinda, CA	550	NA	1
Maxxam Inc	213-474-6264	Los Angeles, CA	519	250	1
McCarthy Brothers Co	314-968-3300	St Louis, MO	1000	NA	5
McDevitt & Street Co Inc	704-525-8110	Charlotte, NC	1000	NA	2
Mellon Stuart Holding Co Inc	412-323-4600	Pittsburgh, PA	750	NA	1
Mission Viejo Realty Group Inc	714-837-6050	Mission Viejo, CA	NA	NA	NA
MMR Holding Corp	504-293-2701	Baton Rouge, LA	250	200	4
Morris Affiliated Companies	417-887-0333	Springfield, MO	400	NA	2
Mortenson, M A Co Inc	612-522-2100	Minneapolis, MN	500	NA	1
National Real Estate Service Ltd	604-685-3474	Vancouver, BC Can	170	NA	4
New England Tile Corp	617-826-5144	Hanover, MA	550	NA	2
New Plan Realty Inc	212-869-3000	New York, NY	245	300	1
NPS Group Inc	201-865-6550	Secaucus, NJ	550	NA	5
NVR Limited Partnership Inc	703-761-2000	McLean, VA	1000	500	4
Oceanic Properties Inc	808-548-4811	Honolulu, HI	NA	NA	NA
Oxford Development Co Inc	301-654-3100	Bethesda, MD	550	NA	5
Pacific Scene Inc	619-299-5100	San Diego, CA	550	NA	1
Pamplin, R B Corp	503-248-1133	Portland, OR	500	NA	5
Paragon Group Inc	214-891-2000	Dallas, TX	750	NA	2
PCL Construction Group Ltd	403-435-9711	Edmonton, AB Can	1071	308	4
Pepper Companies	312-266-4703	Chicago, IL	500	NA	1
Perini Corp	508-875-6171	Framingham, MA	849	374	3
Peters, J M Co	714-833-9331	Newport Beach, CA	300	250	1
Phelps Co Inc	303-353-7000	Greeley, CO	600	NA	3
PHM (Pulte Home) Corp	313-661-1500	West Bloomfield, MI	834	590	2
Raymond International Inc	713-623-1500	Houston, TX	1100	NA	2
Re Max Ltd	416-542-2400	Mississauga, ON Can	425	NA	7
Rockefeller Group Inc	212-698-8676	New York, NY	1000	NA	5
Royal LePage Real Estate Ltd	416-862-0611	Toronto, ON Can	554	405	8
Ryan Homes Inc	412-276-8000	Pittsburgh, PA	750	NA	1
Ryland Group Inc	301-730-7222	Columbia, MD	881	458	3
Schlott, Richard Realty Inc	201-633-5000	Wayne, NJ	3300	NA	4
Schneider Inc	412-257-6000	Bridgeville, PA	550	NA	11
Shurfine Central Corp	312-681-2000	Northlake, IL	825	NA	2
Slattery Group Inc	516-484-5858	Roslyn, NY	240	200	2
Southmark Corp	214-241-8787	Dallas, TX	2838	9161	33
Spanos, A G Construction Inc	209-478-7954	Stockton, CA	715	NA	2
Standard Pacific Corp	714-546-1161	Costa Mesa, CA	450	200	1
Steuart Investment Co Inc	202-537-8940	Washington, DC	550	NA	1
Sverdrup Corp	314-436-7600	St Louis, MO	400	NA	4
Swinerton & Walberg Inc	415-421-2980	San Francisco, CA	550	NA	5
Taubman Co Inc	313-258-6800	Bloomfield Hills, MI	3000	NA	1
Taubman Investment Co	313-258-7600	Bloomfield Hills, MI	1000	NA	10
TDC Development Corp	213-433-9931	Long Beach, CA	1100	NA	2
Tishman Realty Corp	212-957-5400	New York, NY	750	NA	1

Major Group: Business Service   Industry: Real Estate/Bldg

Organizations Listed by Industry

Organization	Phone	City / State or Province	Revenue ($ mil)	Assets ($ mil)	Emp (thous)
Toll Brothers Corp	215-441-4400	Horsham, PA	200	256	2
Trammell Crow Corp	214-742-2000	Dallas, TX	1500	NA	6
Tridel Enterprises Inc	416-661-9290	Downsview, ON Can	340	595	2
Trizec Corp	403-269-8241	Calgary, AB Can	1014	7325	6
Trump Organization Inc	212-832-2000	New York, NY	1000	NA	10
Tucson Realty & Trust Inc	602-577-7000	Tucson, AZ	550	NA	1
Turner Corp	212-878-0400	New York, NY	3196	920	10
Turner Development Corp	813-963-0786	Tampa, FL	NA	NA	NA
UDC Universal Development Corp	312-726-1885	Chicago, IL	400	200	1
Unicorp American Corp	212-972-6100	New York, NY	266	250	1
US Home Corp	713-877-2311	Houston, TX	736	943	2
Vantage Companies Inc	214-631-0600	Dallas, TX	550	NA	2
Walbridge, Aldinger & Co Inc	313-591-6000	Livonia, MI	500	NA	1
Webb, Del E Corp	602-468-6800	Phoenix, AZ	350	300	4
Wimpey, George Canada Ltd	416-233-5811	Toronto, ON Can	340	213	1
Zachry, H B Co Inc	512-922-1213	San Antonio, TX	500	NA	5

Industry: Real Estate/Bldg   Number: 135

Major Group: Business Service   Industry: Business Service

Organization	Phone	City / State or Province	Revenue ($ mil)	Assets ($ mil)	Emp (thous)
AAR	312-439-3939	Elk Grove, IL	384	329	4
Adia Services Inc	415-324-0696	Menlo Park, CA	400	200	3
Advo System Inc	203-285-6100	Windsor, CT	500	300	6
Agency Rent-A-Car Inc	216-349-1000	Solon, OH	227	351	3
Alexander & Baldwin Inc	808-525-6611	Honolulu, HI	702	1070	3
Alza Corp	415-494-5222	Palo Alto, CA	84	262	1
AM International Inc	312-558-1966	Chicago, IL	821	777	8
Amerco (U-Haul) Inc	602-263-6011	Phoenix, AZ	750	NA	15
American Building Maintenance Ind Inc	415-864-5150	San Francisco, CA	582	172	32
American Water Works Co Inc	609-346-8200	Voorhees, NJ	512	1737	4
Amfac Inc	415-772-3400	San Francisco, CA	2200	1400	19
Amgen Corp	805-499-5725	Thousand Oaks, CA	78	207	1
AMI American Medical International Inc	213-278-6200	Beverly Hills, CA	3111	832	46
ARA Holding Co	215-238-3000	Philadelphia, PA	4000	1500	110
Armor All Products Corp	714-533-1003	Irvine, CA	163	150	1
Ask Mr Foster Travel Inc	818-988-0181	Van Nuys, CA	550	NA	2
Asplundh Tree Experts Inc	215-784-4200	Willow Grove, PA	500	NA	6
Audits & Surveys Inc	212-627-9700	New York, NY	275	NA	4
Avnet Inc	516-466-7000	Great Neck, NY	1817	1153	11
Ayer, N W Inc	212-708-5000	New York, NY	1100	NA	2
Banta, George Corp	414-722-7777	Menasha, WI	300	200	3
Bates, Ted Worldwide Inc	212-297-7000	New York, NY	450	NA	5
Bearings Inc	216-881-2838	Cleveland, OH	543	223	4
Beverly Enterprises Inc	818-793-2911	Pasadena, CA	2025	1845	106
Blair, John & Co	212-603-5000	New York, NY	750	NA	7
Block, H & R Inc	816-753-6900	Kansas City, MO	794	677	4
Boise Cascade Office Products Corp	312-773-6400	Itasca, IL	NA	NA	NA
Bozell Jacobs Kenyon Inc	212-727-5000	New York, NY	1650	NA	4
Browning Ferris Industries Inc	713-870-8100	Houston, TX	2067	1872	20
Burnett, Leo Co Inc	312-565-5959	Chicago, IL	2200	NA	4
Cantrex Group Inc	514-335-0260	Montreal, PQ Can	425	213	2
Carlson Marketing Group Ltd	416-236-1991	Toronto, ON Can	255	85	1
CDI Corp	215-561-1750	Philadelphia, PA	734	NA	8
Centex Corp	214-559-6500	Dallas, TX	1460	1039	5

Major Group: Business Service   Industry: Business Service

Organizations Listed by Industry

Organization	Phone	City / State or Province	Revenue ($ mil)	Assets ($ mil)	Emp (thous)
Centocor Inc	215-296-4488	Malvern, PA	60	153	1
Cetus Corp	415-420-3300	Emeryville, CA	45	274	1
Charter Medical Corp	912-742-1161	Macon, GA	1200	NA	12
Chem-Nuclear Systems Inc	803-256-0450	Columbia, SC	NA	NA	NA
Chemical Waste Corp	312-572-8800	Oak Brook, IL	700	876	6
Comdisco Inc	312-698-3000	Rosemont, IL	1309	3488	2
Crawford & Co	404-256-0830	Atlanta, GA	300	200	5
D'Arcy Masius Benton & Bowles Inc	212-758-6200	New York, NY	2750	NA	7
Deluxe Check Printers Inc	612-483-7111	St Paul, MN	1196	786	17
Donnelley, R R & Sons Co	312-326-8000	Chicago, IL	2878	2346	21
Elrick & Lavidge Inc	312-726-0666	Chicago, IL	825	NA	8
Federal Express Corp	901-369-3600	Memphis, TN	3883	3009	49
Fleming Companies Inc	405-840-7200	Oklahoma City, OK	10467	2559	25
Flightsafety International Inc	718-565-4100	Flushing, NY	183	451	2
Foote, Cone & Belding Inc	312-751-7000	Chicago, IL	520	350	4
Foster, L B Co	201-533-1100	Pittsburgh, PA	262	107	1
GATX Corp	312-621-6200	Chicago, IL	587	2605	2
Gelco Corp	612-828-1000	Eden Prairie, MN	1000	2500	7
General Aviation Services Co	214-406-2000	Dallas, TX	NA	NA	NA
Genetech Corp	415-952-1000	S San Francisco, CA	262	669	2
Genetics Institute Inc	617-876-1170	Cambridge, MA	30	197	1
Geneva Management Inc	703-522-2300	Arlington, VA	550	NA	1
Genuine Parts Co	404-953-1700	Atlanta, GA	2942	1141	15
Grainger, W W Inc	312-982-9000	Skokie, IL	1535	936	7
Graphic Industries Inc	404-874-3327	Atlanta, GA	270	200	2
Greyhound Corp	602-248-4000	Phoenix, AZ	3305	5034	37
Handleman Co	313-362-4400	Troy, MI	532	284	3
Harland, John H Co Inc	404-981-9460	Decatur, GA	333	295	6
Henley Group Inc	603-926-5911	Hampton, NH	1036	4503	2
Horsehead Industries Inc	212-972-2100	New York, NY	750	NA	3
IMS International Inc	212-371-2310	New York, NY	500	400	6
Inspiration Resources Corp	212-503-3100	New York, NY	1436	842	6
International Lease Finance Corp	213-658-7871	Beverly Hills, CA	213	1765	1
International Technology Corp	213-378-9933	Torrance, CA	265	300	2
Interpublic Group of Companies Inc	212-399-8000	New York, NY	1192	1601	14
ISS International Service Corp	212-382-9800	New York, NY	250	150	4
IU International Corp	302-571-5000	Philadelphia, PA	1500	900	15
JWP Corp	914-935-4000	Purchase, NY	350	250	3
K & E Holding Inc	212-880-2000	New York, NY	275	NA	3
Kelly Services Corp	313-362-4444	Troy, MI	1269	326	5
Kinder Care Centers Inc	205-277-5090	Montgomery, AL	936	6087	15
Krueger, W A Co	602-948-5650	Scottsdale, AZ	400	300	3
Laidlaw Industries Inc	312-439-6686	Hinsdale, IL	1200	600	5
Marley Co Inc	913-362-5440	Mission Woods, KS	500	NA	5
McJunkin Corp	304-348-5211	Charleston, WV	400	NA	1
McKesson Corp	415-983-8300	San Francisco, CA	7283	2255	17
Mentor Graphics Corp	503-626-7000	Beaverton, OR	301	282	2
Metromail Inc	402-475-4591	Lincoln, NE	NA	NA	NA
Mills, Olan Inc	615-622-5141	Chattanooga, TN	1100	NA	11
Mitre Corp	617-271-2000	Bedford, MA	550	NA	5
Morrison Knudsen Corp	208-386-5000	Boise, ID	1909	746	15
Morse Diesel Inc	212-730-4000	New York, NY	825	NA	6
National Cleaning Contractors Inc	212-689-4050	New York, NY	500	NA	10
National Education Corp	714-474-9400	Irvine, CA	400	200	4
Needham Worldwide Advertising Inc	212-415-2000	New York, NY	1100	NA	2

Major Group: Business Service   Industry: Business Service

Organizations Listed by Industry

Organization	Phone	City / State or Province	Revenue ($ mil)	Assets ($ mil)	Emp (thous)
Ogilvy Group Inc	212-907-3400	New York, NY	575	639	2
Olsten Corp	516-832-8200	Westbury, NY	400	150	2
Omnicom Group Inc	212-415-2000	New York, NY	881	1135	3
Overseas Shipholding Group Inc	212-869-1222	New York, NY	333	1318	2
Pan Am World Services Inc	305-784-7100	Cape Canaveral, FL	NA	NA	NA
Parsons Corp	818-440-2000	Pasadena, CA	1000	NA	10
Pechiney World Trade Inc	203-622-8300	Greenwich, CT	1100	NA	1
Penske, Roger Corp	201-428-7500	Parsippany, NJ	2000	NA	10
PHH Group Inc	301-771-3600	Hunt Valley, MD	1735	4231	5
Policy Management Systems Inc	803-735-4000	Blythewood, SC	217	301	2
Premier Industrial Corp	216-391-8300	Cleveland, OH	566	263	4
Regis Corp	612-929-6776	Minneapolis, MN	550	NA	5
Rent-a-Center Inc	316-689-4100	Wichita, KS	250	200	2
Reynolds & Reynolds Corp	513-443-2000	Dayton, OH	600	399	5
Rollins Environmental Services Inc	302-429-2700	Wilmington, DE	206	214	2
Rollins Inc	404-888-2000	Atlanta, GA	380	147	5
Ryder System Inc	305-593-3726	Miami, FL	5030	6039	45
Saatchi, Saatchi Co	212-661-0800	New York, NY	1500	NA	2
Safecard Services Inc	305-491-2111	Fort Lauderdale, FL	125	222	2
Safety Kleen Corp	312-697-8460	Elgin, IL	417	399	4
Service Corp International	713-522-5141	Houston, TX	616	1667	7
Service Master Industries Inc	312-964-1300	Downers Grove, IL	1531	484	17
SNC Group Inc	514-866-1000	Montreal, PQ Can	375	305	4
SYSCO Corp	713-877-1122	Houston, TX	4385	1021	13
TBWA Advertising Inc	212-725-1150	New York, NY	550	NA	1
Thompson, J Walter Group Inc	212-210-7000	New York, NY	500	NA	5
Tiger International Inc	213-522-6300	Los Angeles, CA	1300	1100	8
Total System Services Corp	404-649-2204	Columbus, GA	56	45	1
TRW Electronic Products Inc	303-475-0660	Colorado Springs, CO	NA	NA	NA
United Parcel Service Inc	203-622-6000	Greenwich, CT	10000	NA	175
Vitt Media International Inc	212-921-0500	New York, NY	250	NA	1
Wackenhut Corp	305-666-5656	Coral Gables, FL	401	150	7
Waste Management Inc	312-654-8800	Oak Brook, IL	3566	4879	35
Wells Rich Greene Inc	212-303-5000	New York, NY	550	NA	2
Wetterau Inc	314-524-5000	Hazelwood, MO	4156	799	14
Wheelabrator Technologies Inc	508-777-2207	Danvers, MA	1205	1221	10
Woodside Management Inc	617-426-7661	Boston, MA	250	NA	3
Young & Rubicam Inc	212-210-3000	New York, NY	750	NA	10

Industry: Business Service   Number: 127

Major Group: Business Service   Industry: Transport

Organization	Phone	City / State or Province	Revenue ($ mil)	Assets ($ mil)	Emp (thous)
ACI Holdings Inc	714-752-8576	Newport Beach, CA	500	250	3
Air Express International	203-655-7900	Darien, CT	500	200	3
Airborne Freight Corp	206-285-4600	Seattle, WA	768	329	7
Allied Van Lines Inc	312-681-8000	Broadview, IL	600	200	5
American Carriers Inc	913-451-2811	Overland Park, KS	475	250	5
American President Companies Ltd	415-272-8000	Oakland, CA	2131	1711	5
American President Trucking Co	415-272-8000	Oakland, CA	NA	NA	NA
Arkansas Best Corp	501-785-6000	Fort Smith, AR	750	400	8
Automotive Carrier Div	313-258-2000	Bloomfield Hills, MI	NA	NA	NA
Brink's Inc	203-655-8781	Darien, CT	NA	NA	NA
Canadian Pacific Express Ltd	416-498-8850	Toronto, ON Can	383	213	3
Carolina Freight Corp	704-435-6811	Cherryville, NC	651	347	10

Major Group: Business Service   Industry: Transport

Organizations Listed by Industry

Organization	Phone	City / State or Province	Revenue ($ mil)	Assets ($ mil)	Emp (thous)
CF AirFreight Inc	415-855-9100	Palo Alto, CA	NA	NA	NA
Chemical Leaman Corp	215-363-4200	Exton, PA	250	150	2
Colonial Pipeline Co Inc	404-261-1470	Atlanta, GA	550	NA	1
Consolidated Freightways Inc	415-494-2900	Palo Alto, CA	2689	1536	29
Crowley Maritime Corp	415-546-2500	San Francisco, CA	1000	NA	5
CSL Group Inc	514-288-0221	Montreal, PQ Can	349	207	5
DHL Airways/Worldwide Express Inc	415-593-7474	Redwood City, CA	1500	NA	15
Emery Air Freight Corp	203-762-8601	Wilton, CT	1223	733	17
Fednav Ltd	514-878-6500	Montreal, PQ Can	340	595	1
HAL (Hawaiian Air) Inc	808-525-5511	Honolulu, HI	354	167	3
Harper Group Inc	415-978-0600	San Francisco, CA	283	250	2
Hunt, J B Transportion Services Inc	501-659-8800	Lowell, AR	393	301	3
Illinois Central Gulf Railroad Co	312-565-1600	Chicago, IL	750	1500	5
International Shipholding Corp	504-529-5461	New Orleans, LA	300	200	1
Laidlaw Transportation Ltd	416-336-1800	Burlington, ON Can	1006	1391	15
Leaseway Transportation Corp	216-464-3300	Beachwood, OH	1500	1100	20
Lykes Brothers Steamship Co Inc	504-523-6611	New Orleans, LA	550	NA	2
Mayflower Group Inc	317-875-1000	Carmel, IN	750	NA	2
McLean Industries Inc	212-593-3325	New York, NY	1000	1500	8
North American Van Lines Inc	219-429-2511	Fort Wayne, IN	NA	NA	NA
Northwest Pipeline Corp	801-584-7308	Salt Lake City, UT	NA	NA	NA
Overnite Transportation Co	824-231-8000	Richmond, VA	550	450	8
PIE Nationwide Trucking Corp	904-798-2000	Jacksonville, FL	750	NA	7
Preston Corp	301-673-7151	Preston, MD	594	338	8
RLC Corp	302-429-2700	Wilmington, DE	450	400	3
Roadway Services Inc	216-384-8184	Akron, OH	2185	1193	27
Santa Fe Pacific Pipelines Inc	213-614-1095	Los Angeles, CA	NA	NA	NA
Schneider National Inc	414-497-2201	Green Bay, WI	500	NA	5
Sea Land Corp	201-632-2000	Edison, NJ	2000	NA	10
Smith International Inc	713-443-3370	Houston, TX	250	200	2
Soo Line Corp	612-347-8000	Minneapolis, MN	570	905	5
Southern Pacific Transport Corp	415-541-1000	San Francisco, CA	2412	4709	23
Stingray Pipeline Co	713-627-5400	Houston, TX	NA	NA	NA
Stolt Tankers & Terminals Inc	203-625-9400	Greenwich, CT	400	500	1
Sun Carriers Inc	215-891-7100	Media, PA	750	600	9
TIC United Corp	214-559-0580	Dallas, TX	275	NA	2
Trailer Train Corp	312-853-3223	Chicago, IL	515	1268	1
Trailways Inc	214-744-6500	Dallas, TX	275	NA	3
Transcon Inc	714-385-1591	Orange, CA	322	114	4
Trimac Ltd	403-298-5100	Calgary, AB Can	288	NA	3
United Van Lines (Unigroup) Inc	314-326-3100	Fenton, MO	750	250	3
XTRA Corp	617-367-5000	Boston, MA	250	300	2
Yellow Freight System Inc	913-345-1020	Overland Park, KS	2016	1021	28

Industry: Transport   **Number: 55**

Major Group: Business Service   **Industry: Accounting**

Organization	Phone	City / State or Province	Revenue ($ mil)	Assets ($ mil)	Emp (thous)
Arthur, Andersen & Co Inc	312-580-0069	Chicago, IL	3000	NA	30
Arthur, Young & Co Inc	212-407-1500	New York, NY	2000	NA	25
Clarkson Gordon Ltd	416-864-1234	Toronto, ON Can	191	NM	3
Collins, Barrow, Maheu, Noiseux Ltd	403-298-1500	Calgary, AB Can	85	NM	1
Coopers & Lybrand Inc	212-536-2000	New York, NY	2500	NA	30
Coopers & Lybrand Ltd	416-869-1130	Toronto, ON Can	170	NM	3
Deloitte Haskins & Sells Ltd	416-861-9700	Toronto, ON Can	170	NM	3

Major Group: Business Service   Industry: Accounting

Organizations Listed by Industry

Organization	Phone	City / State or Province	Revenue ($ mil)	Assets ($ mil)	Emp (thous)
Deloitte, Haskins & Sells Inc	212-790-0500	New York, NY	2000	NA	25
Doane Raymond Associates Ltd	902-421-1734	Halifax, NS Can	128	NM	2
Ernst & Whinney Inc	216-861-5000	Cleveland, OH	2000	NA	30
Grant Thornton Inc	312-856-0001	Chicago, IL	250	NA	3
Leventhal, Kenneth Inc	213-277-0880	Los Angeles, CA	400	NA	5
Peat Marwick Main & Co	212-758-9700	New York, NY	4000	NA	30
Peat Marwick Main & Co	416-863-3300	Toronto, ON Can	128	NM	2
Price Waterhouse & Co Inc	212-489-8900	New York, NY	2250	NA	25
Price Waterhouse Ltd	416-863-1133	Toronto, ON Can	170	NM	2
Thorne Ernst & Whinney Ltd	416-864-9520	Toronto, ON Can	213	NM	4
Touche Ross & Co	212-489-1600	New York, NY	1750	NA	20
Touche Ross Ltd	416-599-5399	Toronto, ON Can	170	NM	3
Ward Marlette Ltd	416-340-8390	Toronto, ON Can	106	NM	2

Industry: Accounting　　　**Number: 20**

Major Group: Business Service　　　**Industry: Consulting**

Organization	Phone	City / State or Province	Revenue ($ mil)	Assets ($ mil)	Emp (thous)
Bain & Co	617-572-2000	Boston, MA	400	NA	3
Battelle Memorial Institute Inc	614-424-6424	Columbus, OH	700	NA	10
BDM International Inc	703-821-5000	McLean, VA	275	NA	4
Bell Laboratories of AT&T	201-582-3000	Murray Hill, NJ	2000	NA	20
Black & Veatch Inc	913-339-2000	Kansas City, MO	275	NA	3
Booz, Allen & Hamilton Inc	212-697-1900	New York, NY	500	NA	4
Boston Consulting Group Inc	617-973-1200	Boston, MA	300	NA	3
CRS Sirrine Inc	713-552-2000	Houston, TX	478	186	3
Day & Zimmermann Inc	215-299-8000	Philadelphia, PA	500	NA	6
DSC Communications Corp	214-519-3000	Plano, TX	340	429	3
Ebasco Services Inc	212-839-1000	New York, NY	900	NA	5
Epstein, A & Sons International Inc	312-454-9100	Chicago, IL	350	NA	1
Flow General Inc	703-893-5915	McLean, VA	250	200	2
Grey Advertising Inc	212-546-2000	New York, NY	450	150	3
Hay Group Inc	215-875-2300	Philadelphia, PA	300	NA	3
Kearney, A T Inc	312-648-0111	Chicago, IL	300	NA	3
Little, Arthur D & Co Inc	617-864-5770	Cambridge, MA	400	NA	3
Lockheed Engineering & Sciences Div	713-333-5411	Houston, TX	NA	NA	NA
LVI Group Inc	212-337-6600	New York, NY	474	220	2
McCann Erickson Worldwide	212-697-6000	New York, NY	250	NA	2
Mercer, William M Meidinger Inc	212-997-7171	New York, NY	300	NA	3
Planning Research Corp	703-556-1000	McLean, VA	654	547	7
Proudfoot, Alexander Inc	407-697-9600	West Palm Beach, FL	300	NA	3
Research Cottrell Inc	201-685-4000	Somerville, NJ	500	NA	2
Russell, Frank Co	206-572-9500	Tacoma, WA	165	NA	1
Sargent & Lundy Inc	312-269-2000	Chicago, IL	550	NA	5
Science Applications Intl Inc	619-454-3811	La Jolla, CA	750	NA	8
SRI International Inc	415-326-6200	Menlo Park, CA	300	NA	3
Stone & Webster Inc	212-290-7500	New York, NY	324	565	4
Strategic Planning Associates Inc	202-778-7000	Washington, DC	28	26	1
TAD Technical Services Inc	617-868-1650	Cambridge, MA	350	NA	3
Telecomm Plus International Inc	407-997-9999	Boca Raton, FL	300	NA	3
Temple, Barker & Sloane Inc	617-861-7580	Lexington, MA	275	NA	3
Towers, Perrin, Forster & Crosby Inc	212-309-3400	New York, NY	500	NA	5

Industry: Consulting　　　**Number: 34**

Major Group: Business Service　　　**Industry: Consulting**

Organizations Listed by Industry

Organization	Phone	City / State or Province	Revenue ($ mil)	Assets ($ mil)	Emp (thous)
Major Group: Utilities		**Industry: Utility**			
Alabama Power Co	205-250-1000	Birmingham, AL	NA	NA	NA
Alberta Power Ltd	403-420-5035	Edmonton, AB Can	340	1275	2
Allegheny Power System Inc	212-752-2121	New York, NY	2171	1031	6
American Electric Power Co Inc	614-223-1000	Columbus, OH	4841	2762	23
Arizona Public Service Co	602-250-1000	Phoenix, AZ	1442	5991	9
Arkansas Power & Light Co	501-371-4000	Little Rock, AR	1357	3928	5
Arkla Inc	318-226-2700	Shreveport, LA	1996	3249	6
Associated Electric Co-op Inc	417-881-1204	Springfield, MO	550	NA	2
Atlanta Gas Light Co	404-584-4000	Atlanta, GA	976	1221	4
Atlantic Energy Co	609-645-4100	Pleasantville, NJ	676	1660	2
Atmos Energy Corp	214-934-9227	Dallas, TX	323	600	2
Baltimore Gas & Electric Co	301-234-5000	Baltimore, MD	1864	5126	9
Bay State Gas Co	617-828-8650	Canton, MA	350	NA	2
Boston Edison Co	617-424-2000	Boston, MA	1203	2817	4
British Col Hydro & Power Authority Ltd	604-663-2212	Vancouver, BC Can	1689	8332	6
Brooklyn Union Gas Co	718-403-2000	Brooklyn, NY	899	1257	4
Cajun Electric Power Cooperative Inc	504-291-3060	Baton Rouge, LA	275	NA	1
Canadian Utilities Ltd	403-420-7121	Edmonton, AB Can	978	2231	1
Canadian Western Natural Gas Co	403-245-7110	Calgary, AB Can	255	340	1
Carolina Power & Light Co	919-836-6111	Raleigh, NC	2273	7504	10
Catalyst Energy Development Inc	212-949-0040	New York, NY	400	1200	1
Centerior Energy Corp	216-622-9800	Cleveland, OH	2038	11573	9
Central & South West Corp	214-754-1000	Dallas, TX	2512	8110	10
Central Hudson Gas & Electric Co	914-452-2000	Poughkeepsie, NY	438	1046	2
Central Illinois Light Co	309-672-5271	Peoria, IL	434	924	2
Central Illinois Public Service Co	217-523-3600	Springfield, IL	616	1678	3
Central Louisiana Electric Co	318-484-7400	Pineville, LA	920	NA	5
Central Maine Power Inc	207-623-3521	Augusta, ME	654	1211	3
Central Power & Light Co	512-881-5300	Corpus Christi, TX	812	3000	3
Cilcorp Inc	309-672-5271	Peoria, IL	471	1096	2
Cincinnati Gas & Electric Co	513-381-2000	Cincinnati, OH	1386	3361	5
Citizens Utilities Co	203-427-8953	Stamford, CT	302	1033	2
City Public Service Inc	512-227-3211	San Antonio, TX	1100	NA	5
Cleveland Electric Illuminating Co	216-447-3103	Cleveland, OH	NA	NA	NA
CMS Energy-Consumers Power Co	313-436-9261	Dearborn, MI	2943	8305	11
Columbia Gas System Inc	302-429-5000	Wilmington, DE	3128	5641	11
Columbus Southern Power Co	614-223-1000	Columbus, OH	778	2067	3
Commonwealth Edison Co	312-294-4321	Chicago, IL	5613	17822	18
Connecticut Light & Power Co	203-665-5123	Belden, CT	NA	NA	NA
Connecticut Natural Gas Co	203-727-3000	Hartford, CT	255	300	7
Consolidated Edison New York Inc	212-460-4600	New York, NY	5109	9552	19
Consolidated Natural Gas Co	412-227-1000	Pittsburgh, PA	2468	4109	8
Constellation Operating Services Inc	301-783-2827	Baltimore, MD	NA	NA	NA
Delmarva Power & Light Co	302-429-3011	Wilmington, DE	768	1915	3
Detroit Edison Co	313-237-8000	Detroit, MI	3102	10060	10
Diversified Energies Inc	612-372-4664	Minneapolis, MN	764	819	5
Dominion Resources Inc	804-755-5700	Richmond, VA	3344	9495	15
DPL (Dayton Power & Light) Corp	513-224-6000	Dayton, OH	1044	2338	4
Duke Power Co	704-373-4011	Charlotte, NC	3627	8891	21
Duquesne Light Co Inc	412-393-6000	Pittsburgh, PA	1063	3877	4
Eastern Enterprises Inc	617-647-2300	Weston, MA	672	1087	4
Eastern Utilities Associates Inc	617-357-9590	Boston, MA	374	1203	1

Major Group: Utilities   **Industry: Utility**

Organizations Listed by Industry

Organization	Phone	City / State or Province	Revenue ($ mil)	Assets ($ mil)	Emp (thous)
El Paso Electric Co Inc	915-543-5711	El Paso, TX	639	1975	3
El Paso Natural Gas Co	915-541-2600	El Paso, TX	1447	3279	3
Enron Corp	713-853-6161	Houston, TX	5708	8695	8
Enserch Corp	214-651-8700	Dallas, TX	2739	2970	19
Entergy Corp (Middle South Utilities)	504-529-5262	New Orleans, LA	3565	15942	15
Equitable Resources Co Inc	412-261-3000	Pittsburgh, PA	406	1069	2
Florida Power & Light Co	305-552-3552	Miami, FL	NA	NA	NA
Florida Progress Corp	813-895-1700	St Petersburg, FL	2002	4304	8
FPL (Florida Power & Light) Group Inc	407-694-6300	North Palm Beach, FL	5854	11793	19
Gaz Metropolitain Inc	514-598-3444	Montreal, PQ Can	808	1020	2
General Public Utilities Corp	201-263-6500	Parsippany, NJ	2834	6415	4
Georgia Power Co	404-526-6000	Atlanta, GA	NA	NA	NA
Gulf Power Co	904-444-6381	Pensacola, FL	NA	NA	NA
Gulf States Utilities Co	409-838-6631	Beaumont, TX	1415	6858	5
GW Utilities Ltd	416-363-3300	Toronto, ON Can	680	1020	4
Hawaiian Electric Industries Inc	808-543-5662	Honolulu, HI	732	2683	4
Houston Industries Inc	713-228-2474	Houston, TX	3649	10219	10
Houston Lighting & Power Co	713-229-7267	Houston, TX	500	NA	2
Hydro Quebec Ltd	514-289-2211	Montreal, PQ Can	4510	26998	19
ICG Utilities Ltd	416-491-1880	Toronto, ON Can	510	638	1
Idaho Power Co	208-383-2200	Boise, ID	412	1609	2
IE Industries Inc	319-398-4411	Cedar Rapids, IA	250	640	2
Illinois Power Co	217-424-6600	Decatur, IL	1285	6053	5
Indiana Energy Inc	317-926-3351	Indianapolis, IN	250	600	2
Indiana Michigan Power Co	219-425-2111	Fort Wayne, IN	983	3993	4
Inland Natural Gas Co	604-684-0484	Vancouver, BC Can	255	383	1
Interstate Power Co	319-582-5421	Dubuque, IA	274	540	2
Iowa Illinois Gas & Electric Inc	319-326-7111	Davenport, IA	496	1242	2
Iowa Public Service Co	712-277-7500	Sioux City, IA	600	1100	2
Iowa Resources (Iowa Power & Light) Inc	515-281-2900	Des Moines, IA	344	1168	2
Ipalco Enterprises Inc	317-261-8261	Indianapolis, IN	609	1752	2
Jersey Central Power & Light Co	201-455-8200	Morristown, NJ	NA	NA	NA
Kansas City Power & Light Co	816-556-2200	Kansas City, MO	737	2647	3
Kansas Gas & Electric Co	316-261-6611	Wichita, KS	526	2443	3
Kansas Power & Light Co	913-296-6300	Topeka, KS	1166	1777	5
Kentucky Power Co	606-327-1111	Ashland, KY	258	600	1
Kentucky Utilities Co	606-255-1461	Lexington, KY	560	1108	2
Laclede Gas Co	314-342-0500	St Louis, MO	450	800	2
Long Island Lighting Co	516-933-4590	Hicksville, NY	2138	8326	6
Louisiana Power & Light Co	504-366-2345	New Orleans, LA	1400	4500	3
Louisville Gas & Electric Co	502-566-4011	Louisville, KY	660	1763	5
Madison Gas & Electric Co	608-252-7000	Madison, WI	250	300	1
Manitoba Hydro Electric Board Ltd	204-474-3311	Winnipeg, MB Can	485	2754	4
MCN (Michigan Consolidated Natgas) Corp	313-965-2430	Detroit, MI	1750	2200	4
MDU Resources Group Inc	701-222-7900	Bismarck, ND	344	977	2
Memphis Light Gas & Water Inc	901-528-4151	Memphis, TN	1100	NA	5
Metropolitan Edison Co	215-929-3601	Reading, PA	656	1594	2
Midwest Energy Co	712-277-7400	Sioux City, IA	570	1092	2
Minnesota Power & Light Co	218-722-2641	Duluth, MN	460	1484	2
Mississippi Power & Light Co	601-949-6442	Jackson, MS	684	1555	2
Mississippi Power Co	601-864-1211	Gulfport, MS	NA	NA	NA
Monongahela Power Co	304-366-3000	Fairmont, WV	NA	NA	NA
Montana Power & Light Co	406-723-5421	Butte, MT	444	1926	4
Narragansett Electric Co	401-941-1400	Providence, RI	NA	NA	NA
National Fuel Gas Co	212-541-7533	New York, NY	769	1177	5

Major Group: Utilities   **Industry: Utility**

Organizations Listed by Industry

Organization	Phone	City / State or Province	Revenue ($ mil)	Assets ($ mil)	Emp (thous)
Natural Gas Corp of California	415-972-7000	San Francisco, CA	NA	NA	NA
Nevada Power Co	702-367-5000	Las Vegas, NV	409	1014	2
New Brunswick Elect Power Comm Ltd	506-458-4444	Fredericton, NB Can	737	2419	3
New Electric Transmission Corp	603-225-5528	Concord, NH	NA	NA	NA
New England Electric System Inc	508-366-9011	Westborough, MA	1461	3111	5
New Jersy Resources Inc	201-938-1480	Wall, NJ	350	700	2
New Orleans Public Service Co	504-595-3100	New Orleans, LA	NA	NA	NA
New York State Electric & Gas Inc	607-347-4131	Ithaca, NY	1340	4693	5
Newfoundland & Labrador Hydro Electric	709-737-1400	St Johns, NF Can	282	1857	1
Niagara Mohawk Power Corp	315-474-1511	Syracuse, NY	2801	7076	11
NICOR (Northern Illinois Gas) Corp	312-242-4470	Naperville, IL	1509	2100	4
NIPSCO Northern Indiana Pub Serv Co	219-853-5200	Hammond, IN	1526	3685	5
Northeast Utilities Inc	203-665-5000	Berlin, CT	2279	6765	9
Northern States Power Co	612-330-5500	Minneapolis, MN	2007	4496	8
Nova Scotia Power Corp	902-428-6221	Halifax, NS Can	411	1254	2
Ohio Edison Co	216-384-5100	Akron, OH	2143	7556	8
Ohio Power Co	216-456-8173	Canton, OH	1387	3494	8
Ohio Valley Transmission Corp	502-566-4011	Louisville, KY	NA	NA	NA
Oklahoma Gas & Electric Co	405-272-3000	Oklahoma City, OK	1098	2521	4
Oneok Inc	918-588-7000	Tulsa, OK	571	958	2
Ontario Hydro Corp	416-592-5111	Toronto, ON Can	4488	27758	32
Orange & Rockland Utilities Corp	914-352-6000	Pearl River, NY	486	922	2
Pacific Enterprises Corp	213-895-5000	Los Angeles, CA	5932	6866	13
Pacific Gas & Electric Co	415-781-4211	San Francisco, CA	7646	21068	27
Pacific Gas Transmission Co	415-781-0474	San Francisco, CA	NA	NA	NA
Pacificorp Corp	503-464-6000	Portland, OR	3519	11396	14
Panhandle Eastern Corp	713-664-3401	Houston, TX	1262	2973	3
Pennsylvania Electric Co	814-533-8111	Johnstown, PA	761	1760	4
Pennsylvania Power & Light Co	215-770-5151	Allentown, PA	2214	7525	8
Pennsylvania Power Co	412-652-5331	New Castle, PA	NA	NA	NA
Peoples Energy Corp	312-431-4000	Chicago, IL	1117	1408	3
Philadelphia Electric Co	215-841-4000	Philadelphia, PA	3229	11863	11
Pinnacle West Capital	602-222-6951	Phoenix, AZ	0	15054	17
Portland General Electric Co	503-226-8333	Portland, OR	762	2511	3
Potomac Edison Co	301-790-3400	Hagerstown, MD	NA	NA	NA
Potomac Electric Power Co	202-872-2456	Washington, DC	1350	4146	5
Primark Corp	703-790-7600	McLean, VA	108	259	1
PSI Public Service Co of Indiana	317-839-9611	Plainfield, IN	1043	2129	4
Public Service Co of Colorado	303-571-7511	Denver, CO	1685	2984	7
Public Service Co of New Hampshire	603-669-4000	Manchester, NH	603	2704	3
Public Service Co of New Mexico	505-848-2700	Albuquerque, NM	842	2393	4
Public Service Co of Oklahoma	918-599-2000	Tulsa, OK	604	1211	2
Public Service Enterprise Group Inc	201-430-7000	Newark, NJ	4395	11690	15
Puerto Rico Telephone Inc	809-782-8282	San Juan, PR	550	NA	5
Puget Sound Power & Light Co	206-454-6363	Bellevue, WA	783	2356	2
Questar Corp	801-534-5000	Salt Lake City, UT	486	1026	2
Rochester Gas & Electric Corp	716-546-2700	Rochester, NY	774	1823	3
Salt River Project Inc	602-236-5900	Phoenix, AZ	1100	NA	5
San Diego Gas & Electric Co	619-696-2000	San Diego, CA	2076	3533	4
Santa Fe Energy Corp	713-783-2401	Houston, TX	NA	NA	NA
Saskatchewan Power Corp	306-566-2121	Regina, SK Can	774	2733	3
Savannah Electric & Power Inc	912-238-2251	Savannah, GA	NA	NA	NA
SCANA (So Carolina Elec & Gas) Corp	803-748-3000	Columbia, SC	1083	2887	4
SCECORP Southern California Edison Co	818-302-1297	Rosemead, CA	6253	14866	17
Sierra Pacific Resources Co	702-689-3600	Reno, NV	408	1244	2

Major Group: Utilities   Industry: Utility

Organizations Listed by Industry

Organization	Phone	City / State or Province	Revenue ($ mil)	Assets ($ mil)	Emp (thous)
Sonat Inc	205-325-3800	Birmingham, AL	1392	3139	7
Southeastern Michigan Gas Corp	313-987-7900	Port Huron, MI	300	500	1
Southern California Gas Co	213-689-2345	Los Angeles, CA	5339	5027	28
Southern Co	404-393-0650	Atlanta, GA	7235	19729	31
Southern Indiana Gas & Electric Co	812-424-6411	Evansville, IN	290	450	1
Southern Natural Gas Co	205-325-7410	Birmingham, AL	1400	1700	2
Southern Union Co	214-748-8511	Dallas, TX	191	370	1
Southwest Gas Corp	702-876-7011	Las Vegas, NV	558	3679	2
Southwestern Electric Power	318-222-2141	Shreveport, LA	742	1889	2
Southwestern Public Service Co	806-378-2121	Amarillo, TX	794	1667	2
Superior Water, Light & Power Co	715-394-5511	Superior, WI	NA	NA	NA
TECO Energy (Tampa Elec) Inc	813-228-4111	Tampa, FL	1034	2315	4
Tennesse Valley Authority Inc	615-632-2101	Knoxville, TN	5322	25823	12
Texas Eastern Corp	713-759-3131	Houston, TX	3481	5444	8
Texas Utilities Co	214-653-4600	Dallas, TX	4154	16058	16
Texas Utilities Electric Co	214-812-1200	Dallas, TX	NA	NA	NA
TNP Texas New Mexico Power Co	817-731-0099	Fort Worth, TX	366	435	1
Toledo Edison Co	419-249-5000	Toledo, OH	628	4135	3
Toronto Hydro Ltd	416-595-6400	Toronto, ON Can	394	293	1
Trans Alta Utilities Corp	403-267-7110	Calgary, AB Can	818	3134	3
Trans Canada Pipelines Ltd	403-269-5611	Calgary, AB Can	2779	4270	2
Transco Energy Co	713-439-2000	Houston, TX	2774	3527	5
Transok Inc	918-583-1121	Tulsa, OK	NA	NA	NA
Tucson Electric Power Co	602-622-6661	Tucson, AZ	543	2840	2
UGI Corp	215-337-1000	King of Prussia, PA	425	350	2
Union Electric Co	314-621-3222	St Louis, MO	2029	5827	9
Union Enterprises Ltd	416-964-6300	Toronto, ON Can	1131	1275	6
Union Gas Ltd	519-352-3100	Chatham, ON Can	1148	1190	3
United Illuminating Co	203-787-7200	New Haven, CT	519	2365	2
Utah Power & Light Co	801-535-2000	Salt Lake City, UT	100	3125	5
Utilicorp United Inc	816-421-6600	Kansas City, MO	600	1200	3
Virginia Electric & Power Co	804-771-3193	Richmond, VA	NA	NA	NA
Washington Energy Co	206-622-6767	Seattle, WA	345	589	1
Washington Gas Co	703-750-4440	Washington, DC	698	923	3
Washington Water Power Co	509-489-0500	Spokane, WA	543	1378	1
West Texas Utilities Co	915-674-7000	Abilene, TX	302	737	2
Western Massachusetts Electric Co	413-785-5871	West Springfield, MA	NA	NA	NA
Wicor Inc	414-291-7026	Milwaukee, WI	850	650	6
Williams Companies Inc	918-588-2000	Tulsa, OK	1673	3567	8
Wisconsin Bell Telephone Co	414-549-7300	Milwaukee, WI	NA	NA	NA
Wisconsin Energy Co	414-277-2345	Milwaukee, WI	1541	2849	6
Wisconsin Gas Co Inc	414-291-7000	Milwaukee, WI	825	NA	3
Wisconsin Public Service Corp	414-433-1598	Green Bay, WI	604	843	3
WPL Holdings (Wisconsin Power Co)	608-252-3311	Madison, WI	601	1026	3

Industry: Utility   **Number: 206**

Major Group: Food Processing   **Industry: Beverage**

Organization	Phone	City / State or Province	Revenue ($ mil)	Assets ($ mil)	Emp (thous)
Alleco Inc	301-341-6000	Hyattsville, MD	1000	600	4
Anheuser Busch Companies Inc	314-577-2000	St Louis, MO	9705	7110	40
Brown Forman Inc	502-585-1100	Louisville, KY	1355	932	9
Carling O'Keefe Breweries Canada Ltd	416-675-3960	Rexdale, ON Can	468	425	4
Coca Cola Consolidated	704-551-4400	Charlotte, NC	328	150	2
Coca Cola Corp	404-676-2121	Atlanta, GA	8338	7450	40

Major Group: Food Processing   Industry: Beverage

Organizations Listed by Industry

Organization	Phone	City / State or Province	Revenue ($ mil)	Assets ($ mil)	Emp (thous)
Coca Cola Enterprises Inc	404-676-2100	Atlanta, GA	3874	4669	11
Coors, Aldolph Co	303-279-6565	Golden, CO	1522	1571	10
Dr Pepper/Seven Up Inc	214-824-0331	Dallas, TX	500	NA	1
General Cimema Corp	617-232-8200	Chestnut Hill, MA	2324	1898	26
General Cinema Beverages Inc	617-739-2950	Chestnut Hill, MA	NA	NA	NA
Heileman, G Brewing Co Inc	608-785-1000	LaCrosse, WI	1500	1200	7
Jim Beam Brands Inc	312-948-0395	Deerfeild, IL	NA	NA	NA
Johnson Coca Cola Bottling Inc	615-899-3449	Chattanooga, TN	750	NA	5
Miller Brewing Co	414-931-2000	Milwaukee, WI	NA	NA	NA
PepsiCo Inc	914-253-2000	Purchase, NY	13007	11135	235
Seagrams, Joseph E & Sons Inc	212-572-7000	New York, NY	3000	6000	10
Stroh Brewery Co	313-446-2000	Detroit, MI	2000	NA	10

Industry: Beverage   **Number: 18**

Major Group: Food Processing   **Industry: Food Processing**

Organization	Phone	City / State or Province	Revenue ($ mil)	Assets ($ mil)	Emp (thous)
ADM Milling Co	913-381-7400	Shawnee Mission, KS	NA	NA	NA
AG Processing Inc	402-334-8010	Omaha, NE	825	250	1
Alberta Wheat Pool Ltd	403-290-4910	Calgary, AB Can	788	1497	2
Amalgamated Sugar Co	801-399-3431	Ogden, UT	440	750	5
American Crystal Sugar Co	218-236-4400	Moorhead, MN	550	NA	2
American Grain Inc	515-223-3700	Des Moines, IA	2750	NA	1
American Maize Products Co	203-356-9000	Stamford, CT	548	420	3
Amstar Corp	212-489-9000	New York, NY	1250	1500	5
Andersons Inc	419-893-5050	Maumee, OH	600	NA	1
Archer Daniels Midland Co	217-424-5200	Decatur, IL	6798	4398	9
Armour Food Co	402-978-4000	Omaha, NE	NA	NA	NA
Associated Milk Producers Inc	512-340-9100	San Antonio, TX	3300	500	3
Aurora Eby Brown Co Inc	312-897-8674	Aurora, IL	550	NA	1
Austin Co Inc	615-638-4124	Greeneville, TN	550	NA	1
Bacardi Import Corp	809-795-1560	San Juan, PR	750	NA	2
Bartlett Agricultural Enterprises Inc	816-753-6300	Kansas City, MO	650	NA	2
Basic American Foods Inc	415-981-5590	San Francisco, CA	550	NA	5
BAT US Inc	502-581-8000	Louisville, KY	5500	NA	16
Beatrice Foods (BCI Holdings Inc)	312-782-3820	Chicago, IL	7500	5000	42
Becker Milk Co	416-698-2591	Scarborough, ON Can	340	170	3
Beef America Inc	402-397-2000	Omaha, NE	1000	NA	2
Best Foods Baking Group Inc	201-808-3000	Fairfield, NJ	NA	NA	NA
Borden Inc	212-573-4000	New York, NY	7244	4440	33
Bristol Meyers Canada Inc	416-362-4281	Toronto, ON Can	298	213	2
Bunge Corp	212-943-6600	New York, NY	5500	NA	3
Busch Agricultural Resources Inc	314-822-6565	St Louis, MO	NA	NA	NA
Calcot Ltd Inc	805-327-5961	Bakersfield, CA	1100	NA	2
California & Hawaiian Sugar Inc	415-356-6000	Concord, CA	825	250	3
California Almond Growers Inc	916-442-0771	Sacramento, CA	550	NA	3
Campbell Soup Co	609-342-4800	Camden, NJ	4869	3610	48
Campbell Soup Co Canada	416-251-1131	Toronto, ON Can	302	147	2
Campbell Taggert Inc	214-358-9211	Dallas, TX	NA	NA	NA
Canada Packers Inc	416-869-6049	Toronto, ON Can	2739	711	12
Cargill Inc	612-475-7575	Minnetonka, MN	40000	NA	45
Cargill Ltd	204-947-0141	Winnipeg, MB Can	947	274	1
Carlson Companies Inc	612-540-5000	Minneapolis, MN	4000	NA	50
Castle & Cooke Inc	213-824-1500	Los Angeles, CA	2469	1922	42
Central Soya Co	219-425-5100	Fort Wayne, IN	1650	500	3

Major Group: Food Processing   **Industry: Food Processing**

Organizations Listed by Industry

Organization	Phone	City / State or Province	Revenue ($ mil)	Assets ($ mil)	Emp (thous)
Chilewich Sons Inc	212-344-3400	New York, NY	1000	NA	1
Chiquita Brands Inc	513-784-8000	Cincinnati, OH	NA	NA	NA
Chock-Full-O-Nuts Corp	212-532-0300	New York, NY	200	200	3
Citrus Hill Manufacturing Co	513-983-1100	Cincinnati, OH	NA	NA	NA
Co-op Atlantic Ltd	506-858-6000	Moncton, NB Can	298	85	1
Co-operative Federee de Quebec Ltd	514-383-6450	Montreal, PQ Can	1057	235	5
Coca Cola Bottling Co of New York	203-625-4000	Greenwich, CT	500	NA	2
Coca Cola Bottling of Chicago Inc	312-775-0900	Chicago, IL	500	NA	2
Conagra Inc	402-978-4000	Omaha, NE	9475	3043	43
Connell Ltd (Avondale Foods) Ptr Inc	617-567-2600	East Boston, MA	1500	NA	5
Connell Rice & Sugar Inc	201-233-0700	Westfield, NJ	1100	NA	2
Consolidated Beef Industries Inc	414-437-4311	Green Bay, WI	500	NA	1
Consolidated Grain & Barge Co Inc	314-658-9200	St Louis, MO	550	NA	1
Continental Baking Co	314-982-1000	St Louis, MO	NA	NA	NA
Continental Grain Co	212-207-5100	New York, NY	13000	NA	12
CPC International Inc	201-894-4000	Englewood Cliffs, NJ	4701	3342	39
Culbro Corp	212-561-8700	New York, NY	942	396	5
Culinar Inc	514-288-3101	Montreal, PQ Can	441	189	5
Curtice Burns Inc	716-325-1020	Rochester, NY	695	377	6
Dairymen Inc	502-426-6455	Louisville, KY	2420	250	4
Darigold Inc	206-284-7220	Seattle, WA	825	NA	3
Dean Foods Co	312-678-1680	Franklin Park, IL	1552	499	7
DeKalb Corp	815-758-3461	DeKalb, IL	230	203	5
Del Monte Foods Corp	305-520-1000	Coral Gables, FL	NA	NA	NA
DiGiorgio Corp	415-765-0100	San Francisco, CA	1046	226	5
Dole Packaged Foods Inc	415-986-3000	San Francisco, CA	NA	NA	NA
Dominicks Finer Foods Inc	312-562-1000	Northlake, IL	2000	NA	10
Dubuque Packing Co Inc	402-397-2000	Omaha, NE	880	NA	3
El Paso Products Co Inc	915-333-7200	Dallas, TX	660	NA	2
Entree Corp	414-271-2768	Milwaukee, WI	396	200	5
Farm Fresh Inc	405-765-6656	Norfolk, VA	750	NA	5
Farmstead Foods Corp	507-377-4200	Albert Lea, MN	750	NA	3
FDL Foods Inc	319-588-5400	Dubuque, IA	825	NA	4
Finevest Services	203-629-8750	Greenwich, CT	2000	NA	12
Fleishman Kurth Malting Co	414-384-7400	Milwaukee, WI	NA	NA	NA
Flowers Industries Inc	912-226-9110	Thomasville, GA	737	434	9
Folger's Coffee Co	513-983-1100	Cincinnati, OH	NA	NA	NA
FPI Fishery Products International Ltd	709-570-0000	St Johns, NF Can	312	263	9
Friona Industries Inc	806-247-3991	Friona, TX	440	NA	1
Gainers Ltd	403-471-0611	Edmonton, AB Can	318	170	2
Gallo, Ernest & Julio Winery Inc	209-579-3111	Modesto, CA	1000	NA	5
General Foods Corp	914-335-2500	White Plains, NY	NA	NA	NA
General Foods Ltd	416-441-5000	Don Mills, ON Can	643	392	4
General Mills Inc	612-540-2311	Minneapolis, MN	5179	2672	74
Georgia Crown Distributing Corp	404-568-4580	Columbus, GA	500	NA	1
Gerber Products Co	616-928-2000	Fremont, MI	1068	697	15
Gillett Group Inc	615-292-0045	Nashville, TN	1250	NA	5
Godiva Chocolatier Inc	212-486-8750	New York, NY	NA	NA	NA
Gold Kist Inc	404-393-5000	Atlanta, GA	2200	650	11
Golden State Foods Corp	818-793-3135	Pasadena, CA	1000	NA	4
Granada Corp	713-783-1310	Houston, TX	825	NA	2
Group Olympia Ltd	514-771-0400	St Simon de Bagot, PQ Ca	357	170	1
Hartz Mountain Corp	201-481-4800	Harrison, NJ	1250	NA	5
Harvest States Cooperatives Inc	612-646-9433	St Paul, MN	3300	NA	2
Heinz, H J Co	412-456-5700	Pittsburgh, PA	5244	3605	39

Major Group: Food Processing   Industry: Food Processing

Organizations Listed by Industry

Organization	Phone	City / State or Province	Revenue ($ mil)	Assets ($ mil)	Emp (thous)
Heinz, H J Co of Canada	416-226-5757	Willowdale, ON Can	362	207	2
Hershey Foods Corp	717-534-4000	Hershey, PA	2168	1765	12
Hill's Pet Products Inc	913-354-8523	Topeka, KS	NA	NA	NA
Hiram Walker Gooderham Worts Ltd	519-254-5171	Windsor, ON Can	1309	NA	6
Hormel, George A & Co	507-437-5611	Austin, MN	2293	707	7
Hudson Foods Inc	501-636-1100	Rogers, AR	450	250	5
Hyplains Dressed Beef Inc	316-227-7135	Dodge City, KS	275	NA	1
IBC Holdings (Interstate Bakeries Corp)	816-561-6600	Kansas City, MO	855	646	10
IBP Corp	402-494-2061	Dakota City, NE	9068	1154	18
Idle Wild Foods Inc	617-757-7761	Worcester, MA	1000	NA	4
Indiana Farm Bureau Coop Assn Inc	317-631-8361	Indianapolis, IN	1320	250	1
International Multifoods Corp	612-340-3300	Minneapolis, MN	1874	716	9
Interstate Milk Producers Inc	215-322-0200	Southampton, PA	550	NA	2
Jimmy Dean Meat Co	214-638-1190	Dallas, TX	NA	NA	NA
Kahn's & Co	513-541-4000	Cincinnati, OH	NA	NA	NA
Kane Miller Corp	914-631-6900	Tarrytown, NY	500	NA	3
Kellogg Co	616-966-2000	Battle Creek, MI	4349	3298	23
Kraft Ltd	514-341-5000	Montreal, PQ Can	700	372	3
Labatt, John Ltd	519-673-5050	London, ON Can	4341	2157	18
Lance Inc	704-554-1421	Charlotte, NC	408	256	3
Land O'Lakes Inc	612-481-2222	North Arden Hills, MN	2180	750	6
Leaf Inc	312-940-7500	Bannockburn, IL	275	NA	3
Lever Brothers Co Inc	212-688-6000	New York, NY	2750	800	13
Lipton, Thomas J Inc	201-567-8000	Englewood Cliffs, NJ	1430	1000	7
Lykes Brothers Inc	813-223-3981	Tampa, FL	750	NA	5
MacAndrews & Forbes Inc	212-688-9000	New York, NY	2500	NA	25
Manitoba Pool Elevators Ltd	204-947-1171	Winnipeg, MB Can	595	82	1
Maple Leaf Mills Ltd	416-484-7400	Toronto, ON Can	723	340	4
Mars Inc	703-821-4900	McLean, VA	8000	NA	20
Marubeni Canada Ltd	416-368-1171	Toronto, ON Can	1162	425	1
Mayer, Oscar Foods Corp	608-241-3311	Madison, WI	NA	NA	NA
McCain Foods Ltd	506-392-5541	Florenceville, NB Can	1275	6800	10
McCormick & Co Inc	301-771-7301	Hunt Valley, MD	1184	770	10
MEI Diversified Inc	612-339-8853	Minneapolis, MN	250	150	1
Michigan Livestock Co Inc	517-337-2856	East Lansing, MI	275	NA	1
Michigan Milk Producers Association Inc	313-474-6672	Novi, MI	550	150	1
Mid America Dairymen Inc	417-865-9641	Springfield, MO	1650	300	4
Milk Marketing Inc	216-826-4730	Strongsville, OH	825	NA	1
Miller, E A Inc	801-245-6456	Hyrum, UT	1100	NA	4
Missouri Farmers Association Inc	314-874-5111	Columbia, MO	550	NA	1
Molson Companies	416-675-1786	Toronto, ON Can	2070	1160	11
Monfort of Colorado Inc	303-353-2311	Greeley, CO	1600	250	5
Moorman Manufacturing Co	217-222-7100	Quincy, IL	550	NA	5
MorningStar Foods Inc	214-360-4700	Dallas, TX	1000	NA	5
Morrell, John & Co	513-852-3500	Cincinnati, OH	NA	NA	NA
Morton Salt Co	312-807-2665	Chicago, IL	NA	NA	NA
Moyer Packing Co Inc	215-723-5555	Souderton, PA	500	NA	2
Mrs Paul's Kitchen Inc	215-483-4000	Philadelphia, PA	NA	NA	NA
Nabisco Brands Inc	201-503-7100	Parsippany, NJ	NA	NA	NA
Nabisco Brands Ltd	416-598-2600	Toronto, ON Can	699	704	4
National Beverage Corp	305-857-3300	Fort Lauderdale, FL	500	NA	1
National Sea Products Ltd	902-422-9381	Halifax, NS Can	477	343	8
Nestle Enterprises Ltd	416-429-4411	Don Mills, ON Can	521	229	2
Nestle USA Inc	914-251-3000	Purchase, NY	2200	NA	11
Ocean Spray Cranberries Inc	508-747-1000	Plymouth, MA	625	400	3

Major Group: Food Processing Industry: Food Processing

Organizations Listed by Industry

Organization	Phone	City / State or Province	Revenue ($ mil)	Assets ($ mil)	Emp (thous)
Ore-Ida Foods Inc	208-383-6100	Boise, ID	500	NA	2
Pacific Resources Inc	808-547-3111	Honolulu, HI	1050	700	11
Packerland Packing Co Inc	414-468-4000	Green Bay, WI	550	NA	2
Pepperidge Farm Inc	203-846-7000	Norwalk, CT	NA	NA	NA
Pepsi Cola Canada Ltd	416-964-1313	Toronto, ON Can	259	211	2
Pepsico Foods International	214-956-3700	Dallas, TX	NA	NA	NA
Perdue Farms Inc	301-543-3000	Salisbury, MD	1500	NA	15
Pet Inc	314-621-5400	St Louis, MO	NA	NA	NA
Pierce, S S Co	607-243-7171	Dundee, NY	600	400	7
Pilgrams Pride Corp	214-856-7901	Pittsburg, TX	550	NA	5
Pillsbury Co	612-330-4966	Minneapolis, MN	6191	3840	100
Pioneer HiBred International Inc	515-245-3500	Des Moines, IA	400	587	5
Prairie Farms Dairy Inc	217-854-2547	Carlinville, IL	330	NA	1
Procter & Gamble Inc	416-730-4711	Toronto, ON Can	891	719	3
Purdel Cooperative Agro Alimentaire	418-736-4363	Bic, PQ Can	255	85	2
Quaker Oats Co	312-222-7111	Chicago, IL	5330	2975	31
Ralston Purina Co	314-982-1000	St Louis, MO	5876	4044	57
Redpath Industries Ltd	416-865-0400	Toronto, ON Can	600	416	4
Riceland Foods Inc	501-673-5500	Stuttgart, AR	825	250	3
Rich Products Corp	716-878-8000	Buffalo, NY	750	NA	5
Robin Hood Multifoods Inc	416-496-1515	Willowdale, ON Can	366	129	2
Rymer Foods Inc	312-419-0060	Chicago, IL	350	250	3
Sara Lee Corp	312-726-2600	Chicago, IL	11206	5663	105
Sara Lee Corp of Canada	416-860-0048	Toronto, ON Can	255	213	3
Saskatchewan Wheat Pool Ltd	306-569-4411	Regina, SK Can	1508	680	4
Savannah Foods & Industries Inc	912-234-1261	Savannah, GA	917	395	2
Schreiber Foods Inc	414-437-7601	Green Bay, WI	1000	NA	5
Schwans Sale Enterprises Inc	507-532-3274	Marshall, MN	600	NA	6
Scoular Corp	402-390-3030	Omaha, NE	1500	NA	1
Seaboard Corp	617-332-8492	Boston, MA	448	400	2
Seagram Co Ltd	514-849-5271	Montreal, PQ Can	4298	8242	19
Seneca Foods Corp	716-385-9500	Pittsford, NY	800	600	8
Simplot, J R Co	208-336-2110	Boise, ID	1500	NA	10
SIPCO (Swift Independent Corp)	214-573-2333	Dallas, TX	3000	300	10
Smithfield Foods Inc	703-357-4321	Smithfield, VA	916	131	4
Smoot Grain Co	913-827-8734	Decatur, IL	NA	NA	NA
Smucker, J M Co	216-682-0015	Orrville, OH	353	188	3
Snacks & International Consumer Products	614-225-4000	Columbus, OH	NA	NA	NA
Southern States Cooperative Inc	804-281-1000	Richmond, VA	967	382	3
Staley Continental Incorporated	312-981-1696	Rolling Meadows, IL	3100	1745	10
Staplecont Inc	601-453-6231	Greenwood, MS	550	NA	1
Star Kist Seafood Co	213-590-3605	Long Beach, CA	500	NA	2
Sun Diamond Growers of California Inc	415-463-8200	Pleasanton, CA	660	250	1
Sunkist Growers Inc	818-986-4800	Sherman Oaks, CA	1100	250	2
Superiors Brand Meats Inc	216-832-7491	Massillon, OH	550	NA	5
Sweet Life Foods Inc	203-623-1681	Suffield, CT	1000	NA	3
TCC Beverages Ltd(Coca Cola Sys Canada)	416-424-6000	Toronto, ON Can	745	539	5
Tejon Ranch Corp	805-248-6774	Lebec, CA	14	42	1
Thorn Apple Valley	313-552-0700	Southfield, MI	593	103	4
Tri Valley Growers Inc	415-445-1600	San Francisco, CA	550	NA	1
Tyson Foods Inc	501-756-4000	Springdale, AR	1936	889	16
Unilever (United States) Inc	212-888-1260	New York, NY	5400	4500	41
Unilever Canada Ltd	416-964-1857	Toronto, ON Can	774	394	6
Union Equity Cooperative Exchange Inc	405-233-5100	Enid, OK	550	NA	1
United Brands Co	513-579-2115	Cincinnati, OH	3503	1436	40

Major Group: Food Processing   Industry: Food Processing

Organizations Listed by Industry

Organization	Phone	City / State or Province	Revenue ($ mil)	Assets ($ mil)	Emp (thous)
United Cooperatives of Ontario Ltd	416-890-8500	Mississauga, ON Can	416	153	1
United Grain Growers Ltd	204-944-5411	Winnipeg, MB Can	748	277	2
Universal Foods Corp	414-271-6755	Milwaukee, WI	721	404	5
Valhi Corp	214-386-4110	Dallas, TX	1000	800	8
Van Munching & Co Inc	212-265-2685	New York, NY	550	NA	1
Vlassic Foods Inc	313-851-9400	West Bloomfield, MI	NA	NA	NA
VS Services Ltd	416-255-1331	Toronto, ON Can	298	85	5
Wakefern Food Corp	201-527-3300	Elizabeth, NJ	3300	NA	4
Weight Watchers International	516-939-0400	Jericho, NY	500	NA	2
Wilbur Ellis & Co Inc	415-772-4000	San Francisco, CA	750	NA	5
Williams, Roger Foods Inc	401-942-4000	Cranston, RI	550	NA	1
Wilson Foods Corp	405-525-4545	Oklahoma City, OK	1324	219	7
Winn Enterprises Inc	714-637-2730	Los Angeles, CA	1000	500	10
Wisconsin Dairies Cooperative Inc	608-356-8316	Baraboo, WI	550	150	1
WLR Foods Inc	703-867-9221	Hilton, VA	371	300	3
Wrigley, William Jr Co	312-644-2121	Chicago, IL	891	440	6
Xcan Grain Ltd	204-949-1388	Winnipeg, MB Can	383	85	1

Industry: Food Processing   Number: 220

Major Group: Food Processing   Industry: Tobacco

Organization	Phone	City / State or Province	Revenue ($ mil)	Assets ($ mil)	Emp (thous)
American Brands Inc	203-698-5000	Old Greenwich, CT	11980	12201	85
American Tobacco Co	203-325-4900	Stamford, CT	NA	NA	NA
Grand Met USA Inc	201-573-4000	Montvale, NJ	2200	NA	21
Imperial Tobacco Ltd	514-932-6161	Montreal, PQ Can	1637	NA	7
Liggett Group Inc	919-683-9000	Durham, NC	2000	1500	15
Lorillard Corp	212-545-2000	New York, NY	2100	1500	5
Philip Morris Companies Inc	212-880-5000	New York, NY	31742	36960	155
Reynolds, R J Tobacco Co	919-741-5000	Winston-Salem, NC	NA	NA	NA
RJR Nabisco Inc	404-770-6000	Atlanta, GA	15766	16861	120
Rothmans Inc	416-449-5525	Don Mills, ON Can	352	338	3
Standard Commerical Tobacco Co	919-291-5507	Wilson, NC	935	559	5
Universal Leaf Tobacco Co Inc	804-359-9311	Richmond, VA	2104	943	14
UST United States Tobacco Co	203-661-1100	Greenwich, CT	565	549	3

Industry: Tobacco   Number: 13

Major Group: Retail   Industry: Retail/Food

Organization	Phone	City / State or Province	Revenue ($ mil)	Assets ($ mil)	Emp (thous)
Acme Markets Inc	215-568-3000	Philadelphia, PA	NA	NA	NA
Affiliated Foods Inc	817-281-4417	Keller, TX	1100	NA	1
Albertson's Inc	208-385-6200	Boise, ID	6773	1591	50
Albrecht, Fred W Grocery Co Inc	216-733-2861	Akron, OH	275	NA	3
Almac's Corp	401-438-2700	East Providence, RI	500	NA	2
Alpha Beta Co	714-738-2000	La Habra, CA	NA	NA	NA
American Drug Stores Inc	312-572-5000	Oak Brook, IL	NA	NA	NA
American Seaway Foods Inc	216-663-5500	Edford Heights, OH	550	NA	2
American Stores Co	801-539-0112	Salt Lake City, UT	18478	7010	165
Arden Group Inc	213-638-2842	Compton, CA	351	250	3
Associated Food Stores Inc	801-973-4400	Salt Lake City, UT	660	NA	3
Associated Grocers Inc	206-762-2100	Seattle, WA	1100	NA	2
Associated Grocers of Colorado Inc	303-297-9121	Wheatridge, CO	550	NA	1
Associated Wholesale Grocers Inc	913-321-1313	Kansas City, KS	1870	NA	2
Bayless, A J Markets Inc	602-731-6800	Tempe, AZ	550	NA	3

Major Group: Retail   Industry: Retail/Food

Organizations Listed by Industry

Organization	Phone	City / State or Province	Revenue ($ mil)	Assets ($ mil)	Emp (thous)
Big Bear Inc	614-464-6500	Columbus, OH	900	500	9
Big V Supermarkets Inc	914-651-4411	Florida, NY	600	NA	3
Borman's Inc	313-270-1000	Detroit, MI	1050	600	11
Boys Market Inc	213-258-8080	Los Angeles, CA	550	NA	4
Brookshire Grocery Co	214-534-3000	Tyler, TX	750	NA	5
Bruno's Inc	205-940-9400	Birmingham, AL	1982	592	6
Butt, H E Grocery Co	512-270-8000	San Antonio, TX	2250	NA	15
C & S Wholesale Grocery Inc	802-257-4371	Brattleboro, VT	600	NA	1
Calgary Cooperative Assn Ltd	403-253-0345	Calgary, AB Can	382	86	3
Canada Safeway Ltd	403-260-8600	Calgary, AB Can	3291	821	22
Casey's General Stores Inc	515-263-3700	Des Moines, IA	419	200	4
Cenex Corp	612-451-5151	Inver Grove Heights, MN	1100	NA	2
Certified Grocers Midwest Inc	312-585-7000	Chicago, IL	1100	NA	2
Certified Grocers of America Inc	213-726-2601	Los Angeles, CA	2750	NA	3
Circle K Corp	602-253-9600	Phoenix, AZ	2657	1536	25
Core Mark International Inc	604-273-7721	Richmond, BC Can	2032	431	3
Cullum Companies	214-661-9700	Dallas, TX	1000	NA	10
Cumberland Farms Corp	617-828-4900	Canton, MA	2200	NA	12
DeBartolo, Edward J Co Inc	216-758-7292	Youngstown, OH	1000	NA	10
Delchamps Inc	205-433-0431	Mobile, AL	800	350	6
DeMoulas Super Markets Inc	508-851-7381	Tewksbury, MA	1000	NA	9
Dillon Co	316-663-6801	Hutchinson, KS	2000	NA	20
Eagle Food Center Corp	309-787-7700	Milan, IL	1000	NA	10
First National Supermarkets Inc	216-587-7100	Maple Heights, OH	1650	NA	16
Food Emporium	212-579-3400	Bronx, NY	1000	NA	10
Food Lion Inc	704-633-8250	Salisbury, NC	3815	1089	36
Foodarama Supermarket Corp	201-462-4700	Freehold, NJ	500	300	7
Furr's/Bishop's Cafeterias Inc	806-792-7151	Lubbock, TX	300	200	10
Furrs Inc	806-763-1931	Lubbock, TX	1250	NA	10
Gateway Foods Corp	608-785-1330	LaCrosse, WI	2250	NA	6
General Host Corp	203-357-9900	Stamford, CT	467	533	6
General Nutrition Inc	412-288-4600	Pittsburgh, PA	361	136	6
Giant Eagle Inc	412-963-6200	Pittsburgh, PA	1500	NA	14
Giant Food Inc	301-341-4100	Landover, MD	2987	983	25
Golub Corp	518-355-5000	Schenectady, NY	1000	NA	10
Grand Union Co	201-890-6000	Wayne, NJ	3100	750	25
Great Atlantic & Pacific Co of Canada	416-239-7171	Toronto, ON Can	1020	425	20
Great Atlantic & Pacific Tea Co	201-573-9700	Montvale, NJ	10068	2640	92
Green, B & Co Inc	301-247-8300	Baltimore, MD	600	NA	1
Grocers Supply Co Inc	713-747-5000	Houston, TX	1000	NA	2
Grocery Supply Co Inc	214-885-7621	Sulphur Springs, TX	550	NA	2
GSC Enterprises Inc	214-885-7621	Sulphur Springs, TX	500	NA	1
Hannaford Brothers	207-883-2911	Scarborough, ME	1000	500	10
Holly Farms Corp	901-761-3610	Memphis, TN	1583	757	15
Hughes Markets Inc	213-227-8211	Los Angeles, CA	1000	NA	5
Hy Vee Food Stores Inc	515-774-2121	Chariton, IA	1800	NA	10
Ingles Markets Inc	704-669-2941	Black Mountain, NC	550	NA	5
Jewel Food Stores	312-531-6000	Melrose Park, IL	NA	NA	NA
Kash n Karry Food Stores Inc	813-621-0200	Tampa, FL	1000	NA	5
Kay Jewelers Corp	703-683-3800	Alexandria, VA	420	275	5
Keith, Ben E Co	817-332-9171	Fort Worth, TX	550	NA	1
Kelly, Douglas & Co	604-661-1200	Vancouver, BC Can	1785	404	15
King Kullen Grocery Inc	516-333-7100	Westbury, NY	600	NA	6
Kohl's Food Stores	414-771-8000	Milwaukee, WI	1000	NA	10
Kraft Inc	312-498-4000	Glenview, IL	10000	6000	45

Major Group: Retail   **Industry: Retail/Food**

Organizations Listed by Industry

Organization	Phone	City / State or Province	Revenue ($ mil)	Assets ($ mil)	Emp (thous)
Kroger Co	513-762-4000	Cincinnati, OH	19100	4200	150
Loblaw Companies	416-922-8500	Toronto, ON Can	7336	1881	33
Lucky Stores Inc	415-833-6000	Dublin, OH	7000	1750	80
Malone & Hyde Inc	901-325-4200	Memphis, TN	4400	NA	21
Marsh Supermarkets Inc	317-759-8101	Yorktown, IN	900	600	9
Mayfair Super Markets Inc	201-352-6400	Elizabethtown, NJ	600	250	5
McDonald's Restaurants of Canada Ltd	416-443-1000	Don Mills, ON Can	987	447	54
McLane Co Inc	817-778-7500	Temple, TX	2000	NA	3
Meadowdale Foods Inc	313-943-3300	Detroit, MI	500	NA	2
Metro Richelieu Ltd	514-353-5000	Montreal, PQ Can	1870	484	17
Minyard Food Stores Inc	214-462-8700	Coppel, TX	500	NA	5
Nash Finch Co	612-929-0371	St Louis Park, MN	1700	500	8
National Convenience Stores Inc	713-863-2200	Houston, TX	1073	600	11
Niagara Frontier Services Inc	716-823-3712	Buffalo, NY	825	NA	5
Oshawa Group Ltd	416-236-1971	Islington, ON Can	3634	572	19
Pantry Inc	919-774-6700	Sanford, NC	275	NA	2
Penn Traffic Inc	814-536-4411	Johnstown, PA	1180	NA	10
Piggly Wiggly Southern Inc	912-537-9871	Vidalia, GA	825	NA	7
Provigo Incorporated	514-866-9781	Montreal, PQ Can	7175	1363	14
Publix Super Markets Inc	813-688-1188	Lakeland, FL	4200	1000	22
Quiktrip Corp	918-836-8551	Tulsa, OK	550	NA	2
Raleys Inc	916-444-8150	Broderick, CA	1000	NA	6
Randalls Food Markets Inc	713-497-8191	Houston, TX	1000	NA	10
Red Apple Companies Inc	212-580-6800	New York, NY	750	NA	7
Red Owl Holdings Inc	612-932-2132	Hopkins, MN	750	NA	3
Richfood Inc	804-746-6000	Mechanicsville, VA	1100	NA	2
Riser Foods Inc	216-292-7000	Bedford Heights, OH	1057	228	10
Roundy's Inc	414-547-7999	Pewaukee, WI	2000	500	5
Ruddick Corp	704-372-5404	Charlotte, NC	1400	700	11
Rykoff Sexton Inc	213-622-4131	Los Angeles, CA	1143	326	5
Safeway Stores Inc	415-891-3000	Oakland, CA	13612	4372	100
Safeway Texas Corp	713-460-5000	Houston, TX	750	NA	3
Save Mart Supermarkets Inc	209-577-1600	Modesto, CA	500	NA	3
Schnuck Markets Inc	314-344-9600	Bridgeton, MO	1000	NA	10
Schwegmann Giant Super Markets Inc	504-947-9921	New Orleans, LA	500	NA	5
Scotty's Inc	813-299-1111	Winter Haven, FL	551	315	6
Services Group of America	206-623-5023	Seattle, WA	1500	NA	5
Shaws Supermarkets Inc	508-378-7211	East Bridgewater, MA	1100	NA	11
Smith Management Corp	801-974-1400	Salt Lake City, UT	1100	NA	5
Sobeys Inc	902-752-8371	Stellarton, NS Can	893	213	9
Southland Canada Inc	604-299-0700	Burnaby, BC Can	448	145	6
Southland Corp	214-828-7011	Dallas, TX	9000	NA	50
Spartan Stores Inc	616-878-2000	Grand Rapids, MI	1650	NA	4
Steinberg Inc	514-931-9131	Montreal, PQ Can	3897	1296	36
Super Food Services Inc	513-294-1731	Dayton, OH	1573	224	2
Super Rite Foods Inc	717-232-6821	Harrisburg, PA	757	450	3
Super Valu Stores Inc	612-828-4000	Eden Prairie, MN	10296	2305	41
Supermarkets General Corp	201-499-3000	Woodbridge, NJ	6000	NA	30
Topco Associates Inc	312-676-3030	Skokie, IL	2200	NA	1
Tops Markets Inc	716-823-3712	Buffalo, NY	1000	NA	4
Twin County Grocers Inc	201-287-4600	Edison, NJ	1100	NA	2
United Grocers Inc	503-653-6330	Milwalkee, OR	825	NA	3
URM Stores Inc	509-467-2620	Seattle, WA	550	NA	3
Village Super Markets Inc	201-467-2200	Springfield, NJ	600	300	4
Vons Companies Inc	818-579-1400	El Mone, CA	3300	NA	19

Major Group: Retail **Industry: Retail/Food**

Organizations Listed by Industry

Organization	Phone	City / State or Province	Revenue ($ mil)	Assets ($ mil)	Emp (thous)
Waldbaum Inc	516-582-9300	Central Islap, NY	1800	1000	14
Wegmans Food Markets Inc	716-328-2550	Rochester, NY	1000	NA	5
Weis Markets Inc	717-286-4571	Sunbury, PA	1189	596	15
Westfair Foods Ltd	204-786-7941	Winnipeg, MB Can	1233	340	2
Weston, George Ltd	416-922-2500	Toronto, ON Can	9206	2955	55
White Swan Co	817-284-4844	Fort Worth, TX	500	NA	3
Winn Dixie Stores Inc	904-783-5000	Jacksonville, FL	9008	1514	40
Young's Markets Inc	213-629-5571	Los Angeles, CA	600	NA	3

Industry: Retail/Food **Number: 133**

Major Group: Retail **Industry: Retail/Merch**

Organization	Phone	City / State or Province	Revenue ($ mil)	Assets ($ mil)	Emp (thous)
Abercrombie & Fitch Inc	614-479-6500	Columbus, OH	NA	NA	NA
Ace Hardware Corp	312-990-6600	Oak Brook, IL	1100	250	2
Alexander's Inc	212-869-0368	New York, NY	700	NA	9
Allied Stores Corp	212-764-2000	New York, NY	4000	5000	25
Amcena Inc	212-391-4141	New York, NY	550	NA	5
Ames Department Stores Inc	203-563-8234	Rocky Hill, CT	3363	1700	21
Amway Corp	606-676-6000	Ada, MI	1500	NA	10
Anthony, C R Co Inc	405-235-3711	Oklahoma City, OK	500	NA	5
Arbor Drugs Inc	313-643-9420	Troy, MI	300	150	4
Audio/Video Affiliates Inc	513-274-3737	Dayton, OH	200	150	2
Audiovox Corp	516-231-7750	Hauppauge, NY	275	150	1
Auto Zone Corp	901-325-4600	Memphis, TN	500	NA	5
Baker, J Inc	617-364-3000	Boston, MA	250	200	3
Bean, L L Corp	207-865-4761	Freeport, ME	500	NA	3
Belk Store Services Inc	704-372-8900	Charlotte, NC	1750	NA	30
Bergner, P A & Co Inc	414-347-4141	Milwaukee, WI	550	NA	5
Best Buy Co	612-831-4552	Minneapolis, MN	400	300	2
Best Products Co Inc	804-261-2000	Richmond, VA	2000	1000	15
Big B Inc	205-424-3421	Bessemer, AL	271	150	2
Birks, Henry & Sons Ltd	613-236-3641	Ottawa, ON Can	314	234	5
Blair Corp	814-723-3600	Warren, PA	500	159	4
Blockbuster Entertainment Inc	214-341-7700	Dallas, TX	300	100	1
Bradlees Stores Inc	617-770-8000	Braintree, MA	990	NA	13
Brendle's Inc	919-835-3400	Elkin, NC	261	150	3
Brooks Fashion Stores Inc	212-714-8600	New York, NY	275	NA	2
Builder Marts of America Inc	803-297-6101	Greenville, SC	500	NA	4
Builders Square Inc	512-731-0500	San Antonio, TX	750	NA	7
Burns Food Ltd	403-265-8140	Calgary, AB Can	680	NA	3
Businessland Inc	408-437-4156	San Jose, CA	750	NA	9
Caldor Inc	203-846-1641	Norwalk, CT	NA	NA	NA
Canadian Tire Co	416-480-3000	Toronto, ON Can	2245	1301	6
Caremark Inc	714-851-2311	Newport Beach, CA	200	150	1
Carson, Pirie, Scott & Co	312-641-7000	Chicago, IL	1023	666	18
Carter Hawley Hale Stores Inc	213-620-0150	Los Angeles, CA	2617	1672	33
Cato Corp	704-554-8510	Charlotte, NC	250	150	22
Cavenham (USA) Inc	203-655-6211	Darien, CT	2750	500	21
Channel Home Centers Inc	201-887-7000	Whippany, NJ	750	NA	10
Charming Shoppes Inc	215-245-9100	Bensalem, PA	725	407	6
Chevron USA Inc	415-894-7700	San Francisco, CA	NA	NA	NA
Child World Inc	617-588-7300	Avon, MA	807	400	4
Circuit City Stores Inc	804-257-4292	Richmond, VA	1721	587	10
CML Group Inc	508-264-4155	Acton, MA	450	150	3

Major Group: Retail **Industry: Retail/Merch**

Organizations Listed by Industry

Organization	Phone	City / State or Province	Revenue ($ mil)	Assets ($ mil)	Emp (thous)
Cole National Corp	216-449-4100	Cleveland, OH	1250	NA	11
Commtron Corp	515-226-3000	Des Moines, IA	450	150	1
Computer Factory Inc	914-347-5000	Elmsford, NY	275	NA	3
Computer Innovations Distribution Inc	416-793-9000	Mississauga, ON Can	298	170	1
Consolidated Stores Corp	614-224-1297	Columbus, OH	601	286	5
Consumers Distributing Co	416-245-4900	Rexdale, ON Can	1105	425	11
Costco Wholesale	206-828-8100	Kirkland, WA	2000	1200	5
Cotter & Co	312-975-2700	Chicago, IL	2200	NA	3
CVN Companies Inc	612-559-8000	Minneapolis, MN	700	300	4
CVS Inc	401-765-1500	Woonsocket, RI	NA	NA	NA
Dairy Mart Convenience Stores Inc	203-741-3611	Enfield, CT	717	400	6
Dart Group Corp	301-731-1200	Landover, MD	406	250	5
Dayton Hudson Corp	612-370-6948	Minneapolis, MN	12204	6523	150
Dillard Department Stores Inc	501-376-5200	Little Rock, AR	2558	2068	23
Dollar General Corp	502-237-5444	Scottsville, KY	590	300	7
Dress Barn Inc	203-327-4242	Stamford, CT	200	100	3
Drug Trading Co	416-288-1100	Scarborough, ON Can	373	213	1
Dylex Ltd	416-586-7000	Toronto, ON Can	1697	595	18
E-Z Serve Inc	817-267-1777	Bedford, TX	550	239	5
Eby Brown Companies	312-242-1919	Aurora, IL	750	NA	1
Eckerd, Jack Corp	813-397-7461	Largo, FL	3000	NA	30
Econocom·USA Inc	901-762-9200	Memphis, TN	550	NA	1
Edison Brothers Stores Inc	314-331-6000	St Louis, MO	1000	500	22
Eighty Four Lumber Co	412-228-8820	Eighty Four, PA	1100	NA	5
Fabri Centers of America Inc	216-464-2500	Beachwood, OH	291	200	3
Family Dollar Stores Inc	704-847-6961	Charlotte, NC	669	291	6
Farm House Foods Corp	414-271-5050	Milwaukee, WI	751	195	8
Fay's Drug Co	315-451-8000	Liverpool, NY	527	300	6
Fedco Inc	213-946-2511	Santa Fe Springs, CA	825	NA	11
Federated Department Stores Inc	513-579-7000	Cincinnati, OH	11118	6009	64
Filene's Inc	617-357-2978	Boston, MA	NA	NA	NA
Florsheim Shoe Co	312-559-2500	Chicago, IL	NA	NA	NA
Fox, G Co	203-522-1920	Hartford, CT	NA	NA	NA
Franklin Mint Corp	215-459-6000	Media, PA	550	NA	5
G&G Shops Inc	212-279-4961	New York, NY	NA	NA	NA
GAP Stores Inc	415-952-4400	San Bruno, CA	1252	481	14
Gendis Inc	204-474-5200	Winnipeg, MB Can	575	262	7
Genovese Drug Stores Inc	516-420-1900	Melville, NY	366	200	4
Gibson Greetings Inc	513-841-6600	Cincinnati, OH	404	326	4
Gordon Food Service Corp	616-530-7000	Grand Rapids, MI	500	NA	3
Gordon Jewelry Corp	713-222-8080	Houston, TX	400	NA	5
Grafton Group Ltd	416-461-9411	Toronto, ON Can	543	275	4
Greenman Brothers Inc	516-293-5300	Farmingdale, NY	267	150	2
Grossmans Inc	617-848-0100	Braintree, MA	1100	NA	11
Groupe Videotron Ltee	514-281-1212	Montreal, PQ Can	298	213	1
Groves, S J & Sons Co Inc	612-546-6943	Minneapolis, MN	550	NA	5
Growmark Inc	309-557-6000	Bloomington, IL	2200	NA	1
Hallmark Cards Inc	816-274-5111	Kansas City, MO	2250	NA	20
Hallmark Electronics Corp	214-343-5000	Dallas, TX	500	NA	2
Hancock Fabrics Inc	601-842-2834	Tupelo, MS	300	200	3
Hardware Wholesalers Inc	219-749-8531	Fort Wayne, IN	825	250	1
Harris Wholesale Corp	919-977-1054	Solon, NC	1000	NA	1
Hechinger Co	301-341-1000	Landover, MD	1019	681	6
Hecht's Inc	703-558-1200	Arlington, VA	NA	NA	NA
Heck's Inc	304-755-8331	Nitro, WV	300	200	5

Major Group: Retail   **Industry: Retail/Merch**

Organizations Listed by Industry

Organization	Phone	City / State or Province	Revenue ($ mil)	Assets ($ mil)	Emp (thous)
Heilig Meyers Co	804-359-9171	Richmond, VA	352	150	3
Highland Superstores Corp	313-451-3200	Plymouth, MI	911	700	5
Hill's Department Stores Inc	617-821-1000	Canton, MA	1671	1000	14
Holiday Companies Inc	612-830-8700	Minneapolis, MN	1000	NA	5
Home Depot Inc	404-433-8211	Atlanta, GA	1999	699	9
Home Interiors & Gifts Inc	214-386-1000	Dallas, TX	400	NA	2
Home Shopping Inc	813-572-8585	St Petersburg, FL	730	540	6
Hook SupeRX Stores Inc	317-353-1451	Indianapolis, IN	1400	NA	14
House of Fabrics Inc	818-995-7000	Sherman Oaks, CA	338	200	3
Hudson's Bay Co	416-861-6112	Toronto, ON Can	3971	2966	40
Humiston Keeling Corp	312-943-6066	Chicago, IL	400	NA	1
Intermark Inc	619-459-3841	La Jolla, CA	721	400	7
Intertan Corp	817-332-7181	Fort Worth, TX	600	400	6
Itoh, C & Co Canada Ltd	604-683-5764	Vancouver, BC Can	937	425	1
Jacobson Stores Inc	517-764-6400	Jackson, MI	357	250	5
Jamesway Corp	201-330-6000	Secaucus, NJ	783	400	8
Jitney Jungle Stores Inc	601-948-0361	Jackson, MS	500	NA	5
Jordan Co	212-460-1920	New York, NY	750	NA	7
K & B Inc	504-586-1234	New Orleans, LA	550	NA	5
K Mart Canada Ltd	416-792-4400	Brampton, ON Can	1278	530	33
K Mart Corp	313-643-1000	Troy, MI	27301	12126	200
KayBee Toys Inc	413-499-0086	Pittsfield, MA	NA	NA	NA
Ketchum & Co	201-815-2800	Clark, NJ	300	150	1
Kinney Shoe Corp	212-553-2000	New York, NY	NA	NA	NA
Kinney Shoes of Canada Ltd	416-742-3590	Weston, ON Can	367	156	5
Kohls Department Stores	414-784-4480	Brookfield, WI	400	NA	4
Lands End Inc	608-935-9341	Dodgeville, WI	456	151	2
Lane Bryant Inc	212-930-9482	New York, NY	NA	NA	NA
Lazare Kaplan International Inc	212-972-9700	New York, NY	350	100	2
Lechmere Inc	617-935-8320	Woburn, MA	NA	NA	NA
Lerner Stores Inc	212-736-1222	New York, NY	NA	NA	NA
Levitz Furniture Corp	305-994-6006	Boca Raton, FL	1000	NA	8
Limited Inc	614-475-4000	Columbus, OH	4071	2145	17
Longs Drug Stores Corp	415-937-1170	Walnut Creek, CA	1925	508	11
Lord & Taylor Inc	212-391-3344	New York, NY	NA	NA	NA
Lowe's Companies Inc	919-651-4000	North Wilkesboro, NC	2517	1086	15
Lumbermens Merchandising Inc	215-293-7000	Wayne, PA	1000	NA	4
Luria, L & Son Inc	305-557-9000	Hialeah, FL	250	100	2
Macy, R H & Co Inc	212-560-3600	New York, NY	5800	NA	70
Maritz Inc	314-827-4000	Fenton, MO	1000	NA	5
Marshall's Inc	508-721-3300	Wakefield, MA	NA	NA	NA
May Department Stores Co	314-342-6300	St Louis, MO	11525	8144	80
Meijer Inc	616-453-6711	Grand Rapids, MI	2000	NA	20
Melville Corp	914-253-8000	Harrison, NY	6780	2736	97
Mercantile Stores Co Inc	302-575-1816	Wilmington, DE	2266	1452	21
Merchants Distributors Inc	704-322-2822	Hickory, NC	1000	NA	2
Merry Go Round Enterprises Inc	301-828-1000	Baltimore, MD	299	200	4
Mervyn's Inc	415-785-8800	Hayward, CA	NA	NA	NA
Meyer, Fred Inc	503-232-8844	Portland, OR	2074	NA	21
Michaels Stores Inc	214-580-8242	Irving, TX	250	200	3
Microage Inc	602-968-3168	Temple, AZ	400	100	4
Microamerica Inc	508-480-0780	West Marlboro, MA	300	150	1
Montgomery Ward & Co Inc	312-467-2000	Chicago, IL	4800	3000	40
Morse Shoe Inc	617-828-9300	Canton, MA	600	NA	6
Musicland Group Inc	612-932-7700	Minneapolis, MN	500	NA	3

Major Group: Retail   **Industry: Retail/Merch**

Organizations Listed by Industry

Organization	Phone	City / State or Province	Revenue ($ mil)	Assets ($ mil)	Emp (thous)
NBI Inc	303-444-5710	Boulder, CO	400	200	4
Neiman Marcus Co	617-232-0760	Chestnut Hill, MA	1200	1300	13
New Process Corp	814-723-3600	Warren, PA	325	200	1
Newmark & Lewis Inc	516-681-6900	Hicksville, NY	250	150	3
Nichols, S E Inc	212-206-9400	New York, NY	350	250	4
Nordstrom Inc	206-628-2111	Seattle, WA	2328	1572	33
Office Depot Inc	407-994-2131	Boca Raton, FL	300	150	3
Pace Membership Warehouses Inc	303-364-0700	Aurora, CO	1271	750	3
Pamida Corp	402-339-2400	Omaha, NE	500	NA	5
Pay Less Drug Stores	503-682-4100	Wilsonville, OR	1500	NA	15
Pay N Pak Inc	206-854-5450	Kent, WA	500	NA	2
Payless Cashways Inc	816-234-6000	Kansas City, MO	1750	800	13
Penney, J C Co	214-591-1000	Dalla, TX	14833	12254	180
Pep Boys/Manny Moe Jack Inc	215-229-9000	Philadelphia, PA	656	582	4
Perry Drug Stores Inc	313-334-1300	Pontiac, MI	600	400	7
Petrie Stores Corp	201-866-3600	Secaucus, NJ	1242	1134	7
Pharma Plus Drugmarts Ltd	416-483-4611	Toronto, ON Can	319	110	2
Pic N Save Corp	213-537-9220	Dominguez, CA	402	262	4
Pier 1 Imports Inc	817-878-8000	Fort Worth, TX	415	300	4
Prange, H C Co Inc	414-459-4800	Sheboygan, WI	275	NA	3
Price Co	619-581-4600	San Diego, CA	4162	993	8
Racetrac Petroleum Corp	404-434-0400	Atlanta, GA	500	NA	1
Radio Shack Inc	817-390-3011	Fort Worth, TX	NA	NA	NA
Rapid American Corp	212-621-4500	New York, NY	2200	1500	42
Revco Drug Stores Inc	216-425-9811	Twinsburg, OH	2500	1000	25
Riklis Corp	212-735-9500	New York, NY	3000	NA	50
Rite Aid Corp	717-761-2633	Harrisburg, PA	2486	1224	28
Rose's Stores Inc	919-492-8111	Henderson, NC	1439	436	17
Ross Stores Inc	415-790-4400	Newark, CA	626	NA	5
Ruffin Corp	316-942-7940	Wichita, KS	750	NA	1
Schottenstein Stores Inc	614-221-9200	Columbus, OH	500	NA	5
SCOA Industries Inc	617-821-1000	Canton, MA	1671	899	16
Seaboard Lumber Sales Co	604-684-3171	Vancouver, BC Can	428	88	1
Sears Canada Ltd	416-362-1711	Toronto, ON Can	3430	2229	50
Sears Roebuck & Co	312-875-2500	Chicago, IL	50252	77952	400
Service Merchandise Co Inc	615-251-6666	Nashville, TN	3093	1711	27
Service Star Corp	412-283-4567	East Butler, PA	880	250	2
Servistar Corp	412-283-4567	East Butler, PA	1000	500	1
ShopKo Stores Inc	414-497-2211	Green Bay, WI	NA	NA	NA
Silcorp Ltd	416-678-9700	Mississauga, ON Can	614	200	2
Simpsons Ltd	416-861-9111	Toronto, ON Can	553	383	6
Sotheby's Holdings Inc	212-606-7000	New York, NY	349	503	1
Spiegel Corp	312-986-8800	Oak Brook, IL	1100	900	6
Star Market Co	617-661-2200	Cambridge, MA	NA	NA	NA
Stop & Shop (SSC Holdings) Inc	617-770-8000	North Quincy, MA	4400	NA	45
Strawbridge & Clothier Inc	215-629-6000	Philadelphia, PA	904	650	5
Sunbuy Inc	514-335-0260	Montreal, PQ Can	298	85	1
Syms Corp	201-902-9600	Secuacus, NJ	283	200	2
Target Stores Inc	612-370-6073	Minneapolis, MN	NA	NA	NA
TBC Corp	901-363-8030	Memphis, TN	450	200	3
Tech Data Corp	813-539-7429	Clearwater, FL	275	150	1
Texaco USA Inc	713-650-4000	Houston, TX	NA	NA	NA
Three Beall Brothers Inc	214-586-9823	Jacksonville, TX	550	NA	5
Thrifty Corp	213-251-6000	Los Angeles, CA	NA	NA	NA
Thrifty Oil Co	213-923-9876	Downey, CA	1000	NA	1

Major Group: Retail   **Industry: Retail/Merch**

Organizations Listed by Industry

Organization	Phone	City / State or Province	Revenue ($ mil)	Assets ($ mil)	Emp (thous)
Tiffany Corp	212-755-8000	New York, NY	290	250	1
TJX Corp	508-651-6000	Natick, MA	1921	1000	22
Toys R Us Inc	201-845-5033	Rochelle Park, NJ	4001	2555	28
Trans World Music Inc	518-452-1242	Albany, NY	268	225	3
US Shoe Corp	513-527-7000	Cincinnati, OH	2343	1111	46
USA Petroleum Corp	213-452-6200	Santa Monica, CA	2200	NA	1
Valcom Inc	402-392-3900	Omaha, NE	400	200	1
Waban Inc	508-651-6500	Natick, MA	2000	750	15
Wal Mart Stores Inc	501-273-4000	Bentonville, AR	20649	5132	200
Walden Book Co Inc	203-356-7500	Stamford, CT	500	NA	5
Walgreen Co	312-940-2500	Deerfield, IL	4884	1512	35
Warren Equities Inc	212-751-8100	New York, NY	500	NA	1
Wawa Inc	215-358-8000	Wawa, PA	400	NA	4
Waxman Industries Inc	216-439-1830	Cleveland, OH	250	125	1
Wholesale Club Inc	317-842-0351	Indianapolis, IN	402	250	2
Wickes Companies Inc	213-452-0161	Santa Monica, CA	4777	4417	62
Wickes Lumber Co	312-367-6540	Vernon Hills, IL	1000	NA	5
Winkelman Stores Inc	313-451-5353	Plymouth, MI	NA	NA	NA
Wolohan Lumber Corp	517-793-4532	Saginaw, MI	300	150	1
Woodward & Lothrop Inc	202-347-5300	Washington, DC	550	NA	5
Woodward's Ltd	604-684-5231	Vancouver, BC Can	577	238	4
Woolworth, F W Canada Ltd	416-361-2111	Toronto, ON Can	1722	566	27
Woolworth, F W Co	212-553-2000	New York, NY	8088	3535	65
Zale Corp	214-580-4670	Irving, TX	909	1126	10
Zayre Corp	508-390-1000	Framingham, MA	1921	1462	19
Zeller's Inc	514-483-7600	Montreal, PQ Can	1573	595	12

Industry: Retail/Merch   **Number: 233**

Major Group: Consumer Service   Industry: Airline

Organization	Phone	City / State or Province	Revenue ($ mil)	Assets ($ mil)	Emp (thous)
Aero Mexico SA	305-591-1494	Miami, FL	1650	NA	16
Air Canada Ltd	514-879-7000	Montreal, PQ Can	2912	2921	24
Alaska Air Group Inc	206-433-3200	Seattle, WA	814	730	6
America West Airlines Inc	602-894-0800	Phoenix, AZ	743	639	5
AMR (American Airlines) Corp	817-355-1234	Ft Worth, TX	8824	9722	68
Braniff Airline Corp	214-358-6011	Dallas, TX	250	100	2
Continental Airlines Corp	713-630-5000	Houston, TX	NA	NA	NA
Delta Air Lines Inc	404-765-2600	Atlanta, GA	6915	5748	38
Eastern Airlines Inc	305-873-2211	Miami, FL	4402	3673	37
Midway Airlines Inc	312-838-0001	Chicago, IL	400	300	4
NWA (Northwest Airlines) Inc	612-726-2111	St Paul, MN	5650	4372	36
Pan Am Shuttle Inc	718-803-6607	Flushing, NY	NA	NA	NA
Pan American Corp	212-880-1234	New York, NY	3569	2149	20
Pattison, Jim Industries Ltd	604-688-6764	Vancouver, BC Can	1384	678	8
Piedmont Aviation Inc	919-767-5100	Winston Salem, NC	3000	1718	20
PS Group Inc	619-546-5001	San Diego, CA	216	692	1
PWA (Canadian Airlines) Corp	403-294-2000	Calgary, AB CAN	1850	1806	14
Southwest Airlines Co	214-353-6100	Love Field, TX	860	1308	6
Texas Air Corp (Continental Airlines)	713-658-9588	Houston, TX	8752	8199	63
Trans World Airlines Inc	212-692-3000	New York, NY	4000	3500	29
UAL Inc (United Airlines)	312-952-4000	Elk Grove Townshp, IL	8982	6701	66
US Air Group Inc	703-892-7000	Arlington, VA	5707	5345	24
Wardair International Ltd	416-671-3100	Mississauga, ON Can	441	673	3

Industry: Airline   Number: 23

Major Group: Consumer Service   Industry: Airline

Organizations Listed by Industry

Organization	Phone	City / State or Province	Revenue ($ mil)	Assets ($ mil)	Emp (thous)
Major Group: Consumer Service		**Industry: Drugs**			
Abbott Laboratories Inc	312-937-6100	Abbott Park, IL	4937	4825	39
AL Laboratories Inc	201-947-7774	Fort Lee, NJ	250	200	1
Allergan Inc	714-752-4500	Irvine, CA	NA	NA	NA
American Home Products Corp	212-878-5000	New York, NY	5501	4611	45
Bard, C R Inc	201-277-8000	Murray Hill, NJ	758	531	8
Baxter Travenol Laboratories Inc	312-948-2000	Deerfield, IL	6861	8550	64
Becton, Dickinson & Co	201-848-6800	Franklin Lakes, NJ	1709	2067	21
Bergen Brunswig Corp	714-385-4000	Orange, CA	3486	889	6
Bristol Meyers Co	212-546-4000	New York, NY	5973	5190	35
Carter Wallace Inc	212-758-4500	New York, NY	514	400	3
Ciba Geigy USA Corp	914-478-3131	Ardsley, NY	3300	NA	16
Erbamont Inc	203-967-4882	Stamford, CT	1100	NA	11
Forest Laboratories Inc	212-421-7850	New York, NY	101	194	1
Fort Dodge Laboratories Inc	515-955-4600	Fort Dodge, IA	NA	NA	NA
Groupe Pharmaceutique Focus Inc	514-254-4937	Montreal, PQ Can	315	95	1
ICN Pharmaceuticals Inc	714-545-0100	Costa Mesa, CA	166	465	2
Johnson & Johnson Corp	201-524-0400	New Brunswick, NJ	9001	7119	81
Key Pharmaceuticals Inc	201-298-4000	Kenilworth, NJ	NA	NA	NA
Lilly, Eli & Co	317-261-2000	Indianapolis, IN	4070	5263	31
Lyphomed Inc	312-390-6500	Rosemont, IL	128	286	1
Marion Labratories Inc	816-966-5000	Kansas City, MO	752	554	4
Merck & Co Inc	201-574-4000	Rahway, NJ	5940	6128	32
Miles Laboratories Inc	219-264-8062	Elkhart, IN	1650	NA	16
Mylan Laboratories Inc	412-232-0100	Pittsburgh, PA	96	109	1
Norwich Easton Pharmaceuticals Co	607-335-2111	Norwich, NY	NA	NA	NA
Owens & Minor Inc	804-747-9794	Richmond, VA	732	190	1
Pfizer Inc	212-573-2323	New York, NY	5385	7638	41
Robins, A H Co Inc	804-257-2000	Richmond, VA	934	1075	8
Rorer Group Inc	215-628-6000	Fort Washington, PA	1042	1388	8
Rugby Darby Group Inc	516-536-3000	Rockville Center, NY	400	NA	2
Sandoz USA Inc	212-307-1122	New York, NY	1650	NA	13
Schering Plough Corp	201-822-7000	Madison, NJ	2969	3426	22
Searle, G D & Co	312-982-7000	Skokie, IL	NA	NA	NA
Shaklee Corp	415-954-3000	San Francisco, CA	628	435	3
Sigma Aldrich Corp	314-771-5765	St Louis, MO	300	226	2
SmithKline Beckman Animal Health Product	215-251-7400	West Chester, PA	NA	NA	NA
Smithkline Beckman Corp	215-751-4000	Philadelphia, PA	4749	5017	42
Squibb Corp	609-921-4000	Princeton, NJ	2586	3083	18
Sterling Drug Inc	212-907-2000	New York, NY	2300	1724	21
Syntex Corp	415-885-5050	Palo Alto, CA	1272	1444	9
Upjohn Co	616-323-4000	Kalamazoo, MI	2746	3139	21
Warner Lambert Co	201-540-2000	Morris Plains, NJ	3908	2703	33
Wyeth-Ayerst Laboratories Inc	215-644-8000	Frazer, PA	NA	NA	NA

Industry: Drugs   **Number: 43**

Major Group: Consumer Service		**Industry: Food/Lodging**			
American Restaurant Group Inc	714-721-8000	Newport Beach, CA	500	NA	15
Best Western International Assn Inc	602-957-4200	Phoenix, AZ	1100	NA	1

Major Group: Consumer Service   Industry: Food/Lodging

Organizations Listed by Industry

Organization	Phone	City / State or Province	Revenue ($ mil)	Assets ($ mil)	Emp (thous)
Canteen Inc	312-701-2000	Chicago, IL	NA	NA	NA
Cara Operations Ltd	416-962-4571	Toronto, ON Can	468	298	6
Chili's Inc	214-980-9917	Dallas, TX	285	200	10
Chubb Corp	201-580-2000	Warren, NJ	3980	9741	12
Church's Fried Chicken Inc	512-735-9392	San Antonio, TX	420	301	13
Collins Foods International Inc	213-827-2300	Los Angeles, CA	1024	394	13
Commonwealth Holiday Inns Ltd	416-675-2030	Rexdale, ON Can	255	255	10
Continental Companies Inc	305-445-2493	Maimi, FL	500	NA	8
Denny's Inc	714-739-8100	La Mirada, CA	1650	NA	63
Dobbs Houses Inc	901-766-3600	Memphis, TN	500	NA	2
Domino's Pizza Inc	313-668-4000	Ann Arbor, MI	1000	NA	15
Evans, Bob Farms Inc	614-491-2225	Columbus, OH	395	219	12
Foodmaker (Jack in the Box) Inc	619-571-2121	San Diego, CA	825	NA	26
Four Seasons Hotels Ltd	416-449-1750	Toronto, ON Can	513	167	10
Hilton Hotels Corp	213-278-4321	Beverly Hills, CA	954	1893	18
Holiday (Inn) Corp	901-762-8600	Memphis, TN	1597	2139	45
Horn & Hardart Co	702-369-9500	Las Vegas, NV	499	400	6
Hyatt Corp	312-750-1234	Chicago, IL	2500	NA	40
Intercontinental Hotels Corportion	201-307-3300	Montvale, NJ	550	NA	8
International Dairy Queen	612-830-0200	Bloomington, MN	265	150	5
Investors Management Corp	919-781-9310	Raleigh, NC	500	NA	10
Jerrico (Long John Silvers Res) Inc	606-263-6000	Lexington, KY	635	428	18
Karcher, Carl Enterprises Inc	714-774-5796	Anaheim, CA	446	300	12
Kentucky Fried Chicken Inc	502-456-8300	Louisville, KY	NA	NA	NA
Loews Corp	212-545-2000	New York, NY	10865	25829	22
Loews Hotel Corp	212-545-2000	New York, NY	NA	NA	NA
Luby's Cafeterias Inc	512-654-9000	San Antonio, TX	254	185	5
Marmon Group Inc	312-372-9500	Chicago, IL	3500	NA	25
Marriott Corp	301-897-9000	Washington, DC	7370	5981	230
McDonald's Corp	312-575-3000	Oak Brook, IL	5566	8159	175
McKinsey & Co Inc	212-909-8400	New York, NY	500	NA	3
Morrison Inc	205-344-3000	Mobile, AL	829	299	15
Motel 6 Lmtd Ptnrship	214-386-6161	Dallas, TX	450	200	8
Pacific Holding Co Inc	213-208-6055	Los Angeles, CA	1000	NA	10
Piccadilly Cafeterias Inc	504-293-9440	Baton Rouge, LA	276	150	8
Pizza Hut Inc	316-681-9000	Wichita, KS	NA	NA	NA
Ponderosa Steak Houses Inc	513-454-2400	Dayton, OH	550	NA	11
Pratt Hotel Corp	214-386-9777	Dallas, TX	250	300	4
Prime Motor Inns Inc	201-882-1010	Fairfield, NJ	410	904	5
Ramada Inc	602-273-4000	Phoenix, AZ	477	705	15
Restaurant Enterprises Group Inc	714-863-6300	Irvine, CA	1250	NA	30
Ryan's Family Steak Houses Inc	803-879-1000	Greer, SC	234	142	5
Scott's Hospitality Inc	416-977-6001	Toronto, ON Can	906	728	24
Service America Corp	203-964-5000	Stamford, CT	1000	NA	10
Shoney's Inc	615-361-5201	Nashville, TN	782	404	12
Sizzler Restaurants International Inc	213-827-2300	Los Angeles, CA	311	86	5
Spartan Food Systems Inc	803-579-1220	Spartanburg, SC	NA	NA	NA
Taco Bell Inc	714-863-4501	Irvine, CA	NA	NA	NA
Tasty Baking Co	215-221-8500	Philadelphia, PA	250	200	2
TCBY Enterprises Inc	501-225-0349	Little Rock, AR	200	150	1
TGI Friday's Inc	214-450-5400	Dallas, TX	340	400	4
TW Service Inc	201-712-0500	Paramus, NJ	3574	2106	120
Vicorp Restaurants Corp	303-296-2121	Denver, CO	315	250	13
Wendy's International Inc	614-764-3100	Dublin, OH	2902	777	42

Industry: Food/Lodging   Number: 56

Major Group: Consumer Service   Industry: Food/Lodging

Organizations Listed by Industry

Organization	Phone	City / State or Province	Revenue ($ mil)	Assets ($ mil)	Emp (thous)
Major Group: Consumer Service		**Industry: Leisure Time**			
AMC Entertainment Inc	816-221-4000	Kansas City, MO	318	300	6
American Greetings Corp	216-252-7300	Cleveland, OH	1275	1088	21
Anthony Industries Inc	213-724-2800	Los Angeles, CA	250	NA	2
Bally Manufacturing Corp	312-399-1300	Chicago, IL	1941	2867	17
Bayliner Marine Corp	206-435-5571	Arlington, WA	550	NA	4
Berrie, Russ & Co Inc	201-891-7500	Oakland, NJ	278	212	3
Brunswick Corp	312-470-4700	Skokie, IL	3282	2092	29
Buena Vista International Inc	818-560-1000	Burbank, CA	NA	NA	NA
Buena Vista Pictures Distribution Inc	818-560-5000	Burbank, CA	NA	NA	NA
Caesars New Jersey	609-348-4411	Atlantic City, NJ	343	300	3
Caesars World Inc	213-552-2711	Los Angeles, CA	902	831	11
Carnival Cruise Lines Inc	305-599-2600	Miami, FL	900	NA	10
Cineplex Odeon Corp	416-596-2200	Toronto, ON Can	592	485	3
Circus Circus Enterprises Inc	702-734-0410	Las Vegas, NV	512	524	9
Club Corp of America	214-243-6191	Dallas, TX	500	NA	6
Columbia Pictures	212-751-4400	New York, NY	1616	3565	10
CPI Inc	314-231-1575	St Louis, MO	328	250	5
Delaware North Companies	716-881-6500	Buffalo, NY	1500	NA	35
Disney, Walt Co	818-840-1000	Burbank, CA	3438	5109	39
Disney, Walt World Inc	407-824-4024	Buena Vista, FL	NA	NA	NA
Disneyland Inc	714-824-4024	Anaheim, CA	NA	NA	NA
Eastman Kodak Co	716-724-4000	Rochester, NY	17034	22964	145
Fleetwood Enterprises Inc	714-351-3500	Riverside, CA	1406	514	11
Fuji Industries Inc	212-943-4435	New York, NY	1100	NA	2
Golden Nugget Inc	702-385-7111	Las Vegas, NV	175	1038	2
Griffin Corp	212-753-1230	New York, NY	500	NA	5
GTG Entertainment Co	212-888-7830	New York, NY	NA	NA	NA
Hasbro Inc	401-727-5000	Pawtucket, RI	1358	1112	8
Huffy Corp	513-866-6251	Miamisburg, OH	350	300	3
Johnson Worldwide Associates Inc	414-631-2000	Racine, WI	300	200	2
King World Productions Inc	201-522-0100	Short Hills, NJ	280	117	2
Lionel Corp	212-818-0630	New York, NY	412	400	3
Live Entertainment Inc	805-499-5827	Newberry Park, CA	352	131	3
Lorimar Telepictures Inc	212-686-9200	New York, NY	750	1400	5
Mattel Inc	213-978-5150	Hawthorne, CA	990	693	20
MCA Inc	818-777-1000	Universal City, CA	3024	4115	16
MCA Records Inc	818-777-4302	Universal City, CA	NA	NA	NA
MGM United Artists Communications Inc	213-281-4000	Beverly Hills, CA	675	1365	7
Milton Bradley Co	413-525-6411	East Longmeadow, MA	250	NA	2
Minstar Inc	612-339-7900	Minneapolis, MN	1300	1150	10
National Amusements Corp	617-461-1600	Dedham, MA	1250	NA	10
New World Entertainment	213-444-8100	Los Angeles, CA	279	200	1
New York-Off Track Betting Inc	212-704-5000	New York, NY	1100	NA	2
Orion Pictures Corp	212-758-5100	New York, NY	469	350	3
Outboard Marine Corp	312-689-6200	Waukegan, IL	1605	1141	13
Paramount Pictures Corp	213-468-5000	Los Angeles, CA	1000	NA	8
Pathe Communications	213-658-2100	Beverly Hills, CA	371	798	2
Playskool Inc	401-727-5576	Pawtuckett, RI	250	NA	2
Polaroid Corp	617-577-2000	Cambridge, MA	1863	1957	13
Resorts International Inc	305-891-2500	North Miami, FL	456	1035	9

Major Group: Consumer Service   Industry: Leisure Time

Organizations Listed by Industry

Organization	Phone	City / State or Province	Revenue ($ mil)	Assets ($ mil)	Emp (thous)
Sea Ray Corp	615-522-4181	Knoxville, TN	NA	NA	NA
Showboat Inc	702-385-9123	Las Vegas, NV	295	250	3
Summa Corp	702-791-4000	Las Vegas, NV	550	NA	5
TriStar Pictures Inc	212-751-4400	New York, NY	350	750	2
United Artists Corp	303-321-4242	Denver, CO	842	1904	3
Universal City Studios Inc	818-777-1000	Universal City, CA	NA	NA	NA
US Marine & Bayline Co	206-435-5540	Arlington, WA	NA	NA	NA
Vestron Inc	203-968-0000	Stamford, CT	275	200	1
Warner Communications Inc	212-484-8000	New York, NY	4206	4598	31
Worlds of Wonder Inc	415-659-4300	Fremont, CA	300	214	2

Industry: Leisure Time   Number: 60

Major Group: Consumer Service   Industry: Publishing/Com

Organization	Phone	City / State or Province	Revenue ($ mil)	Assets ($ mil)	Emp (thous)
ABC Television Network Group Div	212-456-7777	New York, NY	NA	NA	NA
ACCO World Corp	312-480-9700	Northbrook, IL	260	220	3
Advance Publications	718-981-1234	Staten Island, NY	2500	NA	20
Affiliated Publications Inc	617-929-2000	Boston, MA	534	425	4
American Television & Communications Inc	203-328-0600	Stamford, CT	800	600	2
Ameritech Publishing Co	313-524-7300	Troy, MI	NA	NA	NA
Ampex Corp	212-759-6301	New York, NY	600	NA	5
Arcata Corp	415-781-4200	San Francisco, CA	750	NA	10
BCE PubliTech Inc	416-964-1374	Toronto, ON Can	659	510	6
BellSouth Advertising & Publishing Corp	404-982-7400	Atlanta, GA	NA	NA	NA
Belo, A H Corp	214-745-8730	Dallas, TX	385	720	2
Cablevision Systems Inc	516-364-8450	Woodbury, NY	493	1171	2
Capital Cities--Amer Broadcasting Co Inc	212-456-7777	New York, NY	4773	6089	20
CBS Inc	212-975-4321	New York, NY	2778	4407	20
Central Newspapers Inc	317-633-9027	Indianapolis, IN	500	NA	5
Century Communications Inc	203-966-8746	New Canaan, CT	150	300	1
Chris-Craft Industries Inc	212-421-0200	New York, NY	251	909	1
CIP Inc	514-878-4811	Montreal, PQ Can	1637	1573	8
Comcast Corp	215-665-1700	Philadelphia, PA	449	2371	3
Commerce Clearing House Inc	312-940-4600	Riverwoods, IL	625	355	7
Continental Cablevision Corp	617-742-9500	Boston, MA	600	NA	5
Cox Enterprises Inc	404-843-5000	Atlanta, GA	1750	NA	14
CSA Press Inc	508-568-0301	Hudson, MA	NA	NA	NA
Diamandis Communications Corp	212-719-6000	New York, NY	550	NA	1
Directories America Inc	913-491-7000	Overland Park, KS	NA	NA	NA
Donnelly Directory Corp	914-933-6400	Purchase, NY	NA	NA	NA
Doubleday & Co Inc	212-984-7561	New York, NY	990	NA	9
Dow Jones & Co	212-416-2000	New York, NY	1603	2112	11
Dun & Bradstreet Corp	212-593-6800	New York, NY	4267	5024	90
Encyclopedia Britannica Inc	312-347-7000	Chicago, IL	600	NA	2
ESL Inc	408-738-2888	Sunnyvale, CA	NA	NA	NA
Freedom Newspapers Inc	714-542-4415	Irvine, CA	400	NA	5
Gannett Co Inc	703-284-6000	Arlington, VA	3314	3793	30
Great American Commmunications Co	513-579-2177	Cincinnati, OH	382	1965	3
Harcourt Brace Jovanovich Inc	305-345-2000	Orlando, FL	1782	3233	14
Harlequin Enterprises Ltd	416-445-5860	Don Mills, ON Can	298	NA	2
Harte Hanks Communications Inc	512-344-8000	San Antonio, TX	600	1000	7
Hearst Corp	212-262-5700	New York, NY	2000	NA	15
Heritage Communications Inc	515-246-1440	Des Moines, IA	900	700	2
Heritage Today Corp	704-542-6000	Charlotte, NC	330	NA	3

Major Group: Consumer Service   Industry: Publishing/Com

Organizations Listed by Industry

Organization	Phone	City / State or Province	Revenue ($ mil)	Assets ($ mil)	Emp (thous)
Home Box Office Inc	212-522-1212	New York, NY	NA	NA	NA
Houghton Mifflin Co	617-725-5000	Boston, MA	368	262	2
International Data Corp	508-875-5000	Framingham, MA	400	NA	4
International Thomson Organisation Ltd	416-977-8700	Toronto, ON Can	3987	3776	23
Journal Communications Co Inc	414-224-2000	Milwaukee, WI	400	NA	4
JPM Industries Inc	312-598-1300	Bridgeview, IL	200	200	1
Katz Communications Inc	212-572-5500	New York, NY	1100	NA	2
Ketchum Communications Inc	412-456-3500	Pittsburgh, PA	550	NA	1
Knight Ridder Inc	305-376-3800	Miami, FL	2083	2357	20
Landmark Communications Inc	804-446-2000	Norfolk, VA	350	300	4
Lee Enterprises Inc	319-383-2202	Davenport, IA	252	308	3
Lin Broadcasting Corp	212-765-1902	New York, NY	226	582	2
Little, Brown & Co Inc	617-227-0730	Boston, MA	NA	NA	NA
Los Angeles Times Inc	213-237-3700	Los Angeles, CA	NA	NA	NA
MacLean Hunter Ltd	416-596-5000	Toronto, ON Can	1107	1356	11
Macmillan Inc	212-702-2000	New York, NY	956	937	10
McClatchy Newspapers	916-321-1000	Sacramento, CA	400	200	6
McGraw Hill Corp	212-512-2000	New York, NY	1818	1758	16
Media General Inc	804-649-6000	Richmond, VA	756	859	11
Media News Group Inc	214-720-5800	Dallas, TX	750	NA	7
Meredith Corp	515-284-3000	Des Moines, IA	678	646	4
Metromedia Inc	201-348-3244	Secaucus, NJ	750	NA	5
Million Market Newspaper/Times Mirror	212-692-7100	New York, NY	NA	NA	NA
Multimedia Inc	803-298-4373	Greenville, SC	440	405	6
National Broadcasting Co	212-664-4444	New York, NY	NA	NA	NA
National Geographic Society Inc	202-857-7000	Washington, DC	550	NA	3
New York Times Co	212-556-1234	New York, NY	1701	1915	11
Oklahoma Publishing Co Inc	405-232-3311	Oklahoma City, OK	750	NA	7
Pacific Bell Directory Inc	415-995-4400	San Francisco, CA	NA	NA	NA
Park Communications Inc	607-272-9020	Ithaca, NY	160	267	2
Pergamon Holding Corp	914-592-9141	Elmsford, NY	825	NA	8
Providence Journal Inc	401-277-7000	Providence, RI	550	NA	5
Pulitzer Publishing Co	314-622-7000	St Louis, MO	391	227	4
Putnam Publishing Group Inc	212-576-8900	New York, NY	NA	NA	NA
Quebecor Inc	514-282-9600	Montreal, PQ Can	1093	1225	11
Readers Digest Assn Inc	914-769-7000	Pleasantville, NY	1500	NA	6
RKO General Inc	212-764-7000	New York, NY	NA	NA	NA
Rogers Communications Inc	416-864-2373	Toronto, ON Can	304	946	4
Scripps Howard Inc	513-977-3000	Cincinnati, OH	1000	546	10
Scripps, E W Corp	302-478-4141	Wilmington, DE	1215	1556	8
SFN Companies Inc	312-657-3900	Glenview, IL	440	NA	4
Simon & Schuster Inc	212-698-7000	New York, NY	500	NA	3
Southam Inc	416-927-1877	Toronto, ON Can	1406	1057	16
Southwestern Bell Publishing Inc	314-957-2261	St Louis, MO	NA	NA	NA
Storer Communications Inc	305-899-1000	Miami, FL	825	NA	5
Telecommunications Inc	303-721-5500	Denver, CO	1709	6296	8
Thomson Newspapers Ltd	416-864-1710	Toronto, ON Can	1027	1708	13
Time Inc	212-586-1212	New York, NY	4507	4913	20
Time-Life Books Inc	703-838-7000	Alexandria, VA	NA	NA	NA
Times Mirror Co	213-972-3700	Los Angeles, CA	3333	3476	28
Torstar Corp	416-367-2000	Toronto, ON Can	813	702	5
Treasure Chest Advertising Inc	818-914-3981	Glendora, CA	550	NA	5
Triangle Publications Inc	215-293-8500	Radnor, PA	1100	NA	3
Tribune Broadcasting Co	312-222-3939	Chicago, IL	NA	NA	NA
Tribune Co	312-222-9100	Chicago, IL	2335	2942	17

Major Group: Consumer Service   **Industry: Publishing/Com**

Organizations Listed by Industry

Organization	Phone	City / State or Province	Revenue ($ mil)	Assets ($ mil)	Emp (thous)
Turner Broadcasting System Inc	404-827-1700	Atlanta, GA	652	1838	6
United Cable Television Inc	303-779-5999	Denver, CO	261	697	2
USA Today Inc	212-715-2100	New York, NY	NA	NA	NA
Viacom International Inc	617-461-1600	Dedham, MA	1258	3980	4
Warner Brothers Inc	818-954-6000	Burbank, CA	NA	NA	NA
Warner Publishing Inc	212-484-2900	New York, NY	NA	NA	NA
Washington Post Co	202-334-6600	Washington, DC	1368	1422	7
Western Publishing Group Inc	212-688-4500	New York, NY	551	450	3
Westinghouse Broadcasting Co	212-307-3000	New York, NY	NA	NA	NA
Wiley, John & Sons Inc	211-285-0600	New York, NY	258	20	2

Industry: Publishing/Com   Number: 105

Major Group: Consumer Service   Industry: Health Care

Organization	Phone	City / State or Province	Revenue ($ mil)	Assets ($ mil)	Emp (thous)
American Healthcare Management	214-387-9181	Dallas, TX	471	NA	8
Basic American Medical Corp	317-783-5461	Indianapolis, IN	284	300	4
Cobe Laboratories Inc	303-232-6800	Denver, CO	250	200	2
Community Psychiatric Centers Inc	415-397-6151	San Francisco, CA	347	478	4
Crownx Inc	416-928-7722	Toronto, ON Can	2480	7641	30
Detroit Medical Center Inc	313-745-5192	Detroit, MI	989	NA	12
Diasonics Inc	415-872-2722	San Francisco, CA	350	200	2
Epic Healthcare Group Inc	214-869-0707	Irving, TX	1000	NA	10
FHP International Corp	714-963-7233	Fountain Valley, CA	504	182	1
Ford, Henry Health Care Corp	313-876-2600	Detroit, MI	1280	NA	15
Healthcare International Inc	512-346-4300	Austin, TX	400	400	4
Healthco International Inc	617-423-6045	Boston, MA	444	300	3
HealthTrust Corp	615-383-4444	Nashville, TN	1500	NA	20
Hospital Corp of America	615-327-9551	Nashville, TN	4111	5388	86
Humana Inc	502-580-1000	Louisville, KY	3435	3422	49
IPCO Corp	914-682-4500	White Plains, NY	225	150	3
Kaiser Permanente Medical	415-428-5000	Oakland, CA	5584	4161	50
Kendall Co	617-574-7000	Boston, MA	750	NA	10
Lifetime Corp	617-330-5080	Boston, MA	377	200	6
Manor Care Inc	301-681-9400	Silver Spring, MD	534	797	19
Maxicare Health Plans Inc	213-568-9000	Los Angeles, CA	1839	992	15
Medco Containment Services Inc	201-794-9010	Fair Lawn, NJ	502	344	4
Mediq Inc	609-665-9300	Pennsauken, NJ	300	200	5
Mercy Health Services	313-489-6010	Farmington, MI	1512	NA	19
Moore Medical Corp	203-225-2225	New Britain, CT	250	150	1
National Health Laboratories Inc	619-454-3314	La Jolla, CA	314	315	3
National Medical Enterprises Inc	213-479-5526	Los Angeles, CA	3202	3507	85
National Patent Development Co	212-826-8500	New York, NY	265	300	1
Oakwood Hospital Corp	313-593-7000	Detroit, MI	253	NA	3
Oral-B Laboratories Inc	415-598-5000	Redwood, CA	NA	NA	NA
Pacificare Health Systems Inc	714-952-1121	Cypress, CA	250	200	1
Puritan Bennett Corp	913-661-0444	Overland Park, KS	250	100	2
Recarey Enterprises Inc	305-854-4000	Miami, FL	550	NA	4
Republic Health Services Inc	214-851-3100	Dallas, TX	500	NA	5
Scherer, R P Corp	313-649-0900	Troy, MI	350	300	5
Sherwood Medical Co	314-241-1673	St Louis, MO	NA	NA	NA
St John Health Corp	313-343-4000	Detroit, MI	318	NA	3
Summit Health Ltd	213-201-4000	Los Angeles, CA	400	250	7
United Healthcare Corp	612-936-1300	Minnetonka, MN	435	210	5
Universal Health Services Inc	215-768-3300	King of Prussia, PA	860	543	14

Major Group: Consumer Service   Industry: Health Care

Organizations Listed by Industry

Organization	Phone	City / State or Province	Revenue ($ mil)	Assets ($ mil)	Emp (thous)
University of Michigan Hospitals Inc	313-936-4000	Ann Arbor, MI	511	NA	6
US Healthcare Inc	215-628-4800	Blue Bell, PA	739	271	10
US Surgical Corp	203-866-5050	Norwalk, CT	300	250	3
West Co	215-935-4500	Phoenixville, PA	250	200	3
William Beaumont Hospital Inc	313-551-5000	Royal Oak, MI	545	NA	7

Industry: Health Care   Number: 45

Major Group: Consumer Service   Industry: Consumer Service

Organization	Phone	City / State or Province	Revenue ($ mil)	Assets ($ mil)	Emp (thous)
Alamo Rent-a-Car Inc	305-522-0000	Fort Lauderdale, FL	400	NA	4
American Protection Industries Inc	213-442-5700	Los Angeles, CA	750	NA	5
Avis Corp	516-222-3000	Garden City, NY	1000	NA	13
Braman Enterprises Inc	305-576-6900	Miami, FL	750	NA	1
Budget Rent-a-Car Inc	312-580-5000	Chicago, IL	512	500	5
Curry Corp	914-725-3500	Scarsdale, NY	500	NA	1
Hertz Corp	201-307-2000	Park Ridge, NJ	2000	3400	15
National Car Rental Inc	612-830-2121	Minneapolis, MN	750	NA	10

Industry: Consumer Service   Number: 8

Major Group: Consumer Prd   Industry: Personal Care

Organization	Phone	City / State or Province	Revenue ($ mil)	Assets ($ mil)	Emp (thous)
Alberto Culver Co	312-450-3000	Melrose Park, IL	605	303	5
Avon Products Inc	212-546-6015	New York, NY	3063	2460	28
Block Drug Co Inc	201-434-3000	Jersey City, NJ	369	356	3
CCL Industries Ltd	416-756-8500	Willowdale, ON Can	720	496	6
Chesebrough Ponds Inc	203-222-3000	Greenwich, CT	3400	1500	25
Church & Dwight Co	609-683-5900	Princeton, NJ	400	150	1
Clairol Inc	203-632-1500	Stamford, CT	NA	NA	NA
Clorox Co	415-271-7000	Oakland, CA	1260	1156	6
Colgate Palmolive Co	212-310-2000	New York, NY	4734	3218	25
CPL Industries Inc	201-568-2303	Tenafly, NJ	NA	NA	NA
Faberge Inc	212-307-8000	New York, NY	600	300	4
First Brands Corp	203-790-2900	Danbury, CT	1000	NA	5
Gillette Co	617-421-7000	Boston, MA	3581	2868	29
Helene Curtis Industries Inc	312-292-2121	Chicago, IL	629	325	4
Imasco Ltd	514-937-9111	Montreal, PQ Can	5101	4514	60
Ingram Industries Inc	615-793-5000	Nashville, TN	1250	NA	7
International Flavors & Fragrances Inc	212-765-5500	New York, NY	840	882	4
Jafra Cosmetics Inc	805-496-1911	Westlake Village, CA	NA	NA	NA
Johnson, S C & Son Inc	414-631-2000	Racine, WI	2500	NA	12
Lauder, Estee Cosmetics Ltd	416-292-1111	Scarborough, ON Can	1488	595	5
Minnetonka Corp	612-448-4181	Chaska, MN	210	180	1
Neutrogena Corp	213-642-1150	Los Angeles, CA	178	93	1
Noxell Corp	301-785-7300	Hunt Valley, MD	522	330	2
Plough Inc	901-320-2801	Memphis, TN	NA	NA	NA
Princess House Inc	617-823-0713	North Dighton, MA	NA	NA	NA
Procter & Gamble Co	513-562-1100	Cincinnati, OH	19491	14820	75
Revlon Group Inc	212-572-5000	New York, NY	1815	1000	16
Richardson Vicks Inc	203-834-5000	Wilton, CT	NA	NA	NA
Schering Corp	201-822-7450	Kenilworth, NJ	NA	NA	NA
Shulton Inc	201-340-6000	Clifton, NJ	NA	NA	NA
Tambrands Inc	516-437-8800	Lake Success, NY	563	465	4

Industry: Personal Care   Number: 31

Major Group: Consumer Prd   Industry: Personal Care

Organizations Listed by Industry

Organization	Phone	City / State or Province	Revenue ($ mil)	Assets ($ mil)	Emp (thous)
Major Group: Consumer Prd		**Industry: Apparel/Textiles**			
Albany International Corp	518-445-2200	Menands, NY	275	NA	3
Amoskeag Co	617-262-4000	Boston, MA	1500	1000	25
Angelica Corp	314-991-2934	St Louis, MO	328	NA	3
Avtex Fibers Inc	215-251-7700	Berwyn Park, PA	275	NA	3
Baddaur Inc	901-365-8880	Memphis, TN	275	NA	2
Bernard, Chaus Inc	212-354-1280	New York, NY	280	150	3
Blue Bell Inc	919-373-3400	Greensboro, NC	1100	NA	5
Brown Group Inc	314-854-4000	St Louis, MO	1707	728	30
Burlington Coat Factory Inc	609-387-7800	Burlington, NJ	282	NA	3
Burlington Industries Inc	919-379-2000	Greensboro, NC	3000	2300	25
Cintas Corp	513-489-4000	Cincinnati, OH	205	180	3
Claiborne, Liz Co Inc	212-354-4900	New York, NY	1184	629	10
Cone Mills Corp	919-379-6510	Greensboro, NC	750	NA	10
Coronet Carpets Inc	514-293-3155	Farnham, PQ Can	383	170	2
Crown Crafts Inc	404-629-7941	Calhoun, GA	150	100	2
Crystal Brands Inc	203-254-6200	Southport, CT	400	300	3
Dan River Inc	804-799-7000	Danville, VA	500	NA	5
Delta Woodside Industries Inc	803-232-8300	Greenville, SC	500	500	4
Dixie Yarns	615-698-2501	Chattanooga, TN	600	250	10
Dominion Textile Inc	514-989-6000	Montreal, PQ Can	1034	1228	14
Dunavant Enterprises Inc	901-369-1500	Memphis, TN	1500	NA	2
Esprit de Corp Inc	415-648-6900	San Francisco, CA	1000	NA	2
Farah Inc	915-593-4444	El Paso, TX	350	250	4
Fieldcrest Cannon Inc	919-627-3000	Eden, NC	1338	812	22
Fruit of the Loom Inc	312-876-1724	Chicago, IL	1005	1830	15
General Felt Industries Inc	201-843-0900	Saddle Brook, NJ	400	NA	4
Genesco Inc	615-367-7000	Nashville, TN	463	265	6
GFI Knoll International Holdings Inc	201-843-0900	Saddlebrook, NJ	1650	NA	11
Gitano Orit Imports Inc	212-819-0707	New York, NY	550	NA	1
Gore, W L & Associates Inc	302-738-4880	Newark, DE	500	NA	5
Greenwood Mills Corp	803-229-2571	Greenwood, SC	250	NA	3
Guilford Mills Inc	919-292-7550	Greensboro, NC	550	300	6
Hanes Hosiery Inc	919-744-2011	Winston-Salem, NC	NA	NA	NA
Hartmarx Corp	312-372-6300	Chicago, IL	1174	734	16
Health Tex Inc	203-661-2000	Greenwich, CT	275	NA	3
Horizon Industries Inc	404-629-7721	Calhoun, GA	350	200	3
Interco Inc	314-863-1100	St Louis, MO	2012	1775	38
Jordache Enterprises Inc	212-279-7343	New York, NY	825	NA	3
JPS Textile Group Inc	803-271-9919	Greenville, SC	750	NA	10
Kellwood Co	314-576-3100	Chesterfield, MO	754	447	15
L'eggs Products Inc	919-768-9540	Winston-Salem, NC	NA	NA	NA
LA Gear Inc	213-822-1995	Los Angeles, CA	450	300	4
Lee Apparel Inc	913-384-4000	Merriam, KS	NA	NA	NA
Leslie Fay Inc	212-221-4000	New York, NY	683	363	6
Levi Strauss & Co Inc	415-544-6000	San Francisco, CA	3000	NA	30
Marcade Group Inc	212-944-0877	New York, NY	287	200	2
Milliken & Co	212-819-4200	New York, NY	2400	NA	20
Nike Inc	503-641-6453	Beaverton, OR	1203	709	6
Oshkosh B'Gosh Inc	414-231-8800	Oshkosh, WI	253	139	3
Oxford Industries Inc	404-659-2424	Atlanta, GA	591	223	8

Major Group: Consumer Prd   Industry: Apparel/Textiles

Organizations Listed by Industry

Organization	Phone	City / State or Province	Revenue ($ mil)	Assets ($ mil)	Emp (thous)
Palm Beach Inc	513-241-4260	Cincinnati, OH	400	NA	5
Pannill Knitting Co	703-638-8841	Martinsville, VA	275	200	4
Phillips Van Heusen Corp	212-541-5200	New York, NY	641	323	7
Playtex Corp'	203-356-8000	Stamford, CT	750	NA	8
Polo/Ralph Lauren Corp	212-974-6868	New York, NY	1000	NA	2
Reebok International Ltd	617-580-1600	Canton, MA	1791	1063	13
Reeves Brothers Inc	212-315-2323	New York, NY	550	NA	5
Reitman's Canada Ltd	514-384-1140	Montreal, PQ Can	300	149	5
Russ Togs Inc	212-642-8500	New York, NY	260	150	3
Russell Corp	205-234-4251	Alexander City, AL	531	561	13
Salant Corp (Manhattan Inds)	212-221-7500	New York, NY	370	184	4
Shaw Industries Inc	404-278-3812	Dalton, GA	958	546	5
Springs Industries Inc	803-547-2901	Fort Mill, SC	1825	1118	19
Stevens, J P & Co Inc	212-930-2000	New York, NY	1660	941	27
Stride Rite Corp	617-491-8800	Cambridge, MA	379	243	3
Tultex Corportation	703-632-2961	Martinsville, VA	350	300	8
United Merchants & Manufacturers Inc	212-930-3900	New York, NY	646	412	10
Vanity Fair Inc	212-582-6767	New York, NY	NA	NA	NA
VF Corp	215-378-1151	Wyomissing, PA	2516	1760	30
Walton Monroe Textiles Inc	404-267-9411	Monroe, GA	500	NA	5
Warnaco Inc	203-579-8272	Bridgeport, CT	750	NA	10
West Point-Pepperell Inc	404-645-4000	West Point, GA	1740	1850	31
Westpoint Pepperell Inc	404-645-4000	West Point, GA	2151	2454	41
Wolverine World Wide Inc	616-866-5500	Rockland, MI	324	184	5
World Carpets Inc	404-278-8000	Dalton, GA	275	NA	2

Industry: Apparel/Textiles   Number: 75

Major Group: Govt & Non-Prof   Industry: Federal Govt

Organization	Phone	City / State or Province	Revenue ($ mil)	Assets ($ mil)	Emp (thous)
Agriculture Canada	613-995-8963	Ottawa, ON Can	2040	NM	11
Canada Mortgage & Housing Corp	613-748-2000	Ottawa, ON CAN	758	8109	3
Canada Post Corp	613-952-1524	Ottawa, ON Can	2525	2235	61
Canadian Department of Defense	613-995-2534	Ottawa, ON Can	20298	NM	120
Canadian Wheat Board	204-983-0239	Winnipeg, MB Can	1750	3488	1
Congress of the United States of America	202-224-3121	Washington, DC	2139	NM	17
Correctional Service of Canada	613-993-7501	Ottawa, ON Can	1530	NM	11
Department of Justice Canada	613-995-2569	Ottawa, ON Can	510	NM	1
Employment & Immigration Canada	819-994-6313	Hull, PQ Can	4080	NM	24
Energy, Mines & Resources Canada	613-995-4510	Ottawa, ON Can	1020	NM	5
Environment Canada	819-997-2800	Hull, PQ Can	1530	NM	9
Export Development Corp	613-598-2500	Ottawa, ON Can	565	5893	1
External Affairs Canada	613-996-9134	Ottawa, ON Can	1020	NM	4
Federal Aviation Administration	202-366-4000	Washington, DC	5000	NM	15
Fisheries & Oceans Canada	613-993-0600	Ottawa, ON Can	1020	NM	6
Health & Welfare Canada	613-957-2991	Ottawa, ON Can	2040	NM	9
Indian & Northern Affairs Canada	819-997-0380	Hull, PQ Can	1020	NM	5
Northwest Territories Power Corp	403-465-3377	Edmonton, AB Can	1020	NM	5
OECD European Common Market	202-785-6323	Washington, DC	250	NM	1
President of the United States of Amer	202-395-3080	Washington, DC	12335	NM	1
Public Works Canada	613-998-7724	Ottawa, ON Can	1190	NM	8
Revenue Canada, Customs & Excise	613-957-0275	Ottawa, ON Can	2040	NM	10
Revenue Canada, Taxation	613-957-0275	Ottawa, ON Can	2550	NM	17
Royal Canadian Mint Ltd	613-992-2348	Ottawa, ON Can	878	108	1
Statistics Canada	613-990-8116	Ottawa, ON Can	765	NM	5

Major Group: Govt & Non-Prof   Industry: Federal Govt

Organizations Listed by Industry

Organization	Phone	City / State or Province	Revenue ($ mil)	Assets ($ mil)	Emp (thous)
Supply & Services Canada	819-997-6363	Hull, PQ Can	2040	NM	10
Transport Canada	613-996-5861	Ottawa, ON Can	5610	NM	21
United Nations	212-963-1234	New York, NY	2000	NM	4
United States Agency for Intl Develpmnt	202-647-1850	Washington, DC	750	NM	5
United States AMTRAK Natl Rail Passenger	202-383-3000	Washington, DC	1000	NM	10
United States Central Intelligence Agncy	703-351-1100	Washington, DC	2000	NM	10
United States Courts	202-479-3000	Washington, DC	1541	NM	9
United States Dept Health & Human Serv	202-245-6296	Washington, DC	11000	NM	43
United States Dept Housing & Urban Dev	202-655-4000	Washington, DC	3261	NM	13
United States Dept of Agriculture	202-447-2791	Washington, DC	50842	NM	104
United States Dept of Commerce	202-377-2000	Washington, DC	3152	NM	86
United States Dept of Defense	202-545-6700	Washington, DC	3000	NM	28
United States Dept of Education	202-245-3192	Washington, DC	25886	NM	5
United States Dept of Energy	202-586-5000	Washington, DC	12404	NM	16
United States Dept of Justice	202-633-2000	Washington, DC	6882	NM	80
United States Dept of Labor	202-523-8165	Washington, DC	31379	NM	18
United States Dept of State	202-647-4000	Washington, DC	4437	NM	26
United States Dept of the Air Force	202-545-6700	Washington, DC	107800	NM	931
United States Dept of the Army	202-545-6700	Washington, DC	85700	NM	1110
United States Dept of the Interior	202-343-3171	Washington, DC	2953	NM	9
United States Dept of the Navy	202-545-6700	Washington, DC	109500	NM	1113
United States Dept of the Treasury	202-566-2000	Washington, DC	13000	NM	156
United States Dept of Transportation	202-366-4000	Washington, DC	27772	NM	64
United States Environmental Protect Agcy	202-382-2090	Washington, DC	4787	NM	15
United States General Services Admin	202-655-4000	Washington, DC	3360	NM	19
United States Information Agency	202-655-4000	Washington, DC	1400	NM	9
United States Internal Revenue Service	202-566-5000	Washington, DC	11101	NM	67
United States Natl Aerospace & Space Adm	202-453-1000	Washington, DC	13148	NM	24
United States Nuclear Regulatory Comm	301-492-7000	Washington, DC	500	NM	3
United States Office of Personnel Mgt	202-632-5491	Washington, DC	850	NM	5
United States Panama Canal Commission	202-634-6441	Washington, DC	1400	NM	9
United States Postal Service	202-268-2000	Washington, DC	36000	NM	802
United States Small Business Admin	202-653-6554	Washington, DC	437	NM	4
United States Social Security Admin	301-594-1234	Baltimore, MD	15000	NM	71
United States Veterans Administration	202-233-2300	Washington, DC	29963	NM	206

Industry: Federal Govt   Number: 60

Major Group: Govt & Non-Prof   Industry: State/Prov Govt

Organization	Phone	City / State or Province	Revenue ($ mil)	Assets ($ mil)	Emp (thous)
Alabama, State of	205-261-2500	Montgomery, AL	8068	NM	80
Alaska, State of	907-465-2111	Juneau, AK	6726	NM	26
Arizona, State of	602-255-4900	Phoenix, AZ	7324	NM	53
Arkansas, State of	501-371-3000	Little Rock, AR	4219	NM	44
California, State of	916-322-9900	Sacramento, CA	73542	NM	328
Colorado, State of	303-866-5000	Denver, CO	8200	NM	62
Connecticut, State of	203-240-0555	Hartford, CT	8599	NM	62
Delaware, State of	302-736-4000	Dover, DE	1907	NM	21
Florida, State of	904-488-1234	Tallahassee, FL	23940	NM	139
Georgia, State of	404-656-2000	Atlanta, GA	13455	NM	98
Hawaii, State of	808-548-2211	Honolulu, HI	2818	NM	48
Idaho, State of	208-334-2411	Boise, ID	1915	NM	19
Illinois, State of	217-782-2099	Springfield, IL	27399	NM	155
Indiana, State of	317-232-4000	Indianapolis, IN	11256	NM	59
Iowa, State of	515-281-5011	Des Moines, IA	6603	NM	59

Major Group: Govt & Non-Prof   Industry: State/Prov Govt

Organizations Listed by Industry

Organization	Phone	City / State or Province	Revenue ($ mil)	Assets ($ mil)	Emp (thous)
Kansas, State of	913-296-0111	Topeka, KS	5872	NM	54
Kentucky, State of	502-465-2500	Frankfort, KY	7295	NM	71
Louisiana, State of	504-342-6600	Baton Rouge, LA	10882	NM	106
Maine, State of	207-289-1110	Augusta, ME	2648	NM	25
Maryland, State of	301-269-6200	Annapolis, MD	11308	NM	94
Massachusetts, State of	617-727-2121	Boston, MA	15502	NM	94
Michigan, State of	517-373-1837	Lansing, MI	24491	NM	156
Minnesota, State of	612-296-6013	St Paul, MN	13023	NM	75
Mississippi, State of	601-359-3100	Jackson, MS	4929	NM	50
Missouri, State of	314-751-2151	Jefferson City, MO	9593	NM	74
Montana, State of	406-444-2511	Helena, MT	2282	NM	21
Nebraska, State of	402-471-2311	Lincoln, NE	3721	NM	34
Nevada, State of	702-885-5000	Carson City, NV	2436	NM	16
New Hampshire, State of	603-271-1110	Concord, NH	1921	NM	21
New Jersey, State of	609-292-2121	Trenton, NJ	20700	NM	105
New Mexico, State of	505-827-4011	Sante Fe, NM	4168	NM	42
New York, State of	518-474-2121	Albany, NY	64568	NM	288
North Carolina, State of	919-733-1110	Raleigh, NC	12205	NM	107
North Dakota, State of	701-224-2000	Bismarck, ND	1949	NM	19
Ohio, State of	614-466-2000	Columbus, OH	24229	NM	151
Oklahoma, State of	405-521-2011	Oklahoma City, OK	7409	NM	72
Oregon, State of	503-378-3131	Salem, OR	7165	NM	56
Pennsylvania, State of	717-787-2121	Harrisburg, PA	27163	NM	144
Province of Alberta	403-427-2711	Edmonton, AB Can	12240	NM	71
Province of British Columbia	604-387-1337	Victoria, BC Can	11220	NM	59
Province of Manitoba	204-945-3744	Winnipeg, MB Can	4080	NM	18
Province of New Brunswick	506-453-2240	Fredericton, NB Can	2550	NM	32
Province of Newfoundland	709-737-3612	St Johns, NF Can	2244	NM	22
Province of Nova Scotia	902-424-2700	Halifax, NS Can	2958	NM	21
Province of Ontario	416-965-3535	Toronto, ON Can	26520	NM	123
Province of Prince Edward Island	902-892-3428	Charlotetown, PE Can	444	NM	4
Province of Quebec	418-643-1430	Quebec City, PQ Can	27540	NM	105
Province of Saskatchewan	306-565-6291	Regina, SK Can	4080	NM	23
Puerto Rico, Territory of United States	809-724-2030	San Juan, PR	5000	NM	90
Rhode Island, State of	401-277-2000	Providence, RI	2569	NM	25
South Carolina, State of	803-734-1000	Columbus, SC	6425	NM	74
South Dakota, State of	605-773-3011	Pierre, SD	1535	NM	17
Tennessee, State of	615-741-2001	Nashville, TN	8799	NM	79
Texas, State of	512-463-4630	Austin, TX	35579	NM	229
Utah, State of	801-533-4000	Salt Lake City, UT	4240	NM	37
Vermont, State of	802-828-1110	Montpelier, VT	1351	NM	13
Virginia, State of	804-786-0000	Richmond, VA	12101	NM	119
Washington, District of Columbia	202-727-1000	Washington, DC	3238	NM	52
Washington, State of	206-753-5000	Olympia, WA	11219	NM	97
West Virginia, State of	304-348-3456	Charleston, WV	4006	NM	43
Wisconsin, State of	608-266-2111	Madison, WI	12463	NM	76
Wyoming, State of	307-777-7220	Cheyenne, WY	2684	NM	13

Industry: State/Prov Govt   Number: 62

Major Group: Govt & Non-Prof   Industry: Local Govt

Akron, City of	216-375-2345	Akron, OH	250	NM	3
Alameda County	415-272-6691	Oakland, CA	950	NM	6
Albuquerque, City of	505-768-3000	Albuquerque, NM	382	NM	5

Major Group: Govt & Non-Prof   Industry: Local Govt

Organizations Listed by Industry

Organization	Phone	City / State or Province	Revenue ($ mil)	Assets ($ mil)	Emp (thous)
Allegheny County Government	412-355-6940	Pittsburgh, PA	925	NM	8
Anaheim, City of	714-999-5166	Anaheim, CA	339	NM	2
Anchorage, City of	907-264-4431	Anchorage, AK	790	NM	4
Arlington, City of	817-459-6121	Arlington, TX	250	NM	3
Atlanta, City of	404-658-6100	Atlanta, GA	596	NM	7
Austin, City of	512-499-2250	Austin, TX	795	NM	9
Baltimore, City of	301-396-4892	Baltimore, MD	1464	NM	29
Baton Rouge, City of	504-389-3100	Baton Rouge, LA	298	NM	5
Bexar County Government	512-220-2496	San Antonio, TX	330	NM	3
Birmingham, City of	205-254-2277	Birmingham, AL	237	NM	3
Boston, City of	617-725-4500	Boston, MA	1179	NM	21
Broward County Government	305-357-7000	Fort Lauderdale, FL	675	NM	5
Buffalo, City of	716-855-4841	Buffalo, NY	510	NM	10
Charlotte, City of	704-336-2244	Charlotte, NC	250	NM	4
Chicago, City of	312-744-3300	Chicago, IL	2581	NM	43
Cincinnati, City of	513-352-3250	Cincinnati, OH	431	NM	6
Cleveland, City of	216-664-2220	Cleveland, OH	531	NM	10
Colorado Springs, City of	303-578-6600	Colorado Springs, CO	458	NM	4
Columbus, City of	614-222-7671	Columbus, OH	420	NM	6
Cook County Government	312-443-5500	Chicago, IL	3900	NM	23
Corpus Christi, City of	512-880-3100	Corpus Christi, TX	250	NM	3
Cuyahoga County Government	216-443-7000	Cleveland, OH	1250	NM	8
Dade County Government	305-375-4176	Miami, FL	2300	NM	22
Dallas County Government	214-749-8011	Dallas, TX	750	NM	5
Dallas, City of	214-670-4054	Dallas, TX	859	NM	14
Denver, City of	303-575-2721	Denver, CO	808	NM	11
Des Moines, City of	515-283-4944	Des Moines, IA	250	NM	2
Detroit, City of	313-224-3400	Detroit, MI	1763	NM	19
El Paso, City of	915-541-4766	El Paso, TX	250	NM	2
Erie County Government	716-846-8500	Buffalo, NY	250	NM	2
Fort Worth, City of	817-870-6117	Fort Worth, TX	338	NM	5
Fresno, City of	209-488-1561	Fresno, CA	250	NM	2
Grand Rapids, City of	616-456-3160	Grand Rapids, MI	250	NM	2
Harris County Government	713-221-5000	Houston, TX	1200	NM	10
Hennepin County Government	612-348-3000	Minneapolis, MN	1400	NM	9
Honolulu, City of	808-523-4111	Honolulu, HI	506	NM	8
Houston, City of	713-222-3141	Houston, TX	1434	NM	21
Indianapolis, City of	317-236-3600	Indianapolis, IN	557	NM	11
Jackson, City of	601-630-1776	Jackson, MS	250	NM	2
Jacksonville, City of	904-630-1776	Jacksonville, FL	1003	NM	8
Jersey City, City of	201-547-5202	Jersey City, NJ	400	NM	3
Kansas City, City of	816-274-2595	Kansas City, MO	503	NM	7
King County Government	206-344-4100	Seattle, WA	825	NM	5
Las Vegas, City of	702-386-6241	Las Vegas, NV	250	NM	3
Lexington, City of	606-258-3110	Lexington, KY	250	NM	2
Long Beach, City of	213-590-6707	Long Beach, CA	623	NM	5
Los Angeles County Government	213-974-1411	Los Angeles, CA	12100	NM	70
Los Angeles, City of	213-485-3311	Los Angeles, CA	4254	NM	42
Louisville, City of	502-587-3061	Louisville, KY	250	NM	5
Maricopa County Government	602-262-3518	Phoenix, AZ	1300	NM	11
Memphis, City of	901-576-6000	Memphis, TN	1439	NM	19
Mesa, City of	602-834-2388	Mesa, AZ	250	NM	3
Miami, City of	305-579-6010	Miami, FL	279	NM	4
Middlesex County Government	617-494-4000	East Cambridge, MA	250	NM	1
Milwaukee County Government	414-278-4222	Milwaukee, WI	1300	NM	12

Major Group: Govt & Non-Prof   **Industry: Local Govt**

Organizations Listed by Industry

Organization	Phone	City / State or Province	Revenue ($ mil)	Assets ($ mil)	Emp (thous)
Milwaukee, City of	414-278-2200	Milwaukee, WI	592	NM	9
Minneapolis, City of	612-348-2100	Minneapolis, MN	636	NM	4
Mobile, City of	205-438-7395	Mobile, AL	250	NM	2
Nashville, City of	615-259-6047	Nashville, TN	1027	NM	16
Nassau County Government	516-535-3000	Mineola, NY	3600	NM	20
New Orleans, City of	504-586-4000	New Orleans, LA	645	NM	11
New York, City of	212-566-1300	New York, NY	27197	NM	339
Newark, City of	201-733-6400	Newark, NJ	313	NM	5
Norfolk, City of	804-441-2679	Norfolk, VA	405	NM	9
Oakland County Government	313-858-0480	Pontiac, MI	725	NM	4
Oakland, City of	415-273-3141	Oakland, CA	396	NM	4
Oklahoma City, City of	405-231-2424	Oklahoma City, OK	352	NM	4
Omaha, City of	402-444-5000	Omaha, NE	250	NM	2
Orange County Government	714-834-3100	Santa Ana, CA	2800	NM	15
Philadelphia, City of	512-686-2181	Philadelphia, PA	2692	NM	31
Phoenix, City of	602-262-7111	Phoenix, AZ	782	NM	9
Pittsburgh, City of	412-255-2626	Pittsburgh, PA	329	NM	6
Portland, City of	503-248-4120	Portland, OR	309	NM	4
Raleigh, City	919-890-3050	Raleigh, NC	250	NM	2
Richmond, City of	804-780-7977	Richmond, VA	250	NM	2
Riverside, City of	714-782-5551	Riverside, CA	250	NM	2
Rochester, City of	716-428-7045	Rochester, NY	413	NM	7
Sacramento, City of	916-449-5407	Sacramento, CA	250	NM	3
Salt Lake City, City of	801-535-7704	Salt Lake City, UT	250	NM	2
San Antonio, City of	512-299-7060	San Antonio, TX	1202	NM	12
San Bernadino County Government	714-387-2020	San Bernadino, CA	1650	NM	10
San Diego County Government	619-531-5700	San Diego, CA	2550	NM	15
San Diego, City of	619-236-6330	San Diego, CA	766	NM	8
San Francisco, City of	415-554-3456	San Francisco, CA	2079	NM	25
San Jose, City of	408-277-4237	San Jose, CA	518	NM	4
Santa Ana, City of	714-647-6910	Santa Ana, CA	250	NM	3
Santa Clara County Government	408-299-2323	San Jose, CA	1825	NM	11
Seattle, City of	206-625-4000	Seattle, WA	721	NM	8
Shreveport, City of	318-226-6250	Shreveport, LA	250	NM	2
St Louis County Government	314-889-2000	Clayton, MO	650	NM	4
St Louis, City of	314-622-3201	St Louis, MO	532	NM	8
St Paul, City of	612-298-4323	St Paul, MN	296	NM	3
St Petersburg, City of	813-893-7117	St Petersburg, FL	250	NM	3
Suffolk County Government	516-360-4000	Hauppauge, NY	2050	NM	12
Tampa, City of	813-223-8251	Tampa, FL	300	NM	4
Tarrant County Government	817-334-1441	Ft Worth, TX	300	NM	3
Toledo, City of	419-245-1001	Toledo, OH	250	NM	2
Tucson, City of	602-791-4201	Tucson, AZ	327	NM	4
Tulsa, City of	918-596-7777	Tulsa, OK	250	NM	3
Virginia Beach, City of	804-427-4111	Virginia Beach, VA	378	NM	10
Wayne County Government	313-224-0286	Detroit, MI	825	NM	5
Wichita, City of	316-268-4331	Wichita, KS	292	NM	3

Industry: Local Govt   **Number: 105**

Major Group: Govt & Non-Prof   **Industry: Govt Authority**

Organization	Phone	City / State or Province	Revenue ($ mil)	Assets ($ mil)	Emp (thous)
Bonneville Power Administration	503-230-5000	Portland, OR	2050	NM	5
New York Power Authority	212-468-6000	New York, NY	1250	5100	10
Port Authority of New York & New Jersey	212-466-7000	New York, NY	2350	5500	20

Industry: Govt Authority   **Number: 3**

Major Group: Govt & Non-Prof   Industry: Govt Authority

Organizations Listed by Industry

Organization	Phone	City / State or Province	Revenue ($ mil)	Assets ($ mil)	Emp (thous)

Major Group: Govt & Non-Prof   Industry: Membership Org

AFL-CIO American Federation of Labor	202-637-5000	Washington, DC	1000	NM	5000
Amalgamated Clothing & Textile Workers	212-242-0700	New York, NY	250	NM	350
American Enterprise Institute	202-862-5800	Washington, DC	500	NM	2
American Fed of Musicians of US & Canada	212-867-1330	New York, NY	250	NM	250
American Fed of State, Cnty & Muni Emp	202-429-1130	Washington, DC	500	NM	1100
American Federation of Government Emp	202-737-8700	Washington, DC	250	NM	250
American Federation of Teachers	202-879-4400	Washington, DC	500	NM	700
American Postal Workers Union	202-842-4200	Washington, DC	250	NM	350
Associated Actors & Artistes of America	212-869-0358	New York, NY	250	NM	220
Brookings Institution	202-797-6000	Washington, DC	500	NM	2
Communications Workers of America	202-728-2300	Washington, DC	500	NM	700
Democratic National Committee	202-863-8000	Washington, DC	1000	NM	5
Electric Power Research Institute Inc	415-855-2000	Palo Alto, CA	275	NA	2
Fraternal Order of Police	502-452-2828	Louisville, KY	250	NM	200
Graphic Communications Intl Union	202-461-1400	Washington, DC	250	NM	200
Hotel & Restrauant Employees Intl Union	202-393-4373	Washington, DC	250	NM	330
International Assn of Machinists & Aerospace	202-857-5200	Washington, DC	500	NM	800
International Brotherhood Electrical Workers	202-833-7000	Washington, DC	500	NM	1000
International Brotherhood of Teamsters	202-624-6800	Washington, DC	1000	NM	2000
International Union of Electronic & Elec	202-296-1200	Washington, DC	250	NM	200
International Union of Operating Engineers	202-429-9100	Washington, DC	300	NM	375
Laborers' Intl Union of North America	202-737-8320	Washington, DC	250	NM	450
National Assn of Letter Carriers	202-393-4695	Washington, DC	250	NM	300
National Education Association	202-833-4000	Washington, DC	1000	NM	1700
Rand Corp	213-393-0411	Santa Monica, CA	500	NM	2
Republican National Committee	202-863-8500	Washington, DC	1000	NM	5
Retail, Wholesale & Dept Store Union	212-684-5300	New York, NY	250	NM	200
Service Employees International Union	202-898-3200	Washington, DC	500	NM	850
United Assn of Plumbing & Pipe Fitting	202-628-5823	Washington, DC	250	NM	325
United Auto Workers	313-926-5000	Detroit, MI	1000	NM	1200
United Brotherhood of Carpenters America	202-546-6206	Washington, DC	500	NM	600
United Food & Commercial Workers Union	202-223-3111	Washington, DC	1000	NM	1400
United Mine Workers of America	202-842-7200	Washington, DC	250	NM	200
United Paperworkers Intl Union	615-834-8590	Nashville, TN	250	NM	250
United Steelworkers of America	202-638-6929	Washington, DC	500	NM	900

Industry: Membership Org   Number: 35

Major Group: Govt & Non-Prof   Industry: University

Alberta, The University of	403-432-3111	Edmonton, AB Can	234	NM	29
Arizona State University	602-965-9011	Tempe, AZ	196	318	45
Auburn University	205-826-4000	Auburn University, AL	171	330	21
Boston University	617-353-2000	Boston, MA	257	211	31
Brigham Young University	801-378-4418	Provo, UT	330	396	29
British Columbia, The University of	604-228-2211	Vancouver, BC Can	327	NM	28
Calgary, The University of	403-220-5110	Calgary, AB Can	234	NM	21
California State Univ Fullerton	714-773-2011	Fullerton, CA	110	84	26
California State Univ Long Beach	213-498-4158	Long Beach, CA	139	271	36
California State Univ Los Angeles	213-224-0111	Los Angeles, CA	108	132	23

Major Group: Govt & Non-Prof   Industry: University

Organizations Listed by Industry

Organization	Phone	City / State or Province	Revenue ($ mil)	Assets ($ mil)	Emp (thous)
California State Univ Northridge	213-885-1200	Northridge, CA	120	86	30
California State Univ Sacramento	916-454-6011	Sacramento, CA	110	106	26
California State University System	213-590-5731	Long Beach, CA	660	660	210
Columbia University	212-280-1754	New York, NY	431	409	21
Cornell University	607-256-1000	Ithaca, NY	484	608	24
Duke University	919-684-8111	Durham, NC	404	405	13
Eastern Michigan University	313-487-1849	Ypsilanti, MI	91	128	22
Florida State University	904-644-2525	Tallahassee, FL	156	253	23
George Washington University	202-676-6000	Washington, DC	245	256	21
Georgetown University	202-625-0100	Washington, DC	253	255	16
Georgia State Unversity	404-658-2000	Atlanta, GA	80	110	24
Harvard University	617-495-1000	Cambridge, MA	520	5100	19
Houston Community College	713-868-0700	Houston, TX	72	110	28
Illinois State University	309-438-2111	Normal, IL	112	270	24
Indiana University	812-332-0211	Bloomington, IN	315	572	34
Indiana University at Indianapolis	317-635-8661	Indianapolis, IN	278	290	26
Iowa State University	515-294-4111	Ames, IA	316	332	30
Kent State University	216-672-2121	Kent, OH	114	167	22
Laval, Universite	418-656-2131	Quebec, PQ Can	281	NM	31
Long Beach City College	213-420-4111	Long Beach, CA	132	132	26
Louisiana State University	504-388-1175	Baton Rouge, LA	153	349	31
Loyola University of Chicago	312-670-3000	Chicago, IL	194	189	16
Massachusetts Inst of Technology	617-253-1000	Cambridge, MA	556	660	12
McGill University	514-398-4455	Montreal, PQ Can	234	NM	21
McMaster University	416-525-9140	Hamilton, ON Can	187	NM	16
Memphis State University	901-454-2234	Memphis, TN	81	125	23
Miami Dade County Community College	305-596-1211	Miami, FL	165	165	44
Michigan State University	517-355-1855	East Lansing, MI	471	648	46
Montreal, Universite de	514-343-6111	Montreal, PQ Can	234	NM	50
New York University	212-598-3127	New York, NY	553	548	40
North Carolina State University	919-737-2011	Raleigh, NC	210	447	27
Northeastern University	617-437-2000	Boston, MA	147	139	40
Northern Illinois University	815-753-1271	DeKalb, IL	136	229	27
Northern Virginia Community College	703-323-3381	Annadale, VA	59	119	36
Northwestern University	312-492-3741	Evanston, IL	262	361	21
Oakland Community College	313-540-1500	Bloomfield Hills, MI	57	113	30
Ohio State University	614-422-6446	Columbus, OH	641	886	59
Oklahoma State University	405-624-5000	Stillwater, OK	172	207	24
Oregon State University	503-754-0123	Corvallis, OR	180	238	21
Pennsylvania State University	814-865-4700	University Park, PA	383	602	39
Princeton University	609-452-3000	Princeton, NJ	245	471	11
Purdue University	317-749-2108	West Lafayette, IN	332	537	37
Quebec, Universite du	418-657-3551	Sainte Foy, PQ Can	327	NM	31
Rutgers University	201-932-1766	New Brunswick, NJ	351	605	42
San Diego State University	714-265-5200	San Diego, CA	171	145	39
San Francisco State University	415-469-2141	San Francisco, CA	117	106	28
San Jose State University	408-277-2000	San Jose, CA	134	145	28
Saskatchewan, University of	306-244-4343	Saskatoon, SK Can	187	NM	18
Southern Illinois University	618-453-2121	Carbondale, IL	196	146	25
Southwest Texas State University	512-245-2111	San Marcos, TX	62	114	21
St John's University	516-990-6161	Jamaica, NY	330	330	21
Stanford University	415-497-2300	Stanford, CA	649	598	21
State Univ of New York	716-831-2000	Buffalo, NY	230	846	29
Syracuse University	315-423-1870	Syracuse, NY	187	341	23
Temple University	215-787-7000	Philadelphia, PA	350	376	36

Major Group: Govt & Non-Prof   **Industry: University**

Organizations Listed by Industry

Organization	Phone	City / State or Province	Revenue ($ mil)	Assets ($ mil)	Emp (thous)
Texas A & M University	713-845-3211	College Station, TX	392	396	40
Texas Tech University	806-742-2011	Lubbock, TX	143	342	26
Toronto, University of	416-978-2011	Toronto, ON Can	561	NM	54
Tulane University	504-865-5000	New Orleans, LA	158	198	13
University of Illinois at Chicago	312-996-3000	Chicago, IL	396	660	27
University of Southern California	213-743-2311	Los Angeles, CA	381	395	33
University of California Berkeley	415-642-6000	Berkeley, CA	428	751	38
University of California Davis	916-752-1011	Davis, CA	428	516	22
University of California Los Angeles	213-825-4321	Los Angeles, CA	799	583	40
University of Georgia	404-542-3030	Athens, GA	266	352	29
University of Pittsburgh	412-624-4141	Pittsburgh, PA	308	422	33
University of Texas	512-741-3434	Austin, TX	431	814	52
University of Wisconsin	608-262-1234	Madison, WI	607	849	50
University of California San Diego	714-452-2230	La Jolla, CA	415	411	14
University of California San Francisco	415-669-9000	San Francisco, CA	395	371	5
University of Texas at Arlington	817-273-2011	Arlington, TX	86	140	25
University of Wisconsin Milwaukee	414-963-4444	Milwaukee, WI	128	282	29
University of Akron	216-375-7111	Akron, OH	95	196	29
University of Arizona	602-626-4824	Tucson, AZ	374	484	34
University of Chicago	312-753-1234	Chicago, IL	435	356	16
University of Cincinnati	513-475-8000	Cincinnati, OH	381	431	40
University of Colorado	303-492-0111	Boulder, CO	189	255	25
University of Connecticut	203-486-2337	Storrs, CT	176	325	26
University of Florida	904-392-3261	Gainesville, FL	440	573	41
University of Hawaii	808-948-8111	Honolulu, HI	204	361	23
University of Houston	713-749-1011	Houston, TX	211	356	34
University of Illinois	217-333-1000	Champaign, IL	460	777	40
University of Iowa	319-353-2121	Iowa City, IA	415	631	34
University of Kansas	913-864-2700	Lawrence, KS	151	416	27
University of Kentucky	606-258-9000	Lexington, KY	334	326	24
University of Louisville	502-588-5555	Louisville, KY	194	298	22
University of Maryland	301-454-0100	College Park, MD	279	354	41
University of Massachusetts	413-545-0111	Amherst, MA	264	264	30
University of Miami	305-284-2211	Coral Gables, FL	263	260	21
University of Michigan	313-764-1817	Ann Arbor, MI	818	971	39
University of Minnesota	612-373-2851	Minneapolis, MN	748	991	52
University of Missouri	314-882-3387	Columbia, MO	303	249	25
University of Nebraska	402-472-7211	Lincoln, NE	359	451	25
University of New Mexico	505-277-0111	Albuquerque, NM	144	245	27
University of North Carolina	919-962-2338	Chapel Hill, NC	389	427	25
University of North Texas	817-565-2000	Denton, TX	94	118	23
University of Oklahoma	405-624-5000	Norman, OK	167	216	22
University of Pennsylvania	215-898-5000	Philadelphia, PA	580	1201	26
University of South Carolina	803-777-0411	Columbia, SC	166	521	23
University of South Florida	813-974-2011	Tampa, FL	130	187	31
University of Tennessee	615-974-2591	Knoxville, TN	194	661	26
University of Toledo	419-537-4242	Toledo, OH	79	121	23
University of Utah	801-581-7200	Salt Lake City, UT	285	310	29
University of Virginia	804-924-0311	Charlottesville, VA	338	343	21
University of Washington	206-543-2100	Seattle, WA	530	689	39
Virginia Commonwealth University	804-257-0100	Richmond, VA	301	240	23
Virginia Polytechnic Institute	703-961-6000	Blacksburg, VA	226	397	25
Washington State University	509-335-3564	Pullman, WA	212	821	21
Waterloo, University of	519-885-1211	Waterloo, ON Can	187	NM	27
Wayne State University	313-577-2424	Detroit, MI	265	376	31

Major Group: Govt & Non-Prof   **Industry: University**

Organizations Listed by Industry

Organization	Phone	City / State or Province	Revenue ($ mil)	Assets ($ mil)	Emp (thous)
Western Michigan University	606-383-1600	Kalamazoo, MI	127	187	23
Western Ontario, University of	519-679-2111	London, ON Can	281	NM	27
Yale University	203-436-0300	New Haven, CT	350	660	13

Industry: University **Number: 123**

Major Group: Govt & Non-Prof **Industry: University**

GET THE THOMAS DATABASE, TOO!

Use the wealth of information contained in the *Sales Prospecting & Territory Planning Directory* on your own personal computer. Your PC and the *Thomas Database* can create custom prospect and territory listings, personalized mail letters, envelope mail labels, analysis reports, and many other customized applications.

The *Thomas Sales Prospecting and Territory Planning Database* gives you immediate access to over 4,100 listings in North America, including the "invisible buyers" found in government, non-profits, Canadian organizations, and North American headquarters of foreign multinationals. Tap the enormous purchasing power of North America with one database, the most complete database available, *the database that really does have it all!*

And for those of you without appropriate software, you can purchase a copy of *ALPHAworks* with the data already loaded! Not only will you be able to use all the applications described above, but you will also have ALPHA Software's versatile "all in one" product *ALPHAworks*. It supplies you with wordprocessing, spreadsheet, data management, graphics and communications—all in one easy to use product. And the *Thomas Database* will be fully installed in *ALPHAworks*!

ORDER TODAY!

ALPHAworks is a registered trademark of Alpha Software Corp.
dBASE III is a registered trademark of Ashton-Tate Corp.
IBM is a registered trademark of IBM Corp.
Apple is a registered trademark of Apple Computer Corp.

Top 10 Uses of the *Thomas Database:*

1. Plan sales territories

2. Identify key prospects

3. Create phone lists for telemarketing

4. Build your own direct-mail program

5. Organize seminars

6. Execute direct sales calls more effectively

7. Target your marketing campaigns by industry

8. Analyze your market penetration geographically

9. Evaluate your industry penetration

10. Research individual organizations

Name _____

Organization _____

Address _____

City _____ State _____ Zip _____

Phone Number (required) _____

☐ Please send me more information.
☐ Please send _____ copies of the THOMAS DATABASE @$249.95 each.
☐ Please send _____ copies of the THOMAS DATABASE with ALPHAworks software @$399.95 each.
   (Add $7.50 for shipping and handling.)

The *Thomas Database* is available for IBM and compatible personal computers and Apple computers.

FILE FORMAT:
☐ ASCII   ☐ dBASE III
DISKETTE SIZE:
☐ 5.25" High Density, 1.2M
☐ 5.25" Low Density, 360K
☐ 3.5" Low Density, 720K

Method of Payment
☐ Check enclosed

☐ _____
V/MC NO.

Signature

Exp. Date

amacom
American Management Association
135 West 50th Street,
New York, N.Y. 10020

GET THE THOMAS DATABASE, TOO!

Use the wealth of information contained in the *Sales Prospecting & Territory Planning Directory* on your own personal computer. Your PC and the *Thomas Database* can create custom prospect and territory listings, personalized mail letters, envelope mail labels, analysis reports, and many other customized applications.

The *Thomas Sales Prospecting and Territory Planning Database* gives you immediate access to over 4,100 listings in North America, including the "invisible buyers" found in government, non-profits, Canadian organizations, and North American headquarters of foreign multinationals. Tap the enormous purchasing power of North America with one database, the most complete database available, *the database that really does have it all!*

And for those of you without appropriate software, you can purchase a copy of *ALPHAworks* with the data already loaded! Not only will you be able to use all the applications described above, but you will also have ALPHA Software's versatile "all in one" product *ALPHAworks*. It supplies you with wordprocessing, spreadsheet, data management, graphics and communications—all in one easy to use product. And the *Thomas Database* will be fully installed in *ALPHAworks!*

ORDER TODAY!

amacom
American Management Association
135 West 50th Street,
New York, N.Y. 10020

NO POSTAGE
NECESSARY
IF MAILED
IN THE
UNITED STATES

USINESS REPLY MAIL
CLASS   PERMIT NO. 7172   NEW YORK, NY

TAGE WILL BE PAID BY ADDRESSEE

erican Management Association
Box 319
anac Lake, NY 12983-9986